Second Edition

Nutrition, Health, and Safety for Young Children

Promoting Wellness

Joanne Sorte

Oregon State University

Inge Daeschel

Oregon State University

Carolina Amador

Community Health Centers of Benton and Linn Counties

PEARSON

Boston   Columbus   Indianapolis   New York   San Francisco   Upper Saddle River
Amsterdam   Cape Town   Dubai   London   Madrid   Milan   Munich   Paris   Montreal   Toronto
Delhi   Mexico City   São Paulo   Sydney   Hong Kong   Seoul   Singapore   Taipei   Tokyo

Vice President and Editorial Director: Jeffery W. Johnston
Senior Acquisitions Editor: Julie Peters
Development Editor: Bryce Bell
Editorial Assistant: Andrea Hall
Vice President, Director of Marketing: Margaret Waples
Senior Marketing Manager: Christopher D. Barry
Marketing Assistant: Elizabeth Mackenzie-Lamb
Senior Managing Editor: Pamela D. Bennett
Senior Project Manager: Sheryl Langner
Senior Operations Supervisor: Matthew Ottenweller
Art Director: Laura Gardner
Text and Cover Designer: Candace Rowley

Cover Image: Little girl swinging: © Xavier Gallego Morel/Fotolia; Boy eating apple with thumb up: © cmlndm/Fotolia; and Safety cones: © Serp/Shutterstock.
Media Producers: Autumn Benson and Emily Ryan
Media Project Manager: Noelle Chun
Full-Service Project Management: Cindy Sweeney, S4Carlisle Publishing Services
Composition: S4Carlisle Publishing Services
Printer/Binder: Courier/Kendallville
Cover Printer: Lehigh Color/Phoenix/Hagerstown
Text Font: Garamond Book

Library of Congress Cataloging-in-Publication Data
Sorte, Joanne, author.
  Nutrition, health, and safety for young children : promoting wellness / Joanne Sorte, Inge Daeschel, Carolina Amador.—Second edition.
    pages cm
  ISBN-13: 978-0-13-286979-9
  ISBN-10: 0-13-286979-9
  1. Children—Health and hygiene—Textbooks.   2. Children—Nutrition—Textbooks.
I. Daeschel, Inge.   II. Amador, Carolina.   III. Title.
RJ101.S655 2014
618.92—dc23

2012033651

10 9 8 7 6 5 4 3 2 1

PEARSON

ISBN-13: 978-0-13-286979-9
ISBN-10:   0-13-286979-9

I extend loving appreciation to my parents, Jean and Burrell Godard, and to my family: Bruce, Cascade, Matt, Caden, Jerry, Misty, Isabelle, Nate, and Sally, who have taught me many things about nutrition, health, and safety and the joys of playing outdoors.

joanne sorte

I would like to thank my husband Mark and our four children, Ariel, Lea, Kimberly, and Devin, for their love and support throughout the writing of this book.

inge daeschel

I extend genuine appreciation to all children, each of whom bring wisdom, courage, and joy to the world. I would like to also extend an extra special thanks to my family: Scott, Lucia, Oscar, and Felix, who bring me great peace, joy, and awe.

carolina amador

Joanne Sorte has worked as an early childhood professional for over 35 years. She received a bachelor of arts and master of science degrees in human development and family sciences from Oregon State University (OSU). She began her early childhood professional experiences as a home visitor for the Home Base program in Yakima, Washington, directed a preschool program for Lower Columbia College in Longview, Washington, and worked as the family services coordinator for Head Start. Currently she is a Senior Instructor for the College of Public Health & Human Sciences at Oregon State University. Joanne is Director of the Oregon State University Child Development Laboratory which presents a blended early education program model in which children from low-income families par-

From Left: Joanne Sorte, Inge Daeschel, and Carolina Amador

ticipate through support of the Oregon Head Start Prekindergarten Program; children with special developmental needs and children from the general community attend preschool together. She directs the practicum experience for students majoring in childhood development, supervises graduate students, and facilitates research on child development and wellness. She is also an active member of the Oregon Head Start Association. She has coauthored an intervention program for preschool settings with Inge Daeschel, called *Health in Action: 5 Steps to Good Health*, and enjoys assisting early childhood settings to partner with families in improving children's wellness.

Inge Daeschel is a licensed and registered dietitian who is board certified as a specialist in pediatric nutrition. She received her bachelor of science degree in foods and nutrition science at Plattsburgh State University in New York. She completed her dietetic internship at Massachusetts General Hospital in Boston and received her master of science degree in nutrition science from the University of Tennessee at Knoxville. She worked at Duke University Medical Center, first as pediatric dietitian clinician and later as assistant chief clinical dietitian. This position was instrumental in developing her interest in helping families understand the nutritional needs of their children.

She and her family relocated to Oregon where she worked at the Corvallis Clinic and later accepted a faculty position as instructor in the department of Human Development and Family Sciences at Oregon State University (OSU) where she is health and nutrition services coordinator of the OSU Child Development Laboratory and the OSU Oregon Head Start Prekindergarten Program. Inge is also a nutrition consultant providing services to an area hospital, a WIC program, and Early Head Start, Head Start, and Migrant Head Start programs. Her expertise in feeding children is based on personal as well as professional experience, gained raising four children, including one with multiple food allergies. She has coauthored with Joanne Sorte an intervention program called *Health in Action: 5 Steps to Good Health*, which promotes wellness by providing focused messages that address nutrition and physical activity in early childhood programs.

Carolina Amador, M.D.,

is a board-certified pediatrician. She received a bachelor of education degree in speech pathology at the University of Georgia in Athens. She earned her medical degree from the Medical College of Georgia in Augusta and completed her residency in pediatrics at West Virginia University in Morgantown. She worked as chief resident in pediatrics at West Virginia University where she developed a lactation clinic as well as a focus on advocacy for breast-feeding mothers. She has a master's degree in public health from the University of Washington in Seattle with a focus on maternal and child health. She moved with her husband to Corvallis, Oregon, and has worked as a general pediatrician for 10 years and is currently employed by a community health center that serves a large percentage of Hispanics and migrant workers. During these years as a general pediatrician, she has developed professional interests in childhood obesity prevention, health disparities, and Latino health. She has been involved in community events and organizations advocating for children's health including the Oregon State University Oregon Head Start Prekindergarten Program Health Services Advisory Committee, the Benton County Healthy Weight and Lifestyle Coalition, the Benton County Oral Health Coalition, and the Breastfeeding Coalition of Benton County. Throughout her years of education and medical practice, she has participated in several international health experiences in Ecuador, Honduras, Uganda, and Malawi.

This is an exciting and interesting time to be an early childhood educator. There is widespread and enthusiastic confirmation that early childhood professionals play an important role in establishing the foundations of wellness for young children. At the same time, teachers of young children are being held accountable for children's progress in learning more than ever before. This presents both an invitation and a challenge to future early childhood educators. In this second edition of *Nutrition, Health, and Safety for Young Children*, we invite you to explore the wide range of challenges that teachers of young children are facing today, including an increasingly diverse population of young learners, more identified food allergies, concern about the obesity epidemic, the increase in pertussis (whooping cough) cases, focus on serving children with special health care needs in classrooms, new kinds of threats to children's safety, and increased awareness of the need to develop healthy environments and use sustainable practices in early childhood settings. This edition explores these challenges by helping future teachers understand the interrelationships among nutrition, health, and safety and learn to share their knowledge with children and their families.

This practical text provides students with a comprehensive understanding of the nutrition, health, and safety needs of young children from birth into school age. In-text examples, case scenarios, and questions promote thinking about professional situations and give students a glimpse into the everyday classroom environment. These prepare teachers to serve diverse populations of young children in family child care, child care centers, preschools, and elementary school settings.

Our intention is to provide students with a strong understanding of wellness concepts, equipping them to implement healthful practices and teach young children ways to contribute to their own wellness. These skills emerge as students gain insight into the basic approaches used to enhance children's well-being:

Partner with children and families, and nutrition, health, and safety professionals to promote wellness in young children. Students learn that they will work within a network of support to meet children's nutrition, health, and safety needs.

Implement and model appropriate wellness practices. Students will be able to design and use practices that are fitting for children's age and developmental capabilities, in tune with children's developmental, health, and language needs, and responsive to family cultural practices.

Recognize the important contributions of nutrition, health, and safety to children's learning and overall well-being. Students will be ready to:

- Provide wholesome nutrition that promotes optimal growth, development, and learning.
- Attend to children's individual health needs and implement healthful classroom practices that build wellness habits to last a lifetime.
- Establish environments and implement practices that ensure children's physical and emotional safety, creating the foundations that inspire exploration, creativity, and discovery.

We extend a warm invitation to students to join the team of early childhood professionals who cherish the important early years of growth and development, and who celebrate each child's potential for a healthy, happy, and productive future. In the following pages, we describe what is new to this edition, and how this text helps students to *understand, see,* and *teach* wellness concepts.

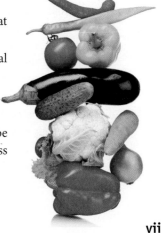

new to this edition

- **Chapters have been merged and material has been streamlined** in order to present the information in 16 chapters, better addressing the flow of topics and supporting instruction. Chapters 1 and 2 (from the first edition) were merged in the new Chapter 1, and Chapters 14 and 15 were combined in the new Chapter 13.

PROGRESSIVE PROGRAMS & PRACTICES

Training Teachers in Healthy Practices

By Tracy Moran and Tom Browning, Erikson Institute and Illinois Action for Children

In November of 2009, the Chicago Board of Health passed a joint resolution recommending new standards for Chicago's center-based child care centers. The goal was to reduce the incidence of childhood obesity and improve overall health. Specifically, the new standards involved limiting children's screen viewing, serving reduced fat milk, and reducing sweetened beverage consumption while also increasing daily physical activity.

A need for training to address overall child wellness was recognized. Local organizations[1] collaborated to provide training seminars for early child care providers. Trainers facilitated brainstorming and discussions about managing challenges related to health and wellness. Topics discussed included motivating providers to be healthier role models, the accessibility and affordability of healthy foods, high crime activity in neighborhoods, and perceived apathy of parents. The seminars resulted in an engaging and comprehensive curriculum designed to positively influence providers' knowledge and behaviors regarding nutrition, physical activity, health, and overall well-being in children.

Participants made many suggestions for promoting physical activity, such as having relay races with plastic eggs on spoons, bowling using partially filled water bottles as bowling pins, taking a walk to learn about nature and the environment, or giving each child a magnifying glass and letting the children explore the outdoor environment.

In 9 months, five trainers conducted 87 trainings with over 1,000 participants. The trainings were held at facilities that were easily accessible via public transportation and located within low-income communities throughout the city and several suburbs. The sessions resulted in a high level of agreement to implement the standards. In evaluation surveys, over half of the providers surveyed reported meeting the standards prior to the training, with the exception of the milk standard. Twenty-eight percent of providers rated the reduced fat milk standard as the most disagreeable and difficult to implement due to perceived cost increases or expected disagreement from children and/or parents.

According to child care provider Maria Salazar, "I started to implement the change from 2% to 1% milk in my day care. I was afraid when I started, but the children have assimilated and taken to the change easily. I have the children stand while putting together a puzzle so that they can be more active throughout the day. They are sleeping better because they are now tired. I also participate in the activities with the children and I love it."

[1]Including The Otho S.A. Sprague Memorial Institute, Erikson Institute, Illinois Action for Children, the Chicago Department of Public Health and the Consortium to Lower Obesity in Chicago Children

- Early childhood professionals from across the country have contributed articles describing **Progressive Programs & Practices** that they have implemented to address issues and concerns in their communities. This new boxed feature in each chapter brings contemporary practices to students who are developing new competencies in applying health, safety, and nutrition information to their work with children and families.

- **Important nutrition updates are presented** including the *USDA MyPlate* approach for planning healthy meals and the *Dietary Guidelines for Americans* (2010 version). Information about the Healthy, Hunger-Free Kids Act of 2010 and the important changes to the school lunch program that reflect current evidence-based practices for feeding young children are also covered.

- **Discussion of health practices is enhanced** for relevance to teachers, including aspects of health screenings, descriptions of common infectious diseases, and classroom management strategies to improve health and wellness for children with special health care needs. In addition, a focus on social and emotional health in early childhood adds to the overall message of attaining mental health and wellness.

- **Safety chapters reflect recently revised practices** including more focus on emergency preparedness, new strategies for implementing cardiopulmonary resuscitation, and expanded discussion of child maltreatment and violence in children's lives.

- Provocative **A Matter of Ethics** scenarios challenge students to consider professional practices and explore how teachers are guided by a professional code of behavior.

- **Ideas are provided for teaching wellness concepts to children with special developmental needs and those who are learning English** to ensure that all children have the opportunity to learn healthy practices.

A Matter of ETHICS

Imagine that you want to have the children in your class make "community soup" an activity where each child is usually asked to bring in a food to contribute to the soup. Making a food contribution might be difficult for some of the low-income families in your class. How might you arrange this activity in a way that respects the dignity and worth of each child and family?

helps students to *understand* wellness concepts

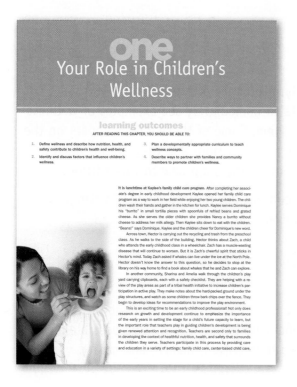

- Through anecdotes, cases, and authentic examples, the authors use a storytelling approach that helps **contextualize** wellness concepts for students. Chapter-opening **scenarios** reveal common situations involving teachers, children, and their families grappling with nutrition, health, and safety issues. These scenarios are woven through each chapter to illustrate the teacher's role.

- The text promotes **culturally responsive** teaching of nutrition, health, and safety concepts, including content about vegetarian, religious, and cultural diets and working with children and families from diverse backgrounds.

- A unique chapter on **children's mental health** explores current thinking about children's emotional health needs. (See Chapter 12.)

- Pedagogical features reinforce concepts and terminology: Learning Outcomes, key terms and glossary definitions, and end-of-chapter Review, Discussion, and Application items.

- Topical features in each chapter—**Nutrition Notes, Safety Segments, Policy Points,** and **Health Hints**—introduce readers to current issues in health, safety, and nutrition to create awareness and develop effective practices.

helps students to *see* wellness concepts . . . and *apply* them

> ▶ Mealtimes are good opportunities for preschool children to practice self-help and social skills. How does the mealtime environment shown in the **video** promote these skills?

- NEW! Videos are embedded directly into pages of the Pearson eText via margin notes. These allow students to immediately see examples of wellness practices in action and learn from them. Some of these videos appear on the MyEducationLab for Health, Safety, and Nutrition, and they are included in assignable exercises on the online site. Others are new to this edition.

- Nutrition chapters break complex content down through clear writing, diagrams, and frequent classroom examples.

> **What if. . .**
> you were assigned to teach 2-year-old toddlers instead of the 3-year-old preschoolers you normally teach? What aspects of children's nutrition would you explore to prepare yourself to feed toddlers appropriately?

- Reflective **What If . . .** situations place students in the classroom to think about how they would solve possible day-to-day challenges related to nutrition, health, and safety.

> **MyEducationLab™**
> Go to Topic 2 (Feeding Children) in the MyEducationLab (www.myeducationlab.com) for your course, where you can:
> - Find learning outcomes for Feeding Children along with the national standards that connect to these outcomes.
> - Complete Assignments and Activities that can help you more deeply understand the chapter content.
> - Apply and practice your understanding of the core teaching skills identified in the chapter with the Building Teaching Skills and Dispositions learning
> - Check your comprehension on the content covered in the chapter by going to the Study Plan in the Book Resources for your text. Here you will be able to take a chapter quiz, receive feedback on your answers, and then access Review, Practice, and Enrichment activities to enhance your understanding of chapter content.

- **MyEducationLab™** content suggested at the end of chapters provides students access to exercises, videos, artifacts, and other resources. Assignable exercises through this Lab (for purchase) can help students see how early childhood professionals convey important health, safety, and nutrition concepts to young children. A Study Plan (pretest and posttest quizzes) reinforces understanding and application.

- The theme of being a good **role model** to children is emphasized throughout.

helps students *teach* wellness concepts to children

- *NEW* Revised Chapter 1, **Your Role in Children's Wellness,** establishes the importance of integrating nutrition, health, and safety concepts throughout learning activities and in the daily curriculum. A suggested activity plan format supports students who need to create learning activities in a practicum or field experience.

- **Teaching Wellness curriculum lesson activities** are provided in each chapter. The activities are presented in developmentally appropriate ways for infants and toddlers, preschoolers, and school-age children. Some of these can be viewed online in video-based assignable exercises in MyEducationLab.

- The content of the text aligns with **NAEYC** professional preparation and program standards. MyEducationLab content aligns exercises with Learning Outcomes, NAEYC professional preparation standards, and Head Start standards.

TEACHING WELLNESS *Will I Like What's Good for Me?*

LEARNING OUTCOME Children will accept a variety of foods.

Vocabulary focus: Try, sample, taste, flavor, taste-test, variety, nutritious, food groups

Safety watch: Ensure that foods are prepared and served appropriately for the age group and the child's abilities, such as serving pureed fruits and vegetables for young infants, or small mashed pieces for older infants. Choose foods that avoid children's food allergies and restrictions.

Prepare foods appropriately for the child's developmental skill, by cooking, straining, mashing, and cutting foods into appropriate pieces, and selecting food textures that the child can manage to avoid choking such as serving pureed fruits and vegetables for young infants, or small mashed pieces for older infants; supervise children closely during the tasting and monitor for cleanliness; avoid any known food allergens or restrictions.

OLDER INFANTS AND TODDLERS

- **Goal:** Older infants will practice selecting and tasting different fruits and vegetables.
- **Materials:** Three or four fruits and vegetables of differing colors prepared appropriately, such as mashed bananas or creamed corn (yellow) cut up soft peaches or mangoes (orange), mashed peas or soft cooked cut up string beans (green), cut up strawberries or watermelon, cooked mashed beets (red), mashed blueberries (blue); plates with small divisions.
- **Activity plan:** The teacher's and child's hands should be washed before beginning. Conduct the activity when the child is calm and ready to explore. Place a small portion of each food in a divided plate for the child and prepare one plate for the teacher. Encourage the child to explore and taste the foods. Demonstrate tasting the foods. Name the

food and talk about the taste and color. Say words that convey pleasure and interest, such as "I like these orange mangoes" or "This red watermelon makes me happy because it tastes so good." Encourage tasting, but do not force. Describe what the child is doing. Say, "You are trying different fruits and vegetables. That is a good way to learn what each food tastes like."
- **How to adjust the activity:** If children are not able to feed themselves, feed the child or guide the child's hand to explore and taste the food. Follow the child's cues and gestures as you select the food to offer. Give the child time to hold the food in her mouth. Allow the child to spit the food out as desired. Reinforce all efforts to explore and taste.
- **Did you meet your goal?** Did the child explore choose and taste a variety of foods?

PRESCHOOLERS AND KINDERGARTNERS

- **Goal:** Children will explore different forms of tomatoes and foods made from tomatoes products, choose products to taste, and identify which ones they like.
- **Materials:** The book *I Will Never Not Ever Eat a Tomato* by Lauren Child; tomatoes of different types (grape, pear, or cherry, Roma, traditional) cut into small pieces (to avoid choking hazard); tomato-based foods (ketchup, salsa, tomato soup, spaghetti sauce); serving bowls; serving spoons; tasting spoons; napkins; large sheet of paper; marking pens.
- **Activity plan:** Set up a tomato taste-testing center. Place each type of tomato and tomato food in a serving bowl. Place the sheet of paper on the wall or table. Draw columns on the paper and label one column for each tomato product. Invite the children to taste each food by serving a small portion onto their plate. Talk about the foods, and ask the children to describe the flavors. Guide the

children to place an "X" in the column for each tomato and tomato food they like. At group time gather the children and read the book. Talk about the themes in the book and reinforce the notion of exploring new tastes and flavors. Talk about the tomato taste-test and review the children's "votes" for each of the tomato foods. Identify the foods that more children liked. Ask the children to tell what they liked about the tomato foods. Ask the children to name four foods made from tomatoes.
- **How to adjust the activity:** Engage all children by learning phrases such as, "I like it" in each child's home language. Link the concept of exploring and trying new foods to taste-tests of other food products, such as foods made from apples or vegetables of different colors.
- **Did you meet your goal?** Did children explore and taste different tomato products?

SCHOOL-AGE CHILDREN

- **Goal:** Children will be able to name the food groups, identify the variety of foods they eat and sort foods into the food groups, and describe what makes foods nutritious or less nutritious.

- **Materials:** The book *MyPlate and You* by Gillia Olsen; red, green, orange, purple, and blue construction paper; markers; scissors; glue; white paper plates; MyPlate poster, magazines with pictures of foods.

- **Activity plan:** Gather children together and introduce the concept of food groups and MyPlate. Read the book and review the MyPlate poster. Identify the different food groups and describe the qualities of foods that make them nutritious or less nutritious. Nutritious foods are rich in vitamins, minerals, and fiber and low in fat. Less nutritious foods are often high in added fat, salt, or sugar or can be low in vitamins and mineral and high in calories. Talk about the importance of eating a variety of foods for a healthful diet. Invite children to cut construction paper into shapes that replicate the MyPlate division of food groups (See www.choosemyplate.gov/downloads/mini_poster_English_final.pdf for sample poster), and glue them onto a paper plate. Guide children to write the name of each food group onto its section on their "MyPlate." Invite children to cut out pictures from magazines or draw pictures of foods they like, and glue them onto the correct food group section. Talk about the goal of showing the variety of foods the child eats from each food group. Ask children to show their "MyPlate" and tell others about the different foods they eat. If some food groups include only one (or few) foods, encourage the children to suggest ideas of other foods that the child could try to increase the variety of foods enjoyed in that food group.

- **How to adjust the activity:** Ensure that there are sufficient scissors, including scissors for children who are left-handed, and adapted scissors who are still developing their cutting skills. If needed offer glue sticks to help children control the gluing process. Provide a paper plate with precut and glued construction paper dividers, and offer precut pictures or clip-art of food to assist children

This child can identify and write the names of the five food groups.

with motor skill challenges—focusing the goal of lesson on sorting a variety of food pictures into food groups and gluing them on the plate. Give assistance to children who are learning English, by reminding them of the food groups, and demonstrating matching foods to food groups as needed.
- **Did you meet your goal?** Can children name the food groups, match foods to the appropriate group, and describe what makes a food nutritious or less nutritious?

MyEducationLab™

MyEducationLab™ is an online homework, tutorial, and assessment product designed to improve results by helping students quickly master concepts, and by providing educators with a robust set of tools for easily gauging and addressing the performance of individuals and classrooms.

MyEducationLab engages students with high-quality multimedia learning experiences that help them build critical teaching skills and prepare them for real-world practice. In practice exercises, students receive immediate feedback so they see mistakes right away, learn precisely which concepts are holding them back, and master concepts through targeted practice.

For educators, MyEducationLab provides highly visual data and performance analysis to help them quickly identify gaps in student learning and make a clear connection between coursework, concept mastery, and national teaching standards. In addition, because MyEducationLab comes from Pearson, it's developed by an experienced partner committed to providing content, resources, and expertise for the best digital learning experiences.

In *Preparing Teachers for a Changing World,* Linda Darling-Hammond and her colleagues point out that grounding teacher education in real classrooms—among real teachers and students and among actual examples of students' and teachers' work—is an important, and perhaps even an essential, part of training teachers for the complexities of teaching in today's classrooms.

In the MyEducationLab for this course educators will find the following features and resources.

Advanced Data and Performance Reporting Aligned to National Standards Advanced data and performance reporting helps educators quickly identify gaps in student learning and gauge and address individual and classroom performance. Educators easily see the connection between coursework, concept mastery, and national teaching standards with highly visual views of performance reports. Data and assessments align directly to national teaching standards, including NAEYC professional preparation standards and Head Start standards, and support reporting for state and accreditation requirements.

Study Plan Specific to Your Text MyEducationLab gives students the opportunity to test themselves on key concepts and skills, track their own progress through the course, and access personalized Study Plan activities.

The customized Study Plan is generated based on students' pretest results. Incorrect questions from the pretest indicate specific textbook learning outcomes the student is struggling with. The customized Study Plan suggests specific enriching activities for particular learning outcomes, helping students focus. Personalized Study Plan activities may include eBook reading assignments, and review, practice, and enrichment activities.

After students complete the enrichment activities, they take a posttest to see the concepts they've mastered or areas in which they still may need extra help.

MyEducationLab then reports the Study Plan results to the instructor. Based on these reports, the instructor can adapt course material to suit the needs of individual students or the entire class.

Assignments and Activities Designed to enhance students' understanding of concepts covered in class, these assignable exercises show concepts in action (through videos, cases, and/or student and teacher artifacts). They help students deepen content knowledge and synthesize and apply concepts and strategies they have read about in the book. (Correct answers for these assignments are available to the instructor only.)

Building Teaching Skills and Dispositions These unique learning units help students practice and strengthen skills that are essential to effective teaching. After examining the steps involved in a core teaching process, students are given an opportunity to practice applying this skill via videos, student and teacher artifacts, and/or case studies of authentic classrooms. Providing multiple opportunities to practice a single teaching concept, each activity encourages a deeper understanding and application of concepts, as well as the use of critical thinking skills. After practice, students take a quiz that is reported to the instructor gradebook and performance reporting.

Iris Center Resources The IRIS Center at Vanderbilt University (http://iris.peabody.vanderbilt.edu), funded by the U.S. Department of Education's Office of Special Education Programs (OSEP), develops training enhancement materials for preservice and practicing teachers. The Center works with experts from across the country to create challenge-based interactive modules, case study units, and podcasts that provide research-validated information about working with students in inclusive settings. In your MyEducationLab course we have integrated this content where appropriate.

Course Resources The Course Resources section of MyEducationLab is designed to help students put together an effective lesson plan, prepare for and begin a career, navigate the first year of teaching, and understand key educational standards, policies, and laws.

It includes the following:

- The **Lesson Plan Builder** is an effective and easy-to-use tool that students can use to create, update, and share quality lesson plans. The software also makes it easy to integrate state content standards into any lesson plan.
- The **Certification and Licensure** section is designed to help students pass licensure exams by giving them access to state test requirements, overviews of what tests cover, and sample test items.

The Certification and Licensure section includes the following:

- **State Certification Test Requirements:** Here, students can click on a state and be taken to a list of state certification tests.
- Students can click on the **Licensure Exams** they need to take to find:
  - Basic information about each test
  - Descriptions of what is covered on each test
  - Sample test questions with explanations of correct answers
- **National Evaluation Series™** by Pearson: Here, students can see the tests in the NES, learn what is covered on each exam, and access sample test items with descriptions and rationales of correct answers. Students can also purchase interactive online tutorials developed by Pearson Evaluation Systems and the Pearson Teacher Education and Development group.
- **ETS Online Praxis Tutorials:** Here students can purchase interactive online tutorials developed by ETS and by the Pearson Teacher Education and Development group. Tutorials are available for the Praxis I exams and for select Praxis II exams.
- The **Licensure and Standards** section provides access to current state and national standards.
- The **Preparing a Portfolio** section provides guidelines for creating a high-quality teaching portfolio.
- **Beginning Your Career** offers tips, advice, and other valuable information on:
  - *Resume Writing and Interviewing:* Includes expert advice on how to write impressive resumes and prepare for job interviews.
  - *Your First Year of Teaching:* Provides practical tips to set up a first classroom, manage student behavior, and more easily organize for instruction and assessment.
  - *Law and Public Policies:* Details specific directives and requirements needed to understand the No Child Left Behind Act and the Individuals with Disabilities Education Improvement Act of 2004.
- The **Multimedia Index** aggregates resources in MyEducationLab by asset type (for example, video or artifact) for easy location and retrieval.

Visit www.myeducationlab.com for a demonstration of this exciting new online teaching resource.

Support Materials for Instructors

The following resources are available for instructors to download on www.pearsonhighered.com. Instructors select Instructor Resources, enter the author or title of this book, select this particular edition of the book, and then click on the "Resources" tab to log in and download textbook supplements.

Instructor's Resource Manual (0-13-287462-8)

The Instructor's Resource Manual provides chapter-by-chapter tools to use in class. In-class activities, discussion questions, and additional resources will reinforce key concepts and applications and keep students engaged.

Test Bank (0-13-287463-6)

These multiple-choice, true-false, and essay questions tied to each chapter provide instructors with a variety of assessment items to evaluate student understanding of chapter content. An answer key is included.

PowerPoint™ Slides (0-13-301386-3)

The PowerPoint slides include key concept summarizations, diagrams, and other graphic aids to enhance learning. They are designed to help students understand, organize, and remember core concepts and theories.

MyEducationLab™ Correlation Guide (0-13-301289-1)

This guide connects chapter sections with appropriate assignable exercises on MyEducationLab.

TestGen™ (0-13-287464-4)

TestGen is a powerful test generator that instructors install on a computer and use in conjunction with the TestGen test bank file for the text. Assessments, including equations, graphs, and scientific notation, may be created for both print or testing online.

TestGen is available exclusively from Pearson Education publishers. Instructors install TestGen on a personal computer (Windows or Macintosh) and create tests for classroom testing and for other specialized delivery options, such as over a local area network or on the web.

The tests can be downloaded in the following formats:
TestGen Testbank file - PC
TestGen Testbank file - MAC
TestGen Testbank - Blackboard 9 TIF
TestGen Testbank - Blackboard CE/Vista (WebCT) TIF
Angel Test Bank (zip)
D2L Test Bank (zip)
Moodle Test Bank
Sakai Test Bank (zip)

Acknowledgments

We would like to thank the many reviewers whose valuable feedback and insights have helped shape and enhance our manuscript: Maria Abercrombie, Chattahoochee Technical College; Marilyn Cavazos, Laredo Community College; Jennifer M. Cave, J. S. Reynolds Community College; Ivy Cobbins, Olive Harvey College; Karen Demchak, Allan Hancock College; Joanne Greata, Lake Sumter Community College; LeAnna Hale, Northeast Lakeview College; Lori Killough, Lord Fairfax Community College; Janette C. Wetsel, University of Central Oklahoma.

We also extend special appreciation to the students, children, and families of the Child Development Laboratory at Oregon State University and to the teachers and staff for their expert advice: Jany Alcala, Shahrnaz Badiee, Amelia Cobarrubias, Dana Crawford, Laura Hickman, Sandi Hunt, Jacquie Keller, Kathleen McDonnell, Wendy McKenna, Jessica Nolen-Morse, Candi Scott, Alexis Tracy, and Cesiah Vega.

We would also like to thank the following individuals for their contribution to MyEducationLab for Nutrition, Health, and Safety for Young Children: Lorraine Breffini, Julie Bullard, Greg Castor, Jeanne Czernowski, Ariel Daeschel, Jennifer England, Connie Gassner, John Harris, Ryan Kral, Debra Pierce, Nikki Reiber, Sharon Reid, Gigi Sims, and Dawn Warneking.

We extend special appreciation to the staff of the Community Health Centers of Benton and Linn Counties for enthusiastically serving underprivileged children in our community and for always offering their time and energy to advocate for children and their families.

Finally, we thank our editors, Julie Peters and Bryce Bell, whose encouragement, expertise, and support made this book possible.

brief contents

contents

part three
Promoting Healthful
Practices   271

8   Creating a Climate of Health and Wellness   272

special features

SAFETY SEGMENTS

POLICY POINTS

part one
Promoting Wellness

1 YOUR ROLE IN CHILDREN'S WELLNESS

one
Your Role in Children's Wellness

learning outcomes

AFTER READING THIS CHAPTER, YOU SHOULD BE ABLE TO:

1. Define wellness and describe how nutrition, health, and safety contribute to children's health and well-being.

2. Identify and discuss factors that influence children's wellness.

3. Plan a developmentally appropriate curriculum to teach wellness concepts.

4. Describe ways to partner with families and community members to promote children's wellness.

It is lunchtime at Kaylee's family child care program. After completing her associate's degree in early childhood development Kaylee opened her family child care program as a way to work in her field while enjoying her two young children. The children wash their hands and gather in the kitchen for lunch. Kaylee serves Dominique his "burrito" in small tortilla pieces with spoonfuls of refried beans and grated cheese. As she serves the older children she provides Nancy a burrito without cheese to address her milk allergy. Then Kaylee sits down to eat with the children. "Beans!" says Dominique. Kaylee and the children cheer for Dominique's new word.

Across town, Hector is carrying out the recycling and trash from the preschool class. As he walks to the side of the building, Hector thinks about Zach, a child who attends the early childhood class in a wheelchair. Zach has a muscle-wasting disease that will continue to worsen. But it is Zach's cheerful spirit that sticks in Hector's mind. Today Zach asked if whales can live under the ice at the North Pole. Hector doesn't know the answer to this question, so he decides to stop at the library on his way home to find a book about whales that he and Zach can explore.

In another community, Sharina and Amelia walk through the children's play yard carrying clipboards, each with a safety checklist. They are helping with a review of the play areas as part of a tribal health initiative to increase children's participation in active play. They make notes about the hard-packed ground under the play structures, and watch as some children throw bark chips over the fence. They begin to develop ideas for recommendations to improve the play environment.

This is an exciting time to be an early childhood professional! Not only does research on growth and development continue to emphasize the importance of the early years in setting the stage for a child's future capacity to learn, but the important role that teachers play in guiding children's development is being given renewed attention and recognition. Teachers are second only to families in developing the context of healthful nutrition, health, and safety that surrounds the children they serve. Teachers participate in this process by providing care and education in a variety of settings: family child care, center-based child care, kindergarten, after-school care, evening child care, and more. Because care and education are intricately intertwined during the early years, we refer to all those who provide care and education to young children as *early childhood teachers*.

Early childhood teachers have much in common. In the opening scenario examples, each teacher demonstrates special enjoyment of very young children and knowledge of child development. Each participates willingly in the full spectrum of responsibilities associated with caring for children, including individualized planning, daily tasks, and classroom management. Each actively embraces the intriguing challenge of providing purposeful experiences to advance children's learning while keeping them safe. Central to these efforts are each child's nutrition, health, and safety. This chapter describes the links between nutrition, health, and safety; offers information about important influences on children's well-being; explores current issues in nutrition, health, and safety; and discusses the important ways that teachers contribute to the development and future potential of young children by teaching wellness concepts.

BUILDING THE FOUNDATIONS FOR CHILDREN'S WELLNESS

Families, early childhood educators, and community members alike envision communities in which wellness is a goal for all people. **Wellness** is a positive state of health and well-being often described by words such as *healthy*, *happy*, and *thriving*. Wellness emerges from healthful practices, such as consuming a nutritious diet, exercising, and sleeping well. Achieving wellness requires access to resources, such as sufficient foods, immunizations, health care, and safe environments. The early childhood years are an important period for building the foundations for wellness. Learning the healthful practices that lead to wellness during the early years is crucial to children's ability to attain optimal development and establish the capacity to learn.

wellness
a positive state of health and well-being

Understanding the Interrelationships Among Nutrition, Health, and Safety

The foundation of healthy growth, development, and wellness are established through the building blocks of nutrition, health, and safety. Each makes a specific contribution to the child's ability to grow and thrive:

- *Nutrition* encompasses the relationship between the nutrients that are eaten, digested, and absorbed and how they contribute to growth and health. A child's **diet**, or the foods and beverages consumed to nourish and support the body and its processes, must meet the child's nutritional demands during the active early years in order for the child to grow appropriately. Serving safe and healthful foods is a common responsibility of early childhood teachers.

- *Health* focuses on physical and mental well-being and the absence of disease. It is achieved through a variety of healthful practices that seek to prevent and minimize illness or disease. Teachers contribute to children's health in many ways, such as encouraging families to obtain childhood immunizations and by teaching children how and when to wash their hands.

- *Safety* centers on keeping children from harm. Safety is increased through practices that reduce the likelihood of unintentional injury or exposure to environmental toxins. Teachers promote safety by creating safe environments, implementing appropriate procedures, and supervising children's safe interactions.

diet
the foods and beverages consumed to nourish and support the body and its processes

MyEducationLab™
Visit the MyEducationLab for *Nutrition, Health, and Safety for Young Children* to enhance your understanding of chapter concepts with a personalized Study Plan. You'll also have the opportunity to hone your teaching skills through video-based Assignments and Activities, as well as Building Teaching Skills and Dispositions lessons.

The interrelationships among these factors become evident as the healthful benefits of one influences the positive outcomes in the others, and as gaps or challenges in one area negatively affect the others. For example:

- In order for foods to be healthful, they must be stored, prepared, and served in a safe and sanitary manner.

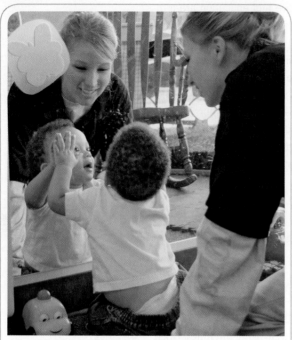

A healthy, thriving child is ready to learn.

- When children consume safe and healthful foods, their bodies are provided with the nutrients needed for optimal development, including learning. A healthful diet also improves the child's ability to fend off illness and to recover from illness and injury when they occur.

- Healthy children grow strong and capable of playing in coordinated and safe ways. Children who are healthy and well nourished are ready to be more attentive in the learning setting and are better able to learn about safety rules and ways to keep healthy through appropriate health practices including eating healthful foods.

Some aspects of the interrelationship are complex. For example, child nutrition impacts the risk for disease in adulthood (Faulk & Dolinoy, 2011; Simopoulos & Milner, 2010). From the moment of conception a child's diet is thought to trigger a predisposition, or tendency, to good or poor health by influencing how specific genes are expressed (*Nutrition and the Epigenome*, 2012). Pregnancy and prenatal development, early childhood, puberty, and old age are times when diet can influence gene function, creating a positive or negative impact on health (Dolinoy, Das, Weidman, & Jirtle, 2007). For example, a mother's diet and rate of weight gain during pregnancy, the birth weight of the infant, and the infant's diet may predict risk for chronic disease in adulthood. It is thought that these factors trigger *epigenetic changes* (changes that have an external rather than a genetic origin) in gene expression that increase the likelihood the child will develop obesity, diabetes, heart disease, or cancer as an adult (Dolinoy et al., 2007; Simopoulos & Milner, 2010; Wang et al., 2012).

Early childhood teachers generally recognize important aspects of the relationships among nutrition, health, and safety, and implement classroom practices to foster positive development. They know that healthy practices need to be learned during early development. Teachers also:

- Share an important responsibility with families to provide the best nutrition possible for infants and children, helping to meet the child's immediate nutritional needs while at the same time protecting the child from future chronic disease.

- Promote positive health practices, and may be instrumental in identifying gaps in a child's health services by providing information and referrals to families.

- Work to ensure children's safe experiences in the early childhood setting.

The impact teachers have on children's lives is truly momentous. Each of the teachers in the opening case scenario embraces this opportunity by addressing the goals of nutrition, health, and safety in the context of their early childhood programs. Kaylee adapts a nutritious lunch to fit the needs of children according to their age and special dietary needs. Hector looks beyond Zach's health concerns, responding to Zach's curiosity by bringing new books into the classroom for exploration and learning. Sharina and Amelia review the playground for safety concerns and consider the need for supports, such as balls, to encourage appropriate active play. Being prepared to put wellness approaches into action requires that teachers be aware of current trends and issues that impact nutrition, health, and safety services in early childhood programs.

Recognizing Trends That Affect Nutrition Services

Renewed attention is being given to the critical role good nutrition plays in preventing disease and promoting health during the early years of development. Current trends and guidelines that influence children's nutritional well-being focus on the prevention of overweight and obesity and redefining children's diets to support good health.

The Obesity Epidemic

The number of children in the United States who are **overweight** or **obese** has increased at an alarming rate since the 1970s. The obesity rate grew from 5% in the 1970s among 2- to 5-year-olds (6.5% for 6- to 11-year-olds), to as high as nearly 14% in 2004 (19% for 6- to 11-year-olds), and has maintained around 11% for children ages 2–5 (19% for 6- to 11-year-olds) through 2010 (US Department of Education 2011; Odgen & Carroll, 2010; Ogden, Carroll, Kit, & Flegal, 2012). The high incidence of obesity among young children has been labeled an *obesity epidemic.* The obesity epidemic is of particular concern because of the serious health consequences that are associated with being overweight or obese at such a young age.

The incidence of overweight and obesity varies from state to state, and even from county to county within states. The rates are highest among low-income preschool-aged children, where 1 in 7 is identified as obese. Obesity rates also vary by racial and ethnic group. In 2009, the highest incidence of obesity was identified among American Indian & Alaska Native children (nearly 21%), followed by Hispanic (18%), non Hispanic white (12%), non Hispanic Black (12%), and Asian/Pacific Island children (12%) (CDC, 2012).

A variety of factors are associated with the obesity epidemic. Trends in family eating behaviors include more snacking, eating meals away from home, and larger portion sizes (Let's Move, 2012). These eating habits are problematic because snack and convenience foods are high in sugar, fats, and calories. Lifestyle factors related to physical activity also contribute to the concern. There has been an increase in sedentary activities such as time spent sitting while watching television and playing computer games which leads to less energy expenditure (American Psychological Association, 2012; Council on Communications and Media, 2011). Early childhood teachers also report that children are being less active, as they spend more time at table activities and less time playing actively outdoors (Sorte & Daeschel, 2006). Taken together, higher calorie diets and lower energy expenditure have tipped the scales resulting in more children who are overweight and obese. This trend adds up to poor health outcomes for young children.

In spite of the recognition of the obesity problem, some people feel that it is too harsh to focus attention on this issue with young children. In addition, many states do not include expectations for encouraging healthy eating or physical activity in licensed child care centers (CDC, 2012). As a result, teachers must use their professional skills to develop classroom nutrition and activity plans that teach healthy habits and put children on course for healthy development and wellness (Figure 1-1).

overweight
an excess of body fat that may lead to obesity; measured by a body mass index score in the 85th to 95th percentile

obese
a medical condition related to the excess accumulation of body fat that may have an adverse effect on health, measured by a body mass index score that is higher than the 95th percentile

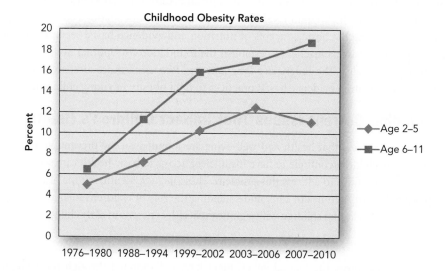

FIGURE 1-1
Trends in Childhood Obesity
Source: Based on: National Center for Health Statistics. Health, United States, 2011: With Special Feature on Socioeconomic Status and Health. Hyattsville, MD. 2012. http://www.cdc.gov/nchs/data/hus/hus11.pdf#075 and Ogden, C. & Carroll, M. (2010). Prevalence of Obesity Among Children and Adolescents: United States, Trends 1963–1965 through 2007–2008. NCHS Health E-Stat. Retrieved June 2012 from http://www.cdc.gov/nchs/data/hestat/obesity_child_07_08/obesity_child_07_08.htm#table1.

Redefining Children's Diets

Recognition is growing among health authorities about the need to address the specific nutritional needs of very young children and promote healthful eating habits during the early childhood years. A variety of resources have been developed to help teachers and families contribute to children's health now and in the future.

Dietary Guidelines for Americans, 2010   The USDA and Department of Health and Human Services promote good nutrition practices for the general population through the *Dietary Guidelines for Americans, 2010* (U.S. Department of Health and Human Services & U.S. Department of Agriculture, 2011). The recommendations address the specific dietary needs of young children and provide key evidence-based diet and physical activity recommendations to direct attention to healthful practices.

Dietary Reference Intakes (DRIs)   The Institute of Medicine of the National Academies of Medicine provides guidance through the Dietary Reference Intakes to address goals for Americans' nutrient intake and offers advice on recommended intake ranges for vitamins, minerals, and calorie-containing nutrients that are important for children's healthful development (Food and Nutrition Service of the USDA, 2011).

MyPlate   MyPlate is the new symbol developed by the USDA to help Americans visually understand what proportion of their meals should come from each of the five food groups (protein, fruits, vegetables, grains, and dairy) (U.S. Department of Agriculture, 2011). MyPlate, like the Food Pyramids before it, is designed to convey the key messages of the Dietary Guidelines for Americans in a simple, easy to understand format. This food guidance system helps families and teachers understand what to feed children to support and maintain health and to promote the development of good eating habits.

Feeding Children   Guidelines for creating a positive nutritional environment for young children also continue to be refined. Feeding guidelines consider how food is presented to young children, describe the roles and responsibilities of teachers and families, ensure food is clean and safe, and confirm the child's right to choose what and how much to eat from the foods that are offered. A variety of health, professional, and government organizations weigh in on guidelines for feeding young children. For example, Head Start, National Association for the Education of Young Children (NAEYC), and USDA child nutrition programs such as the Child and Adult Care Food Program (CACFP) and the National School Lunch Program (NSLP), offer specific recommendations about feeding young children. Understanding the basic concepts of nutrition and evidence-based recommendations for feeding young children helps teachers to establish the foundation for optimal nourishment, a vital component of good health. The *Progressive Programs and Practices* feature discusses a collaborative approach for implementing evidence based practices to fight obesity in young children.

Understanding Current Issues That Impact Children's Health

There is general awareness that health and well-being are founded on the prevention and treatment of illness, yet many children continue to have insufficient access to basic health care services. Current efforts are focusing on ways to address this problem. These include identifying the indicators of well-being, exploring disparities in health care, understanding the role of children's mental health, and addressing the needs of including children with significant health concerns in early childhood classrooms.

Indicators of Well-Being

Since 1997, agencies across the federal government have collaborated through the Federal Interagency Forum on Child and Family Statistics to compile a report on the well-being of children and families: *America's Children in Brief: Key National Indicators of Well-Being* (Federal Interagency Forum on Child and Family Statistics [FIFCFS], 2012). These indicators provide insight into the challenges that must be addressed in order to ensure that each child has the opportunity for healthful development. The indicators for health are discussed next.

PROGRESSIVE PROGRAMS & PRACTICES

Training Teachers in Healthy Practices

By Tracy Moran and Tom Browning, Erikson Institute and Illinois Action for Children

In November of 2009, the Chicago Board of Health passed a joint resolution recommending new standards for Chicago's center-based child care centers. The goal was to reduce the incidence of childhood obesity and improve overall health. Specifically, the new standards involved limiting children's screen viewing, serving reduced fat milk, and reducing sweetened beverage consumption while also increasing daily physical activity.

A need for training to address overall child wellness was recognized. Local organizations[1] collaborated to provide training seminars for early child care providers. Trainers facilitated brainstorming and discussions about managing challenges related to health and wellness. Topics discussed included motivating providers to be healthier role models, the accessibility and affordability of healthy foods, high crime activity in neighborhoods, and perceived apathy of parents. The seminars resulted in an engaging and comprehensive curriculum designed to positively influence providers' knowledge and behaviors regarding nutrition, physical activity, health, and overall well-being in children.

Participants made many suggestions for promoting physical activity, such as having relay races with plastic eggs on spoons, bowling using partially filled water bottles as bowling pins, taking a walk to learn about nature and the environment, or giving each child a magnifying glass and letting the children explore the outdoor environment.

In 9 months, five trainers conducted 87 trainings with over 1,000 participants. The trainings were held at facilities that were easily accessible via public transportation and located within low-income communities throughout the city and several suburbs. The sessions resulted in a high level of agreement to implement the

standards. In evaluation surveys, over half of the providers surveyed reported meeting the standards prior to the training, with the exception of the milk standard. Twenty-eight percent of providers rated the reduced fat milk standard as the most disagreeable and difficult to implement due to perceived cost increases or expected disagreement from children and/or parents.

According to child care provider Maria Salazar, "I started to implement the change from 2% to 1% milk in my day care. I was afraid when I started, but the children have assimilated and taken to the change easily. I have the children stand while putting together a puzzle so that they can be more active throughout the day. They are sleeping better because they are now tired. I also participate in the activities with the children and I love it."

[1]Including The Otho S.A. Sprague Memorial Institute, Erikson Institute, Illinois Action for Children, the Chicago Department of Public Health and the Consortium to Lower Obesity in Chicago Children

Health Insurance   Health insurance coverage is an important indicator of whether families can access preventive care and treatment for their child if the child is sick or injured. In 2010, 7.3 million children ages 0 to 17 (nearly 10% of the age group) had no form of health insurance at some time during the year (FIFCFS, 2012). Without health care insurance families are more likely to forgo preventive health care due to its high cost and may delay obtaining medical treatment until an illness is in an advanced stage.

Access to a Usual Medical Provider   Families who have an identified and accessible source for health care services (sometimes called a *medical home*) are more likely to obtain the preventive and treatment services needed to ensure good health. In the absence of a usual medical provider, families may obtain services at an emergency room or other sources where medical records and familiarity with the child's health history are not available as a resource. In 2010, 5% of children did not have a usual medical provider (FIFCFS, 2012).

Oral Health   Oral health care, including regular brushing and professional dental care, is an important indicator of general health. While yearly checkups

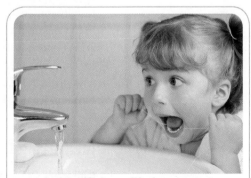

Oral health is a critical component of health and well-being.

are recommended for children over the age of 1, many children do not have access to a dentist. In 2010, 48% of children ages 2 to 4, and 15% of children ages 5 to 17 had not seen a dental care provider in the past year (FIFCFS, 2012). This is of particular concern as cavities are the most common illness in childhood. Untreated oral health care needs can negatively impact children's health and ability to learn and thrive.

Childhood Immunizations   Preventative health care includes obtaining vaccinations for preventable diseases. In 2009, 70% of children ages 19 to 35 months received the recommended immunizations. This leaves 30%, or more than 8 million children, without recommended protection from preventable disease (FIFCFS, 2011).

Disparities in Health Care

Disparities in health care refers to the situation in which some individuals or groups of children are disproportionately at risk for disease and do not have adequate access to health care. Children living in poverty, those who are a member of a minority group, and those being raised by very young parents have the highest risk for health disparities. Poor children typically have less access to health insurance and most often do not have a usual health care provider. They also tend to suffer more often from oral health care problems and are less likely to be immunized.

Children's Mental Health

Young children's mental health has emerged as an area of general health concern. Mental health is considered to be a key component of overall health and well-being—not simply the absence of disease or disorder. It encompasses social and emotional well-being and the ability to cope and function in social settings. The incidence of mental health problems among young children is considered to be at a level of crisis in the United States today. Six percent of parents reported that their child has serious difficulties with emotions behaviors (FIFCFS, 2012). The majority of mental health concerns among young children are never addressed. The lack of access to mental health services, the stigma associated by some to potential diagnosis of mental illness, and the limited number of mental health consultants with expertise in serving very young children are cited as reasons (World Health Organization, 2010). Unresolved mental health concerns introduce risk factors for disease and injury, and restrict children's opportunity to lead normal lives.

Inclusion of Children with Significant Health Concerns

Early childhood classrooms are serving more children with special health concerns than ever before. Asthma and food allergies are becoming more common. For example, more than 9.4% of children under the age of 17 have been diagnosed with asthma (7 million), and nearly 5% of children have significant food allergies (Bloom, Cohen, & Freeman, 2011). More young children with diabetes are being served, as well as many children who have unidentified health needs, such as iron deficiency, obesity, or other health conditions. These trends reinforce the importance of training and supporting teachers to effectively manage children's special health care needs. It is important for teachers to fully understand children's special health needs and know how to appropriately address them in the classroom setting. For this reason early childhood programs are being encouraged to make arrangements with health care consultants to serve as resources for planning appropriate services for children's special health care needs. In the opening scenario, Hector demonstrated his comfort with managing Zach's unique health condition. As he reflected on ways to encourage Zach's curiosity about whales, Hector showed he was able to look beyond Zach's health challenge and recognize the child within.

Identifying Emergent Issues in Child Safety

Children's wellness is directly related to safety in the home and early childhood setting. Emergent issues related to children's safety include managing security in children's settings, implementing regulatory guidelines, and planning for disasters.

Managing Security

In recent years more attention has been given to the need to address security in early childhood settings. Children's programs are located in a variety of spaces throughout communities, with some situated in neighborhoods that introduce particular safety challenges. Families are also bringing pressures to bear on programs to explain how security practices will ensure that no one will be able to take their child from the setting. Custody issues among divorced parents are often part of this concern. While most programs have some method for controlling entry to the early childhood spaces, not all choose to address safety risks by installing coded entry locks or other security devices. Deliberations about this issue continue as families and teachers explore their worries about whether security devices ultimately ensure children's safety, and whether they unduly detract from the comfortable family friendly environments that are the hallmark of early childhood settings.

Regulatory Guidelines

The regulations that govern licensed child care and education settings continue to evolve to address newly identified risks to children's safety. Standards for maximum group size, adult-to-child ratios, rules for supervision of children, and steps for screening staff and volunteers for criminal background are periodically reviewed to ensure they adequately address child safety needs.

Many state licensing agencies are making information available to the public about validated complaints submitted against licensed programs. This invites individuals to report unsafe conditions or problems at early childhood programs that may result in harm to children, and is one way in which regulatory guidelines encourage communities to participate in improving children's safety.

There is also growing scrutiny of the products used in construction of toys and materials for young children. Hazards in the form of toxic paints, small parts that might cause choking, or warnings about the dangers of small magnets if they are swallowed have resulted in toy recalls and new safety standards for products made for children. The *Safety Segment* provides an example. These trends require that teachers continually monitor news about safety practices, potential safety issues in children's settings, and safety recalls. The warnings issued by the U.S. Consumer Product Safety Commission are a good place to start.

Emergency Management Planning

Disasters and emergency events of the past decade have increased awareness of need for emergency management planning for programs serving young children. Emergencies from natural causes, such as severe weather, as well as human-made disasters, such as chemical spills or purposeful attacks, have unfortunately come to the forefront of safety management planning. Coupled with the increasing numbers of children in part- and full-day education settings, it is necessary to make plans to respond appropriately when children's safety is threatened. Greater attention is needed to ensure that teachers and children's programs link with their communities to address the full scope of emergency management planning.

SAFETY SEGMENT   Laws Governing Toy Safety Challenge Innovation

The Consumer Product Safety Improvement Act of 2008 prohibits the sale of toys that contain lead-based products or various chemicals present in some plastics. Manufacturers must prove compliance with the law, which requires testing by independent labs to prove that every accessible toy component meets the guidelines. The laws governing toy safety aim to remove dangerous products present in children's play things, but some say that this will limit toy availability to only mass-produced and marketed items that are often not the kinds of innovative or heirloom materials selected for use in educational settings.

Source: *Consumer Product Safety Act, as Amended H.R. 2715, Public Law 112–128 (August 12, 2011 Version)*, retrieved April 9, 2012, from www.cpsc.gov/businfo/cpsa.pdf.

Supporting Wellness Through National Initiatives

Early childhood teachers, families, health professionals, and policy makers are joining together to promote wellness for young children through policies and national initiatives. These efforts are based on public health approaches that seek to bring citizens together around disease prevention and intervention. Individuals are encouraged to learn and practice positive health behaviors, and the community is charged with taking responsibility for establishing policies and practices that promote individual and community wellness. The *Policy Point* reinforces the notion that healthy child development supports strong communities. Several national initiatives promote these interests. Each places a focus on engaging both individuals and the community in the effort. They are examples of ways citizens and our government work together to address the health and wellness needs of all people.

Healthy People 2020

Healthy People 2020 is the newest wave of an initiative established in 1979 to improve the health and well-being of people across the country. Organized around health objectives gleaned from evidence-based practice, the initiative's goals are to help people of all ages to:

- Attain high-quality, longer lives free of preventable disease, disability, injury, and premature death.
- Achieve health equity, eliminate disparities, and improve the health of all groups.
- Create social and physical environments that promote good health for all.
- Promote quality of life, healthy development, and healthy behaviors across all life stages. (U.S. Department of Health and Human Services [HHS], 2012).

To reach these goals, *Healthy People 2020* organizes 600 objectives within 42 topic areas and 28 health indicator focus areas. Topics that relate to the care and education of young children include those listed in Figure 1-2. The initiative invites the community, from individuals to organizations, to integrate the goals into their daily practices. In this way the project generates multiple approaches to improving the health of young children and their families.

The Healthy, Hunger Free Kids Act of 2010

This legislation reauthorizes federal child nutrition programs such as the National School Lunch and Breakfast programs and the Child and Adult Care Food Program. The bill directs the USDA to increase access to healthy foods for low-income children, address childhood obesity by requiring schools and participating children's programs to offer healthier food options, and expand support for breastfeeding through the WIC program. The reauthorization includes an increase in meal reimbursement rates, the first in over 30 years. This legislation represents a federal commitment to providing better access to healthy foods, educating children to make healthy food choices, and teaching children healthy habits that can improve their health for a lifetime (USDA, 2012).

FIGURE 1-2   *Healthy People 2020* Topics That Aim to Improve Children's Nutrition, Health, and Safety

- Access to Quality Health Services
- Clinical Preventative Services
- Environmental Quality
- Injury and Violence
- Maternal and Child Health
- Mental Health

- Nutrition, Physical Activity, and Obesity
- Oral Health
- Reproductive and Sexual Health
- Social Determinants of Health
- Substance Abuse
- Tobacco

Source: *Healthy People 2020* by the U.S. Department of Health and Human Services, retrieved March 21, 2012, from www.healthypeople.gov/2020/.

National Call to Action

The National Call to Action is a program of the U.S. Department of Health and Human Services that seeks to advance the health and well-being of Americans by promoting oral health and eliminating disease (U.S. Department of Health & Human Services (HHS), 2003). The initiative came about through a collaboration of public and private partners, who identified **oral health** as critical to general health and well-being. Oral health refers to all aspects of dental, gum, and mouth health. The U.S. Surgeon General describes unmet oral health needs as a "silent epidemic" affecting vulnerable people, including poor children and those of racial and ethnic minority groups (HHS, 2003). Partners at all levels of society are challenged to improve health and well-being by:

Oral health
all aspects of dental, gum, and mouth health

- Promoting oral health.
- Improving quality of life.
- Eliminating oral health disparities (HHS, 2003).

Action steps focus on encouraging partners to work for improved understanding of the importance of oral health and on overcoming barriers that limit access to oral health care.

Healthy Child Care America

Healthy Child Care America is an initiative coordinated by the American Academy of Pediatrics that aims to improve the early education, health, and safety of children in out-of-home child care. The effort calls on families, early childhood educators, and health professionals to work together to support children so they enter school healthy and ready to learn. The initiative's purposes include:

- Increasing access to preventive health services.
- Ensuring safe physical environments.
- Promoting a medical home for all children.

Healthy Child Care America serves as a resource for child care providers and families by offering health and safety materials. It works with programs funded through the HHS's Maternal and Child Health Bureau to provide technical assistance and improve children's access to health services (American Academy of Pediatrics, 2007). Central to the Healthy Child Care America initiative is the view that pediatricians and other community partners can work as a team to develop comprehensive services that aid children.

National Health and Safety Performance Standards for Child Care

The National Resource Center for Health and Safety in Child Care and Early Education is a program of the HHS's Maternal and Child Health Bureau. The center is charged with promoting health and safety in out-of-home child care settings nationwide. To achieve this goal, the center provides a resource for families and child care providers called *Caring for Our Children: National Health and Safety Performance Standards: Guidelines for Out-of-Home Child Care Programs*. A sample of the resources that promote health and safety in out-of-home care is listed in Figure 1-3. The performance standards guidelines were established in collaboration with the American Academy of Pediatrics and the American Public Health Association. They serve as standards for the direct provision of services to young children, guidelines for state licensing of early childhood programs, and as a resource for policy development.

National Children's Study

The National Children's Study is an investigation into the effects of environmental influences on the health and development of young children. Several federal agencies are collaborating in the project, including the National Institutes of Health and the U.S. Environmental Protection Agency. The project will follow 100,000 children from across the country from birth to age 21. The goals of the study are to:

- Improve the health and well-being of children.
- Increase understanding of the role that various factors have on health and disease (National Institute of Child Health and Human Development, & National Institutes of Health (NIH), 2012).

> **FIGURE 1-3   Health and Safety Resources Provided by the National Resource Center for Health and Safety in Child Care and Early Education**
>
> - Guides for families, including selecting child care and indicators of quality early childhood programs
> - Guidance publications, such as *Caring for Our Children: National Health and Safety Performance Standards: Guidelines for Out-of-Home Child Care Programs*, that provide standards for typical and special care situations, such as caring for children with special developmental needs, transporting children in child care, and administering medications
> - Web-based resources such as *Healthy Kids Healthy* Care
> - Links to child care information
> - Responses to frequently asked questions
> - State licensing information

Sources: American Academy of Pediatrics, American Public Health Association, National Resource Center for Health and Safety in Child Care and Early Education. 2011. *Caring for our children: National health and safety performance standards; Guidelines for early care and education programs* (3rd ed.). Elk Grove Village, IL: American Academy of Pediatrics; Washington, DC: American Public Health Association. Also available at nrckids.org.

The National Children's Study is designed to reveal the effects of natural and human-made environmental, biological, genetic, and psychosocial factors on different phases of children's growth and development, and to increase understanding of these factors on health and disease. Outcomes from the study will influence the development of health practices and policies that will guide individuals, program practices, and policy development to improve the health and well-being of young children.

Elementary and Secondary Education Act (ESEA)

The ESEA was approved by Congress in 1965 as part of President Lyndon Johnson's *War on Poverty*. Its purpose was to guide the appropriation of money for education and to address the achievement gaps that existed between children raised in poverty and those in households with more abundance. The notion is that the gap can be reduced through equal access to education, high standards, and accountability. The ESEA has been reauthorized every 5 years, most recently in 2001 under the name of the *No Child Left Behind Act*. The ESEA is currently in the process of reauthorization under the name *Blueprint for Reform*. The *Blueprint* continues work toward closing the achievement gap by encouraging state and local innovation through flexibility in the design of educational programming and collaboration with nonprofit partners. The *Blueprint* builds on these key priorities:

- College- and career-ready students
- Great teachers and leaders in every school
- Equity and opportunity for all students
- Raise the bar and reward excellence
- Promote innovation and continuous improvement (U.S. Department of Education, 2010).

The *Blueprint for Reform* encompasses a "cradle through college to career continuum" to develop successful, safe, and healthy students (U.S. Department of Education, 2010, page 31). The initiative reinforces the need for collaboration among families, teachers, and the community. It identifies good teachers as crucial to children's success.

Common Core State Standards Initiative

Launched in 2010, the Common Core Initiative responds to the call of the *Blueprint for Reform* through development of a consistent framework for preparing children and youth in grades K–12 for college and the workforce. The initiative is coordinated by the National Governors Association Center for Best Practices (NGA Center) and the Council of Chief State School Officers (CCSSO). Drawing on the input of teachers and education experts, a set of common standards outline age-related goals for English Language Arts and Literacy, History, Social Studies, Science, Technical Subjects, and Mathematics. Currently 45 states have adopted the Common Core State Standards (NGA Center & CCSSO, 2010). Early childhood education is a partner in this initiative. An effort called the *Connection Project* is working to identify links between the Head Start Child Development and Early Learning Framework and the Common Core State Standards for kindergarten. The goal is to ensure that children enter kindergarten with the skills they need to be successful in school.

Partnership for 21st-Century Skills

The Partnership for 21st-Century Skills is another participant in the effort to improve positive outcomes for children and youth. It was formed in 2002 through the efforts of the U.S. Department of Education, business organizations, and interested individuals. Its mission is to ensure that students graduating from high school in the United States are capable of succeeding in rigorous higher education coursework and prepared to compete in the 21st-century global workforce. The elements identified for a 21st-century education include (The Partnership for 21st-Century Skills, 2011):

- *Core subjects knowledge:* such as reading, mathematics, science, civics, and government.
- *21st-century content:* including civic literacy; global, health, and wellness awareness.
- *Learning and thinking skills:* such as critical thinking, problem solving, and collaboration.
- *Information and communications technology:* the ability to use and develop technology.
- *Life skills:* including leadership, ethics, responsibility, and social responsibility.

Although early childhood education is not a formal partner in this effort, many of the elements align well with the early childhood developmental approach that builds children's capacities to become self-directed learners capable of contributing to their own well-being.

What if. . .
one of your relatives asked you about your plans to be a prekindergarten teacher? How would you describe your responsibilities as a teacher to implement appropriate practices and teach about nutrition, health, and safety?

● FACTORS THAT INFLUENCE CHILDREN'S WELLNESS

Many factors affect children's well-being and ability to learn. Some add interest and richness to children's experiences while others may put children at risk for poor development. Some influences have a general or overarching impact while others encompass trends that are causing changes in how nutrition, health, and safety are addressed in early childhood classrooms. These influences can be complex, and are important for teachers to consider. Teachers have the capacity to enhance the positive potential of desirable influences. They also have the opportunity to mediate or reduce the damaging effects of negative influences, helping children gain the capacity for success that they may not otherwise achieve.

Considering the Contexts in Which Children Grow and Develop

Children do not grow and develop in isolation, nor are teachers the only people concerned about children's healthy growth and development. Children's wellness is heavily influenced by the *contexts*, or settings, in which they live. These contexts include the environment and circumstances that surround the child and affect the child's experiences. Teachers come to understand that family conditions—poverty, the health and education of the child's family, cultural beliefs, and many other factors—interact and contribute to the child's development in positive and negative ways. Urie Bronfenbrenner's (1979) ecological systems theory seeks to explain how the contexts that surround children, and the systems of interaction among the people in those settings, impact children's health and well-being. This theory considers the child as developing within a nested series of surrounding contexts and systems, each connecting and interacting with the others.

One important setting in which children grow and develop is the neighborhood. As you watch this **video**, notice the differences in the two children's understanding of their neighborhoods and the safety considerations in each.

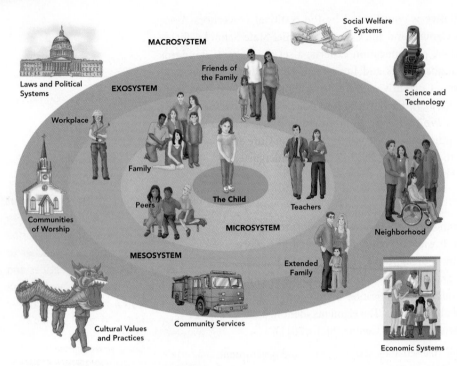

FIGURE 1-4
Bronfenbrenner's Ecological Systems Theory Describes the Contexts That Influence Child Development

Figure 1-4 depicts the child encircled by four types of contexts and systems.

- *Microsystem:* This system includes the environments that immediately surround the child, such as the home, the early childhood setting, and school. Safe and nurturing aspects of this environment positively affect children's health and well-being, whereas hunger or dangers in the environment may interrupt healthy development.

- *Mesosystem:* This system encompasses the connections and interactions that take place in the microsystem. Nurturing parenting and positive relationships with the teacher are examples of positive influences on children's development, whereas domestic violence or disagreements among parents and teachers can negatively affect children's well-being.

- *Exosystem:* This system involves the people and places that provide indirect influences on the child's development, such as the extended family or neighborhood. Children's wellness is enhanced through the supports of extended family members and safe neighborhoods, but is negatively affected by disagreements among the extended family or unsafe neighborhoods.

- *Macrosystem:* This system addresses the influences of the larger social, cultural, political, and economic contexts that provide support for child development or that challenge children's ability to grow and thrive. For example, children's wellness is supported when the society provides access to health care and high-quality early childhood education. Conversely, children's well-being may be threatened in times of economic depression due to reduction in resources such as accessible health care (Bronfenbrenner, 1979).

Early childhood teachers have responsibilities that intersect with all levels of these contextual systems. For example, teachers have direct responsibility for creating and managing the early childhood setting (microsystem). They establish important connections between the early childhood setting and the child's home (mesosystem) by building relationships where families and teachers share knowledge and ideas about how to best promote the child's development.

Finally, teachers extend their professional skills and responsibilities to the larger systems that affect children (the exosystem and macrosystem) by advocating for the needs of children at school board meetings or community planning commissions, and championing the development of policies and local, state, and national initiatives that aim to improve outcomes for young children.

Understanding the Overarching Influences on Children's Wellness

Several factors have a widespread impact on children's wellness, further demonstrating the interconnections of nutrition, health, and safety with children's well-being. These include multicultural factors, diverse family structures, poverty, living conditions, environmental issues, and food insecurity. All are examples of dynamics that influence children's development across the spectrum of nutrition, health, and safety services.

Multicultural Classrooms

Early childhood class groups continue to become more diverse and multicultural. The number of children of Hispanic heritage is growing fastest in nearly all parts of the country. It is anticipated that by 2050, 39% of children will be of Hispanic heritage, up from 24% today (Federal Interagency Forum on Child and Family Statistics [FIFCFS], 2012). In addition, 22% of children nationwide speak a home language other than English (FIFCFS, 2012). These numbers vary depending on the region, with rates as high as 34% of children in the West, and as low as 12% in the Midwest. This information is important because many children who have difficulty communicating in English face challenges in learning and being successful in their future work settings. Figure 1-5 provides a visual depiction of the diverse racial composition of children under age 18 in the United States today.

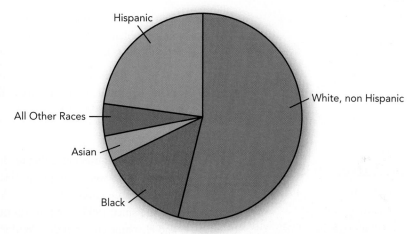

FIGURE 1-5

Racial and Ethnic Composition Among Children Under Age 18 in the United States (2010)

Source: Based on: *America's Children in Brief: Key National Indicators of Well-Being, 2011*, Demographic Background, by the Federal Interagency Forum on Child and Family Statistics, 2010, retrieved from www.childstats.gov/americas children/demo.asp.

Greater cultural and ethnic diversity also brings more variety in family child-rearing practices, many of which interface with the early childhood classroom and influence how children learn. Examples include diet, food choices, dress, hygiene, comfort with health practices, levels of physical activity, expectations for boys and girls, and other aspects such as how sleeping arrangements are managed at home and how napping is arranged in the classroom. Teachers need to be aware that perspectives on children's nutrition, health, and safety vary among the families they serve.

Teachers themselves have beliefs and expectations that are rooted in their own cultural or ethnic perspectives which may impact how and what they teach in the classroom. To best take advantage of multicultural richness, and to ensure that all children have the supports they need to succeed in school, teachers must be competent in embracing cultural diversity and implementing strategies that support teaching all children. Finding ways to invite conversation about diverse approaches and practices, and knowing how to negotiate differing perspectives, are important opportunities for new discoveries that will improve teacher skills and enhance children's learning opportunities.

Diverse Family Structures

Family structures continue to evolve and change, becoming increasingly complex. These changes are important for teachers to consider as notions of the traditional family no longer reflect the home lives of young children today. Family arrangements include various combinations of adults caring for children, such as children raised by teenage mothers, single parents, grandparents, or same-sex parents. Some children join families through adoption or live temporarily in foster care placements. Others divide their time between the homes of their divorced parents or are members of blended families created through remarriage. Families are the most important teachers of young children, yet some family structures may put children at risk for poor developmental outcomes. Examples include (FIFCFS, 2012):

- Children born to unmarried mothers (nearly 41% of all births in 2010) are at risk for the negative impacts of low birth weight, infant mortality, and poverty.
- Children raised in a home with two married parents (65% in 2011) benefit from the financial security and care of two parents, but the numbers of children raised in this family structure continues to decrease.
- Children who join families through adoption (2.5% of children nationwide) benefit from the positive opportunity to be raised in a family, but may face challenges with loss, grief, and identity development, and issues such as fetal exposure to drugs or alcohol.
- Children in families where parental unemployment is a problem face risks from increased family financial stress and potentially lack of medical care and other supports. In 2010 only 71% of children lived in homes where at least one parent was employed year around.

- Children with a parent who is imprisoned (nearly 1.7 million in 2007) experience a disrupted home life and problems associated with a long period of separation from a parent (Allard & Greene, 2011; Glaze & Maruschak, 2010).

Teachers are in a good position to get to know each family as a unique group with challenges that may make it difficult to provide for the child's well-being. With this information teachers plan school experiences that may assist children toward more positive outcomes.

Poverty

Poverty is a significant threat to children's well-being. In 2010, 22% of children under the age of 18 were living in poverty (FIFCFS, 2012). Nearly 10% of children lived in homes whose family income was less than half of the national poverty level, the highest rate since 1994. The poverty numbers are nearly three times higher among Black and Hispanic children than White non-Hispanic children. Overall, many children are encountering poverty's challenges.

The impacts of poverty are particularly disturbing because poverty is a contributor to nearly every negative influence on children's wellness. Children raised in poverty are more likely to experience poor health outcomes. Families living in poverty must make difficult choices, such as paying rent or purchasing food. Low-cost housing is often substandard, and is more likely to have environmental hazards, such as lead-based paint. Children may be malnourished because families are compelled to select low-cost foods rather than make nutritious purchases. Families may not be able to afford preventative or necessary health care. As a result, children living in poverty are more likely to experience cognitive, behavioral, and social-emotional problems that get in the way of learning. This can lead to lower educational attainment and increased unemployment across their lifetime.

A Matter of ETHICS

Imagine that you want to have the children in your class make "community soup" an activity where each child is usually asked to bring in a food to contribute to the soup. Making a food contribution might be difficult for some of the low-income families in your class. How might you arrange this activity in a way that respects the dignity and worth of each child and family?

Housing and Homelessness

Families with young children often struggle to find affordable and safe housing. Nearly 45% of households with children in the United States face problems such as inadequate or crowded housing that costs more than 30% of the family's household income (Federal Interagency Forum on Child and Family Statistics [FIFCFS], 2012). Inadequate housing suggests all manner of deficiencies, including those that put children at risk, such as older homes that contain dangerous lead-based products or housing that is located in unsafe neighborhoods.

Many low-income families face severe housing problems because their housing costs more than 50% of the family's monthly income (FIFCFS, 2012). When housing costs require such a large portion of the family income, the family struggles to meet other basic needs including food and health care. The frequency of moves among these families is especially high, as families who have trouble making rent payments often look for opportunities to save money by finding less expensive housing.

Severe housing problems make family life very stressful. They increase family mobility, cause irregular school attendance which interrupts learning and social connections, and may lead to homelessness. In 2009, 156,000 children were homeless and 346,000 children used homeless shelters or transitional housing on one January test (FIFCFS, 2011). Early childhood teachers must build relationships quickly and work purposefully to reinforce learning opportunities for children who experience such disruptions.

Environmental Considerations

Environmental impacts on children's health and wellness are being more closely considered as information about the potential for negative effects are identified. Due to their small size, high rate of growth, and close interaction with their surroundings, young children are particularly at risk from the effects of environmental toxins. Exposure to lead in the environment is associated with learning and behavior problems, and contaminants in water can lead to health issues including gastrointestinal illnesses. In urban settings children may be at risk from industrial and vehicle contaminants while in rural settings children may be at risk from agricultural sprays.

Air quality is also being closely studied. Air pollutants, including ozone, solid particulates and liquid droplets, sulfur dioxide, and nitrogen dioxide, are known to increase asthma and respiratory problems (FIFCFS, 2012). High levels of carbon monoxide in the air reduce the blood's ability to transport oxygen, which can lead to health problems. In 2010, 67% of children lived in counties where air pollution was above allowable levels. In addition, secondhand tobacco smoke can lead to increased respiratory problems, pneumonia, asthma, and sudden infant death syndrome (SIDS) (FIFCFS, 2012). Because of the overall negative impacts, the U.S. Surgeon General has identified that there is no risk-free exposure to secondhand smoke.

Food Insecurity

The U.S. Department of Agriculture (USDA) reports that more than 23% of children ages 0 to 17 years live in households that are classified as experiencing *food insecurity* (FIFCFS, 2012). Food insecurity refers to not having access to enough food at all times to maintain an active healthy life. Families who are food insecure often make changes in their diets reducing the variety, quality, and desirability of the foods they obtain (Nord, Coleman-Jensen, Andrews, & Carlson, 2010). Many rely on community emergency food sources such as food banks or social service agencies.

In 2010, food insecurity was reported among 44% of families with incomes below the federal poverty level (FIFCFS, 2012). Food insecurity puts children at risk for poor diets and related health concerns.

Hunger may get in the way of children being able to focus and learn. For this reason teachers should look for signs that children are hungry, and assist families to access community resources and the school's lunch program. Many early childhood programs participate in the Child and Adult Care Food Program which supports the children's program to provide healthy foods for children from low-income families.

Advocating for Children's Wellness

Nutrition, health, and safety are crucial to children's wellness, their ability to learn, and ultimately develop to their full potential. Teachers, therefore, must be advocates for addressing negative influences on children's development, and promoters for supporting children's wellness. One way teachers begin is by making a commitment to professionalism. This commitment goes beyond the concept of "do no harm" in that it encourages teachers to purposefully take action to improve children's health and well-being. It means being intentional about the choices made when planning environments and implementing activities for children. It also means using evidence-based practices rather than making choices based on myths or "the way it's always been done."

Making a commitment to professionalism encompasses the expectation that teachers develop the *dispositions* (the values, beliefs, and attitudes) that promote positive outcomes in the children they teach. Dispositions that are of particular importance in teaching include the values of fairness and equity and the belief that all children can learn. Teachers demonstrate these values every day through their words and interactions with children and families.

The decisions and actions of teachers are guided by the NAEYC *Code of Ethical Conduct and Statement of Commitment* (2011). The Code articulates the dispositions, values, beliefs, and attitudes held by professional teachers of young children. It guides teachers to recognize and defend early childhood as a valuable and vulnerable stage of life, while understanding that children develop within the embrace of their families, and respecting the dignity and worth of each individual child (NAEYC, 2011).

The *Code* is also a beginning point for becoming an advocate for children and families. Being an advocate means supporting actions that promote the well-being of children, such as backing

Hunger may get in the way of children being able to focus and learn.

POLICY POINT Advocating for Healthy Child Development Supports Strong Communities

Policies that support healthful child development are founded on scientific research and emerge from the belief that all children can learn. The publications and resources of the Center on the Developing Child at Harvard University help to promote this understanding by reinforcing the notion that healthy growth and development are the foundation for strong communities and economic prosperity, and that science can be used to enhance child well-being.

The mission statement of the Center on the Developing Child presents the notion that equalizing opportunities for all children is essential to creating the responsible and productive citizens on which society depends. Early childhood teachers are important advocates for the development of policies designed to address the issues that put children at risk for failure in school in an effort to "close the gap between what we know and what we do to support positive life outcomes for children" (Center on the Developing Child).

Source: The President and Fellows of Harvard College. 2012. The Center on the Developing Child. Retrieved online April 2012 at: http://developingchild.harvard.edu/.

initiatives to provide more healthful meals in schools, and supporting efforts to provide safe parks and outdoor areas where children can play and families can socialize. Being an advocate is an endeavor that develops over the years. This commitment to professionalism unfolds as early childhood practitioners learn to take on leadership roles in their program and community and work alongside professionals in nutrition, health, and safety to improve children's well-being. The *Policy Point* describes the importance of advocating for healthy child development.

Within the classroom teachers express their commitment to professionalism by recognizing the importance of wellness in the learning process. They put this commitment into action by learning all they can about nutrition, health, and safety, and by putting this knowledge into practice by teaching children the behaviors and practices that lead to wellness.

TEACHING CHILDREN WELLNESS CONCEPTS

While the trends that affect children's nutrition, health, and safety are studied and addressed at national and local levels, important activities that contribute to children's wellness take place right in the early childhood classroom. Teaching children wellness concepts is exceptionally rewarding because early childhood is a time when children develop the capacity to use their learning "tools." Their innate curiosity and motivation to explore make young children capable of learning healthful behaviors and being participants in promoting their own wellness, setting them on a healthy course for the future. To help children reach these desired outcomes, teachers must understand how children learn, know how to use purposeful teaching approaches, and be ready with a "tool-box" of ideas to implement a wellness-focused curriculum.

Understanding How Children Learn

During the *early childhood years*, birth through age 8, many physical and emotional changes occur. Children gain strength, coordination, and control over movement. Complex skills such as walking and speech emerge, and the intricacies of social and emotional development play out as children develop trust and attachment to caregivers. Language blossoms and cognitive problem-solving skills are tested and refined. This wealth of growth and maturation is founded on healthy brain development, encouraged through teaching that helps children construct knowledge, and reinforced by knowledge of the commonly recognized domains of development.

Early Brain Development

At birth the brain is a relatively immature organ. Even so, the newborn child has nearly 100 billion *neurons*, or brain cells, that are ready to assist with growth and development. Children's ability to learn and ultimately to function in society depends on the success of the brain to develop a complex system of neural connections. This brain growth and development is stimulated by experiences and interactions.

As children experience new information, the neurons reach out to one another, interacting and building a network of highly sophisticated connections that link the various parts of the brain. During the infant and toddler years, the brain focuses on organizing the information provided by the sensory systems of sight, touch, taste, smell, and hearing. From age 3 onward, brain development is highly directed toward growing and refining the neural connections. These links influence all aspects of children's functioning and ability to learn, such as recognizing the sounds that form language, coordinating movement, recognizing shapes and letters, and developing the ability to manipulate math functions, control behavior, and manage social interactions (Hawley, 2000; Massachusetts Institute of Technology, 2006; National Institute of Mental Health, 2011).

An important part of the process of evolving brain cell connections is a process called brain *plasticity*. Plasticity refers to the brain's ability to be flexible and change when new information modifies existing neural connections and expands or replaces previous knowledge. For example, young children may first learn to call all four-sided figures a square. With experience they learn that two long sides help to identify the four-sided shape called a rectangle. Later, as they learn to focus on the angled corners of the four-sided figure they learn to distinguish a trapezoid or rhombus. The original understanding of what makes a square remains while the new experiences stimulate and expand new neural connections and new understandings. Brain plasticity provides for these modifications and is an important aspect of the child's ability to learn.

FIGURE 1-6
Exploration and Experience Build the Architecture of the Brain

Children who are provided rich opportunities for learning benefit by developing highly complex webs of neural connections that support future learning. Brain cell connections that are used again and again establish the channels for managing information and making sense of experiences and learning. Figure 1-6 depicts how the brain's complex network of connections evolves through interaction and experience. Practicing skills is a primary way of reinforcing these brain cell connections. In this way experience and learning build the "architecture" of the child's brain (Center on the Developing Child, 2007).

Children who are deprived of learning opportunities, or who experience chronic stress or toxic environments, show diminished neural development in areas of their brains, especially those that control learning and behavior (National Scientific Council on the Developing Child, 2010). A lack of interactions or negative experiences result in closing off or "pruning away" brain cell connections (Hawley, 2000). The consequence is a "use it or lose it" process. Connections that are not used are pruned away to allow the brain to be more efficient, but lack of stimulation can also result in less than optional brain development. In sum, the experiences children have, or don't have, during the formative early childhood years, establish their capacity to learn and set the course for future development.

Constructing Knowledge

Learning occurs when children act on things and interact with people. It unfolds as children follow their interests, select the toys and materials that intrigue them, and practice and repeat skills that are exciting to them. Providing freedom to explore allows children to test new ideas, repeat routines to reinforce existing knowledge, take in information at their own pace, and come to understand new ways of using information. This interactive process is called *play*. Play is the context within which children construct the knowledge base that supports their understanding of the world (Piaget, 1929).

Social interactions and language are important parts of the learning process. The ideas that children share as they talk about what they are doing and give each other ideas and directions keep them engaged and pique their interest in the learning opportunity. Teachers and families also use social interactions and language to help children focus on the significant aspects of an activity, and make meaning from what they have experienced. For example, teachers offer new vocabulary or ask questions that focus children's attention on what they are doing. With a 2-year-old the teacher might say, "See how the soap bubbles wash off your hands? That is the way we wash germs away too!" or with a 7-year-old, a teacher might say, "You were running fast at recess. Is your heart pumping quickly? Can you feel how you are breathing hard? Why do you think your body reacts this way after running?" The teacher's involvement helps the child focus on significant aspects of the learning opportunity. The questions provoke the child to wonder, predict, and offer ideas. Important social aspects of culture are also communicated and practiced through social interaction and language (Vygotsky, 1962).

Teachers guide the learning process by structuring experiences that are familiar and of interest to the child and that offer challenges just beyond the child's current level of understanding and ability. This process is called *scaffolding*. Just as scaffold equipment provides a framework of support during a construction project, scaffolding in teaching refers to providing the series of supports that allow a child to move into new levels of understanding and higher levels of skill. Figure 1-7 depicts the steps involved in scaffolding using the example of a biscuit making activity.

Exploring in the Developmental Domains

Learning in young children, infants through preschool age, is commonly described as occurring through maturation in four developmental areas or *domains*. These include physical, cognitive, language, and social-emotional development. Each domain fosters growth through the contributions of particular learning systems.

Physical Development   Physical development includes overall physical health as well as growth and development of the muscle systems. This includes the large muscles of the arms, legs, and whole body used to accomplish movement, such as running, as well as the small muscles of the hands, fingers, wrist, toes, and eyes used to accomplish manipulation tasks like writing and reading. Learning in the physical domain focuses on:

- Developing muscle strength, control, and stamina to accomplish safe and purposeful movement and manipulation, such as a baby holding its head up, or a child pouring a cup of milk.
- Integrating movement to accomplish a new skill, such as a toddler learning to stand, a preschooler learning to ride a tricycle, or a school-age child learning to dribble a basketball.
- Coordinating movement to accomplish complex tasks, such as focusing the eyes and using hand movements to string a bead, put on clothes, or toss a ball through a hoop.

Cognitive Development   Cognitive development involves learning to make meaning from the world. It includes the maturation of the sensory systems that form the basis of perception and the skills to use this information to learn. Cognitive development includes:

- Developing memory, such as learning to wash hands before sitting down for a snack.
- Using problem-solving skills, such as learning to match shapes.
- Thinking logically, such as knowing that a cat is small and an elephant is big.
- Using symbols, such as understanding gestures, reading signs, drawing, and writing.

Language Development   This domain involves understanding and using language and other forms of communication to gather and exchange information and ideas. It includes:

- Listening and speaking.
- Using language to express needs and to make social connections, such as asking for help with putting on shoes or asking for a turn at the swing.
- Building the foundations for literacy skills such as reading and writing.

Social-Emotional Development   Social-emotional development involves building the skills needed to interact, work, and play successfully with others. This area encompasses how children learn about the world and their place in it. Social-emotional development means:

- Learning to build trusting and caring relationships with others.
- Identifying and expressing feelings in appropriate ways: "I miss my mom, but I know she'll come back after work."

STEP	SCAFFOLDING APPROACH	WHAT A TEACHER MIGHT DO AND SAY	
7	**Introduce a new activity.** Building on the previous task, introduce a slightly more challenging activity. Repeat the scaffolding steps.	Offer a next-step baking activity. Say for example, "It looked like you enjoyed baking biscuits today. Tomorrow the baking center will have a recipe for tortillas. You can let me know if you need any help getting started."	
6	**Observe the children continuing the activity.** Watch how each child proceeds with the task without support.	Continue to be physically near. Watch to ensure each child is proceeding successfully.	
5	**Reduce participation gradually.** Observe how the children proceed with less help.	Watch and respond if a child has questions or asks for help. "Yes, it is normal for the dough to be sticky. Try sprinkling on a spoonful of flour and using the flat part of your hands and fingers to mix at this point. Does that help with cutting the biscuits? Let me know when your pan of biscuits is ready to bake."	
4	**Let children lead—but stay engaged.** Follow each child's interest and efforts. Offer explanations and supportive suggestions as needed.	Offer encouragement: "I see you are measuring. You are right, Step Two says one tablespoon of baking powder." "Do you see the straight area at the top of the container? How can you use it to make sure to measure just one tablespoon of baking powder? That's it!	
3	**Describe the task at hand.** Verbalize what the children are doing. Identify the materials and how they can be used. Ask questions about the task.	Point to the step-by-step recipe cards. Say, "Here are the steps. First get all the things you need: bowl, measuring spoons, stirring spoon, and biscuit cutter. Now measure the flour into your bowl. Yes, one cup of flour."	
2	**Become involved.** Ask the children what they are doing. Request permission to watch and help.	Ask, "Are you getting ready to bake biscuits? Can I help you get started?"	
1	**Observe children at work.** Become aware of what each child is working on. Use your knowledge of the child's strengths, interests, and needs.	Watch the children who are working at the biscuit-making activity. Notice the children who are moving materials around but do not know how to begin.	

FIGURE 1-7

Steps in Scaffolding Children's Learning

Source: Bodrova, E., & Leong, D. J. (2006). *Tools of the mind: The Vygotskian approach to early childhood education* (2nd ed.). Upper Saddle River, NJ: Prentice Hall.

- Developing the ability to make choices, take responsibility for own actions, and be capable of solving problems in social settings: "OK, you be the red guy and I'll be the blue guy. Next time I get red."

Learning across the developmental domains is highly interrelated. That is, successful learning in one domain affects, and is also dependent on, successful learning in the other domains (National Association for the Education of Young Children [NAEYC] & National Association of Early Childhood Specialists in State Departments of Education [NAECS/SDE], 2002; National Scientific Council on the Developing Child, 2007). For example, fine motor skills help children manipulate small blocks. As children build they are able to explore concepts of size comparison and balance, which enhances cognitive development. Competency in the language domain allows a child to communicate with others, building friendships that promote social-emotional development. Skills acquired through maturation and experiences in the developmental domains also set the foundation for successful learning in the kindergarten core curriculum areas including early literacy and mathematics, science, art, social science, health, and well-being. Teachers consider these interrelated aspects as they plan learning activities.

Inspiring a Positive Approach to Learning

Each child has his or her own style of learning. Understanding each child's learning style and supporting them to develop strategies to successfully navigate various learning settings are important ways teachers help children develop a positive approach to learning. A positive approach to learning includes fostering attributes such as:

- Motivation and curiosity—to explore and discover.
- Confidence—to engage in the learning process.
- Focus—to pay attention and notice the details of the lesson.
- Persistence—to keep trying.
- Adaptability—to retain and use new information and concepts in new settings.

Activities that spark children's interest invite them to interact with materials and process ideas and concepts at their own pace, thus reinforcing positive perceptions about learning.

Planning with Purpose

Teaching is an interactive process that requires purposeful and intentional planning, making it more than a gathering of interesting activities that children enjoy. Informed decisions must be made about how to assemble the environment and how to present activities to optimize learning. Purposeful teaching focuses on structuring activities that help children learn desired concepts. It is this purposeful approach that characterizes high-quality teaching and is associated with greater academic gains among young children when they enter kindergarten (Howes et al., 2008). Purposeful teaching involves making a commitment to use evidence-based approaches, by following developmentally appropriate practices, applying a variety of teaching approaches, and including culturally relevant experiences.

Using Evidence-Based Practices

Effective practitioners need to know and understand the interventions and practices that are most successful in providing for children's nutrition, health, and safety. These are called *evidence-based practices*. They include approaches that are credible and reliable in effecting positive change, such as improving a particular skill, promoting knowledge, or achieving a specific quality standard. Reputable sources for evidence-based practices regarding children's nutrition, health, and safety include the National Institutes of Health, Office of the Surgeon General, American Dietetic Association, American Academy of Pediatrics, and Consumer Product Safety Commission. Guidance from credible sources such as these prepares teachers to know what to do, how to do it, and why.

Evidence-based practices specify the particular underlying principles and activities that lead to effective outcomes. Familiar evidence-based practices for early childhood form the basis for **developmentally appropriate practice (DAP)** outlined by the NAEYC (2009a). DAP guides teachers to consider three important aspects as they establish environments and interventions to best meet children's needs:

- The age-related characteristics of children, which allow teachers to predict the activities and experiences that will promote children's development.
- Individual child characteristics learned through observations and interactions with each child, which inform the teacher about the child's strengths, interests, and approaches to learning.
- The impacts of the social and cultural contexts in which the children live, which help teachers formulate meaningful and relevant experiences for children (NAEYC, 2009a).

Staying informed about the practices that are supported by professional consensus also helps teachers avoid following approaches that are heavily based in opinion and personal preference. Planning wellness goals for nutrition is a good example. Nearly everyone has an opinion about food and what constitutes a healthful diet. Many cultural values are related to food with respect to what is eaten and how it is prepared, and families may follow a variety of dietary practices.

The nutrition messages that teachers present should address basic information and behaviors that are commonly understood to advance health and well-being. Focusing on basic practices can often bridge differing points of view. For example, the wellness concept of "Food should be clean and carefully prepared" is a basic practice that everyone would value. Established health and nutrition practices recognize that germs and potential toxins can be found on unwashed fruits and vegetables. Focusing the nutrition wellness lessons on basic and evidence-based concepts gives teacher's confidence that the nutrition message is credible.

Another aspect of evidence-based practice is the purposeful teaching cycle, as depicted in Figure 1-8. This approach puts teachers in the role of research investigators. In order for the evidence-based approach to be successful, it needs to be applied in a way that interests children and fits their readiness to learn. Even as the activities are presented, teachers constantly observe how children participate in and respond to the wellness lessons. Adjustments are made if children are struggling to understand a concept or if they are not interested or engaging in the activity. Observation and evaluation guide teachers to follow up on activities that are especially enjoyed by children, allowing children's interests and ideas to extend the lesson, bringing the teaching process full circle.

Engaging in Developmentally Appropriate Practices

The purposeful teaching plan should be based on developmentally appropriate practices. That is, activities must fit children's developmental capabilities and readiness to learn. Children are most able to learn when the experiences are appropriate for their age, stage of development, and individual maturity level (NAEYC, 2009a;

developmentally appropriate practice (DAP) a teaching approach that addresses the child's age and maturity, individual characteristics, and the context in which the child grows and develops

This **video** describes two aspects of developmentally appropriate practice. Not mentioned is the third aspect, considering children's development within the context of family, neighborhood, society, and culture. As you watch, think about how all three elements of developmentally appropriate practice can be used in planning a wellness curriculum.

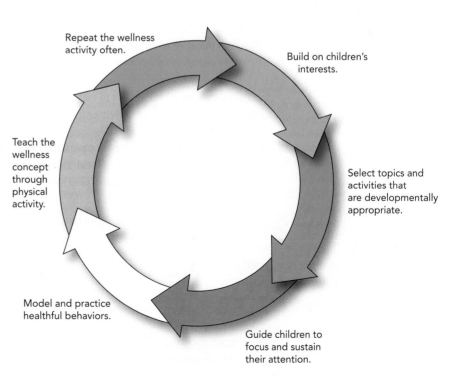

Repeat the wellness activity often.

Build on children's interests.

Select topics and activities that are developmentally appropriate.

Guide children to focus and sustain their attention.

Model and practice healthful behaviors.

Teach the wellness concept through physical activity.

FIGURE 1-8
Essential Elements in Teaching Wellness

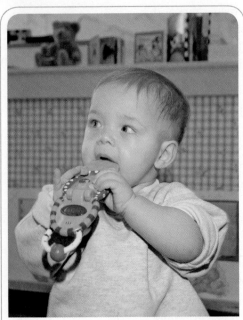

Babies experience their first wellness lessons through a safe and appropriate environment.

Piaget, 1929). Teaching using developmentally appropriate practices matches tasks with the child's level of understanding and skill in order to appropriately scaffold the learning experience. Infants, toddlers and preschoolers, and early elementary age groups each have a specific style and developmental readiness to learn.

Infants   Babies ages birth to 18 months learn foremost through sensory exploration and movement. Piaget (1929) calls this the *sensorimotor period.* Touching toys, bringing a toy to the mouth and exploring its sensations, and moving arms, legs, hands, head, and torso are a baby's method of learning and discovery. Increasing coordination and motor skill development such as rolling over, crawling and walking, and recognition of an *object's permanence* (the continued existence of an object even though it is out of sight) are examples of the ways learning is demonstrated. Teaching infants wellness concepts involves:

- Providing safe opportunities for babies to freely explore using their sensory and motor skills, such as placing toys within reach of the infant's hands and feet.
- Introducing healthful routines, including washing the baby's hands before eating and after diapering.
- Modeling safe interactions, such as guiding the baby to touch another child with gentle motions.

Toddlers and Preschoolers   Children ages 16 months to 5 years of age tend to use their intuitive curiosity as the motivation and method for learning. These children explore the environment without preconceived notions. They use their sensory and motor capabilities to touch and manipulate toys, explore their uses, and begin to organize newly discovered information. For example, a toddler may attempt to sit on a doll house–sized chair, showing awareness of the purpose of the toy, but not yet recognizing the disparity of her size compared to the size of the toy chair. A preschooler may use a block as part of a road for a toy truck or in other play, as a cellphone.

Through play and exploration, children in this age group begin to organize their understanding by using increasingly complex spoken language. They also begin to use symbols to represent ideas, such as drawing pictures of themselves with their family. Piaget (1929) called this the *preoperational period* in recognition of the child's need to experience the environment in order to begin the process of understanding it. Wellness activities for toddlers and preschoolers are promoted by:

What if . . .

you were assigned to teach 2-year-old toddlers instead of the 3-year-old preschoolers you normally teach? What aspects of children's nutrition would you explore to prepare yourself to feed toddlers appropriately?

- Providing ample opportunity for children to explore their ideas by manipulating materials such as real and toy foods and utensils and dramatizing wellness scenarios in dramatic play settings such as getting a shot or receiving a bandage "to stop the blood from the accident."
- Offering planned activities that guide children to learn nutrition, health, and safety rules, such as washing hands before eating or sitting down to eat to avoid choking.
- Using language to support understanding of wellness concepts: "Closing the gate keeps everyone safe" and "Covering your mouth when you cough keeps your friends and teachers healthy."

Early Elementary-Age Children   Children ages 5 to 8 learn best when they can explore ideas in real and tangible ways. Providing actual experiences helps this age group to grasp the facts of an idea. For example, using blocks to explore the math concepts of addition and subtraction helps to ground the concept of quantity in real terms. Collecting the classroom's paper garbage for a week helps children to visualize how much paper is used and clarifies the importance of recycling much more than simply talking about recycling. Planned wellness activities that are rich with hands-on opportunities are important for teaching this group, which Piaget (1929) termed the *concrete operations period*. Wellness activities for elementary school children include:

- Offering individualized activities, such as having children keep a diary of all the foods they have eaten for the day.
- Guiding small group activities, such as inviting children to use a safety checklist to identify any potential dangers in the classroom.
- Identifying healthful alternatives to less healthful activities, such as snacking on apples instead of potato chips.

Because learning emerges in different ways for different age groups, teachers must establish approaches to teaching about wellness that are not just a simplified form of activities that are used with older age groups, but activities that are purposeful and appropriate. Figure 1-9 provides an example of a wellness curriculum that shows how each age group is capable of learning about fruits and vegetables according to their developmental readiness.

Employing a Variety of Teaching Strategies

Curriculum planning provides an opportunity for teachers to apply a variety of teaching strategies that are suitable to convey the intended message and to meet children's needs. Variety does not mean random or haphazard. It refers instead to using a diversity of approaches to engage children's interest and participation. It also allows teachers to fit the teaching approach to the desired wellness message. Some commonly used teaching approaches and their descriptions are listed next.

- *Child-selected play*—allows children to be self-directed as they are free to choose the activities that are of greatest interest to them and to play at that activity until they are ready to make a change. In this

Toddlers: Read books about healthful fruits and vegetables.

Primary-grade children: Conduct a survey about how many times children in the class eat fruits and vegetables on a particular day.

Preschool children: Sort fruits and vegetables by attributes such as color or shape, what grows on a tree, or what grows in the soil.

Kindergarten children: Learn about the ways different families prepare fruits and vegetables.

FIGURE 1-9

Planning a Wellness Curriculum to Fit Children's Developmental Capabilities

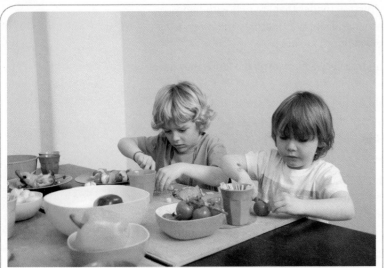

A hands-on cooking activity provides a good way for children to learn about healthy food.

approach the wellness lesson is presented through the materials provided. For example, placing a large plastic model of teeth, a large toothbrush, and fluffy soap bubbles in the sensory table invites children to "practice" brushing teeth, thus exploring a beneficial dental health practice.

- *Teacher-directed activities*—focus on individual children, small groups, or large groups. They are structured and aim to teach a specific skill or involve children in a prescribed process. Teacher-directed activities focus on teaching the skills of listening, responding, and following directions. For example, the teacher may lead a group of children through the steps of taking cover in an earthquake drill, or how to cover a cough.

- *Infusing wellness topics across the curriculum*—includes setting up the environment so that children may explore the wellness message through activities planned for several parts of the classroom. This approach increases the likelihood that all children will come in contact with the wellness message, and allows children to explore the concept from various perspectives. Figure 1-10 describes how teachers might plan a variety of activities around a wellness concept.

- *Hands-on exploration*—allows children to use all of their sensory capabilities and innovative ideas to inspect, touch, manipulate, taste, smell, shake, weigh, and poke. This approach provides

FIGURE 1-10   Infusing Wellness Messages Across the Curriculum

Cognitive Development

- Match real fruits and vegetables to colored construction paper to discover a food rainbow. (Art)

- Conduct cooking activities to sample a variety of foods. Sample the same food prepared in different ways: fresh, juiced, sauced. (Science)

- Create a picture list of different foods. Have children mark the foods they like. Identify most and least liked. (Math)

Physical Development

- Play sorting games using small manipulative toys; define variety; sort matching items; then sort to create groups with variety (no matches). (Fine motor; Math)

- Paint a class mural of foods on butcher paper placed on the wall. (Art)

- Hop to music. Stop the music and ask each child, "What is your favorite: fruit, vegetable, dairy, protein?" (Health and well-being)

Social-Emotional Development

- Read the book and provide props for children to dramatize the story *The Very Hungry Caterpillar* (E. Carle). (Literacy)

- Ask parents for ideas about field trips to places where food is grown, processed, or sold. (Social Studies)

- Invite families to come to school to talk about foods from their family tradition. (Social Science)

Language Development

- Provide a fresh fruit, vegetable, or grain. Ask small groups of children to talk about the food and make a list of different words to describe that food. (Literacy)

- Have children interview their families to learn about each person's favorite foods. (Social Science)

- Create a classroom chart of all the different foods the children eat for a week. (Social Science)

Wellness Concept

- Eat a variety of foods every day.

Note: Cheese, although a dairy product, is considered a meat/protein alternate when counting food components for CACFP. Also, only two components in any combination are required for snacks.

Sources: About Food Safety and Inspection Service, U.S. Department of Agriculture, 2012 from http://www.fsis.usda.gov/about_fsis/index.asp; Foodborne Outbreak Investigations - Key Players in Foodborne Outbreak Response, Centers for Disease Control and Prevention, 2011 from http://www.cdc.gov/outbreaknet/investigations/key_players.html; The FDA Food Code, Food and Drug Administration, 2011 from http://www.fda.gov/Food/FoodSafety/RetailFoodProtection/FoodCode/default.htm.

opportunity for children to experience, internalize, and understand all manner of lessons that would not otherwise be available to them. Talking about the temperature of an ice cube is one approach, but this does not convey the concept of cold with nearly the impact that holding an ice cube provides.

- *Process-oriented activities*—engage children in the enjoyment of using and creatively exploring materials; a goal guides the plan, but the focus is on the process rather than on a particular product. For example, Sue offers a variety of craft supplies for children to self-select on their own. Wilson offers bike helmets and knee pads in his dramatic play setting for the preschool class, allowing children to explore sporting equipment designed to increase safety.

- *Project learning*—refers to a series of related activities that emerge from children's interests and evolve across a period of time until the children determine that the topic has been exhausted. This approach allows children to become invested in a topic, supports participation in their own learning, and teaches persistence. The teacher's role is to nudge thinking by helping children formulate their questions and identify where they can search out the answers. Topics could include an in-depth study of insects, creating a group collage of 100 leaves, or exploring how food gets from a farm to the child's lunch table.

- *Incidental learning*—this kind of teaching occurs when teachers take advantage of situations that arise to teach a concept. An incidental learning situation might include noticing a child watching the birds at the birdfeeder outside the window and taking advantage of the moment to talk about the foods that birds eat to keep healthy, and relate the idea to foods that children eat to grow strong and healthy.

Including Culturally Relevant Approaches

To be most effective, wellness activities should be compatible with the child's family and cultural experiences. The NAEYC (2011) reports that "Continuity between home and early childhood settings supports children's social, emotional, cognitive and language development" (p. 1). This reinforces the notion that children learn best when the early childhood activities and lessons are valued and relevant to their home culture.

Knowledge of each family's approaches to nutrition, health, and safety helps guide teachers to create appropriate wellness activities. For example, learning to take an appropriate serving size during family-style meal service at preschool is one way of practicing healthful eating behaviors. However, a child might be confused by this lesson if the practice at home is for the adult to serve the child. Some families believe that children should eat all that has been served, whereas the classroom approach may be to encourage but never force children to eat. Ways of thinking about what causes disease or how to manage illness can also vary greatly between school and home. Engaging in conversations about such topics helps teachers and families find ways to explore wellness practices in ways that are compatible for both school and home.

Children who are English language learners often benefit from learning new concepts in their home language before or alongside learning them in English. The familiarity of the home language adds credibility to the message and ensures that children fully understand complex issues. This is important when teaching safety skills, such as staying away from poisonous products, using playground equipment safely, or not playing near traffic. Teachers need the support of families and language resource personnel to ensure that each child in the class has access to important wellness information in their home language.

Designing a Wellness Curriculum

An effective wellness program is established by identifying appropriate wellness messages, including nutrition, health, and safety themes, addressing local wellness needs, drafting activity lesson plans, and ensuring that the plans allow all children to be included.

Identifying Developmentally Appropriate Wellness Messages

Most teachers will naturally teach children about the importance of eating healthy foods, washing hands, and covering coughs to keep from spreading germs, and how to stay back from traffic and cross the street with an adult. These are *wellness messages*, or lessons that children are capable of understanding, and that when practiced can become habits that contribute to the child's health and well-being.

Formally designed health and safety goals have been established to help guide the development of a comprehensive program of wellness activities for young children. Wellness goals for children include these examples of capabilities that children will learn to demonstrate (American Association for Health Education, 2007):

- Describe how to prevent communicable disease by showing how to cover coughs.
- Show how friends can influence health behaviors through dramatic play.
- Identify community helpers who are health providers (doctor, dentist, nurse).
- Demonstrate healthy ways to express needs and feelings by giving a puppet show.
- Give an example of a health-related decision (I am hurt, hungry, or sleepy).
- Recognize a healthy activity, like drinking water or brushing teeth.
- Demonstrate a safe behavior sitting and chewing carefully while eating.
- Tell others about a healthy behavior, like telling their family that being active is good.

Appropriate wellness messages encompass the concepts of nutrition, health, and safety and should form the foundation of the curriculum plan. Examples are presented in Figure 1-11.

In addition, some wellness messages may be needed to address safety aspects specific to the community. For example, while avoiding germs is an important wellness concept for all children, staying away from the ocean is an important safety concept for children who live along the coast, and learning to ride the subway safely is important for children who live in the city. The wellness curriculum should be planned to include activities that address such local issues.

Reviewing Activities for Safety

Teachers use the planning process to evaluate each activity for appropriateness and safety. This is especially important when trying new ideas that have been gathered from curriculum resources including the Internet. Each idea needs to be assessed with the specific group of children in mind. Some examples in the planning and safety review process include:

- Consider the credibility of the curriculum resource: Is the source reputable? Is the source selling something?
- Think about the message being promoted: Is the message appropriate for the class? Can the message be adapted to better fit the needs of the children?
- Study each activity for potential dangers: Are the materials used safe and appropriate? Should any adaptations be made to improve safety?
- Imagine how the activity will be set up: Are there potential dangers related to the ways children will be involved?

FIGURE 1-11   Sample Wellness Messages

Nutrition

- Food helps our bodies grow strong and be healthy.
- Our bodies need a variety of foods every day.
- Only eat the food that our family or teachers serve us.
- Drink water every day.

Health

- Germs can make you sick.
- Cover our coughs to keep from spreading germs.

- Wash hands to get rid of germs.
- Parents, doctors, and dentists can help if you get sick.

Safety

- Stay away from things that are hot.
- Follow the rules to keep safe.
- Go to a parent or teacher if you need help.
- Hold hands and cross the street with an adult.

- Anticipate how the activity will be supervised to ensure safety: Is a teacher needed within an arm's length to direct the activity or can children interact with the materials under general supervision?

Thinking about safety issues during the planning process is an important step in presenting safe and appropriate wellness activities.

Drafting Activity Lesson Plans

Planning to teach wellness messages is thoughtfully done to ensure that activities are relevant, organized, and developmentally appropriate. Each activity should have an identified purpose, be thought through from start to finish, and include a method for evaluating whether the goal was achieved. Lesson plans typically include components and actions such as those listed below.

- *Teaching wellness message.* Capture the overall concept in a short summary statement.
- *Learning outcome.* Identify what children will know and be able to do after participating in the activities designed to teach the wellness concept.
- *Vocabulary focus.* List the words that may be new to the children, and that should be defined and explained by the teacher.
- *Safety watch.* Describe the safety issues that must be considered when presenting the activity and offer suggestions to address them.
- *Target age group.* Identify the age group for which the activity is appropriate.
- *Goal.* State the age and developmentally appropriate skill the children will be able to show, or the information the children will be able to tell about as a result of the activity. Use a phrase such as, *children will be able to . . .* and verbs such as, *demonstrate, show, tell, discuss,* or *explain.* Activity goals usually describe a step in the process of achieving the learning outcome.
- *Materials.* List the materials needed to conduct the activity.
- *Activity plan.* Explain what the teacher will do to prepare and teach the activity. Describe the steps of what the children will do.
- *How to adjust the activity.* Describe ways to adjust the activity to meet the needs of all children, such as those who are English language learners, or children who have special developmental or health needs. Give ideas for supports, such as offering adaptive scissors for a child with motor skill challenges, or revising a recipe for a child who has a food allergy.
- *Did you meet your goal?* Draft questions to guide reflection about whether the children achieved the desired goal. Can they show the desired skill or tell about the focus information? Use these observations to recognize aspects of the activity that worked well and those that need to be changed for next time.

Written lesson plans demonstrate how each activity contributes to the overall wellness program. Figure 1-12 provides an example of a wellness activity plan using this approach.

Including All Children: The Individuals with Disabilities Education Act

Many children with developmental challenges participate in today's early childhood classrooms. This has not always been the case. Before the initiation of federal laws ensuring the rights of children with disabilities to a free and appropriate public education, only 1 in 5 children with disabilities received services to address their early education needs. In 1975 Congress enacted the Education for All Handicapped Children Act (Public Law 94-142) enabling young children across the nation to receive *early intervention* (for children birth through age two) and *special education* services (for children ages 3 to 21). These services aim to prepare children and youth for further education, employment, and independent living. Since that time the law has been reauthorized, most recently with the Individuals with Disabilities Education Act (IDEA) of 2004. The IDEA has four main objectives (U.S. Department of Education, 2007):

- To ensure a free and appropriate public education for all children with disabilities.
- To protect the rights of children with disabilities.

FIGURE 1-12   Sample Wellness Activity Lesson Plan

Teaching wellness message: All living things need water.
Learning outcome: Children will learn that their bodies need water to be healthy and grow.
Vocabulary focus: water, oxygen, sweat, nutrients, active play, less active play, thirsty.
Safety watch: Conduct the activity in an open area where children can move safely. Ensure there is space around each child, and monitor that children keep from bumping one another. Supervise the serving of water for cleanliness.
Target age group: Preschool and elementary.
Goal: Children will be able to name the times when it is important to drink water.

Materials: A variety of picture cards showing children engaged in active play (sports, hiking, playing on playground), and less active play (reading, making a puzzle, building with blocks), cups, cold water.
Activity Plan: Gather children in a space where they can move freely. Introduce the activity by talking about how our bodies need water to make healthy blood (so our brains can get the oxygen we need to think); it lets our bodies sweat so we can cool down; it helps with digestion so our bodies get the nutrients we need to grow. Talk about times when your body might get thirsty and you need to drink water (when you wake up in the morning after a long night's sleep, at meal times, when it is hot, and before, during, and after you play hard). Give examples of times when it is less likely that your body will get thirsty (less active play like reading, painting, playing with trucks). After this kind of play it is not as likely that your body will get thirsty, so it is not so important to drink water. Now introduce the game. Show the children the picture cards. Guide them to jump up if they see a picture showing children playing actively (when it is important to drink water) and sit down if they see a picture card showing children being less active (when it is less important to drink water). After children have learned the game, invite one of the children to show the cards. When you are done playing ask the children to sit down and offer them a cup of cold water. Remind them that the body needs water to do its work and to grow. It is especially important to drink water before, during, and after active play.
How to adjust the activity: Prepare to support English language learners by creating a teacher cue card with the words for "jump up" and "sit down" in the children's home languages. Include phonetic spelling to assist with pronunciation as needed. Make adjustments to include children with special developmental needs, such as changing the physical response to stretching arms up when it is important to drink water, and down when it is not so important, or ask the children to suggest a response where everyone can participate. Repeat the directions at intervals for children who need reminders. Allow children to watch if they are uncomfortable responding. Repeat the game at transition or group times so children will become familiar with the concept.
Did you meet your goal? Can you observe each child responding appropriately to the picture cards? Are children able to identify times when it is important to drink water?

- To support states to provide special education services.
- To ensure that early intervention programs are effective.

Currently more than 200,000 infants and toddlers and their families receive early intervention services and 6.5 million children and youth receive special education services each year (U.S. Department of Education, 2010). The majority of these children participate in classrooms with their typically developing peers.

Early childhood teachers participate with families, physicians, and others in identifying children who may be eligible to receive services through the IDEA. Children with observable developmental delays are referred to the local education agency (LEA), which has the responsibility to provide early intervention and special education services. The LEA conducts assessments to determine the nature of the child's developmental delay and to ascertain if the disability hinders the child's educational progress. Children may be identified for service based on hearing, vision, speech, orthopedic or other health impairments, autism, pervasive developmental delay, or other learning disabilities.

When children are identified for special education services, families, teachers, and special education professionals work together to create an *individualized family services plan (IFSP)* for infants and children birth through age 2 or an *individualized education program (IEP)* for children 3 to 21 years of age. These plans describe the child's disability, including how it affects the child's learning. Goals are listed to promote and track the child's educational progress, and plans are made to select an early childhood placement that offers the least restrictive and most appropriate environment.

The IFSP or IEP is a resource for teachers. It helps teachers identify accommodations that may be needed in the classroom, such as special scissors to support children with fine motor delay, adaptive chairs for children with orthopedic impairments, or open floor plans and furnishing arrangements for children who move with a wheelchair. In some cases children are assigned a special education assistant who supports the child's inclusion in the classroom. Specialized instructional approaches may also be required to support children's learning, including wellness concepts. Early intervention therapists can offer ideas for teachers about ways to adapt activities to support children's participation and understanding of the wellness message.

Accessing Supports for Teachers

Many resources are available to provide ideas about wellness topics to explore with young children. Children's literature, curriculum books and Internet resources, and professional development trainings are some familiar supports for teachers.

Children's Literature

Children's books provide a wonderful way to introduce wellness topics. The colorful presentation and engaging characters focus children's attention on specific messages, such as foods to eat for good health, what happens when you visit the doctor or dentist, and ways to keep safe. In response to the growing interest in teaching children wellness concepts, authors and vendors offer picture books on a variety of nutrition, health, and safety topics. As always, teachers need to review these resources to ensure that the message is reflective of current trends in wellness and that the presentation is appropriate for the age and maturity of the children. Teachers often develop a list of their favorite books for teaching particular topics, adding to it when new resources are discovered. A beginning list of children's literature is offered in Figure 1-13. Other lists of appropriate children's literature for wellness topics can be found on the NAEYC and American Dietetic Association websites.

Curriculum Books and Internet Resources

Curriculum books and the Internet provide ready access to a variety of activity ideas and directions for implementing wellness lessons for young children. It is important for teachers to assess the activity ideas, weighing them against the developmental capabilities of the class, and making any needed adaptations. Figure 1-14 provides examples of teacher resources that are particularly suited for a wellness program.

Professional Development Training

Commitment to continuing education is a quality of successful teachers. Accessing professional development opportunities related to children's health and wellness, attending seminars and workshops, and participating in in-service training are all ways to learn about resources to support effective teaching. All early childhood teachers and most elementary school teachers are required to participate in periodic health and wellness training, such as infant and child first aid and cardiopulmonary resuscitation. These trainings often include updates about nutrition, disease, and injury prevention.

Membership in professional organizations is another way to keep current on wellness trends and to learn about resources. Membership in the National Association for the Education of Young Children connects teachers to a multitude of resources and information that are directly applicable to the education of young children. The NAEYC conferences are popular venues for learning and exchanging ideas about teaching young children.

FIGURE 1-13   Children's Literature to Support the Wellness Curriculum

Nutrition

The Very Hungry Caterpillar (E. Carle)

Eating the Alphabet: Fruits & Vegetables from A To Z (L. Ehlert)

Bread Bread Bread (A. Morris & L. Heyman)

Everybody Cooks Rice (N. Dooley)

My Whole Food ABC's (D. Richard)

I Will Never Not Ever Eat a Tomato (L. Child)

Drink More Water (C. Dalton)

Let's Read About Food (C. Klingel)

Dinosaurs Alive and Well; A Guide to Good Health (L. Krasny Brown & M. Brown)

Munching: Poems About Eating (L. Bennett Hopkins)

The Bugabees: Friends with Food Allergies (A. Recob)

Health

Como Cuidar Mis Dientes/Taking Care of My Teeth (T. Debezelle)

Those Mean Nasty Dirty Downright Disgusting but Invisible Germs (J. A. Rice)

Why I Sneeze, Shiver, Hiccup, & Yawn (M. Berger)

My Amazing Body: A First Look at Health and Fitness (P. Thomas)

Germs Are Not for Sharing (E. Verdick & M. Heinle)

Bear Feels Sick (K. Wilson & J. Chapman)

Sleep Is for Everyone (P. Showers)

Cuts, Breaks, Bruises, and Burns: How Your Body Heals (J. Cole)

Today I Feel Silly and Other Moods That Make My Day (J. Curtis)

I Feel Happy and Sad and Angry and Glad (M. Murphy)

Everybody Has Feelings: Todos Tenemos Sentimientos (C. Avery)

Safety

The Allergy Buddy Club; The Green Apple Tales Series on Food Safety (Rice-Andrea)

Safety on the Playground; Safety on the School Bus; Safety Around Strangers (L. Raatma)

Franklin's Bicycle Helmet (E. Moore)

Stop Drop and Roll (M. Cuyler)

Dinosaurs, Beware! A Safety Guide (M. Brown)

Never Talk to Strangers: A Book About Personal Safety (I. Joyce)

Safety First; Series (J. Mattern)

Arthur's Fire Drill (M. Brown)

No Dragons for Tea: Fire Safety for Kids (and Dragons) (J. Pendziwol)

● PARTNERING WITH FAMILIES AND THE COMMUNITY

Creating partnerships with families and community members is an important aspect of the wellness initiative. Parents, who are the first teachers of the young child, have much to share about how their child learns and the goals they have for their child in the early childhood setting. Community members bring expertise to inform the plan. Teachers also want to share the important outcomes that they are fostering as children participate and learn in the early childhood classroom. Working together, families, community members, and teachers create a team to implement mutual goals for children's wellness. This partnership is founded on working together to develop the wellness curriculum, creating strategies to reinforce wellness behaviors at school and home, guiding families to access resources when necessary, and building relationships with community health providers.

FIGURE 1-14   Teacher Resources to Support Wellness Curriculum Development

Nutrition
- The USDA's Choose MyPlate for Preschoolers. www.choosemyplate.gov/preschoolers.html
- USDA/ARS Children's Nutrition Research Center at Baylor College of Medicine. Nutrition Information and Sites Just for Kids. www.bcm.edu/cnrc/
- Kalich, K., Bauer, D., & McPartlin, D. (2009). *Early sprouts: Cultivating healthy food choices in young children.* Redleaf Press.
- USDA Agriculture Library, Food and Nutrition Information Center, Lifestyle Nutrition. http://fnic.nal.usda.gov/nal_display/
- The National Dairy Council's Nutrition Explorations. www.nutritionexplorations.org/

Health
- SPARK Early Childhood Physical Activity Program and SPARK K–6 Physical Activity Program. Available online at www.sparkpe.org

- Kids Health in the Classroom. The Nemours Foundation. http://classroom.kidshealth.org
- National Association of Sport & Physical Education. Available online at www.aahperd.org/naspe
- Smith, C. J., Hendricks, C. M., & Bennett, B. S. *Growing, growing strong: A whole health curriculum for young children* (rev. ed.). Redleaf Press.

Safety
- Feigh, A. *I can play it safe.*
- O'Brien-Palmer, M. *Healthy me: Fun ways to develop good health and safety habits.*
- Safe Kids USA. www.safekids.org/safety-basics/safety-resources-by-risk-area/playground/
- National Resource Center for Health and Safety in Child Care and Education. http://nrckids.org/
- U.S. Consumer Products Safety Commission. www.cpsc.gov/

Collaborating in Curriculum Development

Families and community members are significant resources for teachers when designing a wellness curriculum. A partnership approach helps ensure that the wellness messages glean ideas from important resources and are part of a broader community of health and wellness efforts.

Partnering with Families

Inviting families to participate in the development of the wellness program is an ideal way to gather a variety of suggestions about wellness topics and activities. Often wellness topics emerge from the questions and challenges families face in ensuring their child's good nutrition, or teaching their child a healthy practice, like brushing their teeth. Families bring ideas about their culture and ways of thinking about wellness. They can offer perspectives the teacher may be unaware of, and often parents will volunteer to help plan culturally appropriate activities to teach children and families about nutrition, health, and safety. Families are also uniquely able to provide ideas about how to adapt activities to address children's special developmental needs or challenges.

A variety of perspectives and ideas emerge when teachers encourage families to share personal stories about their family traditions and ways they keep their children healthy. These discussions also offer a forum for discussing conflicting points of view if there is disagreement. When this happens, the group might invite a health provider to participate in the discussion.

Other ways to invite the involvement of all families includes establishing a wellness program message board, blog, or inviting families to e-mail their ideas to add to a bulletin board display. Such activities encourage a climate of participation and sharing which improves the quality of the wellness plan, and expands the idea that everyone shares in the responsibility of teaching children about healthful practices.

Engaging with Community Resources

Community health care professionals are another good source of information and ideas when designing the wellness-oriented curriculum. Physicians, nurses, dentists, hygienists, and other community health providers bring expertise about current health issues, and goals for promoting healthful behaviors. When invited to be part of the wellness team they are often willing to come into classrooms to talk with children and visit with families, or provide a tour of their health facility. They may also be available to offer training for teachers and families, which broadens the impact of the wellness effort.

Some early childhood settings convene a health services advisory committee, made up of parents, teachers, and community health providers, to discuss program health and wellness practices and offer advice about program policies and procedures. In turn, the health care provider gains a better understanding of the important roles that teachers play in providing healthy and safe environments for children and guiding children to develop positive health behaviors. Inviting community partners to engage with early childhood teachers and families creates a partnership of support and understanding across the service systems.

Reinforcing Wellness Concepts at Home and School

The collaborative relationship built between the teacher and families increases the likelihood that wellness concepts taught at school will be reinforced at home. Communication and role modeling are important elements of this collaboration.

Communicating About Wellness Goals

School-to-home communication is an important part of creating a partnership around wellness. When families know what wellness topics are being discussed at school, they can reinforce the ideas at home and encourage their child to show or talk about what they have learned. Examples of common wellness messages to share with families include (NAEYC, 1999):

- Provide nutritious meals.
- Ensure children get sufficient sleep.
- Identify a regular medical provider.
- Obtain recommended immunizations.
- Keep children home when they are sick.
- Encourage physical activity.
- Protect children from harm.

FIGURE 1-15

A Classroom Display of Nutrition, Health, and Safety Pictures Creates a Wellness Newsletter for Everyone to Enjoy

Sharing these ideas may introduce new information for some families or serve as a reminder for families to practice the healthful behaviors at home.

Communicating with families about the topics covered in the wellness curriculum is needed for another important reason. Some wellness topics, especially those that relate to health and safety, have the potential to raise concerns or potentially frighten children. For example, even a carefully presented lesson about evacuating the classroom for a fire drill may introduce worries in children who are mature enough to recognize that a fire *could* happen and that fire is very dangerous. Ongoing communication is important in order for families to recognize when such activities are being discussed, so they can observe for signs of worry and ensure children that the family and the health and safety workers will take care of them. Figure 1-15 provides an example of ways children's artwork can share a wellness message being explored in the classroom.

Sharing Community Health Information

Teachers also serve as a resource for families, informing them of community health issues, such as food safety alerts, new immunization requirements, or product safety issues. To best serve in this role, teachers must keep aware of emergent health issues that could affect both the classroom and the home setting. Having a plan to communicate important wellness information is helpful, such as establishing a special bulletin board for important news or creating a family e-mail list. These outreach efforts

HEALTH HINT   Talking with Families About Children's Health

Sometimes teachers need to communicate concerns about a child's health. When talking with families, remember to:

- Be sensitive; know that most parents really care about their child's health.
- Communicate respectfully.

- Be prepared to carefully and simply state your concern.
- Recognize family challenges.
- Assist with creating strategies for improvement.
- Be a positive member of the child's support network.
- Understand resources in the community to which you can refer the family.

demonstrate the teacher's commitment to child well-being, assist families to develop networks of support, and guide them to access the services children may need.

Providing Guidance When Needed

Sometimes teachers provide guidance for families if there is a concern for a child's unmet health or safety need. Building a strong relationship helps make discussions of health issues a natural part of the teacher and parent relationship. This "normalizes" such conversations making it easier and more comfortable for both teachers and parents to talk about concerns. Teachers may recognize when families are experiencing difficulties that could jeopardize children's well-being. As an example, parents who experience high levels of stress may be less able to take prevention measures to reduce their child's risk of injury or illness (Alemango, Niles, Shafer-King, & Miller, 2008). Engaging in sensitive health discussions may be difficult but is an important part of the teacher and parent relationship. The *Health Hint* offers guidance for communicating with parents when difficult concerns must be shared.

Being Healthful Role Models

Children learn by watching others, including their family and teachers. Helping children learn healthy habits requires that these important role models have knowledge about wellness practices, a healthful attitude, and physical energy. It means letting children see how you put your healthy ideas into practice. Here are ways to set a good example for children (American Academy of Pediatrics, 2007):

- Eat well and stay active.
- Get regular health checkups and recommended vaccinations.
- Join a smoking cessation program if you smoke.
- Ensure positive experiences with food and eating; sit together at meals.
- Participate in physical activities with children. Dance, be active, and play together.
- Model healthful behaviors: wash hands, cover coughs, stay home when ill.

Healthy role modeling enhances wellness activities in the classroom. For example, when teachers demonstrate how to use tongs to serve apple slices, children recognize this as the appropriate way to serve food. When teachers bend and stretch vigorously with musical games, children learn to participate enthusiastically too. When adults wash their hands after sneezing, children see that adults practice the health behaviors they expect of children. Being a healthful role model demonstrates that wellness habits are something you *do*, not just talk about. The *Nutrition Note* provides ideas about ways adults model healthful eating.

Making the commitment to be a healthful role model for young children is one way teachers align with the high standards of the teaching profession. It requires dedicating time and resources to pursue professional development activities that contribute to the teacher's knowledge and understanding of excellence in professional practice. This effort calls on early childhood teachers to be willing to reflect on their current practices, to identify both personal strengths to further enhance and areas where additional professional development is needed. The self-inventory in Figure 1-16 offers a guide for developing professional competencies in nutrition, health, and safety for young children. Successful educators are open to new ideas and approaches that will improve their capacities to be healthful role models as they promote children's abilities to grow and thrive.

FIGURE 1-16   Self-Inventory for Wellness Practices

How much do you know about your own health and well-being? How much do you know about the nutrition, health, and safety practices of young children, from birth to age 8?

Personal Practices	Always	Sometimes	Never	Reflections and Comments
I eat vegetables and/or fruits at every meal.				
I drink skim or 1% milk and choose low-fat cheeses.				
Half of the grains I eat are whole grains.				
I am overweight.				
I feel rested when I wake up each day.				
I smoke.				
I get at least 150 minutes of cardiovascular exercise every week.				
I wash my hands with soap and water after I use the bathroom.				
I eat fast food.				
My vaccinations are up to date.				
I have a primary care physician or a "medical home."				
I get a flu shot each year.				
I have a dental checkup at least once each year.				
I wear a seat belt and avoid talking on a cell phone or text messaging when I drive.				
I follow bicycle safety rules when I am riding on the road.				
I wash fresh fruits and vegetables before I eat them.				
I get 8 hours of sleep most nights.				
When I teach children I dress appropriately so I am comfortable playing outdoors with them.				
I recognize signs of illness and stay home when I am ill.				
I develop friendships and enjoy socializing and laughing with others.				
I have friends/family with whom I can consult when I have concerns.				

FIGURE 1-16 **Self-Inventory for Wellness Practices** (*Continued*)

Young Children's Wellness Practices	I Was Aware of This	I Was Somewhat Aware of This	I Was Not Aware of This	Reflective Questions and Things I Want to Learn About
The medical field recommends that, ideally, infants should be exclusively breast-fed for the first 4 to 6 months.				
It is recommended that adults replace infants' use of a bottle and nipple with a cup after 12 months of age.				
Children age 2 and older should drink skim or 1% milk unless they are underweight.				
Children should be served fruits and/or vegetables at meal and snack times.				
Children should be offered but not forced to eat any food including a "no thank-you bite."				
Fresh fruit should be served rather than juice because it adds fiber to the diet.				
Breakfast is a very important meal and enhances learning.				
Children should have their first dental visit by their first birthday.				
Families are children's first teachers, but teachers can have tremendous influence over young children's health and well-being.				
Being outside in cold weather does not, by itself, give a child a cold.				
Play promotes cognitive development.				
Building relationships with nurturing adults promotes children's development.				
Children should be physically active every day.				
TV viewing should be limited to 1 to 2 hours or less per day and children under age 2 should not view TV at all.				
Even very young children can learn ways to keep safe.				

NUTRITION NOTE   Adults Are Important Models for Healthful Eating

The American Dietetic Association tracks eating practices as a measure of diet trends. A recent survey revealed that adults have increased consumption of these healthy foods in the past 5 years:

- Whole grains.
- Fruits and Vegetables.
- Fish and chicken.
- Foods with health-related benefits such as berries and Omega-3 rich foods.

Overall more adults report that they "have a good attitude toward diet and exercise" and that they "are doing all they can to eat healthfully." This is a promising trend for the health and well-being of both adults and children. Families and teachers who model eating nutritious foods and healthful eating practices encourage children's acceptance of wholesome foods and teach positive eating habits. This contributes to children's wellness.

Source: *Nutrition and You: Trends 2011: Report of Results,* presented at the American Dietetic Association Food and Nutrition Conference and Exposition, September 24, 2011.

● SUMMARY

Wellness is established on the building blocks of nutrition, health, and safety which work together to increase children's abilities to develop and thrive in the educational setting. Teachers are second only to families in guiding children's healthful development, making the study of these wellness components crucial to successful teaching.

Many complex influences affect children's lives and their ability to learn. A growing multicultural society, diverse family structures, food insecurity, and the impacts of poverty are some of the factors that must be understood in order to establish classroom approaches that meet children's needs.

Young children are capable of learning behaviors that will contribute to their well-being throughout life. To optimize this opportunity, teachers must understand how children learn and be capable of planning a wellness program that is relevant and developmentally appropriate for the children they teach.

Teachers, families, and community members are partners in the effort to improve children's wellness by helping them build capabilities to live healthful lives. Teaching wellness is a process of discovery that promises positive benefits long after children have grown beyond the early childhood years.

Never before has the value of the early learning years been recognized with such enthusiasm and intensity. Teachers offer significant contributions to the health and vitality of children, families, and communities making it an exciting time to be a teacher of young children. This text guides teachers to understand the interrelationship of nutrition, health, and safety, and provides background information sufficient for teachers to feel confident in their ability to create learning environments and teaching approaches that will make a significant contribution in children's lives.

KEY TERMS

Developmentally appropriate practice
Diet

Obese
Oral health

Overweight
Wellness

REVIEW QUESTIONS

1. How do nutrition, health, and safety interrelate to affect children's wellness?
2. What factors influence children's wellness and why are these influences important for teachers to understand?
3. What does it mean to teach wellness "across the curriculum" and why is this important?
4. What are the benefits of partnering with families and community members when planning a wellness program?

DISCUSSION STARTERS

1. Consider the term *wellness*. Make a list of words that describe wellness to you. What would wellness look like in a young child? Describe how nutrition, health, and safety contribute to your interpretation of wellness. Share your list and reflections with others.
2. Reflect on the complex influences that impacted the nutrition, health, and safety of children in the community where you grew up. How would you describe the typical family in your home community? Were resources available to assist families who had needs? What community services benefited you during your early development?
3. Identify wellness topics that would be especially important to teach children in the community where you live and explain why. Describe a wellness message that would be appropriate for these children, and discuss some of the teaching strategies and activities you would use to teach your identified wellness message.
4. Consider the cultural diversity present in your community. What aspects of each tradition would contribute to the plans for teaching children about nutrition, health, and safety wellness? What community partners would you invite to help create an appropriate wellness curriculum for young children?

PRACTICE POINTS

1. Gather more information about the National Children's Study. What environmental, biological, genetic, and psychosocial factors are being discussed that may influence different phases of children's growth and development? What connections are being made between these factors and health and disease?
2. Identify an issue in your community that challenges children's wellness. Investigate the topic to learn about the scope or size of the problem, and talk with others to learn what is being done to address the issue.
3. Select a wellness message related to each of the foundations of wellness: nutrition, health, and safety. Brainstorm a list of topics and activities that could be used to teach each message. Work with a teacher to implement one of your activities and reflect on its effectiveness.
4. Contact a child care, Head Start, school, or community health agency to learn if they implement a health or wellness curriculum for young children. Ask how parent and community members are involved in the wellness activities. Learn about any challenges, successes, or lessons learned from their effort.

WEB RESOURCES

Healthy Child Care America
www.healthychildcare.org

National Association for the Education of Young Children
www.naeyc.org

National Scientific Council on the Developing Child
www.developingchild.net

The National Children's Study
www.nationalchildrensstudy.gov

U.S. Department of Education, Building the Legacy: IDEA 2004
http://idea.ed.gov

MyEducationLab™

Go to Topic 13 (Wellness Curriculum) in the MyEducationLab (www.myeducationlab.com)
for your course, where you can:

- Find learning outcomes for Wellness Curriculum along with the national standards that connect to these outcomes.
- Complete Assignments and Activities that can help you more deeply understand the chapter content.
- Apply and practice your understanding of the core teaching skills identified in the chapter with the Building Teaching Skills and Dispositions learning units.

- Check your comprehension on the content covered in the chapter by going to the Study Plan in the Book Resources for your text. Here you will be able to take a chapter quiz, receive feedback on your answers, and then access Review, Practice, and Enrichment activities to enhance your understanding of chapter content.

part two
Promoting Good Nutrition

two
The Foundations of Optimal Nutrition

learning outcomes

AFTER READING THIS CHAPTER, YOU SHOULD BE ABLE TO:

1. Discuss nutritional issues that impact children and how they relate to the changing food environment.

2. Define *malnutrition* and discuss nutrition issues that lead to under- and overnutrition.

3. Discuss the recommended standards and guidelines that promote healthful eating and how to use them in the early childhood education settings.

4. Describe diverse ethnic educational resources that contribute to healthful diets in the early childhood setting.

Luisa arrives early at preschool with 3-year-old Gabriella. They have just come from a doctor's appointment where Luisa learned that Gabriella is overweight and also has iron-deficiency anemia. The doctor told her this means Gabriella does not have enough iron in her blood for healthy development. Luisa is upset and explains to her daughter's preschool teacher, Cecilia, that she can't understand why Gabriella, who is eating enough to become overweight, isn't getting enough iron.

As Cecilia reviews the materials she has about children's nutrition, she remembers that Gabriella receives a vegetarian diet when she is at preschool, and she is enthusiastic about drinking milk and favors cheese and yogurt. The next day Cecilia shows Gabriella's mother a website that discusses the iron content of foods. Luisa realizes that Gabriella is not eating many of the high-iron foods listed and decides to add more of these to her child's diet. She also recognizes that some of Gabriella's favorite foods, the dairy products, are rich in calcium and vitamin D but are not very good sources of iron.

Cecilia says that she will explore whether the preschool lunch can be changed to offer more iron-rich foods in place of some of the cheese entrées that are being served as part of Gabriella's vegetarian diet. Cecilia copies the information about iron-rich foods and provides Luisa with the telephone number of the local Women, Infants, and Children program where she can get more nutritional advice. Luisa leaves the classroom feeling much more positive about the situation and appreciates the collaborative support provided by Cecilia.

Life cannot exist without nutrition. From the moment babies are fed their first meal, the nutrients they consume affect their growth, development, and well-being. **Nutrients** are substances found in foods that are essential requirements of life and thus are necessary for survival and growth. **Nutrition** refers to the relationship between the nutrients found in foods and their influence on the human body. The nutritional environments to which children are exposed both before birth and throughout their early childhood years influence health across the life span (Bernal & Jirtle, 2010; Faulk & Dolinoy, 2011; *Nutrition and the epigenome, 2012*).

Teachers play an important role in creating environments that support children's nutritional health (American Dietetic Association, 2011; Kenney, Henderson, Humphries, & Schwartz, 2011). Some teachers plan menus, select foods, and manage food preparation and service in the early childhood setting. In settings for older children, teachers are typically much less engaged in direct food service, but are equally involved in recognizing the important health impacts of good nutrition on children's ability to participate, to pay attention to lessons, and to learn.

In the chapter-opening case scenario, Cecilia, a busy teacher, takes time to discuss Luisa's concerns about her child's nutrition. When Cecilia learns that Gabriella has a nutritional deficit, she helps Luisa to discover ways to address her child's nutritional needs both at home and at school. Cecilia demonstrates a basic knowledge of nutrition and recognition of the resources that are available to support appropriate planning for children's diets. Her knowledge about the significance of nutrition to good health and learning makes an important contribution.

This chapter introduces the science of nutrition and provides an overview of current nutrition issues faced by children and their families. This prepares teachers to recognize and address the diet concerns of young children. We discuss important standards and evidence-based recommendations that form the basis for nutrition guidelines for feeding infants, toddlers, preschoolers, and early primary school-age children. This basic nutrition knowledge equips teachers to do the following:

- Understand how nutrition impacts children.
- Identify food sources of nutrients.
- Recognize the components of a healthful diet.
- Plan healthful menus.
- Use the various education and nutrition information guidelines.
- Develop personal eating habits that influence teachers' health and enhance their ability to serve as role models for children.
- Recognize creditable sources of nutrition information.

This chapter also presents a summary of food guidance systems created for different populations so that you will understand the rich diversity of ethnic foods served to young children and how they contribute to a healthful diet.

nutrients
substances found in foods that are essential requirements of life and, thus, are necessary for survival and growth

nutrition
refers to the relationship between the nutrients found in foods and their influence on the human body

phytochemicals
natural compounds found in plants that may protect against disease and support good health

antioxidants
natural compounds found in plants that may protect cells from damage and thereby decrease the risk of cancer

UNDERSTANDING HOW NUTRITION AFFECTS CHILDREN

Optimal nutrition provides children with the building blocks they need for healthful growth and development. Providing optimal nutrition for children in the early childhood setting relies on teachers who have an appropriate understanding of the components of good nutrition and recognition of the factors that sidetrack families from providing the foods that children need for healthful growth and development.

Identifying Optimal Nutrition

Optimal nutrition refers to the best possible nourishment for children. It is based on access to an appropriate amount and combination of foods in the diet, including dairy products, grains, fruits, vegetables, meats, and protein alternates such as beans and legumes. Consuming these foods provides children with the essential nutrients such as proteins and important vitamins and minerals. Optimal nutrition includes eating foods that provide **phytochemicals** and **antioxidants**, which are natural compounds found in plants that may protect against disease. It also entails eating the right combination of energy- or calorie-providing nutrients (the carbohydrates, fats, and proteins) so that the needs of growth are balanced with that of physical activity. Too little energy from food means children will not grow adequately; too much energy from food and children will face problems with obesity.

In the early childhood setting, optimal nutrition means eating healthful meals that meet the standards set by government and health agencies, and that are offered in appropriate ways and at times of the day to support children's energy needs. It includes carefully selected snacks, the types

MyEducationLab™
Visit the MyEducationLab for *Nutrition, Health, and Safety for Young Children,* to enhance your understanding of chapter concepts with a personalized Study Plan. You'll also have the opportunity to hone your teaching skills through video-based Assignments and Activities, as well as Building Teaching Skills and Dispositions lessons.

Teachers who understand and support the optimal nutrition of young children help them acquire the nutritional building blocks needed to thrive.

of foods served at school events, and the recipes used in cooking activities. Finally, good nutrition is fostered by teachers who eat healthy foods *with* children and participate in activities as active role models.

Collaborating with Families

Most parents are genuinely concerned about how their children eat and have a strong commitment to the types of foods they serve at home. Factors such as family socioeconomic status, rural versus urban living, family lifestyle, ethnicity, and religious traditions have some bearing on the foods families give their children to eat. The early childhood program may be the family's first experience entrusting others with the feeding of their children and their first exposure to food provided in group settings. Parents want to know what their child will be eating and want to participate in ensuring that their child is cared for appropriately. Teachers, such as Cecilia, understand these concerns. They invite parents to share important information about the child's needs. They are also prepared to describe the menus and ways foods are offered to children to help parents build confidence in the teacher's ability to appropriately provide for their child's well-being.

Children come to early childhood classes with unique nutritional needs that are influenced by their age, activity level, genetics, and sometimes the presence of disease or illness. Teachers like Cecilia accommodate the nutritional needs and special diet requirements of each child in their classes and establish a common ground with families to ensure that the meals served are nourishing, mutually acceptable, and, as much as possible, within the constraints of budget and school policy. Creating collaborative relationships with families to meet children's nutritional requirements sets a tone that supports good health and fosters positive food experiences.

Teachers are also important resources for parents when it comes to feeding young children. The early childhood years provide a window of opportunity for establishing habits that lead to a lifetime of healthful eating and wellness (American Dietetic Association, 2011). During these years children explore flavors and textures and develop comfort and familiarity with foods that are frequently served. They begin to establish preferences for these familiar foods, including how they are prepared and served. They learn to appreciate the variety of foods offered, which becomes a standard for what they expect when meals are served in the future. They develop confidence that food will be available to them and that they can trust their families and teachers to satisfy their hunger.

Teachers support the development of good eating habits by establishing predictable schedules for food service and relaxed and comfortable mealtimes. Teachers help families learn to be advocates for children's optimal nutrition by encouraging parents to push for schools and early child care programs to serve nutritious foods and to promote physical activity to support good health. For example, when school budget cuts result in decisions that eliminate physical education programs, teachers can provide families with the guidance they need to effectively communicate their opinions with school authorities. Teachers can direct interested families to participate in school health advisory councils and wellness committees so that parents have input into the nutrition and health standards established for their schools and school districts.

Recognizing Challenges to Nutrition

Teachers share with parents an important role in shaping the health of young children. They teach children about food and nutrition, and must be able to address childhood nutrition issues such as occurred in Gabriella's case. To be prepared to effectively manage this complex responsibility, teachers must be able

What if . . .

a child joined your class who was identified as very underweight and both parents were developmentally delayed? How would you address the nutritional needs of this child and ensure the family understood how to meet the child's needs at home too?

to recognize aspects of the changing food environment that challenge children's diets and learn about ways to work with families to ensure children have the opportunity to experience optimal nutrition.

During the past 30 years, there has been a shift in the way Americans eat. These changes represent challenges to good nutrition and have the potential to compromise children's health.

Disappearing Family Meals

Meals that are prepared at home and served and consumed by the family are important to children's nutrition. Children eat more fruits, vegetables, whole grains, and calcium-rich foods and less soda and fried foods when meals are prepared at home (Adams, 2011; Spear, 2006). In addition, family meals help children develop a sense of family connection and social support that helps them do well in school (Academy of Nutrition and Dietetics, 2012). However, sit-down family meals are not occurring consistently in the home setting. Recent survey data show that 17% of families with children 5 years of age or younger eat three or less meals together per week as a family and that only 28% of family meal occasions include children (Murphy, 2012; Sloan, 2012). A trend more recently observed is that some parents are preparing separate meals for children based on their preferences and then preparing a second meal for themselves (Sloan, 2012). Children also skip meals such as breakfast or dinner on occasion and rely on snacks to fill the gap (American Dietetic Association Foundation, 2011). Kitchens have become more like 24-hour commissaries with foods purchased based on family schedules and individual preference rather than for family meal occasions (Sloan, 2012). The good news and perhaps a sign of the economic times is that the percentage of families eating meals at home increased from 52 to 73% in 2010 (American Dietetic Association Foundation, 2011). It appears that more families are eating at home but they are not always eating together. The disadvantage of preparing separate food for children based on their preferences and not always eating meals together as a family is that it limits children's opportunity to learn about and try new foods and decreases the opportunity for the adults in children's lives to act as role models.

Using Convenience Foods

Families that choose to eat at home often look for convenient and quick-to-prepare foods. One reason for this is the time constraints experienced by working parents. Sixty percent of families have dual incomes, and about 5% of all employed people hold more than one job. In addition 64% of employed women are mothers with children under age 6 (U.S. Department of Labor U.S. Bureau of Labor Statistics, 2011). These families are strapped for time and often resort to quick mealtime solutions when feeding their children. For example, 58% of consumers surveyed indicate time was the most important criterion for selecting what foods to purchase (Sloan, 2012). Another factor influencing the preparation of family meals is that many individuals lack basic cooking skills and have not learned how to "cook from scratch" (Jarratt & Mahaffie, 2007). Those parents that report they do have good cooking skills often still choose to use convenience foods which have become a normal part of many meals prepared for children (Chenhall, 2010). Prepackaged, heat and serve, and frozen foods can offer convenience but often at a nutritional cost. Many can be high in fat, sugar, and sodium content and may lose a portion of their beneficial nutritive properties such as vitamins and fiber during processing.

The reliance on convenience food is also evident in the lunches children bring from home. Children's lunches often include prepackaged lunch meals, store-bought cookies, chips, or soft drinks. Home-packed lunches often do not provide the variety of fruits, vegetables, whole grains, and

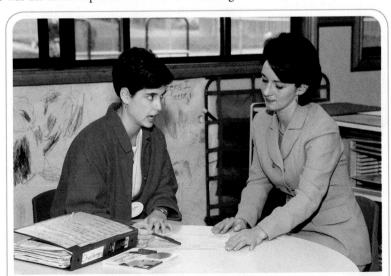

Teachers who take the time to describe menus and address the nutritional concerns of children in their programs create a bond of trust with families about the care of their children.

FIGURE 2-1   Healthy Lunch Box Ideas for Preschoolers and School-Age Children

Monday:
Turkey with cold roasted sweet potato slices on whole grain bread*
Orange Wedges
Zucchini and summer squash sticks

Tuesday:
Peanut butter and banana on a whole grain sandwich thin**
Low fat cottage cheese with chives (to use as dip)
Red and green pepper strips

Wednesday:
Sliced low fat cheese, leafy dark green lettuce rolled up on a whole grain tortilla

Sliced mangoes and strawberries
Broccoli florets

Thursday:
Tuna salad in a whole grain pita with spinach leaves
Kiwi slices
Carrot match sticks

Friday:
Lentil soup with shredded low fat cheese***
Whole grain corn bread square
Sliced melon
Diced tomatoes and cucumbers
(All meals served with non-fat milk)

*Keep cold foods safe: Lunches should be packed in an insulated box or bag with an icepack and refrigerated at arrival to school

**Replace with sunflower seed butter if peanut allergies are a concern

***Keep hot foods safe: Soups and leftover casseroles can be sent to school cold with an icepack and heated up or kept in an insulated container such as a thermos that will keep it appropriately hot. Temper the container or thermos with hot water before placing hot food inside.

dairy products needed to support good nutrition in young children (Sweitzer et al., 2010; Sweltzer, Briley, & Robert-Grey, 2009). Teachers who understand nutrition requirements and standards can provide helpful nutrition education to families to ensure that home-packed lunches are nutritious. Figure 2-1 provides menu ideas that can be shared with families on how to prepare safe and healthy meals for the lunch boxes of preschool and school-age children.

Eating Away from Home

Busy families sometimes rely on meals provided by fast-food restaurants. Children are attracted to fast-food establishments because of the exciting environment and promotional toys that are offered. Parents are attracted to the low-cost menu items. However, families may not always recognize the high nutritional price they pay for these quick meal solutions. Children who eat fast food receive larger portions than they would consume at home, and fewer options for fruits, vegetables, and milk are available. Fast-food meals also tend to be high in sodium content and higher in total fat (including the less healthy saturated and *trans* fats). In addition, children drink more soft drinks when eating at restaurants. Soft drinks contain 10 to 12 teaspoons of sugar per 12-ounce cup or can and have minimal nutritionally redeeming qualities. This is especially problematic because when soft drinks are consumed they take the place of more nutritious foods and beverages (Meinke & University of Nebraska-Lincoln Extension in Lancaster County, 2009). Researchers have shown that eating frequently at fast-food restaurants can lead to obesity and living close to fast food restaurants increases the likelihood of eating more fast food (Boone-Heinonen et al., 2011; U.S. Food and Drug Administration, 2011e; Krukowski, Eddings, & West, 2011). The Patient Protection and Affordable Care Act of 2010 is a law that now requires nutrition labeling of menu items for chain restaurants and similar retail food establishments with 20 or more locations, and vending machines

Because of time and cost, fast food is a convenient and inexpensive way to feed busy families. What are the consequences for today's children?

that will aid families in making healthier food choices when eating out. Once the proposed rule is implemented by the FDA calorie content of menu items will need to be clearly identified and additional nutrition information on nutrients of concern, such as fat and sodium, will need to be made available on request (U.S. Food and Drug Administration, 2011e).

In spite of increasing awareness about an obesity epidemic and the recent challenging economic times, families' reliance on fast food for quick, inexpensive meals continues. For example, McDonald's Corporation (2012) reported a 7.5% increase in sales in the United States in the last quarter of 2011 (McDonald's Corporation, 2012). Teachers may observe families dropping off children with a fast-food breakfast or offering them a fast-food meal or snack when picking them up at the end of the day. While supervising children at play, teachers may observe play themes such as this one:

> Meredith, a preschool teacher, notices Tristan playing in the dramatic play area. He sits in a chair outside the playhouse and leans toward the "window." In an official tone he orders, "A hamburger and fries!" When Tristan's not ordering fast food at play, he frequently asks Meredith if they are going to have a hamburger and fries at lunch. Later, Tristan's mother tells Meredith that she is worried about Tristan's weight. After talking with Meredith, Tristan's mother decides to limit trips for fast-food meals and prepare more meals at home.

> **What if . . .**
> you ask a child in your class what he had for dinner the previous night and he says, "The same thing I have every night—fried chicken and French fries." How would you respond? How might you approach the child's family to discuss more nutritious options?

Struggling with Food Affordability

The economy of the past few years has left many parents struggling to purchase sufficient food to meet the needs of their families. There are many family wage earners who have lost jobs and remain unemployed. Some may no longer be receiving unemployment benefits. Others who have found positions may be earning lower wages. Another compounding problem is the increasing cost of food (Food Research and Action Center, 2012). All these factors contribute to the difficulties families face putting adequate food on the table. Being able to afford food has become a problem for some middle-class as well as low-income families. For example, in a 2011 survey conducted in New York City; 32% of families with incomes in the $50,000–74,999 range and 16% of families with incomes in the $75,000 and above range reported difficulty affording food, which was an increase from the previous year (Quets & Spota, 2011). These families do not qualify for the Supplemental Nutrition Assistance Program (SNAP or formerly the Food Stamp Program) or other nutrition assistant programs available to lower income families. Participation in SNAP rose to 15% of the U.S. population, which represents a 76.6% increased rate of participation over the past 5 years (Coleman-Jensen, Nord, Andrews, & Carlson, 2011). Economizing strategies used by families in all income ranges when purchasing food include buying less healthy foods, including less fruits and vegetables, dairy, meat, poultry, and fish. In 2010, estimates indicated that 24% of U.S. children live in food insecure households (Child Trends, 2012). Teachers who are aware of these trends can link families to child nutrition programs and community resources that provide emergency food assistance.

Identifying New Wellness Opportunities

Emerging interest in wellness has created a heightened awareness around food production and nutrition practices. Many families are paying special attention to the foods they serve, and school settings are focusing on wellness policies.

Growing Interest in Sustainable Food Practices

Some families have made a gradual shift in how they think about food purchased for their children. Many families are interested in supporting sustainable food practices such as:

- Choosing pesticide or hormone-free food that is processed minimally.
- Selecting foods that are grown and produced locally, which reduces pollution.
- Buying fair trade products (Sloan, 2012).

What if . . .

you were approached by a parent who tells you that their family eats only organic food and requests a "natural foods diet" for their child? How would you respond?

Some families, such as Gabriella's, are environmental vegetarians, who choose a vegetarian lifestyle because they believe the production of animal foods is not sustainable. Parents who select organic or sustainable foods or both may bring this preference to the school setting. They may confront teachers with food requests that are difficult to fulfill in an institutional food service setting where food costs and availability must be factored into menu planning. These situations present an opportunity for collaboration with families. Together teachers and families can explore the challenges of meeting new requests and identify opportunities for change. New ideas offered by concerned parents can be the motivating factor for improving menus and providing a fresh look to established mealtime routines.

Increasing Interest in Wellness in the School Environment

Children spend a significant amount of time in early childhood settings and at school, where they may eat breakfast, lunch, and an afternoon snack. As a result they consume a sizable portion of their daily food intake in the education setting (Story, 2009). Health authorities and parents have become increasingly interested in promoting wellness in settings that serve young children, which could lead to improvements in the diets offered.

A major shift in the school food environment can be credited to the Healthy, Hunger-Free Kids Act of 2010. This act provides additional funding to improve access to healthy foods and represents the first increase in reimbursement rates above cost of living increases to programs in over 30 years (U.S. Department of Agriculture Food and Nutrition Service, 2012c). The bill gives the USDA the authority to have oversight of all food served at school including vending machines, á la carte lunch items and foods sold at school stores. It also updates and improves nutrition standards, and helps advance the use of local foods by helping communities to develop farm to school connections and establish school gardens. See the Progressive Programs and Practices feature, *A National School Garden and Farm to School Program*, to see how schools can obtain help changing school environments and implementing school gardens while at the same time addressing childhood obesity and food insecurity. Other factors such as improved wellness policies and a heightened level of awareness regarding the negative features of foods used for rewards in the classroom or to support fund-raising efforts are welcome trends that are beginning to have an impact on the quality of diets offered to children in schools.

UNDERSTANDING MALNUTRITION

Negative nutritional trends affect the food environment both at home and in the school setting. In fact, the overall quality of the diet consumed by children in the United States does not meet national dietary standards and recommendations for maintaining good nutritional status. As a result, many children are poorly nourished (Story, 2009). When children's diets do not contain the right combination of nutrient-rich foods, **malnutrition** can develop. Malnutrition refers to an imbalance in the diet of one or more vital nutrients that support appropriate growth and development. The two types of imbalance are:

- **Undernutrition**, in which children do not get enough calories, protein, or other nutrients.
- **Overnutrition**, in which children receive an excess of nutrients required for normal growth, development, and metabolism (Shine Dyer & Rosenfeld, 2011).

In the opening case scenario Gabriella faces both aspects of malnutrition: iron-deficiency anemia due to insufficient iron intake, and obesity due to too many calories in the diet. Researchers suggest that undernutrition and overnutrition can occur simultaneously when children eat foods low in nutrients such as iron, but high in calories (Cepeda-Lopez et al., 2010). Gabriella is not alone. Researchers, using a survey tool to assess quality of U.S. diets called the Healthy Eating Index 2005, found that although meat and grain food groups were consumed in recommended amounts, fruits, vegetables, and milk are still lacking in U.S. diets. The survey also found that people are still eating too much sodium, saturated fat, and calories from solid fats and added sugars (Reedy, Krebs-Smith, & Bosire, 2010). Although

malnutrition
an imbalance of one or more vital nutrients in the diet that support appropriate growth and development, resulting in undernutrition or overnutrition

undernutrition
a type of malnutrition in which individuals do not get sufficient calories, protein, or other nutrients to meet their bodies' needs

overnutrition
a type of malnutrition in which individuals consume too many calories

PROGRESSIVE PROGRAMS & PRACTICES

A National School Garden and Farm to School Service Program

By Debra Eschmeyer, FoodCorps, Inc.

FoodCorps is a national nonprofit organization that seeks to combat childhood obesity, food insecurity, and diet-related disease while training the next generation of farmers and public health leaders. The centerpiece of our work is an AmeriCorps service program that launched in ten states in 2011. Our service members are investing a year of paid public service conducting nutrition education, building and tending school gardens, and sourcing local food for school meals in high-obesity, limited-resource communities.

The child at risk for obesity and the child facing food insecurity is, ironically, often one and the same. FoodCorps addresses the root cause of both: lack of access to healthy food. In keeping with the directives of the National Prevention Council, FoodCorps is not a response to obesity's symptoms, but a strategic plan to build community-based school environments that make healthy choices the norm, not the exception.

Under the Kennedy Serve America Act signed into law in 2009, AmeriCorps is slated to triple in size by 2017. FoodCorps leverages federal funds and partners with local groups to provide schools with the people power to change their food environments. And it does so without burdening already overtaxed teachers, administrators, or school lunch budgets.

Tapping into the groundswell of interest in food, farming, and health, we recruit emerging leaders for a year of public service. Serving under the direction of partner organizations in public schools, our service members implement a three-ingredient recipe for healthy kids:

1. Knowledge: we teach children what healthy food is and where it comes from

2. Engagement: we create hands-on opportunities to grow fresh food in school gardens and engage parents, volunteers, teachers, and business leaders in the school food environment

3. Access: we work with local farmers to bring high-quality food into the school cafeteria

Because of this grassroots approach, the solutions FoodCorps service members foster remain durable, even after management of their projects is passed to new service members and eventually to the community itself.

In our first year of service in the field in 300 schools, our 50 service members have taught more than 50,000 children,

built or restored 500 school and community gardens, recruited 1,700 volunteers to help improve school food, and harvested 11,000 pounds of garden-fresh produce for food-insecure children and families. Beyond the statistics, the stories our service members share with us—of salsa taste-tests and broccoli biology lessons and local food and farmer days in the school lunchroom—are inspiring. Meanwhile, the places we work see protection of green space, renewal of vacant lots and concrete schoolyards, and revival of vibrant economies for farmers and food producers.

"We get very excited to eat things we usually don't like, like broccoli, spinach, peas, and carrots . . . we grew it, so we like it a lot more."—Eva, age 10

"This is the first time I'm ever trying it (broccoli). My mom usually tries to get me to eat it, but I'm going to give it a shot today."—middle school student in Des Moines, Iowa

"See?! I like every fruit and vegetable there is! And I eat all of it!"

"The kohlrabi is just a hit," said Christopher Chemsak, FoodCorps service member. "They love to pull it out of the ground and say, 'Can we cut this up?' I think it's harvesting something they helped grow. The kids get so excited about carrots with the green leafy stems still attached on top that they fight over them. They take pride in having been a part of the growing and harvesting process, which is really the most beautiful part to me, when I can help them reconnect with the direct source of their food."

educational leaders, school districts, and individual schools have made moderate progress improving the school healthy eating environment, children still do not meet national dietary guidelines (Kraak, Story, & Wartella, 2012). For example, the Third School Nutrition Dietary Assessment Study found that children, when evaluated separate from the total population, are not eating enough fruits, vegetables, dairy products, and whole grains and are consuming too many high-calorie, low-nutrient-containing foods and beverages (Story, 2009). This highlights the need and supports Healthy People, 2020 goals to improve fruit, vegetable, whole grain, low-fat milk intake and decrease foods that are high in added sugar, sodium, and solid fats in the diets of young children (U.S. Department of Health and Human Services, 2012). Teachers become part of the solution to this nutritional paradox by understanding the difference between undernutrition and overnutrition and helping families address some of the more common conditions that may occur due to these aspects of malnutrition.

Recognizing Undernutrition

Although diets in the United States include an abundance of food for many people, the nutritional well-being of children can be compromised by nutrient deficiencies, or undernutrition. Undernutrition may be the result of poor dietary choices, serious illness, or lack of financial resources to provide sufficient amounts of healthful foods.

Insufficient Calorie Intake

Some infants and children do not consume sufficient calories to grow properly. They often appear significantly thinner or smaller compared to other infants and children of the same age. Physicians follow growth by measuring weight, length or height, and head circumference and comparing these measurements to standard growth charts. If children vary significantly from established growth patterns, they may be diagnosed with **failure to thrive**, a condition in which a child's growth rate slows down or comes to a halt. Infants or children with failure to thrive experience a drop-off in the rate of weight gain first, followed over time by a faltering of growth in height.

Failure to thrive may also be due to an underlying medical condition, such as heart, lung, or digestive problems. Sometimes growth failure can be related to psychological, social, or financial problems within the family. Undernutrition can occur in families who:

- Experience emotional problems.
- Experience economic problems such as unemployment or homelessness.
- Are involved in substance abuse.
- Lack knowledge about appropriate feeding.
- Use poor feeding techniques or have established a poor feeding relationship with their child (Johns Hopkins Children's Center, 2012a; Johns Hopkins Children's Center, 2012b).

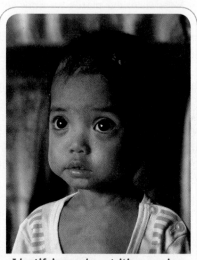

Identifying undernutrition requires looking beyond the child's height and weight. Consider the child's living situation, economic situation, and whether the child has a history of medical or psychological problems.

failure to thrive
a condition in which the growth rate slows down or comes to a halt; may be due to an underlying medical condition, such as heart, lung, or digestive problems or related to psychological, social, or financial problems within the family

psychosocial
refers to psychological and social factors that affect well-being

supplemental food programs
federal food programs that provide nutrition assistance for at-risk populations such as children, low-income families, and the elderly

When undernutrition is recognized, teachers work in conjunction with health care providers and families to provide nutrition support to children who are not growing properly. Specially prepared infant formulas, supplemental high-calorie beverages, and nutritious high-calorie snacks may be prescribed. If the problem is **psychosocial**, teachers can help families access appropriate support services such as those provided by doctors, dietitians, social workers, or qualified mental health advisers. A psychosocial concern refers to psychological or social factors that affect a child's well-being. For example, if a mother does not interact well with her baby because of postpartum depression and, therefore, doesn't respond appropriately to her baby's hunger cues, a psychosocial feeding problem can result.

Teachers can refer parents to **supplemental food programs** (federal food programs that provide nutrition assistance) such as the Special Supplemental Nutrition Program for Women, Infants, and Children, more commonly known as the WIC program. WIC serves low-income women, infants, and children up to age 5 by providing nutritious foods, such as milk, soy milk, whole-grain bread, cereals, brown rice, eggs, cheese, canned fish, juice, beans, peas, peanut butter, fruits, vegetables, baby foods, and formula, to supplement their diets (U.S. Department of Agriculture, Food and Nutrition Service, 2012b). In addition, food resources can be obtained from the Supplemental Nutrition Assistance Program (SNAP), formerly called the Food Stamp Program, which helps low-income families buy healthy foods (U.S. Department of Agriculture, Food and Nutrition Service, 2012a).

Iron-Deficiency Anemia

Iron-deficiency anemia is a condition in which, due to lack of iron in the diet, a person's body does not make enough healthy red blood cells to accomplish the goal of transporting oxygen in the bloodstream. It is one of the more common nutrient deficiencies among children in the United States (U.S. National Library of Medicine & National Institutes of Health, 2010). Researchers estimate that approximately 9% of children 1 to 3 years of age are iron deficient and that toddlers of Hispanic descent have an even higher incidence of 13.9% (Baker, Greer, & The Committee on Nutrition, 2010).

The signs of iron deficiency include sleepiness, irritability, difficulty concentrating, pale skin, headache, brittle nails, a sore tongue, and problems with memory and learning (Fretham, Carlson, & Georgieff, 2011; U.S. National Library of Medicine & National Institutes of Health, 2010). In addition, when children are deficient in iron, their immune system is less able to fight off infections, leading to illness and decreased school attendance. Of greatest importance is the association of iron-deficiency anemia with cognitive, socioemotional behavioral, and motor skill developmental delays (Georgieff, 2011). When young children do not receive enough iron in their diet, the development of the central nervous system may be significantly delayed and brain development may also be compromised (Baker et al., 2010; Beard, 2008). A window of opportunity may be available when these adverse effects can be corrected. The window, however, is age and time sensitive. If left untreated, the health concerns associated with iron-deficiency anemia, may be irreversible (Baker et al., 2010; Beard, 2008). Sufficient iron in children's diets is also important because it offers protection against lead poisoning. When iron levels are low, lead from the environment is more readily absorbed. The *Health Hint* describes the iron, lead, and calcium connection.

Children ages 1 to 3 are at higher risk for iron deficiency if they are:

- at the younger end of the age range
- of Hispanic descent

> **What if . . .**
> you suspected that a child in your class was not getting sufficient food due to the family's economic difficulties? How would you address this issue with the family? What food resources in your community would you recommend to them?

iron-deficiency anemia
a common single-nutrient deficiency of iron that results in the body making fewer red blood cells with less hemoglobin than normal; causes sleepiness, impaired growth and development, and increased risk of infection in young children

---

HEALTH HINT The Iron, Lead, and Calcium Connection

Industrialized society has created a lead burden that is evident worldwide. Lead is a heavy metal that can have significant health consequences when children are exposed to it in their environment. Urban environments, in particular those with older dilapidated multiple-dwelling buildings, create high-risk situations in terms of lead exposure because lead-containing paints often flake off in the older buildings. Children can get lead poisoning by breathing and swallowing dust that contains lead.

What are some effects of too much lead in children?

- It Increases the risk of anemia because it inhibits the production of heme, the oxygen-carrying component of hemoglobin in the red blood cells.
- It causes central nervous system damage in children who are exposed.
- It can result in impaired intellectual function and developmental delays including problems with speech and language.

- It can cause behavioral problems.
- It can damage the kidneys.

How does children's nutritional status impact the risk for lead toxicity?

- Children who are iron deficient absorb more lead.
- Children who go a long time without eating absorb more lead.
- A diet high in fat content promotes more lead absorption.
- A high-calcium diet protects by competing with lead for absorption.

What can early childhood educators do to protect children from lead poisoning?

- Establish lead-free classroom environments.
- Provide meals that are high in iron and calcium, and low in fat.
- Refer the family to a health care professional for a blood lead test, if the child is at risk for iron deficiency or environmental lead exposure.

Sources: R. D. Baker and F. R. Greer, *The American Academy of Pediatrics Clinical Report Diagnosis and Prevention of Iron Deficiency and Iron-Deficiency Anemia in Infants and Young Children (0–3 Years of Age)*, 2010, *Pediatrics*, *104*(1): 110. California Department of Public Health, Childhood Lead Poisoning Prevention Branch, *Frequently Asked Questions about Lead Poisoning*, 2010, retrieved from http://www.cdph.ca.gov/programs/CLPPB/Pages/FAQ-CLPPB.aspx#simplesteps; KidsHealth from Nemours, *Protecting Your Family*, 2009, retrieved from http://kidshealth.org/parent/medical/brain/lead_poisoning.html#.

- born prematurely
- overweight or obese
- from low-income families
- consume milk, a beverage that is low in iron to the exclusion of iron-rich solid foods (Baker et al., 2010; Brotanek, Gosz, Weitzman, & Flores, 2008; Fretham, Carlson, & Georgieff, 2011; Queen Samour & King, 2012; Ziegler, 2011)

In the opening case scenario, Gabriella faces three risk factors for iron deficiency. She is an overweight child and is of Hispanic descent. In addition, Gabriella consumes a diet that is low in iron content due to her vegetarian food choices. She prefers cheese and milk products instead of iron-rich beans, peas, lentils, and leafy green vegetables. For Gabriella the risk factors compound, resulting in her iron deficiency.

Teachers are in a good position to watch for the symptoms of iron deficiency. Teachers affiliated with Head Start programs are more likely to be aware of children who have low iron levels because of the Head Start–mandated requirement that medical and nutritional screens be conducted. These screenings often include an evaluation of children's iron status.

Vitamin D and Health

rickets
a nutritional deficiency caused by a lack of vitamin D; can cause bones to form improperly, resulting in severe skeletal deformities

vitamin D
a nutrient (fat-soluble vitamin) that aids in calcium absorption; can be obtained from dietary sources such as fortified milk and yogurt, but can also be produced in the skin in response to sunlight

Historically, investigations by researchers at the turn of the century focused on the role of vitamin D in preventing **rickets**, a nutritional deficiency caused by a lack of vitamin D. **Vitamin D** is a nutrient that can be obtained from dietary sources but is also produced in the skin in the presence of sunlight. A severe deficiency of vitamin D can affect the absorption of calcium and phosphorus from the gut, which in turn causes bones to form improperly, resulting in severe skeletal deformities. At the turn of the 20th century, rickets was rampant among poor children living in the industrialized cities of North America where lack of exposure to sunshine, especially during the winter months, in combination with poor diets often caused as many as 80% of children to suffer from this bone deforming malady (Holick, 2010). With the discovery of the beneficial role of vitamin D came the clear understanding of how to cure this form of undernutrition. The public health initiative that resulted in adding vitamin D to milk in the 1930s appeared to have effectively eradicated vitamin D deficiency in the United States (National Institutes of Health, Office of Dietary Supplements, 2011). However, it has been recognized in more recent years that low vitamin D status is still a problem in the United States, (Holick, 2010; Queen Samour & King, 2012). In addition, health authorities now understand that vitamin D has many functions in the body and is needed for more than just bone health. For example, vitamin D may play a role in the prevention of cancer, heart disease, infectious diseases, and autoimmune disorders (National Institutes of Health, Office of Dietary Supplements, 2011; Queen Samour & King, 2012). The incidence of vitamin D deficiency is estimated to be about 1% for U.S. children 1–8 years of age. In addition, 10% of children fell into the "at risk for deficiency" category (Looker et al., 2011). Children most likely to be impacted are babies who were exclusively breastfed without vitamin D supplementation in the past 6 months, children who have immigrated from Asia, Africa, and the Middle East, and children not exposed to sufficient sunlight especially if they live in a temperate climate, used sunscreen, and/or are dark skinned and obese children (Holick, 2010; National Institutes of Health, Office of Dietary Supplements, 2011). The dietary recommendation for vitamin D was doubled by the American Academy of Pediatrics for infants, children, and adolescents in 2008 (Wagner, Greer, & the Section on Breastfeeding and Committee on Nutrition, 2008).

Teachers can contribute to children's health and reduce the risk of vitamin D deficiency in young children by ensuring that children are offered vitamin D–fortified milk or vitamin D and calcium–fortified soy milk at meal and snack times instead of juice that is not fortified or soft drinks. Other foods to encourage that are good sources of vitamin D include fortified yogurt, fortified cereals, and fortified fruit juices. Salmon, tuna, and sardines are naturally excellent sources of vitamin D (National Institutes of Health, Office of Dietary Supplements, 2011).

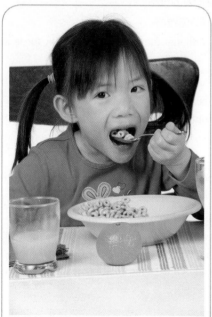

Selecting cereal, milk, and orange juice fortified with vitamin D gives an excellent boost to children's diets.

Addressing Undernutrition

In the United States there is a blending of public and privately funded programs that can help address undernutrition in young children. For example the USDA has oversite over five programs that serve the nutritional needs of children:

- National School Lunch Program,
- School Breakfast Program,
- Child and Adult Care Food Program,
- Summer Food Service Program, and
- Fresh Fruit and Vegetable Program (U.S. Department of Agriculture, Economic Research Service, 2011).

Both the National School Lunch Act (1946) and the School Breakfast Program (1966) were enacted by Congress to help protect against dietary deficiency diseases and to improve the nutrition of low-income children (Story, 2009). The goals of the Healthy Hunger Free Kids Act of 2010 include improving access to and enhancing the nutrition standards of these programs. As previously mentioned, other government-sponsored nutrition programs that families can be linked to in the community include the Special Supplemental Nutrition Program for Women, Infants, and Children (WIC), which in addition to providing meal packages for pregnant and postpartum women and children provides nutrition services to almost half of all infants born in the United States, and the Supplemental Nutrition Assistance Program (SNAP) (U.S. Department of Agriculture, Economic Research Service, 2011). Privately funded nutrition networks that can support the nutritional needs of low-income families include food pantries, soup kitchens, and emergency food assistance programs. These programs act as a nutrition safety net for young children. Teachers need to be knowledgeable about these resources and understand the importance of addressing any form of undernutrition if it is identified so they can help families access resources, as Cecelia did in the opening case scenario.

Recognizing Overnutrition

Consuming excessive calorie-rich foods also plays a role in the quality of diet and health of young children. Overnutrition is a form of malnutrition caused by an imbalance of calories consumed when compared to calories needed for growth and activity. Overnutrition causes children to become overweight or obese. Today's changing nutrition environment and more sedentary lifestyles are factors in overnutrition and have resulted in an epidemic of obesity in young children. In fact, obesity is the number-one form of malnutrition in the United States today. Among preschool children aged 2–5, obesity increased from 5.0% to 12.1% during 1976–1980 and 2009–2010 and from 6.5% to 18% among those aged 6–11. Overall about 12.5 million children age 2–19 are obese in the United States (Odgen, Carroll, & Centers for Disease Control and Prevention, 2010; Ogden, Carroll, Kit, & Flegal, 2012).

Identifying Obesity in Children

Obesity is identified and defined based on measurements of children's heights and weights that are plotted on growth charts. Conducting height and weight screenings during the beginning of a program's year is a procedure that can help screen for children who are underweight or overweight and obese. The Centers for Disease Control and Prevention (CDC) provides growth charts to assist in screening and identifying children who are at risk for overweight and obesity from age 2–20. (See the Chapter Resources on MyEducationLab for growth charts.) The charts show percentile curves that represent the range of distribution of heights and weights typical in young children in the United States (Centers for Disease Control and Prevention, 2010).

In children over age 2 another criterion used to determine appropriate rate of growth is the **body mass index (BMI)**. Although heights and weights give a comparison for norms based on age, the BMI is not age specific. Instead, the BMI assesses body weight relative to height to determine the risk for overweight or obesity. The CDC makes it easy for teachers to calculate and plot BMIs for individual children and also by class with their online BMI tool for schools (see the Web Resources listing at the

body mass index (BMI)
a calculation that evaluates weight in relation to height to assess whether an individual is obese or underweight. In young children BMI is also a measure of growth. It is calculated by dividing the weight of a person by the height squared

end of the chapter). Figure 2-2 shows different BMI measurements for a 5-year-old boy. This figure illustrates how BMIs are used to identify obesity, overweight, healthy weight, and underweight in young children.

For infants and toddlers under age 2, growth is also evaluated by monitoring weight, length, and weight relative to length using the World Health Organization (WHO) growth charts, which better reflect growth in infancy by describing growth patterns among children who were predominantly breastfed for at least 4 months and still breastfeeding at 12 months (Centers for Disease Control and Prevention, 2010). These measurements should be recorded regularly throughout the year to ensure that proper growth is occurring. (Growth charts are discussed in more detail in Chapter 9.)

If excessive weight gain is identified, sharing this information with parents can set a course for change and obesity prevention. In dealing with weight issues in young children an "ounce of

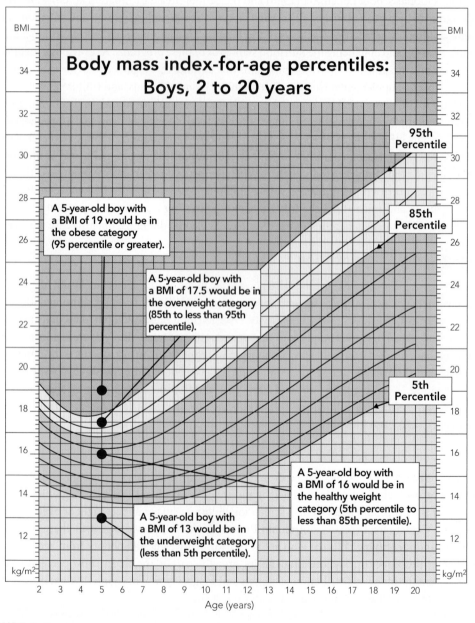

FIGURE 2-2

What Is the BMI? This growth chart indicates how children are identified as obese, overweight, healthy weight, and underweight using the BMI calculation.

Source: Based on *Healthy Weight: Assessing Your Weight: About BMI for Children and Teens*, by the Centers for Disease Control and Prevention, 2012, retrieved from http://www.cdc.gov/healthyweight/assessing/bmi/childrens_bmi/about_childrens_bmi.html.

prevention is truly worth a pound of cure" because children who are obese when young are more likely to grow up to be overweight and obese adults. A fat baby is no longer regarded as a healthy baby, and children do not always grow out of their "baby fat."

The Health Consequences of Obesity

Being overweight or obese during childhood is of great concern because of the immediate as well as the long-term health consequences. Obese children suffer from problems such as **sleep apnea** (a sleep disorder in which a person's breathing pauses during sleep), asthma, and orthopedic problems that interfere with learning and contribute to a higher incidence of absenteeism (Spruyt & Gozal, 2012; U.S. National Library of Medicine National Institutes of Health, 2012; University of Washington, 2012). Being obese at a young age and over a long period of time can have a significant adverse impact on health and longevity (Olshansky et al., 2005). Figure 2-3 summarizes the health risks for children who are overweight or obese.

Unfortunately, the health-related consequences of obesity can become self-perpetuating. Consider this scenario:

> At age 8 Colin was significantly obese. During his third-grade year he developed a hip abnormality in which the growing end of the thigh bone slipped from the ball of the hip joint, a condition often linked to obesity. Colin experienced considerable pain and ultimately required surgery to realign the joint. Colin missed school and when he was able to return he used a wheelchair for 6 weeks. During this time he was unable to participate actively in physical education classes. His weight increased because of this inactivity. Although his teacher tried to help him catch up with his class assignments, his condition was painful, making it hard for him to progress in his schoolwork.

In this scenario, Colin's obesity caused both health and learning problems.

> ### What if . . .
> you had a family whose cultural traditions valued heavy babies and young children and felt this was a sign of good health? How would you address the sensitive subject of obesity?

sleep apnea
a sleep disorder in which a person's breathing pauses during sleep

---

FIGURE 2-3   Health Problems Associated with Obesity in Children

Heart-related risks:
  High blood cholesterol levels
  High blood pressure
  Increased risk of heart attack or stroke
    as adults

Endocrine-related risks:
  Insulin resistance
  Type 2 diabetes

Cancer-related risks:
  Breast cancer
  Colon cancer
  Cancer of the esophagus
  Kidney cancer

Gastrointestinal-related risks:
  Nonalcoholic fatty liver disease
  Gall bladder disease

Lung-related risks:
  Asthma
  Obstructive sleep apnea syndrome (a sleep
    disorder in which there are frequent
    breathing interruptions during sleep)

Orthopedic-related risks:
  Bow legs
  Slipped capital femoral epiphysis (the
    ball of the thigh bone slips off the
    thigh bone)
  Arthritis

Mental health-related risks:
  Depression
  Low self-esteem
  Face social stigmatization and
    discrimination

Sources: U.S. Department of Health and Human Services, The Surgeon General's Vision for a Healthy and Fit Nation. Rockville, MD: U.S. Department of Health and Human Services, Office of the Surgeon General, 2010. http://www.surgeongeneral.gov/library/obesityvision/obesityvision2010.pdf; Policy Statement: Prevention of Pediatric Overweight and Obesity, American Academy of Pediatric Committee on Nutrition, 2003 reaffirmed 2007, *Pediatrics 112*(2) 424–430; U.S Department of Health and Human Services, National Institutes of Health National Cancer Institute Fact Sheet: Obesity and Cancer Risk Fact Sheet: National Cancer Institute, 2012. Retrieved from http://www.cancer.gov/cancertopics/factsheet/Risk/Fs3_70.pdf.

The Psychosocial Impact of Obesity

Children who are obese often experience low self-esteem, depression, and poor peer interactions (Nevin-Folino, 2003; updated 2008). Researchers in one study revealed that obesity affected health-related quality-of-life indicators such as physical, psychosocial, emotional, social, and school functioning. The effects were comparable to those reported for children diagnosed with cancer and who were undergoing treatment (Schwimmer, Burwinkle, & Varni, 2003). In addition, obese children were four times more likely than healthy children to do poorly in school.

The psychosocial consequences to children are significant. Children who are obese face stigmatizing attitudes by the adults who care for them such as health professionals, teachers, PE teachers, and parents as well as their peers. The impact of the negative stereotyping and marginalization by their peers is particularly painful for obese children and can become apparent in preschoolers as early as age 3. Students become sensitized to obesity, preferring nonobese friends and attributing negative personality traits such as laziness and sloppiness to obese children (O'Dea and Eriksen, 2010; Schwimmer et al., 2003). Teachers should be particularly attuned to the challenges faced by children who are overweight and obese whose struggles with self-esteem increase as they mature.

The Role of Inadequate Physical Activity

Lack of sufficient physical activity contributes to the other side of the coin of obesity, inadequate **energy expenditure** (the amount of calories burned), which compounds the problem of overnutrition. Maintaining a healthy weight requires a fine balance between calorie intake and energy expenditure. Some practices in early childhood and school settings may contribute to inadequate physical activity among young children, such as:

- Providing little space for safe indoor or outdoor active play.
- Offering insufficient opportunities for physical activity in daily programming.
- Devoting most of the school day to academic achievement, as mandated by some school districts, at the cost of time for exercise.
- Neglecting training of teachers in after-school programs who are able to promote and model physical activity (Coleman, Geller, Rosenkranz, & Dzewaltowski, 2008).
- Withholding recess as a form of punishment or as a means to have children catch up on assignments.
- Eliminating physical education classes due to funding constraints, which decreases opportunities for exercise and also decreases the focus on teaching physical activity skills that support active lifestyles.

Teachers are in a good position to encourage activity in young children by increasing the amount of time in the daily schedule devoted to outside play and incorporating physical activity into daily routines, as follows:

- Plan walking field trips and scavenger hunts in the community.
- Include a physical activity center during self-select time.
- Provide activities using portable playground equipment, such as balls and hoops.
- Plan school events with a physical activity theme, such as a field day, sock hop dance, walk or bike to school day, walking club, parent–child activity night.
- Offer fund-raisers that encourage physical activity such as a jog-a-thon, fun run, or family walking obstacle course.
- Promote noncompetitive sports and cooperative games so that all children—regardless of skill level and ability—will want to participate.
- Plan time for both structured and unstructured play.
- Integrate physical activity into lesson plans (Lee, Srikantharajah, & Mikkelsen, 2010).

energy expenditure the amount of energy or calories used by the body during rest and physical activity

This **video** shows Walk and Bike to School Day, a collaborative effort between a school and community. What are some other kinds of school and community activities that provide children with opportunities to increase their physical activity?

The National Association for Sport and Physical Education (NASPE) is a professional organization and national authority on physical education, sports, and physical activity. The NASPE has established general physical activity guidelines for children in two main age divisions: birth to age 5 and ages 5 to 12 (see Web Resources). These age-specific physical activity recommendations give teachers parameters to consider as they strive to achieve physically active environments for the children in their care. Important standards are listed for each age group. For example, it is recommended that toddlers (1- to 2-year-olds) receive 30 minutes of structured physical activity each day and preschoolers (3- to 4-year-olds) 60 minutes. Toddlers and preschoolers should participate in at least 60 minutes or more of unstructured play per day as well. NASPE also recommends that, unless sleeping, young children should not be sedentary for more than 60 minutes at a time.

Inactive lifestyles contribute to the rising incidence of obesity.

Guidelines are also offered on how to promote the physical activity of infants by creating safe settings that do not limit movement, but do stimulate babies to explore their environment (National Association for Sport and Physical Education, 2009). The NASPE website provides links to excellent resources that help teachers incorporate physical activity into the early childhood education setting.

Food Insecurity and Obesity

In the United States one in four children in 2010 lived in homes that experienced food insecurity at some point during the year (Child Trends, 2012). **Food insecurity**, or consistently having too little food to eat due to financial constraints, can predispose low-income children to overweight and obesity. Although it seems contradictory, hunger and obesity can exist side by side. The rationale behind this association is not completely understood; however, food insecurity can lead to less expensive, less healthy food choices that are limited in variety. In addition, children who do not have a consistent source of food may overeat when food is available (Child Trends, 2012). Low-income families often have to choose high-fat, energy-dense, inexpensive food to maximize their calories per dollar spent. They also face additional risk factors for obesity such as limited access to healthy and affordable foods, and lack of safe and accessible recreational facilities, parks, and walking trails that support physical activity (Food Research and Action Center, 2011).

food insecurity
the lack of access to enough food to prevent hunger at all times due to lack of financial resources

Teachers need to understand that children who are obese and who eat larger than normal serving sizes may be reacting to the stress of food insecurity. They should consider how they might support these children who struggle with the stigma of obesity and poverty. Here is how one teacher approached this situation:

> Vanessa, a preschool teacher, carefully supervises Kimberly during mealtime, especially when oranges are on the menu. Kimberly, who is overweight, frequently serves herself more orange wedges than the one-half orange portion planned for each child. This became a problem during the family-style meal service when the other children at the table did not get their share of oranges. Vanessa, who was concerned about Kimberly's weight, mentioned this behavior to Kimberly's father Mark. Mark explained that the family could not afford to buy fresh fruit very often and admitted that Kimberly had never had oranges before coming to school. Vanessa recognized that Kimberly's family was suffering from food insecurity. During the meal service she showed Kimberly how to count out her portion. Then she arranged for Kimberly to have more oranges if she wanted after everyone was served.

Addressing Obesity

Helping children learn healthful eating habits and encouraging enjoyment of physical activity are two ways in which teachers can promote a proactive approach to the challenges of the obesity epidemic. It is important for educators to stay abreast of evidence-based approaches to achieve these goals. Teachers and their early childhood programs are partners with families and communities in

POLICY POINT Supporting Policy Changes That Impact Obesity

Many teachers feel a strong need to advocate for change in their school or community to fight the obesity epidemic. To start, they need information to "shake things up." To influence decision makers, they need information that relates specifically to their state.

The Oregon Health Sciences University, with support from the U.S. Department of Health and Human Services, developed a website called the Data Resource Center for Child and Adolescent Health at www.childhealthdata.org. This resource offers state-by-state data on the incidence of obesity and discusses what each state is doing to address the obesity epidemic. Another website that provides state-by-state data on the food environment is the USDA's Economic Research Service website found at www.ers.usda.gov/ which includes the Food Environment Atlas and Food Desert Locator. This website provides state and county information that relates to a community's ability to access nutritious foods and participate in physical activity, the incidence of food insecurity, and other socioeconomic information. These powerful facts can provide the impetus teachers need to support change that improves the wellness of young children.

Source: *Childhood Obesity Action Network, State Obesity Profiles,* by the National Initiative for Children's Healthcare Quality, the Child Policy Research Center, and the Child and Adolescent Health Measurement Initiative, 2009, retrieved on April 6, 2012, from http://www.childhealthdata.org/browse/snapshots/obesity-2007; *Your Food Environment Atlas,* U.S. Department of Agriculture Economic Research Service, 2010. http://maps.ers.usda.gov/FoodAtlas/.

promoting healthy lifestyles for children. Classroom approaches that help teachers be proactive in addressing the concerns of obesity include the following:

- Provide an environment that supports wellness, such as offering nutritious meals and providing space and equipment for physically active play.
- Integrate nutrition concepts into program curriculum and activities. For example children can study different kinds of beans, learn how whole-grain bread is made, and participate in growing a vegetable garden.
- Introduce games that promote physical activity, such as "Duck, Duck, Goose" or "Four Square."
- Invite parents to help plan menus, to share ideas about nutrition activities and games, and to promote these wellness approaches at home.
- Be a good wellness role model. Eat with pleasure the healthful meals served to children. Model enjoyment of physical activity and participate in active games with the children.

Teachers who have insight into the challenging and changing nutrition environment in the United States have the tools necessary to formulate a plan for protecting the health and well-being of young children in their care. See the *Policy Point* for information on supporting policy changes that impact obesity.

USING RECOMMENDED STANDARDS TO GUIDE HEALTHY EATING

Knowledge of nutrition is crucial in supporting good health in adults and children alike. Teachers and parents select and plan a healthy diet for the children in their care and, therefore, must understand the components of food that contribute to a balanced diet. Researchers and experts in the field of nutrition have established guidelines and standards to ensure that teachers know how to plan appropriate menus and serve foods that support healthy development.

Understanding Dietary Reference Intakes

Dietary Reference Intakes (DRIs)
a listing of daily estimated nutrient requirements; used to assess diets for adequacy at the nutrient level

The **Dietary Reference Intakes (DRIs)** established by the Institute of Medicine of the National Academies are one of the important standards used to guide development of a healthful diet. They were developed in phases starting in 1997 through 2011, and continue to evolve using the most recent research on nutrition to establish evidence-based reference values that specify the amount of nutrients needed in the diets of adults, children, and population groups to maintain good health (Committee to Review Dietary Reference Intakes for Vitamin D Food and Nutrition Board & Institute of Medicine of the National Academies, 2011; Otten, Pitzi-Hellwig, & Meyers, 2006). (DRIs are listed in Web Resource and can be found in the Chapter Resources on MyEducationLab). The nutrients reviewed within the DRI guidelines include those that are considered essential nutrients because they either cannot be made in the body or cannot be made in sufficient quantities to meet the body's needs; consequently, the nutrients must be consumed in the diet.

The Dietary Reference Intakes form the basis for diet recommendations made by health and government authorities. They are used as a foundation for the development of public policies that address the health and wellness of children in the United States. For example, the *Dietary Guidelines for Americans, 2010* and the MyPlate base their diet recommendations on meeting the nutrient goals established by the DRIs. In addition, the National School Lunch and the School Breakfast Programs have updated their standards for meal planning to reflect the DRIs and Dietary Guidelines for Americans (U.S. Department of Agriculture, Food and Nutrition Service, 2012c). The Dietary Reference Intakes are the guiding force when researchers assess the nutritional quality of children's diets. Studies that link iron-deficiency anemia to insufficient iron intake could not draw these conclusions without the DRIs, the yardstick for healthy diets. To understand the DRIs, it is helpful to become familiar with how the nutrients are divided into different categories, as discussed next.

Classification of Nutrients

Nutrients are classified into six major categories: protein, fat, carbohydrates, vitamins, minerals, and water (Figure 2-4). Food provides energy or calories from proteins, fats, and carbohydrates (macronutrients) and essential nutrients such as vitamins and minerals (micronutrients).

Macronutrients Proteins, fats, and carbohydrates are **macronutrients** that are needed in large amounts in the diet. **Carbohydrates** and **fats** are predominantly used as sources of fuel for the body. **Proteins** can also be used as fuel; however, they are preferentially used to regulate body processes and serve as building blocks for body structures such as muscles, organs, and blood.

The balance of macronutrients in the diet as well as the total amount provided by the diet is very important. Too many calories from the macronutrients will cause excessive weight gain, whereas too little may result in insufficient growth. Macronutrients are found in the typical foods children consume during a day. For example, a tuna sandwich served at lunch contains protein (in the tuna), carbohydrates (in the bread), and fat (in the mayonnaise). Most foods are a combination of macronutrients. Bread contains mostly carbohydrates, but does have some protein, and its fat content can

macronutrients
nutrient category that includes protein, fats, and carbohydrates; they are the energy- or calorie-providing nutrients and are needed in large amounts in the diet

carbohydrates
macronutrients in the form of sugars and starches that provide the body with energy

fats
macronutrients that provide the most concentrated source of energy for the body; also used to cushion the organs and to insulate the body

proteins
essential macronutrients that function as the building blocks for body structures such as muscles and organs; can also be used as a source of energy when necessary

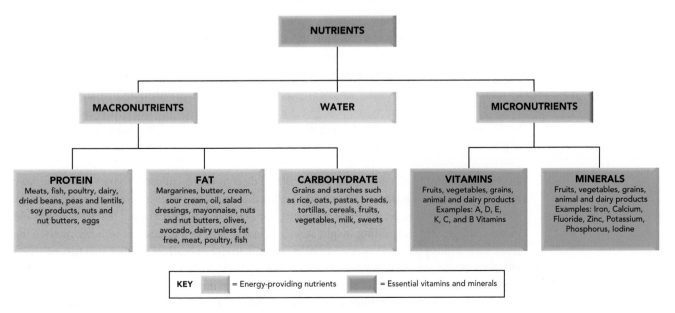

FIGURE 2-4
Classification of Nutrients

vary considerably as in the case of a high-fat croissant. The milk served at mealtime is also a combination of protein, fat, and carbohydrates unless the milk is fat free.

micronutrients
nutrient category that includes vitamins and minerals that are required in much smaller amounts than macronutrients, but are essential because the body cannot synthesize them and will not function properly without them. Children will not thrive without these nutrients in spite of sufficient calorie intake

Micronutrients The **micronutrients** include **vitamins** and **minerals**. The body requires micronutrients in much smaller amounts than macronutrients, but they are essential for children to thrive. It is with the assistance of micronutrients that energy from the macronutrients can be processed. Micronutrients promote growth and development. Each micronutrient has a unique role. Micronutrients are found in all different types of foods but some foods have a higher concentration of certain micronutrients. For example, milk is a natural source of calcium and is fortified with vitamin D, whereas citrus fruits and kiwis are high in vitamin C. Food that contain a significant amount of micronutrients per calorie of food consumed is called nutrient dense.. For example, a fresh fruit cup with strawberries, blueberries, and bananas served with non-fat light yogurt and a slice of whole grain toast is more nutrient dense than a couple of doughnuts or croissants for breakfast in the morning.

vitamins
an organic or carbon-containing class of essential micronutrients that are not made in the body or made in sufficient amounts to support the body's needs and, therefore, must be obtained from the diet

Water Water is essential for survival because all systems in the body need water to carry on life processes. Water transports nutrients in the bloodstream and flushes the body of wastes. It helps the body maintain proper temperatures through perspiration. Children obtain water from the beverages they drink, but also get water from foods that they eat such as fruits and vegetables.

Components of the Dietary Reference Intakes

minerals
an inorganic or non–carbon-containing class of micronutrients that are required in small amounts and must be obtained from the diet

The Dietary Reference Intakes include five component parts. The first four components establish recommendations for consuming micronutrients. The fifth component establishes guidelines for the macronutrients (Otten, et al., 2006). The components are as follows:

- *Recommended Dietary Allowances (RDAs):* Evidence-based nutrient goals that meet the needs of almost all healthy individuals including infants and children.

- *Adequate Intakes (AIs):* Same as the RDAs, but kept distinct because the evidence-based research is not as strong.

- *Estimated Average Requirements (EARs):* These nutrient recommendations meet the needs of 50% of the population and are used to assess food intakes of groups and provide standards for research conclusions.

- *Tolerable Upper Intake Levels (ULs):* These are the highest nutrient intake levels that pose no risk. They are used to ensure food safety by providing standards for individuals taking supplements or consuming fortified foods.

- *Acceptable Macronutrient Distribution Ranges (AMDRs):* AMDRs provide recommendations for protein, fat, and carbohydrate consumption, expressed as a percentage of total calorie needs. AMDRs are used to promote health and decrease the risk of chronic disease by providing guidelines on what proportion of the diet should consist of fats, carbohydrates, and protein.

Young children up to age 3 have a higher AMDR for fats than older children and adults. This is because they have smaller stomachs and a rapid rate of growth, both of which result in a need for higher calorie foods. This influences diet recommendations such as serving whole milk to most children up to age 2, and then switching to skim or 1% milk for children older than 2 years of age (see the *Nutrition Note*).

Some parents, in an effort to provide healthful diets to young children, restrict foods that have higher fat contents. Teachers can share with families that restricting fat excessively in young children's diets can negatively impact their rate of growth. For example, a teacher noticed that a 14-month-old in her program was not gaining weight as well as in the past. In a discussion with her mother, the teacher learned the baby was weaned from breast milk to rice milk when her daughter turned 1 year old. A referral to a dietitian revealed that rice milk was not an ideal choice because of its low fat and protein content. A switch back to whole milk resulted in an improved rate of weight gain.

Other families may worry about picky eaters who make limited food choices and wonder if they are getting enough nutrients. They may wonder if giving them multivitamins is appropriate. The *Safety Segment* describes the importance of using caution when offering multivitamins. Teachers,

NUTRITION NOTE Fats for Infants

Fat is an important nutrient for infants and toddlers who have high energy needs because of their rapid growth. These young children have a small stomach capacity and can meet their nutritional needs for growth and development only by eating calorie-dense fats. The fat intake requirement of infants is greater than at any other time in life, with infants needing 45% to 55% of their calories to come from fat.

Fats serve not only as a source of energy but as an aid in the absorption of the fat-soluble vitamins A, D, E, and K. Fat is also a source of *essential fatty acids*, which are vital in supporting optimal brain growth and development in infants. It is very important for adults who care for infants and toddlers to recognize the important role fat plays in early development.

Sources: "Low Fat Diets for Babies," Hassink, S. G., *American Academy of Pediatrics*, 2012, HealthyChildren.org at http://www.healthychildren.org/English/ages-stages/baby/feeding-nutrition/pages/Low-Fat-Diets-For-Babies.aspx; "Dietary (n-3) Fatty Acids and Brain Development," by S. M. Innis, 2007, *Journal of Nutrition, 137*(4), pp. 855–859; and "Lipid Requirements of Infants: Implications for Nutrient Composition of Fortified Complementary Foods," by R. Uauy and C. Castillo, 2003, *Journal of Nutrition, 133*(9), pp. 2962S–2972S.

when asked, should refer concerned parents to their health care providers for recommendations about multivitamin use.

In summary, the Dietary Reference Intakes reflect a variety of goals established by nutrition experts. These goals include ensuring that diets are adequate, but not excessive, in nutrient content and are protective of long-term health. Although teachers may not need to refer often to the DRIs, familiarity with them, and recognition of the science that is behind such resources, reminds teachers of the importance of nutrition and diet to healthy growth and development.

Evaluating Daily Values and Reading Food Labels

Another nutrient-based guidance system is one that teachers see every day: the **daily values (DVs)**, which are located on the label of almost all foods purchased and consumed. Daily values indicate what percentage of the daily recommended amount of a nutrient is met when a portion of a food is consumed. For example, a label may show that a serving of food meets 20% of the daily recommended amount of iron. This means 80% more iron must be consumed in other foods to meet the total daily value. The total daily value is based on a 2,000-calorie diet. Figure 2-5 shows an example of DVs displayed on a food label.

The daily values were established as a standard for measuring the contribution of a food item or supplement to the diet. The daily values are different from the Dietary Reference Intakes in that

daily values (DVs)
dietary reference values that are used on food labels and represent the requirements of an "average" individual, unlike Dietary Reference Intakes, which have reference values that represent different age and gender categories

SAFETY SEGMENT Keep Children Safe from Multivitamin Overdoses

The Dietary Reference Intakes (DRIs) provide guidance on the amount and types of essential nutrients individuals need to consume to maintain a healthy diet. Sometimes children may not eat as well as they should. Families may consider giving multivitamins to their children to make sure nutrition goals are met. Should children take multivitamins? Most healthy children do fine without dietary supplementation. Their needs are less than those of adults, and they may be consuming foods that are fortified such as breakfast cereals or juices.

Teachers should direct families with concerns to discuss the use of multivitamins with their doctor or dietitian. If they are

advised to take multivitamins, they should select ones that are designed for children. Caregivers should be careful about how they are dispensed. Many multivitamins can look and taste like candy, and children who take too many put themselves at risk.

The American Academy of Pediatrics and the American Dietetic Association agree that vitamin and mineral supplements (except for vitamin K in the newborn infant and vitamin D for the breast-fed infant, and non–breast-fed infants, and children who drink less than 32 ounces of formula or milk per day are not needed for most healthy children and that it is always better to meet nutrient needs with foods rather than in pill form.

Sources: *Vitamin D: On the Double*, Healthychildren.org, American Academy of Pediatrics, 2012, at http://www.healthychildren.org/English/healthy-living/nutrition/pages/Vitamin-D-On-the-Double.aspx; *Pediatric Nutrition Handbook*, 6th edition, edited by R. Kleinman, 2009, Elk Grove, IL: American Academy of Pediatrics; *Position of the American Dietetic Association: Nutrient Supplementation* by the American Dietetic Association, 2005, *Journal of the American Dietetic Association, 109*(12), pp. 2073–2085.

The nutrient content of a product cannot be assessed without knowing its serving size and how many servings are in a box.

Divide fat calories by total calories $\times$ 100 to get %fat calories. Healthy diets aim for more foods that have 30% calories or less from fat.

Information on fat and cholesterol content is particularly important for those concerned about heart health or weight. *Trans* fat and saturated fats and cholesterol should be kept as low as possible. Remember that just because a food announces its *trans* fat free does not mean it is low in saturated fats.

The sodium content of U.S. diets tends to be higher than desirable. A food is considered low sodium if it has 140 mg or less per serving.

The total carbohydrate figure includes fiber and sugar. The sugar includes natural sugars as well as added. This product is higher than some because it is a cereal with raisins. Look for foods that are rich in fiber. High fiber is 5 g or more per serving.

Children and adults should consume a diet rich in these nutrients. This product has been fortified and is a good source of iron. The DV for iron is 18 mg. At 25% this cereal provides 4.5 mg of iron per serving. 5% or less of DV is low and 20% or more is high in a particular nutrient.

Here are the standard intakes by which the %DV is derived. The complete list of the standard nutrients content for a 2,000-calorie diet can be found at: www.fda.gov/Food/ResourcesForYou/Consumers/NFLPM/ucm274593.htm)

Ingredients are listed from highest to lowest concentration. Allergy information is provided.

Nutrition Facts

Serving Size 1 cup (59g/2.1 oz)
Servings per Container About 12

Amount per Serving	Cereal
Calories	190
Calories from fat	15

	% Daily Values*
Total Fat 1.5g	2%
Saturated fat 0g	0%
Trans fat 0g	0%
Cholesterol 0mg	0%
Sodium 350mg	15%
Potassium 360mg	10%
Total Carbohydrate 45g	15%
Dietary fiber 7 g	28%
Sugars 19g	
Other carbohydrates 19g	
Protein 5g	
Vitamin A	10%
Vitamin C	0%
Calcium	2%
Iron	25%

*Daily Values are based on a 2,000 calorie diet. Your daily values may be higher or lower depending on your calorie needs

	Calories	2000	2500
Total fat	Less than	65g	80g
Sat fat	Less than	20g	25g
Cholesterol	Less than	300mg	300mg
Total carbohydrates		300g	350g
Fiber		25g	30g

Ingredients: Whole wheat, bran, sugar, raisins
CONTAINS: WHEAT

FIGURE 2-5

Sample Label for a High-Fiber Cereal

Sources: U.S. Food and Drug Administration, updated 2012. Retrieved from http://www.fda.gov/Food/ResourcesForYou/Consumers/ucm266853.htm. Eating Healthier and Feeling Better Using the Nutrition Facts Label U.S. Food and Drug Administration Appendix A: Definitions of Nutrient Content Claims, updated 2011. Retrieved from http://www.fda.gov/Food/GuidanceComplianceRegulatoryInformation/GuidanceDocuments/FoodLabelingNutrition/FoodLabelingGuide/ucm064928.htm.

they are not as age and gender specific. Instead, they represent what has been determined to be the average intake range of most people in the United States. The requirements for children age 4 and older, teenagers, adults, and the elderly were examined and averaged into one set of values. That is, the daily values are designed for an "average" person; they are a "one-size-fits-all" recommendation. This approach is appropriate to meet the needs of most people; however, some individuals may need less than the DV-recommended amounts of nutrients and some might need more. Infants and young children, for example, would need less than the daily value on a typical food label. Because infants and children have lower nutrient needs than the daily value listed for a 2000 calorie diet., teachers need to recognize that meeting 100% daily value is not a goal for them. Rather, daily values can best be used to understand the nutritional composition of a food. For example, a food that contains 5% or less of the daily is low in a particular nutrient. If it contains 20% or more of a nutrient it is considered a high source of that nutrient (U.S. Food and Drug Administration, 2012).

The daily values are in the process of being updated to reflect the new Dietary Reference Intakes and to take into consideration the nutrient requirements of children and pregnant and breast-feeding women (Institute of Medicine, 2009; Schneeman, Trumbo, Ellwood, & Satchell, 2006).

Food Label Requirements

In 1990 the Nutrition Labeling and Education Act (NLEA) established clear food labeling requirements. What was once a system riddled with misleading claims and unrealistic portion sizes is now an organized and accessible nutrition report within a nutrition information facts panel. The content of labels must now include:

- *Serving size and servings per container:* Listed in both the U.S. system of measurement (1/2 cup) and metric amounts (120 mL) or in amounts commonly consumed (6 crackers).

- *Nutrient amounts per serving:* Includes calories, fat calories, total fat, *trans* fats and saturated fats, cholesterol, sodium, potassium, total carbohydrates, fiber, sugar, and protein (**trans fats** are a type of unhealthy fat found in food that promotes heart disease).

- *Nutrients: as a percentage (%) of daily values:* Includes total fat, *trans* fats, saturated fats, cholesterol, sodium, total carbohydrate, fiber, vitamin A, vitamin C, calcium, and iron.

- *Ingredients:* Listed in order of highest to lowest concentration.

- *Warnings:* Lists possible allergens (briefly discussed in next section).

- *Nutrition claims:* Uses a standardized approach, such as what constitutes "low fat" or "high fiber" (see Table 2-1).

trans **fat**
a type of unhealthy dietary fat that is created when oils are partially hydrogenated; when found in food can promote heart disease

TABLE 2-1   Understanding Nutrient Content Claims

Nutrient	Per Serving
SODIUM	
Sodium free	Less than 5 mg
Very low sodium	35 mg or less
Low sodium	140 mg or less
Reduced sodium	25% lower than regular
CALORIES	
Calorie free	Less than 5 calories
Low calorie	40 calories or less
Reduced	25% lower than regular
FAT	
Fat free	Less than 0.5 g
Low fat	3 g or less
CHOLESTEROL	
Cholesterol free	Less than 2 mg
Low cholesterol	20 mg or less
SATURATED FAT	
Saturated fat free	Less than 0.5 g
Low saturated fat	1 g or less
Reduced saturated fat	25% less than regular
***TRANS* FAT**	
Trans fat free	Less than 0.5 g
FIBER	
High fiber	5 g or more

Source: Appendix A: Definitions of Nutrient Content Claims: Guidance for Industry: A Food Labeling Guide U.S. Food and Drug Administration, 2011, retrieved April 9, 2012, from http://www.fda.gov/Food/GuidanceComplianceRegulatoryInformation/GuidanceDocuments/FoodLabelingNutrition/FoodLabelingGuide/ucm064911.htm.

- *Health claims:* Claims that have been approved by the FDA for listing on food labels to describe a link between the food and health (U.S. Food and Drug Administration, 2011c).
- *Structure/Function claims:* Describes the effect a dietary ingredient has on the structure or function of the body such as "calcium builds strong bones" (U.S. Food and Drug Administration, 2011c).

Overall, the information provided on food labels helps consumers determine how the food contributes to the daily total nutritional intake and how a food's nutritional content compares to that of other foods. Teachers are likely to use label-reading skills when they comparison shop, looking for nutrient-rich foods to use in any type of food preparation for children, whether for lunch meals, snacks, or food-related school activities.

Reading Labels for Food Allergens

The Food Allergen Labeling and Consumer Protection Act, approved in 2004 and initiated in 2006, mandates that eight major foods or food groups—milk, eggs, fish, crustacean shellfish, tree nuts, peanuts, wheat, and soybeans—be included on the food label to help people with food allergies recognize products they may need to avoid.

Gluten free is a term that can voluntarily be included on labels. **Gluten** is a type of protein found in the grains of wheat, rye, barley, and possibly oats. Gluten causes symptoms in adults and children with **celiac disease**, a genetic gastrointestinal disorder (U.S. Food and Drug Administration, 2011a). Allergy information is shown on the bottom of a food label (in Figure 2-5 notice the statement "CONTAINS").

Special Labeling for Infant/Toddler Foods

The FDA and USDA have established slightly different labeling regulations for foods such as infant cereals and baby foods that are targeted toward children under the age of 2 and children ages 2 to 4. For example, labels may not contain information about fats and cholesterol. These regulations were developed in recognition of the specific nutrient needs of very young children. Special labeling for children's foods ensures that adults who care for children avoid making the mistake of inadvertently restricting certain nutrients such as fat and cholesterol that are needed for young children to grow properly (U.S. Food and Drug Administration, 2011b; U.S. Food and Drug Administration, 2011d).

Label reading is an important skill for teachers who may be gatekeepers for the types of food schools purchase for their meal service or foods uses for cooking activities. Label reading helps teachers to:

- Make decisions about the nutritional contribution of different foods.
- Ensure children get foods that are rich in healthful vitamins, minerals, and fiber.
- Select foods low in saturated fats, *trans* fats, and cholesterol (if over age 2).
- Avoid foods that are high in sodium.
- Select appropriate foods for children with food allergies or sensitivities, cultural food preferences, and special diets.

Using the *Dietary Guidelines for Americans, 2010*

The *Dietary Guidelines for Americans, 2010* is a collaborative effort of the Department of Health and Human Services (HHS) and the USDA (U.S. Department of Health and Human Services & U.S. Department of Agriculture, 2011). The guidelines are issued every 5 years to address the needs of people 2 years of age and older, offering recommendations for the general public as well as special populations such as children, the elderly, and pregnant women. The key points of the current dietary guidelines are described in Figure 2-6.

The dietary guidelines provide overall lifestyle recommendations that include dietary guidance and recommendations for physical activity. In addition the guidelines promote the development of healthy eating patterns that support achieving and maintaining a healthy weight. The principles of

---

What if . . .

a parent informed you that she did not want her healthy child to consume any foods with gluten? How would you negotiate a common ground with the parent and the child who might object to having to eat something different than what the other children in the class get to eat?

---

gluten
a type of protein found in the grains of wheat, rye, and barley that causes symptoms in adults and children with celiac disease. Oats are sometimes avoided as well on a gluten-free diet

celiac disease
a genetic gastrointestinal disorder that is characterized by an immune response to gluten that damages the gastrointestinal tract and leads to malabsorption

FIGURE 2-6   *Dietary Guidelines for Americans, 2010*

Overarching Goals

1. Maintain calorie balance over time to achieve and sustain a healthy weight.
2. Focus on consuming nutrient-dense foods and beverages.

Key Recommendations

1. Balance calories to manage weight.
   - Improve eating and physical activity behaviors.
   - Control total calorie intake to manage body weight.
   - Increase physical activity and reduce sedentary behaviors.
   - Maintain appropriate calorie balance at each stage of life.
2. Reduce certain foods and food components.
   - Reduce sodium intake to less than 2,300 mg and for those over 51 years of age, and those of any age who are African Americans or who have hypertension, diabetes, or chronic kidney disease, reduce sodium intake to 1,500 mg.
   - Consume less than 10% of calories as saturated fat by replacing with monounsaturated and polyunsaturated fats.
   - Consume less than 300 mg per day of dietary cholesterol.
   - Keep *trans* fatty acids as low as possible.
   - Reduce the intake of calories from solid fats and added sugars.
   - Limit the intake of foods that contain refined grains especially those that contain added sugars, solid fats, and sodium.
   - If alcohol is consumed it should be consumed in moderation.
3. Increase certain foods and food components.
   - Increase vegetable and fruit intake.
   - Increase variety of vegetables (orange, red, dark green vegetables and beans/peas).
   - Consume at least half of all grains as whole grains.
   - Increase fat free or low fat milk and milk products.
   - Choose a variety of protein foods (seafood, lean meats, poultry, eggs, beans and peas, soy products, and unsalted nuts and seeds).
   - Increase the use of seafood by choosing it to replace some meat or poultry in the diet.
   - Use oils to replace solid fats where possible.
   - Choose foods that provide more potassium, dietary fiber, calcium, and Vitamin D in the diet.
4. Build healthy eating patterns.
   - Select an eating pattern that meets nutrient needs over time at an appropriate calorie level.
   - Account for foods and beverages consumed and assess how they fit within a total healthy eating pattern.
   - Follow food safety recommendations when preparing and eating foods.

Source: Dietary Guidelines for Americans, 2010, by the U.S. Department of Health and Human Services and the U.S. Department of Agriculture, 2011 retrieved April 11, 2012 http://www.health.gov/dietaryguidelines/dga2010/DietaryGuidelines2010.pdf.

food safety are also stressed (U.S. Department of Health and Human Services & U.S. Department of Agriculture, 2011).

The dietary guidelines highlight that consuming nutritious foods, rather than supplements, is the foundation for good health. They also stress the importance of making smart choices from all food groups in order to obtain the most nutrients per calorie consumed. Figure 2-7 provides guidelines for selecting foods that are nutrient dense in relation to their calorie content such as whole grains, fruits, vegetables, nonfat or low-fat milk and low-fat dairy products, lean meats, poultry, seafood, beans, peas, nuts, and seeds. **Nutrient-dense foods** are foods that are high in vitamin and mineral content compared to their calorie content. Select unprocessed foods lower in sodium, solid fat, and added sugar content. Consider how the dietary guidelines with their focus on nutrient-dense foods were put to use by Kerrin in her family child care program:

nutrient-dense foods
foods that are high in vitamin and mineral content while relatively low in calorie content

> Kerrin decided to review the dietary guidelines before writing the menus for her child care program. She felt she was doing very well because she chose many nutrient-dense fruits and vegetables to place on her menu. She realized, however, that the guidelines recommended that at least half of the grains offered to children be whole grains. She decided to take steps to increase the whole-grain portions offered on her menus. She switched to the exclusive use of whole-grain bread products, brown rice, and whole-grain cereals. She also decided to combine nutrient-dense foods such as chicken stir fry over brown rice and sweet potato muffins, yogurt, and berry smoothies. These changes enhanced the nutritional quality of the menu and were well received by the children.

Choose Fresh Fruits
(or frozen without sugar)
such as citrus fruits,
mangos, berries, melons,
papaya, bananas, kiwis,
peaches, nectarines, plums

Choose Fresh Vegetables (or frozen
without sauces) such as dark green
and deep orange vegetables as well
as tomatoes; red, green, and yellow
peppers; red cabbage

Select Whole, Basic, Unprocessed Foods

**Select Lean Cuts of Meat, Skinless
Poultry and Fish, and Use More
Alternative Protein Sources** such
as dried beans, peas and lentils,
soy products, and nuts or nut butters

Select Low-Fat Dairy Products
such as skim or 1% milk (age 2
and older), low-fat cheeses
and plain yogurt with fresh fruit

Select Whole Grains
such as oats, brown rice,
whole grain breads, rolls
and cereals, barley, corn
tortillas

FIGURE 2-7
Components of a Nutrient-Dense Diet

Together the dietary guidelines and the Dietary Reference Intakes are the primary contributors to the policies that guide federally supported child nutrition programs. These guidelines can also be used more directly by teachers for:

- Planning menus.
- Implementing good nutrition and health education activities and lessons (see the *Teaching Wellness* feature).
- Developing parent education programs.
- Selecting topics for newsletters, posters, and bulletin board displays.
- Making healthy decisions about what to eat and how to plan their own active lifestyle to enhance health.

Overall the dietary guidelines primary goal is to promote and protect the health of the current and future generations of U.S. citizens. Everyone plays a role in achieving this goal including individuals, families, teachers and health care professionals, and policy makers (U.S. Department of Health and Human Services & U.S. Department of Agriculture, 2011).

Using the Choose MyPlate Food Guidance System

The MyPlate icon is the USDA's replacement for the MyPyramid Food Guidance System which was felt to be too complicated for many people to quickly interpret and apply. The MyPlate recommendations are more easily understood because the visual illustration of a place setting that includes an image of a plate divided into four color-coded sections (purple for protein, red for fruits, orange for grains, green for vegetables, and a blue side dish for dairy) shows not only what to eat but the

TEACHING WELLNESS   Eating Fruits and Vegetables Keeps Me Healthy

LEARNING OUTCOME   **Children will experience the sensory aspects (touch, smell, taste) of fruits and vegetables.**

Vocabulary focus: Touch, smell, taste, texture, odor, fragrance, flavor, names of foods, vitamins, minerals, fiber, names of rainbow colors.

Safety watch: Be aware of children's food allergies or restrictions; avoid serving these foods. Prepare foods appropriately to ensure food safety and to avoid potential for choking. Monitor for cleanliness and safety as children participate.

INFANTS AND TODDLERS

- **Goal:** Babies who are eating finger foods, and toddlers will touch, smell, and taste fruits and vegetables.
- **Materials:** Paper or plastic cups, plate or tray, fruits and vegetables (such as bananas, berries, oranges, green beans, zucchini, squash, carrots, potatoes).
- **Activity plan:** Cook firm vegetables until soft enough to pierce with a fork. Cut foods into tiny pieces no larger than ¼ inch. For babies and toddlers, offer foods one at a time based on the child's feeding plan. Offer familiar foods first and then add new foods to explore. Place a small portion of cut food on a tray or plate. Cover the food with a cup turned upside down. Show the child that a food is under the cup. Encourage the child to pick up the cup and discover the food underneath. Show the child that it is ok to touch the food. Describe touching, smelling and tasting the food, such as, "This is a fruit called banana. Let's touch it." Pretend to touch the banana and say, "It is soft. Let's smell the banana." Pretend to smell the food and

say, "The banana smells good! Let's taste the banana!" Pretend to taste the food and say, "The banana tastes sweet!" Next time try a different food.

- **How to adjust the activity:** To support children who are learning English create picture cards depicting the food to be explored. Include the name of the food in English as well as the child's home language (also spelled out phonetically for all kids if needed). Say the name of the food in both English and the home language. Support children with special developmental needs by guiding their hands as they touch the food, and moving the food to the child with your clean and gloved hand. Provide ample time for touching and smelling according to the child's needs, and never force children to taste the food. Reinforce each child's effort by remarking, "You are getting to know about fruits and vegetables by smelling, touching, and tasting these foods. That is a good way to learn."
- **Did you meet your goal?** Did the child explore—touch, smell, and taste—the offered foods?

PRESCHOOLERS AND KINDERGARTNERS

- **Goal:** Children will explore the texture, smell, and flavor of various fruits and vegetables that learn about why these foods are good for them.
- **Materials:** The children's book *Eating the Alphabet: Fruits & Vegetables from A to Z*, by Lois Ehlert; 6 fresh fruits and vegetables depicted in the book, 6 cups, foil, serving bowl, small plates, spoons, napkins, a serving tray, and paper towels.
- **Activity plan:** Select 6 foods and cut them into bite-size pieces. Place a small spoonful of each food into a cup, cover with foil, and poke a few small holes in the foil with a fork. Place the remaining portion of each food into serving bowls. Set all on a tray. Cover the serving bowls with paper towels so the foods are a mystery. Invite children to gather for the activity. Explain that there are many fruits and vegetables—enough for each letter of the alphabet. Read the children's book. Encourage children to name the fruits and vegetables as you read. Teach children by saying, "Fruits and vegetables are good for our bodies. Eating a variety of fruits and vegetables helps us feel good and gives our bodies the energy we need to keep healthy so that we can run and play and so our bodies grow strong." Name a fruit or vegetable from the book and

ask children to jump up high if they have tried the food that was named. Vary the movement each time a new food is named. Invite children to gather at a table. Ask them to smell the foods that are hidden in the foil-covered cups and try to identify them by the smell. Then ask the children to remove the foil to discover the food inside the cup. Uncover and pass the serving bowls of foods. Invite children to serve themselves a piece of each food. Encourage them to describe the texture, smell and flavor of each food. Identify which food is a fruit and which is called a vegetable. Encourage children's efforts by saying, "You are really exploring these fruits and vegetables by using your senses to touch, smell, and taste them." Reinforce why these foods are important to eat.

(Continued)

- **How to adjust the activity:** Use picture cards with the food names included in English and the other home languages of children in the class. Repeat the names of each food in all languages spoken by children in the class. Reinforce the message by using gestures as you speak to communicate touching, smelling, and tasting the foods. Be aware that some children may have an aversion to touching certain foods or textures. Provide time for children to explore. Ensure that each child can readily reach the cups to smell, and serve the foods to taste them. Do not force children to touch, smell, or taste.

- **Did you meet your goal?** Are children able to describe the texture, odor, and flavor of each food? Can the children describe why eating fruits and vegetables is important?

SCHOOL-AGE CHILDREN

- **Goal:** Children will learn that a healthy meal includes a "half plate" of fruits and vegetables. They will be able to identify a color combination of fruits and vegetables that is very healthy (rich in Vitamin A) and describe why fruits and vegetables are an important part of the diet.

- **Materials:** MyPlate Mini Poster (retrieve from: www.choosemyplate.gov/downloads/mini_poster_English_final.pdf), picture or poster showing many fruits and vegetables, construction paper for each color of the rainbow (red, orange, yellow, green, blue, purple), magazine pictures depicting brightly colored fruits and vegetables (or stickers of fruits and vegetables), small white paper plate, crayons or marking pens, scissors, glue.

- **Activity plan:** Gather children together and show them the MyPlate Mini Poster. Briefly review the different food groups. Point out that the poster shows that a healthy meal includes enough fruits and vegetables to fill half the plate. Describe the benefits of these foods by saying, "Fruits and vegetable are very high in vitamins, minerals and fiber. These are all important for the body to grow." Explain that a very healthy group of fruits and vegetables are those that are dark green, orange or red such as, spinach, broccoli, mangos, papayas, cantaloupe, carrots, sweet potatoes, red peppers and tomatoes. Invite the children to make a rainbow placemat using the colored construction paper. Provide a small paper plate to glue to the placemat. Ask the children to fill half of their plate with pictures of fruits and vegetables for each color of the rainbow, by cutting and pasting pictures, drawing a picture of a food, or writing in the name of the food or food group with a marker of the food group's color. Remind them to be sure to include some dark green and orange or red foods.

- **How to adjust the activity:** Label a piece of construction paper for each color of the rainbow with the name of the color in English as well as the home languages of the children in the class. Name the colors of the rainbow in all languages. Prepare the craft activity to suit the developmental needs of children in the class. Allow ample time for children to work. Offer adaptive scissors, glue sticks or tape, previously cut out pictures, or stickers depicting fruits and vegetables, to assist all children to be successful.

- **Did you meet your goal?** Are children able to fill their half of their plate with a rainbow of fruits and vegetables? Did they include dark green, orange, or red choices? Can they describe why fruits and vegetables are healthy foods?

FIGURE 2-8
ChooseMyPlate

Source: U.S. Department of Agriculture's ChooseMyPlate, USDA, 2012, retrieved April 17, 2012, from http://www.choosemyplate.gov/index.html.

proportions recommended. For example, the fruits and vegetables portion takes up half of the plate (Figure 2-8).

The goal of MyPlate, like its predecessor the MyPyramid, is to combine the specific nutrient recommendations of the Dietary Reference Intakes and the general messages of the *Dietary Guidelines for Americans, 2010* and translate them into practical guidelines for building a healthy diet. The MyPlate system includes much of the information formerly found on MyPyramid.gov such as how individuals can achieve personal health and nutrition goals and offers recommendations and strategies for young children ages 2 to 5, children ages 6 to 11, and adults (U.S. Department of Agriculture, 2012). The system focuses on the importance of both diet and physical activity to enhance health and is individualized for different age categories of children. For example, Figure 2-9 illustrates sample 1,400-calorie meal and snack patterns that meet the nutritional needs of 4-year-old boys and girls who are active 30–60 minutes per day.

The MyPlate guidance system offers a solution to healthy eating that is personalized, easy to understand, and positive. According to the USDA, the overall goals of the MyPlate system are to encourage adults and children to:

- Balance calories by enjoying foods but eating less and avoiding oversized portions.

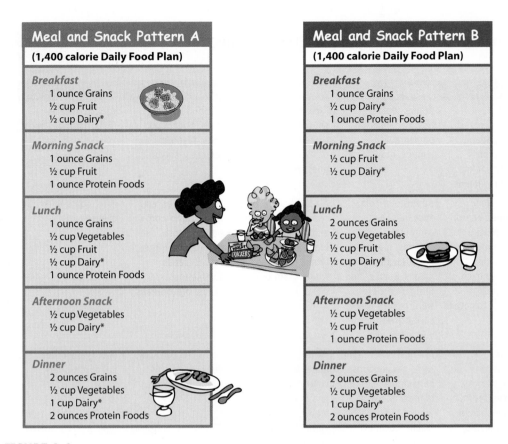

Meal and Snack Pattern A

(1,400 calorie Daily Food Plan)

Breakfast
1 ounce Grains
½ cup Fruit
½ cup Dairy*

Morning Snack
1 ounce Grains
½ cup Fruit
1 ounce Protein Foods

Lunch
1 ounce Grains
½ cup Vegetables
½ cup Fruit
½ cup Dairy*
1 ounce Protein Foods

Afternoon Snack
½ cup Vegetables
½ cup Dairy*

Dinner
2 ounces Grains
½ cup Vegetables
1 cup Dairy*
2 ounces Protein Foods

Meal and Snack Pattern B

(1,400 calorie Daily Food Plan)

Breakfast
1 ounce Grains
½ cup Dairy*
1 ounce Protein Foods

Morning Snack
½ cup Fruit
½ cup Dairy*

Lunch
2 ounces Grains
½ cup Vegetables
½ cup Fruit
½ cup Dairy*

Afternoon Snack
½ cup Vegetables
½ cup Fruit
1 ounce Protein Foods

Dinner
2 ounces Grains
½ cup Vegetables
1 cup Dairy*
2 ounces Protein Foods

FIGURE 2-9

1,400 Calorie Meal and Snack Patterns for Preschoolers
Source: USDA ChooseMyPlate retrieved April 17, 2012, from
http://www.choosemyplate.gov/downloads/1400cals.pdf.

- Increase in the diet healthy foods such as whole grains, vegetables, fruits, and fat-free or low-fat dairy products.

- Reduce foods that are higher in sodium, added sugar, and solid fats such as highly salted processed foods, cakes, cookies, candies, sweetened soft drinks, and high-fat meats such hotdogs, bacon, and sausage (U.S. Department of Agriculture, 2012).

Other resources available on the MyPlate website include a 10 Tips Nutrition Education Series, educational materials and lessons that support nutrition and physical activities messages in the classroom setting.

ETHNIC FOOD GUIDANCE SYSTEMS

The U.S. population is becoming increasingly multicultural. Consequently, teachers must be responsive to the cultural influences on children's diets as well as other aspects of school life. Various resources are available to support teachers as they become familiar with the food guidance systems from other countries. For example, Figure 2-10 illustrates an example of a Chinese food guide. Other examples of food guidance systems from different countries or representing different ethnic groups can be found in the web resource section. Many of the

FIGURE 2-10

A Food Guide Pagoda from China

Fats and
Oils, 25g

Milk and
Milk Products, 100g
Bean and
Bean Products, 50g

Meat and Poultry,
50–100g
Fish and Shrimp, 50g
Eggs, 25–50g

Vegetables, 400–500g
Fruits, 100–200g

Cereals, 300–500g

China

Source: Based on an illustration from the Chinese Nutrition Society, http://www
.cnsoc.org/asp-bin/EN/?page=8&class=42&id=149.

FIGURE 2-11   Modifying MyPlate for a Sampling of Ethnic Groups

Ethnic Group	Vegetables	Fruits	Grains	Protein	Dairy
Mediterranean	Eggplant, artichokes, squash, tomatoes, grape leaves, onions, mushrooms, okra, cucumbers, greens	Grapes, dates, figs, persimmons, pomegranate, lemons, grapefruit	Rice, bulgur, couscous, freekeh (green wheat), pasta, pita bread, pilaf, risotto	Seafood, poultry, lamb, beef, pork, nuts, fava beans, legumes, seeds	Yogurt, cheese, (feta, ricotta), milk
Navajo	Carrots, celery, corn, green beans, hominy, Navajo spinach, onion, potatoes, chili peppers, spinach, squash, squash blossoms, tomatoes	Apples, apricots, avocados, bananas, cantaloupe, casabas, grapes, kiwi, Navajo melon, raisins, sumac and juniper berries, watermelon, wax currant, wolfberry, yucca bananas	Alkaad (cake), blue corn bread, mush and dumplings, fry bread, kneel down bread, tortillas, whole grain bread	Mutton, deer, elk, fish, prairie dog, poultry, pork, deer, rabbit, pinon nuts, squash seeds, tumble mustard seeds, pinto beans	Milk, goats milk, cheese
Vietnamese	Artichoke, asparagus, broccoli, cabbage, carrots, cauliflower, corn, cucumbers, dauhu, eggplant, garlic, gia, green beans, leeks, mang, mung beans, onions, potatoes, raumuong (water spinach), squash, sweet potatoes, tomatoes	Mangosteen, dragon fruit, persimmons, banana, carambola, grapes, guava, jejube, lemon, lit chi, coconut, lychee, mango, orange, pandeo, papaya, pineapple, watermelon	Banh trang (rice paper wrapper) cellophane noodles, cha gio (egg roll), mein, mung beans, vermicelli, rice, rice noodles, xoi (sweet rice dish)	Beef, chicken, crab, duck, pork, shrimp, squid, fish. Eggs, tofu	Milk (valued but not traditional)

Sources: Mediterranean Grains: The History and Healthful Preparation of Four Old and Emerging Varieties, by Nour El-Zibdeh, *Today's Dietitian* Vol. 12 No. 6 p. 36, 2010
Mediterranean Fruits, FruitsInfo.com, 2012. http://www.fruitsinfo.com/mediterranean_fruits.htm.
Navajo Food, 2011. http://navajo-arts.com/food-navajo.html.
Indiana's Food for the Hungry, Modifying the Food Pyramid: Mexican American, Puerto Rican, Navajo, Jewish http://www.cfs.purdue.edu/safefood/nutrition/modifypyramid4.html.
Modifying the Food Pyramid: African American, Asian Indian, Chinese American, Vietnamese American http://www.cfs.purdue.edu/safefood/nutrition/modifypyramid3.html.
Vietnamese family health: What we eat to grow.http://vietfamilyhealth.org/nutrition/Nutrition_WhatWeEat_Online.pdf.
(All sources retrieved April 15, 2012)

 Early childhood educators use literature to help children learn about different cultures. As you watch this **video**, think about children's books that describe cultural differences in food, eating, and mealtimes. Which of these books are offered in languages other than English?

recommendations are similar to those of the USDA food guidance system in that eating a variety of nutritious foods in appropriate portions is encouraged. Figure 2-11 shows how the MyPlate can be modified to accommodate typical food choices for a sampling of ethnic groups.

Providing Bilingual Educational Materials

The MyPlate website does provide many of its materials in Spanish including their 10 Tips Nutrition Education Series. Although the MyPyramid approach has been archived by the USDA, the information shared is still very valid. There are many educational materials currently available in translated versions that help convey important nutrition concepts. For example, the Pyramid has been translated into 36 different languages thanks to the New Education for New Americans project at Georgia State University (Georgia State University, 2004). The "Good Food for Kids," series, found at the same web resource, explains key nutrition messages important for young children. These materials are versatile tools teachers can use when educating families on nutrition-related topics. The Canadian government publishes *Canada's Food Guide*, which is available in 18 different languages including 7 Native American languages (Health Canada, 2011). The Southeastern Michigan Dietetic Association has information on food choices in the MyPyramid format for a variety of cultural groups (Southeastern Michigan Dietetic Association, 2004). This information, presented in English, helps teachers understand traditional ethnic food choices. The National Agricultural Library, USDA has an excellent link to resources for understanding cultural and ethnic foods practices and nutrition recommendations for educators. See web resources.

Teaching English Language Learners

Appropriate teaching practices guide how nutrition concepts are presented for all children, with special consideration given to those who are English language learners. Strategies that promote understanding of the nutrition message include the following:

- Have children learn by participating in hands-on activities, such as cooking activities and taste tests.
- Use a range of foods, recipes, and food preparation and cooking methods to reflect a variety of cultural approaches.
- Base the activity on a bilingual children's picture book with a focus on nutrition.
- Use visuals such as real food, food models, or pictures of food whenever presenting a verbal message.
- Speak clearly. Show and explain concepts in more than one way.
- Invite parents and others to visit the class to demonstrate a nutrition concept, to engage children in a cultural food tradition, and to be role models promoting the value of cultural diversity.
- Plan field trips to local businesses such as ethnic supermarkets, restaurants, and bakeries to experience how traditional foods are made.

Teachers, who promote healthful eating from a multicultural perspective need to challenge themselves to explore new ideas and ways of planning appropriate and healthful menus for young children. They should also educate themselves about the nutrition traditions of alternate cultures. The resources that guide teachers and families with important nutritional information provide the structure to guide decision making about the selection and presentation of foods. The actual foods selected, however, and the lessons taught about nutrition evolve from the teacher's knowledge of the needs of all children in the group, including their cultural traditions. This highlights the important role that teachers play in selecting and serving healthful foods in the early childhood setting and in presenting nutrition wellness activities that assist all children to learn valuable nutrition lessons.

> ## What if . . .
>
> a parent from an Asian culture expressed concern that there were not enough menu items that appealed to her child? For example, the parent noticed that rice was not offered very often. How would you respond?

● SUMMARY

Good nutrition is the foundation for good health and optimal learning. Yet many young children are poorly nourished. The changing food environment has resulted in decreased time spent sharing family meals and more reliance on fast foods, restaurant dining, and convenience foods. In addition, some families struggle with food affordability. These changes have had a negative impact on the quality of children's diets. In spite of many positive trends, including the goal of supporting more sustainable food practices and the desire to improve the school food environment, children's diets still do not meet recommendations for fruit, grain, and dairy groups and are higher in fat and sodium content than advised by the *Dietary Guidelines for Americans* (Wood & Child and Nutrition Division, Food and Nutrition Service, 2008).

Planning a healthful menu and serving appropriate foods are important for children's health and ability to learn. Children who do not eat nutrient-rich foods can face undernutrition, overnutrition, or both—especially if families face food insecurity. Consuming too few or too many nutrients negatively impacts learning and development and may have lifelong health consequences. In addition, over-consuming food coupled with decreased physical activity has resulted in an obesity epidemic among young children that threatens their long-term health and wellness. Recognizing nutritional problems during the early years offers the opportunity for modifications to be made to improve children's health outcomes. This positive contribution involves teachers, families, and health care providers.

The food guidance systems are important resources that help teachers create an environment that fosters good nutrition and health. The Dietary Reference Intakes, which are established levels of nutrient requirements, and the daily values found on food labels provide specific information on nutrient requirements to help guide food selection and menu planning. The Dietary Reference Intakes are the basis of the *Dietary Guidelines for Americans, 2010*, which provides general advice on nutrition and physical activity. The MyPlate educational tool takes the guesswork out of healthful eating by providing simple to use guidance on how to construct a nutrient-dense, high-quality diet. Teachers can use this information to establish classroom practices that promote good health and wellness in young children as well as to guide their own personal health goals. The food guidance systems are adaptable to a variety of ethnic food practices, and many are available in languages other than English so that increasingly teachers have tools they need to overcome language barriers and to protect the health of all children in their care.

KEY TERMS

Antioxidants	Gluten	Phytochemicals
Body mass index (BMI)	Iron-deficiency anemia	Proteins
Carbohydrates	Macronutrients	Psychosocial
Celiac disease	Malnutrition	Rickets
Daily Values (DVs)	Micronutrients	Sleep apnea
Dietary Reference Intakes (DRIs)	Minerals	Supplemental food programs
Energy expenditure	Nutrient-dense foods	*Trans* fats
Failure to thrive	Nutrients	Undernutrition
Fats	Nutrition	Vitamin D
Food insecurity	Overnutrition	Vitamins

REVIEW QUESTIONS

1. List three ways in which the food environment has changed in the past 20 years and summarize the impact of these changes on children's diets.
2. Define malnutrition as it relates to under- and overnutrition and provide an example of each.
3. Discuss three standards that act as guides to healthy eating and provide an example of how each might be used.
4. Describe how to use ethnic food guidance systems and other educational resources as a guide for promoting healthful eating from a multicultural perspective.

DISCUSSION STARTERS

1. Explain how food insecurity can lead to obesity. How can teachers help alleviate food insecurity if they identify this problem in children's families?
2. How can teachers address the obesity epidemic in their programs?
3. How can teachers implement the principles of the *Dietary Guidelines for Americans, 2010* and the MyPlate food guidance system in their classrooms? How would you do this for toddlers, preschoolers, and school-age children?

PRACTICE POINTS

1. Gabriella is exactly 4 years old. She weighs 48 lb and is 44 inches tall. Using the CDC BMI website listed in the Web Resources section, calculate her BMI. Today is 1/1/present year. Her birth is 1/1/present year–4. Using the growth charts in the Book Specific Resources on MyEducationLab (also available on the CDC growth chart website listed in the Web Resources section) determine what the percentile is for her height, weight, and BMI. What weight classification would you give her? What does this tell us about Gabriella?

2. Suppose you were like Gabriella and consumed a vegetarian diet and wanted to assess if your iron intake was sufficient. Go to ChooseMyPlate website: www.choosemyplate.gov/supertracker-tools/supertracker.html and select the SuperTracker to determine how your diet below rates. What changes might you make to improve your iron intake?

Breakfast:	1 flour tortilla with 2 ounces of cheese
	½ cup orange juice
	1 cup milk, 2%
Snack:	1 cup milk, 2%
	¼ cup teddy graham crackers
Lunch:	1 slice whole wheat bread with 1 ounce of cheese
	1 cup tomato soup
	1 sliced kiwi
	1 cup of milk, 2%
Snack:	1 apple
Dinner:	½ cup rice, white
	2 ounces cheese
	1 cup salad with 1 tablespoon Italian dressing
	1 flour tortilla
	1 cup apple juice

3. Refer to the breakfast cereal food label shown in Figure 2-5. Explain three nutritional qualities that make this a healthy food choice. What might you be concerned about?

WEB RESOURCES

American Academy of Pediatric Nutrition: What Every Parent Needs to Know, American Academy of Pediatrics 2012, Editors Dietz, W. H., Stern, L., and the American Academy of Pediatrics
http://wdn.ipublishcentral.net/www_aap_org/viewinside/2364091620214

CDC Growth Charts and BMI Calculator
www.cdc.gov/GrowthCharts
http://apps.nccd.cdc.gov/dnpabmi/

ChooseMyPlate.gov
http://www.choosemyplate.gov/

Data Resource Center for Child and Adolescent Health, Childhood Obesity State Report Cards
www.childhealthdata.org/content/ObesityReportCards.aspx

Dietary Guidelines for Americans, 2010
www.health.gov/dietaryguidelines/2010.asp

Institute of Medicine of the National Academy, Dietary Reference Intakes
www.iom.edu/Activities/Nutrition/SummaryDRIs/DRI-Tables.aspx

National Association for Sport and Physical Education
www.aahperd.org/naspe

The Food and Nutrition Information Center of the National Agricultural Library of the USDA, 2011
www.nal.usda.gov/fnic/pubs/ethnic.pdf

USDA Food and Nutrition Information Center Dietary Guidance; Ethnic/Cultural Food Pyramids, 2011
http://fnic.nal.usda.gov/nal_display/index
.php?info_center=4&tax_level=3&tax_subject=256&topic_id=1348&level3_id=5732

Your Food Environment Atlas (USDA)
www.ers.usda.gov/FoodAtlas/

MyEducationLab™

Go to Topic 1 (Basic Nutrition) in the MyEducationLab (www.myeducationlab.com) for your course, where you can:

- Find learning outcomes for Basic Nutrition along with the national standards that connect to these outcomes.
- Complete Assignments and Activities that can help you more deeply understand the chapter content.
- Apply and practice your understanding of the core teaching skills identified in the chapter with the Building Teaching Skills and Dispositions learning units.

- Check your comprehension on the content covered in the chapter by going to the Study Plan in the Book Resources for your text. Here you will be able to take a chapter quiz, receive feedback on your answers, and then access Review, Practice, and Enrichment activities to enhance your understanding of chapter content.

three
The Science of Nutrition

learning outcomes

AFTER READING THIS CHAPTER, YOU SHOULD BE ABLE TO:

1. Define nutrition science.

2. Identify the steps in the process of digestion.

3. Explain how nutrients are absorbed and identify the accessory organs involved in absorption.

4. Describe the function of carbohydrates, proteins, and fats and the food groups in which they are found.

5. Define the role of vitamins and minerals and other important components of the diet and their interactions in supporting the growth, development, and health of infants and children.

6. Summarize how the knowledge of nutrients can be used to plan healthful diets for young children and teach them nutrition concepts.

Jamal is a 5-year-old kindergartner who is noticeably small for his age. During health screening day his teacher, Tonya, notices that his weight falls in the 5th percentile range when plotted on standard growth charts. She puts a notice for his family with his height and weight measurements in his backpack. As she thinks about Jamal, it occurs to her that since the first day of school he has frequently complained of being tired, has been irritable, and often has difficulty concentrating in class. She wonders if there is a connection to his poor rate of growth.

The next day Jamal's mother, Aiesha, tells Tonya she has scheduled an appointment with the doctor to find out why Jamal is so thin. She tells Tonya that she suspects his poor growth is related to his sensitive stomach and that he frequently has bloating and diarrhea. The fact that his growth has recently stalled worries her.

A couple of weeks later, Aiesha shares important news with Tonya. Jamal has been to a specialist where tests reveal he has celiac disease. Aiesha was told that celiac disease is an inherited condition in which an immune response to gluten, a protein found predominantly in wheat, barley, and rye, causes damage to the lining of the small intestine. This damage interferes with digestion and absorption, which is why Jamal is so thin. Aiesha was also told that the cornerstone to his treatment is diet.

Aiesha gives Tonya a list of foods Jamal can and cannot eat. She asks Tonya if the school will be able to provide Jamal with gluten-free meals. She also wonders if he will feel left out at mealtime because he can't eat the same foods as the rest of the children. Tonya reassures Aiesha that there are others in the school who require special diets, including a child in first grade who also has celiac disease. She explains that to accommodate children with special diets, a special allergen-free table is available where children may sit together and get assistance from lunchroom staff. Perhaps Jamal may want to join this group at mealtime.

Tonya then calls the director of food services about the need for a gluten-free diet. She also notes that the classroom parents rotate bringing packaged crackers and fruit for snacks. Aiesha agrees to bring in a couple of boxes of gluten-free crackers to have on hand for Jamal. After her discussion with Tonya, Aiesha feels confident that her son will receive appropriate and appealing meals at school and that he will begin to gain weight.

DEFINING NUTRITION SCIENCE

Nutrition science is the study of how food provides nourishment to support the growth, maintenance, and repair of the human body. Understanding the science of nutrition helps teachers learn about healthful eating for themselves and the children in their care. The responsibility of feeding young children is important because they are nutritionally vulnerable and dependent on adults to make choices and provide for them. For example, infants and children need more calories for their size compared to adults because they are growing. When they are not consuming the right types and amounts of food, nutritional problems can develop quickly. If children face the additional stress of an illness or disorder such as celiac disease, the nutritional concerns can increase significantly.

The information shared in this chapter explains why the substances found in food are necessary for good health. Step-by-step descriptions explain how the body digests and absorbs food in order to generate the energy needed to function. Sometimes the process of digestion and absorption is complicated by health conditions. We discuss disorders that young children may experience in the process of digestion and absorption so that you, as an early childhood educator, will feel prepared to handle a variety of feeding challenges. In addition, we explain why different food groups are important to maintain a healthful diet and discuss the role of the essential macronutrients (carbohydrates, protein, and fats) and micronutrients (vitamins and minerals). Finally, the information in this chapter will provide you with the background fundamentals you need to teach nutrition concepts to young children and support young children who have digestive disorders.

nutrition science
the study of how foods provide nourishment to support the growth, maintenance, and repair of the human body

UNDERSTANDING THE PROCESS OF DIGESTION

To understand why specific foods are needed in the diet, we need to start at the beginning and look at what happens to food once it is consumed. The overall goal of eating is to take the nutrients found in food and transport them from the outside of the body to the inside, where they are used to maintain body functions. The nutrients found in food are essential for young children because they:

- Provide energy.
- Are necessary for growth.
- Repair and maintain the body.
- Regulate body processes.
- Affect how genes are expressed (turned on or off) and therefore affect overall health.

We turn now to a discussion of the digestion process. Teachers who understand this process will have a better understanding of why nutrients and balanced diets are so important for infants and young children. This knowledge helps develop strategies to ensure all children are well nourished.

MyEducationLab™

Visit the MyEducationLab for *Nutrition, Health, and Safety for Young Children*, to enhance your understanding of chapter concepts with a personalized Study Plan. You'll also have the opportunity to hone your teaching skills through video-based Assignments and Activities, as well as Building Teaching Skills and Dispositions lessons.

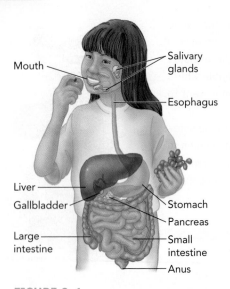

FIGURE 3-1

The Digestive System

digestion
the mechanical and chemical breakdown of foods into smaller nutrient components to make it available for absorption

gastrointestinal tract
the mouth, esophagus, stomach, and small and large intestines; part of the body where foods are digested and changed to nutrients in anticipation of being absorbed

The Digestion Process

Digestion is the mechanical and chemical breakdown of foods into smaller nutrient components, making the nutrients available for absorption. Multiple steps take place when turning the cereal with milk served for breakfast at school into the fuel children need to start the day. The process takes place in the digestive system, which is made up of the **gastrointestinal tract** and other accessory organs that aid in digestion. This multiple-organ system is the gateway for all nutrients into the body.

Problems in the digestive system can have catastrophic consequences for infants and children. For example, Jamal was not getting adequate amounts of nutrients to sustain growth and development because his digestive system was compromised by the celiac disease. Jamal needs the help of his teacher and food service staff to plan meals he can eat at school, using foods that avoid further damage to his gastrointestinal tract. This highlights the need for teachers to understand normal digestion and absorption so they can troubleshoot when issues related to food intake arise in the feeding of infants and children.

The gastrointestinal tract is like a long, tube-shaped conveyor belt with food pushed along the length of it by the wavelike contractions of the intestinal muscles. As Figure 3-1 illustrates, food undergoes both mechanical and chemical changes within the digestive tract to ready it for absorption, which occurs predominantly in the small intestine.

As food moves along this conveyor belt, it is chopped, churned, and mixed with enzymes, acids, and mucus, which slowly change it into smaller absorbable substances. Attached to the gastrointestinal tract are accessory organs, such as the salivary glands, liver, and pancreas, that secrete a variety of components that also aid in the digestion process (Table 3-1).

The Mouth

The start of all digestive action takes place in the mouth. The mechanical process of chewing physically breaks food down into small pieces. This allows saliva (spit) to begin its work. Saliva released from the salivary glands contains digestive **enzymes**, which start the chemical breakdown of food.

TABLE 3-1   The Parts of the Gastrointestinal Tract and Their Functions

	Accessory Organs	Chemical Secreted	Functions
Mouth	Teeth	None	Mechanically chop food into small pieces.
	Tongue	Lingual lipase	The tongue moves food around in the mouth. The lipase begins fat digestion.
	Salivary glands	Saliva, enzyme amylase	Saliva moistens foods; the amylase begins carbohydrate breakdown.
Esophagus	None	None	Provides passageway from mouth to stomach.
Stomach	None	Gastric juices that include:	The stomach acts as a holding unit for food as it is churned and mixed, and produces secretions.
		Acids	Create an acidic environment so that enzymes can work.
		Enzyme pepsin	Causes protein breakdown.
		Mucus	Binds and mixes food, protects stomach.
Small intestine		Intestinal juices and mucus	The secretions cause the chemical breakdown of proteins, fats, and carbohydrates to substances that can be absorbed; protects and lubricates the intestine.
	Liver and gallbladder	Bile	Bile emulsifies fats and helps in fat breakdown.
	Pancreas	Pancreatic juices	The juices cause chemical breakdown of proteins, fats, and carbohydrates to substances that can be absorbed.
Large intestine, rectum, and anus	None	None	Absorb water; store and eliminate stools.

Sources: Based on Lubey, S. *Lubey's Biohelp: The Human Digestive System*, retrieved May 1, 2012, at http://home.roadrunner.com/~lubehawk/BioHELP!/biotopcs.html; *Williams' Essentials of Nutrition and Diet Therapy* (pp. 188–194) by E. D. Schlenker, 2007, St. Louis: Mosby Elsevier.

Enzymes are proteins that speed up chemical reactions. Saliva keeps the tongue moist so that taste buds can work more effectively. The moist chewed-up food forms a mass, which is pushed to the back of the mouth by the tongue, ready to be swallowed. The teacher's role in this first step of digestion is to decide the types of foods to offer children that match their ability to chew. This reduces the risk of choking.

Textures of Foods

Textures of food play a role in children's ability to chew and swallow. This ability depends on the child's age and whether the child has conditions that interfere with chewing. For example, infants who are learning to swallow their first nonliquid foods are offered puréed textures. This provides a gradual introduction of new textures to manage. By around 10 months, teeth begin to appear and side-of-the-mouth chewing develops. Foods with more texture are well received at this time. Food textures may need to be altered for children who have difficulty chewing because of motor development delays. The *Teaching Wellness* feature provides an activity that will help children understand how their mouth helps jump-start the process of digestion.

Protecting Teeth

Foods provide both dental risks and benefits. These risks and benefits need to be considered when selecting foods in order to protect the teeth, the greatest tool of the mouth. Although foods provide the nutrition needed to strengthen teeth, some foods can cause dental decay. Dental decay is an infectious process in which various plaque-forming bacteria turn the carbohydrates that children eat into acid. This acid causes the loss of calcium from the teeth, resulting in decay.

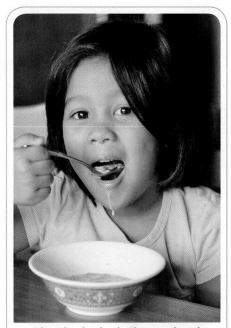

Digestion begins in the mouth and proceeds through multiple steps before the food consumed can be used for energy.

enzymes
proteins produced by the body's cells to speed up chemical reactions

Protecting teeth starts as soon as they erupt. For infants, this means that babies should not be put to bed with bottles filled with beverages such as milk, infant formula, fruit juice, or fruit drink or allowed to access a filled bottle or sippy cup all day (American Dental Association, 2010). Ongoing, repeated exposure to the sugars contained in these beverages puts infants at risk for baby bottle tooth decay. *Baby bottle tooth decay* is the development of early dental cavities that is extensive and particularly damaging to the front teeth, although any teeth can be involved.

Untreated dental decay can cause suffering and pain and affect the ability to eat, speak (impaired language development), and concentrate in the school setting (Centers for Disease Control and Prevention Division of Oral Health, 2011). Nutritional factors that increase the risk of dental decay include a high intake of fruit juices and soft drinks, delayed weaning from the bottle, access to toddler cups throughout the day, and the intake of sticky foods such as raisins, granola bars, and carbohydrate foods, such as bread, crackers, and cookies, that get stuck in the teeth. These factors result in prolonged exposure of the tooth surface to the acids that cause tooth decay.

By contrast, the foods that protect teeth include milk and cheese. These dairy products may be helpful in neutralizing acids produced by bacteria in the mouth and also provide calcium, phosphorus and magnesium, which help to build strong teeth in young children (Mayo Clinic, 2011). Fluoride found in fluoridated water is another nutrient that protects teeth by making tooth enamel strong and preventing bacteria from making acids that damage teeth (Centers for Disease Control and Prevention, 2011). Well water and bottled water may not be good sources of fluoride. The xylitol found in some sugar-free gums, mints, and toothpastes is also effective in reducing the incidence of cavities by decreasing bacteria in the mouth and helping strengthen teeth (Hirsch, Edelstein, Frosh, & Anselmo, 2012). Teachers help children protect their teeth by teaching them the basics

What if . . .

you needed to plan the menu for your family child care program, which serves infants through preschool-age children? What modifications in texture might you need to take into consideration? What do you need to do to ensure modified foods are appealing to all age groups?

Teaching families about infant dental hygiene and the risks of putting babies to bed with bottles can help prevent baby bottle tooth decay.

TEACHING WELLNESS   Digestion Begins in the Mouth

LEARNING OUTCOME   **Children will gain an understanding of how tasting and chewing food begins the digestion process.**

Safety watch: Be aware of children's food allergies or restrictions. Adjust foods used as needed. Monitor for cleanliness in food activities.

OLDER INFANTS AND TODDLERS

- **Goal:** Children will explore moist and dry foods and learn about chewing foods to make them easier to swallow.
- **Materials:** A plate for each child, chopped plums, unsalted saltine crackers.
- **Safety watch:** Cut the plum into pieces no larger than ¼ inch. Supervise eating. Offer a sip of water if the cracker is too dry for the child to chew and swallow.
- **Vocabulary focus:** Plum, cracker, taste, chew, moist, swallow.
- **Activity plan:** For infants who are eating solid foods and toddlers, offer a plate with small pieces of fresh plum and an unsalted cracker. Encourage the child to pick up a piece of food and taste it. Name the food, and say words to add interest such as, "That is a plum. Does it taste sweet? Sour? Is it smooth and moist in your mouth?" or "Does the cracker feel dry in your mouth?" Describe the process of chewing. Say, "The cracker is crunchy. You are using your teeth to chew the cracker to make it easy to swallow. When you chew, the cracker gets wet and soft so you can swallow it. You are tasting and chewing. This is how we help our food be ready to swallow." Talk about chewing and swallowing at meal times.
- **How to adjust the activity:** Offer familiar foods first. Create support cards with the names of the tasting foods and the vocabulary words in the child's home language. If needed, spell out each word phonetically to assist with pronunciation. Ensure all children are able to pick up the offered foods. Allow children time to explore the foods. Encourage but do not force children to taste the foods.
- **Did you meet your goal?** Did the children explore the offered food by chewing and tasting? Did they hear you talk about chewing the food to make it easier to swallow?

PRESCHOOLERS AND KINDERGARTNERS

- **Goal:** Children will learn that digestion starts in the mouth as food is chewed and mixed with saliva.
- **Materials:** Large model of teeth, the book *The Very Hungry Caterpillar* by Eric Carle, snack supports: plates, napkins, plastic knives, washed bananas (in the peel), stick pretzels, raisins, broccoli, peanut butter (or whipped light cream cheese if there are peanut allergies), cups, milk in small pitchers.
- **Safety watch:** Supervise children as they create their caterpillar snack to ensure cleanliness and safety.
- **Vocabulary focus:** Incisors, molars, saliva, swallow, digestion.
- **Activity plan:** Gather children. Read *The Very Hungry Caterpillar*. As you read invite the children to name the foods the caterpillar eats. Help children recognize that the caterpillar grows larger as he eats. When finished, summarize that eating healthy food helps all living things grow and develop. Explain that like the caterpillar, we people use our teeth to bite and chew foods. We have teeth for biting (incisors) and teeth for grinding and chewing (molars). Show these teeth on the model and discuss how the teeth have different shapes for their different purposes. Describe that we use our tongues to move food as we chew. Our saliva, the moisture our mouth makes, helps the food become soft and slippery as we chew so we can swallow the food. These are steps in digestion that happen in our mouths.

Invite children to create a hungry caterpillar for snack. Provide each child a plate, knife, and half of a banana. Pass small bowls filled with the other snack building foods. Guide children to peel the banana, place it on their plate, and cut it into five pieces. Describe the steps to spread one side of each banana piece with peanut butter, and stick the pieces together. Use the peanut butter to stick two raisins to the front banana to represent eyes. Show children how to stick the pretzel sticks into the sides of each banana piece to represent legs and place two into the front piece to represent antennae. Place a piece of broccoli in front of the caterpillar to "eat." Take a picture of children with their caterpillar snack. Pass cups and milk, and invite children to eat their caterpillar snack.

As you eat, talk about biting, chewing, and swallowing the different foods. Help children identify the foods that take more or less chewing before they are ready to swallow. Say, "We chew food so it is easy to swallow it. The food that is chewed goes into our stomach and helps us feel full. It gives us energy to play, think, and grow."

- **How to adjust the activity:** for English learners, use the model teeth to demonstrate biting and chewing food while describing what is happening in English (and alternate languages if possible). Create prompt cards for the focus vocabulary words in the home languages of children in the class. Be purposeful to ensure that each child has a chance to name a food the caterpillar in the book eats—in English or their home language. Support children with mobility challenges to create the caterpillar snack. Offer tongs, short handled butter knives, or other tools to help all children be successful. Provide time for children to eat their "caterpillar" snack.

- **Did you meet your goal?** Can children explain what happens in the mouth to start digestion?

As you watch this **video** on the caterpillar activity, think about what children are learning.

SCHOOL-AGE CHILDREN

- **Goal:** Children will learn that digestion is the way the body breaks down food so it can use the food's nutrients, and that digestion starts in the mouth and continues in the stomach.

- **Materials:** Saltine crackers, mirror, bowl of quick-oats oatmeal, cups, spoons, pitchers with warm water, bowl of raisins.

- **Safety watch:** Supervise for safety and cleanliness as children use the mirror and mix and mash the oatmeal.

- **Vocabulary focus:** Saliva, digestion, stomach, vitamins, minerals, fiber.

- **Activity plan:** Gather children at work tables. Describe how digestion starts in the mouth and continues in the stomach. Offer each child a saltine cracker. Ask them to chew for 30 seconds but not swallow the cracker. Pass a mirror around and ask them to inspect the cracker mash in their mouths. When everyone has had a turn, ask the children to continue chewing and swallowing their cracker. Talk about what happened in their mouths while they chewed—their teeth crushed the cracker and their mouth's made saliva or "spit" to help the cracker mash be soft and wet enough to swallow. Explain that when we chew and swallow food we begin the first stage of digestion. Ask children to imagine what it might feel like to swallow the cracker without moisture in their mouths! Now offer each child a spoon and cup, and guide them to serve themselves two heaping spoonfuls of dry quick oats. Ask them to taste a spoonful of dry oats. Is it easy to eat? *Now guide, then pour ¼ cup of warm water over the oats in their cup, and use their spoon to mash and stir the mix. Ask the children to inspect and describe the mash made in their "stomach mixer" cups. Explain that the stomach uses the same mixing and mashing actions to continue the digestion process until the food is a soft wet mash which helps the body get ready to absorb the nutrients in food (vitamins, minerals, and fiber) when it moves from the stomach into the small intestines. Pass a bowl of raisins and invite children to mix in some raisins and eat their "stomach mixer" snack.

  Summarize that our teeth crush the food, our saliva moistens the foods and makes it easier to swallow, and our stomachs do the next step of mixing and mashing so our bodies can get the food energy it needs for us to play, work, think, and grow.

- **How to adjust the activity:** Provide picture card prompts for the steps of the activity to guide English learners and children who may need frequent reminders of the directions. Offer a bowl or a cup with a handle to provide greater stability for a child with motor coordination challenges.

- **Did you meet your goal?** Can children explain the purpose of digestion? Are they able to identify what happens in the mouth and stomach during the process of digestion?

of oral hygiene. Including tooth brushing as part of the daily routine ensures that the first step of digestion is not hampered by dental decay. Teachers are also important resources for families. For example, they can provide guidance to help children receive needed dental services, as described in this example:

Three-year-old Devin attends the Head Start program. Although he attends school regularly, he is often irritable and tired. He does not smile and he does not eat well. One day his teacher, Lea, notices that Devin has a swollen cheek. She is concerned and asks Devin to let her look in

This **video** shows Super Smile Day, a special event held at a school. Notice the different activities for both children and families in order to promote oral health. What other activities might be included?

his mouth. She sees that Devin's front teeth are visibly decayed, but he says that a back tooth is hurting him.

Lea calls Devin's mother, Andrea, and learns that Devin still takes a bottle to bed. Lea tells Andrea that she thinks Devin is suffering from painful cavities. She strongly encourages Andrea to schedule an emergency dental exam. She helps her locate a dentist who will provide the service at a reduced cost for children enrolled in the Head Start program. The exam reveals that two of Devin's teeth are infected. Devin receives extensive dental treatment. When it is completed, Lea notices that he has an entirely different demeanor. He is happy, smiles, and eats with enthusiasm. He is ready to learn now that he is no longer in pain.

Swallowing and the Esophagus

Next in the process of digestion is swallowing. After the mass of chewed food is swallowed, it enters the esophagus, a tube that connects the mouth to the stomach. The food mass is pushed by wavelike contractions to the stomach. The entrance into the stomach is controlled by a small muscle called the lower esophageal sphincter. The sphincter is like a gate that opens and shuts, letting food in and gas out (as burps), as needed.

Swallowing Difficulties

Swallowing food is a simple process that occurs without effort for most individuals. However, the process of chewing and swallowing uses a multitude of muscles and must be synchronized with breathing. Some children have a condition called **dysphagia**, which is the inability to swallow foods or liquids easily. Many conditions are associated with dysphagia such as prematurity, developmental disabilities, cerebral palsy, and Down syndrome.

dysphagia
a disorder characterized by the inability to swallow foods or liquids easily

Teachers and families need to be aware that swallowing difficulties can result in significant feeding challenges. Feeding times may be prolonged and the child may choke, cough, or gag, which is unpleasant and frightening for the child and requires the extra attention of teachers. The consequences of dysphagia can include poor nutrition, **aspiration** (when food or liquids are inhaled into the lungs), and pneumonia (Kleinman, 2009). Teachers often become part of a team, which includes families, health care professionals, and early intervention staff, to work together to achieve the goals of safe eating and good nutrition. Figure 3-2 provides a checklist for teachers who work with children who have swallowing disorders.

aspiration
occurs when food or liquids get into the lungs instead of into the stomach

Reflux

Sometimes infants and children experience difficulty keeping food in the stomach. This happens when the lower esophageal sphincter is relaxed, causing spitting up or **gastroesophageal reflux (GER)**.

gastroesophageal reflux (GER)
reflux of stomach contents into the esophagus

FIGURE 3-2   Teacher's Checklist: Caring for Children with Swallowing Disorders

❏ **Positioning:** Does the child need special positioning and an adaptive feeding chair? The correct position is essential in promoting safe swallowing during feeding.

❏ **Oral aversion:** Is the child involved in a desensitization program to help him overcome aversion to flavors, textures, consistencies, and temperatures of foods? What is the teacher's role?

❏ **Nutrition plan:** Is a modification of food consistency needed? Does special menu planning need to happen before the child can come to school? Are supplements required?

❏ **Adaptive feeding equipment:** Does the child need tube feeding equipment, positioning seats, or special cups, plates, bottles, nipples, or plates?

❏ **Skill building:** Are there exercises that focus on developing oral motor skills and or adaptive swallowing skills? What are the teacher's responsibilities?

Source: Based on *Pediatrics Nutrition Handbook, 6e*, edited by R. Kleinman, 2009, Elk Grove, IL: American Academy of Pediatrics Committee on Nutrition.

As many as 67% of 4-month-old infants with GER spit up at least once a day after a feeding (Campanozzi et al., 2009). Often called "happy spitters," these infants grow well and do not experience any pain or compromise to their growth. The spitting up usually resolves by 12 to 14 months without any negative consequences (Reuter-Rice & Bolick, 2012).

When spitting up is chronic and severe, however, it is called **gastroesophageal reflux disease (GERD)**. GERD is a condition that causes the contents of the stomach to back up into the esophagus. GERD can cause pain and heartburn. Heartburn is a burning sensation experienced when the esophagus is exposed to stomach acids. GERD can cause small amounts of stomach contents to be aspirated or inhaled into the lungs. It can trigger asthma and pneumonia (Reuter-Rice & Bolick, 2012). The *Safety Segment* discusses the recommended sleep position for infants with GERD.

Infants who frequently reflux to the point of vomiting may not get enough nutrients, leading to poor growth. The use of specially thickened formulas or the addition of rice cereal or another commercial thickening agent to formula or liquids can sometimes help decrease the incidence of vomiting, thus allowing infants to gain weight. Adding cereals to liquids in bottles is not advised, however, unless recommended by a health care provider because it may displace more vital nutrients in formula such as protein and result in too rapid weight gain (Queen Samour & King, 2012).

Teachers can help reduce some of the symptoms infants experience by supporting the baby in an upright position during and after feeding. Medications can also be prescribed by a physician to help alleviate symptoms and ensure good nourishment. Suggestions for managing GER and GERD and other digestive conditions are listed in Table 3-2.

gastroesophageal reflux disease (GERD) severe reflux of stomach contents into the esophagus that causes pain, heartburn, indigestion, and when associated with excess vomiting, can result in poor growth in young children

The Stomach

Once food reaches the stomach, it is mixed with stomach acids, secretions, and enzymes, which begin to break down the protein in the food. The stomach's role is to squeeze and churn the food and move it further along the digestive tract. Although food generally flows from the stomach to the small intestine, sometimes it comes back up when children vomit. Whereas reflux is usually burping of stomach contents, vomiting is a much more violent event. A child vomiting in the classroom always creates a disruption.

The first question that may come to mind for teachers when they are considering a vomiting episode is "Should this child go home?" Vomiting can be caused by gastrointestinal infections or other factors such as allergies, medications, overeating, and motion sickness. Schools and preschools have policies about illness that are shared with families through parent handbooks or preschool websites. The National Resource Center for Health and Safety in Child Care and Early Education (American Academy of Pediatrics, American Public Health Association, National Resource Center for Health and Safety in Child Care and Early Education, 2011) recommends that if children have two or more episodes of vomiting within 24-hours, should be sent home. In practice, since it is often difficult for a teacher to know how often a child has vomited within a 24-hour period, parents are called. A

What if . . .
a mother, rushing to go to work, told you that her child vomited before coming to school? The mother is not concerned because she feels it was related to roughhousing with a sibling right after eating breakfast. How might you handle this situation? Would you allow the child to stay?

SAFETY SEGMENT   Gastroesophageal Reflux Disease

Infants with gastroesophageal reflux disease (GERD) may vomit frequently, and choking can be a concern to caregivers, especially when they consider sleep positions. The American Academy of Pediatrics (AAP) agrees with the North American Pediatric Society for Pediatric Gastroenterology, Hepatology and Nutrition, which recommends that like all infants, infants with GERD need to be placed on their backs to sleep (not on their stomachs or side) to prevent sudden infant death syndrome (SIDS) (Vandenplas et al., 2009). Having babies sleep on their stomachs is considered only in the rare occasions when the risk of death due to GERD outweighs the potential increased risk of SIDS (Task Force on Sudden Infant Death Syndrome, 2011). Ultimately if an infant has GERD the baby's medical provider should recommend the appropriate sleeping position.

TABLE 3-2   Common Childhood Disorders of the Gastrointestinal Tract

Disorder	Symptoms	Nutrition Risk Factors	Tips for Teachers*
Celiac disease	Gas, bloating, abdominal pain, and diarrhea or constipation, poor appetite, fatigue, weight loss.	Poor growth, malabsorption, anemia, increased risk for osteoporosis.	Very close attention must be paid to diet. Avoid food containing gluten, such as wheat, barley, rye, and oats (unless the oats are gluten free). Set up meeting with families, teacher, and food service staff to review diet, label reading and discuss the use of special gluten-free products.
Constipation	Constipation is the painful passage of stool that is hard and dry.	Poor appetite.	*Infants with constipation:* Refer family to health care professional for advice. *Children with constipation:* Encourage them to gradually consume more foods high in fiber content such as fruits, vegetables, and whole grains, drink sufficient fluids, and be physically active.
Diarrhea	Watery stools that occur three or more times per day, cause stomach cramping, and are not explained by change in diet.	Dehydration. *Signs of dehydration:* dry mouth and tongue, decreased amount of dark-colored urine, or in babies and young children, decrease in the number of wet diapers, dry skin, crying without tears, and excessive sleepiness.	Infants and children who are sick with diarrhea should be sent home. Maintaining adequate hydration is important. On the return to school offer a regular diet and avoid excess juice and high-fat foods.
Gastroesophageal reflux disease (GERD)	Occurs when stomach contents back up into the esophagus (spitting up or vomiting).	Poor growth, food refusal, difficulty eating.	Thickened formula may be recommended. Feed and keep infants in an upright position (at least 30 minutes after a meal). Avoid overfeeding, tight diapers, and car seat positioning.
Lactose intolerance	Noninfectious diarrhea, gas, and bloating caused by the inability to break down lactose, the sugar found in milk, due to an insufficiency of an enzyme called lactase.	Children on a lactose-free diet may need calcium and vitamin D supplementation if unable to tolerate any dairy products.	Milk products should be limited or restricted based on individual tolerance. Substitute lactose-free milk or fortified soy milk in the school setting.
Swallowing disorders	Coughing, choking, or gagging during feedings.	Malnutrition, aspiration (getting food or liquids into the lungs), pneumonia, and difficult mealtime behavior.	Assessment of oral motor capabilities by a speech or occupational therapist to provide teacher/families guidelines on positioning, food consistency, etc. Should be included as written guidelines in the IFSP or IEP. It is very important to have a proper feeding chair that supports the swallowing process.
Vomiting	Vomiting is the forceful emptying of the stomach's contents through the mouth.	Dehydration (see signs of dehydration listed for diarrhea).	Infants and children who experience two or more incidences of vomiting within the previous 24 hours should be sent home. Maintaining adequate hydration is important. On the return to school, offer regular diet but avoid excess juice and high-fat foods.

*Children identified with a special health condition that warrants a modification in diet or special feeding technique require written instructions from the child's parents/guardians and health care provider. Teachers can consult with a registered dietitian. When children are sick, teachers should not hesitate to call their parents/guardians. Young children can get very sick quickly and teachers or parent/guardians may need to call health care providers or refer families for expert care and professional advice.

Sources: American Academy of Pediatrics, American Public Health Association, National Resource Center for Health and Safety in Child Care and Early Education. 2011. *Caring for our children: National health and safety performance standards; Guidelines for early care and education programs,* 3rd edition. Elk Grove Village, IL: American Academy of Pediatrics; Washington, DC: American Public Health Association; Also available at http://nrckids.org. Kleinman, R. (Ed.). (2009). *Pediatric nutrition handbook* (6th ed.), Kleinmann, R., (Ed.). Elk Grove Village, IL American Academy of Pediatrics; Digestive Diseases: A–Z List of Topics and Titles, National Digestive Diseases Information Clearinghouse, retrieved April 29, 2012, from http://digestive.niddk.nih.gov/ddiseases/a-z.asp; The Academy of Nutrition and Dietetics, Pediatric Nutrition Care Manual, 2011. Digestive Topics A–Z The North American Society of Pediatric Gastroenterology and Hepatology and Nutrition http://www.naspghan.org/wmspage .cfm?parm1=444.

decision as to whether a child should go home is made based on the child's history of illness, the incidence of similar illnesses in the classroom, and whether there was a possible noninfectious source of illness such as twirling too long on the tire swing.

UNDERSTANDING THE PROCESS OF ABSORPTION

The transport of nutrients from the gastrointestinal tract into the body is called **absorption**. The primary site of absorption is the small intestine. When food has been broken into sufficiently small units, it is ready to be transported into the body via the circulatory system.

The Small Intestine

When the stomach has completed churning and breaking food into smaller pieces, it releases it into the small intestine. The small intestine is an approximately 20-foot-long tube where the most significant part of chemical digestion occurs (U.S. National Library of Medicine, National Institutes of Health, 2012). It is designed in such a way as to absorb as many nutrients as possible. To accomplish this, the inside of the small intestine has a series of folds that are lined with **villi**. The fingerlike villi are, in turn, lined with **microvilli** so that the total area involved in absorption is larger in size than a tennis court (Shills, Shike, Ross, Caballero, & Cousins, 2006).

Intestinal enzymes, acids, bile, and pancreatic juices further digest the major nutrients, breaking down carbohydrates, proteins, and fats and making them ready for absorption. When the nutrients are finally small enough to be absorbed, they enter the circulatory system (National Institute of Diabetes and Digestive and Kidney Diseases, National Institutes of Health, 2008). Once in the circulatory system they are transported to various cells of the body. Table 3-3 shows the food sources and final breakdown products of carbohydrates, protein, and fats. The products that are not absorbed by the small intestine are collected in the large intestine.

The Large Intestine

The large intestine is the last section of the digestive system. Its primary role is to absorb water and some minerals and vitamins from the products not absorbed in the small intestine. Anything that cannot be digested, such as fiber, collects in the rectum until it is expelled via the anus as a bowel movement.

Understanding Problems Related to Absorption

Providing children with a variety of foods from each of the food groups at mealtime is the best way to ensure a healthy, balanced diet. However, children can face nutritional problems in spite of eating a good diet if they have trouble with absorption. These problems can be significant enough to impact a child's growth and development. Teachers are the child's link to responsible care when parents are not available. Understanding factors that impact nutritional health ensures that teachers can effectively care for children with health concerns. Children who are physiologically comfortable will be more apt to learn. Parents feel confident leaving their child in the care of a teacher who understands and is able to respond to their child's unique needs.

absorption
the transport of nutrients from the small intestine into the circulatory system

villi
located on the surface of the folds of the small intestine; is where absorption takes place

microvilli
located on the surface of the villi, further expanding the surface area to enhance absorption of nutrients

TABLE 3-3   Macronutrient Sources and the Breakdown Products of Digestion

Macronutrient	Selected Sources	Primary Breakdown Products	Role of Nutrient
Protein	Meats, fish, poultry, cheese, milk, eggs	Amino acids	Growth and repair; can be used as energy if necessary
Fats	Oil, margarine, butter, mayonnaise, salad dressing	Fatty acids and glycerol	Stored energy source. Aids absorption of vitamins A, D, E, K
Carbohydrates	Grain products, fruits, vegetables, milk	Simple sugars: fructose, glucose, and galactose	Body's main energy source

Understanding Malabsorption

malabsorption
occurs when damage to the small intestine's lining results in difficulty absorbing nutrients, leading to diarrhea and sometimes weight loss

When the small intestine's lining becomes damaged, it is difficult to absorb nutrients. This condition is called **malabsorption** and can happen in a number of different circumstances. Diet-related conditions of malabsorption can often be modified by changes in diet.

Celiac Disease This genetic autoimmune condition is caused by the body's response to a group of proteins referred to as *gluten* found in wheat, rye, and barley. The symptoms of celiac disease vary and the condition is sometimes hard to diagnose; however, it is characterized by damage to the small intestine. The most common features include malabsorption with resulting gas, bloating, stomachache, and diarrhea. Children can experience weakness, weight loss, joint pain, and loss of appetite. The malabsorption can lead to anemia and increased risk for **osteoporosis** (weak bones), as well as generalized malnutrition (Queen Samour & King, 2012). As we saw at the beginning of the chapter with Jamal, children with celiac disease can also experience irritability, inability to concentrate, and depression, which can adversely affect a child's ability to learn (University of Maryland School of Medicine, 2012).

osteoporosis
condition that results in porous, weak bones that break easily

In Jamal's situation his celiac disease caused damage to his gastrointestinal tract, resulting in an inability to absorb nutrients, which led, in turn, to poor growth. Jamal had to give up gluten-containing bread, pasta, pizza, muffins, and cookies, among other things that he liked to eat. His mother knew it was essential for Jamal to follow a special diet. She also knew that, although it might be difficult for him to make changes in his diet, he would adjust once he began to feel better.

Recent research has shown that there appears to be a milder form of intolerance to gluten that does not cause damage to the small intestine and is not an autoimmune disorder but does cause symptoms similar to celiac disease that go away when gluten is removed from the diet (Sapone, Lammers, Casolaro, Cammarota, Giuliano, De Rosa, et al., 2011). This condition is called gluten sensitivity and, regardless of the difference in diagnosis, it still results in the elimination of gluten-containing foods from the diet (Sapone, Bai, Ciacci, Dolinsek, Green, Hadjivassiliou, et al., 2012). Teachers who have children in their classrooms with celiac disease or gluten sensitivity will need to fully understand how to prevent gluten exposure from both dietary and non-dietary sources. For example some play dough, pastes, and paints may contain gluten. See the resource section for more information about celiac disease and gluten-free diets.

lactose intolerant
term used to define an individual who experiences gas, bloating, and diarrhea because of an inability to break down the lactose found in milk

Lactose Intolerance   One of the enzymes in the small intestine is called lactase. Lactase helps digest the sugar in milk, called lactose. In comparison to a milk protein allergy, which is an immune response that triggers serious and sometimes life-threatening symptoms, children who are **lactose intolerant** simply do not make sufficient lactase. When they consume too many dairy foods or beverages with lactose, they develop gas, bloating, and diarrhea (Queen Samour & King, 2012).

The degree of lactose intolerance varies. Some children may be able to tolerate up to a cup of milk or yogurt per day. Yogurt with active live cultures and aged cheese are generally better tolerated than milk. Infants who are lactose intolerant can do well with either a lactose-free or soy formula. The incidence of lactose intolerance is also higher in certain ethnic populations. For example, it is estimated that 20% of African American, Asian, and Hispanic children under the age of 5 have some evidence of lactose malabsorption (Queen Samour & King, 2012).

Some children can develop a secondary lactose intolerance because of damage to the small intestine, which results in not enough lactase being available to aid in digestion. For example, if children have had gastroenteritis or "stomach flu," they may develop a temporary lactose intolerance until the small intestine heals. It is also not uncommon for children like Jamal who have celiac disease to be lactose intolerant.

The consequences of exposure to lactose are not as dire or dangerous as those of food allergies. Consequently, some children may be willing to suffer the consequences of lactose intolerance in order to eat a food they desire. Teachers and parents should clarify a feeding plan for children with lactose intolerance. It is also important for teachers to understand the effects of lactose intolerance and recognize how they may affect a child. For example:

Jesse, a third grader, requests a pass to the restroom about a half hour after lunch. He is gone for 15 minutes. When he returns to the classroom the substitute teacher is upset and issues a referral to the principal's office. She assumes Jesse was taking advantage of the fact that she was not his usual teacher and had simply wasted time in the bathroom and halls. Jesse turns beet red and emphatically states, "I was using the bathroom!" He explains to the principal as he sits down to discuss the referral: "The only thing I did wrong was drink chocolate milk. I really like it but it doesn't like me. It gives me a stomachache." A quick look at his health files confirms lactose intolerance. Jesse's referral is immediately rescinded although it takes a little more time for his pride to be restored.

The symptoms of lactose intolerance can be quickly resolved by avoiding foods high in lactose content. Milk is a high-lactose food. Using lactose-reduced milk or vitamin D and calcium–enriched soy milk in place of regular milk will solve most children's problems. A conversation with families helps teachers to understand the degree of lactose sensitivity. Other dairy products such as yogurt, cheese, and ice cream also contain lactose and may or may not need to be eliminated depending on the degree of sensitivity. Less obvious sources of lactose that teachers need to consider include pancake or cake mixes, processed meats, and boxed potato products.

Diet-Related Diarrheas   Diarrhea can be caused by factors such as viruses and bacteria, but sometimes children eat or drink something that triggers diarrhea. Diarrhea is characterized by watery stools that occur with increased frequency and stomach cramping.

Certain foods can cause diarrhea in young children. For example, many foods contain sugar alcohols (a type of sugar substitute) that are not completely digested and absorbed by the body. Sugar-free gum, candy, and cookies may contain sugar alcohols. These foods pass into the large intestine and are fermented by bacteria, which can cause diarrhea when children eat too much. The following terms are an example of some of the sugar alcohols that can be found in the list of ingredients on labels when used in foods: sorbitol, mannitol, xylitol, maltitol, maltitol syrup, lactitol, erythritol, isomalt, and hydrogenated starch hydrolysates (International Food Information Council, 2009).

Other causes of diarrhea include the following (American Academy of Nutrition and Dietetics, 2011; Ball, Bindler, & Cowen, 2010):

- Excess juice consumption, particularly apple and pear juices, which are naturally high in sorbitol.
- Consumption of drinks with caffeine such as tea or soft drinks.
- Diets that are excessively high in fiber.
- Overfeeding.
- The introduction of new foods that the child does not tolerate.
- Foods that are malabsorbed because of Crohn's disease (a disease that causes inflammation of the digestive tract) or irritable bowel syndrome (a dysfunction of the large intestine).

When a child has a bout of diarrhea, teachers must review the symptoms, consider the classroom incidence of diarrhea, and obtain family input before deciding whether to send a child home or not. Sometimes it is unclear whether a child is ill. Loose stools may not always be indicative of a major gastrointestinal illness; they could instead indicate a mild change in stool patterns. Figure 3-3 provides guidance in determining when to send children home if they have loose stools.

Diarrhea that is caused by viruses or bacteria may also be accompanied by vomiting. This combination creates a more critical condition because dehydration can occur.

Understanding Constipation

Sometimes too much water is absorbed in the large intestine and constipation occurs. Constipation is the painful passage of stools that are hard and dry. This problem sometimes happens when children feel shy about using the bathroom at the early childhood or school programs or develop a fear of pain from passing hard stool because of problems with constipation in the past. Some children with special health care needs can be prone to constipation because of abnormal anatomy or function of the intestinal tract, low muscle tone, medications, or inability to communicate needs

What if . . .

you had a toddler in your program with lactose intolerance whose family was inconsistent in restricting lactose. This was causing this child to have periodic bouts of diarrhea that were affecting potty training. How would you discuss this subject with the parents?

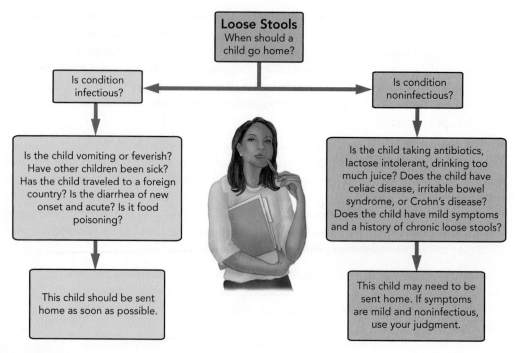

FIGURE 3-3
What to Consider When a Child Has Loose Stools

(Yang, Lucas, & Feucht, 2010). Constipation in young children can be caused by lack of fiber in the diet, inadequate fluid intake, and insufficient physical activity. When the amount of fiber in the diet is insufficient, the waste products of digestion and absorption move more slowly through the large intestine and, consequently, more water is reabsorbed, causing drier stools. Adding fiber and water to the diet allows for easier passage of stools. Physical activity also stimulates the movement of stool through the gastrointestinal tract.

Teachers can help prevent constipation by providing children with:

- Opportunities to drink water between meals, especially on warm days.
- Sufficient time for physical activity.
- Nutritious foods rich in fiber.
- Easy access to toilet facilities.

Aiding Digestion and Absorption

To ensure that children receive the most nutrition from their foods, teachers must create an environment that enhances and supports the natural rhythms of eating. Children feel confident about eating when they know that meals will be presented within a reasonable time frame and include foods they enjoy. The stomach generally empties in 2 to 4 hours. Planning meals and snacks every 3 to 4 hours is appropriate for most children. In fact, the Child and Adult Care Food Program (CACFP), a child nutrition program that is designed to reimburse programs for nutritious meals served to children, requires specific mealtime scheduling so that meals are not served too close together or too far apart.

The sight, aromas, and taste of food can be very important to children. These factors stimulate the production of saliva and gastric juices and can contribute to muscular activity of the gastrointestinal tract, inducing hunger pains. It is essential to provide appealing meals that stimulate the senses and whet the appetite to ensure adequate intake. For some low-income families, the meals provided at school are the best chance for their children to eat healthy, balanced meals. Making sure desirable, appetizing foods are served supports a healthy diet.

Emotional upset can interfere with digestion. This occurs because under stress the body makes fewer digestive enzymes. In addition the wavelike movements of the gastrointestinal tract that move food along are limited by stress. For these reasons, meals should be provided in a calm environment with limited distractions. To avoid stress and anger at mealtimes, plan enough time so that children can eat in a relaxing manner. In the elementary school setting, the timing of meals before outside breaks can result in a rush to finish eating. Planning sufficient time for meals as well as outdoor play provides the best balance for health and nutrition.

THE FUNCTION OF MACRONUTRIENTS

Through the process of digestion, food is converted into components that can be readily absorbed. The macronutrients (carbohydrates, proteins, and fats) as their name suggests, are needed in large amounts because they supply energy. This energy is used for physical activity and the repair and replacement of cells but also for growth and development in children. In this section we discuss energy as well as the composition of food and macronutrients. This information will help you put into focus the rationale behind diet recommendations for young children.

Understanding Energy

Food provides energy for the body. Food energy is measured in the form of calories. A **calorie** represents the amount of energy released from food when it is metabolized by the body. Different macronutrients provide different amounts of calories. The calories per gram of protein, fats, and carbohydrates are as follows:

- Protein   4 calories
- Carbohydrates   4 calories
- Fats   9 calories

Children need energy to run and play as well as to maintain body functions such as breathing and pumping blood. The energy released from these nutrients when they are metabolized provides the fuel needed by the body.

Nutrient Composition of Foods

Food is a complex mixture of carbohydrates, proteins, fats, vitamins, and minerals. When children drink a glass of milk, they are consuming protein, fat (unless it's skim milk), and carbohydrates. The meat in a roast beef sandwich contains protein and fats, whereas the whole-grain bread contains some protein but mostly carbohydrates, as illustrated in Figure 3-4. The mayonnaise on the sandwich is predominantly fat, whereas the lettuce and tomato have small amounts of carbohydrates. When children eat a piece of fruit, they are consuming carbohydrates.

Foods can be grouped together based on similar nutrient composition. The MyPlate system uses these food groups to explain healthy meal choices (U.S. Department of Agriculture, 2012). Understanding the composition of food can be helpful when working with children who require special diets. For example, when planning meals for children with diabetes, teachers should understand the sources of carbohydrates in the diet. Eating an appropriate amount from each food group ensures that the body has sufficient energy, vitamins, and minerals to sustain life. Achieving the right balance between calories consumed and calories burned is one of the primary goals of healthy eating.

Releasing or Storing Energy

The metabolism of nutrients is a balancing act in which energy is either being released for immediate use or stored so that it is available at a later time. This releasing and storing occurs simultaneously

What if . . .

your class has an early lunch period, which is right before recess, and you observed on more than one occasion your third-grade students rushing through lunch and throwing food away in an effort to quickly get outside to play? How would you resolve the problem?

calorie
a unit of measurement of the amount of energy that is released from food when it is metabolized by the body

FIGURE 3-4
Macronutrients

Milk, Meat, and Whole Wheat Bread Are a Combination of Macronutrients While Mayonnaise Is Mainly Fat and Fruits Are Mostly Carbohydrates from the moment of conception to the end of life. For example, when children play soccer, they use energy to contract their muscles, move their body, pump blood, breathe faster, and perspire to keep cool. When they stop for a snack of orange wedges, they use energy to digest and absorb the oranges. At the same time energy is also being used to maintain and repair the body and build muscles as they exercise. Growth will continue to occur even while children play soccer, provided there is enough energy available in the diet. If children eat more oranges than they need immediately for fuel, energy will be stored in the liver, muscles, and fat cells for later use.

The releasing and storing of energy cannot be accomplished without the presence of vitamins, minerals, and water. The finely tuned metabolic processes of life are interrelated and codependent. Often vitamins and minerals have more than one role.

Determining Energy Needs

Children's energy (calorie) needs change as they grow and vary depending on age, whether they are boys or girls, and what size they are. Calorie needs also vary according to children's level of activity. Children playing soccer have greater energy needs than do classmates who sit on the sidelines and watch the game. The amount of energy children need depends on many variables; however, most children are able to self-regulate their energy needs and maintain appropriate growth. A closer evaluation of energy needs by health care professionals may be needed when children are underweight or overweight. The baseline of calories needed to sustain life and maintain the body's function such as breathing, pumping blood, and repairing cells, is called the **basal metabolic rate (BMR)**. Calories needed to digest and absorb food and for physical activity are added to the BMR to obtain the **total energy expenditure**, or the amount of calories a child burns each day. When this information is determined, the child's diet is reviewed to ensure that enough, but not too much, food energy is being consumed in the diet to balance the child's energy needs.

Children have high calorie needs in relation to their size because of the energy requirements for growth. The Dietary Reference Intakes (DRIs) list the calorie requirements of children by age (see Web Resources) (Otten, Pitzi-Hellwig, & Meyers, 2006). Other factors that can influence calorie needs are illness and fever. For instance, Jamal's calorie needs are increased because he is experiencing malabsorption and has damage to his intestinal tract. He must also compensate for the loss of nutrients due to diarrhea and use extra calories for repair of his intestinal tract.

Teachers who feed children must take into consideration their differing needs for calories and serve age-appropriate portion sizes. Providing healthful diets and an environment that supports physical activity ensures that the balance of using and storing energy is maintained, and that proper growth and excess weight gain is avoided.

Carbohydrates

Carbohydrates provide the body's most abundant source of energy. They are found in grains, fruits, vegetables, milk products, and sweets. Cultures throughout the world rely on carbohydrates to provide their predominant source of nourishment. Each culture's carbohydrate choice is based on geography, terrain for farming, and cultural traditions. Rice, beans, maize, wheat, potatoes, barley, cassava, and quinoa are just some of the variety of plants that provide inexpensive energy sources for people of the world. These plant sources of carbohydrate are important because they provide an ongoing source of glucose. Glucose, a simple sugar, is the common fuel for all cells and the only source of energy for the brain. The different types of carbohydrates include simple sugars and complex carbohydrates and are illustrated in Figure 3-5.

Sugars

Six different sugars play a role in children's diets. They are divided into two groups based on whether they occur as a single sugar unit or are bonded together as two units.

Monosaccharides The simplest type of sugar consisting of single sugar units are **monosaccharides**. They include glucose, fructose, and galactose. Glucose and fructose occur naturally in some foods such as fruits and honey. Galactose is a simple sugar made by animals and found in the milk they produce. All sugars and starches must be broken down to monosaccharides via digestion to be absorbed and metabolized in human cells (Goodman, 2010; Sizer & Whitney, 2011).

basal metabolic rate (BMR) a measurement of the baseline calories individuals need to sustain life and maintain the body's functions such as breathing, pumping blood, and repairing cells

total energy expenditure a measurement of the number of calories needed by individuals; includes the basal metabolic rate plus the calories used for physical activity and the digestion and absorption of food

monosaccharides these are the simplest type of sugar consisting of single sugar units and include glucose, fructose, and galactose

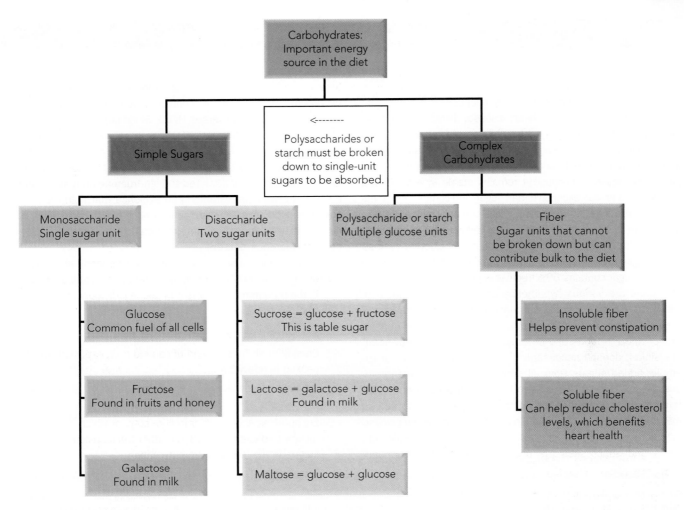

FIGURE 3-5
Types of Carbohydrates

Disaccharides   Two single sugar units, when bonded together, are called **disaccharides**. They include sucrose, lactose, and maltose. Table sugar is sucrose. It consists of fructose and glucose units that are bonded together. Lactose is milk sugar. It consists of galactose and glucose sugar units. Maltose consists of two glucose units.

disaccharides
these are sugars that contain two single sugar units, which are bonded together. They include sucrose, lactose, and maltose

Conflicting Role of Sugar in the Diets of Young Children   Teachers and families often have very strong preferences about whether sugar should be included in the diets of young children. Teachers must make judgments about how to manage these concerns, as described in the following scenario:

> Hallie, a teacher in a kindergarten/first-grade blended class, has a parent who feels that graham crackers contain too much sugar and should not be offered as a snack in class. Another parent has complained because Hallie does not allow cupcakes to be served for celebrations such as birthdays. A third parent does not permit her child to eat canned fruit at snack time because it contains high-fructose corn syrup. Each parent has strong feelings about sugar. Hallie tries to accommodate their preferences while at the same time considering the school's policies.

Opinions about sugar can be put into perspective by reviewing the recommendations of health authorities and federal guidelines. The Institute of Medicine's DRIs recommend that sugar not exceed 25% of total calories (Otten, et al., 2006). Added sweeteners such as sucrose and fructose are generally recognized as safe (known as GRAS) by the Food and Drug Administration (FDA), yet health concerns exist about the increased use of added sugars in the diets of young children as discussed in the *Health Hint* (American Academy of Nutrition and Dietetics, 2012b).

HEALTH HINT   High-Fructose Corn Syrup: Are There Health Risks?

Does high-fructose corn syrup (HFCS) increase the risk of obesity and the chronic diseases associated with obesity because of the way it is metabolized? Does it cause heart disease, diabetes, and accumulation of damaging fat in the liver? Some studies suggest this is the case, although research has had conflicting results. HFCS is used in food products such as soft drinks, canned fruits, and processed desserts because it remains stable in acidic foods and drinks, it is less expensive than sugar, and comes from a reliable and plentiful U.S. crop: corn. It was originally called HFCS to distinguish this type of corn syrup from regular corn syrup which is 100% glucose. However it is similar in composition to sucrose (table sugar) and honey in that it contains about 42–55% fructose whereas sugar contains 50% fructose and honey about 49%.

There are various hypotheses as to why HFCS may contribute to obesity. Originally correlations were made that linked the rise of obesity to a time frame that also saw an increased use of HFCS in foods and beverages. Although this may seem plausible it doesn't necessarily show cause and effect. For example, added sugars from all sources particularly when combined with solid fats have been linked with obesity and other related health concerns. Another theory suggests that fructose may impact appetite regulation in a negative way. When glucose is absorbed, it triggers the release of the hormones insulin and leptin and suppresses the production of ghrelin—hormonal responses that inhibit appetite. This does not occur when fructose is absorbed. There is speculation that this may lead to overeating. However, some confusion surrounds studies that focus on pure fructose versus HFCS. Since sugar has about the same amount of fructose as HFCS, it is important to remember that cutting back on sugar naturally will reduce fructose in the diet. The American Academy of Nutrition and Dietetics evaluated numerous studies related to high fructose corn syrup and found there was consistently little evidence that high fructose corn syrup differed from sugar in how it affects metabolism, hunger, satiety, and calorie intake (American Academy of Nutrition and Dietetics, 2012b).

Can evidence-based recommendations be made about high-fructose corn syrup? Not yet because research is still ongoing.

In the meantime, teachers can take a judicious approach to high-fructose corn syrup and all added sugars by:

- Not offering soft drinks to young children.
- Serving fresh fruit instead of canned fruit, especially fruits packed in heavy syrup.
- Avoiding excessive use of processed desserts, snack bars, and sweets.
- Encouraging a diet higher in fiber content which is a natural way to decrease HFCS and other fructose-containing sugars in the diet and promote satiety.

Sources: American Academy of Nutrition and Dietetics. (2012). Position of the Academy of Nutrition and Dietetics: Use of nutritive and nonnutritive sweeteners, *Journal of the Academy of Nutrition and Dietetics, 112*(3), 739–757. International Food Information Council Foundation, 2011. *Questions and Answers about Fructose*, Food Insight. White, J. S. (2008). Straight talk about high-fructose corn syrup: What it is and what it ain't. *American Journal of Clinical Nutrition, 88*(6), pp. 1716S–1721S. Lustig, R. H. (2010). Fructose: Metabolic, hedonic, and societal parallels with ethanol. *Journal of the American Dietetic Association 110*(9), 1307–1321. Elliot, S. Keim, N., Stern, J., Teff, K., & Havel, P. (2002). Fructose, weight gain, and the insulin resistance syndrome. *American Journal of Clinical Nutrition, 76*, 911–922.

The body does not distinguish between a unit of glucose obtained by eating a jelly bean versus a unit of glucose obtained by eating a slice of whole-grain bread when it comes to metabolizing that glucose for energy. However, teachers need to consider other concerns related to the inclusion of foods that contain sugar. For example, a jelly bean is simply calories, whereas the slice of whole-grain bread is rich in fiber, vitamins, and minerals. Eating foods high in sugar content such as sugar-sweetened beverages, sweets, and sweetened grain products may displace needed nutrients in the diet of young children and therefore compromise diet quality (American Dietetic Association, 2008). For example, children who consume "worms in the dirt" (chopped chocolate cookies on top of chocolate pudding and threaded with gummy worms) during a midmorning cooking activity may not eat their lunch of turkey sandwiches with milk, apple, and carrot sticks. Consequently, they will get fewer of the recommended nutrients important for growth and development. Other concerns about food high in added sugars is that they are usually higher in energy density and lower in essential nutrients and dietary fiber (American Academy of Nutrition and Dietetics, 2012b). There is also strong evidence that drinking sugar-sweetened beverages contribute to overweight and obesity in children (U.S. Department of Agriculture, 2010). In addition, frequent exposure to sugary, sticky foods and sweetened beverages is linked to an increase in dental cavities (Roberts & Wright, 2012).

Sugar occurs naturally in some foods such as fruit and milk. Sugar content of food can be identified using the nutrition facts label which indicates the total grams of sugar in a product. However, since this includes naturally occurring sugar such as that contributed by fruit or milk, it is challenging to identify how much is added sugar. This requires looking at the list of ingredients for words that mean added sugar such as:

- high fructose corn syrup or corn sweeteners
- words that contain "ose": fructose, dextrose, glucose, maltose, sucrose
- brown sugar
- honey
- molasses
- evaporated cane juice
- fruit juice concentrate

It important to remember that ingredients are listed from highest to lowest concentration on the label so a food item that has added sugars at the beginning of the list or lists several types of added sugar may contain more added sugar than is desirable.

Taken together, there is concern when children's diets exceed the recommended level for sugar intake. For this reason, schools are taking steps to reduce children's intake of high-calorie soft drinks at school as discussed in the *Policy Point*.

One concern that can be alleviated is the link between sugar and behavior. Researchers have found that in general there is no link between hyperactivity and sugar intake in the general population of children (Benton, 2008; Queen Samour & King, 2012). Some research, however, suggests that a small number of children with attention deficit/hyperactivity disorder (ADHD) may show improvement of symptoms if sugar in their diet is restricted (Millichap & Yee, 2012).

What if . . .

other teachers in your school offered candy as a reward to children who are keeping on task? What type of nonfood methods might you suggest as an alternative to motivate students?

POLICY POINT   Reducing High-Calorie Soft Drink Consumption in Schools

In May 2006, the Alliance for a Healthier Generation, a joint initiative of the American Heart Association, the William J. Clinton Foundation, and the American Beverage Association, announced new school beverage guidelines that voluntarily remove high-calorie soft drinks from all U.S. schools starting in the 2009–2010 school year.

Although guidelines for preschool programs are not available, the recommendations for children in primary school allow the following:

- Bottled water.
- Up to 8 ounces of milk or juice.
- Regular or flavored milk or USDA acceptable soy milk alternative that is fat free or low fat that provides up to 150 calories per serving.
- 100% juice that provides up to 120 calories per 8-ounce serving and 10% of the daily value for three vitamins and/or minerals.

These guidelines have become the standard of practice for the soft drink beverage industry and will be used as a basis for establishing contract arrangements with elementary, middle, and high school programs. They are applicable to the school setting, including before- and after-school programs and also include all beverages sold outside the context of school breakfast and school lunch programs (i.e., vending machines, snack carts, à la carte menu items).

These guidelines do not cover sporting events, school plays, and so on, where parents are present or are selling soft drinks as boosters. They do not supersede state legislation, school district policies, or local initiatives, which may be more restrictive. For example, schools may choose not to allow sugar-sweetened soft drinks at school plays or other after-school events that include parents.

This initiative has been a step in the right direction in that it shows that both schools and industry are making a concerted effort to reduce the intake of calorie-rich, nutrient-poor beverages. Has the initiative been effective or not? The American Beverage Association states that these guidelines including those established for middle schools and high schools have resulted in an 88% reduction in beverage calories shipped to schools since 2004. These guidelines, as well as school wellness policies, appear to be having an impact.

Sources: American Beverage Association & the Alliance for a Healthier Generation. (2009). *School Beverage Guidelines.* Retrieved May 6, 2012, from http://www .ameribev.org/nutrition-science/school-beverage-guidelines/the-guidelines/; American Beverage Association. (2011). News Releases: School Beverage Guidelines. Retrieved May 6, 2012, from http://www.ameribev.org/nutrition-science/school-beverage-guidelines/news-releases/; Terry-McElrath, Y. M., O'Malley, P. M., & Johnston, L. D. (2012). Factors affecting sugar-sweetened beverage availability in competitive venues of US secondary schools. *Journal of School Health, 84*(1), 44–55.

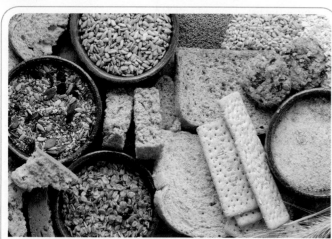

The complex carbohydrates found in dietary sources include starch and fiber.

The goal is for children to consume sugar in moderation and within the context of an otherwise healthful diet. Teachers set the tone in the classroom for healthful eating by raising the level of awareness among parents as well as children. For this reason many children's settings limit foods that are perceived as "sweets." Healthful food choices can include foods that are sweet tasting. Teachers should however select foods with nutritionally redeeming qualities such as sweet potato or carrot muffins, and zucchini bread made with whole grains, oatmeal raisin cookies, and plain yogurt served with ripe strawberries, raspberries, or blackberries. Overall the goal for children and their families is to learn a mindful and moderate approach to eating.

Complex Carbohydrates

Complex carbohydrates are the second category of carbohydrates. They include two different types: starch and dietary fiber. The *starches,* also called **polysaccharides**, consist of multiple glucose sugars linked together in chains. Breaking starches down to simple sugars (glucose) through the digestive process makes them available for absorption in the small intestine.

Fiber is a type of carbohydrate that cannot be used as energy because humans lack the digestive enzymes to break it down. However, dietary fiber does provide significant health benefits. The recognized health benefits depend on the type of fiber being consumed: insoluble or soluble (American Academy of Nutrition and Dietetics, 2012a).

Insoluble Fiber A type of fiber that comes from the structural components of plant cell walls and does not dissolve in water is referred to as **insoluble fiber**. Wheat bran, rice bran, whole-wheat breads, crackers, cereals, and the seeds in berry fruits are examples of this insoluble fiber. Eating foods with insoluble fiber aids digestion. Insoluble fiber acts like a sponge to draw water into the stool. Softer, bulkier stools move through the gastrointestinal tract more quickly, which helps children maintain regular bowel habits and avoid constipation.

Soluble Fiber A fiber that readily mixes with water, forming gels and giving foods a thickened consistency, is called **soluble fiber**. Oatmeal, oat bran, and beans are examples of soluble fiber sources (American Academy of Nutrition and Dietetics, 2012a). Soluble fiber offers significant health benefits. It binds with cholesterol in the diet so that less cholesterol is absorbed, protecting children from heart disease. It also delays stomach emptying, making children feel full longer, and may aid in weight control.

Whole grains are a type of carbohydrate in which all parts of the grain, including the germ, endosperm, and bran, are consumed. For example, oatmeal, brown rice, whole wheat, and corn are examples of whole grains. Whole grains are healthy for children because they are rich in fiber, vitamins, and minerals and contain naturally occurring phytonutrients that reduce the risk for cancer, diabetes, and heart disease and promote healthy weight management and gastrointestinal health (Jonnalagadda et al., 2011).

Adding more fiber to early child care program menus can be easily accomplished with a few simple adjustments in food selection that focus on whole grains and more fresh fruits and vegetables. Figure 3-6 shows examples of both a high-fiber and a low-fiber breakfast.

Proteins

Proteins are the basis of life in humans. Without proteins the body cannot grow, reproduce, or repair itself. Proteins are organic compounds that contain carbon, hydrogen, oxygen, and nitrogen. Proteins are essential in all life processes and are particularly important to young children because they are growing.

polysaccharides
complex carbohydrates that consist of multiple glucose sugars linked together in chains. Also called starch

insoluble fiber
a type of dietary fiber that does not dissolve in water. It comes from the structural components of plant cell walls and is found in wheat bran, rice bran, whole-wheat breads, crackers, cereals, and the seeds in berry fruits. This type of fiber prevents constipation

soluble fiber
a type of dietary fiber that readily mixes with water to form gels. It gives foods a thickened consistency and is found in oatmeal, oat bran, and beans. It can bind with cholesterol, thus inhibiting cholesterol absorption, which can protect against heart disease

Breakfast A	Fiber (grams)	Breakfast B	Fiber (grams)
½ cup Raisin bran	5.5	½ cup Puffed rice	0.2
1 cup milk, skim	0	1 cup milk, skim	0
Whole-grain bread	2.2	White bread	0.6
1 Tbsp peanut butter	1	1 Tbsp cream cheese	0
1 cup strawberries	3.3	1 cup orange juice	1.0
Total	**12 grams**		**1.8 grams**

FIGURE 3-6   A High-Fiber and Low-Fiber Breakfast
Source: U.S. Department of Agriculture. (updated 2011). National Nutrient Data Base for Standard Reference. Retrieved May 6, 2012, from http://ndb.nal.usda.gov/.

Defining the Function of Proteins

Proteins have three primary roles: growth and repair of the body, regulation of the processes within the body, and energy:

1. *Proteins are necessary for growth and repair.* Proteins form structures in the body such as skin, bones, organs, and muscles. Insufficient protein during growth can impede brain development and function (Otten, et al., 2006).

   Proteins consumed in the diet are digested into amino acids, which when absorbed are used to make body protein that needs to be replaced. For example, when a red blood cell dies, a new red blood cell will be made from the amino acids furnished by the diet.

2. Proteins control body functions. This is managed through a system of regulatory processes. Enzymes, hormones, antibodies, and red blood cells are just a sampling of the protein-based components that help the body maintain vital functions. When children fight off a cold, antibodies (a type of protein found in the blood that fights infections) come to their rescue. When they eat lunch, protein-based enzymes break the food down for digestion and absorption. The multitude of uses for protein in the body explains why it is so important for children to have sufficient amounts in their diet.

3. Proteins can be used for energy if need be. Protein, however, is a fuel of last resort because of its importance in other body functions such as growth and development. Too much protein in the diets of children is not stored as protein, but instead is converted into body fat.

Understanding Amino Acids

Amino acids are the biological compounds that act as building blocks for all proteins. Twenty different amino acids combine in innumerable ways to build the vast array of proteins found in humans. The process for converting dietary protein into human protein is as follows:

1. Plant or animal protein is consumed.
2. Protein is broken down into amino acids in the small intestine.
3. Amino acids are absorbed and recombined in different sequences according to the type of human protein needed (such as skin cells, hormones, muscle).

Essential, Nonessential, and Conditionally Essential Amino Acids

How well children are able to build proteins for their body depends on whether

> **What if . . .**
>
> a parent believed his overweight child needed to follow a low carbohydrate diet? What are the disadvantages of such a diet for young children? How would you handle this diet request?

amino acids
biological compounds that act as the building blocks for all proteins

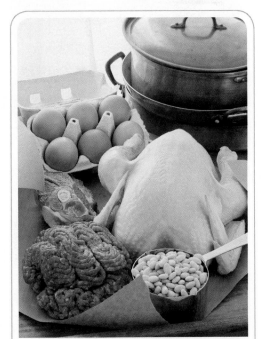

Eggs, meat, poultry, and beans are excellent sources of protein in the diet.

the right amount and type of amino acids are available. Amino acids can be categorized based on the need to have them provided in the diet:

- Essential amino acids: the nine amino acids the body cannot make. It is "essential" that these amino acids be provided by the diet.
- Nonessential amino acids: the five amino acids the body can readily make.
- Conditionally essential amino acids: amino acids the body is sometimes able to make, but sometimes must be provided by the diet in times of illness or stress (Otten, et al., 2006; U.S. National Library of Medicine National Institutes of Health, 2011).

The Quality of Protein   All the essential amino acids must be available in the diet to make the body's protein. If one particular essential amino acid is low in the diet, the body will make protein only until it runs out of this amino acid in spite of the fact that other amino acids are readily available. Similar to missing a link in a chain, if one link is missing the chain simply cannot be put together. When a food is low in a particular amino acid, that amino acid is called the **limiting amino acid**. The presence or absence of a limiting amino acid determines the quality of the protein:

limiting amino acid
an essential amino acid that is lacking in a dietary protein source, thereby limiting protein synthesis

- *High-quality protein:* Protein that comes from animal sources has all the essential amino acids or links needed to make human protein chains. These are called high-quality proteins and include milk, eggs, cheese, meats, fish, and poultry. All protein from animal sources is high quality except for gelatin. Soy protein is also a source of high quality protein.

- *Lower quality protein:* Some foods provide lower quality proteins because they do not contain much protein or have a limiting amino acid. For example, fruits and many vegetables are generally not good sources of protein. Other foods of plant origin can add significant amounts of protein to the diet, but are limiting in an amino acid. For instance, grains are low in some amino acids and legumes are low in others. However, if they are combined over the course of the day, enough essential amino acids are available to make the necessary links to form the proteins needed by the body (Sizer & Whitney, 2011). These foods are said to contain **complementary protein** because, in combination, they provide all the amino acids necessary to build human protein.

complementary protein
proteins that are low in different amino acids but can be combined to provide enough total essential amino acids to form all the amino acids necessary to build human protein

Traditionally, people from all cultures have learned to match foods that provide complementary proteins. Examples include:

- Red beans and rice.
- Peanut butter and whole-grain bread.
- Bean burritos.
- Falafel (made from chick peas) and whole-wheat pita.
- Hummus (chick peas and ground sesame seeds) and whole-wheat crackers.
- Tofu or other soy products and rice.

Supplementing a lower quality protein (one with a limiting amino acid) with small amounts of high-quality animal protein will result in a complete protein combination that provides all the essential amino acids such as adding cheese to a beans dish.

Defining Protein Requirements

The Dietary Reference Intake for protein requirements changes as children grow. For example, children's protein needs are 13 grams per day for 1- to 3-year-olds and 19 grams for 4- to 8-year-olds (Otten, et al., 2006). To put this into perspective, 1 cup of milk has about 8 grams of protein on average, a 1-ounce serving of meat/poultry provides 7 grams of protein, and a slice of bread from the grain group provides about 3 grams of protein. Totaled together, 18 grams is enough to meet just about all the protein needs of young children. The typical U.S. diet provides ample protein. The Child Adult Care Food Program (CACFP) requires 1.5 ounces of protein to be served for lunch

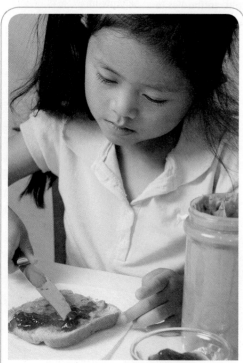

Some of children's favorite foods consist of complementary proteins.

for 3- to 5-year-olds. This represents about 10 grams of protein. To get a sense of what this portion represents, visualize half of a deck of cards. Although this may seem like a small portion, for a child it provides more than enough protein.

Fats

The fats are the most concentrated source of calories in the diet. Although too much fat is not beneficial because of its link to obesity, there is a role for healthful fats in children's diets. Fats provide **essential fatty acids** (linoleic acid and alpha-linolenic acid) that cannot be made by the body and must be obtained from the diet. Essential fatty acids are needed for normal growth and development (Simopoulos, 2011). They also help control inflammation and blood clotting and are important in promoting good vision and maintaining a healthy immune system (Birch et al., 2010; Linus Pauling Institute at Oregon State University, 2012; U.S. National Library of Medicine & National Institute of Health, 2012). Lack of essential fatty acids in infants may impact brain development and can result in learning problems (U.S. National Library of Medicine & National Institute of Health, 2012). Fats help with the absorption of the fat-soluble vitamins A, D, E, and K and provide a concentrated source of energy to support growth in infants and young children (Otten, et al., 2006). Fats also add flavor and satiety to foods. Some fats also promote heart health.

Types of Dietary Fat

Dietary fats are often referred to as "good" fats and "bad" fats. Good fats are those that reduce the risk of heart disease and are called unsaturated fats. They include **polyunsaturated fats** and **monounsaturated fats**, and both reduce the risk for heart disease by lowering blood cholesterol levels and decreasing inflammation (Weber & Noels, 2011). The polyunsaturated fats include two types: omega-6 fatty acids and **omega-3 fatty acids**. Corn oil, safflower oil, sunflower or corn, nuts, and seeds are rich in omega-6 fatty acids while fattier fish such as salmon, tuna, mackerel, and sardines as well as plant oils such as canola, soybean oil, and flaxseed oil are rich in omega-3 fatty acids (American Academy of Nutrition and Dietetics, 2012a).

The "bad" dietary fats are those that increase the risk of heart disease. They include the **saturated fats** and *trans* **fatty acids**. Saturated fats come predominantly from animal sources, but also include coconut oil, palm oil, and palm kernel oil. *Trans* fatty acids are formed during food processing when liquid oils are made solid through the process of hydrogenation. Although both types of fat increase the risk of heart disease, *trans* fatty acids are especially harmful (American Heart Association, 2012a). **Dietary cholesterol** is a fat-like substance that is found in foods of animal origin. Cholesterol is also made in the body. Increased levels of cholesterol in the bloodstream are associated with the risk for heart disease. Although eating a diet high in cholesterol-containing foods is linked to elevated blood cholesterol levels, the impact is not as significant as that caused by *trans* fats and saturated fats. Table 3-4 lists types of dietary fats and dietary cholesterol, fats, their dietary sources, and their impact on the risk for heart disease.

Dietary Fats and Health

The health impact of dietary fats is linked to how cholesterol and fats are transported in the blood. Just as oil and vinegar don't mix, neither do fats, cholesterol, and blood. To transport fat and cholesterol to where they are needed in the body, the liver packages them in a lipoprotein "coating." One of the lipoproteins that transports cholesterol in the blood is **low-density lipoprotein (LDL)**, also commonly called LDL cholesterol or "bad" cholesterol. Elevated LDL cholesterol levels in the bloodstream are a marker for heart disease. LDL deposits cholesterol within the artery walls, which accumulates causing the formation of a plaque. These deposits are made of cholesterol and other fatty compounds that clog the arteries in a process called atherosclerosis which can increase the risk for a heart attack (Harvard School of Public Health, 2012). In addition, atherosclerosis can trigger inflammation, which may further contribute to heart disease (Ridker, 2012).

Another common lipoprotein is **high-density lipoprotein (HDL)**. This is called the "good cholesterol" because the higher the levels the lower the risk for heart disease. HDL may pick up

---

essential fatty acids
a type of fatty acid that cannot be made by the body and must be obtained from the diet; needed for growth and maintaining a healthy immune system

polyunsaturated fats
unsaturated fats with two or more double bonds in their chemical structure that come predominantly from plant sources (such as corn oil, safflower oil), are liquid at room temperature, and reduce the risk of heart disease

monounsaturated fats
unsaturated fats with one double bond in their chemical structure (such as olive oil and canola oil) that also come from plant sources, are liquid at room temperature, and reduce the risk of heart disease

omega-3 fatty acids
polyunsaturated fats that are found in fish and also plant oils such as canola and flaxseed oil; protect against heart disease

saturated fats
fats found predominantly in animal sources that are solid at room temperature and are detrimental to heart health

***trans* fatty acids**
fats formed during the process of hydrogenation in which liquid oils are made solid and are especially harmful to heart health

dietary cholesterol
a fat-like, waxy substance that is found in foods of animal origin that plays a role in the risk for heart disease when consumed in excess

low-density lipoprotein (LDL)
a class of lipoprotein that transports cholesterol in the bloodstream; when elevated, it can increase the risk of heart disease

high-density lipoprotein (HDL)
a class of lipoprotein that transports excess cholesterol from the bloodstream back to the liver where it is excreted; associated with lower risk for heart disease

TABLE 3-4   Types and Sources of Dietary Fats and Dietary Cholesterol

Types of Fat or Cholesterol	Example of Dietary Sources	How They May Impact Risk for Heart Disease
Polyunsaturated fats	Corn oil, safflower oil, sunflower oil, soybean oil	Reduce
Omega-3 fatty acids	Flax oil, canola oil, soybean oil, fatty types of fish	Reduce
Omega-6 fatty acids	Fattier fish such as salmon, tuna, mackerel, herring, trout, and sardines and canola oil, flaxseed and flaxseed oil, walnuts and walnut oil, corn, safflower, sunflower, and soybean oils	Reduce
Monounsaturated fats	Olives, avocados, olive oil, canola oil, peanut oil, nuts and seeds	Reduce
Saturated fats	Cheese, meats, poultry, milk (except nonfat), cream, butter, coconut oil, palm oil, palm kernel oil	Increase
Trans fats	Stick margarine, vegetable shortening, some commercial baked goods such as pastries and doughnuts, commercially fried foods such as French fries	Increase
Dietary cholesterol	Cheese, meats, poultry, milk, butter, eggs, liver	Increase

Sources: Harris, W. S., Mozaffarian, D., Rimm, E., et al. Omega-6 fatty acids and risk for cardiovascular disease: A science advisory from the American Heart Association Nutrition Subcommittee of the Council on Nutrition, Physical Activity, and Metabolism; Council on Cardiovascular Nursing; and Council on Epidemiology and Prevention. *Circulation,* 2009 (updated 2011), retrieved from http://my.americanheart.org/professional/General/Omega-6-Fatty-Acids-in-the-Hierarchy-of-Cardiovascular-Protection_UCM_433122_Article.jsp. Harvard School of Public Health, 2012. The Nutrition Source Fats and Cholesterol: Out with the Bad, In with the Good, retrieved from http://www.hsph.harvard.edu/nutritionsource/what-should-you-eat/fats-full-story/index.html. Mayo Clinic, 2011. Dietary fats: Know which types to choose, retrieved from http://www.mayoclinic.com/health/fat/NU00262. *Dietary Reference Intakes: The Essential Guide to Nutrient Requirements,* 2006, by the National Academy of Sciences, courtesy of the National Academies Press, Washington, DC.

excess cholesterol in the circulatory system and bring it back to the liver where it can be excreted. This theory has undergone some reevaluation because recent research suggests that not all subclasses of HDL cholesterol are equally protective and that elevated HDL cholesterol may be a marker for improved heart health but may not actively reduce the risk of heart disease (Jensen, Rimm, Furtado, & Sacks, 2012; Voight et al., 2012). Regardless, HDL cholesterol still remains an important indicator of the risk for heart disease (Davis, 2012).

The key to a heart-healthy lifestyle is to:

- Substitute healthy dietary fats (polyunsaturated and monounsaturated) for unhealthy fats (*trans* fat and saturated fats).
- Limit the amount of cholesterol consumed.
- Maintain a healthy weight.
- Exercise regularly.

Teachers should understand that the biggest influence on blood cholesterol levels is the mix of fats in the diet—more so than the amount of cholesterol found in foods. The *Nutrition Note* takes a look at the role of saturated and *trans* fats in children's diets.

Implications of Dietary Fats in Children's Diets

Thinking about heart disease in infants and young children may seem premature. However, as teachers plan what they should feed young children, they must consider the foods that will foster children's healthful growth and development. They also need to consider the importance of nutrition as it relates to disease prevention. It has been estimated that as many as 50% of primary school–age children have one or more risk factors for heart disease (Reed, Warburton, & McKay, 2007). Furthermore, children may inherit a genetic predisposition to elevated blood cholesterol levels.

The type of fat consumed in the diet plays an important role in supporting the health of all children. Consequently, as teachers plan meals and cooking activities, they should focus on the use of healthy fats. For example, when making biscuits with children, teachers should select a recipe that uses oil instead of shortening and, when margarine is used, be sure to select a brand that does not have *trans* fatty acids.

NUTRITION NOTE The Role of *Trans* Fats and Saturated Fats in Children's Diets

As of January 1, 2006, the U.S. Food and Drug Administration requires that *trans* fats be listed on food labels. Why might this create problems in children's diets? With the initiation of this labeling law food companies have had to find replacements for *trans* fats. There has been concern that *trans* fat might be replaced with saturated fats, which, like *trans* fats, stimulate the production of LDL or bad cholesterol. A recent study compared the composition of 5,000 U.S. cookie and cracker products before and after the *trans* fat law was implemented. The use of partially hydrogenated vegetable oil (a source of *trans* fats) in chip products did decrease without a corresponding increase in saturated fat content. However, that was not the case with cookie products where sometimes *trans* fats were replaced with saturated fats such as palm oil and palm kernel oil. Although many food manufacturers have made favorable changes in the types of fats used in commercially prepared food items, it is still important for teachers to look for both *trans* fat and saturated fat content when checking the labels. Review the food label shown here to compare the fat composition of various types of desserts.

Compare Desserts!*
Keep an eye on Saturated Fat, *Trans* Fat and Cholesterol!

Granola Bar ±
Nutrition Facts
Serving Size 1 bar (33g)
Servings Per Container 10

Amount Per Serving
Calories 140   Calories from Fat 45

% Daily Value*
Total Fat 5g — 8%
  Saturated Fat 1g — 5%
  Trans Fat 0g
Cholesterol 0mg — 0%

Saturated Fat : 1g
+ *Trans* Fat : 0g
Combined Amt.: 1g

Cholesterol: 0% DV

Sandwich Cookies ±
Nutrition Facts
Serving Size 2 cookies (28g)
Servings Per Container 19

Amount Per Serving
Calories 130   Calories from Fat 45

% Daily Value*
Total Fat 5g — 8%
  Saturated Fat 1g — 5%
  Trans Fat 1.5g
Cholesterol 0mg — 0%

Saturated Fat : 1g
+ *Trans* Fat : 1.5g
Combined Amt.: 2.5g

Cholesterol: 0% DV

Cake, Iced and Filled ±
Nutrition Facts
Serving Size 2 cakes (66g)
Servings Per Container 6

Amount Per Serving
Calories 280   Calories from Fat 140

% Daily Value*
Total Fat 16g — 25%
  Saturated Fat 3.5g — 18%
  Trans Fat 4.5g
Cholesterol 10mg — 3%

Saturated Fat : 3.5g
+ *Trans* Fat : 4.5g
Combined Amt.: 8g

Cholesterol: 3% DV

*Nutrient values rounded based on FDA's nutrition labeling regulations.
± Values for total fat, saturated fat, and trans fat were based on the means of analytical data for several food samples from Subramaniam, S., et al., "Trans, Saturated, and Unsaturated Fat in Foods in the United States Prior to Mandatory trans-Fat Labeling," Lipids 39, 11-18, 2004. Other information and values were derived from food labels in the marketplace.

Sources: Van Camp, D., Hooker, N. H., & Lin, C. J. (2012). *Changes in fat contents of US snack foods in response to mandatory* trans *fat labeling*. Public Health Nutrition, 15, 1130–1137. doi: 10.1017/S1368980012000079; *Trans Fat Now Listed with Saturated Fat and Cholesterol on the Nutrition Facts Label*, by the U.S. Food and Drug Administration, updated 2011, retrieved May 16, 2012, from http://www.fda.gov/Food/ResourcesForYou/Consumers/NFLPM/ucm274590.htm; Mozaffarian, D., & Jacobsen, M. F. *Correspondence: Food Reformulations to Reduce Trans Fatty Acids*. (2010). *New England Journal of Medicine*. 362: 2037–2039.

Remember, however, that during infancy and the toddler years, restricting fat and cholesterol is not advised by health care professionals because of the calories these children need for growth. The position of the American Academy of Pediatrics and Institute of Medicine of the National Academies is that young children should make a gradual transition from receiving 50% of their calorie needs from fat during infancy to 30% to 35% during the ages of 2 to 3 (American Academy of Pediatrics, Hassink, S., 2012; Otten, et al., 2006). By the time children are ages 4 and older, a diet more closely aligned with the adult requirements of 25% to 35% is recommended (American Heart Association, 2012b).

Summary of the Role of Macronutrients

The goal of a healthful diet is to achieve a beneficial balance of macronutrients. Foods are a combination of proteins, fats, and carbohydrates. When children eat foods in a manner that supports MyPlate recommendations, they are ensured balanced diets that contain an appropriate percentage of calories from carbohydrates, fats, and proteins. The diet will have sufficient protein for the growth and repair of the body. It will have enough fat to meet calorie needs, but not have too much, thereby decreasing the risk of heart disease and obesity. It will have ample carbohydrates to meet energy needs and provide sufficient fiber for good health.

VITAMINS AND MINERALS AND OTHER IMPORTANT DIETARY COMPONENTS

Vitamins and minerals are components in food that are required in small amounts to sustain body processes. They are referred to as micronutrients. Vitamins and minerals are needed to release and utilize the energy found in protein, fats, and carbohydrates. They help transport oxygen, fight infections, build body structures such as bones and teeth, and keep the body working efficiently and in good repair. Vitamins and minerals may also play an important role in preventing chronic diseases such as high blood pressure, heart disease, stroke, and cancer (Drake, 2011; U.S. Department of Health and Human Services & U.S. Department of Agriculture, 2011). The goal of all nutrient guidance systems is to encourage the intake of a varied and balanced diet, thereby ensuring children consume the micronutrients needed to sustain health. It is best to obtain the micronutrients from foods as opposed to vitamin pills, which may not provide all the beneficial nutrients.

Vitamins

The body requires 13 essential vitamins, as listed in Table 3-5. Vitamins are organic compounds found predominantly in the foods we eat. The exceptions are vitamin D, which can be made by the body when the skin is exposed to sunlight, and vitamin K, which is produced by microorganisms in the gastrointestinal tract (Sizer & Whitney, 2011). Vitamins are essential. Without them humans cannot process and use energy from the proteins, fats, and carbohydrates we consume. Vitamins can be categorized into two groups: water soluble and fat soluble.

Water-Soluble Vitamins

water-soluble vitamins vitamins that dissolve in water and are therefore not stored in the body, (B vitamins and vitamin C)

The **water-soluble vitamins** include all the B vitamins and vitamin C. These vitamins dissolve in water and are absorbed directly into the bloodstream. Unlike fat-soluble vitamins (discussed next), water-soluble vitamins cannot be stored in any significant amount in the body. Therefore, the B vitamins and vitamin C should be consumed on a daily basis. Excess water-soluble vitamins are excreted in urine and, therefore, the risk for toxicity from overconsumption is low.

coenzymes compounds that help enzymes in their activities and are used in processes that release energy

Water-soluble vitamins often act as **coenzymes**, or partners that help enzymes, to regulate all types of body processes, including those that produce energy (Anderson & Young, 2012). For example, the B vitamins act as coenzymes in the metabolism of proteins, fats, and carbohydrates.

Fat-Soluble Vitamins

fat-soluble vitamins vitamins that dissolve in fat and are therefore stored in the body (vitamins A, D, K, and E)

The **fat-soluble vitamins** include vitamins A, D, E, and K. These vitamins dissolve in fat and are stored in the body until needed. This means they do not need to be consumed every day. The absorption of fat-soluble vitamins is enhanced by fat in the diet. For example, vitamin A in a fresh spinach salad is absorbed better when the salad is eaten with an oil-based salad dressing.

Children like Jamal, who experience malabsorption of dietary fats, are more likely to have poor absorption of fat-soluble vitamins. Because fat-soluble vitamins are stored, children are less likely to develop a deficiency of these vitamins. However, they are at more risk for toxicity if overconsumption occurs.

Minerals

Minerals are substances that originate from the earth. Minerals come from plants and animal foods and from water. The minerals in the ground are absorbed by plants and become part of the food chain. Like vitamins, minerals initiate and regulate processes within the body. They are essential for growth because they are part of body structures such as bones and teeth.

TABLE 3-5   Vitamins

	Functions	Good Food Sources*	Symptoms of Excess Intake	Symptoms of Deficiency
WATER SOLUBLE				
Thiamin (B$_1$)	Helps metabolize carbohydrates and some amino acids for energy. It is necessary for the normal functioning of the heart and nervous system.	Enriched, fortified, or whole-grain products such as breads and cereals, wheat germ, pork, ham, liver, legumes, and nuts, fortified meat substitutes.	None reported.	Symptoms include loss of appetite, weight loss, mental changes, muscle weakness, heart failure, nerve problems. Leads to beriberi.
Riboflavin (B$_2$)	Helps metabolize protein, fat, and carbohydrates for energy and is needed for growth and red blood cell production.	Animal protein such as meat, liver, eggs, and milk products, enriched bread and fortified cereals, green leafy vegetables.	None reported.	Sore throat, mouth, and tongue with cracks at the corners of mouth.
Niacin (B$_3$)	Helps metabolize carbohydrates, protein, and fat for energy. It is beneficial for the digestive system and skin.	Animal protein such as meat, liver, poultry, fish, milk products, and eggs, enriched, fortified, or whole-grain products such as breads and cereals, legumes.	None reported from dietary sources. Niacin used as a medication to improve blood fat levels can cause flushing and liver injury.	Leads to pellegra: symptoms include rash, vomiting, diarrhea, bright red tongue, depression, apathy, and memory loss.
Pyridoxine (B$_6$)	Helps metabolize proteins and maintains blood sugar levels by releasing glucose from stored glycogen, helps make the hemoglobin found in red blood cells.	Meat, fish, poultry, starchy vegetables, bananas, livers, fortified soy-based meat substitutes, and cereals.	Neurologic disorders and numbness.	Convulsions, loss of weight, depression, confusion, skin problems, microcytic anemia.
Pantothenic acid	Helps metabolize proteins, fats and carbohydrate for energy, and synthesize fatty acids.	Poultry, meat, fish, eggs, broccoli, milk and yogurt, potatoes, whole grains, legumes.	None reported.	Deficiency is rare.
Biotin	Helps metabolize proteins, fats, and carbohydrates for energy.	Widely available in foods, especially liver, egg yolk, milk, avocado, yeast, and meat.	None reported.	Deficiency is rare but can be associated with eating a large amount of raw egg whites (egg whites have avidin, which binds with biotin). Skin conditions, loss of appetite, depression, hair loss.
Folate or folic acid	Involved in protein metabolism, red blood cell formation, and DNA and new cell synthesis.	Liver, leafy green vegetables, beans, legumes, seeds, fortified breads and cereals, citrus fruits and juice.	Excess masks vitamin B$_{12}$ deficiency, which can cause neurologic damage.	Macrocytic anemia, poor growth, swollen tongue. Women who are deficient have increased risk of giving birth to infants with neural tube defects.
Vitamin B$_{12}$	Involved in the metabolism of fatty acids and amino acids. Helps form red blood cells and maintains the central nervous system.	Found in animal foods, meat, fish, poultry, cheese, milk, eggs, or fortified soy products.	None reported.	Leads to anemia and neurologic problems, depression, confusion, and dementia.

(Continued)

TABLE 3-5   Vitamins (*Continued*)

	Functions	Good Food Sources*	Symptoms of Excess Intake	Symptoms of Deficiency
Vitamin C	Involved in collagen formation. Improves wound healing, resistance to infection, and iron absorption.	Fruits and vegetables: especially citrus fruits, tomatoes, potatoes, kiwi fruit, peppers, broccoli, strawberries.	Increased incidence of kidney stones, gastrointestinal distress.	Leads to scurvy: symptoms include bleeding gums, decreased wound healing, easy bruising, swollen and painful joints.
FAT SOLUBLE				
Vitamin A	Important for normal vision, growth, immune function, formation of skin and mucous membranes, gene expression and reproduction, bone growth.	There are two types: *Preformed:* liver, dairy products, fish, fortified margarine. *Carotenoids:* orange fruits and vegetables (carrots, sweet potatoes, cantaloupe), dark green vegetables.	Toxicity only from preformed vitamin A: nausea, vomiting, headache, dizziness, blurred vision, lack of muscular coordination; excessive intake during pregnancy leads to birth defects.	Night blindness, blindness, poor growth, impaired resistance to infection.
Vitamin D	It aids in the absorption and raises the levels of calcium and phosphorus in the blood, which promotes bone maintenance and formation.	Can be made in the skin in the presence of sunlight. *Food sources:* fatty fish, fortified milk, orange juice and cereals, infant formula. Breast milk is not a rich source and, therefore, supplementation is recommended in exclusively breast-fed infants.	High blood levels of calcium, calcification of soft tissues such as kidneys, blood vessels, nausea, vomiting, and poor appetite.	Leads to faulty bone growth and rickets in children and under-mineralized bones in adults.
Vitamin E	Acts as an antioxidant protecting cell membranes and is involved in immune function.	Vegetable oils, whole grains, wheat germ, fortified cereals, nuts, green leafy vegetables, meats, poultry, fish, eggs.	None reported with naturally occurring vitamin E; excessive supplementation can lead to impaired blood clotting.	Very rare but can lead to nerve and muscle damage, vision problems, and weakened immune system and in premature infants hemolytic anemia.
Vitamin K	Involved in blood clotting and bone metabolism.	Produced by gastrointestinal tract bacteria. Dark green leafy vegetables, broccoli, vegetable oils, and margarine.	None reported.	Rare, but when it does occur, it can lead to impaired blood clotting. Vitamin K does not cross the placenta effectively; therefore, infants are provided vitamin K supplementation at birth.

*Breast milk and formula are good sources of vitamins unless indicated otherwise.

Sources: *Dietary Reference Intakes: The Essential Guide to Nutrient Requirements*, edited by J. J. Otten, J. Pitzi-Hellwig, and L. D. Meyers, 2006, Washington, DC: National Academies Press; *An Evidence-Based Approach to Vitamins and Minerals-Health Benefits and Intake Recommendations*, 2nd edition, by J. Higdon and V. J. Drake, 2012, New York: Thieme Publishing Group; Medline Plus: Vitamins, *U.S. National Library of Medicine National Institutes of Health*, 2012. Retrieved from http://www.nlm.nih.gov/medlineplus/ency/article/002399.htm; Vitamin and Mineral Fact Sheets, 2011, Office of Dietary Supplements, National Institute of Health. Retrieved from http://ods.od.nih.gov/factsheets/list-VitaminsMinerals/; *Manual of Pediatric Nutrition*, 4th edition, edited by K. M. Hendricks and C. Duggan, 2005, Hamilton, Ontario: B. C. Decker, Inc.; and *Pediatric Nutrition Handbook*, 6th edition, edited by R. Kleinman, 2009, Elk Grove, IL: American Academy of Pediatrics.

Minerals are divided into two groups, the macrominerals and the microminerals, based on how much is required in the diet:

- **Macrominerals:** calcium, phosphorus, magnesium, sodium, chloride, sulfate, and potassium. The requirement for macrominerals is 100 mg/day or more.
- **Microminerals:** iron, zinc, iodine, fluoride, selenium, manganese, copper, chromium, molybdenum, and cobalt. The requirement for microminerals is 15 mg/day or less (Mahan, Escott-Stump, & Raymond, 2012).

Table 3-6 illustrates the role of selected macrominerals and microminerals and describes the symptoms that children might exhibit if their bodies do not have enough or receive too much of these important nutrients.

A subcategory of the macrominerals includes the **electrolytes**. Electrolytes such as chloride, potassium, and sodium play an important role in helping to regulate fluids in and out of the body's cells. These minerals also help transmit nerve impulses. That is, they send messages to the brain for muscles to contract and relax. During gastrointestinal upset, diarrhea and vomiting can cause a loss of electrolytes and water. This can quickly result in dehydration. **Dehydration** is the dangerous lack of water in the body that can occur when insufficient fluids are consumed or when the body experiences excessive loss of fluids through vomiting and diarrhea.

A diet high in sodium content is not recommended for young children. High sodium intake is associated with high blood pressure in salt-sensitive individuals. The *Dietary Guidelines for Americans, 2010* emphasizes the importance of not eating too much salt (U.S. Department of Health and Human Services & U.S. Department of Agriculture, 2011).

macrominerals
minerals needed in larger amounts (100 mg/day or more)

microminerals
minerals needed in smaller amounts (15 mg/day or less)

electrolytes
a subcategory of minerals that help regulate fluid movement in and out of the body's cells and help transmit nerve impulses

dehydration
a dangerous lack of water in the body due to not drinking enough or losing too much by perspiring, vomiting, and/or diarrhea

Water

The macronutrients and micronutrients receive a lot of attention when discussing a healthy diet. Little attention, however, is given to the importance of water in the diet. Adults cannot survive more than 3 to 5 days without water, and young children even fewer days. Water accounts for about 60% of the adult's body composition and 78% of the infant's body (U.S. Geological Survey, 2012). Water performs myriad functions:

- Water regulates body temperature through perspiration.
- Water transports nutrients and oxygen as a component of blood.
- All chemical reactions of the body take place in water.
- Water helps to remove waste products from the body (Sizer & Whitney, 2011).

Decreases in the water content of the body can have immediate consequences. Individuals feel tired, experience headaches, and find it difficult to concentrate. Insufficient water can lead to dehydration and death.

Because of their higher water composition, infants and children are more sensitive to fluctuations in water status. Diarrhea, vomiting, and fever can quickly lead to dehydration. Providing a liquid rehydration solution such as Pedialyte can restore fluid and electrolytes. Teachers must make sure that infants and children are well hydrated, especially on warm days when children are active. A new CACFP requirement established in 2011 to reflect a new provision of the Healthy Hunger Free Kids Act of 2010 stipulates that child care centers, family day care homes, at-risk afterschool programs, and shelters participating in CACFP must have water readily accessible for children during the day (Oregon Department of Education, 2012). An added advantage to providing children with water is the fluoride (in fluoridated communities), a mineral that protects teeth from the risk of dental decay.

What if . . .
you noticed that your program's menu frequently offered a combination of high-sodium menu items such as a ham sandwich served with a pickle and canned soup? What recommendations might you make? Can you think of healthier food options?

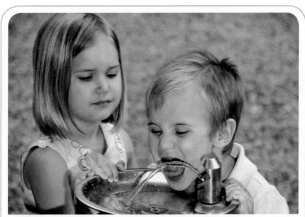
Offering water at routine times, especially during warm weather, helps children maintain a healthy fluid balance.

TABLE 3-6   Selected Minerals

	Functions	Good Food Sources	Symptoms of Excess Intake	Symptoms of Deficiency
MACROMINERALS				
Calcium	Is a component of bones and teeth, important for growth, involved in blood clotting, nerve impulse, muscle contractions.	Milk and milk products, sardines, clams, oysters, tofu, kale, broccoli, greens, calcium-fortified orange juice, and soy milk.	Decreases absorption of other minerals, impairs kidney function.	Increases risk of fractures and osteoporosis.
Phosphorus	Involved in the formation of bones and teeth and in energy metabolism, is important in growth and maintenance of tissues, maintains acid-base balance of body fluids, is part of cell membranes and genetic materials of cell.	Dairy foods, meat, fish, and almost all other foods.	Blood levels can become elevated when kidneys are not functioning well or when calcium regulation is dysfunctional.	Rare.
Magnesium	Involved in bone health, and a plethora of enzymatic reactions, including those involved in energy metabolism, protein synthesis, and maintaining blood sugar levels. Involved in the contraction and relaxation of muscles.	Green leafy vegetables, whole grains, nuts, legumes, tofu.	None from food sources. Excess supplementation can cause diarrhea, severe hypotension, confusion, muscle weakness, difficulty breathing, and irregular heartbeat.	Rare: hypocalcemia, muscle cramps and seizures, loss of appetite, nausea, vomiting, fatigue, and weakness.
Sodium and chloride	Maintains fluid balance, regulates blood pressure, involved in the function of nerves and muscles.	Salt, cured and processed foods, condiments such as soy sauce, ketchup, steak sauce.	High blood pressure in salt-sensitive individuals, which is a risk factor for heart disease, stroke, and kidney disease.	Rare: Extreme exercise in hot temperatures can cause sodium depletion with symptoms of confusion, headache, vomiting, and seizure.
Potassium	Maintains fluid balance and regulates blood pressure. Is involved in the function of nerves and muscles, maintains heartbeat.	Fruits and vegetables.	Blood levels can become elevated when kidneys are not functioning well (hyperkalemia) which can lead to muscle weakness, temporary paralysis, and cardiac arrhythmia.	Hypokalemia (low blood potassium) can occur in people taking diuretics, or who have severe vomiting or diarrhea, which can lead to fatigue, muscle weakness, stomach pain, and, if severe, to cardiac arrhythmias.
MICROMINERALS				
Iron	Involved in the transport of oxygen as part of red blood cells and helps with energy metabolism and needed for growth, reproduction, and immune function.	Meat, poultry, fish, fortified breads and cereals, beans, peas, lentils.	Acute toxicity, gastrointestinal distress. Accidental overdose of supplements containing iron is the largest cause of fatal poisoning in children under the age of 6.	Iron-deficiency anemia, weakness, pale skin, delayed cognitive development, increased risk of infection, fatigue, irritability.

(Continued)

TABLE 3-6 Selected Minerals (*Continued*)

	Functions	Good Food Sources	Symptoms of Excess Intake	Symptoms of Deficiency
Zinc	Is essential for growth and development and plays a role in wound healing and immune response. It impacts the senses of taste and smell.	Red meats, liver, eggs, dairy products, some seafood, vegetables, whole grains, fortified breakfast cereals.	Excess supplementation may cause diarrhea, stomach cramps, and vomiting; can suppress the immune system.	Slow growth, poor appetite, slow wound healing, loss of hair, infections, problems with sense of taste and smell.
Iodine	Is an essential component in thyroid hormones, which regulate enzymes and metabolic processe.	Seafood, iodized salt, processed foods that use iodized salt.	Thyroiditis, thyroid suppression.	Goiter, mental retardation, cretinism, hypothyroidism, delay in growth and development.
Fluoride	Is necessary for the health of teeth and bones. Protects against dental caries.	Fluoridated water.	Enamel and skeletal fluorosis.	Dental decay.
Selenium	Functions as a coenzyme and acts as an antioxidant.	Meat, organ meats, seafood, cereals, dairy products, fruits and vegetables depending on the selenium content of the soil where they were grown.	Hair and nail brittleness and gastrointestinal disturbances, rash, fatigue, nervous system abnormalities, garlic breath.	Enlarged heart, impaired immune system.

Sources: *Dietary Reference Intakes: The Essential Guide to Nutrient Requirements*, edited by J. J. Otten, J. Pitzi-Hellwig, and L. D. Meyers, 2006, Washington, DC: National Academies Press; *An Evidence-Based Approach to Vitamins and Minerals–Health Benefits and Intake Recommendations*, 2nd edition, by J. Higdon and V. J. Drake, 2012, New York: Thieme Publishing Group; Medline Plus: Minerals, *U.S. National Library of Medicine National Institutes of Health*, 2012. Retrieved from http://www.nlm.nih.gov/medlineplus/minerals.html; Vitamin and Mineral Fact Sheets, 2011, Office of Dietary Supplements, National Institute of Health. Retrieved from http://ods.od.nih.gov/factsheets/list-VitaminsMinerals/; *Manual of Pediatric Nutrition*, 4th edition, edited by K. M. Hendricks and C. Duggan, 2005, Hamilton, Ontario: B. C. Decker, Inc.; and *Pediatric Nutrition Handbook*, 6th edition, edited by R. Kleinman, 2009, Elk Grove, IL: American Academy of Pediatrics.

Phytochemicals

Phytochemicals are newcomers to the realm of nutrition science, but preliminary research suggests that these chemicals offer significant health benefits. Phytochemicals are found in fruits and vegetables. Diets rich in these foods offer protection from chronic diseases such as cancer, heart disease, stroke, high blood pressure, and urinary tract infections, to name just a few. The research is still new; however, the following is known about phytochemicals:

- Eating more fruits and vegetables provides vitamins, minerals, and phytochemicals.
- A single food will often contain many different phytochemicals. For example, kale contains three phytochemicals, isothiocyanates associated with lower cancer risk and lutein and zeaxanthin which may prevent the development of cataracts (Higdon & Drake, 2009).
- Foods that are rich in color are likely to be rich in phytochemicals. This includes carrots, pumpkins, sweet potatoes, winter squash, spinach, collards, kale, cantaloupe, red peppers, papayas, tomato products, watermelon, blue berries, and purple grapes.
- Eating a variety of foods will maximize the benefits of phytochemicals.

Children can learn about the importance of food components such as phytochemicals.

Consider how Sayaka shares the importance of eating a variety of fruits and vegetables rich in phytochemicals:

Sayaka introduces her second-grade class to the concept of phytochemicals by presenting a variety of brightly colored vegetables on the science table. She places child-safe pumpkin cutters

What if . . .

you were taking your class on a walking field trip and the day turned out to be unseasonably warm? How would you ensure each child has access to enough water?

phytochemicals
health-promoting substances obtained from a diet rich in fruits and vegetables

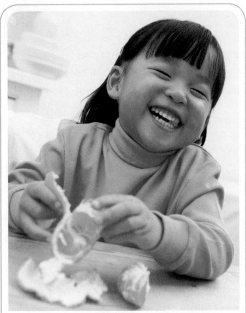

Eating a variety of rich-colored fruits and vegetables provides vitamins, minerals, and phytochemicals.

on the table with the foods and invites children to "dissect" the vegetables. The children are guided to study the structure and color of each food. Sayaka tells them about phytochemicals and how these chemicals protect the body from disease. Then she guides the children to plan a menu that includes one of the brightly colored vegetables. The children present their menus to the group and tell why they have selected each item on their menu.

Important Vitamins and Minerals for Children

All vitamins are important for children to consume. However, vitamins involved in growth need special consideration. Oftentimes, vitamins and minerals work in concert to provide the combination of nutrients needed to perform important roles in the body.

The Teamwork of B Vitamins

The B vitamins work together in important body processes. As discussed earlier, protein is used to produce enzymes that jump-start and speed up the chemical reactions that occur in the body, sometimes by a factor of a million or more (Berg, Tymoczko, & Stryer, 2008). To do this, the enzymes must join with the molecules involved in a reaction. Coenzymes support them in this role. The B vitamins, in addition to other roles, often act as coenzymes in metabolic processes assisting in the release of energy from the macronutrients. Some of the B vitamins also prevent certain types of anemia. Folic acid helps prevent neural tube defects.

Vitamin A

Vitamin A is generally recognized for its role in vision. The "old wives' tale" that carrots are good for the eyes is true. Vitamin A, found in carrots, sweet potatoes, and dark leafy green vegetables, will not correct near- or farsightedness, but this vitamin is required for vision. Vitamin A is needed to make a pigment of the eye that is very sensitive to light and aids vision. In addition to its role in vision, vitamin A also supports growth of bones and the overall body and helps maintain a healthy immune system.

Children in developing countries throughout the world still experience deficiencies in vitamin A and the resulting blindness and increased risk of severe infection or death that occurs if left untreated. The World Health Organization estimates that 250,000 to 500,000 vitamin A–deficient children become blind every year and half of them die within 12 months of becoming blind (World Health Organization, 2012). Vitamin A deficiency is usually not a problem in the United States, but can occur in children who experience malabsorption. For example, Jamal who has celiac disease is more likely to be at risk for vitamin A deficiency. Figure 3-7 lists sources of vitamin A that appeal to children.

FIGURE 3-7 Child-Friendly Sources of Vitamin A

- **Infants:** pureed peaches, apricots, mangoes, or commercially prepared pureed carrots, sweet potatoes, and squash.
- **Toddlers:** milk, eggs, shredded cheese, diced cooked carrots, mashed sweet potatoes with crushed pineapple, diced peaches, mango or apricot yogurt parfait, diced cantaloupe, steamed broccoli with cheese sauce, vegetable soups made with peas, carrots, sweet potatoes, and/or spinach, pumpkin custard.

- **Preschoolers and older:** milk, eggs, cheese, carrot sticks, carrot raisin salad, spinach and grapefruit salad, sweet potato, pumpkin, or carrot muffins or bread, homemade baked sweet potato fries, mango or peach smoothie, raw broccoli or red pepper strips with low-fat dip, homemade cream of spinach or kale soup, cantaloupe slices, peas and carrots, cottage cheese with cubed peaches, mangos or papaya, salad with dark green leafy lettuces, baked sweet potato, apricots, frozen homemade fruit pops made with peach or apricot nectar.

Vitamin A toxicity is a more likely concern in the United States. This can be caused by well-meaning parents who oversupplement or provide more than the Tolerable Upper Intake Levels (UL) of vitamin A. This is of particular concern because the U.S. food supply consists of many vitamin-fortified foods and beverages. In addition, children who mistake chewable or "gummy" style multivitamins for candy are also at risk for toxicity. Too much vitamin A can cause skin rashes, loss of appetite, problems with bones, liver damage, and even death (Higdon & Drake, 2012). Because vitamin A is one of the fat-soluble vitamins, excess amounts are stored in the liver, which increases the risk of toxicity.

Vitamin D, Calcium, Phosphorus, and Magnesium

Vitamin D is required for healthy bone development, as are the minerals calcium, phosphorus, and magnesium. Calcium, phosphorus, and magnesium also play a key role in the structure of teeth. These three minerals account for 98% of the body's mineral content (Kleinman, 2009). They are priority nutrients for children because of their importance for bone growth and maintenance. Vitamin D stimulates the intestinal absorption of calcium and phosphorus. Vitamin D is synthesized in the skin through exposure to sunlight. Certain factors can limit this synthesis. For example, children who are dark skinned or use sunscreen will make less vitamin D.

Vitamin D deficiency may be more common than previously recognized, and although there is not complete consensus among health authorities as to the scope of the problem and the impact on other aspects of health, there has been a consensus in the need for sufficient intake to promote proper mineralization of bone (Abrams, 2011; Holick et al., 2012; Rosen et al., 2012). A vitamin D deficiency can cause rickets, a condition that results in the softening of bones in young children. Teachers can influence the consumption of these important bone-building nutrients by offering milk and dairy products and other foods that are good sources of vitamin D, calcium, phosphorus, and magnesium. The intake of these nutrients can be increased in children's diets in the following ways:

- Offer cold cereal with milk.
- Prepare hot cereal and cream soups with milk instead of water.
- Offer vitamin D–fortified regular or Greek yogurt.
- Substitute calcium and vitamin D fortified soy milk or orange juice when children have a milk allergy or lactose intolerance.
- Make smoothies using milk, yogurt, and fruit.
- Offer fatty fish such as tuna, sardines, and salmon.

Iron and Vitamin C

Iron and vitamin C are another important vitamin and mineral team that are linked together in function. Lack of iron in children's diets results in iron-deficiency anemia, which is a particular concern among older babies and toddlers as they transition from breast milk and formula to solids. Because the consequences of iron-deficiency anemia are linked to adverse effects on both motor and cognitive development, teachers must understand dietary strategies for making the most of the iron found in children's diets (Kleinman, 2009).

The iron content of a food does not reflect the amount of iron that will be absorbed. Studies show that plant sources of iron (**nonheme iron**), such as beans, peas, lentils, and green leafy vegetables, are not as well absorbed as the animal sources of iron (**heme iron**) found in meats, poultry, eggs, and fish (Higdon & Drake, 2012).

Certain dietary strategies, however, can help balance meals for better iron absorption. Vitamin C, for example, enhances the absorption of nonheme iron. Figure 3-8 provides some nutritious ideas for pairing iron with vitamin C–rich foods. In addition, just a little bit of meat in a meal containing nonheme iron will enhance overall iron absorption (Hurrell & Egli, 2010). A bean and beef burrito, for example, is a food combination that promotes nonheme iron absorption. Foods can also impede iron absorption. For example, diets that have a very high fiber content and the tannins found in tea can inhibit iron absorption.

nonheme iron
a type of iron that is not readily absorbed by the body; found in plants

heme iron
a readily absorbed form of iron found in meats

FIGURE 3-8   Food Combinations That Support Iron Absorption

Vitamin C and Nonheme Iron Combinations
orange wedges and enriched cereal
salsa and burritos
tomato sauce and chili beans
sliced strawberries and a peanut butter on
whole-wheat sandwich
kiwi and orange tossed spinach salad

Meat and Nonheme Iron Combinations
ham and pea soup
pork and baked beans
ground beef and bean burrito

Teachers can ensure that young children start off on the right foot when it comes to iron intake by following suggestions such as these recommended by the American Academy of Pediatrics Committee on Nutrition (Dee et al., 2008; Kleinman, 2009).

- Introduce iron-fortified infant cereal or strained meats around 6 months of age.
- Supplement iron for those breast-fed infants who are not able to consume enough iron from foods.
- Do not feed infants younger than 12 months regular cow, goat, or soy milk.
- Avoid serving young children excessive amounts of milk, which can decrease their appetite for high-iron foods.

◼ IMPLEMENTING NUTRITION SCIENCE

In Chapter 2 we discussed different food guidance systems, such as the Dietary Reference Intakes and the USDA's Choose *MyPlate,* to provide teachers with an understanding of the standards that form the basis for food recommendations. In this chapter, we supplied basic nutrition information that covers the digestion, absorption, and classification of nutrients. Teachers need to understand this information for several important reasons. Meeting children's nutritional needs is an obvious primary goal. Understanding how diet recommendations impact personal health is also important for teachers. In addition, teachers who understand nutrition can promote nutrition principles across cultural food preferences. Finally, effective teachers need to understand the nutrition principles they are teaching.

Meeting the Nutritional Needs of Children

Teachers who understand the principles of nutrition have a stepping stone to knowing what to feed children and how to address their nutritional concerns. Teachers can best understand how to meet children's needs by evaluating each child's nutrition and health histories with attention directed to:

- Evidence of overnutrition or undernutrition.
- Health conditions that impact nutrition such as celiac disease or diabetes.
- The need for special diets.
- Food likes and dislikes.
- Cultural food preferences.

This type of information used in conjunction with the above-mentioned resources helps teachers plan healthful menus and address the nutritional needs of all children in their care. See the Progressive Programs and Practices feature *Helping Hungry Children through the Weekend* to see how teachers and volunteers collaborate to address a nutritional concern of children identified in their community.

What if . . .

a mother in your program was breast-feeding her 6-month-old and wanted you to provide cow's milk to the baby while in your care whenever she did not have a sufficient amount of pumped breast milk available? What would you advise?

PROGRESSIVE PROGRAMS & PRACTICES

Helping Hungry Children Through the Weekend

By Jennifer Moore and Todd Morrone, Food4Kids Backpack Program of North Florida, Inc.

One in four children in Alachua County, Florida, are affected by poverty and live in food-unstable (food insecure) households despite the resources of Free and Reduced-Price Lunch/Breakfast, afterschool snacks, food stamps, and other programs that target hunger. The county had multiple church, individual, and community-supported food assistance programs. Although these programs addressed low-SES population schools, none had the goals or resources to expand and address the need at the county level.

The Food4Kids Backpack Program of North Florida, Inc., founded by Jennifer Moore and Todd Morrone, targets children who are "chronically hungry" and at risk of not receiving food over the weekend when other resources are not available. Teachers, staff, and administration at participating schools can refer children into the program when they witness regularly exhibiting behaviors or symptoms of chronic hunger, such as stealing or hoarding food, rushing food lines Monday morning and quickly eating all food served, excessive tardiness and/or absences, extreme thinness, or inability to concentrate. After parental consent is obtained, all school-age children in the home are provided with the equivalent of seven meals each weekend. Every Friday, a rolling backpack full of child-friendly nonperishable food items are discreetly distributed to the enrolled student. Allergies, homelessness, or lack of electricity are taken into consideration and adjustments to packing are made as needed. The empty backpack is returned to school on Monday to be refilled for the next weekend.

Food4Kids is run completely by volunteers and partners with the school to identify and distribute the backpacks to the recipients. Each school is assigned a coordinator to manage the program at the school and work closely with the staff and volunteers to follow the program model. The schools, as well as the local food bank, provide storage space. Volunteers transport food supplies monthly and pack food weekly, and a local television network donates public service announcements to help increase community awareness and support. Community organizations have become involved with organizing food drives, while businesses serve as official drop-off locations for food donations and display marketing materials and information to

their patrons. Some businesses and churches have dedicated employees, members, and resources to help support a school. Girl Scout troops have initiated food drives and collected items to donate. Marketing concepts, such as the ability to sponsor a child, host a food drive, or volunteer time and talent, have been created to allow everyone to participate to their ability and interest. Key components of the program's business model are to reduce administrative costs by decentralizing, innovative fundraising, and partnering with other community groups who want to contribute.

In just 2 years, the program has grown from serving one school to 14 and feeds over 300 children each weekend that may have otherwise gone hungry. The community donated over 23,000 pounds of food for the program during the 2011–2012 school year alone. Partnerships with individuals, organizations, and businesses have been formed to help sustain and expand the program. Food4Kids is now serving children in a neighboring county and working to establish county networks to help impact childhood hunger beyond just Alachua County.

Promoting Personal Health

Teachers work hard and must cope with stress and the time constraints of their profession. In addition, teachers have the added responsibility of making sure children are kept safe while in their care. When teachers don't eat well, exercise, and get enough sleep, they compromise their own resiliency. Teachers need to take care of themselves so that they can provide optimal care and education for children. Teachers who exercise and eat healthfully promote their own wellness and are prepared to be vital educators and positive role models for children.

In this video a teacher describes foods to be served during a school's Southeast Asian lunch. What strategies does she use to discourage children's negative comments and increase their respect for culturally different foods?

Understanding Cultural Food Choices

Understanding cultural food preferences and belief systems regarding food choices is an important part of providing nutritional care for children. Minimizing personal cultural biases and preconceived opinions is important in effective communication. For instance, infants starting solids in the United States rely on infant cereals, strained meats, and fruits and vegetables as first foods. They then gradually transition to foods with more texture. Infants from Hispanic families are more likely to be introduced to foods such as rice, soups, tortillas, and beans as early as 6 to 12 months of age (Mennella, Ziegler, Briefel, & Novak, 2006). This is a cultural difference rather than a "wrong way" of feeding infants.

Having respect for a culture while providing nutritional care creates a collaborative approach between teachers and parents that ultimately benefits the child. Understanding basic nutrition principles helps teachers to promote healthful diets that explore and honor cultural preferences. Here is how one teacher puts this philosophy into action:

> Miguel, a 24-month-old, is a selective eater and does not like many of the foods Brittany offers at her family child care program. Brittany asks Miguel's mother, Diana, what types of foods Miguel enjoys. Diana tells Brittany that Miguel's favorite dish at home is caldo de pollo. Brittany is not familiar with the ingredients so Diana explains the recipe for the chicken and vegetable soup. Later that week Brittany serves caldo de pollo for lunch and all the children, including Miguel, enjoy the nutritious food.

Teaching Nutrition Concepts

Understanding nutrition science helps teachers to effectively teach nutrition concepts, and teaching nutrition concepts is no longer an option when it comes to good health. For example, the California Department of Education feels nutrition is so important that they have drafted nutrition competencies for children prekindergarten through grade 12 (see Web Resources) (California Department of Education, 2011). These competencies are aligned with the national and state health education standards. There are eight overarching nutrition competencies that relate to understanding basic nutrition concepts, analyzing nutrition influences, assessing valid nutrition information, and using strategies for practicing and promoting nutrition-enhancing behaviors. The competencies offer suggestions on how these goals will be met for the various grade levels. For example, the first competency, entitled *Essential nutrition concepts,* includes content standards for kindergartners, some of which are listed below:

1. Know the six nutrient groups and the functions
   - Identify foods of plant origin
   - Classify plant foods such as fruits, vegetables, and grains
   - Identify the variety of foods of animal origin
2. Know nutrition and health guidelines
   - Name a variety of health foods and explain why they are necessary for energy and good health
   - Identify a variety of healthy snacks
   - Describe tools used to measure servings of food
3. Identify the physiological process in digestion, absorption, and metabolism of nutrients
   - Describe food by using senses: taste, touch, sight, smell, and sound (California Department of Education, 2011).

This example highlights the growing expectation for teachers to present activities and lessons that teach developmentally appropriate nutrition concepts that can be reinforced across grade levels, and shows another way in which the understanding of nutrition science promotes effective teaching.

What if . . .

you were a teacher of a kindergarten/first grade blended class and planned to teach about dairy products? What nutrition concepts do you feel are appropriate for this age? How would you modify the lesson to take into consideration the age range of children in the classroom?

● SUMMARY

Nutrition science is the study of how food provides nourishment to the body to support its growth, maintenance, repair, and reproduction. The consequences of poor nutrition are evident in both immediate and long-term health. Nourishing young children is an important responsibility. Because of this, teachers must fully understand and embrace the basic principles of healthful eating. Teachers have a responsibility to impart accurate and unbiased information in their promotion of health and nutrition concepts.

Teachers may find that understanding the science of nutrition is enhanced by an awareness of how food is digested, absorbed, and metabolized. The digestive process can be challenged, however, by a variety of health issues that can result in malabsorption and poor growth. When teachers understand these processes and the potential for disorders, it helps them partner with parents to provide a calm feeding environment that meets the dietary needs of children.

Food can be categorized into six major groups: proteins, fats, carbohydrates, vitamins, minerals, and water. The energy-providing macronutrients include protein, fats, and carbohydrates. Vitamins and minerals are micronutrients that sustain body processes and are needed to release and utilize the energy found in protein, fats, and carbohydrates. Water is a vital nutrient. It transports nutrients and oxygen as a component of blood, and all chemical reactions of the body take place in water. Phytochemicals are health-promoting substances found in food that may offer protection from chronic diseases such as cancer, heart disease, and stroke. Teachers who learn the principles of nutrition are able to translate recommendations into healthful meals for children and choose healthful diets for themselves. They are also able to take cultural food differences into account when planning meals. Teachers who understand the foundations of nutrition are able to effectively teach nutrition concepts.

KEY TERMS

Absorption
Amino acids
Aspiration
Basal metabolic rate (BMR)
Calorie
Coenzymes
Complementary protein
Dehydration
Dietary cholesterol
Digestion
Disaccharides
Dysphagia
Electrolytes
Enzymes
Essential fatty acids

Fat-soluble vitamins
Gastroesophageal reflux (GER)
Gastroesophageal reflux disease (GERD)
Gastrointestinal tract
Heme iron
High-density lipoprotein (HDL)
Insoluble fiber
Lactose intolerant
Limiting amino acid
Low-density lipoprotein (LDL)
Macrominerals
Malabsorption
Microminerals
Microvilli
Monosaccharides

Monounsaturated fats
Nonheme iron
Nutrition science
Omega-3 fatty acids
Osteoporosis
Phytochemicals
Polysaccharides
Polyunsaturated fats
Saturated fats
Soluble fiber
Total energy expenditure
Trans fatty acids
Villi
Water-soluble vitamins

REVIEW QUESTIONS

1. Explain the process of digestion, including the role of each part of the gastrointestinal tract and the breakdown products of foods.
2. Describe the physical characteristics of the small intestine that enhance the absorption of nutrients and relate this to two conditions in which absorption can be impaired.

3. List six nutrient categories and explain the roles of each of the macronutrients.

4. Explain the role of vitamins and minerals in the diet and elaborate on the differences between water-soluble and fat-soluble vitamins and macrominerals and microminerals.

5. Provide three reasons why it is important for teachers to understand nutrition science.

DISCUSSION STARTERS

1. Imagine that the parents of the second graders in your classroom have complained that the school's food menu has too many solid fats, added sugars, and processed high-sodium foods and not enough fiber. How would you address this issue? Who would you involve in this conversation?

2. The process of digestion involves the mechanical and chemical breakdown of food. What are some examples of the mechanical breakdown of food? What are some examples of chemical breakdown? What are the breakdown products of the macronutrients?

3. Select one of the eight overarching nutrition competencies developed by researchers at the UC Davis Center for Nutrition in Schools in collaboration with the California Department of Education found on the following website: http://cns.ucdavis.edu/content/Competencies/NutrEdComp.pdf. Select a specific content area within the competency and explain how you would teach a concept and what levels of expectations you might have for kindergarten and third-grade children.

PRACTICE POINTS

1. What would happen if a child in your program had diarrhea? How would you decide whether she should go home or stay at school? What foods or beverages should she avoid until she feels better and no longer has diarrhea?

2. A 3-year-old who has celiac disease is going to start school soon. Plan a lunch menu and snack menu for his first day at school.

3. Develop a Teaching Wellness lesson for a third-grade class that teaches a concept from the competency and content area you selected for the last discussion starter (question 3).

WEB RESOURCES

California Department of Education Nutrition Competencies for California's Children
    cns.ucdavis.edu/resources/curriculum/index.cfm

Celiac Disease Foundation
    www.celiac.org/

Celiac Sprue Association
    www.csaceliacs.org/index.php

Dietary Reference Intakes
    http://fnic.nal.usda.gov/dietary-guidance/dietary-reference-intakes

National Digestive Diseases Information Clearinghouse
    http://digestive.niddk.nih.gov

MyEducationLab™

Go to Topic 1 (Basic Nutrition) in the MyEducationLab (www.myeducationlab.com) for your course, where you can:

- Find learning outcomes for Basic Nutrition along with the national standards that connect to these outcomes.
- Complete Assignments and Activities that can help you more deeply understand the chapter content.
- Apply and practice your understanding of the core teaching skills identified in the chapter with the Building Teaching Skills and Dispositions learning units.

- Check your comprehension on the content covered in the chapter by going to the Study Plan in the Book Resources for your text. Here you will be able to take a chapter quiz, receive feedback on your answers, and then access Review, Practice, and Enrichment activities to enhance your understanding of chapter content.

four
Feeding Infants

learning outcomes

AFTER READING THIS CHAPTER, YOU SHOULD BE ABLE TO:

1. Describe the importance of establishing a nurturing and supportive feeding relationship.

2. Describe how to support families in the feeding of infants from birth to 6 months of age.

3. Discuss how developmental milestones for infants ages 6 months to 1 year guide decision making about the progression of offering solid foods.

4. Describe concerns and methods for feeding infants with special needs.

5. Discuss cultural influences on feeding practices.

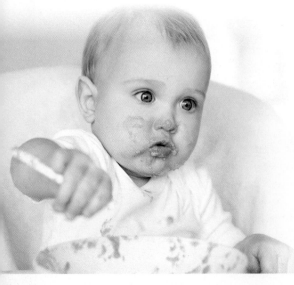

Amelia, a family child care provider, has just been introduced to baby Manuel. His mother Lucia is dropping him off at Amelia's house for the first time. Manuel is 3 months old and is being transitioned from breast milk to formula by his mother who is returning to work part time. She feels she may not have the accommodations at her workplace to express (pump) breast milk and has decided to introduce formula. Manuel has just begun to accept the bottle. Lucia admits she wishes she didn't have to use formula because Manuel has such a sensitive stomach, especially since she started cereal 2 weeks ago. She started solids a little early to make sure Manuel has enough to eat when he starts child care. After sharing information about Manuel's normal routine, she nurses him and after he falls asleep, she places him in his assigned crib and goes to work.

Amelia checks on Manuel who naps for almost 3 hours. She begins lunch for the other children. When a toddler cup is knocked to the floor, Manuel wakes up with a start and begins to cry. Amelia is busy feeding another infant. By the time she gets to Manuel he is extremely upset. She tries to give him his bottle, but he is so upset he sputters and chokes on the formula. Halfway through the bottle he throws up and begins to cry again. She tries giving him cereal, but he pushes it out with his tongue. It seems to Amelia that Manuel may be in pain as he pulls his legs up and continues screaming. When Lucia comes to pick him up an hour later she is surprised to see teacher Amelia pacing the floor with her very upset son. She takes Manuel and immediately sits down to nurse him. As Manuel settles down, both Amelia and Lucia admit that he has had a challenging first day.

Early childhood teachers are frequently called on to ease the child's transition into the early childhood group. Knowing about a child's pattern of eating is very important in that process, especially for infants who are less able to communicate about their needs. As demonstrated in the opening case scenario, teachers and families need to work together to plan a successful transition and to continue to communicate about children's nutritional needs.

In this chapter we explore feeding practices for infants, including ways to create positive eating experiences. We also discuss resources that can assist teachers to build child wellness through healthy nutrition in the early childhood setting. We focus on feeding issues that sometimes arise during specific developmental stages and offer strategies to support the optimal nourishment of infants during critical times of growth and development. Understanding the fundamentals of infant nutrition is especially important in the face of the increasing incidence of overweight and obesity in young children. Decisions made about feeding can have ramifications on the rate of weight gain of infants and result in lifelong consequences.

Not every infant can adapt to the standard approach to feeding. Flexibility and accommodations may be needed for babies with special needs. In addition, cultural food practices can sometimes create a need to rethink how teachers feed young children. For example, the progression of infant feeding from breast milk or formula to solids may vary from one culture to another. Understanding these differences ensures that teachers are prepared to manage the nutritional needs of young children in their care.

● THE BALANCE OF NURTURE AND NUTRIENTS

Infants need a nurturing feeding relationship and appropriate nutrition in order to grow and thrive. The **feeding relationship** established between infants and their families and caregivers is an important contributor to successful growth and development. A good feeding relationship is established when teachers and parents are responsive to infants' feeding cues, such as hunger and satisfaction. A warm, caring relationship supports effective feeding. In turn, good feeding supports good nutrition, which is critical during infancy because of the rapid rate of growth that occurs during the first months after birth.

Babies learn about the world through their senses. When infants are talked to and held by their teachers, this verbal and tactile stimulation contributes to the "wiring of their brains," or their neurological development. The combination of holding, talking, and smiling at babies while they eat is how babies learn. Later, as foods are introduced, babies learn about their environments through the aromas, colors, tastes, and textures of the foods to which they are exposed. As the opening case illustrates, without an effective feeding relationship, providing nourishment can become a challenge even when a baby is hungry. The feeding relationship is half of the equation that teachers balance when nourishing infants. It is also essential for teachers to understand what to feed infants.

Feeding infants follows a progression that evolves as children develop. The needs of infants are particularly important because the consequences of inappropriate feeding are significant. The nutritional needs of infants are influenced by how well mothers are nourished prior to and during pregnancy. For example, women who gain too much or too little weight during pregnancy may give birth to infants who were over- or undernourished in the uterine environment (Kleinman, 2009; Retnakaran et al., 2012). Both of these scenarios may cause changes in their metabolism that put these infants at increased risk for obesity later on in life (Phelan et al., 2011). Women who have anemia during pregnancy are more likely to have infants with low iron stores. Iron deficiency may affect the development of the central nervous system and is linked to developmental delays in young children, including deficits in cognitive and motor skills development. These detrimental effects may be long lasting and some may be irreversible (Baker, Greer, & The Committee on Nutrition, 2010; Lozoff, 2011). In addition, some infants, such as those who are born prematurely, have nutrition-related health concerns. The medical complications associated with being born early may prevent babies from growing well while hospitalized, so families need to ensure a healthy rate of growth when premature infants are sent home. The unique feeding and nutritional needs of these children

feeding relationship
the relationship established when teachers and families are responsive to infants' feeding cues; supports effective feeding and good nutrition

MyEducationLab™

Visit the MyEducationLab for *Nutrition, Health, and Safety for Young Children* to enhance your understanding of chapter concepts with a personalized Study Plan. You'll also have the opportunity to hone your teaching skills through video-based Assignments and Activities, as well as Building Teaching Skills and Dispositions lessons.

An increasing amount of research in recent years focuses on the important relationship between nutrition and infant brain development. As you watch this **video**, consider the potential negative effects of poor nutrition in infancy.

may require teachers to prepare special transitional formulas or offer fortified breast milk that is higher in calories per ounce.

Finally, teachers also assist families of well-nourished infants to maintain feeding practices to help their babies continue to grow and thrive. The special nutrient needs of each infant must be recognized in order to provide an appropriate feeding plan. In this chapter, we discuss the feeding strategies for infants in two age categories: birth to 6 months of age and 6 to 12 months of age.

FEEDING INFANTS: THE FIRST 6 MONTHS

The first 6 months of life are a time of significant growth and development. At birth infants do not have a fully developed gastrointestinal tract, immune system, nervous system, or brain (Kleinman, 2009). Good nutrition is essential to support the continued development of these vital systems. In fact, the development that occurs during the first year is unparalleled by any other time in the child's life. By around 5 months of age, most infants have doubled their birth weight. By the end of the first year, birth weight is increased by approximately 200%, and length by 50% (Mahan, Escott-Stump, & Raymond, 2012). The size of the brain doubles by age 1 and triples by age 6 reaching 93% of its adult size (Perneczky et al., 2010; Sinclair & Dangerfield, 1998). To achieve this rapid rate of growth and provide needed support for optimal brain development, a sufficient supply of calories and nutrients is needed.

Infants need only breast milk or formula for the first 4 to 6 months of life, and because an infant's stomach is small, frequent feedings are needed. Breast milk is ideal because it is easily and quickly digested and provides ideal proportions of essential nutrients.

The Breast-Fed Infant

Breast milk is the gold standard for the nourishment of infants because it contains the perfect combination of nutrients to support optimal growth and development. In a few situations, however, the use of breast milk is not acceptable, such as when mothers are HIV positive or taking illegal drugs or certain prescribed medications (Kleinman, 2009). Unlike formula, the nutrient content of breast milk changes over time to meet the maturing infant's needs and when fed exclusively to babies will support growth until 6 months of age (Kleinman, 2009; Queen Samour & King, 2012).

Benefits of Breast Milk

Breast milk is recommended as the infant food of choice by a number of health organizations including the American Academy of Pediatrics, the World Health Organization, and The Academy of Nutrition and Dietetics (formerly the American Dietetic Association) (Eidelman, Schandler, & American Academy of Pediatrics, 2012; World Health Organization, 2011; American Dietetic Association, 2009). The consensus recommendation is to maintain exclusive breastfeeding for about the first 6 months and continued breastfeeding as complementary foods are introduced to at least the first year of life. (The WHO encourages breastfeeding until age 2 or older.) This is because breast milk offers unique nutritional and non-nutritional benefits that protect the health and promote the optimal growth and development of infants (Eidelman et al., 2012).

The nutritional benefits of breast milk are significant. The type of fat found in breast milk is easily absorbed by the baby and its composition appears to be ideally suited to promote brain and vision development (Kleinman, 2009). The protein composition of breast milk is also more easily digested than that of formula and it provides just the right amount to promote growth. Breast milk also contains enzymes that help in the absorption of the fats, carbohydrates, and protein found in breast milk.

colostrum
the first milk produced by the nursing mother; it is rich in antibodies and other protective factors to help keep infants healthy

The advantages of breast milk are not limited to nutrition. **Colostrum**, the first milk produced by the nursing mother, is very rich in protective factors. Various components in breast milk, including antibodies, help prevent illness and infection, allergic disease such as asthma, and protect against a number of chronic conditions such as obesity and Type 1 and Type 2 diabetes. Figure 4-1 shows the decreased risk of illness for a variety of health conditions (related to the duration of breastfeeding) as compared to infants who are fed commercial formula. The decreased risk for common childhood illnesses—ear infections, respiratory infections, and gastroenteritis (commonly known as the

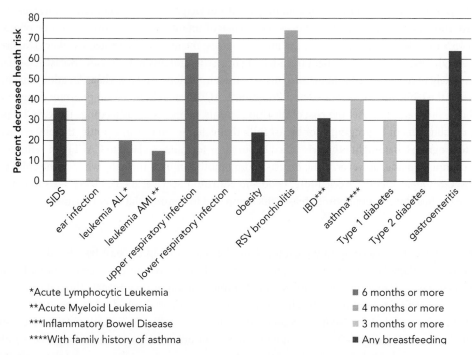

*Acute Lymphocytic Leukemia
**Acute Myeloid Leukemia
***Inflammatory Bowel Disease
****With family history of asthma

■ 6 months or more
■ 4 months or more
■ 3 months or more
■ Any breastfeeding

FIGURE 4-1

The Percent Decreased Health Risk Related to Duration of Exclusive Breastfeeding

Sources: Based on American Academy of Pediatrics (2012). "Policy Statement Breastfeeding and the Use of Human Milk," *Pediatrics, 129*(3) pp. e827–e841 (doi:10.1542/peds.2011-3552). Ip, S., Chung, M., Raman, G., Chew, P., Magula, N., DeVine, D., Trikalinos, T., & Lau, J. *Breastfeeding and maternal and infant health outcomes in developed countries.* (2007). Rockville (MD): Agency for Healthcare Research and Quality (US); (Evidence Reports/Technology Assessments, No. 153.) from http://www.ahrq .gov/downloads/pub/evidence/pdf/brfout/brfout.pdf; American Academy of Pediatrics. (2012). "Executive Summary: Breastfeeding and the Use of Human Milk," *Pediatrics, 129*(3) pp. 600–603 from www2.aap.org/breastfeeding/files/ . . . /Breastfeeding-2012ExecSum.pdf.

"stomach flu" vomiting and diarrhea)—ranges from 50% to 72% (American Academy of Pediatrics, 2012f). This is significant and has an important impact on infant health that can be especially appreciated by working mothers and their employers.

It's not just the antibodies found in breast milk that protect infants. Breast milk contains other bioactive compounds that stimulate the development of the gastrointestinal tract, the largest organ of the immune system. For example, human milk oligosaccharides found in breast milk help to establish beneficial microbial populations in the infant gut (Li et al., 2012). This is important because the beneficial microorganisms protect the infant from infection by harmful bacteria and strengthen the immune system so that it can fight off chronic health problems like food allergies and asthma (University of Illinois College of Agricultural, Consumer and Environmental Sciences, 2012). The benefits of breast milk can be life saving for premature infants who have a greater risk for developing necrotizing enterocolitis (NEC), which is a serious infection and an inflammation of the intestines that causes destruction of parts of the bowel. In severe cases it can result in the surgical removal of the damaged part of the intestine. In spite of aggressive treatment the estimated mortality rates for NEC are about 25% (Eisner, 2011). The cause of NEC is not completely understood; however, researchers estimate that the risk of developing it is 77% less for premature infants fed breast milk while in neonatal intensive care units (American Academy of Pediatrics, 2012f).

The research suggests that breast-fed infants, particularly those born prematurely, perform better on IQ tests administered later in childhood and have overall better cognitive performance than children who do not receive breast milk in infancy (Guxens et al., 2011; Isaacs et al., 2010; Kramer et al., 2008). In addition, there is some indication that breastfeeding may protect against developmental delays and support the attainment of gross motor skills and language development (Dee, Li, Lee, & Grummer-Strawn, 2007).

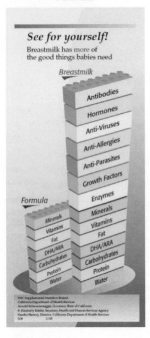

Comparing Human Milk to Formula:

See for yourself!

Breastmilk has more of the good things babies need

FIGURE 4-2

The Beneficial Qualities of Breast Milk

Source: Used courtesy of the WIC Supplemental Nutrition Branch of the California Department of Health Services.

Breast milk also plays a role in maintaining healthful weight of young children. Numerous studies have shown that breastfeeding reduces the chance of infants becoming overweight or obese by about 15% to 25% and that the longer the mother nurses, the greater the protective effect (Koletzko et al., 2009). Teachers directly benefit from having breast-fed infants in their care. Breast-fed infants are less likely to have colds, ear infections, urinary tract infections, and diarrhea. An additional benefit is that the Child and Adult Care Food Program (CACFP), a child nutrition program designed to reimburse programs to offset the cost of nutritious meals, supports breastfeeding. The CACFP provides reimbursement to programs for breast milk that is fed to infants in a bottle, thereby reducing costs to programs that might otherwise need to purchase formula. A claim to CACFP for reimbursement cannot be made, however, if the breast-feeding mother nurses the baby while at the child care setting (U.S. Department of Agriculture, Food and Nutrition Service, 2000). Figure 4-2 summarizes some of the healthy components of breast milk compared to commercial infant formula.

Rates of Breastfeeding

The frequency of breastfeeding in the United States has increased in the past two decades. In 1972, 22% of U.S. mothers began breastfeeding their infants at birth (Wright & Schanler, 2001). In 2008 provisional data gathered by the CDC National Immunization Survey reveals this rate increased to about 75%. This does not meet the current health objectives established by *Healthy People 2020*, which aims for a goal of 81.9% of all women initiating breastfeeding (Centers for Disease Control and Prevention, 2011b). In addition, although the rate of breastfeeding is improving, the number women who are exclusively breastfeeding (no solids, no water, and no other liquids) their infants at 3 months of age is only 35%. Lower rates of breastfeeding initiation in the United States occur among mothers who are non-Hispanic black women, of lower socioeconomic status, under the age 20, and/ or women who are unmarried (Centers for Disease Control and Prevention, 2011b).

Cultural Influences on Breastfeeding Practices

Cultural perspectives are factors in whether women breast-feed their infants and for how long. Foreign born Hispanic women living in the United States are more likely to initiate breastfeeding and breastfeed longer than Hispanic mothers who have spent all of their lives in the United States (Gill, 2009; Sparks, 2011). Although non-Hispanic black women have lower rates of breastfeeding initiation in the United States, in recent years, this group has shown the greatest improvement, going from 36% in 1993–1994 to 65% in 2005–2006 (McDowell, Wang, & Kennedy-Stephenson, 2008). Additionally, more foreign-born mothers living in the United States breast-feed compared to U.S.-born women (Pak-Gorstein, Haq, & Graham, 2009). This reflects the U.S. culture in which breastfeeding, although promoted, may be considered an option rather than the norm for feeding infants.

Culturally specific beliefs can have both positive and negative influences on breastfeeding practices among nursing women. For example, Islamic women aim to breast-feed their infants for 2 years; religious guidance supports them in this practice (Shaikh & Ahmed, 2006). However, the traditional garb worn by Islamic women decreases their exposure to the sun, and may lead to vitamin D deficiency among the mothers. In turn, this may result in vitamin D deficiency among infants who receive breast milk low in vitamin D (Allali et al., 2006; Haggerty, 2011). During the month of Ramadan, fasting is practiced by Muslims from sunup to sundown. Although religious guidance exempts breastfeeding women, some choose to fast for spiritual reasons in spite of their recognition that it can impact milk supply and can lead to more supplemental feedings (Al-Oballi Kridli, 2011). Some Hispanic mothers feel that breast milk can be negatively affected by situations that precipitate strong anger (*coraje*) or shock (*susto*) in their lives. They may choose not to breast-feed or to stop breastfeeding for fear the milk will be harmful to the baby. Asian mothers also believe that "vital energy" is required for the production of breast milk and that when the body is "imbalanced" the mother's milk can become unhealthy for the baby (Pak-Gorstein et al., 2009). Native American populations have a history of lower initiation rates of breastfeeding (about 65% in 2005). However, in recent years there has been

What if . . .

while you were feeding a 2-month-old baby a bottle of breast milk, the mother arrived at the program and wanted to nurse the baby instead? How would you respond to this request? Could this feeding be counted as a reimbursable CACFP meal? How might you get a definitive answer?

a resurgence in reconnecting to traditional values and roles and, along with this trend, there has been an increased recognition of the importance of breastfeeding with breastfeeding rates beginning to improve (74% in 2007) (Centers for Disease Control and Prevention, 2011a). Figure 4-3 from the U.S. Department of Health and Human Services, Office on Women's Health shares both the practical benefits of breastfeeding in a way that connects to the spirituality of the Native American culture and is a message that can resonate for any mother considering whether to breastfeed. When promoting breastfeeding to women of Native American heritage it is important to consider the influence of extended family members such as grandmothers, aunts, and fathers. Support from family can enhance successful changes in infant feeding practices including initiation of breastfeeding (Dellwo, Houghton, & Graybeal, 2001; Horodynskia, Calcaterab, & Carpenter, 2012).

Teachers who learn about the cultural perspectives of breastfeeding that guide families' decisions are better able to understand and support the establishment of healthful feeding practices. This can be accomplished by fostering close communication about the care of infants and approaching varying beliefs and practices with sensitivity and respect. Teachers who include family members in interactive and supportive discussions about breastfeeding may increase the likelihood and length of time mothers choose to breast-feed.

Supporting Breast-Feeding Mothers

Teachers are an important part of the nursing mother's support system. They can have a positive impact on helping nursing mothers continue to breast-feed. The WHO highlights this influential role in promoting positive infant-feeding practices and the importance of caregivers supporting breast-feeding mothers who return to work (World Health Organization, 2010; World Health Organization & UNICEF, 2003). In addition, the Centers for Disease Control and Prevention in their goal of promoting the health of mothers and their infants developed a Breastfeeding Report Card which includes an evaluation of state and national trends in breastfeeding data. One of the indicators they evaluate is a state's child care regulations that support breastfeeding based on the National Resource Center for Health and Safety in Child Care and Early Education best care standards (Centers for Disease Control and Prevention, 2011a; National Resource Center for Health and Safety in Child Care and Early Education, University of Colorado Denver, 2011). More women may be likely to request assistance from child care providers in helping them maintain breastfeeding as a result of the Patient Protection and Affordable Care Act. This health insurance reform legislation was passed by Congress and signed into law by President Obama in 2010. Section 4207 of this act requires employers to provide break time and a private place that is not a bathroom for nursing mothers to express breast milk, for as long as 1 year after a child's birth (United States Breastfeeding Committee, 2011). In addition, this act ensures that breast-feeding women are given the support and counseling they need from trained health care providers such as lactation consultants and that they are provided with breast-feeding equipment such as breast pumps. The reason these types of services are provided for women is because breastfeeding is such an effective preventative step mothers can take to protect their health and the health of their infants (U.S. Department of Health and Human Services, 2012).

Research shows that women who have a sense of "confident commitment" are more likely to be successful in breastfeeding (Avery, Zimmermann, Underwood, & Magnus, 2009). Teachers who share in the care of infants can offer positive support for this commitment. The National Association for the Education of Young Children as well as other health authorities provides specific guidelines

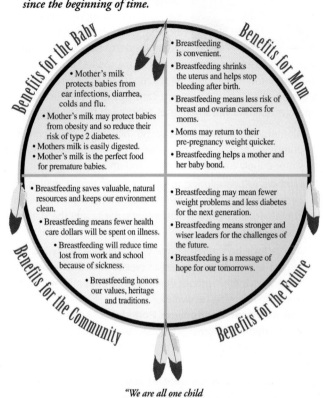

Babies are born to be breastfed

Breastfeeding has kept our people and traditions strong since the beginning of time.

Benefits for the Baby
- Mother's milk protects babies from ear infections, diarrhea, colds and flu.
- Mother's milk may protect babies from obesity and so reduce their risk of type 2 diabetes.
- Mothers milk is easily digested.
- Mother's milk is the perfect food for premature babies.

Benefits for Mom
- Breastfeeding is convenient.
- Breastfeeding shrinks the uterus and helps stop bleeding after birth.
- Breastfeeding means less risk of breast and ovarian cancers for moms.
- Moms may return to their pre-pregnancy weight quicker.
- Breastfeeding helps a mother and her baby bond.

Benefits for the Community
- Breastfeeding saves valuable, natural resources and keeps our environment clean.
- Breastfeeding means fewer health care dollars will be spent on illness.
- Breastfeeding will reduce time lost from work and school because of sickness.
- Breastfeeding honors our values, heritage and traditions.

Benefits for the Future
- Breastfeeding may mean fewer weight problems and less diabetes for the next generation.
- Breastfeeding means stronger and wiser leaders for the challenges of the future.
- Breastfeeding is a message of hope for our tomorrows.

"We are all one child spinning through Mother Sky."
– Shawnee proverb

FIGURE 4-3

A Breastfeeding Guide for American Indians and Alaska Native Families
Source: U.S. Department of Health and Human Services, Office on Women's Health, An Easy Guide to Breastfeeding for American Indians and Alaska Native Families, retrieved June 1, 2012 from http://www.womenshealth.gov/publications/our-publications/breastfeeding-guide/Breastfeeding-Guide-NativeAmerican-English.pdf.

POLICY POINT   Supporting Breastfeeding in the Early Childhood Setting

Sunshine Child Care Center recognizes the nutritional and health benefits of breastfeeding and is committed to supporting mothers who wish to breast-feed or provide expressed breast milk for their infants. To promote and support this philosophy, it is a breastfeeding-friendly program that offers a comfortable, culturally attuned environment that adheres to the following policy:

1. Mothers will be provided a private place to breast-feed or pump breast milk that has access to a comfortable chair, a water supply for hand washing, and an electrical outlet.

2. Mothers will be allowed to keep pumped breast milk in the center's refrigerator. All breast milk will be stored in clean containers and labeled with infant's name and the date milk was expressed.

3. All staff will be trained on the breastfeeding policy including the appropriate handling of breast milk. The information used to establish proper handling of breast milk will come from the following resources:

   The American Academy of Pediatrics (AAP)
   www.healthychildren.org/English/ages-stages/baby/ breastfeeding/Pages/Storing-and-Preparing-Expressed-Breast-Milk.aspx

   Centers for Disease Control and Prevention (CDC)
   www.cdc.gov/breastfeeding/recommendations/handling_ breastmilk.htm

   Caring for Our Children: National Health and Safety Performance *Standards* (CFOC)
   http://nrckids.org/CFOC3/HTMLVersion/Chapter04 .html#4.3.1.3

   NAEYC recommendations (as outlined in Health Standard 5.B.09):
   www.naeyc.org/files/academy/file/AllCriteriaDocument.pdf

4. The storage of breast milk will follow the most recent recommendations of AAP, CDC, CFOC, and NAEYC. If these recommendations are not uniformly consistent, the more recent and stringent guideline will be used:

   Storage and handling recommendations:

   · If possible, used expressed breast milk within 24 hours.
   · Breast milk will be discarded if not used within 48 hours.
   · Breast milk that will not be used within 24 hours will be frozen.
   · Breast milk will be thawed in the refrigerator or by placing in a bowl of warm water. It should NOT be microwaved which can create hot spots that may burn baby's mouth and destroy some of the beneficial qualities of breast milk.
   · Thawed breast milk will be stored no more than 24 hours.
   · Frozen breast milk will be stored no more than 3 months at 0°F (−18°C).
   · Do not refreeze thawed breast milk.
   · Any breast milk that has set out over an hour or that has been fed over an hour's period of time should be discarded.
   · Do not save milk from a bottle that was partially consumed.

5. All staff will receive training on how to sensitively coordinate infant feeding with the breastfeeding mother's work schedule.

   · Staff will help ease mother and baby's transition to work by developing a feeding plan.
   · Staff will try not to feed baby just before mother arrives.
   · Staff will try not to waste breast milk.

6. Breastfeeding will be supported and promoted by sharing resource information for mothers and posting flyers that highlight the Sunshine Child Care Center's commitment to breastfeeding. The policy will be made available to parents in the parent handbook.

7. The program director will be responsible for maintaining and updating the policy and ensuring compliance standards are met.

Sources: Storing and Preparing Expressed Breast Milk, by American Academy of Pediatrics, 2011 retrieved June 2, 2012, from http://www.healthychildren.org/English/ ages-stages/baby/breastfeeding/Pages/Storing-and-Preparing-Expressed-Breast-Milk.aspx; Centers for Disease Control and Prevention, http://www.cdc.gov/breastfeeding/ recommendations/handling_breastmilk.htm; Caring for our Children: National Health and Safety Performance Standards 2012 retrieved June 2, 2012, from http:// nrckids.org; *Academy for Early Childhood Program Accreditation: Standard 5: NAEYC Accreditation Criteria for Health Standard,* by the National Association for the Education of Young Children, 2012, retrieved June 2, 2012, from http://www.naeyc.org/files/academy/file/AllCriteriaDocument.pdf; *Model Health Breastfeeding Promotion and Support Policy for Child Care Programs,* by Public Health: Seattle and King County, 2012, retrieved June 2, 2012, from http://www.kingcounty.gov/healthservices/health/ child/childcare/modelhealth.aspx; and *Ten Steps to Breastfeeding Friendly Child Care Centers,* by the Wisconsin Department of Health Services, 2009, retrieved June 2, 2012, from http://www.dhs.wisconsin.gov/health/physicalactivity/pdf_files/BreastfeedingFriendlyChildCareCenters.pdf.

on how to support breastfeeding in early childhood settings (National Association for the Education of Young Children, 2012). A sample program policy in support of breastfeeding is presented in the *Policy Point* feature. Creating a policy such as this reinforces the program's commitment to families and outlines the responsibilities of teachers and other program staff.

The first step in supporting nursing mothers may occur before babies are enrolled. For families who have made the decision to have their infant attend a program, teachers can provide advice on how to ease baby's transition from nursing at the breast to accepting breast milk in a bottle. Figure 4-4 offers suggestions to help babies become accustomed to drinking breast milk from a bottle as well as breastfeeding.

> **FIGURE 4-4   Tips to Share with Parents About Transitioning Babies from the Breast to the Bottle**
>
> 1. **Start early but not too early:** Infants become used to what they know and can develop a strong nipple preference for the breast. At around 4 weeks of age, babies have mastered breast-feeding and the mothers' milk supply is usually well established. This is a good time to try offering a bottle of breast milk as babies are still generally open to this option.
> 2. **Be consistent:** Offer breast milk in a bottle every day or every other day to keep babies used to the bottle's nipple.
> 3. **Ask for help:** Babies are more likely to accept a bottle from another family member or friend, rather than the mother.
> 4. **Choose the right time:** Babies should not be too hungry or too upset.
> 5. **Be patient; don't let the situation escalate:** Keep offering the bottle using gentle encouragement. Babies will gradually get used to the nipple. If there is too much pressure and tension surrounding this transition, babies may begin to get upset as soon as they see the bottle.

Sources: *Making the Transition from Breast to Baby Bottles,* by W. C. Fries, 2011, retrieved June 3, 2012, from http://www.webmd.com/parenting/baby/bottle-feeding-9/weaning-from-breast; and *Starting Solid* Foods, by the American Academy of Pediatrics, 2011, retrieved June 3, from http://www.healthychildren.org/English/ages-stages/baby/breastfeeding/pages/Introducing-the-Bottle.aspx.

Breastfeeding support is particularly important for mothers who are returning to work and dealing with new schedules, lack of sleep, and obstacles in the work environment. Although the decision to go back to work does not tend to influence breastfeeding initiation, the timing of when women stop breastfeeding is often linked to their return to their jobs (Ogbuanu, Glover, Probst, Liu, & Hussey, 2011). Teachers can be a vital source of support during this crucial time. They can help by accommodating the nursing mother's need to breast-feed by arranging a comfortable and private place for mothers to nurse when they drop off and pick up their babies. Welcoming mothers who stop by during the day to nurse during their lunch breaks is also an effective means of assisting mothers in maintenance of their breast milk supply and commitment to breastfeeding.

Linking pregnant and nursing mothers to community organizations and resources that promote and support breastfeeding is another important contribution that teachers make. For example, in the opening case scenario Manuel had a difficult first day because a good transition plan was not in place. Amelia and Lucia recognized that they could explore ways to provide Manuel breast milk in spite of Lucia's return to work. Amelia provided the phone numbers for various resources: a lactation consultant, a dietitian, the county Women, Infants, and Children (WIC) office, and La Leche League. She told Lucia that these resources would help her find information and guidance on pumping breast milk for Manuel. They sat down and discussed how to coordinate Manuel's feedings with Lucia's work schedule. Lucia decided to use her half hour break at work to pump breast milk for Manuel so that instead of offering formula, Amelia could feed him expressed breast milk. Lucia also planned to nurse Manuel just before she left and as soon as she came to pick him up at the end of the day. They tried and experienced success with these new strategies. An added benefit was that Manuel's stomach distress went away. All three partners in this feeding relationship were happy with the new plan.

> **What if . . .**
> you were caring for a breast-fed infant who was crying and hungry, but you knew the mother was due to arrive within a half hour and liked to breast-feed when she got there? How would you manage this situation?

Safe Handling of Breast Milk

Teachers must take special precautions to safely handle, store, and serve breast milk provided by mothers to feed their infants. Teachers need to be sure to wash their hands before handling breast milk. Breast milk is not considered to be body fluid but rather food by the CDC, so universal precautions such as wearing gloves when handling breast milk are not necessary and it can be safely stored in a refrigerator as other foods (Centers for Disease Control and Prevention, 2010). Breast milk should be provided in clean containers, such as sturdy plastic bags designed for storing breast milk that fit directly into the bottle. Breast milk stored in soiled containers should not be accepted. Containers should be clearly labeled with the baby's name and the date that the milk was expressed.

What if . . .

you noticed that a bottle of breast milk in the refrigerator was not labeled with the date it was expressed by the mother who dropped it off? What would you do?

fore milk
the watery, nutrient-rich breast milk that is first released when the baby begins nursing

hind milk
milk from the back of the breast that is rich in fat and calories and is secreted at the end of nursing or expressing breast milk

When the infant arrives at the early childhood setting the breast milk should be stored in the refrigerator immediately and until the baby is ready for a feeding. Refer to the Policy Point, which includes storage and handling guidelines for breast milk. By using safe handling techniques, breast-feeding mothers and caregivers of breast-fed infants can maintain the quality of expressed breast milk and the health of the baby.

Unlike formula, breast milk is not a standard product. Initially when babies are first born, colostrum-rich milk can be pale to bright yellow in color. Mature breast milk can vary in color depending on the foods or supplements the mother consumes and the fat content. The fat in breast milk will rise to the top of the storage container. The amount of fat varies depending on how much **fore milk** and **hind milk** is expressed. Fore milk is the watery, nutrient-rich milk that is first released when the baby begins nursing. Hind milk is milk from the back of the breast and is rich in fat and calories and is secreted at the end of nursing or expressing breast milk. Simply shaking the bottle of breast milk gently ensures that the fat is redistributed in the milk and made available to the infant. Mothers should be encouraged to express and save breast milk in small 2-oz volumes as well as larger volumes to provide teachers an option when baby wants just a little more. This helps prevent the waste of this valuable food.

Nutrients of Importance for Breast-Fed Infants

Although breast milk is a perfect form of nutrition designed to meet the needs of most healthy infants, some dietary considerations when using breast milk require special attention as the infant matures.

Vitamin D   Breast milk is not a rich source of vitamin D, an important vitamin that enhances calcium absorption and facilitates the building of strong bones and teeth. Vitamin D is produced in the body when skin is exposed to sun. However, infants and young children, particularly those who have minimum exposure to sunlight and those who are dark skinned, are at risk for developing rickets, a deficiency disease associated with abnormal bone mineralization and development. Therefore, the AAP recommends providing 400 IU vitamin D supplements for all breast-feeding infants (American Academy of Pediatrics, 2011).

Vitamin B$_{12}$ A lack of vitamin B$_{12}$ can be a concern for infants of breast-feeding mothers who are vegan (vegetarians who do not consume any foods of animal origin including dairy products or eggs). This can result in a form of anemia as well as impaired neurological development. Vegan mothers are encouraged to take vitamin B$_{12}$ supplements (Roed, Skovby, & Lund, 2009).

Iron   Prior to birth babies lay down stores of iron in their liver. In addition, the iron in breast milk is easily absorbed and is sufficient until around 6 months of age. But by 6 months of age (or earlier in premature infants), an infant's iron reserves are depleted. Insufficient iron can negatively impact growth and cognitive development. Babies who are iron deficient or anemic are likely to be tired and cranky and are at increased risk for illness due to a compromised immune function. For these reasons, it is important to introduce iron-rich foods such as iron-fortified cereal and meats to supplement the infant's dietary intake of iron from breast milk (Przyrembel, 2012). Introducing whole cow's milk at this age is not recommended because it can cause intestinal bleeding, which also increases the risk of anemia (Kleinman, 2009).

Zinc   Zinc is an important mineral for growth and a well-functioning immune system. Zinc in breast milk is easily absorbed and meets the needs of infants until about 6 months of age. The older breast-fed infants' need for zinc can be met with the introduction of strained meats and zinc-fortified cereals (American Academy of Pediatrics, 2012e; Kleinman, 2009).

Note that the infant's need for iron and zinc coincides with the typical introduction of solid foods. Delaying introduction of solids can result in suboptimal intake of these nutrients.

The Formula-Fed Infant

Some babies receive their nutrition through formula, which is a manufactured product used as a substitute for breast milk. Although breast milk is the best form of nourishment, babies can also thrive on infant formulas. Mothers may choose to use infant formula for several reasons. For example, women who are infected with HIV or have active tuberculosis should not breast-feed (Mahan et al., 2012). Although many medications women take are acceptable, some are unsafe and can pass into the breast milk and have a negative impact on the baby. In these cases mothers should be advised to consult with their health care provider to discuss their concerns.

Some mothers also worry that breast milk may contain possible contaminants such as chemicals and pesticides and, therefore, may choose not to breast-feed. A recent study suggests that more than three-quarters of breast-feeding mothers who were interested in knowing if their breast milk was contaminated said they would wean early if they learned their breast milk contained a harmful substance (Geraghty, Khoury, Morrow, & Lanphea, 2008). The *Safety Segment* provides reassuring background information regarding the relative risks of breast milk contamination. However mothers choose to feed their infants—through breastfeeding, infant formula feeding, or some combination—they should be supported in their decision.

Types of Infant Formula

Like breast milk, infant formula is designed to meet the nutrient needs of infants until 6 months of age. A variety of infant formulas are available. Infant formulas may differ in the type of carbohydrate, protein, and fat they contain. Several of the different types of infant formula are discussed next.

Modified Cow's Milk–Based Formulas Modified cow's milk is the most commonly used commercial formula. It is composed of cow's milk that has been altered to provide the best composition

SAFETY SEGMENT   Breast Milk and Environmental Contaminants

Breast milk is the ideal form of nutrition for infants and is recommended by leading health authorities. However, mothers and caregivers may wonder if breast milk is safe considering the potential risk for contamination from environmental pollutants. Pollutants can be found in the air, water, and food supplies. Mothers consume foods or beverages that contain these contaminants, which can be stored in the body and transferred via breast milk to the infant during breastfeeding.

The health risk of these contaminants is not clearly understood because of the difficulty in determining whether the pollutants are related to prenatal exposure before a baby is born or after a baby is born and breast-fed. Fortunately, the levels of these contaminants have been decreasing in the environment with the advent of regulatory restrictions on their production and use that began 30 to 40 years ago. In 2001 the Stockholm Convention, an organization focused on decreasing global environmental pollution, created an international treaty that brings worldwide cooperation to solving these problems. These actions have had positive results. In recent studies, Swedish women showed a significant decline in the amount of breast milk contaminants and U.S. pregnant women also showed decreased levels of exposure to these types of contaminants. It is important to note that to date, effects of contaminated breast milk on an infant has only been seen in a situation in which the mother herself was ill from a toxic exposure.

In spite of the concern about environmental pollutions, breastfeeding is strongly recommended by the World Health Organization and CDC because the tremendous benefits of breastfeeding far outweigh the potential risks.

Sources: "Persistent Organochlorine and Organobromine Compounds in Mother's Milk from Sweden 1996–2006: Compound-specific Temporal Trends," by S. Lignell, M. Aune, P. O. Darnerud, S. Cnattingius, and A. Glynn, 2009, *Environmental Research, 109*(6), pp. 760–767; "Environmental Contaminants in Breast Milk," by K. Nickerson, 2006, *Journal of Midwifery & Women's Health, 51*(1), pp. 26–34; Fact Sheet: What Is the Stockholm Convention? by the Stockholm Convention, 2011, retrieved June 3, 2012, from http://chm.pops.int/Portals/0/LiveContent/1847/Images/f4b.JPG; "Serum Concentrations of Selected Persistent Organic Pollutants in a Sample of Pregnant Females and Changes in Their Concentrations During Gestation," by R. Y. Wang, R. B. Jain, A. F. Wolkin, C. H. Rubin, and L. L. Needham, 2009, *Environmental Health Perspectives, 117*, p. 1244. *Chemicals in breast milk: Not a risk*, by the American Academy of Pediatrics, 2011, retrieved June 3, 2011, from http://www.aap .org/en-us/about-the-aap/aap-press-room/aap-press-room-media-center/Pages/Breastfeeding-and-Chemicals.aspx; and *Exposure to environmental toxins: Do chemicals in the environment pass to infants through breast milk?* by the Centers for Disease Control and Prevention, 2010, retrieved June 4, 2012, from http://www.cdc.gov/ breastfeeding/disease/environmental_toxins.htm.

of protein, fat, and carbohydrates in an easily digested form. Some cow's milk formulas are lactose free, to support the feeding of the rare infant who is lactose intolerant. This product is not appropriate for infants who are allergic to milk because it contains cow's milk protein. Thickened cow's milk–based formulas are available for infants who suffer from gastroesophageal reflux disease. These products contain added rice starch that when exposed to stomach contents thickens, which may reduce the spitting up and help the baby keep the formula down (Adler & Dickinson, 2009).

Soy-Based Formulas   Soy-based products were developed in the 1960s for infants who are allergic to cow's milk or have lactose intolerance. The substitution of soy formula for infants with a cow's milk allergy is less accepted these days based on research that reveals as many as 30–64% of infants who do not tolerate cow's milk formula (the type of intolerance that causes enterocolitis, or inflammation of the small intestine and colon) are also unable to tolerate soy formula. In addition 10–14% of infants with a cow's milk protein allergy will go on to develop a soy milk protein allergy (Bhatia & Greer, 2008; Queen Samour & King, 2012). Soy-based formulas are often used by families who are vegetarian.

Hypoallergenic Formulas   Hypoallergenic formulas contain protein that has been broken down into smaller components such as peptides and amino acids, making them less likely to cause an allergic response and are easier to absorb. These products were developed for children with cow's milk or soy allergies and for infants who have gastrointestinal or liver disease that results in problems with absorption.

There are two types of hypoallergenic formulas. The extensively hydrolyzed formulas have the protein broken down into amino acids and small peptides, whereas the amino acid–based or elemental formulas designed for extremely sensitive infants contain only amino acids. These formulas are very expensive and are only selected with careful consideration by health care providers. Another type of formula contains partially hydrolyzed protein. The protein in this type of formula is not broken down extensively and, therefore, should not be used when infants have a cow's milk protein allergy (Academy of Nutrition and Dietetics, 2012; Kleinman, 2009).

Premature Formulas   These formulas are designed to support the increased nutritional needs of the premature infant. They provide higher calories, more protein, and increased levels of some vitamins and minerals per ounce compared to standard formulas (Queen Samour & King, 2012). For example, standard formulas and breast milk contain 20 calories per ounce, whereas premature formulas contain 22 to 24 calories per ounce. Some very low birth weight infants may need to consume a more concentrated formula or a formula to which additional ingredients such as carbohydrate and fat have been added to increase the caloric density. When preparing formula in any way that deviates from standard mixing directions on the label, a prescription from the health care provider is needed.

Follow-Up Infant Formulas   These formulas are designed to meet the needs of older infants and toddlers (9 to 24 months) who have begun to eat solids but may not be eating enough to meet all of their nutritional requirements. Although nutrient content varies depending on brand, the follow-up formulas tend to be higher in iron, calcium, and vitamins than whole milk. The AAP states that although these products are nutritionally adequate they do not have a significant advantage over breast milk or formula in combination with a healthy diet (Kleinman, 2009).

All infant formulas undergo scrutiny by the U.S. Food and Drug Administration (FDA). The vitamin and mineral content of formula is standardized based on FDA regulations that specify the nutrient level requirements to ensure that all formulas fed to infants are safe and nutritionally complete (Food and Drug Administration, 2011). Selection of the infant formula is made by the infant's family in consultation with their health care provider. The decision is guided by identifying formula that is most appropriate for the baby. Infants should receive the same type and form of formula in the early childhood setting that is used in the home setting.

Formula Intolerance

formula intolerance
results when infants have difficulties and symptoms that appear to be related to the formula they are consuming

Formula intolerance occurs when infants have difficulties and symptoms that appear to be related to the formula they are consuming. Teachers need to keep families informed when babies show signs of excessive gas, bloating, diarrhea, abdominal pain, vomiting, excessive crying, rash, or allergic symptoms.

It is often challenging for families and teachers to recognize when babies are unable to tolerate their formula. Normal infant behavior includes crying, vomiting, gas, and diarrhea. Often well-meaning mothers will switch formulas in an attempt to solve these perceived problems. A recent study showed that mothers were more likely to switch formulas based on perceived formula intolerance as compared to physicians, indicating that sometimes mothers will make unnecessary and sometimes expensive changes in formula use that may not be warranted (Berseth, Mitmesser, Ziegler, Marunycz, & Vanderhoof, 2009). Over time, teachers gain experience with many infants. They are able to reassure families about normal infant behavior and direct them to health care providers if they have concerns about formula intolerance.

Forms of Infant Formula

Infant formula is available in three different forms:

- *Ready-to-feed:* This is usually the most expensive form and requires no preparation.
- *Canned concentrate:* This formula requires water to be added to a concentrate.
- *Powdered:* This is the least expensive form of formula and requires a powder to be mixed with water.

The type of formula is selected by families is based on need for convenience and cost considerations. A child care program may have a policy of only offering ready-to-feed formulas if this is mandated by state licensing requirements or if they do not have adequate space for formula preparation.

Safe Preparation of Infant Formula

Safe and sanitary procedures must be used when preparing infant formula. Formula and water must be measured exactly. Inaccurate measurements can lead to dangerous problems. If formula is prepared with too much water, it will be too low in calories and nutrient concentration to meet the needs of the baby, resulting in poor growth. If the formula is too concentrated, diarrhea and dehydration can result and may cause excess calorie intake. Guidelines for preparing formula will vary depending on the form used (ready to feed, liquid concentrate, or powder). Figure 4-5 provides general guidelines for preparing formula using standard liquid concentrated formula. If powdered formula is used, it is important to use the scoop provided in the can because scoops can vary slightly in size depending on the brand or type of formula. Powdered infant formula must be carefully handled because it cannot be sterilized. It is important to read the manufacturer's directions when preparing formula.

The National Resource Center for Health and Safety in Child Care and Early Education is a valuable resource for early childhood education programs. It provides an online book on health and safety standards entitled *Caring for Our Children: National Health and Safety Performance Standards: Guidelines for Out-of-Home Child Care Programs*, Third Edition (American Academy of Pediatrics, American Public Health Association, and National Resource Center for Health and Safety in Child Care and Early Education, 2011). This resource provides guidance in establishing policies and procedures within the early childhood setting including guidelines for infant formula preparation as well as many other aspects related to providing nutritious meals for children. The World Health Organization also provides guidelines for the safe preparation of powdered infant formula in child care settings. See resources at the end of the chapter.

Understanding the Feeding Relationship

One of the many pleasures in caring for children is feeding young infants. Their complete satisfaction is rewardingly apparent as they suck and swallow the breast milk or formula offered to them. This is an important time for teachers and infants to connect, one on one, in a relaxed and comfortable

FIGURE 4-5

Preparation Checklist for Standard Liquid Concentrated Iron Fortified Infant Formula (using glass or hard plastic bottles)*

Source: USDA Infant Nutrition and Feeding: A Guide for the use of WIC and CSF programs, WIC Works Resource System, 2009, retrieved June 10, 2012, from http://wicworks.nal.usda.gov/infants/infant-feeding-guide.

*Directions for the preparation of ready to feed and powdered infant formula can also be found at this website.

setting. Designate a special place to feed infants such as a rocking or comfortable chair to enjoy the time socializing with the baby. Looking into infants' eyes and allowing them to gaze back at you builds positive bonds of trust and appreciation. It is during this interaction that teachers learn to recognize the feeding cues babies give to indicate when they are hungry or full.

Feeding Cues

Teachers should be able to recognize feeding cues in order to satisfy the needs of the infant. Although developmentally, infants share common traits, they also exhibit a wide variety of individual characteristics and rates of maturation that affect cues, making each feeding relationship a unique experience. Infants are born with the instinctual ability to cry when they are hungry. However, babies cry for a variety of reasons. The caregiver must learn the nuances of the message the baby is trying to convey. This understanding is important because babies are completely reliant on the adults in their lives to meet all of their physical and emotional needs.

Signs of Hunger and Satiety

Successfully reading hunger and satiety (fullness) cues can reduce infants' stress and enhance the feeding relationship. A baby's inability to verbalize means the teacher must rely exclusively on body language and behavior to recognize any needs. Although each infant will have unique ways of expressing needs, a variety of common signs may suggest when babies are hungry or full. Table 4-1 provides a list of common behaviors associated with hunger and fullness in infants.

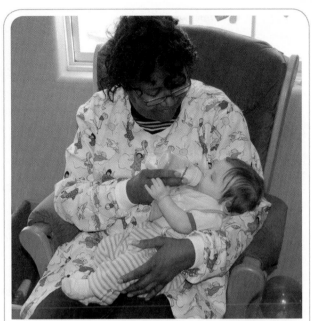

A close feeding relationship between teacher and child enhances the baby's growth and development.

Some babies become very anxious when hungry. They can work themselves into such a spell of frustrated crying that when they finally receive the breast or their bottle they may sputter or gulp air, which in turn leads to gas, stomach distention, spitting up, and even more crying. Recall in the opening case scenario that Manuel became very upset on his first day because he woke up in a new environment and had his feeding delayed. On top of that, he wanted the breast for comfort and

In this **video**, an early childhood educator is feeding an infant. Notice the cues given by the baby during the feeding. How does the caregiver respond?

TABLE 4-1	Understanding Hunger and Fullness Cues in Infants
Hunger Cues	**Fullness Cues**
EARLY CUES	
Alert and looking at caregiver	Stops sucking
Increased arm and leg motions	Seals lips together
Mouthing lips, fingers, or fists	Turns face away
Rooting	Spits out or plays with nipple
Grunting sounds	Falls asleep
Opens mouth wide	Limbs are relaxed
Fussing	
Making sucking motions with the mouth	
Reaching to mother or the breast	
LATE CUES	
Appears tense	Baby arches back and turns face away
Frantic crying	Baby gets irritable with repeated attempts to offer bottle
Trembling	Crying

Sources: Infant feeding, 2012, California Department of Public Health, retrieved June 10, 2012, from http://www.cdph.ca.gov/ programs/NutritionandPhysicalActivity/Documents/MO-NUPA-InfantFeedingGuidelines.pdf; *Infant Nutrition and Feeding: A Guide for Uses in the WIC and CSF Programs*, by the National Agricultural Library, 2009, retrieved June 10, 2012, from http://www.nal .usda.gov/wicworks/Topics/FG/Contents.pdf; and *Child of Mine: Feeding with Love and Good Sense*, by Ellyn Satter, 2000, Boulder, CO: Bull Publishing Company.

Recognizing babies' early signs of hunger prevent the need for them to use later signs of hunger and crying.

was offered the unfamiliar bottle with formula instead. He worked himself into such a frenzy that he swallowed air, causing him to spit up. The best way to avoid such frantic behavior is to be attuned to and respond quickly to early feeding cues. If Amelia had been able to respond to Manuel immediately, he may have been more accepting of the bottle.

Similarly, babies' fullness cues should not be disregarded in an effort to have them finish a bottle or clean a plate. This can cause infants to fuss and struggle. If the conflict persists, it will likely result in poor eating habits (over- or under-eating) and compromise the feeding relationship (Hurley & Black, 2011). In turn, a teacher's or parent's lack of sensitivity to infants' fullness cues can result in overfeeding, setting the stage for excess weight gain and obesity (Black & Aboud, 2011; Hurley, Cross, & Hughes, 2011; Worobey, Lopez, & Hoffman, 2009). With time and experience, as well as input from families, teachers and infants settle into a routine and an effective feeding relationship ensues. The *Teaching Wellness* feature provides examples of ways in which teachers can help older infants and young children identify their signs of hunger and fullness.

Feeding Infants from a Bottle

Infants should always be fed on demand. It is inappropriate to impose a feeding schedule on infants in an early childhood setting unless this has been authorized by a health professional for medical reasons. Teachers should not put infants in a crib with a bottle. Bottle-propping puts babies at risk for choking, earaches, and dental caries. It also decreases time spent in bonding and socializing. Instead, teachers should feed one baby at a time so they can easily and quickly interpret and be responsive to feeding cues.

Formula or breast milk is often accepted better if warmed, but this is not necessary. The USDA Food and Nutrition Service, in their infant nutrition and feeding guide, provides guidance for caregivers who feed infants breast milk or formula from a bottle (U.S. Department of Agriculture, 2009). (See Web Resources.) They advise that teachers should wash hands before feeding infants. Babies should be held comfortably, positioning them so that their heads are held higher than their trunks and they are facing the teacher. This helps prevent choking and promotes the opportunity for social interaction. The bottle should be tilted so that the milk moves into and fills the nipple. Keeping the nipple full helps prevent the infant from swallowing excessive air. Touching the nipple to the infant's mouth stimulates the sucking reflex as feeding begins. There are many types of nipples that families can select based on personal preference or need as illustrated in Figure 4-6.

Periodically, babies need to take a break to be burped. This is accomplished by holding the baby upright against the teacher's shoulder and gently patting on the baby's back until air has been expelled. Feeding continues until babies provide cues that they are full. This time should be calm and comfortably paced, not rushed. Spitting up after a feeding is

FIGURE 4-6

Examples of Different Types of Nipples

Flat-topped nipple

Standard nipple

Orthodontic nipple

Medela SpecialNeeds feeder nipple

TEACHING WELLNESS   I Feel Hungry, I Feel Full

LEARNING OUTCOME   Children will be able to communicate when they are hungry and when they are full.

Vocabulary focus: Hungry, eat, full, finish, stomach growling

Safety watch: Ensure that foods are prepared and served appropriately for the age group and the child's abilities, such as serving puréed fruits and vegetables for young infants, or small mashed pieces for older infants. Choose foods that avoid children's food allergies and restrictions.

INFANTS

- **Goal:** Babies will learn the concepts of hungry and full through the use of baby sign motions.
- **Materials:** Fruits and vegetables of different colors, such as puréed foods for young infants who have recently started solids, or small mashed pieces of banana and cooked carrots for older infants; sign language glossary that includes terms for *full* (bend elbow and hold hand and arm straight across the body; keep hand and arm parallel and lift up under the chin) and *hungry* (shape hand as if holding a cup; place hand on upper chest with palm facing chest, and slide it downward), see the Web Resource: Babies and Sign Language, Free Baby Sign Language Dictionary and Glossary, www.babies-and-sign-language.com/glossary-photos.html.
- **Activity plan:** Talk to the baby while preparing the meal. Ask, "Are you hungry? Do you want to eat?" Use sign language hand motions for *hungry*. Serve baby the meal. Allow baby to help self-feed if appropriate. When the baby stops eating (closes mouth, turns away head, or acts disinterested in eating) ask, "Are you full?" while making the sign for feeling *full*. Do this routinely before and after mealtimes. Add new sign motions for words such as *eat*, *finish*, *thirsty*.
- **How to adjust the activity:** Learn the focus vocabulary words in the child's home language and use them along with English when giving the sign motions. Reinforce the meaning of each vocabulary word frequently.
- **Did you meet your goal?** Can you observe the infant attending to your words and motions as you talk and make the signs for hungry and full?

TODDLERS, PRESCHOOLERS, AND KINDERGARTNERS

- **Goal:** Children will be able to describe the signs of hunger and fullness.
- **Materials:** The children's book *Lunch* by Denise Fleming; three or four fruits and vegetables that are referred to in the book (watermelon, blueberries, peas, carrots); flat trays filled with paint (offering the colors of the selected foods); large mural-sized sheet of white paper; tubs with warm water; paper towels.
- **Activity plan:** Place the paper on the floor with the paint trays near one end, and the tubs of water and towels at the other end. Gather the children and talk about how it feels to be hungry and full. Demonstrate the sign language hand motions. Ask children to describe how they feel when they are hungry (stomach rumbles and makes noise, mouth waters) and full (stomach feels tight and bigger; no more growling and rumbling). Tell them it is important to learn to recognize our body's cues of hunger and fullness. Read the book *Lunch*. Talk about how the mouse feels at the beginning of the book and at the end. Use the sign language terms for hungry and full. Talk about

This toddler shows she is hungry by reaching and crying. She is happy when she receives her food and uses sign language to indicate when she is full.

(Continued)

the colors of the foods and tell about how the foods help the body. Invite children to remove their shoes and socks. One at a time, ask each child to identify their favorite food on the tray. Guide the child to step in the tray with paint that matches the color of the favorite food, and then walk across the paper just as the mouse does in the book. Hold the child's hand to avoid slipping. Engage the other children by asking them to count the child's steps. Help the child to wash and dry their feet and put socks and shoes on (an assistant is helpful here). Use clean water to wash each child's feet. While eating lunch together, remind the children of the feelings associated with hunger and fullness. Summarize that it is good to "listen" to our body as it "tells" us when we are hungry and when it is time to stop eating

- **How to adjust the activity:** Repeat the information frequently, at meal time or when washing hands for the meal so all children will learn the message. Use the signs for *hungry* and *full*, and picture cards to reinforce the concepts.
- **Did you meet your goal?** Can children describe the cues for hunger and fullness?

SCHOOL-AGE CHILDREN

- **Goal:** Children will be able to identify the signs of hunger and fullness and describe the basic steps of digestion.
- **Materials:** The book *Chewy, Gooey, Rumble, Plop* by Steve Alton, stethoscopes.
- **Activity plan:** Plan the activity in the morning. Gather the children and read the book. Talk about why we eat food and what happens to food once it's eaten. Review the basic steps in digestion presented in the book. Discuss how the body sends signals when it is time to eat and when it is time to stop eating. Have children think about these signals and tell how it feels to be hungry and full. Identify three areas of the room: "hungry," "not hungry or full," and "full." Direct the children to think about how they feel right now, and go to that area. Ask children in the "hungry" area what it is that makes them feel they are hungry (how do they feel). Ask why they might be feeling that way. Did some skip breakfast? Introduce the idea that being hungry can make it hard to concentrate at school. Ask children in other areas to describe how they feel, and tell why they may not be feeling hungry. Guide the children to use the stethoscopes to listen to their stomachs and the sounds of digestion. Summarize why it is important to pay attention to the body's signals for hunger and fullness.

- **How to adjust the activity:** Some children benefit from repeating the lesson frequently. Engage all learners by asking children to show through movement or dance the steps of digestion, and show what it feels like to be hungry and full. Support English language learners by repeating the vocabulary words often, and reminding everyone of the steps of digestion.
- **Did you meet your goal?** Can children identify and describe hunger and fullness signs? Can they describe the basic steps of digestion?

normal. However, if there is projectile vomiting or vomiting of large volumes of breast milk or formula, the family should be encouraged to obtain advice from their health care provider.

Communicating with Parents

Communicating with parents is an important teacher responsibility. A baby's behavior cannot be fully understood unless it is put into the context of the child's most recent experiences. For example, it is important for parents to share information such as how well the baby is sleeping at night, when the baby was last fed and changed, and if a baby is teething. This helps the teacher understand the infant's needs. Teachers cannot effectively read the signs of the infant if they don't know "what's up." For instance, in the opening case scenario, it might have been an easier first day for Manuel and Amelia, his caregiver, if his mother Lucia had mentioned that Manuel had slept poorly and been up a good part of the night before.

Similarly, teachers need to share information such as what and how much the infant eats and the frequency of diaper changes so the family feels informed. One way to ensure detailed communication is to send home a note with families at the end of each day. Figure 4-7 provides an example. Another effective communication approach is to use a notebook with a section for writing comments back and forth between the teacher and family.

What if . . .

you had a mother who was consistently behind schedule when dropping off her infant and frequently left without sharing important details such as when her baby was last fed? How might you ensure better communication?

FIGURE 4-7 **Sample Parent Update Form**

Baby's Day at Sunshine School

Baby's name _____

Baby slept from _____to_____   Baby's mood was _____
                 _____to_____   _____

Today:
Baby drank _____ bottles or ounces of formula   Baby ate the following solids:_____
Baby drank _____ bottles or ounces of breast milk   _____
Baby drank _____ bottles or ounces of _____
Baby was last fed _____ (what baby had) at _____ AM or PM (time)

Baby had diaper changed at _____ AM/PM   Baby had diaper changed at _____ AM/PM
  • wet   • wet
  • stool   • stool
  • both   • both

Baby had diaper changed at _____ AM/PM   Baby had diaper changed at _____ AM/PM
  • wet   • wet
  • stool   • stool
  • both   • both

Baby needs the following items:
Baby wipes   Diapers   Formula   Breast milk
Extra clothes   Other _____
Additional comments: _____

Source: Based on *Infant Toddler Daily Communication Form*, by North Dakota Child Care Resource and Referral, retrieved from http://www.ndchildcare.org/ providers/ supporting-children-families/docs/Written%20Daily%20Communication.pdf.

How Often and How Much to Feed a Baby

Teachers feel more secure that they can meet infant needs if they have a general idea of how often and how much babies should be fed. Babies usually develop a routine for eating that is influenced by their weight, age, whether they receive breast milk or formula and whether they are eating solids. In general, newborns who are breast-fed tend to eat every 1½ to 3 hours or about 8 to 12 times per day for the first 6 weeks. By the time they are 4 to 6 months old, they consume greater volumes of breast milk, and feedings gradually decrease to 5 or more feedings per day (Kleinman, 2009). Newborns receiving formula typically need 8 to 12 feedings per day, although some will be hungry less often because formula takes longer to digest than breast milk. By 4 to 6 months the number of formula feedings decreases to five to eight bottles per day (although it can sometimes be more) as infants mature and are able to hold greater volumes in their stomachs (Queen Samour & King, 2012). With the introduction of solid foods, infants begin to need less breast milk or formula.

This information provides general feeding guidelines. However, it is important that infants be fed on demand. This means they are provided breast milk or formula whenever they are hungry. A rigid schedule for feedings only creates stress for both babies and caregivers. In addition, infants experience growth spurts, at which time the demand for formula or breast milk may increase. Table 4-2 provides information on the typical feeding expectations for infants, illustrating the wide range of feedings per day and amount of breast milk or formula consumed.

The expectations for infant meal quantities outlined by the CACFP are also shown in in the Appendix, which demonstrates the range of breast milk and formula intake on a per meal basis. The CACFP provides this information as a guideline for meeting reimbursement requirements. The CACFP supports demand feeding, however, by allowing flexibility in when the feeding is served (when the baby is hungry) and how much is offered (feed until the baby is full).

TABLE 4-2   Feeding Guidelines for Infants

Age	Approximate Number and Volume of Feedings (Breast Milk or Formula) per Day[a]	
	Number of Feedings/Day	Amount(oz)/Feeding[b]
0–4 mo	8–12	2–6
4–6 mo	4–8	6–8
6–8 mo	3–5	6–8
8–12 mo	3–4	6–8

[a]Formula and breast milk contain the same amount of calories per ounce; therefore, expressed breast milk's range of intake is comparable to that of formula.

[b]Recommendations do not include the introduction and amounts of solid foods to offer infants. See the Appendix for the CACFP Infant Meal Plan which provides solid food recommendations.

Sources: American Academy of Nutrition and Dietetics, *The Pediatric Nutrition Care Manual*, 2012; and Queen Samour, P., & King, K., *Pediatric Nutrition*, 4th edition, 2012. Boston: Jones and Bartlett Learning.

Inappropriate Infant Feeding Practices

Teachers work closely with families. At times, teachers may learn that families are not feeding infants in ways that are healthy and appropriate. In this case, teachers can take the opportunity to gather resources and educate families about safe and healthy feeding practices. Providing and reviewing educational materials on infant feeding are positive ways to introduce these concerns. The family's medical provider is also a valuable resource. The following sections illustrate some of the common poor feeding practices.

Adding Cereal to Formula in the Bottle

Sometimes families feel that the addition of infant cereal to formula in the bottle will increase a baby's likelihood to sleep through the night. Research has shown that this is not the case and can create problems. For example, cereal in the bottle can lead to choking (Nemours, 2012). The early introduction of solid foods, including cereals, also increases the risk of acquiring allergies (American Academy of Pediatrics, 2012d). When infants are ready for solid foods, they are ready to learn to eat from a spoon. Putting cereal in a bottle delays this natural developmental opportunity. Putting cereal in the bottle also throws off the balance of nutrients in the feeding by displacing the nutrients of breast milk or formula with infant cereal. This may result in the intake of excessive calories, putting the baby at risk for overweight and obesity (American Academy of Pediatrics, 2012g). If bottles containing formula (including those with added cereal) are given to infants when they are put to bed, the formula can pool in the mouth and create an ideal environment for cavity-causing bacteria. The bacteria use this liquid for food and secrete an acid that can damage teeth (National Institute of Dental and Craniofacial Research & National Institute of Health, 2011).

When researchers delved into the reasons why mothers added cereal to the bottle, some reported that they did not recognize cereal as a solid. Others indicated that feeding decisions were influenced by grandparents (Heinig et al., 2006). These reasons provide opportunity for discussion and problem solving to identify the practices that are best for babies. The *Nutrition Note* discusses the influence of grandparents in feeding infants and offers suggestions on how teachers can collaborate with grandparents to support healthful infant feeding practices.

Putting the baby to bed with a bottle can result in increased risk of cavities and choking. It is also a missed opportunity for socializing.

Finishing the Bottle

Some parents and teachers may encourage a baby to finish the bottle to avoid wasting formula or breast milk. This disrupts the infant's ability to self-regulate intake by altering responsiveness to internal cues of hunger and satiety, putting them at risk for developing obesity (U.S. Department of Agriculture, 2009). The infant's feeding cues should be respected. When the baby is full, the feeding is stopped and the extra formula or breast milk is discarded.

Using Honey in the Bottle or on the Pacifier

The inappropriate feeding practice of putting honey in a baby's bottle can have very severe outcomes. A serious foodborne illness called **infantile botulism** can occur in infants as a result of consuming honey (Division of Communicable Disease Control, Center for Infectious Diseases, California Department of Public Health, 2011). This illness occurs because infants' digestive systems are not fully developed. This

Grandparents are often vital members of the team of adults caring for infants and can provide valuable information to teachers when they drop off their grandchildren.

allows the *C. botulinum* spores to grow, and eventually releases a potent toxin causing illness. This rare foodborne illness can cause a progression of symptoms that lead to paralysis and death if not identified early and treated.

Avoiding honey is imperative until after the baby's first birthday (American Academy of Pediatrics, 2012c). This includes foods to which honey has been added such as yogurt with honey. The California Department of Health's Infant Botulism Treatment and Prevention Program states that because each manufacturing process differs, it is unable to make recommendation on the likelihood that the honey-containing foods may contain botulism spores (California Department of Public Health, 2011). Older children and adults have more mature gastrointestinal tracts and do not experience harm from honey.

Although honey has been considered the culprit for infant botulism, note that in most cases no source of the botulism illness can be found. In these cases it is believed that the illness was acquired through swallowing invisible airborne dust that contains the botulism spores (Division of Communicable Disease Control, Center for Infectious Diseases, California Department of Public Health, 2011). This emphasizes the importance of keeping pacifiers and other items young babies put in their mouths clean, especially when they are dropped on the ground.

Many cultures consider honey an acceptable source of nourishment to be given to babies to cleanse the system shortly after birth and before the initiation of breastfeeding or as a component of foods offered as babies get older (Pak-Gorstein et al., 2009). Teachers can create awareness of the risk by providing access to resources. The California Department of Public Health's Infant Botulism Treatment and Prevention Program has created a website and brochure that explains the risk factors associated with this rare but deadly food poisoning (Division of Communicable Disease Control, California Department of Public Health, 2010).

Offering Alternate Milks

Families may choose to feed their babies with a product other than breast milk or infant formula. This is not advised because only breast milk and infant formula can meet the nutritional needs of infants. Researchers estimate that even though cow's milk is not recommended for young infants, approximately 17% of families give their infants cow's milk by the time they are 10½ months of age (Grummer-Strawn, Scanlon, & Fein, 2008). Milk produced by cows should not be served until a baby has reached 12 months of age. Consuming cow's milk can lead to iron-deficiency anemia. This occurs because the content of iron in cow's milk is low, and cow's milk can cause intestinal blood loss in some infants. Cow's milk is also too high in protein, sodium, and potassium for infants, which puts stress on the kidneys. Finally, cow's milk is not supplemented with vitamins and minerals that babies need (Kleinman, 2009; Queen Samour & King, 2012).

infantile botulism
a serious illness that results from ingesting *Clostridium botulinum* spores that germinate and release a deadly toxin in the gastrointestinal tract

NUTRITION NOTE   Grandparents and Infant Feeding Decisions

Parents have the ultimate responsibility for making decisions regarding the care and feeding of their infants. Grandparents play a wonderful and important role in the lives of their grandchildren, but sometimes can exert significant influence on feeding decisions, especially when parents are young or inexperienced. Many grandparents may share child-rearing responsibilities and be involved in dropping off and picking up children.

Grandparents have a natural interest in the child's well-being, but may not be aware that guidelines for feeding infants have changed since they were parents. For example, grandparents may have introduced solids earlier with their children than is currently recommended by health care professionals. Adding cereal to the bottle was a more common practice in the past. Grandparents may feel a heavy baby is a healthy baby. Grandmothers may not be supportive of breastfeeding if they did not breast-feed themselves. Parents may make appropriate decisions about feeding that are not supported by grandparents, creating tension that can spill into the early childhood setting. For example, a grandparent may admit to feeding strained meat to an infant whose parents are vegan.

It is important for teachers to respect boundaries and recognize that, unless grandparents have legal custody or guardianship of their grandchildren, the parents have the final say about what to feed their children. However, teachers can help manage these influences by creating a strong bond of communication among all the family members involved in the infant's care.

Teachers can provide sources of information for grandparents on feeding and food safety such as the following web resources:

WIC Works Sharing Center at http://wicworks.nal.usda .gov/children where the following handouts are available:

· *Grandparents Play an Important Role*

· *A Special Message for Grandparents*

North Dakota State University Education and Extension Service also has a handout entitled *Seniors and Food Safety: When Grandparents Take Care of Grandchildren* at www.ag.ndsu .edu/pubs/yf/foods/fn703.pdf.

These messages also help guide grandparents to be part of the infant's support team:

✓ Learn and follow new child care practices and recommendations, especially those that relate to infant feeding.

✓ Support the infant's family in their efforts to provide the best nutritional options for your grandchildren.

✓ Follow infant hunger and fullness cues. Allow infants to decide when they want to eat and how much.

✓ Give infants the gift of healthful diet. As they begin their transition from breast milk or formula to solids, offer only nutritious foods and beverages.

✓ Spoil your grandbabies with loving attention instead of rewarding them with food.

✓ Share the message of good nutrition with other family members.

Goat's milk should also not be used for the same reasons. In addition, goat's milk is very low in folic acid, which can lead to a form of anemia (Queen Samour & King, 2012). Alternative vegetarian beverages designed for consumption by adults such as soy beverages, rice beverages, and other vegetarian milk substitutes are not acceptable for infants. These beverages may be too low in fat and they are not supplemented appropriately to meet the vitamin and mineral needs of infants. The protein content of rice milks and other vegetarian milk substitutes, except soy milk, is also very low and malnutrition has been reported in infants fed these types of beverages (U.S. Department of Agriculture, 2009). It is important for teachers to offer guidance if parents suggest the use of alternative milks before a baby reaches his or her first birthday.

● FEEDING THE INFANT: 6 MONTHS TO THE FIRST BIRTHDAY

Between 6 and 12 months of age, babies' bodies and diets undergo a significant transformation. The maturation of the gastrointestinal tract allows the infant's diet to evolve from the exclusive intake of liquids to the consumption of adult-like solid foods. Babies are gradually exposed to myriad aromas, flavors, and textures that come with the introduction of **complementary foods**. Complementary foods are any foods or beverages introduced to babies' diets that are in addition to breast milk or formula.

complementary foods
any food or beverage introduced to babies' diets that is in addition to breast milk or formula

Introducing Complementary Foods

As infants grow, their need for additional vitamins and minerals requires the introduction of additional foods and beverages. However, the ideal time for infants to start complementary foods has been a topic of ongoing discussion among different health organizations (Kleinman, 2009). Introducing solids too early can result in increased risk for choking, eczema, and food allergies. Early introduction of solids may also displace the valuable nutrients found in breast milk and formula with the less needed nutrients found in the complementary foods, thus interfering with proper growth (Grummer-Strawn et al., 2008; U.S. Department of Agriculture, 2009). Early introduction of solids is associated with an increased risk of developing obesity (Dattilo et al., 2012). For example, a recent study revealed that for formula-fed infants the introduction of complementary foods before 4 months of age led to a six-fold increased risk of obesity at 3 years of age (Huh, Rifas-Shiman, Taveras, Oken, & Gillman, 2011).

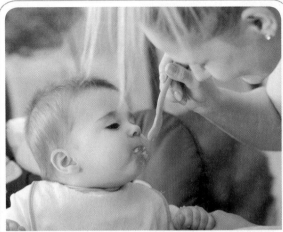

Babies should begin eating when they demonstrate developmental signs of readiness, usually between 4 and 6 months of age.

The "window of opportunity" for introducing complementary foods *and* advancing flavors and textures occurs somewhere between 4 and 6 months of age through 10 months of age. Providing a gradual transition in food textures during this time frame decreases the risk of rejection of foods with more texture and consistency at a later date (Butte et al., 2004; Coulthard, Harris, & Emmett, 2009). Infants who are exposed to a variety of foods and textures are more accepting of new textures and new foods than those who are not (Blossfied, Collins, & Delahunty, 2007). For example, offering a baby puréed commercial infant bananas first, then well-mashed ripe bananas, and finally ripe bananas cut up into ¼-inch pieces is an example of a progression of textures. If this advance in texture does not occur, as babies get older, they may refuse more lumpy textures. For example, one study found that infants not exposed to lumpier textures by 9 months of age ate less of many of the food groups including fruit and vegetables and were reported as having more long-term feeding problems at 7 years of age than infants who were introduced to textures between 6 and 9 months of age (Coulthard et al., 2009).

When introducing complementary foods, offering infants many different-flavored foods such as a variety of puréed meats, vegetables and fruits may increase their willingness to try new foods as they get older. Interesting too is research that suggests infants whose mothers eat a variety of foods during pregnancy tend to be more open to trying new foods. Changes in the flavor of the amniotic fluid that surrounds the baby before birth promote greater food acceptance when the baby begins eating solid foods. Breast-fed infants are also more likely to try different foods. This is because breast milk flavor changes with the types of food mothers consume (Mennella, Jagnow, & Beauchamp, 2001; Mennella, Lukasewycz, Castor, & Beauchamp, 2011). Pregnant and breast-feeding women who eat a healthy diet with a variety of foods keep their infants well-nourished and contribute to success when the infant begins to eat solid foods.

Reflect back on the opening case scenario. The stomach pain and gas Manuel experienced were related to the switch from breast milk, which is easily digested, to formula. Manuel was also started on cereal at 3 months of age. This was too early for his immature digestive tract. The diet changes left him gassy and fussy. His situation illustrates the impacts of starting babies on solid foods too soon.

The World Health Organization, the American Academy of Pediatrics, and the Academy of Nutrition and Dietetics recommend exclusive breastfeeding for around the first 6 months of life and adding solids when the baby is 6 months old (Academy of Nutrition and Dietetics, 2012; American Academy of Pediatrics, 2012; World Health Organization, 2011). Ultimately the decision to start complementary foods is linked to the infant's physiological, nutritional needs and developmental signs of readiness. Teachers and families can use signs of infant readiness as guidelines when considering the introduction and progression of solid foods in babies' diets.

Linking Developmental Skills to Feedings

Transitioning from liquids to puréed solids, from puréed solids to textured foods, and then to the self-feeding of table foods are all eating achievements linked to developmental milestones. Infants are born with the instinctual skills that help them to survive. They know to turn reflexively toward the breast

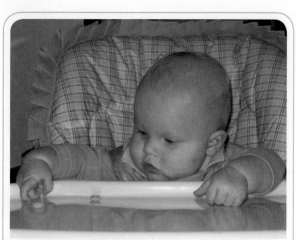

The ability of an infant to grasp cereal with his hand (palmar grasp) and pick up individual oat cereal rings with the thumb and index finger (pincer grasp) indicates he is ready to try new textures and should be given opportunities to self-feed.

or bottle when their mouth or cheek is brushed by the nipple (rooting reflex) and will begin to suck when something touches the roof of their mouth (sucking reflex). When the lips are touched, the tongue comes out of the mouth (tongue thrust reflex). These reflexes help to ensure infants can latch onto a bottle or breast. In addition, infants possess a gag reflex, which is activated when food is placed in the back of the mouth and results in the ejection of the food.

Infants' development and growth can help determine when to initiate semisolid foods. For example, it is time to introduce complementary foods when infants develop the oral motor skills to consume semisolid foods safely (Queen Samour & King, 2012). The tongue thrust and gag reflexes gradually start to diminish. Infants are able to keep food in their mouth and move it around with their tongues and they begin to use an up-and-down chewing motion. Other signs of readiness include the ability to sit with support, and to indicate hunger by opening the mouth or leaning in or fullness by closing the mouth or leaning away (Academy of Nutrition and Dietetics, 2012; Queen Samour & King, 2012). Just like any other milestones, the developmental readiness for starting solid foods has an age range and although some infants may be ready to eat solids earlier (around 4 to 5 months), in general most will be ready to start complementary feedings at around 6 months of age (Cattaneo et al., 2011). A recent review of many research studies revealed that, in terms of long-term health outcomes, the available evidence is not sufficient to define the exact age at which complementary food should be introduced into babies' diets. However the data are strong enough to advise against the introduction of complementary food before the age of 12 weeks because of the increased risk of gastrointestinal and respiratory infections, allergy and eczema, and perhaps obesity. In addition, delaying the introduction of complementary food beyond the age of about 26 weeks may increase the risk of nutritional insufficiency, particularly for children from low-income families (Przyrembel, 2012). The WIC program supports these recommendations and does not offer in its food packages complementary foods to infants until they are 6 months of age (U.S. Department of Agriculture, Food and Nutrition Service, 2012a). Many teachers may have more experience feeding infants than first-time parents. The teacher's role is to help families learn to recognize the signs of developmental readiness in their infants.

Table 4-3 provides helpful information for determining the types of foods to introduce based on developmental milestones. It shows the link between the developmental stages and appropriate progression of foods for infants and toddlers. The physical and eating skills are provided as a guide to selecting complementary foods. A visual relationship between the introduction of complementary foods and the transition in food texture and feeding styles is illustrated in Figure 4-8. This figure offers guidance on when to change textures and when to introduce finger foods and the use of cups.

Understanding What to Feed Infants

Communication between families, teachers, and health care providers becomes important during infants' transition to solids. It is the family's responsibility to introduce new foods gradually into the baby's diet. Research does not support the introduction of complementary foods in any specific order. However, the American Academy of Pediatrics recommends infant cereals and puréed meats as important first foods because they introduce key nutrients, iron and zinc, which are important minerals in the diets of breast-fed infants (Kleinman, 2009).

The current practice for caregivers who feed infants is to introduce puréed meats late in babies' diets. When puréed meats are served, they are often mixed in commercial infant dinners. These combination meals have far less zinc and iron than puréed meats alone. Teachers can share with families the benefits of

What if . . .

you had limited experience with babies and were assigned to provide care in an infant class? What questions or worries might you have about feeding babies? What resources could you turn to for advice?

TABLE 4-3 Infant Feeding Guidelines: Birth to 12 Months

Age Range	Development Feeding Characteristics	Key Recommendations	Infant Feedings
Birth to around 6 months	Instinctual reflexes present at birth through around 5 months include: • rooting reflex to help seek out source of nourishment • suck-swallow-breathe reflex coordinates breathing with feeding • gag reflex occurs when food is placed in the back of the mouth • tongue thrust occurs when lips are touched that allows sucking but not swallowing from a spoon or cup	1. The ideal goal is for infants to exclusively breastfeed for the first 6 months. 2. Begin transition to solids when infants exhibit readiness skills.	Breast milk and/or formula
	Infants develop readiness skills for the introduction of solids (around 4–6 months) that include: • ability to hold head up and sit with support • put fingers in mouth • open mouth to receive food • move food in the mouth with tongue to aid in swallowing • remove food from spoon with lips • indicate hunger by moving toward food and fullness by turning head away • tongue thrust and gag reflex start to diminish	1. A traditional first solid food is infant cereal which provides iron and zinc, nutrients needed by breast-fed babies by around 6 months 2. For most infants, it does not matter which type solid baby food is offered first 3. Introduce single-ingredient new foods and wait 3–5 days before introducing another new food to observe for allergic reactions 4. Do not offer juice or water as all the liquid baby needs come from breast milk or formula 5. Do not offer honey through the first year of life due to the risk of botulism foodborne illness	Fortified infant cereal, puréed vegetables, meats, fruits

Around 6 to 12 months	Infants continue to develop feeding skills that support the introduction of solids with more textures (around 6–9 months) such as:
	• sits unsupported
	• is able to position food in the mouth and move food between jaws for chewing
	• uses an up and down chewing motion
	• begins to reach for food and feed self
	• takes food off spoon readily
	• drinks from a cup with some spilling
		1. Breastfeeding recommended for at least the first year of life
		2. Infant moves through 4 stages of textures
		  • Puréed
		  • Mashed (puréed with a few lumps)
		  • Chopped (more lumpy)
		  • Small pieces of food (no more than ¼-inch thick)
		3. Be sure infants have mastered one texture before moving on to another
		4. Infants should begin to drink liquids from a cup
		5. Do not add sugar, salt, spices, gravies, or butter to infant foods
			Introduce a variety of healthy foods of appropriate transitional texture such as meats, cereals, vegetables, fruits, eggs and fish, beans, tofu, cottage cheese, plain yogurt, rice, and noodles

	Infants begin to master chewing and take more of a role in self feeding (around 9–12 months): • begins to use a rotary motion for chewing food • is able to move food from side to side of mouth • mashes food using the tongue and jaw • uses the thumb and finger in a pincher grasp to pick up food • feeds self finger foods • starts to use a spoon to self-feed • curves mouth around a cup	1. Introduce finger foods. 2. Offer a variety of new foods during this window of opportunity. 3. If a new food is rejected, offer it again. It may take 10 tries or more before infant accepts a new food.	Introduce a variety of healthy foods of appropriate transitional texture such as meats, cereals, vegetables, fruits, eggs and fish, beans, tofu, cottage cheese, plain yogurt, rice, and noodles

Sources: American Academy of Pediatrics, 2012, Ages and Stages: Switching to Solid Foods from healthychildren.org. American Academy of Pediatrics, American Public Health Association, National Resource Center for Health and Safety in Child Care and Early Education. 2011; *Caring for our children: National health and safety performance standards; Guidelines for early care and education programs. 3rd edition.* Elk Grove Village, IL: American Academy of Pediatrics; Washington, DC: American Public Health Association. Also available at http://nrckids.org. California Nutrition and Physical Activity Guideline for Adolescents: Infant Nutrition, 2012, by California Department of Health from http://www.cdph.ca.gov/HealthInfo/healthyliving/childfamily/Documents/MO-NutritionAndPhysicalActivityGuidelines.pdf; *Pediatric Nutrition Handbook*, 6th edition, edited by R. E. Kleinman, 2009, Elk Grove Village, IL: American Academy of Pediatrics; "The Start Healthy Feeding Guidelines for Infants and Toddlers," by N. Butte, K. Cobb, J. Dwyer, W. Graney, and K. Rickard, 2004, *The Journal of the American Dietetic Association, 104*(3), pp. 442–454; Infant Nutrition and Feeding: A Guide for Use in the WIC and CSF Programs, 2009; U.S. Department of Agriculture, Food and Nutrition Service, Special Supplemental Nutrition Program for Women, Infants and Children, 2009, Washington, DC: U.S. Department of Agriculture from http://wicworks.nal.usda.gov/infants/infant-feeding-guide; and Key Changes in WIC Recommendations, 2009, California WIC program from http://www.cdph.ca.gov/programs/wicworks/Documents/NE/WIC-NE-InfantFeedingGuidelines-ComparisonOfInfantFeedingRecommendations.doc.

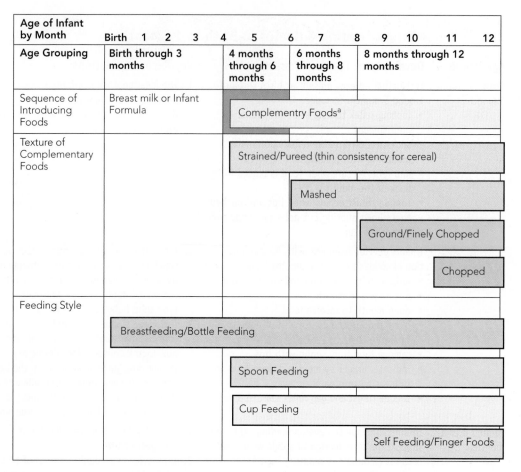

Age of Infant by Month	Birth 1 2 3	4 5 6	7 8	9 10 11 12
Age Grouping	Birth through 3 months	4 months through 6 months	6 months through 8 months	8 months through 12 months
Sequence of Introducing Foods	Breast milk or Infant Formula	Complementry Foods[a]		
Texture of Complementary Foods		Strained/Pureed (thin consistency for cereal)		
			Mashed	
				Ground/Finely Chopped
				Chopped
Feeding Style	Breastfeeding/Bottle Feeding			
		Spoon Feeding		
		Cup Feeding		
				Self Feeding/Finger Foods

FIGURE 4-8

Relationships Between the Introduction of Complementary Foods and the Transition in Texture and Feeding Styles

Special note: ▭ represents the age range when most infants are developmentally ready to begin consuming complementary foods. The American Academy of Pediatrics section on breastfeeding recommends exclusive breastfeeding for the first 6 months of life. The AAP Committee on Nutrition recommends that, in developed countries, complementary foods may be introduced between ages 4 and 6 months. This is a population-based recommendation and the timing of introduction of complementary foods for an individual infant may differ from the recommendation.

[a]Complementary foods include infant cereal, fruits, vegetables, and meats and other protein-rich foods modified to a texture appropriate for the infant's developmental readiness.

Source: From *Infant Nutrition and Feeding: A Reference Handbook for Nutrition and Health Counselors in the WIC and CSF Programs*, National Agricultural Library, 2008, retrieved September 20, 2009, from http://www.nal.usda.gov/wicworks/Topics/Infant_Feeding_Guide.html#guide.

introducing fortified cereals and meats earlier in their babies' diets especially if they are breast-fed. Formula-fed infants receive the iron and zinc they require because these nutrients are included in the formula.

Single-ingredient foods should be introduced into infants' diets one at a time with a wait period of 3 to 5 days before introducing the next new food. This way, if an allergy develops it is easier to identify the food that has caused it (Kleinman, 2009). For example, after introducing rice cereal and offering it with success for 4 days, an infant might then progress to another cereal. Once all of the cereals have been introduced, meats might be a logical next step for breast-fed infants. Commercially prepared infant fruit or yogurt desserts or smoothies, unlike puréed single-ingredient fruits, are not as desirable because they often contain added sugar in the form of concentrated fruit juice and other ingredients such as rice flour. Infant dinners contain a variety of mixed ingredients that make it difficult to determine the food source that triggers an allergic reaction. In addition, ounce

---

FIGURE 4-9 Infant Food Checklist

Baby's name _____

General guidelines to remember:

- Introduce the new food.
- Offer it for approximately 3 to 5 days before introducing another new food.
- Watch for signs of allergic reaction.
- Remember: Babies do not need fat, sugar, spices, or salt added to foods.

Check the appropriate boxes when you want your baby's teacher to begin a new food at school that the baby has been exposed to at home and tolerates.

Infant Cereal

❏ Rice cereal ❏ Barley cereal ❏ Oatmeal

Strained Meats/Poultry

❏ Strained chicken ❏ Strained turkey ❏ Strained beef or veal

Strained Vegetables

❏ Green beans ❏ Sweet potatoes ❏ Peas
❏ Squash ❏ Carrots ❏ Spinach

Strained Fruits

❏ Peaches ❏ Prunes ❏ Guava
❏ Applesauce ❏ Apricots ❏ Papaya
❏ Pears ❏ Mango ❏ Prunes
❏ Bananas
❏ Finger foods _____
_____
_____

---

per ounce they may not be as nutritious as single ingredient commercial baby foods. The CACFP does not reimburse for baby food combination dinners or baby foods in the dessert or jarred cereal with fruit category, and the WIC program only offers single-ingredient baby food in their infant meal packages, although combinations of single ingredients such as apple-banana are allowed (Oregon Department of Education, 2009; U.S. Department of Agriculture, Food and Nutrition Service, 2012b). A notebook entry or chart checklist system in which parents communicate the acceptability of a new food to the caregiver can be a helpful way to share which foods have been introduced. Figure 4-9 provides an example.

Fruit juice should not be offered to infants before 6 months of age because it can blunt their appetite for other foods including breast milk or formula. If juice is given to babies after they reach 6 months of age it should be 100% juice, limited to no more than 4 ounces per day and introduced in a cup rather than a bottle. The disadvantages of introducing juice into the diets of babies include the risk for excessive weight gain and dental caries. In addition the sorbitol found in juices can also lead to diarrhea, gas, abdominal distention, and diaper rash. Water is not necessary in most situations before infants are 6 months of age because their fluid needs are met by breast milk or formula. Once solids are introduced to the diet or when days are hot small amounts of water can be offered to infants with advice from their physicians (American Academy of Pediatrics, 2012b).

Some caregivers, with a goal to providing nutritious basic whole foods for babies, choose to make home-prepared baby food. This is an acceptable alternative that is cost effective and offers increased flexibility regarding types of ingredients and textures; however, food safety is an important consideration. Home-prepared infant foods should be made from fresh ingredients, cooked until soft and tender, puréed, and stored promptly. Safe methods of food preparation and storage are particularly important in preparing foods for infants. Figure 4-10 provides guidelines on preparing and storing baby food that can be shared with families. The *Health Hint* describes some of the precautions to consider when preparing infant foods.

Making your own baby food is easy

Homemade baby food is good for your baby. It will help your baby get used to the foods your family eats, and you always know what is in it!

Did you know that you can help your baby get a good start with solids using the foods and utensils you already have home?

Try these simple steps:

1 You will need a clean fork, potato masher, food processor or blender.

2 To make sure your fresh fruits and vegetables are clean and safe, scrub them, peel off the skin and remove stems, pits and seeds.

3 Prepare meats by removing bones, skin and visible fat.

4 Cook hard or tough foods until soft.

5 Cool to room temperature.

6 Mash, purée or blend food by adding small amounts of cooking water, breast milk, or formula until mixture is smooth.

Even if you like foods sweet or salty, your baby will prefer the natural flavor of foods—avoid adding sugar, salt or syrups to baby's food.

> Never use honey in your baby's food—honey can make your baby very sick.

Keeping your baby food safe

The safest way to feed your baby is to put the amount of food your baby will eat into a small bowl.
Throw away anything that is left over in the bowl.

Feeding your baby directly from the container will cause the food to spoil quickly.

Storing

- If you have any baby food leftover, you can store it in the refrigerator for up to two days in a container with a tight-fitting lid.

- If you want to keep your baby food longer, you can then put the container in the freezer.

- One good way to store baby food in individual portions is to freeze it in an ice cube tray. Once it is frozen, transfer the cubes to a plastic bag and return them to the freezer.

 DHS
Oregon Department
of Human Services

FIGURE 4-10
Making Baby Food
Source: Used with permission from the Oregon WIC program www.healthoregon.org/WIC.

HEALTH HINT   Is Homemade Baby Food Always Best?

Many families and early childhood teachers enjoy preparing baby food from fresh ingredients. They like the idea of knowing exactly what the infant is eating. They may make this choice because they prefer organic ingredients, have an abundance of fresh produce from home gardens, or want to save money. Making baby food is a healthful choice; however, adults who care for young children must be aware that chemicals, called nitrates, are found in some foods and water. Nitrates can be toxic to infants. Infants who consume unsafe levels of nitrates develop a type of anemia known as "methemoglobinemia" or "blue baby syndrome." The nitrates impact hemoglobin, a component of red blood cells, so that oxygen is not picked up as readily. The lack of oxygen in the blood causes a bluish cast to the skin. Babies younger than 3 to 6 months of age are particularly susceptible.

Where do the nitrates come from? Formula prepared with well water contaminated with high levels of nitrates can be the source of this condition. Families and family child care settings with wells should be sure to check the nitrate level in their well water. Some vegetables tend to be high in nitrate content. These include beets, carrots, green beans, spinach, turnips, collard greens, and squash. Preparing infant foods using these vegetables should be avoided during the first year of life. Commercially prepared baby foods are monitored for nitrate content and do not pose a risk. Additionally, infants do not receive high levels of nitrates in breast milk regardless of a mother's diet.

Sources: Basic Information About Nitrate in Drinking Water by U.S Environmental Protection Agency, 2012, from http://water.epa.gov/drink/contaminants/basicinformation/nitrate.cfm; "Vegetable-borne Nitrate and Nitrite and the Risk of Methaemoglobinaemia," by Thomas Chan, 2011, *Toxicology Letters, 200*(1), 107–108; Infant Nutrition and Feeding: A Guide for Use in the WIC and CSF Programs by U.S. Department of Agriculture, Food and Nutrition Service, Special Supplemental Nutrition Program for Women Infants and Children, 2009, from http://wicworks.nal.usda.gov/infants/infant-feeding-guide; Starting Solid Foods, by the American Academy of Pediatrics, 2008, from http://www.aap.org/bookstore/brochures/br_solidfoods_2008_sample.pdf; "Drinking Water from Private Wells and Risks to Children by Walter J. Rogan, Michael T. Brady, the Committee on Environmental Health, and the Committee on Infectious Diseases, *Pediatrics 2009, 123*(6), pp. e1123–e1137 (doi: 10.1542/peds.2009-0752); "Infant Methemoglobinemia: The Role of Dietary Nitrate in Food and Water," by F. R. Greer, M. Shannon, Committee on Nutrition, and Committee on Environmental Health, 2005, *Pediatrics, 116*(3), pp. 784–786; and "Methemoglobinemia Caused by the Ingestion of Courgette Soup Given in Order to Resolve Constipation in Two Formula-Fed Infants," by F. Savino et al., 2006, *Annals of Nutrition & Metabolism, 50*(4), 368–371.

In summary, health experts have reached a general consensus on the following key points about introducing complementary foods:

- There is no evidence to support introducing foods in a particular order.
- There is no nutrition-related rationale to adding complementary foods before age 4 months.
- There is support for adding puréed meats or iron and zinc–fortified cereals to the diets of breast-fed infants at 4 to 6 months (American Academy of Pediatrics, 2012a; Kleinman, 2009).

Understanding How to Feed Solids to Infants

An important goal for teachers and families is to create a feeding experience that continues to foster the feeding relationship. Feed babies at a pace that is comfortable for them. When feeding infants solid foods, consider the following practical recommendations:

- The teacher's hands should be washed before preparing and serving the meal, and the infant's hands should be washed before eating.
- Teachers should have space identified for feeding infants that includes high chairs with removable trays that can be easily sanitized.
- Babies should have specifically assigned and labeled high chairs.
- Babies should be placed in a high chair when fed unless they have special needs or disabilities. Sitting up straight with feet supported promotes proper swallowing and helps reduce the risk of choking.
- Use plastic-coated baby spoons with food placed on the tip of the spoon to make it easier to access and swallow.
- Place food in a small bowl for serving. Don't feed babies directly from a jar because this will contaminate the baby food.
- Always supervise the baby in the high chair. Never leave baby unattended.
- Remember, babies have small stomachs and, therefore, require small but frequent meals and snacks.

The CACFP provides other helpful guidelines on suggested meals and snack routines for infants (see the Appendix, CACFP Meal Pattern Requirements for Infants and Children).

Offering Finger Foods

The introduction of finger foods gives infants an opportunity to practice their developing fine motor skills. Finger foods can be introduced into diets when infants can sit up, have developed the **pincer grasp** (the ability to pick up items using the thumb and forefinger) and can bring this food to their mouth. In addition, oral motor skills such as using the jaw to mash foods and moving food around from side to side in the mouth are indicators that babies are ready to eat finger foods. This generally occurs around 8 months of age. Finger foods should be soft enough for babies to chew using their gums.

pincer grasp
the developmental ability of infants to pick up items using thumb and forefinger

Cooperation between teachers and families is important as the infant is exposed to new textures, shapes, and sizes of food. A system should be in place to track what finger foods the infant has been fed. Cooked fruits and vegetables can be excellent first finger foods. NAEYC guidelines recommend cutting foods for infants into pieces no larger than $1/4$-inch squares to prevent choking. Teachers are also encouraged to evaluate each baby's chewing and swallowing skills when preparing and offering finger foods (NAEYC—Academy for Early Childhood Program Accreditation, 2012). As babies grow older and are exposed to wheat and milk, breads, cereals, and small pieces of cheese can be added to the diet. Some examples of finger foods are listed in Figure 4-11. When serving finger foods, the teacher can promote social interaction and introduce cognitive and language skills by, for example, counting the pieces of food or identifying their colors or flavors.

Feeding Concerns in Older Infants

Older infants accomplish the transition from a milk-based diet to regular soft foods over an amazingly short period of time. Sometimes during this transition infants are challenged when the adults who care for them make inaccurate assumptions about the types of foods or beverages

FIGURE 4-11 Examples of First Finger Foods

Fruits: Remove skin, seeds, or pits

- Diced or mashed ripe banana
- Diced ripe peaches, plums, or pears
- Diced mango or papaya or melon
- Diced canned fruits packed in their own juice such as peaches, pears, or apricots

Vegetables

- Cooked and diced sweet or white potatoes, peeled
- Cooked and diced green beans or semimashed peas, and lima beans
- Cooked and diced broccoli or cauliflower
- Soft cooked and diced zucchini and summer squash

Grains and starches

- Toast wedges or plain soda crackers
- Soft cooked pasta
- Cereal rings

Protein foods

- Shredded or small cubes of cheese (¼ to ½ inch depending on age)
- Tender pieces of chicken or turkey cut into pea-sized pieces and served with gravy

that should be offered. Teachers can share with families feeding practices that keep their babies healthy and safe.

Reducing the Risk of Choking

When planning meals for infants, it is particularly important to consider whether the food prepared might pose a choking risk. Although Chapter 7 discusses choking risks in young children and provides a list of high-risk foods to avoid, this section addresses the specific choking concerns of infants. Infants are new eaters and are developing oral motor skills at different rates.

Learning how to swallow solids and manipulating a challenging array of foods within the mouth are aspects of infants' developmental growth and maturity. It is important for teachers to be vigilant when textured foods are introduced. Teachers can reduce the risk of choking by ensuring infants are fed in a calm environment with limited distractions. For example, wiping off infants' faces before they swallow their last bite or putting food into their mouths while they are crying or laughing places babies at risk for choking. Likewise, medications for teething pain should not be applied before meals because gums, mouth, and throat can become numb. This can make swallowing more difficult.

Food items used for teething can pose a risk too. For example, chicken bones, raw carrots, frozen bananas, bagels, and whole apples are not recommended. The following foods have characteristics that cause concern about choking in infants:

- Slippery foods that are round such as grapes and cooked carrots.
- Easy to inhale foods such as sunflower seeds, peanuts, raisins, popcorn, and corn kernels.
- Sticky, chewy foods such as peanut butter, fruit leathers, and gummy candy.
- Firm food that can wedge in the throat such as hotdogs, whole bananas, and bagels.
- Hard, dry foods such as pretzels and chips (Mayo Clinic, 2011).

As older infants advance their eating skills, textured foods can be mixed with softer foods to aid in swallowing. For example, adding puréed carrots to rice, puréed sweet potatoes to finely diced turkey, or puréed peaches to alphabet pasta provides healthful, easy-to-swallow combinations.

Teachers may experience family members who don't support or understand the risks of specific foods. For instance, a parent might say, "Oh, my baby does fine with grapes. She knows how to chew them" or "I always give him popcorn and he never chokes on it." It is an important responsibility of teachers to inform families if they notice feeding practices that put young infants at risk. For example, consider the following situation:

Brittany, an 11-month-old baby, had not been coming to Patty's program for the past week. Her mother called to inform Patty that although Brittany was home and doing well, she had spent the past week in the intensive care unit being treated for pneumonia. Brittany had inhaled a sunflower seed that she grabbed from a bowl at a family picnic a couple of weeks before. Her mother thought Brittany had coughed it out, but the seed had remained in her lung and became a source of infection. A pediatric surgeon was able to remove the seed.

Brittany was lucky that she did not die. Because of the hazards of choking, early childhood programs should establish policies that prohibit foods that are choking risks from being served. The policy should include a descriptive list of foods that are not acceptable to serve to infants due to choking risk.

Introducing Foods That Are Low in Nutritional Quality

Eating habits are established early, and infancy is a critical time for starting these habits off right. However, sometimes adults who care for infants introduce solids that are low in nutritional quality or foods that are high in calories in relation to the nutrients they offer. A better choice is to offer foods that have **high nutrient density**. Nutrient density describes foods that have a high percentage of nutrients per serving size, but are not excessively high in calories. For example, mashed bananas are nutrient dense because they are a rich source of vitamin C, potassium, and fiber and are low in fat and salt. Single-ingredient puréed infant foods are nutrient dense. The CACFP reimburses for only the use of infant foods that contain a single ingredient such as 100% fruit, and 100% vegetables with the exception of puréed meats, which can contain gravy but cannot be offered in a mixed commercial infant dinner (Oregon Department of Education, 2009).

Studies conducted on the eating habits of U.S. infants provide some astounding trends. As many as 50% of infants are exposed to French fries, candy, cookies, or cake by 1 year of age. In addition, 15% were consuming sweetened drinks such as soda or juice drinks (Grummer-Strawn et al., 2008). Introducing these foods at such a young age may establish preferences that contribute to excess fat and calorie intake among young children. These figures reveal that families need positive reinforcement and guidance in helping their infants establish healthful eating habits. Teachers play an informative role in helping families navigate the introduction of solid foods into the diet of babies and encouraging the introduction of age-appropriate soft-cooked and puréed or mashed whole foods such as fruits, vegetables, and unprocessed meats and poultry. Program policies and procedures and CACFP guidelines set the tone for early childhood settings and create a nutritional ambiance that can favorably impact families' perceptions about foods.

Infants Learning About Food and Eating

Eating is a learning process. Infants learn about food if they are allowed to examine it. This may mean exploring the food by looking, touching, poking, squishing, smelling, and tasting it. Through these explorations infants are learning how to move food in their mouth, to chew, and to swallow. Allowing babies to self-feed when they indicate readiness is also a learning experience. It is also important not to force the intake of any foods. Babies are cautious about new foods and it may require up to 10 or more exposures before a new food is accepted (U.S. Department of Agriculture, 2009). This learning process requires adults to be understanding and patient as new foods are introduced and to respect the baby's feeding cues for hunger and fullness.

An important part of the learning process is to expose infants to a wide variety of foods. This increases the likelihood that they will be open to eating new foods and learn to enjoy a balanced diet as they grow older. It is very important for teachers to model good eating behaviors because babies

What if . . .
while unpacking a home-prepared lunch for an 11-month-old you discovered a choking hazard (a cold hotdog packed in a baggie) as part of the meal. What would you do? Are there other concerns you might have about serving a hotdog to this infant?

high nutrient density describes foods that have a high percentage of nutrients per serving size, but are not excessively high in calories

What if . . .
you saw a 7-month-old eating a French fry as she was carried by her mother into the classroom? What are the concerns and what would you do?

Babies should be allowed to fully experience the food they are fed. Let them play with the food. The feel of the food as well as the taste and smell of food all contribute to babies' learning experiences.

and children learn from what they see teachers do and what they hear teachers say. Consider the following scenario:

> Mary is in charge of the infant class. She takes a sip of the soft drink she has sitting on her desk. Jeremy, an 11-month-old, points to her can of soft drink but Mary says, "No, this is not for you, Jeremy." Jeremy starts crying just as Rosalie, his mother, comes in to pick him up. Mary explains why Jeremy is crying. Rosalie replies, "Well, I always share my soft drink with him. He loves it." What can Mary say?

Setting a good example and being a good role model are not always easy tasks. It requires a great deal of personal reflection and introspection to recognize when the behaviors modeled in front of children and families are not ideal. The best approach is to learn from situations like the one Mary experienced, and identify a better approach for next time.

FEEDING INFANTS WITH SPECIAL HEALTH CARE NEEDS

Infants with health-related conditions sometimes face significant feeding challenges that can impact growth and development. These conditions may include developmental disorders and physical disabilities. Teachers and families, along with health care professionals, form a team in helping infants with health issues maintain a nutritious diet with sufficient calories for growth. They also strive to help infants acquire eating skills and behaviors that support good nutrition.

Infants with Feeding Problems

Infants are born with the instinctual ability to obtain nourishment from the breast or bottle by latching on, sucking, swallowing, and breathing in a synchronized manner. Infants with developmental delays, however, may not always be effective eaters. Feeding problems become apparent as they struggle with nursing or bottle feedings and perhaps fail to gain weight appropriately. **Feeding problems** are defined by the American Academy of Pediatrics as developmental disorders related to the mouth (Kleinman, 2009). Swallowing problems are abnormalities in the swallowing process. An infant who struggles with liquids and coughs or chokes during meals has symptoms of a swallowing disorder. Infants who gag on foods that need to be chewed, have a strong preference for smooth or crunchy foods, but have no problems with liquids also show symptoms of a feeding problem (Kleinman, 2009).

Feeding problems can be either sensory or motor based (Kleinman, 2009). For example, some babies may have issues with oral sensitivity. Infants with **oral hyposensitivity** have less feeling within the mouth and are, therefore, less conscious of where food is once it is placed inside their mouths. **Oral hypersensitivity**, on the other hand, describes a condition in which infants are overly aware of foods placed in or near their mouths. For these babies, food brought near or into the mouth can cause a gag or bite-down reflex. These conditions can make mealtimes challenging for both baby and caregiver (The Children's Hospital at Westmead, 2003; Yang, Lucas, & Feucht, 2010). Babies with **oral motor delays** may have difficulties chewing due to weak chewing muscles. They may also have problems moving food around within the mouth due to uncoordinated tongue movement. This can result in choking or gagging and slow and labored eating (Kleinman, 2009; Yang, Lucas, & Feucht, 2010). Teachers who suspect feeding issues or have concerns about an infant's ability to consume solids should confer with families and consider referral to an early intervention team and the infant's health care provider. Collaboration with speech, physical, or occupational therapists can help identify and provide assessments of infants' feeding issues (Yang, Lucas, & Feucht, 2010).

feeding problems
developmental disorders related to the mouth

oral hyposensitivity
an oral motor condition in which infants have less feeling in the mouth and are not entirely aware of where food is when it is placed within the mouth

oral hypersensitivity
an oral motor condition in which infants are overly aware of foods placed in or near their mouths

oral motor delay
a developmental delay that can result in weak oral muscles and tongue movement such that difficulties occur in chewing

Feeding Premature Infants

Premature infants may have special feeding needs. Infants are considered premature if they are born before 37 weeks of gestation. These fragile infants may have different nutritional requirements than the baby born full term. Premature infants should receive breast milk if possible. Breast milk offers immunological protection and improved developmental outcomes compared to formula. In premature infants (but not necessarily near-term infants), expressed breast milk can be fortified with special milk fortifiers to meet the higher protein, vitamin, and mineral requirements of growth (Academy of Nutrition and Dietetics, 2012; Kleinman, 2009). Premature infants who are not breast-fed are given special formulas developed to meet the higher nutrient needs necessary for appropriate growth.

If families want teachers to prepare the formula in any way that deviates from standard mixing directions on the label or to add fortifiers to breast milk, a prescription from the health care provider with a clearly written recipe is required. In some cases a demonstration by the parent on how to prepare formula may be helpful. Teachers should rely on the guidance of health care providers and parents on when to introduce solid foods for premature infants. As a rule, the introduction of solids for these infants should be based on developmental readiness, which may need to be based on the baby's due date or **corrected age** as opposed to date of birth. A baby's corrected age is the number of weeks the baby was born early subtracted from his current age in weeks. For example, an infant who enters a child care center when he is 3 months old but was 3 weeks premature would have a corrected age of 2 months 1 week, or 9 weeks old. Generally infants who are premature begin solids when they demonstrate signs of developmental readiness around 4–6 months old corrected age (Academy of Nutrition and Dietetics, 2012). Premature infants are at greater risk than full-term infants for developing iron-deficiency anemia because their bodies have lower stores of iron. They should be fed a variety of foods rich in iron content when they are ready.

Feeding Infants with Cleft Lip and Cleft Palate

Cleft lip and **cleft palate** are birth defects of the lip and mouth that contribute to particularly complex swallowing problems. During the first few weeks of pregnancy, the sides of the lip and mouth begin developing and eventually come together. In some cases the sides of the mouth or lips do not fuse properly, creating a cleft palate or cleft lip or both. A cleft lip is generally not problematic for babies because they can generally still suck and swallow. A cleft palate, however, consists of an opening in the roof of the mouth. Babies born with a cleft palate may not be able to suck successfully and are at increased risk of poor intake (Academy of Nutrition and Dietetics, 2012). This problem can be overcome with the use of special bottles that allow formula or breast milk to be squeezed into the infant's mouth. Elongated nipples can also be used to help with sucking and swallowing (see Figure 4-6, the Medela SpecialNeeds Feeder nipple). Figure 4-12 illustrates how to position a baby with cleft lip or cleft palate when feeding. Feeding in the upright position prevents breast milk or formula from getting in the nose.

A cleft lip is surgically closed at about 6 weeks to 3 months of age and a cleft palate is repaired at about 9–12 months; therefore, caregivers should make sure infants are well nourished prior to surgery (Academy of Nutrition and Dietetics, 2012). Children with cleft lip and palate can be fed an adequate diet with the use of a few simple strategies such as those outlined in Figure 4-13. Sometimes infants born with cleft lip and cleft palate require alternative feeding strategies. See the Progressive Programs and Practices feature that shows how an early Head Start program supports the family of an infant with significant feeding challenges.

● FEEDING INFANTS FROM DIFFERENT CULTURES

The introduction of solids into the diets of infants is an important and celebrated event in many cultures. For example, one of children's first rites of passage in the Hindu religion is *annaprashana*. This ceremony celebrates the

corrected age
the number of weeks a baby is born early subtracted from the baby's current age in weeks

cleft lip
a birth defect in which the lip does not grow together

cleft palate
a birth defect that consists of an opening in the roof of the mouth

FIGURE 4-12

Position for Feeding a Baby with Cleft Lip or Cleft Palate

45°

FIGURE 4-13   Tips for Teachers: Feeding an Infant with a Cleft Lip or Cleft Palate

- Have parents demonstrate the use of special feeding equipment. If an elongated nipple with flexible bottle is used, practice squeezing the bottle in the sink to get an idea of the correct rate of flow.
- Have parents present the first time you feed the infant.
- Feed infants in an upright position to prevent milk from going up into the nose and ear canals (see Figure 4-12).
- Select a comfortable seat and try to reduce distractions. Infant feeding may take longer.
- Pay extra attention to burping because more air may be swallowed while feeding.
- Be supportive of the mother who pumps and feeds the baby breast milk.
- Remember: The progression of solids in babies with cleft lip or cleft palate is the same as for comparably aged infants.

baby's first taste of solid food, a sweet rice dish prepared with milk. The baby sits in the lap of a family member and is fed the rice dish in a celebratory event that includes family and friends (Rajendran, 2011). Families of the Jewish faith may also participate in a weaning celebration. This is a family affair that occurs at home and can include a religious blessing and songs. Someone other than the mother, such as the father, a sibling, or grandfather, has the honored role of feeding the baby solids for the first time (Diamant, 2005). In the United States, families might honor the start of feeding solids in a more casual way by taking photos of their baby's first bite of solid food and writing an entry about the event in the child's baby book or blog.

These types of meaningful celebrations create emotional connections to special foods. Many families subsequently have strong preferences for the traditional foods they prepare and those preferences extend to the food they choose to offer infants. For example, U.S. infants are traditionally offered dried infant cereal as the first solid food choice. This is followed by an orderly progression of puréed vegetables, followed by puréed fruits, and finally puréed meats and poultry. This was considered best practice until recent evidence-based research revealed that there is no reason to introduce solid foods in any particular order and that puréed meats with their zinc and iron content have particular benefits for breast-fed infants (American Academy of Pediatrics, 2012a; Kleinman, 2009). This example points out that all cultures can have traditions that include healthful and less than healthful trends.

In general, most cultures have traditional first foods that include some type of grain mixed with water, broth, or milk to create a gruel or porridge that is fed to infants (Katz, 2003). Asian families, for example, may prepare congee, a thick rice-based soup to which a variety of ingredients can be added such as tiny pieces of meat or fish (Kittler, Sucher, & Nelms, 2012; Ramachandran, 2004). Hispanic families may choose to offer bean broth with small pieces of soaked tortilla, mashed beans, rice, and broth-based soups (Mennella, Ziegler, Briefel, & Novak, 2006). In the United States, rice, barley, and oatmeal are commercial baby cereals that are offered as traditional first foods.

Cultural food choices can have an impact on the health of infants. For example, in Lebanon, where sesame is a traditional component of the diet, allergies to this seed can be more severe than peanuts, leading researchers to ask, "Is sesame the 'Middle Eastern' peanut?" (Irani, Germanos, Kazma, & Merhej, 2006). Mercury poisoning was found in Chinese infants residing in Australia who were consistently fed contaminated fish in a traditional fish congee (fish mixed with a rice porridge) as an infant complementary food (Corbet & Poon, 2008). Some cultural traditions involve the adult chewing foods until it becomes gruel-like in composition, making it easier for babies to swallow. There have been rare reports of hepatitis B and HIV transmitted by this practice (Centers for Disease Control and Prevention, 2009; Gaur et al., 2009).

These cultural practices point out the need for teachers to understand and respect the basis of food choice in different cultural groups. At the same time teachers have an important responsibility to ensure the safety and nutritional quality of foods offered to the infants in their care. Both families and teachers share a common goal, which is to support the optimal health and development of the infants in their care.

PROGRESSIVE PROGRAMS & PRACTICES

Caring for Caden

By Pam Woitt, Home Based Educator (HBE) and Madeleine Sprague, RD, Kidco Early Head Start, Albany, Oregon

Jessica and Robyn were 17 and 18 years old, respectively, and still seniors in high school when their baby, Caden, was born. Taking care of an infant can be challenging for teenagers but even more so for Jessica and Robyn as Caden was born with cleft palate and Pierre Robin syndrome. With Pierre Robin the lower jaw is smaller than a normally developed jaw and his tongue would fall back into his throat. He could not swallow and had difficulty breathing.

Caden spent 3 weeks in the hospital. A feeding tube was put into his nose to help him receive needed nutrition and to help with his breathing. Robyn and Jessica were trained how to replace the tube and how to use a special bottle to feed Caden before being sent home from the hospital.

A lot of people would be intimidated by the special care Caden needed but Robyn and Jessica did what needed to be done without any complaining or expecting others to do it for them. They jumped right in and fed Caden, changed the tubes, and started back in with their schooling. Robyn started back to school full time and Jessica was able to get a tutor to come and work with her a few days a week. Both were committed to graduating on time.

Jessica had enrolled in Early Head Start during her seventh month of pregnancy and the Home Based Educator (HBE) provided weekly home visits. These visits focused on preparing for impending parenthood, prenatal health concerns, the relationship with her partner, and the birth process. After Caden was born, the home based educator kept in frequent contact with Robyn and Jessica. She visited, offered support, and helped connect them with resources in the Portland area for food and clothing since they had not been prepared for a lengthy hospital stay away from home.

The parents followed through with everything that they needed to do to better provide for Caden. They signed up for and were able to receive SSD for Caden. The HBE informed them about the Ride Line transportation service to help get them back and forth to doctors' visits in Portland. These parents used all resources available to them.

Robyn and Jessica worked very hard to keep up with their studies and kept in frequent contact with their school counselors. They kept all their scheduled home visits with the HBE and they never hesitated to ask questions. With the help of the HBE, they filled out five scholarship applications. They received

all five scholarships plus a few they hadn't even applied for. Robyn didn't simply graduate; he overcame having to take extra classes to make up for those that didn't transfer from his previous school and even raised his GPA in the process. Jessica was able to complete all her classes working with the tutor. Graduation was a very proud moment for their friends and family!

Robyn said that Early Head Start was important in helping them fulfill their goals because they knew that the HBE believed in them and was there to offer support by educating them on parenthood, child development, nutrition, and providing encouragement and connections for taking care of a child with a disability.

Caden is now 18 months old and has recently had jaw distraction surgery to bring out his lower jaw, surgery to fix his cleft palate, and he's had his feeding tube removed. He is able to eat regular food now, which gets a little bit easier every day. All this has taken place during Robyn and Jessica's first year of college. They have been able to, once again, keep up with their studies and get Caden back and forth to all their appointments. Robyn has recently gotten his driver's license and they no longer need the assistance of Ride Line.

Robyn and Jessica are great examples that when you have the support of family and community and choose to use that support, you can accomplish anything!

● SUMMARY

The impact of good nutrition during infancy is profound. Infants who receive too much or too little nourishment can suffer consequences that are immediate and long term. Growth and development can be negatively impacted, increasing the risk of chronic disease in adulthood.

Breastfeeding is the preferred feeding of choice and should be supported in early childhood education settings. Infants who are breast-fed should be introduced to fortified infant cereal and puréed meats and poultry around 6 months of age to help meet their needs for dietary sources of zinc and iron. Formula-fed infants can be fed one of several different types of formulas that run from standard to highly specialized products. Selecting which formula to use as well as the time at which to introduce solids is a decision shared by families and their child's health care provider.

When feeding infants breast milk, formula, or solid foods, teachers need to develop a supportive feeding relationship. Teachers need to be sensitive to feeding cues and recognize signs of hunger and fullness. . . . A nurturing relationship between teachers and infants helps create a climate of understanding and trust, which in turn supports effective feeding.

This helps infants develop healthy attitudes toward foods and supports self-regulation of food intake. This means teachers allow infants to dictate when and how much they eat. Teachers also promote healthful eating habits by routinely exposing infants to a wide variety of nutritious foods. Teachers encourage infants to experience healthful eating by permitting them to use all their senses when they eat: to see, touch, smell, taste, and even play with food during meals and snack times. The social-emotional development of infants is fostered by caring interactions with adults who are responsive to infants' emotional and physical needs.

Teachers have an important responsibility to work with families and their health care providers to accommodate infants with special needs. They also must make conscientious efforts to understand different cultural practices related to feeding infants. Close communication between teachers and families is the cornerstone of collaborative care and facilitates the optimal nourishment of infants.

KEY TERMS

Cleft lip
Cleft palate
Colostrum
Complementary foods
Corrected age
Feeding problems

Feeding relationship
Fore milk
Formula intolerance
High nutrient density
Hind milk
Infantile botulism

Oral hypersensitivity
Oral hyposensitivity
Oral motor delays
Pincer grasp

REVIEW QUESTIONS

1. Provide examples of infant feeding cues and describe how they relate to a trusting feeding relationship.
2. Describe the benefits of breastfeeding and how a teacher can support the breastfeeding mother. Compare this to the responsibilities of providing infant formula that is safely prepared, stored, and fed to infants.
3. Explain the progression of infant foods and how this progression relates to infants' developmental skills.
4. Provide an example of an infant's special need that may cause a feeding problem. Describe how to meet the infant's nutritional needs.
5. Describe cultural factors that influence infant feeding decisions.

DISCUSSION STARTERS

1. How would you support a nursing mother who is returning to work but has a position with an inflexible schedule and a boss who is unsympathetic to the mother's breastfeeding goals?
2. A mother is hearing contradictory advice from friends, relatives, and health care professionals about introducing solid foods in her infant's diet. How would you help this mother without adding to the confusing advice she has already received?
3. A mother is feeding her infant a cultural dish that contains honey. How do you manage this situation in a culturally sensitive way while considering the safety of her infant?

PRACTICE POINTS

1. Baby Matt is 6 months old. He is currently being exclusively breast-fed. His mother Jenna is wondering how to begin solids. This is her first baby and she doesn't want to make any mistakes. She is returning to college and will be leaving Matt at Fran's home child care program four mornings per week. Jenna asks Fran for advice. Using your knowledge of infant nutrition, discuss how you will decide on an infant feeding progression that will meet Matt's needs. List the questions you might ask Jenna as you gather information for developing a feeding plan.

2. Using CACFP meal patterns for infants found in the Appendix, design a menu for a 10-month-old infant.

3. You are responsible for developing an activity for an infant class. You want the focus to be on exploring the tastes, colors, and texture of foods. Your class has a 6-month-old, an 8-month-old, and two 10-month-old infants. Plan an activity and explain the decisions you made as you prepared this lesson.

WEB RESOURCES

American Academy of Pediatrics
www.aap.org

Centers for Disease Control and Prevention: Breastfeeding
www.cdc.gov/breastfeeding/index.htm

Infant Nutrition and Feeding: A Guide for Use in the WIC and CSF Program
http://wicworks.nal.usda.gov/infants/infant-feeding-guide

La Leche League
www.llli.org

National Resource Center for Health and Safety in Child Care and Early Education
http://nrc.uchsc.edu

Womenshealth.gov Breastfeeding
www.womenshealth.gov/breastfeeding/

World Health Organization (WHO) Guidelines for the safe preparation, storage, and handling of powdered infant formula
www.who.int/foodsafety/publications/micro/pif2007/en/index.html

MyEducationLab™

Go to Topic 2 (Feeding Children) in the MyEducationLab (www.myeducationlab.com) for your course, where you can:

- Find learning outcomes for Feeding Children along with the national standards that connect to these outcomes.
- Complete Assignments and Activities that can help you more deeply understand the chapter content.
- Apply and practice your understanding of the core teaching skills identified in the chapter with the Building Teaching Skills and Dispositions learning units.
- Check your comprehension on the content covered in the chapter by going to the Study Plan in the Book Resources for your text. Here you will be able to take a chapter quiz, receive feedback on your answers, and then access Review, Practice, and Enrichment activities to enhance your understanding of chapter content.

five

Feeding Toddlers, Preschoolers, and School-Age Children

learning outcomes

AFTER READING THIS CHAPTER, YOU SHOULD BE ABLE TO:

1. Define the nutritional needs of toddlers and discuss how to manage eating issues typical of this age group.

2. Describe characteristics of preschool children's diets and factors that enhance how preschoolers learn about food and nutrition.

3. Define how to create a quality nutritional environment for school-age children that supports the dietary guidelines and enhances the goals of the school lunch program.

Laura, a teacher in the toddler class, is concerned about Michaela, an 18-month-old who attends her child care program. Michaela is a petite child who was born 4 weeks premature and has a history of poor growth. Her mother Hanna has strong ideas about what and how much Michaela should eat. She insists that Laura make sure Michaela eats all of her school lunch. She tells Laura, "Unless I watch her like a hawk she won't eat and the doctor says she needs to gain weight." Laura has tried a variety of ways to get Michaela to eat. She has used stickers on a chart. She has offered a special dessert if Michaela eats her entire meal. Michaela is often resistant and mealtimes have become stressful. Laura doesn't feel good about this, but she understands how important it is for Michaela to eat enough to gain weight. She is concerned that sometimes the only nourishment Michaela will consume is her milk.

The situation comes to a head when Michaela, in a fit of frustration, throws her lunch plate to the floor. Laura, with Hanna's enthusiastic agreement, requests a meeting with their program's dietitian, Christina, who oversees their food service. Christina recognizes that in spite of everyone's good intentions, Michaela is not eating well. She also knows that using forceful techniques for getting children to eat during mealtimes often backfires. She commends both Hanna's and Laura's efforts on behalf of Michaela to provide her with a healthful diet, but points out the missing link for success—allowing Michaela to decide what she is going to eat and how much. Hanna is very worried that this approach won't work but agrees to a trial period. At first Michaela does eat less but as she sees that both her mother and teacher are not pressuring her to eat, she begins to feel free to explore her food. Michaela is still not a big eater but things are improving. Laura feels better about the approach and mealtimes are less stressful. Hanna is pleased that her relationship with her daughter is better because they are no longer battling about food.

Children undergo tremendous growth and developmental change during their first year of life. They enter the toddler years having completed the transition from a single-ingredient, liquid-based diet to a multitude of solid foods, from being fed to self-feeding, and from basic instinctual communication to increasingly determined and directive requests for food. Their nutritional needs are in transition, too. Toddlers, preschoolers, and school-age children are not growing as rapidly as infants and, therefore, their eating style changes from a somewhat indiscriminant ingestion of calories to a more selective mode of eating in which preference plays an increasingly important role. Preschoolers continue to advance in the textures and complexity of foods they consume because better chewing skills allow them to eat most foods found in adult diets. School-age children learn to make independent food choices and put into practice the eating habits they acquired when younger.

The multitude of steps taken by caregivers to positively influence children's nutritional well-being can be sabotaged if children are given messages that undermine the nutritional care and guidance they have previously received. For example, children receive confusing mixed messages when they come to school sporting events where soft drinks, candy bars, and chips are served after learning about making healthful nutrition choices from their teachers and school food service staff.

To address these issues, we focus this chapter on the nutritional requirements unique to three age groups: toddlers, preschoolers, and school-age children up to age 8. We review child nutrition programs that are implemented in the school setting and discuss how they set the stage for healthy diets. We also describe methods for managing the unique challenges that can complicate feeding and impact children's nutritional status. Finally, we provide strategies for using the classroom and cafeteria environments to support healthful nutrition messages. These approaches ensure that wholesome nutrition habits and patterns take firm root, providing children with a lifelong foundation of healthful eating.

FEEDING TODDLERS

Feeding toddlers (children from 12 to 36 months) is different from feeding infants. The complacent attitude of infants with their easy acceptance of food can change when these children become toddlers. Appetites that were once consistent in infants become sporadic and selective in toddlers. In addition toddlers establish their autonomy by asserting themselves at mealtimes. Toddlers, like Michaela, are often ready and willing to do battle about what they will and will not eat. The wise caregiver remains neutral, does not overreact, and continues to offer nutritious foods in a supportive manner.

According to the Academy of Nutrition and Dietetics (2012), caregivers should:

- Allow toddlers to explore foods as they become increasingly independent in their food choices.
- Promote pleasure and success while eating.
- Avoid succumbing to unreasonable demands.

Caregivers are also responsible for providing a healthful balanced diet that meets the nutritional needs of toddlers. To accomplish these goals, teachers need to understand the nutritional requirements of toddlers, recognize characteristics of toddler diets, and know how to feed toddlers in culturally appropriate ways.

Understanding the Nutritional Needs of Toddlers

Toddlers need the same variety in their diets as adults. They have made the transition from strained infant foods to soft table foods. To address these changes, some adjustments to texture and size of pieces need to be made so that foods are easy and safe for toddlers to eat. As the amount of solid food eaten increases and begins to provide more of the nutrient needs of the toddler, the role of milk in the diet decreases. However, breast-feeding still has an important role, so teachers should support the mother who is committed to breast-feeding.

MyEducationLab™

Visit the MyEducationLab for *Nutrition, Health, and Safety for Young Children* to enhance your understanding of chapter concepts with a personalized Study Plan. You'll also have the opportunity to hone your teaching skills through video-based Assignments and Activities, as well as Building Teaching Skills and Dispositions lessons.

Supporting Extended Breast-Feeding

Mothers who continue to nurse their toddlers after their first birthday give their child the precious gift of time. Time is a commodity that is often hard to come by for women who work or go to school. **Extended breast-feeding** allows mothers and toddlers to reconnect after being apart and contributes to toddlers' social and emotional well-being by providing a special peaceful time of comfort and reassurance.

The health benefits of breast-feeding outlined in Chapter 4 continue to provide advantages to toddlers. Breast milk continues to offer immunological protection and in addition appears to develop a greater concentration of immune components as babies mature (American Academy of Family Physicians, 2012; Stein, Boies, & Snyder, 2004). This may reflect natural adaptations in breast milk to accommodate the greater likelihood of toddlers being exposed to infections as they grow older. The *Safety Segment* provides an example of the benefits of breast-feeding during a flu pandemic. These are important reasons for teachers to support the efforts of breast-feeding mothers.

Toddlers do best when they are provided an array of healthful foods offered in a supportive manner. Allow toddlers to feed themselves but offer assistance when needed.

extended breast-feeding practice of mothers who continue to nurse their toddlers after they have reached 1 year of age

Balancing Toddler Diets

Often the quality of toddlers' diets will vary from day to day based on their food preferences and what they choose to eat. Caregivers can enhance the likelihood of toddlers eating well by planning meals that include a variety of wholesome foods. Fruits and vegetables in an assortment of rich colors are more likely to add nutrients such as vitamins A and C, potassium, and fiber to the diet. Meats, poultry, and fish are rich sources of iron and zinc, and dairy products are excellent sources of vitamin D and calcium. A balanced diet for toddlers includes high-iron foods as well as fruits and vegetables rich in vitamin C, which aids in iron absorption.

Understanding Portion Sizes for Toddlers

Children's appetites should dictate portion size. One rule of thumb to use when deciding how much to serve at meals is that children need about 1 tablespoon of food from each food group per

SAFETY SEGMENT   Breast Milk Protects During Flu Season

Teachers may not recognize the true gift they provide infants and toddlers in their care when they support mothers who are breast-feeding. Even mothers may not fully understand how fortunate they are to be breast-feeding their babies and toddlers when infectious disease strikes because breast milk offers immunological protection for infants. It is so beneficial that the U.S. Department of Health & Human Services (Flu.gov) and the Centers for Disease Control and Prevention (CDC) encourage mothers to nurse their children even if they become ill with influenza. They recommend that mothers who are sick use a breast pump to express their breast milk and have a healthy caregiver feed the breast milk to their child. The CDC makes the following recommendations for breast-feeding mothers who are sick with an influenza virus:

- Have a healthy caregiver available to take care of your infant and provide pumped breast milk if possible.

- Do not stop breast-feeding if you are ill because a mother's milk is made to help her child fight diseases.

- Breast-feed often and limit formula feeding if your child takes supplemental formula.

- Use everyday precautions to limit the spread of infection such as washing hands often and using proper cough etiquette (cough into elbow).

- If you are taking medication to prevent the flu because you have been exposed to the virus, you should continue to breast-feed your baby at the breast as long as you do not have symptoms of the flu such as fever, cough, or sore throat.

Source: Flu FAQ: Should I stop breastfeeding my baby if I think I have come in contact with the flu? 2010, retrieved July 4, 2012, from http://answers.flu.gov/questions/4401; The Centers for Disease Control and Prevention, 2011. Responding to Influenza: A Toolkit for Prenatal Care Providers. Retrieved July 4, 2012, from http://www.cdc.gov/flu/pdf/freeresources/pregnant/2011_influenza_prenatal_toolkit_withposters.pdf.

FIGURE 5-1   **Sample Breakfast, Lunch, and Snack Menu Using CACFP Guidelines for Toddlers**

MEAL	PORTION SIZE
Breakfast	
Oatmeal	¼ cup
Mixed berries	¼ cup
Milk, whole	½ cup
Lunch	
Milk, whole	½ cup
Simmered diced turkey with au jus	1 ounce (the size of a small matchbox)
Mashed sweet potatoes	2 tablespoons
Diced kiwi	2 tablespoons
Whole-grain bread	½ slice
Trans-fat-free margarine	½ teaspoon
Afternoon Snack	
Pizza muffin:	
Whole-wheat English muffin	¼ muffin
with tomato sauce and	1 tablespoon
cheese, shredded	½ ounce
Water	

year of age (Academy of Nutrition and Dietetics, 2012). The Child and Adult Care Food Program (CACFP) provides specific guidance regarding appropriate portion sizes for toddlers. Figure 5-1 provides a sample menu for toddlers using the CACFP guidelines for children ages 1 to 2. The menu includes foods rich in vitamins and minerals for meals and snack times. Menu planning is discussed in more detail in Chapter 6.

Teachers are often surprised at the small portions recommended for children. Usually these amounts are sufficient for most children; however, the CACFP recommendations describe minimum portions and some children may require or desire more food. It is important to serve enough food so that children feel satisfied. In the opening case scenario, Michaela's mother, Hanna, was very concerned about how much her daughter was eating. A helpful strategy that Laura might use is to show Hanna examples of the normal portion sizes for toddlers. This way Hanna's expectations for Michaela will be reasonable.

The CACFP provides guidance on portions and food groups via meal patterns. In an effort to ensure the CACFP is in alignment with the *Dietary Guidelines for Americans, 2010*, the USDA has requested that the Institute of Medicine evaluate the program. Initial recommendations are offered in the report, *Child and Adult Care Food Program Aligning Dietary Guidance for All* and when implemented will likely include larger servings from vegetable and fruit groups (Committee to Review Child and Adult Care Food Program Meal Requirements & Institute of Medicine, 2011).

Recognizing Characteristics of Toddlers' Diets

Teachers who care for toddlers must make decisions about what foods are nutritious and also safe for children to eat. Even when teachers do not plan the menus, they must be in tune with characteristics that influence the diets for toddlers. This includes considering the textures and consistency of food served, timing meals appropriately, and understanding the impacts of development on children's diets and eating capabilities.

What if . . .

you sat down to eat and someone served you a mixing bowl full of cooked rice? How would you feel? How do you think toddlers feel if very large servings are offered to them?

Modifying Food Textures and Consistency

The textures and consistencies of food need to be adjusted for toddlers, especially as they begin to master table foods. Meats, poultry, and other foods need to be chopped into small bite-size pieces no larger than 1/2 inch for toddlers through age 2 (National Association for the Education of Young Children, 2012). The skin should be removed from fruits, and soft, easy-to-mash foods should be offered. Extra sugar, salt, and spices are not necessary.

Mixing textured foods with foods that have smoother consistencies can make them easier for toddlers to swallow. For example, young children do well with casseroles, stews, and spaghetti sauces over pasta. Choosing soft foods that don't fall off spoons such as cooked cereal, refried beans, cottage cheese, and yogurt can help toddlers feel more successful when they eat. Foods that fall off the spoon easily such as peas and gelatin should be avoided.

Timing of Meals

Toddlers still have small stomachs. They are, however, ready to shift from the demand feeding of infancy to more scheduled meals. Offering three meals plus snacks every 2 to 3 hours provides toddlers ample opportunity to refuel. This routine is also helpful because of toddlers' variable appetites. In fact, the NAEYC recommends that meals and snacks be least 2 hours but not more than 3 hours apart (National Association for the Education of Young Children, 2012). This is helpful information to share with families whose toddlers are selective eaters. In the opening case scenario, one strategy Laura can use to reassure Hanna about her daughter's eating habits is to explain the toddlers' need for frequent meals and snacks. This way Hanna will know that even if Michaela doesn't consume very much at mealtime, she will soon have another opportunity to eat. Michaela may be more motivated by hunger to eat her snack later on.

Understanding Impacts of Development

Children's developmental skills influence their ability to negotiate biting, chewing, and swallowing certain foods. For example, a 14-month-old toddler will have different eating skills than a 19-month-old. The 19-month-old may have no problems managing thinly cut zucchini sticks, whereas the 14-month-old will do better if the zucchini is steamed and cut into small pieces. Toddlers' willingness to eat also changes as they grow and develop. This willingness is impacted by a variety of factors, including the child's growth rate, preference for "sameness," and changes in the child's perceptions of taste.

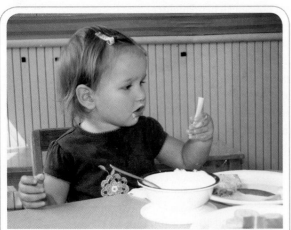

Teachers need to evaluate the eating skills of children and make decisions about the appropriateness of food served. This 19-month-old has no problems managing the zucchini sticks.

Decrease in Growth Rate   A toddler's rate of growth is slower than during the infant period. Because of this the child's food intake decreases. This natural decrease in eating is sometimes seen as having a poor appetite or being picky.

The Need for "Sameness"   Toddlers are busy maturing, developing, changing, and learning many new skills. Sometimes routine foods provide comfort and security during times of rapid change and development (Zero to Three, n.d.). Toddlers may feel secure and comfortable with their mashed potatoes mixed with peas and want to hold off on trying new foods.

Changing Taste Perceptions   Taste buds are located on the roof of the mouth, the cheeks and tongue. Research suggests that there are variations in the ability to taste bitter. Some children may taste bitter more strongly than others and therefore their food preferences are not within their control (Hayes et al., 2011; Nova, 2009; Schwartz, Issanchou, & Nicklaus, 2009). Spinach, broccoli, Brussels sprouts, cabbage, and grapefruit may have flavors that are too strong for some toddlers. Teachers need to be patient and understand that eating patterns are influenced by a toddler's stage of development. The following Nova website explains the genetics behind taste perception: www.pbs.org/wgbh/nova/body/science-picky-eaters.html.

Understanding How to Feed Toddlers

Toddlers experience significant developmental transitions as they strive to establish their independence. They are increasingly mobile and may occasionally show their autonomy through challenging behavior. "No" may become a well-used word in their vocabulary. Teachers recognize that these responses are natural expressions as toddlers begin to learn to make their own decisions. Sometimes these first steps in learning to make choices show up in the realm of eating. Teachers are better able to help promote positive eating habits if they recognize and anticipate potential feeding challenges and are prepared to address them.

Selective Eaters

Selective eaters are children who accept a very limited variety of foods, eat small portions, and may not be very interested in eating. This eating pattern is sometimes called picky or finicky. Selective eating, however, is relatively common in the toddler age group and is considered normal.

selective eaters
children who make very limited food choices

Before labeling children as selective eaters, teachers should reflect on normal toddler eating behavior and recognize that children's previous eating patterns are undergoing changes as they mature. Some selective eaters limit food choices to such an extent that teachers may become concerned about the nutritional adequacy of the child's diet. The best way to determine if the problem is a significant issue is to assess the child's growth patterns using a growth chart. If children are growing at a normal rate, then they are getting sufficient calories to grow and develop in spite of their selective eating habits. For many toddlers choosy eating is a temporary phase. For a few it can become a long-term pattern that may require intensive intervention using a team approach that includes health care providers, families, and teachers (Davis, Cocjin, Mousa, & Hyman, 2010; Harding, Faiman, & Wright, 2010; Zero to Three, n.d.).

food neophobia
term used to describe fear of new foods

Food Neophobia

Food neophobia refers to fear of new foods. Toddlers are often suspicious of new foods. This fear may be an adaptive behavior that has historically protected young children from eating poisonous substances (Monneuse, Hladik, Simmen, & Pasquet, 2011). In three different studies that looked at pairs of twins and their fear of new foods, a strong genetic tendency toward food neophobia was observed. The inheritability rate ranges from 66% to 78% with one study showing a difference in heritability rates for males and females, 45% and 61%, respectively (Cooke, Haworth, & Wardle, 2007; Knaapila et al., 2007; Knaapila et al., 2011) In other words, children may inherit their fear of new foods from their relatives. A mother, for example, may very well be accurately assessing the situation when she states, "He eats just like me. I was always a picky eater."

In spite of this likely genetic tendency, if children are introduced to a variety of new food early on and given ample exposure to these new foods, it can help overcome their hesitations about trying something new. Teachers understand that various and repeated exposures to any new concept help children to learn. The same holds true for learning to accept new foods. It may take 15 to 20 exposures or more before young children are confident enough to try new foods (Satter, 2012a). Toddlers also benefit from having role models (parents, teachers, and particularly peers) who demonstrate pleasure in eating a variety of foods (Johnson, van Jaarsveld, & Wardle, 2011; O'Connell, Henderson, Luedicke, & Schwartz, 2012).

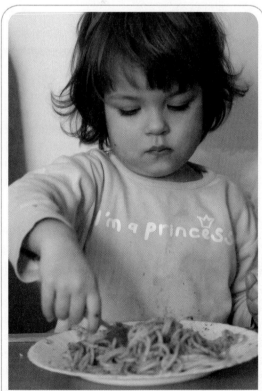

The division of feeding responsibility allows children to master the acceptance of a new food on their own time line.

FIGURE 5-2   Strategies for Encouraging the Selective Eater

Estrategias

Strategies for the eating challenge "I don't like vegetables!"

- Seat the child next to a child or teacher who likes vegetables.
- Offer vegetables as a first course: salad or vegetable sticks or vegetable soup.
- Add vegetables to foods: grated carrots to spaghetti sauce or zucchini or pumpkin to quick bread.
- Provide enjoyable opportunities to explore foods: classroom gardens, taste tests, cooking activities.
- Serve vegetables with condiments: low fat ranch dressing or yogurt.
- Serve vegetables in child friendly ways: make a smoothie using fruits and vegetables.
- Minimize strong cooking odors that detract from the enjoyment of eating vegetables like overcooked broccoli.

Strategies for the eating challenge "I don't like meat!"

- Add meat to combination dishes: chicken stir fry, beef and bean burrito.
- Offer high protein alternates: peanut butter, beans, peas and lentils, tofu, tempeh, and eggs.
- Offer fork-tender meats such as braised beef or pork or chicken stew.

- Serve meats with condiments: catsup, barbeque sauce, salsa, low fat cheese.

Strategies for the eating challenge "I don't like milk!"

- Serve milk cold and with a straw.
- Provide yogurt or low fat cheese as calcium rich alternatives.
- Serve calcium and vitamin D fortified soy milk.
- Use milk in meal preparation: Use milk in hot and cold cereals, cream soups or smoothies.

Strategies for the eating challenge "I refuse to eat a meal!"

- Ask child to sit at the table and visit with the group; allow children to eat the amount they want (even if the amount is nothing).
- Do not offer alternatives to the meal (except for required special diets).
- Do not offer any food until the next snack or meal time.

Strategies for the eating challenge "I will only eat certain favorite foods (food jag)"

- Continue to offer the basic program menu food items.
- Avoid rewards for eating particular foods.
- Be patient. Food jags usually go away.

Another strategy is to offer new foods along with foods toddlers already like. For example, 2-year-old Shawn, who attends a family child care program, does not like many vegetables. When his teacher Ruby offers him vegetables she also offers diced soft fruits because she knows Shawn really likes fruit. This takes the pressure off Shawn because there is something available that he likes to eat. He is able to try the new food without the pressure of hunger. Figure 5-2 provides additional ideas for teachers to help remove pressure while giving toddlers time to learn and get used to new foods.

food jag
the persistent eating by young children of a limited number of favorite foods for a period of time

Food Jags

A **food jag** occurs when toddlers select a very limited number of favorite foods to eat and reject all others, including foods they liked in the past. Sometimes a well-loved favorite will suddenly no longer have appeal and another food will take its place. Teachers and families who recognize a food jag should try to focus on what the children are still eating rather than focusing on what they are no longer eating. It may become evident that, although the child's food selections are limited, there may be three or four choices from each food group that the child still accepts. Teachers should not draw attention to this eating behavior because it may prolong the food jag. Just as in the case of the selective eater, it is important to offer a variety of foods from each of the food groups.

Teachers may be concerned about conflicts with CACFP recommendations and reimbursement guidelines when children experience food jags and refuse to eat a

What if . . .

you had a toddler in your classroom who refused to sit at the table for breakfast? What if your program director was pressuring you to have all the children sit down together so the meals can be counted for CACFP reimbursement purposes? How would you handle this?

POLICY POINT   The Child and Adult Care Food Program and the Picky Eater

Children's programs can obtain CACFP reimbursement only if all of the required food groups, including fat free or low fat (1%) milk, are offered at each meal. Teachers may be concerned that children need to consume foods from all food groups in order to receive reimbursement. This is not the case. As long as the appropriate foods are served, programs are able to count the meals as reimbursable. But what if a child can't drink milk?

- If a child has a medical reason for not drinking milk, such as lactose intolerance or milk allergy, a health authority can provide documentation that allows the program to make an appropriate substitution with non-dairy beverages that are nutritionally equivalent to milk and still receive CACFP reimbursement. For more details see www.fns.usda.gov/cnd/Care/Regs-Policy/policymemo/2011/CACFP-21-2011.pdf.

- If the child simply doesn't like milk, programs can still claim a reimbursement if the milk was offered but refused.

- If, however, families request that no milk be served and ask that juice be offered instead, the program cannot get CACFP reimbursement for that meal.

- If a child prefers and a family requests whole milk or 2% the program cannot claim reimbursement for meals in which the higher fat milk is served.

  What about the child who refuses to eat a meal?

- If the child sits down and is offered a meal but chooses not to eat, the program can still receive reimbursement for this meal.

- If the child refuses to sit down at the table for a meal, the program cannot receive reimbursement.

---

particular food group. The *Policy Point* discusses how to navigate the CACFP when children are selective eaters or during a food jag.

Families and teachers may also become concerned that the quality of the child's diet is inadequate. Families who are concerned about a prolonged food jag can obtain advice and reassurance from the child's health care provider.

Division of Responsibility in Feeding

Responsibility for healthful eating is shared between teachers and children. Teachers are responsible for what children eat, when they eat, and where they eat. Children are responsible for whether they eat and how much (Satter, 2008). Teachers provide leadership and structure in eating, while keeping a focus on the nutritional quality of the diet. Children's responsibility relies on their innate ability to select and eat the amount of foods needed to maintain growth and a healthful weight (Satter, 2008).

When teachers seek to impose their will on children, negative repercussions may result. Children may become compliant and potentially overeat, or display defiance and not eat enough. Children should not feel pressured to try a new food. Teachers may be surprised to learn that this means not even requiring children to take a "no thank-you bite" or clean their plate. Allowing children to regulate their own food intake preserves the feeding relationship and helps children become competent eaters. Competent eaters are children who feel positive about foods and eating, are able to accept an increasing variety of different foods, and understand their internal food cues. Competent eaters know when they are hungry and when they are full (Satter, 2008).

In the opening case scenario, Hanna and Michaela had not established a division of feeding responsibility. This was because Hanna did not trust Michaela to eat enough and the doctor confirmed her fears. In her well-intentioned goal of trying to get Michaela to eat, she applied pressure and was met with resistance. Laura contributed to the problem too by taking on Hanna's role as food enforcer when Hanna wasn't there. With input from the dietitian, Laura and Hanna were able to pull out of the food battle and allow Michaela the freedom of choice. Figure 5-3 provides a summary of how teachers can support the division of feeding responsibility in the early childhood and school settings.

A Matter of ETHICS

You observe a parent who comes early for pickup at your half-day preschool program specifically to observe how much her child eats at lunch. The parent hovers at the entrance but you notice that as soon as the parent appears the child tends to slow down and stop eating. Generally the child eats as other children do; some days more and some days less and is growing fine according to growth charts. This parent is very concerned about the child getting the "right" foods to eat. You feel this pattern of pressure related to feeding may be going on at home, too. Families and teachers have a common interest in the well-being of children. The NAEYC Code of Ethical Conduct discusses the ethical responsibility to families. How do you support the parent and bring about the goals of communication, cooperation, and collaboration between classroom and home with this parent? The Code stresses the importance of providing parents access to the child's classroom but in this case you feel it might be interfering with the child's meal. How would you navigate through this sensitive situation?

FIGURE 5-3   Division of Responsibility in Feeding

Teachers' Responsibilities: What, When, and Where

- Provide young children with structure when eating meals.
- Meals should be routine and include snacks in between meals.
- Meals and snack should be consumed in a designated area.
- Avoid menu substitutions or "short-order cooking" unless there is a medical reason.
- Serve family-style meals with the teacher socializing and modeling healthful eating.
- Avoid food or drinks between meals or snacks except for water.
- Minimize distractions so teachers and young children can enjoy eating together.

Children's Responsibility: How Much and Whether

- Allow children to self-serve while assisting them to take what they will realistically eat. Do not restrict how much they eat except as it relates to fair distribution of food between all children at the table. There should be enough food available however to allow them to have more of any food if they want it.
- Avoid the "no thank you" bite which is a control tactic that interferes with food acceptance because it takes away the child's joy in mastering a new food and puts pressure on the child.
- Let children decide what they would like to eat.
- Let children decide how much they want to eat from the food adults have put on the table.

Source: Adapted with permission from *Child of Mine: Feeding with Love and Good Sense.* Copyright © 2005 by Ellyn Satter, MS RD LCSC BCW, owner Ellen Satter Associates. www.EllynSatter.com.

Weaning from the Bottle

Some toddlers struggle with the transition to solid foods. They find comfort in the bottle and prefer to get their calories from milk or juice. Excessive milk or juice consumption, however, can blunt the appetite for solid foods. In the opening case scenario, a contributing factor to Michaela's poor food intake was her reliance on milk. Her preference for milk and her mother's concern that Michaela consume some form of nutrition prevented Michaela from taking interest in her food. Although milk is a rich source of nutrients, including calcium, it does not meet all the vitamin and mineral needs of young children. For example, milk is not a good source of iron. Children who drink too much milk may not eat enough nutritious foods rich in iron, which can lead to anemia.

It is also important for children to wean from the bottle to reduce the risk of dental cavities and avoid a lag in the development of appropriate feeding skills. The American Academy of Pediatrics recommends weaning children from a bottle by 12 to 15 months of age (Kleinman, 2009). Teachers can help support weaning by collaborating with families and making sure a consistent message is sent to toddlers both in the home and program setting. Figure 5-4 provides strategies teachers and families can use to support the weaning process.

Switching to Whole Milk

It is very important for infants to receive breast milk or formula during their first year of life. Once they reach their first birthday, they are ready to make the transition from formula to whole milk. Breast-fed toddlers may also be offered whole milk; however, mothers may choose to continue to breast-feed. The CACFP and Women, Infants, and Children (WIC) programs recommend that toddlers receive whole milk until 2 years of age (U.S. Department of Agriculture Food and Nutrition Service, 2011a; U.S. Food and Drug Administration Food and Nutrition Service, 2009). Fat free, 1%, and 2% milk may be too low in fat content to support an adequate rate of weight gain and growth. The fat and cholesterol in whole milk may support neurological development. The

Delayed weaning from the bottle creates risks for dental cavities because of the constant exposure of teeth to beverages that contain sugar.

FIGURE 5-4   Strategies for Weaning from the Bottle

When:

Offer formula or breast milk from a cup starting at 6 months and begin the weaning process by around 12 months.

How:

1. Select one meal or snack time to introduce a cup. Use the cup at this meal for 1 week. Discuss with parents which meal to start substituting a cup for a bottle.
2. Every week substitute a cup for a bottle at another meal. Coordinate with parents which meal and what type of cup to use.
3. Assist the child to hold the cup and sip the liquid.
4. A toddler may still need assistance with self-comfort measures. Offer alternatives such as a pacifier, stuffed animal, and extra hugs and cuddles.
5. A consistent approach should be used at home and school.

Source: Based on UCSF Benioff Children's Hospital FAQ Baby Bottle Weaning. Copyright 2002–2012 by the Regents of the University of California at http://www.ucsfbenioffchildrens.org/education/baby_bottle_.

fat in whole milk also aids in vitamin A and D absorption. However, points of view differ concerning the fat content in milk provided to toddlers. The *Health Hint* describes some of the questions raised by health authorities regarding the type of milk that should be offered to toddlers.

Exploring Cultural Differences in Feeding Toddlers

Teachers, families, and the children who attend early childhood programs come from a wide array of cultural backgrounds. Teachers who are familiar with their own cultural perceptions and seek out information and knowledge about other cultures are better able to understand and support the differences in how children are introduced to food. They are also better able to appreciate the family eating habits. For example, people eat food with their hands in Bangladesh, India, Nepal, and Pakistan, whereas people in Asian countries use chopsticks and spoons (Luitel, 2006). Some cultures sit on the floor to eat meals or serve themselves from a communal bowl. Understanding family eating practices helps teachers recognize these influences on toddlers' feeding skills and behaviors at mealtimes.

Nutrition practices in food selection can vary as well. In China, Korea, Japan, and Southeast Asia, and in Western African cultures, milk is not used as a beverage and limited milk is used in cooking (Ishige, 2012; Maritz, 2011). This places toddlers at risk for vitamin D deficiency. In Hispanic cultures milk is often considered an ideal food and it is believed that children can never drink too much milk. Weaning from the bottle is often delayed, putting Hispanic children at risk for iron-deficiency anemia (Brotanek, Schroer, Valentyn, Tomany-Korman, & Flores, 2009).

Teachers need to use culturally sensitive approaches when discussing family food practices and agree on the

> ### What if . . .
> a 2-year-old child from India in your class wouldn't use eating utensils? What would you do?

Children's cultural practices may influence how they eat and when they are served meals.

HEALTH HINT The Fat Content of Milk: What's Best for Children?

The general consensus among health authorities is that when children reach 2 years of age, the fat content of the milk they consume should be gradually decreased from whole milk (4% butterfat content) to fat-free milk. This goal is promoted in an effort to introduce a heart-healthful diet and prevent obesity in children. But recommendations become less clear for toddlers between 1 and 2 years of age. Issues under consideration include the following:

- Some health authorities discourage lower-fat (2% or 1%) or fat-free milk for children between 1 and 2 years of age because it is believed that fat and cholesterol in a child's diet are beneficial for central nervous system development and provide adequate calories for growth.

- The American Academy of Pediatrics and the National Heart, Lung, and Blood Institute suggests that 2%, 1%, or fat-free milk can be offered to children between the ages of 1 and up to age 2 depending on a child's rate of growth, appetite, other sources of fat in the diet and the nutrient

density of other foods consumed, and the child's risk for obesity and heart diseases.

- The American Heart Association, whose mission is focused on preventing coronary artery disease, also advises 2% milk for children after age 1.

- The CACFP (in accordance with the requirements established by the Healthy Hunger Free Kids Act of 2010), allows only fat-free or low-fat (1%) milk to be served to children age 2 and older. Children between age 1 and up to 2 years of age, however, are served whole milk.

- The WIC program also provides whole milk to children between age 1 and up to 2 years of age.

Teachers should follow the guidelines provided by governmental agencies and the recommendations of the USDA Food and Nutrition Service and be open to individualizing practices for toddlers if advised by the child's health care provider and in collaboration with families.

Sources: *Dietary Guidelines for Americans, 2010,* by the U.S. Department of Health and Human Services and U.S. Department of Agriculture, 2011, retrieved July 9, 2012, from http://www.cnpp.usda.gov/Publications/DietaryGuidelines/2010/PolicyDoc/Chapter5.pdf; "Dietary Recommendations for Children and Adolescents: A Guide for Practitioners: Consensus Statement from the American Heart Association," by the American Heart Association, 2005, *Circulation, 112*(13), pp. 2061–2075 updated online June 20, 2012, at http://www.heart.org/HEARTORG/GettingHealthy/Dietary-Recommendations-for-Healthy-Children_UCM_303886_Article.jsp; "Expert Panel on Integrated Pediatric Guideline for Cardiovascular Health and Risk Reduction" 2012, *Pediatrics, 129*(4), pp. s1–s44 by the American Academy of Pediatrics from http://pediatrics.aappublications.org/content/129/4/e1111.full.pdf+html; "The Start Healthy Feeding Guidelines for Infants and Toddlers," by N. Butte et al., 2004, *Journal of the American Dietetic Association, 104,* pp. 442–454; "Lipid Screening and Cardiovascular Health in Childhood," by S. R. Daniels, F. R. Greer, and the Committee on Nutrition, 2008, *Pediatrics, 122*(1), pp. 198–208; USDA Memo CACFP 21-2011—Revised Child Nutrition Reauthorization 2010: Nutrition Requirements for Fluid Milk and Milk Substitutions in the Child Adult Care Food Program Questions and Answers from http://www.fns.usda.gov/cnd/care/regs-policy/policymemo/2011/CACFP-21-2011.pdf; and Women, Infant Children Laws and Regulations, 2012. Retrieved July 15, 2012, from www.fns.usda.gov/wic/PDFfiles/WICRegulations.pdf.

approaches that will be used in the school setting. Teachers should also support healthful traditional food practices and find ways to incorporate diverse foods in the children's menu at school. This can be accomplished by planning menus that include foods that reflect cultural preferences or special cultural occasions, and planning social events such as potlucks where families can share special cultural dishes to promote cultural awareness.

Understanding the Teacher's Role in Promoting Healthful Eating Habits

The foremost nutrition goal for feeding toddlers is to establish a foundation of eating habits that supports immediate growth and long-term health. Teachers can achieve this goal by linking developmental skills to feeding skills and by being good role models.

Linking Developmental Skills to Feeding Skills

Teachers develop a keen understanding of child development. They assess and recognize signs of readiness for advancing skills in all realms of children's lives including eating. They understand that children develop eating skills at different rates. Being attuned to children's development helps teachers make decisions about what and how to feed toddlers. It also prepares teachers to use a variety of strategies to encourage healthy eating habits. Table 5-1 describes the link between physical, social–emotional, and intellectual development and approaches to feeding toddlers. The *Teaching Wellness* feature provides specific examples of ways teachers can help children experience new foods while they learn about nutrition.

TABLE 5-1   Developmental Influences on Toddlers' Eating and Relevant Teacher Strategies

Development Physical	Feeding Strategies for 12- to 24-Month-Olds
Rate of growth decreases.	Toddlers are more selective and eat less than infants. Offer variety and age-appropriate portions.
Toddlers tend to eat frequently throughout the day.	Smaller frequent meals are more common. Snacks are desirable and necessary. Avoid daylong access to bottles or toddler cups filled with calorie-containing beverages. This can cause problems with dental decay and decrease appetite for food.
Begins to walk by 12–15 months.	Attention span can be short when it comes to eating as toddlers desire to practice new motor skills. Distractions should be kept to a minimum. They are expending calories as they move and grow, and adequate calorie intake is important.
Most can hold cup and feed self with spoon but still spill on occasion.	They should be allowed to self-feed but assistance should be available when they need it. Offer finger foods and other options that will stay on a spoon (yogurt, cottage cheese, oatmeal, etc.).
Social-Emotional	
Toddlers want to be more independent.	Allow them to select what they want to eat. Offer choices but not too many. They may refuse a food. Do not pressure toddler about which food to eat or force food intake. It may take several exposures before they are ready to try it. Allow them to practice eating skills and to select age-appropriate foods from a healthful array offered by caregivers.
Frustration can occur when they try out activities they can't quite do yet which leads to temper tantrums.	Provide gentle guidelines for mealtime behavior. Never feed a crying child. Offer meals that are easy for toddlers to eat to promote feelings of success rather than frustration (for example, green peas can be mashed to make them easier to eat).
Become aware of their possessions and sharing can be challenging.	Each child should have his or her own high chair and when old enough to sit at the table his or her own space and place setting. Family-style meal service helps toddlers learn to take turns and share food from a common serving bowl.
Remembering rules is still not possible.	In a positive manner remind about mealtime rules such as washing hands, sitting down together, not licking the serving spoon, etc.
They are developing a sense of self and start to feel emotions such as pleasure, jealousy, affection, pride, and shame.	Help them to feel proud of their eating skills. Do not offer blame when spills occur. Recognize eating skill achievements such as "You are learning to drink from a cup."
They become more fearful as they begin to learn about the world.	Toddlers may be afraid to try new foods. Offer food without pressure. It takes many exposures before toddlers will accept a new food. Offer a new food along with a food that they like.
They benefit by having routines and schedules.	There should be a schedule for when and how meals and snacks are served. Mealtime procedures should follow a typical beginning, eating, and ending sequence of events.
Cognitive	
Toddlers are curious and eager.	Offer many different types of foods with various flavors, textures, tastes, and smells. Allow them to touch, taste, squeeze, drop, and overall experience the food. Food may go in the mouth and out again. Allow children enough time to discover the different qualities of foods by allowing time for touching, smelling, and tasting it. Toddlers learn through these exploratory activities.
When they want something, they will point to it.	Be responsive to toddlers' communication attempts. When they point at a food, verbalize their request: "You are pointing at the yogurt. Do you want yogurt?" Teaching basic sign language can help toddlers communicate when they are hungry and when they are full.
They can identify familiar objects or pictures by name and begin to use two-word sentences.	Identify foods, eating utensils, and other toddlers sitting at the table by their names to facilitate language skill development. Read children's books that have themes in which children can identify different types of food. Use typical words associated with mealtimes such as *please* and *thank-you*.
They begin to use items for their intended function.	Demonstrate for toddlers how to use spoons and forks. Assist them when they drink beverages from a cup. Offer them a napkin to wipe their face.
Toddlers are very active.	Toddlers cannot sit for very long. Mealtimes vary but 20 to 30 minutes provides time for eating while not stretching mealtime beyond toddlers' limits. Do not allow toddlers to leave the table with food (either in the mouth or carried in the hand) because this can pose a choking risk.

Sources: The National Network for Child Care–NNCC, by C. Malley, 1991. University of Connecticut Cooperative Extension System, *Toddler Development (Family Day Care Facts series). Amherst, MA: University of Massachusetts, retrieved July 16, 2012, from N.C. Division of Child Development and Early Education, 2008; Infant-Toddler Foundations, retrieved July 16, 2012, from http://ncchildcare.dhhs.state.nc.us/pdf_forms/dcd_infant_toddler_early_foundations.pdf; American Academy of Pediatrics, 2011. Ages and Stages Developmental Milestones 12 months, retrieved July 16, 2012, from HealthyChildren.org; Medline Plus, 2010. Toddler Development, retrieved July 16, 2012, from http://www.nlm.nih.gov/medlineplus/ency/article/002010.htm.

TEACHING WELLNESS   *Will I Like What's Good for Me?*

LEARNING OUTCOME Children will accept a variety of foods.

Vocabulary focus: Try, sample, taste, flavor, taste-test, variety, nutritious, food groups.

Safety watch: Ensure that foods are prepared and served appropriately for the age group and the child's abilities, such as serving pureed fruits and vegetables for young infants, or small mashed pieces for older infants. Choose foods that avoid children's food allergies and restrictions.

Prepare foods appropriately for the child's developmental skill, by cooking, straining, mashing, and cutting foods into appropriate pieces, and selecting food textures that the child can manage to avoid choking such as serving pureed fruits and vegetables for young infants, or small mashed pieces for older infants; supervise children closely during the tasting and monitor for cleanliness; avoid any known food allergens or restrictions.

OLDER INFANTS AND TODDLERS

Goal: Older infants will practice selecting and tasting different fruits and vegetables.

Materials: Three or four fruits and vegetables of differing colors prepared appropriately, such as mashed bananas or creamed corn (yellow), cut up soft peaches or mangoes (orange), mashed peas or soft cooked cut up string beans (green), cut up strawberries or watermelon, cooked mashed beets (red), mashed blueberries (blue); plates with small divisions.

Activity plan: The teacher's and child's hands should be washed before beginning. Conduct the activity when the child is calm and ready to explore. Place a small portion of each food in a divided plate for the child and prepare one plate for the teacher. Encourage the child to explore and taste the foods. Demonstrate tasting the foods. Name the

food and talk about the taste and color. Say words that convey pleasure and interest, such as "I like these orange mangoes" or "This red watermelon makes me happy because it tastes so good." Encourage tasting, but do not force. Describe what the child is doing. Say, "You are trying different fruits and vegetables. That is a good way to learn what each food tastes like."

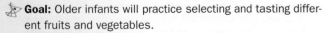

- **How to adjust the activity:** If children are not able to feed themselves, feed the child or guide the child's hand to explore and taste the food. Follow the child's cues and gestures as you select the food to offer. Give the child time to hold the food in her mouth. Allow the child to spit the food out as desired. Reinforce all efforts to explore and taste.

- **Did you meet your goal?** Did the child explore choose and taste a variety of foods?

PRESCHOOLERS AND KINDERGARTNERS

- **Goal:** Children will explore different forms of tomatoes and foods made from tomatoes products, choose products to taste, and identify which ones they like.

- **Materials:** The book *I Will Never Not Ever Eat a Tomato* by Lauren Child; tomatoes of different types (grape, pear, or cherry, Roma, traditional) cut into small pieces (to avoid choking hazard); tomato-based foods (ketchup, salsa, tomato soup, spaghetti sauce); serving bowls; serving spoons; tasting spoons; napkins; large sheet of paper; marking pens.

- **Activity plan:** Set up a tomato taste-testing center. Place each type of tomato and tomato food in a serving bowl. Place the sheet of paper on the wall or table. Draw columns on the paper and label one column for each tomato product. Invite the children to taste each food by serving a small portion onto their plate. Talk about the foods, and ask the children to describe the flavors. Guide the

children to place an "X" in the column for each tomato and tomato food they like. At group time gather the children and read the book. Talk about the themes in the book and reinforce the notion of exploring new tastes and flavors. Talk about the tomato taste-test and review the children's "votes" for each of the tomato foods. Identify the foods that more children liked. Ask the children to tell what they liked about the tomato foods. Ask the children to name four foods made from tomatoes.

- **How to adjust the activity:** Engage all children by learning phrases such as, "I like it" in each child's home language. Link the concept of exploring and trying new foods to taste-tests of other food products, such as foods made from apples or vegetables of different colors.

- **Did you meet your goal?** Did children explore and taste different tomato products?

SCHOOL-AGE CHILDREN

- **Goal:** Children will be able to name the food groups, identify the variety of foods they eat and sort foods into the food groups, and describe what makes foods nutritious or less nutritious.

- **Materials:** The book *MyPlate and You* by Gillia Olsen; red, green, orange, purple, and blue construction paper; markers; scissors; glue; white paper plates; MyPlate poster, magazines with pictures of foods.

- **Activity plan:** Gather children together and introduce the concept of food groups and MyPlate. Read the book and review the MyPlate poster. Identify the different food groups and describe the qualities of foods that make them nutritious or less nutritious. Nutritious foods are rich in vitamins, minerals, and fiber and low in fat. Less nutritious foods are often high in added fat, salt, or sugar and can be low in vitamins and mineral and high in calories. Talk about the importance of eating a variety of foods for a healthful diet. Invite children to cut construction paper into shapes that replicate the MyPlate division of food groups (See www .choosemyplate.gov/downloads/mini_poster_English_final .pdf for sample poster), and glue them onto a paper plate. Guide children to write the name of each food group onto its section on their "MyPlate." Invite children to cut out pictures from magazines or draw pictures of foods they like, and glue them onto the correct food group section. Talk about the goal of showing the variety of foods the child eats from each food group. Ask children to show their "MyPlate" and tell others about the different foods they eat. If some food groups include only one (or few) foods, encourage the children to suggest ideas of other foods that the child could try to increase the variety of foods enjoyed in that food group.
- **How to adjust the activity:** Ensure that there are sufficient scissors, including scissors for children who are left-handed, and adapted scissors who are still developing their cutting skills. If needed offer glue sticks to help children control the gluing process. Provide a paper plate with precut and glued construction paper dividers, and offer precut pictures or clip-art of food to assist children

This child can identify and write the names of the five foods groups.

with motor skill challenges—focusing the goal of lesson on sorting a variety of food pictures into food groups and gluing them on the plate. Give assistance to children who are learning English, by reminding them of the food groups, and demonstrating matching foods to food groups as needed.

- **Did you meet your goal?** Can children name the food groups, match foods to the appropriate group, and describe what makes a food nutritious or less nutritious?

Teachers as Role Models

Toddlers seek to imitate the adults in their lives. This means that teachers are important role models, and that children are watching what you eat. Teacher behaviors influence the choices they make. In addition, modeling pleasant interactions during mealtime introduces toddlers to appropriate eating behaviors. Providing opportunities for toddlers to self-feed and self-serve promotes competence and accomplishment.

Teaching Toddlers About Nutrition

Toddlers are curious and learn best when abstract concepts are a part of everyday tangible experiences. Some of the diverse ways that toddlers learn about food and eating occur when they are exposed to healthful, colorful meals rich in aromas, tastes, and textures. Participating in family-style meal services helps toddlers to establish positive mealtime behaviors and develop social skills such as sharing, passing food, and saying "please" and "thank-you." Mealtime in the classroom provides opportunities for toddlers to practice fine motor skills, such as spreading, pouring, and grasping foods with tongs. Mealtime is also an important time to introduce diverse foods and familiar foods prepared in different ways. Helping with cleanup fosters self-help skills as children put dishes into a tub and wipe their place at the table after they eat.

Children learn about food through dramatic play. This little boy has also learned about food safety and is appropriately wearing gloves while pretending to handle fresh produce.

Classroom activities provide opportunities for children to have direct hands-on experiences with food-related topics. Activities that introduce toddlers to nutrition concepts include simple food preparation tasks that allow them to stir, cut soft foods, pour ingredients into a bowl, wash fruits and vegetables, and knead dough. These experiences allow toddlers to taste, smell, and touch different foods. Children's books with food-related themes, dramatic play with food props, and creative activities that include food topics are all appropriate ways to teach toddlers about foods and nutrition. These approaches help toddlers to establish positive eating habits that support them as they move into the preschool years.

● FEEDING PRESCHOOLERS

Franklin is 4 years old. During the health screening at preschool, it was determined that he is overweight. His teacher, Madeline, shares this information with his family by sending home a note that reports his height and weight measurements. The following day Franklin's mother, Lenora, stops to talk to Madeline. She is very concerned. Several people have commented on Franklin's weight and she feels frustrated. The note from the health screening is the final straw. Lenora vows to start Franklin on a diet the next day. She insists Franklin not receive any more snacks. Madeline understands Lenora's frustration. She obtains Franklin's growth chart from his school file and brings it to the meeting to share with Lenora. The chart shows that Franklin is at the 90th percentile but he has been growing at the same rate during the past 2 years. Together they identify some resources that Lenora can review, and Madeline recommends that Lenora check with Franklin's health care provider before making any drastic changes in his diet. Lenora feels reassured by Madeline's practical approach. She decides to check with the medical care provider at Franklin's next well-child checkup. In the meantime she will focus on making sure the choices offered at home model the types of healthful foods provided at school.

During the eager-to-please preschool years, children experience a decreased rate of growth that can result in unpredictable eating behaviors. Children's body fat naturally decreases as they leave the toddler years and enter the preschool years. This means that preschooler children's appetites, like those of toddlers, can be sporadic. Preschool children may eat well one day but need encouragement to sit and eat the next. As their experience with foods expands, they also develop distinct preferences. To support preschoolers in their efforts to develop positive eating habits, teachers need to understand the nutritional needs and characteristics of the diets of this age group, understand how to create positive mealtime experiences, and be prepared with strategies to teach children healthful nutrition concepts.

Understanding the Nutritional Needs of Preschool Children

Preschool-age children rely on a high-quality diet to support growth and development. The goal is to balance their nutrient needs with their calorie requirements and energy expenditure. This is best accomplished by providing a variety of foods rich in tastes, colors, and textures while establishing habits that promote an active lifestyle. Teachers can find dietary advice about feeding preschool-age children from several sources including the federal government's MyPlate food guidance system (see Figure 5-5) which offers health and nutrition information for preschoolers, the CACFP, and the *Dietary Guidelines for Americans, 2010* (U.S. Department of Agriculture, 2012a; U.S. Department of Agriculture, Food and Nutrition Service, 2011b; U.S. Department of Health and Human Services & U.S. Department of Agriculture, 2011). Each of these sources encourages the provision of a variety of foods from each of the five food groups. The MyPlate food guidance system simplifies the recommendations of the *Dietary Guidelines for Americans, 2010* into a visual icon that helps Americans age 2 through adulthood make healthy food choices (U.S. Department of Agriculture, 2012b; U.S. Department of Health and Human Services & U.S. Department of Agriculture, 2011). The MyPlate offers the following selected messages:

- Balance calories to manage weight. For preschoolers this means preventing obesity by maintaining healthy eating habits and an active lifestyle and reducing sedentary behaviors such as spending too much time in front of the TV or computer.

- Reduce foods that are high in salt, added solid fats, and sugars. Preschool age children are learning healthy eating habits. Foods like cakes, cookies, pies, candy, ice cream, soft drinks, and high-fat meats such as regular ground meat, hotdogs, bacon, sausage, and fried chicken are foods for occasional use. When planning menus or selecting snack choices evaluate labels for sodium content in foods like soups, crackers, breads, and frozen meals and choose the foods that are lower in salt.

- Increase the consumption of healthy foods rich in nutrients by ensuring half the plate contains a variety of colorful vegetables and fruits, offering more whole grains and switching to fat-free or low-fat (1%) milk. See Figure 5-5 which illustrates these messages in the MyPlate icon.

FIGURE 5-5
MyPlate
Source: http://www.choosemyplate
.gov/print-materials-ordering/
graphic-resources.html.

Teachers play a very important role in helping children to learn about food. Exposing children to a variety of nutritious foods sets the tone for healthy eating across their life span. Preschool children also need to consume foods that provide all needed nutrients including vitamins and minerals. Researchers who surveyed a large sampling of families and caregivers to assess the diet and food consumption patterns of young children found that although most of the nutrient needs of preschoolers were being met, potassium, vitamin E, and fiber were sometimes below recommended requirements (Butte et al., 2010). The U.S. Department of Agriculture also indicates that potassium, fiber, calcium, and vitamin D are nutrients of concern in American diets (U.S. Department of Health and Human Services & U.S. Department of Agriculture, 2011). Recent studies reveal that the content of meals served in child care centers and family child care programs is still often high in saturated fats, added sugars, and foods high in salt content (Ball, Benjamin, & Ward, 2008; Benjamin Neelon, Vaughn, Ball, McWilliams, & Ward, 2012; Dwyer, Butte, Deming, Siega-Riz, & Reidy, 2010). It is important to recognize the role of teachers and program policies in promoting good nutrition. A recent study for example of 429 child care providers working in child care centers, preschools, and family day care homes, showed that in general sites that participate in CACFP, particularly those that are Head Start programs, are more likely to provide more nutritious options (more fruits, vegetables, whole grains, less sweets, sweetened beverages, and snack-type foods) compared to those sites that were not participating in CACFP (Ritchie et al., 2012). Both CACFP and Head Start programs have in place standards and requirements that offer guidance to teachers regarding healthy diet and nutritious meals. In addition, teachers and programs that make changes in menu planning can have a very positive impact. For example, researchers showed that when new high-fiber lunch entrees were added to the menu, children's daily fiber intake improved and that children readily accepted the new menu items (Zuercher & Kranz, 2012).

In addition to providing guidance on healthy meals, the MyPlate website is also an excellent educational resource for teachers to share with families to promote understanding of the nutritional needs of young children (see Web Resources section at the end of this chapter). The USDA provides sample menus for meals and snacks that are appropriate for preschool-age children (Figure 5-6). They also share healthy eating tips and offer easy to understand posters that include the MyPlate icon and important nutrition messages.

For example, in the preschool case scenario, the resources that Madeline shares with Lenora include the menu guidelines shown in Figure 5-6 as well as information that describe the portion sizes recommended by the CACFP. In addition, Madeline points out that health care providers generally do not place young children on weight-loss diets but instead stress the importance of following healthy eating guidelines and being physically active. Lenora begins to feel more confidence in the way she feeds Franklin and the way Franklin eats when she examines these resources. Later that month when Lenora takes Franklin to his health care provider she learns that although Franklin is above average in size, because he is growing steadily rather than excessively, his growth rate is actually fine.

These patterns show one way a 1200 calorie Daily Food Plan can be divided into meals and snacks for a preschooler. Sample food choices are shown for each meal or snack.

Notes for using the Meal and Snack Ideas.

Breakfast	Breakfast Ideas		
1 ounce Grains ½ cup Fruit ½ cup Milk*	Cereal and Banana *1 cup crispy rice cereal* *½ cup sliced banana* *½ cup milk**	Yogurt and Strawberries *½ cup plain yogurt** *4 sliced strawberries* *1 slice whole wheat toast*	Applesauce Topped Pancake *1 small pancake* *¼ cup applesauce* *¼ cup blueberries* *½ cup milk**

Morning Snack	Morning Snack Ideas		
1 ounce Grains ½ cup Fruit	1 slice cinnamon bread ½ large orange	1 cup toasted oat cereal ½ cup diced pineapple	Frozen Graham Cracker Sandwich *2 graham crackers (4 squares)* *½ cup mashed banana*

Lunch	Lunch Ideas		
1 ounce Grains ½ cup Vegetables ½ cup Milk* 1 ounce Meat & Beans	Open-faced Chicken Sandwich and Salad *1 slice whole wheat bread* *1 slice American cheese** *1 ounce sliced chicken* *½ cup baby spinach (raw)* *¼ cup grated carrots*	Soft Taco (meat or veggie) *1 small tortilla* *½ cup salad greens* *¼ cup chopped tomatoes* *¼ cup shredded cheese** *1 ounce cooked ground beef or ¼ cup refried beans*	Bagel Snake *1 mini whole grain bagel* *¼ cup sliced cherry tomatoes* *¼ cup diced celery* *1 ounce tuna* *½ cup milk**

Afternoon Snack	Afternoon Snack Ideas		
½ cup Vegetables ½ cup Milk*	½ cup sugar snap peas ½ cup yogurt*	½ cup veggie "matchsticks" (carrot, celery, zucchini) ½ cup milk*	½ cup tomato juice 1 string cheese*

Dinner	Dinner Ideas		
1 ounce Grains ½ cup Vegetables ½ cup Milk* 2 ounces Meat & Beans	Chicken & Potatoes *2 ounces chicken breast* *¼ cup mashed potato* *¼ cup green peas* *1 small whole wheat roll* *½ cup milk**	Spaghetti & Meatballs *½ cup cooked pasta* *¼ cup tomato sauce* *2 meatballs (2 ounces)* *½ small ear corn on the cob* *½ cup milk**	Rice & Beans with Sausage *½ cup cooked brown rice* *¼ cup black beans* *¼ cup bell pepper* *1 ounce turkey sausage* *¼ cup broccoli* *½ cup milk**

*Offer your child fat-free or low-fat milk, yogurt, and cheese.

FIGURE 5-6
MyPlate Sample Menu Meal Pattern for Preschoolers
Source: From http://www.choosemyplate.gov/downloads/PatternA1200cals.pdf.

Recognizing Characteristics of Preschool Children's Diets

Preschool-age children have developed many eating skills and are able to eat most of the foods that adults eat. They enjoy socializing at mealtimes and are eager to participate in serving themselves. They develop confidence as they master tasks such as spreading jam on a slice of bread and pouring milk from a small pitcher into a cup. As teachers promote these skills, various aspects of the preschool diet need to be considered to ensure that children receive safe and nutritious meals. The textures and consistencies of foods still play a part in the preschool diet. Appropriate scheduling of meals, attention to portion sizes, and establishing approaches that encourage children to accept new foods are all important areas of focus when feeding preschool children.

Food Textures and Consistencies

Preschool children have completed the teething process and are ready to eat most solid foods. But chewing and swallowing skills are still developing, so special attention must be given to foods that could represent a choking hazard. Foods that are difficult to chew, such as meats, still need to be cut up into small pieces to avoid choking. Round cherry tomatoes or grapes, because of their shape, present a choking risk. However, by chopping fresh tomatoes or quartering the grapes, this risk is avoided. Cutting raw vegetables, such as carrots, into thin strips makes them easier for children to bite and chew safely. Supervision at mealtime is crucial. Teachers may need to remind preschool children to stay seated when they eat to decrease the risk of choking.

Scheduling Meals and Snacks

Preschool children become accustomed to eating meals and snacks at predictable times. As with toddlers, providing three meals and three snacks at intervals of every 2 to 3 hours provides active preschoolers with a consistent energy source throughout the day. Snacks should be planned to provide important nutrients and also be low in added fat and sugars. For example, a corn, bean, and salsa dip served with whole-grain corn tortillas provides a rich assortment of nutrients compared to cookies and a fruit punch drink.

Avoiding Portion Distortion

Teachers may unknowingly offer children larger portions than desirable in an effort to make sure children have sufficient food for growth. This is problematic and potentially unhealthy. Researchers have found that children consume more calories when large portions are offered, especially as they enter the preschool years (Burger, Fisher, & Johnson, 2011; Fisher, Liu, Birch, & Rolls, 2007; Piernas & Popkin, 2011). Research suggests when children are allowed to serve themselves they choose smaller portions and may consume as much as 25% fewer calories (Orlet Fisher, Rolls, & Birch, 2003). Providing the opportunity for preschool children to serve themselves through family-style meal service, with guidance from teachers, puts a focus on their internal hunger and fullness cues that may help prevent excess calorie intake, thereby reducing the risk of obesity. Using child-sized plates and bowls also prevents portion distortion. (See Figure 5-7 for examples of how portions have increased in recent years.)

Bagel
Calorie difference: 210 calories

3-inch diameter
140 calories

6-inch diameter
350 calories

Cheeseburger
Calorie difference: 257 calories

333 calories

590 calories

Soda
Calorie difference: 165 calories

6.5 ounces
85 calories

20 ounces
250 calories

French Fries
Calorie difference: 400 calories

2.4 ounces
210 calories

6.9 ounces
610 calories

FIGURE 5-7
Portion Distortion
Source: From www.nhlbi.nih.gov/ health/public/heart/obesity/ wecan/learn-it/distortion.htm.

Creating a Child-Friendly and Healthful Diet

Creating a child-friendly diet focuses on selecting and preparing foods that encourage children to try a variety of foods. The USDA MyPlate, CACFP, and the *Dietary Guidelines for Americans, 2010* provide advice about nutrition as well as how to balance the different food groups. However, creativity is needed to select and prepare foods that children will accept while at the same time teaching them about nutrition.

To address this, teachers can focus on offering new foods at a specific meal, selecting foods from the different food groups, and paying attention to particular nutrients. For example, teachers might focus on the role of fiber in the menu. They can influence the consumption of high-fiber foods by reviewing menus, rethinking snacks, and planning cooking activities that use fiber-rich foods. They can plan ways to enhance preschoolers' acceptance of these foods by frequently exposing children to foods high in fiber. In addition, they can increase the likelihood that children will try new foods by incorporating this nutrition concept into a variety of class activities. For example:

- Observe what happens to dried beans (which are high in fiber) when they are left in water. *Concept:* Fiber is good for us because it holds water and keeps us regular.
- Study celery and onion skins through a magnifying glass to observe fiber. *Concept:* Plants provide us with fiber.

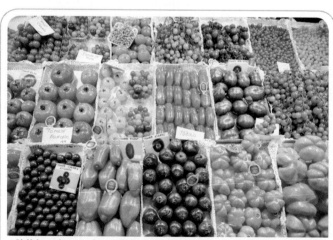

Children learn about fiber by going to the Farmer's Market and seeing different types of fruits and vegetables. They can also learn that there can be many types of the same vegetable to try and they often have different flavors.

- Taste different high-fiber breads and cereals. *Concept:* Fiber is found in grains and tastes good.
- Prepare a fruit salad of apples, pears, melons, and berries. *Concept:* Fiber is found in the skin and seeds of fruits.
- Sample a variety of different tomatoes. *Concept:* Fiber is found in vegetables and sometimes there are many types of the same vegetable to taste and try.

Understanding the Teacher's Role in Creating a Positive Mealtime Experience

A positive mealtime experience enhances children's comfort and offers a relaxed environment for eating and trying new foods. Teachers help create this positive environment by creating a comfortable space and establishing routines that children can be a part of. Mealtimes should be considerate of cultural traditions and should encourage visiting and conversation. Teachers are important role models during mealtimes.

Arranging the Mealtime Environment

A comfortable physical environment supports meal service and enhances the eating experience. Space for children to eat should be adequate without being crowded. Chairs and tables should be child sized so that children can sit comfortably and focus on eating. Silverware, cups, plates, and serving utensils should be sized to match the children's motors skills (American Dietetic Association, 2011).

The environment should be free of hazards such as food-warming units, electrical cords, and large containers of hot foods. Tables should be properly sanitized before and after use. The food served should be visually appealing and prepared in such a way as to promote children's success when eating. Decorate the setting with a changing array of posters or food-related displays that convey nutrition education messages while adding color and interest to the space.

Establishing Comfortable Routines

Teachers set the tone for mealtimes by establishing routines that convey appropriate expectations and help the meal service to flow easily and enjoyably. Children learn to predict their responsibilities and tasks, which provide them with a sense of security and comfort about mealtime. For example, children can wash their own hands, help set the table, serve themselves family style, and help with cleanup.

Considering Cultural Traditions

Mealtimes are important for nourishing children, but they also convey social and cultural values. Mealtime practices vary across different social groups in terms of how children participate, the timing of meals, the items served, and the sequence of food presentation. Children obtain cultural knowledge about food and eating by their active observation and participation in mealtime routines and socialization (Ochs & Shohet, 2006). Teachers should be aware that children's cultural traditions and experiences may differ from the practices in the classroom setting. In the United States a cultural norm at mealtimes is that everyone sits down together before anyone starts to eat. Children who start to eat before everyone is seated are reprimanded and considered impolite. This practice is reinforced by the CACFP program guidelines, which state that everyone must be seated at the table with the adult present and all food components available before eating starts (Oregon Department of Education, 2009). In China, however, older generations are often served before younger generations, and in formal social occasions children may be excluded until older adults are finished eating (Ochs & Shohet, 2006). Other strategies that can be used to support family traditions are to have healthy options on the menu that reflect the cultural preferences of children and their families (Johnson-Askew, Gordon, & Sockalingam, 2011). Preserving ethnic food traditions can have benefits to all cultural groups, and acculturation may not be a one-way exchange. For example, one study showed that

Mealtimes are good opportunities for preschool children to practice self-help and social skills. How does the mealtime environment shown in the video promote these skills?

What if . . .

you want to focus on encouraging breakfast in your program? How would you implement a child-friendly breakfast menu and teach preschoolers about the breakfast meal?

Mexican-American children are 12 times more likely to meet the recommended levels of dried bean consumption compared to Non-Hispanic children (Van Horn, 2012). This is an ethnic traditional food that has health benefits for all children when supported on the menu.

Encouraging Conversation

Another very important aspect of meals is the opportunity they provide for language development. Talking and visiting during mealtime helps children learn new vocabulary and how to listen and tell stories (Fishel, 2010). It is also an important way children acquire command of culturally relevant knowledge, and conversation contributes to the language and cognitive skills that support children's ability to learn to read and write (Snow & Beals, 2006). Teachers encourage visiting by actively listening to children, restating and elaborating on what children have said, and asking probing questions during mealtime conversations. How would you include children who are English learners in conversations while eating?

Supporting Children's Internal Cues of Hunger and Fullness

Infants and toddlers are generally in tune with their internal cues for hunger and satiety. They will eat when they are hungry and stop when they are full (Fox, Devaney, Reidy, Razafindrakoto, & Ziegler, 2006). Children are born with this innate ability. It's like an internal thermostat that regulates their intake. It turns on when they are hungry and kicks off when they are full. If the caregivers in their lives trust and respect this ability children will eat just the right amount of food. As children enter their preschool years, however, they are more easily influenced by environmental cues such as the presence of desirable food, the time of day, and the portion size (Burger et al., 2011; McConahy, Smiciklas-Wright, Mitchell, & Picciano, 2004; Rolls, Engell, & Birch, 2000). And since they are eager to please they can also be influenced by caregivers' verbal communication at mealtimes that either support or override their "thermostat" or self-regulation of food intake. When teachers use comments that validate children's expressions of hunger and fullness, they support children's sensitivity to calories consumed and reinforce their innate self-regulation skills (Ramsay et al., 2010). If they disregard children's fullness or hunger cues, problems can arise. For example, if caregivers encourage children to eat more, there is a possibility that children may eat in the absence of hunger, which can contribute to eating more calories than they need (Birch, Fisher, & Davison, 2003; Satter, 2012c). Alternatively if families or teachers pressure less compliant children to eat more food, some may "dig in their heels" leading to greater resistance to eating, mealtime battles, and possibly poor weight gain (American Dietetic Association, 2011; Satter, 2012b). Also, rigidly restricting the amount and type of food a child consumes for health reasons or because of concerns about weight can lead to the exact opposite eating behavior; overconsumption of calories (Satter, 2012c; Tan & Holub, 2011). Some researchers feel that there are parallels between how adults foster children's emotional self-regulation (helping them to tolerate frustration, curb aggressive impulses, and express emotions in socially acceptable ways) and self-regulation of food intake. For example, if a child is crying and demanding something from another child a teacher might respond by saying "Kyle you are very upset and it is OK to be angry but it's not OK for you to shout at David. Let's relax for a moment and then in your speaking voice tell me and David what's bothering you." This comment validates his feelings and lets him know an acceptable way to share his concerns and to resolve the problem. How would Kyle feel, however, if the teacher said to him, "There's no reason for you to shout and cry! No one likes a cry baby"? This belittling response demonstrates a lack of acceptance of Kyle's feelings and does not help him learn to communicate and manage this strong emotion in a constructive way. Similarly, consider the teacher who says to a child asking to be excused at the end of a meal "Dylan you can't be full. You hardly touched your lunch. Finish your meal or you can't leave the table." This teacher does not acknowledge a child's satiety. Over time, this punitive approach may diminish a child's ability to self-regulate food intake (Frankel et al., 2012). A teacher who asks "Are you full Dylan? If so, you can leave the table" helps the child to evaluate satiety before leaving the table. Teachers and caregivers who are aware of these influences may, through thoughtful conversation, role modeling, and insightful interactions, help children maintain their

What if . . .

a child in your class seems to always put more on his plate than he can eat? What strategy might you use to address this situation?

TABLE 5-2   Supporting Children's Self-Regulation of Food Intake

Phase of the meal	Comments that can override children's internal self-regulation cues (Not supportive)	Comments that support children's internal self-regulation cues (Supportive)
Beginning of the meal	Take one of each item. You need to take a carton of milk. That's not enough. You need to take more.	Are you hungry? How much would you like? Are you thirsty? Would you like some milk? There is more if you are hungry.
During the meal	Take at least three bites and then you can go outside. You eat when I tell you to eat! That's it? Drink some more milk. You want some more? You can go play once you eat your chicken and broccoli.	Are you feeling full? Is your tummy telling you it's time to eat? There is more milk in the pitcher if you are still thirsty. You can have more if you are still hungry. If you are full you can leave the table. *Conoce hablar con vocabulario nuevo*
At the end of the meal	Lunchtime is over. A clean plate is a happy plate. You want more? I think you have had enough.	Is your tummy full? Are you too full to eat the rest of the food on your plate? There is more in the bowl if you are still hungry.

Source: S. A. Ramsay, L. J. Branen, J. Fletcher, E. Price, S. L. Johnson, M. Sigman-Grant, 2010, "Are you done?" child care providers' verbal communication at mealtimes that reinforce or hinder children's internal cues of hunger and satiation, *Journal of Nutrition Education and Behavior*, 42(4), 265–270; L. A. Frankel, S. O. Hughes, T. M. O'Connor, T. G. Power, J. O. Fisher, and N. L. Hazen, 2012. Parental influences on children's self-regulation of energy intake: Insights from developmental literature on emotion regulation, *Journal of Obesity*, vol. 2012 Article ID 327259. doi:10.1155/2012/327259.

ability to recognize hunger and satiety cues and successfully self-regulate their food intake (Frankel et al., 2012). Table 5-2 provides examples of mealtime phrases that may either override or support children's self-regulation of energy intake. Recognizing children's hunger and satiety cues reinforces the division of feeding responsibilities approach which specifies that teachers and parents are responsible for the what, where, and when of feeding children while children are responsible for how much and whether to eat (Satter, 2012c).

Being a Good Role Model

Preschooler children watch and copy the behaviors of their teachers—a reminder of the importance of being a good role model. Teachers are role models for children when they sit and eat with them and consume the same foods that they are served. This encourages children to try new foods and learn about healthy eating habits (American Dietetic Association, 2011; Erinosho, Hales, McWilliams, Emunah, & Ward, 2012). An important aspect of modeling for preschool children involves helping children learn to make decisions about food by providing opportunities for children to serve themselves and choose what and how much they eat. This provides the practice children need to support good decision making during the school years when the selection and eating of food becomes less supervised. It is important for teachers to remember that forcing a child to eat a food can create food aversions. Even teachers trying to be good role models may not be able to eat all the foods that are offered because of food restrictions, allergies, previous negative experiences, or preferences. Consider this situation:

Mac, a 68-year-old retiree, volunteers 3 days a week in a Head Start classroom. He confesses to the teacher, Mindy, that he finds eating lunch with the children a challenge. Mindy is surprised because the children generally interact well with Mac during mealtimes. He quickly reassures her that it isn't the children he finds challenging, it's eating the vegetables! He says vehemently, "I just can't eat cabbage, broccoli, or cauliflower. I know I should be a better role model but my mother forced me to eat them when I was a kid and I just can't do it." Mindy reassures him that no one, including volunteers, is pressured to eat something they don't like.

Children may notice that a teacher does not eat a certain food and ask why. Food allergies are a factor of health and safety and should be explained to children as clearly as possible by saying, "My doctor has helped me to learn that my body cannot accept eating peanuts. This is only true for some people, not everyone." Food restrictions related to cultural or religious practices can be explained by stating, "In my culture we choose not to eat cheese." When teachers do not like a food that is served they might respond by saying in a neutral way, "I don't care for broccoli when it is cooked. I like it better raw." These examples are a reminder that teachers are people, too.

Being a good role model is not always easy, and teachers must learn how to navigate situations where their personal preferences challenge their ability to be the perfect role model. Sharing information simply and clearly and modeling how to try and eat as many foods as possible communicate an attitude of being open to new flavors and experiences.

Teaching Preschoolers About Nutrition

Preschoolers are full of questions and want to master new experiences. The most effective learning opportunities are those in which children are active participants. Nutrition concepts should be integrated into the daily routine. Certain themes can teach children a breadth of information about nutrition.

Learning About the Origins of Food

Preschool children may not have a clear understanding of where food comes from. When asked, they may say that food comes from the kitchen, restaurant, or grocery store. Concepts such as the origin of food, how seeds grow into plants, where milk comes from, how food gets from the farm to the table, or how grains of wheat become loaves of bread may be new. Teachers can introduce these concepts in many ways such as through field trips, school gardens, and classroom cooking activities.

Field Trips   Taking preschoolers outside the classroom extends learning to real-life situations and experiences. Field trips, because of their novelty, often create very memorable moments that enhance acquisition of knowledge. A trip to the dairy barn, milk processing plant, and grocery store shows

Preschoolers benefit from hands-on activities in which they use their senses. As you watch this **video**, think about this teacher's use of hands-on and sensory experiences in teaching children about nutrition. How does she include English Language Learners in the lesson?

Field trips extend the learning to real-life situations.

PROGRESSIVE PROGRAMS & PRACTICES

Gardens as Learning Environments

By Vanessa Thompson, Head Start of Lane County, Oregon

Head Start of Lane County is the leading birth-to-five early childhood program in Lane County, Oregon. We have rural and urban sites, from the mountains in Oakridge to Florence on the sea, and in the fertile Willamette Valley. Our mission is "Ensuring that our youngest children have a solid foundation for life." We do this by promoting school readiness, by focusing on the health, education, nutrition, and social needs of young children. Gardens are an extension of our learning environments. With some inspiration and tools, children can be practicing pre-math, science, and literacy skills while playing outside in the garden too (i.e., counting, measuring, sorting, classifying, labeling, and documenting, to name a few).

We have created low maintenance gardens at all 17 sites, despite challenges like concrete, vandalism, and weeds. When school is out of session, enthusiastic staff members have assumed garden maintenance responsibilities, such as watering and harvesting, as part of the agency's wellness program.

According to teacher Jan Olguin, "The time we play outside is very important for fitness and so is eating healthy food. When children are involved in the growing of vegetables, they eat more of them!"

Children plant year round—in the fall they plant fava beans, clover, and oats. In the spring they pull up the cover crop and plant carrots, radishes, peas, and other vegetables. Indoor planting also occurs to allow children to witness root growth, to cut the grass they grew, and marigolds to send home to plant after they grow larger. In addition, children play games at circle using fruit and vegetables, such as nutrition bingo, and the "Guess What's Missing" game, where picture cards of food on that day's menu are shown to the children. One card is then removed and the children guess what's missing.

children the sequence of steps involved in getting milk from the farm to the table. Tasting different types of milk (whole, low-fat, skim, or goat's milk) while discussing the nutrients they contain and their health benefits is meaningful because children get to experience a lesson through multiple senses.

School Gardens Planting and growing a school or classroom garden provides an opportunity for children to experience the surprise and delight of pulling a carrot out of the ground or picking and shelling a fresh pea for the first time. Children are better able to develop a clear picture of the origin of food when they plant seeds, watch them grow, tend to the plants, and then have the pleasure of eating what they have produced. See the *Progressive Programs & Practices* feature that tells how a Head Start Program shares with children the delight of growing food in classroom gardens.

Food and nutrition concepts are brought to life as children learn about plants, insects, and rain, and also learn about cooperating, persevering, and waiting for food to grow. Gardens foster learning about the cycle of life and sustainability through composting, compatible planting, and careful use of water. Whether the facility offers space for a garden plot, raised garden bed, or a garden planted in large containers at the edge of the playground, city and country dwellers alike learn about nature, the environment, and healthful nutrition through participation in school gardens.

Classroom Cooking Activities Cooking activities teach many concepts and are of great interest to children because they get to sample what they have made. Literacy is promoted as children view simply illustrated directions and sequential steps. Math skills are practiced through measuring and weighing foods. Science concepts are introduced as children see how ingredients interact when mixed together. The origin of a food item is enhanced when children experience the steps of food preparation. For example, making corn tortillas by grinding dried corn, mixing, and baking offers opportunity to study where the corn was grown and how it was dried.

Activities That Support Nutrition Education

Activities that teach children about food and nutrition are popular in the preschool classroom. They can be infused in many activities. Themes can be reinforced by offering related activities at various learning centers. Pizza is an example of a food that uses products from each food group. The activities listed below relate to pizza, a five-food-group food.

- *Dramatic play props for an Italian restaurant:* chef's hat, aprons, pizza delivery boxes, pizza pans, plastic pizza cutters, checkered tablecloth, plastic food models of pizza, spaghetti, salad, milk.
- *Math props:* a cash register and play money.
- *Literacy props:* menu, paper to record "pizza orders," telephone to receive take-out orders.
- *Creative materials to "make" pizza:* colored paper to cut and paste to make paper pizzas with a tan crust, green and red peppers, brown mushrooms, yellow pineapple and cheese, black olives.
- *Blocks to create a food group plate:* magazine with food pictures for children to cut and paste to boxes, creating boxes for each food group (grains, fruits, vegetables, dairy, meat) which can be stacked on a large circle drawn onto a butcher paper that is divided into food group categories.
- *Science exploration center with ingredients to make pizza:* whole-wheat flour, yeast, salt, and warm water, measuring cups and spoons, bowls, and pizza sauce and toppings.

> **What if . . .**
> you wanted to extend the pizza theme by planning a manipulative activity and a game that promotes large motor skills? What activities would you develop?

FEEDING SCHOOL-AGE CHILDREN

It is "Sock Hop" dance night for the children of Locust Grove School and Paul and Jose, two third-grade boys, are having a fantastic time at this 1950s-style event. The Parent–Teacher Association (PTA) has obtained donations for the cake-walk contest. Soft drinks, cotton candy, and buttered popcorn are available for all to eat. The PTA is also selling candies and gift wrap as a fundraiser. Paul has won a whole iced cake that he proudly shows to his teacher, Anne, who is supervising the dance. Anne is a member of the School Health Advisory Council, which includes the principal, teachers, and parents with interest in nutrition and wellness. Anne is exasperated by the excess of "junk food" at the dance. She tries to respond positively to Paul but feels the school's wellness goals are not always being met. She wonders how she will be able to convey her health and nutrition concerns to other staff and families. As she reminds Paul to be careful walking with that big cake, she comes up with a great idea. She will invite a member of the PTA to join the School Health Advisory Council. This will help create a connection between these groups who have the best interests of kids in common.

Primary school-age children become captains of their own ships when it comes to eating. They are now in a larger environment and experience less supervision at mealtimes. A school cafeteria is rife with activity and throwing away parts of a packed lunch or choosing not to select or eat certain components of a school lunch menu are decisions that primary school-age children can make. Here is where they get to practice all the nutrition-related decision-making skills they learned in their home and early childhood programs.

In spite of this newfound freedom, teachers continue to have important responsibilities to positively influence children's ideas and decisions about food. Teachers need to understand the nutritional needs of this age group and recognize the characteristics of diets that support growth and development. They also need to understand how to create a positive nutritional environment and know how to teach nutrition and wellness concepts.

Understanding the Nutritional Needs of School-Age Children

School-age children's rate of growth is slow and steady compared to infancy, preschool, and the adolescent years that are yet to come. Their nutrient requirements increase with their increasing size and are reflected by larger portions in the CACFP food guidance system's recommendations. Children are able to accommodate longer time periods between meals.

The school-age years are a time when children's food choices are increasingly influenced by peer groups and media advertising. Maintaining a steady rate of growth can be hampered by societal influences such as decreased opportunities for physical activity, increased time in front of TVs and computers, and increased exposure to processed, easy-to-prepare convenience foods, fast foods, and snack items that can lead to excess weight gain. Understanding these influences helps teachers understand the challenges that children face related to eating and being active.

Recognizing Characteristics of School-Age Children's Diets

School-age children have usually worked out the kinks of eating and experience fewer food-related feeding problems than toddlers and preschoolers. During this time children become more responsible for selecting their own foods. If they are not pressured, school-age children can manage their internal hunger and satiety cues sufficiently to support growth and maintain normal weight. This success relies on an environment that supports healthful eating and avoids pressures related to food acceptance. Teachers contribute to this positive environment by being alert to the timing of meals and recognizing the importance of breakfast and the school lunch program.

Timing of Meals

A pattern of three meals with three snacks per day is still advised for school-age children. In most kindergarten and first-grade classroom settings, children consume snacks in the morning at school. By the time children are in second and third grade the morning snack is discontinued. Teachers should be sensitive to the hunger cues among children in their classroom to determine whether to plan snacks as part of the morning routine. The type of snack is important. A recent survey conducted by the American Dietetic Association Foundation found that most children snack after school and found the higher the rate of snacking the lower the overall quality of the diet especially if snacks take the place of meals such as breakfast or dinner. This is because many of the snack foods consumed after school are higher in added sugar and solid fat and lower in vitamins and minerals such as cakes, cookies, pies, doughnuts, and sweetened beverages (American Dietetic Association and the American Dietetic Association Foundation, 2011). Teachers who serve nutrient-dense snacks that are low in solid fat and sugar such as fruits, vegetables, low-fat dairy foods and whole grains make a positive contribution to children's nutrient needs and act as role models for children and their families. In addition to contributing important nutrients, studies show that healthy midmorning snacks may help children concentrate, improve memory, and fill in nutrient gaps by providing them with some of the vitamins, minerals, proteins, and calories they need for growth and development (Benton & Jarvis, 2007; Martinez & Shelnutt, 2010; Muthayya et al., 2007).

The Importance of Breakfast

Some school-age children eat breakfast at home while others participate in the School Breakfast Program. Other children may skip breakfast because of hectic family lifestyles, early morning time constraints, or the family's lack of familiarity with the School Breakfast Program. It is estimated that approximately 20% of children are breakfast skippers (Deshmukh-Taskar et al., 2010). Eating breakfast boosts children's intake of key vitamins and minerals, improving the chances that children will meet their daily nutrient requirements (Food Research & Action Center, 2010; Rampersaud, 2009). Children who skip breakfast may be more at risk for obesity because, by the time they are able to eat, they are so hungry they may make poor choices and overeat (Coppinger, Jeanes, Hardwick, & Reeves, 2012; Deshmukh-Taskar et al., 2010). In addition, prolonged fasts, such as occur when the breakfast meal is skipped, may increase the insulin response to food offered later in the day, promoting fat storage and weight gain (Rampersaud, Pereira, Girard, Adams, & Metzl, 2005).

School Breakfast Program   The School Breakfast Program (SBP) is a child nutrition program administered by the federal Food and Nutrition Service that offers cash subsidies from the USDA for every meal served by participating school districts (U.S. Food and Drug Administration, 2012d).

Thanks to the Healthy Hunger-Free Kids Act and input from experts at the Institute of Medicine, standards for both the SBP and National School Lunch Program (NSLP) have recently been improved. Participating schools must provide breakfasts that align with the most recent dietary guidelines and the Dietary Reference Intakes to promote healthy meals consistent with the latest evidence-based research (U.S. Food and Drug Administration, 2012a).

The SBP is an important core child nutrition program that becomes even more valuable during difficult economic times when families may struggle to afford meals for their children. Some children are not hungry when they first wake up. The SBP gives them another opportunity to eat a nutritious meal a little later in the morning (Food Research & Action Center, 2010). The SBP and lunch program are available free of charge to children whose family income is 130% or less than the federal poverty level. A reduced-price option is also available to families whose income is between 130% and 185% of the established federal poverty level (U.S. Food and Drug Administration, 2012d). This makes the SBP accessible to many children and families.

Impact of Breakfast on Learning   Breakfast is a significant meal not only because it helps children maintain a balanced diet, but also because it can impact learning. Studies show that children who eat breakfast experience benefits such as:

- Increased math and reading scores.
- Improved speed and memory in cognitive tests (Centers for Disease Control and Prevention, 2012; Food Research & Action Center, 2010; Rampersaud, 2009).
- Improved school behavior and attentiveness, which supports the overall educational environment.

Children who do not eat breakfast are at a disadvantage academically. Teachers need to share this important information with families, and help them explore options for providing morning meals for their school-age children.

In the school-age case scenario, Anne is the teacher representative for the Health and Wellness Council at her school. She brings her concern to one of the monthly meetings. She has noticed that many children, regardless of family income level, are skipping breakfast and coming to school hungry. The school district food service manager, also a member of the committee, decides to offer the children a free breakfast once a month as a way to increase families' awareness of the School Breakfast Program. The committee decided to coordinate this with walk and bike to school events so that children can take advantage of a healthy breakfast when they arrive at school. This is an excellent way to convey the message that nutrition and physical activity are both important components of wellness.

> **What if . . .**
> you noticed a child was consistently coming to school hungry in the morning and you suspected there were financial concerns at home? How would you address this problem?

Providing School Lunch

Lunch is usually the largest meal offered when children are at school. It plays a major role in children's diets through programs such as the National School Lunch Program.

National School Lunch Program   The National School Lunch Program (NSLP) is another core child nutrition program offered by the USDA Food and Nutrition Service that provides nutritious lunches for children attending school. The Healthy, Hunger-Free Kids Act, 2010 resulted in important reform for the NSLP. For the first time in over 30 years, the USDA has had the opportunity to make significant improvements to the nutritional quality of lunches offered to children (U.S. Food and Drug Administration, 2012b). Like the SBP, to receive federal subsidies, school lunches must also align with the most recent dietary guidelines and DRIs (U.S. Food and Drug Administration, 2012a).The recent changes to the school lunch program standards and how they are now more closely aligned with the dietary guidelines is shown in Table 5-3. School lunches must provide nutritious meals that keep fat at 30% of total calories or less and are reduced in sodium, saturated fat, and *trans* fat content. Daily calories offered at lunch must fall into a 550–650 minimum and maximum range. This supports the Dietary Guidelines goal of balancing calories to manage weight and prevent obesity (National Food Service Management Institute, 2012).

TABLE 5-3	**Aligning the National School Lunch Program with the Dietary Guidelines for Americans**

Dietary Guidelines Recommendations	National School Lunch Program Requirements (Kindergarten Through Grade 5)
Maintain calorie balance over time to achieve and sustain a healthy weight	Weekly average calorie range for lunch: 550–650
Food and food components to reduce • Reduce sodium to 1,500 mg for children • Reduce saturated fat to 10% or less than 10%, cholesterol to 300 mg or less and reduce *trans* fats and calories from solid fats • Limit added sugars	Menu planning requirements • In a stepwise fashion, sodium content in school lunches will be reduced to less than or equal to 640 mg. • Weekly average of saturated fat content must be less than 10%. Food labels should indicate zero *trans* fat per serving. Milk must be fat free or 1%. • Serve unflavored milk, 100% full-strength juice may be served but cannot exceed half the fruit requirement per week. No snack-type fruit product like fruit drops, leather, or strips. Frozen fruit cannot contain added sugar.
Food and food components to increase • Increase vegetable and fruit intake • Increase whole grains • Choose a variety of lean protein foods.	Menu planning requirements • There is a weekly requirement for dark green, red/orange, legumes, starchy, and other vegetables. Vegetable and fruit requirement per lunch is increased from ½ cup to 1¼ cup. • Half the grains served must be whole grains and by 2014 all grains must be whole grains. • Lean meats, seafood, poultry, beans/peas, yogurt, tofu, nut butters, and nuts. Daily minimum and weekly ranges established.
Build healthy eating patterns • Choose foods that provide calcium, vitamin D, potassium, and dietary fiber, nutrients of concern in U.S. diets • Remember that beverages count	Meal planning requirements • Follow above mentioned meal planning requirements. • Water must be made available to children. Juice is limited to half the fruit requirement per week and must be 100% fruit juice, milk must be fat free or 1% and unflavored.

Sources: U.S. Department of Agriculture, 2012. Comparison of Current and New Regulatory Requirements under final rule Nutrition Standards in the National School Lunch and Breakfast Programs, retrieved July 27, 2012, from http://www.fns.usda.gov/cnd/governance/legislation/comparison.pdf; U.S. Department of Agriculture and U.S. Department of Health and Human Services, *Dietary Guidelines for Americans*, 7th ed. Washington DC. U.S. Government Printing Office, 2010; The University of Mississippi National Food Service Management Institute, 2012. *The New Meal Pattern Training Participant Guide*, retrieved July 27, 2012, from http://nfsmi.org/documentlibraryfiles/PDF/20120627021105.pdf; U.S. Department of Agriculture, 2012. Final Rule Nutrition Standards National School Lunch and School Breakfast Programs, http://www.fns.usda.gov/cnd/governance/legislation/dietaryspecs.pdf.

Like the School Breakfast Program, the NSLP is available free of charge to children whose family income is 130% or less than the federal poverty level and at reduced price to families whose incomes are between 130% and 185% of the established federal poverty levels. The USDA also provides a variety of other programs to support the nutritional health and wellness of school-age children:

- *Team Nutrition:* This program provides technical support and training for food service employees at school as well as nutrition education opportunities for children and teachers (U.S. Department of Agriculture Food and Nutrition Service, 2012b).

- *Healthier US School Challenge:* This program promotes and recognizes positive change in school nutrition and health environments. It provides guidelines for improving nutrition and physical activity in the school setting. When schools comply with these recommendations, they are recognized by monetary award and are certified as Bronze, Silver, Gold, or Gold of Distinction Schools (U.S. Department of Agriculture Food and Nutrition Service, 2012a). In 2010, First Lady Michelle Obama incorporated the HealthierUS School Challenge into her Let's Move initiative.

- *Let's Move:* The Let's Move program goals were established with the intent to solve the childhood obesity epidemic within a generation. Through integrated strategies this initiative aims to put children on the path to good health by providing support, resources, and action steps to families, caregivers, schools, community leaders, chefs, and health care providers. Let's Move encourages the development of environments that support healthy nutrition and physical activity choices (Let's Move, 2010). *Chefs Move to School* is part of the *Let's Move* initiative and partners chefs with schools and school personnel to help with menu ideas, culinary training, and teaching children about healthy meals (Chefs Move to Schools, 2012). See Web Resources.

- *Summer Food Service/Seamless Summer Programs:* These programs continue to provide nutritious school lunches throughout the summer break in communities where 50% or more of the children served are eligible for free or reduced meals year-round, ensuring that low-income children have access to nutritious meals (U.S. Department of Agriculture Food and Nutrition Service, 2012).

- *Farm to school programs:* The Healthy, Hunger-Free Kids Act of 2010 established this program in order to improve children's access to locally grown and produced foods via regional farmers and other producers. Grant awards provide funding to support these efforts as well as hands-on educational and experiential activities that include school gardens, field trips to local farms, and cooking classes (U.S. Food and Drug Administration Food and Nutrition Service, 2012).

Teachers make a positive impact on children's nutrition and the wellness climate of schools by endorsing and participating in initiatives such as these.

What is a Recess Before Lunch Policy?

Where students go to recess first, then eat lunch.

Montana schools are reaping the benefits:

★ Improved student behavior on the playground, in the cafeteria and the classroom.

★ Students waste less food and drink more milk. This leads to increased nutrient intake.

★ Improved cafeteria atmosphere.

★ Children are more settled and ready to learn.

Tips For Getting Started:

★ Build support within your community and school staff.

★ Realize that adapting the schedule is a work in progress.

★ Develop a hand washing routine.

★ Schedule adequate time for students to eat (at least 25-30 minutes.)

★ Decide where to store cold lunches for easy access.

★ Take care of lunch money prior to recess.

★ Practice this new routine with the students. Spend as much time in the lunchroom as possible during first few weeks.

★ Be committed, even through a trial period, to stick with it. Expect some resistance.

FIGURE 5-8

Benefits of Recess Before Lunch

Source: Used with permission from http://opi.mt.gov/Programs/ SchoolPrograms/School_Nutrition/ MTTeam.html, Montana Team Nutrition Program, Montana State University and School Nutrition Programs, Office of Public Instruction, Helena, Montana, 2012.

School Lunch: Before or After Recess?   The timing of school lunch has become an issue of importance in many schools. The predominant practice in primary schools is to eat lunch and then participate in outdoor recess. Yet research shows that children who eat lunch after recess eat better, waste less food, and behave better (Montana Team Nutrition Program, 2009; Rainville, Wolf, & Carr, 2006). Many children rush through lunch to go outside to play. For children from low-income families, this can mean missing a vital opportunity for a nutritious meal. Teachers may consider advocating for offering lunch after recess if they notice children are coming back from recess hungry (Figure 5-8).

Understanding the Teacher's Role in Creating a Quality Nutrition Environment

Perspectives about the quality of children's nutritional environment have shifted in recent years. Increased concern about the health of children in the United States due to increasing rates of childhood obesity and decreasing rates of activity have led to a greater awareness of the need to provide more healthful meals, more physical activity, and foods that are produced and purchased in more sustainable ways. This thinking has led to the development of a school wellness movement. These initiatives have been supported by a number of recently enacted programs and initiatives that place a high degree of importance on good nutrition and physical activity.

School Wellness Policy

In 2004, the Child Nutrition and WIC Reauthorization Act was signed into law. This act made it mandatory for schools to establish a school wellness policy by January 2006. With the advent of this requirement, a new mind-set was put into place related not only to the foods being served but also to

What if . . .

you noticed groups of children sitting on the bench during recess? What ideas do you have to encourage them to be more active?

the overall quality of the school environment in supporting health practices. This law has shifted the focus of food service from not only providing adequate nutrient intake but also to providing meals that promote healthful eating habits in an effort to prevent chronic diseases such as obesity, diabetes, high blood pressure, heart disease, and stroke. As a result, federally sponsored school nutrition programs have made major strides to revamp their menus to address the new health and nutrition guidance systems. The Healthy, Hunger-Free Kids Act of 2010, expands the role of wellness policies within school districts. The act encourages the participation of physical education teachers and school health personnel in the development, implementation, and review of wellness policies and requires a system of evaluation and public updates on the content and degree of compliance to goals of the wellness policies (U.S. Food and Drug Administration Food and Nutrition Service, 2011).

The school wellness policy must also address the importance of physical activity for improving the health climate of the school setting. The importance of physical education classes, recess, and before- and after-school opportunities to participate in sports activities are reemphasized in this approach. Figure 5-9 summarizes the requirements for establishing physical activity goals that must be included in the school wellness policy. Overall the message is clear: Schools must enhance the school environment to promote healthy food choices and increase levels of physical activity. Nutrition and physical activity are two sides of the same coin; without one or the other, children's health and wellness are compromised.

In addition, school wellness policies must address the provision of food that occurs outside the realm of traditional school food service. Food is served in a variety of situations in the school setting. For example, food is commonly available at after-school programs and school social and sporting events. Food is often used as a reward in the classroom setting as well. The case scenario highlighted some of the problems associated with providing foods at school events that contradict school wellness policy goals. Teachers, administrators, and parents need to develop policies that are supportive of healthy eating. The *Nutrition Note* gives an example of how teachers can avoid using food as a reward to reinforce behavior or reward academic achievement in the classroom setting. Guidelines from the Food and Nutrition Service for establishing policies that address these issues are offered in Figure 5-9 and can help teachers to envision how they can foster good nutrition in all settings of the school environment.

NUTRITION NOTE   Avoid Using Food as a Reward

Rewarding children with food to reinforce behavior or reward academic achievement is not good practice and the repercussions are not always obvious. Negative consequences of using food as a reward include the following:

- Creating value for the food being used for reward: Children begin to think "This candy must be very special if it's used by my teacher to get me to do something."
- Encouraging children to eat when they are not hungry, creating a link between food and behavior rather than food and hunger: This promotes a pattern of children rewarding or comforting themselves with food and predisposes them to obesity in the future.

- Sabotaging children's diet: Children may be less likely to eat a healthy lunch or snack.
- Promoting eating between meals and snack times: This increases the risk for obesity and dental caries.
- Exposing children to high-fat and -sugar, low-vitamin and -mineral foods: This creates a taste for these foods.

More effective and healthful ways to acknowledge positive behaviors include:

- Assigning children a leadership opportunity, such as passing out books or leading a song.
- Allowing children to choose the story at group time.
- Offering a walk with the teacher.
- Providing an extra 5 minutes of outside playtime.

FIGURE 5-9   School Wellness Sample Policy Guidelines

Physical Activity Goals

- Students are given opportunities for physical activity:
  - during the school day through PE classes.
  - daily recess periods for elementary school students.
  - the integration of physical activity into the academic curriculum.
  - through a range of before- and/or after-school programs such as intramurals, interscholastic athletics and physical activity clubs.
- Schools are required to:
  - work with the community to create ways for students to walk, bike etc. safely to and from school.
  - encourage parents and guardians to support their children's participation in physical activity, to be physically active role models, and to include physical activity in family events.
  - provide training to enable teachers, and other school staff to promote enjoyable, lifelong physical activity among students.

Nutrition Education and Promotion Goals

- Students in grades pre-K-12 receive nutrition education that is:
  - interactive and teaches the skills they need to adopt healthy eating behaviors.
  - offered in the school dining room as well as in the classroom, with coordination between the foodservice staff and teachers.
  - provides consistent nutrition messages throughout schools, classrooms, cafeterias, homes, community and media.
  - integrated into the health education or core curricula (e.g., math, science, language arts).
  - is provided by staff who have nutrition education appropriate training.
- Schools will:
  - use district health education curriculum standards and guidelines that include both nutrition and physical education.
  - link nutrition education activities with the coordinated school health program.
  - conduct nutrition education activities and promotions that involve parents, students, and the community.

Goals for All Foods and Beverages Available During the School Day

- The school district will set guidelines for foods and beverages:
  - in a la carte sales in the food service program on school campuses.
  - sold in vending machines, snack bars, school stores, and concession stands on school campuses.
  - sold as part of school-sponsored fundraising activities.
  - served at parties, celebrations, and meetings during the school day.
- The school district makes decisions on these guidelines based on nutrition goals, not on profit making.

Goals for Other School-Based Activities

- The school district provides an environment that:
  - is a clean, safe, enjoyable meal environment for students.
  - provides enough space and serving areas to ensure all students have access to school meals with minimum wait time.
  - includes drinking fountains available so that students can get water at meals and throughout the day.
  - encourages all students participate in school meals program and protect the identity of students who eat free and reduced price meals.
  - ensures an adequate time for students to enjoy eating healthy foods with friends in schools.
  - schedules recess for elementary schools before lunch so that children will come to lunch less distracted and ready to eat.
  - prohibit the use of food as a reward or punishment in schools.
  - will not deny student participation in recess or other physical activities as a form of discipline or for classroom make-up time.
- The school district ensures:
  - that all schools' fundraising efforts are supportive of healthy eating.
  - school or district-owned physical activity facilities open for use by students outside school hours.

(Continued)

FIGURE 5-9   School Wellness Sample Policy Guidelines (Continued)

- encourage parents, teachers, school administrators, students, foodservice professionals, and community members to serve as role models in practicing healthy eating and being physically active, both in school and at home.
- encourage all students to participate in school meals programs.

- that a system is in place for informing and updating the public including parents of the content and implementation of wellness policy goals.
- that a method of periodically assessing and reporting progress made in achieving the goals of the school wellness policy and that there are designated school official(s) that are responsible for ensuring wellness policy goals are achieved.

Sources: Based on Local School Wellness Policy, 2012, by USDA Food and Nutrition Service, retrieved July 28, 2011, from http://www.fns.usda.gov/tn/healthy/wellnesspolicy_requirements.html; Local School Wellness Policy Requirements, 2004, by USDA Food and Nutrition Service, retrieved July 28, 2012, from http://www.fns.usda.gov/tn/healthy/wellnesspolicy2004_requirements.html.

What if . . .

the physical education teacher in your school did not feel appropriately trained to include a child with cerebral palsy in her class? What ideas would you have to offer?

Children with Special Needs   All children are entitled to wellness. Some children with special developmental or health needs may experience challenges that make achieving wellness particularly relevant. Some may have conditions that predispose them to being underweight, whereas others will be more prone to obesity.

Teachers must communicate with families and health care providers to determine how to best meet children's goals for healthful weight. Some children may follow special diets to manage health conditions. On occasion, attending to these medical needs can compromise the overall quality of the child's diet. For example, meeting the nutritional needs for calcium in a child with a milk, egg, and soy allergy may prove difficult. Children on gluten-free diets may not be offered enough variety at school to ensure they eat enough. Teachers cannot make medical recommendations but they can encourage collaboration among families, school nutrition personnel, and health care providers to ensure that children's special nutritional needs have been appropriately addressed. Teachers can also step back from the details and determine whether routine wellness goals are being met.

Children from Culturally Diverse Backgrounds   Promoting wellness goals benefits all children but may be particularly important for children from diverse cultural backgrounds. Some ethnic groups suffer disproportionately more from chronic health conditions related to nutrition and obesity. For example, when using body mass index as an indicator, the incidence of obesity is estimated at 31.2% among American Indian/Native Alaskan children, 22% for Hispanics, 20.8% for blacks, 15.9% for whites, and 12.8% in Asians (Anderson & Whitaker, 2009). Efforts to promote wellness among all children must be addressed in culturally appropriate ways. Strategies include:

- Communicating school wellness goals, policies, and educational materials in the home languages of children attending the school.
- Incorporating healthful ethnic dishes in the school menu.
- Providing translation services at parent education seminars.

The Cafeteria as a Learning Lab

Part of the technical assistance offered to schools to support the implementation of school wellness policies is access to resources that help teachers learn about and effectively convey nutrition and health messages. This includes taking advantage of the school cafeteria as a learning lab. Resources, educational materials, and ideas to support nutrition education in the cafeteria are provided by the *Healthy Meals Resource System* (U.S. Food and Drug Administration, 2012c). Activities that use the cafeteria as a learning center include:

- Offering taste tests of new foods and recipes.
- Displaying food sculptures.
- Conducting nutrition poster contests.
- Providing cafeteria kitchen tours.
- Preparing healthful recipes.
- Inviting important guest visitors to promote good nutrition and physical activity.

Understanding the Teacher's Role in Promoting Healthful Eating Habits

Teachers continue to be an important influence in supporting good eating habits in school-age children. They enhance their influence by sharing nutrition information with families and advocating for the children in their care.

Communicating with Families

Teachers and school administrative staff have responsibilities to share nutrition and health information that supports healthful eating in the home environment. This can be accomplished by providing nutrition and health-related articles in school newsletters or on the school menus sent home with children. Schools can post the lunch menu on the school website and provide nutrient analysis for menu items. Information about carbohydrate content for children with diabetes, and alternative menu options for children with special nutritional needs or preferences can also be

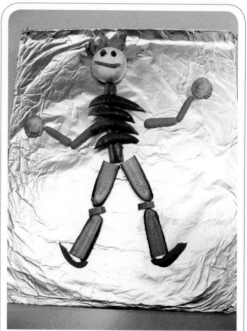

The school cafeteria becomes a learning lab when children are exposed to nutrition-related activities such as creating food sculptures.

provided. Teachers and schools can offer parent education programs on nutrition and sponsor family events that promote physical activity. These activities promote a partnership approach to helping school-age children eat healthy and be active.

Teachers as Advocates

Teachers are important advocates for healthy school environments. They promote healthful nutrition and wellness among school-age children by advocating for nutritious menus and supporting the school breakfast and lunch programs. Teachers continue to serve as role models for healthful eating and physical activity behaviors. Eating school lunch with children and participating in physically active games and events during recess send important messages to young children.

In the case scenario Anne did not criticize Paul's prize of a large cake. Instead she encouraged him to put the cake aside and join her and the other children on the dance floor where he had fun while exercising. The next day when Paul came back to school Anne asked him if his family was excited about the cake. He told her he'd had one piece of cake, but it didn't taste good. His mother gave him permission to throw it away if he wanted to and he did. At the next School Health Advisory Council meeting Anne asked members to consider devising policies specific to social events at school and it was agreed to ask a PTA member to serve on their School Health Advisory Council.

Participating in school committees that support healthy eating and physical activity provides opportunities for teachers to advocate for policies and programs that fit the developmental learning of school-age children while fostering healthy habits that contribute to children's health and wellness.

Helping Families Access Nutrition Services

Sometimes children have nutritional needs that cannot be solved easily. Families may need to obtain consultation with health care providers who have expertise in the field of nutrition. The scrutiny of children's weight by health care authorities in face of the obesity epidemic has brought the issue of overweight into the spotlight for many families (see Chapter 3 for a discussion on obesity). Families may turn to teachers with their concerns. Teachers can direct families to appropriate health care providers and support their recommendations in the early childhood setting.

anorexia nervosa
an eating disorder that is caused by a distortion of body image, characterized by the severe restriction of food intake resulting in significant, and sometimes life-threatening, weight loss

bulimia nervosa
an eating disorder that entails periods of binge eating followed by purging activities such as vomiting, using laxatives, or excessive exercising

The focus on the obesity epidemic has revealed another health care concern relating to weight: eating disorders. Eating disorders represent an extreme dysfunction in eating habits that develop gradually and eventually become an uncontrollable conflict about food consumption that can negatively impact the growth, development, and health of children (Kleinman, 2009; Mahan, Escott-Stump, & Raymond, 2012). Two commonly recognized types of eating disorders include anorexia nervosa and bulimia nervosa. **Anorexia nervosa** is caused by a distortion of body image and is characterized by the severe restriction of food intake resulting in significant weight loss. **Bulimia nervosa** entails binge eating followed by purging activities such as vomiting, using laxatives, or excessive exercising. Although eating disorders are typically considered an adolescent issue, more young children are being identified with eating disorders at earlier ages (Mahan et al., 2012; Pinhas, Morris, Crosby, & Katzman, 2011). These are psychological disorders that result in medical complications that can be life threatening (Queen Samour & King, 2012). Dieting, a society that values thinness, and mass media influences appear to be common precipitators of eating disorders (American Academy of Pediatrics, 2012; Field et al., 2008). Some of the warning signs or risk factors associated with the development of eating disorders include a history of dieting and food avoidance, a preoccupation with weight and food, body image distortion (they feel fat even though they are significantly underweight), and denial of the symptom severity (Pinhas et al., 2011). It is important for teachers to support nutritious diets to promote good health and avoid focusing on weight or appearance when discussing healthful eating with children. For example, it is appropriate to comment on healthful food choices such as, "It's great to see you drinking water instead of soda, Waverly" while on the other hand it's detrimental to state, "Maria, if you drink that soft drink you're going to get fat." It is paramount that children develop a positive body image. A moderate approach that puts more emphasis on some foods and less emphasis on others and that avoids rigid restrictions of any food teaches children how to eat well and with enjoyment.

Teaching School-Age Children About Nutrition

The school-age years are an important time for teaching children about nutrition and wellness. The 2004 Child Nutrition and WIC Reauthorization Act focuses on nutrition education by requiring school wellness policies to include a systematic approach to nutrition education. Figure 5-9 provides a summary of the components of the school wellness policy that addresses the requirements for providing nutrition education in schools.

Nutrition education needs to be integrated into all aspects of the school environment. Nutrition messages should be incorporated into math, reading, and health curricula. Teachers may be concerned that teaching nutrition will require a new curriculum and take time from the daily schedule to teach a new subject. Instead, this perspective requires a shift in mind-set (Huber, 2009). Any lesson plan can integrate physical activity and nutrition concepts. It is a matter of looking at lesson plans through a wellness lens. Refer to Figure 5-10 and consider how nutrition concepts can be interwoven into this unit on herbs and leafy greens. Many helpful resources are available such as the U.S. Department of Agriculture National Agricultural Library's Curricula and Lesson Plans website (see the Web Resources section).

Teaching Basic Nutrition Concepts

A useful curriculum for teaching basic nutrition concepts to school-age children is the USDA's ChooseMyPlate website which has nutrition tips, recipes, information, and lesson plans for the MyPlate and MyPyramid for Kids food guidance systems. The MyPlate icon was developed to replace the less user friendly MyPyramid and consequently revising and updating of nutrition lessons plans to reflect this change are under way at the USDA. The goals of the lessons are to introduce the concept of food groups and teach students how to identify the foods they eat in their diets. Understanding these basic nutrition concepts helps children to categorize foods and understand the role of food in maintaining good health.

Measuring Cup

Anna

FIGURE 5-10
Incorporating Nutrition Education into Primary-Grade Curricula

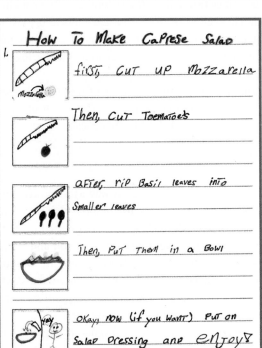

How To Make Caprese Salad

1. first CUT UP Mozzarella

Then, CuT Toematoe's

After, riP Basil leaves into smaller leaves

Then, PuT Them in a Bowl

OKay, now (if you want) PuT on salad Dressing and enjoy

Basil

Basil is used in Soap. if you have a mosquito Bite you can Rub basil on it so it gets better.

mosquito Bite

how to Transplant a herb
step 1 get a herb plant.

step 2 pinch The sides fo the plant.

step 3 Then Tank it out Of The Pot.

step 4 Then put it in a Biger Pot and Some Soil intel it Covers The roots.

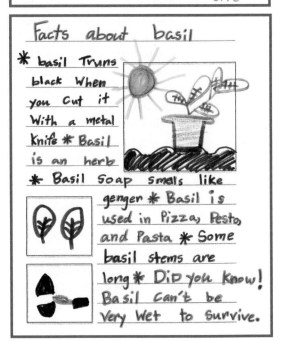

Facts about basil

* basil Truns black When you Cut it With a metal Knife * Basil is an herb
* Basil Soap smals like genger * Basil is used in Pizza, Pesto, and Pasta * Some basil stems are long * DiD you Know! Basil Can't be Very Wet to survive.

Using an Integrated Nutrition Curriculum

Many nutrition and health curricula support an integrated approach to learning. For example, the North Carolina Nutrition Education and Training Program developed an integrated curriculum called *Food for Thought* (see Web Resources). Lesson plans are available for kindergarten through grade 5 on nutrition-related topics. These lessons focus on integrating healthy eating and physical activity with math and English language arts. The lesson plans include objectives, teacher resources, and teacher input sections that help teachers organize their nutrition lessons.

Another curriculum called *Cooking with Kids* addresses goals established by a local student nutrition advisory council to improve school food (see Web Resources). The bilingual curriculum introduces the concepts of food and culture through taste testing and cooking lessons. The cafeteria participates as well by serving *Cooking with Kids* recipes throughout the school year. The cooking lessons focus on preparing recipes from five different regions of the world. Each lesson begins by using a map to identify where the recipe originated and then provides the history of the foods and how they are grown, as well as the nutritional contributions of the ingredients used in preparing the recipe.

Teachers have access to a tremendous amount of support from a variety of resources as they strive to promote nutrition and health messages in the school environment. The extent of these resources emphasizes the importance placed on nutrition issues as health and education authorities team up to help solve the obesity epidemic and promote wellness.

Teaching About Sustainable Nutrition

Sustainable nutrition is the consumption of food that is grown in such a way as to protect the environment. Sustainable nutrition practices focus on encouraging the use of foods that have had minimal processing, packaging, and transportation, thereby decreasing the energy used in their production. In addition, careful sustainable growing practices are used to protect soil and water resources. Children are increasingly concerned about the environment. Teachers have the unique role and responsibility of helping children develop the collective skills to create a sustainable community. Teaching about sustainability empowers students. It also helps them understand the connection between the careful management of the environment and its impact on the economy and the livability of their community. Teachers can integrate sustainability concepts throughout the nutrition lessons they teach and relate these ideas to the school environment as well as the community at large.

Sustainability as a core practice has been successfully adopted by a number of schools. For example, in Vermont, two pilot schools are participating in the *Sustainable Schools Project*. This foundation-funded project is a dynamic new model for school improvement and civic engagement. The program helps schools use sustainability as an integrating context for curriculum, community partnerships, and campus practices (Sustainable Schools Project, 2012).

The project supports teachers by providing assistance with curriculum consultations and training and linking teachers to community partners and projects. It also helps them identify funding sources. This type of support can greatly enhance teachers' ability to foster an in-depth and meaningful approach to sustainability.

● SUMMARY

The diets of toddlers and preschool-age children are in transition as eating skills develop. Children learn about foods through experience and repeated exposures. A varied and balanced diet is important to promote positive eating habits and to help children explore and accept a wide range of foods. Toddlers are busy acquiring new eating skills. Teachers support these efforts by understanding toddlers' nutritional requirements and knowing how to feed them to address selective eating patterns, food neophobia, and food jags as toddlers learn about eating.

Preschool-age children have mastered many new eating skills and do well with routinely scheduled meals and snacks. The division of feeding responsibility helps preschool children learn to become autonomous eaters. This is supported by teachers who understand feeding responsibilities: Children choose whether they eat and how much, while teachers are responsible for what children eat, when, and where. Teachers need to understand general nutrition concepts and be familiar with the food guidance systems that support appropriate feeding practices such as the Child and Adult Care Food Program and the USDA's MyPlate food plans for preschoolers and children.

Children in kindergarten through third grade are still growing at a steady pace and need healthy, balanced diets that meet their growth needs. Teachers need to advocate for each child to receive breakfast at home or school and to support the school lunch program. School-age children have more freedom than younger children to make their own decisions when eating in the school setting, so nutrition education, eating practices, and being physically active continue to be important wellness messages.

Teachers are also important advocates for school-age children. As advocates, teachers contribute to school wellness policies by encouraging healthful practices related to food and physical activity across the school environment and in all school-related activities. Teachers continue to be powerful role models for children of all ages. Demonstrating healthful eating and physical activity behaviors and environmental responsibility makes a positive contribution to children's future health.

KEY TERMS

Anorexia nervosa
Bulimia nervosa

Extended breast-feeding
Food jag

Food neophobia
Selective eaters

REVIEW QUESTIONS

1. Describe the nutritional needs of toddlers and discuss how to manage challenging eating issues typical of this age group.
2. Discuss the types of developmental skills that must be considered when serving foods to toddlers.
3. Discuss the transitions in the feeding relationship between caregivers and preschool-age children and how teachers can support these transitions by providing nutritious food in a positive supportive environment.
4. Using the dietary guidelines as a framework, discuss the nutritional needs of school-age children and how the National School Lunch program's new requirements support these goals.
5. Describe how to integrate nutrition, physical activity, and sustainability into planned curriculum for school-age children.

DISCUSSION STARTERS

1. Describe how you would encourage a toddler who is a selective eater and has multiple food allergies to broaden his food choices. How would you approach an older child who is average weight but doesn't eat much at lunch time?
2. Outline plans for a field trip to help preschool children learn where bread comes from. Where would you take the group? What aspects of bread production would you focus on?
3. Imagine that your elementary school has decided to embrace the concepts of sustainability. Discuss how to incorporate this into classroom routines as well as lesson plans.

PRACTICE POINTS

1. Using the CACFP guidelines for toddlers in the Appendix, plan menus for a breakfast, a lunch, and a snack.

2. Create a math activity for preschool-age children that integrates nutrition and sustainability concepts.

3. Using MyPlate and the Dietary Guidelines for Americans as resources, develop a school wellness policy for an elementary school. Would your policy suit the needs of a school that serves predominantly low-income families or families with a Hispanic or Native American cultural tradition?

WEB RESOURCES

CDC Local Wellness Policy Tools and Resources
www.cdc.gov/HealthyYouth/healthtopics/wellness.htm

Chefs Move to Schools
www.chefsmovetoschools.org/

ChooseMyPlate
www.choosemyplate.gov/

Cooking with Kids Curriculum
http://cookingwithkids.net/

Ellyn Satter's Division of the Responsibilities of Feeding
www.ellynsatter.com

Food and Nutrition Information Center: Toddler Nutrition and Health Resource List
www.nal.usda.gov/fnic/pubs/bibs/gen/toddler.pdf

Let's Move
www.letsmove.gov/

North Carolina Division of Public Health: Eat Smart Move More: Food for Thought Curriculum
www.eatsmartmovemorenc.com/FoodForThought/FoodForThought.html

School Health Guidelines to Promote Healthy Eating and Physical Activity-Recommendations and Reports
www.cdc.gov/mmwr/pdf/rr/rr6005.pdf

USDA Local School Wellness Policy
www.fns.usda.gov/tn/healthy/wellnesspolicy.html

USDA National Agricultural Library Curricula and Lesson Plans
http://fnic.nal.usda.gov/professional-and-career-resources/nutrition-education/curricula-andlesson-plans

Zero to Three
www.zerotothree.org

MyEducationLab™

Go to Topic 2 (Feeding Children) in the MyEducationLab (www.myeducationlab.com) for your course, where you can:

- Find learning outcomes for Feeding Children along with the national standards that connect to these outcomes.
- Complete Assignments and Activities that can help you more deeply understand the chapter content.
- Apply and practice your understanding of the core teaching skills identified in the chapter with the Building Teaching Skills and Dispositions learning units.

- Check your comprehension on the content covered in the chapter by going to the Study Plan in the Book Resources for your text. Here you will be able to take a chapter quiz, receive feedback on your answers, and then access Review, Practice, and Enrichment activities to enhance your understanding of chapter content.

six
Menu Planning

learning outcomes

AFTER READING THIS CHAPTER, YOU SHOULD BE ABLE TO:

1. Explain the four phases of menu planning.

2. Describe menu planning requirements and resources for child care settings.

3. List three broad program goals that support the development of healthful menus.

4. Explain the procedure for building a menu.

5. Discuss strategies for managing young children's special dietary considerations.

Jeanine places a set of old menus on her kitchen table and begins the process of planning a new set of menus for the upcoming week. Feeding 3- to 5-year-olds has its challenges. Every week she plans menus, shops, and prepares food for a group that includes one finicky eater, a child who is allergic to milk, another who is overweight, and one who for religious reasons does not eat pork. Included in the mix is a 3-year-old vegetarian whose well-intentioned mother makes many menu suggestions that Jeanine tries to accommodate even though it puts a strain on her food budget. Jeanine participates in the Child and Adult Care Food Program, a federal child nutrition program that provides funding to offset the cost of meals and snacks. This helps but completing the paperwork to meet the program's reimbursement requirements is time consuming.

Jeanine wants to plan nutritious meals but there are so many recommendations to consider she wonders where to start. She recalls how last week none of the children ate the mashed sweet potatoes she served and thought with regret of all that wonderful vitamin A going down the kitchen disposal. Such waste is also not cost effective! Jeanine realizes she needs to rethink her approach to menu planning. Her goals are to plan nutritious menus that are appealing to children, meet families' expectations, and fit her food budget constraints. At the same time she wants to streamline her menu planning process and make sure she meets the unique needs of each child in her program. She organizes her materials and begins.

The best health recommendations are useless unless they can be applied easily to daily life routines. This is true when creating routines for early childhood programs as well. For example, in the case scenario Jeanine struggles with the weekly planning of healthful menus for a small group of young children who have a wide range of nutritional needs. If you were responsible for Jeanine's program, how would you translate diet guidelines into menus that promote healthful eating and obesity prevention in young children? How would you feed this group of 3- to 5-year-old children nutritious meals that meet all of their needs? First you need a plan.

In this chapter we describe a systematic way to develop appropriate menus. We begin by discussing the resources available for developing menus that meet quality recommendations and are appealing to children. We discuss how to establish and promote broad program-wide nutrition-related wellness goals through effective menu planning. We detail a step-by-step procedure for writing and implementing menus and define strategies for purchasing, storing, and preparing foods to keep menus cost effective. All of this work is for naught, however, if children don't eat what is offered. To address this, we discuss strategies that support children as they explore new foods. We also provide tactics for adapting menus for children with special dietary needs and religious or cultural preferences. Taken together, this information will help you plan menus that support appropriate growth and development in young children.

● HEALTHFUL MENU PLANNING

The menu forms the foundation of nutritional health in the home and guides many other aspects of food management in the children's setting, such as food purchasing, storing, preparation, and service. Developing a healthful, cost-effective menu requires an understanding of nutrition goals, evidence-based nutrition practices, and food budgeting. The task of menu planning may seem daunting as these many aspects are addressed and balanced. A good menu, however, can save time and money and—as with any other skill—menu planning becomes easier with practice. Menu planning is made simpler by using a four-phase approach:

- *Phase 1:* Understand child nutrition and food program requirements.
- *Phase 2:* Establish broad program nutrition goals.
- *Phase 3:* Write menus using a step-by-step approach.
- *Phase 4:* Adapt menus to support special dietary needs or food preferences.

The first phase of menu planning includes understanding specific program requirements. Teachers need to be aware of existing nutrition, licensing, and funding directives when planning menus in early childhood settings. For example, the *Dietary Guidelines for Americans, 2010* and the Dietary Reference Intakes (DRI) are food guidance systems that form the foundation for federal food program recommendations, including the Child and Adult Care Food Program, the National School Lunch Program, and the School Breakfast Program (U.S. Department of Agriculture, Food and Nutrition Service, 2012b; Institute of Medicine, 2008; Murphy, Yaktine, Suitor, & Moats, 2011). These established requirements provide teachers direct guidance in menu planning.

The second phase of menu development focuses on determining how well menus address nutrition wellness goals established for the early childhood setting. In the opening case scenario, Jeanine is committed to offering many different fruits and vegetables in her class. Based on her familiarity with the *Dietary Guidelines for Americans, 2010*, she understands the importance of offering a wide variety of fruits and vegetables to children when they are young. She chooses *Tasting the Fruits and Vegetables We Read About* as a theme in her curriculum that focuses on learning about the foods discussed in different children's books and plans to start with *Eating the Alphabet* by Lois Ehlert.

The third phase of menu planning involves the steps associated with menu writing and implementation, putting the concepts of the previous two phases into action. This is a creative process in which teachers are encouraged to take into consideration the flavors, textures, colors, and aromas of foods when designing menus that tempt the palates of young children.

MyEducationLab™

Visit the MyEducationLab for *Nutrition, Health, and Safety for Young Children* to enhance your understanding of chapter concepts with a personalized Study Plan. You'll also have the opportunity to hone your teaching skills through video-based Assignments and Activities, as well as Building Teaching Skills and Dispositions lessons.

Finally, the fourth phase of menu development focuses on how to adapt menus to support alternative or special diets so that all children, regardless of health concerns or cultural preferences, receive a healthy balanced diet. These four phases of menu planning provide teachers with an approach to creating healthful, appealing menus that are easy to use and cost effective.

● UNDERSTANDING REQUIREMENTS FOR MENU PLANNING

Young children grow and develop quickly during the early childhood years. They rely on their families and teachers to ensure that they get the nutritious foods they need every day. Planning healthy meals that appeal to children and accommodate their needs is a key component of this responsibility. This goal is considered so important in early childhood settings that a variety of established requirements must be met for licensed programs and those funded by state or federal agencies. Failure to provide healthy menus may jeopardize children's nutritional needs and may also put the children's program or school at risk for having its license revoked or funding rescinded. Therefore, early childhood educators must:

- Understand the teacher's role in menu planning.
- Determine the types of guidelines and how to apply them to menu planning.
- Develop a system to organize these resources so that they are easily accessible.

These steps ready teachers for actual menu writing. However, teachers first must consider their specific program and the role they play in the menu planning process.

Identifying the Teacher's Role

The teacher's role in menu planning varies depending on the style of the early childhood setting. Most settings offer snacks and meals or supervise children as they eat food brought from home. Teachers who work in large child care centers and primary school settings are usually not responsible for writing menus. Such organizations usually rely on food service professionals to plan menus. In contrast, teachers in family child care settings and small child care centers are often involved in menu planning.

Although teachers may not always be directly involved in preparing menus, an understanding of the concepts and requirements for menu planning helps teachers reinforce healthful eating practices and educate children and their families about nutrition. The menu is a focal point for teaching children about foods and nutrition and can provide families with a tool for their own menu planning.

Understanding healthful menu planning has other benefits. Teachers are often the link between children with special food-related concerns and food service staff. Recognizing how special food needs impact the menu helps teachers know how to advocate for accommodations. They can make sure the correct menu items are served to all children, especially those who require special diets. If teachers plan classroom cooking activities in which the food prepared replaces a meal or snack, they need to know how to make appropriate menu substitutions. Teachers in primary schools typically have direct responsibility for planning and supervising snacks served in the kindergarten or early primary classes in which young children often get hungry between meals. All teachers benefit by being prepared to plan appetizing, nutritious menus.

Understanding Menu Planning Resources

Many resources are available to guide menu planning for young children. Some agencies, such as funding authorities, provide a list of nutritional requirements that food service in children's settings must meet to secure financial reimbursement. Health organizations offer diet advice based on evidence-based research, which is summarized in guidelines. Food safety is another factor covered by various licensing requirements. These requirements and guidelines direct the types of food choices teachers make when planning menus. A successful menu is appealing to children and in compliance with the regulations for meeting children's nutritional needs. Examples of the different types of authorities and the agencies and programs that fall under their oversight are found in Table 6-1. By adhering to the authorities' recommendations and regulations, teachers can understand the parameters that guide menu writing.

TABLE 6-1   Menu Planning Resources

Types of Authorities	Types of Agencies	Types of Programs
Health authorities	Government agencies, health care organizations	Maternal and Child Health Bureau American Public Health Association American Academy of Pediatrics U.S. Department of Agriculture and the Department of Health and Human Services • 2010 Dietary Guidelines for Americans • ChooseMyPlate.gov American Dietetic Association American Medical Association
Licensing authorities	State child care licensing agencies, Food and Drug Administration, Public Health Service, state public health divisions, county health departments	National Resource Center for Health and Safety in Child Care and Early Education Local, state, and federal regulators who inspect programs that are involved in food service using the FDA Food Code, which contains food safety rules
Accreditation authorities	National agencies that set professional standards for early childhood education programs	National Association for the Education of Young Children (NAEYC) National Association for Family Child Care (NAFCC) National Early Childhood Program Accreditation (NECPA) National After School Association (NAA)
Funding authorities	Federal or state agencies that provide funding for early childhood education programs, child nutrition programs, Administration for Children and Families, Office of Head Start	Child and Adult Care Food Program (CACFP) National School Lunch Program (NSLP) School Breakfast Program (SBP) After School Snack Program (ASSP) Federal and State Head Start and Early Head Start Programs

Sources: Based on *Caring for Our Children: National Health and Safety Performance Standards: Guidelines for Out-of-Home Child Care Programs,* 3rd ed., by American Academy of Pediatrics, American Public Health Association, and National Resource Center for Health and Safety in Child Care, 2011, Elk Grove, IL: American Academy of Pediatrics; *Food Code,* 2009 updated 2011, U.S. Department of Health and Human Services, Public Health Service and Food and Drug Administration, College Park, MD from www.fda.gov/Food/FoodSafety/RetailFoodProtection/FoodCode/FoodCode2009/default.htm; and *Health.gov,* the Office of Disease Prevention and Health Promotion, Office of the Assistant Secretary for Health, Office of the Secretary, U.S. Department of Health and Human Services, Office of Disease Prevention and Health Promotion, 2012, from health.gov.

Understanding Funded Menu Planning Systems

Three child nutrition programs provide the template for menu planning in early childhood settings: the Child and Adult Care Food Program, which guides menu planning for prekindergarten programs; the National School Lunch Program and the School Breakfast Program, which guides menu planning for schools. Each offers information on how to prepare menus that meet the federal assisted meal program prerequisites for reimbursement.

The Child and Adult Care Food Program (CACFP)

The CACFP is a federal child nutrition assistance program funded by the Food and Nutrition Service of the USDA. The CACFP aims to increase the quality and affordability of early childhood programs by providing funds for healthy meals and snacks. It also allows participating programs to provide nutritious meals to low-income children (U.S. Department of Agriculture, Food and Nutrition Service, 2011b). Participating programs are eligible to receive reimbursement for either two meals and one snack per day or one meal and two snacks. Early childhood education programs can participate in CACFP if certain eligibility criteria are met.

Eligibility for Participation   Licensed or approved nonprofit public or private child care centers, Head Start programs, family child care homes, after-school programs, and homeless shelters are eligible to participate in the CACFP. For-profit child care programs may be eligible to participate in the CACFP if 25% of the children enrolled qualify for free or reduced-price meals or subsidized child care payments (Title XX of the Social Security Act funding). All children enrolled in Head

What if . . .

a child in your program refused to drink milk? What would you do? How do you think this would impact CACFP reimbursement?

Start are eligible for free meals regardless of family income level (U.S. Department of Agriculture, Food and Nutrition Service, 2011b).

To receive CACFP reimbursement, participating programs must maintain accurate records, including menus planned, foods purchased and served, and numbers of children who ate at each meal. Teachers must record exactly how many children eat at each meal while the meal is served, which is called a point-of-service meal count. The CACFP reimbursement is paid directly to programs. Many child care programs, unlike primary school settings, do not charge separately for meals. The amount of reimbursement to programs is determined using guidelines that are based on the household income of each enrolled child. The classification of families' income as eligible for free, reduced, or paid meals, therefore, does not reflect what families are charged but rather determines the degree of reimbursement the program receives from the CACFP funding authority.

Benefits of CACFP CACFP helps offset food and food service administrative expenses, making child care more affordable. The CACFP also provides yearly training for teachers to learn about nutrition for infants and children, and also menu planning. The CACFP's system for menu planning helps teachers understand which food groups need to be served and in what amounts for each specific age group to meet children's nutritional requirements. Even programs that do not participate in the CACFP find that the CACFP guidelines provide an excellent framework for drafting menus.

meal patterns
a guide to inform menu planners which food groups, or components, need to be offered and in what amounts for breakfast, lunch, supper, and snack for infants and children

components
term used by the CACFP to describe food groups; includes milk, grains/breads, meats/meat alternates, and fruits/vegetables

CACFP Program Requirements The CACFP guides meal-by-meal menu planning with specific requirements for infants and young children. Also called **meal patterns**, these meal-by-meal breakdowns provide menu planning templates for various age categories. The meal patterns outline the food groups, or **components**, that need to be offered and the amounts of each food required to qualify as a CACFP-approved breakfast, lunch, supper, or snack. All required food components must be served at the same time. The food group components for children's meals include milk, grains/breads, meats/meat alternates, and fruits/vegetables. It is important for teachers to remember that the CACFP portions represent the minimum portion to serve. Very active children and older children usually need larger portions to satisfy their hunger. Sufficient food should be available to meet these needs. Table 6-2 illustrates CACFP meal patterns for children in three different age categories

TABLE 6-2   CACFP Meal Pattern Requirements for Children

Food Components	Ages 1–2	Ages 3–5	Ages 6–12[1]
BREAKFAST: SELECT ALL THREE COMPONENTS FOR A REIMBURSABLE MEAL			
1 milk			
fluid milk	½ cup	¾ cup	1 cup
1 fruit/vegetable			
juice,[2] fruit and/or vegetable	¼ cup	½ cup	½ cup
1 grains/bread[3]			
bread or	½ slice	½ serving	1 slice
cornbread or biscuit or roll or muffin or	½ slice	½ serving	1 serving
cold dry cereal or	¼ cup	⅓ cup	¾ cup
hot cooked cereal or	¼ cup	¼ cup	½ cup
pasta or noodles or grains	¼ cup	¼ cup	½ cup
LUNCH OR SUPPER: SELECT ALL FOUR COMPONENTS FOR A REIMBURSABLE MEAL			
1 milk			
fluid milk	½ cup	¾ cup	1 cup

(Continued)

TABLE 6-2   CACFP Meal Pattern Requirements for Children *(continued)*

Food Components	Ages 1–2	Ages 3–5	Ages 6–12[1]
2 fruits/vegetables			
juice,[2] fruit and/or vegetable	¼ cup	½ cup	¾ cup
1 grains/bread[3]			
bread or	½ slice	½ serving	1 slice
cornbread or biscuit or roll or muffin or	½ slice	½ serving	1 serving
cold dry cereal or	¼ cup	⅓ cup	¾ cup
hot cooked cereal or	¼ cup	¼ cup	½ cup
pasta or noodles or grains	¼ cup	¼ cup	½ cup
1 meat/meat alternate			
meat or poultry or fish[4] or	1 ounce	1½ ounces	2 ounces
alternate protein product or	1 ounce	1½ ounces	2 ounces
cheese or	1 ounce	1½ ounces	2 ounces
egg[5] or	½	¾	1
cooked dry beans or peas or	¼ cup	⅜ cup	½ cup
peanut or other nut or seed butters or	2 Tbsp.	3 Tbsp.	4 Tbsp.
nuts and/or seeds or	½ ounce	¾ ounce	1 ounce
yogurt[6]	4 ounces	6 ounces	8 ounces
SNACK: SELECT TWO OF THE FOUR COMPONENTS FOR A REIMBURSABLE SNACK			
1 milk			
fluid milk	½ cup	½ cup	1 cup
1 fruit/vegetable			
juice,[2] fruit and/or vegetable	½ cup	½ cup	¾ cup
1 grains/bread[3]			
bread or	½ slice	½ slice	1 slice
cornbread or biscuit or roll or muffin or	½ serving	½ serving	1 serving
cold dry cereal or	¼ cup	⅓ cup	¾ cup
hot cooked cereal or	¼ cup	¼ cup	½ cup
pasta or noodles or grains	¼ cup	¼ cup	½ cup
1 meat/meat alternate			
meat or poultry or fish[4] or	½ oz.	½ oz.	1 oz.
alternate protein product or	½ oz.	½ oz.	1 oz.
cheese or	½ oz.	½ oz.	1 oz.
egg[5] or	½	½	½
cooked dry beans or peas or	⅛ cup	⅛ cup	¼ cup
peanut or other nut or seed butters or	1 Tbsp.	1 Tbsp.	2 Tbsp.
nuts and/or seeds or	½ oz.	½ oz.	1 oz.
yogurt[6]	2 oz.	2 oz.	4 oz.

[1]Children age 12 and older may be served larger portions based on their greater food needs. They may not be served less than the minimum quantities listed in this column.

[2]Fruit or vegetable juice must be full-strength. Juice cannot be served when milk is the only other snack component.

[3]Breads and grains must be made from whole-grain or enriched meal or flour. Cereal must be whole-grain or enriched or fortified.

[4]A serving consists of the edible portion of cooked lean meat or poultry or fish.

[5]One-half egg meets the required minimum amount (one ounce or less) of meat alternate.

[6]Yogurt may be plain or flavored, unsweetened or sweetened.

Source: From USDA Food and Nutrition Service Child and Adult Care Food Program at http://www.fns.usda.gov/cnd/care/programbasics/meals/meal_patterns.htm.

(ages 1–2, 3–5, and 6–12). It's important to recognize when planning menus that the breakfast and snack pattern calls for fruit or vegetable or of both whereas at lunch there must be two different choices from the fruit/vegetable group.

Meal pattern requirements for infants are very specific. They outline the minimum amounts of breast milk or formula and other age-appropriate infant foods that must be served to meet CACFP guidelines. The infant meal patterns show teachers the progression of how foods are introduced and served to infants over the first year of life. They also offer guidelines about how much breast milk or formula infants generally consume. Table 6-3 provides guidance on infant meal patterns from birth through 11 months of age.

CACFP guidelines and recommendation are in transition. The Institute of Medicine (IOM), at the request of the USDA, asked a panel of health authorities to review CACFP meal requirements. Their report offers recommendations to ensure meals served to children are in better alignment with the *Dietary Guidelines for Americans, 2010* and the Dietary Reference Intakes (DRIs) (Murphy et al., 2011). The Healthy, Hunger-Free Kids Act of 2010, Public Law 111-296, introduced to improve nutrition and reduce childhood obesity, includes requirements that implement some of the IOM recommendations. For example, currently skim or low-fat milk (1%) must be served to children once they reach age 2 and water must be readily accessible for children to drink during the day and especially at meal times. Other changes to meal patterns that place a focus on offering more whole grains; dark green, orange, and red vegetables; and less sodium are forthcoming (U.S. Department of Agriculture, Food and Nutrition Service, 2011a). The CACFP information from the USDA will be updated during this transition process. The most current information can be found at www.fns.usda.gov/cnd/.

TABLE 6-3   CACFP Meal Pattern Requirements for Infants

Birth Through 3 Months	4 Through 7 Months	8 Through 11 Months
Breakfast		
4–6 fluid ounces of formula[1] or breast milk[2,3]	4–8 fluid ounces of formula[1] or breast milk[2,3]; 0–3 tablespoons of infant cereal[1,4]	6–8 fluid ounces of formula[1] or breast milk[2,3]; and 2–4 tablespoons of infant cereal[1]; and 1–4 tablespoons of fruit or vegetable or both
Lunch or Supper		
4–6 fluid ounces of formula[1] or breast milk[2,3]	4–8 fluid ounces of formula[1] or breast milk[2,3]; 0–3 tablespoons of infant cereal[1,4]; and 0–3 tablespoons of fruit or vegetable or both[4]	6–8 fluid ounces of formula[1] or breast milk[2,3]; 2–4 tablespoons of infant cereal[1]; and/or 1–4 tablespoons of meat, fish, poultry, egg yolk, cooked dry beans or peas; or ½–2 ounces of cheese; or 1–4 ounces (volume) of cottage cheese; or 1–4 ounces (weight) of cheese food or cheese spread; and 1–4 tablespoons of fruit or vegetable or both
Snack		
4–6 fluid ounces of formula[1] or breast milk[2,3]	4–6 fluid ounces of formula[1] or breast milk[2,3]	2–4 fluid ounces of formula[1] or breast milk[2,3], or fruit juice[5]; and 0–½ bread[4,6] or 0–2 crackers[4,6]

[1]Infant formula and dry infant cereal must be iron-fortified.
[2]Breast milk or formula, or portions of both, may be served; however, it is recommended that breast milk be served in place of formula from birth through 11 months.
[3]For some breastfed infants who regularly consume less than the minimum amount of breast milk per feeding, a serving of less than the minimum amount of breast milk may be offered, with additional breast milk offered if the infant is still hungry.
[4]A serving of this component is required when the infant is developmentally ready to accept it.
[5]Fruit juice must be full strength.
[6]A serving of this component must be made from whole-grain or enriched meal or flour.

Source: From USDA Food and Nutrition Service Child and Adult Care Food Program at http://www.fns.usda.gov/cnd/care/programbasics/meals/meal_patterns.htm.

Teachers should easily recognize the value of these meal service patterns as they plan menus. Planning healthy menus is not left up to chance in programs that use CACFP guidelines.

CACFP Creditable Foods High-quality food is a priority of the CACFP. For example, CACFP guidelines recommend that foods from the grain group be either enriched or whole grains. If a food does not meet CACFP specifications it is not considered a **creditable food**. A creditable food is one that meets CACFP guidelines and is eligible for reimbursement. A **noncreditable food** does not meet the CACFP's quality standards and is not eligible for reimbursement. An example of a noncreditable food in the milk group is yogurt, which does not meet the standard of identity for fluid milk. Yogurt can however be credited as a food choice in the meat/meat alternate group. Some but not all soy milks have a composition that meets nutrient standards established by the USDA that allows them to be creditable as a milk substitute. Incentives to use both creditable foods and accurate menu planning tactics are strong. When programs use noncreditable food items in place of creditable foods or make mistakes in menu planning, they cannot claim reimbursement for that meal. Figure 6-1 shows two lunch meals. The meal on the right does not meet CACFP standards because juice was served at lunch instead of the required milk.

FIGURE 6-1
CACFP Standards Require That Milk Be Provided with Breakfast and Lunch

creditable food
food that meets CACFP guidelines and is eligible for reimbursement

noncreditable food
food that does not meet quality standards established by the CACFP and when served in place of a creditable component makes a meal or snack ineligible for reimbursement

The National School Lunch Program (NSLP) and School Breakfast Program (SBP)

The NSLP and SBP are USDA programs designed to improve children's health and well-being by providing access to nutritious meals. All public and private schools and residential child care institutions are eligible to participate in the NSLP program if they agree to offer a nonprofit school lunch program that meets all federal regulations and is available to all children (U.S. Department of Agriculture, Food and Nutrition Service, 2012b). The NSLP and SBP are managed by each state's education authority, which establishes agreements with schools, institutions, and other facilities.

Primary grade school teachers are generally unlikely to plan menus. However, they should be aware of the type of menu planning system in place at their schools so that they can support goals that promote the development of positive eating habits. Teachers who support the NSLP and SBP help create a healthful school nutrition environment and enhance opportunities for nutrition education.

Like the CACFP, the NSLP and SBP are in transition. The new nutrition standards were revealed in January 2012 and are designed to more closely align with the *Dietary Guidelines for Americans, 2010* and the DRIs. The nutrition guidelines for the NSLP changed the fall of 2012. **Nutrient targets** have been established by the Institute of Medicine and provide the scientific basis for developing the new meal standards. **Meal requirements** include both standards for menu planning (what is *offered* to students) and for meal components that must be selected by students. Like the CACFP, the NSLP and SBP have goals that are met by a food-based approach that includes major food groups and subgroups. The new standards include recommendations for both daily and weekly requirements and also provide the establishment of minimum and maximum calorie ranges for meals offered to children based on different age group categories. Additional goals include reducing sodium content of meals; keeping saturated fat content of meals to less than 10%; offering more dark green, orange, and red vegetables; and requiring labeled foods to contain zero grams of *trans* fats per serving (Stallings, Suitor, & Taylor, 2010). Table 6-4 provides an example of new school lunch guidelines for the kindergarten through grade 5 age group. An illustration of how these beneficial changes impact the quality of food components offered on the school lunch menu can be seen in Figure 6-2.

nutrient targets
new requirements for the amounts of nutrients and dietary components to be provided by school meals that are offered to children, and they are the scientific basis for developing meal standards

meal requirements
a set of standards for menu planning that aims for consistency with dietary guidelines and provides standards for meals as selected by the student

TABLE 6-4   Sample of the New National School Lunch Standards

Recommended as Offered Meal Standards for Lunch (Grades K–5)		
	Meal Pattern Amount of Foods	
	Per Week	**Minimum per day**
Fruits (cups)	2.5	0.5
Vegetables (cups)	3.75	0.75
Dark green	0.5	
Orange/red	0.75	
Legumes	0.5	
Starchy vegetables	0.5	
Other	0.5	
Additional vegetables to reach total	1	
Grains, half must be whole grain-rich (oz. eq)	8–9	At least one 1 oz. eq
Meats, beans, cheese, yogurt (oz. eq)	8–10	At least one 1 oz. eq
Fat-free milk or low-fat milk (cups)	5	1
Daily Amount Based on the Average for a 5-Day Week		
Min-max calories	550–650	
Percent saturated fat	<10%	
Sodium (mg) by year 2020	≤640	
Trans fat	Nutrition label must specify zero grams of trans fat per serving	

Source: *Final Rule: Nutrition Standards in the National School Lunch and School Breakfast Program.* U.S. Department of Agriculture, Food and Nutrition Service, 2012a, from http://www.fns.usda.gov/cnd/Governance/Legislation/nutritionstandards.htm.

FIGURE 6-2

School Lunch Menus Before and After the New Nutrition Standards

Source: U.S. Department of Agriculture Food and Nutrition Service, 2012, http://www.fns.usda.gov/cnd/healthierschoolday/pdf/HHFKA_BeforeAfterMealsChart.pdf.

Other ways that teachers can influence the quality of meals served to children is to participate in school district wellness committees or school health advisory councils where input on menus, wellness policies, and opportunities for nutrition education are sought. These opportunities bring teachers, families, and school food service personnel together to discuss health and nutrition issues, including goals for menu planning. Supporting healthful practices is everyone's responsibility.

Head Start/Early Head Start Programs

Head Start is another federal agency that provides funding conditional on meeting specific nutrition standards. Head Start is administered by the Office of Head Start (OHS), Administration for Children and Families (ACF), and the U.S. Department of Health and Human Services (U.S. Department of Health and Human Services, Administration for Children and Families, 2011). Head Start and Early Head Start grantees are guided by the **Head Start Performance Standards**, which outline performance measures for all aspects of the program. Teachers who work with menus in the Head Start setting must become familiar not only with CACFP guidelines, but also with the Head Start standards for menu planning. A section in the Head Start Performance Standards entitled *Child Nutrition* outlines the standards that relate to program nutrition services (Head Start Performance Standards Title 45, Volume 4, U.S.C. Section 1304.23, 1998). A few of these are summarized below:

Head Start Performance Standards
federal regulatory guidelines that provide oversight on all aspects of Head Start and Early Head Start program administration

- All children's nutritional needs must be met, including those with special diets and children with disabilities.
- Programs must serve foods that broaden a child's food experience, including cultural and ethnic foods.
- One third of a child's daily nutritional needs must be met in part-day programs and one half to two thirds in full-day programs.
- Programs must participate in the CACFP and portion sizes must meet CACFP guidelines.
- Foods served must be high in nutrients and low in fat, sugar, and salt.

These Head Start Performance Standards support CACFP requirements. They also help programs to provide meals that are more closely aligned to the *Dietary Guidelines for Americans, 2010*.

USDA Schools/Child Nutrition Commodity Program

The Food and Nutrition Service of the USDA manages the distribution of **commodity foods** through the USDA Schools/Child Nutrition Commodity Program (U.S. Department of Agriculture, Food and Nutrition Service, 2011d). Commodity food, also called USDA foods, are foods that the federal government has legal authority to purchase from American farmers and distribute to support farm prices. The food is made available to state agencies and Indian Tribal Organizations and is distributed through a variety of venues including the CACFP. Early childhood programs participating in CACFP are eligible to receive these foods. Commodity foods typically include some fresh but predominantly canned and frozen fruits, fruit juices, and vegetables, frozen or canned meats, poultry and tuna fish, cheese, dry and canned beans, peanut butter, vegetable oils, rice, pasta products, flour, cornmeal, and oats (U.S. Department of Agriculture, Food and Nutrition Service, 2011d). Programs using commodity foods should have a list of these foods on hand when planning menus.

commodity foods
foods that the federal government has legal authority to purchase from American farmers and distribute to support farm prices. These foods are used to support nutrition assistance programs including child nutrition programs

Organizing Resources

Remembering the many details of menu planning is not necessary if resources are well organized and accessible. In the opening case scenario, Jeanine recognizes the need to improve her approach to writing menus. She starts by compiling recommendations and regulations for meal service and menu planning in a notebook. She also creates a computer "folder" to organize her electronic resources. She finds it helpful to review and refer to these resources while she drafts her menus. Jeanine's resource files include information that pertains to her family child care program and to the age group she serves:

- An electronic bookmark to the USDA's MyPlate (U.S. Department of Agriculture, 2011a).
- A copy of the *Dietary Guidelines for Americans, 2010* (U.S. Department of Health and Human Services & U.S. Department of Agriculture, 2011).
- Position paper of the American Dietetic Association, *Benchmarks for Nutrition Programs in Child Care Settings* (American Dietetic Association, 2011b).
- State licensing guidelines for food preparation and service.
- CACFP guidelines (U.S. Department of Agriculture, Food and Nutrition Service, 2011b) and handbook: Nutrition & Wellness Tips for Young Children: Provider Handbook for the Child and Adult Care Food Program, 2012 (see web resources).
- A link to the Special Supplemental Nutrition Program for Women, Infants, and Children (WIC) Works Resource System, which provides guidelines for feeding children from infant to age 5, information on ethnic foods, and food preparation advice including thrifty recipes (WIC Works Resource Team, 2010).

Teachers who are drafting menus for their Head Start program might also include this item in their notebooks:

- Head Start Performance Standards for Nutrition (U.S. Department of Health and Human Services Food and Nutrition Service & Administration for Children and Families, 2009).

A program serving infants and toddlers benefits by including:

- The USDA's Infant Nutrition and Feeding: A Guide for Use in the WIC and CSF Programs (U.S. Department of Agriculture, 2009).

A teacher in a large child care center involved in menu planning will also need:

- A copy of the National Association for the Education of Young Children (NAEYC) Health Standards 5A (*Promoting and Protecting Children's Health and Controlling Infectious Disease*) and 5B (*Ensuring Children's Nutritional Well-Being*), which provide standards for feeding infants, food safety, timing of meals and snacks, and guidance on foods that cause choking (National Association for the Education of Young Children, 2012).
- The contact number for a registered dietitian who can evaluate menus if the program does not participate in the CACFP.

In her menu planning, Jeanine uses the USDA's Choose MyPlate website as a resource to learn more about nutrition goals and healthy food choices within the different food groups. She determines that the MyPlate website provides a Healthy Eating for Preschoolers Daily Food Plan for Preschoolers (Figure 6-3) (U.S. Department of Agriculture, 2012). She reviews the food plan to determine age-appropriate daily amounts of food from each food group recommended for the children her program serves. She then turns to the CACFP meal patterns to give her the framework for putting MyPlate recommendations into practice during the time frame children are in her care. She reviews the CACFP meal patterns to learn which food group components need to be served at breakfast and lunch. She also learns that variety is important especially when serving fruits and vegetables. She understands that non-fat or low-fat milk is a requirement for children age 2 and over. She reviews guidelines that explain how to determine which grains qualify as whole grains so that she can ensure that the grain choices she offers meets this recommendation (Murphy et al., 2011).

She learns from the American Dietetic Association's position paper titled *Benchmarks for Nutrition Programs in Child Care Settings*, which references Head Start Performance Standards, that children in part-day programs (4 to 7 hours) should be served meals that meet one third of their daily nutrient needs, while those in full-day programs (8 hours or more) should receive at least half to two thirds of their daily requirements (American Dietetic Association, 2011b; U.S.

What if . . .

you were not responsible for menu planning in your preschool program and noticed that the portions provided were often very large? What might be your concerns? What resources would you use to understand appropriate portion sizes for the children you serve?

Healthy Eating for Preschoolers

Daily Food Plan

Use this Plan as a general guide.

- These food plans are based on average needs. Do not be concerned if your child does not eat the exact amounts suggested. Your child may need more or less than average. For example, food needs increase during growth spurts.

- Children's appetites vary from day to day. Some days they may eat less than these amounts; other days they may want more. Offer these amounts and let your child decide how much to eat.

Food group	2 year olds	3 year olds	4 and 5 year olds	What counts as:
Fruits	1 cup	1–1½ cups	1–1½ cups	**½ cup of fruit?** ½ cup mashed, sliced, or chopped fruit ½ cup 100% fruit juice ½ medium banana 4-5 large strawberries
Vegetables	1 cup	1½ cups	1½–2 cups	**½ cup of veggies?** ½ cup mashed, sliced, or chopped vegetables 1 cup raw leafy greens ½ cup vegetable juice 1 small ear of corn
Grains Make half your grains whole	3 ounces	4–5 ounces	4–5 ounces	**1 ounce of grains?** 1 slice bread 1 cup ready-to-eat cereal flakes ½ cup cooked rice or pasta 1 tortilla (6" across)
Dairy Protein Foods	2 ounces	3–4 ounces	3–5 ounces	**1 ounce of protein foods?** 1 ounce cooked meat, poultry, or seafood 1 egg 1 Tablespoon peanut butter ¼ cup cooked beans or peas (kidney, pinto, lentils)
Choose low-fat or fat-free	2 cups	2½ cups	2½ cups	**½ cup of dairy?** ½ cup milk 4 ounces yogurt ¾ ounce cheese 1 string cheese

FIGURE 6-3
Healthy Eating for Preschoolers Daily Food Plan
Source: *Health and Nutrition Information for Preschoolers*. USDA ChooseMyPlate.gov, 2012. http://www.choosemyplate.gov/preschoolers/HealthyEatingForPreschoolers-MiniPoster.pdf.

Department of Health and Human Services Food and Nutrition Service, & Administration for Children and Families, 2008). She also notes that she does a good job of meeting other recommended benchmarks in her child care program such as using low-fat cheese and avoiding foods that are high in sugar or salt content. Jeanine decides to check the National Resource Center for Health and Safety in Child Care and Early Education website to refresh her memory on national and state health and safety performance standards. She is reminded that in her home state she is required to participate in a food safety course to obtain a food handler's card and that her menus should follow CACFP guidelines.

Having these resources easily accessible helps teachers like Jeanine streamline their menu writing, create a menu that successfully meets the nutrient needs of young children, and support the reimbursement requirements for federally funded child nutrition programs.

● ESTABLISHING PROGRAM NUTRITION GOALS

Menu planning and the selection and service of foods reflect the early childhood setting's goals for wellness and nutrition. Using nutrition as a way to improve health and prevent illness and disease is a common theme. When endorsed by teachers and supported by the total program environment, this goal can promote healthful lifestyles and dietary changes that are sustainable into adulthood. Healthful nutrition is especially important during early childhood when lifelong eating and physical activity patterns are being established. Teachers are uniquely positioned to have a significant impact on beneficial eating habits in young children that support wellness and health.

Promoting Healthful Eating Habits Through Menu Planning

Early childhood education programs influence many aspects of children's lives. For example, research demonstrates the effectiveness of the early childhood setting as a means of preventing and achieving improvement in overweight and obesity in children (Hesketh & Campbell, 2010; Llargues et al., 2011; Vos & Welsh, 2010). This impact is considered so important that the National Resource Center for Health and Safety in Child Care and Early Education created a new set of national standards, *Preventing Childhood Obesity in Early Care and Education* (2010), describing evidence-based best practices that focus on obesity prevention for early care and education (National Resource Center for Health and Safety in Child Care and Early Education, 2010). In addition, at the request of U.S. Department of Health and Human Services, this Center reviewed state child care regulations for obesity prevention content in an effort to strengthen regulations nationally (National Resource Center for Health and Safety in Child Care and Early Education, University of Colorado Denver, 2011). Teachers who plan menus need to carefully consider not only the nutrient requirements of meals but also the dietary practices that protect children's health especially as it relates to obesity prevention.

Health authorities have been considering these issues and look to research to establish evidence-based recommendations. Evidence-based practices shift the basis of decision making from historical practices to those supported by the best available science. A good example of evidence-based guidelines and a starting point for teachers to consider when establishing program nutrition wellness goals is the *Dietary Guidelines for Americans, 2010*. Using the dietary guidelines as a guide, there are concrete things programs can do to promote healthful eating in the early childhood classroom.

Offering Children More Fruits and Vegetables

Fruits and vegetables are rich in vitamins, minerals, and fiber and, with a few exceptions, are low in fat and always cholesterol free. Consequently, eating fruits and vegetables can lead to lowered total fat, saturated fat, and cholesterol intake and a higher intake of nutrients protective against heart disease, high blood pressure, obesity, and certain cancers (American Dietetic Association, 2004; Annema, Heyworth, McNaughton, Iacopetta, & Fritschi, 2011; Flock & Kris-Etherton, 2011; Liu, 2003; U.S. Department of Agriculture Nutrition Evidence Library, 2010). Fruits and vegetables are also rich in vitamin A, which helps maintain and protect healthy vision (Harvard School of Public Health, 2011b). Teachers who identify the goal of adding more fruits and vegetables to menus sometimes face a dilemma. How do they get children to eat what's good for them?

Enticing Children to Eat More Fruits and Vegetables   The flavor of foods is the primary basis by which young children decide whether or not to eat or drink something (Harvard School of Public Health, 2011b). Children respond to certain tastes differently than adults because their sensory system for taste is not yet fully developed. Infants and young children tend to like sweet-tasting foods more than adults and bitter-tasting foods less (Beauchamp & Mennella, 2011; Harvard School of Public Health, 2011b). Infants, however, may not be as discriminating between tastes and are

more accepting of the introduction of new foods than toddlers or preschoolers (Schwartz, Chabanet, Lange, Issanchou, & Nicklaus, 2011). There may in fact be a time-sensitive period of flavor learning in which infants and young children, if exposed frequently to new foods such as fruits and vegetables, begin to eat more of them and learn to like their flavors (Beauchamp & Mennella, 2011; Forestell & Mennella, 2007). This information can be used to advantage. Teachers and families should be partners in making sure infants are exposed to a wide variety of fruits and vegetables when they are young to create an acceptance that will last into older years (Guidetti & Cavazza, 2008).

Neophobia, or the fear of new foods, peaks in children between 2 to 6 years of age (Birch & Anzman-Frasca, 2011). In response to this reluctance teachers and families may begin to limit the types of foods offered to those that children like, as a way to ensure that children get enough to eat. Young children, however, learn through experience. By offering foods repeatedly, children will learn over time to accept a new food (Birch & Anzman-Frasca, 2011; Satter, 2011). It is always important to remember to offer different foods, but not force children to eat them. Forcing causes stress and tension around mealtime and may end up creating food aversions (Satter, 2011).

Menu Planning Strategies to Include More Fruits and Vegetables Teachers can use a variety of strategies in menu planning to increase children's interest in fruits and vegetables. Consider these tactics:

- Plan to serve fruits and vegetables with flavors, textures, and smells that appeal to children. For example, overcooked broccoli has a less desirable texture and aroma than raw broccoli.
- Serve foods that are visually appealing. Offer salads with lots of color instead of plain iceberg lettuce.
- Offer various forms of fruits and vegetables. Fresh, frozen, canned, and dry varieties all count toward good nutrition.
- Plan menu items into which shredded or pureed vegetables or fruits can be added such as pizza, spaghetti, chili, meatloaf, quick breads, and muffins.
- Serve foods using different methods of preparation such as shredded carrot raisin salad, steamed carrots, mashed carrots, carrot soup, or carrot muffins.
- Select menu items that combine various vegetables or fruits such as soups, stir-fried vegetables, or fruit salads.
- Introduce a new fruit or vegetable frequently, and serve it along with familiar foods. Realize that it can take up to 15 to 20 exposures before children accept new foods (Satter, 2011).
- Use classroom cooking activities to introduce children to new fruits and vegetables.
- Add dips that have nutritious qualities to the menus, such as sliced vegetables with salsa and sliced fruit with yogurt, to increase the likelihood that children will try them.
- Focus on nutrition by offering variety when planning menus.

  ✓ Daily, offer a fruit or vegetable rich in vitamin C (citrus fruits, kiwis, strawberries, mangoes, red peppers, and tomatoes).

  ✓ Include dark green, orange, and red vegetables on the menu often (broccoli, spinach, kale, collard green, carrots, sweet potatoes, winter squashes, tomatoes, and red peppers).

  ✓ Include more protein and fiber-rich legumes on the menu (such as black beans, garbanzo beans, kidney beans, lentils, pinto beans, soy beans, and split peas).

Whole foods are foods that have undergone minimal food processing and have no ingredients added to them that detract from a healthful diet.

These strategies help set the stage for getting children to try more fruits and vegetables. There is one tactic, however, that is easy and costs next to nothing to implement. *Teachers and families simply need to eat their fruits and vegetables at mealtimes, too.* Modeling, especially with enthusiasm, is a very effective strategy for improving children's willingness to try new foods (American Dietetic Association, 2011b; Guidetti & Cavazza, 2008).

Encouraging Whole Basic Foods

whole basic foods
foods with only one ingredient such as milk; fresh fruits and vegetables, including dried beans, peas, and lentils; whole grains; nuts; eggs; fresh meats; poultry; and fish. Whole foods have undergone minimal food processing

Whole basic foods are foods that are unprocessed or minimally processed and usually contain only one ingredient. Milk, fresh fruits and vegetables including dried beans, peas, and lentils, whole grains, nuts, fresh meats, poultry, and fish are all basic nutrient-rich foods to which no salt, sugar, or fat has been added (Sizer & Whitney, 2011). Whole foods have no ingredients added to them that detract from a healthful diet. For example, consider a fresh potato. It is naturally rich in potassium, vitamin C, and fiber. When it is turned into a potato chip, it loses its vitamin C and fiber and gains excess sodium and fat. Compared to a fresh potato, the potato chip is a less-than-desirable food choice.

whole grains
grains that contain all parts of the grain kernel including the bran, endosperm, and germ after the grain is milled

Select Whole Foods Rich in Dietary Fiber Whole foods, such as whole grains, legumes, fresh fruits, and vegetables are rich in nutrients including dietary fiber. Fiber has health-promoting qualities and reduces the risk of some chronic diseases. For example, certain types of fiber are effective at preventing constipation while other types of fiber help reduce cholesterol levels. **Whole grains** are rich in essential vitamins, minerals, and fiber. They also contain high levels of antioxidants, which are helpful in reducing the risk for cancer, heart disease, and other diseases (Carlsen et al., 2010; Harvard School of Public Health, 2011a). Whole grains are foods that contain all parts of the grain kernel including the bran, endosperm, and germ, even after the grain is milled (Figure 6-4). In contrast,

refined grains
grains that have the bran and germ removed during the milling process, which reduces the fiber and nutrient content

refined grains have had the bran and germ removed in the milling process, which reduces the fiber and nutrient content. Examples of refined grain products include white bread, pasta, and white rice.

A good rule of thumb to remember when purchasing whole-grain products is to look for items that list the "whole-grain" ingredient first on the ingredient list or that state they are 100% whole grain. A grain food that contains the FDA-approved health claim, "Diets rich in whole grain foods and other plant foods and low in total fat, saturated fat, and cholesterol may reduce the risk of heart disease and some cancers" on the label is another indication that the product is a significant source of whole grain and qualifies the grain as an acceptable choice for Child Nutrition Programs like the CACFP (Murphy et al., 2011). The *Dietary Guidelines for Americans, 2010* advises that at least half the total number of recommended servings of grains consumed should be whole grains (U.S. Department of Health and Human Services and U.S. Department of Agriculture, 2011). The NSLP new requirements have set these recommendations as minimal requirements for menu planning starting in 2012 with a transition to all whole grains by 2014 (U.S. Department of Agriculture, Food and Nutrition Service, 2012a).

Whole grain kernel

Bran
"Outer shell" protects seed
Fiber, B vitamins, trace minerals

Endosperm
Provides energy
Carbohydrates, protein

Germ
Nourishment for the seed
Antioxidants, vitamin E, B-vitamins

FIGURE 6-4

Components of a Whole Grain
Source: HealthierUS School Challenge Whole Grains Resource guide http://www.fns.usda.gov/tn/healthierus/HUSSCkit_pp25-35.pdf.

Choose Whole Foods That Are Naturally Low in Sodium Eating too many foods high in salt or sodium can be a risk factor for high blood pressure. Highly processed foods are often high in sodium content. For example, a half cup of canned chicken noodle soup has between 800 and 1,100 mg of sodium per cup. The *Dietary Guidelines for Americans, 2010* recommends Americans, including children, consume 2,300 mg of sodium or less per day while those individuals who are over 51, of African American descent, or who have high blood pressure, diabetes, or chronic kidney disease should limit their sodium to 1,500 mg per day (U.S. Department of Health and Human Services, & U.S. Department of Agriculture, 2011). Selecting fresh fruits and vegetables, fresh meat, fish, and poultry instead of cured options and limiting high-sodium condiments such as soy sauce, salad dressings, and pickles are all good strategies for planning healthful menus.

Menu Planning Strategies to Include Whole Foods Adding whole foods to program menus may require revising current menus to minimize highly processed foods. Strategies for adding more whole foods to menus include the following:

Plan to use more whole-grain foods such as:

- Whole-grain breads, English muffins, bagels, and whole-grain corn tortillas.
- Side dishes like brown rice, bulgur, and whole-wheat pasta.
- Whole-grain cooked and cold cereals for breakfast and snacks.

- Serve fresh, plain frozen vegetables or low-sodium canned vegetables in place of regular canned vegetables or frozen vegetables with sauces.
- Serve fresh fruit in place of juice or canned fruits.
- Serve fresh or frozen plain meat, fish, or poultry instead of processed chicken patties, fish sticks, or highly processed cold cuts like salami or bologna.
- Serve homemade soups to which barley, brown rice, or legumes are added.
- Serve vegetarian meals such as salads with kidney beans, vegetarian chili, frijoles with whole grain tortillas, or hummus with whole-grain pita bread.

The goal of adding whole foods to the menu is to increase options that appeal to children's taste and also fit into the program's budget and the kitchen's food preparation capacity.

What if . . .
you wanted to introduce whole foods into children's diets? What whole foods might appeal to young children?

Limiting Solid Fats and Extra Fats When Planning Menus

Young children are growing and have high calorie needs. Fats can be part of a healthful diet when used to meet these needs. However, fats affect health in many ways. For example, individuals who eat a diet high in solid fats, including saturated fats and *trans* fats, may increase their risk for heart disease. Eating too many foods to which fats have been added, such as fried foods or foods prepared with heavy sauces or gravies, makes it challenging to avoid excess calorie consumption. Too many calories can lead to an unhealthy rate of weight gain (U.S. Department of Health and Human Services & U.S. Department of Agriculture, 2011).

With some thoughtful consideration the menu can become an ideal tool for keeping the dietary fat content of meals within recommended ranges. The menu must be planned to achieve a balance between low-fat and high-fat foods. In addition, the menu should substitute the more healthful unsaturated fats for saturated fats. Several strategies help to accomplish this:

- Serve only nonfat and low-fat milk (age 2 and older).
- Offer low-fat dairy products such as low-fat cheeses and fat-free yogurts.
- Use more heart-healthy oils, including olive, canola, and peanut oils, and select foods that contain heart-healthy fats such as avocados and nut and seed butters.
- Use broth-based soups instead of cream-based soups.
- Use oven-baked sweet potato fries made from fresh potatoes tossed with a small amount of olive oil.
- Avoid the *trans* fatty acids found in some margarines, shortenings, crackers, cookies, pies, doughnuts, some chips, and fried fast foods.
- Serve heart-healthy fish on the menu such as tuna, salmon, and sardines.

When teachers use these strategies to plan menus they set standards of practice that support excellence in menu planning.

Creating Menus That Support Sustainability

Interest in the use of sustainable practices and sustainability is growing. This idea has relevance to menu planning and food service. Sustainable practices are those that meet current needs without compromising the ability of future generations to meet their needs (United Nations Department of Social and Economic Affairs Division for Sustainable Development, 2009). Sustainability also encompasses the interconnectedness of human and natural systems. It is the linking of social, economic, and environmental goals to create practices that support the perpetuation of these systems.

In selecting foods and planning menus, the concept of sustainability involves asking questions such as "What are the environmental consequences of using this product, this procedure, or this vendor when making decisions about menus?" or "Does my choice negatively affect other systems or people?" There is general consensus that many human activities are not sustainable. Early childhood programs make

What if . . .
you wanted to support sustainability in early childhood settings? How would you approach this goal? How might teachers' sustainability practices influence young children?

a commitment to health and wellness, not just for the present, but also for the future. This commitment to well-being is naturally attuned to concepts of sustainability. The following sections discuss sustainable practices in relation to menu planning and food service.

Using Locally Grown Produce

One way to support sustainability when planning menus is to purchase foods that are grown locally. This means identifying and purchasing from growers located within the state or a less than 400-mile radius of the program (Martinez et al., 2010). Foods should also be cultivated using sustainable agricultural practices that are environmentally friendly and socially responsible. This means foods are produced with soil and water conservation, pesticide reduction, and wildlife habitat conservation in mind. They are also produced in environments that support safe and fair working conditions and that provide healthy and humane care of livestock (Allen, Benson, Shuman, & Skees-Gregory, 2011).

Selecting Environmentally Responsible Products

Along with the foods selected during menu planning are all of the products used to implement meal service. Selecting cleaning products that are environmentally friendly is a desirable sustainable practice. For example, sanitizers used for cleaning tables and other surfaces should be safe, leave no harmful residue for children, and should not cause negative impacts on the environment when washed down the drain. Selecting reusable food service materials is another sustainable practice. Disposable plastic silverware and Styrofoam plates are less desirable than reusable products. Products that come wrapped in individual packaging are less desirable because of the quantity of packaging material. Purchasing items in bulk is more sustainable.

Recycling and Composting

Recycling and composting are practices that contribute to sustainability. For example, establishing recycling stations in classrooms or cafeterias for milk cartons contributes to sustainability and is a good way for children to be involved with this concept. Children can participate in recycling activities and learn about the phases of production that end with recycling. Programs or schools should consider the purchase of *Earth tubs* or other composting units used to compost cafeteria food waste (Green Mountain Technologies, 2012). Children can see how compost changes over time and can be used to enrich gardens.

Planting School Gardens

A school garden is an excellent way to contribute to sustainability, while offering a range of other learning opportunities. Planting a garden provides opportunities to discuss climate, weather, soil, growing practices, insects, growing cycles, and food. When children tend gardens they are physically active, which reinforces health goals. Eating homegrown fruits and vegetables helps children learn where food comes from and inspires them to try the fruits and vegetable they helped to grow.

At Sunnyside Environmental School, an inner-city school located in Portland, Oregon, every grade level has its own garden. The first- and second-grade classes create a "snacking" garden of vegetables that can be picked and eaten for immediate gratification (Anderson, 2009). The school's focus integrates academics with hands-on learning about horticulture, outdoor education, and the environment, giving inner-city children an opportunity to learn in the natural setting. The *Teaching Wellness* feature discusses planning a school garden with children of different ages. In addition see the Progressive Programs and Practice feature which shows how schools in Berkeley, California, embrace school gardens.

Partnering with Children and Families

Obtaining ideas from children, their families, and other program staff is another important resource for menu planning. Teachers have the opportunity to observe meal service in the classroom, which provides insight into details that are helpful for selecting menu items. By noticing children's response

TEACHING WELLNESS   Planting a Three Sisters' Native American Garden

LEARNING OUTCOME   **Children will be able to describe how seeds planted in the ground grow into the vegetables we eat.**

Safety watch: Be aware of children's allergies and avoid known allergens as you interact with the garden and foods. Monitor children closely as they interact with the tools and activities. Ensure that children wash their hands after participating.

INFANTS AND TODDLERS

- **Goal:** Babies and toddlers will experience the look, color, smell, and feel of a vegetable garden.
- **Materials:** Identify a nearby vegetable garden, or establish a program garden area, strollers, and vegetable examples (carrots, potatoes, green beans, lettuce leaves).
- **Vocabulary focus:** Garden, vegetables, brown, earth, green, leaves, smell, touch, carrot, potato, bean, tomato.
- **Activity plan:** Walk with infants and toddlers through the garden at different times during the growing season. Talk about what you see in the vegetable garden. Encourage children to look, touch, and smell appropriate aspects of the garden. Talk about the colors of the garden and the smell of recently turned dirt. Smell and touch the leaves of appropriate plants. Watch as water is used to sprinkle the garden. Describe the names of vegetables that grow in a garden. Serve an appropriate garden vegetable for a snack and talk about how the food grows from the earth.
- **How to adjust the activity:** Prepare vocabulary cards for the focus vocabulary words in English and the home languages of children in the group. Assist all children to appropriately explore the garden through sight, smell, and touch.
- **Did you meet your goals?** Can you observe babies and toddlers looking at and reaching out to touch the plants? Do toddlers repeat the names of the smells, textures, and vegetables grown in the garden?

PRESCHOOLERS, KINDERGARTNERS, AND SCHOOL-AGE CHILDREN

- **Goal:** Children will plant a Native American Three Sisters' Garden and understand the steps of planting and growing foods.
- **Materials:** A 4' × 6' (or larger) gardening bed in a sunny area, child-sized gardening tools (such as a shovel, hoe, rake, watering can, wheelbarrow), seeds (corn, squash, and pole beans), access to water, the children's book *Corn Is Maize* by Aliki, the resource book *Native American Gardening: Stories, Projects and Recipes for Families* by M. J. Caduto and J. Bruchac.
- **Vocabulary focus:** corn, maize, squash, beans, soil, seeds, germinate, sprout, harvest.
- **Activity plan:** Prepare a garden area for planting. Use the book *Native American Gardening* listed above as a resource, and read an account of the tale of the Three Sisters found online at www.ncmuseumofhistory.org/collateral/articles/F05.legend.three.sisters.pdf.

  Gather the children and read the book *Corn Is Maize*. Describe how the Native Americans traditionally planted corn, beans, and squash together, and called these the "three sisters." Explain to the children that the Native Americans learned that these three plants help each other grow. The corn provides shade for the small bean plants and becomes the poles for the beans as they grow. The beans add nutrients back into the earth. The squash makes a shady ground cover that helps the soil retain moisture. The prickly spines on the squash leaves keep away animals that like to eat corn. Talk about what is needed for seeds to grow: soil to grow in, water for the seeds to drink, and sunlight, which provides the food for growth. Working with small groups, invite children to use their hoes to make a circular mound of dirt about 18 inches across the bottom tapering to 10 inches across the top. Level off the top so that it makes a flat circle. Plant six corn seeds in each quarter of the circle, about 6 inches apart. Pat the soil and keep evenly moist while the corn seeds begin to grow. When the corn has grown to about 6 inches in height, plant 8 pole bean seeds around the edge of the circle about halfway down the mound. Finally, plant six squash seeds around the lower edge of the mound. Pat the soil over the seeds. Wash hands when done. During the growing season, work with the children to keep the soil evenly moist while these seeds germinate and to tend the garden by pulling weeds. Provide an ear of corn, several fresh beans, and a squash for children to open and study.

- **How to adjust the activity:** Create picture cards depicting each of the foods that are planted. Tape on a seed for each food, and include the name of the food in English and each home language of children in the class. Make adjustments, such as providing a trowel with a large handle for a child who struggles to grip, or ensuring that children who travel in a wheelchair can move into the garden area by placing a large piece of plywood over the soil for a firm surface. Take photos of all children participating at different points of the planting and growing process and post these to reinforce the steps of planting and growth.
- **Did you meet your goals?** Did children participate in planting and caring for the garden? Are children able to identify the steps in planting and growing food?

(continued)

SCHOOL-AGE CHILDREN

- **Goal:** Children will plant a Native American Three Sisters Garden and describe the steps of planting and growing foods and how to use them to plan a healthful menu.
- **Materials:** Gardening materials and resource book as described above, lined paper, pencils, recipe books.
- **Vocabulary focus:** soil, seeds, germinate, sprout, harvest, recipe, menu.
- **Activity plan:** Involve children in planting a Three Sister Garden at school as described above. Read the stories in the book *Native American Gardening*, such as "The Bean Woman" (p. 61) or "Onenha, The Corn" (p. 1). During the growing season, assist children to create and keep a weekly garden journal describing the planting, tending, and growing process: what they do to tend the garden and what they observe. In preparation for harvest, guide children to research recipes that include corn, beans, and squash and create a menu that meets CACFP guidelines. Print out the selected recipes, invite the children to illustrate them, and include the recipes with their garden journal to take home at the end of the growing season.
- **How to adjust the activity:** Assist children who are learning English by posting pictures of gardening, planting, tending, and harvesting activities labeled in English. Encourage children with special developmental needs by providing adaptive pencils or pens, journal pages on clipboards for easier control, and offering ample time and support to create journal entries. Ensure the garden area is accessible

to children who travel by wheelchair. Consider a raised bed garden for easier access if indicated.

- **Did you meet your goals?** Did children participate in planting and tending the garden? Are children able to describe how seeds grow into plants that produce food? Can they plan a healthful menu using corn, beans, and squash?

to menu items and the amount of food left on their plates, teachers become aware of trends. This insight can be used to develop or revise menus that will enhance food acceptance. Talking with family members to find out what they see as successful versus less successful menu items both at school and in the home setting is another useful source of information. The *Health Hint* describes the partnership between teachers, families, and children in planning menus. Whether teachers are creating a brand-new menu from scratch or revising a menu currently in place, input from these sources can be invaluable.

WRITING MENUS

With a good understanding of the requirements for children's menus and knowledge of nutrition wellness goals, teachers are ready to gather the tools they need and begin to make decisions about the menu.

Gathering Tools for Menu Planning

Once teachers envision the type of menu they wish to produce, it is helpful to organize and review the resources discussed in the previous section that help support menu writing. Other useful resources to include in a menu planning notebook are:

- Old menus and cost analysis of the menus, if available.
- Menu templates (see Figure 6-5).

PROGRESSIVE PROGRAMS & PRACTICES

Healthful Learning in an Edible Schoolyard

By Kyle Cornforth, Martin Luther King, Jr. Middle School, Berkeley, CA

Martin Luther King, Jr. Middle School in Berkeley, California, is invested in promoting student wellness. The school board in Berkeley maintains an innovative wellness policy, which aims to promote student and family health through education, garden and cooking classes, nutritious school meals, and core academic content in the classroom. Every student receives a comprehensive education about food and wellness that has three main pillars: a 9-week course focused on a variety of food-related topics; a nutrition services program providing healthy, seasonal meals prepared from scratch; and hands-on lessons in a garden and kitchen classroom at the Edible Schoolyard Berkeley.

The nutrition course "What's On Your Plate?" was developed by King teachers for all sixth-grade students. The course is an interactive and hands-on approach to food science, nutrition, and other healthy lifestyle concepts. One objective of this course is to make students more aware of what they are eating—sugar in sodas, fat in chips, and portion sizes in fast food. The course encourages making healthy choices in the cafeteria through weekly tastings prepared by nutritional services. It also encourages students to try new foods through tastings of seasonal fruits and vegetables.

King Middle School also promotes wellness through the food served in the cafeteria. Meals are prepared from scratch from produce that is mostly local and/or organic, including meat, baked goods, and beverages. Importantly, the cafeterias in Berkeley operate on a balanced budget—income from serving Universal Breakfast and income from student lunches pay for the ingredients and labor it takes to produce school meals that are not only good for student health but also good for the health of the wider economy and community.

The Edible Schoolyard Berkeley hosts the garden and kitchen program at King Middle School. The mission of the

Edible Schoolyard Berkeley is to teach essential life skills and support academic learning through hands-on classes in a 1-acre organic garden and kitchen classroom. Students are taught the skills necessary to growing, tending, harvesting food, and preparing and eating fresh, seasonal, nutritious meals. In addition, classes at the Edible Schoolyard Berkeley are connected to classroom lessons and standards; students come to the garden and kitchen to deepen their learning about world cultures, ancient technologies, and life science concepts. The Edible Schoolyard Berkeley curriculum is fully integrated into the school day and teaches students how their choices about food affect their health, the environment, and their communities.

- A list of foods that reflect the food preferences of culturally diverse populations within the program (see Table 6-5).
- A list of the special diets and food allergies of children in care.
- Recipes and recipe templates (from the program's previously used recipes, USDA website, etc.).
- A list of commodity foods.
- Price lists for suppliers or sales flyers for local grocers.
- A grocery shopping list template.

Once these tools have been gathered, teachers are ready to schedule a block of uninterrupted time to plan menus.

The Cycle Menu

The **cycle menu** offers new foods every day for a set number of weeks and then repeats. The menu items are offered in the same order as the previous cycle. A repeating 4- to 6-week cycle menu is often

cycle menu
menu that offers new foods every day, is planned for a week or longer, and repeats itself

HEALTH HINT   Building Health in the Classroom and at Home Through Menu Planning

Everyone has opinions and ideas about food. Harnessing this interest and energy can be empowering for children's programs and families alike. It can also contribute to health in the classroom and at home through a shared partnership approach. Strategies to accomplish this include the following:

- Match menu offerings with curriculum activities in the classroom. For example, focus on including milk, yogurt, and low-fat cheese on the lunch menu and explore where dairy foods come from by taking a trip to a dairy and watching cows be milked. Taste test different types of dairy products.
- Ask children to offer ideas for menu items. Encourage them to name favorite fruits, vegetables, grains, dairy products, and meats and which ones they would like to try.

- Invite families to participate on a menu review committee. Involving families in the development of menus invites them to contribute ideas and recipes that reflect their culture and family eating practices.

Through a menu planning partnership, children, families, and teachers learn about food preferences, gain knowledge of family cultural and eating practices, and discuss the health benefits of certain foods. Families learn about nutrition by working with teachers who are adhering to nutritional guidelines and requirements. When families are part of a menu planning partnership they are empowered with the knowledge they need to make nutritious food choices at home that support good health for the entire family.

FIGURE 6-5   Sample CACFP-Compatible Menu Template

Week 1	Monday	Tuesday	Wednesday	Thursday	Friday
Breakfast Milk Fruit/Vegetable Bread/Grain Meat/Meat Alternate (optional)					
Lunch Milk Meat/Meat Alternate Fruit/Vegetable (either two of one or one of each) Bread/Grain					
Snack **(any two components)** Milk Fruit/Vegetable Bread/Grain Meat/Meat Alternate					

used in early childhood settings and schools. Cycle menus are time and cost effective. Establishing a cycle menu creates a familiar system for shopping and food preparation. Through experience, teachers learn how much to purchase and prepare, thereby reducing food waste. Cycle menus can be created to incorporate seasonal foods. For example a 4- to 6-week cycle can be offered in the summer to use seasonal produce such as watermelon, peaches, and berries. A winter cycle menu would focus on readily available foods such as oranges, apples, and carrots. Cycle menus can be easily adjusted for variety and flexibility to reflect holidays or other special events.

Teachers need to decide how often to rotate their menus and must consider how to balance familiar well-accepted foods with new food options that broaden taste experiences. For example, in the chapter-opening scenario, Jeanine decides to improve her menu planning practices by switching to a 4-week cycle menu. Although the cycle menu will take time to write initially, in the long run

TABLE 6-5	Culturally Diverse Food Preferences		
Culture	Protein Sources	Grain Sources	Fruit and Vegetable Sources
Asian	Fish, pork, poultry, shellfish, dried beans, tofu, nuts	Rice, cereals, breads, noodles	Cabbage, kimchee, hot peppers, fruit juice
African American	Pork, ham, beef, fish, legumes, dried beans, peas	Rice, cereals, breads, biscuits, corn products such as hush puppies, cornbread, grits	Greens such as collard greens, kale, cabbage, turnips, beets, onions, okra, succotash, carrots, potatoes, yams, sweet potatoes, corn, peaches, melons, apples, bananas
Middle Eastern	Beef, lamb, chicken, lentils, chick peas, pistachios, almonds, fish, black beans, yogurt	Couscous, millet, pita, rice, bulgur	Onions, spinach, cucumbers, artichokes, potatoes, green beans, cabbage, eggplant, okra, squash, olives, figs, apples, apricots, plums, grapes, melons, bananas, tangerines, lemons
Mexican	Beans, poultry, beef, pork, eggs, goat, fish, shellfish, chorizo, menudo	Rice, tortillas (corn and flour), breads	Tomatoes, jicama, yams, cactus, salsa, chilies, sweet potatoes, squash, onions, corn, tomatillos, guava, mango, bananas, oranges, cherimoya, limes

Sources: Based on *Cultural Diversity*, by the National Food Service Management Institute, 2002, retrieved November 6, 2011, from http://www.olemiss.edu/ depts/ nfsmi/Information/Newsletters/Mealtime_memo_index.html#2002; and *Ohioline, Food: Cultural Diversity-Eating in America, 2010* Ohio State University, College of Food, Agriculture, and Environmental Sciences, retrieved November 6, 2011, from http://ohioline.osu.edu/lines/food.html.

she knows that it will save her time and effort once it is complete. She plans to include some of the favorite foods she has used in the past, but will expand the menu to offer a greater variety of fruits, vegetables, and whole grains.

Creating a Budget for Menus

The menu implements the program's food service goals including providing safe, healthful, and appealing meals to young children. The menu also directs the cost of meal service. For example, a menu that includes entirely fresh fruits and vegetables may cost more than one that relies on fresh, canned, and frozen produce. The way to understand the impact of these costs to the overall operation of an early childhood program is to develop a **budget**. A budget is a plan that designates the financial reserves available for purchasing, preparing, and serving foods. It is an itemized summary of expected food service–related expenses matched with the estimated income to cover these expenses. Teachers planning menus must stay within the constraints of the budget allotted for food service expenses.

budget
plan that designates the financial reserves available for food purchasing, preparation, and service of meals

Determining Income Sources for Menu Implementation

The income to support food service operations costs comes from a variety of sources depending on the children's program or school funding design. These sources include:

- Family fees for care and education.
- Child care subsidies for eligible low-income children.
- CACFP reimbursements for meal service.
- Public school district funding.
- Grants such as Head Start funds provided for programs that serve low-income families (Oliveira, 2005).

Sufficient funds are needed to implement an early childhood food program, including the costs of food, equipment, and the salaries of food service staff. The percentage of income needed is estimated to range from 6% to 19% of the total budget (Oliveira, 2005). If the costs for food service exceed 19% of the total program income, teachers should review their menu planning, food purchasing, and food preparation practices and look at ways to control costs.

Using Cost Control Strategies

Cost control strategies must consider all aspects of food program expenses. Besides direct food purchasing expenses, other costs related to food service over which teachers can exert some control include the use of disposable supplies (napkins, straws, dish detergent) and durable items (dishes, silverware, cooking utensils, and food service equipment). Sometimes a very simple change can make a significant difference. For example, consider the following situation:

> Sunshine Preschool food service staff must wear hairnets during food service. One of the teachers noticed that sometimes employees would use as many as three to four hairnets each day, discarding them whenever they left the kitchen for breaks and putting new ones on when they returned. She talked with the program's food service manager about this wasteful practice. The manager reviewed the kitchen supplier's catalogue and found that each hairnet cost about 25 cents. She realized that with five food service employees, the program was spending at least $5 per day on hairnets. The manager looked into the cost of institution caps and found out that they cost $16 each. She ordered five caps at a total cost of $80. She realized that, with this switch to caps instead of hairnets, the program would soon experience cost savings because the expense of the new caps would be repaid in just over 2 weeks.

Considering these types of details helps keep costs within the constraints of the budget. Cost control strategies involve teachers evaluating the menu planning process from its inception all the way to the actual serving of meals.

Control of food service costs can make or break a program's budget. Any expenses that are unnecessary take funds away from other vital areas of the early childhood program. The fundamental basics for food purchasing entail estimating food requirements based on the menu, creating a shopping list, pricing foods to obtain the best bargain, and purchasing food from either large suppliers, wholesale clubs, or local retail grocers.

A budget for purchasing foods for classroom and program activities is also important. A teacher may want to offer an activity that teaches children how orange juice is made using fresh oranges. A cooking activity may form the basis of a family meeting, or refreshments may be served at a family social or staff meeting. Procedures should be in place to communicate the budget available for these activities. Guidelines are also needed to ensure that teachers communicate with food purchasers in a timely manner so that adjustments can be made to the weekly shopping list. This avoids the need for last minute purchasing, which often results in less attention to cost.

The USDA publication *Building Blocks for Fun and Healthy Meals—A Menu Planner for the Child and Adult Care Food Program* recommends the following strategies to help contain food service costs:

- Keep good food records especially as they relate to food costs.
- Be a bargain hunter when it comes to buying foods:
  - Purchase locally and know what's in season.
  - Use commodity foods when available.
  - Shop from a grocery list and use coupons.
  - Shop at large discount stores.
  - Compare the cost of packaged items with the cost to purchase in bulk.
  - Purchase reusable food service supplies rather than disposable when possible. (This strategy supports sustainability as well as budget goals.)
  - Prevent food waste through spoilage by using proper storage strategies.

- Use **standardized recipes**. Standardized recipes are tried-and-true recipes that leave less room for error. See web resources.
- Aim to prepare exactly what is needed. This helps avoid excess leftovers and costly substitutions if food runs out and helps to ensure CACFP guidelines are met so that full reimbursement can be claimed.

standardized recipes recipes that have been tested for quality, accuracy, and yield, which results in consistent, predictable food products

Building Menus

An organized approach is important when making food selections. Deciding on menu choices and serving sizes requires the planner to consider the age and nutritional needs of children in the program. For example, will the menu serve older infants and toddlers as well as preschool-age children? Can food items be altered to accommodate the younger eaters? How will food be apportioned? Can the menu accommodate children on special diets? These types of questions guide menu development.

 School meals provide children with opportunities to try new foods and learn about different foods in cultures. As you watch this **video**, consider the teachers' ideas about building menus that promote nutrition, as well children's knowledge.

Starting the Day with Breakfast

Foods traditionally offered at breakfast contribute significantly to the total day's intake of vitamins, minerals, and fiber and overall can enhance the quality of a child's diet. Breakfast foods include fortified cereals, enriched and whole-grain breads, fruits, and protein foods like eggs, cheese, and milk. When breakfast is skipped it is very difficult to make up these nutrients at other meals (Affenito, 2007; Hoyland, Dye, & Lawton, 2009). In addition, research has shown that eating breakfast is a simple practice that may have a positive effect on how well children do in school. One review study found that when breakfast was consumed, children showed an increase in cognitive function, attention, and memory (Hoyland, Dye, & Lawton, 2009). Children who eat breakfast may also be more likely to maintain a healthful weight (Rampersaud, 2008). In spite of its many benefits, not all programs serve breakfast because it is assumed that children have eaten before coming to school. Instead many programs serve a midmorning snack. Programs eligible to participate in the CACFP may find it cost effective to switch from serving a morning snack to serving breakfast. The reimbursement for the breakfast meal is larger than that for the morning snack, and with a few changes in the menu, the switch can be easily accomplished.

The breakfast menu can be constructed following CACFP guidelines. Selections are made from the three required components: milk, fruits/vegetables, and starches/grains. A meat/meat alternate component can be offered but is considered optional. Teachers involved in menu planning can support nutrition-related goals by offering menu items such as whole-grain fortified cereals and whole-grain breads and items that increase the variety of fruits and vegetables served, especially those rich in vitamin C and vitamin A such as oranges, grapefruits, strawberries, kiwis, melons, mango, and tomatoes. In addition, breakfast foods that are high in solid fats, *trans* fat, and added sugar and sodium such as bacon, sausage, sweetened cereals, and breakfast pastries and doughnuts should be avoided. Milk service (nonfat or low-fat) is required by the CACFP; therefore, menus will include fresh, frozen (unsweetened), or canned fruits (packed in its own juice) instead of juice for breakfast. Offering whole fruits or vegetables is desirable whenever possible. Figure 6-6 provides a breakfast template that includes a 1-week menu for preschool-age children. This template provides guidance on portions to be served to meet CACFP requirements as well as information on the amount of food needed to serve a class of 20. This menu uses simple to prepare foods that can be used in a program with limited capacity for extensive cooking.

Selecting the Main Entrée for Lunch

The lunch meal is the largest meal offered at most programs and contributes significantly to children's overall energy and daily nutrient intake. A meat/meat alternate selection is needed to establish a CACFP-compatible lunch meal. The main entrée is often selected first because this menu item tends to be the highlight of the meal and is usually the most expensive menu item. The following considerations are useful when planning a cycle menu for lunch:

- How often should a particular entrée be served during the menu cycle?
- If an entrée is offered more than once a month, how can the side dishes be changed to ensure variety?
- How often will hot versus cold entrées be served? During the summer, sandwiches and chef's salads might be well received, whereas stews and soups may be preferred during the winter months.

FIGURE 6-6   Sample Breakfast Menu for 3–5 year olds

Spring Menu					
Week 3 of 6	**Monday**	**Tuesday**	**Wednesday**	**Thursday**	**Friday**
Breakfast **Milk** **Fruit/Vegetable** **Starch/Grain** **Meat/meat alternate which is optional at breakfast**	milk, nonfat strawberries Wheat Chex® yogurt, nonfat	milk, nonfat kiwi red peppers whole-grain bread scrambled egg	milk, nonfat applesauce blueberries oatmeal	milk, nonfat banana oat rings cereal	milk, nonfat tomatoes black beans orange slices corn tortilla cheddar cheese
Required portions	¾ c milk ½ c strawberries ⅓ c cereal ½ c yogurt	¾ c milk ¼ c kiwis ¼ c peppers ½ slice bread ¾ of an egg	¾ c milk ¼ c applesauce ¼ c blueberries ¼ c oatmeal	¾ cup milk ½ banana ⅓ cup cereal	¾ c milk ⅛ c tomatoes ⅛ c black beans ¼ of an orange ½ tortilla ½ oz cheese, lowfat
SPECIAL DIRECTIONS	Hull and slice strawberries and serve on top of yogurt.	Peel and slice kiwi. Prepare eggs with peppers following standardized recipe.	Add applesauce to oatmeal to sweeten. Sprinkle blueberries on top.	Bananas can be sliced and served on top of cereal.	Prepare bean and cheese burrito following standardized recipe. Slice oranges.
TOTAL AMOUNT OF FOOD TO SERVE PER CLASS BASED ON A 20-CHILD CLASS	1 gal of milk 10 c of berries 7 c of cereal 10 c of yogurt	1 gal of milk 5 c kiwis 5 c of peppers 10 slices of bread 15 eggs	1 gal of milk 5 c of blueberries 5 c of applesauce 5 c of oatmeal	1 gal of milk 10 bananas 7 c cereal	1 gal of milk 5 c of tomatoes 5 c of beans 5 oranges 10 corn tortillas 10 oz of cheese
Special diets: 1 lactose-free diet in Room 115	Substitute soy milk for nonfat milk and soy yogurt for regular yogurt.	Substitute soy milk for nonfat milk.	Substitute soy milk for nonfat milk.	Substitute soy milk for nonfat milk.	Substitute soy milk for nonfat milk. Substitute beans for cheese.
1 no strawberries in Room 117	Substitute apple for strawberries.				

If a **commercially prepared entrée** (a processed main course item to which ingredients may have been added) is chosen for the menu, it must be identified by the Child Nutrition (CN) Labeling Program. This is a voluntary federal program that supports labeling disclosure for the Child Nutrition Programs (U.S. Department of Agriculture,

FIGURE 6-7 A Sample Child Nutrition (CN) Label

— CN —

CN   This 3.00 oz serving of raw beef patty provides when, cooked 2.00 oz equivalent meat for Child Nutrition Meal Pattern Requirements. (Use of this logo and statement authorized by the Food and Nutrition Service, USDA 05-84.)   CN

— CN —

Source: From *Building Blocks for Fun and Healthy Meals—A Menu Planner for the Child and Adult Care Food Program*, by the U.S. Department of Agriculture, Food and Nutrition Service, 2000, retrieved February 27, 2012, from http://teamnutrition.usda.gov/Resources/appendm.pdf.

Food and Nutrition Service, 2011c). A CN label is required by the CACFP on foods that contribute to the meat/meat alternate component of the menu for reimbursable meals. Processed foods such as breaded fish and chicken products, frozen hamburger patties, pizzas, burritos, and garden burgers are examples of foods that require a CN label. A CN label clearly identifies how a product can be counted in the CACFP meal component requirements (Figure 6-7). Notice how the CN label communicates how much is needed of a processed product to meet protein equivalents when planning meals that adhere to CACFP requirements.

Consider the decisions a teacher might make while selecting an entrée for the menu. To meet CACFP requirements, the lunch menu requires a protein source for the entrée. Spaghetti is a versatile and nutritious choice. Even toddlers are able to eat this main dish without difficulty. The sauce for the spaghetti can be made with ground turkey, a more economical protein choice compared to ground beef. Lean ground turkey is also low in fat and rich in iron. In addition, the tomato sauce is an excellent source of vitamin C, which helps with iron absorption. Children will consume lots of vegetables with this entrée if green peppers, mushrooms, and chopped zucchini and summer squash are added to the tomato sauce. This menu item is also easy to adapt for children with special diets. For example, spaghetti is acceptable for children following milk-free diets if the sauce is prepared without cheese. Some sauce can be reserved and prepared without ground turkey for children following vegetarian diets. Adding shredded mozzarella cheese provides an appropriate protein source for the vegetarian. The addition of solid fats, sugar, and salt should be kept to a minimum as recommended by the *Dietary Guidelines for Americans, 2010*.

commercially prepared entrée
a processed main course item to which ingredients may have been added

Selecting Side Dishes for Lunch

After the entrée is selected, the side dishes such as starches/grains, fruits, and vegetables need to be chosen to round out the menu. Side dishes contribute to the menu's balance both in nutrition and sensory appeal. Variety in the selection of the side dishes is important to ensure that children get all the nutrients they need for good health. It is also important to consider whether the flavors and textures within a meal are varied and complementary. When too many similar flavors, such as strong, spicy, or sweet, are offered in the same meal, "mouth boredom" can occur. For example, a lunch with many sweet components, such as a peanut butter and jelly sandwich, spiced apples, carrot raisin salad, and milk may be unappealing even to children with the most tenacious sweet tooth.

Visual balance is important too. Menu selections should represent food components that look appealing as evidenced by a variety of colors, shapes, and sizes. Figure 6-8 shows two different planned lunches. The contrast of colors in Lunch 2 is more likely to encourage the appetite in both children and teachers. This is desirable because it is much easier for teachers to model good eating behaviors when they truly enjoy the meal.

Side dishes, such as the starches/grains and fruits and vegetables, can often be used to introduce children to new foods. Young children who may be leery of unfamiliar foods do better when new foods are offered with familiar favorites. However, children often require repeated exposures before they are willing to try a new food (Cooke, Haworth, & Wardle, 2007; Harris, 2008; Satter, 2011).

VS.

Lunch 1   Lunch 2

FIGURE 6-8

Variety and Contrast in Flavor, Texture, and Visual Appeal Inspire a Good Appetite

Children who have an opportunity to prepare foods in classroom cooking activities are more likely to try something new. The *Nutrition Note* describes ways to build children's interest in new foods. In addition, when teachers and peers consume a new food, it enhances children's willingness to try something different, too (O'Connell, Henderson, Luedicke, & Schwartz, 2012; Wardle & Cooke, 2008).

NUTRITION NOTE   Building Interest in New Foods

Children are enthusiastic about cooking activities, and it is also fun for them to taste the results of their cooking projects. Cooking with children provides opportunities to teach about foods: where food comes from; how food smells, tastes, and feels; and how to prepare different kinds of food. Cooking also engages children in activities that help to develop motor skills as they use their arms, hands, and fingers. Children have different developmentally appropriate "kitchen skill" levels depending on their age. Understanding children's skill levels helps teacher to direct students to activities that help them feel successful. Kitchen skills for different age categories of children are found in the table below.

Cooking Skills	1-year-olds	2-year-olds	3-year-olds	4- to 5-year-olds
Listening: Learns when you talk about the steps and identify the ingredients and utensils used to prepare a recipe	X	X	X	X
Smelling, tasting, and feeling: Experiences food by smelling, tasting and touching ingredients	X	X	X	X
Practices by doing: Plays with pots, pans, plastic bowls, and large spoons	X	X	X	X
Washing: Can scrub produce and wipe tops of cans and tabletops		X	X	X
Tearing: Pulls apart lettuce and bread into pieces		X	X	X
Dipping: Can dunk fruit and vegetable pieces into dips		X	X	X
Pouring: Pours liquids into mixtures and stirs ingredients together			X	X
Kneading: Can knead dough			X	X
Spreading: Is able to use a knife to spread peanut butter on bread			X	X
Juicing: Will squeeze citrus fruits to make juice				X
Peeling: Can use a peeler with carrots or potatoes				X
Mashing: Can mash soft fruits and vegetables				X
Measuring: Measures ingredients using spoons and cups				X
Rolling and cutting: Can use a rolling pin and a cookie cutter				X

Sources: *Cooking with Children*, by the California Department of Health Services, retrieved from http://www.wicworks.ca.gov/education/nutrition/kidsRecipes/cooking_w_index.htm *Cooking with Preschoolers* by Kids Health from Nemours, retrieved from http://kidshealth.org/parent/growth/learning/cooking_preschool.html?tracking=P_RelatedArticle.

Grains/Starches   Variety in the type of starch or grain side dish selected is important at mealtimes. For example, if spaghetti is offered one day followed by lasagna the next, the menu becomes boring. The menu needs to alternate the presentation of whole-grain breads, brown rice, and whole-wheat or corn tortillas to provide enough variety to maintain interest.

Fruits and Vegetables   When selecting fruits and vegetables for the menu, vary the way the food is prepared and served. Some vegetables, such as broccoli, cauliflower, spinach, carrot sticks, and pepper strips, may be better accepted if they are served raw with low-fat dip. If shopping is done once a week, perishable fresh produce should be served early in the weekly menu. Some flexibility may be needed; for example, if the bananas are green on Monday and the kiwi fruit is hard on Tuesday, they should be used later in the week.

Selecting Beverages

Beverage selections are also important to the nutritional value of meals. The beverages that meet the requirements for CACFP reimbursement are milk for breakfast and lunch, and either milk or juice (but not both) for a snack. CACFP-acceptable milk alternatives such as certain soy milks should be available for children who are lactose intolerant or allergic to milk. The CACFP also requires that children have unlimited access to water throughout the day. Water should also be available for events such as walking trips, field days, and family social events. In addition, it is important for children to stay hydrated in the winter months when heavy clothing and strenuous outdoor activities coupled with heated inside environments can increase the need for fluids.

Rounding Out the Day with Snacks

The snack is an important meal for young children. Snacks provide a "second chance" to obtain nutrients missed at meal times. The CACFP requires that snack menus include two components from any of the four food groups (milk, fruits/vegetables, cereals/grains, and protein/protein alternate) to meet reimbursement requirements. Although 100% fruit juice may be served as part of a healthy snack, priority should be given to fresh fruits and vegetables, which provide added fiber and nutrients and are more likely to help children feel full longer. Figure 6-9 provides examples of easy-to-prepare, child-friendly snacks that include at least two food groups. Snacks are more likely to be prepared and served under the direction of teachers than any other meal. As with lunch and breakfast, a variety of factors influence the choice of snacks, including the age of the children in the program and the availability of kitchen space and staff for food preparation. Which components are used in these snack combinations?

Transitioning to New Menus

Once the cycle menu for breakfast, lunch, and snacks has been completed, a systematic evaluation of the menu is conducted to ensure that menu planning goals have been met. Figure 6-10 provides a checklist for reviewing the menus and determining if they

What if . . .
you were planning the side dishes to accompany a spaghetti entrée for lunch? What type of whole foods (fruits, vegetables, whole grains) and beverages would you select?

What if . . .
you were planning snacks for your program? What types of healthy and appealing snacks might you consider for infants, toddlers, preschoolers, and school-age children?

FIGURE 6-9   Nutritious Snack Combinations

Low-fat cheese and whole-grain crackers
Peanut butter on thin sliced apples
Whole-grain cold cereal with banana and 1% milk
Whole-grain waffles topped with applesauce
Whole-grain English muffin mini pizza
Baked sweet potato wedges with sliced turkey strips

Low fat cheese quesadilla topped with chopped tomato salsa
Whole-grain raisin bread with sliced low-fat Swiss cheese
Banana dipped in yogurt and crushed cereal
Turkey and low-fat cheese rollup served with carrot match sticks
Fruit salad topped with vanilla yogurt and low-fat granola cereal

Note: Cheese, although a dairy product, is considered a meat/protein alternate when counting food components for CACFP. Also, only two components in any combination are required for snacks.

FIGURE 6-10   Sample Menu Evaluation Checklist

Sunshine Preschool Program

Date: 4/1/2012

Menu planner: Maren

Age of students: 3- to 5-year-olds

Are food components/food groups being met?

❏ Breakfast

   ❏ Milk component (nonfat or low fat)

   ❏ Fruit or non-starchy vegetable component (no juice)

   ❏ Bread/grain group

   ❏ Optional items: Meat/meat alternate component, *trans* fatty acid-free margarine, jam, jelly, low-fat cream cheese

❏ Lunch

   ❏ Meat/meat alternate component

   ❏ Fruit component: no juice

   ❏ Vegetable component: (1/2 cup total combined with fruit)

   ❏ Bread/grain component

   ❏ Milk component (nonfat or low-fat)

   ❏ *Optional foods*: salad dressing, low-fat vegetable dip, mayonnaise, salsa, ketchup

❏ Snacks contain two components of four components and focus on variety

❏ At least half the grains are whole grains

❏ There is wide variety within the components groups especially within the fruit/vegetable group.

   Dark green vegetables are offered frequently (at least two times per week)

   Orange/red vegetables are offered frequently (at least three times per week)

   Legumes are offered at least once per week (or can count as meat alternate)

   At least three different fruits and five different vegetables are offered weekly.

❏ Menus contain a variety of flavors, contrasting colors, shapes, textures, temperatures, and forms.

❏ Menus are culturally appropriate.

❏ Menus are able to accommodate special diets.

❏ Menus reflect input from children, parents, and staff.

❏ Menus support sustainability when possible (local seasonal foods, foods from program garden).

❏ Special occasions are represented.

❏ Menu items can be accommodated by the food preparation staff, equipment, and facilities.

❏ Menu items are foods appropriate for the age group.

❏ Recipes are available.

❏ Breakfast, lunch, and snack menu items avoid repetition of foods on any given day.

❏ Nutritional goals that support dietary guidelines and recommendations are met.

❏ A fresh fruit or raw vegetable is offered daily.

❏ A good source of vitamin C is offered each day.

❏ At least four different entrees are offered each week and they are moderate in fat content.

❏ Two or more sources of iron are offered each day.

❏ Water is available and accessible throughout the day.

Sources: Based on USDA Child and Adult Care Food Program Center Manual, Oregon Department of Education, updated 2009, retrieved November 9, 2011, from http://www.ode.state.or.us/search/page/?id=3285; *Healthier US School Challenge: Recognizing Excellence in Nutrition and Physical Activity*, USDA Food and Nutrition Service, updated 2012, retrieved September 29, 2012, from http://www.fns.usda.gov/cnd/healthierschoolday/pdf/5_HUSSCCriteria.pdf ; Committee to Review Child and Adult Care Food Program Meal Requirements, Food and Nutrition Board, Child and Adult Care Food Program: Aligning Dietary Guidance for All, 2010, retrieved November 9, 2011, from http://books.nap.edu/openbook.php?record_id=12959.

are ready to be implemented. Staff involved in food preparation and service should participate in the menu review at this point. A food service employee might recognize a potential problem with equipment or food storage. A cook might recognize a food preparation procedure that takes more time than is advisable. This input provides the opportunity to revise the menu plan as needed before it is put into use.

Implementing a new menu can initially create some "bumps in the road." Food purchasing may involve a bit of trial and error as amounts of food needed for new recipes are estimated and tried. Opportunities to try out new recipes before they are used in the new menu can be very helpful but may require some additional start-up time. The transition to the new menu can be eased by:

- Notifying families of the new menus in advance.
- Modeling an adventuresome attitude while trying new foods.
- Observing children's reaction to new menu options.

Through careful planning the new menu can set the tone for healthy eating habits and have a beneficial impact on the nutritional status of children and teachers alike.

Using Meal Service to Enhance Menu Acceptance

Learning to eat is a developmental process that is acquired over time. Infants are entirely dependent on adults to provide what is best for them nutritionally. As children mature the teacher's role shifts from making food decisions for children to supporting them as they strive to achieve eating independence. This is accomplished by supporting children's development of eating skills and by providing an environment in which children are able to make their own healthful food selections within the context of the nutritious options provided by well-planned menus.

Supporting the Development of Eating Skills

The menu also makes important contributions to children's opportunities to gain eating and self-help skills. Appropriate menu items encourage children to learn to feed themselves. Finger feeding is an important developmental stage in learning to self-feed. As children learn to manipulate a spoon and fork, the menu must reflect foods prepared in ways that children can manage. Eating oatmeal with a spoon is a good first step. Peas may be too challenging for toddlers and preschoolers to eat with a fork.

When planning menus for a wide range of ages (infants to preschoolers), the adaptability of foods served should be considered. For example, thin-sliced apple wedges are a good choice for toddlers and older, whereas unsweetened applesauce would be a better choice for an 8-month-old infant. Teachers should allow children to feed themselves as much as they are able even though this is sometimes a messy business. Spills are to be expected and should be treated in an unconcerned manner. Teachers should respond with encouragement as children try new foods or textures or learn a new self-feeding skill: "Look how well you are using your spoon today" and "Great job, Jake. You tried the beans! Aren't they yummy?" Planning meals that challenge children to learn new skills without frustration is an extra dimension in menu planning.

Eating utensils, tables, and chairs should be age appropriate in size. Children should be able to sit with their feet touching the ground. The table should be at a comfortable height and there should be ample room at the table for children to maneuver. The room should be at a pleasant temperature with good lighting and distractions should be minimized. Parents coming in to pick up children after lunch should be encouraged to avoid entering the room until meal service is done. If there is a television in the family child care home, it should not be on during meal service. Teachers should not be talking on the phone during meal service but rather at the table interacting with children.

Enhancing the Social Experience for Children

Mealtimes should be relaxed and enjoyable. Teachers create this comfortable atmosphere by establishing guidelines for acceptable eating behavior. This includes offering meals on a routine schedule and allowing enough time so meals are not rushed. The expectations for eating etiquette should be introduced and reinforced, such as washing hands before eating, helping set the table, waiting until everyone is seated before beginning to eat (if age appropriate), and helping clean up after the meal. Mealtimes are also important social times as children talk and visit with each other and their teachers.

Selecting a Type of Meal Service

Meal service can be accomplished in a variety of ways in the early childhood or school setting, including the following:

- *Restaurant-style meal service* involves portioning food out on plates before it is served to children at the table. This is an efficient method that guarantees each child receives the correct portion and may help contain costs by minimizing food waste.
- *Cafeteria-style meal service* entails children making food choices while moving through a cafeteria line. This method allows children to select what they want to eat, but does not allow them to determine the amount. This style of service is common in the primary school setting.

> **What if . . .**
> you observed that children were disinterested in the menu offerings because they were the same every week? What suggestions might you make to the director or food service authority at your program? What resources could you use to support your point of view?

> This **video** shows a group of preschoolers transitioning to lunch. What strategies are used by the teachers to create a mealtime environment that is comfortable for children?

- *Family-style meal service* involves placing foods and beverages in serving containers on the table. Children serve themselves, choosing what they will eat and how much. In this approach, teachers sit with children to model appropriate eating behaviors, assist with meal service when needed, and provide conversation as well as educational activities focused on foods (Connecticut State Department of Education, Bureau of Health/Nutrition, Family Services and Adult Education, 2010).

The advantage of family-style meal service is that it involves children in the process of food service and uses mealtime as an educational experience. Family-style meal service is also a comfortable and nonthreatening way to introduce new foods. It provides opportunity for teachers to introduce the food choices of the day and to model how children may serve themselves. This gives children time to decide what to select based on their preferences. Children find the assurance they need to try new foods by observing what other children and teachers are eating. Family-style meal service also allows children to make their selections based on how hungry they feel. They learn to recognize hunger and satiety cues because they can take a small serving size with the knowledge that they can have more if they so desire (Connecticut State Department of Education, Bureau of Health/Nutrition, Family Services and Adult Education, 2010). Family-style meal service also helps children to practice fine motor skills as they dish out foods and pour beverages. Children learn to make choices, take turns, share, and "not lick the spoon."

Regardless of the type of meal service, it is important for teachers to sit with children, modeling healthy eating practices and encouraging social interactions.

Managing Foods from Home

Many children's programs ask families to provide the foods for snacks or have children bring their own lunches from home. Teachers may find it difficult to manage the food children bring to school. Part of the challenge faced when children bring food from home is the inconsistency in what is provided and how it impacts the program's nutrition. For example, what should teachers do if families send soda pop in their child's lunch box or perishables that may pose a food safety risk? Developing policies and procedures for home-prepared meals helps establish a partnership with families to support the healthful eating environment teachers wish to create for all children.

One helpful resource is the NAEYC's standards for program accreditation. The NAEYC recommends that foods brought from home to be shared with other children must consist of whole fruits or commercially prepared packaged foods (NAEYC, 2012). Home-baked items may be delicious and healthful, but can pose food safety risks if appropriate food preparation and storage practices are not followed. Children with allergies are also put at risk when there is no list of ingredients for teachers to read. Even when store-bought foods with labels are brought from home an allergic child can be put at risk in situations that are outside regular meal service. Consider the following situation:

> A special Valentine event was planned by Maren, a preschool teacher in a program that included a child with a peanut allergy. Maren was always very careful about Brianna's allergy and made sure meals served were peanut-free. When she planned the school cooking activity for the day, a whole-grain heart-shaped biscuit, she made sure the recipe contained peanut-free ingredients. She even asked parents not to make cupcakes, cookies, or other treats for the class. What she didn't count on was the Valentine's Day cards that children brought from home to share with other children in the program. Many of the cards had candy attached. Brianna brought home her decorated bag full of Valentine's cards. She found a chocolate peanut candy that had been tucked into a card she received and promptly ate it. She ended up in the emergency room shortly thereafter. She was well enough to come to school the next day but it had been a scary and upsetting experience for all involved.

It is important to communicate with families the goals for maintaining the safety of food brought from home and the kinds of food allergies or food restrictions that are present in the class group. A sample policy is described in the *Policy Point*. Reviewing the food-from-home policies with families before children start the program helps families make healthful choices for foods sent from home. A list of recommended

What if . . .

a parent arrived at school with a plate full of homemade cupcakes to celebrate a child's birthday? How would you handle this? How would you draft a program policy to address this issue?

POLICY POINT   Sample Policy for Foods Brought from Home

To manage food safety and to reduce the risk of exposing children to certain allergens, it is the policy of this program that all food served to children will be provided by the program. Food from home is not allowed.

Exceptions will be provided as follows:

1. *To address special dietary needs due to a medical condition that cannot be accommodated by the program's menu, for example, multiple food allergies.*
   - A note is required from the medical provider.
   - The note must explain the medical condition and what diet restrictions are necessary.
2. *In response to religious dietary restrictions that cannot be accommodated by the program's menu.*
   - A note from the parent is required to be on file.
   - The note will list the foods the child cannot eat.

When lunch is brought from home because of medical or religious reasons noted above, families will be encouraged to support the nutrition goals of the program by providing a balanced meal. The program will provide milk or a milk substitute.

- Because the program serves children with peanut and nut allergies, it is requested that no foods made from peanut or nut products be brought into the center.
- No soft drinks, candy, chips, or sugary desserts, such as cupcakes, are allowed.
- For safety, food must be brought to school in a lunch box or brown bag that has an ice pack to keep food appropriately chilled. The lunch box or brown bag should be labeled with the child's name and date and will be stored in the refrigerator located in the kitchen until meal service.
- The program will provide the family with the Child and Adult Care Food Program guidelines for snacks and lunches to assist with planning healthful food from home meals.

Source: *Standard 5: Health Topic 5.B: Ensuring Children's Nutritional Well-Being, Criterion 5.B.02 and Criterion 5.B.05,* 2009, Washington, DC: National Association for the Education of Young Children.

foods is useful to guide food selections when families are asked to contribute to the snacks for the classroom. This provides an opportunity to reinforce the program's food safety and nutrition goals. These approaches ensure that foods brought from home contribute to the nutritional well-being of children and protect children who, for cultural or health reasons, cannot eat the traditional foods brought in for snack times.

CREATING MENUS THAT SUPPORT ALTERNATIVE OR SPECIAL DIETS

Some children cannot consume the standard infant formula or the typical menu offered at a program or school. They may have food allergies or special medical conditions, or the family may have cultural, religious, or philosophical beliefs that require a special diet. Acting in partnership with families, teachers, food service staff, and administrative staff need to find ways to accommodate children's special diet needs.

Planning Menus for Children with Food Allergies

Managing special diets can be challenging, especially when children must follow allergen-restricted diets. It is estimated that about 8% of children in the United States have food allergies (Gupta et al., 2011). Each classroom is likely to have one or two children with food allergies.

Understanding Food Allergies

Food allergies occur when the body's immune system responds inappropriately to the exposure of typically harmless proteins found in certain foods. Once these proteins are identified as foreign bodies, or allergens, the body produces defense molecules called

Planning menus that can accommodate children with special diets is especially crucial for children who have food allergies.

immunoglobulin E (IgE) antibodies. This initial response creates a situation whereby the body is now sensitized to the allergen. When the offending food is consumed again, IgE antibodies defend the body from the allergen "invaders" and cause specific white blood cells called mast cells located throughout the body to release chemicals, including histamine, into the bloodstream. These chemicals cause the myriad of symptoms associated with allergies (Nemours, 2011; U.S. National Library of Medicine, the National Institutes of Health, 2010).

anaphylaxis
a severe, life-threatening reaction that can lead to a drop in blood pressure, loss of consciousness, and death if untreated

Symptoms can include hives; rash; swelling of the mouth, tongue and throat; red and tearing eyes; wheezing; difficulty breathing; coughing; shortness of breath; trouble swallowing; vomiting; diarrhea; and **anaphylaxis** (Food Allergy Anaphylaxis Network, 2011; NIAID-sponsored expert panel et al., 2010). Anaphylaxis is a severe life-threatening reaction that can lead to a drop in blood pressure, loss of consciousness, and death if untreated.

These symptoms describe immediate IgE-mediated reactions. Some children, however, can experience other food disorders that are not IgE mediated that result in an assortment of delayed symptoms that occur hours or days after exposure making identification of a food allergy more challenging (Berni Canani, Di Costanzo, & Troncone, 2011).

The only way to prevent allergic reactions is to avoid the offending food (NIAID-sponsored expert panel et al., 2010). This means that special menu decisions must be made to omit foods that contain allergens from the diet of children with that particular food allergy. In addition, teachers need to be prepared to manage a severe food allergy reaction in the event that an accidental exposure occurs. A food allergy action plan must be developed by the family and health care provider for emergency response at school (see the Food Allergy and Anaphylaxis Network (FAAN) Web Resource). A food allergy action plan identifies symptoms and specifies how to treat the allergic reaction in case of an emergency. Epinephrine is the product used most often to manage anaphylaxis. It is administered by injection (Figure 6-11). The FAAN website also lists the responsibilities of schools, families, and children for managing food allergies and creating a safe environment for children with allergies.

Early childhood teachers in family child care settings must also remember to have a plan for the care of other children while the teacher provides care for a child experiencing an allergic reaction. Feeding children with allergies is a serious responsibility. The consequences of making a mistake with their diet can be life threatening. It is important for families to share information about children's allergies with teachers and food service staff before the child attends the program. This provides time to make appropriate adjustments to the menu, an important aspect in creating a safe environment. Teachers may be very busy during meal service in the early childhood classroom, and in elementary settings teachers are usually not present when children eat. In addition, food products are used in a variety of other ways in early childhood programs. It is important to be aware of times when an allergen exposure might occur. If everyone involved in food service is informed about a child's food allergy, the likelihood that a food service error will happen is reduced. The *Safety Segment* provides an example of how one preschool program communicates about special diet requirements for children with food allergies. It is also important to listen to children who have life-threatening allergies. Even very young children are often well aware of what they can and cannot eat.

FIGURE 6-11
Epinephrine Injector

Infants with Food Allergies

Individuals involved in menu planning usually adapt the daily menu to accommodate children with food allergies. How menus are adapted varies depending on the age of the child. Allergies may begin to appear in infants when solid foods are introduced and they are exposed to new foods. Foods should be introduced one at a time, waiting for 3 to 5 days before the next new food is offered. In this way, if allergy symptoms develop, it is easier to identify the offending food (Kleinman, 2009). Families should provide teachers with a list of foods that have successfully been introduced. It is important for this list to be updated periodically to add new foods the infant tolerates (American Academy of Pediatrics, American Public Health Association, National Resource Center for Health and Safety in Child Care and Early Education, 2011). Menus planned for infants emerge from the

SAFETY SEGMENT Communicating About Allergy Diets

Special diets need careful planning. Foods need to be handled safely to avoid cross-contamination, and the foods need to be distributed to the correct child. Good communication and safety checks along the way help prevent food "accidents." Below is an example of the steps involved in managing peanut allergies.

Sunshine Preschool receives food through an agreement with a vendor. The vendor is the local school district's food service. Food is prepared offsite and sent via heated and chilled carts to the preschool program. One classroom has two children severely allergic to peanuts. What can the teacher do to ensure that these children are safe from potentially life-threatening allergens?

1. *School district food service:* The teacher or preschool dietitian contacts the school district kitchen that provides food for the center. Information about a child's food allergy is communicated prior to the child attending the class. A peanut-free menu is requested and all labels and recipes are checked for peanut-containing products. The school district kitchen ensures that containers and packaging for special peanut-free diets are labeled.

2. *The preschool:* The preschool decides to eliminate peanuts or peanut products from the menu. Staff members and families are asked to not bring peanut products to school. A list of children who are on special diets includes the two children with peanut allergies. This list is posted on the kitchen bulletin board and each teacher is given a copy. Staff is oriented to not make any substitutions for the peanut-free diet without prior approval from the dietitian. Staff members receive training on how to administer a rescue medication via an epinephrine injector.

3. *The classroom:* Assistant teachers are assigned to be in charge of serving and supervising service of special diets. The assistant teacher is asked to sit with the children who have food allergies at mealtime. Children with special diets are served first. A Food Allergy Emergency protocol is developed by the child's health care provider and is posted in the classroom near the phone so that all staff will know what to do and who to call in case of an emergency.

Checklist for Managing Food Allergies in the Classroom

Activities or lesson plans:

- ☐ Do any cooking activities use foods with potential allergens?
- ☐ Are food items with potential allergens used in other activities (sensory tables with corn meal, pasta, or rice, sorting and stringing pastas, made-from-scratch play dough)?

Field trips:

- ☐ Are allergen-free foods available for lunch and snacks?
- ☐ Does the emergency kit include children's medications (i.e., epinephrine injector) and an up-to-date Food Allergy Action Plan?
- ☐ Does everyone know who is carrying the child's medication?
- ☐ Does someone have a cell phone?

Lunchroom procedures:

- ☐ Is there a plan in place for assuring the child receives the correct food from food service?
- ☐ What practices are used to remove all traces of allergens during cleanup?
- ☐ Are kitchen staff informed and trained on food allergies?
- ☐ Is there sufficient supervision of the child with allergies during meal service to ensure that the correct food is selected and served and that children are not sharing food?

Social events:

- ☐ Are foods with allergens coming into the classroom from outside sources for classroom celebrations, picnics, etc.?

Teacher's absence:

- ☐ Is there a plan in place to ensure allergen safety when the teacher is absent?
- ☐ Is backup staff trained to supervise food service for children with allergies?

Classroom environment:

- ☐ Does more than one class use the same classroom (AM and PM classes)?
- ☐ Are both teachers aware of the allergies of each other's students?

list of well-tolerated foods. If a food allergy is identified, the offending food is eliminated from the infant's diet.

The teacher must closely follow recommendations from the family and health care provider for elimination of food allergens. This information should be documented in an individualized care plan. Families should be closely involved in identifying appropriate menus for infants with allergies. The family should approve the menu and, with the family's consent, the child's special diet should be posted where it is easily accessible in areas where food is prepared and served and any other area that the child typically uses (*Standard 5: Health Topic 5.B: Ensuring Children's Nutritional Well-Being, Criterion 5.B.05* (NAEYC, 2012). It is also imperative to carefully read food labels. Foods selected for purchase for infants should be single-ingredient foods to prevent inadvertent exposure to an allergen. Some infant foods that might appear

Children with allergies often have symptoms such as hives, a rash, and swelling of the mouth and throat.

FIGURE 6-12
Example of Labeling Special Diet Items

to be single-ingredient products can have hidden sources of potential allergens. For example, some infant meats and poultry are prepared with gravy that contains cornstarch, a potential allergen (U.S. Food and Drug Administration, 2009).

Supports should be provided for breast-feeding mothers (*Standard 5: Health Topic 5.B: Ensuring Children's Nutritional Well-Being, Criterion 5.B.09*) (NAEYC, 2012). This is especially important because exclusively breastfeeding until infants are 4–6 months of age may offer protection from the development of food allergies (Ferdman, McClenahan, & Falco, 2010; NIAID-sponsored expert panel et al., 2010). Breast-fed infants who have a family history of allergies are less likely to develop skin rashes or a milk allergy in the first 2 years of life compared to infants who drink regular formula (Greer, Sicherer, Burks, & and the Committee on Nutrition and Section on Allergy and Immunology, 2008). Sometimes breast-fed babies become exposed to allergens in mother's breast milk. If this occurs the mother may have to restrict consumption of certain foods (Greer et al., 2008). In these situations teachers must be sure to not offer stored breast milk that predates the start of the mother's elimination diet.

Extra care is also needed when preparing infant formula to avoid cross-contamination. Strategies to avoid cross-contamination include the following:

- Formula should be prepared in specifically identified containers, using specific mixing utensils.
- Bottles should be cleaned with specific bottle brushes and thoroughly rinsed.
- Special hypoallergenic formulas should be labeled so that bottles are not inadvertently given to the wrong infant. The label on the formula should be double-checked before feeding the infant.

Toddlers, Preschoolers, and Primary-Grade Children with Food Allergies

The challenge in planning menus for children with food allergies is ensuring that the foods offered are allergen free while still meeting nutritional recommendations. In addition it is important to create enough variety so that children do not become bored with the substitutes offered. Using whole basic foods instead of processed foods may reduce the risk of allergen exposure for children who have multiple allergies. For example, children who have egg and wheat allergies can consume fresh baked chicken without fear of allergen exposure, whereas prepared chicken strips or nuggets will most likely contain these allergens.

As with infant diets, food for young children should be prepared and served to avoid cross-contamination. Food purchased for children with allergies should be labeled with the child's name and date and properly stored. In addition, special diet items must be labeled when served so that children receive the correct allergen-free foods (Figure 6-12). Menus for children with allergies should be approved by families and posted so that all staff involved know that children with special diets will be served. During meal service, young children should be supervised so that they do not inadvertently consume other children's food. School-age children should be cautioned about sharing lunches.

When the menu is carefully planned to accommodate food allergies and food service safety checks are a routine part of food service and preparation, teachers minimize the risk of accidental exposure to food allergens. If exposure does occur, teachers can be confident that there is an allergy action plan in place.

Planning Menus for Children with Diabetes

Children with diabetes have special dietary needs that require close coordination between families and teachers. They must be served meals and snacks that meet their nutritional needs and at the same time maintain appropriate blood sugar levels. Teachers who have children with diabetes in the class need specialized training by a diabetes educator about the effects of physical activity, diet, and insulin on blood glucose levels. They also must be trained in the treatment of diabetes emergencies (American Diabetes Association, 2011a).

A Matter of ETHICS

A child in your program has a severe nut allergy and you ask families not to bring any nut products into your program. A mother of a child who enjoys peanut butter and jelly sandwiches for lunch complains that her child's rights are being ignored. What is the best course of action to take to resolve this ethical dilemma?

Understanding Type 1 and Type 2 Diabetes

There are two types of diabetes: **Type 1** and **Type 2**. Both types result in elevated blood sugar levels but the cause of these conditions is very different. In children with type 1 diabetes, the cells in the pancreas that make insulin are destroyed by the immune system and therefore insulin injections are required. Children who have type 2 diabetes often still make insulin; however, their bodies are less effective at using it and over time insulin production can eventually decrease. Children with Type 2 diabetes often are overweight or obese and this extra body fat makes it harder for the cells of the body to respond to insulin (National Diabetes Education Program, 2011). A visual explanation of the differences between Type 1 and Type 2 diabetes can be observed by viewing the flash animations at http://kidshealth.org/parent/videos/in_diabetes_vd.html. Teachers who understand the difference between Type 1 and Type 2 diabetes will have a better understanding of how to manage the special diets that are the cornerstone of treatment.

Type 1 diabetes
a condition that results in the inability of glucose to get from the circulatory system or bloodstream into the cell where it can be used as energy; requires insulin to correct

Type 2 diabetes
a condition that is often associated with overweight and obesity that results in elevated blood sugar due to the decreased ability of the cells to use insulin effectively

Understanding the Diet for Type 1 Diabetes

A very important aspect to consider when planning menus and providing meal service for children with Type 1 diabetes is the amount of carbohydrate-containing foods served at meal and snack time. This is because it is predominantly the carbohydrates (starches/grains, fruits, milk, and sweets) in a diet that are broken down to glucose during digestion. In addition, because the goal is to balance blood glucose or sugar levels with the need for insulin, the timing of meals and snacks is very important. Regular meal and snack times help prevent high or low blood sugar levels.

Although children with Type 1 diabetes do not require special foods, it may be helpful to have on hand sugar substitutes and sugar-free beverages (American Diabetes Association, 2011b). The special diets of children with Type 1 diabetes vary depending on the child's age and calorie requirements. Teachers will know how much to serve and when based on the child's **meal plan**. A child's meal plan is developed and reviewed by health care professionals such as dietitians to help children with diabetes. This individualized plan reflects the child's personal and cultural food preferences (American Dietetic Association, 2011a). The family receives the meal plan instructions and is typically the resource for communicating the meal plan to the teacher. In addition, the management of all aspects of a child's diabetes, including diet, is outlined in Diabetes Medical Management Plan and the 504 Plan (see Web resources). To accommodate children who have diabetes, families need to:

meal plan
a diet guidance tool developed by health care professionals such as dietitians to help children with diabetes and their families know what amount of carbohydrates they should eat and when so that their blood sugar level stays within an acceptable range

- Provide and review the child's meal plan and snack schedule.
- Provide instructions on what to do when food is offered at classroom parties or other special events.
- Provide the supplies needed to treat low blood sugar reaction such as a source of glucose.

For their part in accommodating children with diabetes, teachers need to:

- Learn the carbohydrate content of foods offered on the menu and understand the portions that are allowed per the child's meal plan.
- Provide families with information on portion sizes and calorie, carbohydrate, and fat content of meals served at school.
- Ensure regular mealtimes. If a meal is delayed, a backup plan for providing food is necessary to prevent the child with Type 1 diabetes from having a low blood sugar reaction.
- Review foods planned for special events and receive approval from families about the particular food items and amounts that should be served.
- Plan appropriate foods for meals away from the program, such as picnics or field trips.
- Develop strategies and obtain guidance from families on what to do if a child refuses to eat.
- Obtain training and guidance on what foods to feed or medication to administer (glucagon) if the child's blood sugar levels get too low.
- Make provisions in case the teacher is absent. A substitute teacher must be trained in diet and diabetes management (American Diabetes Association, 2012).

What if . . .

a child in your class has diabetes and the lunch meal is late? You wonder if you should provide the child with diabetes an emergency snack while the other children continue to wait. How would you manage this?

Teachers may be called on to check children's blood sugar levels, make decisions about the amount of food to serve based on the child's blood sugar level, and administer insulin. All information pertaining to these types of decisions is included in the Diabetes Medical Management Plan and the 504 Plan.

Understanding the Diet for Type 2 Diabetes

The overall goals of diet therapy are similar to the goals for children with Type 1 diabetes, which include providing a nutritious diet that minimizes elevations in blood sugar levels by focusing on the carbohydrate content of meals. However, lifestyle changes that promote healthy weight and encourage physical activity are also very important objectives (American Dietetic Association, 2011a; National Diabetes Education Program, 2011). Children with Type 2 diabetes are often treated with lifestyle changes first; however, sometimes they will need oral medications and insulin to keep blood sugar levels in good control.

Planning Menus for Children Who Are Overweight or Obese

A healthful menu requires little modification to accommodate children who are overweight. Most children identified as overweight or obese will continue to eat from the regular menu unless a physician has determined a specially structured diet is a medical necessity (Academy of Nutrition and Dietetics, 2012). Children who are significantly obese may be referred to a multidisciplinary obesity care team. In this case, families may provide more specific diet recommendations from their health care team. Only a select group of children with significant obesity-related health issues will require this type of intervention (Academy of Nutrition and Dietetics, 2012; Skelton & Beech, 2011).

Close monitoring of a child's blood sugar level is done by pricking the finger and using a glucose meter to determine if the blood sugar is within the acceptable range.

Many of the strategies available for managing overweight or obesity among children also address prevention. Attention is given to improving health rather than focusing only on weight. This protects both the physical and social/emotional well-being of young children (August et al., 2008; Weight realities division of the Society of Nutrition Education, Center for Weight and Health, U.C. Berkeley, 2003). A well-planned menu is an effective tool for implementing nutrition recommendations and teaching children and their families what constitutes a balanced meal. The American Academy of Pediatrics, the Academy of Nutrition and Dietetics, and the USDA recommend the following evidence-based nutrition practices for preventing and treating overweight and obesity:

- Limit the intake of sugar-sweetened beverages, soft drinks, and juice.
- Encourage the intake of sufficient fruits and vegetables.
- Eat breakfast daily.
- Provide appropriate portion sizes.
- Limit calorie-dense and high-fat foods at meal and snack times.
- Serve non-fat or low-fat milk to children age 2 and older (American Dietetic Association, 2010a; Davis et al., 2007; U.S. Department of Agriculture, 2010).

In the chapter-opening scenario Jeanine's goal was to create a system for menu planning. Developing a 4-week cycle menu was the first step in her plan. She then found that by switching to nonfat milk, adding more fruits and vegetables, and limiting juice, she was able to create a more healthful nutrition environment for all the children, including the child in her class who was overweight.

Planning Menus for Children with Special Needs

Children with disabilities or special health care needs may have special diet requirements and may be at increased risk for nutritional problems. For example, they may have one or more nutritional risk factors that can impact their rate of growth or take medications that interfere with nutrient absorption or their appetite (American Dietetic Association, 2010b). In addition, these children may have unique feeding concerns, such as problems with chewing and swallowing. This highlights the need for careful discussion of menus and the adjustments that may be needed to ensure that the child's dietary needs are well understood. Directions for meeting the child's nutrition and feeding needs in the classroom setting should be obtained from the child's health care provider.

In some situations teachers may require specialized training. For example, if a child requires **tube feedings**, teachers will need to be trained in tube feeding administration before the child attends. With tube feeding, a liquid supplement is fed via a tube that enters the stomach or small intestine. This method is used when a child is not able to eat solid foods or the amount that can be eaten is insufficient in volume for the child to achieve adequate nutritional intake. Training would be provided by a qualified health care professional. A medical statement needs to be on file documenting the need for the special diet and describing the recommended feeding practices. Figure 6-13 is a sample form that can be used for any child requiring a special diet (Food and Nutrition Service & United States Department of Agriculture, 2001).

tube feedings
a method of feeding used when eating solid foods is not possible or insufficient in volume to achieve adequate intake. A liquid supplement is fed via a tube that goes into the stomach or small intestine

---

FIGURE 6-13   Eating and Feeding Evaluation: Children with Special Needs

PART A		
Student's Name	Age	
Name of School	Grade Level	Classroom

	Yes	No
Does the child have a disability? If yes, describe the major life activities affected by the disability.	Yes	No
Does the child have special nutritional or feeding needs? If Yes, complete Part B of this form and have it signed by a licensed physician.	Yes	No
If the child is not disabled, does the child have special nutritional or feeding needs? If Yes, complete Part B of this form and have it signed by a recognized authority.	Yes	No

If the child does not require special meals, the parent can sign at the bottom and return the form to the school food service.

PART B
List any dietary restrictions or special diet.
List any allergies or food intolerances to avoid.
List foods to be substituted.
List foods that need the following change in texture. If all foods need to be prepared in this manner, indicate "All." Cut up or chopped into bite size pieces: Finely ground: Pureed:
List any special equipment or utensils that are needed.
Indicate any other comments about the child's eating or feeding patterns.

Parent's Signature	Date:
Physician or Medical Authority's Signature	Date:

From *Accommodating Children with Special Dietary Needs in School Nutrition Programs—Guidance for Food Service Staff*, p. 34, 2001, Alexandria, VA: USDA Food and Nutrition Service, retrieved December 15, 2012, from http://www.fns.usda.gov/cnd/Guidance/special_dietary_needs.pdf.

There are many factors to consider when adapting menus for children with special health and development needs. Children with special needs may have varying requirements for calories to maintain an appropriate rate of growth. Some children may find it difficult to eat enough calories to support growth because of increased calorie requirements, oral-motor problems, or developmental delay of feeding skills, while other children may face increased risk for obesity due to poor muscle tone or decreased physical activity. Some children may experience reflux, diarrhea, or constipation (Samour & King, 2012). Table 6-6 provides a summary of the nutritional and related health concerns of children with special health care needs.

TABLE 6-6 Nutritional Concerns of Select Health Care Conditions

Special Health Care Condition	Impact on Eating and Diet	Impact on Growth/Nutritional Status/Overall Health	Implications for Teachers
Attention deficit hyper-activity disorder (ADHD)	Medications can decrease appetite.	Some children experience weight loss or reduced growth rate.	Provide high-calorie, nutrient-dense foods. Offer three meals with three snacks.
Autism spectrum disorder	Difficulty with changes in routine including meal times. Medications can interact with nutrients and impact nutritional status. Limited food acceptance due to sensitivities related to taste, texture, odor, and temperature of foods.	Some children experience weight loss or reduced growth rate. Some families try special diets (e.g., gluten- and milk-free diet) with restrictions that can increase the risk of inadequate intake.	Provide a routine schedule for meal times with three meals and three snacks. Introduce new foods with foods that are liked. Avoid distractions. If weight is low provide high-calorie, nutrient-dense foods.
Cerebral palsy	Oral motor problems that can result in prolonged feeding time and decreased food intake. Medications can interact with nutrients and impact nutritional status.	Children may experience inadequate calorie intake resulting in poor growth. Calorie needs can be higher with hypertonia/spasticity resulting in decreased weight or lower with hypotonia resulting in increased weight gain. Constipation is common.	May need specialized feeding equipment, adjustment in food textures or tube feedings, extra time for feeding. If underweight provide high-calorie, nutrient-dense foods. If overweight provide lower calorie, nutrient-dense foods. Provide fiber-rich foods and adequate liquids.
Down syndrome	Poor suck in infancy. Short stature results in decreased energy needs.	At risk for poor growth initially but increased risk later on for obesity. Constipation is common.	Watch for adequate growth the first year and later provide low-calorie, fiber-rich foods, adequate liquids, and physical activity.
Fetal alcohol syndrome	Poor suck and difficult to feed.	Children may experience inadequate calorie intake resulting in poor growth.	Provide high-calorie, nutrient-dense foods. Offer three meals with three snacks. Tube feeding may be needed.
Epilepsy and seizure disorder	Medications can interact with nutrients and impact nutritional status.	Constipation can occur.	Offer nutrient-dense foods rich in fiber and adequate liquids. Some children may need special diets for seizure control that are coordinated with family and health care providers.
Muscular dystrophy	Muscle weakness can lead to chewing and swallowing problems that result in prolonged feeding time and decreased food intake.	Children may experience inadequate calorie intake resulting in poor growth. Sometimes obesity occurs when ability to walk is reduced resulting in decreased calorie needs. Appetite can be increased due to medication.	May need specialized feeding equipment, adjustment in food textures or tube feedings, and extra time for feeding. If underweight provide high-calorie, nutrient-dense foods. If overweight provide lower calorie, nutrient-dense foods.
Spina bifida	Swallowing problems, may develop allergy to latex.	Sometimes obesity occurs when ability to walk is reduced resulting in decreased calorie needs. Constipation can occur.	If overweight provide lower-calorie, nutrient-dense foods. If there is a latex allergy avoid bananas, kiwi, water chestnuts, and avocados.

Sources: *Journal of the American Dietetic Association*, 2010, *110*(2). Position of the American Dietetic Association: Providing Nutrition Services for People with Developmental Disabilities and Special Health Care Needs; *Pediatric nutrition in chronic diseases and developmental disorders: Prevention, assessment and treatment*, 2nd ed., edited by S. W. Ekvall, & V. K. Ekvall, 2005, New York: Oxford University Press; *Pediatric nutrition care manual*, American Dietetic Association, 2011, www.nutritioncaremanual.org; and Bagnell, A., & Davies, T. (2008). *Muscular dystrophy campaign: Nutrition and feeding*, http://www.muscular-dystrophy.org/.

Adjustments to the way food is offered may also be needed. These include:

- *Food texture:* Food may need to be ground or pureed.
- *Food consistency:* A commercial thickener may need to be added to liquids.
- *Special equipment:* Special equipment such as a feeding chair or special plate and eating utensils may be necessary.
- *Commercial supplements:* Supplements used to boost calorie intake or for tube feeding.
- *Calorie level:* High-calorie or low-calorie foods may be needed.
- *Mealtimes:* More time may be needed for consuming meals.

Families, the child's medical team and early intervention specialists are good resources for guidance about managing children's eating concerns. During mealtimes teachers should observe children with special eating concerns carefully, watching for chewing, swallowing, and other eating problems. The NAEYC (National Association for the Education of Young Children, 2012) recommends that staff keep a daily record documenting the type and amount of food consumed by children with special needs and provide this information to families. Any concerns should be shared because children may need to be referred to a feeding clinic that offers the services of a physician, an occupational or speech therapist, and a dietitian.

Planning Menus for Children with Vegetarian Diets

A vegetarian diet is one in which the child's primary source of nutrition comes from plant foods. There are different types of vegetarian diets. Teachers need to understand which type of vegetarian diet a child requires so that they understand the type of substitutions to make on program menus. Table 6-7 describes four types of vegetarian diets and the foods that are avoided and consumed.

Infants with Vegetarian Diets

The age of a child influences vegetarian menu planning decisions. A vegetarian diet can safely meet the nutritional needs of infants. At first infants are either breastfed or provided regular formula. Soy formula is an option for infants whose families avoid all animal sources of food including milk. Solid foods are introduced gradually, following the same guidelines recommended for non-vegetarian infant diets. In place of meat or poultry protein sources, eggs, dairy products such as cottage cheese and yogurt, and protein-rich vegetable foods such as pureed legumes, tofu, and soy yogurts are offered. Infant cereal is particularly beneficial especially for breast-fed infants because it is rich in iron and zinc, nutrients generally found in meat products. Infants following a vegetarian diet require attention to maintain adequate nutrient intake. A feeding progression chart that follows CACFP guidelines for infants on vegetarian diets is provided in Table 6-8. Nut or peanut butter are good vegetarian foods, but should not be given by the spoonful to children younger than 4 years of age due to the risk of choking (U.S. Department of Agriculture, 2011b). Bread and peanut butter can form a glob in the roof of the mouth, which can make it difficult to swallow.

Toddler, Preschool, and Primary-Grade Children with Vegetarian Diets

Young children whose vegetarian diet includes milk, other dairy products, and eggs receive a diet that supports growth. It can be more challenging to meet the nutrient needs of children on vegan diets. Sometimes the fiber content of a plant-based vegan diet provides so much bulk that children become full before

TABLE 6-7	Types of Vegetarians	
Type of Vegetarian	**Avoids**	**Consumes**
Lacto-ovo	Meat, poultry, fish	Eggs, milk and dairy products, foods of plant origin
Ovo-vegetarian	Meat, poultry, fish, dairy	Eggs, foods of plant origin
Lacto-vegetarian	Meat, poultry, fish, eggs	Milk and dairy products and foods of plant origin
Vegan	Meat, poultry, fish, eggs, and dairy	Only foods of plant origin

Source: Based on "Types of Vegetarian Diets" Pediatric Nutrition Care Manual, American Dietetic Association, 2011, available at www.nutritioncaremanual.org.

TABLE 6-8   CACFP Meal Pattern for Vegetarian Infants

Birth Through 3 Months	4 Months Through 7 Months	8 Months Through 11 Months
Breakfast		
4–6 fluid ounces of breast milk or iron-fortified formula for all meals. (Soy formula can be used for non-breastfeeding vegan infants.)	4–8 fluid ounces of breast milk or iron-fortified formula for all meals. (Soy formula can be used for non-breastfeeding vegan infants.) 0–3 T iron-fortified infant cereal	6–8 fluid ounces of breast milk or iron-fortified formula for all meals. (Soy formula can be used for non-breastfeeding vegan infants.) 2–4 T of iron-fortified infant cereal and 1–4 T of fruit or vegetable or both
Lunch or Supper		
4–6 fluid ounces of breast milk or iron-fortified formula for all meals. (Soy formula can be used for non-breastfeeding vegan infants.)	4–8 fluid ounces of breast milk or iron-fortified formula for all meals. (Soy formula can be used for non-breastfeeding vegan infants.) 0–3 T of infant cereal and 0–3 T of fruit or vegetable or both	6–8 fluid ounces of breast milk or iron-fortified formula for all meals. (Soy formula can be used for non-breastfeeding vegan infants.) 1–4 T of egg yolk, cooked dry beans, peas, or lentils or ½–2 ounces cheese or 1–4 ounces of cottage cheese and 1–4 T of fruit or vegetable or both Note: Soy yogurt, tofu, and soy cheese can add protein to the vegan infant's diet; however, they do not count as a creditable protein alternate for CACFP reimbursement.
Snack		
4–6 fluid ounces of breast milk or iron-fortified formula for all meals. (Soy formula can be used for non-breastfeeding vegan infants.)	4–6 fluid ounces of breast milk or iron-fortified formula for all meals. (Soy formula can be used for non-breastfeeding vegan infants.)	2–4 fluid ounces of breast milk or iron-fortified formula for all meals. (Soy formula can be used for non-breastfeeding vegan infants.) 0–½ bread or 0–2 whole-grain or enriched crackers

Source: Adapted from Child and Adult Care Food Program Meal Patterns, available at http://www.fns.usda.gov/cnd/care/programbasics/meals/meal_patterns.htm.

their nutrient needs are met. One way to ensure sufficient calories and protein for growth is to provide nutrient- and calorie-dense foods. This is especially important for children who are selective eaters. Food products that increase calories in the diet include nut butters (assuming there are no allergies), oils, and avocado. Whole soy milk should be offered for toddlers from age 1 until 2 years of age rather than fat-free or low-fat soy milk and it should be fortified with calcium and vitamin D. The CACFP provides guidelines for acceptable soy milks that more closely align with the nutrients in cow's milk. Soy beverages must contain 8 grams of protein, 100 IU of vitamin D, 500 IU of vitamin A, and 276 mg of calcium per 8 ounces to be a creditable milk substitute (Murphy et al., 2011). Rice milk and nut milks are not generally acceptable because, although enriched with calcium, vitamin D, and vitamin A, they are typically lower in protein content. It is important to compare labels and make informed decisions when selecting beverages.

Several aspects are important to consider when planning menus to meet vegetarian diet needs:

- Select vegetarian protein products that are fortified with calcium, iron, vitamin D, zinc, and vitamin B_{12}.
- Use meat substitutes such as soy burgers, soy cheese, vegetarian deli slices, bean loaves, nut butters, and tofu to maintain variety in the menu.
- Avoid gelatin products made from pork, such as marshmallows, gummy candies, and gelatin desserts.
- Plan healthy vegetarian snacks, such as whole-grain crackers with cheese or nut butters, whole grain corn tortillas with beans, pita bread triangles with hummus, or yogurt mixed with fresh fruit.

What if . . .

children in your class noticed that a child was being served a special diet? How would you respond to their questions?

Respecting the philosophical beliefs of families and providing them with the means for sustaining these practices in early childhood programs are important.

Planning Menus to Reflect Cultural Preferences

The traditions associated with eating are some of the most deeply ingrained behaviors of life. Many cultural traditions, customs, and beliefs are associated with food practices and affect the family's preferences for their child's diet in the early childhood setting. Making adjustments to menus for children based on family cultural practices requires close communication with families.

Each culture's food practices can have health and nutrition advantages and disadvantages for children. For example, traditional Asian meals are low in meats and rich in vegetables, which contribute to a reduced incidence of heart disease, bowel cancer, and breast cancer (Hill & The Ohio State University, 2010). Middle Eastern diets are high in olive oil, which contributes to that population having, in general, lower blood pressures (Nolan & The Ohio State University, 2010). Ethnic and cultural diets can also have negative features. For example, a study of Mexican American preschoolers showed that children's intake of calories, fat, and saturated fat exceeded recommendations, putting them at risk for obesity and its associated health risks such as diabetes (Mier et al., 2007). This may reflect a degree of acculturation to mainstream American dietary practices because traditional Hispanic diets may be higher in fruits and vegetables and healthy higher fiber carbohydrates such as beans and corn products (Ghaddar, Brown, Pagán, & Díaz, 2010; Ewing & The Ohio State University, 2010). African American "soul food" is rich in green leafy vegetables such as collards, kale, mustard, and turnip greens and high-fiber beans such as black-eyed peas and red beans. However, the diet also relies on fried and seasoned meats and whole-milk products, resulting in a higher than recommended fat and sodium intake (Edwards, 2003; Kulkarni, 2004; The Ohio State University, 2010).

Teachers also need to be aware that infant feeding practices vary among different cultural and ethnic groups. For instance, in one study, 6- to 11-month-old children of Hispanic heritage were more likely than white infants to be eating fresh fruits, baby cookies, and foods such as soups, rice, and beans that are traditional foods in their culture (Mennella, Ziegler, Briefel, & Novak, 2006). Feeding practices may also differ from the goals of the early childhood setting. For example, some cultures give sugar water or tea to infants or add other foods to bottles of formula (Nevin-Folino, 2003; updated 2008; Zhang, Fein, & Fein, 2011). When planning to meet cultural preferences, teachers need to work closely with families to identify foods from the cultural tradition that can be included in the menu while also meeting the goals for healthful menus.

Planning menus that reflect the cultural backgrounds of children in the class or school is one way of demonstrating **cultural competency**. Cultural competency refers to the respectful understanding and appreciation of cultural differences and similarities among groups and the ability to use this understanding to effectively interact with people across cultures. Strategies to support cultural sensitivity in the early childhood setting include the following:

cultural competency
the respectful understanding and appreciation of cultural differences and similarities among groups and the ability to use this understanding to effectively interact with people across cultures

- Plan menus that include culturally diverse food options.
- Offer classroom cooking activities for children to prepare and taste foods that represent a variety of traditions.
- Offer opportunities for parents to learn about healthful ethnic cooking by using a grain staple, such as rice, in a variety of ethnic recipes.
- Provide information, such as menus, in the various home languages of children present in the class.
- Read children's books on eating that reflect culturally diverse settings.
- Conduct field trips to grocery stores, supermarkets, and bakeries, including visits to culturally diverse establishments.

Teachers are respected sources of authority and information in many cultures. In response to this respect, teachers should provide accurate information about diet and nutrition that is reputable and culturally sensitive.

What if . . .

you wanted to include activities that explored cultural diversity in your class curriculum? What themes would you use? What foods could you include on the menu to reinforce your theme?

Planning Menus to Address Religious Beliefs and Practices

Religious beliefs, customs, traditions, and practices hold deep meaning to the families who adhere to them. In some cases religious belief systems and practices influence the diet choices of children. For example, some religious groups refrain from eating certain meats. Hindus do not eat beef, and people of Islamic and Jewish faiths may avoid pork and pork products. Devout Seventh Day Adventists avoid all meats. Teachers need to work closely with families to identify food restrictions and preferences based on religious customs or practices. Table 6-9 summarizes common religious food practices among eight different religious groups.

The Islamic Religion

Adherents to Islam follow religious writings that recommend a mother breast-feed her infant until 2 years of age if possible (Nevin-Folino, 2003; updated 2008). Modesty is an important aspect of this religion. Providing a private location for Islamic mothers who are breastfeeding helps support them in maintaining this feeding relationship. The traditional dress and head covering of Islamic women cover most of their body. This puts them and their infants at risk for vitamin D deficiency if the infants are exclusively breastfed.

TABLE 6-9 Religious Practices That Influence Food Choice

Religious Group	Meat	Poultry	Fish	Shellfish	Dairy	Fruits/Vegetables/Grains	Other
Buddhist	Avoided by most	Avoided by most	Avoided by most	Avoided by most	Permitted	Onion, garlic, chives, or leek or root vegetables are avoided by some. Most but not all are vegetarian.	No set dietary laws. Great variation in customs.
Hindu	Avoided by most. No beef, and pork is often avoided.	Avoided by most	Avoided by most	Avoided by most	Permitted	Use of these foods is encouraged. Some may avoid onions, garlic and mushrooms. Most but not all are vegetarian.	No set dietary laws. Great variation in customs. No alcohol, coffee, or tea.
Islam	Ritual slaughter laws. No pork.	Ritual slaughter laws	Permitted	Avoided by some	Permitted	Permitted	No alcohol. Coffee and tea avoided by most.
Judaism (Kosher diet)	Ritual slaughter laws. No pork.	Ritual slaughter laws.	Must have fins and scales	Forbidden	Dairy cannot be served with meat.	Fresh fruits and vegetables are naturally kosher.	Great variation in Kosher practice.
Mormonism	Use in moderate amounts.	Permitted	Permitted	Permitted	Permitted	Use of these foods is encouraged.	No coffee, tea, or alcohol.
Roman Catholic	Avoided by some on Fridays especially during certain religious days.	Permitted	Permitted	Permitted	Permitted	Permitted	Fish may be consumed when meat is avoided.
Seventh Day Adventist	Avoided by most. No pork.	Avoided by most	Avoided by most	Forbidden	Milk and eggs permitted	Use of these foods is encouraged. Most are vegetarian.	No coffee, tea, or alcohol.

Sources: Framingham State College, Buddhism, 2009, www.framingham.edu/food-nutrition/documents/buddhism.pdf; KITTLER/SUCHER, Food and Culture, 5e. © 2008 Brooks/Cole, a part of Cengage Learning, Inc.; American Dietetic Association, Cultural Food Practices, Pediatric Nutrition Care Manual, 2011; and Central Mosque.com, The Fiqh of Halal and Haram Animals, 2003, http://www.central-mosque.com/fiqh/fhalal1.htm. FaithandFood.com, 2009, http://www.faithandfood.com/index.php.

Many Muslims consume a *halal* diet, which means they consume foods that are lawful or permitted according to the Quran (Islamic Food and Nutrition Council of America, 2011). Only the flesh of animals or poultry killed in a humane way while speaking the name of God can be eaten, such as beef, veal, turkey, chicken, goat, and lamb. The Halal diet avoids pork and pork products such as the gelatin used in marshmallows, gummy candies, and gelatin desserts (American Dietetic Association, 2011c).

The Jewish Religion

The Jewish religion also has rules about how animals are butchered. According to Jewish law all blood must be drained from the meat for it to be considered *kosher*. Kosher symbols are used on processed foods to designate that they have been prepared in accordance with dietary laws. Milk and meat cannot be consumed at the same meal (American Dietetic Association, 2011c). The term *pareve* on a label indicates foods that contain neither meat nor dairy products. These foods are therefore considered neutral and can be served with either meat or milk. Pareve foods include eggs, fish, grains, fruits, and vegetables. Pork and pork products are not permitted in the kosher diet. Fish with fins are permissible, but shellfish are not. Eggs and fish can be eaten with either milk or meat. During food preparation and service, the cooking and eating utensils are also kept kosher. This means that those of the orthodox faith have available two sets of serving ware and cooking utensils for the separate preparation of meat and milk. The restriction that prohibits drinking milk and eating meat or poultry in the same meal is in conflict with the Child and Adult Care Food Program and the School Lunch Program requirements for milk and meat components served at lunch and supper. To address this, the USDA Food and Nutrition Service provides three options for Jewish schools, institutions, and sponsors to select from and still be in compliance with regulations:

Option I: Serve an equal amount of 100% juice in place of milk with lunch or supper. Programs operating 5 days per week may substitute juice for milk twice per week for lunches and twice for suppers, but no more than once each day.

Option II: Serve milk at an appropriate time before or after the meal service period, in accordance with applicable Jewish dietary law.

Option III: Serve the supplement (snack) juice component at lunch or supper. Serve the lunch milk component as part of a supplement (snack) (U.S. Department of Agriculture, Food and Nutrition Service, 2006).

When planning menus it is helpful to determine a local source for special dietary products such as kosher or halal foods.

Labeling of foods makes it easier to determine if a food is acceptable for a child following Jewish or Muslim dietary laws.

The Seventh Day Adventist Religion

This religion encourages the lacto-ovo vegetarian diet. Eggs and dairy are permitted although egg yolks are limited to three per week. The use of whole grains is encouraged. This diet is healthy for children as long as there are not too many high-fiber foods to interfere with the consumption of adequate calories. Menu planning for these children would follow the guides for the lacto-ovo vegetarian diet.

● SUMMARY

A well-planned menu is the foundation for creating a healthful nutrition environment in early childhood settings. An organized approach to menu planning ensures that nutritious meals are designed. This involves writing menus that demonstrate understanding of food program requirements and program nutrition goals and that support alternative and special diets. Many resources are available to assist teachers and food service personnel to plan nutritious meals that meet the recommendations of health, licensing, accreditation, and funding authorities. Program nutrition goals ensure that children receive appropriate foods and take into consideration quality-of-life issues such as sustainability.

A cycle menu is typically selected for early childhood settings. This helps organize the process of menu development, purchasing, and food service. It also helps family child care settings, programs, and schools establish and maintain cost-effective practices. The process of menu development includes selecting entrées, side dishes, and beverages that offer variety in taste, texture, and visual appeal. Once established, the basic menu is adjusted to accommodate special dietary needs.

Careful menu development is important. Children receive a large portion of their daily requirement of nutrients in the early childhood setting. They rely on adults to help them learn about making good food choices. Mealtime offers opportunities for children to participate in relaxed social discussions and guides children to learn self-help skills such as serving their own food and clearing their dishes. Children with special dietary concerns or cultural or religious preferences depend on their teachers to ensure they receive the appropriate meal. Families who send food from home also benefit from the information provided by programs that helps them make healthful choices for the child's lunch and snacks. Overall, careful menu planning contributes to children's health and wellness, and establishes healthful eating practices that children can sustain throughout life.

KEY TERMS

Anaphylaxis
Budget
Commercially prepared entrée
Commodity foods
Components
Creditable food
Cultural competency

Cycle menu
Head Start Performance Standards
Meal patterns
Meal plan
Meal requirements
Noncreditable food
Nutrient targets

Refined grains
Standardized recipes
Tube feedings
Type 1 diabetes
Type 2 diabetes
Whole basic foods
Whole grains

REVIEW QUESTIONS

1. What is the four-phase approach to planning menus?
2. What types of resources should a teacher have on hand and which funded menu planning system should a teacher be familiar with when planning menus for preschooler and kindergarten age children?
3. What are some important nutrition goals that promote the development of healthy menus?
4. Describe the process for building a menu.
5. What adjustments to the menu might be needed to accommodate health conditions and religious or cultural traditions?

DISCUSSION STARTERS

1. Discuss the following situations. How would you deal with each scenario in such a way that a child's accidental exposure to an allergen is avoided?
    a. A young child might trade or share foods with a child who has allergies.
    b. Food service staff forget to prepare the special diet.
    c. Cross-contamination of foods occurs such that some allergen gets into an otherwise acceptable food.
    d. The teacher is absent. How would the substitute know who has allergies and special dietary requirements?
    e. Foods from home are brought in for a celebration and a toddler with allergies is reaching for something he should not have.
2. A group of parents is upset about the school lunch menu. Some are concerned that there are too many processed foods, not enough whole grains, and too much canned fruit instead of fresh fruit. How would you approach this dilemma?
3. A 4-year-old in your program is obese. His mother tells you she has placed him on a diet and he can only eat the foods she packs for him from home. The boy cries during lunch because he can't eat what the other children are eating and he is hungry. How do you handle this situation?

PRACTICE POINTS

1. You have been asked to join the School Health Advisory Council to develop a new policy that focuses on the development of a more sustainable food service. List the steps you would take to develop and implement the new policy. How would you involve staff, families, and children?

2. Using the Figure 6-5 menu template, develop a weekly menu for 3- to 5-year-old children for breakfast, lunch and snack. Use the Figure 6-10 Sample Menu Evaluation Checklist to check your menu.

3. Using the four phases of menu planning, list important program requirements, establish two broad program goals, and develop a 1-day breakfast menu that will meet the needs of a preschool Head Start program that includes Hispanic children. Adapt the menu for a child with milk allergy.

WEB RESOURCES

American Academy of Pediatrics: Healthy Children
https://healthychildren.org

American Diabetes Association: Diabetes 504 plan
www.diabetes.org/assets/pdfs/schools/504-adanasndredf-2007.pdf

Diabetes Medical Management Plan
www.diabetes.org/assets/pdfs/schools/dmmp-form.pdf

Food Allergy and Anaphylaxis Network's Food Allergy Action Plan
www.foodallergy.org/actionplan.pdf

Institute of Medicine of the National Academies: Dietary Reference Intakes
www.iom.edu/Reports/2006/Dietary-Reference-Intakes-Essential-Guide-Nutrient-Requirements.aspx

National Food Service Management Institute: Measuring Success with Standardized Recipes
www.nfsmi.org/ResourceOverview.aspx?ID=88

USDA recipes for schools
http://www.nfsmi.org/Templates/TemplateDefault.aspx?qs=cElEPTEwMiZpc01ncj10cnVl

U. S Department of Agriculture and U.S. Department of Health and Human Services: *Nutrition and Wellness Tips for Young Children: Provider Handbook for the Child and Adult Care Food Program*
http://teamnutrition.usda.gov/Resources/nutritionandwellness.html

U.S. Department of Agriculture: ChooseMyPlate
http://www.choosemyplate.gov/

U.S. Department of Agriculture Food and Nutrition Service Child Nutrition Programs
www.fns.usda.gov/CND, which includes links to:
 Child and Adult Care Food Program, National School Lunch Program and School Breakfast Program

U.S. Department of Health and Human Services: *Dietary Guidelines for Americans, 2010*
www.health.gov/dietaryguidelines/2010.asp

MyEducationLab™

Go to Topic 3 (Menu Planning) in the MyEducationLab (www.myeducationlab.com) for your course, where you can:

- Find learning outcomes for Menu Planning along with the national standards that connect to these outcomes.

- Complete Assignments and Activities that can help you more deeply understand the chapter content.

- Apply and practice your understanding of the core teaching skills identified in the chapter with the Building Teaching Skills and Dispositions learning units.

- Check your comprehension on the content covered in the chapter by going to the Study Plan in the Book Resources for your text. Here you will be able to take a chapter quiz, receive feedback on your answers, and then access Review, Practice, and Enrichment activities to enhance your understanding of chapter content.

learning outcomes

AFTER READING THIS CHAPTER, YOU SHOULD BE ABLE TO:

1. Identify the hazards responsible for foodborne illness.

2. Define the role of federal, state, and county food safety regulations and guidelines that impact on food service in the early childhood setting.

3. Explain how to implement a food safety system in the early childhood setting using the principles of the Hazard Analysis and Critical Control Point system and standard operating procedures.

4. Describe how to minimize food contamination risk at each stage of food handling in the early childhood setting.

5. Explain food safety precautions that need to be considered during an emergency and define strategies for managing food defense.

6. Learn how to teach concepts of food safety to young children.

Lacey's class of preschool children enjoys an eventful day. Lacey and Joan, teachers at Sunshine Preschool, have scheduled a field trip for their class groups to an area supermarket. They observe how meat is ground and packaged. They watch as bread and rolls are made and baked in large ovens in the bakery. At the end of the visit, they get to sample fresh warm bread and sliced oranges. When the children return to preschool, they eat lunch (turkey sandwiches, green salad, sliced watermelon, and milk), which was prepared in the school kitchen. Just as lunch is ending, Lacey is surprised by Kimberly's mother who arrives bearing a platter of homemade frosted cupcakes in celebration of Kimberly's fourth birthday.

The next morning Lacey gets the first inkling that something is wrong. A third of the children in the class are absent. Several parents call in reporting similar symptoms: vomiting, stomach cramps, and diarrhea. Lacey talks to the director, Jill, who decides to notify the health department of a suspected outbreak of a foodborne illness.

The health sanitarian begins to investigate the situation. The trip to the supermarket is determined to not be the source of the problem. The supermarket manager and workers have food safety training certification; they follow state and federal food safety guidelines and have consistently passed local sanitation inspections. The children who had toured the area where meat was prepared had washed their hands before eating the snacks. Also the children in Joan's class have not gotten sick.

The food service at the preschool is also reviewed. The director of food service shows the sanitarian their Hazard Analysis and Critical Control Point food safety plan in which documentation confirms that proper safety procedures have been used in preparing the lunch. This confirmation and the fact that only the children in Lacey's class are experiencing symptoms similarly rules out the preschool food service as the source of the problem. Next, the sanitarian interviews Kimberly's mother. Ultimately the homemade cupcakes are identified as the culprit in this outbreak of foodborne illness. It is discovered that the frosting on the cupcakes was made with raw egg whites. Salmonella food poisoning was later confirmed by laboratory tests.

Lacey is upset that this has occurred in her class. She takes pride in providing a healthy, safe environment for the children in her care. She constantly sanitizes surfaces and carefully supervises children as they wash their hands before meals. She had been caught unaware when Kimberly's mother brought in the cupcakes and had allowed them to be served against her better judgment. After this event she learns that serving food made in a home kitchen is against the preschool policy. She decides that she needs to rethink her practices on food safety. She is glad to learn that Jill intends to follow up by offering a food safety in-service training for both teaching and food service staff.

Food is a source of nutrition; however, in some situations it can also become a source of illness. **Foodborne illness** is the sickness that results from the consumption of contaminated foods. It is estimated that foodborne illnesses account for approximately 48 million illnesses per year, which represents about 1 in 6 Americans and resulting in about 3,000 deaths per year (Centers for Disease Control and Prevention, 2012b). According to the Centers for Disease Control and Prevention (CDC) the incidence of key foodborne diseases is greatest in children less than 5 years of age (Centers for Disease Control and Prevention, 2011c). Understanding how foods become contaminated and the hazards they pose in the early childhood setting helps teachers prevent situations that put children and staff at risk for a foodborne outbreak. Infants and young children are particularly at risk for food poisoning because their immune systems are not yet fully developed (Mayo Clinic, 2010). In addition, their bodies produce fewer stomach acids compared to adults. Stomach acids offer protection from some infectious microorganisms (Pelton, 2011). For these reasons young children are at greater risk than adults for becoming sick when exposed to contaminated food, and the illness can become severe and even life threatening. In fact, one of the risk factors identified by the CDC for certain specified bacterial illnesses is attendance at a child care center (Centers for Disease Control, 2008; Jones et al., 2007).

Part of teachers' daily routines often involves the handling of food for children. This entails special responsibilities. In the opening case scenario, Lacey followed food-safe practices in the classroom. However, the weak link that resulted in foodborne illness occurred when oversight of food preparation was left to an individual who was outside the umbrella of the program's food safety procedures. The scenario illustrates the importance of the teacher's role in making informed decisions about food preparation within the program setting and with *any* risky situation that may lead to foodborne illness. Children may be at risk when served food prepared by an individual who has not received food safety training in a home kitchen that has not been inspected and approved by an appropriate health regulatory agency.

In this chapter we provide information to help you understand how to effectively manage food safety. We discuss the nature of foodborne illness. We also describe the food safety requirements mandated by federal and state regulations that provide the foundation you need to develop and implement an evidence-based food safety program. We also discuss food safety related to emergencies and food defense to help you be prepared to deal with unplanned events. Finally, we discuss how teachers can help young children learn food safety concepts.

● IDENTIFYING HAZARDS THAT CAUSE FOODBORNE ILLNESS

Contamination occurs when something hazardous to health is present in food or drink. Food and beverages can become contaminated by a variety of agents including those that are biological in origin, such as germs. Chemical agents such as pesticides and cleansing agents can accidentally end

foodborne illness
an illness caused by eating food that has been contaminated by biological, chemical, or physical contaminants

MyEducationLab™

Visit the MyEducationLab for *Nutrition, Health, and Safety for Young Children* to enhance your understanding of chapter concepts with a personalized Study Plan. You'll also have the opportunity to hone your teaching skills through video-based Assignments and Activities, as well as Building Teaching Skills and Dispositions lessons.

contamination
occurs when something hazardous to health is present in food or drink

Teachers who work with children often handle food, so they must understand the food safety risks associated with feeding young children.

up in food and pose a health risk as well. Physical hazards to food safety include items that fall into foods such as fingernails, insects, metal shavings, nails, and glass (Environmental Services Department, Maricopa County Arizona, 2011; Wallace, Sperber, & Mortimore, 2010). A review of the different types of food hazards provides insight into the causes of foodborne illness.

Recognizing Biological Hazards

Biological hazards include microorganisms that contaminate food and cause serious illness when consumed. These germs, which are too small to be seen by the naked eye, include bacteria, viruses, parasites, and fungi. Germs that contaminate food are by far the greatest hazard to health and occur more often than chemical and physical contamination (National Restaurant Association, 2010).

Understanding how microorganisms create illness prepares teachers to identify risky food safety situations and prevent foodborne outbreaks from occurring. Microorganisms damage the human body in three different ways: via infection, intoxication, or toxin-mediated infection (Brown, 2011).

biological hazards
living microorganisms that contaminate food and cause foodborne illness

Infection

Infection is most familiar because it is a process that occurs routinely in the early childhood setting. Children "catch a cold" or a "flu bug" and the infection runs its course. A foodborne illness that is classified as an infection is similar in that there is an exposure to germs. The exposure, however, occurs via food instead of by coughing or sneezing. The germs grow in the body and create symptoms such as fever, vomiting, and diarrhea until the body's immune system destroys the pathogens and children are once again healthy.

Table 7-1 defines the three different categories of foodborne illness and provides some examples of microorganisms that cause sickness as well as steps teachers can take to prevent an outbreak from occurring. *Salmonella*, the microorganism responsible for the outbreak in Lacey's class, falls into the infection classification. Because the egg white in the frosting was not cooked, *Salmonella* bacteria were able to proliferate, especially because the cupcakes were stored at room temperature.

Intoxication

Intoxication refers to foodborne illness caused by microorganisms that grow on the food and release toxins (poisons) into it. This in turn produces the symptoms of illness. This type of food poisoning can be very dangerous when the toxin is not destroyed by cooking or the toxin is highly lethal. For example, the microorganism responsible for the foodborne illness called *botulism* creates a toxin that causes paralysis and is considered one of the most dangerous biological hazards known to man (U.S. Department of Agriculture Food Safety and Inspection Service, 2011c). Strategies teachers can use to avoid the production of toxins in food are listed in Table 7-1.

What if . . .

food arrived in the classroom from the kitchen and you noticed the hamburgers appeared pink in the center and undone? What would you do to ensure children do not get a foodborne illness? What would you do if a child has already taken a bite?

Toxin-Mediated Infection

The final classification of foodborne illness is the toxin-mediated infection, which has features of both infection and intoxication. When food containing a harmful microorganism is consumed, the germs begin to reproduce and then release toxins in the gastrointestinal tract (Brown, 2011). For example, *Escherichia coli* (*E. coli*) is a diverse group of bacteria that includes both harmless and illness-producing strains. The *E. coli* O157:H7 strain produces a toxin-mediated infection (Shiga toxin) and has gained media attention because of the outbreaks associated with ground beef, spinach, hazelnuts, and Romaine lettuce (Centers for Disease Control and Prevention, 2012a). Another strain of Shiga toxin-producing *E. coli* (*E. coli* O104:H4) resulted in

De enfermedades mas comunes de los niños

TABLE 7-1   A Sample of Foodborne Illnesses and Prevention Strategies for Teachers

Pathogen	Type of Illness	Common Sources	Symptoms	Prevention Strategies for Teachers

Campylobacter jejuni	Infection	Raw chicken, unpasteurized (raw) milk	Diarrhea, stomach pain, fever	1. Serve chicken that is thoroughly cooked
				2. Do not serve raw milk
				3. Practice good personal hygiene (hand washing)
				4. Avoid cross-contamination
				  • Keep raw food of animal origin separate from ready to eat food.
				  • Use separate cutting boards for foods of animal origin and produce
				  • Thoroughly clean work area and utensils after preparing raw food of animal origin.

Clostridium botulinum: foodborne	Intoxication: caused by toxin in the food	Home or commercial canned foods that are not processed appropriately, food from damaged cans	Weakness, dizziness, problems with vision, speaking, swallowing, breathing	1. Do not use home canned foods in your program 2. Do not use food from damaged cans
Clostridium botulinum: infant botulism (infants less than 12 months of age)	Toxin-mediated infection: caused by spores of the bacteria that grow in the intestine and release toxins	Honey	Constipation, weakness, weak crying, loss of head control	1. Do not feed honey to infants less than 12 months of age 2. Do not serve food containing honey such as honey yogurt to infants less than 12 months of age
Clostridium perfringens	Toxin-mediated infection	Meat, poultry, gravy, temperature abuse of prepared foods	Severe diarrhea, stomach pain	1. Make sure food is properly cooked, cooled, and reheated 2. Foods should be held at proper temperatures 3. Leftover foods should be refrigerated promptly and divided into small quantities for refrigeration
Escherichia coli, Shiga toxin producing (*E. coli 0157:H7*)	Toxin-mediated infection	Raw or undercooked beef, unpasteurized (raw) milk or apple cider, contaminated foods such as sprouts, leafy greens	Diarrhea (can be bloody), stomach pain, vomiting, kidney failure and death in severe cases	1. Check that meat is thoroughly cooked before serving it 2. Do not serve raw milk or apple cider or sprouts 3. Practice good personal hygiene 4. Avoid cross-contamination (see above)
Norovirus	Infection	Leafy greens, fresh fruits, and shellfish, foods exposed to this virus	Diarrhea, vomiting, and stomach pain	1. Do not come to work or handle food if sick 2. Practice good personal hygiene 3. Carefully wash fruits and vegetables, and cook shellfish
Salmonella	Infection	Raw or undercooked eggs, poultry, or meat, dairy products, and produce such as spinach, sprouts, melon	Diarrhea, vomiting, fever, and stomach pain	1. Do not come to work or handle food if sick 2. Do not serve poultry and meat that is not well-cooked or raw milk products 3. Use pasteurized eggs in cooking activities 4. Produce should be thoroughly washed. Avoid raw sprouts 5. Avoid cross-contamination (see above)
Staphylococcus aureus	Intoxication	Foods contaminated by handling (sliced meat, egg, tuna, chicken salads, pastries, sandwiches), unpasteurized (raw) milk	Diarrhea, vomiting, and stomach pain	1. Practice good personal hygiene 2. Do not prepare food if you have infection of the nose or eye or on your hands/wrists 3. Make sure food is properly cooked, cooled, and reheated 4. Foods should be held at proper temperatures 5. Leftover foods should be refrigerated promptly and divided into small quantities for refrigeration

Sources: A–Z Index for Foodborne, Waterborne, and Mycotic Diseases, Centers for Disease Control and Prevention, 2012, from http://www.cdc.gov/nczved/divisions/dfbmd/diseases/index.html; *Essentials of food safety and sanitation*, 4th ed., by D. McSwane, N. R. Rue, and R. Linton, 2005, Upper Saddle River, NJ: Pearson; *Servsafe coursebook*, 5th ed., National Restaurant Association, 2010, Chicago, IL; *Bad bug book: Introduction to foodborne pathogenic microorganisms and natural toxins*, United States Food and Drug Administration, Center for Food Safety and Nutrition, 2008, from http://www.cfsan.fda.gov/~mow/intro.html.

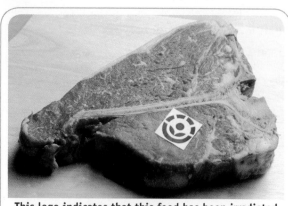

This logo indicates that this food has been irradiated as a method of food preservation.

4,321 cases of illness and 50 deaths in Germany in the spring and summer of 2011 and was eventually linked to the ingestion of raw sprouts (Buchholz et al., 2011). When food containing *E. coli* is cooked to appropriate temperatures, the microorganisms are destroyed and foodborne illness does not occur. The risk of illness, however, remains for food that is not cooked prior to meal service such as the sprouts.

Fresh fruits and vegetables have increasingly been identified as sources of foodborne illness. The use of fresh manure for fertilizing, unsanitary water for cleaning, and unsanitary food-processing practices are all factors that increase the risk of foodborne outbreaks from produce (Centers for Disease Control and Prevention, 2012b; Hunting & Gleason, 2012). Although washing produce can help reduce the number of pathogens, it will not completely eliminate the risk.

Food irradiation can be used to control spoilage and eliminate germs that cause foodborne illness (U.S. Environmental Protection Agency, 2011b). The FDA (U.S. Environmental Protection Agency, 2011c) has approved the use of irradiation as a means to make certain fresh produce and meats safer from contamination by microorganisms such as *E. coli*. Labels must indicate when food has been irradiated by displaying the irradiation logo.

Irradiation of food is a controversial method of food preservation. Some consumers are concerned that irradiated food may become radioactive and, therefore, dangerous to eat. However, the source of radiation used in food preservation is too low to add radioactivity to foods and has been determined by the FDA to be safe. Remember that irradiation is just one tool in the arsenal of options available to fight foodborne illness. The FDA emphasizes that, "no preservation method is a substitute for safe food handling procedures" (U.S. Environmental Protection Agency, 2011c).

Recognizing Chemical Hazards

chemical hazards unnatural chemicals that are present in foods and pose a health risk when consumed

physical hazards items that fall into foods that may cause injury or illness

Chemical hazards are contaminants in foods that pose a health risk when consumed. Chemical contamination can occur during the growing, harvesting, processing, and storage of foods. Examples of chemical contaminants that come in contact with food during growing and harvesting include pesticides and fertilizers. During processing, chemical contaminants in food include lubricants, cleansing detergents, polishes, and sanitizers (National Restaurant Association, 2010). Chemical contamination can also occur when food is not appropriately stored. In the early childhood setting, a potential risk for chemical contamination occurs when cleaning agents are stored near food. Chemical agents can spill onto foods causing contamination. There is also a chance for mistaken identity when cleaning agents are stored in containers that look similar to items of food (Figure 7-1).

Recognizing Physical Hazards

Physical hazards are items that get into foods that may cause injury or illness. Examples include glass, rocks, metal shavings, staples, bandages, insects, hair, fingernails, and jewelry. In a children's program physical contaminants might include beads, glitter, or beans and rice from sensory tables that are mistakenly returned to a food preparation area. On-site strategies that can minimize the risk of physical contamination of foods include wearing caps or hairnets, removing jewelry when preparing and serving food, maintaining kitchen equipment, and practicing pest control. In addition, teachers should carefully clean tables that are used both for school activities and eating before and after any type of meal service to avoid the chance of introducing physical contaminants to food.

Understanding the type of contaminants found in food reveals the number of ways food can become unfit for human consumption. Fortunately, the United States has one of the safest food supplies in the world (U.S. Department of Agriculture Food Safety and Inspection Service, 2011b). This is due in part to federal, state, and local agencies that oversee regulations that keep foods wholesome

FIGURE 7-1

Food and Cleaning Agents Should not be Stored Together Because of the Risk of Chemical Contamination and the Potential for Mistakenly Using the Wrong Product

and safe. These regulatory agencies also step into action when food products from other countries are found to be unsafe. For example, in September 2008, infant formulas produced in China were found to contain melamine, a contaminant that causes kidney stones, kidney failure, and in some cases death (Zhang et al., 2010). The U.S. Food and Drug Administration (FDA) immediately released a health information advisory clarifying that infant formula producers in the United States do not use imported formula or milk products from China and confirming that the nation's formula supply is safe (U.S. Food and Drug Administration, 2008). The FDA requires all companies in the United States that produce infant formulas to register with the FDA and adhere to clearly defined nutrition and labeling requirements. Companies must also undergo annual inspections of their manufacturing plants (U.S. Food and Drug Administration, 2008). These types of careful regulations support food safety for the most vulnerable segment of our population: infants.

Recognizing Food Allergens and Intolerances as a Special Type of Hazard

Some children face an additional food safety risk that is unique to them and harmless to most others: food allergies. Children with food allergies are at risk for exposure to allergens, which can have life-threatening consequences. In Chapter 6 you learned about the various aspects of food preparation and menu planning that must be taken into consideration for children with food allergies. Food allergies are also a food safety issue. Teachers must read food labels carefully to determine if the allergens are present in the foods being offered to the child with allergies. Although the Food Allergen Labeling and Consumer Protection Act (FALCPA) requires that the eight major food allergens (milk, wheat, egg, soy, fish, shellfish, peanuts, tree nuts) be listed on food labels, there are more than 160 known food allergens that can trigger allergic reactions (U.S. Food and Drug Administration, 2012a). Careful label reading is especially important for children who suffer less common allergies. For example, consider the following situation:

> Jan, a teacher in a toddler classroom, discovered how important it is to check on potential food allergens. A 2-year-old in her class has a mild allergy to cranberries. The toddler began to display irritability and stomach discomfort. The child's father believed it was caused by something eaten at school. Jan asked the food service manager to check the labels of all products used to prepare meals for any form of cranberries. The next day the food service manager reported back. In an effort to use up extra cranberry sauce, the cook had been mixing it with grape jelly and was serving it with breakfast. The vendor stopped this practice when its effects were identified.

Children with celiac disease can also face a food safety risk. Celiac disease is intolerance to gluten-containing foods such as wheat, rye, barley, and possibly oats. For these children consuming gluten-containing foods causes damage to the lower gastrointestinal tract. Although not as potentially life threatening as food allergies, careful label reading is still important. In August 2008, voluntary labeling identifying gluten content went into effect, making it easier to identify gluten in some foods (U.S. Department of Health and Human Services Food and Drug Administration, 2011).

Reading labels is just one aspect of ensuring food safety for children who require special diets. Teachers must also be watchful for **cross-contamination**. Cross-contamination in the context of food allergies occurs when a nonallergenic food comes into contact with an allergen during cooking, baking, or meal service. For example, if ham is sliced on the same slicing machine used to slice cheese, this will create a situation of cross-contamination that puts children who are allergic to milk at risk when they eat the meat. Cross-contamination can also occur if children share eating utensils, bottles, cups, or food. Teachers who are careful label readers and use safe practices when preparing food for children with allergies and celiac disease create a safe food environment for all children in their care. See the *Progressive Program & Practices* feature which describes how a school district in Corvallis, Oregon minimizes the risk of cross-contamination of peanut products in their central kitchen and cafeterias.

In this **video**, you'll hear teachers describing precautions used in their programs to ensure food safety. What specific steps are taken to protect children with food allergies?

What if . . .

you had a new child entering your program who needed a gluten-free diet? What information would you need to gather before the child enters your program? What would you do if you were unsure whether a food item contained gluten?

cross-contamination
the transfer of harmful microorganisms from one food to another food or from an infected person to food. It can also refer to food contaminated with an allergen

PROGRESSIVE PROGRAMS & PRACTICES

Addressing Food Allergies

By Sharon Gibson, Corvallis School District Food and Nutrition Services

The Corvallis School District Food and Nutrition Services provide approximately 5,000 meals in seventeen schools and an array of other community programs daily. A small, but increasing, percentage of these meals are for children who have food allergies or intolerances.

One major food allergy with significant consequences is associated with peanuts or peanut oil. Even though PB&J sandwiches are served in the cafeterias, special precautions are taken at the Central Kitchen where they are prepared in a secluded area to avoid cross-contamination, and then individually wrapped in cellophane. Once they are delivered to the schools, only one student worker is assigned to hand them out and to not touch any other food or area. Many cafeterias designate a peanut-free zone where children can sit without concern. The lunches children choose to bring from home often contain a PB&J sandwich so the complete elimination of foods containing peanuts in the cafeteria setting is not feasible. There are ways, however, to decrease the likelihood of peanut exposure.

Concerned parents communicate with their child's school about the severity of their allergies and establish a food allergy action plan with input from the child's physician. They also educate their children to be constantly aware of any potential hazards in their environment.

School staff must do their part as well. Carefully scrubbing down lunch tables, prohibiting the sharing of food and eliminating home-made celebration snacks where ingredients are unknown are the best precautionary practices to decrease

the risk of allergen exposure. When children are offered nutritious, allergen-free meals in a safe school setting they are less distracted and have the energy and attention to learn at school.

UNDERSTANDING FOOD SAFETY REGULATIONS AND GUIDELINES

Rules to keep food safe originated in ancient times. For example, some of the religious food laws and practices discussed in the previous chapter may have had their foundations in food safety. Rules and regulations that govern food safety protect children from illness and harm and are especially important in settings that serve this vulnerable age group. Food safety is regulated by federal, state, and county agencies. For example, it is not only convenient but a requirement that all establishments in which food service occurs must have hand washing sinks (National Restaurant Association, 2010).

Federal, State, and County Roles in Food Safety Regulations

Federal food safety laws are established by Congress and implemented through regulations imposed by federal agencies. For example, recently the House of Representatives and the Senate passed the FDA Food Safety Modernization Act, which President Obama signed into law on January 4, 2011 (U.S. Department of Health and Human Services, 2011). This law provides a strong mandate for strengthening food safety systems (producing, processing, transporting, and preparing) using scientific evidence and puts a focus on prevention strategies, more oversight of imported foods, increased inspection of facilities, and a strengthened role of the FDA in food recalls (U.S. Department of Health and Human Services U.S. Food and Drug Administration, 2011). Food safety regulations outline the specific legal requirements related to various categories of food safety (U.S. Department of Agriculture Food Safety and Inspection Service, 2011a; Marriott & Gravani, 2006). The federal food safety regulations provide the model for state and county guidelines for all establishments that serve food, including early childhood settings. Figure 7-2 summarizes the roles of federal agencies in overseeing the safety of the U.S. food supply. The predominant responsibility for monitoring and investigating foodborne illness, however, rests with city or county and state health agencies (Centers for Disease Control and Prevention, 2011a). State agencies work with the FDA and other federal agencies to implement food safety standards for foods produced within the state's borders. State or county health agencies conduct inspections at restaurants, grocery stores, retail food establishments, child care centers, and schools (Orange County North Carolina, 2011).

Impact of Food Safety Regulations

Federal food safety regulations have a direct impact on early childhood programs. For example, the Child Nutrition and WIC Reauthorization Act of 2004 mandates that all schools participating in the National School Lunch or School Breakfast Program must obtain food safety inspections twice a year (U.S. Department of Agriculture, Food and Nutrition Service, 2009a). In addition, funding sources such as Head Start and the Child and Adult Care Food Program have food safety standards in place such that if a program receiving their funds is not in compliance, the program risks losing its funding. Child care licensure by state agencies is contingent on passing health inspections that include an evaluation of food production sites. Efforts such as these implement food safety regulations and improve the quality of food service in children's settings.

FIGURE 7-2 **The Roles of Federal Programs That Oversee Food Safety** *Rercurso cap. 8*

acenuas ysus fonclones

Centers for Disease Control and Prevention (CDC) ✓

- Leads investigations of outbreaks that involve large numbers of the population over multiple states or are foodborne illnesses that are severe or unusual.
- Coordinates PulseNet, a national network of public health and food regulatory agency laboratories that identify foodborne bacteria.

Environmental Protection Agency (EPA) ✓
Proteccion aubiental
- Prevents air, water and land pollution.
- Helps avert chemical contamination of food through regulation of pesticide use.
- Sets national standards and develops regulations to support environmental laws.

U.S. Department of Agriculture's (USDA) Food Safety and Inspection Service (FSIS)

- Regulates and sets the standards for the food safety of meats, poultry and egg products.
- Investigates and announces recalls of any outbreak of foodborne illness related to meats, poultry and egg products.

Food and Drug Administration (FDA) ✓

- Assures that all foods (except meats, poultry and egg products) are safe, wholesome, sanitary and properly labeled.
- Investigates any outbreak of foodborne illness (except meats, poultry and egg products) and issues mandatory recalls of any outbreak of foodborne illness related to all foods except meats, poultry and egg products.
- Regulates the food service industry through the publication and enforcement of the FDA Food Code, a set of national food safety standards.
- Implements the FDA Food Modernization Act of 2011 by creating stronger prevention and regulatory controls for the U.S. food supply as well as imported foods and is mandated to create an integrated national food safety system in partnership with other federal, state and local agencies.

Sources: About Food Safety and Inspection Service, U.S. Department of Agriculture, 2012, from http://www.fsis.usda.gov/about_fsis/index.asp; Foodborne Outbreak Investigations—Key Players in Foodborne Outbreak Response, Centers for Disease Control and Prevention, 2011, from http://www.cdc.gov/outbreaknet/investigations/key_players.html; The FDA Food Code, U.S. Food and Drug Administration, 2011, from http://www.fda.gov/Food/FoodSafety/RetailFoodProtection/FoodCode/default.htm; About FDA, U.S. Food and Drug Administration, 2011, from http://www.fda.gov/AboutFDA/default.htm; Background on the FDA Food Safety Modernization Act (FSMA) U.S. Food and Drug Administration, 2011, from http://www.fda.gov/Food/FoodSafety/FSMA/ucm239907.htm; and U.S. Environmental Protection Agency, 2011a, Our Mission and What We Do; U.S. Environmental Protection Agency, 2011, from http://www.epa.gov/aboutepa/whatwedo.html.

Teachers and others who prepare and serve food in school settings must be familiar with the agency that monitors food safety in the child's setting. In most cases this agency is the local health department. The health department is a program's ally in creating a food safe environment. Creating a strong working relationship with the county health department sanitarians has many benefits because:

- They assist programs in developing effective food safety policies and standard operating procedures.
- They are a resource for food safety and foodborne illness-related questions and issues.
- They conduct inspections that support school goals for promoting food safe environments.
- They investigate foodborne illness outbreaks and assist programs in developing steps to control the spread of infection.
- They help programs identify when a foodborne outbreak needs to be reported to state or federal health agencies (Food Safe Schools, 2004).

Teachers and health department personnel have a common goal: children's health and safety. A close working relationship reduces the likelihood of food safety problems. If a concern is identified, health department personnel can provide timely expert advice to limit an illness outbreak. In the opening case scenario, the health department was a key resource. With the sanitarian's help the program was able to identify the source of illness. The *Health Hint* provides an additional example of the benefits of collaboration between the health department and children's programs or schools when the potential for illness threatens.

What if . . .

there was a suspected foodborne illness in your program? Who would you contact? What additional training would you need to be able to identify the signs of a potential foodborne illness? How would you try to minimize the spread of illness?

DEVELOPING A FOOD SAFETY SYSTEM

Program inspection by regulatory agencies helps create an environment of knowledge and accountability, which is necessary to support food safety goals. However, an even more important goal for programs is to develop a system of self-inspection that implements the most up-to-date food safety recommendations and monitors the safety of foods. The regulations that pertain to food safety are ever-changing based on new technologies and public demand in response to food safety events. For example, after an *E. coli* 0157:H7 outbreak in 1993 that occurred in the Pacific Northwest as a result of hamburgers that were not cooked to proper internal temperatures

HEALTH HINT Managing a Foodborne Illness Outbreak

An outbreak of Norwalk virus was linked to a local fast-food establishment where a recently ill employee had handled lettuce without gloves. Within days, a number of families in the preschool classroom reported their child had been diagnosed with Norwalk virus. One child spent the night in the hospital due to dehydration.

The teacher called the health department for advice. In addition to providing information about the symptoms of Norwalk virus and methods of transmission, the following preventive steps were recommended:

- Inform all staff not to come to work if they are sick.
- Direct food service staff to take extra precautions when handling dirty dishware.

- Wash and sanitize toys and surfaces in the classroom using a chlorine bleach solution.
- Remind teachers, food service staff, and children to wash hands frequently, especially after using the toilet and changing diapers and before eating or preparing food.
- Send home an illness notice explaining the signs and symptoms of Norwalk virus. Notify families that no child or staff should return to the program until 72 hours after their last symptoms.

Although a few additional cases occurred in the program, the spread of the illness was limited due to the health department's expert advice and the teacher's quick action.

Sources: *Norovirus: Technical Fact Sheet, Centers for Disease Control and Prevention,* 2010, from http://www.cdc.gov/ncidod/dvrd/revb/gastro/norovirus-factsheet.htm; *Making the News in Benton County: Norwalk-Like Virus Health Alert,* Benton County Health Department, April 27, 2006, from http://www.co.benton.or.us/read_article .php?d=&p=72.

(the outbreak caused 400 illnesses and four deaths), a more evidence-based approach to food safety was demanded, resulting in the development of the **Hazard and Analysis Critical Control Point System** approach (U.S. Department of Agriculture, Food Safety and Inspection Service, 2011a).

The HACCP is a proactive, preventive system for tracking food through the many phases of production, processing, preparation, and service and evaluating the potential for exposure to contamination. The origin of HACCP has its roots in the U.S. space program where scientific principles were used to ensure that foods fed to astronauts during space missions were absolutely safe (Goodrich, Schneider, Schmidt, & University of Florida, IFAS Extension, 2008). The FDA and the USDA require the use of HACCP procedures in certain food-processing industries. For example, the use of HACCP is mandatory in plants processing seafood, fruit juice, meat, and poultry (FDA, 2011b).

HACCP procedures can be adapted to any establishment that is involved in food service, including schools. In fact, the Child Nutrition Reauthorization Act of 2004 required the HACCP food safety system to be implemented in all school district food services by 2006 (Iowa State University Extension, 2009) . Schools represent the first retail food service establishment in which HACCP was mandated. Currently early childhood programs such as child care centers can voluntarily participate in HACCP food safety programs and use the state and local health departments to understand local food safety requirements (Riggins & Barrett, 2008). Understanding and implementing HACCP also supports the National Association for the Education of Young Children (NAEYC) accreditation goals for food safety as described in Health Standard 5.B.03 (National Association for the Education of Young Children, 2012).

Some early childhood programs contract with local school districts to provide their food. Food received from public school kitchens has been prepared using HACCP food safety recommendations. Whether a program receives meals through a contracted meal service, prepares food on site, or serves meals prepared in a home kitchen, it is important to understand and implement HACCP food safety recommendations.

Understanding HACCP Principles

HACCP is a plan for organizing safety measures to ensure that all feasible strategies are used to keep food safe. If, for example, a cook called in sick and a teacher was pulled from the classroom to prepare lunch for 50 children, how would the teacher know what to do to make sure food was safely prepared? If a HACCP system is in place, all the procedures involved in preparing a meal (cooking, serving, and cooling foods) have been analyzed and hazardous foods identified. Any risky steps in food preparation have been labeled *critical control points*. This designation is a warning that extra attention is needed to maintain food safety. This warning comes with guidelines, or *critical limits*, that list specific criteria that must be met for food to remain safe (e.g., the temperature a food must reach before it can be served). To make sure that the HACCP guidelines are consistently met, a monitoring system must be in place that can be verified as effective. This monitoring system outlines what needs to be done when guidelines are not met (corrective actions) and includes procedures for documentation and record keeping. The HACCP plan of action described above is based on seven basic principles that are summarized in Figure 7-3 and discussed in more detail next (U.S. Food and Drug Administration, 2011b).

It is important to understand these principles because staff who work in early childhood program or school settings are responsible for keeping food safe from the time it enters the program until it is served. Teachers are a part of the system of accountability.

Principle 1: Hazard Analysis

The first principle of hazard analysis involves evaluating the processes used to prepare foods that might cause safety issues and identifying foods on the menu that are most likely to be hazardous because of their ability to sustain microbial growth if contaminated. Foods that can readily support the growth of microorganisms that cause spoilage or illness when improperly handled are called **potentially hazardous foods**. An equivalent term that the FDA is transitioning into use is **TCS foods** which stands for foods that need time and temperature control for safety (U.S. Food and

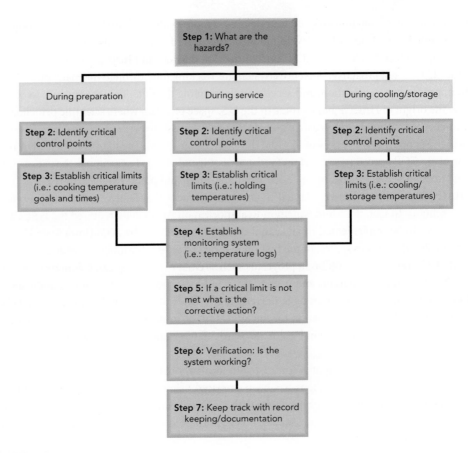

FIGURE 7-3
The Seven Steps of HACCP

Drug Administration, 2012b). Pathogens such as bacteria need certain conditions to flourish, such as moist foods that are rich in protein or carbohydrates and contain little or no acid. These types of foods will support the growth of microorganisms within a certain temperature range and time period of exposure to that temperature range (usually about 2 to 4 hours for bacteria) (National Restaurant Association, 2010).

Some potentially hazardous or TCS foods are listed in Figure 7-4. Recognizing which foods are potentially hazardous is important, so that appropriate management strategies for monitoring food

---

FIGURE 7-4   Examples of Potentially Hazardous Foods

- Raw or heat-treated foods of animal origin: meat, poultry, fish, shellfish, and crustaceans.
- Milk and egg products (such as custards and cream fillings).
- Leafy greens and tomatoes that have been cut.
- Heat treated foods of vegetable origin: cooked rice, pasta, potatoes, vegetables, and beans.

- Cut or sliced melons.
- Raw sprouts.
- Unprocessed garlic and oil mixtures.
- Any foods with a water, protein, and lower acid content (neutral or slightly acid pH) that make them more likely to support microbial growth.

Sources: The FDA Food Code, U.S. Food and Drug Administration, 2011, from http://www.fda.gov/Food/FoodSafety/RetailFood-Protection/FoodCode/default.htm; *Servsafe coursebook*, 5th edition, 2010, Chicago, IL: National Restaurant Association.

FIGURE 7-5
Lunch Menu with Potentially Hazardous Foods Identified

safety can be established. For example, some of the foods served for lunch in Lacey's classroom in the opening case scenario were potentially hazardous. The turkey on the sandwich, the watermelon, and the milk are foods that require careful management. Foods less likely to cause illness are the orange slices and bread served at the supermarket during the field trip because oranges are acidic and bread is low in moisture content. Both time and temperature factors came into play when the cupcakes covered with an egg-based frosting were allowed to sit at room temperature overnight. Potentially hazardous food should not be left at room temperature for more than 2 hours or 1 hour if the temperature is 90°F (32°C) or above (American Academy of Pediatrics, American Public Health Association, National Resource Center for Health and Safety in Child Care and Early Education, 2011; U.S. Department of Agriculture Food Safety and Inspection Service, 2011d). Teachers can prepare to monitor potentially hazardous foods by circling them on the menu so that they can quickly identify which foods need to be observed more closely (McSwane, Rue, & Linton, 2005) (Figure 7-5).

Once hazardous foods on the menu are identified it is important to consider how these foods are handled during food preparation. Each food item has a different type of risk associated with its preparation process. Risk is related to the number of times the food item moves through the **temperature danger zone**, the temperature at which microorganisms such as bacteria are more likely to grow, 41 to 135 degrees Fahrenheit (5 to 57 degrees Celsius) (Figure 7-6) (U.S. Department of Health and Human Services, Public Health Service, U.S. Food and Drug Administration, 2011).

In an effort to promote food safety in all types of establishments where food is consumed, the FDA created a simplified variation of the HACCP food safety system that the USDA promotes for use in schools. It is called the **process approach** (U.S. Department of Health and Human Services Food and Drug Administration Center for Food Safety and Applied Nutrition, 2006). This approach establishes guidelines for the processes different foods undergo when being prepared. The USDA identifies these food processes as follows:

- *Food preparation with no-cook process:* The food is not cooked and does not enter the temperature danger zone. Examples of foods that are subject to this process include cold cuts, tuna salad, and cheese.
- *Food preparation for same-day service:* The food is heated and served the same day and goes through the temperature danger zone once. Examples include hamburgers, French toast, and scrambled eggs.
- *Food preparation using complex food preparation:* Food is cooked, chilled, and reheated, going through the temperature danger zone two or more times (U.S. Department of Health and Human Services Food and Drug Administration Center for Food Safety and Applied Nutrition, 2006). Examples include soups, spaghetti sauce, casseroles, and dried beans (that are cooked, chilled, and later used in a burrito recipe).

The overall goal of the process approach is to allow menu planners to group foods according to how they are prepared and served, evaluate the risks, and develop strategies to minimize the

temperature danger zone the temperature range between 41° and 135°F (5° and 57°C) at which microorganisms such as bacteria are likely to grow

process approach the process of grouping menu items by the method of food preparation into three different processes that are distinguished by the number of times the food item goes through the food temperature danger zone

FIGURE 7-6
Food Temperature Danger Zone

time food spends in the temperature danger zone, thereby decreasing the chance of foodborne illness. Food service personnel are responsible for overseeing the process approach for foods served in early childhood centers and schools. Family child care providers, and those serving children in occasional groups, need to identify hazardous foods as well as the process used in preparation to minimize food safety risks when planning menus or cooking activities that use food in the classroom setting. Teachers also support the process approach by ensuring that food delivered to the classroom has been held at appropriate temperatures prior to service and is served immediately to children.

Principle 2: Identify the Critical Control Points

critical control points (CCPs)
points in time during food processing, preparation, and service at which control can be exerted to minimize the development of a food hazard risk

Critical control points (CCPs) are points in the procedure of food processing, preparation, and service at which food handlers can control, or reduce, food hazard risks (McSwane et al., 2005). The points at which control can be established occur during the critical steps in preparing recipes or when holding food prior to meal service. Tools used to manage CCPs include thermometers, refrigerators and refrigeration carts, freezers, ovens, warming carts, and steam tables. For example, a CCP for a program that receives food from an off-site kitchen includes taking the temperature of the delivered food and only accepting it if it is delivered at an appropriate temperature. The temperature of food is measured at the time of delivery to ensure that it is still safe to eat.

Principle 3: Establish Critical Limits

critical limit (CL)
an indicator used to establish whether or not the control measure identified for a critical control point is actually controlling the food safety risk. Critical limits must be measurable, accurate, realistic, and based on evidence-based research

Food Code
a food safety model developed by the USDA and FDA to be used by state and county regulatory agencies to develop rules to prevent foodborne illness

To ensure safety, **critical limits (CLs)** must be identified for each CCP identified in food processing. The CL is an indicator of whether the control measure is actually managing the identified food safety risk. Critical limits must be measurable, accurate, realistic, and based on evidence-based research (Schmidt & Newslow, 2009). CLs include the temperatures and times for cooking, holding, cooling, and reheating foods and ingredients in a recipe. For example, a teacher who has children prepare burritos for a classroom cooking activity needs to know the appropriate temperature to hold this food if the activity includes families joining children later for lunch.

The CL represents the highest and lowest range for a food safety standard established for a critical control point. This information is available in the **Food Code**. The Food Code is a set of food safety guidelines established by the FDA and the USDA to promote food safety (U.S. Department of Health and Human Services, Public Health Service, U.S. Food and Drug Administration, 2011). For example, the code identifies the critical limit for baking chicken as follows: It must reach an internal temperature of 165°F (74°C) for 15 seconds and maintain a temperature above 135°F (57°C) until the chicken is served (U.S. Department of Health and Human Services, Public Health Service, U.S. Food and Drug Administration, 2011). The USDA website provides standardized recipes for child nutrition programs that offer guidance on food preparation steps and also identifies CCPs and their recommended CLs (U.S. Department of Agriculture Food and Nutrition Service, 2009b). See Figure 7-7.

Principle 4: Establish a Monitoring System

A monitoring system is needed to ensure that food is checked during all aspects of its flow through the processing system—from delivery through storage, food preparation, and service. Examples of monitoring methods include recording the temperature of foods at delivery and during cooking, cooling, and reheating. The temperature maintained by heating and cooling equipment is also measured. A monitoring system is a crucial aspect of the HACCP plan because deviation from an established critical limit, such as food temperatures during cooking, needs to be identified and action taken to avoid a potentially hazardous food safety situation. Figure 7-8 shows appropriate cooking temperatures for foods.

corrective action plan
a plan of action that must be taken immediately if a lapse occurs in the critical limits established for a critical control point of a menu item

Principle 5: Establish a Corrective Action Plan

A **corrective action plan** outlines the steps that must be taken immediately if there is a lapse in the identified critical limit for a particular menu item's critical control point. In the early childhood

FIGURE 7-7 Example of a Bean Burrito Recipe That Uses HACCP with Critical Control Points and Critical Limits

Ingredients

Ingredients	**Amounts for 50 Servings**
Dried kidney beans	7 pounds
Onions, chopped	¾ cup, 2 Tablespoons
Tomato paste	3 cups, 2 Tablespoons
Granulated garlic	1 Tablespoon
Water	1 quart
Chili powder	3 Tablespoons
Cumin	2 Tablespoons
Pepper	2 teaspoons
Paprika	1 Tablespoon
Onion powder	1 Tablespoon
Low-fat cheese, shredded	3 pounds
Tortillas	50

Directions:

1. Soak beans overnight in 12¼ quarts of water. Cover and refrigerate.
2. Drain beans and add again 12¼ quarts of water and 1 tablespoon salt.
3. Boil gently for 2 hours until tender.
4. Use immediately or cool to 70°F (21°C) within 2 hours and from 70°F (21°C) to 41°F (5°C) or lower within an additional 4 hours.
5. Combine onions, tomato paste, chili powder, cumin, paprika, onion powder, and pepper. Blend and simmer in 1 quart water for 15 minutes.
6. Puree beans until smooth in consistency. Combine with ingredients in step 5 and shredded cheese.
7. Steam tortillas until warm.
8. Place ½ cup beans onto tortilla and fold.
9. Place on a pan, seam side down.
10. Heat to 165°F (74°C) or higher for at least 15 seconds.
11. Hold for hot service at 135°F (57°C) or higher.

Note: Red indicates a critical control point or a step in the recipe that deserves careful attention. Blue indicates a critical limit or standard that must be met for the food to remain safe. If beans are chilled and used at a later time to make the bean burritos, this represents a complex process of food preparation.

Source: USDA Recipes for Child Care by the U.S. Department of Agriculture, Food and Nutrition Service, Child Nutrition Programs June 2009, from http://www.fns.usda.gov/tn/Resources/childcare_recipes.html.

setting, for example, it might be discovered that the hot food holding cart had been unplugged and the bean burritos had not been held at the required temperature. The corrective action would be to discard the burritos.

Principle 6: Establish Procedures for Verification

Verification procedures are needed to verify, or make sure, that the food has been managed according to the five principles listed above. This step ensures that the HACCP plan is working. Conducting inspections observing food storage, production, and service procedures are all methods of verification. The program director can accomplish this by doing spot checks when foods are delivered to see if food handlers are taking temperatures or by monitoring temperature logs.

verification procedures procedures used to determine if a HACCP system is working effectively; can include a review of records, inspections, and so forth

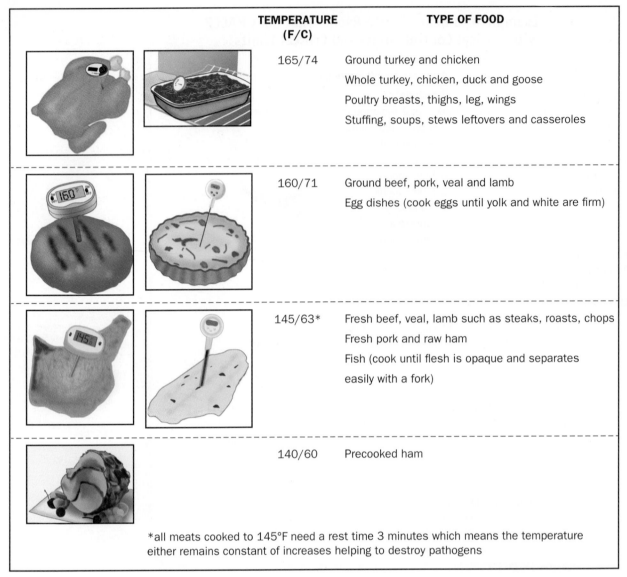

		TEMPERATURE (F/C)	TYPE OF FOOD
		165/74	Ground turkey and chicken
			Whole turkey, chicken, duck and goose
			Poultry breasts, thighs, leg, wings
			Stuffing, soups, stews leftovers and casseroles
		160/71	Ground beef, pork, veal and lamb
			Egg dishes (cook eggs until yolk and white are firm)
		145/63*	Fresh beef, veal, lamb such as steaks, roasts, chops
			Fresh pork and raw ham
			Fish (cook until flesh is opaque and separates easily with a fork)
		140/60	Precooked ham

*all meats cooked to 145°F need a rest time 3 minutes which means the temperature either remains constant of increases helping to destroy pathogens

FIGURE 7-8
Recommended Cooking Temperatures for Food
Source: Use A Food Thermometer U.S. Department of Agriculture & Food Safety and Inspection Service, 2011, from http://www.fsis.usda.gov/Fact_Sheets/Use_a_Food_Thermometer/index.asp#chart; Safe Minimum Cooking Temperatures, FoodSafety.gov, 2011, from http://www.foodsafety.gov/keep/charts/mintemp.html; and USDA Blog » Cooking Meat? Check the New Recommended Temperatures, U.S. Department of Agriculture, 2011, from http://blogs.usda.gov/2011/05/25/cooking-meat-check-the-new-recommended-temperatures/.

Principle 7: Maintain a System of Record Keeping

Record keeping is an important aspect of the HACCP process. Written records confirm that each required step is conducted appropriately. For example, in the opening case scenario, the sanitarian was able to rule out the school food service as a source of infection in Lacey's class by looking at HACCP logs and records. Taking the temperature of foods at delivery and recording the temperature on a temperature receiving log or on the delivery invoice are also methods that ensure this step is conducted.

Any teacher who consistently handles and prepares food must participate in a food safety plan. In some settings, teachers may not work directly with food and may not need to routinely consider the HACCP procedures. However, understanding how the food safety system works in the early childhood setting or school ensures that teachers are prepared to be a vital link in the chain that supports food safety and protects young children.

Understanding Standard Operating Procedures

Although the HACCP system provides specific strategies for handling foods to prevent foodborne illness, the system cannot be effective if certain general food safety practices are not part of the routine procedures of the food service operation. For example, policies for maintaining a clean kitchen, wearing head coverings during food preparation, sanitizing the kitchen work surfaces and children's eating surfaces, and basic hand washing guidelines are all examples of general food safety procedures that support safe food handling. In the HACCP food safety system, these are called **standard operating procedures (SOPs)** (Iowa State University Extension, 2010).

Standard operating procedures are important in early childhood settings. Programs and schools often have policies and procedures based on best practices that address food safety and sanitation. However, SOPs differ from general school policies in that they are written in a consistent HACCP format, which includes a description for monitoring, implementing corrective action, verification, and record keeping. In a review of trends that affect food safety in retail food service, including schools and child care centers, researchers found that the three most common risk factors for foodborne outbreaks are:

- Improper holding times and temperatures of foods.
- Poor personal hygiene.
- Cross-contamination (the transfer of harmful germs from one food to another, from an infected person to food, or from dirty equipment to food) (U.S. Food and Drug Administration, 2010).

Establishing food safety programs and complying with basic SOPs eliminate these types of risk factors. In the upcoming section we review general food safety and SOPs that apply to the early child care setting by evaluating the flow of food within a program.

● PREVENTING CONTAMINATION AT EACH STAGE OF FOOD HANDLING

Teachers directly involved in the purchase, storage, preparation, and service of foods, such as those who work in the family child care setting, require a detailed commitment to ensuring food safety. All teachers who handle food for young children need to understand the risks associated with each phase of the flow of food. The flow of food refers to everything that happens to food from the moment it is purchased and delivered to a program until it is ready to be served (Figure 7-9) (National Restaurant Association, 2010).

Minimizing Contamination Risk During Food Purchasing

Purchasing food is the first step in bringing food into the early childhood setting. Although teachers in the family child care setting have more direct responsibility for food safety when purchasing foods for their programs, there may be times when teachers in child care centers or schools also purchase food for classroom cooking activities, snacks, and special social events. All teachers need to consider food safety issues when they buy food for the classroom. A very important consideration is whether the food comes from an approved and reputable source. Reputable suppliers include those that are inspected and follow local, state, and federal laws (National Restaurant Association, 2010). The following tips provide guidance on determining whether foods come from acceptable sources:

- Food must come from a supplier that carries USDA-inspected and -approved meats and poultry and other FDA-approved processed foods.
- Food must be transported in such a way that perishable foods are kept safe.
- Food cannot be home canned.

A Matter of ETHICS

A concerned teacher has been giving leftover food from lunch to needy families in his classroom. Consider this ethical dilemma by reflecting on the risks of food insecurity versus food safety. How does the first principle in the Ethical Responsibilities to Children in the NAEYC Code of Ethical Conduct "Above all, we shall not harm children" guide your thinking?

standard operating procedures (SOPs) written procedures related to food service tasks that help to maintain food safety

What if . . .

you observed a staff member who is sick working with food? How would you manage this situation?

FIGURE 7-9
An Example of Food Flow
Source: Adapted from TrainCan, Inc.: BASICS.fst® *Food Safety Training and Certification,* 2004, http://www.traincan.com.

- Food cannot be prepared in a kitchen that has not been inspected by the health department (U.S. Food and Drug Administration, 2012b; McSwane et al., 2005).

Allowing families to bring food from home to share with all children introduces a food safety risk because the home kitchen is not an approved source of food. The intentions of families who bring homemade treats to school, such as the mother who brought cupcakes in the case scenario at the beginning of the chapter, are well meaning. However, these foods pose a safety risk and must not be allowed in the early childhood classroom. In addition these foods can undermine the healthful school food environment that early childhood programs strive to achieve.

FIGURE 7-10 Food Safety Checklist for Purchasing Food

- ☑ Purchase only the amount that can be safely stored.
- ☑ Keep raw meats, poultry and seafood separate from other foods in the shopping cart, grocery bag, and refrigerator.
- ☑ Place foods such as milks, raw meat, poultry, and seafood into the shopping cart last.
- ☑ Check to make sure eggs aren't cracked and containers and cans aren't damaged.
- ☑ Select produce that is fresh and free of bruises or cuts.

- ☑ Carefully evaluate expiration or dates on cans and boxes of food paying special attention to bags or containers of salads or cut fruits and vegetables (select items with the latest date).
- ☑ Only purchase bagged salads or precut produce that is refrigerated or surrounded by ice.
- ☑ Use a cooler to store groceries that require refrigeration especially when driving long distances.

Sources: Food Safety for Your Family, Kids Health: The Nemours Foundation, 2012, from http://kidshealth.org/parent/firstaid_safe/home/food_safety.html#; and Raw Produce: Selecting and Serving it Safely, U.S. Food and Drug Administration, 2011, from http://www.fda.gov/Food/ResourcesForYou/Consumers/ucm114299.htm.

Families can be included in the sharing of foods in other ways. Families may offer recipes for inclusion in the program or school menu. Additionally, children's programs can arrange for a family member to prepare a recipe using food purchased by the program from approved sources in the program's kitchen under the supervision of a worker who has a food handler's card.

Preventing foodborne illness requires a proactive approach. A variety of strategies assist teachers when purchasing groceries for their programs. Figure 7-10 provides a checklist of safety tips that support safe practices when shopping for food.

Minimizing Contamination Risk When Receiving and Storing Food

When food arrives at an early childhood program either as a bulk delivery of goods or as cooked meals from a vendor, it must be carefully inspected to determine if the food is fresh and wholesome and free from spoilage. As discussed earlier, testing the temperature of foods is a critical aspect of this inspection.

A food thermometer is an important tool for food safety. To be effective, the thermometer must be routinely calibrated to ensure accurate readings are obtained. A thermometer can be calibrated using the ice-point method:

- Insert the thermometer probe into a cup of crushed ice.
- Add enough cold water to remove any air pockets that might remain.
- Allow the temperature reading to stabilize before reading temperature.
- Temperature measurement should be 32°F ($\pm$2°F) (or 0°C [$\pm$1°C]).

Figure 7-11 illustrates the ice-point method of calibrating thermometers. Temperatures should be taken as soon as food arrives to ensure foods sent are heated or chilled to appropriate temperatures.

In early childhood settings and schools, meals are often delivered from a contracted source called a vendor. The food service operations of a school district often act as vendors for early childhood settings in the community, and the school kitchen has the primary cooking responsibility. A key element to ensuring that safe food is sent by the vendor involves creating a detailed contract in which conditions and expectations specify food safety responsibilities, as discussed in the *Policy Point*.

In addition teachers must communicate with vendors about special diet requirements so that children receive the correct menu item. For example, a child in teacher Jaime's class is vegan (eats no animal foods) and another child has a milk and soy allergy. Jaime must make sure that the vegan

FIGURE 7-11

Calibrating a Thermometer Using the Ice-Point Method

POLICY POINT   Food Safety and Vended Meal Service

An early childhood program that contracts for vended meal service shares responsibility for food safety with the vendors providing the meals. Teachers who work within this setting must support food safety goals to ensure that children are served food that is wholesome. The teacher is the last responsible individual to inspect the food before it is given to children to eat. To ensure that there is a mutual understanding of food safety responsibilities, it is important for programs to establish food safety stipulations within the contract. The contract should include the following:

✓ A specific time and receiving process is designated for delivery of food.

✓ The conditions for delivery of food are outlined, including the use of a sanitary truck with appropriate warming and chilling containers and the delivery of meals in containers that meet local health standards.

✓ The vendor is in compliance with all federal, state, and county health and sanitation requirements and HACCP principles.

✓ Food temperatures at delivery are designated for hot and cold foods.

✓ Conditions for rejection and substitution of unsafe foods are included in the contract.

✓ Production records for total amounts and portion sizes are made available.

✓ Requirements for the accommodation of special diet requests and food labeling of special diets are stipulated.

✓ Access to the following information is included within the contract:

· Standardized recipes.

· Nutrition and CN labels for processed foods.

Sources: Child nutrition and school health CACFP guide for registered food vendors, Nevada Department of Education, 2010 from http://www.doe.nv.gov/CACFP.htm; and Materials & resources for the national school lunch program: Guidelines for contracting vended meals, Wisconsin Department of Public Instruction, 2011, from http://dpi.wi.gov/fns/market1.html.

child receives soy milk and the child with allergies is given rice milk. Because both milk products appear the same once they are poured into glasses, Jaime will only serve them if they are clearly labeled.

Once food has arrived, been inspected, and accepted, staff involved in food preparation must give a high priority to prompt and proper storage. Potentially hazardous foods that sit in the receiving area or a kitchen for an extended period of time can quickly spoil and become unsafe to eat. Such foods must be stored under the correct conditions as soon as possible.

Three types of storage that require special consideration are refrigeration, freezer, and dry goods storage. Figure 7-12 describes food storage recommendations for each of these storage situations. How foods should be stored and at what temperature are important considerations. Germ growth is dependent on the amount of time the food product remains within the temperature danger zone. Consider the thoughtfulness of Shahrnaz, a teacher of twenty preschoolers who really does not like to waste food. The CACFP program guidelines stipulate that ¾ cup milk be served for breakfast. The entire amount must be made available to children at mealtime. Running down the hall to a kitchen to get more milk is not allowable by the CACFP. The milk that is delivered to the classroom is served in 16-ounce pitchers. Not all the children drink ¾ cup serving so a considerable amount of milk is discarded. The CACFP will allow a gallon of milk as a reserve source in the classroom if teachers choose to serve less in the pitchers. Shahrnaz knows, however, that leaving a gallon jug of milk at room temperature for too long a period of time is a food safety risk so this was not a viable option to her. Shahrnaz's solution was to request a small refrigerator for the classroom. She now fills the pitchers with less milk (making it easier for children to pour) and refills with milk from the gallon in the refrigerator if needed. She monitors the temperature in the refrigerator on a daily basis and records this on a temperature log. She accomplished her goal and sets a good example for her preschoolers.

It is important to also monitor the informal storage of foods that are not menu related. For example, teachers may store crackers, coffee, hot chocolate, nondairy creamer, and other similar foods in a cupboard for social events or staff meetings. These foods can pose a risk because there is generally no system for monitoring dates of expiration. Food that sits in cupboards for long periods of time can become a source of rodent or insect infestation.

FIGURE 7-12   Food Storage Recommendations

Refrigeration Storage

- Perishable foods should be stored at 41°F (5°C) or colder.
- The temperature in refrigerators should be checked daily and recorded on a temperature log.
- All foods should be labeled and dated.
- Special diet items should be labeled with both the date and the child's name.
- Refrigerator shelves should be cleaned weekly.
- Raw meats and poultry should be stored on the bottom shelves and separate from other foods.
- Medications that require refrigeration should be stored away from food in a locked box within the refrigerator.
- Refrigerators in food service areas should be used exclusively for storing foods for children. (Staff should not store personal foods in the refrigerator.)

Freezer Storage

- Foods that are frozen should be stored in moisture-proof wrap, bags, or containers at temperature of 0°F (–18°C) or colder.
- Freezer temperatures should be measured daily and recorded on a temperature log.
- Frozen food items should be thawed in the refrigerator.

Dry Goods Storage (Canned, Jarred, or Packaged Items)

- Dry storage should be located in a room that is cool, dry, and has a room temperature that is maintained between 50° and 70°F (10°and 21°C).
- Food should be keep 6 to 8 inches off the ground.
- Food should be rotated so oldest items are used first.

Sources: *Caring for Our Children: National Health and Safety Performance Standards: Guidelines for Out-of-Home Child Care Programs*, 3nd edition, 2011, Elk Grove Village, IL: American Academy of Pediatrics; *Essentials of Food Safety and Sanitation*, 4th edition, by D. McSwane, N. R. Rue, and R. Linton, 2005, Upper Saddle River, NJ: Pearson; and *Mealtime Memo for Child Care: Safe Food Storage*, National Food Service Management Institute, 2005, from http://www.nfsmi.org/documentlibrary-files/PDF/20080610114058.pdf.

The amount of time a food is in storage affects both food safety and food quality. A system of food rotation needs to be in place to ensure that previously purchased foods are used first. A common method used in the food service industry is **first in, first out (FIFO)**. Newly purchased foods are stored and older products are rotated so that they are used first. For example, consider Lewke, a teacher shopping for her family child care program. She has in her cart perishables such as eggs, milk, cheese, and fresh produce. In addition she has frozen foods such as peas, waffles, juices, canned corn, tomato sauce, and canned fruits. Once she returns home she evaluates what she currently has on hand and discards any food that is past its expiration date. When storing the newly purchased foods, she labels foods with the date of purchase. She has a food storage rack in her pantry that helps her rotate her canned foods. New food is placed behind previously purchased food making it easy for her to remember which food to use first.

first in, first out (FIFO) inventory system in which foods that were previously purchased are rotated and newly purchased foods are stored such that older foods are used first

Minimizing Contamination Risk During Food Preparation

Every foodborne illness is preventable. Prevention is a key aspect of keeping food safe during preparation. Three important concepts that support food safety during food preparation and service are maintaining personal hygiene, preventing cross-contamination, and avoiding the temperature danger zone.

Maintaining Personal Hygiene

The human body harbors many microorganisms, which are usually harmless. They live in our lower gastrointestinal tract, mouth, nose, and scalp. These microorganisms

What if . . .

your school sponsored a yearly potluck picnic? What food safety challenges does the potluck-style social raise? How might you arrange the picnic to increase food safety? Who is responsible for the safety of the food that is eaten?

This **video** shows preschoolers washing their hands before a meal. How do the teachers help the children engage in proper hand washing?

usually do not make us sick but can contaminate foods and, if conditions are right, grow exponentially to create a foodborne illness. It is very important for teachers who work with food to maintain consistent and scrupulous personal hygiene. One of the most important aspects of personal hygiene is hand washing.

Hand Washing   Hand washing is the simplest and most effective way to decrease the incidence of foodborne illness. A study on the impact of hand washing on the health of school-age children found that washing hands effectively reduced the risk of diarrhea, conjunctivitis (pink eye), and influenza by 30%, 67%, and 50%, respectively, and reduced overall the rate of school absenteeism (Talaat et al., 2011). Teachers also benefit when they wash their hands. For example, a recent study found that there was about a 7% decreased incidence of acute illness in typical work environments when staff was asked to practice good hand washing procedures (Savolainen-Kopra et al., 2012). These findings clearly support the importance of frequent hand washing by both teachers and children as an effective means of reducing the risk of foodborne illness and any infectious disease.

Teachers involved in the care of infants need to be particularly careful with hand hygiene. For example, in a family child care setting, in a short span of time teachers may change diapers, wipe runny noses, prepare formula, and organize meals for young children. Hands that are not properly washed become a source of biological contamination of food and increase the risk of foodborne illness.

Hand washing specific to food safety is one of the standard operating procedures recommended by health authorities to support HACPP in the school food service environment (National Food Service Management Institute, 2005). Figure 7-13 provides an example of a standard operating procedure for hand washing for staff working with food and children.

In addition, sinks designated for hand washing only are required to minimize the potential for cross-contamination (U.S. Food and Drug Administration, 2012b) (Figure 7-14). For example, consider the potential for contamination if lettuce is washed in the same sink that was just used by a teacher who changed an infant's diaper. Hands should be dried using a single-use (disposable) paper towel or hand dryer. Drying hands on cloth towels or aprons is not acceptable because these can become soiled and are a potential source of cross-contamination.

Wearing Appropriate Attire   Appropriate attire is important for maintaining food safety. Teachers who handle food should not wear jewelry, watches, or rings during food preparation because of the risk of biological contamination. Even with proper hand washing, microorganisms remain on the surface and crevices of these personal items. In addition, gemstones, backs of earrings, and jewelry clasps can come apart and become a physical contaminant of food.

Appropriate attire includes easy-to-clean clothes and head coverings such as a cap or hairnet to contain hair. Long hair should be restrained with a clip. An apron can help protect clothing from getting soiled with food or germs from food preparation activities. Ready-to-eat foods should not come in contact with bare hands (U.S. Food and Drug Administration, 2012b). Disposable gloves and serving tongs, ladles, or spoons are appropriate food service tools when working with ready-to-eat foods. Disposable gloves are a useful food safety tool; however they can become contaminated just as readily as hands and must be changed as often as hands should be washed.

Reporting Infectious Disease   One of the primary methods for cross-contamination or transferring germs in food preparation is an infectious staff member who comes to work when sick and contaminates food during the food-handling process. This is an extreme health hazard.

Legal requirements are in place for reporting about food service workers who have a confirmed illness or have been exposed to *Salmonella typhi*, *Shigella*, *E. coli* O157:H7, hepatitis A, or norovirus or who have symptoms such as vomiting, diarrhea, jaundice, sore throat, or infected cuts, pimples, or boils (U.S. Food and Drug Administration, 2012b). Food service workers or teachers who have been ill or exposed to the illnesses listed above must report this to the program director who, depending on state requirements, will share this information with local health authorities. Food service workers and teachers who have contracted the above illnesses should not return to work until they have written approval from a medical provider.

cleaning
the removal of dirt, grime, and food particles using soap and water and friction with the goal of reducing risk of biological, physical, and chemical contamination

FIGURE 7-13   Standard Operating Procedure for Hand Washing

PURPOSE: To prevent foodborne illness by contaminated hands.

SCOPE: This procedure applies to staff who handle, prepare, and serve food.

INSTRUCTIONS:

1. Train program staff on using the procedures in this SOP.
2. Follow state or local health department requirements.
3. Post hand washing signs or posters in a language understood by all food service staff near all hand washing sinks, in food preparation areas, and in restrooms.
4. Use designated hand washing sinks for hand washing only. Do not use food preparation, utility, and dishwashing sinks for hand washing.
5. Provide warm running water, soap, and a means to dry hands. Provide a waste container at each hand washing sink or near the door in restrooms.
6. Wash hands:
   - Before starting work.
   - During food preparation.
   - Before putting on or changing gloves.
   - After using the toilet.
   - After changing diapers or assisting children with toileting.
   - After sneezing, coughing, or using a handkerchief or tissue or wiping children's noses.
   - After touching hair, face, or body.
   - After smoking, eating, drinking, or chewing gum or tobacco.
   - After handling raw meats, poultry, or fish.
   - After any cleanup activity such as sweeping, mopping, or wiping counters, putting away toys, sanitizing children's tables.
   - After touching dirty dishes, equipment, or utensils.
   - After handling trash.
   - After taking a break.
   - After handling animals.

7. Follow proper hand washing procedures:
   - Wet hands and forearms with warm, running water at least 100°F (38°C) and apply soap.
   - Scrub lathered hands and forearms, under fingernails with a nail brush, and between fingers for at least 20 seconds. Rinse thoroughly under warm running water for 5 to 10 seconds.
   - Dry hands and forearms thoroughly with single-use paper towels.
   - Turn off water at the faucet using paper towels when touching the faucet.
   - Use paper towel to open door when exiting the restroom.
   - Double hand washing by early childhood staff who handle food should occur after coughing, sneezing, having contact with body fluids, or using the bathroom. After using the bathroom or assisting a child in the bathroom, the first hand washing will take place in the restroom; the second at the designated hand washing sink in the work area before continuing work with food.

MONITORING:

Administrative staff will visually observe the hand washing practices of the staff involved in food service during all hours of operation.

CORRECTIVE ACTION:

1. Retrain any staff member found not following the procedures in this SOP.
2. Ask staff members who are observed not washing their hands at the appropriate times or using the proper procedure to wash their hands immediately.

VERIFICATION AND RECORD KEEPING:

The administrator will observe staff and document whether hand washing procedures are being effectively used.

DATE IMPLEMENTED:_____ **BY:**_____

Sources: HACCP-Based Standard Operating Procedures (SOPs), National Food Service Management Institute, U.S. Department of Agriculture and Food and Drug Administration, 2005 http://sop.nfsmi.org/HACCPBasedSOPs/WashingHands.pdf; Food Code 2009, U.S. Department of Health and Human Services, Public Health Service, Food and Drug Administration, 2009 from http://www.fda.gov/Food/FoodSafety/RetailFoodProtection/FoodCode/FoodCode2009/default.htm; and Food Safety Basics: A Reference Guide for Food Service Workers, Julie Garden-Robinson, NDSU Extension Service, January, 2012 from http://www.ag.ndsu.edu/pubs/yf/foods/fn572.pdf.

Preventing Cross-Contamination

Using sanitizing methods during food preparation helps to minimize cross-contamination. Cleaning and sanitizing have distinct purposes:

- **Cleaning** refers to the removal of dirt, grime, and food particles using soap, water, and scrubbing. Although cleaning reduces the risk of biological contamination, it does not destroy all germs.
- **Sanitizing** involves the use of heat or sanitizing solutions to reduce the risk of contamination by killing microorganisms. After surfaces and equipment have been cleaned, they are then ready for sanitizing.

sanitizing
process used to reduce the risk of contamination by reducing microorganisms to safe levels by heat or sanitizing solutions

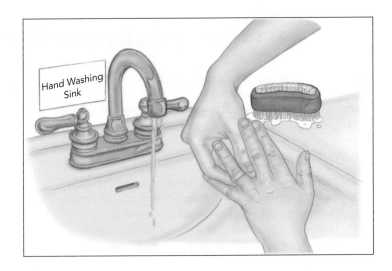

FIGURE 7-14
Teachers Must Wash Hands in Designated Hand Washing Sinks

⏵ The teacher in this **video** is demonstrating the steps for properly sanitizing the classroom. As you watch, think about why sanitizing is critical in food safety, as well as reducing infectious diseases.

Methods of Sanitizing Typically, in the kitchen setting items sanitized by food handlers include food preparation and service surfaces, dishware, cookware and utensils, thermometers, food service equipment, and doorknobs and handles. Sanitizing is accomplished by:

- Washing dishware, cookware, and utensils in hot water (171°F [77°C] or hotter for at least 30 seconds).
- Using chemical sanitizers such as bleach or other chemical products approved by local regulatory agencies (Garden-Robinson, 2012).

Both sanitizing methods are used when washing dishes in a three-compartment sink. The three-compartment sink procedure is described in Figure 7-15. The three-sink method is used when a facility does not have an appliance that washes and sanitizes dishes.

Preparing and Using Bleach Solutions Sanitizing with bleach solutions is often done because it is inexpensive, kills most germs, can be used in many different situations and in appropriate concentrations, and does not leave a residue that needs to be washed off (American Academy of Pediatrics, American Public Health Association, National Resource Center for Health and Safety in Child Care and Early Education, 2011).

Bleach solution dilutions of between 50 and 200 parts per million or about 1 Tbsp. 5.25% sodium hypochlorite unscented bleach per gallon water are recommended as an option for cleaning food service contact surfaces (countertops, high chair trays, dining table, and equipment) (American Academy of Pediatrics, American Public Health Association, National Resource Center for Health and Safety in Child Care and Early Education, 2011; U.S. Food and Drug Administration, 2012b). The amount of bleach to add to water, however, is dependent on the temperature, pH, and hardness of the water and therefore it is important to contact local regulatory agencies for guidance on preparing a solution and to check concentration with chlorine test strips (U.S. Food and Drug Administration, 2012b; National Restaurant Association, 2010). Recently in many states the concentration of bleach solutions sold in stores has changed to an 8.25% sodium hypocholrite bleach solution. Teachers need to check the bleach bottle labels to determine which concentration they are using. The National Resource Center for Health and Safety in Child Care and Early Education provides guidance for making the correct bleach solution at http://cfoc.nrckids.org/Bleach/Bleach.cfm. Health authorities generally agree that leaving the bleach solution on the surface for 2 minutes significantly reduces microbial contamination. A stronger dilution is recommended for disinfecting spills of body fluids such as blood, feces, and vomit. For this purpose, using about 1 tablespoon bleach to 1 quart of water with 2 minutes of contact time is sufficient for disinfecting (American Academy of Pediatrics, American Public Health Association, National Resource Center for Health and Safety in Child Care and Early Education, 2011). Bleach

TABLE 7-2 Sample Cleaning Schedule

Items to Clean	Cleaning Activity	How often	Mon	Tues	Wed	Thurs	Fri
STOVE	Clean burners	After use	X	X	X	X	X
	Clean outside	Daily	X	X	X	X	X
	Clean inside	Weekly					X
	Clean hood	Weekly					X
REFRIGERATOR AND FREEZER	Defrost/clean	As needed			X		
	Wipe outside	Daily	X	X	X	X	X
	Wipe inside	As needed/weekly					X
FOOD PREP SURFACES	Clean	Before & after use	X	X	X	X	X
	Sanitize	Before & after use	X	X	X	X	X
SINKS	Clean	After use and end of day	X	X	X	X	X
	Sanitize	Before and after use	X	X	X	X	X
CUPBOARDS & STORAGE AREAS	Wipe & organize	As needed			X		
EATING SURFACES	Clean	Before & after use	X	X	X	X	X
	Sanitize	Before & after use	X	X	X	X	X
EQUIPMENT (can opener, mixer, etc)	Clean	After use	X	X	X	X	X
DISH MACHINE	Clean	Daily	X	X	X	X	X
TRASH	Non-recyclables	Daily	X	X	X	X	X
	Recyclables	Daily	X	X	X	X	X
FLOOR	Mop	As needed and at end of day	X	X	X	X	X

Sources: Based on Benjamin, SE, ed. *Making Food Healthy and Safe for Children: How to Meet the National Health and Safety Performance Standards—Guidelines for Early Care and Education Programs.* Second Edition. Chapel Hill, NC: The National Training Institute for Child Care Health Consultants, Department of Maternal and Child Health, The University of North Carolina at Chapel Hill; 2012. Cleaning and Sanitizing for Food Business. Clutha District Council, New Zealand, 2008. Food Code 2009, U. S. Department of Health and Human Services, Public Health Service, Food and Drug Administration, 2009 http://www.fda.gov/Food/FoodSafety/RetailFoodProtection/FoodCode/FoodCode2009/ucm188064.htm#part4-6.

should never be mixed with ammonia or any other cleaning agents because toxic fumes can result. For safety, bottles containing bleach solutions must be clearly labeled and stored out of the reach of children.

A sanitizing routine is needed to ensure that surfaces and equipment are safe for food. It is not sufficient to clean and sanitize when a piece of equipment "looks" soiled. For example, a can opener can appear clean even though the blade may have been exposed to food multiple times during the day. A cleaning schedule, such as the one shown in Table 7-2, helps create an appropriate routine.

Safe Food Production at Each Stage of Food Preparation

Biological contamination is a risk during all phases of food preparation such as thawing, cooking, holding, and cooling, and the risk increases substantially when temperature abuse occurs. Once again, temperature control plays an important role in ensuring food safety.

Thawing Food Foods should be thawed overnight in the refrigerator in a drip-pan. Food can also be thawed under cool running water of 70°F (21°C) or less or in the microwave but only if it is going to be cooked immediately. Food being thawed should never reach temperatures above 41°F (5°C) (National Food Service Management Institute, 2009).

FIGURE 7-15

Procedure for Sanitizing Dishware Using the Three-Sink Method

1. Wash items in water that is at least 110°F (43°C).
2. Rinse in water that is at least 110°F (43°C).
3. Sanitize in hot water (171°F (77°C) for 30 seconds or chlorine bleach solution for at least 60 seconds).
4. Air dry.

Sources: HACCP *in Your School*, by A. Fraser, October 2007, from http://www.foodsafetysite.com/resources/pdfs/schoolhaccp/SchoolHACCPManual.pdf; and *Essentials of Food Safety and Sanitation*, 4th edition, by D. McSwane, N. R. Rue, and R. Linton, 2005, Upper Saddle River, NJ: Pearson.

Preparing Food   Food safety relies on careful preparation. Cross-contamination is one critical aspect to avoid. An important strategy is to keep raw meats, poultry, eggs, and seafood separate from ready-to-eat foods. Jan, a teacher who cares for children in her home, uses color-coded cutting boards. She uses a red cutting board for preparing raw meats, and a green one for fresh produce. When she prepares salad she doesn't have to worry that her lettuce will come in contact with bacteria from the hamburger patties she prepares on the red cutting board. She also knows it is not a good idea to "eyeball" a food to see if it looks done. One in four hamburgers turns brown before it reaches an internal temperature that kills germs (U.S. Department of Agriculture Food Safety and Inspection Service, 2011e). Jan uses a thermometer to check the internal temperature of foods. She also refers to the USDA standardized recipes because they tell her what temperatures her foods must reach to minimize the risk of foodborne illness.

Using microwave ovens to cook food may be convenient, but additional factors must be considered. Microwave ovens vary, and heating is not always consistent. To make sure there are no cold spots in food that might harbor bacteria, food should be covered, rotated, and stirred during heating and then allowed to sit for indicated stand times.

Cooling Food   Sometimes food is prepared ahead to serve on another day. Food that is prepared in advance must be chilled in a timely manner so that it does not stay in the temperature danger zone for an excessively long period of time. Consider this example:

> Rosalind stays late to prepare soup for the family social event that will be held the following day. Although she uses a USDA-approved standardized recipe, she does not follow proper cooling instructions before refrigerating the soup. The next morning, the health inspector makes an unexpected visit to her children's center. The inspector measures the temperature of the refrigerated soup and finds that it is still 50°F (10°C). The health inspector tells Rosalind that the soup has not been chilled quickly enough for it to be safe and, therefore, the soup must be discarded. The inspector makes some recommendations for the future, telling her that soup can be cooled using shallow 2- to 4-inch-high steam table pans with an ice paddle (a hollow plastic paddle that can be filled with water) and frozen and then placed in the soup to chill it quickly.

Reheating Food   Methods for reheating foods are also important to food safety. Reheated foods must reach an internal temperature of 165°F (74°C), which should be sustained for at least 15 seconds to kill bacteria (Garden-Robinson, 2012). The time it takes to reheat foods should not exceed 2 hours. Longer reheating times increase the risk of microorganisms proliferating.

Practices related to keeping and reheating leftover food for service in children's programs is governed by state and local health authorities. If local health regulations allow leftovers to be served, a careful management plan is needed. Any food that is being stored as leftovers should be carefully labeled, including the name of the food, the amount prepared, and the date of preparation. Leftovers should only be reheated once.

Minimizing Contamination Risk During Food Service

Ensuring safety during food service in the children's settings offers special challenges. Keeping heated food sufficiently hot prior to meal service is important. In school settings children often pass through a lunch line where food is served onto trays by food service workers. This format allows the food in the cafeteria to be held in heating units such as steam tables. This food must be monitored to make sure proper temperatures are maintained. Salad bars also create a food safety risk. Purchasing equipment that contains sneeze guards or food shields reduces the risk of contamination from coughs or sneezes. Salad ingredients are highly perishable and must be kept at 41°F (5°C) or below for proper cold holding.

Children's programs also use family meal–style service, which provides the opportunity for children to gain important self-help skills such as selecting and serving their own food. This approach requires that teachers supervise children to avoid cross-contamination as they serve themselves and pass the serving dishes. It is not unusual for children to want to lick the serving spoon, use the same serving spoon for different menu items, or put their used forks into a serving dish when they want another serving. This can result in biological contamination and also put children with food allergies at risk.

It is also important to monitor how long food is maintained at room temperature while waiting to be served. To ensure food safety at the time of service, meals are planned on a regular schedule, with routines that help children to be washed and ready to eat when food is ready, and meal tables cleaned and sanitized. It is also important to ensure that food is not too hot for consumption. For example, foods that are heated in a microwave oven can have hot spots that may cause burns to the mouth. Soups and stews may be hot and could pose a burning risk if spilled.

Another aspect of food service safety involves ensuring that children on special diets receive the correct meals. Having a system in place for serving children with special diet requirements is helpful because mealtimes can be very busy. For example, Elisa, a preschooler teacher, finds it helpful to serve the children with special diets first. She posts a list in the classroom that includes the children's names and their special diet needs. The program's dietitian has provided a menu that lists special diet substitutions, and Elisa always double checks to make sure the correct foods are being served.

Understanding the food safety risks related to each phase of the flow of food through a program from purchasing and storage to food preparation and service helps teachers to minimize the chances of a foodborne illness. Figure 7-16 provides a checklist that can be used by teachers to make sure all aspects of food safety are being considered on a routine basis.

Understanding At-Risk Situations in Early Childhood Settings

Although rules and regulations exist that govern food preparation in schools at any age level, feeding young children poses unique challenges. Children's physical and social-emotional development provides the basis for making many decisions that relate to feeding and safe nourishment. In addition, early childhood teachers may work with children from a variety of age groups and must understand children's needs in a variety of settings. It is important to recognize that some food safety issues are unique to the early childhood setting.

Food Safety and Feeding Infants

Infants have a special need for a safe food supply because the immaturity of their immune system puts them at greatest risk for foodborne illness. Infant feeding and handling and storage of breast milk were discussed in earlier chapters. Some additional food safety guidelines to consider when feeding infants are listed below:

- Don't leave baby food solids or liquids at room temperature for more than 2 hours (U.S. Food and Drug Administration, 2011c).
- Check formula and baby food to make sure they have not exceeded their "use by" dates.
- Discard any jar of baby food if the safety button on the lid has popped.
- Don't put a bottle back in the refrigerator if the baby doesn't finish it.
- Do not heat breast milk, formula, or baby food in the microwave oven because uneven heating can lead to hot spots, which can burn the baby's mouth and throat and can destroy protective protein and vitamin components of breast milk (American Academy of Pediatrics, 2011).
- Do not feed baby directly from the jar. This introduces germs from the baby's mouth into the jar of food creating a food safety risk if food is refrigerated for later use.
- Do not feed babies honey until age 1 and older due to the risk of botulism.

Ensuring that infants receive their own mother's breast milk is another important component of food safety when feeding infants. The *Nutrition Note* discusses this topic and offers guidance on what to do if an infant drinks the wrong milk.

Food Safety and Feeding Toddlers and Preschoolers

Choking is a potential hazard for young children. It is the leading cause of unintentional injury and death of children especially those under age 3 (American Academy of Pediatrics, 2010). Specific foods introduce safety risks for young children because they have characteristics associated with choking. Foods that can get lodged in the throat or lung are round, hard, small, thick, and sticky

FIGURE 7-16   Sample Food Safety Checklist

Date_____   Reviewer_____

Directions: On a daily basis evaluate food safety by using the following checklist. Record any corrective action taken and file.

HAND HYGIENE	Yes	No	Corrective Action
A standard operating procedure for hand washing is posted.	❏	❏	_____
Teachers ensure children wash hands before and after preparing food and eating meals.	❏	❏	_____

SAFE FOOD PREPARATION	Yes	No	Corrective Action
All food comes from approved sources.	❏	❏	_____
Food is kept out of the temperature danger zone.	❏	❏	_____
· Temperature of hot food being held is at or above 135°F (57°C).	❏	❏	_____
· Temperature of cold food being held is at or below 41°F (5°C).	❏	❏	_____
· Thermometers are available and accurate.	❏	❏	_____
· Food is cooked to the required safe internal temperature for the appropriate time.	❏	❏	_____
Procedures are in place to prevent cross-contamination.	❏	❏	_____
· All equipment, food preparation and service areas are washed, rinsed, and sanitized before and after use.	❏	❏	_____
· Disposable gloves or serving utensils are used to avoid touching ready-to-eat foods with bare hands.	❏	❏	_____
· Raw animal foods are kept separate from ready-to-eat foods.	❏	❏	_____
· Classroom food activities using ready to eat food do not include mixing and consuming ingredients that have been handled by multiple children.	❏	❏	_____
· Cooking activities with children do not include the use of raw egg or other raw animal foods.	❏	❏	_____
· Procedures are in place for handling food allergies.	❏	❏	_____

HOLDING AND STORAGE	Yes	No	Corrective Action
Temperature for refrigerator, freezer, and dry storage area is monitored daily including classroom and staff refrigerators.	❏	❏	_____
All food is properly wrapped, labeled, and dated including special diets.	❏	❏	_____
The FIFO (first in, first out) method of inventory management is used.	❏	❏	_____
All leftover food served to children is discarded after meal service.	❏	❏	_____

CLEANING AND SANITIZING	Yes	No	Corrective Action
Dish machine is working properly.	❏	❏	_____
Water temperatures are correct for wash and rinse and sanitizing.	❏	❏	_____
Tableware and utensils are allowed to air dry.	❏	❏	_____
Children's tables are washed, rinsed, and sanitized before and after meals.	❏	❏	_____
Cleaning cloths are stored in sanitizing solution while in use.	❏	❏	_____

Sources: HACCP-*Based* SOPs: *Food Safety Checklist,* by the National Food Service Management Institute, 2005. For a complete list, go to http://sop.nfsmi.org/Records/FoodSafetyChecklist.pdf; and Food Safety Basics: A Reference Guide for Foodservice Operators by Julie Garden-Robinson, NDSU Extension Service, 2012, http://www.ag.ndsu.edu/pubs/yf/foods/fn572.pdf.

(peanut butter), smooth, compressible or dense, or slippery and large enough to obstruct an airway (American Academy of Pediatrics, American Public Health Association, National Resource Center for Health and Safety in Child Care and Early Education, 2011). Hotdogs, which are just the right size to lodge in the throat of a child, cause more choking deaths than any other food (American Academy of Pediatrics, 2010). The following foods should not be served to children under age 4 (American Academy of Pediatrics, 2010; American Academy of Pediatrics, 2012; American Academy of

NUTRITION NOTE Feeding Breast Milk to Another Mother's Baby

Breast milk is considered the gold standard for infant nutrition. Teachers who support mothers who choose to breast-feed provide an invaluable service to both mother and baby. Breast milk, however, must be handled appropriately to avoid food safety problems.

Teachers who follow proper procedures for handling breast milk will rarely feed a baby the wrong bottle of breast milk. However, a bottle can be put down by one infant and picked up by another. If a baby consumes another infant's bottle of breast milk, this must be treated as an accidental exposure to a bodily fluid and a potential exposure to hepatitis B, hepatitis C, or HIV.

The National Resource Center for Health and Safety in Child Care and Early Education and the CDC recommend that the teacher notify the parents of the baby who consumed the wrong milk, the infant's medical provider, and the mother whose

breast milk was consumed. The mother whose milk was consumed by the wrong child should be asked if she has had a blood test for hepatitis B, hepatitis C, or HIV test and if she would be willing to share this information with the family whose infant was exposed. If she has not been tested, she should be asked if she would be willing to take a blood test and follow-up test 6 months later and share the results with the baby's family. Depending on the response to these questions the medical provider may recommend blood tests for the baby who consumed the wrong milk.

Although the risk of transmission of HIV in breast milk is very low, the follow-up procedures and testing that occur as a result of feeding the wrong breast milk to an infant highlight the importance of following careful food safety procedures when feeding babies breast milk.

Source: American Academy of Pediatrics, American Public Health Association, National Resource Center for Health and Safety in Child Care and Early Education, 2011. Caring for our children: National health and safety performance standards; *Guidelines for early care and education programs.* 3rd edition. Elk Grove Village, IL: American Academy of Pediatrics; Washington, DC: American Public Health Association. Also available at http://nrckids.org.

Pediatrics, American Public Health Association, National Resource Center for Health and Safety in Child Care and Early Education, 2011; Washington State Department of Health, 2011):

Hot dogs, sausages, and meat sticks

Nuts and seeds

Large pieces of meat or cheese

Beef jerky

Whole grapes

Hard, gooey, or sticky candy

Popcorn

A large serving size of peanut butter

Raw vegetables including carrot sticks or rounds and raw peas

Whole kernel corn

Hard pretzels, chips

Small, dried fruits such as raisins

Rice cakes

Gum

Food offered to toddlers and preschool-age children should be cut into age-appropriate pieces of ½ inch or less (¼ inch or less for infants). Children should be seated while eating and teachers should supervise mealtimes closely. NAEYC *Standard 5.B.14* provides guidance on foods that pose a choking risk (National Association for the Education of Young Children, 2012).

Food Safety and Children with Special Needs

Some children with special developmental needs may have food preparation and service requirements that are different than other children. These differences may create unique food safety concerns. For example:

- Children with developmental impairments may be at increased risk for choking and require alternative food textures and/or thickeners added to beverages.
- Children with special needs may require tube feeding, which requires careful handling.

- Service of foods to children with special developmental challenges may take longer as the child negotiates the eating process.
- During meal service, temperatures of foods may enter food temperature danger zones longer or more often due to the need to transport special single-serving portions, which are harder to maintain at appropriate temperatures, and prolonged feeding times. Reheating of foods may be more common to support meal service (Krueger, 2008).

As with all food service, specialized equipment used in food preparation for children with special needs such as blenders or food processors must be properly cleaned and sanitized. Any special feeding devices such as adaptive eating utensils, plates, and bowls must also be properly cleaned and sanitized.

Some children with identified special developmental needs may require a medical statement or guidance from a medical provider, describing the disability and how it affects the child's diet, including what to omit and what to substitute (American Academy of Pediatrics, American Public Health Association, National Resource Center for Health and Safety in Child Care and Early Education, 2011). Teachers may need to obtain training to know how to respond if a child's disability interferes with swallowing or if choking is a potential concern. Teachers need to ensure that all children have access to quality, balanced, wholesome meals that meet their unique requirements. Teachers also need to make sure they understand any required diet modifications.

Food Safety and Food Brought from Home

Some families may ask to bring their child's food from home rather than have meals prepared by the early childhood program. Such a request may be made for children whose diet restrictions are complex. In considering such a request, teachers need to be aware of the health regulations in their area. Many state and local health authorities discourage or prohibit sending meals from home. Foods from home may increase the risk of foodborne illness. Where permitted, a written agreement between families and the children's program should be established (American Academy of Pediatrics, American Public Health Association, National Resource Center for Health and Safety in Child Care and Early Education, 2011). Guidelines for families who choose to bring food from home include the following:

- Food should always be sent in lunch containers that have frozen ice packs.
- Food should be labeled with the child's name, the date, and the type of food.
- Food should not be shared with other children in the program.

What if . . .
you observed a child sharing food from his lunch box with other children? Isn't a child who shares doing something commendable? How might you explain the safety risks to this child?

Families may wish to share food from home with all children in the program. Programs must carefully weigh the pros and cons of allowing food to be brought from home and be proactive in prevention of foodborne illness by devising policies that support safe food and meet state and county regulations. As discussed in an earlier chapter, the NAEYC accreditation standards recommend that foods brought from home to share with other children must consist of whole fruits or commercially prepared packaged foods (National Association for the Education of Young Children, 2012). In addition, remember the consequences that occurred in the case scenario, when homemade cupcakes were brought into Lacey's classroom.

Food Safety and Cultural Considerations

Teachers who support cultural traditions in the selection of food for early childhood programs create a respectful enriching environment for all children and their families. However, some cultural food traditions may create a dilemma in terms of food safety. For example, the food traditions of the First Nations people of British Columbia include wild foods such as moose, deer, salmon, rabbit, dried berries, and sea weed (B.C. First Nations Head Start, 2003). Their Head Start programs took steps to ensure that traditional foods served met food safety regulations such as consulting with their health inspectors and making sure meats were processed in approved plants and prepared in inspected kitchens.

Some cultural food choices may be associated with increased risk for foodborne illness. For example, some soft Mexican-style cheeses have been linked to Listeriosis, an uncommon foodborne disease which can cause high fever, severe headache, neck stiffness, nausea, and sometimes death

SAFETY SEGMENT   Food Safety on Field Trips

Taking foods on field trips requires careful planning to keep food safe.

1. *Menu planning:* Field trip menus should include foods with low risk for spoiling. Some safe foods to take along on field trips include:

- Boxed juices
- Whole fruit
- Individual canned or plastic fruit cups
- Dried fruit (if age appropriate)
- Whole-grain crackers, breads, bread sticks, and rolls
- Peanut butter sandwiches (if there are no peanut allergies)
- Nuts (if there are no allergies and this snack is age appropriate)
- Trail mix (if age-appropriate ingredients are used)
- Dry cereal
- Baked whole-grain chips

2. *Storing food:* Foods must be maintained at proper temperatures. Store foods that need to be chilled in coolers filled with ice or plastic frozen gel packs. Freeze juice boxes and use them to keep other food cold. Place a thermometer in the cooler to make sure temperatures remain under 41°F (5°C). Foods that need to be chilled include:

- Meat, poultry, fish, or egg salad sandwiches
- Milk
- Cheese
- Yogurt
- Fruits or vegetables that have been peeled or cut
- Salads

3. *Hand washing:* Remember to wash hands and have children wash hands before eating. Premoistened hand wipes are not a substitute for hand washing, but can be used if no soap and running water are available.

Sources: American Academy of Pediatrics, American Public Health Association, National Resource Center for Health and Safety in Child Care and Early Education, 2011. *Caring for our children: National health and safety performance standards; Guidelines for early care and education programs.* 3rd edition. Elk Grove Village, IL: American Academy of Pediatrics; Washington, DC: American Public Health Association. Also available at http://nrckids.org; American Academy of Pediatrics; *Food Safety Standard Operating Procedures* (SOPs), National Food Service Management Institute, 2005, from http://www.nfsmi.org/ResourceOverview.aspx?ID=75; and *Food Safety for Home Child Care Providers: Chill,* New Mexico State University Cooperative Extension Service, 2004, from http://www.childcarefoodsafety.com/chill/chill.html.

(Centers for Disease Control and Prevention, 2011b). Sushi, a Japanese dish made with rice, seaweed, vegetables, and often raw fish, has also been linked to foodborne illness. If made with raw fish, this menu item should never be served to young children (Colorado State University Extension, 2006). Teachers can honor cultural food traditions, but this must be done within the context of food safety policies and regulations.

Food Safety on Field Trips

When children go on a field trip, special challenges must be addressed when serving food away from the school program. These challenges have to do with maintaining proper temperatures and personal hygiene. The *Safety Segment* provides advice on acceptable foods for a field trip.

Food Safety and Classroom Cooking Activities

Children learn about food by touching, tasting, and smelling it. They are often more likely to want to try new foods when they have helped with preparation. Safety management considerations for classroom cooking activities include the following:

- *Raw foods:* Avoid handling raw foods that contain infectious microorganisms. Children making cookies using a recipe that calls for eggs are at risk for salmonella food poisoning. Using a pasteurized egg substitute eliminates this problem.

- *Foods that will not be cooked:* If children participate in preparing foods that will not be cooked, they should only eat the food they have prepared and handled. For example, if the teacher plans an activity in which children make salad, each child should be given the ingredients to make his or her own salad.

- *Potential food allergens:* Teachers must make sure that children with allergies or food intolerances are not involved in activities that lead to exposure. For example, covering a pinecone with peanut butter and birdseed would be a risky project for children with peanut allergies. Making play dough from wheat flour would be hazardous to children with celiac disease.

● THE EMERGENCY PLAN AND FOOD DEFENSE

Emergencies cannot be predicted, but children's programs and schools can prepare in advance for potential emergencies. There are two aspects of food safety guide planning for emergencies: ensuring that there is a safe supply of food and water in case of a natural disaster, and making sure that foods are not tampered with or intentionally contaminated as an act of terrorism.

Developing an Emergency Food Plan

An emergency food plan is needed in the event an emergency requires that children and teachers are not able to return to their homes, but must take shelter in the facility. The Federal Emergency Management Agency (Federal Emergency Management Agency, 2012) and the American Red Cross (American Red Cross, 2012) provide guidelines on what foods and how much food and water to store. A 3-day supply of food and water is recommended.

Whereas an effective emergency food plan ensures that children will have access to safe food and water if supplies are interrupted, even an emergency food supply can pose a food safety risk if it is not properly monitored. The FIFO method of food rotation discussed earlier in this chapter is one way to ensure that food on hand is safe. Some examples of emergency foods to store include:

- canned meats, fish, milk, soup, fruit, juice, and vegetables
- ready-to-eat cereals and instant hot cereals
- crackers, granola bars, trail mix
- peanut butter, jelly
- staples such as sugar, salt, pepper (U.S. Department of Homeland Security, 2010)

The emergency food supply should include foods appropriate for the age group of the children served and should include options for children with food allergies and other food restrictions.

Planning for Food Defense

The U.S. Department of Homeland Security has raised awareness that food service establishments may be at risk for intentional contamination of foods by terrorist groups (U.S. Food and Drug Administration, 2011a). To provide **food defense**, which is the assurance that foods are not tampered with or intentionally contaminated as an act of terrorism, food service handlers are the "front line in protecting our food supply" (New York State Department of Health, 2006). For teachers and food services workers, this means being vigilant about who has access to the food that is stored and served to children. Children's programs can implement these strategies:

- Allow only authorized individuals to receive, store, and have access to food preparation areas.
- Know the food delivery personnel and always have someone available to directly receive food.
- Make sure self-service food items are placed in an area that can be supervised by staff.
- Keep buildings and grounds secure by locking doors in delivery, storage, and food preparation areas when not in use and allowing only key or code access.
- Discourage loitering in the program setting or school. Install alarm or video surveillance systems if security problems are an issue.
- Conduct employee background checks to ensure employment of safe teachers and food workers.
- Encourage employees to report suspicious behaviors.
- Train employees on food defense and food safety and on how to recognize potential security risks (New York State Department of Health, 2006; U.S. Food and Drug Administration, 2011a).

These recommendations can heighten awareness of threats to food safety, decreasing the risk that early childhood programs will become targets for deliberate contamination. It is unfortunate that issues of this

---

What if . . .

you were in charge of creating an emergency food plan? How would you plan for children with special diet needs? What might you include in your emergency food supply to address various special diets?

---

food defense
practice of ensuring that foods are not tampered with or intentionally contaminated as an act of terrorism

type need to be considered in the early childhood setting. However, children are vulnerable and have been targeted in the past. It is every program's and school's responsibility to consider all aspects of safety.

TEACHING FOOD SAFETY TO CHILDREN

Although program administrators and teachers bear the responsibility of ensuring a safe food supply, children are capable of helping to create a safe food environment. Teaching children about food safety includes a progression of ideas from basic ideas to more advanced concepts.

Routines in the school setting often are established to keep children safe. These routines also teach children expected behaviors that relate to food safety. Children learn about food safety through these everyday practices, especially if teachers explain the rationale behind the routines. Leading questions are appropriate for preschool-age children and older and could include these:

- We wash our hands because. . . .
- We sneeze into our elbow and not our hands because. . . .
- We pick up the fork by the handle when setting the table because. . . .
- We can put our forks in our mouths, but not the serving spoon, because. . . .
- We share most things, but we only eat or drink our own food because. . . .
- We put milk in the refrigerator because. . . .
- We wash the tables before and after eating because. . . .

Activity-based exploration of food safety topics is appropriate for all children. For example, teaching food safety tips while preparing and sampling food keeps children interested. Singing the "ABC" song once while washing hands teaches children how long to wash their hands in a way that holds their interest. The *Teaching Wellness* feature offers ideas about how to incorporate food safety lessons such as hand washing into the daily curriculum.

Being a good role model and combining simple explanations with consistent reminders help children establish food safety habits that benefit them now and into the future.

> ### What if . . .
> you were asked to teach food safety topics to children in your class? What topics would you select? How would you create a child-directed activity for a food safety topic?

TEACHING WELLNESS   Washing Hands Keeps Me Healthy   *Cap. 8*

Como enseñar a los niños el porque enseñar a lavar las manos

LEARNING OUTCOME   Children will show how to prevent the spread of germs by washing their hands.

Manejando alimentos apropiadamente y

Vocabulary focus: Wash, rinse, dry, hand, palm, fingers, wrist, germs, disease.

Safety watch: Ensure that soaps used are allergen free. Supervise children around water. Monitor the temperature of the water and ensure the floor near the sinks is kept dry to avoid slipping.

INFANTS AND TODDLERS

- **Goal:** Babies will experience having their hands washed and toddlers will be able to wash and dry their hands with help.
- **Materials:** Small tub of warm water, gentle soap, paper towels.
- **Activity plan:** For infants, allow babies to touch and splash hands in a shallow tub of lukewarm water. Say words that convey interest and pleasure, such as "That's it, touch the nice warm water. It feels so nice and clean." Help the baby dip hands in the water and gently stroke hands and between fingers, allowing the infant to touch and splash about. For toddlers, guide the child to wash under slowly

running lukewarm water at a sink. Talk through the process of washing and encourage the child through each step. Say, "First let's get our hands wet, next we add a little bit of soap. That's it. Now we rub the palms, the tops, and between fingers. Now let's rinse away the soap and dry our hands. We turn off the water with this paper towel, throw the towel away and now we are ready to eat." Reinforce the child's efforts by remarking, "You are scrubbing all parts of your hands. That is how we wash away the germs and make our hands clean."

- **How to adjust the activity:** Post a picture guide for washing hands near the sink. For children who are English learners,

(continued)

learn the words for washing hands, using water, and soap. Assist children with special developmental needs to access water, soap, and towels. Point out the picture guide to reinforce the steps of hand washing. Allow the child ample time to move through the hand washing process.

PRESCHOOLERS AND KINDERGARTNERS

- **Goal:** Children will demonstrate appropriate hand washing techniques and tell when it is important to wash hands.
- **Materials:** The book *Those Mean Nasty Dirty Downright Disgusting But . . . Invisible Germs* by Judith Rice; sink; water; liquid soap; paper towels.
- **Activity plan:** Gather the children and read the book using a variety of fun voices and hand gestures. Talk about germs and explain why it is important to wash them off of our hands. Help children identify the times it is important to wash hands (such as, before eating, after sneezing, going to the bathroom, or playing in the sensory table). Describe and act out the steps of hand washing. Invite children to practice washing their hands at the sink:
  - Turn on the water and wet hands.
  - Use one squirt of liquid soap.
  - Rub and wash hands for 20 seconds including between fingers, palms, backs of hands, and wrists. (Count to 20 slowly or sing the *ABC* song once or the *Happy Birthday* song twice.)
  - Rinse hands letting the water run over palms, between fingers, backs of hands and wrists.
  - Dry hands with a paper towel.
  - Use the paper towel to turn off the water, and then throw the towel away.
- **How to adjust the activity:** As children wash, refer to the posted picture guide for washing hands. For English learners or those whose special developmental need requires lots of repetition and reinforcement, point to each step of the picture and repeat the direction in English. Encourage children's efforts as they move through the process. Be sure that the sink, soap, and towels are accessible to all children.
- **Did you meet your goal?** Can children be observed washing hands appropriately? When asked, are children able to identify times when it is important to wash hands?

SCHOOL-AGE CHILDREN

- **Goal:** Children will be able to describe how germs can be spread from one hand to another, demonstrate the steps in hand-washing, and explain how washing helps remove germs that can cause illness.
- **Materials:** Magnifying glasses; five small paint cups; five colors of paint (black, brown, red, yellow, blue); five small paint brushes; paper to cover the table top; a variety of everyday objects (small empty milk carton, pencils, a small ball, a hair brush, plastic toys); hand-washing sink; liquid soap; paper towels.
- **Activity plan:** Cover a table top with paper. Fill paint cups each with a small amount of a different color of paint. Place the filled paint cups, brushes, and objects on the table. Gather a group of five children at the table. Guide them to look at their hands with a magnifying glass and describe what they see. Talk about how you can see skin, wrinkles, and dirt but you cannot see germs with the eyes or a magnifying glass because germs are so small. Explain how germs can hide in the cracks and folds of the skin and describe why germs can be harmful (they carry disease that can make us sick). Offer each child a cup of paint and paint brush, and tell them that you are going to pretend that the paint is "germs". Instruct them to dab paint all over the palm of just one hand. Then ask them to shake or grasp their clean hand with their "germy" painted hand. Next ask them to pick up and move each of the objects to another place on the table for 30 seconds. Now ask them to stop and talk about what you see. Did the (paint) germs spread? How far? Can children detect colors of paint on their hands that are different from the color they painted on? Remind children that germs spread the same way the paint colors have spread around the toys, table, and hands. Guide the children to go the sink and rinse their hands for 2 to 3 seconds. Have them inspect their hands under the magnifying glass. Are the (paint) germs gone or can they still be seen in the cracks of the hand? Guide the children to demonstrate washing their hands using the healthy hand

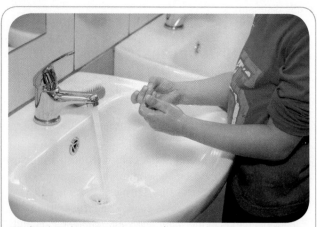

To simulate how germs spread, older children can apply paint to their hands and touch various objects—and wash them thoroughly afterward.

- **Did you meet your goal?** Did babies participate in the hand washing process? Can toddlers move through the steps of appropriate hand washing with help?

washing steps described above. Invite them to inspect their hands again when they have washed their hands carefully. Ask the children what they learned from the activity.

· **How to adjust the activity:** Speak clearly and use hand gestures to communicate the steps in the activity. Provide time for each child to describe what they see happening. Adapt the activity for children with special needs by using short paint brushes with wide handles and small shallow saucers of paint for stability. Ensure that students with wheelchairs are able to move up close to the table so they can reach the objects and move them about on the table. Allow children who choose not to put paint on their hands to sit and watch, and participate with others in describing what is happening as the paint "germs" move from place to place.

· **Did you meet your goal?** Are children able to describe how germs are spread? Can they demonstrate healthy hand washing? Can they explain how hand-washing helps keep people healthy?

■ SUMMARY

Food safety is the responsibility of all staff involved in the purchase, storage, preparation, and service of food to young children. Young children have immature immune systems and are at risk for illness or death when exposed to biological, chemical, and physical contaminants or allergens. Understanding the sources of food contamination that can cause foodborne illness is the first step in creating a food safe environment.

Federal, state, and local health authorities are responsible for establishing and regulating food safety in licensed children's programs and schools. These agencies are a good source of information to guide program-level policies regarding food safety. Teachers need to understand the food safety requirements mandated in their area. The county health department and food safety inspectors are a vital link and valuable resource in maintaining food safety in early childhood programs.

Reducing the risk for foodborne illness is accomplished through the development of a consistent food safety plan. The Hazard and Analysis Critical Control Point (HACCP) system consists of seven principles that guide the food safety program for any establishment that serves food. Schools use an adapted version of HACCP called the process approach. The HACCP process approach provides strategies for preventing contamination of food at each stage of food handling. From the time food is purchased until meals are served, food service workers and teachers have important responsibilities to keep food safe and reduce the risk of foodborne illness.

Food safety is an important consideration for managing potential emergencies and natural disasters. In addition, teachers should be aware of the need to monitor for food defense and prevent potential intentional contamination of food.

Children are partners with teachers and families as they learn about food safety and ways they can participate in keeping food safe in their classroom. Teaching children about food safety helps create a safe food environment. Food safety habits are supported by consistent routines that are offered in age and developmentally appropriate ways, with ample opportunity for hands-on exploration.

KEY TERMS

Biological hazards
Chemical hazards
Cleaning
Contamination
Corrective action plan
Critical control points (CCPs)
Critical limits (CLs)

Cross-contamination
First in, first out (FIFO)
Food Code
Food defense
Foodborne illness
Hazard Analysis and Critical Control
 Point (HACCP) system

Physical hazards
Potentially hazardous/TCS foods
Process approach
Sanitizing
Standard operating procedures (SOPs)
Temperature danger zone
Verification procedures

REVIEW QUESTIONS

1. Discuss three different types of hazards that can impact food safety.
2. Describe four federal programs that oversee food safety.
3. Explain the seven principles that form the basis of the HACCP food safety system.
4. Discuss methods to minimize contamination at each stage of food handling.
5. Discuss how to develop an emergency food plan and prepare for food defense.
6. Describe how to teach children about food safety.

DISCUSSION STARTERS

1. You have been asked by the director of your preschool program to participate on a hazard analysis committee with the goal of developing a food safety system using HACCP. Explain how you would determine the potential hazards and what steps you would take to develop a food safety system.
2. You are preparing a vegetable soup recipe with the preschool-age children in your class. Explain how you would incorporate a food safety message throughout the activity.
3. Explain the precautions and food safety concerns that need to be addressed during the receiving, storing, preparing, and serving of foods in an early child care setting.

PRACTICE POINTS

1. Using the sample breakfast menu found in Chapter 6 (Figure 6-6) identify the foods that are potentially hazardous and the ideal temperatures at which they should be maintained.
2. Identify the critical control points and critical limits in the following recipe:

Arroz con Queso

Ingredients	Serve 50
Enriched white rice, medium grain	2 lbs. 13 oz.
Water	3½ cups
Fresh onions	1 quart
Canned green chilies, mild	12 oz.
Canned jalapeño pepper, chopped	½ cup
Granulated garlic	1 Tbsp. + 1 tsp.
Low-fat plain yogurt	1 quart +1½ cups
Low-fat milk, 1%	1 quart + 1 cup
Salt	2 tsp.
Reduced-fat Monterey jack cheese, shredded	1 lb.
Reduced-fat cheddar cheese, shredded	1 lb.
Canned pinto beans	2 quarts + 1¼ cups
Fresh tomatoes	1 lb. 8 oz.
Reduced-fat cheddar cheese, shredded	1 lb. 3 oz.

Directions	Critical Control Point (yes or no)	Critical Limit
1. Place rice and water in a stockpot. Bring to a boil. Cover and reduce heat to medium. Simmer for 12 minutes or until tender.		
2. Combine onions, chilies, jalapeños, granulated garlic, yogurt, milk, salt, reduced-fat Monterey jack cheese, reduced-fat cheddar cheese, and pinto beans. Add to rice. Spread 5 lbs. 18 ounces in each steam table pan (12″ × 20″ × 2½″); will need two pans.		
3. Bake in conventional oven at 350°F for 35 minutes.		
4. Sprinkle 12 oz. of diced tomatoes and 9½ oz. of reduced-fat cheddar cheese over the top of each pan and bake for 5 minutes until cheese is melted.		
Bonus question: What if dried pinto beans were used and cooked in advance to be used the next day—would there be any critical control points and, if so, what would they be?		

Source: Recipe is from the USDA Recipes for Schools USDA Food and Nutrition Service Team Nutrition Updated November 30, 2011.

Note: For assistance with this practice point, refer to http://teamnutrition.usda.gov/Resources/usda_recipes.html.

3. Your first-grade class is going to the pumpkin patch to select pumpkins. You arranged to have your school food service provide brown bag lunches for this field trip. A mother has volunteered to make pumpkin cookies to bring along. The pumpkin patch farm will demonstrate how apples are turned into fresh cider and will offer children a taste. What are the food safety risks and how would you manage them?

WEB RESOURCES

FDA Food Code
www.fda.gov/Food/FoodSafety/RetailFoodProtection/FoodCode/default.htm

Food Safety.Gov
www.foodsafety.gov/

Iowa State University Extension Standard Operating Procedures for Child Care
www.extension.iastate.edu/HRIM/HACCP/ccflowoffood.htm

The University of Mississippi National Food Service Management Institute
www.nfsmi.org/

USDA Team Nutrition Healthy Meals Resource System
http://healthymeals.nal.usda.gov/nal_display/index.php?info_center=14&tax_level=1

MyEducationLab™

Go to Topic 4 (Food Safety) in the MyEducationLab (www.myeducationlab.com) for your course, where you can:

- Find learning outcomes for Food Safety along with the national standards that connect to these outcomes.
- Complete Assignments and Activities that can help you more deeply understand the chapter content.
- Check your comprehension on the content covered in the chapter by going to the Study Plan in the Book Resources for your text. Here you will be able to take a chapter quiz, receive feedback on your answers, and then access Review, Practice, and Enrichment activities to enhance your understanding of chapter content.

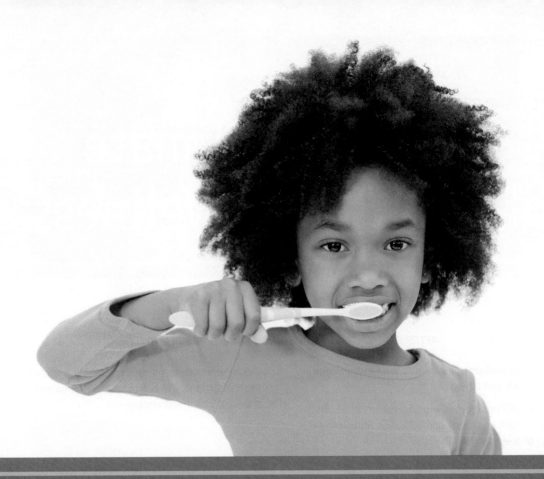

part three
Promoting Healthful Practices

eight
Creating a Climate of Health and Wellness

learning outcomes

AFTER READING THIS CHAPTER, YOU SHOULD BE ABLE TO:

1. Define health and wellness and identify the determinants that impact health and illness.

2. Identify resources that inform the development of health policies in children's programs and schools and describe the components of a written health policy.

3. Describe health disparities and discuss strategies that teachers can use to promote acceptance and tolerance in the early childhood setting.

Cooper is a 7-year-old boy who was born with cystic fibrosis, a hereditary disease that affects the lungs and causes progressive disability. He is a pleasant and hard-working child, and his teacher Deanie gets to know him well. She notices in particular that Cooper enjoys drawing pictures of alligators.

Cooper's mother, Alicia, lovingly and tirelessly cares for him. Alicia is a working single mother who cannot afford health insurance for her family. Because she is unable to afford frequent preventive health care visits and medications for Cooper, he does not receive the care he needs. Consequently, his health care is fragmented and usually consists of urgent care visits.

Cooper's school environment is one of the most consistent aspects of his life. Alicia often turns to Deanie to help her cope with challenges related to being a low-income single parent. Deanie is glad that Alicia is open to discussing Cooper's needs. It encourages her to learn more about ways she can support Cooper in the classroom. Reflecting on the challenges that Alicia faces, Deanie is inspired to plan a children's art show as part of the school open house. Alicia and Cooper are delighted to see his art on display. Deanie takes advantage of the event to introduce Alicia to other parents during the parent meeting. Deanie presents her plans to conduct special health promotion activities in the classroom and then asks the parents for their ideas.

"Every child deserves to be born well, to be physically fit, and to achieve self-responsibility for good health habits" (Bright Futures at Georgetown University, n.d.). These goals highlight the importance of creating surroundings that promote and nurture health and wellness in young children. The study of health and wellness is an important component in the professional development of teachers. Children spend a large portion of their day under the care and guidance of their teacher, and they rely on teachers for significant educational support and attention to their health and well-being. Teachers such as Deanie welcome the opportunity to significantly impact the lives of all children by creating healthy classroom environments and by teaching children to establish healthy habits. They also work to establish a positive and accepting atmosphere that helps each child feel valued and welcome. Together, a healthy environment and an accepting atmosphere create a climate of health and wellness.

In this chapter we introduce the foundations for establishing a climate of wellness. We begin the process by defining health and wellness and discussing the components of health that impact the lives of children. We present strategies for supporting the development of optimal health in young children, and explore the influences of health and culture on children's well-being. Creating a climate of health and wellness is an important teaching goal. The information explored in this chapter will assist you in achieving positive health outcomes for children.

■ HEALTH AND WELLNESS IN THE EARLY CHILDHOOD YEARS

Health and wellness are concepts that combine to create a complete sense of well-being. They are interrelated, but different. Understanding the components and the determinants of health helps teachers to recognize that all children do not have the same opportunity for healthful outcomes.

Defining Health and Wellness

Health is a state of complete physical, mental, and social well-being, not merely the absence of disease or infirmity (World Health Organization, 1948). Health is influenced by aspects such as genetic makeup and environmental influences. **Wellness** on the other hand is broader in perspective. It refers to optimal health and the vitality to enjoy life. Wellness is largely determined by lifestyle choices. These lifestyle choices encompass activities such as selecting healthful foods, obtaining necessary health services, and experiencing safe environments.

Individuals cannot change some aspects of their health, but they can improve their health outcomes by making positive lifestyle choices and focusing on wellness goals. In this way health and wellness are interrelated, and the words are often used interchangeably to reflect a positive state of well-being.

Components of Health

Health is established through positive growth, development, and well-being in two major component areas: physical health and mental health. In young children, physical and mental health are essential to overall health and wellness. Each of these components influences the other.

Physical Health

Physical health refers to the condition of the body. It is established in part, through a diet that provides appropriate nutrition, adequate exercise, and sufficient rest. When these conditions are addressed on a daily basis, children are supported in their efforts to develop good physical health.

Children's physical health may be compromised by either acute or chronic conditions. **Acute conditions** are those that have a sudden onset and short duration. Examples of acute illnesses include infectious diseases, such as upper respiratory infections, or injuries, such as bone fractures or sprains. **Chronic conditions** have a long duration and require ongoing evaluation or treatment. Examples include malformations that are present at birth, called **congenital conditions**—genetic diseases or physical malformations. Many children with chronic illnesses are also at risk for or prone to acute illnesses. In the opening case scenario, for example, Cooper has a chronic condition called **cystic fibrosis**, which causes inadequate growth, frequent lung infections, and premature death. His physical health is also likely to affect his mental health, as well his ability to learn and have healthy relationships in school.

MyEducationLab™
Visit the MyEducationLab for *Nutrition, Health, and Safety for Young Children* to enhance your understanding of chapter concepts with a personalized Study Plan. You'll also have the opportunity to hone your teaching skills through video-based Assignments and Activities, as well as Building Teaching Skills and Dispositions lessons.

health
a state of complete physical, mental, and social well-being and not merely the absence of disease or infirmity

wellness
optimal health and the vitality to enjoy life; is largely determined by lifestyle choices

physical health
level of functioning and well-being individuals feel with respect to their bodies

acute conditions
medical conditions that have a sudden onset and short duration

chronic conditions
medical conditions that have a long duration and require ongoing evaluation and/or treatment

Mental Health

congenital conditions
physical defects or
malformations that are
present at birth

cystic fibrosis
chronic health condition that
causes growth retardation
and frequent pulmonary
(lung) infections and may
lead to premature death

mental health
the ability to function in
developmentally appropriate
ways with respect to self,
family, and peers

determinants of health
risk factors or causative
factors that are associated
with a health problem

risk factors
aspects of health that
contribute to illness or
disease

protective factors
aspects of health that
promote health and wellness

socioeconomic status
a measure incorporating
income, social, and work
status that is a strong
predictor of health

Mental health is the ability to achieve developmentally appropriate tasks, to have a positive sense of self-esteem, and to effectively cope with adversity (Bershad & Blaber, 2011). Mental health is established in the early childhood years through a process of positive social and emotional development. Healthy relationships with caregivers and teachers play a critical role in children's sense of social and emotional well-being.

Physical and mental health impact one another. For example, the presence of a special physical need, such as decreased mobility due to an injury or a physical impairment, may influence a child's mental health. On the other hand, children with mental health conditions, such as depression, may develop unhealthy habits that lead to problems with their physical health. In this chapter's case scenario, Cooper is unable to play actively with his peers because of breathing problems. This separation from typical physical play and interaction may predispose him to depression.

What Determines Children's Health and Illness?

Health and wellness is determined by a combination of many factors related to an individual and his or her environment. One often thinks of health and disease as being determined by an individual's characteristics, such as genetics or as a condition with a biological cause, such as an infection. However, factors external to an individual have a significant impact on health outcomes as well. For example, in the opening case, Cooper's disease is caused by a genetic defect. However, his health outcomes are dependent both on the course of his disease and external factors, such as his relationships with caregivers, family income, and environmental exposures. Understanding how these factors either cause or contribute to disease is important for developing treatment or intervention programs and for promoting health and wellness in the classroom.

These **determinants of health** can either be **risk factors**, which contribute to illness or disease, or **protective factors**, which support health and wellness. Examples of risk factors are poverty, child abuse, having reading disabilities, and living in families that use harsh or inconsistent discipline while examples of protective factors include having skills to manage conflict and relationships and having a warm, supportive relationship with family and caregivers (World Health Organization, 2011). Determinants of health can be categorized into the following: the social and economic environment, the physical environment, and the child's individual characteristics and behaviors (World Health Organization, 2011). These factors are illustrated in Figure 8-1.

Social and Economic Environment

Social factors that influence health include social support networks and social status. Families who have greater support from other family members, friends, and their community experience better health outcomes. Another critical social factor is education level. Lower education levels are associated with poor health.

FIGURE 8-1
Determinants of Health

How a child's family fares economically is another important determinant of health. One of the strongest predictors of health is **socioeconomic status** (SES) (Seith & Kalof, 2011). This measure incorporates income, social, and work status. An important component of SES is family income because children who live in poverty are at a strong disadvantage with respect to health. Examples of these disadvantages include experiencing food insecurity, exposure to secondhand smoke, lead poisoning, and inadequate access to health care. Children living in low-income families are

Problemas de salud comunes

TABLE 8-1   Common Health Problems More Commonly Affecting Children Living in Poverty   Cap. 8

Common Health Problems	Possible Outcomes	Possible Solutions for Teachers
Exposure to environmental toxins	• Lead poisoning • Increased risk for asthma	• Conduct screenings • Educate families
Inadequate access to health care	• Inadequate immunizations • Lack of preventive health care • At risk for untreated illnesses	• Refer to health department or community health center
Mental health problems	• Emotional and behavioral problems • Learning disabilities	• Refer to available services • Provide support to families
Dental problems and inadequate dental care	• Pain • Problems with self-image	• Teach and promote oral hygiene • Promote screening • Refer to dental programs
Chronic conditions that limit a child's ability to fully participate in activities	• Increased absenteeism • Learning problems	• Refer to community resources • Communicate with families

Source: Seith & Isakson, Who Are America's Poor Children? Examining Health Disparities Among Children in the United States, 2011.

also at higher risk for certain diseases such as asthma as well as mental health problems such as poor emotional health, behavioral problems, and learning disabilities (Seith & Kalof, 2011). Table 8-1 lists health problems more commonly seen in low-income families and implications for teachers.

Physical Environment

The physical environment refers to where a family lives, the structure of their neighborhood, and any environmental exposures that exist in that space. Specific characteristics of a healthy physical environment include safe water, clean air, safe houses, safe and toxin-free school environments, and safe communities and roads. The physical environment can contribute to a child's health status. For example, certain children are more likely to develop asthma when exposed to toxins such as air pollution or cockroaches. Or, in the opening case, Cooper suffers from a serious health condition that affects his lungs. Certain toxins or germs in his environment could cause him to develop serious infections that impact his overall health and well-being. This chapter's *Health Hint* describes how housing insecurity influences a child's health.

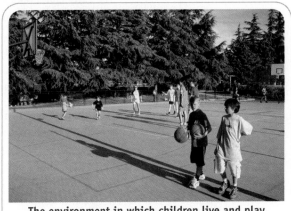

The environment in which children live and play contributes to overall wellness.

HEALTH HINT The Effect of Housing Insecurity on Children's Health

In both children and adults, housing insecurity has been strongly associated with poor health outcomes. *Housing insecurity* refers to high housing costs in proportion to income, poor housing quality, unstable neighborhoods, overcrowding, or homelessness. In children, crowding in homes and moving frequently from one home to another has strong negative associations. Crowding, in particular, is associated with poor mental health, decreased ability to cope with stress, poor parent-child relationships, poor social relationships, and inadequate sleep.

In young children, housing insecurity is also associated with multiple health issues including growth problems and developmental delay. It is also strongly associated with food insecurity, which contributes to further poor health outcomes. Additionally, many families who qualify for housing subsidies do not receive them.

Teachers can support families by screening for these social issues and making appropriate referrals when problems are identified.

Source: Based on Cutts, Meyers, Black, Casey, Cook, & Geppert, 2011.

Individual Characteristics and Behaviors

Characteristics of an individual that influence health include age, gender, and genetic makeup. For example, infants are more susceptible to certain types of infections. Some diseases only afflict males, such as muscular dystrophy. Genetic defects or hereditary diseases can cause certain health conditions.

A child's behavior influences health. Examples of behaviors that influence health are eating habits, level of physical activity, and hand washing habits.

Children's Health in the Context of Their Environments

The ecological systems theory highlights the health impacts of the environments in which children develop (Bronfenbrenner, 1979). In the microsystem, families directly contribute to children's optimal health and development by meeting children's need for nourishment, providing access to healthy lifestyle choices, providing access to health care, and correcting unsafe conditions in the environment. Positive communications between families and teachers (mesosystem) contribute to the continuity in children's care and provide opportunities for parents and teachers to align teaching approaches in the home and school settings that support children's well-being. Maintaining sanitary conditions in the neighborhood (exosystem) contributes to children's health and well-being. A commitment to health goals for all people in the larger community and social systems (macrosystems) ensures the development of public policies that provide for access to health care. Each aspect of the ecological system contributes to the climate of health and wellness that is crucial to children's optimal development and the attainment of good health.

The early childhood setting plays an important role in creating climates of health and wellness through the contexts of Bronfenbrenner's microsystem and mesosystem. When teachers create these healthful environments and develop positive relationships with families, they help to surround children with positive environments in which their needs can be recognized and services can be identified.

Influencing Health and Wellness in the Early Childhood Setting

Learning the skills that promote wellness is a lifelong process that begins when children are very young. Young children depend on adults to make healthy choices for them and to teach them to make choices for themselves. In the early childhood years, children are particularly receptive to aspects in their environment that facilitate learning. They are also vulnerable to forces that obstruct health. Teaching children healthful practices is an investment in a healthy childhood and perpetuates health and wellness into the child's future (American Academy of Pediatrics, American Public Health Association, National Resource Center for Health and Safety in Child Care and Early Education, 2011).

Families and teachers help children establish lifestyles that promote wellness. The early childhood years are a time in which children learn habits and behaviors that positively impact health, such as washing hands and eating a variety of healthy foods. Behaviors that encourage a healthy lifestyle, such as playing actively and getting sufficient sleep, are also introduced and practiced during the early years, setting the stage for health-promoting behaviors across a lifetime.

In addition, many chronic, or ongoing, conditions seen in adulthood such as obesity, heart disease, diabetes, and mental health problems have their roots in early childhood. Parents and teachers play an important role in teaching children lifestyle habits that minimize the potential of such diseases occurring. This is a remarkable and exciting opportunity for teachers to positively affect children's lifelong development. This chapter's *Policy Point* describes how child care policies and characteristics of the child care environment can influence physical activity.

Understanding the determinants of health that impact children guides teachers to establish protective approaches in the classroom. For example, growing up in a poor neighborhood where children are often not free to play outdoors because of unsafe conditions may compromise children's physical health. Teachers address this by providing opportunities for children to play actively in safely supervised outdoor environments. Overall, children who live in disadvantaged neighborhoods

POLICY POINT Characteristics of the Preschool Environment That Influence Physical Activity

The National Association for Sport and Physical Education recommends that all preschool children (ages 3 to 5 years) participate in up to 60 minutes of structured activities *and* 60 minutes of unstructured play every day. Most children's settings do not provide this level of active play. Characteristics of children's environments influence time spent in moderate and vigorous physical activity. Children are more active in:

- Higher quality programs, such as those that have wellness policies.
- Settings with large playground spaces where children can run and be active.
- Schools with more portable equipment, such as balls and hoops that encourage children to plan and direct their own active play.
- Settings that limit the use of electronic media, which contribute to sedentary play rather than active play.

Source: Dowda, 2009; Connecticut State Department of Education, 2010.

often benefit even more than children living in higher income neighborhoods from school health screenings, classroom activities relevant to health promotion, and referral to needed community resources, simply because access to these services outside the school setting is inadequate due to the impacts of poverty and lack of access to usual health care.

Evidence has shown that the child care center or preschool a child attends is associated with the child's level of physical activity. Certain policies and environmental characteristics are associated with a healthier level of physical activity such as the availability of play equipment and activity opportunities, smaller school size, higher education level of staff members, child-initiated play and an outdoor play area that offers more open areas and the presence of vegetation.

The following characteristics in the center's policies have been noted to show increase in physical activity:

- Staff education and training
- Staff behavior on the playground
- Additional training provided to staff related to physical activity in young children
- Reaching out to parents supporting physical activity in the home
- Multiple outdoor recess breaks as opposed to one prolonged break

Careful consideration of the child care and preschool environment can have a significant impact on physical activity in this age group (Gubbels, Kremers, van Kann, & Stafleu, 2011; Trost, Ward, & Senso, 2010).

Although children may come to the classroom with circumstances that are out of the teacher's control, teachers promote children's health by giving them tools to protect themselves, such as warding off germs, practicing safety procedures, or communicating appropriately about their worries and frustrations. Teachers observe children throughout the day and are often the first to know when a child's hunger or thirst is getting in the way of learning. They have the authority to make sure children get outside daily to run and be active, and can institute a policy of brushing teeth after lunch. These practices counterbalance some of the negative factors existing in children's lives.

Teachers also contribute to children's healthful development by getting to know each family's social circumstances and the challenges that may impact children's wellness. Teachers arrange opportunities to:

- Promote the development of positive relationships between teachers and parents.
- Increase parental knowledge of children's cognitive and emotional needs.
- Encourage children's healthy social development and behavior.
- Prevent child abuse.

What if . . .

You were teaching in an area with low-income families? What are some health risks that children in your classroom might encounter? Can you think of some useful activities that you could implement in your setting to positively contribute to their health and well-being?

● CHILD HEALTH POLICIES

health policies
guidelines that define a desired health outcome, such as promoting healthy behaviors or preventing the spread of disease

A climate of wellness in the early childhood and school setting is founded on supportive **health policies**. Health policies are guidelines for classroom practices that promote a desired health outcome. These policies ensure that safe and appropriate health practices are in place. They also help to guide decision making about how to manage confusing or difficult situations. Health policies in the early childhood and school setting demonstrate that children's health is recognized as a vital aspect of well-being. This chapter's *Progressive Programs and Practices* describes how public health collaborating with child care settings can promote health and wellness in the critical years.

Developing Policies to Promote and Protect Health

Health policies are developed to address common health and safety issues in early childhood and school settings. Specific policies are required by national, state, and local agencies that license children's programs. In addition, national agencies that promote quality standards for children's programs make policy recommendations to improve services for children. Accrediting organizations also outline minimum standards for programs they endorse. These groups compel children's programs to develop policies and practices that are designed to achieve health and safety goals. This Chapter's

PROGRESSIVE PROGRAMS & PRACTICES

Creating a Climate of Health and Wellness

By Kathy Cunningham, Boston Public Health Commission

The Boston Public Health Commission conducted the Wellness in Child Care Initiative that trained Boston family child care providers on strategies to promote healthy weight, using the Nutrition and Physical Activity Self-Assessment for Child Care (NAPSACC). The NAPSACC instrument helped to identify strengths and challenges to healthy eating and physical activity within family child care settings. As a result of the trainings, providers implemented wellness action plans to improve nutrition and physical activity at their sites and to engage parents in supporting healthy weight for their children.

Key components of the initiative were to: (1) provide free training to family child care providers, with continuing education credits as an incentive for participation, (2) provide resources for providers to assess their own nutrition and physical activity, and (3) make environmental and policy changes to support healthy weight among children.

We offered the training in two 6-hour sessions. The first workshop gave an overview of the obesity issue with modules on ways to improve healthy eating and strategies for incorporating 60 minutes per day of physical activity. The second workshop included group activity to review their NAPSACC assessment and develop Action Plans for their program. The training also included how to communicate to parents about their policy changes for healthy eating, physical activity, and limited television time. This format supported providers with peer-to-peer opportunities to share strategies that they found positive and to discuss community resources to support policy changes.

The workshops offered child care providers an opportunity to expand their knowledge of healthy foods and ways to offer

these foods to children in fun and interactive ways. Providers also received incentives to support indoor physical activity to reach the recommended 60 minutes per day. Finally, providers were given the opportunity to work on program policies to improve the environments in which children spend a large percentage of their day.

Planning policies and implementing procedures that promote children's health requires attention to safety details. It is important that health policies do not introduce risks or overlook opportunities to improve children's safety. Obtaining advice from knowledgeable individuals helps teachers improve their classroom practices. Program health and safety policies should be reviewed from a variety of health perspectives, including those of:

- Parents
- Community health providers
- Dietitians
- Sanitarians
- Child care licensing workers
- Community safety workers

Safety Segment discusses accessing community members and other individuals to develop child health policies.

Resources for Health Policy Development

A variety of resources are available to guide the development of relevant program health policies. The resources discussed next aim to improve services to young children by establishing best practice goals.

The National Resource Center for Health and Safety in Child Care and Early Education

The National Resource Center for Health and Safety in Child Care and Early Education (NRC) takes the lead in communicating standards that inform child health policies. The NRC is funded by the Maternal and Child Health Bureau of the U.S. Department of Health and Human Services (HHS). The NRC website provides a variety of resources that support health and safety in out-of-home care and education settings:

Health and safety policies help teachers establish healthful environments and implement safe practices in the classroom.

- *Health and safety standards:* The primary information needed to develop policies that promote health and safety in children's programs is available through the *Caring for Our Children: National Health and Safety Performance Standards; Guidelines for Early Care and Education Settings.* Third Edition, 2011 (American Academy of Pediatrics, American Public Health Association, National Resource Center for Health and Safety in Child Care and Early Education, 2011). This resource presents the rationale for policies that guide health practices and sets the standards for quality in healthful programming.
- *Licensure regulations:* The licensing regulations of the 50 states, the District of Columbia, Puerto Rico, and the Virgin Islands are available for review and comparison. The minimum policies that must be established in licensed family child care and early education programs are presented.
- *Standards-based resources:* User-friendly materials on specific subjects provide information for the development of policies such as how to administer medications in children's settings and when to exclude sick children from care.

Health policies are a requirement for licensed programs. They also describe an early childhood program's commitment to health and safety. While program directors and principals usually manage decisions about policies with input from community health providers, teachers should be familiar with policies that guide health practices in their setting.

Office of Head Start

The Office of Head Start provides the *Head Start Performance Standards* (U.S. Department of Health and Human Services, 2009), which outline a variety of nutrition, health, and safety policies for Early

Head Start, Head Start, American Indian/Alaska Native, and Migrant Seasonal Head Start programs nationwide. Head Start programs are required to develop policies and practices related to:

- Child health and development
- Child health and safety
- Child nutrition
- Child mental health

National Association for the Education of Young Children

The National Association for the Education of Young Children (NAEYC) is a professional organization committed to increasing the quality of programs that serve children from birth through age 8. They offer several systems of **accreditation** (endorsement) to acknowledge programs that meet national standards of quality.

accreditation
endorsement or acknowledgment of programs that meet national standards of quality

NAEYC accreditation assesses quality in 10 program standards. Topic areas in the health standards include:

- Promoting and protecting children's health and controlling infectious disease.
- Ensuring children's nutritional well-being.
- Maintaining a healthful environment.

School Wellness Policies

In 2004, Congress passed the Child Nutrition and Women, Infants, and Children (WIC) Reauthorization Act. This act requires that all school districts with federally funded school meal programs develop and implement school wellness policies. The responsibility of developing specific wellness policies is placed on the school districts so that each can address its own unique challenges. The wellness policies must address the following (Centers for Disease Control, 2011):

- Goals for nutrition education, physical activity, and other school-based activities designed to promote wellness.
- Guidelines that all food available on school property must promote health and prevent obesity.
- Guidelines for reimbursable school meals.
- Community involvement including parents, students, and representatives of the school food authority, school board, school administrators, and the public in the development of the school wellness policy.
- Communicate wellness policy updates to the public including parents, students, and community members.
- Plans for measuring implementation of the wellness policies and its effect on school wellness.

Table 8-2 provides a list of common policy topics and examples of practices in early childhood settings.

Components of Health Policies

Written health policies need to be clear, brief, and easy to understand. Guidelines for writing health policies include the following:

1. *State prevention goals.* They are usually written in the form of goals that promote positive health outcomes and prevent specific problems. For example: *Health checks will be conducted daily* or *Children will be supervised by sight and sound.*
2. *Identify steps to achieve the policy goals.* List the steps, or procedures, to take to implement the policy. Procedures should be specific and identify who will do what. For example: *The lead teacher will greet children at the door and conduct a 20-second health check. Identified concerns will be discussed with the parent.*

TABLE 8-2   Developing Policies That Promote Health and Wellness

Policy Topic	Examples
NUTRITION	*Desarrollar Polica que promueun Salud y Bienestar*
Eating environments	• Provide an enjoyable eating environment and offer meals on a regular schedule with time for children to eat. • Encourage students to participate in free or reduced-price meal programs.
Nutrition messages	• Avoid using food as reward or limiting physical activity as a consequence of poor classroom behavior. • Conduct fundraising activities and provide foods provided in vending machines that promote healthy eating philosophy.
HEALTH	
Controlling disease	• Teach children to wash hands and cover their coughs. • Obtain health information and ensure that children are up-to-date with immunizations before enrollment. • Provide information to help parents know when to keep children home from school.
Healthy environments	• Clean restrooms daily and during the day as needed. • Sanitize toys each week or whenever they are put into children's mouth.
SAFETY	
Enrollment information	• Obtain emergency contact, health history, and immunization records before children enroll. • Orient families to arrival and departure procedures.
Planning and supervising	• Purchase toys and materials that meet safety standards. • Review play areas every day; remove hazards. • Supervise children by sight and sound.

3. *Guide response to difficult situations.* Policies must also direct appropriate response to challenging situations. In the health check example, this might include: *If signs of illness are observed, communicate kindly but firmly that the parent must take the child home.*

4. *Ensure procedures are practical and specific to the setting.* Lists of policies established for early childhood and school settings are similar. However, the procedures for implementing each policy may be different to accommodate the particular setting. Health checks in a preschool setting may be conducted as children and parents arrive. Health checks in the school setting may be conducted during an opening circle activity after children are in the classroom.

An important health policy area concerns food allergies. The *Nutrition Note* provides an example related to nut allergies.

Ensuring Policies Are Appropriate for the Setting

Some programs serving young children invite local health consultants to advise on the development of health policies. For instance, Head Start programs convene a Health Services Advisory Committee of parents and professionals to participate in developing and reviewing health policies. This ensures that wellness goals are based on current knowledge and practice.

Obtaining the advice of community health workers also helps to identify policies that are needed to address health and safety concerns unique to a certain community. For example, a preschool situated in an area where air quality may pose a health risk should develop a policy related to outdoor play. The policy should describe how the program will determine when air quality is at an unhealthy level, such as if a smog alert has been issued and where the children will play if an alert has been announced (American Academy of Pediatrics, American Public Health Association, National Resource Center for Health and Safety in Child Care and Early Education, 2011). A school in a metropolitan area where violence is frequently reported might develop policies related to teaching a violence prevention curriculum. The policy would state what curriculum approaches would be used and how often the prevention interventions would be conducted. Health policies should be reviewed periodically, and new policies should be developed when necessary to improve program services.

 This **video** provides a description of the many services provided to children and families through child care. In light of these services, what kinds of health policies would be appropriate in childcare settings?

NUTRITION NOTE   Policies Relevant to Nut Allergies

About 1 in 25 students in school have a food allergy. Among those 16–18% report having a reaction at school. Nut allergies are of particular concern to children's health because of the potential for serious, life-threatening reactions. Many early childhood and school settings have developed policies to address this issue:

- A "no nut" policy may be an appropriate approach for settings that serve children with known nut allergies. This means no nuts of any kind or products prepared with nut oil will be served.
- A policy of "no food sharing" is also important so that children with food allergies do not inadvertently eat foods that contain the allergens.

Studies report that two thirds of fatal allergic reactions occur at school. Comprehensive policies will help minimize the consequences of these allergies occurring at school. A comprehensive policy includes:

- Identifying students with food allergies
- Develop written plans for each student
- Develop a protocol for administering medications
- Monitor the school environment for potential exposure including classroom, cafeteria, buses, activities/field trips
- Communicate the plan to school staff and families, honoring confidentiality as much as possible
- Develop an emergency response plan
- Provide training for school staff
- Monitor and evaluate policy in place

With the increasing prevalence of allergies and the severity of reactions, it is critical for children's settings to have policies that define the symptoms related to acute reaction and procedures for what to do if an allergic reaction occurs. Teachers need to be given training on how to identify and respond to nut allergy emergencies.

Source: Information from Burgden, Martinez, Greene, & Eig, 2011.

Policies Promoting Oral Health

dental caries
tooth decay; is the most common and preventable chronic disease in childhood

Childhood tooth decay, or **dental caries**, is one of the most common and preventable chronic diseases in childhood. Research shows that proper dental care and oral hygiene can significantly decrease dental problems that lead to tooth decay, infection, and illness (Marrs, Trumbley, & Malik, 2011).

Schools can promote oral health through education and dental care services. For children who lack health insurance and are very unlikely to receive usual, regular dental care, such as Cooper at the beginning of the chapter, school-based oral health promotion is the only access to dental care available to promote dental health.

Oral Health Education

Policies that direct teachers to offer oral hygiene education and encourage toothbrushing after meals contribute to better oral health. Teachers are responsible for planning and implementing these health education activities. The goals for oral health education include helping children understand why their teeth are important and how brushing and seeing a dentist help keep teeth healthy.

Collaboration with community partners is helpful. Programs can collaborate with local dentists or with state dental associations. Teachers of toddlers and preschool-age groups might read books about taking care of teeth or dramatize a trip to the dentist using puppets. Preschool settings may also provide toothbrushes and toothpaste for children.

The NAEYC (2005) has identified an emerging practice guideline for accredited early childhood programs that relates to early dental care for infants. The guideline describes how oral health education begins in infancy. The guideline states:

NAEYC Accreditation Criterion 5.A.13: After each feeding, infant's teeth and gums are wiped with a disposable tissue (or clean soft cloth used only for one child and laundered daily) to remove liquid that coats the teeth and gums. (p. 21)

Proper nutrition also contributes to the prevention of tooth decay. Teaching proper nutrition and serving meals rich in whole grains, fruits, and vegetables are ways to promote oral health. Teachers in Independence, Missouri, designated Friday as "Nutrition Day." Teachers incorporated fruits and vegetables into the regular classroom activities. Newsletters were sent to parents with recipes and activities to promote healthy nutrition (Lapin & Smith, 2008). The *Teaching Wellness* feature describes ways to teach children about the importance of brushing teeth.

Dental Care Services

Oral health in children has become a priority for early childhood health. The Office of Head Start initiated the Head Start Oral Health Initiative for Young Children in 2005, providing supplemental funding for programs to improve oral health services for enrolled children. School policies that

---

TEACHING WELLNESS   Brushing My Teeth Keeps My Smile Healthy

LEARNING OUTCOME   Children will learn how to brush their teeth.

[handwritten: Como ayudar al niño a elevarse los dientes,   cap 2]

Vocabulary focus: teeth, gums, germs, plaque, cavity, decay

Safety watch: Ensure children sit or stand quietly and use their toothbrushes safely. Watch that toothbrushes are not exchanged. Be sure children drink fresh water and spit appropriately. Use appropriate toothpaste only with children 2 years of age and older.

INFANTS AND TODDLERS

- **Goal:** To encourage children's willingness to have their gums wiped and teeth brushed.
- **Materials:** Damp washcloth or gauze, small toothbrushes, paper cups fresh water, and paper towels.
- **Activity plan:** For infants without teeth, gently wipe the gums with a clean damp cloth. For infants with teeth and toddlers, use a small, soft toothbrush and fresh water to gently brush teeth and gums. Talk through the process and describe the steps for brushing teeth. Say, "You are keeping your mouth open while I help clean your gums." Say words that teach the steps of brushing, "First let's rub (or brush) the front of your gums (or teeth), and then the sides, the backs, and the tops." Encourage babies and children to help by placing their hands on yours or by guiding their hands to gently rub their gums or brush their teeth. Add interest and extend brushing time by singing a song. Try singing this song to the tune of *Row, Row, Row Your Boat*: "Brush, brush, brush, your teeth, brush them twice a day. This will keep them clean and white and help prevent decay." When finished, offer the children a small drink of fresh water.
- **How to adjust the activity:** For children who are not English speakers, post pictures of babies and toddlers having their gums rubbed and teeth brushed. Talk with parents or dentists for recommendations about modified toothbrushes designed to help brush the teeth of children who have special oral health or physical motor needs.
- **Did you meet your goal?** Were babies willing to have their gums wiped or teeth brushed? Were toddlers willing to participate in brushing their teeth?

PRESCHOOLERS AND KINDERGARTNERS

- **Goal:** To learn to brush teeth appropriately and know that toothbrushing is important.
- **Materials:** A children's book about brushing teeth, such as *Clarabella's Teeth* by An Vrombaut, model of large teeth and a large toothbrush, toothbrushes, paper cups, toothpaste (approved by the American Dental Association), fresh water, sink, paper towels.
- **Activity plan:** Gather a small group at a table. Read a book about brushing teeth. Talk about how brushing teeth removes the food particles that can cause cavities. Demonstrate the steps of brushing teeth using the model teeth and large toothbrush. Provide each child a toothbrush and a paper cup with a pea-sized dab of toothpaste on the edge. Invite children to practice the steps of toothbrushing:
  - Dab the toothbrush against the toothpaste.
  - Hold the toothbrush at a 45-degree angle; brush front, sides, back, and top of each tooth.
  - Gently brush the tongue.
  - Spit toothpaste into the cup.
  - Rinse toothbrush and return to the child's place in the toothbrush rack.
  - Rinse mouth with water and spit into the sink. Dry mouth on towel and discard towel.
- **How to adjust the activity:** For English learners, read a story in English and the child's home language. Post pictures as cues for each step in brushing teeth to help all children understand the steps. Assist a child with special physical needs to be successful by providing modified toothbrushes, or adjustments to help the child sit at the table or stand at the sink.
- **Did you meet your goal?** Are children able to brush teeth appropriately? When asked, are children able to arrange picture cards to show the steps of toothbrushing, or can they tell why it is important to brush teeth?

(Continued)

SCHOOL-AGE CHILDREN

- **Goal:** To learn how to carefully brush teeth and understand that toothbrushing removes germs that cause cavities.
- **Materials:** Toothbrushes, paper cups with dab of tooth-paste, paper cups with water, disposable dentist mirror, plaque-disclosing tablet, sink with running water.
- **Activity plan:** Gather children at a table. Review the steps for brushing teeth. Offer children toothbrushes and cups with toothpaste. Invite them to brush their teeth and spit toothpaste into the cup. Ask the children to look at their teeth with a disposable mirror and describe what they see. Do they see any germs? Talk about how you cannot see germs because they are so small. Germs can hide on their teeth and cause plaque. Plaque sticks to the teeth and causes holes or cavities in the surface of the tooth. It also makes their gums sore. Now ask the children to use the plaque-disclosing tablet. Have the children chew the tablet first on one side of the mouth and then on the other, then spit into a cup. Ask the children to look at their teeth again in their mirror. Do they see red and pink? This shows that the plaque was not brushed away. Encourage children to brush their teeth until the color is brushed away. Offer children a small drink of water to rinse their mouths and guide them to rinse their toothbrush and return them to the toothbrush rack. Help children explain why it is important to take their time when they brush their teeth.
- **How to adjust the activity:** For English learners, provide a story or information for the child to read in their home language, or post pictures that depict and describe the steps of toothbrushing in both English and children's home languages. Include a picture that shows germs and plaque. For children with special developmental needs, obtain modified toothbrushes, adjust how the child sits or stands to brush teeth, or make other accommodations to assist each child to be successful when brushing teeth.
- **Did you meet your goal?** Are children able to show how to brush teeth carefully and describe why brushing teeth is important?

What if . . .

you wanted to teach oral hygiene in your kindergarten class by having the children brush their teeth each day after their snack? What procedures would you need to consider to prevent the spread of germs during toothbrushing? Would you offer toothpaste? Why or why not?

implement dental care services are of great benefit to children. Strategies to provide dental care services in schools include screening for dental problems, collaborating with community members to provide oral health assessments, and promoting school-affiliated or school-based dental care services such as fluoride varnish or dental sealants.

Policies Preventing Disease

Health policies are needed to prevent the spread of disease in early childhood settings. **Infectious diseases** are illnesses that are spread from one child to another. Infectious diseases are commonly spread in any group setting including child care and school settings. To prevent the spread of disease in preschools or primary classroom settings, teachers can employ policies regarding hand washing, room sanitation, and exclusion of children who are ill. Infants and toddlers are particularly vulnerable to infections and, in childhood settings, can have repeated exposures (Sun & Sundell, 2011).

infectious diseases illnesses that are spread from one child to another

● HEALTH PROMOTION AMONG DIVERSE POPULATIONS

Acknowledging the value and belief systems of children and families from culturally diverse backgrounds is a critical aspect of understanding and promoting health and wellness. An individual's race, culture, and ethnic background influence how they perceive health and illness throughout the life span (Spector, 2009). The demographics of infants and children enrolled in schools and early childhood settings have changed significantly during the past several decades. The cultural composition of families in the United States is becoming increasingly diverse. With more children from a variety of backgrounds in schools today, it is important to understand and acknowledge differing perspectives related to health and health promotion.

Disparities in Quality of Health

Not all families experience the same quality of health. These differences are called **health disparities**. The roots of health disparities are complex, but can be due only in part to differences in resources and opportunities to obtain needed health care. An example of a health disparity is that African American children experience higher rates of certain chronic diseases, such as asthma (Seith & Isakson, 2011). The reasons why health disparities exist are complex. Some families have ready access to health care through insurance programs, and they are comfortable using these resources. Others delay accessing medical treatment until health conditions become dire because they do not know how to access the care or cannot afford the cost. Disparities in physical and mental health also occur due to social reasons such as poverty, unsafe neighborhoods, or inadequate education.

Language may be a barrier for some families. Teachers gain a needed perspective about the potential challenges the families face when they build relationships with each child's family. Teachers are usually not health professionals. However, teachers are important links to the resources that are available in the community. Health care professionals and teachers should be aware that these disparities exist and work to help all families access the help they need.

Disparities in the quality of health are deeply related to social causes. For example, children's early nutrition can influence health outcomes as they grow. Children who experience malnutrition will have worse health outcomes. Children whose families are exposed to discrimination may have adverse health outcomes. Children living in unsafe neighborhoods or in impoverished living conditions will have a higher risk of health problems. Again, teachers may not be able to directly influence a child's living conditions or prior history of malnutrition but, through family support and health promotion, the chances of the child having better health will be greater.

Recognizing Stereotypes and Prejudice

Disparities exist in health but also in other settings that serve diverse racial, cultural, and socioeconomic groups, such as classrooms. Teachers come to classrooms with their own backgrounds, beliefs, and past experiences. Although they may be conscious of discriminatory practices and work to avoid them, there are other subtle ways in which children and families of diverse backgrounds are treated differently. Stereotyping and prejudice often lead to intolerance:

- **Stereotyping** results when individuals are labeled based on certain characteristics such as racial or ethnic heritage, age, gender, or socioeconomic background. An example of stereotyping is evident when teachers make the assumption that "all" boys prefer to play with trucks, or "all" children of a particular racial group are good at math or are more expressive. Often individuals are not conscious of the way they stereotype others.

- **Prejudice** refers to a negative attitude toward an individual based on group membership (Institute of Medicine, 2003). Prejudice is fueled by intolerance. It is evident when teachers group children according to certain characteristics rather than by an understanding of each individual child's skills and needs. For example, the teacher may create a seating arrangement that places the low-income children at the front of the room based on her perception that they will not pay attention if they choose their own seats.

Stereotyping and prejudice can result in discrimination or inequality and unfair treatment. Discrimination exists in health care, education, housing, employment, and other aspects of

health disparities
differences in health outcomes and quality of health and health care experienced by people of different incomes, races, or education levels

stereotyping
the labeling of others based on certain characteristics such as racial or ethnic heritage, age, gender, or socioeconomic background

prejudice
a negative attitude toward an individual based on group membership

society. Exposure to discrimination is associated with poor health outcomes (Institute of Medicine, 2003). Not only must teachers embrace children and their families' differences, they should also ensure that there is acceptance and tolerance among all children in their classrooms.

When teachers notice that families are not treated fairly, they can serve as advocates to support families:

Anadelia, a child in Shauna's first-grade class, is missing a needed immunization. Her mother, Consuelo, tells Shauna that she has taken her daughter twice to the local clinic to obtain the shot. Both times they were turned away by the receptionist who told them Anadelia did not need any more shots. Consuelo is concerned because the school nurse has told her that Anadelia will be excluded from class if the immunizations are not brought up to date. Consuelo asks Shauna for help.

Shauna and the school nurse collaborate to help Consuelo obtain an appointment to discuss vaccination details with a nurse or doctor. Consuelo returns to the physician's office where Anadelia receives the needed immunization. Shauna reflects on the situation, and feels frustrated that this family was not given sufficient encouragement to sort out the child's needs on the first visit. Was it because the family is Hispanic?

Promoting Acceptance in the Classroom

Teachers set the standard for acceptance and tolerance in the classroom and among children's families. This is demonstrated when teachers strive to interact equitably with all children and families, regardless of their backgrounds and unique characteristics. Teaching children to understand and appreciate differences is one way to promote acceptance. Activities to introduce this complex concept should begin simply and become more detailed, as shown in the following examples:

Sandi offers toddlers and preschoolers many opportunities to sort and classify objects while introducing the concepts of "same" and "different." To begin, she offers items that have only one aspect that is different, such as square blocks of the same size, in two different colors. Children learn to sort by color. Next she increases the challenge by offering both square blocks and small balls in two colors. In this task children are able to sort by color and shape. Activities such as these engage children in interesting discovery of how objects can have characteristics that are the same and at the same time have aspects that are different: Red blocks and red balls are the same color, but have different shapes.

Al engages older children in exploration of personal characteristics that may be the same (Who has five fingers?) and those that may be different (Who has brown hair?). He and the children make lists of the many ways children in the class are the same and different. They begin to understand that a great variety of similarities and differences exist among people.

From these activities children begin to recognize that personal characteristics and personal choices are sometimes the same and sometimes different. Lessons like these plant the ideas that help children to resist stereotyping: Not all people are the same and not all people like the same thing. They also help children learn to oppose prejudice, as the children begin to see themselves as sometimes members of one group (the group that loves soccer, for example) and sometimes members of another group.

Learning to recognize and enjoy differences and to develop a tolerance of differing points of view is a lifelong process. Teachers who model accepting behaviors and who encourage children to explore these topics offer children the opportunity to develop skills of negotiation, problem solving, and appreciation of the rights of self and others.

Supporting Families Who Do Not Speak English

Communication between teachers and parents is critical to children's well-being. Teachers need to be able to discuss the child's educational progress, describe any observed health concerns, and share

Early childhood teachers often need to provide support during children's peer interactions. As you watch this video, think about the strategies used by this teacher to encourage the children's cooperation and acceptance of each other.

information about behavioral or social issues. Likewise parents need to be able to inform teachers of any health issues or other concerns they may have about the child. Since a growing percentage of children come from families whose first language is one other than English, teachers need a plan to overcome language barriers when communicating with families.

For casual conversations or communicating with families about everyday classroom activities, teachers may be able to involve other family members or even older children as interpreters. When discussing sensitive or confidential issues, however, including health issues, teachers may need to seek the assistance of interpreters to establish needed communication with families. Using English-speaking family members may be convenient, but it does have some disadvantages. Family members may not be objective and may filter information instead of translating exactly what has been said. This is particularly troublesome in situations involving details of the child's health or behavior. Confidentiality may be compromised when family members are used as interpreters, and the quality of information obtained may be compromised.

Trained interpreters offer an appropriate but expensive option. When this is a viable option, trained interpreters have skills that are extremely helpful in communicating important information. Trained interpreters should demonstrate fluency in both languages and recognize the importance of confidentiality. They also have a clear role, which prevents inaccurate transfer of information. When teachers do not have ready access to the assistance of trained interpreters, alternative strategies are needed. These may include:

Teachers play an important role in promoting acceptance in early childhood settings.

- Prioritize when trained interpreters are most needed, such as to assist with family conferences or meetings to plan services for children with special health care needs or when situations arise related to challenging behavioral problems or mental health problems.
- Identify workers at community health service agencies who are bilingual. Establish connections to support families that you refer to those agencies.
- Create or obtain simple printed bilingual messages related to common early childhood situations to share with parents, such as *Your child appeared ill today* or *Several children in this class have become ill with the flu. Please remember to keep your child home when she is sick.*
- Advocate within the early childhood or school setting for the hiring of bilingual teachers who can assist everyone to improve communication with families who are not English speaking.

Although using family members or children as interpreters may be appropriate for much of the information that needs to be conveyed to families such as future early childhood activities and family responsibilities, this practice should be reconsidered when handling information about any aspects of a child's health.

In this **video**, a principal describes some techniques used in her school to encourage the involvement of parents who are English Language Learners. What strategies were successful? What other supports might be provided to encourage health and wellness in the home?

⬤ SUMMARY

Many factors in children's home, school, and community environments influence their health and well-being. Factors related to an individual and their social and physical environment contribute to children's health, whereas lifestyle factors affect wellness. Understanding these aspects of health and wellness helps teachers create a climate of health and wellness in the classroom.

Policies that guide health practices in the early childhood and school settings are promoted by licensing and accreditation agencies. The guidance provided by these groups helps ensure that children have safe and healthy experiences. Policies outline the procedures that create consistency and continuity in health and wellness program services. The presence of policies and procedures reflects the teacher's commitment to health and wellness in the early childhood setting.

As the nation's classrooms become increasingly diverse, teachers must plan health promotion activities that are culturally sensitive and honor differences among families. Health promotion is accomplished through activities and curriculum that introduce children to healthful behaviors. Health-promoting activities can be incorporated into any early childhood experience. Teachers are important role models demonstrating for children what healthy practices look like.

Teachers should understand that racial, cultural, and socioeconomic backgrounds may influence how families respond to health and illness. Families may have different values and beliefs about health and health care. Teachers must understand these differences and build comfortable relationships with families to promote communication about children's health and wellness. Planning activities in the classroom that teach children about differences and how to negotiate different viewpoints is beneficial to children's overall health.

KEY TERMS

Accreditation

Acute conditions

Chronic conditions

Congenital conditions

Cystic fibrosis

Dental caries

Determinants of health

Health

Health disparities

Health policies

Infectious diseases

Mental health

Physical health

Prejudice

Protective factors

Risk factors

Socioeconomic status

Stereotyping

Wellness

REVIEW QUESTIONS

1. Define *health* and *wellness*. Describe how these terms are linked and how they are different.

2. List the components of health. Describe determinants of health and illness.

3. Describe the goals of school health and wellness policies with respect to nutrition and physical activity.

4. Define *health promotion* and provide examples of ways that children can participate in promoting their own wellness.

5. Define *health disparities* and give an example that could impact the health of young children.

6. Provide examples of ways teachers can promote children's understanding and acceptance of differences.

DISCUSSION STARTERS

1. What is your social and cultural background? How do you think your background has affected your quality of health and your access to health care?

2. How can teachers address health disparities in our society?

3. Think about low-income families you have known or worked with in the past. What are some of the challenges they have faced? In what ways do you think children from low-income families are at a disadvantage in our society? Can you think of any advantages or strengths that children might gain from growing up in a low-income family?

PRACTICE POINTS

1. Examine the community in which you live. What is the incidence of poverty in your area? What resources are available to families with low incomes? What gaps in local services may limit the involvement of children from low-income families in school activities?

2. Imagine that you are in charge of a dental health promotion event for your school. What oral health concepts would you focus on? What resources would you tap to obtain expertise? What ideas do you have to include both children and parents in this learning experience? How would you ensure that this event reaches non-English-speaking families in your school?

3. Create a lesson that promotes physical activity for preschool-age children. Make adjustments for children who have special needs that pertain to mobility. How would you teach this lesson to children who speak predominantly Spanish? What aspects of the preschool environment might promote physical activity?

WEB RESOURCES

Model School Wellness Policies
   www.schoolwellnesspolicies.org/

National Center for Child Poverty
   www.nccp.org

National Resource Center for Health and Safety in Child Care and Early Education
   http://nrckids.org

MyEducationLab™

Go to Topic 5 (Health Promotion/Policy) in the MyEducationLab (www.myeducationlab.com) for your course, where you can:

- Find learning outcomes for Health Promotion/ Policy along with the national standards that connect to these outcomes.
- Complete Assignments and Activities that can help you more deeply understand the chapter content.
- Apply and practice your understanding of the core teaching skills identified in the chapter with the Building Teaching Skills and Dispositions learning units.

- Check your comprehension on the content covered in the chapter by going to the Study Plan in the Book Resources for your text. Here you will be able to take a chapter quiz, receive feedback on your answers, and then access Review, Practice, and Enrichment activities to enhance your understanding of chapter content.

nine
Health Screening and Assessment

learning outcomes

AFTER READING THIS CHAPTER, YOU SHOULD BE ABLE TO:

1. Discuss each component of a comprehensive health history.

2. Explain the purpose of immunizations for young children and discuss some of the common concerns families have regarding vaccinations.

3. Describe how to gather and manage confidential health history information.

4. Explain what types of gaps in the health history are frequently identified by teachers.

5. Describe various health screenings and why they help ensure children are able to learn.

6. Explain how teachers monitor children's health in the classroom.

Adelina is a bright 9-month-old infant whose family has recently immigrated from Mexico. Adelina is being enrolled in an infant child care program. Her family is pleased to have a chance to visit with the teacher who explains that during their visit she will ask some questions to learn about Adelina's health and development. After a few moments of visiting, the family provides the records they brought showing that Adelina received vaccinations in Mexico and additional vaccinations in Texas. As they talk, Maria learns that Adelina had a serious illness at 3 months of age that the family describes as an "infection of the brain." They report that Adelina was hospitalized for several weeks, but has otherwise been healthy.

Maria reviews the health history and enrollment materials. Maria asks if the family has any concerns about Adelina's development. The family reports that Adelina has not started making sounds or using other vocalizations appropriate for her age. They are worried because this is different from their experiences with their older children. Together Maria and the family decide that this should be evaluated further. The family also reports that they have recently moved out of an older home that was very run down. They have heard that a physician can do a simple blood test to determine if the baby was impacted by the presence of lead in the older home. Maria records these referrals accordingly.

By the end of the visit Adelina is reaching out to pat Maria's hands and offer her toys. They say good-bye and the family leaves with instructions on where to follow up on the issues that they discussed. They feel excited about their daughter's new care setting, and are pleased that Maria is so helpful and approachable. After they leave Maria reflects on their conversations. She makes a note to check back with the family in a week to see what they have learned from their follow-up plan.

Children come to early childhood classrooms with different health and development experiences. Learning about these aspects of a child's background is an important part of the transition into the classroom. Children's health and development information guides the development of the care and education plan. It ensures that teachers are aware of children's individual health needs. It also focuses attention on concerns such as allergies or hearing or vision problems so that children do not miss important opportunities to learn.

In this chapter we discuss the significance of evaluating children's health to ensure they are ready to learn. We highlight the importance of managing health information and communicating it appropriately. We explore the common ways in which children are assessed and screened for health and development concerns that might impact learning. Finally, we offer suggestions about how daily health assessments can be conducted in the classroom to efficiently and effectively monitor and improve children's health and well-being while they are in the classroom.

health evaluation
an assessment of a child's overall health and well-being
health screening
an evaluation using specific tools to detect potential health concerns
health assessment
an evaluation of health or a description of an aspect of health

● EVALUATING CHILDREN'S HEALTH AND DEVELOPMENT

Early childhood programs and schools are part of children's health and wellness network. Health evaluation tools are used in early childhood programs and schools because these settings provide an important opportunity to assess children at an early age and determine who needs further assistance or referral for services. The early childhood setting may be the first time that some children have had attention given to aspects of health and development that influence learning. In this way early childhood programs provide an important contribution to children's future development and opportunity to learn.

Evaluating and addressing health concerns at an early age set children on a course for optimal development and learning.

Understanding Health Evaluations

A **health evaluation** is an assessment of a child's overall health and well-being. It is a multifaceted process that reviews and considers the many factors that influence children's health. Health evaluations are conducted for several specific purposes:

1. To understand a child's health status so that teachers can make necessary accommodations.
2. To identify known medical conditions or risk factors for illness or injury.
3. To identify children who benefit from further evaluations or referrals.
4. To help families learn about the health of their child and to understand potential hazards to their child's health.
5. To identify gaps in the family's access to needed resources.

The health evaluation process is an important part of early childhood and school services. In order for children to develop and learn optimally, health problems need to be identified and addressed. The approaches to collecting information for an overall health evaluation are discussed in this chapter. Each approach provides guidance for collecting and managing health information.

Health evaluation involves both initial and ongoing approaches. Initial approaches include health screenings and assessments. **Health screenings** are specific methods used to identify health conditions or risk factors for health problems. An example is when children's settings and schools offer health fairs or special health screening events where children's hearing, vision, and oral health are evaluated to detect potential problems. Another aspect of screening involves a review of the health history looking for information that may suggest risk factors associated with diseases such as lead poisoning or dietary habits that put children at risk for anemia or obesity.

Health assessments in early childhood settings are evaluations of overall health and include descriptions of each child's general health. Health assessments also focus on particular aspects of health

MyEducationLab™

Visit the MyEducationLab for *Nutrition, Health, and Safety for Young Children* to enhance your understanding of chapter concepts with a personalized Study Plan. You'll also have the opportunity to hone your teaching skills through video-based Assignments and Activities, as well as Building Teaching Skills and Dispositions lessons.

by evaluating children in relation to others. An example is evaluating children's growth through height and weight measurements that are plotted on growth charts.

Ongoing assessment approaches include daily health checks and continual observation for health and illness indicators. **Daily health checks** involve visual reviews of children soon after they arrive at the classroom. **Continual observation** refers to consistent and thoughtful recognition that children display observable signs that cue teachers to impending illness. Together these approaches ensure that potential problems are identified so that any needed interventions can be implemented.

daily health checks
visual assessment of a child's apparent health conducted at arrival

continual observation
consistent observation for signs of impending illness

Managing Health Information Appropriately

Health information is personal and private information. It must be obtained respectfully, used appropriately, and managed confidentially. In 1996, Congress enacted Public Law 104-191, the Health Insurance Portability and Accountability Act, often referred to as HIPAA. The purpose of this legislation was to improve the effectiveness of the health care system and to maintain the privacy of individual health care information. The act requires that safeguards be in place to ensure that individual health information is managed confidentially and communicated appropriately.

HIPAA requirements are directed primarily to health care providers and insurance agencies. These groups are considered *covered entities*, that is, they are required to follow the HIPAA rules. Child care providers and teachers are not included in the definition of covered entities. However, teachers do come into contact with individual health information and may work with health care providers. For example, collecting health history information as part of the enrollment process provides information about the child's past and current health issues. As they receive this information, teachers and their programs interface with HIPAA-covered entities. Because of this, teachers must ensure that the privacy of child and family health information is protected. This means that children's settings and schools must have policies that describe how confidential information is to be managed and communicated. Health records should be accurate, complete, confidential, and shared appropriately. Policies should provide details about the safeguards to be put in place to maintain confidentiality. Guidelines for appropriate safeguards include the following (Kentucky Cabinet for Health and Family Services, 2011):

- Provide a private space for teachers and families to discuss health issues.
- Keep all written documents out of view when in use; store documents in a secure, locked file.
- Ensure that information stored on computers is password protected, and that computer screens are turned away from public view when in use.
- Require the signature of the parent or other person authorized by the parent for the release of children's health information.

health history
a summary of a child's previous health experiences

Health information must be managed privately and confidentially.

Defining the Health History

Each child's early development and health experiences are unique. A **health history** is a summary of the child's previous health experiences. It includes the child's medical history, immunization records, information about previous injuries, and a history of the child's development. The health history provides an overall view of the child's physical and mental health and development. A comprehensive, or complete, health history includes the following information and topics that, taken together, create a thorough picture of children's health experiences:

- Basic details such as the child's name, birth date, names of the parents or guardian, and family contact information.
- A list of past illnesses.
- A summary of any chronic, or continual, health conditions.
- The child's record of immunizations given and when.
- A history of significant injuries or accidents the child has had.
- A summary of the child's behaviors or personal style that might make the child more prone to accidents or may influence his ability to learn.

- Information about the health and wellness of the child's family, including medical and mental health conditions and challenges.
- A summary of the child's developmental history, such as a timeline of when the child achieved key developmental milestones.
- Information about the child's mental health, including social and emotional well-being.
- Information about the child's nutritional background, to identify nutritional risks such as over- or undernutrition and access to healthy balanced meals.
- A summary of the child's oral and dental health history.
- A summary of resources the family is currently using, and gaps in access to medical care.

Knowing these details of children's early life helps teachers to be watchful for aspects that may have negative consequences for growth, development, and learning. Requirements for obtaining health histories within early childhood programs vary according to the type of program and the age of the children in the program. Head Start standards for obtaining health histories represent a comprehensive model that best exemplifies how to obtain information and promote health. Not all teachers will obtain all components of a health history. However, it is important to understand why each component, discussed next, is important to the health and wellness of a child.

Early Development

Prenatal and early development set the stage for later development. The health history briefly explores this information, identifying significant aspects that may continue to influence the child's development.

Pregnancy and Birth History Information about the mother's pregnancy and birth history helps identify risks for children's development. Questions include whether the mother had any health problems during the pregnancy or during delivery. Some maternal medical conditions cause congenital defects in children. For example, babies of mothers with diabetes are at risk for heart defects. Mothers who contract **rubella**, a serious viral infection, during pregnancy are at risk for having a baby with a hearing loss.

The health history also explores aspects related to the child's birth to learn if the child was a **premature infant** (born more than 3 weeks early) or if the child experienced any problems at birth or during the first few days of life. A child's birth weight is also of interest. Low-birth-weight babies are at risk for developmental delays, poor school performance, seizures, and hearing or visual impairments. Figure 9-1 provides sample questions to ask when exploring health issues related to pregnancy and birth.

Developmental History A comprehensive health history includes discussions that help teachers learn about the child's progress with respect to **developmental milestones**. Developmental

rubella
a viral infection that can cause fetal defects when contracted during pregnancy

premature infant
an infant born more than 3 weeks early, or less than 37 weeks' gestation

developmental milestones
physical abilities or tasks that most children are able to achieve by a certain age range

> ## A Matter of ETHICS
>
> You are a kindergarten teacher in a public school and have a child enrolled in your class who is prone to frequent skin infections. The child's parent reports that he is under the care of a medical provider who confirms that the condition is not contagious. However, some of the other families in the class keep asking you for details and are concerned about their child playing with this boy. They suggest that he should attend a special class. What is the problem that you need to address? How does the NAEYC Code of Ethical Conduct advise you in this situation? What responsibilities do you have to this child, the community, and society in general related to matters such as this?

FIGURE 9-1 Pregnancy and Birth History

Asking questions about health problems during pregnancy and delivery helps identify potential problems with children's growth and development. Questions include the following:

1. Did the mother have any health problems during pregnancy or during delivery?
2. Was the child born more than 3 weeks early or premature?
3. What was the child's birth weight?
4. Did the child have any problems at birth or in the first days of life?

Source: Adapted from *Head Start Child Health Record*, by the U.S. Department of Health and Human Services, Administration of Children and Families, retrieved December 1, 2011, from http://eclkc.ohs.acf.hhs.gov/hslc/resources/ECLKC_Bookstore/Child%20Health%20Record.htm.

milestones are physical abilities or tasks that most children are able to achieve by a certain age range. For example, most children are able to walk on their own by age 2. A few children may walk as early as 9 months. Many children are walking at 1 year of age. Some children show a pattern of reaching developmental milestones earlier than the typical age range. Some develop quickly in some areas of development and more slowly in others. Here are two examples:

- Hal reports that his child began speaking at a very young age but did not begin to walk until well after the first birthday. He has noticed that the child is more interested in reading and less interested in playing outside.
- Kayla describes her child as very coordinated and active. She remembers that her child was running around the house at 9 months of age and still prefers to play all ball games rather than doing homework.

Understanding the individual child's pace and pattern of development helps teachers anticipate how to structure learning activities so each child will thrive in the classroom.

Information from a developmental history also helps detect the possibility of developmental problems or delays. The signs of developmental disability are highly variable depending on cause, type, and severity of the delay. Some developmental delays are apparent soon after birth. Others emerge during early childhood and into the early elementary years. Teachers spend many hours with children. They become acquainted with the range of behaviors that are typical for certain ages that enables them to recognize gaps in development through observation of the child in the classroom. Using a developmental milestones checklist is another way to engage families in discussion about a child's developmental history. Checklists, like the one shown in Figure 9-2, guide families to recognize possible indicators of developmental delay.

History of Illness and Disease

The health history helps teachers and families identify and discuss any serious diseases that require special health care or that would affect participation in the classroom. Plans for managing chronic illnesses in the classroom can then be developed and discussed.

Illnesses and Hospitalizations   Significant illnesses and hospitalizations are important aspects of children's health experiences. Some may have long-term consequences, such as meningitis, which may cause hearing loss or cognitive delays. In the opening case scenario Adelina's mother reported that her child had been hospitalized for an "infection of the brain" which may have been meningitis. The description of this illness along with the mother's report that Adelina made very few vocalizations might indicate that the child suffers from hearing loss. Serious injuries also have the potential to cause developmental problems. For example, a child who has experienced a serious leg fracture may have damaged the growth center in the bone, resulting in growth retardation of the leg and causing physical limitations.

Chronic Health Conditions   The health history should explore chronic or persistent health conditions such as allergies, asthma, or digestive issues. These are important aspects of a child's health that may need special attention in the classroom setting. For example, a teacher could ask if the child has ever been diagnosed with **asthma** or has had a history of breathing problems or chronic cough. Asthma is one of the most common chronic medical conditions in childhood and causes inflammation in the lungs in response to environmental agents such as cigarette smoke, pollens, or infections. Chronic conditions may require specific treatment plans that involve administering medications in the classroom. Discussing this aspect of the health history helps reveal these needs so plans can be established. This chapter's *Progressive Programs and Practices* illustrates how chronic health conditions can impact every aspect of the early childhood environment and how teachers can play a big role in the activities of the day.

asthma
the most common chronic medical condition in childhood causing chronic inflammation in the lungs in response to environmental agents such as cigarette smoke, pollens, or infections

Medications and Treatments   This aspect of the health history directs teachers and families to discuss and document any medications the child is taking. If medications need to be given when children are in the classroom, special documentation, training, and procedures are needed. Directions

PROGRESSIVE PROGRAMS & PRACTICES

Giving Caleb a Voice!

By Laurie Katz, The Ohio State University, Franklin County Board of Developmental Disabilities' Early Childhood Education and Family Center

Five-year-old Caleb starts to chuckle and smile as he sees "Curious George," one of his very favorite characters, while he plays a game on the computer that moves a school bus to George. Although most young children would play this game using their hands to move the mouse, Caleb has limited control of his arms and hands. Caleb plays this game while he sits in his wheelchair with two head switches attached. Caleb uses his switches to "drive" the bus. These switches enable Caleb to take turns and have fun with his classmates at the computer. He also sees that his actions can cause change.

This is no simple task for Caleb, a child born with cerebral palsy and considered medically fragile. While Caleb can vocalize (i.e., cries, laughs, fusses, grunts, produces some vowel/open sounds such as "ahhhh"), his level of motor involvement limits his ability to produce words. In the past, he primarily communicated his needs by holding his breath when he didn't like something. His family and the professionals at the Franklin County Board of Developmental Disabilities' Early Childhood Education and Family Center located in Columbus, Ohio, have worked together for about four years to give Caleb a voice, control over his environment, and a sense of belonging in his community.

The center is part of an extensive partnership combining numerous agencies that enroll children from birth–kindergarten-age who are developing typically and with special needs and their families. The center's philosophy is based on *all children* learning together and influenced by the Reggio Emilia approach and other research-based early childhood practices in which each child is perceived as a unique individual with developmental, family, and cultural histories that shape his or her approach to learning. Important health and wellness programs support each child's growth such as movement activities including dance, yoga, fitness groups, and jumping for exercise. Whole body activities are used to develop motor skills and self-awareness. Wellness and nutrition are strong features of these programs that involve children learning about cooking, gardening, and outdoor explorations.

The professionals at the center of Caleb's life at school include a speech and language pathologist (SLP), physical and occupational therapists, classroom teachers and assistants, an adaptive physical educator, and medical personnel who work together to provide Caleb with the needed education services to increase his independence with his peers and the community. His team of professionals is continually challenged to find ways to accommodate Caleb's strengths and needs so he can access and learn with his peers using the same curriculum. They work together helping Caleb interact in socially appropriate ways predominantly through nonverbal and augmentative communication, to increase his understanding of language and expressive abilities to interact and make choices.

Sandy, (SLP): "Getting to know Caleb and working with him and his family during the past few years has been an amazing adventure! It has both challenged and inspired me to seek further training in augmentative/alternative communication, to find more effective ways to support and expand his communication skills for a wide variety of purposes. Caleb has helped me learn how to really 'listen' to him. I've learned that it's not about what I or someone else thinks he should say, but about providing him a way to have and express his own 'voice.' We are in the process of getting him a new, more sophisticated communication device but we know that regardless of what he uses: pictures, gestures, facial expressions or a high-tech speech device, Caleb will always let us know that he has something to say.

Another example of Caleb's use of augmentative communication involved his class making smoothies. Although he was unable to physically add the ingredients, he could assist by giving the directions and pressing another switch to turn on the blender and mix up the smoothies when his classmates asked. By providing simple assistive technology accommodations (such as switches), Caleb was able to actively engage in social interactions with his peers, touch the glass to feel the cold, and smell the smoothies."

Stacy, Caleb's mother, is very grateful for the work of these professionals and believes it's best to have as many professionals as possible working together to help Caleb whether it's in their home or the center.

FIGURE 9-2   Indicators of Developmental Delay

Age 4 to 7 Months

- Excessive stiffness of muscles.
- Floppy or very loose muscle tone.
- Head falls back when pulled up to sitting position.
- Reaches with one hand rather than both hands.
- Does not show interest in faces.

Age 8 to 12 Months

- No crawl.
- Does not stand with support.
- No babbling by 9 months.
- Has no words such as 'mama' or 'dada'.
- Does not show interest in objects by pointing.

Age 12 to 24 Months

- Does not understand simple instructions by 2 years of age.
- Does not speak at least 15 words by 18 months.
- Not walking by 18 months.
- Does not push a wheeled toy by 2 years of age.
- Does not mimic actions or words by age 2.

Age 24 to 36 Months

- Persistent drooling or unclear speech.
- Little interest in playing with or observing other children.

- Does not point to or show objects of interest to others.
- No pretend play.
- By age 3, has made no progress in self-care or toilet training.
- Frequently falls or has difficulty climbing or descending stairs.

Age 3 to 4 Years

- Cannot jump, ride a tricycle, or throw ball overhand.
- Does not show interest in playing with other children.
- No fantasy play.
- Seems withdrawn on a consistent basis.
- Shows violent behaviors such as hitting or biting.
- Is exceedingly shy or fearful around other children.

Age 4 to 5 Years

- Exhibits overly impulsive behavior when angry or upset.
- Very easily distracted and cannot concentrate on single activity for more than 5 minutes.
- Unable to stack a tower of six to eight blocks.
- Unable to accurately give her first and last name.
- Does not talk about daily activities.
- Exhibits extremely fearful, timid, or aggressive behavior.

Source: Shelov, 2009.

from the child's health care provider must be obtained that outline the timing and dose of medications needed and how the medications are given. Teachers must document what was given, when, and whether there were any side effects. This information should be available to the family.

Immunization Status

immunizations
vaccinations are given to individuals to trigger the person's immune response, which helps prevent infection

Immunization records are an important part of the health history. **Immunizations** are important because they prevent the incidence and spread of disease. This is of special significance as children enter group settings where infections frequently occur.

Many states have strict policies regarding children who have not had up-to-date immunizations.

Immunization Requirements An advisory committee at the government's Centers for Disease Control and Prevention (CDC) outlines the immunizations that are recommended for children and adults. The recommendations include the age at which a vaccine should be given, the number of doses, the time between doses, and safety measures related to the administration of the vaccines. Individual states are responsible for establishing laws that outline the specific immunization requirements for children who participate in child care or school settings. These requirements vary from state to state (Centers for Disease Control and Prevention, 2011). Most routine vaccinations are given during the first 6 years of life. After age 6, only flu shots may be required until age 12 when routine vaccinations are given again. The family should obtain a document of the child's immunization status and provide it to the early childhood program or school well in advance of attendance. Immunization records are then reviewed by the staff to determine if the child's immunization status meets state requirements and, therefore, if the child is eligible to begin school.

Family Concerns About Immunizations   A small number of families may choose not to vaccinate or only to partially vaccinate based on a number of concerns. Misconceptions can lead to some of these concerns. The following are common misconceptions (American Academy of Pediatrics, 2009):

- Family believes that it is better to get "natural" immunity by being exposed to the disease rather than being vaccinated.
- Giving too many vaccines at once is harmful to a child's immune system.
- Vaccines cause illnesses such as autism or autoimmune disorders.

Families may express their concerns about immunizations to their child's teacher. Teachers should be prepared to give accurate information or refer families to an appropriate resource. Another concern that families often express relates to the presence of **thimerosal** in vaccines. Thimerosal is a mercury compound that was widely used as a preservative in vaccinations. The *Safety Segment* discusses the use of thimerosal in vaccines.

Potential Reactions Following Vaccination   Some vaccines can produce **adverse reactions**—or side effects. Three types of vaccine side effects have been identified (Centers for Disease Control and Prevention, 2011):

1. *Local reaction:* This is the most common and least severe side effect. Local reactions are characterized by pain, swelling, and redness at the site of the injection.
2. *Systemic reaction:* This reaction is characterized by generalized symptoms including fever, malaise, fatigue, muscle pain, headache, and loss of appetite. These symptoms can occur because of the vaccine or because of a concurrent viral infection. Systemic reactions are sometimes seen after immunizations that use live vaccines such as MMR and varicella (chicken pox).
3. *Allergic reaction:* Allergic reactions are very rare but can be life threatening. They occur in less than 1 in 500,000 doses. Signs of allergic reaction to immunizations may include trouble breathing, weakness, wheezing, hives, and swelling of the throat. If any of these reactions is noticed, emergency medical assistance should be obtained immediately.

If a teacher or parent has concerns about any symptoms following a vaccination, a follow-up appointment with the child's health care provider should be scheduled.

thimerosal
a mercury compound that was widely used as a preservative in vaccinations

adverse reactions
side effects

local reaction
the most common type of side effect after vaccination; characterized by pain, swelling, and redness at the site of the injection

systemic reaction
a type of reaction following vaccination; characterized by generalized symptoms such as fever, malaise, fatigue, muscle pain, headache, and loss of appetite

allergic reaction
rare but life-threatening reaction following vaccination

What if . . .
on the first day of preschool a late-enrolling child arrived with immunization records in hand that were not up to date? How would you handle this situation?

SAFETY SEGMENT   Thimerosal and Vaccines

Thimerosal is a mercury compound that was used in vaccines that came from multidose vials. It is a preservative that prevents bacterial growth and contamination. After 1990, as vaccines were being added to the routine schedule for infants, the amount of total thimerosal given exceeded limits reported by the Environmental Protection Agency. This level that exceeded limits was detected in 1999 but at that time, no data suggested any harm to infants. As a *precaution,* the CDC recommended that vaccine manufacturers eliminate the use of thimerosal in vaccines for children.

Considerable concern has been raised regarding a suspected association between thimerosal and autism. Numerous studies focusing on the relationship between thimerosal and autism and other neurological disorders have not shown any relationship.

Source: Centers for Disease Control and Prevention, 2011.

Salud de los niños y las conductas de riesgo

Child Safety and Risk-Taking Behaviors

Gathering information about the child's style and behavioral characteristics helps identify the child's potential for injury. Injuries are the single leading cause of death among children (Borse et al., 2008). In a classroom setting, it is the teacher's responsibility to ensure that each child is safe and secure. Knowing about the child's safety behaviors guides planning for the types of activities offered and helps identify any special supervision the child may require. Asking about the child's physical activity habits includes questions such as these: Does the child tend to take risks? Has the child had any major accidents, fractures, or head injuries that were associated with risk-taking behavior? Conversations with families about child safety behaviors also provide an opportunity to talk about ways to promote health and safety at home. Questions to explore with families include the following:

- Is the family car equipped with appropriately installed car seats or booster seats?
- Are all medications or poisons such as cleaning supplies or chemicals stored out of the child's reach?
- Does the home have a swimming pool, lake, irrigation canal, or other open water source nearby? Have appropriate measures been taken to prevent unsupervised entry into these areas?
- Does the family feel safe in their neighborhood?
- If the family owns guns, are all guns locked up and unavailable?

Exámenes sobre la nutrición

Nutrition Screening

The nutritional health history identifies aspects of children's dietary habits and special dietary needs. Here are some important aspects of the nutritional health history discussion:

- Are there barriers to providing the child healthful foods?
- Is the child's diet nutritious and appropriate for the child's age?
- What are the child's eating habits?
- Does the child have any special dietary needs, food restrictions, or food allergies?
- Is the child growing appropriately?

Discussing the family's ability to provide healthful food for the child may reveal challenges the family faces. This provides an opportunity for teachers and families to explore community resources that may be of support. Such conversations also identify whether a child has suffered from periods of malnutrition (overnutrition and undernutrition) that may have interrupted normal growth and development.

Health Issues Related to Nutrition Other health issues related to nutrition are also discussed, such as diabetes and how it should be managed in the class setting. Some children have challenges related to the physical aspects of eating, such as chewing and swallowing. Food allergies are also an important consideration. Food allergies must be carefully explored so teachers have all the information they need to implement a safe environment. These issues are discussed and strategies are developed for safety at mealtime.

The history also addresses children's individual and age-appropriate feeding needs. It provides an opportunity for families to describe what the child typically eats, how much, and the usual eating schedule. Figure 9-3 provides sample questions to ask when gathering information about children's history and to promote conversations about children's dietary needs.

Special Diets and Food Preferences The nutritional history also informs teachers about family preferences for special diets or food restrictions. Special diets may be followed for religious or cultural reasons. Food preferences may be influenced by a variety of factors including access to food, presence of food insecurity, ethnicity of family, or level of **acculturation**. Acculturation refers to the social, psychological, and behavioral changes that are associated with adapting to a new culture (Dave, Evans, Saunders, Watkins, & Pfeiffer, 2009). This chapter's Nutrition Note discusses the effect of acculturation. Immigration can influence a family's health behaviors, including the way in which they adjust to dietary changes. Some families may struggle to find familiar foods in the groceries and supermarkets in their new community. They may also be impacted by unhealthy dietary habits of their new environment. For example, young children of Hispanic families tend to consume less fruits and vegetables as they become acculturated to the United States (Dave et al., 2009).

acculturation
the social, psychological, and behavioral changes associated with relocation

FIGURE 9-3 Sample Nutrition Screening Questions

For Infants

✓ Is the baby breast- or bottle feeding?
  · If breast-feeding, will you provide breast milk for your baby?
  · If bottle feeding, what type of formula?
✓ How often does your baby eat?
✓ If formula feeding, how much does your baby eat?
✓ If formula feeding, is your baby on a special formula and are there special directions for preparing it?
✓ How long does it usually take to feed your baby?
✓ How does your baby let you know when she is hungry?
✓ How does he let you know when he is full?
✓ Does your baby eat anything other than breast milk or formula? If so, what and how often?
✓ Does your baby have any problems when feeding?
✓ *If age appropriate:* Has your baby had any problems with the introduction of solid foods?

For Preschool and School-Age Children

✓ What foods does your child like? What foods does your child dislike?
✓ Are there any foods your child should not eat for medical, religious, or personal reasons?
✓ Is your child on a special diet?
✓ What is your child's usual meal schedule?
✓ Does your child eat breakfast?
✓ How much and what type of milk does your child drink?
✓ How much juice does your child drink?
✓ Have there been any recent changes in your child's diet?
✓ Does your child have trouble chewing or swallowing?
✓ Does your child eat or chew things that aren't food?
✓ Do you have any concerns about your child's eating?
✓ Do you eat meals at home together as a family?

Source: Adapted from *Head Start Child Health Record*, by the U.S. Department of Health and Human Services, Administration of Children and Families, retrieved December 1, 2011, from http://eclkc.ohs.acf.hhs.gov/hslc/resources/ECLKC_Bookstore/Child%20Health%20Record.htm.

These discussions are important opportunities to not only learn about a child's habits but also to promote healthy dietary behaviors.

Oral Health History

Gathering information about the child's oral health provides an opportunity to explore dental problems the child has experienced. It explores the answers to questions such as these:

- Has the child ever had a dental examination or screening?
- Are the child's teeth brushed regularly?
- Does the child brush her or his teeth?
- Has the child had any dental surgery or other procedures?

The oral health history also identifies if the child is at risk for dental disease. For example, infants who are given juice regularly and young children who drink soft drinks are at high risk for developing cavities because of the high sugar content in these beverages. This is especially problematic if babies are put to bed with bottles containing juice.

The oral health history also identifies the family's water source and whether the water is a good fluoride source. **Fluoride** is a mineral recommended for children 6 months to 6 years of age. Fluoride helps to prevent dental disease. Some public water systems have fluoride added to the water system. If the child is drinking well water or water from another nonpublic source, the child may not be getting the fluoride needed to prevent dental disease. In some cases a physician will prescribe fluoride drops as a preventive measure.

Mental and Emotional Health History

[handwritten: Historia de la salud mental y emocional]

Assessing children's social and emotional development through a mental health history is an important part of ensuring a child's overall health and well-being. Social and emotional problems that go unrecognized can persist into adulthood, interrupting normal development.

What if . . .

you discover that a 5-year-old in your class has never seen a dentist? When you explore this with the family you learn that it is the parents' fear of the dentist that keeps them from making an appointment. What guidance can you provide to ensure the child gets the oral health care that is needed?

fluoride

mineral recommended for children 6 months to 6 years of age for the prevention of dental disease

NUTRITION NOTE   The Effects of Acculturation on Nutrition in Hispanic Populations

Acculturation refers to changes in behaviors and ways of thinking that occur when families join a new culture. For example, acculturation impacts eating behaviors and the use of traditional foods. This impact on the diet is more pronounced the longer the family lives outside their native country. Interestingly, research has shown that the health of a recently immigrated Hispanic individual is much better than the typical U.S. Caucasian person. The adoption of the U.S. diet along with other obesity-related behaviors has negative effects as immigrants become more acculturated.

Changes due to acculturation on the diets of Hispanic families who have immigrated to the United States include:

• A decrease in the use of traditional foods.

• An increase in the use of traditional foods in a new way.

• An increase in the use of foods from the host country.

For many Mexican families, dietary acculturation has replaced a diet rich in beans, fruits, vegetables, and grains with a diet composed of highly processed and sugary foods. An acculturated diet leads to higher intake of high-fat milk, soda, and increased fast-food including pizza and French fries.

These trends suggest that acculturation can be a risk factor for unhealthy eating behaviors. Early childhood teachers promote healthful nutritional practices by preserving healthy traditional behaviors. They also support children's wellness by assisting families to choose positive dietary options as they integrate aspects of the American diet.

Source: Based on Batis, Hernandez-Barrera, Barquera, Rivera, & Popkin, 2011.

The mental health history focuses the discussion on a variety of social and emotional health indicators:

- The child's ability to interact positively with others.
- The child's ability to manage emotions, such as anger or frustration.
- The child's interest in playing with other children.
- Ways the child copes with change and stress.
- Problems or worries the child may have.

One common topic in the mental health history involves discussing the child's style when transitioning into a new environment. Three behavior styles are often discussed (Thomas & Chess, 1977):

- *Easy and adaptable:* Describes children who adapt readily to new situations.
- *Difficult and emotional:* Describes children who display high levels of emotion in new situations.
- *Slow to warm up:* Describes children who withdraw from new situations at first and instead spend time observing before they gradually adapt.

Discussions about these behavior styles help identify the kinds of supports a child may need when beginning in the early childhood setting and when learning the daily classroom routine. Families can also describe other aspects of the child's style or temperament such as the child's adaptability, typical moods, intensity of reaction, and activity level. These characteristics guide teachers to fit their teaching and management approaches to the individual needs of the child.

The mental health history also includes exploration of ways the family soothes the child when the child is worried or hurt. In programs that care for infants, questions should focus on the infant's patterns such as whether the child cries frequently or has fussy periods. Teachers should also ask families about the strategies they use at home. It is common to ask questions about the child's habits during the mental health history. Examples of questions to spark conversation about social-emotional development are shown in Figure 9-4.

Family Health and Wellness

Health and wellness practices within the family impact children's health. Understanding the context that surrounds the child provides clues to the child's healthful development. It also offers an opportunity for teachers and families to discuss resources the family may need and ways the classroom environment can contribute to the child's healthy development.

FIGURE 9-4   **Sample Questions for a Mental Health History** *Salud mental*

✓ Does your child sleep less than 8 hours or have trouble sleeping at night?

✓ Is your child learning to use the toilet? Or, does your child manage toileting by herself?

✓ Can your child dress and undress herself?

✓ Does your child have any worries or fears?

✓ Does your child enjoy playing with children her age?

✓ Does your child experience temper tantrums or have any challenges controlling behavior?

✓ Does your child enjoy fantasy play? Is your child able to recognize the difference between fantasy and reality?

✓ Have there been any changes in your child's life in the last 6 months such as a move, family divorce, or death in the family?

✓ Are you or your family having any problems that might affect your child?

✓ Is your child interested in new experiences?

Sources: Adapted from *Head Start Child Health Record*, by the U.S. Department of Health and Human Services, Administration of Children and Families, retrieved December 20, 2011, from http://eclkc.ohs.acf.hhs.gov/hslc/resources/ECLKC_Bookstore/Child%20Health%20Record.htm; and *The Complete and Authoritative Guide: Caring for Your Child; Age Birth to Age 5,* by the American Academy of Pediatrics, 2009, New York: Bantam Books.

Family Medical History   It is important to know when a parent has a chronic medical condition because these are sometimes inherited or passed down to a child. Teachers should also be aware of situations when families who are ill have difficulties caring for their child. It may be necessary to provide referrals and support for families to obtain the services they need.

Home Environment   Aspects of the home environment help identify conditions that may be unhealthy for children. Children who live with or are exposed to smokers are vulnerable to the effects of secondhand smoke. Drug production and drug use expose children to toxic products and put children in dangerous situations. Older houses introduce risk for lead exposure from paint and other deteriorating building products that contain lead. Unsafe neighborhoods surround children with dangers that may, among other things, limit the child's ability to play outside.

Family Dynamics   The relationships that exist among family members impact children's mental health. Dynamics associated with poverty, job loss, single parenthood, and homelessness contribute negatively to children's mental health. For example, children of mothers with depression compounded by living in poverty have higher rates of emotional difficulties in early childhood (Melchior, 2011). Teachers are an important resource for families who face such needs. Referrals to resources and local support programs are a crucial component of the family support network.

> **What if . . .**
> a mother disclosed to you that her husband sometimes used a back room to cook "meth"? She says she doesn't want her child to be near that, but she doesn't have anywhere else to go. How would you respond? What child health and safety questions might this information suggest? What resources would you refer this mother to?

OBTAINING CHILDREN'S HEALTH HISTORY

Health information is sensitive information. It is important for teachers to obtain health-related details with understanding and tact. Information should be gathered in an efficient way and should be meaningful and useful for the setting. It should be used to establish individualized care and service and to inform the development of wellness activities in the classroom.

Gathering Health History Information

In some settings the health history is obtained by having the family complete a written form and return it with a record of the child's immunizations. Written forms may be brief and concise or more detailed. In other settings, teachers, health staff, or program directors might meet with families to discuss and record health information. Some programs conduct home visits in which teachers and families talk in the home setting. Regardless of how the information is collected, attention to details ensures that an appropriate health history is obtained and that the information is used to improve the child's experience in the classroom. Here is how one teacher prepared for the health history visit:

> Dashay knows that families are sometimes nervous about meeting with the teacher to share health information. He works to create a welcoming environment by moving a small table near the window where a group of houseplants offers home-like comfort. He positions two chairs at the table but has others nearby in case many family members come to participate. On the floor nearby he places a tub of brightly colored toys. He sets several out onto the rug with some picture books about "going to school" and some pillows for children to sit on. He is ready when the family arrives, and greets them with a big smile.

Often the process of gathering and discussing the child's health history is completed quickly. If a child has no unusual health or development concerns, the discussion may be very brief. Some children may have health issues that are addressed easily and for whom a plan is developed with no further follow-up needed. A few children may have more complex health considerations that require special discussions, planning, and training. For these children it is important to provide sufficient time to establish a thorough health and safety plan. For each child, the health history sets an important course of action for safe and appropriate services.

Selecting Purposeful Questions

The health history information that is gathered needs to be easy to understand and specific so that useful information is discovered. When only one general question is asked about the child's health, the response may not reveal needed information. For example, if asked, "Does your child have any medical problems?" the parent may simply answer, "No" even when the child might have asthma or frequent breathing problems, allergies, or a history of seizures. A child with one of these conditions may be stable and not experiencing any current problems, so the family may not raise it as a concern.

Using a series of questions can prompt the family to recall past or ongoing health problems. A standard comprehensive health history form is used in many settings, such as Head Start programs, to ensure that specific information is gathered. Children's programs may adapt information to create their own health history format including special questions that have relevance in the particular community or with the specific group of children and families served.

> ▶ This **video** shows a parent-teacher conference. What steps have been taken by the teacher to ensure the mother's comfort and participation during the conference? How might these same strategies be used in a meeting to discuss a child's health history?

Gathering Information Before Children Attend

Ample time should be provided to gather and discuss a child's health history *prior* to the child's attendance. Sometimes this may mean slowing down the enrollment process so that all important information is shared and discussed. Families may need to be reminded that the teacher needs to know about the children's health in advance so that adjustments to the program can be made if needed. Gathering all health information before a child attends is a safety measure. It ensures that important discussions occur and are not overlooked.

Building Comfortable Relationships

Families need to feel comfortable in order to fully share information about their child. This is especially true if the child's history is sensitive or if traumatic events have occurred in the past. Spending a few minutes explaining the purpose of the health history helps everyone focus on the goals of the discussion:

- To share important information about the child's health.
- To identify whether special arrangements are needed to assist the child in the classroom.
- To ensure that appropriate strategies are planned.

> **What if . . .**
>
> a family failed to inform the director or teacher about their child's seizure disorder until the first day of school? What if the parent brought along medication that the child needed to take in the event of a seizure? How would you handle this situation?

Documenting Information Accurately

Health history information needs to be recorded clearly and objectively. Families may not know the medical name of a condition or infection. They may use a description rather than a medical term. For instance, in the opening case scenario, Adelina's family reported that the child had an "infection of the brain."

Health information should be recorded just as the family reports it. Teachers should not add their own speculation or guesses about the condition the family describes. This way the health record documents the facts as the family understands them. This allows teachers to formulate an understanding of the child's health status based on what is known. Then the teacher may ask the family to obtain additional information from the health care provider to clarify what is not understood.

Asking for Clarifying Information

Teachers should be sure they understand the information shared about the child's health. It is important to know if health issues have been resolved or if treatment is continuing. It is helpful to know how a child's chronic health issues are being managed in the home. It is important to know if a food restriction is related to preference or an allergy that could cause a dangerous reaction. Teachers listen carefully to the information that is provided by the family and reflect on how the child's health needs can be managed in the classroom.

Identifying Impacts on the Child's Participation

As the details of the health history are discussed, implications for the child's participation in the classroom are noted and a detailed plan is developed. For example, if the child needs to receive medication during the day, a plan for administering the medication must be developed. This usually involves:

- Obtaining instructions from the child's health care provider.
- Training the teacher to identify when and how to administer the medication.
- Establishing protocols for storing medication and recording when the medicine was given.

Similarly, plans for managing allergies, special health care situations, and emergencies should be discussed.

Confirming Who May Access Health Information

Because children's health information is private, it is important to clarify who is allowed to have access to the records. In children's programs, this would typically include the classroom teachers and appropriate program staff such as the dietitian, nurse or health consultant, and those who manage children's records. To confirm this, a consent form is signed by the appropriate family member, and the form is stored in the child's file. A sample of such a consent form is shown in Figure 9-5.

Promoting Health and Wellness

Discussing children's health provides a good opportunity for teachers to share information that promotes family well-being and supports children's participation in the setting. Many health promotion topics are appropriate for all families, especially as children prepare to transition into a program or school. Teachers are attuned to the topics that are helpful to address when gathering health history information such as the following:

- Offering healthful food at meals and snack times.
- Feeding children breakfast or arriving early to participate in the school breakfast program.

FIGURE 9-5 Sample Consent to Access Child Health Information

Evergreen Children's Center PARENT/GUARDIAN CONSENT FORM

Child's Name_____

Birth Date_____Gender _____

Parent/Guardian Name _____

Evergreen Children's Center may share health and medical records, and educational development information about my child with:

- **Community Early Intervention/Early Childhood Special Education**
- **Local School District**

(Please initial below)

_____I have discussed with my child's teacher how and why information about my child may be provided to the agencies listed above.

_____I understand that my child's information will only be released to the agencies listed above.

_____I understand that my child's information will be used by staff within the Evergreen Children's Center to provide appropriate services.

_____I understand that I may revoke this consent at any time.

_____I have received a copy of this completed form.

My child's teacher has discussed this consent form with me. I understand what has been discussed and I give my permission for my child's information to be shared as described above.

Parent/Guardian Signature_____Date _____

Printed Name_____

Teacher Signature_____Date_____

Printed Name_____

_____

Source: Based on Permission to Share Information form from the Office of Health and Human Services, Massachusetts; and U.S. Department of Education, Family Education Rights and Privacy Act (FERPA).

- Ensuring children obtain a full night's sleep.
- Providing sufficient opportunity for active play.
- Dressing children appropriately for the weather and for active play.
- Encouraging the use of sunscreen during outside play.
- Decreasing screen time (television and computers).
- Increasing time spent reading together.
- Teaching children to brush their teeth.
- Teaching children to be safe pedestrians.

Other health promotion topics are situation specific and emerge during the health history discussions:

- Reducing children's exposure to violence and ways to accomplish this among families who live in challenging neighborhoods.
- Reducing children's exposure to stress in families where job loss or adult illness adds difficulties.
- Creating smoke-free environments for children if family members smoke.

Health and wellness promotion is accomplished by partnering with families. Teachers and family members are important role models for children. Together they create a team approach to improving health and wellness in the home and classroom.

Identifying Missing Information

The health history discussion between the early childhood program or school staff member and the appropriate family member concludes with a brief referral summary that highlights any gaps in needed information. In some cases, the family may need to pursue additional immunizations or obtain directions from the child's medical provider about administering a needed medication in the early childhood setting. The family may need to seek clarification about restrictions for a food allergy, or training and guidance about developing a protocol for serving a child with diabetes. The referral summary should clearly list the specific information required and when it is needed.

● REVIEWING THE HEALTH HISTORY

After obtaining the health history, it is reviewed to identify aspects that impact the child in the classroom. An individual trained to recognize gaps in information or aspects that need follow-up or further assessment should conduct this review. Some early childhood settings may have a dietitian or health consultant conduct this review. Others may train teachers or program personnel to manage this responsibility.

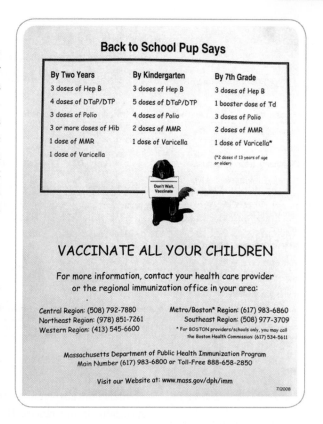

Back to School Pup Says

By Two Years	By Kindergarten	By 7th Grade
3 doses of Hep B	3 doses of Hep B	3 doses of Hep B
4 doses of DTaP/DTP	5 doses of DTaP/DTP	1 booster dose of Td
3 doses of Polio	4 doses of Polio	3 doses of Polio
3 or more doses of Hib	2 doses of MMR	2 doses of MMR
1 dose of MMR	1 dose of Varicella	1 dose of Varicella*
1 dose of Varicella		(*2 doses if 13 years of age or older)

Don't Wait. Vaccinate

VACCINATE ALL YOUR CHILDREN

For more information, contact your health care provider or the regional immunization office in your area:

Central Region: (508) 792-7880
Northeast Region: (978) 851-7261
Western Region: (413) 545-6600

Metro/Boston* Region: (617) 983-6860
Southeast Region: (508) 977-3709
* For BOSTON providers/schools only, you may call the Boston Health Commission: (617) 534-5611

Massachusetts Department of Public Health Immunization Program
Main Number (617) 983-6800 or Toll-Free 888-658-2850

Visit our Website at: www.mass.gov/dph/imm

7/2008

Screening Immunization Reports

Children's immunization records are compared to the list of vaccinations required for the child's age by the particular state. This review can be done by an individual who is familiar with the terminology and the local requirements. Table 9-1 illustrates the standard federal immunization schedule for young children.

If a child is missing a needed vaccination, the program or school contacts the family and guides them to obtain the immunizations before the child attends the early childhood setting or school. Some immunizations are offered as a series of several shots that must be spaced over specified intervals of time. As guided by the health professional, children may begin receiving a vaccination series before entering the early childhood program, and then complete the series at the recommended intervals while attending. The child's immunization record at the school should be updated as additional vaccinations are received to document that the needed series has been completed.

Exclusion Dates

Most states require that all children enrolled in child care and schools have updated immunizations. In an effort to improve compliance, some states establish immunization exclusion dates. If a child's immunization record is incomplete, families receive a warning letter from the state immunization registry. The letter alerts families that the child will be excluded from school on a certain date if documentation of updated immunizations is not provided.

Exemptions

For the vast majority of children, vaccinations are given according to a prescribed schedule. This typical immunization schedule ensures that children will have all the required immunizations in time for early childhood or school entry. However, a small percentage of children may be on a modified immunization plan.

TABLE 9-1 Childhood Vaccination Schedule
Recommended Immunization Schedule for Persons Aged 0 Through 6 Years—United States, 2012 (For those who fall behind or start late, see the catch-up schedule [Figure 3])

Vaccine ▼ Age ▶	Birth	1 month	2 months	4 months	6 months	9 months	12 months	15 months	18 months	19–23 months	2–3 years	4–6 years	
Hepatitis B[1]	Hep B	HepB			HepB								Range of recommended ages for all children
Rotavirus[2]			RV	RV	RV[2]								
Diphtheria, tetanus, pertussis[3]			DTaP	DTaP	DTaP		see footnote[3]	DTaP				DTaP	
Haemophilus influenzae type b[4]			Hib	Hib	Hib[4]		Hib						Range of recommended ages for certain high-risk groups
Pneumococcal[5]			PCV	PCV	PCV		PCV				PPSV		
Inactivated poliovirus[6]			IPV	IPV		IPV						IPV	
Influenza[7]					Influenza (Yearly)								
Measles, mumps, rubella[8]							MMR		see footnote[8]			MMR	Range of recommended ages for all children and certain high-risk groups
Varicella[9]							Varicella		see footnote[9]			Varicella	
Hepatitis A[10]							Dose 1[10]				HepA Series		
Meningococcal[11]							MCV4 — see footnote [11]						

This schedule includes recommendations in effect as of December 23, 2011. Any dose not administered at the recommended age should be administered at a subsequent visit, when indicated and feasible. The use of a combination vaccine generally is preferred over separate injections of its equivalent component vaccines. Vaccination providers should consult the relevant Advisory Committee on Immunization Practices (ACIP) statement for detailed recommendations, available online at http://www.cdc.gov/vaccines/pubs/acip-list.htm. Clinically significant adverse events that follow vaccination should be reported to the Vaccine Adverse Event Reporting System (VAERS) online (http://www.vaers.hhs.gov) or by telephone (800-822-7967).

State laws also regulate modifications and exemptions to the immunization requirements based on certain circumstances. Three types of immunization exemptions are available: *medical, religious,* and *philosophical*. All 50 states allow medical exemptions; all states except West Virginia and Mississippi allow religious exemptions; and only 20 states allow philosophical exemptions (National Conference of State Legislatures, 2011). Families can request a modification or exemption from the immunization requirements under these options.

Medical Exemptions Medical exemptions are granted when children have certain medical conditions, have compromised immune systems, or are taking specific medications. A vaccine can also be excluded from a children's immunization schedule if they have had a severe allergic reaction. Modifications or delays in vaccinations for medical reasons are allowed when recommended by a health care provider. Such exemptions should be documented in the child's health record.

Religious Exemptions Some families claim exemption for religious reasons. The religious exemption laws are intended for families who hold sincere objections to vaccinations based on their religious beliefs. The specific religious exemption requirements vary from one state to another. For example, some states require families requesting a religious exemption to be members of the First Church of Christ or Christian Scientists.

Philosophical Exemptions These exemptions are intended for families who have personal or moral beliefs that contradict immunizing their children (National Conference of State Legislatures, 2011). States that allow these exemptions have higher rates of vaccine-preventable diseases such as measles and **whooping cough**, which is a highly contagious respiratory infection that can be fatal to infants and young children (Omer, Salmon, Orenstein, deHart, & Halsey, 2009).

Ensuring Children Have a Medical Home

The review of the health history may reveal that a child does not have an identified **medical home**. The term *medical home* refers to the location where the family obtains regular health care for their

What if . . .

a family in your program has misplaced their child's immunization records? They don't want to bother searching for the documentation, so they tell you that they want to claim a religious exemption. What issues does this approach raise? How would you manage this situation?

whooping cough
a highly contagious respiratory infection that can be fatal to infants and young children

medical home
place where a child obtains preventive health care, sick health care, immunizations, and coordination of medical care

child, including regular checkups, immunizations, and care when the child is sick. Typically, the medical home provider is a physician, nurse practitioner, or physician's assistant. Ideally, the medical home provider offers family-centered services that are accessible and culturally attuned (American Academy of Pediatrics, n.d.).

Under some circumstances, teachers may have the opportunity to assist families in finding medical care services if needed. A list of medical providers or clinics in the community is a helpful resource. In addition, teachers can guide families to overcome any obstacles they may face in trying to obtain necessary health care. Obstacles may include the family's lack of health insurance, cultural and language barriers, or a limited number of providers who serve families with Medicaid.

Many communities have community health centers or clinics that provide comprehensive primary health care regardless of the patient's insurance status or ability to pay. These clinics are often designed to serve a high-need community or a medically underserved population and can be an excellent medical home resource. Teachers may also collaborate with medical consultants, school nurses, or other community resources to help families.

> Infant Health Supervised Visits are conducted with many families of newborns. As you watch this **video**, think about how such visits connect families with a medical home, ensure timely immunizations, and help to create safe and healthy home environments.

Confirming Children Have Well-Child Exams

The health history is also reviewed to identify if the child has had regularly scheduled **well-child checkups** with the health care provider. The focus of well-child exams is on preventive health care. Well-child care involves:

- A review of the child's health history.
- Screening tests.
- Examinations.
- Treatments to prevent disease, including immunizations.
- Education and counseling to promote health and wellness.

well-child checkups
health care visits provided for children to ensure that health and development are progressing normally

Families of children who have not had periodic well-child exams should be encouraged to schedule a checkup as part of the enrollment expectations. Head Start Performance Standards require that programs support families to obtain comprehensive health exams for their child. Table 9-2 lists the recommended timing for well-child visits for all children.

Making Referrals

When gaps in the child's health care are discovered, follow-up is initiated through the **referral** process. Referrals are recommendations that direct families to needed resources. Common reasons for making referrals include encouraging the family to get a well-child exam, follow up on missing immunizations, or obtaining a vision exam. Another frequent referral in the early childhood setting is

referral
process of obtaining assistance for a family after identifying a need

TABLE 9-2 Well-Child Checkup Schedule	
Infants (0–12 Months)	**Children Older Than 1 Year of Age**
✓ Newborn visit	✓ 15 months
✓ 2 months	✓ 18 months
✓ 4 months	✓ 2 years
✓ 6 months	✓ 3 years
✓ 9 months	✓ 4 years
✓ 12 months	✓ 5 years and yearly thereafter

referring families to agencies that provide early intervention assessment for suspected developmental delays. Families may also raise questions about children's health that are beyond the scope of the teacher's knowledge and expertise. Any time a concern is identified that requires outside assistance, a referral is appropriate.

Teachers are an important referral resource when families face difficulties providing sufficient housing, food, or transportation. Sharing information about community support services benefits the family and contributes to the child's well-being. In addition, teachers who recognize that families are facing such difficulties are better able to understand how to support the family and care for the child's well-being in the classroom. Families also benefit from social connections, such as a supportive network of family and friends. Teachers help build social networks among families in the class by sponsoring family socials, game days, and parent and child community service activities. These social networking activities contribute to positive outcomes for children.

Referrals are made in collaboration with families. Together, the teacher and family member identify and record the specific aspects of concern. A written summary supports families when they take their questions to the health care provider. For example, in the opening case scenario Maria and the family have identified two areas for possible follow-up. The observation that Adelina is not making vocalizations concerns both Maria and the family, suggesting that an evaluation of Adelina's hearing is needed. The family has also described living in an older home that was in poor condition. They are aware that building materials in older homes often contain lead, a product that is harmful to young children. They decide to ask that Adelina be evaluated for possible lead poisoning. Together, the teacher and Adelina's family summarize their concerns and the family is prepared with specific goals as they follow up with their medical provider.

CONDUCTING OTHER HEALTH EVALUATIONS

In addition to the health history, additional health evaluations are conducted to screen for normal health and development. These include physical health, mental health, and developmental evaluations. Some evaluations are conducted for all children. Others are done to follow up on specific concerns. Teachers or trained volunteers may conduct the evaluations. Some may require the expertise of those with specialized skills, including nurses, dietitians, and counselors. In addition, evaluations of children's health include input through growth measurements, vision screenings, and assessment for risk of lead poisoning. All contribute to the understanding of the child's health status and the design of the teaching environment.

Growth Measurements

Growth is one of the most important indicators of normal health and development in children. Height, weight, head circumference, and body mass index are the most important growth measurements. A trained person using reliable measuring devices can do these measurements. Because many children lack access to regular health care, the growth measurements obtained in the school may become an essential resource for identifying health concerns.

Growth charts are graphs that demonstrate normal values for children of all ages. Charts published by the CDC consist of a set of percentile curves and are used as a tool to monitor the growth of children over time. In April of 2006, the WHO published growth charts that are also now in use. Growth charts published by the WHO should be used for children ages 0 to 2. After age 2, CDC growth charts should be used. See this chapter's *Health Hint* for a summary of the growth charts available.

Height and Weight

The most common measurements taken are height and weight. In infancy, height is often referred to as *length*. Growth is reviewed by plotting height and weight measurements on standard growth charts. These charts are easily obtained from the CDC's website as well as many other online resources.

HEALTH HINT Childhood Growth Charts

Monitoring growth in children is an important component of health screenings. Normal growth can be an indicator of health and wellness. Two sets of growth curves exist for children, one published by the CDC and another by WHO. From the 1970s until 2006, the CDC published the only growth charts available. Although they were widely used, there were concerns that they lacked racial diversity and the infant sample from which the data were extrapolated were almost exclusively formula fed.

In April 2006, WHO published growth charts that described the growth of healthy children when they were growing under optimal environmental conditions. The CDC growth charts were more of a reference, describing how certain children grew in a certain place and time (how children in the United States grew between 1963 and 1994).

Most recent recommendations suggest use of the WHO growth standards for assessing growth in children less than 24 months of age, regardless of type of feeding. After 2 years of age, the CDC growth charts should be used. Data from WHO growth charts are available only through age 6, whereas CDC growth chart data continue into adulthood. These new recommendations should give health screeners more accurate information and identify children who are truly outside the normal range.

Source: Centers for Disease Control and Prevention, 2010.

Standardized growth charts are available for children ages 0 to 36 months and ages 2 to 20 years. Growth charts for boys and girls can be found in the Book Specific Resources on MyEducationLab. The charts are designed as a tool to determine if growth is within the normal range. If there is any question that a growth measurement is below or above the normal range, the child should be referred to a health care provider for additional evaluation.

Body Mass Index

Body mass index (BMI) is a measure of body fat. It is calculated based on height and weight. BMI is an inexpensive, reliable method used to screen for underweight or obesity. BMI is calculated by multiplying weight in pounds by 703 and dividing by height in inches squared. This number is then plotted on BMI charts, which are provided for boys and girls ages 2 to 20 years. The chart shows the categories that determine if the child is underweight, normal weight, overweight, or obese. Children whose BMI falls in the underweight, overweight, or obese categories should be referred for evaluation by a medical professional. BMI charts for boys and girls can be found in the Book Specific Resources on MyEducationLab. In addition, many BMI calculators for children and adults are available online.

The use of the BMI measurement is being explored as a tool to screen for risk for obesity and to encourage schools to focus on teaching and modeling healthy lifestyles. The AAP and CDC recommend the use of BMI as a screening tool for children beginning at age 2. The *Policy Point* discusses controversies involved with BMI screening in schools.

Oral Health Assessments

Conducting oral health assessments in the early childhood setting or school is highly beneficial for children who do not have access to dental care. Dental caries, or cavities, is one of the most common chronic diseases in childhood. Dental caries is the formation of cavities or tooth decay caused by abnormal growth of bacteria in the mouth. Identification and treatment of dental caries in early life are important to overall physical health. It is recommended that all children have a dental visit by their first birthday if they are at high risk for caries and all children by 24 months of age (American Academy of Pediatrics, 2011).

Many children do not receive these recommended dental examinations. Higher risk groups include children in low-income families, children with special health care needs, and certain racial/ethnic groups such as blacks and Hispanics (Child and Adolescent Health Measurement Initiative, 2007). The

Schools in the United States are mandated to screen for hearing and vision. However, there are no national guidelines regarding measuring children's body mass index (BMI) even though obesity is so widespread among children. Currently, seven states require or recommend BMI screening in schools. Little is known about the outcome of reporting BMIs to parents. Does this actually promote healthier behaviors?

Case studies in Florida demonstrated that parents were very uncomfortable discussing the topic with their child. Some parents of overweight children reported trying to use food restriction to control their child's weight in response to the BMI letter or even increased use of negative comments regarding child's weight. These unhealthy behaviors, of course, could be potentially harmful to the child's emotional development and may not address the underlying problem. It is unclear if these unintended consequences of reporting BMI are due to the way that the information was delivered to the parent or to other factors.

Because of lack of clarity regarding the risks and benefits of BMI screening in school, it is important for teachers and other staff to be aware of the unintended consequences and carefully plan on how the information will be delivered to the parents. It may also be helpful to give families suggestions regarding follow up and need for further evaluation if results of BMI screening are not within the normal range for age.

Source: Based on Kaczmarski, DeBate, Marhefka, & Dale, 2011.

federal Head Start program ensures that enrolled children receive comprehensive health care screenings including dental screenings. Head Start serves as a model for supporting early childhood programs to provide the health assessments young children need.

Many children's programs are able to arrange with a local dentist or dental hygienist to conduct dental screenings at the children's setting. For some children these may be the only dental examinations they receive over the course of many years. If additional care is identified, children are referred to their dental provider or community services for further evaluation and intervention.

Accessibility to dental services is often a problem for low-income children. Teachers can share with families options for obtaining dental treatment. For example, "Give Kids a Smile" is an annual component to National Children's Dental Health Month and is observed on the first Friday in February. "Give Kids a Smile" is an American Dental Association event that draws on the volunteer services of dentists to provide dental treatment to low-income children who do not have access to care (American Dental Association, 2011). Many school districts also make arrangements for dental van services where children receive dental examinations and cleanings as well as other forms of treatment for dental caries.

Oral health assessments also provide opportunities to educate children and families about caring for their teeth. Families are notified in advance and permission is obtained for children to participate in dental screenings conducted in the children's setting. Once completed, families are provided a report of the findings. This is a good time to share information with families about how to promote oral health and prevent dental caries.

Hearing and Vision Screenings

Specific tools are also used to screen for hearing and vision disorders. Hearing and vision screenings are often conducted in school settings where large numbers of children can be evaluated. Optimal development and learning are influenced by the child's ability to accurately hear and see. Screening for hearing and vision loss is an important aspect of assisting children to be able to learn.

Hearing Screening

Permanent hearing loss is the most common congenital condition in the United States, affecting 30 infants born every day (Russ, White, Dougherty, & Forsman, 2010). Hearing loss can occur in both ears or just in one ear. It can be mild, moderate, severe, or profound. Milder forms of hearing loss are more difficult to detect because children often compensate by using other sensory stimuli such as watching the environment closely for cues.

This **video** shows children undergoing hearing and vision screenings. Think about the strategies used by the specialists to increase children's comfort during these assessments.

Because hearing loss is difficult to detect during the first few months of life, universal hearing screenings for newborns were implemented through the Early Hearing Detection and Intervention (EHDI) program. Most newborns have a hearing screen within the first few days of life before leaving the hospital. Before this program was implemented, many children with hearing loss were not recognized for many months or even years. Children born outside of the United States or children born outside of a hospital may not have received a hearing screen at birth.

Vision Screening

Vision disorders are common in childhood and can lead to long-term disabilities. It is estimated that 1 in 5 school-age children have some type of vision problem (Basch, 2011). Vision screening is an efficient and cost-effective way to identify children who need further evaluation. For this reason, vision screening has been mandated as a part of federal programs including the Early Periodic Screening, Diagnosis, and Treatment (EPSDT) Program and Head Start. Vision screening is important because when detected early, vision problems can be treated. Vision problems that go untreated can lead to vision loss or blindness. Vision screening can detect the most common vision problems including:

amblyopia
a disorder that involves abnormal interaction between the eyes causing unfocused vision

strabismus
malalignment of the eyes

refractive disorders
visual conditions that cause problems with focusing

colorblindness
the inability to distinguish between some colors

- *Amblyopia:* when one eye does not recognize information properly causing a discrepancy in the visual acuity compared to the other eye.
- *Strabismus:* when the eyes are not aligned with each other.
- *Refractive disorders:* conditions that cause problems with focusing; usually corrected with glasses.
- *Colorblindness:* the inability to distinguish between certain colors.

Vision screening done as part of a health care exam includes assessing how well the child tracks movement, fixates on a point, and responds to light. Familiar methods in the early childhood and school setting include having a child cover one eye while looking at a chart with symbols. The child is asked to match or identify the symbol, such as a letter or picture on the chart. These screening methods include directions for how to conduct the screening and indicators that suggest the child be referred for additional vision assessment. In addition to this form of vision screening, teachers can detect visual problems by noticing and reporting symptoms of visual disturbances. Signs of visual problems that teachers may notice include the following (Prevent Blindness America, 2011):

- Eyes don't line up.
- Rubbing eyes frequently.
- Tilting head to look at items.
- Holding objects close to eyes or trouble reading.
- Blinking more than usual.
- Squinting eyes or frowning.

Screenings are highly effective ways to identify children with treatable hearing or vision conditions.

If teachers notice these symptoms, they should refer the child's family to a health care provider for further evaluation. The activities in the *Teaching Wellness* feature contribute to children's learning about hearing and vision.

Screening for Communication Disorders

Children with communication disorders have better outcomes if they are diagnosed and treated early (Heward, 2013). Formalized screening for communication disorders varies among different types of early childhood programs. Regardless of standard screening practices in early childhood programs, input from families and teachers is important for identifying children with communication disorders.

For a child whose first language is not English, the teacher must attempt to ascertain if a communication disorder is actually present or if the child functions normally in his or her own native

TEACHING WELLNESS Health Care Checkups

LEARNING OUTCOME **Children will be more comfortable with the idea of visiting a medical provider and will know what to expect during a checkup.**

INFANTS AND TODDLERS

- **Goal:** To introduce information about health care checkups and visiting the doctor.
- **Materials:** *Time to See the Doctor* by Heather Maisner and Kristina Stephenson (2004, Kingfisher Publications).
- **Activity plan:** Read the book to the children. Point to aspects in the pictures that show what is found in the doctor's office. Talk about the child who is worried about the checkup and how he becomes more confident. Talk about what the doctor does and why.
- **Did you meet your goal?** Are the young children interested in the book? Do they follow along and anticipate the story? Do they talk about the activities that occur during the checkup? Can they answer, "What is the doctor doing?"

PRESCHOOLERS AND KINDERGARTNERS

- **Goal:** To reduce children's worries about health care checkups through dramatic play exploration.
- **Materials:** Dramatic play props for the health care setting, including a doctor's kit with stethoscope, thermometer, blood pressure gauge, reflex hammer, bandages, and examination gloves.
- **Activity plan:** Provide the props and space for the children to create a doctor's office and conduct imaginative play. Provide picture books about visiting the doctor, such as:
  - *Biscuit Visits the Doctor,* by Alyssa Satin Capucilli (2008, HarperCollins Publishers)
  - *Corduroy Goes to the Doctor,* by Don Freeman and Lisa McCue (2005, Penguin Group)
  - *My Friend the Doctor,* by Joanna Cole and Maxie Chambliss (2005, HarperCollins Publishers)
  - *Elmo's World: Doctors!* by Naomi Kleinberg (2008, Random House Children's Books)
  - *La Doctora Maisy* (Spanish-language edition), by Lucy Cousins (2005, Lectorum Publications)
  - *Going to the Doctor,* by Anne Civardi, Michelle Bates, and Stephen Cartwright (2006, EDC Publishing)
  - *Doctor Ted* by Andrea Beaty and Pascal Lemaitre (2008, Atheneum Books for Young Readers).
  - *Going to the Hospital,* by Fred Rogers (1997, Putnam and Grosset Group)
- **How to adjust the activity:** Invite a medical provider to visit the classroom and talk about what to expect. Take pictures of children playing in the dramatic play area. Create a picture board and have children describe what happens when you visit the doctor. Have children talk about their experiences.
- **Did you meet your goal?** Observe children at play in the dramatic play area. Do they dramatize their experiences at the doctor's office? Do you hear them talking about worries or comforting their "patients"? When asked, are children able to describe with accuracy the kinds of things that happen at the exam?

SCHOOL-AGE CHILDREN

- **Goal:** To learn about the work that doctors and other medical providers do and communicate it to others.
- **Materials:** Materials to make posters such as large paper, marking pens, paints. Library books that describe the work of doctors and other medical providers, such as:
  - *What Does a Doctor Do?* by Felicia Lowenstein Niven (2005, Enslow Publishers)
  - *A Day in the Life of a Doctor,* by Heather Adamson (2004, Capstone Press)
  - *Keeping You Healthy: A Book about Doctors,* by Ann Owen (2004, Picture Window Books)
  - *Médico,* by Heather Miller (2003, Heinemann Library)
  - *If You Were a Doctor,* by Virgina Schomp (2001, Benchmark Books)
- **Activity plan:** Provide picture books and other library resources. Ask children to research information about the different things that doctors do. Have individuals or small groups of children create a poster to display describing how medical workers help us.
- **How to adjust the activity:** Have children create posters to share with preschool-age children and send them to early childhood programs. Take a field trip to a nearby preschool program. Have the children describe their posters to the preschoolers.
- **Did you meet your goal?** Do children display their knowledge of the work of medical providers through their posters and conversations? Do the posters effectively communicate this information?

language. When assessing children for disabilities, the Individuals with Disabilities Education Act (IDEA) requires that the assessment be conducted in the child's native language (Heward, 2013).

Lead Screening

Lead is a chemical element commonly found in the environment. It has been a component of vehicle emissions and lead paint. Lead poisoning can cause permanent neurological damage and it is entirely preventable. Though the prevalence of lead in the environment has decreased, it is still a public health problem, primarily affecting children in urban settings.

The major source of lead exposure is the lead-based paint present in buildings constructed before the 1940s. Lead-based paint and contaminated dust present in homes with deteriorating surfaces are the most common sources (Warniment, Tsang, & Galazka, 2010). Lead-based paint is most dangerous when the paint is deteriorating, and paint flakes and dust are introduced into the environment. It is ingested via a hand-to-mouth route or it can be inhaled. Inhalation is especially a problem when homes containing lead are being remodeled. Here are some other sources of lead exposure (Warniment et al., 2010):

- Soil and dust.
- Imported toys, jewelry, cosmetics, candy.
- Contaminated water pipes, solder, valves, and fixtures containing lead.
- Vinyl mini-blinds.
- Pottery/ceramics.
- Industrial sources: from parents with occupational exposures such as battery, construction, or ceramics workers or furniture refinishers.

Symptoms of lead poisoning can be nonexistent or vague so it is difficult to diagnose based solely on the child's history (Warniment et al., 2010), which is why screening is so important. Screening for lead exposure in the early childhood setting is done as part of the health history using a checklist. Screening for lead toxicity is done in the medical setting using a blood test. The AAP and CDC recommend targeted blood-level screenings for lead (Warniment et al., 2010). Children who are enrolled in Medicaid and children who are found to be at risk for lead exposure using the checklist are referred to a medical provider to be screened using the blood test. In the past, most children with elevated lead levels were enrolled in Medicaid programs, which is why the CDC recommends screening all Medicaid-eligible children at 1 or 2 years of age. Figure 9-6 is an example of a checklist to use in screening for lead exposure.

FIGURE 9-6 Lead Screening Checklist

If the answer is yes to any of these questions, the child is considered to be at risk of excessive lead exposure and should be referred to a medical provider for blood lead test screening.

Does your child:

- ❏ Spend time in buildings built before 1950, including child care centers, preschools, or the homes of babysitters or relatives?
- ❏ Live in or regularly visit buildings built before 1978 with recent, ongoing, or planned renovation or remodeling?
- ❏ Have a brother or sister, housemate, or playmate being followed up or treated for lead poisoning?

- ❏ Frequently come in contact with an adult whose job or hobby involves exposure to lead, such as construction, auto repair, batteries, welding, pottery, or other trades?
- ❏ Live near an active lead smelter, battery recycling plant, or other industry likely to release lead?
- ❏ Does your family use pottery or ceramics for food or drink that are made in other countries?
- ❏ Has your child used any traditional or imported home remedies such as Azarcon, Alarcon, Greta, Rueda, Pay-loo-ah, or Kohl?
- ❏ Was your child adopted from or did your child live in another country?

Source: Adapted with permission from *Lead Poisoning Prevention Program*, by the Oregon Department of Human Services, retrieved December 20, 2011, from http://www.oregon.gov/DHS/ph/lead/docs/parentquest.pdf.

Another important source of lead exposure in more recent years has been toys. The risks of exposure to lead in toys exist for toys that are imported or old toys that are passed down or bought used (Centers for Disease Control and Prevention, 2009). Specific questions about toys are generally not included in lead screening questionnaires because of the difficulty in identifying which toys contain lead. The U.S. Consumer Product Safety Commission issues recalls on toys that have potentially exposed children to lead (Centers for Disease Control and Prevention, 2009). If families or caregivers have *any* concerns about possible lead exposure, regardless of the lead screening questions, the child should be referred to a health care provider for lead testing.

Developmental Screening and Assessment

Detecting developmental problems early in life is important so that intervention strategies can be implemented. Developmental screening is a service to children and families that is conducted to discover if the child's development is progressing as expected. Screening activities are provided soon after the child joins the early childhood program or school.

A plan should be in place to implement screening activities thoroughly and effectively. The screening plan should be (Early Head Start National Resource Center, 2009):

- *Systematic:* purposefully conducted.
- *Comprehensive:* include observations and discussion of developmental history.
- *Sensitive:* considerate of family characteristics, relationships, and other environmental or situational factors.

Screening tools for developmental progress should be considered as part of the larger process of evaluation. Teachers have access to another powerful assessment tool: their ability to conduct meaningful observations. The early childhood setting offers an environment in which children's development can be seen in a natural setting. Teachers take advantage of this opportunity by conducting observations of children at play and in interactions with others. Knowing about developmental milestones allows teachers to identify behaviors that may benefit from further evaluation.

Both screening and observational assessment are conducted by teachers, or other program personnel, who are familiar to the child and who have received orientation and training on appropriate approaches. Developmental screenings and assessments are conducted using tools that have been validated and are culturally appropriate. The process involves families by first discussing identified concerns. Next, teachers obtain permission from the family to conduct a formal screening and assessment.

When information has been gathered the teacher and family need to decide how to use the information. They discuss the findings and identify the next step. If a developmental concern is suspected, the child is referred to a developmental specialist for additional evaluation. The screening and assessment process also includes identifying the child's strengths and competencies and ways to promote the next steps in development. In this way developmental screening serves two purposes:

1. To identify possible developmental delays early so that intervention strategies can be planned and implemented.
2. To identify children's strengths and needs to inform the development of appropriate classroom curriculum.

Screening and assessment of infants and toddlers is especially challenging. Children in this age group are growing and maturing at a fast rate, and the tools used to conduct developmental assessments are variable in quality. Other challenges are present when assessing this age group, including these (Early Head Start National Resource Center, 2009):

- Developmental areas are closely connected, making it difficult to separate and identify the source of specific concerns.
- Developmental delays in this age group can be very subtle.

- Infants and toddlers have limited ability to express themselves or to tell what they think and know, which limits the ability to identify delays through expressive language.

These challenges make ongoing observation especially important. Documentation of developmental observations provides a method for tracking concerns and recognizing when growth occurs or when it is delayed.

Recognizing normal developmental patterns and milestones for each child is important for all ages. By knowing and understanding typical developmental patterns, teachers are prepared to recognize abnormal behaviors and patterns that fall outside expected development. Like *red flags*, recognition of behaviors that do not align with expected development attracts the teacher's attention and highlights the need for further exploration.

In many cases, the early childhood teacher is the first person to mention to families that their child may be experiencing a developmental delay or concern. Families may have strong emotional reactions to this information. Teachers should be sensitive to these feelings and prepare carefully for such meetings. Teachers are partners with families in supporting child development wherever the child is on the continuum of developmental skills and competencies. Developmental screening and assessment provide information for purposeful curriculum planning. Teachers are *not* responsible for diagnosing developmental delays; however, they are important sources of referral and support for families if developmental concerns are suspected.

> ## What if . . .
> you notice a child who has difficulty speaking so others can understand him? What kinds of special observations might you make? How would you approach the family with your concerns? What referrals would you make? What resources in your community would you utilize?

Conducting Daily Health Checks

Keeping attuned to children's health every day is a part of the teaching process that also includes continual observation and reflection. Daily health checks are a natural part of this process. The daily health check is a planned approach to direct teacher attention to the child's health. Teachers conduct these checks to determine if the child shows signs of illness, injury, or other health concerns. The American Academy of Pediatrics, American Public Health Association, and National Resource Center for Health and Safety in Child Care and Early Education (2011) recommends that daily health checks include the following:

- Changes in behavior or appearance from the previous day.
- Skin rashes, itchy skin or scalp.
- Temperature if the child appears ill.
- Complaints of pain or not feeling well.
- Other signs or symptoms of illness.
- Reports of illness or injury.

Daily health checks can be done efficiently and accurately during the greeting time. They are typically conducted by the teacher as the child arrives in the classroom or soon thereafter. The process involves:

- Stopping briefly to focus attention on the child.
- Looking at the child, observing for signs of illness or disease.
- Listening to the parent and child, paying special attention to information that suggests illness.

A description of this kind of approach is outlined in Figure 9-7.

During the health check the teacher watches for signs of good health such as pink skin, bright eyes, and easy breathing. The teacher also observes for indications of health problems such as irritability and asks the family if there are any concerns. If the child appears ill, the teacher needs to be prepared to explain to the family members the symptoms that are observed and discuss arrangements for the child to be taken home.

The daily health check and any symptoms of illness or concerns regarding a child's health should be recorded on a tracking chart. The *National Health and Safety Performance Standards* (American Academy of Pediatrics, American Public Health Association, National Resource Center for Health

FIGURE 9-7   Stop-Look-Listen Daily Health Check

Stop

Greet each child at arrival and take a moment to really observe the child.
Have a small conversation. Ask kind questions, such as "How are you feeling?" "Did you sleep
well last night?" "Did you eat breakfast today?"

Look

Observe these aspects:

	Signs of Good Health	Possible Signs of Illness
❑ Skin color	Pink and fresh; typical skin color for individual child	Flushed, feverish, or pale?
❑ Skin appearance	Smooth and calm	Rashy with sores or swelling?
❑ Eyes	Bright and alert	Red with discharge or dull with dark circles?
❑ Nose	Clear and clean	Dripping with nasal discharge?
❑ Ears	Does the child look comfortable	Rubbing and holding ears?
❑ Hair	Clean and combed	Unclean and badly tangled?
❑ General appearance	Does the child look interested in play	Droopy, listless, irritable, or restless?

Listen

Pay attention to what you hear:

	Signs of Good Health	Possible Signs of Illness
❑ Breathing pace	Even breathing	Fast breathing or panting?
❑ Breathing sounds	Quiet and smooth	Coughing, spitting, or congested?
❑ Parent reports	No concerns are mentioned	Child has been given medication before school?
		Child would not eat breakfast or has had a stomachache?
		Child has had diarrhea or has vomited recently?
		Child is acting unusually weepy?
		Child has been injured?

FOLLOW UP by asking more about any concerns.

DECIDE if the child is healthy. If signs of illness are present, child should return home.

and Safety in Child Care and Early Education, 2011) recommends that the daily health check be charted in a way that is convenient for teachers to use, and that provides a picture of the overall class group's health. Two sample formats are shown in Figure 9-8. These charts make it easy to notice the pattern of symptoms of illness and subsequent absences. As total classroom attendance numbers drop due to illness, the chart also demonstrates the rate of disease spread among the children. These charts should be kept for at least 3 months to help track the spread of communicable diseases. They also provide the teacher and program with information to reflect on the effectiveness of disease prevention strategies, such as extra cleaning and sanitizing of the classroom.

Ongoing Observation

Observing children and monitoring them for signs of illness is the second part of continual health evaluation in the classroom. Through observation, teachers establish an understanding of each child's typical appearance and style of behavior so that signs of illness are more easily recognized.

FIGURE 9-8 Daily Health Check and Attendance Tracking Chart

Option 1: Attendance and daily health check information overlap.

Month: *February*	Date									
Child's Name		**1**	**2**	**3**	**4**	**5**	**6**	**7**	**8**	**9**	**10**
Asma M.			SL	C, V	A	A					
Shay R.						C			A		
Liliana T.						C, V			A	A	A
Riki H-G.									C, V	A	A

Option 2: Attendance and daily health check are recorded separately.

Month: *February*	Date									
Child's Name		**1**	**2**	**3**	**4**	**5**	**6**	**7**	**8**	**9**	**10**
Asma M.					A	A					
			SL	C, V							
Shay R.									A		
					C						
Liliana T.									A	A	A
					C, V						
Riki H-G.									A	A
								C, V		

Attendance:

Mark if present

Mark if absent   A

Codes for Symptoms:

B = behavior change	I = report of injury	ST = sore throat
CP = chicken pox	L = lice	SR = skin rash
C = coughing	P = complaint of pain	T = suspected temperature
D = diarrhea	SL = sleepy or withdrawn	V = vomiting

Source: American Academy of Pediatrics, American Public Health Association, National Resource Center for Health and Safety in Child Care and Early Education, 2011.

Signs of illness that are identified through observation include unusual fussiness and crying, listless-ness or sleepiness, disinterest in food, paleness, or flushed cheeks. Observation is also important once an illness has been identified. In this situation, the teacher pays special attention to signs of illness spreading to other children.

The observations of children's health that teachers provide are important to families. Families rely on teachers to share feedback about how their child is doing in the class group when they are not present. They need to know if the teacher has detected signs of illness. Sometimes signs of ill-ness are sudden, and require teachers to contact the family member to take the child home due to illness. Other times the cues of potential illness are shared with families at the time of departure. A clear description of the signs of illness is important so the family can continue to monitor the child at home. Ongoing observations respect the needs of young children to have teachers who are their advocates for health and wellness.

● SUMMARY

Health evaluation is an important aspect of early childhood development and education. Whether caring for infants and toddlers, nurturing the needs of preschoolers, or supporting school-age children, the teacher–child relationship involves being aware of children's health and wellness. Incorporating health screenings into the children's settings is a highly effective and efficient way to access large numbers of children. Identifying and addressing health and development problems early sets children on a course for improved outcomes and optimal learning.

Health screenings and assessments are initial steps in the process of health evaluation. They provide important information about the wide range of influences on children's health and contribute to an understanding of gaps that may exist in health care.

Collecting children's health history offers an opportunity to obtain health information in partnership with families. The information that is discussed guides the plan of services for the child in the classroom and provides opportunities to promote wellness in the family setting. Conducting assessments such as growth measurements, hearing and vision screenings, nutrition screenings, and developmental assessments ensures children get help for identified needs.

Health information is private and sensitive. It should be gathered and managed confidentially and appropriately. Understanding the status of children's health, promoting health and wellness in the family, and referring children to needed services improves physical and mental health outcomes for all children.

KEY TERMS

Acculturation
Adverse reactions
Allergic reaction
Amblyopia
Asthma
Colorblindness
Continual observation
Daily health checks
Developmental milestones

Fluoride
Health assessments
Health evaluation
Health history
Health screenings
Immunizations
Local reaction
Medical home
Premature infant

Referral
Refractive disorders
Rubella
Strabismus
Systemic reaction
Thimerosal
Well-child checkups
Whooping cough

REVIEW QUESTIONS

1. Who should know the details about a child's medical history?
2. Describe the three types of exemptions to the required immunizations that are legally allowed in some states.
3. What are the symptoms of visual problems in children?
4. Describe risk factors for lead poisoning.
5. Explain how to perform a daily health check in an early childhood program.

DISCUSSION STARTERS

1. A significant percentage of families in the United States lack affordable health insurance. Furthermore, even families with public health insurance have difficulty finding regular health care. How might lack of regular medical care influence health screenings in the early childhood setting?

2. Early childhood educators may interact with families who have concerns about vaccinating their children. How might a child who has not been completely vaccinated influence the health of other children in the early childhood setting?

3. As more schools incorporate BMI measurements into health screenings, some children will be identified as overweight or obese. When families are notified about their child's BMI, how do you think they will respond to these screenings? How do you feel about schools using obesity screening tools? Do these screenings have any unintended consequences?

PRACTICE POINTS

1. A 5-year-old child enrolling in kindergarten in your state is unvaccinated. The family has applied for a religious exemption. Find the laws in your state about vaccinations. Determine what vaccinations are required and if religious exemptions are allowable.

2. Various formats are used to obtain health history information. Contact early childhood programs or the school district in your community to learn how they collect this information. Explore the Internet for sample health history formats and compare them.

3. Conduct the Stop-Look-Listen Daily Health Check (see Figure 9-7) with a child or peer teacher. Are you able to determine potential health concerns using this format?

4. Research information about conducting classroom vision screenings. What materials are available? What is the cost? Is special training required to use the materials? If possible, obtain vision screening materials and conduct a vision screening with a peer teacher or friend.

WEB RESOURCES

Centers for Disease Control and Prevention, About BMI for Children and Teens
www.cdc.gov/healthyweight/assessing/bmi/childrens_BMI/about_childrens_BMI.html

Childhood Immunization
www.nlm.nih.gov/medlineplus/childhoodimmunization.html

Children's Vision Screening
www.preventblindness.org/vision_screening/childrens_vision_screening.html

Health and Mental Health Services, School Health Screening Programs
www.nationalguidelines.org/guideline.cfm?guideNum=4-18

Immunization Action Coalition, State Information
www.immunize.org/laws

National Network for Immunization Information, Immunization Issues
www.immunizationinfo.org/immunization_issues.cfm

MyEducationLab™

Go to Topic 6 (Health Appraisal/Screening) in the MyEducationLab (www.myeducationlab.com) for your course, where you can:

- Find learning outcomes for Health Appraisal/ Screening along with the national standards that connect to these outcomes.

- Complete Assignments and Activities that can help you more deeply understand the chapter content.

- Apply and practice your understanding of the core teaching skills identified in the chapter with the Building Teaching Skills and Dispositions learning units.

- Check your comprehension on the content covered in the chapter by going to the Study Plan in the Book Resources for your text. Here you will be able to take a chapter quiz, receive feedback on your answers, and then access Review, Practice, and Enrichment activities to enhance your understanding of chapter content.

ten
Managing Infectious Disease

learning outcomes

AFTER READING THIS CHAPTER, YOU SHOULD BE ABLE TO:

1. Describe the infectious disease process, including route of transmission.

2. Describe common symptoms of illness seen in children and how these are managed in early childhood programs.

3. Describe classroom practices that prevent or minimize the spread of infections.

4. Identify some of the more common infectious diseases and describe when children should be excluded from school because of them.

5. Describe some of the unique health challenges of children who are internationally adopted or refugees.

Mark is a healthy and vibrant 6-year-old who usually plays very actively during recess. Today his first-grade teacher, Mary Beth, notices that Mark is unusually quiet and not playing. She asks him if something is bothering him. He says he does not feel well and that his "tummy hurts." Mary Beth tells the other playground monitors that she is going to take Mark to the school office. The school nurse evaluates him and finds he has a fever. She notifies Mark's family who come to take him home. The nurse recommends that Mark see his primary care provider.

The next day Mark is absent from school. His mother calls and tells Mary Beth that Mark has been diagnosed with strep throat and that he will be out of school for at least another day. Mary Beth knows that strep throat is contagious, but she is not sure if she should report this to the other families in the class. She e-mails the school nurse for advice. The nurse returns a notice for families alerting them to the signs of strep throat.

At story time Mary Beth talks with the children about ways to keep healthy. She reads *Germs Make Me Sick!* by Melvin Berger to help explore the topic. Mary Beth demonstrates how the children can cover their coughs by coughing into the crook of their arms. They also talk about how to carefully wash their hands and when to wash their hands to keep germs away. At the end of the day Mary Beth hears Calvin declare, "When Mark gets back let's tell him about how to be healthy!"

Children are exposed to many illnesses during the early childhood years. Illness is more common for children who participate in group settings because of the potential for spreading germs. Children are naturally curious, and their exploration of the world involves touching and handling toys and surfaces. These behaviors cause them to put their hands and objects in their mouths, creating easy entry for germs. Teaching young children naturally involves caring for children when illness occurs in the early childhood setting as well as employing strategies to prevent the spread of infection.

Teachers like Mary Beth become familiar with individual children and are able to recognize changes in the child's behavior or appearance that may be clues to sickness. They also know that they are responsible for assisting children when illness occurs, supporting families to get the medical help the child needs, and teaching children ways to keep themselves healthy. To help prepare you for these important aspects of teaching, this chapter describes the basic process of disease transmission and ways to prevent illness from spreading. We discuss some of the symptoms of common diseases and how to manage them in the early childhood setting. Some children such as children who are internationally adopted or who have recently immigrated to the United States may face special health concerns. These needs are also discussed.

Throughout the chapter, when we refer to *disease*, we are talking about illnesses, infections, viruses, and other maladies that cause children to get sick. Teachers are not trained medical professionals and should not offer diagnoses or treatment for health care problems. However, the guidance that is provided here contributes to the specialized set of skills that prepares teachers to care appropriately for children when illness occurs at school.

UNDERSTANDING THE INFECTIOUS DISEASE PROCESS

Diseases caused by infections can interrupt the body's functioning. Usually, the body is able to call into action the intricate biological responses of the immune system to detect and fight off disease. In the process of fighting off infections, a child can become ill and manifest a wide array of symptoms in response to infections. **Infectious diseases** are illnesses or conditions caused by germs, and they can cause symptoms related to many body systems.

Infectious diseases are common in childhood and can be a worrisome aspect of teaching. Children rely on their teachers to comfort and nurture them, and their classmates depend on the teacher to help keep them from getting sick. Teachers who understand the disease process are better able to address these responsibilities by reducing the frequency of disease and minimizing its impact.

The Causes of Infectious Diseases

Microscopic organisms are present in huge numbers throughout the environment and can cause diseases. They include viruses, bacteria, fungi, and parasites that invade the body and cause illness. Each of these organisms exists in one form or another virtually everywhere on earth. In their infectious forms, each is a cause for disease and potentially, death. We commonly refer to these infectious agents as **germs**.

Viruses

A **virus** is a type of infectious germ that invades human tissue and causes illness. The body's immune system is highly effective at killing off most viruses. Illnesses caused by viruses include chicken pox, measles, the common cold, influenza, and human immunodeficiency virus (HIV). Usually diseases caused by viruses are allowed to improve on their own. Through this healing process the body's systems develop a certain level of immunity to similar viruses in the future. Most viruses cause mild infections but can rarely cause serious medical complications.

MyEducationLab™
Visit the MyEducationLab for *Nutrition, Health, and Safety for Young Children* to enhance your understanding of chapter concepts with a personalized Study Plan. You'll also have the opportunity to hone your teaching skills through video-based Assignments and Activities, as well as Building Teaching Skills and Dispositions lessons.

infectious diseases
diseases caused by microorganisms that are spread from person to person or animal to person

germ
an organism or infectious agent that can potentially cause disease

Disease is caused by viruses, bacteria, fungi, and parasites–commonly referred to as germs.

virus
a type of infectious germ that invades human tissue and causes illness

bacteria
infectious germs that invade human tissue and cause illness; sometimes treated with antibiotics

fungi
a type of germ that can commonly cause skin infections or allergic reactions

parasite
infections that invade the body and live within human tissue for extended periods of time

communicable diseases
infections that are spread from one person to another

mode of transmission
the route by which an infection is spread

Bacteria

Like viruses, **bacteria** are infectious germs that cause illness. Some bacteria are useful in digestion and in certain familiar processes such as making yogurt from milk, but other bacteria can cause disease. These harmful bacteria are the cause of many respiratory illnesses, such as bacterial pneumonia and tuberculosis, and diseases such as tetanus. Bacteria are a major cause of disease and death worldwide. Bacterial infections are often treated with antibiotics.

Fungi

Fungi are germs that are the cause of common illnesses such as ringworm or athlete's foot. Other examples of fungi are mushrooms, mold, and baker's yeast. Other fungi are used to grow special molds for making cheese. The spores of some fungi can cause allergies.

Parasites

Parasites are infectious agents that feed on or enter the body tissue. They can live on and within human tissue for extended periods of time. Examples of parasitic diseases include head lice, scabies, intestinal worms, malaria, and parasites such as *Giardia*, which are contracted from drinking contaminated water.

How Disease Is Spread

Infectious diseases are spread from person to person or from an animal or insect to a person. The most frequent infections among young children are **communicable diseases**, which are spread from one person to another. Disease is spread in different ways, called **modes of transmission** (see Figure 10-1). Most infections are transferred by one of the four common modes of transmission, as discussed next.

Droplet Transmission

Airborne Transmission

Contact Transmission

Bloodborne Transmission

FIGURE 10-1
Common Modes of Transmission

Infections Spread by Direct or Indirect Contact

This is the most common mode of transmission in the early childhood setting. Direct contact occurs by direct person-to-person contact while indirect refers to transmission via a contaminated object or contaminated hands. Contaminated hands are the most common way infections get transmitted in early childhood settings (American Academy of Pediatrics, American Public Health Association, National Resource Center for Health and Safety in Child Care and Early Education, 2011).

Typical actions such as these occur in everyday play and provide the opportunity to spread disease. For example, Cherice, who is coming down with a cold, may sneeze directly onto Aiden while they are playing with blocks. Or she may turn away and sneeze onto some blocks that are touched a few minutes later by Karl, who has just joined the play. When Karl picks up the blocks and later scratches his nose or puts his fingers into his mouth, the germs are indirectly transmitted to him. Most common respiratory and diarrheal infections are spread by direct or indirect contact.

Infections Spread by Droplet Transmission

This occurs when a person coughs or sneezes, propelling droplets of contaminated fluid that land on another person's eyes, nose, or mouth. Examples of infections transmitted by this mechanism include influenza, whooping cough, and strep throat, which are all discussed later in the chapter (American Academy of Pediatrics, American Public Health Association, National Resource Center for Health and Safety in Child Care and Early Education, 2011).

Infections Spread by Airborne Transmission

Similar to droplet transmission, **airborne transmission** involves much smaller microscopic droplets that travel through the air via air currents and over a longer distance. Examples include chicken pox, measles, and tuberculosis (American Academy of Pediatrics, American Public Health Association, National Resource Center for Health and Safety in Child Care and Early Education, 2011).

airborne transmission occurs when infected particles are sneezed or coughed into the air and inhaled by another person

Infections Spread by Bloodborne Transmission

Bloodborne transmission occurs through contact with contaminated blood. In this situation, the infection can be transmitted only if the infected blood comes into contact with an uninfected person's bloodstream through a wound. This might happen if a child comes into contact with infected blood from a wound such as a bite, nosebleed, bleeding from excessive scratching of irritated skin, or injury (American Academy of Pediatrics, 2009). This mode of transmission is very uncommon in early childhood and school settings.

bloodborne transmission occurs when infections are spread by contamination with blood

The Incubation Period

Illness does not always occur immediately after contact with an infectious germ. Sometimes illness is not evident until a few hours, days, or even up to a few months in rare cases. The time between the child's first exposure to an infectious agent and when the first symptom of illness appears is called the **incubation period**.

Each infectious agent has a typical incubation period. Recognizing that the incubation period for familiar diseases may vary provides important information. For some diseases, the incubation period is the time when the child is most infectious to others. When an illness has been diagnosed, teachers who are knowledgeable about the illness's incubation period are then able to identify other children who may have been exposed to the disease. Knowing about incubation periods also helps teachers know how long to watch for the spread of the disease and to recognize when the potential risk for additional cases is likely to be over.

incubation period period of time between a child's first exposure to an infectious germ and the time when the child's first symptom appears

In the opening case scenario, Mary Beth understands that other children may have been exposed to strep throat. She takes steps to counteract the possible spread of the disease by teaching the children how to cover their coughs and wash their hands carefully. She also shares information with parents about the symptoms of strep throat. In addition, Mary Beth will also watch for signs of strep throat over the next 2 to 5 days, the typical incubation period for this disease.

The period of contagiousness can also vary and be different or similar to the incubation period. Local health departments and health care providers can be excellent resources for teachers when potential outbreaks or questions arise. Table 10-1 outlines modes of transmission, incubation periods, and symptoms associated with the infectious diseases discussed in this chapter.

Capítulo 10

TABLE 10-1 Childhood Infections: Mode of Transmission, Incubation Period, and Symptoms

Infectious Disease	Mode of Transmission	Incubation Period	Symptoms
Chicken pox	Airborne, droplet	10–21 days	Fever, cough, rash
Common colds	Droplet	Variable	Fever, runny nose, cough, congestion
Conjunctivitis (pinkeye)	Droplet	Variable	Eye drainage, redness of eyes
Coxsackie virus (hand, foot, and mouth disease)	Droplet	3–5 days	Fever, blisters in the mouth, refusal to eat, rash on palms and soles, diaper rash
Croup	Droplet	Variable	Fever, barky cough, runny nose
Ear infections	Usually Not communicable	Variable	Fever, earache
Fifth disease	Droplet	4–28 days	Fever, headache, muscle aches, rash
Group A strep (strep throat)	Droplet	Several hours to 4 days	Fever, sore throat, rash
Haemophilus influenzae type b (Hib)	Droplet	Unknown	Fever, upper respiratory infection, meningitis
Head lice	Direct contact	10–14 days	Itching of scalp
Hepatitis A	Direct or Indirect contact	15–50 days	Fever, nausea, abdominal pain
Hepatitis B	Bloodborne	45–160 days	Inflammation of the liver
Hepatitis C	Bloodborne	6–7 weeks	Inflammation of the liver
Human immunodeficiency virus (HIV)	Bloodborne	12–18 months	Wide range of symptoms
Influenza	Airborne or droplet; depends on the strain	1–4 days	Fever, muscle aches, sore throat, cough, headache
Measles	Airborne, droplet	7–18 days	Fever, pinkeye, runny nose, rash
Methicillin-resistant *Staphylococcus aureus* (MRSA)	Direct contact	Variable	Skin infections
Pertussis (whooping cough)	Droplet	4–21 days	Initial: fever, runny nose, cough Later: Numerous bursts of cough, sometimes with the characteristic whoop
Pinworms	Direct or Indirect contact	Variable	Itching around anus
Respiratory syncytial virus (RSV)	Droplet	2–8 days	Fever, runny nose, cough, difficulty breathing
Ringworm	Direct contact	Unknown	Rash
Rotavirus	Direct or Indirect contact	1–2 days	Fever, vomiting, diarrhea
Scabies	Direct contact	4–6 weeks	Rash, itching
Streptococcus pneumonia	Droplet	1–3 days	Ear infections, pneumonia, meningitis
Tetanus	Direct contact through open wound	4–21 days	Severe muscle contraction, spasm, seizures
Tuberculosis	Droplet, airborne	2–12 weeks	Chronic cough

Sources: American Academy of Pediatrics, 2009; Centers for Disease Control and Prevention, 2010.

Symptoms of Disease

Each disease has its own set of symptoms. Understanding symptoms of illness can guide teachers to be watchful and ready to take appropriate action to care for a child. Symptoms that are frequently associated with disease include the following:

- *Fever*, which may be evident by the child's brightly flushed cheeks.
- *Cough*, especially if the cough is new.
- *Rash*, such as a newly emerging flush on the skin.
- *Vomiting*, especially when vomiting occurs with no other likely explanation.
- *Changes in the child's typical behavior*, such as being very quiet or not engaging in typical play.

In the opening scenario, it was Mark's atypical behavior that caught his teacher's attention. Following her observations, and after talking with Mark, Mary Beth decided that it was highly likely he was becoming ill. She felt reasonably confident that it was in Mark's best interest to see the school nurse for further assessment. Most children's programs do not have a nurse available to assist with determining a course of action for a child who gets sick at school. In these settings, teachers must use their best judgment to determine if the child can be cared for in the setting or if the parent should be contacted.

A description of the symptoms the teacher observed provides helpful information for families and medical providers. It is not appropriate for the teacher to suggest a medical diagnosis or offer a plan of treatment. However, it is appropriate for the teacher to provide a summary of the symptoms that were observed, to inform the family of the intensity of those symptoms, and to recommend that the parent seek medical evaluation. Symptoms provide clues to help medical providers diagnose the disease and create an appropriate treatment plan.

Symptoms of Common Infections

Among the many diseases that children may experience, three groups of infections are most common. These include infections with symptoms of diarrhea, respiratory illness, or skin infections and rashes.

Acute Infectious Diarrhea

Diarrhea is the frequent and excessive discharge of watery feces. It is experienced in young children as discomfort and soiled diapers and clothing or as a frequent need to use the bathroom. Infectious diarrhea is caused by both viruses and bacteria. The infection is transmitted from person to person usually by direct or indirect contact. Infectious diarrhea outbreaks are more common among children who participate in early childhood group settings than among those who do not, especially in programs that include children in diapers. Periodic training of staff in hygiene and proper diapering and toileting reduces the risk of outbreaks (American Academy of Pediatrics, American Public Health Association, National Resource Center for Health and Safety in Child Care and Early Education, 2011).

Because of this frequency of occurrence and the potential for the spread of infectious diarrhea, its management and prevention are especially important. Frequent hand washing is essential for children and teachers. If a child develops diarrhea, the teacher should inform parents how many episodes the child experienced. It is particularly important to notice if any blood is present in the child's stool. Other symptoms such as fever, vomiting, or rash should also be reported.

Respiratory Tract Illnesses

Symptoms of respiratory tract illnesses involve the nose, sinuses, ears, throat, and lungs. Respiratory diseases are extremely common in young children. Familiar respiratory infections include the common cold, ear infections, **pharyngitis** (an infection of the throat), **sinusitis** (a sinus infection), and **pneumonia** (a lung infection).

This **video** shows a teacher talking to a young girl who is feeling ill. How does the teacher evaluate the child's symptoms?

diarrhea
the frequent and excessive discharge of watery feces

What if . . .

several children in your class developed diarrhea? What policies would you implement to minimize further spread of the illness? What resources in your community would you turn to for assistance if it became a large outbreak of infectious diarrhea?

pharyngitis
infection of the throat
sinusitis
sinus infection
pneumonia
lung infection

These illnesses are most often spread by sneezing, coughing, or drainage from the nose. Symptoms of respiratory tract illness include fever, nasal congestion, runny nose, sore throat, ear pain, cough, or difficulty breathing. Some of these infections are associated with skin rashes as well. Studies report that the incidence of respiratory infections is increased in children attending child care programs but can be reduced with consistent hand washing and appropriate cough etiquette (American Academy of Pediatrics, American Public Health Association, National Resource Center for Health and Safety in Child Care and Early Education, 2011).

Families should be contacted and children should be referred to their medical provider if they exhibit symptoms such as uncontrolled coughing, difficulty breathing, or wheezing (American Academy of Pediatrics, American Public Health Association, National Resource Center for Health and Safety in Child Care and Early Education, 2011). During the initial days of respiratory illness, children may be uncomfortable or in pain. Although they may be receiving treatment and do not have a fever, they should stay at home simply because they are not feeling well and are unable to participate in normal school activities.

The symptoms of runny nose and cough are not uncommon in young children, especially during the winter months. These symptoms alone should not exclude children from attending early childhood programs. If teachers have concerns, parents should be notified. Collaboration with a health care provider may be helpful to determine if exclusion is necessary. Many of these children can safely be included. See this chapter's *Nutrition Note: Vitamin D and Infectious Diseases* for some interesting information regarding vitamin D and respiratory infections.

Skin Infections and Contagious Rashes

Skin infections are caused by viruses, bacteria, and fungi. They are a common symptom of several diseases. Sometimes respiratory tract infections are associated with skin infections. Chicken pox is one example. Initially, the disease starts with mild respiratory symptoms, then progresses to the characteristic skin rash.

Inclusion or exclusion of children with skin rashes depends on the underlying cause. Teachers may need to rely on the recommendations from the child's health care provider when determining if exclusion is appropriate. Frequent hand washing helps minimize potential spread.

● PREVENTING AND CONTROLLING INFECTIOUS DISEASE

Because children participating in group settings have the potential to be exposed to a wide range of diseases, it is especially important for teachers to be purposeful in implementing strategies to reduce the incidence of illness. Strategies include the following:

- Recognizing national public health policies.
- Complying with medical interventions, such as required immunizations.

NUTRITION NOTE Vitamin D and Infectious Diseases

Every type of tissue in the body uses vitamin D for various purposes. Though it is not clear what levels of vitamin D are considered normal, it has been shown that low levels of vitamin D are associated with higher risk of respiratory infections, higher rates of asthma, eczema, and food allergies.

Over 90% of vitamin D in the body is produced by exposure to sunlight. It is difficult to ingest enough vitamin D from the diet so deficiency is common even in children. Because of the widespread deficiency, it is reasonable that all children receive supplementation with vitamin D, especially in areas where there is limited exposure to sunlight during certain seasons. This, of course, must be balanced with the risks of sun exposure: sunburn and skin cancer. Supplementation begins during infancy and should continue throughout the childhood years.

Source: Based on Bozzetoo, Carraro, Giordano, Boner, & Baraldi, 2012.

- Following recommended practices for the classroom that are provided by licensing and accreditation agencies.
- Establishing and practicing prevention strategies that are established and implemented at the local level by the children's program or school.

We now look at some of the more common prevention strategies: immunizations, health assessments for teachers, and classroom practices to reduce the spread of disease.

Immunizations

The immunizations that are required for entry and participation in early childhood and school settings are put in place to stop the spread of potentially dangerous diseases. Requirements for children's immunizations are typically regulated by federal or state agencies that have oversight for early childhood settings and schools. Immunization requirements are useful to teachers because they help in establishing healthful environments for young children. Immunizations have been proven to be the most effective method of disease prevention among groups of children.

Health Assessments for Teachers

Preemployment and ongoing health appraisals for teachers help reduce the potential for spread of disease between teachers and children and assist in keeping teachers healthy. Health assessments assist in detecting infectious disease that teachers may introduce into the classroom. For example, some infectious diseases such as tuberculosis can be "silent," meaning the adult has no symptoms. The *National Health and Safety Performance Standards* recommend that teachers obtain a health assessment before employment, which may include the following items (American Academy of Pediatrics, American Public Health Association, National Resource Center for Health and Safety in Child Care and Early Education, 2011):

- *Health history:* to establish an understanding of the adult's general state of health.
- *Physical and dental exam:* to screen for illness and to recognize if dental decay is evident. The germs that cause dental decay are infectious and can be communicated to young children.
- *Vision and hearing screening:* to identify the need for glasses or hearing assistance.
- *Tuberculosis (TB) screening:* to identify whether the teacher is a potential carrier of TB. Standards related to TB screening are specific to regional health recommendations depending on the risk of TB in the local area. Many programs require a TB test prior to employment and again if the teacher has a known exposure.
- *Review of occupational health hazards:* to clarify risks to the teacher in the children's setting and to identify any accommodations that might be needed.
- *Assessment of limitations:* to identify issues that may require modifications in the workplace, such as regular break times for a teacher who needs to test and manage her own insulin treatment for diabetes.
- *Review of immunization:* to determine if any are lacking or needed. Those of particular importance include hepatitis A, hepatitis B, tetanus (TdaP), influenza, chicken pox, measles, and pertussis.

Some infections, such as hepatitis A and chicken pox, are common among children and can easily be spread to an adult. These infections are often more serious for adults than children.

There is an increasing prevalence of whooping cough (pertussis) among older children and individuals whose immunity from previous vaccination is waning. For this reason the tetanus booster vaccine for adults now includes pertussis vaccination (TdaP). Teachers should receive TdaP instead of the former tetanus booster (dT) (Centers for Disease Control and Prevention, 2011). Yearly influenza vaccination is recommended for staff caring for children of any age (American Academy of

A Matter of ETHICS

One of the families in your class has a philosophical opposition to giving their children any vaccinations, so the child in your class has not received any. The family has completed the appropriate paperwork for an exemption. Do you have a personal bias for or against their decision? What specific issues might you be concerned about? How does the Code of Ethical Conduct guide you in this matter? Given your professional responsibilities, what plan might you establish with the family in case the child is exposed to a vaccine-preventable disease at preschool? What steps could you take to minimize exposure to disease for all the children in your class?

Pediatrics, American Public Health Association, National Resource Center for Health and Safety in Child Care and Early Education, 2011).

Teachers need to be concerned about their own health. Teachers who may be pregnant should be aware that some childhood illness can have negative impacts on the unborn child. The *Safety Segment* addresses these situations.

Finally, teachers are not only susceptible to infection, but they can spread infection, just as children can. When certain symptoms are present such as fever or vomiting, teachers should stay home and avoid exposing others. If a specific diagnosis has been made, such as strep throat, teachers should follow the same recommendations that are made for children.

Classroom Practices for Controlling the Spread of Disease

Purposeful health practices that are routinely followed in children's settings can significantly decrease the frequency of infections. These include such practices as hand washing, conducting daily health checks, sanitizing toys and classrooms, following careful diapering and toileting policies, implementing universal precautions when needed, and teaching children preventive health practices.

Hand Washing

Children need clear instructions and frequent reminders about washing their hands thoroughly. In this **video**, a teacher gives a lesson in handwashing. What do the children learn from this lesson?

Hand washing is the single most important way to reduce the spread of disease. Unwashed or improperly washed hands are the primary source for the spread of disease. Studies have shown that proper handwashing can significantly reduce the spread of diarrheal and respiratory illnesses in child care programs (American Academy of Pediatrics, American Public Health Association, National Resource Center for Health and Safety in Child Care and Early Education, 2011).

When to Wash Hands All children and teachers should wash their hands at routine times during the day, such as at arrival or before eating, as well as at other times when germs can be transmitted. Children and teachers should wash their hands at the following times (American Academy of Pediatrics, American Public Health Association, National Resource Center for Health and Safety in Child Care and Early Education, 2011):

- On arrival at school or when coming in from outdoor play.
- When moving from one classroom to another, for example, when a teacher moves from leading one group to another.
- Before:
  - Eating or feeding a child.
  - Whenever handling food for a child or for themselves.
  - Giving medication to a child.
  - Playing in the water table, or other water play when more than one child is participating.
- After:
  - Using the toilet.
  - Diapering or helping a child use the toilet.

- Assisting children to wipe or blow their noses.
- Contacting body fluids such as mucus (from sneezing), blood, and vomit.
- Handling animals (see the *Health Hint, Infections and Animals*).
- Playing in the water table or sandbox.
- Cleaning or sanitizing.
- Handling garbage.

Supporting Children to Wash Their Own Hands Children are capable of washing their hands effectively if the appropriate supports are available. This includes providing a child-sized sink or an appropriate step stool so children can reach the water. Warm, running water is needed to encourage scrubbing and to remove soil and germs. Liquid soap should be provided because it is easier for children to use (see Figure 10-2). Disposable towels are recommended to avoid the spread of germs. Children should be taught to turn the faucet off with a paper towel because this helps reduce the spread of germs from the faucet back to the child's hands.

Once children have been taught how to effectively wash their hands, the teacher's role is primarily to supervise for safety. For children who cannot wash their hands independently, a teacher can safely cradle a child in one arm or provide support for a child to stand while they wash hands. Teachers should wash their own hands after assisting children. For children who cannot be held and cannot stand, it is appropriate to use an alcohol-based hand sanitizer as an alternative (American Academy of Pediatrics, American Public Health Association, National Resource Center for Health and Safety in Child Care and Early Education, 2011).

START ➡

1. Wet hands

2. Soap
(20 seconds)

3. Scrub backs of hands, wrists, between fingers, under fingernails.

4. Rinse

5. Towel dry

6. Turn off taps with towel

FIGURE 10-2

Hand Washing Is the Single Most Important Way to Reduce the Spread of Disease
Source: Based on steps from La Crosse County Environmental Health (n.d.).

HEALTH HINT Infections and Animals

Interaction with animals is a fun and valuable teaching tool, but animals can introduce certain types of infections. To minimize risk of infection:

- All animals should be fully vaccinated.
- Teachers and children should wash hands after handling pets.
- Animal contact should occur in designated areas.
- No food should be allowed in animal contact areas.
- Classroom animals should not be allowed to roam or have contact with wild animals.

- Parents should be informed in advance about the presence of animals. Teachers should consult with parents about children's special health care needs, especially for children with immune problems. Cat allergies are common and can be particularly problematic.
- Aquariums and cages should not be cleaned in sinks that are used for food preparation.
- Children under the age of 5 should not have contact with baby chicks or ducks, reptiles, or ferrets because of increased risk for certain types of infections.

Source: Centers for Disease Control and Prevention, 2011.

Conducting Daily Health Checks

Daily health checks are an important way to prevent the spread of disease. Teachers should be prepared to conduct the daily health check as soon as possible after the children arrive. The purpose of the check is to identify children who are ill and who may need to be excluded from participation, which can reduce the transmission of infectious diseases (American Academy of Pediatrics, American Public Health Association, National Resource Center for Health and Safety in Child Care and Early Education, 2011). For example, teachers should monitor the class group for 2 weeks (the incubation period) following a confirmed case of chicken pox. Teachers should document the findings from the daily health checks to assist in tracking and monitoring illnesses in the classroom.

Cleaning and Sanitizing

Cleaning and sanitizing are important actions in preventing the spread of disease. Young children touch and share many objects throughout the day. They deposit germs either directly onto others or indirectly onto surfaces and objects. Because of this, any surface that a child can reach, including floors, should be sanitized regularly to minimize contamination with infectious germs.

Cleaning products should be safe for use in the classroom setting. The bleach and water solutions for cleaning and sanitizing discussed elsewhere in this text are appropriate for use in children's settings. More detailed recommendations for cleaning and sanitizing specific areas and items in early childhood settings are found in the *National Health and Safety Performance Standards*.

Teachers carry the primary responsibility for a healthy classroom environment. This requires teacher's commitment to ensuring clean and sanitary spaces and equipment. It also means that teachers need to have a positive disposition toward what can sometimes be a tedious task: cleaning. Several approaches can help:

- Post a cleaning and sanitizing reminder chart to ensure that the schedule is achieved.
- Provide a "wash me" bucket for collecting toys that have been in children's mouths. The toys in the bucket are then sanitized after class.
- Stock the cupboard with disposable towels for wiping doorknobs and cupboard handles.
- Obtain laundry bags for gathering dramatic play clothing at the end of each week so the clothing can be laundered.
- Be prepared to increase the frequency of cleaning and sanitizing when the number of children with illness is unusually high.

Diapering and Toileting

Sanitary practices are especially important when changing diapers or assisting children at the toilet. Settings that provide care for children who wear diapers typically require the use of disposable

FIGURE 10-3   Diaper Changing Procedures

1. **NEVER** leave the child unattended at the changing table.
2. Have all needed supplies available at the changing table. Wash hands.
3. Place the child on the changing table, avoiding contact of soiled diaper with surrounding surfaces and clean clothing.
4. Unfasten soiled diaper, leaving it under child. Clean the child's diaper area and genitalia using appropriate wipes. Clean from front to back. Use a fresh wipe each time removing urine or stool.
5. Remove soiled diaper without contaminating surfaces. Enclose the diaper in a disposable bag.
6. Slide the fresh diaper under the child and fasten.
7. Wash the child's hands and return the child to the supervised area.
8. Clean and sanitize the diaper changing area.
9. Wash your hands. Record diaper change in child's daily log.

Source: American Academy of Pediatrics, American Public Health Association, National Resource Center for Health and Safety in Child Care and Early Education, 2011.

diapers. Exceptions may be made for children who have a medical reason, such as an allergic reaction to disposable diapers. Figure 10-3 describes appropriate diaper-changing procedures. This procedure should be posted in all diaper-changing areas. A child should **never** be left unattended on the changing table.

Settings that serve children who are learning to use the toilet are discouraged from using potty chairs (or non-flushable toilets) because sanitation is difficult. If potty chairs are used, they should be easy to sanitize, used only in the bathroom area, and used on a surface that does not absorb moisture and is easy to clean. They should also be used in areas where toilets and other potty chairs are out of reach and where a sink is designated to sanitize only potty chairs (American Academy of Pediatrics, American Public Health Association, National Resource Center for Health and Safety in Child Care and Early Education, 2011). Ideally, settings serving children ages 2 to 5 should provide child-sized toilets. This makes children more comfortable and helps them learn to manage their own toileting.

When assisting children with toileting, teachers should guide the child in removing their garments and help them use the toilet. Teachers should assist with wiping as needed, remembering to wipe from front to back. Young children may need help with arranging and fastening their garments. Then both the child and the teacher should thoroughly wash their hands. Sinks and toilets should be cleaned and sanitized daily.

Using Standard Precautions

The **Standard Precautions** are a set of guidelines created to prevent the spread of infections from exposure to blood and body fluids. They were developed by the CDC for use in hospitals and other health care settings. The basic principle is that all blood, body fluids, secretions, excretions (except sweat), nonintact skin, and mucous membranes potentially contain germs that can cause infections. Standard Precautions include two important practices relevant to early childhood settings (American Academy of Pediatrics, American Public Health Association, National Resource Center for Health and Safety in Child Care and Early Education, 2011):

Standard Precautions a set of guidelines defined by the CDC for use in hospitals and other health care centers to prevent the spread of disease through blood and body fluids

1. Using barriers, such as disposable gloves, when caring for children when blood or body fluids as stated above may be present.
2. Cleaning and sanitizing surfaces to prevent the transmission of infections by touching surfaces that have been contaminated by blood.

Teachers should wear gloves whenever an injury involves blood, such as a cut, scrape, or bloody nose. Once the bleeding has been stopped, any surfaces that have been exposed to blood must be sanitized. Consider this scenario:

Tom is in the play yard bouncing a ball to Lena. He hears a crash and looks to see that Jimmy has tipped over on the trike. Tom moves quickly to Jimmy who has crawled out from under the trike. He can see that Jimmy's lip is bleeding. As he hurries to Jimmy, Tom reaches into his pocket and pulls out a pair of disposable gloves. He puts them on as he arrives at Jimmy's side. "Hey Jimmy," Tom says as he crouches down to gently hug Jimmy. "That looked like a pretty big bump! Let's go inside and take a good look at it."

Tom was prepared for this accident, and he knew immediately to use Standard Precautions. Many teachers find it useful to place a pair of gloves in their pocket for emergencies such as this. Another strategy is to tape pairs of gloves at various locations on the classroom wall, and in logical locations in outdoor play areas. Each classroom should have a ready supply of disposable gloves as well as disposable toweling and appropriate sanitizing solutions. Even when gloves are used to manage injuries that involve blood, hand washing is still crucial. After use, the gloves should be removed and discarded in a sanitary manner, and hands should be washed.

Teaching Children Preventive Health Practices

Teachers help children be partners in disease prevention by guiding them to develop self-help skills and by teaching age-appropriate and developmentally appropriate prevention practices. Teaching disease prevention practices has a dual purpose: It helps to reduce the spread of disease immediately and educates children about ways to improve their wellness in the future. The *Teaching Wellness* feature offers examples for the classroom.

As discussed in Chapter 1, infusing the daily curriculum with health messages is the best way to engage and educate children about wellness. This includes offering activities that have a health

TEACHING WELLNESS Germ Stoppers

Como podar los germenes

LEARNING OUTCOME   **Children will learn how germs spread and how to stop them.**

INFANTS AND TODDLERS

- **Goal:** To introduce the child to the concept of germs.
- **Materials:** Paint, paintbrush, and paper; paint smocks as appropriate.
- **Activity plan:** Make handprints on paper. Have the toddler paint her hand and pat it against a piece of paper. Keep making handprints until there is not enough paint to make a mark on the paper. Talk about how germs are so small we cannot see them, but that they stick to our hands like paint and spread to others. Have the child look at her hand to see if any paint can still be seen. Talk about how children can wash their hands to take germs away just as washing removes paint.

- **How to adjust the activity:** Have children carry a basket of small blocks ("germs") and "spread" them to places around the room. Tell them these are the germs. When all have been spread around the room, ask the children to "clean" the germs away by gathering them back into their baskets.
- **Did you meet your goal?** Were children able to experience how germs can be spread like paint is spread? Listen to what children say about the activity to assess if children are beginning to discover the concept of germs and their spread.

PRESCHOOLERS AND KINDERGARTNERS *AND* SCHOOL-AGE CHILDREN

- **Goal:** To learn how germs are spread and ways to stop them.
- **Materials:** Paint, paintbrush, paper towels.
- **Activity plan:** First, talk with children about how germs are spread by touching. Then have a small group of children stand in a line. Have one child paint his hand. Then ask that child to shake hands with the next child in line. Have this child shake hands with the third child in line, continuing until each child has shaken hands. Have the children compare their hands to see how many handshakes continued to pass along the paint. Review the concept of spreading germs by touching.

- **How to adjust the activity:** Have the children paint their hands, spreading the paint on generously. Then have the children wash their hands at the sink. Provide paper toweling for each child. Have the child bring their paper towels to the circle. Have each child show their paper towel. Do any show signs of paint? Talk about how much hand washing is needed to appropriately and thoroughly wash away germs.
- **Did you meet your goal?** Were children able to experience and understand how germs are spread through touching? Were children able to experience and understand how hand washing can reduce the spread of germs, and that careful and thorough hand washing is needed to completely clean away germs?

focus. It also means purposefully teaching age-appropriate disease prevention practices and ways that children can help reduce the spread of germs. Topics for teaching prevention messages include:

- How and when to wash my hands.
- How to blow my nose.
- How my body gets sick.
- How my body tells me I am sick.
- How to cover my cough.
- How to keep my sickness to myself.
- How to take care of myself when I am sick.

Topics such as these should be explored in different ways, through literature and activities. They should be repeated at appropriate intervals to reinforce the ideas. Activities like those suggested in the *Teaching Wellness* feature help children explore concepts, such as how germs are spread, in ways that are appropriate and relevant.

Partner with Parents

Parents are also important participants in disease prevention and management. To be effective partners, they need teachers to provide them with information about program health practices and ways that parents help keep children and classrooms healthy. Several practices support this effort:

- To begin the partnership, provide preenrollment information about immunization requirements and advise parents to obtain health and dental screenings for their child.
- Communicate the program's commitment to health and wellness in parent handbooks, bulletin boards, etc.
- Ensure that families provide contact information and let them know how they will be contacted in case their child becomes ill at school. This information should be updated regularly.
- Orient families to classroom health practices, such as having children wash their hands at arrival and conducting daily health checks. Tell families how they will be notified of illnesses in the classroom.
- Provide information about when to keep children home from school due to illness.
- Inform families about how the program will care for children who become ill at school.

Managing Challenges

Illness in the classroom can be disruptive as teachers work to continue the daily routine and activities while caring for a sick child. Being prepared for such situations is important as a management strategy, but also to ensure that germs and disease are not unnecessarily spread. Obtaining supportive supplies in advance and having resources readily available are important ways to prepare to appropriately care for sick children. Programs should have policies that address situations like epidemics or pandemics as discussed in this chapter's *Policy Point*.

Establish an Isolation Area

Sick children need to be removed from the general class group activities to prevent spread of germs and to allow them to rest appropriately until a family member or emergency contact person can come to get them. An isolation area should be identified in the program facility or in a quiet area of the classroom. A pad and blanket should be readily available to provide a comfortable place to rest. These items should be clean and ready for use, and they should be cleaned and sanitized after use. Ill children should be supervised at all times while they are resting. In some settings this may mean that the isolation area is simply a corner of the room where the teacher can supervise the ill child as well as other children in the space. When children leave the class, they should be "signed out" on a sign-in/out sheet to document who picked them up and when.

POLICY POINT Epidemic? Pandemic? Who Sets Policy in Disease Emergencies?

Teachers know to call 911 when there's an emergency in the early childhood setting. But where do teachers get information when disease threat is widespread? Epidemics (situations where the incidence of disease is higher than expected) and pandemics (situations where infectious disease becomes geographically widespread) have the potential to impact programming in children's settings and schools. Emerging diseases can spread across the world with great speed. When this happens health authorities must work quickly to identify the infectious agent, discover medical treatment to reduce its effect, and communicate methods to prevent spread of disease.

In recent years, concern about avian flu prompted health authorities to plan management strategies for a potential pandemic health crisis. The H1N1 flu (swine flu) outbreak of 2009 tested the strength of such plans. Early childhood programs have taken steps to model their own policies for disease prevention and communication after these efforts. However, when health crises are emerging, teachers and parents need to know where to turn for current information. Several important resources are available:

- The World Health Organization (WHO) monitors the world-wide incidence and spread of disease. The WHO provides updates as emergencies develop and offers guidance for individuals and communities (www.who.int/en).
- The Centers for Disease Control and Prevention is the national agency for up-to-date information on pandemic

disease. The CDC provides information about how to plan for pandemic health emergencies and guidance about what schools and child care programs need to do when pandemic disease is occurring (www.cdc.gov).

- Local health authorities are the go-to agencies for providing local updates and advice for an emergency response to health crises. During pandemic events public health agencies will make recommendations on prevention strategies and will ultimately direct decisions related to program and school closures. Local health authorities also have personnel available to answer questions and provide individualized advice.

Children's programs also need to do their part by establishing program and school-level policies for health emergencies. Policies should include:

- How health crisis information will be communicated to families.
- How program or school-level decisions related to closures will be made.
- How families will be notified in the event of a school closure.
- How decisions related to reopening the program will be made.

Teachers who are prepared become part of the network of disease prevention efforts that is needed to protect the health of young children and their communities.

Early childhood settings should implement clear policies about the attendance of children who are sick. As you watch this video, think about the policies established at this school and how they minimize the spread of infectious diseases.

Record Illness Information

It is helpful to have an illness recording form available for immediate use. Such forms help to document the child's illness and release from school. The teacher should follow the program or school protocol for recording the child's illness. Helpful information to record includes:

- Child's name.
- Date and time of day.
- Symptoms observed.
- Who provided care for the child.
- Who was contacted to pick up the child.
- Who picked up the child from care or school and when.

Be Prepared to Send Sick Children Home

A child's illness can cause disruption in the family work schedule. Some families may not have a backup plan to care for an ill child at home. Families may be stressed about losing their job if they take time off to care for their child. These are realistic concerns that families need to manage. It is helpful to orient families to the program policies related to sick children, so they are alerted in advance to the need to pick up and care for their child if illness occurs.

Teachers should be understanding about the challenges families face, but be firm when children are too ill to attend. If families bring a child back to school too soon following an illness, the daily

FIGURE 10-4   Sample Health Alert for Parents

HEALTH ALERT for Parents: Pinkeye

Please observe your child for pinkeye (conjunctivitis).

Pinkeye has been identified in our classrooms. Pinkeye can be alarming because it may make the eyes extremely red and can spread rapidly. Pinkeye (conjunctivitis) can be caused by infections (such as bacteria and viruses), allergies, or substances that irritate the eyes. It is a fairly common condition and usually causes no long-term eye or vision damage. **But if your child shows symptoms of pinkeye, it's important to contact your doctor.**

Avoid the spread of pinkeye at home. Children get pinkeye by touching an infected person or something an infected person has touched, such as a used tissue. If pinkeye is diagnosed in one eye, it can also spread it to the other eye by touching. Teach and help your child to wash his or her hands often with warm water and soap.

If you think your child has pinkeye, it's important to contact your doctor to try to determine what's causing it and to learn how to treat it.

health check assists teachers to recognize if the child is still too ill to attend school. Some programs have sufficient staff to receive children who are no longer contagious but still recovering from illness. Sometimes families request that their child rest in the classroom rather than go outside for recess or play time. These decisions are made at the program level depending on the capacity to provide individualized supervision.

Have Illness Notifications Available

When children are diagnosed with an infectious condition, teachers need to communicate with other families to alert them to the illness. These notices also guide families in how to monitor their own child for symptoms of the disease. Having basic health alert flyers on hand is an important time-saver for teachers who want to distribute correct information as soon as possible. Figure 10-4 provides a sample health alert for pinkeye.

● RECOGNIZING AND MANAGING INFECTIOUS DISEASE

Preventing and controlling infections in early childhood settings requires teachers to have a basic understanding of communicable diseases that are common among young children. Although teachers are not responsible for diagnosing illnesses, those who are able to identify the symptoms of disease are better prepared to understand and control its spread. Teachers can also help families obtain health evaluations when necessary. Infectious diseases can be categorized as either vaccine-preventable diseases, which should occur infrequently, or other infections that are not vaccine preventable and are more common in the children's setting. Rarely, teachers will care for a child who has a bloodborne disease. In this section we briefly describe these diseases and offer insight into whether children should be excluded from the children's setting.

Vaccine-Preventable Diseases

Vaccine-preventable diseases are those that are prevented by immunization. These diseases have decreased in prevalence during the past several decades because of efforts to increase the number of children who are immunized. For this reason, teachers may never see a child with one of the vaccine-preventable diseases. However, many vaccine-preventable diseases are highly contagious, and some can cause very serious disability or death.

Outbreaks of these diseases that do occur may result in clusters of individuals being struck with the illness. More expansive outbreaks are labeled **epidemics**. An epidemic is declared when the

epidemic
situation in which the incidence of disease is substantially higher than what is expected in that population

number of people with the infection is substantially higher than what would normally be expected in that population. Next we provide brief summaries of these diseases to help teachers learn to recognize them in the rare event that they occur in the children's setting.

Pertussis (Whooping Cough)

pertussis
a bacterial upper respiratory infection that is highly contagious and can be fatal to infants and young children; also called *whooping cough*

Pertussis, also known as *whooping cough*, is a highly contagious and dangerous bacterial disease, especially for infants. Symptoms include bursts of uncontrolled coughing and wheezing that create the characteristic "whooping" sound. During these coughing spasms the child may turn blue and have severe respiratory distress.

The symptoms of pertussis often last several weeks. Children diagnosed with pertussis should be excluded from school, and the community health authority should be notified. The immunity provided by the pertussis vaccine tends to fade as individuals age. Therefore, periodic booster shots are required. Teachers should check with their health care provider, and obtain the pertussis booster along with the tetanus booster shot. Any teacher diagnosed with pertussis should be excluded from the classroom until a course of antibiotics has been completed. Here is an example scenario:

> Mary Jean is an observant teacher. She pays close attention to the health and well-being of the children in her class. On this day while working in the teacher's room, she surprises herself as she listens to her coworker cough. She remarks, "Michael, if I didn't know better, I would say that you are suffering from whooping cough!" This remark is enough to send Michael to get a checkup at the Immediate Care Clinic. He calls in later to report that he has been diagnosed with whooping cough.

Strong evidence demonstrates that protection provided by the pertussis vaccination wanes over time. In fact, older children or adults who have not received recent boosters are the source of most infections in children (American Academy of Pediatrics, 2009).

Haemophilus influenzae Type b

haemophilus influenzae type b (Hib)
a bacterial infection that can cause severe respiratory problems or meningitis

Haemophilus influenzae **type b (Hib)** causes **meningitis**, a severe infection of the membranes covering the brain. It occurs most commonly among infants. It can also cause other serious life-threatening respiratory infections.

meningitis
severe infection of the membranes covering the brain

- If a case of Hib infection is reported within an early childhood program, the families of each child should be notified as well as the local health authorities.

  - Children who have not been immunized due to special exceptions should be excluded from school until health authorities determine there is no longer a risk for infection (American Academy of Pediatrics, American Public Health Association, National Resource Center for Health and Safety in Child Care and Early Education, 2011).

chicken pox
viral infection that causes fever and rash

Chicken Pox

Chicken pox is a common childhood condition, especially in unvaccinated children. The chicken pox rash usually progresses from the head to the toes. The majority of the pox, or lesions, appear on the trunk (Centers for Disease Control and Prevention, 2011). The rash is characterized by itchy red bumps that rapidly progress to fluid-filled lesions. Teachers may notice the bumps on the back of the child's neck or on the cheeks.

- Children with chicken pox should be excluded from school until all the lesions have dried and crusted over.
- Rarely, chicken pox can cause severe complications that require intense medical treatment.

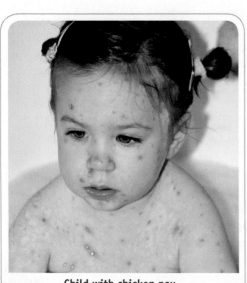

Child with chicken pox.

- Teachers should share with parents that *aspirin not be used to treat infants and children for chicken pox influenza (or any other suspected viral illness).* Aspirin use is associated with a serious complication called **Reye's syndrome**. Reye's syndrome can cause inflammation of the brain and liver and is potentially fatal.

Measles

Measles is an acute, highly contagious infectious disease. It is characterized by cough, runny nose, pinkeye, and rash. The measles rash begins on the face and head and spreads to the body. If a case of measles is confirmed, the child should be excluded from the classroom until a medical provider approves the child's return to the classroom.

Tetanus

The **tetanus** bacteria form spores that are deposited in soil where they can survive for months or even years. The spores are also found in the intestines and feces of many animals, including horses, sheep, cattle, dogs, cats, rats, guinea pigs, and chickens (Centers for Disease Control and Prevention, 2011). The bacteria usually enter the body through a puncture wound caused, for example, by stepping on a contaminated nail.

- Children should be guided to wash their hands after playing in the dirt and after visiting ranches, farms, and fairs where they may come into contact with infected animal feces.
- In case of injuries causing puncture wounds or cuts, documentation of an updated tetanus vaccine should be confirmed.
- Teachers should periodically receive a tetanus booster to maintain their own immunity.

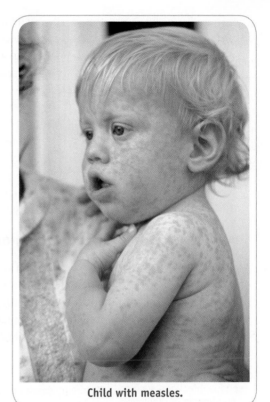

Child with measles.

Influenza (The Flu)

Influenza, also called "the flu," is a highly contagious respiratory disease that is caused by a virus. Symptoms include fever, sore throat, muscle aches, cough, headache, and fatigue. Although school-aged children (ages 5–18) do not have an increased risk of complications of influenza, they have the highest attack rates and serve as a major source of transmission of influenza (Centers for Disease Control and Prevention, 2011).

- Children should be excluded until the symptoms of the flu resolve.
- Hand washing and sanitization practices in the classroom should be monitored.
- All persons older than 6 months of age should be vaccinated. If there is vaccine shortage, focus will be on children 6 months to 4 years old and household contacts/caregivers of children less than 5 years old.
- Teachers should also protect themselves from the disease by obtaining a yearly flu vaccination.

Hepatitis A

Hepatitis A is an acute infection of the liver. Symptoms include fever, diarrhea, abdominal pain, or yellow discoloration of the skin (jaundice). Some children may be exposed and infected with this disease and do not develop symptoms but can still transmit the infection (Centers for Disease Control and Prevention, 2011). These children are called *carriers* because they can expose others to the disease even though they do not display the symptoms. The use of standard policies for diapering and toileting when caring for children and following hand washing procedures helps to interrupt the spread of this hidden disease.

Rotavirus

Rotavirus is a virus that causes infectious diarrhea. Symptoms include fever, vomiting, and watery diarrhea. It is spread through **fecal–oral transmission**, making it especially contagious among

Reye's syndrome
severe inflammation of the brain and liver caused by giving aspirin to children with certain viral infections

measles
an acute, highly contagious infectious disease that causes fever, rash, and pinkeye

tetanus
a bacterial infection acquired when wounds or lacerations are contaminated with soil that contains the infectious germ

influenza
a highly infectious virus that causes fever, muscle aches, sore throat, cough, and headache; also called simply "the flu"

hepatitis A
a viral illness of the gastrointestinal tract that causes fever, malaise, nausea, abdominal pain, and, in some individuals, dark urine and jaundice

rotavirus
a common cause of infectious diarrhea in children; symptoms include fever, vomiting, and diarrhea

What if . . .

a child in your class has just contracted a second bout of illness involving vomiting and diarrhea? The child's parent has called you to ask why her child is sick again. She wants to know why you have not stopped the spread of this illness. How would you respond?

children under the age of 2 and in settings in which children wear diapers. Children infected with rotavirus shed viral particles in the stool beginning 2 days before, during, and for up to 10 days after the onset of symptoms of the disease (Centers for Disease Control and Prevention, 2011).

Streptococcus Pneumoniae

Streptococcus pneumoniae is a bacterium that commonly causes respiratory infections, ear infections, pneumonia, infection of the bloodstream, and less commonly, meningitis in young children. The symptoms depend on the type of infection. It is transmitted by direct or indirect contact with respiratory secretions. The prevalence of disease has decreased since widespread vaccination was instituted in children in 2000.

Other Common Communicable and Infectious Diseases of Childhood

Many diseases of childhood are not vaccine preventable. These infections are common in settings where children have frequent and prolonged contact with one another such as child care, preschool, and classroom settings. Each of the common infectious diseases has its own set of characteristics and implications for management in the children's setting. Exclusion recommendations vary for each disease, as described in Table 10-2.

Common Colds

Common colds are upper respiratory infections that are caused by more than 200 viruses. Viruses causing the common cold are spread by respiratory modes of transmission, such as sneezing. People with colds often carry the virus on their hands and can infect others in this way for up to 2 hours (Pappas & Hendley, 2012). Colds are also spread through direct contact from nose blowing or contact with germs on surfaces. Some cold viruses can survive on contaminated objects for up to 1 day.

On average, children younger than age 6 experience 6 to 8 colds per year, causing a significant number of missed school days (Pappas & Hendley, 2012). Teachers often experience frequent respiratory illnesses during the first few years that they teach young children.

- The best way to interrupt the cycle of infection is to wash hands frequently in the classroom and to ensure that toys and surfaces are sanitized.
- Teachers should also wash their hands immediately when they return to their homes to help reduce the spread of the cold virus.

Conjunctivitis (Pinkeye)

Conjunctivitis, also called *pinkeye*, is a condition in which the lining of the eye becomes inflamed. Causes include bacterial and viral infections, allergies, chemicals, or trauma. Bacterial and viral infections usually cause white or yellow discharge from the eye, which may cause the eyelids to stick together in the morning. When a child has symptoms of pinkeye, teachers should:

- Contact the child's parents and refer the child to a health care provider.
- Monitor other children and teachers for signs of pinkeye.
- Disinfect any contaminated articles.
- Notify parents to watch for signs of pinkeye.
- Ensure that proper hand washing procedures are being followed.
- Exclude children with symptoms until they have been seen by a health care provider and approved for readmission.

Croup

Croup is a common upper respiratory infection that causes fever, cough, and in some cases, difficulty breathing. It can also cause noisy breathing called

fecal–oral transmission occurs when microscopic amounts of infected feces are transferred to another person's mouth either directly or indirectly (surfaces, objects, etc.)

Streptococcus pneumoniae a bacterium that causes respiratory infections that can lead to invasive or more serious infections such as pneumonia or meningitis

common cold upper respiratory infection that is generally caused by viruses and will not respond to treatment with antibiotics

conjunctivitis condition in which the lining of the eye becomes inflamed due to bacterial or viral infections, allergies, chemicals, or trauma; also called *pinkeye*

croup a viral upper respiratory infection causing fever, runny nose, and barky cough

Pinkeye is a common infection among children.

Exclvir alos enfermos   Enfermedades infecciosas

TABLE 10-2 Exclusion Guidelines

Condition	Length of Time Child Should Be Excluded
Fever (>101 orally or >100 axillary)	When fever has ended or when health care provider recommends
Common colds	No exclusion required
Diarrhea, not contained by child using toilet	When diarrhea resolves or when health care provider recommends
Cough without a fever and not associated with a communicable disease	No exclusion required
Vomiting illness	24 hours after last bout of vomiting; when health care provider recommends
Persistent or intermittent abdominal pain	When pain resolves; when health care provider recommends
Mouth sores with drooling	When health care provider recommends
Rash with fever or behavior change	When health care provider recommends
Purulent (draining) conjunctivitis (pinkeye)	After treatment is initiated
Head lice	No exclusion required
Scabies	After treatment is completed
Tuberculosis	When health care provider recommends
Impetigo	24 hours after treatment is initiated
Streptococcal infection (strep throat)	24 hours after treatment is initiated
Chicken pox	When all sores are dried and crusted
Pertussis (whooping cough)	5 days after treatment has been completed; when health care provider recommends
Mumps	5 days after onset of salivary gland swelling; when health care provider recommends
Hepatitis A	1 week after onset of jaundice and/or illness; when health care provider recommends
Measles	4 days after onset of rash; when health care provider recommends

Sources: American Academy of Pediatrics, 2012; and American Academy of Pediatrics, American Public Health Association, National Resource Center for Health and Safety in Child Care and Early Education, 2011.

stridor. Many different types of viruses cause croup. Incubation periods vary according to the virus, but will be in the typical range of 1 to 3 weeks. Its mode of transmission is droplet.

The cough associated with croup is very distinctive and described as *barky* or similar to the sound of a seal. Stridor and difficulty breathing most often occur during the night, but teachers should watch for these symptoms and notify families if they occur. Children should only be excluded based on the presence of fever or other reasons that prevent the child from participating comfortably, such as breathing difficulty.

Group A Strep Infections

A **group A strep infection** is caused by bacteria that cause three common infections in childhood: strep throat, scarlet fever, and impetigo. Transmission occurs by contact with infected respiratory secretions. The virus is most contagious when children are acutely ill. Symptoms generally include fever, sore throat, and possibly a rash. Children should be excluded from school until they have been treated with antibiotics for 24 hours and no longer have a fever (American Academy of Pediatrics, 2012). It is especially important to recognize strep throat because, if left untreated, other complications can occur such as **acute rheumatic fever**, a serious complication that affects the heart.

Scarlet fever is a condition characterized by fever, sore throat, and a scarlet rash that has texture like sandpaper. Scarlet fever is often treated with antibiotics. **Impetigo** is a skin rash composed of blisters with honey-yellow scabs. Impetigo spreads in children's settings through direct contact with infected individuals or from toys. Children with impetigo should be excluded from the classroom or early childhood setting until 24 hours after treatment has started. Exposed lesions should be covered (American Academy of Pediatrics, 2012).

stridor
noisy breathing

group A strep infection
infection with bacteria that causes three common infections in childhood: strep throat, scarlet fever, and impetigo

acute rheumatic fever
a serious complication of strep infection that affects the heart

scarlet fever
a type of strep infection characterized by fever, sore throat (not always), and a scarlet rash that has a texture like sandpaper

impetigo
a type of strep infection that causes a skin rash marked by pustular lesions

Ear Infections

Ear infections are common infectious diseases of childhood. Bacteria or viruses that infect the eardrum cause ear infections. Infants and children younger than age 3 are at highest risk. Ear infections are not contagious. Therefore, children with ear infections and that accompanying earaches do not need to be excluded from school unless they are too ill to participate in normal activities. If other symptoms such as fever are present, the child may have another illness that is contagious. The child should be separated from the group and parents should be notified.

Fifth Disease

Fifth disease is so called because it is considered the "fifth" of the six common infectious childhood diseases causing a skin rash. The others include measles (first), scarlet fever (second), rubella (third), fourth disease (not recognized today), and roseola (sixth). Symptoms of fifth disease include fever, head and muscle aches, and the characteristic skin rash. Fifth disease is recognized by its intensely red rash, which appears on the cheeks. This is sometimes called "slapped-cheek" rash. As the illness progresses, the rash becomes more diffuse and has a lacy pattern that appears on the trunk. By the time the rash appears, the child is no longer contagious and should not be excluded from the early childhood setting (American Academy of Pediatrics, 2012).

Fifth's disease has a characteristic 'slapped cheek' rash.

Pinworms

Pinworm infection is a common intestinal parasitic infection in young children. Usually if a child is infected with **pinworms**, others in the family are infected as well. Transmission occurs by ingesting microscopic eggs by either the fecal–oral route or by contact with contaminated objects such as toys, bedding, clothing, or toilet seats. Symptoms include itching around the anus, vulva, or genital area, although some children have no symptoms (American Academy of Pediatrics, 2012). Pinworm infections can be difficult to control in early childhood settings. Hand washing is the most effective way to prevent its spread.

Respiratory Syncytial Virus

Respiratory syncytial virus (RSV) is a viral upper respiratory infection that causes fever, runny nose, cough, and possibly wheezing in some children. Transmission is through contact with contaminated secretions. Contaminated droplets can live on surfaces for several hours. The incubation period is 2 to 8 days. Most children have an initial RSV infection during their first year of life. It is common for children to become reinfected later (American Academy of Pediatrics, 2012). RSV in older children and adults looks more like a common cold. Most healthy children with RSV have an uncomplicated upper respiratory infection. Younger infants and premature infants are at higher risk for developing breathing difficulties and requiring hospitalizations for complications.

RSV occurs in epidemics during the winter and spring. Careful cleaning of surfaces and frequent hand washing are the best ways to prevent infection. Exclusion and notification of parents should occur in children with a fever or with breathing difficulties.

Tuberculosis

Tuberculosis (TB) is a potentially harmful lung infection. It is spread through respiratory and airborne transmission when tiny droplets are propelled through the air from coughing or sneezing. Symptoms include fatigue, fever, and chills. Children are most often exposed to TB from infectious adults. For this reason, many children's programs and schools require that teachers be screened for TB as a requirement of employment.

Infections and Acute Illnesses Involving the Skin

Some infections that are highly contagious in children's settings and schools primarily affect the skin. Head lice, scabies, and ringworm are examples of skin-related infectious diseases. Skin infections are often distinguished by the type and color of the rash they cause.

ear infections
infections of the eardrum; some of the most common infectious diseases of childhood

fifth disease
viral illness characterized by fever, headaches, and muscle aches followed by the skin rash

pinworms
a common intestinal parasitic infection in young children

respiratory syncytial virus (RSV)
a common upper respiratory infection that occurs in children and adults most commonly during the winter and spring months

tuberculosis (TB)
an infection that is transmitted by air droplets and can affect many different parts of the body, most commonly causing lung infections

Head Lice

Head lice is an infestation of the hair and scalp that occasionally causes skin discomfort. It is transmitted most commonly by direct contact with the hair of an infested person. It is rare for lice to be transmitted by sharing personal belongings such as combs, hairbrushes, and hats. Lice do not transmit other infections (Frankowski & Bocchini, 2010).

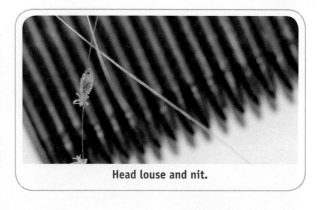

Head louse and nit.

Adult lice and nits (egg casings) are usually most visible behind the ears and near the nape of the neck. Itching is the most common symptom of head lice, but many children have no symptoms at all. Head lice should not be considered a health hazard and are not responsible for the spread of other diseases.

Although head lice do not represent a serious health problem, this infection often causes disruption in the classroom. When an incidence of head lice is discovered, teachers are faced with trying to contain the spread. Parents may respond with disgust when they learn of the presence of lice. To attain better control of this infection, some health authorities have recommended a *no-nit* policy for early childhood programs. This approach requires that children must stay out of school if they have any lice, eggs, or nits in their hair. Nits are the egg casings that may contain a developing louse or they may be empty and not infectious. They can remain visible for up to 6 months on the hair shaft. Consequently, many children have been incorrectly diagnosed with an ongoing head lice infestation and excluded from the classroom. They may have also received unnecessary and potentially toxic repeat treatments of *delousing* pesticides. No-nit policies have not been shown to be effective in controlling head lice infestations and are not recommended (American Academy of Pediatrics, 2012; Frankowski & Bocchini, 2010). It is also important to remember that over-the-counter and prescription treatments for head lice can be quite toxic and are actually considered pesticides.

Rather than excluding children for head lice, early childhood programs and schools are gaining a new perspective on this annoyance. These thoughts are useful when establishing a policy related to head lice (Frankowski & Bocchini, 2010):

- Head lice are a health annoyance rather than a health emergency.
- Head lice are not associated with poor hygiene and poverty. They are opportunistic, moving from head to head without regard to socioeconomic status.
- If head lice are discovered, children do not need to be sent home immediately; a few hours at school will not make a significant difference.
- Families of infected children should be notified. Treatment should be implemented only after infestation has been confirmed. All other families should be notified so they can monitor their children for evidence of lice.
- Treatment for head lice can be started by families using over-the-counter shampoos and other hair treatment products designed to kill head lice. If head lice persist despite this treatment, parents should be encouraged to call their child's health care provider for advice.
- Children can return to school when treatment has been completed.

Some families may refuse to treat their child for head lice. This may be due to a lack of understanding of how to obtain and use lice treatment procedures or lack of funds to purchase the products. Some families may not want to treat their child with chemical pesticides. Teachers should try to help families access information and guidance. Community health authorities or pharmacists may be able to guide them to use treatment methods that meet their needs. Ultimately, the negative impact of missed school days may be more problematic than head lice.

Scabies

Scabies is a skin infection caused by adult female mites that burrow into the skin, causing an intensely itchy, red, and bumpy rash. The rash typically occurs between the fingers, on wrists and

head lice
an infestation of the hair and scalp that is transmitted most commonly by direct contact with the hair of infested people

scabies
a skin infection caused by adult female mites that burrow into the skin, causing an intensely itchy, red, bumpy rash that is seen in a snake-like pattern

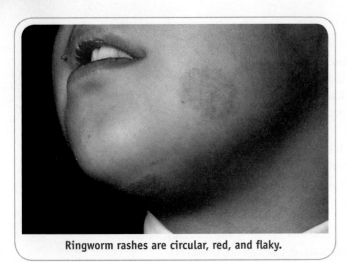

Ringworm rashes are circular, red, and flaky.

elbows, waistline, thighs, genitalia, and buttocks (American Academy of Pediatrics, 2012). Scabies is transmitted through prolonged, personal contact, such as household contacts. Children should be excluded until they have received treatment. Any bedding and clothing the child has used should be washed, including dramatic play clothing. Family members often need treatment as well.

Ringworm

Ringworm is a skin infection caused by a common fungus. It appears as a red and scaly skin rash that has a raised circular shape with healthy skin in the middle. No worm is involved in this condition. It is the shape of the rash that gives the infection its name. Ringworm is transmitted by direct contact with infected humans, animals, or objects. It can occur on the scalp, causing hair loss. Treatment usually involves application of an antifungal cream for several weeks. Children infected with ringworm do not need to stay home from school. Hand washing and maintaining cleanliness in the environment are the most effective ways to prevent spread of the infection.

ringworm
an infection of the skin caused by a fungus

Coxsackie Virus (Hand, Foot, and Mouth Disease)

coxsackie virus
a common childhood respiratory virus causing fever, mouth sores, and skin rash

The **coxsackie virus**, also called *hand, foot, and mouth disease*, causes blisters on the hands, feet, and mouth. It is spread through contact with hands and surfaces that are contaminated with infected droplets from the mouth and nose. Symptoms include fever, loss of appetite, and sore throat, followed by sores in the mouth and gums. A nonitchy rash appears first on the hands and soles of the feet.

The virus spreads easily, but exclusion is not usually recommended because exposure to others has already occurred by the time symptoms are recognized. Children should stay home if the symptoms are painful and they are not able to fully participate with the class. Hand washing and sanitizing surfaces are the most important management strategies.

Bite Wounds

staph infections
a potentially dangerous type of bacteria that is normally found in the skin but can cause infections under certain circumstances

Bite wounds are included here because of their potential to cause infection. Bite wounds are relatively common in children's settings. Bites that do not break the skin should be managed with comfort care and guidance to address the cause of the bite. Bites that break the skin are more serious. Around 10% to 15% of human bites become infected (American Academy of Pediatrics, 2012). Teachers should carefully wash the bite wound, using Standard Precautions, and monitor the child's behavior. Parents should be contacted and encouraged to seek medical evaluation. Bite wounds should be monitored for signs of infection including increasing tenderness, pain, redness, and swelling.

methicillin-resistant *Staphylococcus aureus* (MRSA)
a potentially dangerous type of bacterial skin infection that is resistant to many types of antibiotics

Staph Infections

Staph refers to a type of bacteria that can cause infections and disease. Thirty different types of *Staphylococci* (staph) can infect humans. Many of these bacteria are naturally found in the mouth and nose and most often do not cause infection. However, sometimes breaks in the skin allow the bacteria to enter the body and cause a **staph infection**. **Methicillin-resistant *Staphylococcus aureus* (MRSA)** is a potentially dangerous type of bacterial skin infection that is resistant to many types of antibiotics. It is spread mostly by direct contact with an open wound and, less commonly, by touching items that have touched an infected wound (American Academy of Pediatrics, 2012).

MRSA skin infections are characterized by red, swollen, and painful pimples or boils that usually drain pus. Frequent skin-to-skin contact and potential for children

What if . . .

a child in your toddler group bit another child, creating a bloody wound on the skin? How would you respond to the child who did the biting? What strategies would you use to reduce the risk of this child biting in the future?

to touch contaminated surfaces makes early childhood classrooms likely settings for the spread of infections such as MRSA (Centers for Disease Control, 2010).

- Teachers should be watchful for signs of infection on children's hands and arms.
- Any skin cuts and scrapes should be kept clean and dry. Infected wounds should be covered with clean, dry bandages.
- Children should not share clothing or other personal items if an infection is suspected.

Special attention to hand washing practices is important, and disposable towels should be used. Children who have an identified MRSA infection should not be excluded unless it is not possible to cover the wound.

Bloodborne Infections in the Early Childhood Setting

Bloodborne infections such as hepatitis B or C and HIV are not common in early childhood. The risk of transmission even with contact with blood is low. However, because of the seriousness of these diseases, teachers must have a general understanding of precautions for preventing transmission. Consider this scenario:

> During the middle of the kindergarten year, a new child joins the class. Natasha has been teaching for many years, but this is the first time a child has been accompanied by the school nurse and two other people. They stay through the first full day and tend to drop in to observe the child now and then. The child also has a special health emergency protocol that requires Natasha to contact the school nurse and parents anytime a child in the class is diagnosed with a communicable illness. Natasha wonders if the child has some kind of serious disease. She feels uncomfortable but doesn't know why.

Some diseases tend to cause a great deal of alarm. To address such concerns, teachers need to gather information and learn more about the risks of infection. Using Standard Precautions when managing injuries when blood is present is an important way to increase safety and prevent the spread of bloodborne diseases. In this section we discuss some of the bloodborne diseases that, although uncommon, may occur among young children in child care and school settings.

Hepatitis B

Hepatitis B is a virus that causes chronic inflammation of the liver and can lead to cancer of the liver. Some children who are infected with hepatitis B experience few symptoms but are carriers of the disease. This is more common in children who were not born in the United States.

The virus is spread through contact with blood and body fluids. It can be transmitted from an infected mother to her baby through labor and delivery. Children infected with hepatitis B should not be excluded from the early childhood setting unless they demonstrate high-risk behaviors. Behaviors and situations that may cause spread of the virus include aggressive behaviors (frequent biting or scratching), generalized weeping skin lesions, or bleeding problems (American Academy of Pediatrics, American Public Health Association, National Resource Center for Health and Safety in Child Care and Early Education, 2011).

Parents of children who are infected with hepatitis B are not required to share information about their child's status. If a child is a known carrier or it is unknown and they do exhibit high-risk behaviors, the program director together with a health care provider or local public health authority can determine the appropriateness of having the child participate in the early childhood setting.

Hepatitis C

Hepatitis C infection in children is very rare. It is a virus that causes chronic inflammation of the liver and it is transmitted through blood and body fluids. Exclusion of children from early childhood programs is not recommended (American Academy of Pediatrics, 2012). The risk of transmission by exposure through a skin wound is greater than that of hepatitis B but less than that of HIV

hepatitis B
a virus that causes chronic inflammation of the liver and can lead to cancer of the liver

hepatitis C
a virus that causes chronic inflammation of the liver that is transmitted through blood and body fluids

(American Academy of Pediatrics, American Public Health Association, National Resource Center for Health and Safety in Child Care and Early Education, 2011).

Human Immunodeficiency Virus

human immunodeficiency virus (HIV)
a virus that is transmitted through blood and body fluids; most common form of transmission in children is from mother to fetus or baby

Human immunodeficiency virus (HIV) is a virus that is transmitted through blood and body fluids. Modes of transmission include sexual contact, use of contaminated needles, and mother-to-child transmission during pregnancy or the birth process (American Academy of Pediatrics, 2012). More than 90% of children with HIV in the United States acquired HIV through their mother. Child sexual abuse can be another way children are infected with HIV.

Children infected with HIV pose a challenge in the early childhood setting because management and treatment of their disease is often complex. The infected child is susceptible to infection and steps should be taken to ensure the health and safety of all children so that transmission is prevented. The *National Health and Safety Performance Standards* recommend that the admission of children with HIV be considered on a case-by-case basis, depending on the health, behavior, development, and immune status of the child (American Academy of Pediatrics, American Public Health Association, National Resource Center for Health and Safety in Child Care and Early Education, 2011). The AAP (2009) outlines the following specific recommendations for children with HIV in the school setting:

- School-age children should be allowed to participate without restrictions except in rare cases in which the child has an increased likelihood of exposing others. In these situations, children should be evaluated individually.

- The only people who need to know that the child has HIV are the parents, other guardians, and the physician. The number of people who are aware of the child's condition should be kept to a minimum. The parents have the right to decide whether or not to inform the school.

- All early childhood programs should adopt routine policies for handling blood and blood-contaminated fluids.

- Children with HIV are at increased risk for serious infections or complications from infectious diseases. The child's family should be notified immediately if the child is exposed to an infectious illness.

- More specific guidelines exist for children with HIV participating in athletics.

Although adults with HIV may work with children, Standard Precautions should be taken. The affected adult should also be cautious about possible exposures to infectious diseases.

● INFECTIOUS DISEASES IN IMMIGRANT AND INTERNATIONALLY ADOPTED CHILDREN

refugees
noncitizen immigrants who cannot return to their country due to persecution

In 2008, more than 17,000 children were adopted from outside the United States (Sweet, Sutherland, Ehresmann, & Lynfield, 2011). The highest numbers of adoptions come from China, Ethiopia, Russia, South Korea, and Guatemala (Centers for Disease Control and Prevention, 2010). In addition, a much smaller group of children came to the United States as **refugees**, immigrants who cannot return to their country due to persecution. Little may be known about the health histories of these children. However, these children may have unique risk factors for infectious disease.

Unknown Health History

Certain infectious diseases and illnesses should be ruled out in children with unknown health histories. Although children born in the United States may also have unknown health histories, the health history of children from international backgrounds is more often incomplete and sometimes unknown. Therefore, these children should have regular medical care during which common diseases can be evaluated and addressed.

Having an unknown health history can complicate entry into early childhood programs. Children who come to the United States through international adoption must have a medical examination in their country of origin before coming to the United States. A physician designated by the U.S. State Department must perform the examination, which screens only for selected infectious diseases and serious physical or mental defects that would prevent the issuing of a permanent visa (American Academy of Pediatrics, 2012). Also, children who are adopted internationally are not required to have documentation showing basic immunizations. Adoptive parents must pledge to obtain basic immunizations for their new children.

Records of immunization and history of family disease may not be available. This lack of information can pose a problem for enrollment in an early childhood setting or school. Parents who are adopting children and those who are supporting refugee families need the support and guidance of a medical provider. The health professional will ensure the child receives a full medical evaluation and plan for obtaining the immunizations needed for entry into the children's program.

Common Diseases Among Immigrant and Internationally Adopted Children

Many internationally adopted children are diagnosed with infectious diseases. This is due to the wide array of infectious agents and diseases to which children from international backgrounds may have been exposed. Other countries also do not use the same vaccinations that are required in the United States. Across the world, nutrition, living conditions, prevalence of various diseases, and access to health care vary greatly. Teachers should be aware that these children may have unique health challenges that go undetected. For example, many children from international backgrounds may have no symptoms associated with an infectious disease, making diagnosis more difficult.

A list of infectious diseases that are seen among children from international backgrounds is shown in Figure 10-5. Descriptions of some of these illnesses are given next to assist teachers in recognizing infections among children from international communities.

Viral Hepatitis

The prevalence of hepatitis B infection in internationally born children ranges from 1% to 5% (Centers for Disease Control and Prevention, 2010). Vaccination is highly recommended unless the child's health care provider has deemed it medically unnecessary. Also, many internationally born children have acquired hepatitis A earlier in life; however, it is recommended that these children also obtain the vaccine unless testing determines it is not needed.

Intestinal Infections

The prevalence of intestinal infections in recently adopted children has been found to be as high as 51% (Centers for Disease Control and Prevention, 2010). Screening is recommended after arriving to the United States. These infections are caused by bacteria, viruses, and parasites. When teachers notice any unusual symptoms related to abdominal pain, abnormal appetite, or abnormal stools, parents should be notified and encouraged to have the child evaluated. For the vast majority of these infections, treatment is effective and simple.

Tuberculosis

The risk of tuberculosis is 4 to 6 times greater in adopted children (Centers for Disease Control and Prevention, 2010). All children who were not born in the United States should be screened for tuberculosis.

Cap. 10

FIGURE 10-5   Common Diseases Among Internationally Adopted Children

Bacterial diseases:
- Salmonella
- Syphilis
- Tuberculosis

Viral diseases:
- Typhoid fever
- Cytomegalovirus
- Hepatitis A, B, and C
- HIV

Other diseases:
- Lice
- Scabies
- Intestinal worms (parasites)
- Giardia
- Malaria
- Impetigo

Source: Centers for Disease Control and Prevention, 2010.

PROGRESSIVE PROGRAMS & PRACTICES

Overcoming Infectious Outbreaks

By Eileen Marma, Public Health Nurse, Benton County Health Department, Corvallis, OR

Preventing the spread of infectious diseases and protecting people from exposure is the primary work of a public health nurse in the communicable disease program. The nurses respond to calls from early childhood teachers who have questions about controlling illness in the early childhood setting. The nurses provide information about what to tell parents, and whether a child needs to be excluded from the classroom during the contagious period.

What Challenge Did You Face?

Barbara, a director at an early childhood center that served 72 children called to report that the number of children who were ill had climbed from 1 to 12 within 3 days and she wanted to quickly get this situation under control. She described the symptoms of stomach distress with abrupt onset, which sounded like Norovirus. Norovirus is a highly contagious virus that occurs in settings that bring people together, such as classrooms. It causes gastroenteritis, with symptoms of vomiting and diarrhea, cramps, fatigue, and headaches. It often strikes during the fall and winter months. An outbreak involving 30–50% of the classroom is not unusual. However, it is often overwhelming for the teacher to deal with children getting sick in the classroom if the teaching assistants are also out sick. An affected person may be ill for 24 hours but remains contagious for at least 72 hours after the last symptom of vomiting or diarrhea. Thus, if the ill child or adult returns to the classroom before 72 hours have passed they continue to spread the virus. Without a doctor's diagnosis or laboratory tests, Norovirus is usually suspected as the main cause because it is very common and contagious. Other similar viruses may be stopped using the same precautions.

How Did You Meet the Challenge?
What Was the Teachers' Role?

After Barbara's phone call, I visited the center with an Environmental Health Specialist, who knew the center and made inspections every 6 months. We took written information for teachers and all parents about Norovirus, including how to limit its spread, how to clean up areas infected by vomit, and how long to stay home after symptoms stop. Barbara showed us the classrooms, pointed out a couch that a child had vomited on, and described the precautions they had been using, such as washing toys after toddlers had played with them.

We suggested getting rid of the couch, using a strong bleach solution for cleaning all common surfaces, steam cleaning the carpets, having children wash their hands upon arrival at school, and instructing parents to keep ill children at home for 72 hours after the last symptoms had disappeared. We discussed that the teacher's role in such an outbreak is to recognize a child's symptoms early, report this to the supervisor, and ask the parent to get a diagnosis. If no diagnosis or doctor's visit is made, appropriate precautions should still be taken.

What Was the Outcome?

The teachers worked vigilantly on the suggestions and enforced the stay home for 72 hour rule. A fact sheet on "Tips for Parents on Coping with Norovirus" was sent home that day. When there have been no new ill persons for 4 days during an outbreak, it is considered finished. The teachers and children were, therefore, back in the classrooms, playing and learning.

Barbara commented that it is very important for the early childhood teacher to develop a comfortable relationship with the EH specialist. She also noted that it really helps when the children's center has policies and procedures developed for the most common infectious diseases among young children. "When a child has symptoms, we quickly turn to the protocol to take appropriate precautions."

HIV Infections

The risk of HIV among internationally born children depends on the country of origin and individual risk factors. It is recommended that all immigrant children should have an HIV test, even if they have had one in their country of origin.

Skin Infections

It is not uncommon for children born outside the United States to arrive with various skin infections such as impetigo, scabies, or fungal infections. Teachers should be observant for signs of infection, and children should be referred for medical treatment.

Other Infectious Diseases

Outbreaks of certain infections, such as measles, have been reported among internationally adopted children. Often, adoptions from the orphanages where children were living are temporarily suspended until the outbreak is controlled. Typically these illnesses are resolved before these children enroll in child care, preschool, or school.

Culture and Management of Infectious Diseases

Families from diverse cultures often have culturally based perspectives about the cause and treatment of infections and disease. For example, Native American families may view illnesses as a result of a disruption of the spirits and may not identify germs as the cause of infections (Ball, Bindler, & Cowen, 2012). Families may turn to religion, herbs, acupuncture, and a variety of other traditional healing practices for illnesses. It is important for teachers to communicate with families in order to protect the health of the child, control disease spread, and honor the family's beliefs.

Regardless of race or ethnicity, each family has its own set of personal and philosophical beliefs about treatment of disease. Personal preferences and beliefs may lead families to use nontraditional forms of medicine. **Complementary and alternative medicine (CAM)** refers to the use of healing practices that are not considered part of conventional medical practices. Examples include herbs, vitamins, homeopathic remedies, and nutritional supplements. Estimates of the use of CAM practices with children are as high as 60% and more common in children with special health care needs and children who are partially vaccinated or unvaccinated (Ben-Arye, et al., 2011).

The use of CAM is typically integrated with traditional medical practices. Examples of CAM that teachers may see with respect to infections are the use of herbal remedies such as eardrops for ear infections or supplements like echinacea or vitamin C for common colds. If families ask teachers to administer any supplement or medications, regardless of the type, the proper procedure for the administration of medicines should be followed in each case.

complementary and alternative medicine (CAM) healing practices that are not considered part of conventional medical practices

> ## What if . . .
> a parent provided you with a baggie of supplements to give their child at lunch time? How would you begin a conversation with the family about their request?

● SUMMARY

Young children are especially vulnerable to infectious disease. They need to explore and touch their environments as they learn about their world. This is their natural style of study. But frequent touching of toys, objects, and surfaces may introduce children to germs that can cause infection. Children rely on their teachers and families to protect them from disease when they can, and to care for them if sickness occurs.

Diseases can be caused by infectious agents that are transmitted easily in early childhood and school settings. Some infections cause symptoms such as diarrhea, respiratory illness, rashes, fever, and vomiting, and these symptoms may be experienced when children are in the classroom. Teachers who recognize these signs of illness are prepared to separate children from the group and care for them until their family is contacted. Teachers also need to be aware of their own risk for contracting infections and take steps to keep disease free.

A variety of preventive practices help teachers to reduce the spread of disease in the classroom. Immunizations, hand washing, and daily health checks are just a few of the ways that teachers help to control infections. Standard Precautions, involving the use of gloves and careful cleaning and sanitization practices, are important strategies to protect children from bloodborne and other diseases. Teachers also have an important responsibility to teach children how they can be participants in keeping themselves healthy. This is an important goal of wellness and provides children with healthful skills that they can use in the future.

Although teachers are not usually medical professionals and should not be diagnosing disease or offering recommendations for treatment, it is important for them to be aware of the many infections that commonly occur among young children. Recognition of symptoms of disease helps teachers plan management strategies in the classroom that interrupt the spread of disease. Some children may be at greater risk for disease. Children from international settings may have been exposed to diseases that are less frequent in the United States. Teachers become keenly aware of children's typical behaviors and may be the first to recognize when illness is developing. They are important participants in the process of caring for children when infections occur.

Overall, infectious disease is a common occurrence during the early years. When teachers participate in reducing the spread and incidence of disease, they are contributing to children's health and well-being. Fewer days ill results in more days of exploration and learning for young children.

KEY TERMS

Acute rheumatic fever	Group A strep infection	Pinworms
Airborne transmission	*Haemophilus influenzae* type b (Hib)	Pneumonia
Bacteria	Head lice	Refugees
Bloodborne transmission	Hepatitis A	Respiratory syncytial virus (RSV)
Chicken pox	Hepatitis B	Reye's syndrome
Common cold	Hepatitis C	Ringworm
Communicable diseases	Human immunodeficiency virus (HIV)	Rotavirus
Complementary and alternative medicine (CAM)	Impetigo	Scabies
	Incubation period	Scarlet fever
Conjunctivitis	Infectious diseases	Sinusitis
Coxsackie virus	Influenza	Standard Precautions
Croup	Measles	Staph infections
Diarrhea	Meningitis	*Streptococcus pneumoniae*
Ear infection	Methicillin-resistant *Staphylococcus aureus* (MRSA)	Stridor
Epidemic		Tetanus
Fecal–oral transmission	Mode of transmission	Tuberculosis (TB)
Fifth disease	Parasite	Virus
Fungi	Pertussis	
Germs	Pharyngitis	

REVIEW QUESTIONS

1. Describe the four modes of transmission for infections. Name two infections that are transmitted by each mode.

2. Describe strategies teachers can use to control the spread of infections.

3. Influenza is still seen in early childhood settings despite vaccination. Describe the mode of transmission and symptoms for this infection.

4. How are head lice transmitted? What policies in early childhood can minimize disease spread?

DISCUSSION STARTERS

1. As discussed in Chapter 1, we know that the quality of child care has an impact on children's overall health and wellness. What impact do you think the quality of child care has on the control of infectious diseases?

2. Opinions vary related to allowing children to attend school when they have head lice. What are the policies related to head lice in the early childhood and school programs in your area? Do you think a "no-nit" policy should be imposed?

3. HIV is an infectious illness that harbors a significant amount of stigma even in children. Although confidentiality is well established for this illness, a family may choose to be open about their child, or a school-age child may discuss his or her infection with friends. How do you think this might influence the child's relationships with his or her peers? How do you think teachers or other staff members would react to the news that a child with HIV is in the classroom?

PRACTICE POINTS

1. Explore the child care licensing requirements in your area. Are preemployment health assessments required for teachers?

2. Call the local health authority to learn about the requirements for teachers with respect to screening for tuberculosis. Is the TB skin test required?

3. Imagine that a child in your Head Start classroom has been sent home with a fever and is diagnosed with chicken pox a few days later. Draft a policy that addresses notification of parents as well as controlling the spread of this infectious disease.

WEB RESOURCES

Centers for Disease Control and Prevention, Influenza
www.cdc.gov/flu

Centers for Disease Control and Prevention, National Center for Infectious Diseases,
Infectious Disease Information: Childhood Diseases
www.cdc.gov/ncidod/Diseases/children/diseases.htm

MyEducationLab™

Go to Topic 8 (Infectious Diseases) in the MyEducationLab (www.myeducationlab.com) for your course, where you can:

- Find learning outcomes for Infectious Diseases along with the national standards that connect to these outcomes.
- Complete Assignments and Activities that can help you more deeply understand the chapter content.
- Apply and practice your understanding of the core teaching skills identified in the chapter with the Building Teaching Skills and Dispositions learning units.

- Check your comprehension on the content covered in the chapter by going to the Study Plan in the Book Resources for your text. Here you will be able to take a chapter quiz, receive feedback on your answers, and then access Review, Practice, and Enrichment activities to enhance your understanding of chapter content.

eleven
Teaching Children with Special Health Care Needs

learning outcomes

AFTER READING THIS CHAPTER, YOU SHOULD BE ABLE TO:

1. Explain special health needs and discuss how these needs affect children's health, functional status, and family dynamics.

2. Identify the goals of inclusion and describe how educating classmates about children's special health care needs helps to create a climate of welcome for all children.

3. Describe the kinds of information needed before teachers administer medications in the early childhood setting.

4. Discuss how partnering with families supports both children and teachers in the inclusive classroom.

5. Identify at least five special health care needs and discuss general strategies teachers can use to support children in the classroom.

Jeremy is a 5-year-old African American boy who will join Mary's kindergarten class in the fall. His medical history is complicated. He was born extremely prematurely, at 25 weeks gestation, with a birth weight of less than 2 pounds. He stayed in the hospital for nearly 2½ months after his birth. The ventilator was required for 6 weeks to assist him with breathing and he had bleeding around his brain, which was significant but not uncommon for his degree of prematurity. Consequently, Jeremy now has several medical problems that impact his learning. He has cerebral palsy, which mainly affects his lower limbs. He also has asthma and a visual impairment requiring corrective lenses, and he has recently been diagnosed with attention deficit disorder.

Mary has had experience with many children who have special developmental needs, but Jeremy's health history is unique. She wonders how his medical problems will impact his learning in the classroom and what resources are available through the school to learn more about these health conditions. She wants to learn more about Jeremy so she can start planning how to help him adjust to the classroom setting. Mary makes notes of her questions. Then she gathers her notebook and walks down the hall to the school library where Jeremy's kindergarten transition meeting is scheduled in a few minutes. One school year is ending, but Mary is already starting to think about next fall and the important experience that is ahead for this young child.

Teaching young children is an exciting profession that combines the enjoyment of helping young children grow and discover their world with the responsibility of ensuring children's health and well-being. This responsibility adds challenge and focus to the endeavor. For many teachers like Mary, the most rewarding aspect of their work comes from crafting individualized approaches that support the learning of children with unique needs.

In this chapter we will discuss children's special health care needs and explore the ways in which a child's exceptional health care needs affect his or her development and the context of the family. We will also discuss laws related to children who have special health needs and briefly explore treatments that are used to improve children's health outcomes. Finally, we will describe the various health needs and discuss some of the ways these conditions are managed in the early childhood and school setting. Understanding children's special health care needs and making purposeful adjustments to the classroom setting are crucial aspects of teaching that characterize the teacher's role in helping children reach their full potential.

UNDERSTANDING CHILDREN'S SPECIAL HEALTH CARE NEEDS

More children with chronic medical conditions are enrolled in early childhood programs and included in school classrooms than ever before. Nearly every early childhood classroom includes **children with special health care needs**. This highlights the need for teachers to be prepared to serve children who have a variety of medical needs and to prepare their classrooms and curriculum to support these learners.

Defining Special Health Care Needs

Children with special health care needs are those who "have or are at risk for a chronic physical, developmental, behavioral, or emotional condition and who also require health and related services of a type or amount beyond that required by children generally" (U.S. Department of Health and Human Services, Health Resources and Services Administration, Maternal and Child Health Bureau, 2008). This definition encompasses a wide assortment of medical diagnoses with a range of symptoms and severity that have an impact on education.

Meeting the needs of children with special health conditions is a high national priority as reflected in *Healthy People 2020* (U.S. Department of Health and Human Services, 2012). To support children with special health care needs so they can develop to their full potential, their health care and educational needs must be widely addressed: at home, at school, and in the community. Children's special health care diagnoses, treatments, and educational interventions and outcomes are unique for each child and change as the child grows and develops.

Teachers make a significant contribution to the education and development of children with special health care needs. They do this by being:

- *Capable and willing*—to learn about the child's unique health care and educational needs.
- *Adaptable and able*—to envision and implement appropriate adjustments in the classroom and curriculum.
- *Reflective and responsive*—to identify successful educational interventions and put them into practice when needed.

In the opening case scenario, Mary demonstrated these engaging and proactive characteristics. When she learned she would be teaching a child with special health care needs, she quickly began to outline the kinds of information she would need to be effective as Jeremy's teacher.

Prevalence of Children with Special Health Care Needs

In 2005–2006, 13.9%, or more than 10 million U.S. children, had a special health care need. Nearly 22% of U.S. households had at least one child with a special health care need (U.S. Department of Health and Human Services, Health Resources and Services Administration, Maternal

children with special health care needs children who have or are at risk for a chronic physical, developmental, behavioral, or emotional condition and who also require health and related services of a type or amount beyond that generally required

MyEducationLab™

Visit the MyEducationLab for *Nutrition, Health, and Safety for Young Children* to enhance your understanding of chapter concepts with a personalized Study Plan. You'll also have the opportunity to hone your teaching skills through video-based Assignments and Activities, as well as Building Teaching Skills and Dispositions lessons.

and Child Health Bureau, 2008). The two most common special health conditions are asthma and allergies. The increase in the number of children with special health care needs in classrooms is due to both increased inclusion as well as a growing prevalence of certain conditions. Inclusion of children increased significantly after the Individuals with Disabilities Education Act (IDEA) was adopted.

The incidence of some health conditions has increased as well. For example, the prevalence of premature infants like Jeremy in the opening case scenario is increasing. Although the survival rates for premature infants are higher, some of these babies are left with medical conditions such as cerebral palsy, intellectual disabilities, or other disabilities that will impact the child's ability to learn.

Children with special health care needs (CSHCN) represent a diverse group. Special health care needs are present in families of all income levels, races, ethnicities, religions, and cultures. Black, non-Hispanic children have higher rates of special health care needs than children of other ethnicities (Oswald, Bodurtha, Gilles, Christon, & Ogston, 2011). Prevalence rates for some health conditions vary according to geographic areas. In the southeastern United States, sickle cell anemia is much more common than in West Virginia, where cystic fibrosis is a more prevalent condition.

Functional Status

functional status
term used to describe the characteristics that are most important to parents and teachers: how well a child can function in the community, in the classroom, and in relationships

Functional status describes the characteristics that are most important to parents and teachers: how well a child can function in the community, in the classroom, and in relationships. The World Health Organization advocates for emphasizing children's functional status and capabilities rather than focusing on children's limitations and disability. This puts the focus on the child and not on the special health care condition or disability. One way this is addressed is through simple vocabulary. When discussing children who have special medical conditions the child's name is used first, followed by the identifying characteristic. The phrase *children with diabetes* reinforces the concept of thinking of children as people with many complexities, qualities, and abilities. The phrase *diabetic children*, by comparison, puts more (and unnecessary) focus on the medical condition and limitations.

To achieve positive functional status, children with special health care needs may require specialized health care services. These services include prescription medications, special diets, medical equipment, or frequent use of health care services. Specialized services may be offered within the health care system or through special educational services. Here are some examples of specialized health care services:

- Specialist care (pediatric cardiology, pulmonology, neurology).
- Mental health care.
- Dental care.
- Physical therapy, occupational therapy, speech therapy.
- Preventive care.
- Eyeglasses/vision care.
- Prescription medications.

Down syndrome
a genetic condition that causes mental and physical challenges

When children have unmet health care needs, many aspects of their lives are affected. A child with **Down syndrome**, a genetic condition that causes intellectual and physical challenges, needs regular vision care because of the high likelihood of needing corrective lenses or other treatment. Without these interventions, the child's health, wellness, and learning are negatively impacted.

Nearly 14% of children less than 18 years of age have special health care needs and the prevalence is increasing. Despite the wide range of diagnoses and functional limitations among CSHCN, they all have an increased need for services (Strickland et al., 2011). Despite needing additional health care services, CSHCN are at risk for receiving disparities in the health care they receive (Oswald, et al., 2011).

Many CSHCN also have limited capability to participate in the activities of daily living. These challenges are called **functional limitations**. About 85% of families of CSHCN report at least one functional limitation. The following are the most common (Lollar, Hartzell, & Evans, 2012):

- Difficulty breathing or other respiratory problems
- Difficulty with learning, understanding, or paying attention
- Feeling anxious or depressed
- Speaking, communication, or being understood

Any of these or other functional limitations will impact the educational setting.

Impact on Families

Special health care needs can add complexity to family life, depending on the type and degree of the child's challenges. Some families may be better able to cope than others depending on socioeconomic status and other family stressors. Families with children who have special health needs have added financial stress even if health insurance is available. These stresses have an impact on children's education.

Children with special health care needs may have different types of functional limitations.

functional limitations challenges that limit a child's ability to participate in activities of daily living

Financial Issues

Financial problems often pose additional challenges to families with CSHCN. Children living in low-income families are more likely to have certain health conditions such as asthma, emotional and behavioral problems, learning disabilities, and obesity (National Center for Child Poverty, 2011). Over 19% of families of CSHCN identify a significant financial burden. Families of CSHCN have increased expenses due to health care services, special foods, equipment, utilities (heating, water), clothing, and medications (Lindley & Mark, 2010; Parish, Rose, Dababnah, Yoo, & Cassiman, 2012). Families of children who have more complex health care needs experience even more financial burden as well as unemployment. Over half of these families report financial difficulties and employment loss (Kuo, Cohen, Agrawal, Barry, & Casey, 2011).

Despite being insured, many families of CSHCN still report that their health insurance does not meet their child's needs (Lindley & Mark, 2010). For example, not all prescription medications and therapies are covered by insurance. The consequences of these challenges can be apparent in schools. For example, a child with asthma who does not have an inhaler because her family could not afford it could have symptoms in school that affect her participation and learning.

Educational Impact

Because the health of children is so closely connected to their educational performance, children with special health care needs face unique educational challenges. Identified challenges include more days absent from school, poorer student engagement, behavioral problems, and lower academic achievement (Forrest, Bevans, Riley, Crespo, & Louis, 2011).

Attendance is also more of a problem for CSHCN. Irregular attendance places children at a disadvantage in the classroom where learning builds on previous lessons the child may have missed. These issues double the negative impact on learning for children with special health care needs: The health challenge itself may impact the child's ability to learn and also reduce the child's participation and attendance. Special attention is needed to build on the child's capacity to learn and to address gaps that may occur with irregular attendance.

What if . . .

a child in your classroom shows symptoms of asthma? The family has not accessed medical advice, so you have no guidance about how to manage the child's needs in the classroom. You have called the child's family to pick him up early from school, but this means the family member had to leave work and will lose pay because of the missed time. How will you manage this situation? What resources are available to you?

● PLANNING INCLUSIVE CLASSROOMS

Children with medical conditions bring special health-related issues and needs to the early child-hood setting. These needs include a range of activities such as administering medications and making accommodations in the classroom environment. Because children's health care needs permeate all aspects of their lives, it is important for teachers to understand them and learn how best to address each situation so that children will have more positive health outcomes.

Ensuring Access to Education

The federal Individuals with Disabilities Education Act describes the requirements regarding provision of services to children with disabilities across the nation. Children with special health care needs are identified for service through the IDEA when their health condition interrupts their ability to learn. The IDEA ensures that children with disabling conditions are able to participate in and be supported to progress in general education. The IDEA describes other health impairment as follows:

> Other health impairment means having limited strength, vitality, or alertness, including a heightened alertness to environmental stimuli, that results in limited alertness with respect to the educational environment, that:
>
> - Is due to chronic or acute health problems such as asthma, attention deficit disorder or attention deficit hyperactivity disorder, diabetes, epilepsy, a heart condition, hemophilia, lead poisoning, leukemia, nephritis, rheumatic fever, sickle cell anemia, and Tourette syndrome; and
> - Adversely affects a child's educational performance.

Three specialized plans describe the services available:

- *Individualized family services plan (IFSP):* This early intervention plan for children ages 0 to 3 years is intended to support and provide services that are targeted to improving the child's developmental progress.
- *Individualized education program (IEP):* This plan is for children in the school setting ages 3 to 21 years who need special education services due to cognitive, motor, social, and communication impairments.
- *Individualized health plan (IHP):* This plan is developed for students who have medical conditions that require management or treatment in the school setting. The IHP may be written as a component of the child's IEP.

Early childhood teachers and schools rely on the support of the local education agency (LEA) charged with administering and overseeing the implementation of the IDEA in the state or locality. This is often the public board of education or other authority that is responsible for evaluating children for participation in early intervention services and for providing needed services. This agency participates with families and schools to create a plan that meets the child's educational needs and addresses the impact of special health conditions.

Some early childhood programs benefit from training provided by the LEA to implement the child's education and health plan. The guidance of a medical consultant is also beneficial. Some school districts have school nurses available to see children and advise teachers in the care of a child with special health needs in the school setting. The *Policy Point* discusses the role of school nurses as a resource for children with special health care needs, their families, and teachers.

Supporting Appropriate Inclusion

The trend for providing services to CSHCN has moved to an inclusion model. Inclusion focuses on educating children to the greatest extent possible in typical classrooms. The goals of inclusion are access, participation, and support (Division for Early Childhood & National Association for the Education of Young Children, 2009).

Federal laws do not require inclusion, but the IDEA does require that children be educated in the least restrictive environment appropriate to meet their unique needs (U.S. Department of

▶ Early intervention involves special services and inclusive classroom experiences for young children with special needs. As you watch this video, notice the different kinds of services that may be provided. How is inclusion beneficial to both children with special needs and those who are typically developing?

POLICY POINT The Role of School Nurses for Children with Special Health Care Needs

One of the goals of *Healthy People 2020* is to ensure that schools have one school nurse for every 750 students. Even more nurses are recommended for schools enrolling a high number of children with special health care needs. School nurses are directly involved with children's existing and potential health problems. They provide screening and referral for health conditions. School nurses also provide case management services and collaborate with family and community members regarding children's health. Most importantly for children with special health care needs, the school nurse is the health expert for the teams developing the individualized education program (IEP).

School nurses support teachers regarding services for children with special health care needs by:

1. Assessing health complaints. This is particularly important for children who are at risk for acute illnesses such as asthma, cystic fibrosis, and diabetes.
2. Administering medications.
3. Identifying and managing children's health care needs that affect educational achievement.

Recent economic constraints have reduced the number of nurses assigned to schools, hindering the *Healthy People 2020* goal. Early childhood professionals and administrators are important advocates for this service and other forms of school health care support.

Source: Council on School Health, 2008; Healthy People 2020, 2012.

Education, n.d.). Teachers are important participants in making placement decisions for children with special health care needs. Along with families and the representatives of the LEA, each classroom is evaluated as a potential educational placement. Decisions are based on the needs of the child, her or his peers, and the classroom's ability to meet those needs.

Teachers may be asked to monitor the child's health status and provide individualized care. Some needs may address making relatively minor changes in the environment. Others may include changing diapers, suctioning a **tracheostomy tube** (a surgically placed tube that allows air and oxygen to enter the lungs through the neck), or feeding a child with a **gastrostomy tube**, a tube placed through the abdominal wall into the stomach in order to feed children who are unable to eat orally.

Most teachers have not received education about serving children's health needs and may need specialized training to build confidence. They need access to resources to turn to for consultation. In addition, they need to be oriented to strategies that can help support children's access to the environment and participation in the learning activities. Teachers are part of a service team that plans, implements, and evaluates the effectiveness of services provided for children with special needs. They follow the guidance provided by the medical professionals and most often have either daily or periodic support of early intervention specialists and therapists. One aspect of inclusion that falls under the teacher's responsibilities is creating an environment in which all children are welcomed and encouraged to thrive.

tracheostomy tube
a surgically placed tube that allows air and oxygen to enter the lungs through the neck

gastrostomy tube
a tube placed through the abdominal wall into the stomach in order to feed children who are unable to eat orally

Administering Medications

Many children with special health care needs are given prescription medications. They may require medications during the school day. To safely manage this, early childhood settings should have a written policy describing how medications are to be administered. Persons administering medications should be familiar with the policy and receive appropriate training to ensure safety. Recommended standards are available to guide best practice procedures for medication administration. For example, the *National Health and Safety Performance Standards* recommend that medication administration be allowed when a health care provider orders a prescription or over-the-counter medicine with permission from the parent/guardian.

Because medication errors can occur easily, all schools and child care facilities should use a standard form that explains the details of medication administration. A standard form for this purpose is shown in Figure 11-1. Guidelines for the administration of medications include the following

FIGURE 11-1   Medication Administration Permission Form

Medication Permission and Administration Permission Form

The staff of the King Avenue Child Development Center has been asked by
(Parent/Guardian) _____ to administer medication to
(Child) _____ during the school day.
In order to comply with this request and in accordance with our state law, we need the
following information from you.

MEDICAL PROVIDER INFORMATION

Health care provider signature _____ Date _____
Health care provider name _____
Address _____
Phone _____
Fax _____

DIRECTIONS FOR ADMINISTRATION OF MEDICATION

Child's name _____ Date of birth _____
Name of medication _____
Purpose of medication _____
Starting date _____ Ending date _____
Dosage _____
When to give medication _____
Time(s) to be given _____
How medication is given: By mouth _____ By injection _____ Other _____

Special instructions

_____

Signs or symptom(s) to watch for _____
Possible side effects or reactions _____
Adaptations suggested for the classroom _____

_____

When to call the parent or health care provider regarding symptoms or if the child fails to
respond to treatment

_____

_____

Signs that urgent care is needed _____

_____

PARENT PERMISSION

*I request and authorize the King Avenue Child Development Center to administer this
medication in accordance with the instructions provided by my child's medical provider.*

_____

_____

Parent or Guardian Signature   Date

_____   _____

Parent or Guardian Name   Phone

_____   _____

_____

(American Academy of Pediatrics, American Public Health Association, National Resource Center for Health and Safety in Child Care and Early Education, 2011):

- Orders specifying medical need, medication, dosage, and length of time medication is given should be provided by health professional.
- Medications should be labeled and in the original container, and label should include child's name, date filled, prescribing clinician's name, pharmacy name and phone number, dosage instructions, and warnings.
- Observe, report, and document any reactions or side effects from medications.
- Document the time and amount of medicine given, and the name of the person administering the medication.

Partnering with Families

Communicating with families is essential to appropriate education and care of children with special medical conditions. Developing partnerships with families has a positive impact on children's education and well-being. When children have special health care needs, communication is of even greater importance. Establishing a good working relationship starts when children with health needs are enrolled and are preparing to join the class. Enrollment materials gather many details about a child's condition and special health considerations. Review of the health history further clarifies aspects of the child's need. However, discussing the plan for the child's entry into the early childhood environment directly with a family member is the most important component of a successful transition.

Families may understandably have many worries about their child with special health care needs. They need to feel assured that the teacher is aware of their child's condition and is ready to assume responsibility for the child's safety and well-being. Direct conversation helps to build trust between the family and the teacher. It also contributes to a greater understanding of the relevant issues and strategies. Language and culture are important considerations when building this trusting relationship. Sometimes teachers may tend to communicate less with families who are not English speakers. Some parents may struggle to explain their child's complex health condition and needs. Teachers are responsible for ensuring that every family has the support they need to fully discuss their child's special health care needs. For example, it is not appropriate to use other children in the family as interpreters, so arranging for translation services or encouraging the family to invite a trusted friend to assist with the discussion are examples of ways to ensure full communication and to build an effective partnership.

muscular dystrophy
a progressive disease of the muscles causing progressive weakness, susceptibility to pulmonary infections, and premature death

Once children are enrolled, teacher and family communication focuses on exchanging information about the child's health and well-being during the school day. Families of children with asthma need to know if the child has been coughing, having difficulty with physical activity, or refusing to use the inhaler. A family whose child has **muscular dystrophy**, a genetic condition that causes progressive weakness, needs to know if the child is experiencing emotional problems due to his challenges. Similarly the teacher needs to be informed about any changes in the child's health status or experiences at home that might impact the child's participation in classroom activities.

To facilitate communication with families in her preschool, Janna creates a small notebook for each child with special health care needs. The notebook is placed in the child's cubby-locker. At orientation she describes how the notebook is for both the teacher and the family to record notes for the other. When Janna wants to communicate a health-related message she writes a note in the log. When the family picks up the child, they check the notebook to read the teacher's message. Similarly the family can leave a message for the teacher. This

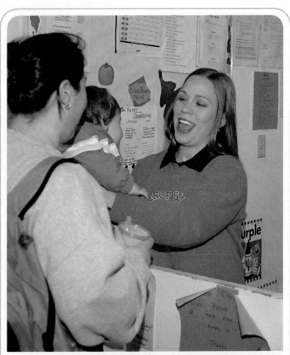

Families need reassurance that their child with special health care needs will be safe in the early childhood setting.

method helps Janna remember to tell the family about important health observations. Karin uses a different approach. The children in her second-grade class ride the bus, so she does not see families very often. Karin communicates with families about children's special medical needs through e-mail.

Educating Classmates

Some children's medical conditions are apparent, others may not be obvious. When teachers realize, however, that classmates are aware of a child's special health care needs, they plan activities to educate classmates about the medical condition. Young children may view aspects that are unique about a child's appearance, behavior, or interaction in the classroom as "different" or "strange." This is due to children's natural interest and curiosity in things that are different and the potential to be confused and possibly frightened by new situations. Children may be naturally curious about why a child receives medication or a special diet or why a child does not participate in running games. They may also have fears and wonder, "Could that happen to me?" When curiosity or fear is displayed in a negative way, the child with special health care needs may suffer socially.

The potential for negative social interactions is an important reason for educating classmates about a child's medical condition and special needs in the classroom. Sometimes classmates pester or make fun of children with medical conditions. They might imitate the child's movements or laugh at the child's efforts. Teachers need to be aware of these potential reactions and be prepared with strategies to address them.

Children who begin to wear corrective lenses while they are attending the early childhood program may become the center of interest and attention. Sometimes this interest takes a negative course. For example, another child may reach out to grab at the child's new glasses. Or children may call the child names or say the child looks "weird." Teachers must anticipate and intervene in such situations, describing how corrective lenses help the child to see and explaining that the glasses are precious and important tools for the child. Teachers might have a pair of corrective lenses available to let the other children touch and try on. This approach addresses children's curiosity and invites conversation and questions about vision problems and how they are managed.

In a similar way young children are capable of learning about other medical conditions. When the mystery is removed, children become accustomed to the management of the health need in the classroom; the novelty of the disability wears off, and children are more likely to treat the child with the special health care need in a typical way. Talking with classmates about a child's special health needs helps to address curiosity, lack of understanding, and fear and builds the desired sense of normalcy. This is an important aspect of creating class groups that are caring communities.

Educating classmates about children's special health care needs requires attention to developmentally appropriate messages. Very young children require short and clear explanations such as "I am helping Jax to feel better" or "D'shay needs to take this medicine to help him feel better. You can watch if you want." Older children are capable of learning more details about a condition and the activities that support the child in the classroom. Strategies to support such discussions include the following:

- Begin by discussing experiences that are familiar to the classmates. Ask children if they have ever been sick. Talk about what that felt like. Help children identify ways their family helped them to feel better, such as resting, eating healthy foods, or taking medicine.

- Show the connection between children's common experiences and the child's special health care need. Name the child's medical

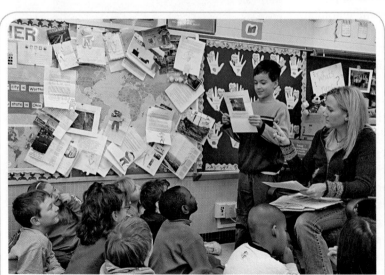

Educating classmates about a child's medical condition addresses children's curiosity and increases understanding of the activities used to manage the special health care need in the classroom.

condition and briefly explain what it is and how it is somewhat similar to other children's health experiences. Talk about how the chronic condition is managed or treated. Identify the ways you help the child care for his or her condition in the class. Explain how the treatment helps the child.

- Talk about how the child developed the special medical condition. Explain if the child was born with the condition or if it was the result of an accident. Clarify whether the condition is contagious.

- Invite children to ask questions. Treat each question as an expression of legitimate interest and concern. Help children learn how to form questions about health.

- Discuss inappropriate interactions with the child if any have been observed. Talk about ways that children can advocate for appropriate treatment of those who have special conditions.

- Include the child with the special health care needs as a leader in the discussion if appropriate. Help the child with special health needs gain strategies and skills for describing and talking about her or his own medical conditions with others.

- Engage family members in classroom discussions. Many families may choose to lead the discussion about their child's needs. You can assist in this process by ensuring that the family member is familiar with appropriate ways to communicate complex information to the particular age group.

- After holding such discussions, observe children's interactions in the class. Reflect on whether the classroom discussion was helpful in supporting positive interactions among the children with special health care needs and their classmates.

When communicating about a child's special health care need, teachers should avoid drawing undue attention to the child's limitations. Rather the goal is to reinforce the similarities that help children to befriend one another. For example, Paula has cerebral palsy. In the classroom she moves with the support of her walker. When the class takes a field trip to the library, Paula's classmates take turns pulling her in a wagon. Paula sits near the back of the wagon to make room for the bag of books the class is returning to the library. As they travel, they talk together about their favorite books and the topics they want to explore next. When they return to the classroom with their new bag of books, Sam turns to Paula and says, "Thanks for carrying the books." The *Teaching Wellness* feature provides other ideas to support recognition of sameness among classmates.

Supports are available to help teachers guide discussions about particular medical conditions. Picture books are a good way to introduce conversation about children's special medical conditions. Reading books such as those suggested below as part of the year-round reading options reinforces the message that special health care needs are part of the everyday world, just like caterpillars and butterflies! Here are some examples of books for young children with special health needs:

- *Lara Takes Charge* (for kids with diabetes, their friends, and siblings) by Rocky Lang and Sally Huss.
- *Taking Asthma to School* (Special Kids in School, Vol. 2) by Kim Gosselin.
- *Taking Food Allergies to School* by Ellen Weiner, Kim Gosselin.

MANAGING SPECIAL HEALTH CARE NEEDS

Learning about chronic health conditions in early childhood equips teachers to be attuned to their impact on children's health and learning. Familiarity with the causes and impacts of special health needs also supports teachers in enrollment conversations with families. It prepares teachers to identify information they need to support the child's positive transition and participation in the classroom.

In the following sections we provide an overview of a variety of medical conditions that affect young children. Examples of strategies used to manage each medical condition in the classroom are

Dental caries are common and an important health condition of early childhood.

provided as a first step in understanding the many ways teachers support children with special health care needs. These suggestions do not replace the guidance provided by health care providers and early intervention specialists. Because most teachers do not have medical training, teachers work in partnership with medical providers, early intervention specialists, and families. This partnership carries the responsibility of planning, implementing, and monitoring appropriate management strategies to support the appropriate inclusion of children with special health care needs in the classroom environment and to address health needs that arise in the early childhood setting.

Conditions Related to the Immune System

Children's **immune systems** are responsible for controlling infections and responding to foreign substances that enter the body. Dental caries, asthma, environmental allergies, and eczema are common health conditions associated with the immune system.

Dental Caries

immune system
responsible for controlling infections and responding to foreign substances that enter the body

Dental caries affects 24% of children ages 2–5 years. Over 55% of Mexican American children, 43.4% of African American children, and 38.6% of non-Hispanic White children are affected (Kawashita, 2011). Texas and California rank the worst for caries and Hispanics are most at risk (California Dental Association, 2011). This condition is a destruction of the tooth enamel caused by an interaction of bacteria, inappropriate feeding practices, lifestyle habits, and individual factors. Both primary and permanent teeth are affected and can be destroyed by the decay. The consequences of the disease are not just limited to the teeth, but can have widespread health effects over the course of a lifetime. These are risk factors for dental caries (Kawashita, 2011):

- Poor maternal dental health or hygiene
- Frequent and prolonged consumption of sugared beverages
- Insufficient exposure to fluoride
- Poverty and ethnicity
- Lack of dental insurance coverage

It is also interesting to note that transmission of harmful oral bacteria has been documented in groups of children in child care or preschool (Kawashita, 2011).

Over half of children with caries are from families living in poverty. Even children covered by Medicaid have low rates of receiving adequate preventive dental care. Fewer than one in five children with Medicaid have a preventive dental visit every year (Bugis, 2012).

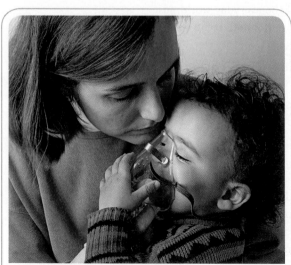

A nebulizer is used to treat asthma in infants, toddlers, and young preschool children.

Classroom Management Strategies The early childhood setting is an important place to promote and practice oral health. The following oral hygiene activities should be followed routinely in child care settings (American Academy of Pediatrics, American Public Health Association, National Resource Center for Health and Safety in Child Care and Early Education, 2011):

- All children should have their teeth brushed at least once during their time there.
- Children should be given water after snacks and meals if brushing is not possible.

Oral health promotion is an important aspect of teaching young children. This can be achieved by encouraging the following (American Academy of Pediatrics, American Public Health Association, National Resource Center for Health and Safety in Child Care and Early Education, 2011):

- Teachers can encourage parents to establish dental care within 6 months of the first tooth erupting

TEACHING WELLNESS Same and Special

LEARNING OUTCOME   Children will be able to identify characteristics of similarity and aspects of uniqueness.

INFANTS AND TODDLERS

- **Goal:** To introduce the concepts of *same* and *different*.
- **Materials:** Typical classroom manipulative toys, the book *It's OK*, by Todd Parr (Little, Brown Kids, 2004).
- **Activity plan:** Take advantage of incidental learning opportunities to describe the concepts of same and different. For example, when playing with cube blocks, set aside a pair of green cube blocks and one red cube block. Place the green cube blocks together and say, "Look. These are the same." Then pair a red and green block, and say, "These are different. See? One is green and this one is red."
- **How to adjust the activity:** As children become familiar with the concepts of same and different, ask them to choose a matching item from a group. Hold a blue block and ask the child to find one that is the same. Then ask the child to find one that is different. Read and talk about the book *It's OK*.
- **Did you meet your goal?** Did the children listen to the questions? Can the children find objects that match?

PRESCHOOLERS AND KINDERGARTNERS

- **Goal:** To explore the concepts of *same* and *different* and to discuss the concept of uniqueness and the notion of being special.
- **Materials:** Provide an array of creative materials such as yarn pieces, fabric scraps, magazine pages, construction paper, scissors, glue; the book *We Are All Alike, We Are All Different*, by the Cheltenham Elementary School Kindergartners and Laura Dwight (Scholastic, 2002).
- **Activity plan:** Offer the creative materials during free exploration time. Let children know that you will invite them to show their creations at group time. During group time ask each child to talk about his or her creation. Then lay the pictures on the floor next to each other. Standing around the pictures, invite the children to talk about what is the same and what is different. Talk about aspects of uniqueness and describe how being different is a way of being unique or special.
- **How to adjust the activity:** Read the book *We Are All Alike, We Are All Different*. Use the book to introduce a discussion about same/special characteristics among people. As children dictate, make lists of all the things children can identify that are the same about people and all the things that are different. Talk about ways being the same is interesting and ways that being unique is interesting. Use other books to explore more aspects of same and special:
  - *Why Am I Special?* by Melissa Langer (2006)
  - *The Family Book*, by Todd Parr (Little, Brown Young Readers, 2003)
  - *Me I Am!* by Jack Prelutsky and Christine Davenier (Farrar, Straus and Giroux, 2007)
  - *I Am Special*, by Charlotte Lisi and David Ortega (Trafford Publishing, 2006)
- **Did you meet your goal?** Are children able to recognize and identify characteristics that make things the same and different? Are children able to list characteristics of similarity and difference among people?

SCHOOL-AGE CHILDREN

- **Goal:** To explore the concepts of *same* and *different* and to discuss the concept of uniqueness and the notion of being special.
- **Materials:** Colored plastic mosaic tiles of various shapes, colors, and sizes; the book *This Is My Hair*, by Todd Parr (Little, Brown, 2000).
- **Activity plan:** Provide colored plastic mosaic tiles of various shapes. Invite a small group of children to sort all the colored tiles by attribute: all the yellow triangles here, all the blue squares there, and so on. Ask the children to take one of each shape (or if there are enough take two or more of each shape) to create a design. When children have finished, ask them to look at each other's designs. Are they the same? Different? Talk about how each child had the same shape, color, and number of tiles but each creation is unique and special.
- **How to adjust the activity:** Read the children's book *This Is My Hair*. Have the children draw a picture using the author's illustrative style that depicts their unique style. Display the drawings and conduct an "Illustrator's Interview": Ask each child to describe aspects of their drawing that are similar to others, but to also identify aspects that are unique. Talk about same and special characteristics among children in the class. Provide other books to read about these concepts:
  - *We're Different, We're the Same*, by Bobbi Kates (Random House Books for Young Readers, 1998)
  - *It's OK to Be Different*, by Todd Parr (Little, Brown Young Readers, 2004)
  - *I Just Am*, by Tom Lambke and Bryan Lambke (Five Star Publications, 2006)
  - *I Am Special*, by Linda Schwartz (Creative Teaching Press, 1978)
- **Did you meet your goal?** Are children able to describe characteristics that make things the same and different? Are they able to discuss aspects of unique and special?

wheeze
a high-pitched whistling
sound made while breathing;
commonly occurs in children
with asthma

trigger
stimulus that starts an
asthma attack

albuterol
medication commonly used
to open the airways when
children have symptoms
of asthma at the onset of
an episode or as a rescue
medicine

- Children greater than 3 years can be taught about tooth decay and appropriate dietary practices to prevent decay
- Provide education to families on good oral hygiene and avoidance of behaviors that lead to decay

Asthma

Asthma is a respiratory disease characterized by intermittent attacks of difficult breathing. It causes chronic inflammation of the small airways within the lung, resulting in a narrowing or obstruction of the airways. This narrowing causes children to cough or experience shortness of breath. Children with asthma may also **wheeze**, creating a high-pitched whistling sound while breathing.

Asthma is the most common chronic disease in childhood affecting 9% of children ages 0 to 17 years (Ball, Bindler, & Cowen, 2012). Families living in porverty, minorities (especially African Americans), and children in urban areas have a higher risk of developing severe asthma, experience more hospitalizations from asthma, and have higher death rates due to asthma (Centers for Disease Control, 2012). It is the leading cause of missed school days and accounts for 13 million missed days per year (Environmental Protection Agency, 2010).

Triggers are specific stimuli that cause an asthma attack (Table 11-1). Examples of triggers include exercise, infections, fragrances, allergens, food additives, pollutants, weather changes, and emotions (Ball et al., 2012). Every child with asthma has different triggers.

Classroom Management Strategies Teachers may be asked to assist children with asthma by administering medications. Two categories of medications are commonly used to treat asthma. One type is used *as needed* to open the airways when the child has symptoms. **Albuterol** is an example of an as-needed medication. Nearly all children with asthma use this type of medication. The frequency of use depends on the severity and control of the child's illness. The other type of medication is used daily even when the child is not having symptoms to *prevent* episodes. **Inhaled steroids** are examples of *prevention* medications.

Asthma medications are administered either as a solution with a nebulizer or with an inhaler and spacer. A **nebulizer** is a small electronic device that distributes a solution into aerosol droplets, or spray, for the

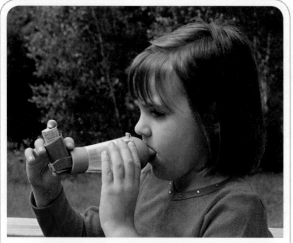

Inhalers and spacers are used for preschoolers and older children.

TABLE 11-1 Common Asthma Triggers

Indoor allergens	Animal dander, dust mites, cockroaches, molds Cleaning products
Outdoor allergens	Pollens from trees, grasses, weeds Molds Air pollutants Cold or dry air School bus exhaust
Other irritants	Tobacco smoke Strong odors or fumes from paint, hair spray, perfumes
Health Conditions	Cold, flu, viruses Sinus infections Nasal allergies Reflux
Exercise	More common in cold weather
Foods or food additives	Some children have specific food triggers

Sources: Centers for Disease Control, 2012; Environmental Protection Agency, 2010.

child to inhale. An inhaler with a spacer also administers medication to be inhaled but requires more coordination on the part of the recipient. To use an inhaler, the child must be able to put the inhaler in her or his mouth and inhale.

Typically, nebulizers are used more often for infants and toddlers, and inhalers are used for preschoolers and older children. To most effectively receive the medication, inhalers should *always* be used with a **spacer** regardless of age of the child. A spacer is a plastic tube that attaches to the inhaler and holds the aerosolized medication in a confined space while the child breathes in the droplets. Asthma medications may need to be administered several times per day.

Children with asthma may receive more than one medication and the frequency of use may change. Periodic communication with the child's family and health care provider may be necessary to understand any changes in the prescribed plan.

Teachers are also important sources of recognizing when a child's asthma is uncontrolled and when a child is experiencing an **asthma attack**. Symptoms of uncontrolled asthma and asthma attacks are similar. Figure 11-2 lists symptoms for both circumstances. Asthma attacks can be life threatening. Even when receiving treatment for asthma, children can still experience an asthma attack if exposed to a trigger. If symptoms of uncontrolled asthma or an asthma attack are observed, emergency treatment as directed by the child's medical provider should be followed immediately, and the family should be notified as soon as possible.

The CDC has also recognized that schools play an important role in the overall health of children with asthma by encouraging schools to become asthma-friendly. This is done by providing a safe and supportive learning environment for children with asthma and by developing policies that allow children to more effectively manage their asthma in the early childhood setting (Centers for Disease Control, 2012).

Environmental Allergies

Environmental allergies occur as a result of a complex interaction between environmental exposure and genetics. They are often referred to as hay fever or seasonal allergies, although they can be due to seasonal or year-round causes. The list of potential stimuli or triggers for allergies is very long. Common examples are tree and grass pollens, dust, mold and mildew, and pet dander. Environmental allergies are a common health problem, affecting 20% to 40% of children (Milgrom & Leung, 2011). The risk of developing allergies increases with early exposure to foods or formula during infancy as described in the *Nutrition Note*.

A Matter of ETHICS
A 3-year-old child enrolled in your class has moderate to severe asthma. His parents are divorced and they disagree on the management of the child's asthma in the classroom. The boy's mother wants to use conventional medical treatment while the father wants to use homeopathic treatments. You get different instructions about what to do depending on who drops the child off at preschool. What are the issues here and how can the NAEYC Code of Ethical Conduct and your state's program licensing requirements help you determine what to do? How do you think it is best to communicate with the family?

inhaled steroids a type of medication used to prevent episodes of asthma attacks; is used daily even when the child is not having symptoms

nebulizer a small, electric device that is used to distribute medication as aerosolized droplets for inhalation by the child

spacer a plastic, hollow tube that attaches to an inhaler and holds aerosolized medication in a confined space while the child inhales the medication

asthma attack episodes of asthma in which symptoms worsen and require immediate treatment to control breathing; characterized by shortness of breath, fast breathing, or worsening cough

FIGURE 11-2 Symptoms of Uncontrolled Asthma and Asthma Attacks

Symptoms of inadequately controlled asthma:
- Persistent cough, especially with physical activity
- Prolonged symptoms after a respiratory tract infections
- Frequent respiratory tract infections
- Need for frequent use of albuterol or rescue inhaler

Symptoms of an asthma attack:
- Frequent or uncontrollable coughing
- Unable to speak in sentences
- Increased use of shoulders or abdominal muscles for breathing
- Audible wheezing
- Shortness of breathe, especially if at rest

NUTRITION NOTE   Early Dietary Practices and Relationship to Allergies and Asthma in Children

Allergic diseases are becoming more prevalent. During the past several decades, asthma has increased by 160%, eczema is two to three times more common, and the incidence of peanut allergy has doubled. To reduce the risk of future allergic disease, the American Academy of Pediatrics recommends breastfeeding exclusively for at least the first 4 months of life. Other allergic disease prevention practices are being studied. These include:

- Monitoring the diet of the pregnant and lactating mother. The mother's diet may be a factor in the child's future development of allergies. At this time, however, studies do not support the exclusion of certain foods, such as peanuts, during pregnancy or lactation.
- Using specialized "hydrolyzed" formulas in formula-fed children who have a strong family history of allergic disease. Hydrolyzed formulas are "predigested," meaning the

protein content has been broken down to make the product more digestible. There is evidence that allergic disease can be prevented or delayed by using hydrolyzed formulas instead of cow's milk–based formulas. It is still unclear if this effect is long lasting or not.

- Delaying solid food introduction until at least 4 months and preferably 6 months of age. For children who are at high risk for allergies, earlier AAP recommendations encouraged delaying introduction of eggs until 2 years and peanuts until 3 years of age; however, recent studies suggest the evidence supporting these recommendations is still inconclusive.
- Encouraging exclusive breastfeeding until 4–6 months of age. Exclusive breastfeeding has been shown to have the strongest beneficial effect for prevention of allergies and eczema.

Source: Silvers, et al., 2012; Kramer, 2012.

Chronic allergies are very common and can impact quality of life. Common symptoms of environmental allergies include runny nose, watery eyes, cough, headache, and fatigue.

Classroom Management Strategies   One of the most important ways teachers can aid children with allergies is to help them avoid known triggers. Adjustments can be made for indoor and outdoor activities. Keeping the indoor environment clean to reduce dust and dry to discourage mold and mildew reduces these triggers. Children who have an allergy to grass can be encouraged to play in the area of the playground that has mulch instead of grass or to run and walk in the grassy area rather than sitting on or touching the grass.

Eczema

Eczema is a condition that causes inflammation and itching of the skin. It is characterized by chronically dry skin with periodic episodes of more intense skin rashes that are red, peeling, and very itchy. The most common areas for the rash are the face, backs of hands and feet, and skin folds (back of knees and in front of elbows). Children with eczema may scratch constantly and have difficulty sleeping because of itching. Infants with eczema may be irritable and move about as they are trying to fall asleep. Children with eczema are prone to skin infections because the integrity of the skin is compromised.

Eczema varies in severity and tends to come and go. It is quite common, affecting 20% of infants and children (Ball et al., 2012). Most children who have eczema develop it in the first year of life. Eczema can be triggered by food or environmental stimuli. Environmental triggers include dust mites, pet dander, pollens, soaps, detergents, abrasive clothing, and emotional stress.

Classroom Management Strategies   Management of eczema involves avoiding known triggers and judiciously keeping the skin moist with lotions recommended by a medical provider. Teachers may be asked to apply creams or lotions if children experience a flare-up. It is also important to reduce children's contact with strong soaps or detergents by selecting appropriate soap for children to use at the sink.

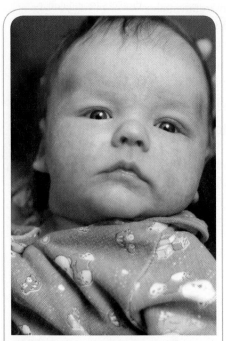

Children with eczema are more likely to contract skin infections.

Conditions Related to the Nervous System

Many chronic health conditions in childhood affect the nervous system or are caused by disorders of the nervous system. Although the effects of these conditions vary, they all have some effect on health and wellness in childhood.

Attention Deficit Disorder and Attention Deficit/Hyperactivity Disorder

Attention deficit disorder (ADD) and attention deficit/hyperactivity disorder (ADHD) are conditions characterized by inattention, impulsivity, or hyperactivity. The causes are not completely understood. Other health conditions are strongly associated with ADD/ADHD, including structural brain abnormalities, history of prematurity, and prenatal exposure to toxins. ADD/ADHD can interfere with the attainment of academic and fine motor skills as well as social and adaptive skills. As a result, children with ADD/ADHD often experience school failure, poor family and peer relations, low self-esteem, and emotional, behavioral, and learning problems (Turnbull, Turnbull, Wehmeyer, & Shogren, 2013).

Estimates of school-age children exhibiting ADD/ADHD range from 6% to 9% (Turnbull et al., 2013). Boys are 2.5 times more likely than girls to be identified (Floet, Scheiner, & Grossman, 2010). Children born prematurely are also at increased risk for acquiring ADD. This could be due to any brain abnormality, such as the intracranial hemorrhage Jeremy's mother reported in the case scenario, or there could be subtle developmental effects on the infant's neurological system.

Three types of conditions fall under the ADD and ADHD categories: *predominantly inattentive* (ADD), *predominantly hyperactive-impulsive* (HD), and *combined* (ADHD). Behaviors and characteristics of children with ADD/ADHD are described in Table 11-2. In addition to frequently displaying these symptoms, the symptoms should be observed in two or more settings, such as at school and at home. In addition, the symptoms must be seen as impairing social or academic functioning. It can sometimes be difficult to distinguish between normal childhood behaviors and ADHD. Children with ADHD may also share some traits associated with giftedness.

Children with ADD often have other conditions that affect learning and behavior such as learning disabilities, behavioral disorders, conduct disorder, mood disorder, anxiety, or depression (Floet et al., 2010). Concerns regarding these other health conditions should be communicated to families and health care providers.

Children with ADD are eligible for development of a behavioral management plan under the IEP process. In 1991, the DOE confirmed that ADHD is considered within the scope of the IDEA (Turnbull et al., 2013). Children with ADHD may also qualify for special education services under the diagnosis of emotional disturbance, which requires a comprehensive evaluation that meets federal and state requirements. Children who do not qualify for services under the IDEA may be eligible under Section 504 of the Rehabilitation Act. ADHD is considered a disability under Section 504 when the child is substantially limited in a major life activity.

Classroom Management Strategies Teachers provide a variety of supports for children with ADD/ADHD. They may be asked to respond to questionnaires that evaluate the child's symptoms in the classroom setting. Adjustments for children may include seating in a quiet area, more time to complete work, and use of materials to aid in organizing and planning, tutoring supports, or modifying homework (Turnbull et al., 2013).

Behavioral therapies may be recommended to assist children to function effectively in the classroom. Some children will also be prescribed medications such as **stimulants** that may need to be administered during the day. These medications are used to increase focus and decrease distractibility in the hopes of improving school performance and relationship building as well as decrease challenging behaviors. Extensive literature demonstrates that the use of these medications is safe and effective (Floet et al., 2010). Several trials of different dosages, medications, and timing intervals may be necessary before identifying the best treatment for an individual child.

stimulants
medications used to increase focus and decrease distractibility for improving school performance and relationship building in children with ADHD

TABLE 11-2 Characteristics of ADD and ADHD

Attention Deficit Disorder
Unable to sustain attention while executing tasks or participating in an activity
Appears to not be listening when spoken to
Fails to follow through with instructions frequently
Fails to finish schoolwork
Loses things frequently
Often forgetful with usual daily activities
Easily distracted

Hyperactive-impulsive type
Constantly fidgeting or moving in their seat
Talks excessively
Leaves seat when it is expected that they stay in their seat
Inappropriately running or climbing
Answers questions before it is time
Cannot wait their turn
Interrupts others constantly
Acts out without thinking
Rushes through activities

Sources: Heward, 2013; Turnbull, Turnbull, Wehmeyer, & Shogren, 2013.

Autism

autism
neurological condition characterized by impairments in social interaction and communication as well as restrictive, repetitive, or stereotypical patterns of behavior

pervasive developmental disorder (PDD)
disorder associated with developmental delays, abnormal or delayed social interactions, and in some circumstances, a restricted range of interests

Autism is the most common condition in a group of developmental disorders called the *autism spectrum disorders* (ASDs). Autism is a condition that involves impaired social interactions, communication problems, repetitive behaviors, and in some circumstances, a restricted range of interests. Other conditions in the ASDs include Asperger's syndrome and **pervasive developmental disorder (PDD)**. The cause of autism is unknown although it appears to have a strong genetic component. The prevalence is about 1 in 110 and it is more common in boys (Ball et al., 2012).

Symptoms   Children with autism exhibit six distinctive characteristics (Turnbull et al., 2013):

- Atypical language development
- Atypical social development
- Repetitive behaviors
- Behavior problems
- Sensory and movement disorders
- Atypical intellectual functioning

Table 11-3 lists more specific characteristics typically seen in children with autism.

Asperger's syndrome
neurological disorder characterized by normal intelligence, poor peer relationships, lack of empathy (similar, to but milder than, autism), language skills that are generally stronger than other types of pdds, and a tendency to overfocus on certain topics or objects (planets, geography)

One of the ASDs is called **Asperger's syndrome**. Children with Asperger's typically have normal intelligence. They display poor peer relationships and lack of empathy (similar to, but milder than, autism), have language skills that are generally stronger than other types of PDDs, and a tendency to perseverate on certain topics or objects.

Controversy exists regarding the cause of the increase in cases diagnosed. Some believe that more frequent diagnosis is due to better recognition of the condition, and that children with the condition in the past were misdiagnosed as being mentally retarded. Others are of the opinion that the rates of autism are increasing. The CDC is conducting ongoing surveillance studies to track prevalence rates to better clarify this issue.

The onset of autism occurs during the first 3 years of life; typically children are diagnosed by age 3. Therefore, many children with autism have been diagnosed by the time they enter the public school system. Children with mild autism or Asperger's syndrome, however, may not be diagnosed until the elementary years.

Classroom Management Strategies   The diagnosis of autism is often made over time, creating a stressful and anxiety-provoking anticipatory period for families. Teachers are part of the support

TABLE 11-3 Characteristics of Children with Autism

Characteristic	Examples
Atypical language development	• Broad range of language abilities • Focusing on one topic • Repeating or echoing • Reversing pronouns
Atypical social development	• Abnormal use of nonverbal language • Lack of relationships with peers • Unable to share enjoyment or interests with others
Repetitive behavior	• Hand and finger mannerisms • Repeating phrases • Persistent attention to parts of objects or toys
Behavior problems	• Self-harm • Aggressive behavior • Tantrums • Destruction of property
Sensory and movement disorders	• Food selectivity • Toe walking • Sleep problems • Abnormal posture
Problems with intellectual functioning	• 75% have intellectual disability

Source: Information from Turnbull, Turnbull, Wehmeyer, & Shogren, 2013.

system for families during this evaluation period. Providing information about autism and offering opportunities for families to discuss their concerns are ways in which teachers can lend support. When children are diagnosed, teachers are important partners in developing an effective IEP. The goals of the IEP are to reinforce children's desirable behaviors, improve social skills and communication, and reduce nonadaptive behaviors such as aggression or inappropriate angry outbursts. Regular routines and a predictable schedule are important, as well as supporting children when schedules vary.

Strategies involve teaching children communication skills, such as helping Mike recognize when Alan is asking to share a toy by saying, "Mike, turn your head to look at Alan. He has a question for you." Teaching children imitation skills is another step in helping children recognize social cues (Schwartz, Billingsley, & McBride, n.d.). Supporting the child to play "Follow the Leader" games is a familiar example of teaching imitation in the early childhood setting. Providing visual cues such as picture cards or pointing to posters that depict an action are often effective ways to support verbal directions. The greatest success occurs when these strategies are consistently used both at school and at home.

Teachers are also an important link to connect families to resources that help them cope with the challenges of autism. There is no cure for autism. However, strategies are available to reduce the impact of symptoms and to improve children's functioning. Interventions provided during the early childhood years are considered critical to improving the symptoms of autism.

Visual cues are often an effective way to support verbal directions for children with autism.

Learning Disabilities

Learning disabilities are defined as a specific and persistent failure to learn age-appropriate academic skills despite normal intelligence, conventional teaching, and adequate sociocultural opportunities. The main characteristic of learning disabilities is a discrepancy between the expected academic

learning disabilities
term used to describe a condition in which there is a specific and persistent failure to learn age-appropriate academic skills despite normal intelligence, conventional teaching, and adequate sociocultural opportunities

achievement based on the child's IQ, which is normal, and the actual achievement. These disabilities are present in 4% of school-age children (Heward, 2013).

Learning disabilities include a number of specific disabilities reflecting difficulties in learning reading, writing, and/or mathematics skills. The most common one is **dyslexia**, a disorder of reading in which children frequently omit, insert, reverse, or substitute words or sounds. The causes are generally unknown, although there is a strong genetic component for certain types of learning disabilities such as dyslexia.

Problems commonly seen in the classroom in children with learning disabilities include the following (Heward, 2013):

- Reading difficulties or learning how to read later than expected.
- Problems with written language including spelling.
- Problems with math.
- Problems with social skills (occurs in about 75% of children with learning disabilities).
- Problems with attention and hyperactivity.
- Behavioral problems.

Classroom Management Strategies   The least restrictive environment as described by IDEA applies to children with learning disabilities. Research demonstrates mixed results with inclusion of children with learning disabilities in the general classroom and some controversy exists. Generally, the quality of education is more important than where the education occurs (Heward, 2013).

Besides specific teaching strategies related to inclusion, input from teachers plays an important role in identification of children with learning disabilities. There is no one test that is diagnostic. Generally, it is a compilation of information gained from parents and teachers along with testing done by the school system that aids in the diagnosis made by specialists.

Cerebral Palsy

Cerebral palsy (CP) is a condition that permanently affects movement and posture, which cause physical limitations. It is caused by problems that occur in brain development before, during, or after birth. Most cases of cerebral palsy are a result of problems that occur before birth and involve anatomical or structural abnormalities of the brain. CP occurs in 1.5 to 2 per 1,000 infants (Ball et al., 2012). Being born prematurely or small for gestational age are risk factors for developing CP.

Children with CP have problems with movement that affect muscle tone and with the signals that promote movement and coordination. Some children have minimal challenges, whereas others experience extensive challenges. Children with CP often experience developmental delays and frequently have other health conditions such as visual problems, hearing loss, speech problems, seizures, feeding difficulties, learning disabilities, and intellectual disability. Children with CP may move with a walker or use a wheelchair. They may have trouble with small motor coordination, making it difficult to hold small items and learn to write. Children with CP may experience difficulties with speech. Different classifications of CP are based on the type of movement difficulties and the part of the body that is affected.

Classroom Management Strategies   Children with cerebral palsy experience a wide variety of type and severity of symptoms. Teachers should learn about the child's needs for adjustments in the classroom environment to accommodate the child's movement in the setting. Understanding how the child communicates is also important because children with CP may use various communication methods such as a picture board, digital communication device, or keyboard. An educational assistant who works with the lead teacher to manage any medical interventions and to modify the learning environment appropriately supports many children with CP in the classroom. Speech and physical therapists are usually partners in supporting the child's educational plan.

dyslexia
a disorder of reading where children frequently omit, insert, reverse, or substitute words or sounds

fetal alcohol syndrome (FAS)
a neurological condition causing a range of physical and developmental outcomes that occur as a result of fetal exposure to alcohol

Fetal Alcohol Syndrome

Fetal alcohol syndrome (FAS) is a neurological condition caused by exposure to alcohol during pregnancy. Alcohol consumption during pregnancy is common and occurs in 1 in 8 pregnancies, while 2% of pregnant women report heavy drinking during pregnancy. About 10% of women who consume alcohol during pregnancy will have an affected baby (Paintner, Williams, & Burd, 2012). This condition has lifelong, severe effects on the fetus, affecting a child's physical, emotional, and neurological development. The prevalence of FAS is reported to be as high as 9.1 per 1,000. The following are characteristics of the disorder (Paintner et al., 2012):

- Abnormalities in the structure of the face.
- Growth deficiency.
- Central nervous system abnormalities including small head circumference, neurological problems, cognitive/developmental deficits, and behavioral/emotional deficits.

The facial abnormalities seen in FAS include a smooth **philtrum** (the fold typically seen between the nose and upper lip), a thin upper lip, and small eyes, which may be obvious in some individuals or very subtle in others. Central nervous system abnormalities range from severe structural abnormalities of the brain to mild cognitive deficits.

Some children exposed to alcohol do not meet the full criteria for FAS. The term *fetal alcohol spectrum disorders* is used to encompass the range of disabilities associated with exposure to alcohol *in utero*, and includes the diagnosis **alcohol-related neurodevelopmental disorder (ARND)**. The ARND diagnosis is often used when there is a history of alcohol exposure, but the child does not meet all of the official criteria for FAS.

Children with FAS often struggle with attention, memory, and learning, which lead to difficulties in school. It is common to see other health conditions such as hearing and vision disorders, seizures, intellectual disability, abnormal relationships with peers, and deficits in judgment and decision making (Paintner et al., 2012).

Classroom Management Strategies In spite of the wide range of potential behavioral challenges, many children with FAS are described as outgoing, friendly, and socially engaging. Most children with FAS do not qualify for special education services. As they plan to successfully teach children with FAS, many teachers find evaluation of children's **executive functioning** to be helpful. Executive functioning refers to children's ability to function in a school setting with respect to planning, organization, and attention.

Teachers focus on teaching skills that build children's self-help skills to navigate through the daily routines of the classroom. Detailed visual cues and prompts are used to make abstract concepts more concrete and to reinforce directions, such as "Time to clean up" or "Time to wash hands." Teachers work to reduce distractions and to help children with FAS focus on tasks and skill-building activities. Teachers also provide immediate feedback for appropriate and inappropriate behaviors.

Intellectual Disability

Intellectual disability is the most common developmental disability. This condition has previously been referred to as cognitive disability or mental retardation, a term that is no longer used because of stigmatization. It is characterized by a significantly below-average score on a test of intellectual ability and by limited ability to function in the tasks of daily life such as self-care, communication, and managing social interactions.

Intellectual disability can result from genetic conditions and developmental causes before birth, as well as injury, infection, or illness occurring at birth or during childhood. The most common causes of intellectual disability are Down syndrome, fetal alcohol syndrome, or fragile X syndrome. These are examples of prenatal influences leading to the condition.

philtrum
the fold typically seen between the nose and upper lip

alcohol-related neurodevelopmental disorder (ARND)
neurological condition covering a spectrum of symptoms that can occur with fetal exposure to alcohol; diagnosis is often used when there is a history of alcohol exposure, but the child does not meet all of the official criteria for FAS

executive functioning
a set of cognitive skills involved in planning, inhibition, concept formation, and reasoning

intellectual disability
significantly subaverage intellectual functioning, existing concurrently with deficits in adaptive behavior and manifested during the developmental period; adversely affects a child's educational performance; previous term used was *mental retardation*

Children with FAS often have subtle characteristics such as a smooth philtrum and a thin upper lip.

Intellectual disabilities are often associated with environmental or biological causes. Environmental causes tend to be exhibited through mild expressions of disability, whereas severe disease is more likely linked to biological causes. Risk factors also exist. Children with mild intellectual disability are much more likely to have mothers who did not complete high school, linking the disability to genetics and to environmental influences such as poverty and other social issues. Poverty is more highly associated with intellectual disability than any other social factor (Turnbull et al., 2013).

Children with intellectual disabilities exhibit a wide range of challenges. **Adaptive behaviors** are challenging for children with intellectual disabilities. Adaptive behaviors refer to the skills children learn in order to function in everyday life. These include language skills, social skills, such as taking turns and sharing, and self-help skills relevant to activities of daily living, such as dressing, bathing, and brushing teeth. There are three aspects of adaptive behaviors (Turnbull et al., 2013):

adaptive behavior
skills children learn in order to function in everyday life including language, social skills, and skills relevant to activities of daily living

- Conceptual skills such as language, reading, writing, understanding of money, and self-direction
- Social skills including following rules, responsibilities, self-esteem
- Activities of daily living

short-term memory
information stored for a few seconds to a few hours

Many children with intellectual disabilities also have problems with **short-term memory**, the information that is stored for a few seconds to a few hours. For example, in the kindergarten classroom, Rachel has been teaching 5-year-old Zane to count by pointing to each block and saying the counting words, "One, two, three, four, five." At the end of the counting session, Zane is able to point and count to five. When asked, "How many blocks all together?" Zane responds, "Five!" The next day, when Rachel prepares to practice the counting lesson using toy animals she discovers that Zane is unable to repeat the counting task from the previous day. She recognizes that Zane associates the counting task with blocks, but he cannot generalize the process when using new props.

Classroom Management Strategies Children with intellectual disabilities vary greatly in the supports needed for successful inclusion in the classroom. Some children may need assistance with many aspects of their participation and to ensure that they are sufficiently supervised for safety. A classroom education assistant may be needed to individually support and teach the child in the larger class group. Children with milder intellectual disabilities may require more modest assistance and can be supported by adapting the typical curriculum. Adaptations may include offering a slower pace for children to explore and try new concepts and providing more specific guidance to ensure directions are understood.

For very young children the focus in the classroom is on developing social interaction and self-help skills. This includes providing specific guidance or age-appropriate modeling and "lessons" about topics such as how to ask for help, how to express needs, how to share a toy, and how to wash hands and serve food. For older children the focus in the class moves toward developing communication and personal care skills and academic skills such as reading, writing, and basic math.

Lead Exposure & Poisoning

Lead poisoning is a condition caused by swallowing an object that contains lead or breathing in dust that contains lead. Lead is toxic to most body systems including the nervous system. Lead can build up in the body over time, causing lead poisoning that can lead to cognitive impairment in young children. Most children with lead poisoning do not have symptoms. Symptoms include gastrointestinal complaints such as loss of appetite, nausea, vomiting, abdominal pain, or constipation. At high levels of exposure, lead poisoning can be lethal and result in **encephalopathy**, brain injury due to a toxin or infection.

encephalopathy
brain injury due to a toxin or infection

The most adverse effect of lead poisoning is its effect on cognition and intelligence. However, lead can have adverse effects on multiple systems in the body. Lead poisoning is completely preventable. During the past few decades, the CDC has lowered the acceptable threshold of levels of lead in the blood stating that no level of lead in blood is safe and the primary focus should be on prevention.

Young children are at risk for lead exposure because of their mouthing behaviors and because they absorb and retain more lead relative to their body weight than adults. Exposure occurs through ingestion or inhalation (Ball et al., 2012). Children who are not well nourished and have nutritional deficiencies, such as a child with an iron deficiency, may be at increased risk for lead poisoning. Lead poisoning is diagnosed through blood testing that is obtained because of concern that the child was at risk for exposure. The prevalence of high lead levels in children ages 1 to 5 is about 1.6%. The primary sources of lead are the following (Ball et al., 2012):

- Lead paint (banned in 1978) present in buildings or homes. Paint may chip and children can ingest or inhale particles
- Airborne lead from gasoline that has contaminated soil
- Parental occupations/hobbies (plumbing, battery manufacturing, refinishing furniture, pottery)
- Water from lead pipes
- Toys

Classroom Management Strategies   Early childhood settings can contribute to prevention of lead poisoning primarily by:

- Establishing classroom environments that reduce exposure to lead.
- Administering lead exposure questionnaires to identify children who may be at risk for lead exposure.
- Educating families about the dangers of lead exposure.

Children who have potentially been exposed to lead sources should be referred to their primary care provider or public health department for further evaluation.

Spina Bifida

Spina bifida is a defect of the vertebral column, or spine, that causes the contents of the spinal cord nervous tissue to protrude and consequently, fail to develop normally. This is also known as neural tube defects. It occurs very early in prenatal development, just weeks after conception. Spina bifida occurs in 1 of every 1,000 births. The degree to which spina bifida affects children's overall health depends on the location of the defect: The higher the defect is in the spinal column, the more severe the effects. Folic acid supplementation during the time of conception and during pregnancy reduces the risk of spina bifida, which has prompted folic acid supplementation of some types of foods such as bread and cereal.

Common health issues associated with spina bifida include (Heward, 2013):

- **Hydrocephalus** (too much fluid around the brain requiring a shunt).
- Seizures.
- Varying degrees of paralysis of lower limbs.
- Varying degrees of bladder and bowel control; some children may require intermittent **catheterization** of the bladder, a process in which a small tube is placed by the caregiver or child through the urethra into the bladder to remove urine.

Children may require surgery to close the gap in the spine soon after birth. Surgery may also be needed to manage problems with the feet, hips, or spine. Some children may need assistive supports for walking, such as crutches, leg braces, or wheelchairs. It is common to have trouble with bladder and bowel control. They may experience problems with perceptual motor skills; cognitive skills such as attention, memory, sequencing, and organization; and hyperactivity or impulse control.

Classroom Management Strategies   Supporting children with spina bifida in the classroom requires that teachers have an understanding of the child's strengths and needs, medical support requirements, and strategies that support inclusion. Details of a child's condition are often determined through psychological and neuropsychological evaluations. Findings of these assessments guide the development of the child's IEP. Teachers work in partnership with the child's medical provider, early interventionists, and families to identify goals and to plan adjustments in the classroom.

The physical spaces need to be reviewed to ensure children will be able to move throughout the classroom and access the outdoor play area. Children may need to be carefully oriented to the

spina bifida
a defect of the vertebral column or spine causing the contents of the spinal cord/nervous tissue to protrude

hydrocephalus
too much fluid in the chambers of the brain, requiring a shunt

catheterization
process of placing a small tube through the urethra into the bladder for the removal of urine

schedule and routines and provided extra time and support when changes in the routine must be made. Some medical supports may be required, such as periodic catheterization to ensure children's bladder health. More than half of children with spina bifida will develop a latex allergy so it is important to keep the classroom latex free including gloves, balloons, and other toys (Ball et al., 2012).

The IEP provides focus for teaching, such as needed skills in verbal communication, social skills and behavior management, motor skills, and academic areas. As with all children with special health needs, the focus in the classroom is on assisting the child to experience positive social interactions with other children and to be a part of all classroom activities.

Conditions That Are Genetic

Genes influence most aspects of health. For example, children with certain genes are more prone to develop allergies or asthma. Other health conditions are caused by defects in specific genes. These conditions may or may not be inherited. In this section we discuss some of the conditions that have strong genetic connections, including cystic fibrosis, sickle cell anemia, diabetes mellitus, and others.

Cystic Fibrosis

Cystic fibrosis (CF) is an inherited disease that affects the lungs and digestive system. A defective gene causes the body to create thick, sticky mucus that clogs the lungs and obstructs the digestive process. This results in progressive respiratory and nutritional problems that lead to severe respiratory infections and premature death. In addition to the chronic respiratory problems, children with CF tend to exhibit poor growth and malnutrition due in part to insufficient pancreatic function.

CF is most common among Caucasians occurring in 1 in 3,200 live births. Among African Americans, CF occurs in 1 in 15,000 births, among Asians the rate is 1 in 31,000, and in Hispanics 1 in 7,000 (Ball et al., 2012). Cystic fibrosis is often diagnosed during the early childhood years and some states have universal screening at birth.

Children with CF display a number of symptoms:

- Persistent coughing, occasionally spitting up thick mucus.
- Shortness of breath and wheezing.
- Frequent lung infections.
- Poor growth and delayed weight gain.
- Difficulty with bowel movements or frequent greasy stools.

Children with CF typically undergo therapy during which the chest is vigorously thumped to dislodge mucus. This kind of treatment may be required during the day. They may also require frequent courses of antibiotics that are sometimes given intravenously. This may or may not require hospitalizations.

In spite of a good appetite, children with CF need to consume a large number of calories to keep up with nutritional requirements. They are typically treated with medications, including inhalers to improve breathing and pills that help them digest food.

Classroom Management Strategies   Most children with CF are eligible for services under the IDEA. Teachers work in partnership with medical providers, early interventionists, and parents to support the inclusion of children with CF in the classroom. Understanding the effects of the disease helps to identify appropriate supports. For example, it is important to recognize that children with CF need to cough frequently and are highly susceptible to respiratory infections.

Administration of medication may be required. Time should be provided to administer or to allow the child to take medications and to conduct activities or treatments to clear the airway. An appropriate space should be identified to help the child feel comfortable.

An emergency medical response plan should be drafted to guide appropriate response when needed. Regular attendance may be an issue for children with CF depending on the severity of the disease. For school-age children, teachers work with families to optimize learning by arranging appropriate homework to make up missed work.

Sickle Cell Anemia

Sickle cell anemia is a genetic condition that is inherited from both parents. It affects the integrity of red blood cells, causing them to have a much shorter life span than they would normally and to be *sickle* shaped, hence the name of the condition. The condition leads to anemia, chronic pain, and susceptibility to infections. It is most common in African American children.

The severity of the disease varies and has improved with earlier diagnosis due to newborn screening, antibiotics, and parent education. The chronic anemia that occurs with sickle cell anemia can lead to developmental delays if not carefully managed. The disease is also characterized by acute pain crises that can be precipitated by dehydration and cold weather. The symptoms include pain, swelling of joints, or abdominal pain. A child with a sickle cell crisis needs urgent medical attention. Many children require blood transfusions and hospitalizations to treat complications of the condition.

Classroom Management Strategies Teachers' main involvement will be to report any complaints of pain or other physical health problems to the parents and school nurse, if appropriate. Children with sickle cell anemia may also miss school days due to illness or hospitalizations, and special considerations should be made to help them make up work. In addition, chronic pain can cause poor peer relationships and problems with self-esteem. Teachers can be an important support system for children and families.

sickle cell anemia
an inherited disorder of red blood cells that causes chronic anemia, pain, and susceptibility to infection

Diabetes Mellitus

Diabetes mellitus is a chronic medical condition that occurs when the body does not produce or appropriately use **insulin**. Insulin is a hormone that breaks down sugars, starches, and fats into food energy. The body's failure to produce insulin results in elevated blood glucose levels, which has detrimental impacts on the body's organ systems. Left untreated or poorly managed, diabetes can result in many long-term health consequences, including nerve damage, loss of vision, kidney failure, heart problems, circulatory problems that may require amputation, and early death.

insulin
hormone secreted by the pancreas that is essential for the metabolism of glucose and fat

Type 1 Diabetes Type 1 diabetes is brought about by a combination of genetics and immunity. Individuals with certain types of genes are prone to develop diabetes. The condition develops when these individuals experience an **autoimmune condition** that causes them to develop antibodies against their own pancreas, resulting in the destruction of cells that produce and secrete insulin. Without sufficient insulin, body cells are not able to use glucose (sugar) to fuel the body. Children with type 1 diabetes require administration of insulin through injection or through an insulin pump.

Children who develop diabetes tend to become ill very quickly. Symptoms include:

autoimmune condition
causes individuals to secrete antibodies against their own organs

- Frequent urination.
- Excessive thirst.
- Fatigue.
- Irritability.
- Blurred vision.

In the early childhood setting, children with diabetes may have a noticeable increase in frequency of urination, requiring more frequent diaper changes, or urinary accidents.

Careful management of diabetes and a healthy lifestyle reduce the impact of the disease and improve children's long-term outlook. Type 1 diabetes is typically treated by testing blood sugar levels, administering injections of insulin, and offering a specialized diet and exercise program. A nutritionally balanced diet is needed, and aspects of the diet must be monitored, such as the kinds and amounts of foods eaten and the timing of meals and administration of insulin injections.

After diagnosis, children with diabetes and their families require a good deal of support and education about the disease. It can sometimes take several weeks to months to establish a treatment regimen, which may be frustrating for families and caregivers. Additionally, as children grow, their regimen will change based on changes in their caloric intake, physical activity, and rate of growth.

For these reasons, children with diabetes require careful monitoring by their medical provider as well as a specialist in diabetes management. See this chapter's *Progressive Programs & Practices* feature for an interesting case scenario involving a child with type I diabetes.

Type 2 Diabetes Type 2 diabetes results from the body's inability to properly use insulin. This type of diabetes is less common among young children than type 1. Type 2 diabetes typically occurs in later childhood and among older people who are obese and who have a strong family tendency toward type 2 diabetes. Type 2 diabetes is influenced by a family history of diabetes, obesity, and sedentary lifestyle. Some racial groups are at greater risk for developing type 2 diabetes, including African Americans, Hispanic/Latino Americans, American Indians, and some Asian Americans and Native Hawaiians or other Pacific Islanders.

Establishing healthy nutritional and physical activity habits early are prevention efforts that may reduce the incidence of type 2 diabetes. Although this condition is uncommon during the early

PROGRESSIVE PROGRAMS & PRACTICES

Accommodating Nate (Type 1 Diabetes)

By Jamie M. Wincovitch, Classroom Teacher at the University Child Development Center, University of Pittsburgh

The University Child Development Center (UCDC), a laboratory school at the University of Pittsburgh, serves children from birth to 5 years of age. We have approximately 160 families at any given time with 12 classrooms.

What challenge did you face?

We had a 2-year-old enrolled who was energetic, full of life, and an amazing communicator. While in a toddler classroom, he started to show symptoms uncharacteristic of his typical behavior. He was easily fatigued, was using the bathroom excessively, and had excessive thirst. Soon after, Nate was diagnosed with type I diabetes.

How did you meet the challenge?
What was the teachers' role?

Nate used an insulin pump (a small battery-operated insulin-delivering device, worn on a belt or in a pocket, with a narrow plastic tube inserted just under the skin and taped in place). All carbohydrates he consumed had to be counted. Although the pump then calculated how much insulin to deliver, a teacher had to decide how much would be delivered immediately and how much would be distributed over time, depending on the fat content and nutritional make up of the food consumed. The classroom teachers were trained extensively by the parents and the Children's Hospital of Pittsburgh on how to make these decisions and care for a child with these diverse needs.

Initially, teachers were nervous about this responsibility, but over time, the process of caring for Nate became second nature. I actually prided myself in my newfound ability to know the carbohydrate count of almost any amount of any food.

To create a classroom climate that was inclusive, we aimed to provide Nate with care that didn't make him feel "different." For example, we put Velcro name stickers on chairs for assigned seating that changed daily. This ensured, discreetly, that Nate

was always near a teacher so she could monitor food intake without forcing him to sit by a teacher every day while other children had free choice. We eat family style, so children are able to scoop their own food onto their plates. We replaced all serving spoons with measuring cups so Nate didn't feel isolated when a teacher recorded how much he consumed.

Nate's blood sugar level had to be tested every few hours (typically 5–6 times daily), which required pricking his finger with a pin, squeezing a small amount of blood onto a glucose testing strip, and inserting it into a blood glucose meter. Nate was very cooperative and verbal, excellent at telling us how he was feeling, which helped notify us of his changing needs.

What was the outcome?

This all sounds so intense and medical, but in reality, Nate was a typical preschool child with typical preschool needs. He sometimes struggled resting quietly at naptime, he loved anything math, and he loved being silly. Yes, the medical part was always present, but as teachers, we worked really hard at making sure Nate was thought of as a preschooler (with type 1 diabetes), NOT a diabetic kid. It makes a BIG difference!

childhood years, it is important for teachers to understand that the habits and sequence of events leading to the condition begin in early childhood. Not only is the prevalence increasing in children, the average age of onset of type 2 diabetes is becoming younger (Shah, Kublaoui, & White, 2009).

Classroom Management Strategies   Children with diabetes typically require no special adjustments for participation in the classroom and academic success. The medical management of the disease in the classroom is the most important area of focus. Management of diabetes requires a clear understanding of the child's medical protocols. Teachers require training on how to test blood sugar levels, how to adjust the kinds and quantities of food served, how to administer insulin injections, and how to recognize and manage emergencies, such as administering glucagon treatments. These practices must be directed by a medical provider. Teachers should receive formal training and supervision as they implement the child's medical plan. Two complications are important to recognize for management of diabetes:

- **Hypoglycemia** occurs when the blood sugar level is low (less than 50 to 60 mg/dL). It can be caused by missed or delayed meals, taking too much insulin, or strenuous exercise (Heward, 2013). Symptoms include faintness, dizziness, blurred vision, drowsiness, nausea, and irritability. Treatment entails giving the child concentrated sugar such as a sugar cube or a glass of fruit juice.

- **Diabetic ketoacidosis (DKA)** is a common, but life-threatening, complication of diabetes. It occurs when blood sugar levels remain high over a period of time as a result of insufficient insulin or sometimes due to illnesses. Symptoms include elevated blood sugars, excessive thirst and urination, unusual odor to breath (smells like acetone/nail polish remover), and lethargy or weakness. Emergency medical personnel should be contacted immediately if DKA is suspected.

The demands of diabetes often influence children's social and emotional well-being, affecting their learning and peer relationships. Table 11-4 shows guidelines that were established by the American Diabetes Association in order to optimize diabetes care in schools.

hypoglycemia
a low blood glucose level measuring less than 50 to 60 mg/dl

diabetic ketoacidosis (DKA)
a fairly common, life-threatening complication of diabetes that occurs when blood sugar levels remain high over some period of time as a result of insulin deficiency

TABLE 11-4   Diabetes in the Early Childhood Setting

Guideline	Details
Medical Management Plan	• Developed by the child's health care provider along with parents • Provides instructions for glucose monitoring, insulin administration, and amount, type, and frequency of meals and snacks • Defines symptoms and treatment for hypoglycemia and hyperglycemia • Provides guidelines for physical activity
Parent Responsibilities	• Provide materials such as insulin, other medications, equipment needed for glucose monitoring, etc. • Provide supplies to treat hypoglycemia • Provide emergency phone numbers • Provide information about meals and snacks
School/Teacher Responsibilities	• Provide appropriate training for persons responsible for child • Ensure accessibility to insulin and meals/snacks as defined in medical plan • Ensure accessibility to trained individual in the case of hypoglycemia • Have backup staff available who are trained to assist child in the case that the usual teacher or nurse is not available • Permission for student to see nurse upon request • Provide a plan for disposal of needles
Student Responsibilities	• Toddlers/Pre-school age: Need an adult to provide all aspects of diabetes care. Involve the child in decisions such as which finger to poke • Elementary age: May be able to check their own glucose but need supervision. Some older children may be able to give themselves insulin

Source: American Diabetes Association, 2012.

Down Syndrome

This **video** shows Carly, a young girl with Down Syndrome. Think about the kinds of accommodations used in the classroom in order to promote Carly's health and wellness.

Down syndrome is one of the most common causes of intellectual disability. Down syndrome is also known as trisomy 21, because it occurs when the child has an extra 21st chromosome. Children with this condition usually have some degree of cognitive impairment, reduced muscle tone, and characteristic facial features, such as almond-shaped eyes, small chin, and flat nasal bridge. Children with Down syndrome often suffer from associated health problems, including:

- Congenital heart disease.
- Gastrointestinal abnormalities.
- Leukemia.
- Alzheimer's disease at an early age.
- Immune problems.
- Thyroid problems.
- Problems with hearing and vision.

Children with Down syndrome are typically very social and friendly. They usually experience delays in speech and communication. Although children may understand much of what they hear, their ability to articulate a response and produce understandable speech may be impaired. Motor skill development is also typically delayed. Cognitive challenges related to problem solving and reasoning are evident.

What if . . .

a child in your classroom has Down syndrome? How would you go about planning ways to educate the class about this child's condition? What resources would you use to guide your planning? What would be your goals for this activity?

Classroom Management Strategies Children with Down syndrome are eligible for services through the IDEA. Often an educational assistant is assigned to support the child with Down syndrome along with other children with special needs in the classroom. Teachers should be well oriented to the child's IEP goals and strategies for successful inclusion. Children with Down syndrome benefit from inclusive learning activities that are social and interactive. The use of visual cues is another important strategy to guide children to develop self-help skills and to reinforce verbal messages. Activities should be planned to help children build fine motor skills and to improve gross motor coordination.

Children with Down syndrome are often exceptionally sensitive to the visual cues and responses of others. They may be quick to recognize disapproval and are sensitive to failure, which may cause them to avoid situations that may be difficult. Teachers should provide tasks with appropriate challenge and supportive encouragement.

Muscular Dystrophy

Muscular dystrophy (MD) refers to a group of genetic diseases that cause deterioration of the muscles resulting in progressive weakness, susceptibility to pulmonary infections, and premature death. It is a relatively rare disease that is diagnosed in 500 to 600 newborns each year. The most common type of MD is Duchenne's. It results from a genetic mutation that is linked to the X chromosome, causing the absence of a protein needed to maintain the integrity of muscle. Only males are affected by MD, although females can be carriers of this gene defect.

Initial symptoms of MD are weakness of the lower extremities, which becomes evident in early childhood, usually by 2 to 6 years of age (Heward, 2013). Families or teachers may notice the child has enlargement of the calf muscles, walks on the toes, falls more than other children his age or has difficulty with climbing stairs (Ball et al., 2012; Heward, 2013). Typically, by the middle of the teenage years, the child is unable to walk. Life expectancy is in the 20s.

Treatment for MD focuses on maintaining as much function as possible. Physical, respiratory, and speech therapies may be offered. Assistive devices are used to support mobility. Some drug therapies may be used.

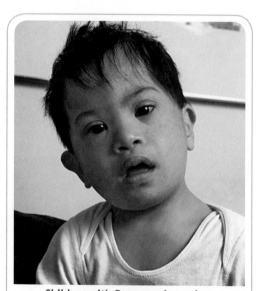

Children with Down syndrome have characteristic facial features.

Classroom Management Strategies Teachers work with early intervention specialists and families to identify the IEP goals for children with MD. Attention to the physical environment is important to allow the child to move easily about the classroom and play yard. Adaptive equipment may be used to support the child's movement. Here is an example:

> Lyle moves with the assistance of an electronic wheelchair. His teacher, Nancy, rearranges the furnishings in her classroom to open pathways for Lyle to move to each activity area. She creates a large open area in the center of the classroom so he can participate easily at group time. At age 3 he is very efficient navigating through the space. His wheelchair has a special attribute that allows him to lower the seat so that he is sitting on the floor. This makes it easy for him to build block structures with his friends and to be at the same height as the other children during group time.

Despite physical health problems, children with MD should receive regular physical therapy and exercise. Outdoor play areas that have firm surfacing are especially important for children who have mobility problems. Teachers are cautioned to never lift these children by the arms because of the increased likelihood of joint dislocations (Heward, 2013). The teacher should provide small motor activities with pieces that come in a range of sizes. This allows the child to select the objects that best fit his ability to grasp and move. Encouraging activities such as hand washing, brushing teeth, and gathering pictures and personal belongings at the end of the day help the child develop organizational and self-help skills.

Seizure Disorders

Seizures are a sign of a brain problem. They occur when the electrical activity in the brain is abnormal. Seizures are the most common pediatric neurological disorder, and they are caused by high fevers, medicines, injuries to the head, and some diseases. Most seizures are relatively harmless, lasting from a few seconds up to 2 minutes. Seizures that last more than 5 minutes are a medical emergency. The types of seizures vary (Ball et al., 2012):

- **Partial seizures** are caused by abnormal activation of a limited number of neurons. Children may have twitching or jerks of only part of their body, one extremity, or the face. These seizures may or may not impair consciousness.
- **Generalized seizures** involve a global, or total, abnormal activation of all neurons. These seizures do impair consciousness. In the past these were called *grand mal seizures.*
- **Absence seizures** cause frequent, abrupt, but brief losses of consciousness often accompanied by eyelid flickering. In the past these were referred to as *petit mal seizures.*

partial seizures
seizures caused by abnormal activation of a limited number of neurons; symptoms typically are related to where the focus is located

generalized seizures
seizures caused by global abnormal activation of all neurons

absence seizures
frequent, brief, abrupt losses of consciousness that are often accompanied by eyelid flickering

Febrile Seizures Some seizures, such as **febrile seizures**, may not represent a seizure disorder. They are caused by fever and occur with the sudden rise in body temperature associated with acute illness. They are usually brief, lasting 1–2 minutes, and are more common among children between 6 months and 3 years of age with a peak incidence of 18 to 24 months. One third of children who experience a febrile seizure will have another one (Ball et al., 2012).

Although most febrile seizures do not indicate an underlying problem or serious infection, they can be a frightening experience for teachers and families. Families should be notified immediately if a child experiences a febrile seizure. A clear description of the event is important for families and medical providers. Because of the risk of recurrence, it is important to control any future fevers. Febrile seizures tend to diminish with age and prognosis is excellent.

febrile seizures
seizures caused by fever

Epilepsy A chronic seizure disorder known as **epilepsy** is defined by having two or more unprovoked, not febrile (fever), seizures. Epilepsy may be caused by problems in brain development, illness, or injury, but in some cases the cause is not known. Epilepsy occurs in about 1% of the population. This chapter's *Health Hint* discusses how epilepsy and other chronic health conditions can have an impact on children's lives and be associated with psychosocial issues.

epilepsy
a chronic seizure disorder that is defined by having two or more unprovoked (not febrile) seizures

HEALTH HINT Chronic Medical Conditions Have an Impact on Children's Lives

Chronic medical conditions such as epilepsy can have a strong impact on the life of families. For example, children with epilepsy have a higher risk of mental health conditions including behavioral disorders, anxiety, and depression. Epilepsy is stressful for families, especially at onset. Parents report a high level of stress and worry associated with watching their child seize. In addition, the unpredictable nature of epilepsy can add to the worry that families experience. Families may wonder what would happen if their child had a seizure at school.

Children with epilepsy also have more problems with academics, even those with normal intelligence. Medications have been proposed as a possible cause but this theory has not been substantiated by research. Families of children with special health care needs will need support and understanding from teachers to assure them that their child is safe and secure. Teachers can carefully document the child's history and what to do if the child experiences an event or worsening of their condition of school. Not only does this ensure that the proper treatment is given, but it also comforts the family and helps relieve their stress.

Classroom Management Strategies A seizure care plan needs to be in place for any child with seizure disorders. Chapter 16 discusses the management of seizures in the classroom. A seizure care plan should include the following information:

- Type and description of the child's seizures.
- Current treatment regimen including medications, schedule, doses, route of administration, and side effects.
- Restrictions from activities including those that could be dangerous to the child should the child have a seizure during the activity and any activities that could precipitate a seizure.
- How to recognize a seizure and recommendations for first aid should a seizure occur.
- Guidelines on when emergency medical help should be obtained for the child.
- Plan to document seizures if they occur including type/frequency of seizures, how the seizure was managed, any relevant observations.
- Plan to support the family of a child with epilepsy.

Teachers also need to be oriented to any medications that need to be given, and a medication administration plan must be in place. Often, medication is not given unless the seizure lasts a certain amount of time, typically minutes. This should be defined by the child's health care provider.

valium
a medication that can be given rectally in the case of acute seizure

Valium is a medication that is often used for acute seizures. It is administered rectally. Teachers follow the protocol for contacting emergency medical services as directed by the medical provider. Management of a seizure disorder may change frequently, especially in young children, requiring the care plan to be reviewed and updated.

Conditions Affecting Communication, Hearing, and Vision

communication
the exchange of ideas, feelings, needs, and desires

Some medical conditions involve the ability to communicate and the use of the hearing and vision sensory systems. **Communication** refers to the exchange of ideas, feelings, needs, and desires (Heward, 2013). It occurs through a variety of avenues including verbal language, facial expressions, written language, body language, and sign language. Effective communication is necessary for all aspects of daily life. Children begin communicating as young infants and progress rapidly in the first few years of life. It is during this time that communication disorders may become apparent.

communication disorder
an impairment in the ability to verbally or nonverbally exchange ideas, desires, or needs

A **communication disorder**, as defined by the American Speech-Language-Hearing Association (ASHA), is "an impairment in the ability to receive, send, process, and comprehend concepts or verbal, nonverbal, and graphic symbols systems" (Heward, 2013, page 283). Conditions affecting hearing and vision can have an adverse impact on aspects of communication. A child born with hearing loss may have difficulty with normal language development. A child with visual problems may not be able to effectively express some forms of nonverbal language. Although many conditions discussed in other sections of this chapter, such as Down syndrome, may involve communication problems, here we focus on children who have disorders specifically affecting communication, hearing, and vision.

Speech and Language Impairments

Speech is the aspect of language that is produced verbally. **Language** is a formal code developed by groups of people for the purpose of communication. Impairments in the speech and language systems interfere with communication. Communication disorders can be caused by damage to a specific organ or part of the body. More commonly, the cause cannot be attributed to any physical condition and some researchers believe that environmental influences may play a role in some communication disorders (Heward, 2013).

Estimates of the prevalence of speech and language impairments vary widely. Current estimates suggest that 2.5% of school-age children receive special education services for speech and language impairment. Additionally, more than half of children receiving special education services for other diagnoses also receive speech and language services (Heward, 2013).

Speech Impairments The term *speech impairment* refers to problems in producing verbal speech. Three types of speech impairments are recognized (Turnbull et al., 2013):

- *Articulation disorders* affect the production of specific speech sounds. Articulation problems make it difficult to understand children's speech.
- *Fluency disorders* affect the rhythm or flow of speech. Stuttering is an example of a fluency disorder.
- *Voice disorders* cause problems with the quality or use of the voice. Voice disorders can cause chronic hoarseness or abnormalities in the air coming through the nasal passage. These disorders are less common in young children.

Language Impairments Language impairments are typically classified as receptive or expressive:

- **Receptive language disorders** are impairments in understanding language. Children with receptive language disorders may have difficulties following directions or understanding spoken language.
- **Expressive language disorders** are impairments in the expression of language, or the use of language to communicate. Expressive language disorders may cause children to incorrectly use words or phrases.

Children with language impairments often have difficulty in school and with social development and peer relationships. They also tend to have more difficulties reading and writing (Heward, 2013).

Classroom Management Strategies Teachers play an important role in identifying children with speech and language impairments. Through interaction and observation, teachers are often able to identify speech and language problems that families may not recognize. In the home it is not unusual for family members to understand the meaning of children's communication by using contextual cues and nonverbal styles of communication. In the classroom setting, a child's challenges with communication may be more evident. Figure 11-3 lists a number of red flags to watch for that cue teachers to recommend that children receive further evaluation for potential communication disorders.

Children with speech and language problems may be eligible to receive early intervention services. Teachers can integrate speech and language goals into the daily curriculum with the help of speech-language pathologists. Consider this example:

> Nephi sets out a display of plastic snakes on the table. He invites Angie to come inspect the toy snakes. First they count the snakes, discovering that there are "seven snakes." Next they inspect the designs on the toy snakes. Some have stripes and some have spots. They count the striped and spotted snakes and find there are "four striped snakes and three spotted snakes." Through this game Nephi helps Angie practice articulating the "s" sounds. They continue to add descriptive words that use the letter "s" sounds, such as "slithering snakes and silly snakes." As other children join the group Nephi suggests that Angie tell the others how to play the counting game using the toy snakes.

speech
the aspect of language produced verbally

language
a formal code developed by groups of people for the purpose of communication

Children with speech and language delays benefit from frequent opportunities to talk about their interests. In this **video**, notice the strategies used by the teacher to keep the child focused on the task, while practicing his communication skills.

receptive language disorders
impairments in the understanding of language

expressive language disorders
impairments in the expression of language

FIGURE 11-3   Identifying Speech and Language Problems

The following indicate that a child needs further evaluation for a speech and language problem:

At < 12 months:

- Rarely requests attention or objects
- Does not use more than one consonant or vowel

12–18 months:

- Does not take turns using vocalizations or utterances
- Does not comprehend single words
- Does not follow one-step commands

18–24 months:

- Does not speak or sign 50 words by age 2
- By age 2, does not begin to use ≥2 word utterances
- Rarely initiates his own language (as opposed to imitating or echoing)

2–3 years:

- Does not engage in small conversations
- Uses only one verb

3–4 years:

- Persons outside the family unable to understand spoken language
- Little or no growth of vocabulary

5 years:

- Has deficits in intelligibility, simple communication with others
- Not interested in learning about printed concepts

Source: Wankoff, 2011.

Hearing Impairment

Hearing impairment is a general term that describes a decrease in ability to hear and discriminate among sounds. Although it is a frequently used term, many people in the Deaf community prefer deaf or hard of hearing. Two kinds of hearing impairment are most common:

- *Conductive hearing loss* refers to the type of hearing loss resulting from problems with the middle ear or eardrum and is usually milder than a sensorineural hearing loss. Conductive hearing loss is most often treated with medications or surgical methods.

- *Sensorineural hearing loss* refers to damage to the acoustic nerves that connect the ear to the brain, or to the inner ear organ called the cochlea. The cochlea is the organ responsible for hearing. This type of hearing loss is permanent and more difficult to treat. The sound of speech from children who have sensorineural hearing loss is often distorted.

Hearing impairment is one of the most common birth defects. Three in 1,000 babies born in America are diagnosed with permanent hearing loss (Heward, 2013). Hearing loss can also develop during childhood and later in life. Hearing impairment can be caused by various factors including genetics, illness experienced by the mother during pregnancy, illness during childhood, and injuries. The use of certain medications may cause hearing loss and some environmental conditions can negatively impact hearing. The *Safety Segment* discusses noise-induced hearing loss.

Early identification of hearing loss is important. Research demonstrates that children who are identified with hearing impairment prior to 6 months of age, and who receive appropriate interventions, have a better chance of developing normal speech and language. Because the early years are so important for the development of speech and language, all states are required to offer a **universal newborn hearing screen** prior to hospital discharge.

universal newborn hearing screen
hearing test done soon after birth that detects hearing loss in newborns

Medical definitions of hearing impairment classify the degree of hearing loss on a spectrum from mild to profound. The following degrees of hearing loss describe the lowest range a child can hear. The following decibel level ranges describe degrees of hearing loss (Ball et al., 2012):

- 0–25 decibels (dB): No hearing loss is present.
- 26–40 dB: Mild hearing loss.
- 41–60 dB: Moderate hearing loss; most conversational speech sounds are missed.

SAFETY SEGMENT   Noise-Induced Hearing Loss in Children

Noise is an important preventable cause of hearing loss in children. Noise exposure destroys cells in the ear that are essential for hearing. Once lost, these cells cannot be regenerated. Noise is a growing concern because of the increasing prevalence of portable music and gaming devices used by children. Other sources of noise include concerts, airplanes, tools, power equipment, and guns. There is even more concern now with extended earpiece use with iPods and similar devices.

Research demonstrates that school-age children are at risk for some degree of hearing loss due to noise exposure. Although the degree of the hearing loss tends to be mild to moderate, it can create challenges for school-age children, particularly in noisy settings like classrooms. In classrooms, even mild hearing loss may reduce how much a child hears and understands directions and lessons. Teachers can make an impact by:

- Recognizing when a child may be having trouble hearing, and referring the child for evaluation.
- Advocating for and implementing policies restricting the use of portable devices and the use of earphones at school.
- Educating parents about noise as a prevalent and preventable cause of hearing loss.

Source: Ball, Bindler, & Cowen, 2012.

- 61–80 dB: Severe hearing loss; no speech sounds can be heard at conversational levels.
- 81–90 dB: Profound hearing loss; no speech sounds heard.
- >90 dB: Deaf; no sounds heard.

After the newborn period, children typically do not receive a hearing screen at preventive health care visits until 4 or 5 years of age. Some early childhood programs incorporate hearing screenings as part of their health services for children and families.

Observation in the early childhood classroom is another way that children may be identified. Teachers may notice symptoms of hearing loss or difficulties in the child's speech development that may suggest hearing impairment. Table 11-5 lists behaviors that suggest hearing loss in infants,

TABLE 11-5 Signs of Potential Hearing Impairment

Age Group	Behavior
Infant	• Diminished or absent startle reflex to loud sound • Awakens only when touched, not when environment is noisy • Does not turn head to sounds by 3 to 4 months • Does not localize sound by 6 to 10 months • Minimal or no babbling
Toddler/preschool	• Unintelligible speech, monotone • Communicates through gesturing • Does not respond to doorbell or telephone • Prefers to play alone and with objects rather than people • Focuses on facial expressions rather than verbal communication
School-age child	• Asks to have statements repeated frequently • Answers questions inappropriately except when looking at speaker's face • Inattention, daydreaming • Poor school performance • Monotone speech • Sits close to TV or turns it up • Prefers to play alone

Source: Ball, Bindler, & Cowen, 2012. Reproduced with permission of Pearson Education, Inc., Upper Saddle River, New Jersey.

preschoolers, and school-age children. It is also important to remember that some children with hearing impairments may not manifest symptoms early in life and can exhibit typical development. This is why screenings are so important. However, if a teacher observes any of the behaviors listed in Table 11-5, the family should be informed and the child referred for evaluation.

Classroom Management Strategies Educational definitions of hearing impairment focus on the impact the hearing loss has on the development and use of speech and language as well as its effects on educational performance. The IDEA identifies two categories under which children may be eligible for services:

- *"Hearing impairment* means impairment in hearing, whether permanent or fluctuating, that adversely affects a child's educational performance but that is not included under the definition of deafness" (U.S. Department of Education, n.d.). A child with a hearing impairment can usually hear and respond to auditory stimuli including speech.

- *"Deafness* means a hearing impairment that is so severe that the child is impaired in processing linguistic information through hearing, with or without amplification, and that adversely affects a child's educational performance" (U.S. Department of Education, n.d.). A child with deafness is prevented from receiving nearly all forms of sound.

Children identified for services by the local education agency may enter the early childhood program with an outline of goals identified in the IEP. The child's IEP and the early intervention team will outline the focus for services in the classroom. The teacher needs to know the style of communication the child is using. Oral approaches include Listening and Spoken Language; visual and gestural systems include Cued Speech and American Sign Language. Some children use a total communication method that combines spoken language and American Sign Language (American Speech-Language Hearing Association, n.d.). The use of sign language also supports the language development of typically developing children.

Families often have strong preferences for a particular mode of communication. Some may prefer the Total Communication method, when a child communicates with both spoken and signed language (Heward, 2013). Sometimes the disability of the child with hearing impairment can be "invisible." Hearing loss cannot be seen, and often children with hearing impairments blend into the classroom so easily that the teacher may forget the child's special health care need. Common strategies used to teach all young children are also appropriate for teaching children with hearing impairments. The focus on seeing and doing and activity-based learning are characteristic learning modes in early childhood that are also appropriate for children with hearing impairments.

Children with hearing impairments rely on their other senses, such as vision, to support learning. Because of their reduced ability to hear, they do not benefit from incidental conversations in the room. A review of the classroom noise level may be necessary to identify ways to reduce background noises. Facing the child when speaking and getting the child's attention before giving directions help to address this challenge. Speaking clearly and simply in a usual tone and volume and avoiding overly long and complex sentences are useful tactics when giving directions. Using appropriate facial expressions and gestures also helps to reinforce verbal messages, as do real-life pictures. The teacher's face and mouth should be clearly visible to the child who may support understanding by reading lips. Teachers also need to know how to check the child's amplification system (hearing aids) *daily* to ensure that it is working appropriately.

vision impairment
an impairment in vision that adversely affects a child's educational performance, even with correction

visual acuity
a measure of how well a child can distinguish forms or discriminate details

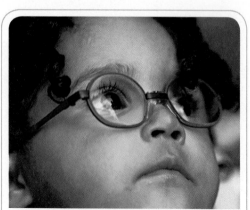

Children with visual impairments rely on their tactile and auditory senses to support learning.

Vision Impairments

The term **vision impairments** refer to conditions in which vision is reduced even when corrected with glasses or contact lenses. Genetics, birth defects, and eye disorders, as well as age-related eye disease, can cause vision impairments. Some of the common causes are refractory errors (nearsightedness and farsightedness), amblyopia, and strabismus. About 2.5% of preschoolers and over 3% of school-age children have vision problems (Ball et al., 2012).

Two kinds of vision impairment are typically recognized: low vision and blindness. These are identified using a test of **visual acuity**, a measure of how well a child can distinguish forms or discriminate details. This is typically assessed by having a child read letters, numbers, or symbols on an eye chart. The measure provides a pair of numbers that compare what the child can see against what a normal eye can see at 20 feet.

- A *normal eye* is scored at 20/20.
- *Low vision* is the term used for measures between 20/70 and 20/400.
- **Blindness** is identified at measures of 20/400.
- *Legal blindness* is measured at 20/200.

For example, a child with low vision (20/70) must stand 20 feet away from an object that a child with normal vision could see clearly at a distance of 70 feet.

blindness
vision of 20/200 or worse even with the best possible correction

Classroom Management Strategies   Children with low vision may not be identified for services by the local education agency. Children with more significant vision loss and blindness are likely to be identified for service and will enter the early childhood classroom with an IEP. These children are likely to receive support services from a vision specialist in addition to the early childhood program, and the specialist may serve as a consultant for the child's teacher.

Children with visual impairments rely on their other senses to support learning. Children with low vision are able to use sight for some activities and also use sound and tactile exploration. For these children it may be useful to assess the lighting in the classroom. Reducing glare and providing color contrasts in some materials may assist the child to visually discriminate among objects. Children who are blind rely primarily on tactile and auditory stimuli.

For children with both types of vision challenges, direct interaction with materials and objects is important to support learning. Sensory activities that allow them to gain vocabulary based on tactile stimuli are good choices. Placing ice cubes in the sensory table where children can feel them melting in warm water is a good way to introduce a discussion of temperature, melting and freezing, solids and liquids, and floating. It is important to maintain appropriate expectations for children with vision impairments so they can be as independent as possible. Other ideas for support include these:

- Speak the child's name when addressing them in the classroom. Children with visual impairments may have a difficult time noticing eye contact.
- Name specific items and events rather than using pronouns like "this" or "that."
- Give verbal warnings prior to handing something to the child.
- Provide appropriate supports for mobility in the classroom.
- When physically showing a child how to do something, put the child's hand over yours rather than the other way around.
- Assign the child appropriate and meaningful classroom "jobs."
- Encourage cooperative group activities so that peer socialization skills can be learned.
- Remember safety while being careful not to overprotect the child.

Children with vision impairments may begin learning tactile codes such as Braille along with their early reading activities in elementary school. Specialized instruction of this kind is usually done by a teaching specialist.

● SUMMARY

Many children have special health care needs. The range of medical needs varies broadly, from the young child with mild environmental allergies to the child with severe cerebral palsy that affects multiple aspects of daily living. Special health care needs can affect the immune system, neurological system, and communication system. Some have more impact on daily living and learning than others. Even those conditions that do not impact cognition may still influence learning, depending on the health and functional status of the child. Teachers work in partnership with others to address the needs of children with health problems.

With the increasing prevalence of children with special medical diagnoses and improved federal regulations that ensure education for all children regardless of their special health care needs, more children are being cared for in early childhood settings at younger ages. This requires the children's program or school to have certain supports in place. Establishing policies and procedures for administration of medications and emergency response protocols are some of the ways programs prepare to serve children with special health care needs. Working as members of the child's educational team provides a network of supports for the child, family, and teachers. Teachers are important resources when identifying goals for inclusion and planning strategies to address these goals in the classroom. Inclusion approaches include creating spaces that are physically and educationally accessible, that invite children to participate as fully as possible, and that support the needs of children with a wide spectrum of medical and educational challenges. Accommodations may also involve making adjustments to the daily routines and how activities are presented so the special learning styles of children with special health needs are addressed.

Children with special health care needs are first of all, children; they are young people interested in being part of a social group where interesting learning activities are available to stimulate their curiosity. Many of the common teaching methods are appropriate for children with special health care needs. For example, activity-based approaches that provide many hands-on experiences are ideal for all children. More specific teaching strategies are designed to fit the needs of individual learners. Together, teachers, families, medical providers, early intervention specialists, and therapists are a part of the community that welcomes and supports children with special health needs.

KEY TERMS

Absence seizures
Adaptive behavior
Albuterol
Alcohol-related neurodevelopmental disorder (ARND)
Asperger's syndrome
Asthma attack
Autism
Autoimmune condition
Blindness
Catheterization
Children with special health care needs
Communication
Communication disorder
Diabetic ketoacidosis (DKA)
Down syndrome
Dyslexia
Encephalopathy
Epilepsy

Executive functioning
Expressive language disorders
Febrile seizures
Fetal alcohol syndrome (FAS)
Functional limitations
Functional status
Gastrostomy tube
Generalized seizures
Hydrocephalus
Hypoglycemia
Immune system
Inhaled steroids
Insulin
Intellectual disability
Language
Learning disabilities
Muscular dystrophy
Nebulizer
Partial seizures

Pervasive developmental disorder (PDD)
Philtrum
Receptive language disorders
Short-term memory
Sickle cell anemia
Spacer
Speech
Spina bifida
Stimulants
Tracheostomy tube
Trigger
Universal newborn hearing screen
Valium
Vision impairment
Visual acuity
Wheeze

REVIEW QUESTIONS

1. How do children's special health care needs affect other aspects of their health and functional status?
2. What are the federal laws that protect the health care needs of children and how do they apply to specific health care needs?
3. In whom and in what geographic regions is asthma more common? What aspects of this illness may be manifested in the early childhood setting?
4. What symptoms would a preschool teacher notice in a child with autism?
5. What aspects of development are affected by fetal alcohol syndrome?
6. How are hearing impairments typically detected?

DISCUSSION STARTERS

1. How might teachers be able to alleviate stressors that families experience when they are caring for a child with a special health care need?

2. As a teacher of a toddler-age group, you notice a child displaying possible symptoms of autism. How do you approach the family with your concerns? How do you prepare for the meeting? To whom do you make a referral?

3. As a teacher in a second-grade classroom, you are teaching a child with a hearing impairment who requires hearing aids. He is able to speak, but the quality of his voice is obviously affected. Other children notice and ask why he sounds different than they do. How do you handle this situation?

PRACTICE POINTS

1. Imagine that a child with type 1 diabetes has enrolled in your third-grade classroom. You know that she checks her blood sugar during the day and receives insulin injections. What other information do you need as she begins attending? Who might you collaborate with in addition to her parents?

2. Oftentimes, children who are suspected as having ADHD are evaluated by the school system before being evaluated by a medical professional. Who evaluates children in your school district? How is the diagnosis made?

3. Call your local health department and ask about the prevalence of lead poisoning in your area. Do preschools in your area conduct lead screening? If so, how?

WEB RESOURCES

Children and Adults with Attention Deficit/Hyperactivity Disorder
www.chadd.org

Managing Asthma in Schools
www.epa.gov/iedweb00/schools/asthma.html

National Survey of Children with Special Health Care Needs
www.cshcndata.org/Content/Default.aspx

Right Under My Nose: A Book for Children with Spina Bifida
www.myspinabifidabook.org

MyEducationLab™

Go to Topic 7 (Chronic Illness/Special Health Care Needs) in the MyEducationLab (www.myeducationlab.com) for your course, where you can:

- Find learning outcomes for Chronic Illness/Special Health Care Needs along with the national standards that connect to these outcomes.

- Complete Assignments and Activities that can help you more deeply understand the chapter content.

- Apply and practice your understanding of the core teaching skills identified in the chapter with the Building Teaching Skills and Dispositions learning units.

- Examine challenging situations and cases presented in the IRIS Center Resources.

- Check your comprehension on the content covered in the chapter by going to the Study Plan in the Book Resources for your text. Here you will be able to take a chapter quiz, receive feedback on your answers, and then access Review, Practice, and Enrichment activities to enhance your understanding of chapter content.

twelve
Children's Mental Health

learning outcomes

AFTER READING THIS CHAPTER, YOU SHOULD BE ABLE TO:

1. Define mental health and discuss the biological, environmental, and developmental factors that influence mental health in young children.

2. Describe the stages of social and emotional development in children ages birth to 8 years of age.

3. Discuss ways in which children's social and emotional development is fostered in the early childhood classroom.

4. Explain how mental health problems are recognized and identify the most common types of mental health problems seen in young children.

5. Discuss strategies used when teaching children with mental health problems and challenging behaviors.

Parent and teacher conferences have been scheduled for the 2- to 3-year-old class group. Meegan is preparing to meet with Heather's parents. She has made a special effort to schedule the conference late in the day to be sure that there will be enough time to discuss her concerns. Meegan is worried about how to talk about the behavior concerns she has observed. Her aggressive behaviors with the other children have not stopped in spite of Meegan's efforts to guide and teach her. Meegan has intervened more than once when Heather grabbed another child around the neck. One time Heather picked up a large block and hit the assistant teacher on the head, and during group time she saw Heather hit Arturo in the face with her hand without even turning to look at him.

Meegan believes the parents have also been experiencing difficult behaviors at home because they have shared that they always take the baby to the grandmother's house if they need to leave Heather at home with a caregiver. To prepare for the conference, Meegan has done some reading about social and emotional development and behavior and explored some of the services that are available in the community. She is uncomfortable about sharing the unpleasant observations she has made, but she feels prepared and hopes that the conversation will go well so that she and the family can develop a plan to help Heather.

Sometimes children struggle as they learn to participate in early childhood settings and classrooms. They may experience problems developing typical social and emotional skills and, as a result, exhibit significant behavior problems in the classroom. These may be signs of delayed social and emotional development, or unrecognized mental health issues. Teachers like Meegan are committed to children's positive growth in all developmental domains. They recognize the importance of emotional health to children's well-being and ability to grow and thrive. They are concerned when children display significant behavior difficulties and need guidance about how to effectively address them.

In this chapter the terms *social and emotional development* and *mental health* are used interchangeably to represent a *positive* state of mental and emotional wellness. This highlights the understanding that just as teachers support children's physical health through purposeful practices, teachers also foster children's mental and emotional health through intentionally established environments and positive relationships and experiences that encourage healthful social and emotional development.

In this chapter we focus on ways that teachers contribute to children's mental health. First we define the terminology we will use to discuss children's mental health and describe the impacts of mental health on children's growth and development. We then provide an overview of healthy social and emotional development and discuss the challenges that occur if development goes off course. Next we describe how social and emotional development is related to learning and success in school and explore how children's mental health is promoted in the early childhood classroom. Finally, we review some of the more common mental health disorders and provide guidance for partnering with families and mental health professionals to design successful interventions when children need special help. Focusing on children's mental health is an important teacher responsibility that builds foundations for children's future success and happiness.

MyEducationLab™

Visit the MyEducationLab for *Nutrition, Health, and Safety for Young Children* to enhance your understanding of chapter concepts with a personalized Study Plan. You'll also have the opportunity to hone your teaching skills through video-based Assignments and Activities, as well as Building Teaching Skills and Dispositions lessons.

UNDERSTANDING MENTAL HEALTH

The early years are a significant period for establishing wellness habits and patterns. This includes fostering children's emotional health as well as their physical health and wellness. Teachers are best prepared to positively impact children's emotional health by understanding mental health, what influences it, how it develops across the early years, and how to recognize typical social and emotional development.

mental health
the capacity to experience and manage emotions, form close and secure relationships, and learn and experience the environment

Defining Mental Health

Mental health refers to children's abilities to understand and manage their emotions and behaviors, to function positively with others in age-appropriate and developmentally appropriate ways, and to form meaningful relationships. It encompasses the capacities to enjoy life and to be flexible, adaptable, and resilient (U.S. Public Health Service, 2000). Just as physical health refers to the presence of bodily wellness and absence of disease, mental health is a positive term that refers to the presence of mental or emotional wellness and the absence of mental illness.

The competencies associated with mental health are observable. For example, in her infant and toddler class, Sharina recognizes healthy social and emotional development, or "good" mental health, when she observes Caitlin laughing and crawling over to interact with Lin Lin. Caitlin shows appropriate interest, enjoyment, and curiosity and expresses this through developmentally appropriate emotions and actions. To Sharina this observation is similar to the height and weight measurements she takes to understand children's physical health. While physical measurements give clues to physical health, observations of children's interactions with their peers and with adults help teachers understand children's mental health.

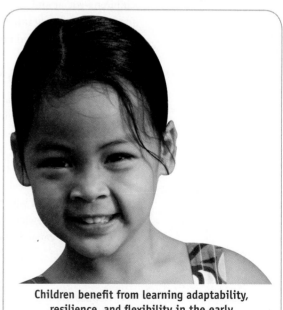

Children benefit from learning adaptability, resilience, and flexibility in the early childhood years.

Positive experiences and interactions in the early years help children to form close and secure interpersonal relationships.

continuum of mental health
the range of behaviors associated with positive social and emotional development, mental health problems, and mental illness

Social and emotional development is a familiar domain of human development. It is also linked to, and considered part of, the **continuum of mental health**. Most early childhood sources consider social and emotional development and mental health to be synonymous, or one and the same (Zero to Three, n.d.). This is helpful in guiding teachers to implement classroom practices that promote social and emotional development and, hence, children's mental health. Teachers should recognize, however, that poor social and emotional development does not automatically suggest that children have mental illness. The continuum of mental health includes behaviors that:

- *Demonstrate positive social and emotional development*, suggesting the children are on course for positive outcomes.
- *Indicate problems with social and emotional development*, also called *mental health problems*, suggesting that further attention is needed to guide the child to more positive mental health habits.
- *Imply potential underlying mental disorders*, or *illness*, suggesting that the child be evaluated by a medical professional for possible mental health diagnosis and services.

Exhibiting behaviors that are typical for the child's age and developmental level indicates that social and emotional development is on course. Behaviors that are not typical are more challenging to understand. They may indicate that a child is simply slower in this area of development or that the child has not had sufficient experiences to practice and attain typical social and emotional skills. These challenging behaviors may also be a sign that the child is *at risk* for more serious problems over time. The most important point is that challenging behaviors be identified and managed early in order to prevent more serious problems later. The boundaries of what behaviors constitute appropriate and inappropriate development are further clouded based on the expectations of social behaviors in different cultures and neighborhoods. For example, behaviors one group considers aggressive may be viewed by another group as a sign of strength.

In spite of the difficulties associated with defining what behaviors suggest mental health problems, teachers are responsible for managing children's behavior and advancing children's development. In this chapter we explore these issues and offer a range of ways teachers play a role in fostering children's social and emotional development. Teachers do not do this work alone. They keep informed of emerging information, partner with families, collaborate with mental health specialists if needed, and design and implement interventions to promote positive mental health.

Current Focus on Children's Mental Health

Recently children's mental health has gained special attention because the number of children displaying significant behavioral challenges in the classroom is increasing. This has raised awareness that mental health problems are evident even among very young children. In 2001, the U.S. Surgeon General released a report on the critical nature of the state of mental health in children in the United States. The report notes that growing numbers of children are experiencing social-emotional difficulties and mental health disorders. Of even more concern is the increasing number of children with these problems who receive no mental health evaluation or treatment. In the report, the surgeon general acknowledged that mental health is a vital component of children's general health and crucial to their capacity for learning. The report (U.S. Public Health Service, 2000) highlights the need to:

- Increase awareness of childhood mental illness.
- Reduce the stigma of mental disorders.
- Strengthen frameworks for the recognition, diagnosis, and treatment of mental disorders and eliminate disparities in mental health.

POLICY POINT **Legislation Impacts Children's Mental Health**

A number of recent federal changes will have an impact on mental health in young children in the coming years. For example, the Children's Health Insurance Program Reauthorization 2009 legislation requires that mental health benefits be equal to medical benefits. This should improve competency of mental health providers as well as increase availability of services. The law also addresses prevention, early intervention, and disparities. Teachers should notice and utilize the increase in services available in schools and communities.

Source: Information from Stagman & Cooper, 2010.

Early childhood teachers interact with many children and need special understanding about how mental health develops and ways to support positive outcomes. This chapter's *Policy Point* also describes recent legislation influencing childhood mental health.

Influences on Children's Mental Health

Children's mental health is influenced by a variety of dynamics that can be apparent even in infancy. These include biological and environmental factors. Particularly with respect to childhood mental health, there is a strong relationship between biological and environmental factors that in turn affect social and emotional development in children.

Biological Factors

Biological factors are traits or characteristics that are specific to the individual child and are related to genetics and proper development of the brain. The importance of these factors begins in utero. Biological factors include:

- *Genetics*, or hereditary factors such as those that influence physical size and appearance, and pace of development.
- *Temperament*, or the child's style and personality, often described as "easy," "slow to warm up," or "difficult."
- *Physical and health attributes*, such as physical anomalies and prematurity.
- *Type of nutrition*, including quality of food.
- *Brain development*: growth and development of the brain.

Brain development significantly influences children's mental health. Although the development of the brain begins at conception and does not end until adulthood, the fastest rate of growth is in utero and during the first few years of life. During this period, an incredible amount of information is learned, and the structures for future learning are established.

Brain development is influenced by experiences with people and the environment. Interactions that are nurturing encourage brain cell development and refine brain cell connections, which set the foundation for positive social and emotional health. Persistent stressful experiences damage normal brain development, causing problems with learning, behavior, and physical and emotional health (Zeanah, Berlin, & Boris, 2011).

These biological factors interact with environmental factors described below creating either positive or negative influences on social and emotional development.

Environmental Factors

Children's social and emotional development is extremely vulnerable to environmental factors such as these:

- Family life situations, including stress, domestic violence, poverty, abuse, neglect, parental drug use or mental illness, the quality of the nurturing relationship, and cultural influences on parenting.

- Community well-being, including community violence, accessible health care, and social service resources.

- Environmental toxins including chemicals such as mercury and secondhand smoke.

- Emotional and social influences, such as quality of **caregiver** bonding and family interactions. Caregivers include parents and other family members such as grandparents, child care providers, and teachers.

caregiver
persons who care for children such as parents, family members, and child care providers

Environmental factors that introduce stress into family life can exert a strong negative influence on children's social and emotional development because anything that affects the parent–child relationship affects the child. Stressors associated with poverty, such as food insecurity, poor housing conditions, or unmet health needs, are examples of factors that add challenge to family life and put children at risk for poor social and emotional development (Spenrath, Clarke, & Kutcher, 2011). This chapter's *Safety Segment* discusses the role of stress on the developing brain. Teachers can help by providing families with ways to cope with the stresses of poverty, including parenting strategies to try at home, and by encouraging parents to build strong and positive relationships with their children. Additionally, the quality of the teacher–child relationship can have a significant impact on social and emotional health outcomes (Biringen, et al., 2012).

Jenna, who teaches infants, knows that some people get frustrated with babies who cry. But she has a special affinity for infants and enjoys trying a variety of approaches to create a strong and positive bond with each child. She is usually highly successful in helping babies establish a strong attachment and develop alternative ways of communicating.

Understanding the Impacts of Mental Health on General Development

Social and emotional development is closely linked to all other forms of development including physical, cognitive, and the development of healthy relationships. When typical milestones in social and emotional development are not achieved, children tend to also have significant challenges in other aspects of development. Social, emotional, and behavior problems during the early years get in the way of learning, and lead to higher incidences of academic problems, aggression, delinquency, and crime in school-age children and adolescents (Stagman & Cooper, 2010).

Children with significant social and emotional challenges are often not able to form close friendships and ultimately may not be capable of assuming the tasks of adulthood, such as maintaining relationships, caring for their own children, and keeping a job. Many of them have more problems with the justice system as they enter the adolescent years (Stagman & Cooper, 2010). If undetected and untreated, mental health challenges are more likely to persist as children get older. Concerns

SAFETY SEGMENT   The Role of Stress on the Developing Brain

For both physical and mental health, risk factors and protective factors exist that impact the outcome for each individual. Protective factors contribute to healthy development. Examples include a child having a meaningful relationship with an adult. Risk factors are factors that increase the likelihood of problems, such as exposure to violence of abuse. Other risk factors related to families include domestic violence, marital discord, history of living in foster care, and family history of substance abuse or mental health problems.

When children are exposed to stress, hormones are released called stress hormones. Evidence shows that high levels of stress hormones impact the developing brain. These effects can lead to problems related to learning, memory, and executive function. This is manifested by an inability to adapt to new situations, inability to regulate and manage emotions, or an inability to manage future adverse events.

Because many of the stressors children are exposed to are related to societal factors such as violence, poverty, and single parenting, policies and programs are needed in schools and communities to educate families about the importance of social and emotional health and to actually promote health in settings where children spend so much time.

Sources: Bershad & Blaber, 2011; Shonkoff & Garner, 2012.

about the potential of long-lasting negative impacts on children's mental health have led to the development of principles that guide mental health services.

In the opening scenario, Meegan doesn't know if Heather's behaviors are an indication of a mental health problem. But she does know that Heather is experiencing challenges that are getting in the way of learning. She hopes that discussing these challenges will open up conversation with Heather's family about ways to help Heather at home and at school.

Characteristics of Social and Emotional Development

Social and emotional development begins at birth and progresses actively during the preschool years. It is highly dependent on healthy interactions and relationships with people including family members, teachers, and peers. Various factors influence and shape children's social and emotional development such as characteristics of the child, family, and community.

Children's social and emotional development occurs in a relatively predictable pattern across the early years. They emerge through children's many interactions with their family, teachers, and classmates, and according to their developmental readiness. Table 12-1 lists social and emotional milestones of infants from birth to 12 months of age. Characteristics of children 1 to 8 years of age are listed in Table 12-2. Overall, social and emotional development shows a progression from self-centered thinking to a greater understanding of being in relationships with others. Understanding the characteristic steps of social and emotional development helps teachers recognize behaviors that are age and developmentally appropriate, providing information to guide the creation of focused and purposeful activities in the classroom.

Infants

Even in the first few months, infants develop signs of healthy social and emotional development. Characteristics typical of the first year of life include (American Academy of Pediatrics, 2009):

- Developing a social smile.
- Imitating movements and facial expressions.
- Expressing communication with face and body.
- Responding to others' emotions and expressing joy often.

After 3 to 4 months of age, infants start becoming less interested in basic needs such as eating and sleeping and more interested in the world around them, providing more opportunities to strengthen relationships with caregivers. These signs of healthful development evolve from children's sense of

The emotional development of toddlers is marked by increasing self-awareness and attention to others' emotions. As you watch this **video**, think about how these aspects of development are connected with the mental health of young children.

TABLE 12-1	Social and Emotional Characteristics of Infants Birth to 12 Months
Age	**Characteristics**
By 6 Months	• Focuses on sights, sounds, and interactions • Communicates needs through expressions, sounds, and movements • Smiles and enjoys playful interaction • Develops attachment when needs are met
6 to 12 Months	• Seeks interaction • Enjoys initiating and imitating sounds and actions • Responds positively to encouragement • Prefers familiar routines • Has preference for parent and regular caregivers • May be shy or anxious with strangers

Source: Information from American Academy of Pediatrics, 2009.

TABLE 12-2 Social and Emotional Characteristics of Children Ages 1 to 8 Years

Age	Characteristics
1–2 years	• Communicates through both words and actions • Uses increasingly complex vocabulary • Identifies and communicates likes and dislikes • Expresses wide range of emotions • May struggle with emotions and behaviors in new settings • Enjoys interacting with toys • Sometimes cooperates; sometimes seeks to be independent • Plays alone and alongside others
3–5 years	• Begins to identify and talk about own emotions • May express fears or be concerned about "monsters" • Enjoys humor including silly words and word games • May be self-centered but beginning to show empathy for others • Responds well to routines; may need support to make changes • Engages in detailed make-believe play; may struggle with fantasy and reality • Expresses self through singing, dancing, arts and crafts • Seeks interaction with other children
6–8 years	• Uses language to share information and describe stories and events • Seeks independence, but still has fears • Develops a sense of right and wrong • Enjoys companionship with adults but prefers to play with other children • Wants to be liked and accepted by peers • Expresses personal interests and preferred play • Develops and repeats intricate play themes and rules of play • Plays cooperative games with designated rules

safety and security. A sense of security emerges from the consistent caregiver's warm, affectionate tone, familiar routines, and positive social interactions.

During infancy, differences in children's temperaments may become more apparent and require that caregivers adjust their interactions for each individual child. Babies of all temperaments need to experience loving, responsive adults, but the manner in which the adults interact with them may be slightly different. For example, more energetic babies may need more patience and gentle guidance from caregivers, whereas calm, sensitive babies may need to be eased into contact with adults and other children (American Academy of Pediatrics, 2009).

Interruptions in normal development can result in significant problems during infancy. For example, infants who experience hardships or difficulties in attachment with the caregiver during this critical period are more likely to demonstrate abnormal expressions of emotions, inattention, and distractibility, disruptions in feeding and sleeping patterns, developmental delays, and abnormal relationships with their peers and caregivers as they grow older (Center on the Developing Child at Harvard University, 2010). This highlights the need to focus on ensuring that infants establish a sense of safety, trust, and security as crucial elements of social and emotional development during the first year of life.

One to Two Years

egocentric
the child's view of self as the center of the world

During the second year of life, children develop an image of their social world, which includes family, friends, caregivers, and acquaintances. Children at this age view themselves to be at the center of the world. This view is described as being **egocentric**. Although other people interest them, children at this age have no idea how these other people think or feel (American Academy of Pediatrics, 2009). For example, 1- to 2-year-old children may play alongside others, but they do not yet interact with purpose or play cooperatively. Characteristics of social and emotional development during the second year of life include (American Academy of Pediatrics, 2009):

- Imitating behaviors of others.
- Being increasingly aware of self as separate from others.
- Being increasingly excited about being around other children.
- Demonstrating increasing independence.
- Beginning to show defiant behaviors.
- Showing more separation anxiety until midyear when it fades.

Interest in exploration is a characteristic of children in the toddler years, creating a "pushing and pulling" situation that can seem confusing. These children desire more independence and may express defiance when exploration is hindered, while at the same time needing to be confident in the caregiver as a source of security. Exploration in toddlers can be encouraged by providing safe, adequate play areas, encouraging children's participation, and using language to label objects, pictures, and ideas. It is important to invite these young children into free exploration within established limits.

Children in this age group need clear and consistent guidance. Typical 2-year-old behavior includes challenges such as aggression. However, these interactions need to be redirected appropriately so that they learn how to manage their emotions. Focused approaches to guidance build on children's natural curiosity and tendency to explore while teaching appropriate boundaries. Teaching children the parameters for play, establishing clear limits for behavior, and guiding children appropriately without harsh punishment or scolding are important strategies that enhance social and emotional development.

Two to Three Years

During the third year of life children continue to be concerned about their own needs. They are still developing awareness of others, and may not understand how others feel. Characteristics of social and emotional development for this age group include:

- Exhibiting more sense of individuality.
- Demonstrating more advanced memory in certain areas.
- Growing in emotional understanding.
- Increasing interest in friendships.
- Increasing development of conscience (sense of right and wrong).

Playing imitation and pretend games are important to social development for this age group. Children 2 to 3 years of age tend to participate in parallel, or side-by-side, play unless they want to play with a toy that is being used by another child. These situations create important opportunities for children in this age group to explore concepts such as sharing and taking turns.

Children at this developmental age seek autonomy and exhibit self-assertion. They are most concerned about their own needs and mostly cannot understand how others feel (American Academy of Pediatrics, 2009). These are complex challenges, and it is natural for children to struggle to maintain emotional balance. Negotiating a plan to share a toy may begin well, but when it comes to deciding who gets the toy first, the negotiation may result in frustration and impatience. A child might exclaim, "I *AM* sharing, but I want to play with the truck first!" Emotionally, the 2- to 3-year-old period is characterized by mood swings, which are an indication that the child is trying to learn how to control actions, impulses, and feelings (American Academy of Pediatrics, 2009).

It is natural for children in this age group to test limits and occasionally lose control. Managing their emotional impulses is difficult; thus, anger and frustration may turn quickly into crying, hitting, or screaming (American Academy of Pediatrics, 2009). Understanding that such behaviors are part of children's natural struggle to gain social and emotional resiliency and competency in difficult situations is important as teachers implement guidance strategies.

Teachers can help children of this age develop healthy emotional skills by setting reasonable and consistent limits that allow children to understand the boundaries for actions and behaviors and begin to take charge of their actions. Offering appropriate encouragement and reinforcement for appropriate behaviors is important. Teachers also need to be prepared to redirect inappropriate behaviors and to help children begin to understand how negative behaviors affect the children around them.

In the chapter opening scenario, Meegan knows that Heather's aggressive behaviors in the classroom won't just go away. She understands that it is her responsibility to identify specific strategies to guide Heather to more appropriate behaviors. At the same time Meegan knows she must try to recognize and understand the challenges that may be limiting Heather's healthful development.

Learning to share is a stage in social and emotional development. Even when very young children agree to share, they still may want the toy first!

Three to Four Years

At ages 3 to 4 years, children's sense of identity and security is stronger and they become more interested in developing relationships with others. Characteristics of social and emotional development for 3- and 4-year-olds include:

- Exhibiting increased interest in interacting with others.
- Using language to communicate wants, needs, and ideas.
- Demonstrating greater ability to manage emotions and regulate behavior.
- Following rules and showing an interest in pleasing others.
- Continuing interest in having a strong relationship with the teacher.

Children in this age group are increasingly interested in associative play, or playing alongside other children and engaging in a similar focus. For example, 3-year-olds might be observed building blocks side by side. They share the same materials and talk about what they are doing, but their play is essentially individual. During this time children start to become more aware of the feelings and actions of others. They notice if another child is upset and can begin to recognize the consequences of their actions.

For example, when Lindsay asks Ben what will happen if he keeps pushing his truck against Karen's block tower, Ben is able to say, "It will fall down." Lindsay follows up by asking, "What do you think Karen thinks about that?" Three-year-olds are becoming more able to take turns, trade toys, and use fewer tactics such as grabbing, whining, and screaming to get what they want (American Academy of Pediatrics, 2009). A vivid imagination begins to develop during this period, enabling children to explore a wide range of emotions including love, anger, protest, and fear. Imaginary friends are common and children may shift rapidly from fantasy to reality. Children continue to need the support of teachers to understand the expectations of behavior and to help them learn ways of managing relationships and emotions.

Four to Five Years

Children become very social at ages 4 to 5 years. They begin to enjoy an active social life and may even have a *best* friend (American Academy of Pediatrics, 2009). Friendships should be encouraged because these are key opportunities for children to practice the social and emotional skills that are involved in building and maintaining relationships. Characteristics of social and emotional development for this age group include:

- Focusing on social interactions.
- Practicing taking leadership roles.
- Exhibiting an increasing ability to understand the perspective of others.
- Demonstrating ability to focus on projects.
- Being literal with rules and needing support to understand flexibility.

Four- and 5-year-old children begin to engage in cooperative play in which elaborate games and rules are established, roles are assigned, and the course of play involves negotiation and give-and-take situations. During this time, children develop increased sensitivity for the feelings of others. They are increasingly able to identify feelings and recognize the impact of their behaviors. Self-confidence is also developing, and children are ready for responsibilities that build their sense of competence such as setting a table or cleaning a play area. This age group continues to need the support and guidance of teachers to ensure that all children are included in play and to find security in consistent expectations about behavior.

Five to Eight Years

Children in kindergarten and elementary school enter a time of industrious exploration of their world and interest in greater independence. Characteristics of social and emotional development for this age group include:

- Increasing interest in autonomy and independence.
- Continuing to judge self on how adults value and respond to what they do.
- Beginning to rely on peers for feedback about what is good and bad.
- Demonstrating individual skills and competencies.
- Communicating emotions, ideas, wants, and needs.

Children in this age group tend to become very involved in projects and enjoy working on them over a period of days, seeing them through to completion. It is also a time in which children begin to build friendships and social connections outside the family, developing friends in the neighborhood and class group.

Cooperative play evolves to a high level as 5- to 8-year-old children carry play themes over from one day to the next. A child may have several good friends, most often children of the same sex, and enjoy frequent contact and "play dates." This is also a time during which children may have heated disagreements that emerge and "blow over" quickly; the child who is an "enemy" on one day may be a "best friend" on the next. Children are growing in their ability to understand the feelings of others. They are able to nurture younger children while looking up to older children as role models.

This age range is also a challenging "between" age. On the one hand, children ages 5 to 8 years are seeking greater independence and find pride in their emergent skills, which may be displayed by tattling when others break the rules, or "pushing back" and showing resistance when given guidance. At the same time, they may still have youthful fears such as death, rejection, or failure, and they can be very sensitive to feedback.

● PROMOTING SOCIAL AND EMOTIONAL DEVELOPMENT

Growing numbers of children spend many hours in early childhood settings during their early years, providing significant opportunities for teachers to promote positive social and emotional development. Programs that plan on supporting social and emotional development can contribute to decreased expulsions due to behavior problems, decrease challenging behaviors, and increase competence with respect to social and emotional health (Smith, Stagman, Blank, Ong, & McDow, 2011). Creating appropriate environments, establishing positive relationships, and implementing strategies that specifically encourage social and emotional development equip children with the skills they need to be successful in kindergarten and build capacities that support children's mental health.

Creating Supportive Environments

Establishing environments that are welcoming and attuned to children's development sets the stage for appropriate social and emotional development. Many studies have suggested that children's social and emotional development is encouraged in early childhood environments that have specific characteristics such as (Biringen, et al., 2012):

- High quality teacher–child relationships.
- High classroom quality.
- Quality of attachment relationship between teachers and infants/toddlers.

Teachers are responsible for creating the welcoming spaces where children play, learn, and thrive. They do this by creating a sense of safety and security, and by arranging the space to avoid unnecessary conflicts, such as providing space for block play and construction that is not in the walkway of the dramatic play center. Other aspects include creating social and quiet areas that allow children to select the setting that meets their needs, and encouraging self-sufficiency by providing toileting areas that allow children to be self-sufficient when age appropriate and labeling tubs and shelves for toys so children can help at cleanup time. Young children recognize environments that are child oriented and child friendly. These attentions to the physical space communicate that children are welcomed and valued.

In this **video**, a teacher helps Alec learn how to manipulate an eyedropper. Think about the different strategies used by this teacher in supporting Alec's learning of a new skill. How do her behaviors communicate caring?

Establishing Caring Relationships

During the early years the child–caregiver relationship has the most important environmental influence on a children's mental health. This relationship exerts positive influence on a child's development when the relationship is responsive and nurturing. Conversely, the relationship can have a negative influence when the relationship is harsh, punitive, or insecure. As a result the quality of the relationship children have with their caregiver can be either a protective factor or a risk factor for social and emotional development.

Recent research has highlighted the value of the teacher–child relationship as making unique contributions to children's social and emotional development (Heller et al., 2011; Biringen, et al., 2012). In the classroom these contributions are put into action through close and nurturing interactions between children and their teachers that demonstrate commitment to building strong and positive reciprocal relationships.

Nurturing Relationships

Building nurturing relationships is a primary component of healthy teacher–child interaction. It encompasses the essential elements of the teacher's contribution to children's positive mental health: respect, responsiveness, appropriate guidance, and positive expectations. For example:

Teachers help young children gain social and emotional skills by setting reasonable limits and providing clear guidelines for behavior.

- Providing interesting challenges and encouraging children's natural interests to explore and discover communicates respect, which enhances each child's feeling of worth.
- Recognizing children's strengths and needs, and responding by purposefully planning activities and experiences to meet those needs, shows value for children and promotes a mutually trusting relationship.
- Communicating appropriate limits and guiding children to positive interactions help children learn how to be positive members of the group and how to build friendships, demonstrating faith in their capabilities.
- Supporting and caring for children through challenging circumstances, and persisting in helping children to learn, expresses confidence in children's competency.

Teachers also serve as models for children regarding how to manage difficult situations. When teachers face challenges with ease, children learn coping strategies rather than defeat. Some children are born with conditions that influence their overall health such as prematurity or heart defects that may challenge their social and emotional development. The effects of these conditions on children's mental health can be modified by the teacher–child relationship. If a child is born very prematurely, the teacher can provide high-quality stimulation and attention in order to maximize that child's potential. This focused interaction communicates to the infant a sense of being valued, demonstrates commitment and love for the child, and models a positive approach to managing challenges.

In her Head Start classroom, Jan tries to model appropriate interactions when she conducts home visits for families of toddlers who have identified special developmental needs. She helps families recognize their child's abilities and accomplishments as they unfold, and encourages them to enjoy their child's unique personality.

Building Attachment

Attachment refers to the bonds of trust, care, understanding, and safety that develop between children and their caregivers. Attachment is a springboard for exploration and future learning. Children who experience the positive bonds of attachment are able to explore and learn with confidence. They know that their caretaker is close and accessible if needed. Without the confidence provided by secure attachment relationships, children may be afraid or remain passive and be unable to initiate and appropriately participate in learning. Children who form strong attachment relationships are better able to manage separation from their families as they enter the early childhood setting, and ultimately are supported to understand themselves as unique human beings (Biringen, et al., 2012; Bowlby, 1969). The quality of the relationship with teachers is associated with academic achievement and social competence (Biringen, et al., 2012).

Secure attachments also build children's perceptions of value and self-worth, which are components of personal safety. For example, children who feel valued are better able to understand the concept of safety rules for themselves and others. The ability to develop an attachment relationship is considered a hallmark of emotional wellness.

attachment
the ability to form close relationships; to bond with others

> ## What if . . .
> a mother of a child in your care blamed family problems on her child's poor social development? How might you explain more healthful ways to approach the child and family's challenge? What ideas do you have to help the parent find support for the family problems mentioned?

Providing Unstructured Play

Free and unstructured play contributes to children's cognitive, physical, creative, expressive, and social and emotional development. It is considered so important to childhood that the United Nations Commission on Human Rights has identified play as a *right* of childhood (Committee on the Rights of the Child, 1991). Children's involvement in play is one aspect of social and emotional development that is easily observed. Through play children are immersed in dynamic interaction and exploration with the objects and people of their world. Play provides opportunities for children to participate in enjoyable activities, use their imaginations, test ideas, practice dexterity, explore outcomes, and gain mastery. Unstructured play, or play that is not directed by adults, is especially important. It allows children to be self-directed in determining the rules and procedures involved in their play themes. This inspires an individual experience of direction and mastery and also encourages social interaction and problem solving. These activities result in a sense of accomplishment and cooperation by using skills that teach resilience and negotiation (Milteer, Ginsburg, Council on Communications and Media Committee on Psychosocial Aspects of Child and Family Health, & Mulligan, 2012). The confidence and resiliency that children develop through child-directed play builds capacities that support them in new situations and challenges. They learn of their abilities to impact the world and apply decision making to outcomes. The *Teaching Wellness* activities provide ideas for setting the stage for children's understanding of their own competencies.

Play also brings children into contact with other people and provides opportunities for them to experience useful social skills such as taking turns, waiting, negotiating, compromising, and sharing (Milteer et al., 2012). Unstructured play allows children to explore according to their own interests and at their own pace. Children who are less verbal, who are learning English, or who have special developmental needs are equally able to engage in and benefit from play when they are allowed to set their own pace and follow their own interests.

TEACHING WELLNESS　I Can Do Things

LEARNING OUTCOME　To develop children's recognition of their own competence by guiding them to realistically identify themselves as people who can do things.

INFANTS AND TODDLERS

- **Goal:** Children experience the teacher describing the child's abilities.
- **Materials:** No materials are needed.
- **Activity plan:** Use everyday activities and experiences to encourage, name, and describe the infant and toddler's emergent skills. Use phrases such as "You are drinking milk from the bottle. You know how to drink milk!" or "I see you are looking at the book. You know how to turn the pages."
- **How to adjust the activity:** Describe the actions of adults, pointing out what the grownup can do, such as "Your mommy knows how to pack your lunch" or "Your dada knows how to zip your coat." As children begin to develop language, spend some quiet time talking with the child and remembering all the things the child did during the day. Summarize the list, saying, "You colored on some paper, you ate your snack, you took your nap. You know how to do many things."
- **Did you meet your goal?** Does the infant enjoy the friendly conversation? Does the toddler begin to respond when the teacher describes "what" the child can do? Does the child provide examples when asked, "Sasha, what do you know how to do?"

PRESCHOOLERS AND KINDERGARTNERS

- **Goal:** Children can identify skills they have and skills they desire.
- **Materials:** Magazine or clip-art pictures showing people doing many different kinds of activities, some of which depict skills children can typically accomplish and some that take training or practice. Be sure to select pictures that show a range of skill activities, people of varying ages, those with special developmental needs, and other features that would be familiar to the children in the group.
- **Activity plan:** Guide the child to look at each picture and place it in the "I can do this now" pile or the "I would like to learn to do this" pile. Invite the child to describe one of her skills in detail (such as brushing teeth or cutting a banana slice). Help the child imagine how she could learn a skill that is in her "like to learn" pile (such as riding a bicycle or baking muffins).
- **How to adjust the activity:** Play a "Can you do this?" game. Take turns asking, "Do you know how to . . . jump?" or ". . . take care of a goat?" Add some silly options: ". . . how to give a hippopotamus a bath?"
- **Did you meet your goal?** Can children realistically identify their current skills?

SCHOOL-AGE CHILDREN

- **Goal:** Children are able to identify many personal skills.
- **Materials:** Paper, pens, stapler.
- **Activity plan:** Guide the children to construct an *I Can Do Things* book that includes drawings and stories about skills they have.
- **How to adjust the activity:** Work with the children to identify different kinds of skill "chapters" for their book, such as Caring for Myself, Caring for Others, and Caring for My World. Periodically encourage children to add to their book.
- **Did you meet your goal?** Is each child able to draw and write about many skills?

Through play, children learn to use words to express emotion and experience the reactions of others. For example, two 4-year-old girls might begin their friendship in this way:

Sophia hears the teacher introduce Althea. "Hey!" said Sophia. "Althea! That sounds like Sophia! I could be your friend!" Althea thinks for a minute and says, "Sometimes my mom calls me 'Thea.'" Sophia exclaims, "Sometimes my mom calls me 'Phia!' I could be your friend forever!"

From individual exploration to games that involve rules and negotiation, children practice and learn many social skills through different types of play. Table 12-3 describes many of these types of play.

Open and unstructured playtime is important throughout the early years. In some settings, however, free playtime is being reduced due to pressures to promote academic skills both in the

TABLE 12-3 Stages of Play

Stages of Play	Examples
Observing	Watching others play
Solitary	Playing independently, following own interests
Parallel	Child playing alongside another child using the same materials, but not interacting
Associative	Child playing with another, using same materials, but play is unorganized—each child follows own interests
Cooperative	Child playing with others in an organized way; interacting and establishing themes, negotiating rules and roles

Source: Engelbright Fox, n.d.

home and in the early childhood and school setting. Academically oriented activities have clear benefits for children's learning. When adult-planned and academically focused activities dominate, children's days may become overscheduled, causing children to feel hurried. The trends that promote attention to academic learning rather than play and social interaction are problematic. Free and unstructured play provides many stress-reducing benefits that contribute to children's resilience and help build social and emotional wellness.

Contributing to School Success

Healthy social and emotional development significantly contributes to children's future academic success. It also eases the transition from preschool into the new environment of kindergarten. During the early years teachers help children develop the foundational skills to be successful learners. Understanding the skills that support school success, recognizing the challenges that some children face, enhancing self-regulation, and fostering positive approaches to learning are important teacher contributions.

Skills for School Success

Enhancing children's social and emotional skills is important to academic success. The Collaborative for Academic, Social, and Emotional Learning (CASEL) has developed a set of skills that provide the foundation (Kendziora, Weissberg, Ji, & Dusenbury, 2011):

1. Awareness of self—the ability to understand one's own feelings and developing self-confidence

2. Self-regulation—the ability to control one's emotions and to handle stress; impulse control; perseverance

3. Social awareness—the ability to understand other's feelings; development of empathy

4. Relationship skills—the ability to make and maintain healthy relationships; development of cooperation; managing conflict

5. Responsibility in decision making—the ability to make decisions while respecting others and understanding safety, social norms, and consequences

Enhancing these social and emotional skills is important not only for promoting healthy and constructive behaviors in the classroom but also contributes to future success in relationships and academics (Kendziora et al., 2011). Children who are socially and emotionally healthy will be ready to start school, participate in relationships, and fully experience learning.

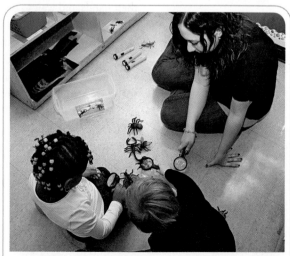

Healthful social emotional development helps children approach learning with curiosity and enthusiasm.

Understanding Problems

Most children transition successfully into kindergarten. They are ready to manage the new routines and navigate the new expectations. However, some children are not prepared for the changes they will experience. Between 8% and 9% of preschool children show evidence of social-emotional and behavioral problems including feelings of anxiety or depression or aggressive and challenging behaviors. These problems are strongly associated with mental health problems and poor academic performance later in life (Kruizinga, Jansen, Carter, & Raat, 2011).

These findings are particularly important because children who do not have the needed social and emotional skills are often the most difficult to teach. They tend to not be interested in learning, lack confidence in their success, and have difficulties cooperating and establishing self-control (Ewing Marion Kauffman Foundation, 2002). They may also display behavior problems as they struggle in the school environment. This is of concern because kindergarten teachers tend to manage classes that are larger than prekindergarten groups and often do so with little or no assistance.

Identifying concerns early on, and finding ways to address them, is important, especially for children who are at risk for behavioral and school problems. An increasing number of children are growing up in stressful circumstances that are associated with negative social and emotional development and its consequences, including low achievement, inattentiveness, psychiatric problems, grade retention, and depressed cognitive development (Ewing Marion Kauffman Foundation, 2002). Teachers can help offset some of these risks by creating opportunities for children to experience success. Here is an example:

> Maxwell invites families to participate at reading time in his second-grade class. He models how to enjoy a book with school-age children and helps children and families practice reading to each other as a way to strengthen their mutual interest in learning and encourage families to appreciate their child's developing skills.

Enhancing Self-Regulation

self-regulation
child's ability to manage his or her own behavior

Self-regulation refers to the ability to manage one's own behavior, which is important to a child's success in group settings. It is natural for very young children to struggle with delaying gratification (that is, waiting for what they want). However, as children prepare to enter kindergarten, they are expected to develop the capacity to regulate their impulses according to the rules of the new setting. For example, with a few gentle reminders, children in kindergarten are expected to learn to raise their hands and wait to be called on rather than calling out an answer to a question. Learning in the school setting relies on children being able to listen to and follow directions given by the teacher rather than rushing forward with the task.

Early childhood teachers can plan many activities to help children learn and practice self-regulation skills during the preschool years. For example, Su Lin recognized at the beginning of the year that many children in her class would run with excitement from one activity to another. She found that providing clear instructions and a predictable daily routine helped the children understand expectations. When they heard the 5-minute warning bell, they were more able to stop their play and participate in cleanup time in order to move on to the next activity of the day. Su Lin continued to offer specific instructions about appropriate behaviors to reinforce her expectations. Over the year she noticed remarkable improvement. Children's ability to self-regulate enabled them to successfully manage the tasks associated with learning and to develop positive social relationships.

Fostering Positive Approaches to Learning

approaches to learning
the attitudes, habits, and learning styles children bring to the learning process

Children's success as learners also depends on the attitudes, habits, and learning styles they bring to the learning process. These are called **approaches to learning**. They include the various qualities, characteristics, and dispositions that help children approach new information and manage new tasks. Qualities associated with positive approaches to learning include (Egertson, 2006):

- Curiosity and openness.
- Persistence and focus.
- Reflection and interpretation.
- Imagination and invention.
- Cognitive problem solving.

Children who approach learning with interest and enthusiasm, and who are comfortable forming questions and focusing on outcomes, are better able to acquire new information and apply new concepts to future settings. These are signs of positive social and emotional adjustment that contribute to children's success in school. Teachers foster these qualities in many ways, such as by offering a variety of opportunities for children to explore new materials and take on appropriate challenges, and by guiding them during unstructured play with intentional and open-ended questions that require reflection and speculation.

> **What if . . .**
> you were asked to be on an early childhood advisory committee for your community? What ideas could you offer to help promote children's success in school? What strategies might you offer to address the gap in social and emotional development experienced by some children?

ADDRESSING CHALLENGES TO CHILDREN'S MENTAL HEALTH

Most children experience normal social and emotional development. They gradually develop interpersonal skills and learn to manage their emotions within the broad range of typical development. However, growing numbers of children are experiencing delays and challenges in social and emotional development that are exhibited through significant behavior problems in the classroom (Smith et al., 2011). Teachers are better able to understand and address children's needs by understanding the prevalence of these concerns, how they are identified, and being familiar with the types of mental health problems that may be experienced by young children.

Understanding the Prevalence of Mental Health Problems

Young children can, and do, experience mental health problems. Between 9% and 14% of children under the age of 6 experience emotional and behavioral problems. The prevalence is much higher in children living in poverty or facing other stressful circumstances such as parental mental health problems (Smith et al., 2011).

In recognition of a growing concern about children's significant behavior issues, diagnostic criteria for identifying early forms of mental health problems among young children have been refined. These tools have been useful in diagnosing mental health problems in children of all ages. Mental health problems include serious emotional disorder, anxiety disorder, disruptive behavior disorder, autism, attention deficit/hyperactivity disorder, and depression. In addition, some children experience multiple mental health problems.

Recognizing Consequences

Mental health problems that begin in early childhood can develop into serious disorders as children age. Over half of lifetime mental health disorders begin in childhood. Children with mental health problems have problems with academic achievement and are at higher risk of becoming involved with the criminal justice system. If problems are treated early, these children will perform better in school, at home, and in society (Stagman & Cooper, 2010).

Even seemingly minor mental health problems can impact children and families. Children with mental health problems often have problems with self-esteem, learning, and relationships with others. They are more likely to experience other health conditions that impact their daily activities and increase their absence from school. Unaddressed behavior concerns are also a problem. Nationally, preschool-age children are expelled from their early childhood setting three times more often than children in K–12 school settings (Stagman & Cooper, 2010). Expulsion interrupts learning time and does not help to resolve children's behavior problems. Families are also affected by children's mental health problems.

Access to help and treatment for mental health problems is also a concern. Between 70% and 80% of children who need mental health services do not receive them. Over 12% of children receive treatment with a mental health provider, while 11% of children receive mental health services in the educational setting. Hispanic and African American children with mental health problems receive fewer services than Caucasian children with the same problems (Stagman & Cooper, 2010).

Identifying Challenges

Children are at risk for mental health problems when their early experiences are negative and threatening and when they do not have adults who are attentive to mediating their fears. Although teachers cannot change children's home environments, they can help children by providing a safe and nurturing school environment and by acknowledging that children face risks to their social and emotional development. For example, as children age, their sense of value and their self-worth are increasingly affected by interactions with peers, sometimes in negative ways. Teachers can help children learn to *test* the reality of negative comments said to them by other children. For example, the *Health Hint* discusses how childhood obesity can be a risk factor for poor social and emotional development.

Observing for Mental Health Problems

Children's difficult behaviors are often the first indication that a problem with social and emotional development may exist. But recognizing behaviors that suggest a mental health problem may not be straightforward. For example, Bob, a teacher in the young preschool room, frequently observes 3-year-old Sasha acting aggressively such as pushing other children in the play yard or knocking over other children's block structures. Bob has been unsuccessful in managing these behaviors and is unsure if they indicate a lack of communication skills or if they are signs of more serious mental health concerns. He is not alone in wondering how to interpret such behaviors.

Difficult behaviors are a common and natural experience in early childhood classrooms. Even typical behaviors can be difficult to manage, and most children will display inappropriate behaviors at one time or another. For young children, understanding how to participate appropriately in the group setting requires learning the rules and cues for appropriate social interaction. Testing limits as children gain this social knowledge is normal. A core responsibility of early childhood teaching involves guiding children through these aspects of social and emotional development and helping them learn to interact appropriately.

Appropriate behaviors are related to normal growth and development; they are behaviors that are expected of most children based on their age and developmental maturity. Behaviors that are considered appropriate change as children age. What is understandable behavior for a 2-year-old is not expected behavior for a 5-year-old. In addition, children who experience special developmental delays may demonstrate behaviors that are understandable given their developmental maturity, but

HEALTH HINT   Obesity and Children's Mental Health

Being overweight continues to be a social stigma that is difficult for children to understand. Obesity in the early childhood years has been associated with problems with peer relationships and teacher-reported emotional problems. They may have trouble developing social relationships and with development of healthy self-esteem, especially in girls.

Teachers can help children by promoting acceptance in the classroom, helping children to recognize and respect differences. Teachers are also in a position to recognize peer relationship problems and discuss them with the family during the early years when it is easier to intervene and prevent further mental health problems.

Source: Information from Sawyer, Harchak, Wake, & Lynch, 2011.

are not age appropriate. For example, 6-year-old Sam, who has a developmental disability, may kick another child who is taking a turn on the bicycle—a behavior commensurate with Sam's special developmental condition, but not typically expected of a 6-year-old. Teachers need to weigh the behaviors that are observed with children's individual age and maturity. Other aspects such as children's culture and nutritional health can also impact behavior.

Understanding Cultural Influences

Children's cultural backgrounds can impact the kinds of behaviors that are considered appropriate. What might be considered appropriate behavior in one culture may not be understood in another. For example, a Korean American child may be taught to hide his emotions, causing his teacher to worry that the child is not capable of expressing and managing his emotions, a possible sign of problems in social and emotional development.

Cultural values also influence family reactions to children's behaviors. For example, parents may allow certain behaviors in the home environment that are not considered appropriate in the early childhood setting. To better understand the cultural framework that influences children's behavior, teachers should discuss these issues with families. This helps everyone understand whether particular behaviors have a recognizable source or whether they indicate signs of problems.

Identifying Sleeping and Eating Habits

Behaviors can also be influenced by children's sleeping and eating patterns. Children who do not receive sufficient rest may show behavior extremes in the classroom. Over one third of school-age children experience poor sleep, which affects many aspects of school readiness such as physical health, social competence, emotional maturity, language skills and learning (Quach, Hiscock, Ukoumunne, & Wake, 2011). What children eat can also influence the way they behave in the classroom, as discussed in this chapter's *Nutrition Note*. For example, children who have not eaten breakfast or who receive a poor diet may demonstrate behaviors such as inability to concentrate, lethargy, and persistent fatigue. Understanding children's sleeping and eating routines can help teachers understand the source of behavioral issues.

Recognizing Warning Signs

To establish successful class groups, teachers must develop a wide range of behavior management approaches and techniques. Sometimes teachers focus so closely on managing behaviors as they occur that they miss the signs that may indicate a more complex problem. To assist teachers to recognize behaviors that have an understandable cause and those that suggest the potential for social and emotional problems, special focus must be given to observing the child's behavior in the classroom setting. Through careful observation teachers look for behaviors that are extreme, such as excessively

This **video** shows a group of teachers discussing children who exhibit attention-seeking behaviors. How are these behaviors related to children's home lives? What strategies might be used by teachers to support these children?

NUTRITION NOTE   Children's Behavior May Be Influenced by What They Eat

What children eat may influence their physical and mental health possibly impacting their behavior. Although the long-term influence of junk food on behavior problems and mental health is still unclear, it is apparent that junk foods can decrease the quality of children's diets. Diets containing high amounts of sugars and processed foods ("junk foods") can displace the consumption of more nutritious foods. As a result, children may have lower intakes of vitamins and minerals and healthy fats such as omega-3 and -6 fatty acids, which contribute to healthy brain development.

Teachers are in a position to suggest and promote healthful food choices for snacks and meals brought from home and program social events. These efforts promote overall health and may contribute to children's abilities to better moderate their behavior in the classroom.

Source: Information from "'Junk Food' Diet and Childhood Behavioural Problems: Results from the ALSPAC Cohort," by N. Wiles, K. Northstone, P. Emmett, & G. Lewis, 2009, *European Journal of Clinical Nutrition*, 63(4), pp. 491–498.

aggressive or withdrawn behaviors, and for emotional responses that are not age appropriate or that seem atypical. Signs of problems in social and emotional development are demonstrated through behaviors that are:

- Inappropriate or dangerous.
- Frequent and reoccurring.
- Persistent.

Making Referrals

A small percentage of children may experience significant behaviors that persist in spite of efforts to guide and manage the behavior concerns. These children may benefit from assessment and evaluation by a behavior specialist or mental health consultant. However, determining when efforts to manage children's behaviors are not making progress and when additional support is needed can be difficult. For example, Hal feels like he is not doing his job as a teacher when Mandy's behavior is not solved by his careful efforts. He feels like the principal will question his teaching skills because the problems persist—in fact, they may be increasing—but he is also struggling because every day is getting harder.

When well-planned intervention strategies are not successful in redirecting children to more positive behaviors, additional supports are needed for both the child and the teacher. To evaluate progress, teachers, families, and others who may be teaming to address the child's needs discuss questions such as these:

- Have the frequency and intensity of the child's behaviors improved?
- Is the child able to successfully navigate most of the activities during the day with relatively little support or does a teacher need to be nearby to prevent aggressive acts or injury?
- Is the child demonstrating more positive behaviors?
- Is growth evident?

Responses that indicate that problems are continuing mean that more information and support are needed. Referring the child to special services is the next step. Community health services or mental health counselors in private practice can provide assessment and evaluation services. Some schools may have counselors or behavior management specialists who provide these services.

The teacher's role in making referrals is to provide concrete descriptions of the behaviors that are problematic and information about what is working. Even after referrals are made, the teacher's responsibility to the child continues through additional efforts to manage and guide behavior. In the example above, Hal finds that talking with other teachers about strategies and support resources is one way for him to boost his confidence and maintain his motivation. Advocating for additional training or the temporary assistance of an aide are other ways that teachers obtain support to better teach children with mental health problems.

Types of Mental Health Disorders

Teachers are an important source of information for parents and health care providers regarding the child's social behaviors and any problems that may be impacting the child's ability to learn and participate effectively in the classroom. However, medical professionals make the diagnosis of mental health disorders. Making a definitive diagnosis of mental health problems is complex. It involves a broad review of biological and environmental factors, children's age and development, and assessments of how children function in the school and home environment.

Understanding some of the mental health disorders that may occur during the early years provides teachers with a general understanding of the range of conditions that may affect children's mental health and behaviors in the classroom. Under the IDEA, the term *emotional disturbance* is used to refer to mental health conditions. The more common mental health disorders identified among young children are discussed in the following sections.

Attention Deficit/Hyperactivity Disorder

Attention deficit/hyperactivity disorder (ADHD) is a condition characterized by restlessness, persistent lack of attention, impulsiveness, and hyperactivity. Behaviors that are associated with ADHD include those that:

- Affect the child in more than one setting, such as at home and at school.
- Are persistent, lasting for a considerable length of time.
- Impair academic or social functioning.

ADHD affects a small percentage of very young children. Prevalence rates and more discussion of symptoms and treatment are included in Chapter 11. Treatment for ADHD includes classroom modifications and medications; however, the appropriateness and effectiveness of treatment strategies continues to be researched.

Anxiety Disorders

Anxiety is a common emotional response, but when it is persistent and experienced with great intensity, it is considered a problem. Anxiety disorder is characterized by excessive worry and/or fear (Turnbull & Turnbull, 2013). Treatment for anxiety disorders may include cognitive problem solving, behavioral therapy, or medications. Cognitive problem solving might include discussing the potential realities of a fear and identifying ways children can manage them, such as helping a child explore a fear of the red light on the smoke detector. Behavioral therapy involves having children gradually face their fears, such as helping a child practice making changes in routines. The various types of anxiety disorders are described next.

Separation Anxiety Although common in infants and children up to 18 months of age, separation anxiety diminishes as children age and is not considered typical of older children. It is characterized by an extreme need to be near the parent or home. Behaviors may include inability to sleep alone or fear associated with separating from the parent when being left in the early childhood setting.

General Anxiety Disorder Children with general anxiety disorder express excessive worry about many things including future events, potential dangers such as earthquakes, or being on time. In the early childhood setting this may be seen when practicing for a fire drill. For example, Cathy, a 4-year-old, may begin displaying anxiety as soon as she sees her teacher bring out the home-style smoke alarm that he will use at group time when they will practice evacuating the classroom. Cathy worries about the loud noise made by the smoke alarm. Her teacher notices her discomfort and sets the alarm in a cupboard until group time. Then he asks Cathy if she would like to push the button to make the alarm sound, putting her in control of the situation, or if she would like to cover her ears, giving her an option to reduce the sound of the alarm.

Social Phobia Children with social phobia suffer from extreme shyness and discomfort in social situations, and they may selectively choose to not speak. Often children with social phobia will speak in the family setting, but not in public. Families can often shed light on this situation. Special sensitivity is needed to build the child's comfort with speaking in the classroom setting. Providing opportunities for the child to "talk" with puppets in a small group setting may be helpful.

Obsessive-Compulsive Disorder Children with obsessive-compulsive disorder (OCD) display obsessive and repetitive behaviors, such as repeated hand washing; insistence on routines, such as having the teacher stand in a certain place at the door during arrival and departure; and having things in their place. Teachers may also notice that children use nonsense words or sounds and that they describe reoccurring thoughts and themes for much longer than they would normally be of interest to most children.

Post-Traumatic Stress Disorder Post-traumatic stress disorder (PTSD) occurs after children have experienced or been exposed to a traumatic experience, such as extreme violence in the home or neighborhood or frequent instances of maltreatment. As a result children may be extremely worried, vigilant, and tense. This can be observed as the child watches others from the edge of play. The teacher might also notice that the child constantly keeps her eye on the teachers and parents as they come and go, noticing the details of what everyone is doing. Children who suffer from PTSD have difficulty relaxing and enjoying their play. Teachers assist by building children's sense of security, as in this example:

> Helena, teacher of the class for 3-year-olds, knows that Zack has experienced violence in his home. Zack and his mother now live in a "safe" house for women and children who have suffered from domestic violence, and he does not get to play outside very often due to their current living situation. Zack appears tense and unable to enjoy playing in the preschool. Helena makes arrangements with her coteachers to take Zack outside to play for 10 minutes on his own at the beginning of every day. She runs and plays ball with him and encourages him to climb and swing. After a few days of this routine, she sees that Zack is relaxing. They agree to invite a small group of children outside to play with him on the next day.

Approaches such as this acknowledge children's struggles and provide an option for working through fears in acceptable ways.

Mood Disorders

Mood disorders are characterized by significant changes in mood, either depressed or elevated or both (Turnbull & Turnbull, 2013). They are complex and are treated with a variety of therapies. Mood disorders include bipolar disorders and depression.

bipolar disorder
a mental health condition characterized by extreme fluctuations in mood and energy

Bipolar Disorder   Extreme fluctuations in mood and energy are characteristics of **bipolar disorder**. Children with bipolar disorder may have long periods of normal behavior, and then swing to highly depressive behaviors and then to extreme manic episodes (high-energy swings) (Ball, Bindler, & Cowen, 2013). The types of behaviors and how they may be exhibited in the classroom are described in Table 12-4.

Bipolar disorder is very rare in the early childhood years and it is thought to be associated with an underlying biological condition; however, it is difficult to pinpoint a specific cause. Treatment for bipolar disorder includes medication and various therapies such as cognitive and behavior therapies and family therapy, which are often combined with medications.

Teachers may be involved in logging children's behaviors in the classroom to help inform medical providers and mental health specialists about the child's participation. Teachers also support children with bipolar disorder by establishing familiar routines and guiding them to manage extreme behaviors by offering appropriate choices.

depression
a mental health condition that causes disturbances in children's relationships; also affects eating and sleeping

Depression   A mental health disorder that causes disturbances in mood is known as **depression**. Children with depression can display a wide range of behaviors including sadness, irritability, anger,

---

TABLE 12-4   Behaviors Associated with Bipolar Disorder

Behaviors	Description	Classroom Examples
Depressive behaviors	• Passivity • Difficulty sleeping or eating • Feeling worthless • Unpredictably switching to manic behavior	• Child shows little interest in toys or other children. • Child appears excessively tired; is not interested in snacks or meals. • Child expresses self-doubt; can't be encouraged to participate.
Manic behaviors	• Excessive high energy • Risky behavior • Unpredictably switching to depressive behavior	• Child makes unusual movements, running, jumping, calling out, moving from activity to activity wildly. • Unusually aggressive • Not sleeping much • Child tests boundaries; climbs and uses toys and equipment without regard to safety.

Sources: Ball, Bindler, & Cowen, 2013; U.S. Department of Health and Human Services; National Institutes of Health; National Institute of Mental Health, 2008.

changes in appetite, fatigue, and recurring unexplained physical complaints (Prager, 2009). Depression can affect many aspects of health and wellness including growth and development, behavioral problems, academic performance, and relationships (Ball, Bindler & Cowen, 2013; Prager, 2009).

The estimates of depression in young children are about 1% to 2%, and it occurs equally among boys and girls (Prager, 2009). Determining the actual cause of depression in young children can be very difficult because no definitive test is available. Evidence suggests that underlying biological causes, such as changes in brain chemistry, might affect a child's mood. Depression can also occur in response to environmental situations such as parental depression and child abuse or neglect (Ball, Bindler, & Cowen, 2013), parental substance abuse, family problems, low socioeconomic or education levels, and loss of a parent or sibling (Prager, 2009). About half of children with depression also have other mental health disorders (Ball, Bindler, & Cowen, 2013).

Medical professionals diagnose depression, giving careful attention to the child's medical history as well as details related to behavior, peer relationships, and behavioral symptoms. The length of time the child's daily functioning has been impaired and the presence of specific symptoms such as sleep disturbances, change in appetite, or thoughts of death are also considered. Sometimes families ask teachers for advice and guidance when they have worries about a child's behaviors, such as the potential for depression. Figure 12-1 shows an example of a drawing done by a child that should raise red flags for a teacher. Although teachers do not make diagnoses, they do have a responsibility to support families by discussing their concerns, referring them to professional assistance, and working to address children's issues in the classroom.

> **What if . . .**
> it is early in the school year and you realize that one of your second graders, Raymond, spends the opening class meeting time staring at the floor. He never participates and when you try to engage him, he shakes his head, indicating that he doesn't want to speak. What can you do to help Raymond engage with you and his classmates?

TEACHING CHILDREN WITH MENTAL HEALTH PROBLEMS

Children who experience mental health problems sometimes display significant behavior challenges. These are behaviors that are problematic, out of the ordinary, frequent, persistent, and sometimes dangerous. Children preschool age and younger may demonstrate frequent and persistent behaviors such as hitting, kicking, biting, and throwing toys or furnishings at other children and teachers. School-age children may display aggressive behaviors such as harming animals, starting fires, or fighting, bullying, and other forms of hostile physical or emotional interactions. Teaching children with these behaviors can be very difficult, because they introduce distress, discord, and upset in the classroom.

FIGURE 12-1
Children's Drawings May Provide Clues to How They Are Feeling. Other Observations Are Needed to Determine If This Is a Sign of Depression

Significant behavior challenges require a great deal of the teacher's attention and energy to manage while at the same time trying to maintain a learning environment for the larger group of children. Sometimes teachers feel that they are only "containing" children's behaviors and not helping them to move on to more positive ways of showing emotions and interacting. Teachers need a range of supports including ways to promote appropriate behaviors, approaches to manage them when they occur, and strategies to direct children from inappropriate to appropriate behaviors. They need to understand the resources that are available to them, such as families and mental health professionals.

Understanding Successful Integration

Many children with mental health problems participate successfully in early childhood classrooms. This success is founded on the attitudes and supports provided by the early childhood setting and teachers, as well as the candid involvement of families.

Characteristics That Support Success

Several characteristics describe programs that support the successful participation in the classroom of children with mental health issues.

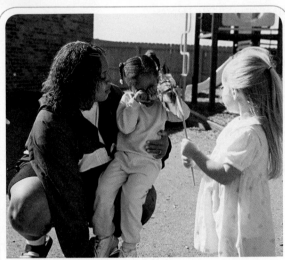

Teachers use many strategies when managing children's challenging behaviors, including helping children recognize appropriate ways to interact.

These include fostering positive attitudes toward the involvement of children with mental health problems and promoting strategic classroom practices by teachers who have understanding and competency with regard to children's social and emotional health (Bershad & Blaber, 2011).

Successfully including children with mental health problems also requires that teachers, families, and program staff all see value in the participation of such children. This requires special efforts to create a common commitment to all children. Teachers are important in promoting this sense of community and acceptance among all children in the class. To accomplish this, they must address two issues: They must establish open and candid communication with the families of children who have mental health problems, and they must encourage other families to be welcoming to children with social and emotional concerns.

Supports Needed from Families

Teachers need the support of families whose children are experiencing mental health problems. These families need to be openly communicative and candid about their child's strengths and challenges so teachers will know how to plan for successful integration and how to manage potential challenges in the classroom. Both teachers and parents may have fears related to the participation of the child in the classroom. They may worry about difficult behaviors that will be hard to manage, or that the child will be unsafe, or not accepted by other children.

Planning a parent–teacher conference before the child joins the class, or soon after, provides the opportunity for families to provide a full description of the child's challenges, how those challenges have been successfully managed in the past, and clarification about any medical treatments that are in place. This sets the stage for open communication and offers opportunity for teachers to describe how they will help the child be successful in the classroom setting.

The successful involvement of children with mental health problems also relies on the positive attitudes of families whose children are typically developing. Creating a classroom motto that "everyone is welcome" is one way to introduce the concept that all children have a place in the early childhood setting. Offering social events that focus on helping families get acquainted builds a sense of common experience and togetherness. Families may be more resilient or "forgiving" when they occasionally observe a child displaying challenging behaviors if they know and appreciate one another.

Finally, all families need to be able to see the concrete ways in which teachers are working to build cooperation and harmony in the classroom. Age-appropriate class group meetings where children discuss classroom rules or make a listing of appropriate behaviors demonstrate that teachers are working to educate all children about how to be an appropriate member of a community.

Strategies for Managing Significant Behavior Challenges

Early childhood programs and schools use a number of different strategies to address the significant behavior challenges that may be exhibited by children with mental health problems. These strategies are most effective when teachers address behavioral concerns as part of a continuum of approaches used for all children. A public health model provides the structure for thinking of behaviors along a continuum, and functional assessment approaches assist in identifying details of children's behaviors.

Using a Public Health Model

A public health model is a useful approach for managing significant behavior challenges in the classroom. The public health model focuses on promoting positive

What if . . .

a parent did not disclose that her child had a mental health disorder until after the child was enrolled in your class? Would this influence your relationship with the child or parent? Upon learning of the disorder, how would you respond?

behaviors and interactions, preventing problems from occurring, and intervening when needed. This approach is designed to impact the mental health for *all* children while providing effective intervention strategies as early as possible to those who need help. This model includes the following components (Bershad & Blaber, 2011):

1. *Promotion strategies,* which promote appropriate development. These strategies are used for everyone. They include activities such as creating nurturing environments and establishing strong teacher and child relationships.

2. *Prevention strategies* are used for everyone, but are especially focused on children at risk for poor social and emotional development. Activities include conducting special social skills curriculum activities about building friendships and knowing about appropriate behaviors.

3. *Treatment/maintenance strategies* are intervention focused. These strategies are used for children who have signs of problems such as persistent and significant behavior challenges. Activities include conducting a functional analysis (described later) and implementing child-specific interventions.

The public health model is especially useful in early childhood settings because it uses a common approach to teach general social and emotional skills for all children while addressing situations when behaviors indicate that positive development is going off course. For this reason early childhood teachers plan activities and curriculum that both implement strategies promoting appropriate behaviors and strategies that transform or change inappropriate behaviors to more acceptable interactions.

Promotion Strategies   Healthy social and emotional development and developmentally appropriate behaviors are fostered by using carefully planned **promotion strategies**. These strategies are used for all children, including those who are experiencing problems. Promotion strategies provide models of appropriate interactions and behaviors. Examples of promotion strategies that are useful for classrooms serving children with challenging behaviors are provided in Table 12-5.

> **promotion strategies**
> strategies used to promote healthy social and emotional behaviors

Other promotion strategies specifically targeted to children with behavior challenges include the following (Hyson & Taylor, 2011):

- Respond to everyday needs with sensitivity
- Create a classroom "community"
- Model behavior that demonstrates caring and empathy
- Prompt and encourage children to be polite and generous
- Support families through education

Transformation Strategies   Children's negative emotions and challenging behaviors are guided to more appropriate actions by using **transformation strategies**. They involve teaching children to recognize what is wrong or inappropriate with the behavior they are exhibiting. For example, a teacher may tell a child that crying and hitting is not appropriate, but asking for a toy is appropriate. As children mature, discussions may include setting goals for increasing appropriate behaviors, as in this example:

> **transformation strategies**
> strategies designed to manage negative emotions and change challenging behaviors

> Anita, a preschool teacher, talks with 4-year old Ted each morning reviewing their discussions about playing kindly, without hitting or pushing. During the day she acknowledges Ted's appropriate interactions with a smile, a wink, or pat on the shoulder. If problems occur during the day, Anita steps in to name them and she and Ted identify better choices. At the end of the day, they briefly summarize, "What went well today?" This requires a good deal of Anita's focus, but she is beginning to see progress over time.

Table 12-6 provides a list of transformation strategies. The suggestions include strategies that teachers can use to help change children's emotional reactions and challenging behaviors.

Conducting a Functional Assessment

When a child's significant behavior challenges are recognized, teachers use a focused process to reflect on, describe, and define what is occurring. This is called **functional assessment**. The Center on

> **functional assessment**
> a process used to reflect on, describe, and define challenging behaviors

TABLE 12-5 Promotion Strategies for Managing Difficult Behaviors

Teachers	Peers	Environment
PROMOTION STRATEGY #1: BUILD RELATIONSHIP WITH EACH CHILD		
• Build relationship with each child based on trust and respect.	• Develop peer relationships with all children in classroom.	• Structure activities so that teachers and children interact frequently and positively. • Provide one-on-one time as available when child first enrolling.
PROMOTION STRATEGY #2: TEAM WITH FAMILIES		
• Encourage consistency between home/school. • Learn about child's home culture. • Determine goals family has for child.	• Peers should not be present when adults discuss challenges. • Children participate in diverse cultural experiences.	• Make time for communication between staff and family. • Document children's notable experiences. • Ensure that activities and expectations are culturally appropriate.
PROMOTION STRATEGY #3: WORK WITH KNOWLEDGE ABOUT EACH CHILD'S INDIVIDUAL CHALLENGES		
• Know what works at home for parents. • Know key events in child's life.	• Plan for therapeutic activities when appropriate.	• Develop individualized activities that support children with challenges. • Incorporate therapeutic activities.
PROMOTION STRATEGY #4: USE A DEVELOPMENTALLY APPROPRIATE CURRICULUM		
• Curriculum should meet needs of all children at the center.	• Engage in common activities that include all children.	• Classroom activities are appropriate for all children.
PROMOTION STRATEGY #5: BALANCE CONSISTENCY AND FLEXIBILITY		
• Create a consistent, predictable day while maintaining flexibility.	• Peers model normal behavior. • Peers receive rewards for healthy social behavior.	• Provide small, structured classroom areas. • Ensure consistent schedules with choices.
PROMOTION STRATEGY #6: ASSIST CHILDREN IN FEELING SAFE AND CALM		
• Teach self-soothing behaviors. • Use artistic expression of feelings. • Remove child to quiet space when overstimulated.	• Peers withdraw to safe place when feeling anxious.	• Maintain appropriate levels of stimulation. • Allows important work to be accomplished in small groups. • Environment and space should promote safety and security.
PROMOTION STRATEGY #7: USE MULTIPLE SENSORY CHANNELS		
• Use physical guidance and touch. • Attach words to positive feelings and actions using illustrations.	• Peers also use varied sensory activities. • Non–English-speaking children learn English more rapidly.	• Provide visual schedules. • Adults should be within reasonable physical proximity.
PROMOTION STRATEGY #8: SUPPORT CHILDREN THROUGH TIMES OF TRANSITION		
• Warn children about transitions. • Spend time with child at drop-off.	• Model appropriate affect and behavior during transitions.	• Build stable staff and consistent staffing patterns. • Provide transitional objects when appropriate.
PROMOTION STRATEGY #9: PROMOTE THE SOCIAL AND EMOTIONAL DEVELOPMENT NECESSARY FOR LEARNING		
• Give opportunities for children to master behavior necessary for learning. • Consider family cultural context when establishing literacy skills. • Seek consultation when behavior is interfering with learning.	• Peers model behavior that promotes learning. • Engage older children in activities such as being a "reading buddy."	• Make books available written in family's home language. • Use activity kits that promote learning at home. • Consultants assist with acquisitions of behaviors necessary for learning.

Source: *Setting the Pace: Model Inclusive Child Care Centers Serving Families of Children with Emotional or Behavioral Challenges,* by E. M. Brennan, J. R. Bradley, S. M. Ama, and N. Cawood, 2003, Portland, OR: Portland State University, Research and Training Center on Family Support and Children's Mental Health. Used with permission.

TABLE 12-6 Transformation Strategies for Managing Difficult Behaviors

Strategies for Teachers and Parents	Examples
Engage in preemptive planning.	• Watch for buildup of negative emotions in children. • Family communicates challenges recently experienced at home.
Develop formal behavior plans through consultation.	• Document incidents. • Use supervision and consultation. • Involve family in planning.
Encourage and assist child to use verbal self-expression.	• Enlist help from speech therapists. • Use signs with children with low verbal skills.
Substitute more appropriate behavior.	• Suggest alternative behaviors in positive terms. • Use art as a vehicle of expression. • Use drawings to illustrate desired behaviors and to indicate negative behaviors.
Foster problem solving.	• Talk through issues with verbal children. • Use drawings to illustrate working through issues. • Use action figures to act out situations.
Employ redirection.	• Use alternate, positive activity to distract child from distressing emotion. • Use alternate physical activity.
Focus attention appropriately.	• Learn behaviors children use to gain attention. • Comfort victims of aggression or children displaying positive behaviors.
Plan for safety of children.	• Plan strategies to keep children safe from their own behaviors and that of others.
Work as a team to address negative behavior.	• Other staff should back up teacher and provide relief. • Use team meetings to plan strategy.
Establish limits and set consequences for negative behavior.	• Emphasize choice with school-age children.
Regulate own emotions.	• Work to not feed children's anger. • Other staff provide back up when necessary.
Engage the school-age child in working through challenges.	• Engage child and family in planning process.

Source: Brennan, Bradley, Ama, & Cawood, 2003. Used with permission.

Social Emotional Foundations for Early Learning at Vanderbilt University promotes the use of functional assessment to facilitate understanding of children's social and emotional problems and how to address them (Fox & Duda, 2008; Homer, Albin, Sprague, & Storey, n.d.). Features of functional assessment include (Fox & Duda, 2008):

- *Describing the child's behaviors:* What? When? Where? How often? Intensity?
- *Recognizing events surrounding the behavior:* What tends to affect the behavior, such as changes in the routine and schedule, sleep challenges, or medical needs?
- *Identifying predictable events:* In what situations are the problem behaviors likely to occur?
- *Summarizing the child's play abilities:* What successes and difficulties does the child experience in play?
- *Understanding the function of problem behaviors:* What does the child get, or avoid doing, because of the behavior?
- *Reflecting on the effectiveness of the problem behavior:* What response does the child get? How quickly?

The goal of functional assessment is to determine the purpose of the problematic behavior, to design interventions to prevent the problem behavior, and to teach the child appropriate skills.

A functional assessment may be conducted individually by the teacher or with a team that may include family members, behavior specialists, or counselors. Teachers conduct and record observations of the child's behavior and keep data to look for patterns of behavior. The team meets to learn about the family's experiences with the child's behavior, to discuss what was observed in the classroom, and to plan appropriate interventions.

This approach is successful in helping teachers and families work together to plan ways to prevent problem behaviors and to increase the effectiveness of managing the behaviors in the early childhood setting and home. Remembering the opening case scenario, Meegan may find that the functional assessment process would be a good next step to explore with Heather's family to address Heather's behavior concerns.

Using a Whole School Approach

The National Center for Mental Health Promotion and Youth Violence Prevention has published information relevant to all schools on how to enhance children's mental health. The primary components of this approach include psycho-social environment, curricula and instruction, and mental health programs and services. This approach emphasizes that not only is the individual and factors within the child important to overall health, but also characteristics of the school, neighborhood, and community are critical components (Bershad & Blaber, 2011).

Psycho-Social Environment

The characteristics of the school that are most important in mental health promotion include the following (Bershad & Blaber, 2011):

- Caring and healthy teacher–student relationships, especially respecting ethnic, cultural, and racial aspects of families
- Maintaining expectations that are high and age appropriate
- Clearly written standards that are implemented throughout the entire school
- Using strategies and interventions that are effective and sensitive to children's needs, including social and emotional needs
- Creating an environment of safety—emotional and physical

This approach, in particular, emphasizes the importance of respecting cultural diversity and minimizing the stigma associated with mental health problems. Parenting styles, expectations of personal boundaries, and gender roles are all aspects that influence cultural and family expectations for children's behaviors. These need to be carefully explored and understood to facilitate an appropriate interpretation of behaviors. It can be challenging to navigate situations where the teacher observes problematic and possibly dangerous behaviors that the family views as "typical" and appropriate. Consider this example:

> Hector has been teaching 3-year-old Davonne to interact with the other children in the class without pushing and hitting. Davonne is beginning to control his impulse to hit by using his words. Davonne's dad arrives to pick him up from the play yard. Davonne's friend Karl runs by and pushes Davonne saying, "Try to catch me!" Davonne clenches his fists and says, "No pushing!" Hector is sorry that Davonne has been pushed, but he is happy to see that Davonne responded appropriately. Before he can get close enough to comfort and encourage Davonne, Davonne's dad grabs up his son and gives him a shake saying, "When someone hits you, you hit them back!" As Hector approaches the pair, quickly trying to summon the words to explain the behavior plan he has been working on, he realizes that Davonne's dad has been left out of the discussion.

evidence-based interventions
specific strategies that have been researched, evaluated, and replicated for the purposes of promoting mental health and preventing problems

Curricula and Instruction

Many programs are now using **evidence-based interventions** to promote health and prevent mental health problems. These are research-based, evaluated, and replicated to address specific factors related to mental health in children (Bershad & Blaber, 2011). Again these interventions should be respectful of language or cultural needs of families and schools. EBIs could be universal (for all students) or designed only for those with risk factors or with actual mental health problems (Bershad & Blaber, 2011). An early childhood program may find it helpful to develop a team of people who develop a plan for EBIs that address specific needs of the program.

Mental Health Programs and Services

Early childhood programs can implement strategies that focus specifically on enhancing mental health. This involves using prevention strategies, such as bullying prevention, developing programs that address specific problems, such as a support group for children of parents with serious physical health problems, and programs for students who have significant mental health problems, such as children with serious aggression (Bershad & Blaber, 2011).

Demonstrating Sensitivity

This is an important aspect of all aspects of early childhood programs, but is especially needed when addressing mental health issues. Parents are often hesitant to discuss mental health issues. Some may feel that mental health issues are not as "real" as physical health issues and believe that people should be able to "fix" their own problems. Families want their children to be accepted by others; they may feel dismayed and embarrassed when their child displays behaviors that are out of the ordinary, aggressive, or problematic. If a mental health issue is identified, parents may wonder if they are to blame. They may find it difficult to reveal this situation to others, and they may not know what to do about it.

Active and supportive communication that includes being sensitive to unique family experiences and perspectives is key to successfully navigating discussions of children's mental health challenges. At times special creativity and problem-solving strategies are needed. For example, language barriers can make communication about children's mental health problems more complex. Discussions may use words and language that are not typically part of everyday communication. Special efforts are needed to ensure clear communication, such as obtaining the support of bilingual family members or qualified interpreters.

At other times teachers may need to approach situations with flexibility, good humor, and understanding. Some children with mental health problems have difficulty being flexible or adapting to rules that are different in different settings. For example, a child may arrive at class wearing a Halloween costume even though the teacher has specifically asked families *not* to send their child to school in costume. The parent may report that the child insisted on wearing the costume, stating that this was the only way they could get the child to school. It is easy to be frustrated when it seems that parents, too, are not "following the rules." However, in this situation, recognizing the challenges the family faces in managing the child's difficult behaviors, and drawing on good humor and understanding rather than frustration, helps the teacher and family negotiate the issue together. This builds a bond of mutual understanding and joint problem solving.

Being Accessible

Engaging with families also requires that teachers be open and approachable when families have questions and need help, and accessible when children's mental health concerns are challenging. Being accessible can be difficult because teachers are usually busy in the classroom during work hours and may not wish to share their telephone number or invite after-hour contacts. Alternative ways to be accessible and responsive to families while maintaining appropriate boundaries include providing a classroom e-mail address or creating a phone or note message system whereby families can ask the teacher to call them. Committing to making contact when such requests are made is an important obligation that teachers need to agree to if such arrangements are offered.

These activities help support the good working relationships that are needed when teachers and families work together to address a child's mental health concern. One teacher offered this summary of accessibility by reporting:

My classroom parents know they can e-mail me when they have concerns about their child. I spend 15 minutes every evening before I go home answering e-mails. This helps us keep in touch, and the families tell me it makes them feel comfortable when they can share their concerns.

One goal of accessibility is to ensure that families are provided supports to help them cope with their child's challenges. This may involve talking about their concerns, finding other supportive people, and helping the family to recognize that the mental health concern is just one of many characteristics of their child.

Mental Health Consultants in Early Childhood Programs

Collaboration with mental health professionals, such as behavior specialists, counselors, nurses, or physicians, provides an important benefit to children who are at risk for or have been diagnosed with a mental health disorder (Heller et al., 2011). Consultation supports teachers and families when they are not able to understand children's behaviors and symptoms and need help managing concerns in the school and home. Together, teachers, families, and mental health professionals can usually design an appropriate management plan to address the challenges and assist children to develop coping strategies. This chapter's *Progressive Programs & Practices* feature describes how mental health consultants can be utilized.

Services provided by mental health consultants include conducting observations of children in the classroom and home setting. Consultation is provided to sort out ways to foster healthy social and emotional development and to manage behavior challenges. The consultant is also an important resource for understanding services that may be available to the child and family in the community, such as public or private family counseling and behavior management "safety net" programs that teach parenting skills and provide respite for families as needed. The mental health consultant may also play a role in helping children's programs establish an environment that promotes social and emotional development as well as develop policies and procedures to promote children's mental health (Heller et al., 2011).

Many consultants can observe classroom environments and offer recommendations to improve the program. They may also offer training for teachers that address the following topics (Heller et al., 2011):

- Establishing positive relationships with children, families, and other staff.
- Creating supportive environments, including schedule/routine, successful transitions, designing appropriate rules.
- Teaching socioemotional skills to young children.
- Strategies to address challenging behaviors.

Providing mental health services in the early childhood setting is a prevention effort that benefits the many children who are enrolled. In this way early childhood teachers and their programs contribute to public health by ensuring that children's social and emotional needs are recognized and addressed. In addition, having access to a behavioral consultant supports teachers to implement successful strategies and greatly reduces the number of children who are expelled from preschool, decreases disruptive and challenging behaviors, and improves the quality of the early childhood program (Heller et al., 2011).

Unfortunately, few early childhood teachers have access to mental health consultants and not all schools have counselors or behavior specialists on staff. Community resources may be available to provide some assistance. Local early intervention services for children with special developmental needs or community health services may offer some supports.

Pursuing professional development training related to children's mental health and advocating for resources to access occasional mental health consultation are other important ways teachers build skills and raise awareness of the importance of children's mental health. Teachers are in a good position to engage in advocacy efforts that bring attention to the need for mental health services for young children.

PROGRESSIVE PROGRAMS & PRACTICES

Promoting Social Emotional Development

By Allison Boothe and Angela Keyes, The Tulane University Institute of Infant and Early Childhood Mental Health

The Tulane University Institute of Infant and Early Childhood Mental Health uses a unique model of early childhood mental health consultation (ECMHC). ECMHC is embedded within Louisiana's Quality Rating and Improvement System, Quality Start, which has a focus on children's social and emotional development. The approach is designed to assist all children, staff, and families involved in center-based child care with the goal of achieving healthy behavioral, social, and emotional development for young children.

Through the ECMHC model, mental health consultants provide services across the state, working with individual centers every other week for 6 months. The mental health consultants strive to form relationships with teachers and directors to assist them with creating supportive environments for young children and building strong teacher-child relationships. With this foundation in place, the mental health consultant works with center staff to design specific interventions for children who exhibit challenging behaviors and provide referrals for families if needed.

Program evaluation has demonstrated that teachers who received the Tulane model of ECMHC believe that they are more efficacious as teachers (Heller et al., 2011). Observation showed that teachers provided increased emotional support for children (e.g., they were more sensitive and showed greater regard for the student's perspective) and increased classroom organization skills (e.g., behavior management) (Heller et al., in press).

The ECMHC model works at two levels: program wide and child specific. For example, one center requested ECMHC to assist in the 2-year-old classroom. The teacher, Ms. Jenny, was struggling with the aggressive behaviors of three children in her class. The mental health consultant spent time in the classroom and worked with Ms. Jenny to create visual schedules and visual class rules to help all children in the class know what to expect during the day. The mental health consultant encouraged Ms. Jenny to discuss the visual schedule and the three simple rules with the children individually and during small and large group activities to help children to learn and remember the rules. Verbal reinforcement was given throughout the day when children followed the rules (e.g., "Wow, Kwan, you used your gentle hands while playing with Esme. You should be really proud of yourself!").

After these supports were in place one child, Jackson, continued to display aggressive behaviors. The mental health consultant observed Jackson closely and met with Ms. Jenny and Jackson's parents. Together they created a behavior management plan for school and home. Jackson's family also acted on a referral provided by the mental health consultant to help Jackson get a behavioral evaluation.

Visual Schedule

Music

Nap

Lunch

Discovery Centers

Teachers who have worked with mental health consultants in their classrooms using the Tulane model have said:

"It is always nice to have a fresh pair of eyes to see things that I may have missed . . . just to see the same situation in a different perspective . . . the idea that all situations have a solution. You just have to figure it out!"

"I had a challenging child in my class and she and I worked together to find solutions to help him. She was very encouraging to me. She taught me to praise good behavior and other children will follow."

References

Heller, S. S., Boothe, A., Keyes, A., Nagle, G., Sidell, M., & Rice, J. (2011). Implementation of a mental health consultation model and its impact on early childhood teachers' efficacy and competence. *Infant Mental Health Journal,* 32: 143–164. doi:10.1002/imhj.20289.

Heller, S. S., Boothe, A., Keyes, A., Nagle, G. A., Vaughn, K., Sidell, M., & Rice, J. (in press). It's all about the relationship: Mental health consultation's impact on classroom interactions. *Early Education and Development.*

● SUMMARY

Social and emotional development and mental health are synonymous. They refer to children's capacities to manage and express appropriate emotional responses and behaviors, to form close relationships, and to explore and learn. Children who are supported to develop these capabilities are able to adjust successfully to new situations and build positive future relationships. They are also more likely to experience success in school.

Social and emotional development is influenced by various factors including children's experiences in the home and early childhood environment. In the classroom, teachers foster children's social and emotional development by creating supportive environments, by nurturing strong attachment relationships, and by providing ample time for children to explore social relationships through unstructured play.

Sometimes children experience mental health problems that are revealed through significant behavior challenges. Working with families and mental health professionals, teachers help to identify strategies to manage children's difficult behaviors in the classroom and promote more appropriate behaviors and interactions. Young children can, and do, experience mental health disorders. Identifying these conditions is important because early intervention can improve emotional and behavioral outcomes and positively affect learning.

KEY TERMS

Approaches to learning
Attachment
Bipolar disorder
Caregiver
Continuum of mental health

Depression
Egocentric
Evidence-based interventions
Functional assessment
Mental health

Promotion strategies
Self-regulation
Transformation strategies

REVIEW QUESTIONS

1. Describe biological and environmental factors that contribute to children's mental health.
2. What essential skills do children need to form positive relationships?
3. Describe characteristics of early childhood programs that can have a positive impact on social and emotional health.
4. What aspects of social and emotional development contribute to school readiness?
5. What are some strategies teachers can use when working with children who exhibit challenging behaviors?

DISCUSSION STARTERS

1. Think of a child of any age who you know or have worked with who exhibited difficult behaviors. Do you know of any risk factors the child had such as poverty or coming from a single-parent household? Can you think of any specific warning signs?
2. Consider a child in the early childhood setting who has been exposed to a significant amount of violence and is displaying severe aggression in the classroom. Can you apply the principles of inclusion described in the chapter? How do you feel about including these children in the classroom? Can you describe advantages and disadvantages to inclusion?
3. Based on what you have read about risk factors that contribute to poor mental health in children, can you think of national policies that either contribute to these risk factors or that help alleviate the stress of these factors on children? What services available in your community help families who are at risk?

PRACTICE POINTS

1. Teachers have endless opportunities in the classroom to promote social and emotional development through establishing healthy relationships and promoting healthy play activities. Can you develop ways in which teachers can engage families in promoting healthy social and emotional development?

2. Mood disorders can interfere with healthy social and emotional development. Can you think of specific ways to help children with mood disorders establish healthy relationships with their peers in the classroom?

3. Develop a list of resources and agencies in your community that can help early childhood programs manage challenging behaviors.

WEB RESOURCES

Children and Mental Health Fast Facts

http://mentalhealth.samhsa.gov/publications/allpubs/fastfact5/default.asp

National Center for Child Poverty: Mental Health in Children

www.nccp.org/publications/pub_687.html

Tulane Institute of Infant and Early Childhood Mental Health

www.infantinstitute.com

Zero to Three: Early Childhood Mental Health

www.zerotothree.org/site/PageServer?pagename=key_mental

MyEducationLab™

Go to Topic 10 (Mental Health) in the MyEducationLab (www.myeducationlab.com) for your course, where you can:

- Find learning outcomes for Mental Health along with the national standards that connect to these outcomes.
- Complete Assignments and Activities that can help you more deeply understand the chapter content.
- Apply and practice your understanding of the core teaching skills identified in the chapter with the Building Teaching Skills and Dispositions learning units.

- Check your comprehension on the content covered in the chapter by going to the Study Plan in the Book Resources for your text. Here you will be able to take a chapter quiz, receive feedback on your answers, and then access Review, Practice, and Enrichment activities to enhance your understanding of chapter content.

part four
Promoting Safety

thirteen
Enhancing Safety Through Appropriate Environments

learning outcomes

AFTER READING THIS CHAPTER, YOU SHOULD BE ABLE TO:

1. Define various aspects of safety and explain the influence of safety on children's growth and development.

2. Explain safety standards promoted by licensing regulations and how they impact children's safety.

3. Describe factors that guide planning for children's programs and discuss strategies for increasing safety and security in children's environments.

4. Plan and create safe and appropriate environments for young children.

5. Explain how to establish safe indoor environments for young children.

6. Select safe and appropriate furnishings, toys, and equipment for young children.

7. Explain how to create safe outdoor environments for young children.

Cass and Everett are looking for child care for their 2-year-old son, Caden. They have heard good things about Sunshine Child Development Center, so they schedule a visit and prepare a list of questions. Barb, the classroom teacher, greets them, gives them a tour of the classrooms and play yard, and describes the curriculum.

Cass likes the colorful environment and the energetic involvement of the children. Everett is impressed by the pretend tide pool touch table and the way the children and teacher are exploring the materials and talking about the oceans. Even so, they have concerns. They have never left Caden in a setting without individual attention and they worry about whether he will be safe. They ask about the teachers, wanting to know about their education and whether they are trained in first aid.

Barb realizes that this family needs reassurance that their son will be well cared for. Barb describes the program's safety policies. She talks about how the room arrangement helps the children play safely while being supervised by the teachers. As they watch, Cass and Everett observe a teacher holding a child who has fallen down. They like the way she comforts the child and then treats the hurt, using gloves and speaking calmly. When they leave, the parents feel confident that they have found a setting that will be a good fit for Caden and for them.

Ensuring children's **safety** is a fundamental responsibility of early childhood teachers. Threats to children's safety exist in all parts of the physical and emotional environments in which children grow and learn. This means teachers need to be proactive and prepared in order to keep children safe. Safety in the early childhood setting *is no accident!* It is established when teachers merge knowledge of child growth and development with recognition of the potential risks to children's safety. Teachers learn to pay attention to the possibility for accidents and are prepared to take the steps needed to reduce risk. Understanding and acting on this information is an important part of the process of becoming a teacher and early childhood professional.

A variety of hazards present risks to children's safety. Among these are accidents caused by risks in the environment, poor supervision and safety management practices, weather and other natural disasters, and violence in the community and in the home. Early childhood teachers are called on to be aware of these risks and capable of establishing safe classrooms and play environments for young children.

In this chapter we describe the importance of safety to children's healthful growth and development and discuss the accidental injuries that occur most frequently during childhood. We explore the safety standards and regulations that guide creation of safe early childhood classrooms and management practices. Finally we identify the characteristics of safe indoor and outdoor classrooms and provide guidance about selecting toys and equipment that are safe and developmentally appropriate for young children.

MyEducationLab™

Visit the MyEducationLab for *Nutrition, Health, and Safety for Young Children* to enhance your understanding of chapter concepts with a personalized Study Plan. You'll also have the opportunity to hone your teaching skills through video-based Assignments and Activities, as well as Building Teaching Skills and Dispositions lessons.

● ENSURING PHYSICAL AND EMOTIONAL SAFETY

Young children grow and mature quickly during the early years. Because of this, teachers need to understand the role of safety in children's typical growth and development. Teachers also need to recognize the influence of development on children's physical ability to navigate safely in the world and their emotional maturity to make safe decisions.

Understanding the Impact of Safety on Healthful Development

Although ensuring children's safety is naturally focused on avoiding harm and pain, it is also a foundational requirement for children's healthful development. Children's physical and emotional requirements must be recognized, their basic needs must be met, and the classroom must be created as a refuge in order for children to grow, thrive, and develop to their full potential.

Attending to Physical Safety Needs

Providing for children's physical safety involves protecting them from bodily harm and injuries such as bumps, bruises, cuts, and scrapes. Any injury that harms children's bodies is a violation of their physical safety. Ensuring physical safety provides children freedom from the threat of harm.

Teachers consider children's physical safety in all aspects of program planning. Safety is foremost when designing facilities and selecting toys for the classroom. It is considered when planning and purchasing food for snacks and meals and when determining how meals will be presented. It is a key consideration

Safe children's environments support healthful development.

safety
protection from harm or danger

when implementing practices to avoid the spread of germs that may lead to disease and illness and when planning daily schedules to allow ample time for children to play actively. Concern for safety compels teachers to notice and remove broken toys and avoid selecting equipment that is too challenging for children's capabilities.

Teachers are generally accustomed to planning safe environments and supervising children to avoid physical harm, and they know that these are essential teaching responsibilities. But physical safety is only one important aspect of a child's well-being that must be considered. Emotional safety is another significant element of a child-safe environment.

Supporting Emotional Safety Needs

Emotional safety refers to children's internal sense of security. It includes the sense of being protected, sheltered, and free from threat or harm—either real or perceived. Attending to emotional safety provides children freedom from fear and violence.

Emotional safety is achieved by protecting children from experiences that damage their spirit and sense of personal worth, and by providing children with experiences that are free from anxiety and fear—experiences where they are free to develop trust and confidence (Cohen, Onunaku, Clothier, & Poppe, 2005). Emotional safety is supported through careful program planning such as offering a favorable teacher-to-child ratio, predictable routines, and developmentally appropriate activities. Supports for emotional safety for infants include responsive and caring relationships where voices are soothing, touch is kind, and the child's needs are met. Preschoolers and older children experience emotional safety when teachers guide them to learn appropriate ways of interacting and when teacher's step in to ensure that no child experiences bullying or intimidation (National Association for the Education of Young Children [NAEYC], 2011; Shonkoff & Phillips, 2000).

Children who feel emotionally safe are able to be responsive to the guidance of the teacher and more capable of following safety rules. They are also more able to be attentive to their environment and open to learning from experiences. This emotional comfort supports development of the *executive functioning skills* of remembering directions, controlling reactions, and being flexible, aspects that form the foundation for cognitive and social abilities (Center on The Developing Child at Harvard University, 2012; Shonkoff & Phillips, 2000). Overall, emotional safety is a component of positive mental health that enables children to establish a sense of personal value or worthiness (Cohen et al., 2005). (See Figure 13-1.)

Addressing Basic Needs

Growth and development are strongly influenced by access to basic needs. These needs are thought to exist in a hierarchy of levels (Maslow, 1954). The first or foundational levels include needs that are crucial for basic survival, such as the physiological (bodily) needs for air, food, water, and shelter, and safety needs, such as physical and emotional protection from violence and aggression. Next are needs related to love and belonging (the need to be cared for and nurtured by others), self-esteem (the need to feel competent and socially acceptable), and finally self-actualization (the need to use and apply knowledge, be able to solve problems, and express one's self creatively). Each level of need must be satisfied before children can go on to meet their needs at the next higher level in the hierarchy.

Meeting children's basic needs builds the foundation on which the more advanced aspects of growth and development depend. When children are in out-of-home care settings, the important task of meeting these needs falls to the teachers and early childhood program. This is a reminder of the important contribution that teachers make to young children's physical and emotional safety, essential aspects of well-being.

FIGURE 13-1

Physical and Emotional Safety Serve as Supports for a Child's Well-Being

CHILD WELL-BEING
Freedom to learn and thrive

PHYSICAL SAFETY
Freedom from threat of harm

EMOTIONAL SAFETY
Freedom from fear and violence

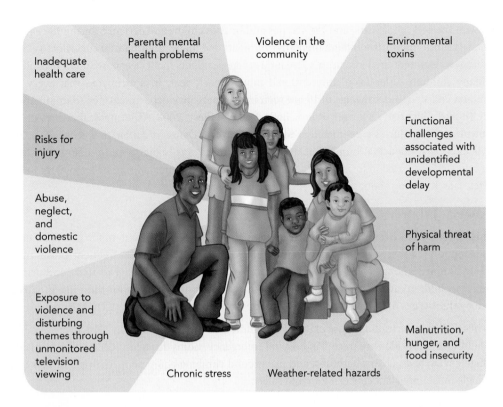

Parental mental health problems

Violence in the community

Environmental toxins

Inadequate health care

Risks for injury

Functional challenges associated with unidentified developmental delay

Abuse, neglect, and domestic violence

Physical threat of harm

Exposure to violence and disturbing themes through unmonitored television viewing

Malnutrition, hunger, and food insecurity

Chronic stress

Weather-related hazards

FIGURE 13-2

The Classroom Is a Refuge from Threats to Children's Physical and Emotional Safety

Source: Based on *From neurons to neighborhoods: The science of early childhood development,* edited by J. P. Shonkoff and D. A. Phillips, 2000, Washington, DC: National Academy Press, retrieved January 19, 2012, from http://www.nap.edu/openbook .php?isbn=0309069882.

Creating the Classroom as Refuge for Children

Some children face many challenges in their daily lives outside the early childhood classroom. As depicted in Figure 13-2, some of these challenges involve negative experiences that can harm children's brain development, such as violence, abuse, and unsafe living conditions (Shonkoff & Phillips, 2000). Early childhood classrooms offer a time and space in which children can be free from worry about their physical and emotional safety, allowing them to relax and learn.

Teachers who create classroom environments that protect children from threats and ensure their physical and emotional safety introduce a vision of a healthy lifestyle that supports children in two ways. First, children are provided a direct opportunity to rest, be nurtured, and learn within the secure environment. Second, seeds are planted for the future; children are given concrete experiences of safe and healthy living that give them hope and broaden their understanding of what their futures can be.

In the opening case scenario, Cass and Everett wanted to know how the teacher will care for and protect their child. Parents like these may not specifically ask about physical and emotional safety or basic needs. Instead they may ask, "How do you keep the classroom secure from intruders?" "What do you do if a child hits?" or "How will you protect my child from bullying?" Teachers need to be prepared to offer concrete examples and confident descriptions of how the classroom is a refuge where children's physical and emotional safety needs are supported and attention to children's well-being is of utmost importance.

Identifying Unintentional Injuries

Injuries during the early years range from incidental accidents and "ouches" to significant injuries that may lead to lifelong disability or even death. These are called **unintentional injuries**. They include the familiar bumps and tumbles that occur as toddlers learn to walk, the skinned knees that seem to

unintentional injury injury from accident

come with the preschool years, and the scrapes and bruises children experience during the early elementary years as they move around their environments and follow their natural curiosity to explore and discover. Unintentional injuries also include severe accidents that cause permanent disability.

Many children suffer from unintentional injuries each year. It is estimated that every year 9.2 million children under the age of 19 are seen in an emergency department due to unintentional injury (Borse, Gilchrist, Dellinger, Rudd, Ballesteros, & Sleet, 2008). The medical cost related to treatment of these injuries is estimated at $17 billion a year (Danseco, Miller, & Spicer, 2000). Even so, it is likely that the actual number of unintentional injuries is higher because many injuries are never reported or treated in formal settings. This highlights the importance of being vigilant to keep children safe. Knowing about the causes of injury is a good first step.

Causes of Unintentional Injury

The incidence and causes of unintentional injuries are tracked by the Centers for Disease Control and Prevention (Table 13-1). Information is compiled to show the 10 most frequent causes of unintentional injury among babies (up to age 1), toddlers and preschoolers (ages 1 to 4), and primary school–age children (ages 5 to 9). Nearly 74% of the unintentional injuries for these age groups are caused by three types of injury (Centers for Disease Control and Prevention [CDC], 2010):

- *Falls:* Falls are the leading cause of injury in children under the age of 9. In 2010, over 1.7 million children nationwide were treated in hospital emergency rooms due to accidental falls: from cribs, high chairs, beds, chairs, bathtubs, and playground climbing equipment. The risk for falls is the single most important concern for child safety.

fall
injury received when a person descends abruptly due to the force of gravity and strikes a surface at the same or a lower level

struck by or against injury
resulting from being hit or by hitting against an object

bite or sting injury
including animal or insect bites or stings from jellyfish, insects, or plants

fatal injury
unintentional injuries that ultimately lead to death

TABLE 13-1 National Estimates of the 10 Leading Causes of Nonfatal Injuries, United States, 2009

Rank	Birth–1 year	1–4 Years	5–9 Years
1	Fall 147,280	Fall 955,381	Fall 631,381
2	Struck by/against 31,360	Struck by/against 372,402	Struck by/against 406,045
3	Bite or sting 10,922	Bite or sting 137,352	Cut or pierce 104,940
4	Foreign body 8,860	Foreign body 126,060	Bite or sting 92,885
5	Fire/burn 7,846	Cut/pierce 84,095	Pedal cyclist 84,590
6	Other 7,036	Overexertion 83,056	Overexertion 77,742
7	Overexertion 6,249	Other specified 62,861	Motor vehicle occupant 58,049
8	Inhalation/suffocation 6,057	Fire/burn 49,896	Foreign body 55,185
9	Cut/pierce 6,049	Unspecified 48,454	Dog bite 43,512
10	Motor vehicle occupant 4,942	Poisoning 41,265	Other transport 39,732
Total	**236,601**	**1,960,822**	**1,594,061**

Source: *National Estimates of the 10 Leading Causes of Nonfatal Injuries Treated in Hospital Emergency Departments, United States, 2009,* by the Centers for Disease Control and Prevention, National Center for Injury Prevention & Control, Office of Statistics and Programming, retrieved January 2012, from www.cdc.gov/Injury/wisqars/pdf/National_Estim_10_Leading_Causes_Nonfatal_Injuries_Tx_Hospital-ED_US2009-a.pdf.

- *Struck by or against injury*: Being struck or striking against objects is the second most frequent cause of treated injury for children under the age of 9, accounting for nearly 22% of the unintentional injuries for the age group. Injuries of this kind occur when babies pull objects over onto themselves, toddlers wobble into the edge of tabletops, or preschoolers and elementary school–aged children accidentally hit each other with toys or sports equipment. The world is full of risks for this kind of injury.

- *Bite or sting injury*: Bites and stings are the third most frequent cause of injury for children 4 and under, and the fourth cause of injury for children ages 5 to 9. This type of injury accounts for almost 7% of the unintentional injuries among children under the age of 9. Bites or stings include human, animal, or insect bites, and insect, jellyfish, or plant stings.

Accidents due to these three causes accounted for nearly 2.9 million treated injuries among young children in 2010 (CDC, 2010).

Teachers need to be generally knowledgeable about the causes of unintentional injury for each age group. This information helps to focus attention on preventive actions.

Defining Fatal Injuries

Some unintentional injuries ultimately lead to death. These are called **fatal injuries**. Table 13-2 depicts the most frequent causes of fatal injuries among young children. For teachers the possibility of a child dying from an injury sustained

Falls are the leading cause of injury among young children.

TABLE 13-2 Ten Leading Causes of Injury Death by Age Group, United States, 2008

Rank	Birth–1 Year	1–4 Years	5–9 Years
1	Suffocation 1,058	Drowning 443	Motor vehicle/traffic 385
2	Homicide 156	Motor vehicle/traffic 346	Drowning 138
3	Homicide: other 98	Homicide: unspecified 192	Fire/burns 111
4	Motor vehicle/traffic 98	Fire/burns 169	Homicide: firearm 44
5	Undetermined: suffocation 46	Suffocation 145	Suffocation 41
6	Drowning 41	Pedestrian 111	Other land transport 28
7	Homicide: suffocation 32	Homicide: other 77	Pedestrian 24
8	Undetermined 28	Homicide: firearm 56	Fall 22
9	Adverse effects 24	Struck by/against 44	Homicide: unspecified 15
10	Fire/burn 22	Fall 38	Struck by/against 13
Total	**1,603**	**1,621**	**821**

Source: *10 Leading Causes of Injury Death by Age Group Highlighting Unintentional Injury Deaths, United States, 2008*, Centers for Disease Control and Prevention, National Center for Injury Prevention and Control. Office of Statistics and Programming, retrieved January 2012, from www.cdc.gov/Injury/wisqars/pdf/Leading_Causes_injury_Deaths_Age_GRoup_Highlighting_Unintentional_Injury%20Deaths_US_2008-a.pdf.

while in the early childhood setting is unthinkable. But the early years are a time of fast growth and rapid change that increase children's vulnerability. Their ability to put themselves at risk can often outpace their judgment. Children rely on the adults in their lives—families and teachers—to keep them safe. One way to be proactive is to recognize the causes of fatal injuries and to take action to reduce children's risk.

Incidence of Fatal Injuries

Fatal injuries are the leading cause of death for children in the United States (Borse et al., 2008); more deaths are caused by fatal injuries than by disease or congenital defects. In 2009, over 3,800 children died from unintentional injuries (Centers for Disease Control and Prevention [CDC], 2009). Deaths due to injury was highest in the 1- to 4-year-old age group (toddlers and preschoolers), followed by infants (birth to 1 year), and school-age children (5 to 9 years of age) (CDC, 2009).

Causes of Fatal Injury

Four primary causes of fatal injury have been identified by the CDC (2009):

suffocation
inhalation, aspiration, or ingestion of food or other object that blocks the airway, causing suffocation

motor vehicle and traffic accidents
death due to injuries sustained when riding as a passenger in a vehicle

drowning
suffocation (asphyxia) resulting from submersion in water or another liquid

burns
severe exposure to flames, heat, or chemicals that leads to tissue damage in the skin or deeper in the body; injury from smoke inhalation to the upper airway, lower airway, or lungs

- **Suffocation** was the leading cause of death due to injury for children under the age of 9 years, accounting for 1,138 deaths in 2009. The majority of deaths caused by suffocation occurred among infants.

- **Motor vehicle and traffic accidents** ranked second in 2009, causing 831 deaths. The highest number of deaths due to motor vehicles and traffic injuries occurred among 5- to 9-year-olds.

- **Drowning** ranked third, causing 614 child deaths in 2009. The highest number of deaths due to drowning occurred in the 1- to 4-year-old age group.

- **Burns** ranked fourth in 2009, causing 282 child deaths, with the highest number occurring among 1- to 4-year-olds.

While the ranking of these four causes of injury may vary from year to year among the age groups, suffocation, vehicle accidents, drowning, and burns persist as significant dangers to young children.

Understanding Risk Factors for Unintentional Injury and Death

A variety of factors influence the incidence of injuries and fatalities due to injury among children (Borse et al., 2008; Danseco et al., 2000). These include children's age, developmental maturity, sex, race, family income, location of residence, and the child's individual risk profile. The association of these factors to actual risk for injury for a particular child is a matter of speculation, as described next.

Children's Age and Developmental Maturity

sudden infant death syndrome (SIDS)
the sudden and unexplainable death of a young child

Age and developmental maturity greatly influence children's risk for injury. Although the number of injuries tends to be higher among preschoolers and young primary school–age children, the number of deaths due to injury is highest among infants and preschoolers (CDC, 2009). The high fatal injury rate for babies is due to the large number of infants who die as a result of **sudden infant death syndrome (SIDS)**. SIDS is the sudden and unexplainable death of a young child and is the leading cause of death of children under the age of 1 year (National Institute of Child Health and Human Development [NICHD], 2012).

Developmental maturity also influences risk. For example, infants who are less mobile may be unable to move away from the dangers that lead to suffocation. As children grow and mature they gain new motor skills and are more able to move themselves into dangerous situations. Their newfound mobility may exceed their ability to recognize and danger. Physically adept 1- to 4-year-olds may put themselves into danger of drowning by exploring water sources. Children in the 5- to 9-year-old age group may be allowed to move about more freely, such as walking and bicycling near traffic, which can put them at risk for motor vehicle and traffic injuries. These examples highlight the importance of adult supervision across the early childhood age range.

At the same time the risks for some injuries decrease as children age and mature. For example, the number of deaths from pedestrian causes drops as children age (CDC, 2008). This suggests that children become more able to understand the dangers and be responsive to educational guidance about staying away from traffic.

Children's Sex

A higher fatality rate due to injury is seen among boys than girls (Borse et al., 2008). This may be because boys are often encouraged to take risks and may be allowed to test their skills more freely, or they may receive less supervision.

Children's Race

Injury rates are higher among White children than among children from other racial backgrounds (Danesco et al., 2000). However, fatal injuries occur more often among American Indian and Alaskan Native children (Borse et al., 2008). Black children are twice as likely and American Indian infants are three times more likely to die of SIDS than White infants (NICHD, 2006). These higher mortality rates due to injury may suggest exposure to more severe injuries or less access to follow-up health care or both.

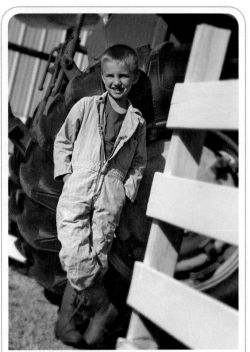

The risk for injury is high among children who live in rural areas.

Family Income

Children from families with very low incomes (below $5,000 per year) tend to have the highest numbers of unintentional injuries (Danseco et al., 2000). Reasons for this may include unsafe conditions in the home due to limited resources, or the community surrounding the low-income housing may introduce more dangers.

Location of Child's Residence

Injury rates, as well as numbers of fatal injuries, are higher for children living in rural areas than for children living in cities (Danseco et al., 2000). Although the numbers of fatal injuries in agricultural settings has decreased in recent years, the number of unintentional injuries has increased (American Academy of Pediatrics [AAP], 2001). Children who live in rural areas are exposed to a variety of risks, including the presence of large animals and farm machinery. These children may be allowed to assume responsibilities that exceed their developmental maturity for understanding safety risks, such as feeding large animals or using equipment, or they may receive less supervision.

Individual Child Risk Profile

Individual children also have their own unique patterns and characteristics that form their risk profile, or individual potential for injury (Wrigley & Dreby, 2005). This includes the child's style, such as how the child approaches a new situation or responds to directions, aspects that may affect their safety in the early childhood setting.

When families enroll their child in a program, they may share information that alerts the teacher to aspects of a child's style that need special attention for safety. A parent might report that the child "Always climbs on things" or "Puts things in her mouth." Teachers use this information along with direct observations to develop an awareness of a child's pattern and style. This information helps identify potential risks that may be significant for that particular child.

> ### What if . . .
> you learned during the enrollment process that a 3-year-old child had experienced two visits to the emergency room as a result of climbing on high shelving in the family's home? What steps would you take to increase the safety of this child in your classroom?

Acknowledging Risk for Injury in Early Childhood Settings

Most reported injuries to young children occur at home (Phelan, Khoury, Kalkwarf, & Lanphear, 2005). Only about 15% of the total reported injuries of young children occur in early childhood settings (Currie & Hotz, 2004). Out-of-home early childhood settings are generally considered to be safe environments for young children; however, accidents do occur and some children's settings are safer than others (Wrigley & Dreby, 2005).

A detailed study examined the numbers of fatal injuries reported in three types of early childhood settings: child care centers, family child care homes (care for small groups of children in the provider's home), and in-home child care (care provided for children in the child's home) (Wrigley & Dreby, 2005). Of the nearly 1,400 fatal injuries reviewed, the fewest (110) occurred in child care centers. In-home child care reported 320 deaths. The most fatalities occurred in family child care homes where more than 700 child deaths were reported.

It was postulated that fewer fatalities occurred in child care centers because of the more open nature of the environment and the presence of two or more teachers. Teachers in child care centers are also easily observed, which may allow supervisors and other teachers to provide advice regarding safety practices, assist with challenges, and offer support when needed. The safety standards required for licensed children's centers are also likely to reduce the frequency of child injury and death. By contrast, teachers in family child care homes and in-home settings usually work alone or with relatively little support. Family child care and in-home settings may also have environmental dangers that are not present in center-based settings.

Implications for Teachers

During the next decade the numbers of children under the age of 5 who participate in out-of-home care and education settings is expected to increase rapidly (Bureau of Labor Statistics, U.S. Department of Labor, 2010). With more children spending more time in out-of-home care, the responsibility for vigilance will also increase. This makes early childhood program safety practices even more important. Teachers need to keep aware of emerging safety trends to ensure that the children are safe.

Understanding the causes and risk factors for unintentional injury equips teachers with important information about the hazards that children face. The next step is to put this information to use by approaching situations with alertness and being ready to assess the situation and take action in relevant ways. Safety standards and regulations are helpful resources.

● USING REGULATIONS TO IMPROVE SAFETY

Early childhood programs and teachers have access to a variety of resources that guide the development of safety policies and practices. These include professional organizations, research institutes, and the state and local regulatory agencies that have oversight for the safety standards that guide programs serving young children. Licensing requirements and accreditation standards help teachers implement the essential elements of safe early childhood classrooms.

Implementing Safety Regulations

A primary resource for safety in early childhood programs is the publication *Caring for Our Children: National Health and Safety Performance Standards: Guidelines for Out-of-Home Child Care Programs*. This 2011 publication is a joint effort of the American Academy of Pediatrics, the American Public Health Association, and the National Resource Center for Health and Safety in Child Care and Early Education. It provides a comprehensive listing of safety standards and recommendations developed from a review of research and the debates and discussions of individuals and associations with concern for child safety. A key recommendation directs each state to establish by law a regulatory agency with authority to protect children through mandatory licensing of all out-of-home care settings. The recommendation advocates for mandatory licensing of all children's programs including both part-time and full-time settings.

The Role of the Regulatory Agency

Each state has a regulatory agency that is responsible for providing a basic level of health and safety protection for children in out-of-home care settings. They are responsible for setting and enforcing minimum standards to reduce the risk of disease, fire, injury, and impairment.

All 50 states and the District of Columbia regulate child care to some extent. While the structure of oversight varies from state to state, all child care regulatory agencies are directed by legislation to:

- Establish standards for out-of-home child care.
- Implement monitoring strategies.
- Enforce the child care regulations.

Licensing Criteria

The criteria that identify what programs must be licensed vary from state to state. Most regulatory agencies identify the following determining factors for mandatory licensing:

- *Group size:* the number of children to be served.
- *Length of the service day:* to separate child care from residential or 24-hour care.
- *Location of care:* centers, family child care homes, and in-home child care.

Regulated child care settings include child care centers, school-based child care settings, and family child care homes (home settings where a provider provides care for a small group of children that are not her own). Child care provided in the child's own home (in-home child care) is not usually regulated.

Some children's programs and facilities may be exempt from the regulatory requirements, such as recreation programs, day camps, and programs where the child's parent is on site, such as child care at sports clubs and in faith-group settings. The National Association for Regulatory Administration (NARA) (2010) estimates that more than 9.8 million child care slots are regulated nationwide. These are located in approximately 330,000 licensed early childhood settings. Of the children who participate in out-of-home child care, 75% attend center-based settings.

Understanding Common Licensing Requirements

Licensing covers a range of requirements that create the basic and minimal foundation for safety of young children in out-of-home care. Child care licensing requirements address licensing applications and fees, facilities, program design and practices, teacher qualifications and orientation, health and nutrition, and the children's educational program.

Licensing Application and Fees

Child care programs that are regulated must apply for a license before starting services. About half of the states require a fee for the license. The fee for center-based care programs is usually based on the number of children in care. Family child care is most often charged a flat licensing fee. Most licenses are valid for a 1- to 2-year period (NARA, 2010).

Facility Requirements

Facility inspections are conducted by a designated agency such as the city or county fire inspector or health department sanitarian. The children's environments are reviewed for safety to identify fire hazards, health and sanitation concerns (water, heat, toileting facilities), emergency facility supports (emergency lighting, exits, evacuation plans), and adherence to local building codes. Minimum square footage requirements, cleanliness, durability and appropriateness of furnishings, and food preparation and service areas are also inspected.

Program Design and Practices

Standards for program design and operation are outlined in the licensing requirements. Guidance is provided for determining child age groupings, class group size, and teacher-to-child ratios. Table 13-3 describes recommendations for maximum group size and teacher-to-child ratios for licensed early childhood programs.

A variety of safety procedures are mandated, such as maintaining child attendance records, planning secure arrival and departure practices, supervising of children, managing guidance and

TABLE 13-3 Class Size and Teacher-to-Child Ratios for NAEYC-Accredited Programs

Child Age Groups	Maximum Class Size	Teacher-to-Child Ratio
Infants (birth to 15 months)	6	1:3
	8	1:4
Toddlers (12 to 38 months)	6	1:3
	8	1:4
	10	1:4
	12	1:4
Toddlers and Twos (21 to 36 months)	8	1:4
	10	1:5
	12	1:6
Preschoolers (2.5- and 3-year-olds)	12	1:6
	14	1:7
	16	1:8
	18	1:9
Preschoolers (4- and 5-year-olds)	16	1:8
	18	1:9
	20	1:10
Kindergartners and young school-age children (5- to 9-year-olds)	20	1:10
	22	1:11
	24	1:12

Source: Based on *Leadership & management: A guide to the NAEYC early childhood program standards and related accreditation criteria,* (p. 29), edited by S. Ritchie and B. Willer, 2005, Washington, DC: National Association for the Education of Young Children.

discipline, conducting emergency evacuation drills, and planning for child safety in special settings, such as field trips, transportation, water activities, and nap time.

Teacher Qualifications and Requirements at Hire

Licensing regulations outline the required qualifications for teachers and program directors, including minimum age, education, and experience. A criminal background screening and reference checks are required before hire. Many states require a preemployment health assessment to rule out the presence of a communicable disease or conditions that cannot be managed through safety practices. Orientation to program safety procedures, emergency response, and child abuse reporting are requirements for pre-employment training.

Children's Health and Nutrition

Regulatory standards mandate health practices to reduce the spread of disease and to ensure child safety in the program setting. These include recommendations for child health exams before enrollment; gathering information about a child's special health, nutrition, and feeding needs; and ensuring children have required immunizations before they participate. The *Health Hint* describes the ways in which immunizations protect children in care and education settings from the effects of disease. A variety of other guidelines promote children's health and safety in child care.

Children's Programming

Licensing standards describe expectations for the design of the children's program. These include the provision of developmentally appropriate activities, communication with families, and always allowing families to access their child and the classroom.

HEALTH HINT Immunizations Keep Children Safe from Disease

The American Academy of Pediatrics pays close attention to the incidence of hospitalization and death for many early childhood diseases. They want parents and early childhood teachers to know the facts about immunizations and safety:

- Immunizations save lives and prevent illness from infectious disease.
- Nearly 100 people die each year from chicken pox. The chicken pox vaccine protects most children from getting the disease.

- Hepatitis A immunization has reduced the incidence of hepatitis A to the lowest numbers ever.
- *Haemophilus influenzae* type b (Hib) used to affect over 20,000 people each year. Since the introduction of the childhood vaccine, only a few hundred cases are identified per year.
- Many childhood diseases are active in other countries. Travelers may unknowingly bring diseases to the United States where they could spread quickly. Immunization keeps children safe.

Sources: *Why Immunizations Are Important,* by the American Academy of Pediatrics, 2000, Common Myths about Immunizations, retrieved October 23, 2009, from www .cispimmunize.org/fam/fam_main.html?http&&&www.cispimmunize.org/fam/myths.html; and "Prevention of Hepatitis A Through Active or Passive Immunization Practices: Recommendations of the Advisory Committee on Immunization Practices," by A. E. Fiore, A. Wasley, and B. P. Bell, May 19, 2006, *MMWR, 55*(RR07), pp. 1–23, retrieved October 13, 2009, from www.cdc.gov/mmwr/preview/mmwrhtml/rr5507a1.htm?s_cidrr5507a1_e.

Monitoring for Compliance

Regulatory agencies must ensure that licensed programs meet the mandatory standards at the time the license is approved and that compliance is maintained on an ongoing basis. Monitoring for compliance and instituting clear sanctions for noncompliance are important aspects of health and safety in early childhood programs.

Conducting Site Visits

Regulatory agencies monitor programs through both prearranged and unannounced site inspections, classroom observations, and review of records. Inspections focus on identifying problems that put children at risk for injury or disease. The most commonly identified licensing violations and examples include (NARA, 2010):

- *Exceeding licensed capacity,* by enrolling too many children for the room and group size.
- *Violating licensing requirements,* by not requiring teachers to be trained in first aid.
- *Lack of suitable staff,* such as hiring teachers who do not meet the required qualifications.
- *Poor care of children,* including gaps in supervision or providing inappropriate activities.
- *Poor administration and record keeping,* such as incomplete emergency records.

Site visits are also used as opportunities to provide technical assistance to help program staff meet and exceed the minimum licensing requirements for keeping children safe.

Investigating Complaints

Child Care regulatory agencies may receive complaints about licensed child care settings from the general public or families of children in care. Common complaints include too many children in care, poor supervision and management of child behavior, and problems related to children's health, safety, and nutrition (NARA, 2010). The licensing agency documents all complaints and decides how to follow up based on knowledge of the early childhood setting and the immediacy of the concern. Unannounced visits and interviews with the program director may be conducted to explore the validity of the complaint.

Some regulatory agencies are now making information about verified complaints and the agency's actions available to the general public through the agency website. This step confirms the seriousness with which regulatory agencies view their role in increasing safety in early childhood settings. It also highlights the importance of vigilance by teachers to ensure that licensing regulations are put into practice every day.

What if . . .

you were teaching in a children's program that was found to be in violation of a licensing requirement related to the teacher-to-child ratio during breaks? What ideas would you have to address this concern?

Responding to Licensing Violations

If licensing violations are discovered, the regulatory agency must determine a course of action. Some violations can be quickly remedied, such as posting emergency procedures. Others may constitute a serious problem that threatens child safety, such as not conducting criminal background checks on program staff. Once the nature of the violation is understood, the regulatory agency determines the appropriate consequence.

Enforcing Consequences

Repercussions are determined based on the severity of the violation. They might include putting the program on probation until the violation has been remedied, withholding licensing, or closing the facility. In some cases programs may have to pay a fine.

In a few cases the violation may be of significant severity that criminal prosecution and imprisonment are the outcome (NARA, 2010). Enforcing health and safety standards is an important way in which the regulatory agency provides for the safety of young children in out-of-home care and education settings.

Implications for Teachers

Understanding health and safety standards and the regulations that guide licensed children's programs is important for teachers. Familiarity helps teachers understand how the standards contribute to health and safety practices in the classroom. It also equips teachers with the information they need to explain to families how all aspects of the program work together to increase children's safety.

Being aware of licensing regulations also helps teachers understand that they are not working alone to ensure children's well-being. They see that they are part of a network of safety provided for young children, and they recognize that safety standards and the regulatory agency are resources for improving program practices to keep children safe.

Moving Beyond Minimum Standards

Public systems to ensure the safety of children in out-of-home care settings are still evolving. The current licensing and regulatory activities, while meeting the basic safety needs of children in child care, may still fall short of the goals for a thorough and effective licensing system. Although research data on strategies that improve child safety are becoming more readily available, regulatory standards do not always keep up. For example, the "Back to Sleep" safety campaign has reduced death due to SIDS by 50% for infants below the age of 1 (NICHD, 2006). New recommendations for a *safe infant sleep environment* include avoiding use of any soft bedding such as blankets, in infant sleep spaces (American Academy of Pediatrics, 2011). In spite of the success of such practices only half of the states currently require that child care centers place infants on their backs to sleep (NARA, 2010). This represents a gap in systematically applying the best safety practices.

Concerns have grown about the large numbers of children's programs that are not licensed and the potential for some of the programs to be harmful (National Association of Child Care Resource and Referral Agencies (NACCRRA), 2008; NAEYC, 1998). Improvements are being called for including (NAEYC, 1998):

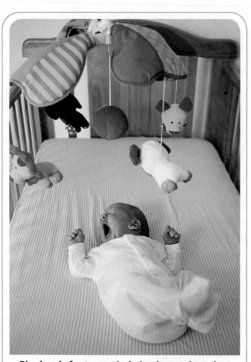

Placing infants on their backs to sleep has greatly reduced the incidence of SIDS.

- Mandatory licensing requirements for all programs that serve young children.
- More comprehensive regulations regarding the skills and education of those working with children.
- Greater focus on research-guided policies.
- More vigorous enforcement of mandatory requirements.

Individual programs can choose to move beyond the minimum regulations. One way is to achieve program accreditation by the NAEYC.

Program Accreditation

NAEYC (2008) accreditation is a comprehensive process that challenges programs to raise the quality of care in early childhood settings. Achieving accreditation is an endorsement that the children's setting and program practices meet important quality standards. All children's settings can voluntarily use the materials provided by the NAEYC to identify aspects of service that can be improved, thus enhancing program quality.

Increasing Quality in Other Ways

Rating systems for child care settings are being developed by states as a way to increase the quality of child care. To date these Quality Rating and Improvement Systems (QRIS) are most often being offered as voluntary steps that programs can take to move beyond minimum standards. A variety of indicators are being implemented, including improving teacher-to-child ratios and managing group size, improving teacher qualifications, enhancing health and safety, and building collaboration across the systems that serve young children and families (Caronongan, Kirby, Malone, & Boller, 2011).

Improving Teacher-to-Child Ratio and Class Size   Improving the teacher-to-child ratio involves either adding another teacher to the classroom or limiting the total size of the group. This increases the likelihood that safety hazards are recognized, thus reducing children's risk for accidents. This step poses a challenge, however, because the cost of providing an additional teacher can be significant and reducing the number of children in a class reduces program income from fees.

Improving Teacher Qualifications   Increasing the expectations for the education and experience of program directors and teachers is another strategy that may improve child safety. NAEYC is moving this way by requiring more specific educational qualifications for administrators of accredited programs. The Office of Head Start and the field of early childhood as a whole advocate for increasing the educational requirements for early childhood teachers and ongoing professional development as ways to promote better outcomes for children.

Enhancing Health and Safety   Increasing the quality of health and safety in programs is accomplished by offering training beyond the minimum requirement of infant and child first aid and CPR (cardiopulmonary resuscitation). Training on when and how to use an epinephrine autoinjection (EpiPen) to treat anaphylactic shock from bee stings is reasonable given the number of unintentional injuries due to bites and stings. Knowing how to respond to seizures and asthma attacks are other beneficial training topics that may enhance a teacher's ability to keep children safe.

Building Collaborative Systems   State QRIS systems are being used to enhance the quality of services provided to young children across program types (such as family child care, center-based child care, Head Start, and state prekindergarten programs) as well as agencies (such as state Child Nutrition Programs and health care). This is accomplished by using the quality indicators to promote discussion and collaboration around the system of services being provided as ways to improve and streamline services.

Exploring the Implications of Increasing Safety Regulations

Mandatory licensing and regulations governing the care of young children are designed foremost to improve the health and safety of children in out-of-home care settings, reduce disease and injury, and increase child well-being. It is particularly difficult then to recognize that stricter standards designed to increase the quality and safety of children's settings have the potential to push some children into more risky situations. How does this happen?

Implementing more rigorous safety standards carries hidden costs. Improving teacher-to-child ratios, increasing teacher education requirements, and providing safety training are all projected to improve children's safety. But these steps ultimately increase the cost of child care. Consequently, some families may no longer be able to afford to enroll their children in licensed care settings. These families may be compelled to seek alternative settings that cost less, which may include settings that are not licensed or regulated. Children's risk for injury may be greater in these unregulated settings (Currie & Hotz, 2004). As a result, the efforts made to increase safety for children in child care may result in more children being placed in unsafe settings.

This also aggravates a current social problem. Affluent families may be able to afford more costly early childhood settings that meet quality, nutrition, health, and safety standards, but the higher cost may make access to such settings even more difficult for low-income families. As regulatory agencies consider stricter standards, and programs work to achieve higher quality, the relative costs and benefits must be explored and reasonable changes implemented.

● PROGRAM AND CLASSROOM SAFETY PLANNING

Ensuring children's physical and emotional safety requires careful planning and preparation at both the program and classroom levels. At the program level safety depends on strong leadership that prioritizes safety and demonstrates a commitment to increasing safety in all aspects of program services. In the classroom, teachers have specific responsibilities to establish safe settings and ensure children's safety as they interact with others in the environment. Program leaders and teachers have different roles, but together they create the system of practices that promote safety for young children.

Understanding Program Responsibilities

Early childhood program leaders, including owners of family child care settings, program directors, coordinators, and principals, are responsible for the systems that support the health and safety of children and staff in the early childhood setting or school. Program leaders carry primary responsibility for the overarching, or program level, aspects of safety. Safety decisions at the program level are broad-based and inclusive. They address physical facilities and program services, policies, and practices.

Providing Safe Facilities

Safe facilities make a significant contribution to children's physical and emotional safety. Program leaders are responsible for providing secure and accessible environments that meet building construction and safety codes. The facilities must also be appropriate for the age groups served, and the kinds of services provided, such as infant care or afterschool programs.

Developing Safety Policies and Procedures

Policies and procedures guide teachers as they do their work. These guidelines need to be relevant and appropriate. If a classroom is supervised by two teachers, the procedures must be designed to be successfully accomplished by two people. Procedures must also be responsive to current issues. If a particularly contagious flu virus has emerged as a health concern, a new safety procedure may need to be developed to include communicating with families about the symptoms of the flu and when to keep children home, and directing teachers what to do if a child develops flu symptoms while at school. The *Policy Point* describes the process of drafting a policy for an emergent issue.

Hiring Safe Personnel

Program leaders must ensure that all the people who work in the program are safe, appropriate, and capable of performing their roles. Making certain that staff have appropriate qualifications and conducting a criminal background screening are ways program leaders address children's safety during the hiring process.

Providing Orientation

Teachers need to be oriented to the program's safety policies and procedures before assuming their responsibilities. This ensures they are aware of their role in implementing safety protocols and

POLICY POINT   Emerging Safety Practices—Do We Need a Policy?

Sometimes early childhood settings are challenged to make policy decisions when the best practice approaches are not yet clear. Developing a new policy and putting it into practice require a thoughtful team approach:

1. **Define the question or problem.**

   Helmets vs. head lice: Which is a more significant risk to health and safety?

   - Head injuries due to bicycle accidents are a significant safety concern.
   - Sharing helmets may increase the risk of spreading head lice.

2. **Get others involved.**

   - Teachers, family members, informed community partners.

3. **Identify the anticipated problems and the potential benefits.**

   - **Problems:** Cost of helmets and cleaning supplies; cleaning helmets between uses may be hard; more

head lice means more program cleaning and management.

   - **Benefits:** Teaches children a safe habit; might avoid injury now and in the future; although head lice are a health annoyance, they are not deadly.

4. **Draft a plan.**

   - Children will wear helmets when riding tricycles or scooters at preschool.
   - We will provide four helmets to share, a cleaning protocol, and supplies.

5. **Implement the new plan for a defined trial period.**

   - We will try the new plan for 6 months.

6. **Reflect on progress and revise the policy.**

   - The kids are wearing the helmets; no lice so far; we will check back in 6 months.

---

assisting in emergencies. Orientation should address safety procedures that are specific to their particular class and individual children, as needed.

Monitoring for Compliance with Safety Rules

Ensuring that the policies and procedures designed to ensure health and safety are effectively implemented is an important program level safety responsibility. Periodic monitoring is a crucial aspect of this process. Monitoring activities may include observing classroom activities and using safety checklists. Program leaders use this information to create action plans for needed training and facility safety improvement.

Building Collaborations with Others

Early childhood programs and schools do not work alone in ensuring the safety of young children. Children's programs are a part of a network of community agencies that provide services to children and families. This means that families and community safety workers, such as firefighters, police, protective service personnel, and social service workers, are all partners in the effort to keep children safe.

Obtaining Insurance and Legal Counsel

Early childhood program leaders are also accountable for anticipating events that may negatively impact children's health and safety. An important way that program leaders arrange support is by purchasing accident and liability insurance and hiring a legal counselor if necessary.

Insurance for Accidental Injury and Death   Accident insurance provides backup coverage for some of the medical costs involved in treating injuries experienced by children while they are at the early childhood program. Depending on the details of the selected plan, accident insurance assists families to pay medical costs as a backup to the family's insurance. In some cases the program accident insurance may be the child's only accident insurance coverage. Obtaining basic accident insurance coverage is a part of the program leader's safety plan.

Liability insurance   Liability insurance supports the program and teachers in the event that a court of law determines they have been negligent in the care and supervision of children (Maine Bureau of Insurance, 2012). In the event of a tragic injury or death, parents or their insurance agencies may present claims against the program or individual teachers asserting that the program or teacher has been careless or negligent in their duties. Programs should purchase the most insurance coverage they can afford (Wyatt, 2001). Lawsuits have been known to award large amounts of money in response to credible suits for loss of a child's life or disability due to injury. Claims related to child care can be made years after the child was enrolled in the program.

Legal Counsel   Program leaders need to know who to turn to for legal guidance. Making arrangements for legal counsel provides the opportunity to obtain advice that can be helpful in creating safe policies and in knowing how to respond in case of tragic events (Perri, 2006). This also provides program leaders with the confidence that legal guidance is only a phone call away.

Clarifying Teacher Responsibilities

Children are the teacher's primary focus and the classroom is the teacher's specific sphere of influence. Teachers are responsible for ensuring children's safety in the classroom at all times. This is a big responsibility. It requires that teachers make a commitment to ensure children's safety, understand and follow program safety procedures, know how to manage safety in the classroom, share safety information with families, teach children safety skills, and take emergency action when necessary. Each of these activities links the program-level safety procedures to actions taken at the classroom level, building a comprehensive system of safe care for young children.

Making a Professional Commitment to Safety

Becoming a teacher means assuming a professional commitment to children's safety. The National Association for the Education of Young Children is the professional organization for those who teach children ages birth to 9 years. Members of NAEYC adhere to the guidelines of the NAEYC Code of Ethical Conduct and Statement of Commitment (National Association for the Education of Young Children [NAEYC], 2011) as a way of demonstrating their professional obligation to provide for the health and safety of young children. The primary principle of the NAEYC Code of Ethical Conduct states:

> Above all, we shall not harm children. We shall not participate in practices that are emotionally damaging, physically harmful, disrespectful, degrading, dangerous, exploitative, or intimidating to children. (NAEYC, 2011, p. 3)

Teachers put these principles into practice by taking a proactive stance to safety in the classroom. They view safety as a primary professional responsibility and structure their teaching and care on safety principles. Assuming a professional identity also involves contributing to program and community efforts to improve safety for children and families. Teachers need to keep current about the risks and causes of injury to young children and know how to identify safety strategies that can make a difference. Advocating in this way requires teachers to study the recommendations of reputable resources and know how to adapt such information to solve problems in the classroom and community.

Implementing Program Safety Practices

Teachers are responsible for learning and implementing the safety procedures of the program. Program-level policies and procedures are useless without concerned follow-through by teachers at the classroom level. A true children's safety team blends the administrative design of policies with thoughtful implementation by teaching professionals.

Program safety procedures need to be followed with care to achieve the desired safety outcome. For example, the evacuation procedure given to Kyra, a first-grade teacher, is very specific about who does what and when. Kyra is notified to prepare the children to respond to the school fire alarm when it sounds. She is directed to lead the children to a designated gathering spot, take a head count to determine whether all children are accounted for, and return to the building when the all-clear bell rings. At the end of the day, Kyra is required to record information about the drill on a pre-scribed form and return it to the office. These steps are conducted by all teachers and classes. This approach ensures that the safety procedure is systematically practiced and provides an opportunity for program leaders to confirm that the evacuation plan works for large groups of children.

In some cases teachers may have more flexibility when it comes to implementing a safety pro-cedure at the classroom level. Talea teaches in a preschool setting. She is directed to conduct an evacuation drill once per month, but is allowed to decide when the drill will occur and how the drill will be introduced and carried out. She must notify her supervisor of when she will conduct the drill, and she must keep a record of each drill to document that she has met the monthly practice require-ment. When Talea plans her drill, she does so as part of a larger unit on safety. She invites the local firefighter education team to visit her class. The firefighters show children the fire truck, talk about their safety equipment, and teach children to "get out and stay out" in case of fire. After the firefight-ers leave, Talea guides the children to pair off and follow the assistant teacher while she activates a home smoke alarm. This way she combines the program requirement to conduct an evacuation drill with a classroom safety education theme, reinforcing the message about why evacuation is important. This approach provides an appropriate mechanism for teachers of very young children to design a drill format that fits the children's developmental understanding.

> ## A Matter of ETHICS
> Emergency drills are important, but sometimes even the drill frightens children. Some teachers may be tempted to skip the drill, or not use the loud smoke alarm during the practice. What aspects of the code of ethics should teachers consider as they create a plan for practicing the fire drill?

Teachers may also be the first to recognize gaps or problems in program safety procedures. Identifying problems in the environment that may introduce risk for injury, recognizing problems in the safety procedures, and advocating for improve-ments are important professional responsibilities of those who teach young children.

Building Secure Relationships

Teachers who are purposeful about developing a caring relationship with each child and who assist children to build social bonds with one another create a sense of inclusion that is beneficial for all children in the class. These activities build strong and trusting teacher and child relationships that support children's willingness to follow safety guidance and respond to safety directions when needed.

Supervising Children

Teachers have the moral and ethical responsibility to recognize children's vulnerability and depen-dency on adults and to provide consistent and thorough supervision without fail (NAEYC, 2011). A common expectation is that children must be supervised by sight and sound at all times (Copple & Bredekamp, 2009). Supervision is the single most important way to keep children safe.

Modeling Safe Behaviors

Teachers are important role models and as such must ensure that their actions always convey appropriate health and safety messages. This includes doing what they expect children to do. For example, responding appropriately during emergency drills, using a ladder to stand on rather than a chair to reach objects that are on high shelves, sitting down and chewing foods carefully at meals, and using words to demonstrate how to ask for help are all examples of ways teachers model appropriate safety behaviors.

Teaching Safety Skills

Teachers are responsible for conveying developmentally appropriate safety messages. With very young children this includes redirecting a child to keep him from hitting on the window with a block while say-ing, "Blocks are for building not for hitting. Show me how you can build with blocks." Being intentional

TEACHING WELLNESS　Pedestrian Safety

LEARNING OUTCOME: Children will be able to move along the sidewalk safely and demonstrate the safety skills of stop, look, listen, and cross with an adult.

VOCABULARY FOCUS: Walking, safety, sidewalk, pedestrian, crosswalk, crossing lights.

SAFETY WATCH: Supervise children carefully on all neighborhood walks.

INFANTS AND TODDLERS

- **Goal:** Infants and toddlers will experience the rhythm associated with walking safely along the sidewalk and safely crossing the street.
- **Materials:** Baby carrier, backpack, or stroller for one or more children.
- **Activity plan:** Take a walk in the nearby neighborhood that is not too busy or noisy. Have toddlers hold hands with a teacher. Walk along the sidewalk. Describe what you are doing and use your body movements to reinforce the messages. Say, "We are walking safely along the sidewalk. The sidewalk is the place for people to move along the street." Stop at a crosswalk. Say, "Now we are getting ready to cross the street. First we stop. We look at the light to know when it is time to move. Do you see the green 'Walk' sign glowing? That means it is time for us to walk right across. We look and listen for cars. We keep watching to make sure it is safe from cars while we walk across. There, we are across the street. That was a safe way to cross."

- **How to adjust the activity:** Use a puppet and pictures to convey the safety message. Learn the words for stop, go, and safety in the languages of children in the class. Reinforce the message frequently. Provide pedestrian safety information for families so they can reinforce the messages at home.
- **Did you meet your goal?** Did children listen to your words and follow your directions? Did you see the toddlers stopping, looking, and listening?

PRESCHOOLERS AND KINDERGARTNERS

- **Goal:** Children will be able to name the safety cues: stop, look, listen, cross with an adult.
- **Materials:** Toy vehicles, people figures, small street signs, blocks, masking tape.
- **Activity plan:** Create a "neighborhood." Place masking tape on the floor in rectangular shapes to resemble neighborhood blocks. Place other materials nearby. Introduce the activity: Talk about the safety rules for crossing the street: stop, look for the crossing sign, watch and listen for cars, cross when it is clear, always cross with a grown-up. Invite the children to create a town. Ask them to teach the people how to cross the street safely. Watch as children play. Ask questions such as "How will this child get to the store? Does she know to stop-look-listen? Does she have a grown up to hold her hand?" If a child in the class uses an alternate method to move about, such as a wheelchair, use inclusive words, such as "move" instead of "walk." At group-time, review the safety message.

- **How to adjust the activity:** Take a neighborhood walk with the children and families. Teach and demonstrate the steps of stop–look–listen-cross with an adult. Guide families to support their child's understanding of the words and concepts, and learn from families how they teach such messages to their child with special developmental needs.
- **Did you meet your goal?** Are children able to identify the steps for safely crossing the street? Are children able to say why it is important to always cross with a grown-up?

SCHOOL-AGE CHILDREN

- **Goal:** Children will be able to name the safety cues: stop, look, listen when crossing the street, and describe how to safely walk along the sidewalk, cross at the crosswalk, and use pedestrian crossing lights.
- **Materials:** Construction paper, scissors, pens, glue, tape.
- **Activity plan:** Provide materials for making pedestrian safety books. Introduce the activity. Discuss the safety cues stop–look–listen, walk along the sidewalk away from the traffic, cross at the crosswalk, follow the crossing signals. Invite children to create a character (a person or animal). Ask them to write and illustrate a book about pedestrian safety to read to the others in the class.

- **How to adjust the activity:** Arrange an opportunity for the children to read their books to younger children. Provide materials for the children to draw bookmarks communicating the pedestrian safety messages.
- **Did you meet your goal?** Are children able to identify the safety cues? Can you observe from their stories that children understand the safety concepts?

is important. For example, teaching preschool and school-aged children skills for pedestrian safety can make a significant impact in helping them avoid the hazards associated with walking near traffic (Agran et al., 2003). The *Teaching Wellness* feature provides examples of ways to teach children about pedestrian safety. It focuses on providing clear guidance about how children should respond without introducing unnecessary worry and reinforces the message that adults help children keep safe.

Sharing Safety Messages with Families

The professional commitment to safety extends beyond the classroom. Teachers extend their commitment by sharing information about injury trends and ways families can help keep children safe, such as sharing the pedestrian safety concepts shared in the *Teaching Wellness* feature, or information about a toy recall. Working together, teachers and families can reduce the potential for injury and make positive contributions to children's physical and emotional health and safety.

Taking Action in Emergencies

While teachers focus a great deal of their attention on working to prevent unintentional injuries, they must also be prepared to respond immediately if they see children in a dangerous situation or if an accident occurs. Teachers prepare themselves to take on this responsibility by participating in emergency response training and focusing attentively on the lessons provided. If an emergency occurs, teachers are then ready to put the program's emergency response plan into action.

● CREATING SAFE AND APPROPRIATE ENVIRONMENTS

Establishing settings that support children's physical and emotional safety is an important task of teaching. It is also a significant responsibility due to the vulnerabilities of the very young children who are served. To meet this challenge many thoughtful decisions must be made to address safety in the **children's environment**, which includes the physical facilities and the materials used to facilitate learning (National Association for the Education of Young Children [NAEYC], 2008). This includes selecting appropriate locations for children's programs, establishing safe classrooms and outdoor facilities, and providing safe toys and equipment. The task can be challenging, given the variety of facilities and schools where young children are typically served. Several aspects guide decision making when creating spaces to care and educate young children: meeting family and community needs, creating spaces that value the developmental needs of young children, and making a commitment to address safety standards in facility development.

children's environment
the physical facility and materials used to facilitate learning

Meeting the Need for Safe Spaces

Early education facilities currently provide out-of-home care and education for a large number of young children. According to the U.S. Census Bureau, in 2010, more than 8.6 million children under the age of 5 participated in some kind of organized child care and education arrangement, and 3.5 million children ages 5 to 14 years received some kind of regular care in addition to their school attendance (U.S. Census Bureau, U.S. Department of Commerce, 2010). Family needs for child care and interest in early education drives much of the need for spaces to house early childhood programs.

Community goals also play a role. The importance of early education as a step in closing educational achievement gaps, is receiving a great deal of attention. Many states are exploring how to provide *universal prekindergarten*, public early childhood programs provided for all 4-year-old children. Such initiatives increase the need for safe and secure early childhood classroom spaces, but challenges must be addressed.

Recognizing Challenges

Addressing family and community needs for facilities to serve young children is complicated. Several aspects contribute to this challenge:

- A wide variety of spaces are needed to address the range of services required and the unique needs of each age group.
- Many early childhood settings must make do with borrowed, rented, or renovated spaces that were not designed to serve young children and are often inadequate.

- Existing early childhood programs usually do not realize sufficient profit to build new facilities.
- Few early childhood professionals have the training to make the important decisions needed to design appropriate facilities or manage the real estate and loan decisions needed to finance the construction of a new facility.

To meet these challenges, national facility development policies and regulations are needed to guide the creation of safe and appropriate early childhood facilities (Sussman & Gillman, 2007).

Implications for Teachers

In order to ensure that the environments created to serve young children are safe and appropriate, early childhood professionals need to be individually aware of the presence of safety standards and learn to access appropriate resources and advocate for the needs of young children. Two resources may offer some guidance:

- Guidance for the construction of federally funded child care settings can be accessed from the U.S. Department of Education's National Clearinghouse for Educational Facilities and the U.S. General Services Administration's (GSA's) Public Buildings Service, Office of Childcare (U.S. General Services Administration, 2003).
- Guidelines for spaces serving young children are provided by the NAEYC's accreditation standards, and the National Resource Center for Health and Safety in Child Care and Early Education provide guidelines (see the Web Resources section at the end of the chapter).

In the long run, for the benefit of young children in the future, early childhood professionals need to advocate for policies that guide the development of spaces that serve young children.

Designing Appropriate Spaces for Children

The child should be the primary consideration when designing and arranging safe and appropriate early childhood environments (NAEYC, 2008). This child-centered approach to design emerges from the perspective that the early years of development are unique, and that the spaces that serve young children should reflect this importance. Commitment to this approach is demonstrated by embracing a belief that young children are valued members of our society. It is enhanced by considering the shortcomings of many early childhood environments, and envisioning appropriate settings that offer sufficient space, are accessible, and reflect cultural values.

Demonstrating Value for Young Children

Decisions made about the design and arrangement of children's spaces are influenced by beliefs regarding the value of children, how children learn, and the role of the teacher and environment in promoting growth and development. These beliefs are based on a philosophical perspective that considers the connection of the space to the activities, experiences, and learning that will occur there. Two approaches provide examples of ways the philosophical perspective about young children influences the development of spaces that serve them.

Maria Montessori   Dr. Maria Montessori (1870–1952) believed that children are capable learners and that there should be careful attention paid to the arrangement of early childhood environments (Montessori, 1966). As a result Montessori-oriented classrooms are orderly environments that promote children's independent learning and invite both individual and group exploration. Toys and materials are carefully arranged on low, open shelving, allowing children to choose what they need and be responsible for returning materials to their place after use. The use of child-sized furnishings is central to this child-centered approach.

Reggio Emilia   The Reggio Emilia approach emerged from the village of Reggio Emilia, Italy, where beliefs embrace the ideal that children are of equal value to others in the community and are the responsibility of the collective group (New, 1993). The value for community is evident in facility design that

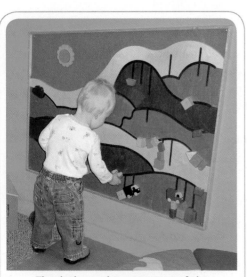

The design and arrangement of the environment send a message of value for young children.

links children to each other by providing common spaces and plazas, as well as to the larger community and world, through the use of carefully placed windows and classroom doorways that connect children to the outdoors (New, 1993). Displays of children's artwork, lovely furnishings, and mirrors are used to promote enjoyment of the indoor and outdoor environments, and invite exploration (Edwards, Gandini, & Forman, 1993; Katz & Cesarone, 1994). In this way the Reggio Emilia approach promotes the idea that the environment is an additional teacher (New, 1993).

Learning from Criticism

Children's environments in the United States are often criticized for showing limited expression of value for the work of young children. Most children's programs are housed in adapted spaces, and programs often do not have the funds to create innovative and beautiful environments. One report claims that early childhood classrooms in the United States tend to be overly busy and crowded spaces (Tarr, 2001), where children are separated from each other and disconnected from the outside world (Greenman, 2005). Some spaces that serve children under the age of 5 are thought to have the look of miniature elementary school classrooms with rows of desks or tables, where the focus appears to be placed on what teachers do in the setting rather than what children experience (Tarr, 2001). These criticisms invite teachers to revitalize their energy around creating safe environments that demonstrate value for young children and nurture children's emotional well-being, as well as keeping them safe.

Envisioning Appropriate Environments

Appropriate environments are established with consideration for children's age, size, and developmental needs (Moore Johnson, 2006). They demonstrate recognition of the ways in which children use their senses to experience and learn from the visual, auditory, aromatic, and tactile attributes of their surroundings. They are also welcoming, comfortable, beautiful, and inspirational. Appropriate environments encourage creativity and exploration and build children's confidence to learn (Greenman, 2005). In sum, appropriate children's spaces:

- Support physical safety and emotional security.
- Convey a sense of welcome and familiarity.
- Provide space for children to ease gradually into the classroom.
- Address children's age, developmental, and educational needs.
- Are culturally appropriate and developmentally accessible.
- Inspire exploration and discovery.
- Support teaching and learning.

Environments that are appropriate for children offer important attributes that are good for teachers, too. Teachers need comfortable spaces that provide flexibility for creative room arrangement, support curriculum delivery, and offer adequate storage (Moore Johnson, 2006). Appropriate environments for teachers contribute to teacher satisfaction, which may reduce the rate of teacher turnover and thus improve the quality of programming for young children. A list of space needs in appropriate early childhood environments is shown in Figure 13-3.

Providing Sufficient Space

Children need enough space to move and play safely. Classroom square footage is considered to be the single most important characteristic of a safe and appropriate children's environment. **Usable square footage** refers to the floor space in a classroom that is not covered by furnishings but is open and accessible. This measurement is used as a basic guide to determine the number of children that may be present in the space at one time. As a result, classroom square footage, along with the furnishings plan, determines the group size for any room in the early childhood setting.

State licensing standards and NAEYC accreditation standards have traditionally identified that each indoor classroom should provide a minimum of 35 usable square feet per child. This is equivalent to a space 5 feet by 7 feet in dimension, or only slightly more than the square footage of two play-pens, causing concern that the small spaces may be stressful for young children. As a result, efforts

The Montessori classroom is characterized by child-size furnishings, order, and some specific learning materials. As you watch this **video**, consider how the Montessori environment is safe and developmentally appropriate.

usable square footage
the amount for floor space that is not covered by furniture but is open and accessible to children

FIGURE 13-3   Typical Space Needs for Early Childhood Settings

Teacher and General Classroom Space Needs

✓ Sufficient square footage for group size
✓ Durable and easy-to-clean floors, walls, and counters
✓ Emergency exits in two directions
✓ Child-sized and adult toileting and hand washing areas
✓ Water fountain or access to fresh drinking water
✓ Food storage, preparation, and service areas
✓ Locked storage and refrigeration for medications
✓ General storage space

Infant Classroom Space Needs

✓ Space for children's belongings (diapers, clothing)
✓ Sufficient space for cribs and high chairs
✓ Movable dividers to separate mobile and nonmobile infants
✓ Diaper changing and hand washing area
✓ Refrigeration for breast milk, infant formula, medications

Toddler Classroom Space Needs

✓ Storage for children's belongings (diapers, clothing, blanket)
✓ Diaper changing and toileting area

✓ Hand washing area near diapering area
✓ Refrigeration for breast milk, infant formula, medications

Preschooler Classroom Space Needs

✓ Coat cubbies; space for child belongings
✓ Space to store cots for napping
✓ Access to child-sized toilets and hand washing
✓ Space to store projects

School-Age Child Space Needs

✓ Lockers for belongings
✓ Appropriate access to gender-specific toilets
✓ Space to store projects

Children with Special Developmental Needs

✓ Accessible toilets, sinks, and furniture
✓ Appropriate floor surfacing, acoustics, and lighting
✓ Storage for adaptive equipment
✓ Sound and light-flashing alarm system

are under way to increase the recommended square footage per child. The GSA (2003) requires a minimum of 45 square feet of usable floor space per child for federally constructed early childhood facilities. The Head Start Technical Assistance Center (National Head Start Facilities Information Services, 2002) and the *National Health and Safety Performance Standards* (American Academy of Pediatrics [AAP], American Public Health Association, & National Resource Center for Health and Safety in Child Care and Early Education, 2011) recommend 50 square feet per child. These variations highlight the trend toward larger space requirements per child.

The goal of providing more square footage per child also creates some challenges:

• Increasing square footage per child adds to the cost of new facility construction.
• Current early childhood settings would need to reduce the number of children served in a particular space which would also decrease the program's income or require the program to increase the cost of care.
• Increased costs might push some children out of the quality care setting.

It is important for teachers to be aware of quality standards discussions, and to weigh in with ideas to reach health and safety goals.

Ensuring Accessibility

Spaces used to provide care and education for young children need to be accessible to all children, including those with special developmental needs as described in the requirements of Section 504 of the Rehabilitation Act of 1973 and the Americans with Disabilities Act (ADA). These guidelines ensure that people with disabilities have access to the buildings, classrooms, play areas, and toilets and sinks. Consideration should also be given to meeting the needs of persons who have special health or developmental needs. For example, children who have hearing impairments are supported when classrooms are constructed with soft surfaces to control for noise and are equipped with fire alarms that signal emergencies with a flashing light in addition to the sound of the alarm. Accessibility guidelines are best addressed as facilities are developed and classrooms are furnished. This way the environment is prepared ahead to include all children.

Creating Spaces That Are Culturally Relevant

Environments send a message about who the people are that use them and what they value. This is communicated by what is in the space and what is not (York, 1991). Including aspects of culture in children's spaces can be a challenge. Teachers have their own experience and knowledge to draw on, but it is easy to overlook ways the environment can reflect the cultural traditions of the children and families who are participating. Teachers need to work together with families to gather ideas and put them into action.

One approach is to select visual materials or pieces of artwork to display, such as paintings, weavings, pottery, and tile work. Choosing work from local artists makes a connection to the community and the local culture. Displaying children's artwork adds another unique expression. Color choices for wall paint and furnishings may convey cultural meaning, and the arrangement of furnishings can help support local customs. For example, placing benches in the lobby or chairs near the door creates a place for families to gather and visit, acknowledging customs that view arrival and departure as important social times. Partnering with families to create culturally relevant spaces communicates that all children and families are welcomed and valued.

> **What if . . .**
> you were new to the community and wanted to learn more about the cultural backgrounds and interests of the children and families you were going to serve? How would you go about getting information directly from the families?

Understanding Building Codes and Facility Requirements

Local building codes specify the requirements for safe facility construction and renovation. Safety regulations address choice of building materials, construction techniques, and requirements for appropriate handrails and barriers around porches and decks to avoid potential falls. Certain restrictions must be addressed for spaces that serve young children in group care settings. Examples include the following (AAP et al., 2011):

- Building materials must be free from hazardous products such as mold or toxic products.
- Basement spaces may not be used to provide services for children under the age of 2.
- Only ground floor spaces may be used if the building is constructed of wood.
- Safety glass must be used for windows and doors or they must be covered with metal mesh safety guards for at least 36 inches from the floor.

Teachers must continue to be vigilant to ensure that any repairs or renovations also follow appropriate safety codes.

Providing Appropriate Utility Services

Programs that serve young children are required to ensure that utility services are safe. These services are typically reviewed during child care licensing site visits and must be monitored to ensure continued safety:

- *Water:* An approved water supply, such as a public water system or well water that has been tested periodically, must be provided to ensure that children are safe from waterborne illnesses caused by bacteria, parasites, or other infectious agents. Salmonella, *E. coli*, and dysentery are three familiar bacterial agents that can be found in contaminated water.
- *Sewer:* A reliable sewer system is important to avoid contaminating the facility and grounds with sewer seepage that can introduce disease.
- *Electrical services:* Sufficient electrical outlets are required to avoid overloading the electrical system. This also ensures that teachers do not use electrical extension cords which can cause a tripping hazard. Emergency lighting is needed in hallways, stairways, and at exits to guide evacuation, if needed.
- *Heating, cooling, and airflow systems:* A system that maintains appropriate temperature and humidity and controls for air pollution is important for health and safety. Fresh air is needed to

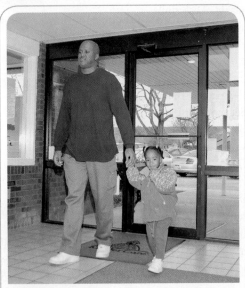

Children and families need safe access into the children's setting or school.

maintain healthy indoor air quality and to reduce the incidence of respiratory problems (AAP et al., 2011).

- *Garbage services:* Periodic removal of garbage is needed to control for insects, rodents, and other pests that may introduce disease in the children's environment.
- *Communication systems:* Telephones or other communication systems are needed to contact emergency services or families in case of child illness or injury.

Providing these utility services is a safety issue. If services fail due to mechanical failure, weather, or other conditions, children are put at risk and program services may need to be suspended.

Creating Safe Areas Around the Building

A safety zone around the building supports safe access. Safe entrances and exits, bicycle parking, and loading zones all contribute to safety as children come to school.

Providing Safe Entrances and Exits   Clearly identified walkways into the building and marked exits increase safety as children move in and out of the building, as well as during emergency evacuation. Walkways should protect children from areas used by cars. Pathways should accommodate strollers, baby carriages, and wheelchairs and be kept clear.

Addressing Parking Lot Safety   Parking areas are a significant source of danger to young children. Nearly one-third of child pedestrian deaths occur when a child darts out from between two cars into the street or parking lot (Savage, Kawanabe, Mejeur, Goehring, & Reed, 2002). Parking areas need to be kept visually open by trimming shrubs and marking walkways through the parking lot with painted stripes, brightly colored traffic cones, flags, or signs. Teachers should teach children and families how to move safely across parking lots.

What if . . .

you observed a child running in and out of parked cars in the parking lot while the parent was talking with another parent? What would you do?

Marking Emergency Exits   Emergency exits are passageways to the outdoors. They should be clearly marked and visible from all areas of the classroom. Access to the exit doors should be kept clear and open at all times. In settings where the exit doors open into a parking lot or other potentially dangerous area, door alarms should be installed to alert the teacher if a child tries to open the door (AAP et al., 2011).

Offering Bicycle Parking   Bicycle parking racks encourage a healthy form of transportation and help keep bikes from being propped near the doors, which can cause a tripping hazard.

Creating Bus Lanes and Passenger Loading Areas   Safe bus loading areas ensure that children move directly from the bus onto a sidewalk rather than into a parking lot, which is dangerous.

Marking Emergency Vehicle Parking Zones   Programs may be required to designate parking zones for emergency vehicles. These spaces are identified with painted stripes and are usually located immediately outside an entrance.

Designating School Zones   Elementary schools often mark the nearby streets as a *school zone* to warn drivers of the presence of young children. This is a good idea near preschool and child care centers, too. If this formal designation is not available, the presence of children can be communicated by placing signs or decorative flags to mark the site as a children's area.

Managing Security

The security of children in the early childhood facility is an important aspect of overall safety. Security refers to keeping children safe from contact with inappropriate or unsafe persons. Families want assurance that teachers are going to keep their children safe from intruders, and teachers want support in case an intruder enters the facility. Security plans help to address these concerns.

Significant attention has been given to ensure that children *stay in* the early childhood facility—that they are protected from being able to wander off. Focus must also be directed to ensure that potential intruders *stay out*—that only approved persons have access to the children's facility and classrooms. Security approaches seek to address both of these concerns without unduly constricting children's opportunities to explore, take on challenges, and learn (Greenman, 2005).

To avoid barricading children from the outside world, teachers look to strategies that are appropriate for the setting. These include identifying security concerns within the local neighborhood, recognizing family issues that may introduce security concerns, and controlling access to the building and classroom. Even with these approaches, it is important to keep alert to the activities and people in the children's environment and supervise children at all times.

Identifying Neighborhood Security Concerns

While safety is a common theme when creating children's classrooms, what works in one neighborhood may not be appropriate or safe in another. Neighborhood factors to consider include nearby traffic patterns, the availability of community services such as police and emergency medical care, the presence of drug and gang-related issues, and the general crime rate. Being aware of such issues helps to prioritize facility and classroom safety goals and the strategies needed to address security concerns.

Understanding Family Security Concerns

Sometimes families have circumstances that threaten the security of the child or other family member, and that spills over into the classroom. Domestic violence or the presence of a restraining order for a family member are issues that may require a special plan for arrival and departure, space for private conversations, and cues about when to call for support for a security concern.

Controlling Facility Access

Controlling access involves managing who comes in and out of the facility and who has access to the classroom, as well as controlling for perceived threats, such as harassment and views of violence. Managing access is a familiar security management approach, but it can be complicated because early childhood programs have a responsibility to ensure that parents and legal guardians have access to their children at any time. This requires a confident understanding of who is approved to enter.

Approaches used to control access depend on the style of the facility and types of security concerns that may be present in the local neighborhood. Strategies include:

- Restricting entry to one doorway and providing a lobby with locked doors into the program service areas beyond which only approved individuals may enter.
- Requiring employees to wear identifying uniforms.
- Requiring all persons in the facility to wear employee or visitor identification tags.
- Installing an electronic keyless entry system with passkeys or passwords available only to approved individuals.

Systems like these communicate attentiveness to security and build a climate of watchfulness. However, it is difficult to determine if they are as effective as hoped in actually improving security. When the security system relies heavily on one identified entryway for the building, attention might be diverted from other potential access areas such as doors that are propped open as supplies are moved in and out or windows that provide access into the building. It is important to identify the level of security that is reasonable for the setting. Here are some examples:

- *Setting 1:* A 4-foot-tall play yard fence meets licensing requirements and adequately prevents children from leaving the play area. In this neighborhood the threat of intruders is considered to be low so the 4-foot fence is sufficient. Teachers pay special attention to supervision at the periphery of the play yard.

> **What if . . .**
> you were asked to describe the childhood accidents that are most typical for your community? How would you respond? Where might you find this information?

- *Setting 2:* A 6-foot-tall solid fence is needed to screen out views of gang activity on the street. Although the solid fence closes off visual access, it also limits the teacher's ability to see if there are potential intruders loitering on the other side of the fence. Teachers consider this as they supervise in the play yard.
- *Setting 3:* Special barriers are planned to screen out the high-rise buildings that surround the play area and overlook the space. Teachers advocate for covered areas to be constructed at strategic locations to screen children from view and the potential of being hit by objects tossed from the buildings. They conduct a walk-through of the playground each day before it is used to ensure that the space is clean and no hazardous debris has been introduced.

Security in children's spaces is reinforced by teachers, families, and program staff who continually observe the children's areas for inappropriate people or potential threats.

Implications for Teachers

Teachers may not be in charge of facility design and management, but they do interface with all aspects of facility safety when teaching young children. This knowledge is also important when creating safe indoor and outdoor environments.

● ESTABLISHING SAFE INDOOR ENVIRONMENTS

Teachers create and maintain safe classrooms where children can grow and thrive. This is accomplished through careful arrangement of the space, selecting furniture that supports children's developmental needs, thoughtful storage of toys and equipment, and continual monitoring to remove potential hazards.

Organizing the Classroom

Children's spaces are arranged with definite purposes and goals in mind. During the planning process, each part of the available space is assigned to support an important classroom activity, such as arrival and departure, toileting and hand washing, and snack and meal service. Areas are also defined to provide specific activities that promote developmental goals. For example, a reading area is often established to support early literacy. Some spaces will overlap, and furnishings may be adjusted during the day to allow flexibility and variation in the activities conducted. Organization is supported by creating a plan for the classroom and addressing the needs of each age group.

space use plan
a map or diagram of a children's space showing how the space will be used and the locations of desired activities, furniture, entrances and exits.

Creating a **space use plan**, or map of the children's environment, is a useful way to show how the space will be arranged for the desired activities. Planning usually starts by identifying basic requirements and then adding the details of activity areas and furnishings. This can be accomplished by drawing the basic layout of the space on a large piece of paper and using smaller circles of paper to identify program activity areas and furnishings. These can be moved around as the space use plan develops. Figure 13-4 provides an example of a preschool or kindergarten classroom space use plan.

Safety aspects to consider when creating a space use plan vary depending on the size of the space and services to be provided. Examples include the following:

- *Identify a doorway for arrival and emergency exits.* Create open gathering areas inside the entry and exit doors. This provides a space to greet families and appropriately supervise children at arrival and departure.
- *Arrange pathways through the room.* Plan logical passageways to support services such as moving lunch into the classroom, and be sure access to the toilets and hand washing areas are open and obvious. Routes to emergency exits need to be kept clear at all times.
- *Provide space for small- and large-group activities.* Plan enough open space for children to gather and move safely during games and dancing.
- *Locate activity areas logically.* Position activity centers to avoid unnecessary conflicts. Locate active dramatic play away from more quiet areas, such as the reading corner.

FIGURE 13-4
Preschool or Kindergarten Classroom Space Use Plan

- *Take advantage of windows.* Use natural light to its best advantage. Place the creative arts areas near a window to encourage themes related to the natural environment.
- *Locate furniture thoughtfully.* Use low shelves to create safe spaces for children to play with toys on the floor. Tall furniture, such as cubbies or shelves, need to be attached to the wall to remove danger of tipping over. Area rugs can help designate play spaces.

Furnishing the Classroom

Furniture is an important aspect of the children's environment. It needs to be selected carefully to ensure that it is durable and appropriate to support children's needs. These decisions support appropriate exploration and learning, and address safety needs.

Choosing Child-Sized Furniture

Child-sized furniture is furniture that "fits" young children. Options typically include:

- Chairs that children can back up to and sit in without climbing.
- Tables that are approximately waist height where children can stand and play with toys without straining.
- Shelves that allow children to reach toys without stretching.
- Toilets that are low and easy for children to sit on unaided.
- Sinks that are sized so children can reach the water faucets without needing a stool or step.

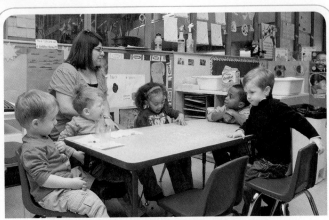
Child-sized furniture promotes independence.

Providing furniture that is child-sized has several benefits. It helps children know they are in a space made for kids, which may smooth the child's transition into the classroom and set the tone for a positive experience. Safety is increased as children are able to use the furniture easily while keeping their feet on the floor. As a result children are able to be more self-sufficient which encourages exploration and the development of self-care skills.

Meeting the Needs of Each Age Group

Each age group has special requirements for the kinds of furniture needed to support children's care needs. Safety is improved when furnishings are selected to meet specific needs rather than trying to "make-do" with less appropriate options.

Infants Furnishings for infant spaces include a crib and high chair for each baby and sturdy changing tables that safely secure the infant, are easy to sanitize, and comfortable for teachers to use. Two comfortable adult-sized chairs are useful when feeding babies. Rocking chairs should be selected to avoid pinch hazards. Carpeting or area rugs that are firm and easy to clean can add color and softness to the environment. Small tubs are helpful for assembling toys. Low room dividers may be useful for dividing spaces for mobile and nonmobile infants.

> This **video** shows an infant-toddler environment. Think about the differnet spaces for feeding, napping, diapering, playing, and learning. What safety considerations should be given to each space?

Mobile Infants and Toddlers Furniture for toddlers and newly mobile infants needs to be low, solid, and sturdy. It should not slip as children pull themselves to a standing position. For example, shelves with rolling casters on the legs should be avoided unless the casters can be locked to keep the shelf in place and avoid rolling. Chairs for toddlers are typically 10 inches high at the seat. Chairs should have a wide base to avoid the potential of having them slip away as the toddler attempts to sit down. Table height should match the toddler-sized chairs. Play kitchens and cubbies with coat hooks should be low and sturdy. Individual cots for naptime should be comfortable, easy to sanitize, and stackable for efficient storage.

Preschoolers Furniture for preschool classrooms should fit children of various sizes. A selection of chairs ranging from 10 to 14 inches high at the seat and tables of varying heights or with adjustable legs, offer flexibility. Shelves should be sturdy and not exceed children's eye height to allow safe access to toys. Other furnishings may include cots, water or sensory tables, painting easels, cubbies for coats, workbenches, small tables for listening centers or science activities, kitchen and dramatic play units, and comfy chairs, cushions, or pillows.

Kindergarten and Elementary Children Chairs for kindergarten and elementary classrooms are usually 16 to 18 inches high. A sufficient number of tables or desks are needed to ensure each child has a place to sit and work. Tables of various sizes are useful for projects and small-group activities. Other furnishings may include water and sensory tables, easels, tub-style shelving units, open shelves, bookshelves, area rugs, cubbies, and lockers or coat hooks.

Evaluating Furniture for Safety

Children's furniture should be strong, durable, and free from splinters or sharp edges. There should be no gaps that could pinch or entrap fingers. No lead-based paint or other toxic products should be used in construction. Soft-surfaced furniture, such as child-sized couches and chairs, should be covered with an easily cleaned material. Furniture for children's environments must be obtained from reputable sources. Furniture purchased from import suppliers should be reviewed to determine if it meets U.S. product safety standards.

What if . . .

you noticed children climbing on a tall shelf to reach the paper supplies? You have reported that the tall shelf is a safety hazard for tipping, but no one has attached it to the wall. What would you do next?

Safely Storing Classroom Supplies

Most early childhood teachers report that there is never enough storage. It seems that creative teaching goes hand-in-hand with collecting teaching materials. Storage must be carefully managed to avoid having toys and materials overflow into the classroom and hallways, creating an appearance of disorganization and lowering the professional appearance of the environment, or causing a safety hazard as materials slide off overloaded shelves or topple when closet doors are opened. Ideally, storage should provide space in the classroom for materials used every day, a common storage space for shared materials, and cupboards or file cabinets for a teacher's personal teaching materials. Special attention must be given to organizing materials, storing medications, restricting access to cleaning supplies, and avoiding infestation.

Organizing Materials

Many storage systems are available to help teachers organize materials. Using labeled boxes or transparent plastic tubs allows teachers to identify needed items and helps when returning materials to the shelves. Organization helps prolong the considerable investment that is made in curriculum materials and makes it more likely that toys are returned to their storage space, helping prevent a tripping hazard if toys are left in walkways.

Securing Medications

Medications that are to be administered to children need to be safely stored in a medication lockbox or locking cupboard. This allows the medication to be easily accessible to the teacher but out of the reach of children. A lockbox may also be needed to store medications in the refrigerator.

Storing Cleaning Supplies

All cleaning supplies, lotions, bleach, and other potentially toxic materials must be stored outside the children's space or in a locked cabinet (AAP et al., 2011). Careful organization of such supplies keeps inappropriate materials from drifting into the children's space which could be dangerous.

Avoiding Infestation of Insects and Rodents

Dried food-related products, such as rice, cornmeal, and birdseed are often used in sensory bins. Such items should be stored in containers with tight-fitting lids to avoid spoilage or infestation by insects or rodents. These materials should be discarded periodically so the bins and storage area can be cleaned thoroughly.

Controlling for Hazards

Managing children's safety also involves making careful decisions about materials that could introduce dangers into the environment, such as plants, wall displays, electrical appliances, and recycling bins. Conducting periodic safety checks is an important way to identify and correct potential hazards.

Choosing Appropriate Plants for the Classroom

Teachers often include softening materials such as flowers and plants to enhance the environment. However, not all plants or plant materials are appropriate for children's spaces. Figure 13-5 lists plants that are appropriate choices for children's settings and those that should not be used because of their poisonous properties.

Creating Safe Wall Displays

Early childhood classrooms are typically bright with children's artwork and posters displayed on bulletin boards and walls. However, posting a large amount of paper can be a fire hazard. Many fire districts do not allow any flammable product to be suspended from the ceiling. The local fire

What if . . .

a parent asked you to store her child's epinephrine autoinjector (EpiPen) in the classroom for emergency use, but your program's practice is to lock the EpiPen with other medications in the director's office? Is the parent's request legitimate? How would you manage this?

FIGURE 13-5   Safe and Poisonous Plants

Safe House Plants to Use in Children's Settings

African violet	Christmas cactus	Jade plant	Spider plant
Aluminum plant	Coleus	Peperomia	Swedish ivy
Anthurium	Corn plant	Prayer plant	Velvet, purple passion
Aphelandra	Dracaena	Rubber plant	Wandering Jew
Baby tears	Emerald ripple	Schefflera	Wax plant
Begonia	Hen-and-chickens	Sensitive plant	Weeping fig
Boston fern	Impatiens	Snake plant	Yellow day lily

Poisonous Plants – DO NOT Use in Children's Settings

House Plants	**Flowers & Shrubs**	**Vegetables**	**Wild Plants**
Bird of paradise	Autumn crocus	Asparagus	Belladonna
Castor bean	Bleeding heart	Potato (green parts)	Bittersweet
Dieffenbachia	Boxwood	Rhubarb leaves	Buttercups
English ivy	Chrysanthemum	Tomato (green parts)	Indian hemp
Holly	Daffodil	**Trees and Shrubs**	Jack-in-the-pulpit
Jequirity bean	Four-o'clocks	Black locust	Jimson weed
Jerusalem cherry	Foxglove	Chokecherry	Larkspur
Mistletoe	Hyacinth	Elderberry	Monkshood
Mother-in-law	Hydrangea	English yew	Mushrooms (some)
Oleander	Iris	Ground ivy	Nightshade
Philodendron	Lily of the valley	Horse chestnut, buckeye	Poison hemlock
Poinsettia	Morning glory	Juniper	Poison oak & ivy
	Rhododendron	Oak	Poison sumac

Sources: Cooperative Extension Service, Home and Garden Education Center, University of Connecticut, *Safe and poisonous houseplants*, retrieved January 19, 2012, from http://www.ladybug.uconn.edu/hotissues/SafeandPoisonousHouseplants.html; Douglas, S. (2007). *Poisonous Plants*. Connecticut Agricultural Extension Service. Retrieved January 19, 2012, from http://www.ct.gov/caes/cwp/view.asp?a=2815&q=376888; and Oregon Health Authority, Public Health, Safe Kids Oregon, *Poisonous plants*. Retrieved January 19, 2012, from http://public.health.oregon.gov/PreventionWellness/SafeLiving/KeepingChildrenSafe/SafeKids/Pages/poisonplants.aspx.

department can provide guidance about the appropriate amount of paper to use in displays. It is also best to attach materials to the wall using tape rather than staples, tacks, or pins that can fall to the floor to be discovered by young children.

Managing Electrical Outlets and Appliances

Electrical outlets can be a shock hazard if a curious child pokes a finger or toy into the socket. This can be avoided by installing outlet covers that close off the outlet when not in use. Classrooms should also be equipped with a sufficient number of electrical outlets. This supports the occasional use of electrical appliances as allowed by licensing requirements and avoids overuse of electrical cords that can cause a trip hazard.

Organizing Recycling and Composting Bins

To support recycling and conservation efforts, many teachers provide collection bins in the classroom. The bins need to be placed out of the walkways and emptied periodically to avoid creating trip or fire hazards.

Conducting Classroom Safety Reviews

Teachers constantly monitor their classrooms to keep them safe. As part of this process, they periodically step outside their teaching roles to take a critical look at the children's environments for

FIGURE 13-6 Safety Checklist for Children's Environments

Safety Feature General Facility Overview	Details and Follow-Up	Initial When Corrected
❑ Entrance and exit routes are clear and open.		
❑ Electrical outlets are covered when not in use.		
❑ All light bulbs are covered.		
❑ Water source is approved and properly maintained.		
❑ Drinking fountains are clean with adequate water pressure.		
❑ Sewage system is in good working order.		
❑ Garbage is collected at least weekly.		
❑ Classrooms receive fresh air; air flow is satisfactory.		
❑ Heating and cooling systems are in good repair.		
❑ Smoke detectors and fire alarms are in working order.		
❑ Storage is free from rodent, insect, and vermin infestation.		
❑ Windows and doors are screened.		
❑ Other:		

Safety Feature Children's Spaces	Details and Follow-Up	Initial When Corrected
❑ Space provides at least 35 usable square feet per child.		
❑ Space is clean and orderly.		
❑ First-aid supplies are properly stored. Location is marked.		
❑ Exits are clearly marked; passageway is clear.		
❑ Telephone numbers for emergency medical care, fire, and poison control are posted by each telephone.		
❑ Classroom equipment is clean and in good repair.		
❑ Classroom cabinets contain no hazardous substances.		
❑ Furniture is sturdy and stable, or attached to the walls.		
❑ Diapering area keeps children safe; area is easy to clean.		
❑ Toilet rooms are clean, well lighted, well ventilated.		
❑ Hand washing sinks are near diapering and toileting areas.		
❑ Soap and paper towels are available.		
❑ Other:		

Source: Based on "Rules for the Certification of Child Care Centers," Child Care Division of the Oregon Employment Department, 2001.

potential hazards. Figure 13-6 provides a sample checklist to use when conducting a safety review of the children's environments. Recording the details of the problem, and following through until the problem has been resolved, complete the safety review process.

Providing Safe Indoor Areas for Active Play

Little attention has been given in recent years to creating indoor spaces where children can be physically active. Research suggests that, over time, early childhood programs have tended to provide fewer opportunities for children to play outdoors while focusing more on sedentary activities indoors (Pate, Pfeiffer, Trost, Ziegler, & Dowda, 2004). In addition, teachers sometimes place restrictions on the activity level and intensity of play indoors because of the closeness of the classroom space. It is common to hear teachers say, "Remember to use your walking feet!" This needs to be

---

FIGURE 13-7   Attributes of Safe Indoor Active Play Areas

- The space has appropriate boundaries and separation from nonactive play areas, cupboards, closets, tables or other protrusions that might have corners children could run against.
- Area is clean and clear of hazards; materials are stored appropriately.
- Walls are relatively smooth.
- The floor surface is relatively smooth and even.
- All windows are screened for safety.
- Area is well lighted; lightbulbs are covered to avoid danger from shattering.

- There are no entrapment or entanglement hazards.
- Equipment and other toys are appropriate for the age of the children.
- Indoor climbing equipment is positioned over safety-approved resilient surfacing mats that extend at least 6 feet beyond the structure.
- Indoor equipment has a maximum height equal to 1 foot per year of age, such as 2 feet for 2-year-olds, 3 feet for 3-year-olds.

Sources: Based on *KidsHealth for Parents: Playground Safety,* Nemours Foundation, 2009, retrieved January 2012, from http://www.kidshealth.org/parent/firstaid_safe/outdoor/playground.html; and *Public Playground Safety Handbook* (Publication No. 325), by the U.S. Consumer Product Safety Commission, April 2008, retrieved January 2012, from http://www.cpsc.gov/CPSCPUB/PUBS/325.pdf.

---

balanced with plenty of opportunity for children to use their "running feet" while engaged in active play both indoors and outdoors.

Indoor active play spaces should offer:

- Sufficient space for the age of the children and the size of the group.
- Space for a variety of movements such as running, playing catch, riding tricycles, dancing, and jumping, as well as group and individual activities.
- Separate spaces for mobile infants, active toddlers, and older children.
- Spaces that are easy to supervise and manage.
- Appropriate storage for equipment, such as a rolling cart for balls so that children can access the toys on their own.
- Access to drinking water from a water fountain or a tray with cups of water.

Figure 13-7 provides a checklist of needed features for safe indoor active play environments.

Providing lots of opportunities for active play in both indoor and outdoor spaces naturally directs children's energies in appropriate ways. As a result, active play may reduce the frequency of roughhousing that can lead to unsafe behaviors in the classroom.

SELECTING SAFE TOYS

Choosing safe and appropriate toys for the early childhood environment is both exciting and challenging. A wide variety of interesting toy options is available, and rigorous marketing is as effective with teachers as it is with children. Sorting through the options and making informed selections for young children is a significant aspect of safety management. Toys should be appropriate, available in sufficient quantity, and meet high safety standards.

Ensuring Toys Are Appropriate

Toys are children's learning tools, representing more than just a fun pastime. Interaction with interesting toys allows children to act on, construct knowledge from, and make discoveries about their world. Toys need to offer developmental challenge and be reviewed to ensure they include appropriate learning characteristics. A sufficient number of toys must be available and there should be options to support children who have special developmental needs. Finally, toys must be available to encourage active play and to teach wellness concepts.

Providing Developmental Challenge

Children's interest in particular toys varies according to their age and stage of development. To be appropriate, toys should attract children's interest, invite safe interaction, and match children's need for challenges (U.S. Consumer Product Safety Commission [CPSC], 2008). Teachers work to understand children's emerging interests in order to provide toys that will help each child to move from one skill level to the next. Attention is given to each age group's developmental capabilities and aspects of potential risk (Telep, 2009).

Infants Children ages birth to 1 year are interested in color contrast, design, and patterns, as well as interesting sounds and textures. Soft toys, rattles, simple musical toys and board books are good choices. Infants naturally explore toys with their mouths, so toys should be checked to ensure there are no small parts that could come loose.

Toddlers Children ages 1 to 3 tend to explore toys with their mouths, hands, and toes, and they are becoming more mobile. They enjoy hand-sized blocks, nesting toys and shape-sorters, puzzles with one to four large pieces, and sturdy push toys. Toys that could introduce dangers to this age group include those that could be pulled over on top of the child, those that have strings, and toys with small parts such as beads, marbles, or magnets.

Preschoolers Children ages 3 to 5 years are eager to try new things and take on new challenges. They enjoy puzzles with increasingly more pieces, blocks and construction toys, dolls and housekeeping, toy vehicles, manipulative toys of all kinds, and riding toys. Children in this age group may display curiosity that exceeds their abilities. Potential hazards include toys that use electricity, toys with strings, those that shoot small parts, and hard toys that may be swung about potentially harming others.

Kindergarten and Elementary Children ages 5 to 8 years have a wide range of interests and are able to explore topics with detail. Their growing capabilities can be supported with increasingly complex puzzles, board games, manipulative building sets, hobbies and collections, and sturdy bikes and scooters. Children in this age group are also eager to test their skills, sometimes beyond their understanding of impacts. Toys to avoid include lawn darts, toys that shoot small parts (including water guns that shoot more than 3 feet), and bikes and sports equipment that are too big. Electrical toys should be closely supervised.

Judging Toy Characteristics

Desirable toys promote child-directed play and self-directed learning. Such toys are self-explanatory, allowing children to explore and figure out what to do on their own. They also offer attributes of self-correction, meaning they have pieces designed to fit in specific ways so children can understand the concept the toy presents.

Toys that promote skills in several developmental areas are also ideal. Small blocks that encourage fine motor skills also offer exploration of spatial awareness and can be used for counting and color and shape recognition, sorting and making patterns, or become part of a dramatic play theme when matched with trucks or people figures. Figure 13-8 provides a list of characteristics to consider when selecting toys.

Offering Enough Toys

Toys need to be available in sufficient quantities so that all children have the opportunity to be actively involved in constructive play, and to avoid undue competition for popular items (Ritchie &

> **What if . . .**
> parents asked you why you do not have some of the more popular fashion dolls or electronic toys in your classroom? How would you explain how toys are selected for your children's setting?

FIGURE 13-8   Toy Characteristics Checklist

Size and shape of parts	❑ Are the attributes of the toy safe, suitable, and appealing for the age group?
Number of parts	❑ Does the number of parts suit the ability of the intended age group?
	❑ Does the toy provide appropriate challenge?
Interlocking nature of parts	❑ Does the connection of the parts suit the interest and ability level of the age group?
Materials	❑ Are the materials the toy is made of suitable for the age group?
Developmental skill needed to play	❑ Do the motor and cognitive skills needed fit the intended age group?
Color/contrast	❑ Does the appearance of the toy invite the child to engage in play?
Cause and effect	❑ Does the toy respond in some way to the child's actions?
Sensory contribution	❑ Does the toy offer unique sensory experiences appropriate for the age group?
Level of realism	❑ Does the toy suit the maturity level of the age group?
Licensing	❑ Is the toy marketed to encourage a licensed product or character?
	❑ Does the licensing interest suit the age group and program goals?
Classic aspects	❑ Does this toy have long-lasting appeal? Will it maintain interest over time?
Robotic or smart features	❑ Does the toy have electronic or robotic appeal? Is it easy to use?
	❑ Does it encourage appropriate cognitive reasoning?
Educational	❑ Does the toy have an educational or cognitive goal that is achievable by the age group and appropriate to the program philosophy?

Source: Based on *Age Determinant Guidelines: Relating Children's Ages to Toy Characteristics and Play Behavior*, edited by T. P. Smith, September 2002, Bethesda, MD: U.S. Consumer Product Safety Commission. Retrieved January 2012, from www.cpsc.gov/businfo/adg.pdf.

Weller, 2005). This is especially important for toddlers and very young children who are still learning to wait for a turn to play. Having a variety of interesting toys available allows teachers to redirect toddlers to appealing alternatives while they are waiting for a turn with the specially desired toy.

Positive social interactions are promoted when several children are able to play side by side with similar toys. For example, a good quantity of blocks moves the play from a solitary activity to a more social activity as children see one another's structures, participate in give and take, and talk about what they are building.

Supporting Children's Special Developmental Needs

Every child needs to be able to access the learning environment through the available toys and materials. To accomplish this, teachers need to recognize barriers that may keep some children from full participation. Sometimes simply noticing a child's struggles will highlight a need, such as the need to provide "lefty" scissors for a child who is left handed. Providing a particular toy with a range of attributes helps make an activity easier or more challenging so children with varying skills can participate. For example, paintbrushes with chubby handles rather than skinny ones may be easier for children whose hand strength and coordination skills are just emerging. Selecting and offering a range of paintbrush styles ensures that there is an option for each stage of development, which benefits all children.

Some toy attributes are especially appropriate for children with special developmental needs:

- Toys with texture and color contrasts and realistic and recognizable designs help children focus on the object and persist with play.
- Toys with large components or raised parts are easier for children with motor challenges to grasp.
- Toys that are sturdy and have nonskid bases will hold still as children play, an attribute that supports children with coordination challenges.

Some toys and equipment are designed to allow the teacher to offer specific assistance. For example, adaptive scissors provide spaces for both the teacher and child to position their fingers in the scissors as they practice the cutting movements together. This helps the child build hand strength and coordination, and teaches the rhythm of cutting. Other times adaptations are made to typical equipment to help children be successful when learning new learning skills. Attaching a wooden block to a tricycle pedal helps a child with low muscle tone learn to push effectively against the pedal to ride the tricycle. Developmentally appropriate toys, adaptive equipment, and adaptations made to typical equipment enhance safety by fitting the challenge of the materials to the child's capabilities. This allows all children to use the toys safely and appropriately.

All children are supported in their learning through thoughtful toy and equipment choices.

Choosing Toys That Encourage Active Play

Teachers also need to select some toys that encourage children to be active both inside and outside. Active play toys include balls, hoops, large blocks, and rolling toys like tricycles and wagons. Seasonal toys, such as child-sized rakes and tubs with handles, invite children to gather and move leaves in the fall. Providing ready access to such toys helps children choose to be active and energetic in positive and appropriate ways. This helps ensure that gross motor development becomes part of the learning opportunities throughout the day.

Using Toys to Teach Wellness Concepts

Toys are important tools for teaching wellness concepts through both child-directed and teacher-directed interaction. For example, safety concepts are naturally promoted by offering traffic signs for use near the tricycle path in the play yard. Figures and trucks that depict emergency personnel provide opportunities to discuss topics such as fire safety and people who help in emergencies. Medical equipment props in the dramatic play area encourage children to explore health care concepts. The *Nutrition Note* offers ideas of toys and equipment that help children explore important nutrition lessons.

Ensuring Toys Are Safe

Teachers are responsible to ensure that all toys provided to children are safe. This involves reviewing each toy against safety guidelines, evaluating toys for potential choking hazards, keeping toys clean, and checking periodically to be sure they continue to be safe for use.

Meeting Safety Guidelines

Toys in the United States are reviewed by the U.S. Consumer Product Safety Commission (CPSC). The CPSC is charged with establishing safety requirements and testing strategies to ensure toy safety, and communicating toy safety labeling requirements. These requirements direct that toys for young children must not contain lead paint, have small parts that could be

NUTRITION NOTE   Toys That Teach Nutrition Concepts

· Play foods representative of many cultures
· Measuring cups and spoons, bowls, whisks, pancake turners, pots, pans, funnels
· Specialty equipment: butter churn, hand-operated food grinder, pasta maker, crank-style apple peeler

· Books with food themes
· Puzzles and matching games with food pictures
· Posters of food, crops, children cooking, and children eating

SAFETY SEGMENT   Toy Labeling Troubles

The U.S. Consumer Product Safety Commission requires that toys designed for use by children under the age of 3 be banned from the market if they contain small parts or are easily broken into pieces. Toys intended for children ages 3 to 6 that contain small parts must be specifically labeled with a choke hazard warning. However, some manufacturers appear to misuse the labeling laws, allowing unsafe toys to enter the market. This is done by marking toys with the choke hazard warning for children ages 3 to 6, even though the toy is typically associated with the play of infants and toddlers. This effectively gets around the ban on small parts in toys for children under the age of 3 through "creative" labeling. For example:

- A series of small-sized children's foam fabric books, with titles such as *I Love My Puppy*, look like board books typically suitable for children as young as 7 months even though they are marked for children ages 3 to 6. The books have Velcro tabs that tear off easily, posing a choking hazard.
- A plastic tea party set looks suitable for children 18 months of age, but the package is marked for children ages 3 to 6. The small plastic utensils are easily broken into small parts, presenting a choking hazard.

Source: Based on *Trouble in Toyland, Attachment A: 2006 Summary of Toy Hazards and Examples of Potentially Dangerous Toys. Potential Choking Hazards.* Boston, MA: U.S. PIRG. Retrieved January 2012, from www.uspirg.org/html/2006DangerousToyList.pdf.

swallowed, or present other hazards. Toys used with young children must be in good repair and durable for use in the busy children's setting. They should have smooth and safe surfaces with no sharp edges or protrusions and no splinters or chipped paint. They should be constructed of nontoxic materials. When working with a mixed-age group of children, teachers must be especially vigilant about the toys that are accessible to the very youngest child. Older children should be taught about the safety hazard and the importance of keeping toys with small parts away from the younger children.

The CPSC prohibits the sale of toys designed for use by children under the age of 3 if the toy contains small parts or is easily broken into pieces that form small parts. However, even with toy labeling laws, unsafe toys still find their way into stores. The *Safety Segment* describes how manufacturers can mislead consumers through misuse of labeling laws.

Some imported toys are not constructed for U.S. markets and are not reviewed against the safety guidelines before they are made available for sale. Imported toys should be evaluated carefully and removed from the classroom if there is concern. In some instances imported toys have been discovered to contain lead and other materials that are toxic to young children. The CPSC provides lists of toys and equipment that have been recalled or pulled off the market due to child injury. This information can be accessed on the CPSC website (see the end-of-chapter Web Resources section). Teachers can also register to receive e-mail notification about toy recalls.

What if . . .

a family brought you a gift of toys from their country for use in the classroom? You know the potential hazards, but how will you respect the generous gesture while also ensuring children's safety?

Toys purchased at garage sales, flea markets, and thrift shops, as well as those donated to the children's program, should be reviewed very carefully. Toys that have been recalled due to safety hazards may have been donated for sale in these settings, unknowingly putting new buyers at risk for purchasing dangerous products. In addition, older toys may not have been constructed to meet the current safety standards. Teachers need to be smart by checking any purchase against the guidelines and toy recall information provided by the CPSC and by carefully reviewing the condition and appearance of each toy. If the toy does not meet a high standard for safety, cleanliness, and appropriateness, it should be discarded.

Avoiding Choking Hazards

Toys provided for babies and very young children should not have small parts that can be swallowed, causing a choking hazard. Toys commonly associated with choking include:

- Marbles, small balls, and beads.
- Toys with small parts, such as wheels on toy cars that can be chewed off.

- Coins and buttons, often used for sorting and counting activities.
- Balloons, which are often associated with celebrations or used as gross motor props. An un-inflated balloon or pieces of popped balloons can cause choking.
- Small magnets that may pose a choking hazard and, if swallowed, can attach to one another inside the body, causing internal damage.

Choke testing devices that are designed to resemble the size of a child's throat, are available to test toys with dangerous small parts. The CPSC tests toys and toy parts using a device that is 1³/₁₆ inches deep with an oval-shaped opening measuring approximately 1³/₈ inches by 2 inches. If any part of a toy fits into the testing device, the toy is considered too small for use with babies and toddlers. This includes toys and rattles that have handles or other protruding parts. If the protruding parts can fit into the space created by the testing device, they can also be inserted far into the child's mouth and cause choking.

A choking hazard is introduced if toys have attached parts that can fit in a choke testing device, such as the wheels on this train.

Providing Clean and Sanitary Toys

Toys need to be free from germs to keep children safe from disease. Everyday play naturally results in toys in mouths, paint on chairs, and sand and dirt sticking to sensory bin toys. This makes it important to clean toys periodically to keep them sanitary and safe for use. Sanitizing toys is especially important for babies and very young children who naturally explore with their mouths.

Many teachers use a "clean-me" tub, where toys are placed during the day if children put them into their mouths, or if they have been dropped on the floor or otherwise been soiled. These toys are washed and sanitized before they are reintroduced into the classroom. Plastic toys can be washed and sanitized in the dishwasher or by using a three-sink method of wash, rinse, and sanitize in a bleach-and-water solution. Other toys should be wiped with a sanitizing solution and left to air dry. Choosing toys that are easy to clean and sanitize is wise, especially for use with children under the age of 5.

How often toys should be routinely cleaned varies according to use and the age of children who use it. If a group of children is experiencing a high number of colds or other communicable illness, toys should be cleaned more often, perhaps daily. The NAEYC has identified periodic cleaning and sanitizing of toys as an emerging practice for accredited programs. This means that the importance of sanitizing toys is moving toward the level of a policy requirement.

Keeping Toys Usable

Toys should be evaluated frequently for safety. Checking toys as they are put away at cleanup time is a good time to notice if parts are coming loose, which could cause a safety hazard. Toys with missing parts, and incidental parts, should be placed in a "missing parts" tub where hopefully they will be reunited. Toys that are broken, worn out, or have missing parts should be discarded. Offering toys, such as puzzles, that have missing parts denies children the full enjoyment of completion. This results in undue frustration and may even "teach" the concept of leaving a job undone.

Storing Toys Appropriately

Each toy should have a specific storage place on a shelf or in a tub. Teachers often use a photograph or line drawing to indicate where each toy should be stored, both in the classroom and in the storage areas. Proper storage helps keep the parts of toys together, prolonging the usable life of the toy. Caring for toys in this way sends a message of respect for the materials that children use for learning and enhances safety by avoiding breakage and by keeping the toys from being a trip hazard.

● CREATING SAFE OUTDOOR ENVIRONMENTS

Outdoor environments bring children into contact with the natural world and provide space for energetic and active play. They include formally designed spaces, such as school yards and public playgrounds, as well as backyards used by family child care homes. Creating safe outdoor play spaces requires attention to many details. These include appreciating the contributions of outdoor play settings to children's development, recognizing potential hazards, organizing the environment, designing appropriate spaces, attending to safety details, choosing safe equipment, storing outdoor materials safely, and monitoring play equipment.

Appreciating the Importance of Outdoor Play Spaces

Outdoor environments offer children opportunities to play and explore in ways that are not available indoors. Play outdoors allows children to feel the seasons, experience the climate where they live, and come into contact with nature and a variety of living things (Greenman, 2005; Rivkin, 1995). These experiences help children develop competencies and comfort in moving safely in the larger world (Trancik & Evans, 1995). They form the foundation of the child's appreciation of the natural world and the role people play in it.

Many children have few opportunities to play outdoors. Neighborhood parks and community outdoor spaces may have been lost due to expansion of housing and development. Some public outdoor sites are not safe for children because they are located too close to traffic or too far from family homes (Rivkin, 1995). Some families simply do not plan time for children to play outside. For many children, the opportunity to play outdoors at the early childhood program or school is the only time they are able to move freely outside.

Teachers who understand this, take the perspective that outdoor environments are extensions of the classroom that provide unique resources and tools for learning. Astute teachers plan outdoor activities in the daily schedule just as they do for the indoor environment.

Recognizing Hazards

In this **video**, teachers discuss supervision of children's outdoor play. As you watch, consider why teachers should be moving around the space and highly aware of children's behaviors during outdoor play.

Teachers need to consider the hazards that are commonly associated with injuries in outdoor settings when they organize the outdoor play setting. The most frequent injuries that occur in the early childhood playground environment involve (CPSC, 1999, 2008):

- Falls—from platforms, slides, swings.
- Collisions—from children running into equipment or being struck by moving equipment.
- Entrapment— gaps that allow the child's head or other body part to enter and get stuck.
- Entanglement—getting caught-up on protruding components, "S"-style hooks, and ropes or straps that children bring into the environment.
- Pinching or crushing—as fingers and other body parts get caught in the equipment.

Even though these hazards are recognized, children's outdoor play spaces are not as safe as they could be and often teachers are unaware of the safety concern (U.S. Consumer Product Safety Commission [CPSC], 1999). This sends an important message to teachers. Safety regulations must be well understood, they must guide decision making whenever play areas are being constructed or rearranged, and keeping current on safety recommendations is important, as restrictions and recommendations continue to evolve and change (CPSC, 2008).

Organizing the Outdoor Environment

Safe outdoor play environments address children's developmental needs, support appropriate supervision, and provide accessible and safe opportunities for active and energetic play. These goals are accomplished by reviewing the site and correcting safety problems, establishing an appropriately sized space with appropriate fencing, and designating spaces for a range of play activities while ensuring needed set-backs for safety (Rivkin, 1995).

Reviewing the Site

Outdoor play spaces need to be carefully assessed to identify hazards, plan for safety, and recognize play opportunities. Potential hazards may include nearby traffic, standing water, poor soil drainage, and exposure of the space to the sun and wind (CPSC, 2008). Safety plans could include identifying the direction to locate slides to avoid the heat of afternoon sun. Opportunities might involve noticing natural pathways that could be used to move children around the area where swings could be placed.

Correcting Safety Problems

The outdoor play area should have no dangerous materials such as garbage, rubbish, metal scraps, or broken glass. The space should be well drained with no standing water. Plants, shrubs, or trees that may have poisonous parts should be removed. The soil should be free of any toxic materials such as paint chips that may contain lead.

Establishing Spaces of Sufficient Size

The NAEYC (2007) recommends that outdoor areas should provide a minimum of 75 square feet per child of usable space. The space should be open for active play and provide visibility for adult supervision.

Fencing the Play Space

Outdoor play spaces should be fenced or have other appropriate barriers to prevent children from wandering into the street, parking lot, or other unsafe location. Fences should be a minimum of 4 feet in height. Gate latches should be self-closing and childproof. Fenced play areas should have at least two exits.

Designating Activity Areas

Defining, clustering, and linking activity areas helps to establish the space as a learning environment while avoiding unnecessary conflicts or hazards.

Defining Learning Spaces Spaces are needed to provide opportunity for all types of active play such as running, climbing, riding, carrying, and building. Open areas for group games and spaces for individual play are ideal. Natural areas and vegetable gardens offer opportunity for exploration and discovery. Strategies to address competing needs include grouping activities and planning transition areas.

Clustering Activities Grouping climbing equipment and swings in one area and planning open space for running games in another area is desirable because it provides opportunity to organize playground surfacing needs and focus areas for teacher supervision (Trancik & Evans, 1995).

Providing Transition Zones Transition zones, which are the entry and exit routes between play areas, provide helpful cues for children. For example, a concrete walkway that divides the grassy area from the climbing equipment, which is surrounded by wood chips, provides a physical reminder that children are moving from one zone to another. This helps children predict the kinds of activities and behaviors that are expected or allowed in each area.

Arranging Safe Setbacks

A setback, or safety zone, is needed around playground equipment. Equipment should be set back from fences and walkways. Climbing and play structures more than 30 inches high should be separated by a space of at least 9 feet to avoid creating overlapping danger zones. Because swings are a significant source of childhood injuries from moving play equipment, they should be made of rubber, plastic, or other soft material and be located away from other play areas. Slides need to be appropriate for the size of children using them. They should face away from busy play areas so that children exiting the bottom of the slide do not hit others. Slides should also be positioned so they are not pointing directly south or west where the sun may heat the surface, causing potential for burns (CPSC, 2008).

This drawing provides a glimpse into the child's vision of a play area that offers a variety of equipment challenges as well as a row of pleasing trees.

> **What if . . .**
> your family child care has only a small space for outdoor play? How will you create play areas for children across the age range of infants to 5 years? What safety aspects should you consider?

Planning Appropriate Spaces

Developmentally appropriate outdoor play areas address the needs of each age group. They support the needs of children with disabilities and invite socialization while also offering semiprivate spaces.

Meeting the Needs of Each Age Group

Outdoor play environments should be appropriate for children's developmental capabilities and offer a series of gradually increasing challenges (CPSC, 2008). In shared-use spaces this may require establishing a separate area for each age group to play actively, providing safety for younger children who are easily bumped and knocked over by older children running by. Pathways, shrubs, and benches are options for separating age group play areas.

Infants Outdoor spaces for infants should provide many sensory experiences without overexposure to sun and wind. Pathways with surface variations add interest as children are pushed in strollers over them. Mobile infants enjoy surfaces that are interesting and safe for crawling, such as concrete aggregate pathways that incorporate rounded stones, areas with rubber mat surfacing, and grassy areas.

Toddlers Spaces for toddlers should offer a variety of walking surfaces, allowing the children to practice walking on regular and less regular surfaces, such as grass, concrete, or rubber mats. Loose-fill surfacing materials, such as pea gravel, wood mulch, or shredded rubber mulch, should not be used in toddler playgrounds because they introduce hazards for eating or aspirating small pieces (CPSC, 2008).

Preschoolers and School-Age Children Outdoor spaces for preschool and older children can offer variety in textures and colors through surfacing materials, trees, plants, and shrubs. This age group enjoys the challenges of sloped areas for running and rolling, and hills and dips in tricycle and bicycle pathways to challenge their riding skills.

Making Spaces Accessible

Children with special developmental needs are more able to actively participate if the outdoor environment has enough space to move safely. Walkways that accommodate wheelchairs and children on crutches should be at least 44 inches wide, and the surfacing should be firm and sturdy (Rivkin, 1995). Teachers should review ramps and slopes to ensure that children can negotiate them.

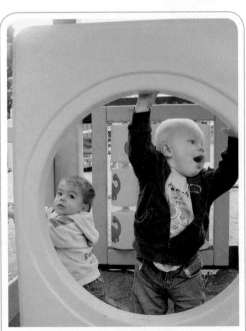

Outdoor equipment supports social interactions as well as active play.

Encouraging Socialization

Outdoor play time is an important opportunity for socializing. Equipping the environment to encourage this is a natural way to bring children together. For example, a large grassy area invites a group of children to play running or ball games. Planning space for a tire swing invites the participation of two to four children, which meets the needs of a small group better than a single swing.

Offering Semiprivate Spaces

Opportunities to enjoy semiprivate spaces in the outdoor environment are also important. Planning space for a playhouse, tunnel, or bench provides an area that is visually open to facilitate supervision, while offering a sense of privacy for child-directed make-believe play. These spaces also contribute to a child's sense of peacefulness and well-being as they offer respite from the noise and action.

Considering Safety Details

Establishing outdoor play areas requires a variety of decisions related to safety attributes, including the choice of safe surfacing materials, planting materials, and attention to air quality and sun exposure.

Selecting Appropriate Surfacing Materials

Falls are the primary concern for injury in outdoor play spaces making the selection of protective surfacing under climbing equipment an important safety decision. Some products that are *not* approved for surfacing under playground equipment are asphalt, concrete, dirt, grass, or wood mulch that has been treated with chromate copper arsenate (CCA). For safety, surfacing materials should meet American Society for Testing and Materials guidelines, ASTM F1292 (U.S. Product Safety Commission, 2008). The two types of approved protective surfacing materials are:

- Unitary surfacing materials which include rubber mats and tiles that are installed in place. Safety-tested rubber mats support access for wheelchairs.
- Loose-fill surfacing materials such as sand, pea gravel, and wood chips. These products are often less expensive but require more maintenance.

Each type of surfacing material has been tested to identify potential product toxicity (such as treated wood or recycled products), accessibility for wheelchairs, and to understand the minimum amount of depth needed of loose-fill surfacing materials needed to protect children in case of a fall (CPSC, 2008). Table 13-4 describes the minimum depths of various loose-fill surfacing materials to protect children in case of falls from different heights. The selected surfacing material should extend at least 6 feet beyond the play equipment.

Including Plants, Shrubs, and Trees

Plants, shrubs, and trees contribute to the beauty and natural appeal of the outdoor environment. They offer variety in color and texture, teach about the seasons, and help to guide travel and designate play spaces. It is important to select and install plants, shrubs, and trees that are safe for young children. Some plant materials have bulbs, roots, leaves, seed pods, berries, or bark that are unsafe for young children.

Considering Air Quality and Sun Exposure

Outdoor play spaces should be located where air quality meets safety levels. Air quality should be checked on a daily basis to determine if pollution levels require that children be kept indoors. In addition, the site should be developed to address the need for shade. Exposure to direct sunlight should be minimized as overexposure can cause painful sunburn and puts children at risk for developing skin cancer later in life (American Academy of Dermatology, 2005). Babies in particular should be kept out of direct sunlight at all times. If natural shade is not available, awnings or covered areas should be made available.

Choosing Outdoor Play Equipment

Play equipment in outdoor environments invites children to try new challenges and develop new skills. Two types of equipment should be offered: *fixed equipment*, such as climbing structures, swings, and slides and *movable equipment*, such as balls, cones, and hoops. Outdoor environments that offer both fixed and movable equipment achieve the status of outdoor classrooms. Safe outdoor environments are established when equipment is developmentally appropriate, offers options for children with special needs, is durable, meets safety requirements, and is installed properly.

TABLE 13-4	**Minimum Compressed Loose-Fill Surfacing Depths**	
Inches	**Of Loose-Fill Material**	**Protects to a Fall Height of (feet)**
9	Wood chips	10
9	Shredded/recycled rubber	10
9	Wood mulch (non-CCA)	7
9	Pea gravel	5
9	Sand	4

Source: *Public Playground Safety Handbook* (Publication No. 325), by the U.S. Consumer Product Safety Commission, April 2008, retrieved November 9, 2011, from www.cpsc.gov/CPSCPUB/PUBS/325.pdf.

Making Developmentally Appropriate Choices

Many fun and challenging options are available for fixed equipment. However, some introduce risk for impact injuries and strangulation. These include trampolines, swinging gates, ropes that are not attached at both ends, heavy metal swings, rope swings, swinging rings, and trapeze bars (CPSC, 2008). Making intentional selections of fixed equipment avoids these hazards.

Play areas that are used by children of various age groups should be selected to reflect each age group's emerging skills in balance, coordination, and reaction time, as well as arm and upper body strength. There should also be sufficient equipment for children at each developmental skill level. This ensures that younger children are not playing on equipment that is too large for them, which exposes them to challenges beyond their abilities (Nemours Foundation, 2012).

Offering Options for Children with Special Developmental Needs

Some play structures provide attributes that are inviting to all children while being especially suitable for children with physical challenges. Interest areas that can be reached from a wheelchair, such as steering wheels or sand and water trays, are safe options. Some swings provide wheelchair access or have seats in which children can be secured as they enjoy the fun. Sufficient space around accessible equipment is needed so adults can assist children as needed.

Selecting Equipment That Is Durable

When making selections it is important to refer to resources that provide guidance for selecting suitable equipment, such as the *Public Playground Safety Handbook* published by the U.S. Consumer Product Safety Commission (2008). Equipment should be constructed of materials that have been used in similar playground settings and have a demonstrated history of durability and safety. The equipment should not contain any products that are known to be toxic. Painted or coated metal options are good choices. Wood used in the construction of play equipment should be naturally resistant to insects and deterioration, such as cedar or redwood, or it should be treated with an appropriate product. Equipment made from wood is resilient and natural but is harder to maintain because of the potential to splinter. Fasteners and connectors should be secure with no protruding hardware that can cause cuts. Moving parts should be covered with shields to avoid entrapment.

Addressing Safety Requirements

The equipment design should include needed safety aspects such as guardrails and barriers, and avoid potential hazards.

Guardrails   Guardrails are required on all platforms, landings, and stairs. They reduce the likelihood of accidental falls, but do not prevent children from purposefully climbing through them.

Barriers   Barriers are required on any elevated walking surface above 18 inches for toddlers, 30 inches for preschoolers, and 48 inches for school-age children (CPSC, 2008). Barriers are designed to prevent children from climbing through.

Entrapment, Pinch, or Crush Points   Play equipment, handrails, guardrails, and fences need to be carefully designed to avoid entrapment, pinch, or crush points. Entrapment can occur if a child's body part becomes lodged between nonmovable parts. Head entrapment can put the child at risk for strangulation. Pinch and crush points refer to openings that could entangle arms, legs, fingers, toes, and clothing. To avoid these hazards, openings should measure less than 3½ inches or be wider than 9 inches. Equipment should also be monitored to be sure that surfaces are smooth with no snag areas that could catch fingers and clothing.

Purchasing and Installing Equipment

Play equipment should be purchased from and installed by an experienced and reputable vendor. The vendor should be able to confirm that the product meets CPSC safety guidelines for children's equipment. The manufacturer's directions for assembly and installation should be strictly followed, and all instructions should be maintained

What if . . .

you identified some problems with rust and rough areas on your swing set? Whom would you contact to help you resolve this safety problem?

on file (CPSC, 2008). The equipment should be evaluated periodically to ensure continued safety, and any problems should be corrected immediately. Teachers are in a good position to monitor playground equipment and to notice and report such problems.

Providing Safe Storage

Storage of outdoor toys and movable equipment is important to maintain the best condition possible for safe play and to protect the investment made in the materials. Weatherproof storage sheds located near the play areas are ideal. This protects equipment made of metal from rusting or deteriorating, which are safety hazards.

Storage units should be well organized, easy to access, and large enough to contain the equipment. These spaces can pose safety hazards when they are overfilled. Tubs of toys positioned on shelves and tricycles hung against the wall may be too heavy for children to access safely. For these reasons, the outdoor storage spaces should be used only by adults and should lock securely.

Providing child-accessible shelving such as a hinged shelving unit that opens and that can be locked when folded closed is a useful option for smaller toys. This allows children to be self-directed as they access the toys they need to develop their play themes.

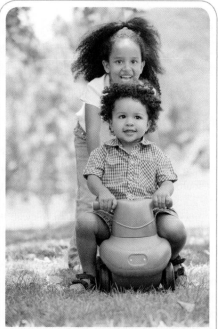

Children are more likely to be active if appropriate toys are accessible to them.

Monitoring for Safety

Ongoing monitoring of the outdoor environment ensures that emergent and incidental dangers are recognized and managed appropriately. Seasonal plant materials, the entry of potential hazards, and effects of weather can introduce problems on a daily basis. Periodic safety checks of the play space help teachers identify and address these and other safety issues.

Supervising Children Near Plant Materials

It is important for children to have access to growing things, but even play near safe plants, shrubs, and trees needs to be supervised. Small seeds can be interesting, but may be poked in the nose or ears and can be very difficult to dislodge. Mushrooms and toadstools in the play area should be removed on a daily basis if needed, even though not all are poisonous. Gloves should be worn to avoid physical contact with the plant and to demonstrate to children that mushrooms and toadstools may be dangerous and should not be touched.

Teachers who engage children in planting gardens should be aware of the parts of fruits or vegetables that might be dangerous. Both safe and unsafe plants can have attractive berries and seed pods that may tempt children to taste them. Teachers need to help children learn to look at but never eat any part of a plant that has not been served to them by their teacher or family.

See the *Progressive Programs & Practices* feature, Safety Measures in a Gardening Experience, for ideas about how the University of Louisiana, Lafayette, Child and Family Studies Early Childhood Lab has implemented a special garden project to help children learn to enjoy vegetables by growing their own.

Watching for Incidental Entry of Hazardous Materials

Teachers need to monitor the outdoor environment for hazards every day. The nests of wasps or hornets should be removed to reduce the potential for stings. If a bat is found hanging under a covered area, children should be kept at a distance until the bat is removed by an appropriate naturalist. Animal excrement should be immediately removed. Teachers should also look over the area to ensure that no garbage, beverage cups, needles, broken glass, or other hazards have been brought into the environment.

Recognizing the Effects of the Weather

Children's safety can also be impacted by the season or weather. Long periods of hot sun can cause drying and splintering of wooden structures. A hot sunny day can raise the temperature of the slide,

PROGRESSIVE PROGRAMS & PRACTICES

Safety Measures in a Gardening Experience

By Mary Sciaraffa, University of Louisiana, Lafayette, Child and Family Studies Early Childhood Lab

In response to the high rate of childhood obesity in Louisiana, a garden project was implemented at the University of Louisiana, Lafayette, Child and Family Studies Early Childhood Lab in collaboration with the UL Dietetics department and the UL Renewable Resource department. The primary educational significance of the garden project, which incorporates life science standards, is to provide children and their families with the knowledge of how to grow their own vegetable garden and to adopt healthier eating habits for a lifetime.

The children learn about the process of growing food and the importance of consuming a variety of vegetables. They learn about planning, planting, caring for (feeding, watering), harvesting, preparing, cooking, tasting, and the importance of eating these "home-grown" vegetables. The children's educational experiences are furthered as they are given a home garden to share with their families.

Ensure a safe gardening experience with children.

- Place the garden away from potential contamination sources as well as any gas or electric lines. Consider fencing the garden to assist teachers in monitoring children.

- The soil and water sources should be free of contaminants (i.e., lead, mold, algae). Contact local extension agents to discuss soil and water tests and help ensure that water containers and procedures are appropriate.

- If using raised garden beds, note that cedar, untreated pine, or fir are naturally durable, weatherproof, and pest-resistant building materials. Do not use nonresidential pressure-treated lumber, used tires, or railroad ties because these contain arsenic, petroleum, and creosote, which are not safe for children's settings.

- Be aware that some plants are naturally poisonous when consumed raw (i.e., rhubarb leaves, lima beans and red kidney beans, potato and tomato leaves and vines, green

tomatoes, eggplant). Check on children's allergies before planting. Teach children to never eat any plant or seed without adult permission.

- Use sturdy child-sized garden tools. Show children the proper use of tools and how to move them safely. For example, when laying tools down, teach children to place rakes and other pointed tools with the tines down and put the tools away when they are no longer needed. If stakes are used, make sure they are taller than the children to avoid eye injuries.

- Chemicals and pesticides should be avoided. Local extension agents can assist in determining child-appropriate pest control methods.

The outdoor garden area provides a wonderful learning opportunity for children. Adults need to pay careful attention to the children and take appropriate safety precautions just as they do in the indoor classroom.

making it an unsafe burn hazard. Freezes can damage trees and shrubs, causing hazards from falling limbs. Teachers need to be observant for safety problems and be ready to correct or report them.

Conducting Periodic Safety Checks

Regular review of the outdoor environment and equipment is important to ensure the play area continues to meet safety expectations. A review by the CPSC (1999) found that 27% of early childhood playgrounds were poorly maintained and that 24% provided unsafe surfacing under children's equipment. This suggests that many children in care are exposed to hazardous conditions that should be corrected. Periodic monitoring helps ensure that teachers recognize and correct safety hazards. Table 13-5 provides a checklist that teachers can use to monitor the safety of the outdoor setting.

TABLE 13-5 Playground Maintenance Checklist

Maintenance Problems	Details and Follow-Up	Initial When Corrected
Play Area Review		
☐ Garbage, debris, broken glass, other hazardous materials		
☐ Gaps in fencing or other safety barriers (entrapment hazards)		
☐ Broken gate latches; latches that do not work		
☐ Cables, ropes, wires in the area (entanglement hazards)		
☐ Decayed or splintered wooden structures, benches, tables		
☐ Trip hazards		
☐ Rust or chipped paint exposing metal on toys, trikes, wagons		
☐ Standing water; problem with drainage		
☐ Sandbox cover missing; sand not protected from animals		
☐ Cracks in plastic equipment		
Play Equipment Assessment		
☐ Sharp points, corners, or edges		
☐ Head entrapment areas		
☐ Crush or shear points		
☐ Corrosion, rust, or deterioration on structural components that connect to the ground		
☐ Damaged equipment or missing components		
☐ Equipment footings are exposed		
☐ Surfacing under equipment is not sufficient		
☐ Other		

Source: *Public Playground Safety Handbook* (Publication No. 325), U.S. Consumer Product Safety Commission, April 2008, retrieved January 2012, from www .cpsc.gov/cpscpub/pubs/325.pdf.

■ SUMMARY

Ensuring children's physical and emotional safety is a fundamental teaching responsibility and crucial to children's wellness. It involves recognizing how safety influences children's healthful development and must be considered in all aspects of teaching. The classroom is an important refuge for children, where they can relax and focus on growing and learning. To create this safe environment and be most effective in their work, teachers need to know about the most common causes of unintentional injury and fatality in young children. In combination with an understanding of individual risk factors for injury, teachers should be prepared to design and implement safe practices in the classroom.

Children's settings and schools are generally safe environments for young children, but accidents can, and do, happen. In response, program leaders and teachers work together to meet or exceed safety standards. Program leaders establish safe and secure facilities and design safety policies to reduce risks. Teachers arrange safe classrooms and indoor and outdoor active play areas. They select appropriate furnishings, equipment, and toys and arrange the environments to avoid hazards. To be effective, teachers keep aware of the unique threats to children's safety in each play space. Teachers continually monitor the play areas for problems and take action when needed to correct issues that are unsafe.

KEY TERMS

Bite or sting injury	Children's enviroment	Falls
Burns	Drowning	Fatal injuries

Motor vehicle and traffic accidents	Struck by or against injury	Unintentional injuries
Safety	Sudden infant death syndrome (SIDS)	Usable square footage
Space use plan	Suffocation	

REVIEW QUESTIONS

1. Describe what is meant by physical safety and emotional safety. Explain how both physical and emotional safety contribute to children's growth and development.

2. Identify three common licensing requirements that contribute to children's safety. Explain how each affects safety in the early childhood setting.

3. Discuss factors that guide planning for children's programs and explain strategies for increasing safety and security in children's environments.

4. List some of the aspects that must be considered when creating safe and appropriate environments. Describe how each contributes to children's safety.

5. Explain some of the steps you would take as a teacher to ensure that your classroom is appropriate for the age group you serve, accessible to all children, and reflective of the cultural heritage of the children in your area.

6. Discuss three important guidelines for selecting safe and appropriate classroom furnishings, toys, and outdoor play equipment for a particular age group.

7. Describe how to create safe outdoor environments for young children.

DISCUSSION STARTERS

1. Consider the aspects of children's age and developmental maturity that influence children's risk for injury. Discuss ways teachers should adapt their supervision practices for each of the following age groups: infants, children ages 1 to 4 years, and children ages 5 to 9 years. Because of the differences in developmental skills, should children be grouped by age? Can a mixed-age class group be safe?

2. Reflect on a children's classroom you have taught in or observed. What policies and actions were in place to ensure children's safety? How would you describe these to prospective parents to help them feel their child would be secure in the environment?

3. Review the various responsibilities teachers have for children's safety. Which responsibility do you feel is most central to ensuring children are safe? Which responsibility do you think is most important to families?

4. Consider the developmental characteristics of each age group: infants, toddlers, preschoolers, and school-age children. Discuss ways you would arrange an appropriate indoor environment for each age group, and explain how your choices address age specific safety risks.

5. Recall early childhood settings where you have worked or classrooms you have observed. Describe the potential safety hazards of each environment and how they were addressed (or not addressed) by the teacher in charge. What aspects of children's safety would you find most challenging to correct?

PRACTICE POINTS

1. Go to the Centers for Disease Control and Prevention web page titled "Injury, Violence & Safety" at http://cdc.gov/InjuryViolenceSafety. Select three topics to explore. Read the "Quick Facts" and "Injury Prevention Tips for Parents and Children." Discuss how this information can guide you as you plan your classroom environment and establish safe supervision practices.

2. Log on to the National Child Care Information and Technical Assistance Center website at http://nccic.acf.hhs.gov/topics/topic/index.cfm?topicId=2. Explore health and safety topics related to

facilities, ratios and group size, and staff qualifications. Identify the requirements for liability and auto insurance for small and large family child care and center-based programs in your state.

3. Consider your responsibilities as a teacher for children's safety. Create a list of safety practices that you feel you are ready to assume. Identify at least three concerns you have related to keeping children safe in your classroom. Find two resources that can help you gain the information and skills you need. What actions will you take to improve your competencies and confidence in each of these areas?

4. Go to the U.S. Consumer Product Safety Commission's website and access the *Public Playground Safety Handbook* at www.cpsc.gov/CPSCPUB/PUBS/325.pdf. Use the Suggested General Maintenance Checklist in Appendix A to conduct a safety review of a playground in your community. Forward your recommendations to the school or public parks office.

5. Explore the types of toys and children's equipment that have been recently recalled due to safety hazards. Access the U.S. Consumer Product Safety Commission's website at www.cpsc .gov/cpscpub/prerel/category/toy.html and summarize the types of hazards that were identified in the 15 most recent toy recalls. Describe how this information helps you with your teaching.

WEB RESOURCES

Centers for Disease Control and Prevention
www.cdc.gov

Head Start Design Guide, Second Edition
www.headstartinfo.org/publications/hs_design_guide/index.htm

National Association for the Education of Young Children
www.naeyc.org

National Association for the Education of Young Children: Code of Ethical Conduct and Statement of Commitment
www.naeyc.org/positionstatements/ethical_conduct

National Child Care Information and Technical Assistance Center
http://nccic.acf.hhs.gov

National Clearinghouse for Educational Facilities
www.edfacilities.org/rl/teachers_workplaces.cfm

National Resource Center for Health and Safety in Child Care and Early Education
http://nrc.uchsc.edu/STATES/states.htm

U.S. Architectural and Transportation Barriers Compliance Board, Guide to ADA Accessibility
www.access-board.gov/play/guide/guide.pdf

U.S. Consumer Product Safety Commission
www.cpsc.gov

U.S. Department of Justice, ADA Standards for Accessible Design
www.ada.gov/stdspdf.htm

MyEducationLab™

Go to Topic 11 (Safe Environments) in the MyEducationLab (www.myeducationlab.com) for your course, where you can:

- Find learning outcomes for Safe Environments along with the national standards that connect to these outcomes.

- Complete Assignments and Activities that can help you more deeply understand the chapter content.

- Apply and practice your understanding of the core teaching skills identified in the chapter with the Building Teaching Skills and Dispositions learning units.

- Check your comprehension on the content covered in the chapter by going to the Study Plan in the Book Resources for your text. Here you will be able to take a chapter quiz, receive feedback on your answers, and then access Review, Practice, and Enrichment activities to enhance your understanding of chapter content.

fourteen

Promoting Safe Practices Through Effective Classroom Management

After teaching third grade for 4 years Jean was assigned to teach full-day kindergarten. She was excited to teach this new age group and approached the start of school with great enthusiasm. But 3 weeks into the year she finds herself exhausted and disheartened.

Her class of 22 students has taken a toll on her confidence. Three of the children are still having separation challenges and cry well into the first hour of the day. Two children have gotten hurt at recess. Manny has kicked children during circle time, and at one point he grabbed Sasha's hair and pulled her under the table. Candida, Olivia, and Sebastian are English learners and tend to fade into the background. Kellis and Mohammed focus well, but they finish their work quickly and tend to start bossing the other children around. Sam, who has Down syndrome, left the classroom at one point and another teacher found him sitting on the floor outside the classroom door. Yesterday, Jean discovered that Emma was trading her lunch with Angie, who has a food allergy. And just this morning Malcomb's mom called and said that she doesn't feel he is being challenged enough.

Jean is an experienced teacher but her class seems unmanageable and she is unsure of where to turn for help. If she contacts her principal, he may feel that she is not doing her job. Jean is bewildered and unsure if the children are even safe, and she certainly is not making progress on her lesson plans!

Any age group of children can present teachers with a variety of individual needs and classroom challenges. How teachers like Jean address these challenges determines the effectiveness of the learning environment and children's safety. In the opening case scenario, Jean is faced with a range of issues that cause her to question her ability to provide a safe class experience. Some are safety issues that should be her first priority; others are more educational or organizational concerns that require thoughtful and intentional intervention. What management approaches will assist teachers like Jean to plan and implement strategies to ensure children's safety?

In this chapter we present a variety of methods that contribute to safety in the early childhood setting. We start by exploring routines that set the stage for safety. Next, we describe supervision strategies to use in indoor and outdoor environments. Finally, we discuss how teachers implement practices that address children's safety needs, and provide strategies to teach appropriate safety messages.

● DEVELOPING SAFE CLASSROOM ROUTINES

Teachers are responsible for ensuring that children are safe in the classroom and during all class activities. They prepare by setting the stage for safety, establishing a daily schedule, planning secure arrival and departure procedures, and supporting safe transportation. Together these approaches create a proactive management plan that places children's safety at the core.

Setting the Stage for Safety

The strategies that build safety in the classroom occur before children arrive. Setting up the environment with appropriate toys and equipment is one example. Others include reflecting on evidence-based safety practices, gathering enrollment information, and orienting families to the classroom's safety procedures.

Using Evidence-Based Safety Practices

Information about the frequency of unintentional injuries and death in young children guides the development of strategies that are effective in reducing disease, injury, disability, and death in children's settings (American Academy of Pediatrics, American Public Health Association, and National Resource Center for Health and Safety in Child Care and Early Education, 2011). Keeping alert to these trends and guidelines helps teachers to know what to do to keep children safe, how to do it, and why.

Most states require that early childhood teachers learn and keep current on recommended safety practices through yearly training and professional development activities. This ensures that classroom safety practices continue to address emerging issues. Teachers who understand and use evidence-based safety practices can feel confident that they are teaching in ways that are consistent with the recommendations of the field (Strain & Dunlap, 2006) and are doing all they can to ensure children's safety.

Gathering Information at Enrollment

Information collected at enrollment provides the details that teachers need to develop appropriate safety practices and prepare to supervise children effectively. Beyond learning about the child's daily rhythms and feeding and nap schedules, teachers need to know about any situations that require special attention to safety and how to contact the family if needed. Ideally teachers have the opportunity to review enrollment materials and meet with families before children attend so that everyone who cares for the child understands any special safety needs (French, 2004). Figure 14-1 lists information that helps teachers better understand how to support children's safe participation. In the opening case scenario Jean would have benefited from this information as a guide to developing supportive classroom practices.

Orienting Families

Inviting families and children to visit before children attend is good practice in support of transition. It is also an important time to introduce classroom safety practices and helps families understand their role in supporting them (American Academy of Pediatrics et al., 2011; National Association for the Education

MyEducationLab™

Visit the MyEducationLab for *Nutrition, Health, and Safety for Young Children* to enhance your understanding of chapter concepts with a personalized Study Plan. You'll also have the opportunity to hone your teaching skills through video-based Assignments and Activities, as well as Building Teaching Skills and Dispositions lessons.

FIGURE 14-1 Enrollment Information That Supports Child Safety

Child Information

- ✓ Child's name and nickname
- ✓ Child's birth date
- ✓ Arrival and departure plan

Contact Information

- ✓ Contact information for custodial parent(s) or guardian(s): name, address, daytime phone numbers, email
- ✓ Emergency contacts: at least one person who lives locally but is not of the immediate family
- ✓ Secondary emergency contact: include a family member or friend that lives outside the community (in community-wide emergencies local communication may be jammed but individuals at a distance may be available to contact)
- ✓ Names of any persons who should never pick up the child from care

Health Information

- ✓ Record of child's immunizations
- ✓ Special health considerations including allergies

- ✓ Food or other restrictions due to religious, cultural, or family practice
- ✓ Information about identified or suspected developmental needs
- ✓ Child's healthcare providers and contact information (medical, dental, other)
- ✓ Child's insurance provider (name of the primary insured, policy or member number)
- ✓ Statement of program emergency medical response plan signed by the parent

Child Comfort Information

- ✓ Feeding and toileting practices (especially for infants and toddlers)
- ✓ Child information to support transition into care:
  - · Favorite toys or games
  - · Child's words for routines
  - · Names of siblings or close friends
  - · Child's comfort strategies
- ✓ Other information (family information that may affect the child in care such as illness of parent or close relative, incarcerated parent)

Sources: American Academy of Pediatrics, 2011; National Association for the Education of Young Children, 2009.

of Young Children [NAEYC], 2009). During the visit safety topics are discussed naturally as children and parents tour the setting. For example, the importance of staying with the group is introduced as children walk into the classroom. Teachers can demonstrate how to wash hands at arrival and show how to walk carefully near the sinks in case the floor is wet to avoid slipping. Safety rules related to use of the swing and slide can be discussed while walking through the playground. This is also an important time to remind families to dress children in clothes suitable for the weather and to provide appropriate shoes or bring boots so outdoor play will be safe and comfortable (AAP et al., 2011; NAEYC, 2009).

Families that do not speak English should be encouraged to bring a trusted family member or friend to assist if a translator is not available. This helps ensure that basic safety rules such as staying with the group and waiting in the classroom until the parent arrives, are successfully conveyed to children and parents. It allows families to ask questions and increases everyone's confidence about security in the setting. When a large percentage of children in a class group speak a language other than English, the program should, for safety and as a matter of good practice, provide at least one teacher who speaks that language.

Establishing a Daily Schedule

A familiar schedule guides the flow of daily activities and supports an organized approach to safe group management. The schedule should offer a predictable plan of activities, create familiar routines, provide smooth transitions, and be flexible enough to manage occasional disruptions.

Designing a Schedule of Activities

The daily schedule is a plan that organizes the class day around a timeline of predictable activities. Children come to learn that as soon as they arrive they are to hang up their coats, wash their hands, and sit down to breakfast. They are able to anticipate that after cleanup they will go outside to play, or come to understand that they will go home after story time. This knowledge helps children develop comfort with moving from one activity to the next, which increases their engagement in productive play.

The daily schedule is typically established around periods of active and quiet playtimes that minimize the number of transitions or interruptions that can cause confusion and potential safety hazards. The schedule for most early childhood programs includes meal and rest times, large-group and story time, outdoor play periods, and times for free-choice play. The schedule should fit children's age and needs. For example, the daily schedule for infants is individualized as teachers follow each child's familiar eating and sleeping patterns (Wittmer & Petersen, 2008). The schedule for toddlers begins to introduce longer blocks of playtime. As children

A predictable schedule helps children know what to expect and encourages cooperation.

mature, they are more able to accommodate a schedule that is designed for the group. Once children learn the rhythm of the daily schedule, they are able to be more self-directed and competent moving through the familiar steps. As children become more self-guided in following cues to move from one activity to the next, teachers are able to focus on supervising the group for safety (Alter & Conroy, 2007).

Creating Familiar Routines

Moving through the daily schedule of activities provides children many opportunities to practice and become familiar with *routines*. Routines are rhythms and habits that are followed every day in the classroom. They help children "know how" to do what is expected in each time period. For example, children in early childhood settings become familiar with the routines of washing their hands before they eat and clearing their plates when they are done with a meal. They learn the routines of getting toys off the shelves to play, and putting them back when they are done. Familiarity with routines helps children learn to guide themselves through the day, which builds a sense of confidence and contributes to their safety in the setting. Figure 14-2 offers examples of routines that become familiar to children in the early childhood setting.

FIGURE 14-2 Sample Daily Routines

- Arrival: greet the teacher; hang up coat; wash hands before play.
- Free play: choose an activity; put toys away when done; choose another activity.
- Clean-up time: listen for the 5 minute warning; put toys in their tub and place tub on the shelf; go to circle.
- Circle time: Sit on the circle marker; listen for directions; raise hand and wait to be called on before talking.
- Going to meals: Listen for the transition song; wash hands; sit at the table; wait for everyone to sit before starting.
- During meals: take turns passing the food; serve myself; wait till the food has been passed to everyone before eating.
- Emergency drills: Listen for the alarm; stop playing; listen and follow the teacher's directions.
- Departure: Wait to be excused; put on coat and get artwork from cubby; wait until a grown-up checks you out; walk out together.

Source: Sorte (from practice).

Implementing Smooth Transitions

Transition refers to the short periods of time during which a child or the group moves from one activity to another. Ending free-choice play and beginning to clean up, or ending story time and preparing to go outside to play, are familiar transitions in the daily schedule. Transition times need to be well planned and managed as they have the potential to introduce disruption in children's behavior that may lead to confusion and increase the potential for unintentional injury (Alter & Conroy, 2007). For example, some children who are reluctant to stop their free play may respond with frustration. Others may seek to avoid cleanup time by running about and knocking toys off tables. Some children might suddenly remember that their parent is gone and begin to cry. What was a calm group of busy children one minute can become a whirlwind the next. The safety concerns that such disruption may cause can be avoided by (Alter & Conroy, 2007):

- Keeping the number of transitions to a minimum by planning large blocks of play time.
- Giving children a 5-minute warning before activities will end, allowing them to prepare.
- Making gradual transitions by directing small groups of children to the next activity.

These approaches show respect for the importance of children's play, teach children to navigate through the period of change, and help keep the group on track.

In the opening case scenario, Jean may benefit from reviewing her daily schedule of activities. She may be able to discover ways to reduce the number of transitions to help address some of the classroom management challenges she is facing.

Addressing Schedule Disruptions

Interruptions to the daily schedule can come from many sources such as late lunch delivery, unplanned emergency drills, or loss of electricity. These situations disturb the flow of activities and cause confusion for teachers and children. When such disruptions occur, effective teachers reassure the children while swiftly assessing the situation. Teachers need to determine the source of the disruption, identify if children's safety is threatened, and sort out strategies to increase safety while the issue is being resolved. For example, teachers can read a story while waiting for lunch, or take charge in the surprise emergency drill by saying, "1-2-3, eyes on me," to gain children's attention and give directions. Emergency lighting sources can be used while waiting for power to be restored. In some settings, the lack of electricity may introduce a safety hazard. The teacher may need to make a judgment about how to respond: Call families to take children home or finish the day without electricity?

Creating Secure Arrival and Departure Procedures

Children arrive and depart from early childhood classrooms in many ways. In some settings children are delivered directly to the teacher at arrival and picked up directly from the teacher at departure. Sometimes children are transported by a bus. School-age children may travel to school on their own. Teachers need to understand the plan for each child. They need to know how and when the child will arrive, who will be bringing the child to the class, and who is authorized to pick up the child. Having this information helps teachers conduct smooth transitions and ensures that children are received and released appropriately.

Ensuring Safety at Arrival and Departure

Teachers should be present to supervise and greet children at arrival and say good-bye at departure. Clear policies are needed to support safety during this exchange (American Academy of Pediatrics [AAP], et al., 2011). For example:

- Young children must be delivered directly to the teacher and not be dropped off outside the building and allowed to "run in" to the classroom.
- Children may not be dropped off or picked up when the program is conducting an emergency evacuation or lockdown, except under the direction of a public safety official.
- Children may not be released to go home with other children without written consent from parents or other authorized individuals.

When moving a group of children from one activity to another, a teacher may use songs or other cues. While watching this **video**, consider how the song guides children's behavior and maintains order in the classroom.

This **video** shows a routine used by parents when they take their children to preschool. Notice the aspects of this routine that ensure safety and help children feel comfortable when parents depart.

FIGURE 14-3   Arrival and Departure Sign-In and Sign-Out Sheet

Note to Families: Please include time of arrival/departure and sign or initial below.

CHILD'S NAME	Monday, October 20		Tuesday, October 21	
	Arrive	Depart	Arrive	Depart
Annette	7:50	5:25	7:45	5:15
	Alice Yates	*Ben Yates*	*Ben Yates*	*Alice Yates*
Arturo	7:45	12:15	7:45	5:45
	Belinda Dee	*Belinda Dee*	*Belinda Dee*	*Belinda Dee*
Maria D.	7:45	12:15	7:45	5:45
	Belinda Dee	*Belinda Dee*	*Belinda Dee*	*Belinda Dee*
Maria M.	7:55	5:15	7:55	5:15
	Marc Mitchel	*Mike Robinson*	*Marc Mitchel*	*Mike Robinson*
Su Lin	7:55	5:25	7:55	5:45
	Seong Yun	*Joon Lee Yun*	*Seong Yun*	*Joon Lee Yun*

Planning child-directed activities at arrival and departure times helps teachers to be accessible to visit with families and to monitor for safety. Setting out activities such as puzzles that children can easily join as they arrive or providing books for children to look at as families arrive to pick them up help create smooth and organized transitions (Hemmeter, Ostrosky, Artman, & Kinder, 2008).

Signing In and Out Most early childhood settings for infants through preschool age require that children be "signed in" upon arrival and "signed out" at departure. This routine documents who delivered or received the child and when, and creates a record of the exchange if there is any confusion. Figure 14-3 provides a sample sign-in and sign-out sheet. Arrival and departure routines can be complicated, especially if several adults participate in transporting the child. A plan is needed to record arrival and departure if families arrive while the class is in the play yard or away from the classroom. Teachers might carry a small notebook in their pocket for parents to sign.

Releasing Children to Appropriate Adults Teachers are responsible for releasing children only to the custodial parent or other authorized adult. The identification of anyone who is authorized to pick up the child but is unknown to the teacher must be checked. Children should not be released to anyone who displays behaviors that could endanger the child due to debilitation by alcohol, drugs, or other impairing conditions (AAP et al., 2011). State requirements differ about how such situations should be managed. At a minimum, teachers should have a plan in place to delay the release of the child while other arrangements are made, such as calling an alternate authorized adult. Teachers may also need to contact the police for advice. Sometimes families authorize an older sibling to pick up a younger child from the classroom. Rules regarding the ages of children who are allowed to pick up younger children from care, and the ages of children who can be released to a minor are not universal. Teachers should consult with their local child care licensing authority for guidance. In addition, teachers should have a plan in place in the event that no authorized adult comes to pick up a child. The local child protective services agency is a resource for helping design a protocol for this situation.

Monitoring Child Attendance

Taking attendance is a familiar safety routine in early childhood classrooms. Teachers need to know who is present and how many total children are in attendance at all times (AAP et al., 2011). Attendance should be recorded immediately as each child arrives and as soon as each child departs to avoid confusion. Throughout the day, teachers should periodically count the number of children to confirm that all are present. This is especially important any time the group moves from one location to another such

Attendance should be recorded as children arrive and checked periodically to ensure that all children are present.

as to and from the play yard, during an emergency drill, when the class gets on and off the bus for a field trip, or after walking down the hallway to the school restroom and back.

Contacting Parents About Child Absence   Monitoring children's absences is also an important health and safety practice. Families should be oriented to contact the teacher in advance if planned absences are anticipated (for a doctor's appointment or trip, for example), and to phone or e-mail if a child is absent due to illness or other unexpected reason. Knowing why children have not come to school helps teachers track the spread of communicable disease and alerts teachers to potential safety concerns.

If children are absent without notification, the teacher should call the family to ask about the reason for the absence. If several children are absent due to illness, teachers recognize the need to conduct additional sanitizing and take other precautions to prevent spread of disease in the classroom. If school-age children are late or absent, program or school safety policies should be in place to ensure that teachers call the family to confirm the child is safe. This is especially important for children who travel to school on their own.

Tracking Midday Interruptions in Attendance   Not all children arrive and depart at the beginning and end of the class day. Some children may arrive late or go home early. A child might leave, for example for a dental appointment, but return again before the school day is complete. Or a child who receives speech services might be taken to participate with a small group in another room. Strategies for recording midday interruptions in children's attendance are important for safety. For example, recording children's departures and arrivals on the attendance sheet, and writing the number of children on a whiteboard, are ways that teachers account for each child and keep aware of the total number of children present (AAP et al., 2011).

Transporting Children Safely

Transportation services have been provided for school-age children and those with special developmental needs for many years (Bluth, 1993). Programs such as Head Start and some child care programs also provide transportation as part of their services (Early Childhood Learning and Knowledge Center [ECLKC], 2008). Teachers are often assigned to supervise children at arrival and departure times and on field trips. They should understand transportation rules, be prepared to support safe transportation practices, and know how to arrange transportation for field trips.

Understanding Child Transportation Regulations

Children are safer being transported in school buses than any other form of motor vehicle (NHTSA, 2011). The strict requirements for school bus construction and people's familiarity with the bright yellow buses used to transport children are two reasons given for the high safety rating.

The use of vans to transport young children is highly discouraged, and in many areas is strictly forbidden, because of a variety of dangers such as fewer regulations for vehicle construction, no requirements that vans stop at train crossings, and the fact that other drivers do not recognize vans as transportation sources for children.

Although federal guidelines direct the safe transportation of young children, each state establishes the specific requirements for transporting children to and from public schools. Some state regulations identify guidelines specific to transporting children younger than 5 years of age such as (NHTSA, 2011; Savage, Kawanabe, Mejeur, Goehring, & Reed, 2002):

- The kinds of child safety restraint systems to be used.
- The maximum number of children who may be transported on a bus (based on age).

What if . . .

you wanted to arrange bus transportation for a field trip? Who would you contact to learn about the regulations in your area?

- The number of adult monitors required to maintain appropriate supervision and their qualifications.
- The procedures used for pickup and drop-off.

Teachers can learn more about these regulations from each state's director of pupil transportation services.

Supporting Safe Transportation Practices

Teachers have an especially important role at bus arrival and departure times. Even though school buses are the safest way to transport children, each year on average, 19 school-aged children are killed in school transportation related traffic crashes (NHTSA, 2011). The majority of these fatalities involve children between 5 and 7 years of age who are hit in the danger zone immediately surrounding the bus. The school bus danger zone consists of the space within 10 feet of the bus, as shown in Figure 14-4. Teachers need to be especially vigilant to ensure that children pass through this danger zone appropriately and do not loiter in this space.

FIGURE 14-4
School Bus Danger Zone

Transportation regulations for young children is evolving as the number of children under the age of 5 who are being transported continues to increase. Teachers are in a good position to observe the program's transportation routines and make recommendations for change if safety concerns are identified.

Arranging Transportation for Field Trips

Many early childhood programs arrange transportation for field trips. Although transportation activities for private programs are not governed by federal guidelines, programs benefit by drafting policies to guide safety planning for field trip transportation. Central to such policies should be the requirement that each child weighing less than 50 pounds must ride in an appropriately installed *child safety seat* and that adult supervision is appropriate for the group (NHTSA, 1999).

Communication with families about transportation for field trips is also very important. When children are to be transported, families need to know:

- Where the group is going—the site and address.
- When the child will be transported—departure and return times.
- How the child will be transported—mode of transportation.
- Who will be driving—describing the qualifications of the drivers.
- Who will be supervising the children and monitoring for safety.

Ultimately, teachers carry the responsibility for planning, communicating, and managing for compliance with program transportation safety rules. Teachers must view the rules as nonnegotiable. In practice this means that if safe and appropriate transportation cannot be achieved, program activities such as field trips and excursions must be cancelled.

● IMPLEMENTING SAFE SUPERVISION PRACTICES

Supervision is crucial to children's safety and is the primary measure of effective teaching. Supervision is the most important way that teachers ensure safe physical interactions and secure emotional environments for young children. Effective supervision decreases the possibility of unintentional injury and increases the likelihood that children will thrive in the setting. To be prepared teachers must understand what constitutes effective supervision, know how to supervise effectively in the classroom and in outdoor activities, be ready with strategies to supervise special events, and able to enforce program safety rules if needed.

Understanding Appropriate Supervision

Supervising children's safety in group settings requires deliberate planning and consistent and careful attention. Teachers must supervise children by sight and sound, clarify individual teacher responsibilities, coordinate supervision with team teachers, reassure children that teachers are watching out for them, and maintain attention and focus.

Supervising by Sight and Sound

Keeping children safe and secure through attentive supervision is crucial. At the most basic level, it is what teachers *do* and what teachers *don't do* on a daily basis that makes the most difference in keeping children secure from harm. The *Code of Ethical Conduct* of the NAEYC (2011a) calls for teachers to supervise children by sight and sound:

- Infants and toddlers must be supervised by sight and sound at all times.
- Preschoolers must be supervised by sight at all times. Preschoolers may be out of sound supervision for short periods of time.
- Kindergartners, in a safe environment, may be out of sight and sound supervision for short periods of time if they are checked on regularly.

Sight and sound supervision is accomplished in different ways, depending on the age group. Infant rooms typically create spaces for sleeping, areas where diapering and feeding take place, and spaces where children play. The room arrangement needs to allow teachers to view and hear children who are participating in each activity. Spaces used by toddlers and older children are usually equipped with low shelving, allowing the teacher to monitor activity by moving about the room. Some states have specific requirements related to supervision of children when they are sleeping. For example, regulations for registered family child care homes address whether children can sleep on a different floor from where the teacher is working.

Teachers must be continually alert to keeping all children in view and paying attention to the sounds of children at play. They must also know how to position themselves in the space, such as (National Association for the Education of Young Children [NAEYC], 2009):

- Standing or sitting where the majority of children are easily in view.
- Being in a position to see the door to prevent a child from walking out.
- Continually scanning the environment to keep aware of the group.
- Periodically walking around the group and changing position.

Supervision also extends to knowing about issues and circumstances that might require special awareness. Table 14-1 describes a variety of supervision scenarios and guides teachers with ideas of what to do and what to avoid.

Assigning Children to Specific Teachers

Young children require close supervision to ensure they are safe. Because of this each child is assigned to a specific teacher who carries primary responsibility for knowing where that child is and what that child is doing at all times. Ideally children are assigned to the same teacher and the same group of children every day (NAEYC, 2009). This supports bonding and familiarity, and allows parents to communicate directly with their child's assigned teacher when changes are needed in the child's care routine. Assigning children to specific teachers reduces the potential for mistakes that could cause safety concerns.

Infants and Toddlers For infants and toddlers, specific and consistent teacher assignments (called *continuity of care*) ensure that the child's feeding and sleeping routines are understood and their emotional and comfort needs are supported. Typically, in infant and toddler settings, each teacher is assigned to a small group of three or four children. For example, a total class group of eight infants and toddlers is led by two teachers. This direct teacher-to-child assignment clarifies who is ultimately responsible for the care and security of each individual child.

TABLE 14-1 Supervision Practices

DO THIS	NOT THIS
DO – Check the classroom and outdoor spaces every day for potential hazards.	DO NOT – Assume that someone else will do this.
DO – Keep children in direct sight and sound at all times.	DO NOT – Leave children unattended.
DO – Teach children to stay with the group at school and on field trips, but keep alert.	DO NOT – Assume that children will remember to watch for the group.
DO – Teach children safety rules for relevant situations.	DO NOT – Transfer inappropriate worry or concern to children.
DO – Learn about children's special family situations (i.e., custody issues, people who should not have access to the child).	DO NOT – Assume that a child's family members or friends are safe people.
DO – Know who the parent has approved to pick up the child from care.	DO NOT – Release the child to anyone not previously approved by the child's parent or guardian.
DO – Require photo identification for approved persons you do not know.	DO NOT – Assume that the child will tell you if the person is "ok" or not.
DO – Understand your role in the security plan for your program.	DO NOT – Assume that security is being taken care of by other people.
DO – Know what to be concerned about; anticipate potential security risks; take appropriate precautions.	DO NOT – Ignore issues that you read about happening "somewhere else."
DO – Step in immediately if you see a person in the facility that you do not know.	DO NOT – Assume that it is alright for people you don't know to be in your classroom, the hallways, or any other part of your secure environment.

Source: Sorte (from practice).

Preschoolers Class groups of 16 to 18 preschool children are usually led by at least two teachers. The teachers work together to provide consistent supervision of the class. Teachers set up the classroom spaces so that children can be easily viewed and heard from all areas of the room.

School-Age Children Kindergarten and elementary school class groups vary greatly in size, ranging from 18 to 24 or more children. Classes are often led by one teacher who is responsible for providing safe activities and consistent supervision. These teachers plan activities and lessons that allow children to be self-directed while the teacher supervises by moving around the room and addressing the needs of individual children.

Children with Special Needs Assigning a teacher to supervise specific children increases the likelihood that each child's special educational supports, language assistance, and allergy or other medical needs are understood and managed consistently and safely (NAEYC, 2009). For example, the *Health Hint* describes information that a teacher needs to provide safe services for a child with

HEALTH HINT Information Teachers Need to Serve Children with Diabetes

✓ General orientation about what diabetes is and how it can be effectively managed in the early childhood and school setting

✓ Detailed training on the child's specific medical plan for daily support

✓ Training on the administration of glucagon and other emergency care steps

✓ Resources to contact for more information, such as those provided by the American Diabetes Association:
  · *Diabetes Medical Management Plan*
  · *Tips to Help Teachers Keep Kids with Diabetes Safe at School*
  · *Solutions for Common Diabetes Management Concerns in the Classroom*

Sources: The American Diabetes Association: Living with Diabetes: *Diabetes medical management plan*. Retrieved February 1, 2012, from www.diabetes.org/living-with-diabetes/parents-and-kids/diabetes-care-at-school/written-care-plans/diabetes-medical-management.html; Living with Diabetes: *A team effort*. Retrieved February 1, 2012, from www.diabetes.org/living-with-diabetes/parents-and-kids/diabetes-care-at-school/a-team-effort.html; and Tips For Teachers of Students with Diabetes: Retrieved February 1, 2012, from www.diabetes.org/assets/pdfs/schools/tentipsforteachers.pdf.

diabetes. For continuity it helps if one or a small team of teachers receives special training and orientation to address these needs. Depending on a child's particular needs, an educational assistant may be assigned to support the child in the classroom. Educational assistants are part of the teaching team and need to understand their supervision responsibilities.

Temporary Groupings Sometimes temporary groups of children are gathered, such as in before- and after-school care, or when classes are merged as children depart at the end of the day. Temporary groups may include children of different ages, and the membership of the group may vary from day to day. Assigning the teachers to specific children helps teachers recognize their responsibilities and focuses the teacher's attention on learning if the child has special safety needs.

Coordinating Supervision with Team Teachers

Groups of children younger than kindergarten age are most often led by a *teaching team* of two or more teachers. Teaching as part of a team requires a deliberate plan for sharing the responsibility of supervision (Kern & Wakeford, 2007). For example, one teacher is assigned to closely supervise the water play activity while the other moves about the room supervising in a general way. Other strategies include assigning each teacher a zone of the room to supervise or dividing tasks where one teacher is observing the group while the other attends to a child's need or sets up lunch. Clarifying the supervision plan ensures that teachers focus on their assigned responsibility and prevents teachers from thinking that "someone else" is watching (Kern & Wakeford, 2007).

Reassuring Children That They Are Safe

Children find comfort in knowing that the teacher is there to keep them safe. Children who feel safe and secure are able to move out into the play setting and enjoy and learn from their interactions in the environment (Bowlby, 1982). They are also more likely to seek the teacher for help if a safety issue arises.

The amount of reassurance required depends on the children's age and maturity, and their need at a particular time. For example:

- Infants benefit from being able to see and hear the teacher, and know that the teacher will attend to their needs.
- Toddlers need reassurance that the teacher is nearby as a physical and emotional safety base.
- Preschool children like to know that the teacher is available to listen to their ideas and concerns and to respond when they have a need.
- School-age children like to know what the rules are and who to go to if they need help.

> **A Matter of ETHICS**
> Children often look to teachers to provide reassurance about their worries. How does the NAEYC Code of Ethical Conduct guide you when a child clings to you and says she does not want to go home?

The reassurance that teachers provide includes being *accessible* (physically near and attentive) and *responsive* (approachable and easy to talk to). These qualities are demonstrated when teachers position themselves physically near and when they engage with children by talking or smiling to show they are available and ready to help if children need them.

Keeping Focused and Alert

Maintaining attention and focus is critical to safe supervision. This means teachers must avoid boredom and distractions such as the following (AAP et al., 2011):

- Talking together or talking or texting on the telephone.
- Daydreaming.
- Cleaning or performing tasks that interrupt appropriate supervision.
- Being overly involved in children's play so that group supervision is forgotten.

Teachers learn to balance interacting with one child while observing the full classroom. For example, when helping a toddler assemble a shapes puzzle, the teacher periodically looks up to scan the remainder of the room, ensuring that all children are playing safely, making eye contact, and smiling at other children.

Supervising Classroom Activities

Supervision in the classroom is an essential aspect of effective classroom management. Supervision and safety are supported by planning developmentally appropriate activities, paying attention to activities that offer special risks such as interactions with animals or water, and by continually monitoring the environment for safety.

Planning Appropriate Activities

Careful planning is needed to balance the number of activities that require direct teacher involvement with the number of activities that children can participate in on their own (Alter & Conroy, 2007). Planning interesting and developmentally appropriate activities helps children to be engaged and involved, and increases their opportunity to be self-directed. This frees teachers to move about the room observing for safety.

Managing Interactions with Animals

Children are very interested and excited about animals, making special planning important to ensure the safety of children and the classroom pet or visiting animal. Child care regulations may limit the types of animals that are allowed in children's settings because of safety concerns (AAP et al., 2011). For example, birds with hooked beaks and animals that may carry salmonella (lizards, frogs, turtles, baby chicks) are typically not allowed. Any visiting animals should be healthy and not aggressive with children.

Teachers carefully arrange interactions between children and animals. For example, as the children sit in a circle on the floor, the teacher may say:

Today Sally's dog, Bess, is coming to visit. We don't want to frighten Bess, so we will sit in a circle quietly while Sally introduces her to us. Sally will invite each of you to come up one at a time to pet Bess.

This approach provides children with the information they need. It communicates:

- What the rule is (sit in the circle; wait until you are called forward).
- What will happen (kids will listen and then have a turn).
- What to do (stay sitting; listen quietly; come forward when invited).
- Who will get to participate (everyone).

When children know what is expected and receive confirmation that each will be able to participate, the experience is more enjoyable and safe for the children and the animal.

Supervising Activities That Involve Water

Water activities can present significant safety concerns including the dangers of drowning and slipping. Careful supervision is essential. For infants and toddlers, teachers provide water play by placing clean water in shallow trays. This avoids the possibility of children "tipping" over into the water. Providing water play in sensory tables for preschoolers and older is popular for exploring "sink and float" concepts. Teachers watch closely for appropriate play, ensure that the floor does not become wet and slippery, and guide children to wash their hands when they are done to avoid spreading germs (U.S. Consumer Products Safety Commission, 2012).

The use of wading pools should be done in compliance with the regulations governing child care in the local area. Some states do not allow wading pools in children's programs.

Monitoring the Environment

Classroom supervision also includes continually monitoring the environment to ensure that safety hazards are corrected. Manipulative toys may be left in the walkway, potentially causing a tripping

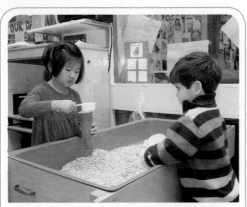

Safety hazards, such as materials spilled from the sensory table, should be cleared away as soon as they are noticed.

hazard or blocking emergency exits. In the course of active play the sand or rice in the sensory-bin may be spilled on the floor introducing a slipping hazard. These issues should be anticipated and avoided through careful room arrangement and by taking safety precautions such as placing safety mats under the sensory table or having a broom and dustpan close by. Careful monitoring ensures that safety problems are corrected right away.

Supervising Outdoor Activities

Special attention is needed when supervising children in outdoor play areas because injuries can happen quickly and have the potential to be severe. Children must be visible at all times, and teachers must be able to hear them to understand if they are in danger or if they are being harassed or bullied. A well-designed outdoor environment should work "with" teachers, supporting the teachers' ability to scan the near and far environments to track for safety (Kern & Wakeford, 2007). Supervising children effectively in outdoor play areas involves planning appropriate activities, using supervision zones to ensure appropriate oversight, and actively teaching.

Planning Outdoor Playtime

Outdoor playtime is learning time. It is not enough to simply give children the opportunity to be outdoors; the playtime must be intentionally planned and prepared to make sure that children have the freedom to move and be active while the teachers are watching for safety. Managing for safety during the outdoor playtime involves selecting an appropriate balance of child-directed and teacher-involved activities, identifying the equipment that will be made available, and organizing where each activity will take place to avoid conflicts. For example, playing ball games away from the swings reduces the likelihood that a child might run under a moving swing to retrieve a rolling ball.

Establishing expectations about safe use of the toys and equipment also helps children be active within the boundaries of acceptable play. A good time to share this information is during the transition as children prepare to go outside. While children gather, teachers talk about the activities and equipment that are available and remind the children of the rules for safe play. Overall, when planning activities for outdoor playtime teachers are responsible for:

- Selecting appropriate and interesting activities that offer challenge and build skills.
- Arranging the needed equipment and supplies.
- Teaching children the rules for safe and acceptable play.
- Encouraging children to be highly active at least part of the time.
- Supervising children for safety at all times.

Being purposeful when planning outdoor activities sets the stage for safe play. It reduces the likelihood of bullying and rough play that may emerge due to boredom.

Using Supervision Zones

What if . . .

you found yourself daydreaming about what you needed to buy at the grocery store when you were supposed to be supervising children at the slide? What could you do to improve your supervision in this important area?

During the outdoor playtime teachers need to allow children to explore and discover without undue intervention, but they must be ready to intervene immediately if unsafe behavior is observed. Teachers might fall into the habit of considering outdoor playtime or recess as "break time." They may cluster at the periphery of the play area, supervising from a distance but not engaging with children except when needed. These practices can be distracting and harmful.

Outdoor play areas are usually large spaces where trees and equipment may block the view, and the sounds of play may make supervision by sight and sound more challenging. Dividing the outdoor play area into "zones" and assigning each teacher to supervise a zone is a good strategy to improve safety (Kern & Wakeford, 2007). This approach helps teachers focus their attention on the specific activities occurring in their zone and increases their attentiveness to guiding children to play appropriately. Periodically rotating teachers to new supervision zones helps refresh attention and reduce supervision boredom.

Teaching Actively

While teachers move about the play area monitoring for safety, they are actively engaged in both teaching and supervising. Teachers observe children's skill development and encourage active play. They offer ideas and questions to spark children's interest in the outdoors and the learning possibilities provided by the setting. These actions demonstrate that supervision occurs naturally as part of the interactive teaching process. As teachers watch and interact with children they are also keeping alert and attuned to the tone of the play. They show by this presence that they are watching to be sure that the rules of safety are being followed and that interactions are positive. This prompts children to play appropriately and sends a message that bullying will be noticed and stopped.

Supervising Special Situations

While classroom and outdoor play are regular parts of the daily schedule, a variety of special situations require teachers to be ready to use their professional experience and common sense to supervise children appropriately. Examples of special situations include field trips, substitutes, visitors, family events, intruders, complicated family issues, and the need to enforce rules and address unsafe behaviors.

Keeping Alert on Field Trips

Moving out of the familiar environment into new settings on field trips has the potential to distract children's attention from teachers and other adults who are guiding and supervising them. Teachers reduce the possibility of unintentional injury by selecting appropriate field trip destinations and by visiting the field trip site in advance to assess the setting for safety concerns. Providing orientation to children and adult volunteers about the safety rules and assigning each child to an adult leader are important strategies for safe supervision.

Ensuring Safety When Substitutes Are Assigned

Any change in group leadership can introduce potential safety concerns. Substitute teachers may not know individual children's needs and must quickly adjust to the classroom schedule. This is addressed by providing appropriate orientation. Introducing the substitute teacher and explaining why the regular teacher is absent helps children understand that the substitute is a leader and person of safety in the class. It may also be wise to adjust the plan for the day to ensure that the majority of activities are child directed. This allows the new teacher to focus on interacting with the children and supervising for safety. Having a "substitute day" lesson plan prepared in advance can help support substitute teachers and improve safety.

Supervising Visitors

Visitors bring welcome assistance and special skills to the early childhood setting, but they can also introduce disruption to safety routines. They need to be oriented to their roles and responsibilities and the safety routines of the classroom. Teachers should introduce the visitors to the children, confirming that they are "teacher-approved" members of the class. It is best if visitors have clear assignments, such as reading with children, filling the paint containers, or supervising the block corner. Visitors should never be left alone with the children and teachers should supervise their interactions at all times.

Sometimes visitors in uniform, such as firefighters with helmets or costumed characters, may visit the children's program. Adults often see these characters as fun and interesting, but children may find them frightening. These visitors should be scheduled only if appropriate for the group. They need to be oriented in advance about ways to appropriately interact with the children. Teachers should always be present to ensure children's comfort and safety.

Families need to know about classroom safety policies.

Guiding Family Events

Gathering families for social and other events is a common way early childhood programs encourage family engagement, yet even such welcome activities can introduce safety concerns. Children may become very excited about having their families with them, and the large group of people adds noise and a sense of confusion in the setting.

There may also be confusion about who is supervising the children—the teacher or the family? It is important for teachers to clearly communicate the goal of the event and who is in charge of supervision. This can be accomplished in the way the invitation is extended:

- If the teacher will supervise the children, parents could be invited to, "Please come watch the class dance and sing favorite songs."
- If parents are to supervise their children, the invitation could say, "Please supervise your children while you enjoy walking through the classroom art show together."

Even when the expectation is that families should supervise their children, teachers should keep aware of safety and be ready to enforce safety rules if needed.

Confronting Strangers

On occasion teachers may need to confront an unknown person in the classroom, hallway, or outdoor play area. Teachers must be prepared to ask about the purpose of that person's presence and be ready to request that the person leave if necessary. A backup plan should be in place if the teacher requires assistance, such as calling for support from other teachers or the program director or principal.

Navigating Complicated Family Issues

Safety challenges may arise as a result of complicated family situations or child custody issues. For example, a parent might report that the noncustodial parent or another adult has a court-ordered temporary restraining order and is not allowed to have contact with the child. Teachers need to know how to handle such situations. In some cases, the temporary restraining order must be reviewed and the limits of the exclusion understood. This is done to ensure that the teacher does not restrict access to the child by one parent simply on the direction of the other parent.

Parents involved in custody battles sometimes ask teachers to record observations about the other parent's behavior with the child. Teachers need to avoid being drawn into family disagreements. Teachers should explain that the school is a safe and neutral place for the child and that recording observations is not an appropriate teacher activity. Developing a relationship of collaboration with families helps when it is necessary to communicate about difficult issues (Olson, 2007).

Enforcing Program Safety Rules

Teachers are responsible for ensuring that program safety rules are followed during all program or school activities. Visitors or family members may introduce unsafe situations or model unsafe behaviors through lack of information, and sometimes they may show outright disregard for the program's safety practices. These situations can catch teachers by surprise. When necessary, teachers must step forward to kindly but firmly enforce the program safety rule. Teachers should persist until unsafe activities stop and safety is restored. Table 14-2 provides examples of potential situations and ideas for responsive action.

Intervening When Families Are Unsafe

Teachers need to act decisively when they observe families using unsafe practices such as transporting children without an appropriate car restraint seat or seat belt or leaving an infant unattended in a vehicle while the parent comes into the classroom. The *Safety Segment* provides information

TABLE 14-2 Situations That Require Responsive Action

Potential Safety Hazard	Responsive Action
A parent parks her bicycle in the walkway to the classroom.	Tell the parent how the bicycle is a safety hazard. Identify a safe place to park the bike.
A child brings in a favorite toy, but it is unsafe for toddlers in the family care home.	Allow the child to enjoy telling you about their toy. Talk about the dangers for the little kids; choose a safe place to store the toy until the end of the day.
A pet is brought into the classroom unannounced.	Inform the pet owner that the pet must be kept outside. Schedule a pet visit following program policies.
A person walks by the play yard and stops to talk with a child at the fence.	Intervene immediately. Redirect the child and ask the person not to talk to children at play. Increase supervision along the fence.
After pick-up, parents stay to talk in the play yard. They do not monitor their children or enforce safety rules.	Approach the parents and explain the safety concerns; ask for their help. Suggest they come early to visit before pick-up.
A parent sends an unfamiliar person to preschool to pick up a child.	Keep the child in care. Contact the parent. Obtain verbal permission to release to the unfamiliar adult. Make a note of the conversation. Require new person to show photo identification.
A parent calls in and asks the teacher to send their child out to the car where they are waiting.	Remind the parent that the child can only be released directly to the parent. Work with the parent to create a workable pick-up plan.

Source: Sorte (from practice).

for families about the dangers of leaving children unattended in cars, a practice that has led to the deaths of many children due to heat suffocation. Teachers need to work with families immediately to resolve the dangerous situation. Families are most often appreciative of guidance that helps them keep their child safe. If families are resistant and the dangerous behavior is repeated, teachers may need to contact the police.

IMPLEMENTING SAFE MANAGEMENT PRACTICES

The early childhood years are a time of rapid change. Children grow from being vulnerable infants to active and involved young children. Greater skills and maturity help children learn how to recognize dangers and keep safe. But children's increasing abilities can also introduce new dangers. This means

SAFETY SEGMENT   Don't Leave Children in Motor Vehicles

Leaving children in motor vehicles is dangerous. Vehicles trap sunlight and heat like a greenhouse. It only takes 10 minutes for the heat inside a vehicle to become life threatening. When parked in the sun a vehicle can reach internal temperatures of up to 131 degrees. Even on mildly warm days of 60 degrees the passenger area of a vehicle can reach 110 degrees. Families need to know these safety rules:

- Never leave a child in an unattended vehicle even with the windows down.

- Sometimes a sleeping child is forgotten. Help busy families avoid mistakes. Tell them to place a needed item like a purse, lunch, or backpack in the backseat where they will see their child when they get out of the vehicle.

- Remind families to always lock the doors of their vehicles at home so children do not enter the car and accidentally lock themselves in.

- Teach children to never play in a vehicle.

- Call 911 if you see a child left unattended in a vehicle.

Sources: National Highway Traffic Safety Association. *Children and Cars: A Potentially Lethal Combination.* Retrieved February 1, 2012, from www.nhtsa.dot.gov/people/injury/enforce/ChildrenAndCars/pages/Unattend-HotCars.htm; Safe Kids, USA. *Preventing Injuries, at home, at play, and on the way: Safety in and around cars.* Retrieved February 1, 2012, from www.safekids.org/safety-basics/safety-resources-by-risk-area/in-and-around-cars/.

that teachers must understand appropriate safety management practices, be attuned to the safety needs of each age group, and prepared with strategies to teach all children safely.

Identifying Appropriate Safety Management Practices

When children's physical skills develop more rapidly than their reasoning skills and knowledge about danger, they may unknowingly put themselves in dangerous situations. For example, once toddlers discover walking, they enjoy testing their new skills by walking up stairs or in the direction of the street—unaware of the potential dangers. It is a mistake to "blame" very young children for acting in unsafe ways simply because they are young and inexperienced. Similarly, it is not helpful to "allow" older children to behave in unsafe ways based on the assumption that they should "know better." Teachers are responsible for using management strategies that keep pace with these changes.

The functions that guide appropriate safety management practices in the classroom are planning, managing and modeling, and teaching about safety.

1. *Planning for safety* includes ensuring that selected activities are suitable for children's physical capabilities, presented so that children can understand the consequences of dangerous behaviors, and supported with appropriate safety directions. For example, by about age 3, most typically developing children can understand that going down the slide is fun, but for safety they need to take turns and "Go down the slide feet first."

2. *Managing and modeling safety practices* are important ways teachers actively demonstrate their commitment to safety in all aspects of teaching. Teachers consider safety when arranging the environment: They model safe and appropriate interactions, such as how to safely put toys away or how to get ready to go outside, and they guide children to interact with the environment and one another in appropriate ways.

3. *Teaching appropriate safety messages* rounds out the spectrum of safety management approaches used in early childhood settings. Safety messages are taught in a gradual and progressive way across the early childhood years. This means that each safety message is introduced in a simple way that focuses on safety rather than dwelling on danger, then is repeated with more detail as children mature, and is reinforced through practice. The *Teaching Wellness* feature provides an example of how safety messages are introduced and gradually reinforced across the early childhood years.

Understanding the Safety Needs of Infants

In the first year of life, children develop from vulnerable infants to enthusiastic crawling or walking explorers. Safety management should encourage and not get in the way of this normal development. Exploration allows the child to gain practical abilities and knowledge as well as confidence that the environment is safe and inviting.

Using Infant Appropriate Safety Practices

In this **video**, a teacher changes a baby's diaper. What measures are taken by the teacher to ensure that the child is safe? Think about how she communicates with the child throughout the routine.

Safety for infants is based on individualized care rhythms such as a familiar schedule for eating and sleeping, as well as a safe environment, kind and caring touch, and appropriate encouraging conversation (NAEYC, 2012). In addition, teachers in infant care settings should:

- Check the environment for safety every day to ensure clean floors, covered electrical outlets, sturdy furnishings, no choking hazards, no rough or sharp surfaces, no blinds with pull strings, no bibs except during feeding, and no pacifiers on strings around necks.
- Label and store the infant's food, personal belongings, high chair, and crib appropriately.
- Place infants on their backs to sleep, alone in cribs with no toys, blankets, or bumper pads.
- Talk and sing to help infants associate the sound and feel of language with positive social connection and safe relationships.

LEARNING OUTCOME   **Children will name and describe safety rules.**

Vocabulary focus: Safety, rules, be careful.

Safety watch: Select appropriate toys and materials for use with each age group. Observe children's play, and reinforce the safety rules in appropriate settings.

INFANTS AND TODDLERS

- **Goal:** Babies and toddlers will experience the safety rule of "Be gentle with one another to keep from getting hurt."
- **Materials:** Play space, appropriate toys including people figures and toy animals.
- **Activity plan:** Set out the toys in a comfortable play space. Invite children to play. As they play demonstrate using words and gestures that convey caring and kindness. Say, "You are touching the toy doggie very gently. See how you can pet the toy doggie with no hurting? That's how we can

take care of him." Redirect rough touching by guiding children's hands and modeling careful touch.
- **How to adjust the activity:** Assist children with motor challenges by moving their hands to stroke a stuffed animal. Repeat the message in both English and the child's home language. Share your class safety rules with families so they can reinforce the concepts at home.
- **Did you meet your goal?** Did children hear kind words and see the teacher modeling care for people and toys?

PRESCHOOLERS AND KINDERGARTNERS

- **Goal:** Children will name classroom safety rules and tell how the rules help keep children safe.
- **Materials:** Large photos of children at play in different school activities (cutting and pasting, eating, climbing steps on the slide). Tape each photo on a large sheet of paper.
- **Activity plan:** Gather children for a group time. Tell them that rules are made to help people keep safe from getting hurt. Show the pictures one at a time. Invite children to think of a safety rule. Help children get started by asking, "Is there a way a person could get hurt when doing this activity?" Guide the children to think of a rule that could help children keep safe. For example, "At cutting activities the rule is to sit down

when cutting. We have this rule so the scissors don't poke anyone." Write the rule on the poster and place them where children can see and talk about them at mealtimes.
- **How to adjust the activity:** Teach and reinforce the safety rule concept by asking the children to look at the photos and act out the safety rule for each setting. Provide time for each child to respond, and reinforce all efforts. Learn and teach the vocabulary words in the home languages of the children. Post the safety rules in multiple languages as appropriate.
- **Did you meet your goal?** Are children able to identify safety practices? Can they explain how the rules help keep children safe?

YOUNG SCHOOL-AGE CHILDREN

- **Goal:** Children will identify rules for several school settings: the classroom, the cafeteria, the bus, outdoors, and field trips. They will be able to explain the rules to others.
- **Materials:** Poster-sized paper, marking pens, tape.
- **Activity plan:** Talk about how rules help people remember to be safe. Create small groups. Ask each group to select a school setting and create a poster listing 2–4 safety rules for that setting. Invite children to illustrate their poster. Gather the children together. Ask each group to tell the others about the rules for each class setting, and how the rules keep children safe. Invite the rest of the class to give feedback and offer additional ideas. Post the posters where others can see the children's work and learn the safety rules.
- **How to adjust the activity:** Monitor the small groups as they work to develop their safety rules. Provide support as needed to ensure that each child has a chance to offer an idea for a rule and add to the illustrations. Provide extra time if needed for children to complete their posters. Support each child's efforts when presenting their poster to the class.
- **Did you meet your goal?** Are children able to identify rules for various school settings and explain the rules to others?

Petee reminds his friends to hold hands and stay together when they go on field trips.

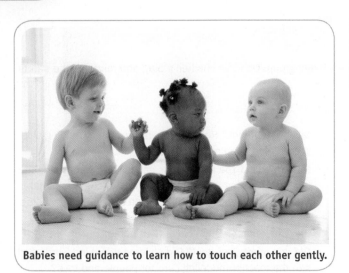

Babies need guidance to learn how to touch each other gently.

Managing for Safety

Managing the behavior of infants is a basic part of the everyday teacher and child interaction. Key management approaches for infant safety include the following:

- Supervise how babies interact with materials. Be sure to sanitize dropped pacifiers and toys and make sure toys that have been in mouths are not exchanged with other babies.
- Guide interactions. Help children touch without grabbing at eyes or earrings, saying, "Pat Lin-Lin's cheek gently like this."
- Protect infants from older and more mobile children who may be playing nearby. This guides older children about how to interact with the baby, while protecting the infant.

Teaching Safety Messages

Teachers of infants convey important safety messages by establishing safe and trusting environments and teaching babies to interact appropriately. Teachers reinforce these positive messages when they:

- Respond to the infant's needs.
- Place the infant to eat and sleep in safe positions.
- Use gentle touching and ensure comforting sounds.

Understanding the Safety Needs of Toddlers

The toddler years (from walking to age 3) are a time of increasingly active movement, exploration, and interest in independence. Teachers should take advantage of this enthusiasm by guiding children to participate safely in their environment and with each other.

Using Toddler Appropriate Safety Practices

Teachers of toddlers should address safety by recognizing that the toddlers' greater mobility may lead them to climb higher, toddle further, and engage with materials in new and inventive ways. Important safety practices for toddlers include the following:

- Review the environment for safety. Be sure child safety locks are used on cupboards and furniture is sturdy so children can pull themselves up to a standing position and balance without worry of furniture tipping over.
- Provide toileting supports, including potty chairs, child-sized toilets, child-accessible sinks or sturdy stepstools, so children can gain toileting skills while being closely monitored.
- Arrange open spaces for play and provide plenty of time for toddlers to move and explore without undue restrictions.
- Monitor toys, sensory bin materials, and food for potential choking hazards.
- Offer finger-food options that promote independence but do not present choking hazards.
- Label and store children's personal items and sleeping mat or cot.

Managing for Safety

Toddlers need close supervision. They have discovered the joys of movement and seek independence, but may have relatively limited ability to communicate and sometimes are not able to achieve the goals they are aiming for. A child might move the helpful teacher's hand away saying, "Alex do it. Alex big boy." Or a child might respond to frustrating situations through familiar toddler behaviors such as scratching or biting, behaviors that cause grief for children, teachers, and parents. The teacher should stay as close as necessary to recognize when such behaviors are about to occur, and be ready to intervene immediately to prevent the problem behavior and redirect the child to productive play. If a problem occurs, management should be clear and direct (NAEYC, 2012):

- Firmly state what the child should do: "No biting!" or "No running to the street!"
- Briefly state why: "Biting hurts" or "Streets are dangerous!"
- Provide an alternative: "You can play with these blocks. At snack time you can bite an apple" or "Here is the safe place to run. Let's go!"

What if . . .

a toddler you were playing and laughing with suddenly reached out and grabbed your glasses? How would you respond?

Teaching Safety Messages

Safety messages for toddlers are taught through modeling safe practices, introducing rules, and teaching words to encourage safe play. This approach helps toddlers see appropriate behavior and connect words with their meaning. For example, the teacher might guide a child's hand to poke a tofu cube with a small fork while saying, "Use the fork to poke the tofu. No poking people." Adding facial expressions that reinforce the "yes" and "no" part of the message increases the likelihood of correct communication. The toddler might repeat back the message, "Poke fu," while nodding his head up and down in affirmation. Other toddler-relevant safety messages taught through modeling actions and words include these:

- *Use gentle touch:* Keep from poking or scratching eyes and faces, or pulling earrings.
- *Stay back from dangers:* Beware of hot stoves, broken glass, unknown animals, and swings.
- *Eat and drink safely:* Sit while eating and drinking; eat slowly and remember to chew.
- *Move about safely:* Watch out for tabletops that stick out at eye level; go down slides feet first.
- *Interact safely in the environment:* Say, "The flower is for touching and smelling, but not eating." Use phrases like "The window is just for looking, not hitting."
- *Play safely:* Say, "Look Jenna, hold the truck down here where it is away from Leon's eyes. Down here is the safe place for your truck."

Safety messages can be introduced to toddlers using storybooks or puppet dramas. Positive and negative facial expressions also help to reinforce meaning.

Understanding the Safety Needs of Preschoolers

Preschool children (ages 3 to 5 years) mature from playing individually or alongside other children to being highly interested in interactive play. They are increasingly able to move, run, and climb quickly and are capable of sustained involvement with activities and inventive dramatic play. Preschool children are also able to learn, implement, and teach others important safety routines. Safety management strategies should respect these increasing capabilities while also empowering children with knowledge to recognize dangers and ways to keep safe.

Using Preschooler Appropriate Safety Practices

Teachers enhance safety for active preschoolers by creating environments where children can test their skills in appropriate ways, encouraging children to try solving problems, and supporting the development of self-help skills (National Association for the Education of Young Children, 2009). Safety practices for preschool-age children include the following:

- Arrange the environment so children can be self-directed. Ensure that furniture is stable and toys are organized on low shelves where children can easily reach them. Store large toys on the floor or bottom shelf so children can get them without danger of pulling them down on themselves.
- Encourage the development of safe self-help skills. Set out tubs for toys, or dirty dishes, so children can pick up after play time, and clear their spaces after meals. The *Progressive Programs & Practices* feature describes how one program works to encourage children's self-help skills by offering a snack area during choice time.
- Label a cubby or hook for the child's coat and a cot or sleeping mat for each child's consistent use. Create labels that use the language the child speaks to encourage literacy awareness.
- Provide access to toileting at will, if possible. Supervise children when they are toileting.

PROGRESSIVE PROGRAMS & PRACTICES

Managing Hunger with the Smart Snack Area

By Roni Cohen Leiderman, Dean, Mailman Segal Center for Human Development of Nova Southeastern University

The Mailman Segal Center for Human Development of Nova Southeastern University, in Ft. Lauderdale, Florida, houses preschool, infant/toddler, and parenting programs. We have 43 classrooms with over 1,000 participating children and families. Our nationally accredited preschool programs and clinical services serve the community and offer a learning laboratory for professional training and development in a variety of fields.

What Challenge Did You Face?

Unlike a home environment, where a young child can request food or drink, children in group care oftentimes are on regimented schedules without easy access to snacks and meals. The challenge we saw with this typical setup was twofold. First, we were not teaching children to pay attention to their body's signals. Very young children modulate their hunger and thirst via signals but as they mature, their food intake is controlled by schedules. The second challenge was how to incorporate healthy eating habits whereby children could have access to healthy food choices throughout the day within the confines of a classic preschool program schedule.

How Did You Meet This Challenge?

We generated possible solutions with parents and staff before deciding on a plan of action. Families in our program take turns being the "snack parent or grandparent" and bring sufficient food items for all the children in their class. We have always given families clear guidelines for healthy snack foods and drinks and ask that sugary, artificially flavored, or high-sodium foods be replaced with whole grains, natural foods, and fresh fruits and vegetables.

After considerable discussion and research, staff suggested a unique snack program to implement quality effective teaching practices and would simultaneously support children's well-being from a nutritional perspective. The idea was to set up a snack table known as the Smart Snack area that would function similarly to other areas of interest (art, manipulatives, imaginative play, etc.). Each day, the family responsible for the snack would work with their child and the classroom staff to put the food, drink, napkins, utensils, and plates on the table. The area would be located near the sink so that children would wash their hands before eating. The snack area would be open during self-selected play and small-group time. Visuals with pictures and simple words would be displayed reminding children to wash their hands, throw out their trash, and clean their area when done as well as offering suggested "recipes." For example, when Maya's mom brought strawberries, whole grain crackers, and cream cheese, sturdy cardboard cards showed step by step how to make a cream cheese and strawberry sandwich. Child-sized pitchers with water and cups would always be available.

At first, parents and teachers had some concerns about the approach: Would children sit and eat too long or in preference to other learning and play areas in the classroom? Would the setting be difficult to monitor?

What Was the Outcome?

During the first few weeks, the children spent a lot of time at the snack table, but as time went on, the approach developed a rhythm of its own. Children began using the snack table less often, an indication that they were eating less for the novelty and were better able to tune into their individual body signals indicating that they were hungry or thirsty. While at the Smart Snack table, rich language developed as did fine motor skills for pouring and spreading. Independence and cooperative skills increased as children shared, negotiated for chairs, and used proper hygiene as modeled by the teachers and posted on the displays. The preschoolers developed an illustrated cookbook of their favorite recipes and the children began to recognize the sight words that were matched to the pictures of the daily snack suggestions.

Even with the success of the Smart Snack program, some teachers would like to return to scheduled snack times. We continue to dialogue and discover ways to handle logistical challenges while maintaining the program. We have a commitment to the children who spend long hours away from home and family. We aim to nurture, protect, teach, and play with the children in our care in ways that foster beneficial habits and pave the way for a healthy future.

Managing for Safety

Preschool teachers need to be constantly alert for potential safety problems. Preschool-age children move independently and quickly and are increasingly interested in social interactions. They can develop intense play themes that may introduce dangers, such as making and eating "stew" from leaves and mushrooms during outdoor play. Or they may follow the unsafe behaviors of other children, such as running up the slide, climbing around equipment and barriers, and jumping from high platforms. Here are some strategies for managing safety for preschoolers:

- Teach children the boundaries for activity and safety.
- Recognize and reinforce safe behaviors with a smile, a wink, or a whisper.
- Guide children to recognize the effect of their unsafe actions. Say, "If you keep riding your tricycle toward the hopscotch area, someone may get hurt."
- Teach children strategies to assert and communicate their needs in unsafe settings. Say, "Tell her you don't want to do that. It is not safe."
- Supervise children's social interactions and intervene in bullying situations.
- Move actively and confidently to correct unsafe behaviors.

Young children are able to understand safety messages such as look but do not touch.

Teaching Safety Messages

Preschool children are growing in their ability to understand the cause and effects of behaviors and are able to understand and learn safety messages. However, teaching preschool children about dangers has the possibility of introducing worries, and ultimately such discussions may convey the message that sometimes things occur that adults cannot control. For example, teaching children to evacuate for a fire drill introduces the concept that fires might happen. Safety messages need to be presented in ways that are appropriate for the child to understand and that avoid overdramatizing worrisome events. Typical safety messages for preschool children include:

- Follow the teacher's directions to leave the classroom in case of emergency.
- Get down and take cover in case of a tornado or earthquake.
- Keep away from dangerous materials (matches and lighters, paints, cleaning supplies, poisons, hot beverages), strange animals, and strangers.
- Eat only the foods given to you by your family or teacher.
- Play safely outdoors and follow the rules of games.

Safety messages can be taught through books and flannel board stories that depict children responding appropriately in potentially dangerous situations. Visits by safety officers such as firefighters and police officers, field trips to locations where safety lessons can be discussed in context such as swimming pools, and dramatic play settings that allow children to explore safety topics are also effective ways to teach about safety.

Teaching safety messages to preschoolers can also begin to introduce self-awareness concepts. For example, as preschool children develop greater language skills, they become more able to communicate about worries, fears, or experiences that threaten them. Teachers support this process by helping children learn to recognize and name their emotions. Pictures showing various facial expressions, such as those in Figure 14-5, can help children identify and learn to express how they feel. Learning to recognize and understand their own emotions and those of others is a developmental task of early childhood.

FIGURE 14-5
Helping Children Identify Emotions

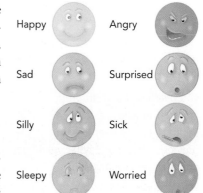

Happy   Angry

Sad   Surprised

Silly   Sick

Sleepy   Worried

Understanding the Safety Needs of School-Age Children

School-age children (ages 5 and older) are more mobile and often are allowed to move independently in their neighborhood and travel on their own to school (Centers for Disease Control and Prevention, National Center for Injury Prevention and Control, 2006). This is also an impressionable age group where heroic television characters and other media-driven images are infused into their experience, potentially confusing children's understanding about realistic abilities. Greater independence can place school-age children in unsupervised settings, increasing the potential for unintentional injury. At the same time these children are capable of learning and following safety rules and telling others about safety. Teachers need to maintain attention to safety practices, while focusing more on teaching children about how to keep safe and supervising from a greater distance.

Using School-Age Appropriate Safety Practices

Safety practices for school-age children continue to focus on safe environments and appropriate activities. Teachers need to avoid thinking that children's greater maturity and capability suggest they know how to keep safe. Safety practices for school-age children include the following:

- Model safe behaviors and establish boundaries for movement and behavior.
- Plan activities that provide appropriate challenge as well as opportunities to learn about safety hazards and ways to keep safe.
- Ensure that children do not have access to dangerous items such as matches, lighters, harmful cleaning products, poisons, alcohol, drugs, firearms, and sharp knives.
- Be aware of peer pressure and the influences of older children who may be intrigued by dangerous items; listen for interest in fire, smoking, firearms, explosives, drugs, alcohol, and other dangerous products, which may be signs of inappropriate interactions.
- Recognize when children are becoming tired and need guidance to stop and rest.

Managing for Safety

Various unsafe behaviors may be exhibited and boundaries may be tested with intensity during the school-age years, making managing for safety a challenge. Behaviors teachers may need to confront include children using materials inventively but unsafely, trying "daredevil" behaviors, and bullying other children by telling them they "can't play." Although these may be typical ways in which children explore and test their skills, they are also examples of times when teachers must help children identify boundaries (Gartrell & Gartrell, 2008). Teachers should reaffirm that inappropriate and dangerous behaviors will not be allowed. Safety management strategies include:

- Focus on behaviors and provide clear messages that communicate the problem and confirm that unsafe behaviors are not allowed. Say, "That tree is dangerous to climb; you need to come down."
- Direct the industriousness and productivity of this age; provide new challenges and opportunities for children to explore.
- Help children build leadership skills; guide them to resolve conflicts and identify safe alternatives.

Teachers redirect unsafe behaviors by providing interesting opportunities for both individual and group activities. Planning a variety of appropriate activities that appeal to everyone, such as crafts, hobbies, information about collecting, and photography, is another useful strategy.

Teaching Safety Messages

Safety messages for school-age children focus on preventive safety themes. Safety topics for this age group include:

- How to ride a bicycle safely (wear a helmet; follow the rules of the road).
- How to be a safe passenger in the car (keeping hands and head inside the car, not distracting the driver) and in the bus (how to get on and off the bus safely).
- How to call 911 for help in case of an emergency.

What if . . .

you overheard a small group of children in your class talking about a gun they had been looking at the previous afternoon? What would you do with this information?

- How to respond if a stranger approaches and who to go to for help.
- Staying away from sick or injured animals.
- Staying away from guns, knives, and other sharp objects.
- Staying away from deep water; don't go swimming without an adult.
- How to safely use e-mail and the Internet.
- How to stay home alone for short periods of time (for older school-age children).

Preventive messages can be more abstract than with younger children because this age group is increasingly able to discuss dangers that they may not have actually experienced. For example, children are capable of learning how to stay away from matches and other things that are hot using the, "I Spy Something Hot" plan (Start Safe Kids USA, 2009).

Group problem-solving approaches, such as classroom meetings, are effective in helping school-age children gain skills to address safety issues (Nast, 2012). Teachers who hold regular classroom meetings can use this opportunity to discuss problems like bullying or unsafe behaviors (National Education Association, 2012). The group process could unfold like this: Children gather in a circle, discuss the problem, and offer solutions by following simple rules such as letting everyone speak, listening, and being respectful (Gartrell, 2006). The teacher should guide the process, providing sufficient time for children to have their point of view heard, while moving children through the process of negotiation. The use of long and drawn-out problem-solving meetings to help children resolve small-scale issues is counterproductive and often ends up with children forgetting what the issue was about. An example of steps in group problem solving is provided in Figure 14-6.

Understanding the Safety Needs of Children with Special Needs

Sometimes, due to lack of information or experience, teachers might be hesitant about how to ensure the safety of children with special developmental needs in the classroom. The Americans with Disabilities Act (ADA) guides teachers to not make assumptions about how a child will behave or what the child can learn simply because the child has an identified disability or special health care need. Instead it is important to consider children's individual safety needs related to the potential of the program to reasonably meet those needs. For example, children may need adaptive supports or special assistance to increase safety, those with food allergies or food restrictions may need special monitoring, and children with special health needs such as diabetes or seizure disorders may require special health and safety routines. Understanding the child's

---

FIGURE 14-6 Sample Group Problem Solving Process

1. Identify the issue. [Tricycles are parked in front of the door.]
2. Talk about why the issue is a safety problem. [The tricycles block the door so people can not come in; people might trip over the tricycles.]
3. Think about ways the problem could be solved. [Not let children ride tricycles? Park the tricycles against the wall? Make "no tricycle parking" signs?]
4. Choose one or two resolutions to try. [Park tricycles against the wall and make "no parking" signs for the door.]
5. Agree on the plan. [Heather and Connor will make signs.]
6. Implement the resolution. [Try it for a few days.]
7. Do a check-up. [Is it working?]

Source: Sorte (from practice).

NUTRITION NOTE   Classroom Activities That Can Introduce Food Allergens

It is estimated that up to 8% of children under the age of 3 have food-related allergies. Food allergies are the most common cause of anaphylactic shock, which if untreated can lead to death. To keep children safe, early childhood teachers need to be cautious to avoid introducing food allergens through curriculum activities.

Common Food Allergens	Activities That May Bring These Allergens into the Classroom
Eggs	• Cooking activities that include eggs (muffins or pancakes)
	• Egg cartons used for craft activities
Cow's milk	• Cooking activities that use milk (bread or smoothies)
	• Finger-painting using pudding made with milk
Peanuts	• Bird feeders made with pinecones, peanut butter, and birdseed
	• Peanuts used in the sensory table or for counting games
Wheat	• Play dough made with wheat flour
	• Cooking and baking activities that use wheat flour
	• Noodle necklaces made with wheat-based pasta
Soy	• Mosaics made with soybeans
	• Tambourines or maracas made using soybeans for "sound"

Source: Based on "Symposium: Pediatric Food Allergy," by S. H. Sicherer et al., 2003, *Pediatrics, 111*(6), 1591–1594.

capabilities, identifying support strategies, and drafting an action plan are logical steps in meeting children's unique safety needs.

Implementing Appropriate Safety Practices

Safety routines for children with special needs are created in collaboration with families, early interventionists, medical providers, and others who advise the teacher about safety accommodations (AAP et al., 2011). Safety routines include:

- Addressing children's need for physical supports by acquiring special equipment such as adaptive scissors or chairs with seat belts for security.
- Supporting children's individual behavior needs by providing extra guidance and supervision during playtime, and using a variety of communication methods such as accompanying gestures to reinforce spoken language or picture schedules to depict what children should do during transition time (put toys away, wash hands, sit down for snack) (Hanline, Nunes, & Worthy, 2007).
- Creating a health management plan specific for each child who has special health needs or allergies.

Monitoring for Food Allergies

Special attention is needed to ensure that all children can participate in activities. The impacts of food allergies for example, extend beyond careful menu planning. Curriculum activities also need to be monitored to ensure that they do not introduce food allergens. The *Nutrition Note* explores some common food allergens and ways they might be brought into the classroom through curriculum activities. Planning cooking activities that are safe for all children is supported by creating a classroom-specific cookbook in which recipes are reviewed and coded according to the dietary restrictions of children in the class, such as nut-free, egg-free, or milk-free.

Managing for Safety

Safety management for children with special needs focuses on the individual child's maturity and ability to understand and recognize danger and follow safety guidance. Teachers need to think individually about a child's unique situation and implement focused strategies that are clear and straightforward. In practice, many of these strategies are appropriate to use with all children. Some examples are listed next.

For children with special developmental needs:

- Use direct and clear language, supplemented by gestures or photographs to communicate and reinforce sequenced responses where appropriate.
- Place danger picture codes or "Stop" signs near boundaries or areas of danger.

For children with specific health concerns:

- Clearly state the safety concern: "You have a special condition called diabetes."
- Describe the purpose of any safety measures: "We need to test your blood sugar levels and choose just the right foods for your snack."
- Help the child know what to expect: "After group time we will go into the quiet corner where we can concentrate while we test your blood. I'll wear gloves and you can sit on the story chair. Then we will join the other children at snack."
- Teach the child to explain his or her health condition to others as a way of fostering normal conversation about the child's specific health safety need: "I have to eat a snack that is just right for my body."

For children who are learning English:

- Talk with families or others who can provide safety words in the child's home language. Create note cards with the directions written phonetically.
- Provide books that present safety issues and are written in the child's home language. Request that the family assist you in teaching the safety message.
- Use clearly spoken English with gestures when giving safety directions. Repeat and demonstrate what is expected. Use inviting and encouraging expressions.

Guidance reminders should be presented clearly, repeated frequently, and followed consistently to avoid confusion. Reminding children of rules that have been discussed previously can seem frustrating to teachers, but should be done kindly and with a steady voice, remembering that for some children learning the safety rules will take longer.

Teaching Safety Messages

Safety messages for children with special needs should be appropriate for the child's developmental ability to understand and accomplish and should be relevant to the child's special situation. The teacher also needs to be able to assess the degree to which the child can recognize, understand, and respond appropriately to danger. Each child's needs may be unique. For this reason teachers should seek guidance and assess the effectiveness of strategies as they are tried, in order to be prepared to teach appropriate safety messages to the child. Examples of safety messages and safety responses for children with special needs include the following:

- *Children with physical disabilities:* Guide children to recognize and avoid safety hazards, such as learning to look for uneven pavement that may cause tripping.
- *Children who have hearing impairments:* Teach children to look at the teacher when she gives safety directions because not doing so might be dangerous. Help children recognize the flashing lights or vibrations of the emergency alarm, and learn to watch for environmental cues such as other people lining up at the door during evacuation drills.

- *Children who have vision impairments:* Teach children where to find the emergency exit and how to recognize the smell of smoke. Practice an evacuation drill using the emergency exit. Keep the furniture pattern consistent and the pathway to the emergency exit clear, as this provides cues that help the child find the exit.
- *Children who move in wheelchairs:* Ensure that the emergency exit is wheelchair accessible. Teach children how to use the emergency exit during an evacuation drill.
- *Children with ADHD:* Teach children to use visual cues, such as a picture of a stop sign on the door, or for an older child, a sign that says "Wait for the teacher" to remind children what to do to be safe. Post rules where children see them easily. Rehearse emergency scenarios.
- *Children with diabetes:* Help the child begin to recognize the warning signs of low blood sugar levels, so they can tell you, "I feel low." Manage the use of glucose tablets or gel, juice, and other emergency foods (as indicated in the diabetes medical management plan) and explain how the foods are used in case of low blood sugar levels.
- *Children with special health concerns:* Help children learn to recognize personal safety hazards and, when age appropriate, how to monitor personal safety, such as teaching a child with asthma to wear a dust mask when sanding wood at the workbench, or guiding and supporting a child with food allergies to not eat certain foods.
- *Children who are learning English:* Teach children the words and gestures for safety, including *stop* and *dangerous.* Enlist the support of the family to help you reinforce the meaning of these safety words.

Managing Challenging Behaviors

Sometimes children's behaviors are intense and dangerous to themselves or others. Challenging behaviors can threaten safety as children test boundaries and rules, such as climbing on furniture or using playground equipment in irrational and unsafe ways. Challenging behaviors can also introduce unsafe situations when children bite, hit, scratch, kick, or bully others. These behaviors can be very damaging for the child who is out of control, the child or teacher who is the target of the behavior, and all the children of the group who are at risk for feeling insecure and unsafe in the setting.

Teachers need to develop guidance strategies to help children be safe and appropriate in the social setting (Fox & Garrison, 2009). *Guidance* is a method of teaching that promotes children's understanding and ability to appropriately manage their behaviors. Guidance is different from *discipline*, which tends to be associated with punitive approaches used to enforce acceptable behavior. Guidance helps children avoid interpersonal conflicts or outbursts during which they might hurt themselves or others (Alter & Conroy, 2007).

Teachers should work closely with families to explore the child's behaviors and to identify guidance approaches that can be reinforced in both the school and home environments (Alter & Conroy, 2007). Such interventions help children learn to manage their behaviors and become more able to listen to and follow directions, both of which are crucial responses in emergency situations. In the opening case scenario, Jean experienced a high level of discouragement due to a variety of challenging behaviors. She needed to summon the courage to reflect on her classroom management style and seek support to help her create a plan for improvement. This is a good example of the efforts that teachers make to manage behaviors safety in the group setting.

Reinforcing Safety Messages

Guiding children to be safe should be central to the early childhood curriculum. Recognizing the safety lessons in daily activities and helping children understand safety as important in their lives are ways teachers reinforce safety messages and prepare children for the future.

Infusing Safety Messages in Everyday Lessons

Reinforcing safety messages through everyday activities helps children begin to recognize that they deserve—and can achieve—safety and security in their lives (Bales, Wallinga, & Coleman, 2005). Learning to stack blocks so the tower does not fall over teaches children about careful touch and the consequences of being rough. Achieving success, such as carrying a cup of water so it does not spill, teaches children the benefits of practice. Teachers support these lessons by helping children recognize the safety skills that they are developing.

Using Teachable Moments

Sometimes unplanned situations can become useful teaching opportunities. For example, while the teacher's first response to an accident is to care for the injury and comfort the child, these situations can also be learning moments if they are handled with understanding. After administering needed first aid, the teacher could hug the child and state, "Bumping heads hurts! Next time if you walk slowly around the corner it will help you see the bookshelf, and keep from bumping your head." This acknowledges the hurt while offering the child a strategy to avoid the accident in the future.

Making Safety Relevant to Children's Lives

Safety messages are most effective if they are relevant and meaningful to children's experiences. If children experience events that make them feel unsafe, such as accidents or frightening storms, teachers can help them discover ways to address their worries such as telling their family when they are scared. Some children witness acts of violence through the media or in their neighborhoods. Storybooks that explore potentially frightening scenarios, describing how the character demonstrates strength and resilience in difficult situations, can support conversations about how children can learn to keep safe.

Safety messages should also be tailored to dangers children might find in or around their home or community. Children in rural settings may benefit from safety messages that relate to farm animals, use of farm equipment, and staying away from irrigation canals. Children in urban areas should be taught about how to safely ride on the subway or use elevators.

Although teachers impart safety knowledge of many kinds, they often do not know in the long run if the safety lessons they teach will, in fact, keep children safe in the future. By using effective management practices, teachers provide a place and a period of time where children can be secure and have a chance to learn, and where the ideas of a safe environment and safe and positive interactions are planted.

● SUMMARY

Effective classroom management in early childhood settings relies on the development of practices that, when used systematically, increase children's safety in the setting. Planning ahead creates the foundation for safety and offers a rhythm to the classroom day where children's safety is of primary importance.

Supervision is crucial to children's safety. Teachers must be prepared to supervise children in a variety of settings and to use appropriate strategies, professional experiences, and common sense to anticipate and address safety concerns.

Teachers also need to understand and address the safety needs of all children. By adapting safety management strategies to fit children's developmental capabilities, and making safety relevant to children's lives, teachers guide children to establish patterns of safety that benefit them now and in the future.

REVIEW QUESTIONS

1. Describe some of the safety management practices that are established even before children attend the class.
2. Name the two key elements of safe supervision. Give examples of situations that require special attention to safety.
3. What is meant by the term *supervision zones* as applied to outdoor environments?
4. Identify some of the safety messages that are unique for children with special developmental or health needs.
5. Describe how safety messages can be infused in the daily curriculum.

DISCUSSION STARTERS

1. Classroom safety routines are important to the development of safety habits in the early childhood setting. Identify a classroom safety routine you think is important and discuss why.
2. Parents often rely on family and friends to help them transport their children to care. Discuss what you would do if "Auntie Janet" came to pick up Meg, a preschooler in your care, but her name is not on your list of persons authorized to pick Meg up from school.
3. Supervising children for safety requires teachers to adapt their strategies to meet the changing needs of children as they grow and mature. Discuss some of the ways in which supervising preschoolers and school-age children are the same and ways that are different.

PRACTICE POINTS

1. Using the Web Resources section as a guide, search the Internet for an article that discusses a current issue related to safe practices for early childhood classrooms.
2. Identify a potential field trip destination for a kindergarten class. Visit the site and make a list of potential safety hazards. Explain how you would ensure children's safety at the location.
3. Create a newsletter for families that communicates the safety rules for your classroom. Provide an explanation for each safety rule that describes how the rule improves safety while also allowing children to explore and learn.

WEB RESOURCES

National Association for Child Care Resource & Referral Agencies
www.naccrra.org

National Association for the Education of Young Children
www.naeyc.org

National Education Association, Promoting Effective Classroom Management
www.nea.org/tools/14367.htm

U.S. Department of Health & Human Services, Early Childhood Learning and Knowledge Center
http://eclkc.ohs.acf.hhs.gov/hslc

Zero to Three
www.zerotothree.org

MyEducationLab™

Go to Topic 11 (Safe Environments) in the MyEducationLab (www.myeducationlab.com)
for your course, where you can:

- Find learning outcomes for Safe Environments along with the national standards that connect to these outcomes.

- Complete Assignments and Activities that can help you more deeply understand the chapter content.

- Apply and practice your understanding of the core teaching skills identified in the chapter with the Building Teaching Skills and Dispositions learning units.

- Check your comprehension on the content covered in the chapter by going to the Study Plan in the Book Resources for your text. Here you will be able to take a chapter quiz, receive feedback on your answers, and then access Review, Practice, and Enrichment activities to enhance your understanding of chapter content.

learning outcomes

AFTER READING THIS CHAPTER, YOU SHOULD BE ABLE TO:

1. Outline the components of an Emergency Response Plan and discuss why it is important for teachers to obtain emergency first aid and CPR training from credible training organizations.

2. Describe the actions to take when assessing a child for signs of injury and discuss the steps of infant and child CPR.

3. Explain what is meant by shelter-in-place, lockdown, evacuation, and relocation, and describe when each of these actions is recommended.

4. Describe ways that teachers help children regain a sense of security and develop resilience following emergencies and disaster events.

Jamal runs a family child care program that serves five children ages 2 to 5 years. Everyone is enjoying being outside. The children select balls from a cart that Jamal rolled out into the grass. Mattie and Tristan toss balls across the grass. Callie and Ahmed, who are older, run after the balls and roll them back. They are laughing as the brightly colored balls bump across the yard.

Jamal smiles as he watches them. Then he hears a crash and turns to discover that 2-year-old Kevin has pulled the ball cart over on top of himself. As Jamal quickly removes the cart, he sees that Kevin has been badly cut. A bright red welt runs from Kevin's forehead across his eyebrow and cheek, and blood is pouring out of his nose and mouth. Kevin's eyes are open and staring, but he is completely silent. Jamal crouches down to assess the situation and puts on the plastic gloves that he always carries in his pocket. The other children gather about him. He calls out to Kevin saying, "Hey, Kevin. Hey, buddy! Are you ok?" Kevin blinks and looks at Jamal. Then he takes in a big breath and begins to cry and reach out to Jamal.

Jamal gently picks Kevin up and, calling for the other children to follow, carries him through to the kitchen where he has the first aid supplies stored. He shifts Kevin to his hip and directs Callie and Ahmed to entertain the younger children in the book corner. Jamal opens sterile gauze pads and presses them to Kevin's nose and mouth. He rocks his body back and forth saying, "It's ok, it's ok now, Kevin. We're going to make it better." Kevin is puffing and whimpering but settles in against Jamal. Jamal picks up the phone and calls Kevin's mother Mimi, who is at work. She says that she will come as soon as she can.

Then Jamal moves to sit with Kevin where they can see the other children playing. He continues to hold the gauze against Kevin's face and distracts him by talking quietly about the story the children are "reading." Kevin's eyes move to watch the other children, but he seems groggy and drowsy. When Mimi arrives she is alarmed by Kevin's appearance. Jamal encourages her to take Kevin to the doctor. They tape the gauze gently against Kevin's cheeks.

After they leave Jamal ties the soiled gauze and latex gloves in a plastic bag, disinfects the nearby surfaces, and washes his hands. Then he helps the other children get ready for nap time. That evening Jamal checks the ball cart and sees that a protective cover for one of the supports has fallen off. It looks like it can be repaired, but he sets the cart in the garage until later when he can work on it carefully. Then he calls Mimi and learns that Kevin needed stitches, but that he should be fine.

Early childhood teachers assume a complex range of responsibilities when caring for and educating young children. They must attend to the small injuries that occur and sometimes must manage more serious emergencies. In order for teachers like Jamal to respond efficiently, they need to be able to recognize when an injury is an emergency. Teachers must have an emergency management plan in place and be prepared with skills and confidence to take action if needed. Teachers must also be prepared for disaster situations and have a plan to supervise children until they can be released to their families.

In this chapter we discuss the planning processes that help teachers prepare to take effective action and describe the steps in basic first aid. This information does not replace the need for teachers to obtain first aid and emergency response training from credible authorities. Together emergency preparedness and periodic training assist teachers to respond effectively to keep children safe.

● PREPARING FOR EMERGENCIES

Any injury to a young child is alarming. The child may be crying and vigorously moving or be unnaturally quiet and still. Blood may be spilling profusely or the child may be blanched and pale. Some emergencies are disasters that can occur without warning, and cause unimaginable destruction. Such events are shocking to witness, and challenging to experience. In these difficult moments teachers are called on to:

- Recognize that a significant incident has occurred.
- Make a focused assessment of the nature of the incident.
- Respond quickly and appropriately.
- Ensure children are safe and cared for.

It can be challenging to remain calm and make decisions in such stressful situations. Even so, the moment an emergency is recognized, the process of effective response begins. Teachers need to be prepared to assess the nature of the emergency and be guided by an emergency response plan. Preparing for emergencies is a way to prevent or reduce harmful impacts to children.

Defining Emergencies

While teachers are responsible for doing all they can to keep children safe from unintentional injury or the effects of illness, serious and unforeseen situations can occur. These situations include emergencies and disasters, which are defined as follows:

- An **emergency** is any situation that threatens the life of the child or that presents risk for permanent injury or disability (National Association of Child Care Resource & Referral Agencies [NACCRRA] and Save the Children, 2010).
- A **disaster** is the result of any event or combination of events that overwhelms the ability to restore safety and order in a short period of time.

MyEducationLab™

Visit the MyEducationLab for *Nutrition, Health, and Safety for Young Children* to enhance your understanding of chapter concepts with a personalized Study Plan. You'll also have the opportunity to hone your teaching skills through video-based Assignments and Activities, as well as Building Teaching Skills and Dispositions lessons.

emergency
any situation that threatens the life of the child or that presents risk for permanent injury or disability

disaster
an event that overwhelms available community emergency response resources and often results in widespread injury, death, and destruction of property

Some emergencies occur as the result of disasters. Several types of emergency situations may threaten children's safety (American Academy of Pediatrics, American Public Health Association, National Resource Center for Health and Safety in Child Care and Early Education, 2011; NACCRRA & Save the Children, 2010). These include:

- *Health emergencies.* These are caused by serious injury, severe health concerns, or potentially deadly disease epidemics, such as avian flu, H1N1, or other pandemic flu illnesses.
- *Natural disasters.* These include events caused by nature, such as hurricanes, tornadoes, wildfires, or floods. They are sometimes referred to as "acts of God."
- *Technological disasters.* These are caused by industrial sources and exposure to hazardous materials. Examples include loss of electricity or water, fires, and chemical or oil spills.
- *Attacks and threats to personal safety.* These acts of violence include threats from guns, sniper fire, bomb threats, kidnapping (missing child), intruders, and acts of terrorism.

All describe situations that require the assistance of specially trained and equipped emergency response and medically trained personnel. Teachers need to be ready to assess the situation. Figure 15-1 lists some of the signs that cue teachers that a child is experiencing a health emergency. When teachers recognize these signs, they must immediately call for emergency assistance and administer first aid until emergency medical personnel arrive. If there is any suspicion that the situation is an emergency, teachers should call for medical assistance.

Creating an Emergency Management Plan

In recent years greater attention has been given to the need for early childhood programs to engage in emergency and disaster planning. The National Commission on Children and Disasters *2010 Report to the President and Congress* recommends that disaster training and emergency preparedness be required as part of the minimum safety requirements of licensed child care programs. Teachers are the first responders when it comes to managing the effects of emergencies and disasters on the children in their care. They need to be prepared to take the lead in managing emergencies that happen in the classroom and capable of working as a team to support the safe management of emergency situations in their center or school. They need training and resources to be able to respond confidently and effectively. To provide the support that teachers need, various agencies have established websites to guide teachers in center and child care home settings to plan and practice appropriate emergency response. The *Policy Point* provides a list of resources that can help teachers

---

FIGURE 15-1   When Is It an Emergency?

An emergency exists if the child:
- Loses consciousness or becomes less and less responsive.
- Has trouble breathing or cannot speak.
- Has confusion, headache, or vomiting after a head injury.
- Has signs of a broken bone.
- Has bleeding that won't stop.
- Is vomiting blood or passing large quantities of blood in the stool.
- Shows signs of shock.
- Has increasingly severe pain.
- Shows signs of dehydration: sunken eyes, lethargy.

Sources: Based on *Caring for Our Children: National Health and Safety Performance Standards: Guidelines for Out-of-Home Child Care Programs*, 3rd ed., 2011, by American Academy of Pediatrics, American Public Health Association, & National Resource Center for Health and Safety in Child Care and Early Education, retrieved April 16, 2012, from http://nrckids.org/CFOC3/index .html; and *Is it a Medical Emergency?* 2009, by KidsHealth, Nemours, retrieved May 11, 2012, from http://kidshealth.org/parent/general/aches/emergencies.html?tracking=P_RelatedArticle#.

develop an appropriate plan to guide effective response in case of emergency, an *Emergency Management Plan* (EMP).

An EMP is a written document developed through a process of careful deliberation and discussion by teachers, families, and community emergency responders. This work is done proactively, before an emergency occurs, which allows decisions to be made before the stress of a crisis situation. While every early childhood program's EMP will address similar topics, the plan is designed to meet the needs and consider the particular characteristics of the site and community. The Emergency Management Plan anticipates potential threats to the program, outlines steps to take to mitigate the potential hazard, identifies how to access emergency resources, addresses site-specific characteristics as well as the special needs of children enrolled, outlines options for taking shelter, and proposes a plan for transporting children if evacuation is required.

Analyzing Potential Emergency Threats

An effective Emergency Management Plan starts with an analysis of potential emergency threats. Health emergencies resulting from sudden injuries such as falls are the most familiar crisis situation in early childhood settings. Teachers work diligently to establish safe environments and supervision practices to reduce the likelihood of such events. Pandemic health issues are detected at the public level and in most cases warnings are communicated as the issue is recognized.

Most geographic areas have some likelihood for natural disasters to occur and in some cases the potential for disaster can be anticipated. For example, natural disasters often occur in a rhythm related to seasons, such as tornadoes and hurricanes, or wildfires caused by drought (NACCRRA, 2010). Areas with industrial plants and major transportation routes for industrial materials have increased potential for chemical or oil spills. In addition, some types of disasters may be linked to one another. For example, earthquakes often cause fires, severe storms can cause mudslides and power outages, and spills of toxic materials may bring on acute illness (NACCRRA, 2010).

Disasters, and the emergencies that follow, have the potential to create barriers to effective response and management. Road closures may block safe evacuation routes or stop families from being able to retrieve children from school or care. For this reason, states and child care regulatory agencies are advocating for early childhood programs to develop plans to guide response in the event of disasters and emergencies (National Commission on Children and Disasters, 2010).

Various resources help keep teachers informed about emerging conditions that have the potential to place children in danger. The Federal Emergency Management Agency (FEMA) provides

POLICY POINT **Early Childhood Programs Need Emergency Preparedness Plans**

The National Commission on Children and Disasters *2010 Report to the President and Congress* highlighted the need for early childhood educators to develop emergency and disaster preparedness plans. Resources that were developed to address this need include:

The Office of Head Start offers tools to support program planning for emergencies including tools on how to plan for specific emergencies in the *Head Start Emergency Preparedness Manual* (ACF-IM-09-09) available at www.headstartresourcecenter.org/assets/files/EPrep%20Manual%20v22.pdf.

The Office of Child Care provides emergency preparedness information and resources to guide emergency response at the *Child Care Resources for Disasters and Emergencies* website: www.acf.hhs.gov/programs/ccb/initiatives/emergency/index.htm.

The National Association of Child Care Resource and Referral Agencies provides a variety of resources for disaster planning and preparation for teachers in child care centers and family child care homes at their *Children and Disasters* website: www.naccrra.org/disaster/.

Source: Based on National Commission on Children and Disasters. *2010 Report to the President and Congress.* AHRQ Publication No. 10-M037. Rockville, MD: Agency for Healthcare Research and Quality. October 2010.

information about the types and dates of disasters that have been declared for each state. This information can be helpful in planning for the types of disasters that might occur. The National Weather Service provides a Storm Watch, Warning, and Advisory map that can be accessed electronically. See the Web Resources for links to these resources. Local emergency personnel are also good resources for learning about the types of dangers that may threaten the community.

Removing Potential Hazards

Preventive actions can be taken to mitigate or reduce the potential for harm. Prevention involves taking a close look at the children's settings to identify possible hazards and making adjustments when possible. Ensuring that light fixtures are well secured to the ceiling, tall furniture is attached to the wall, and heavy items are placed on the floor all help to avoid danger of falling if an earthquake occurs. Knowing how to turn off gas, water, and electricity helps avoid dangers to the facility during severe storms. Removing dangerous tree branches reduces the likelihood that they may be blown into windows in case of high winds. Proactive actions like these help improve positive outcomes.

Identifying How to Access Emergency Resources

An effective Emergency Management Plan is created through collaboration by teachers, school officials, families, and community emergency responders. This interaction is helpful in gleaning the expertise and realistic viewpoints of all partners. It also assists in connecting the early childhood program to the greater community, which ensures that the needs of very young children are considered at both the program and community planning levels.

The effectiveness of the EMP relies on the teacher's ability to connect with emergency responders as quickly as possible. Various aspects aid quick response, including the ability to:

- *Know who to contact in case of an emergency.* Emergency phone numbers for fire, ambulance, and poison control should be posted by each phone and entered into cell phone emergency contact lists.
- *Recognize how quickly emergency personnel are likely to respond.* When support is readily available and quick to respond, teachers can focus on implementing basic first aid and keeping children stable for a shorter period of time. When emergency personnel are at a greater distance, response will take longer and teachers must be prepared to provide care for a longer period of time.
- *Identify options for transporting children to emergency services.* Some communities may have readily accessible medical transport. In other settings teachers may need to rely on air transport to get children to more distant medical centers, or teachers may need to be ready with a plan to transport the child themselves.
- *Create formal arrangements with medical providers for over-the-phone consultation if needed.* When emergency personnel are at a distance, or when immediate response is crucial, teachers need to know who to call for guidance. Posting the contact information of a medical advisor in an easily accessed location is an important support in such situations.

Addressing Site-Specific Characteristics

The Emergency Management Plan must be designed to address the needs of the particular children's setting. For example, child care centers and school-based programs usually have a variety of personnel who can assist with emergency response. In family child care or short-term child care settings, teachers like Jamal may be individually responsible for the care of a small group of children. These teachers must plan to manage emergencies while at the same time supervising the remaining group of children.

Attributes of the facility contribute to the EMP as well. Designating a space where an injured or ill child can be isolated, and equipping the space ahead of time with a cot or sleeping pad, blanket, and first aid supplies, adds to a coordinated response during the first minutes of an injury emergency. Access to both a telephone (landline) and cell phone is advisable to provide options if the electricity is out or the cell phone batteries are dead.

The EMP should also address emergency procedures for each part of the classroom day such as when children are playing inside and outside, are at lunch, or napping. Steps should be outlined for emergency management when children are on a field trip. The pattern of supervision and location of the children need to be considered as emergency procedures are planned.

Planning for Children's Special Needs

Children's age, special medical conditions, and developmental needs must be considered when developing the EMP. Specific evacuation plans are needed for infants and toddlers and children with mobility challenges. First aid kits need to be equipped with copies of individual emergency medical protocols for children who have special health needs. Any medications that have been approved for administration to individual children should be readily available for teachers to access during an emergency. This may require special planning to ensure that these items are accessible to the teacher but out of the reach of children. Foods stored for emergencies need to be selected with children's food restrictions or allergies in mind.

Understanding Options for Taking Shelter

Some emergencies require that teachers and children leave the facility. In other situations staying inside is the safest choice. Knowing when to stay and when to leave are key elements in safety management. Common shelter options are described next:

- *Sheltering-in-place* refers to remaining within the early childhood facility until the emergency is over or until help can arrive. This option is used when the children's facility is essentially safe and secure, and when leaving the facility is either unsafe or not an option due to outside dangers or blocked evacuation routes. Taking **shelter-in-place** is an appropriate choice if exit routes are blocked by floods or downed power lines, for example.

- *Lockdown* refers to sheltering with children in a secure location within the early childhood facility. This option is used when danger from the outside is present and children are threatened even in their own classroom. Lockdown is put into action when the threat is imminent and leaving the facility is unsafe—for example, if there is danger from an intruder in the building or gunfire near the school.

- *Evacuation and Relocation* refer to leaving the facility and traveling to an alternate assembly location. Evacuation is required when it is not safe to remain in the children's facility. Evacuation is used in response to a sudden emergency such as a fire in the facility.

The EMP should describe appropriate preparations and outline the procedures for management of children for each shelter option.

Transporting Children

The Emergency Management Plan should describe options for relocating children to both nearby and distant evacuation sites and describe how children will be transported during evacuation. A nearby assembly location that can easily be reached by walking is a good choice when the emergency is related to the children's facility, such as a fire. The nearby location should provide shelter from the weather and be appropriate for a stay of a few hours.

A transportation plan is needed to prepare for emergencies that require moving children a good distance from the children's setting. Teachers need to consider the number of children to be transported and ways to address children's special mobility needs. Some programs may have vehicles that are always present and available in emergencies. Others may rely on the presence of teacher and staff vehicles. It is recommended that vehicles identified as part of the evacuation plan contain at least ½ tank of gas at all times (Schwartz, 2009). Alternate methods of transportation should also be considered, including using strollers, carts, wagons, wheelchairs, or cribs equipped with wheels.

> **What if . . .**
> a child in your class is known to have an allergy to bee stings? What extra items might you need in your first aid kit to support this child in case of an emergency?

shelter-in-place
tactic of taking shelter in the early childhood setting if the facility is secure and if leaving the facility would put children at risk

Preparing for Action

Emergency preparedness involves taking steps to minimize the negative impact of crisis situations. It includes thinking through all the aspects that contribute to a child's health and safety, and considering as many potential scenarios as possible. A variety of familiar aspects are involved in this part of the plan including identifying roles and responsibilities, assembling emergency supplies, compiling children's emergency information, communicating the plan to families, and posting the emergency procedures.

Identifying Roles and Responsibilities

Emergencies require purposeful and organized action. It is essential that teachers understand their role and the activities for which they are responsible. Each teacher should know:

- Who will call for emergency assistance.
- Who will provide emergency care for an injured child.
- Who will supervise the remaining children.
- Who will take leadership if taking shelter or evacuating is required.
- Who will contact the parents.
- Who will document and report the emergency to appropriate supervisors or emergency responders.

In group settings teachers share the emergency response responsibilities. This inspires confidence among the teaching team and contributes to children's safety during emergencies. Family child care workers such as Jamal need to develop supports in advance, such as identifying a neighbor who will help during a crisis. Teachers in elementary school settings need to know who to call for backup assistance in the classroom in case of an emergency.

Assembling First Aid Kits

The American Academy of Pediatrics (AAP), American Public Health Association, and National Resource Center for Health and Safety in Child Care and Early Education (2011) recommend that children's programs maintain at least one first aid kit at the facility and one to take along on field trips. The AAP and child care licensing agencies specify the first aid supplies that are required for children's settings. Figure 15-2 provides a sample checklist of supplies for the first aid kit.

A first aid kit should be located in each classroom in a place that is out of the reach of children but easily accessible by teachers. The kit should be labeled so it is easy to identify. A "traveling" first aid kit is also needed to take along on trips away from the facility. This first aid kit should include children's emergency contact information and any special medical protocols and supplies for children with special health needs. A backpack that can be hung near the door is a good container for a traveling first aid kit. In addition, any vehicles used to transport children should also be equipped with a first aid kit. The first aid kits should be checked at least monthly and restocked after use.

Creating a Blood Spill Cleanup Kit

Careful cleanup of blood spills or splashes is important to avoid possible exposure to bloodborne diseases. A well-equipped blood spill kit includes protective equipment such as gloves and goggles or other eye protection. Paper towels to absorb the spill and bags to safely dispose of soiled materials should also be included, as well as soap or antibacterial gel for washing hands after cleanup. A spray bottle or bucket is needed to mix disinfectant products, such as the bleach and water solution used to sanitize soiled surfaces.

In the opening case scenario, Jamal was able to quickly attend to Kevin's cut because the emergency supplies he needed were readily available. This supported Jamal's effective management of the injury and reduced confusion so he was better able to direct the remaining children to a safe activity.

Children's programs need at least one first aid kit at the facility and one to take along on field trips.

FIGURE 15-2 First Aid Supplies Checklist

- ❏ Telephone numbers for community emergency care providers and Poison Control center
- ❏ Emergency contact information for children's families
- ❏ Guide to standard first aid care
- ❏ Emergency medications for children with special medical needs
- ❏ Disposable plastic gloves (latex free preferred)
- ❏ Scissors
- ❏ Tweezers
- ❏ Thermometer (non-glass and mercury free)
- ❏ Adhesive-style strip bandages
- ❏ Sterile gauze pads and rolls
- ❏ Adhesive bandage tape
- ❏ Safety pins
- ❏ Triangular bandages
- ❏ Eye dressing
- ❏ Cold pack
- ❏ Water
- ❏ Small plastic or metal splints
- ❏ Liquid soap
- ❏ Flashlight (and working batteries)
- ❏ Pen/pencil and note pad
- ❏ First aid chart or booklet
- ❏ Plastic bags for disposing of soiled materials
- ❏ Cell phone

Source: Based on *Emergency/Disaster Preparedness for Child Care Programs: Applicable Standards from "Caring for Our Children,"* American Academy of Pediatrics, American Public Health Association, and National Resource Center for Health and Safety in Child Care and Early Education, 2011. Retrieved May 18, 2012, from http://nrckids.org/CFOC3/PDFVersion/PDF_Color/CFOC3_ch5.pdf.

Assembling Disaster Emergency Supplies

Emergency supplies need to be available to support children's care if taking shelter-in-place or evacuating to another location is required. Supplies should be sufficient to support extended shelter care for 48 to 72 hours. The *Safety Segment* provides a sample checklist to assist with gathering disaster emergency supplies. Large plastic tubs or rolling garbage cans with lids are good choices for containing disaster emergency supplies. Disaster emergency supplies should be checked periodically, and stored food and water should be rotated every 6 months.

Compiling Children's Emergency Information

Emergency files and information should be readily accessible in case evacuation is required. Emergency records that are needed include:

- *Attendance roster for the day* to ensure all children are accounted for.
- *Child and teacher emergency contact information* to support communication with families.
- *Emergency medical plans for children and staff* to ensure that special health or medical needs are addressed appropriately.

Maintaining emergency information in a current, readily accessible, and portable format takes special attention. Teachers might copy this information on CDs, e-mail the information to a secure location so it is available electronically, and place a packet of printed materials in a re-sealable plastic bag in the traveling first aid kit.

SAFETY SEGMENT   Disaster Emergency Supplies Checklist

Assemble supplies in backpacks, rolling luggage, or large plastic crates with handles.

✓ First aid supplies: first aid kit, hand sanitizers, antiseptic wipes

✓ Clothing and bedding: extra clothing, rain gear, hats, gloves, blankets or sleeping bags

✓ Tools and supplies: paper cups and plates, utensils, manual can opener, plastic sheeting, duct tape, scissors, battery-operated radio, extra batteries, flashlight, cash, tool kit, matches (in a waterproof container), signal flare, whistle, map of the local area, emergency preparedness handbook

✓ Personal care and sanitation supplies: toilet paper, towels, soap, plastic garbage bags, disinfectant or bleach

✓ Special items: formula, bottles, diapers, special medications, games, books, telephone, emergency contact information for children and adults, telephone numbers of local and state emergency agencies

✓ Water: enough for 3 days (at least 1 gallon of water per person per day)

✓ Food: enough for 3 days. Choose nonperishable foods that are lightweight, compact, and do not need refrigeration or cooking, such as canned fruits and meats, high-energy and comfort foods, infant foods.

· Package foods in clean plastic containers with lids.

· Rotate supplies every 6 months.

Source: Based on *Preparing for Disaster* (FEMA 475; A4600), August 2004, Jessup, MD: FEMA and Washington, DC: American Red Cross, retrieved May 9, 2012, from www.fema.gov/pdf/library/pfd.pdf; and *Emergency Preparedness and Response: Chemical Agents: Facts about Sheltering in Place,* August 16, 2006, Atlanta, GA: Centers for Disease Control and Prevention, retrieved December 17, 2012 from www.bt.cdc.gov/planning/shelteringfacts.asp.

Communicating the Plan to Families

Communicating with families once children have taken shelter or been evacuated is crucial, but the process of communication begins during the planning and preparation process. To begin, teachers invite families to participate in developing the Emergency Management Plan. Once the plan is established, they acquaint families with the emergency plans through program orientation meetings, handbooks, newsletters, the program website, and posted emergency procedures. Families want to know:

· Who will care for their children during an emergency.

· Where children will be sheltered in case of evacuation and relocation (address and telephone number).

· How families will be contacted.

Families need to be assured that teachers will give their first attention to the safe care and supervision of children in emergency situations, and that communication with families is seen as a later step in emergency management. This can sometimes be a topic of dispute. In some scenarios a family member may learn from a news report that a fire or other problem has occurred at the school or children's site before teachers have the opportunity to communicate with families. Sharing information with families is very important, but children's safety always comes first.

Posting Emergency Procedures

Emergency procedures should be posted where they can be easily seen and used as a resource during the alarm and confusion of an emergency event. The emergency procedures should briefly list directions about what to do and provide a list of emergency telephone numbers for emergency services. The procedures should also print out information that teachers can read during the stress of an emergency, including the name of the program or school, the address and driving directions to the location, and the telephone number of the classroom. The information should be clear, straightforward, and printed in large bold print so that it can be read from a distance. The procedures should be written in all languages spoken by the teachers or any volunteers who might be assisting. The emergency procedures should be located where everyone will know where to look, such as on the wall near the first aid kit and beside each telephone so the information is readily available to support teachers when making an emergency call. Figure 15-3 provides an example of an emergency procedures poster.

In addition it is helpful to post directions for common first aid procedures on the inside of a cupboard door where the first aid kit is stored or on the wall in the area where first aid care might be

FIGURE 15-3   Sample Emergency Procedures Poster

Head Teacher:

- Administer emergency first aid and CPR.
- Provide child's medical information to emergency personnel.
- Stay with the child at all times.
- Travel with the child to the hospital if needed.
- Transfer responsibility directly to parent or other authorized adult.

Assistant Teacher:

- Call 911. Give directions. Stay on the line.
- Provide supervision for remaining children.
- Contact other program staff for backup.
- Contact the child's family.

Emergency Telephone Numbers

FIRE - AMBULANCE - POLICE: Call 911
POISON CONTROL: Call 9-1-800-222-1222
Emergency Room at Good Health Medical Center: Call XXX-XXXX
Electricity: Call XXX-XXXX Water: Call XXX-XXXX Gas: Call XXX-XXXX
Say, "I'm calling from Kennedy School at 567 NW 160th Street, at the corner of 160th and Adams Boulevard. Take Main Street to Adams, turn north and travel one mile to 160th Street. The building is on the right side of the street. We are in room 107. Our phone number is XXX-XXX-XXXX."

provided. This way the information can be a reminder for a teacher who is working quickly to put on gloves, access first aid supplies, and administer first aid.

Conducting Emergency Drills

Practicing the planned response steps for emergencies is a useful way to determine if the Emergency Management Plan is realistic and workable. Practice builds teachers' familiarity with the actions that will support them in case of an emergency. Managing simulated emergency scenarios also builds a sense of teamwork and confidence among program or school staff—qualities that can be crucial to effective response. Through practice, teachers are able to recognize aspects in their own personal or family lives that could be impacted by a medical emergency at school. For example, teachers may need to travel with an injured child to obtain emergency medical care and, as a result, should have a backup plan for their own children and families. Planning in advance helps teachers avoid being distracted by competing responsibilities.

Implementing Emergency Drills with Children

Familiar emergency drills in early childhood and school settings include fire, earthquake, tornado, and lock down drills. It is also important to practice response drills with children using injury or medical scenarios. One way to conduct such a drill would be for the director to enter the play yard and hand a note to a teacher indicating the beginning of an "Injury Drill." Following the directions on the note, the teachers could select a child to pretend to be injured, and then act through the steps of calling for emergency assistance, conducting first aid, supervising the other children, contacting the child's family, cleaning up after the scenario, and completing the closing report. Questions to consider during a medical emergency drill such as this include the following:

- Are first aid supplies and child emergency contact information easily accessible?
- Is at least one communication source available to call for emergency aid?

- Does the plan provide sufficient supervision for both the "injured" and remaining children?
- Are additional safety precautions needed to reduce danger in the future?

Emergency procedures should be periodically reviewed to be sure that barriers and problems have been corrected and that all supports remain available. Periodically testing the plan through a drill helps ensure that the emergency plan is effective in supporting appropriate response and teachers are ready to keep kids safe. During an emergency is no time to learn that bandages were "borrowed" from the first aid kit for use in dramatic play.

Practicing Emergency Response for Disasters

Disaster emergency drills should also be practiced periodically. One approach is to identify a potential disaster scenario that requires teachers to determine the appropriate shelter or evacuation response and simulate putting a plan into practice. This helps teachers focus on the unique aspects related to taking shelter and offers an alternative to fire drills to teach children how to follow directions in an emergency. Practice helps children gain comfort and familiarity with emergency drills. The *Teaching Wellness* feature offers ideas about how to help children develop skills in focusing on the teacher and following directions.

Practicing disaster emergency response also offers opportunities for teachers to review the emergency supplies and test whether emergency foods and water have been rotated, batteries for flashlights have been replaced, and emergency information is readily available to take if evacuation is needed. These actions help ensure that disaster preparations are organized and useful.

Accessing Emergency Response Training

Training by credible authorities is an essential part of managing emergencies. Infant and child first aid and cardiopulmonary resuscitation (CPR) are the most common training topics for appropriate emergency response. These trainings offer specific information about the injuries and emergency situations that might involve young children and up-to-date guidelines for addressing injuries.

Obtaining First Aid and CPR Training

First aid and CPR training is a key component of effective emergency response. Under the guidance of trained personnel teachers have the opportunity to practice identifying first aid concerns and implementing rescue procedures such as applying bandages and conducting CPR for infants, children, and adults. They learn that changing a child's position to open a blocked airway or stopping blood flow by applying pressure are examples of first aid actions that can save a child's life. Training helps teachers learn ways to get past the fear of doing something wrong by helping them recognize that in an emergency the consequence of *not* responding may be death or serious disability. Periodic training builds teacher confidence and inspires teachers to take appropriate action when needed. Obtaining training from credible sources is crucial for effective response.

Most states require that teachers maintain certification in infant and child first aid and CPR through renewal classes every 2 years. This ensures that teachers refresh their skills and learn about new and emerging safety practices. Sometimes well-learned lessons become outdated as new information is discovered and safety practices are improved.

First aid and CPR certification classes are offered through organizations such as the American Red Cross, the American Heart Association, and hospitals. Larger child care centers or schools may schedule periodic training for staff, but ultimately it is the responsibility of individual teachers to maintain their certification as a part of their professional commitment to keep their skills current.

Accessing Specialized Training

Teachers may also need to participate in specialized training to address potential emergency needs of children who have special health concerns. Specialized training topics may include:

- Use of glucagon for children with diabetes.
- Use of epinephrine autoinjectors (EpiPens) for children with sensitive allergies.
- Special response for children with seizure disorder.
- Emergency response for children with specific developmental concerns, such as potential for choking.

LEARNING OUTCOME Children will be able to show what it means to follow directions (look at the teacher, listen to the words, do what is asked) and tell why following directions is important in emergencies.

Vocabulary Focus: Follow, leader, copy, look, listen, do, safety

Safety Watch: Use motions appropriate for babies to follow,

INFANTS AND TODDLERS

- **Goal:** Babies and toddlers will play follow-me copying activities.
- **Materials:** Play space, colored blocks, two small tubs or containers.
- **Activity plan:** Sit with the child to play copying games. Make motions, facial expressions, or sounds and guide the

child to follow, or copy, what you do. Follow what the baby does; then encourage the baby to follow you.

- **How to adjust the activity:** Help all children focus by using clear movements. Exaggerate movements as needed, and encourage the child with words to look and follow.
- **Did you meet your goal?** Did children to copy and follow actions in play?

PRESCHOOLERS AND KINDERGARTNERS

- **Goal:** Children will demonstrate and define what it means to be the leader and the follower.
- **Materials:** A variety of small toys (5 matching items for each selected toy), such as small blocks, beads, manipulative and sorting toys, construction paper.
- **Activity plan:** Place a piece of construction paper in front of each child. Put the toys in the center of a table. Ask the children to watch and then copy what you do. Choose two toys and place them on your paper. Position the toys in obvious locations, such as near each other in the center, at the edges, or at opposing corners. Guide the children to follow your lead by finding the same toys and placing them on their paper in the same way. As children work, talk through the steps of what it means to follow: listen and look, think about the directions, and copy the placement. Ask the children to return the toys to the middle of the table, and repeat. Invite a child to be the leader. Guide the child to choose and place 3 different toys on their paper.

Ask the others to follow. Ensure each child has a turn to be the leader. Increase the number of toys placed on the paper. Reinforce the concepts of listening to and watching the directions, and being the leader or follower.

- **How to adjust the activity:** Increase visual contrast by using white construction paper so children with vision impairment can see and focus more easily on copying the placement of the toys. Verbally describe the activity to reinforce the need for all children to listen and look as a way of better understanding the directions. Offer toys that all children are able to pick up. Position materials on the table so all children can reach them. Learn the vocabulary words in the home language of children in the class, and use them along with the English words to reinforce the concepts of lead and follow.
- **Did you meet your goal?** What do you observe? Are children able to copy the placement of the toys? Do they demonstrate understanding of lead and follow? When asked can they define the words?

SCHOOL-AGE CHILDREN

- **Goal:** Children will explain what it means to follow directions and tell why it is important to follow directions during an emergency.
- **Materials:** 1-inch-cube blocks; 12-inch × 18-inch poster board pieces (one for each pair of children); current event article from the newspaper describing an emergency or disaster.
- **Activity plan:** Gather children and introduce the topic of the importance of listening and following directions in emergencies. Ask children to pair with another to practice an activity involving giving and following directions. Give each pair a piece of poster board, and ask them to fold it in half and stand it on a table like a screen. Ask the children to sit one child on either side of the screen where they cannot see what the other child is building. Give each child five blocks. Identify one child in each pair to be the leader and one to be the follower. Ask the leader to build a 3-block structure and then give instructions guiding the follower to build one just like it. Give time for the follower to complete their structure. Ask the children to remove

the poster board and compare the structure. Are they the same? Why would they be the same and why would they be different? Reverse the roles and increase the number of blocks. Finish the activity and assemble as a group. Read about an emergency event that has occurred in your community. Talk about how following directions in emergencies is similar to this game; some people must be the leaders and some must be the followers. Identify who are the leaders in an emergency and who are the followers. Discuss why following directions during an emergency is important.

- **How to adjust the activity:** Ensure that all children can grasp and build with the selected blocks. Position an adult near children who may have coordination, hearing or focus challenges, to repeat the lead child's directions and to guide the follower to listen, think, and do what is directed. Ensure that all children are supported and have a chance to be the leader.
- **Did you meet your goal?** Can children describe what it means to follow directions? Are they able to explain why it is important to follow directions during an emergency?

A Matter of ETHICS

Sarah's class includes children who have known allergic reactions to peanut butter. Her director has planned a training to instruct teachers on how to use an EpiPen. Sarah notices that her assistant teacher Erin left the training and was gone for over 30 minutes, missing much of the demonstration and practice. Sarah knows if she reports this to the director it may disrupt her relationship with her assistant teacher, but she is also worried that Erin won't be able to help in case of an allergic reaction. What are the issues here and what course of action would you recommend?

Participating in Community Disaster Response Training

Participating in community disaster preparedness training is a good way for teachers to gain a perspective of the kinds of actions and supports that can be expected in a community-wide emergency event and the roles and responsibilities of emergency responders. These activities also help teachers recognize the ways that early childhood facilities and schools can support their communities in times of disaster by serving as potential evacuation sites or by providing child care for emergency personnel who are working to address the effects of the disaster. When teachers participate in disaster planning they also help raise awareness that children and early childhood programs are vulnerable parts of the population that should be considered in community emergency management plans (National Commission on Children and Disasters, 2010).

● MANAGING EMERGENCIES

Even though teachers may have a strong commitment to children's safety, taking action in emergencies is not always easy or natural. Emergencies can be alarming, disconcerting, and stressful. Teachers may be anxious that they will cause an injured child more pain or may worry that they will make a mistake and be sued for trying to help. Familiarity with the volunteer protection laws, a clear understanding of the teacher's role, knowing how to assess an emergency and use universal precautions, and completing emergency response reports are all aspects that prepare teachers to respond when emergency action is needed.

Understanding the Good Samaritan Doctrine

Good Samaritan doctrine laws designed to encourage people to help in emergencies by protecting rescuers from being sued for providing emergency help

All states and the District of Columbia include in their common laws protections for rescue efforts that are provided in good faith. These protections are referred to as the **Good Samaritan doctrine**. The laws protect rescuers from being sued for wrongdoing when they provide emergency help as long as the helper conducts care activities that are reasonable and prudent, using all the resources available at the time (Rosenbaum, Harty, & Sheer, 2008). The laws that relate to the Good Samaritan doctrine were designed to encourage people to help in emergencies.

In order for emergency assistance to be covered by the Good Samaritan doctrine:

- The help must be a volunteer act.
- The person receiving the help must not object.
- The actions of the helper must be a good faith effort to provide emergency care.

The Good Samaritan doctrine does not provide protection for rescue acts that are unreasonable, careless, or negligent. In the teaching setting, this means that teachers are expected to provide appropriate emergency first aid assistance for the child's immediate needs, but that this care is only administered as a substitute until professional emergency medical help can be obtained. Calling for medical assistance and ensuring the child receives professional care are part of the expectations of teachers under the Good Samaritan doctrine.

Using Universal Precautions

universal precautions a set of precautions designed to prevent transmission of human immunodeficiency virus (HIV), hepatitis B virus (HBV), and other bloodborne pathogens when providing first aid or health care

Many emergency situations involve bleeding injuries. For this reason teachers need to know and use basic universal precautions when providing emergency assistance. **Universal precautions** are a set of safety measures that are designed to prevent the transmission of bloodborne diseases such as human immunodeficiency virus (HIV), hepatitis B virus (HBV), and other bloodborne pathogens (Siegel, Rhinehart, Jackson, Chiarello, & the Healthcare Infection Control Practices Advisory Committee, 2007). Universal precautions are recommended to ensure that health care workers and emergency responders are not themselves harmed when they provide first aid assistance. Universal precautions include the following practices:

- Wear gloves at all accidents involving blood or any other body fluids containing visible signs of blood.
- Use a one-way mask when offering rescue breathing.
- Watch for sharp objects, electricity, toxic fumes, and other hazards at the site of the accident.
- Use appropriate hand washing when providing medical assistance.
- Dispose of contaminated materials appropriately.

These universal precautions outline safe practices both during and after emergency help has been offered.

Universal precautions include wearing protective gloves when caring for any injury that involves blood or body fluids containing visible signs of blood.

Assessing for Signs of Injury

The first few minutes after an injury occurs are of crucial importance to a positive outcome. Brain death, for example, begins within 4 to 6 minutes after sudden cardiac arrest if air and circulation are not restored (Heller & Zieve, 2011a). High-quality CPR chest compressions generate the flow of blood and delivery of oxygen to vital organs. If effective CPR is provided within minutes of cardiac arrest, the chances of survival can be greatly increased (Berg et al., 2010).

Even when children are under the watchful eye of the teacher, it is possible for a serious injury to occur. Sometimes teachers directly observe the accident as it happens. Other times teachers must conduct a quick and concise review of the situation, reach a reasonable judgment about the appropriate response, and swiftly take action. A great deal of information must be quickly managed Also, some actions must be taken simultaneously while other steps can be taken in a logical order (Berg et al., 2010). The following assessments should be done simultaneously.

A *assess the situation*. Look for signs of what may have contributed to the injury. Anticipate the type of injury that may have occurred. For example:

- Is the child lying under climbing equipment that might suggest a fall? If so, the head or back may be injured and the child should not be moved.
- Is furniture tipped over? If so, was the child hit or cut? Has the child twisted a limb?
- Could electricity be involved? If so, do not touch the child until the electricity is turned off.
- Are sharp objects present such as broken glass? If so, look for ways to avoid danger while approaching and assisting the child.

Observe *the child's physical appearance*. Quickly inspect the child from head to toe looking for problems or signs of injury. For example:

- Is the child breathing?
- Is the child bleeding profusely?
- Is the child's body position abnormal or distorted in any way?

Notice *the child's behavior*. Observe how the child is responding and look for signs of distress and concern. For example:

- Is the child moving?
- Is the child crying?
- Does the child respond when spoken to?

This information is used to determine whether the situation is an emergency. It helps teachers decide whether the child should be moved or cared for in place. It guides teachers to reasonably know what should be done and prepare to take action. Table 15-1 provides additional guidance about how a

TABLE 15-1   Accident Settings and Potential Injuries

Setting	Types of Injuries
Climbing equipment	• Fall from equipment (head injury, broken bone?) • Climbing (pinched fingers?)
Tricycle	• Striking against objects (bumps, bruises?) • Falling over in motion (bump to head?)
General outdoor playground	• Trip or fall (skinned knee, bumps, bruises?) • Insects (bites or stings?) • Children running into others or against play equipment (bumps, bruises, scrapes?) • Excessive heat (heat exhaustion or heatstroke?)
Sandbox	• Sand (foreign object in the eye?)
Workbench	• Hammer, nails (crushed finger, cut or pierced?)
Indoor play	• Striking against objects (bumps and bruises?) • Objects falling against child (bumps, bruises, cuts?)
Craft materials	• Exposure to allergens (acute illness or anaphylaxis?)

review of the situation can help teachers consider the context of the accident as they determine the types of injuries that may have occurred and begin to develop a response plan.

In the opening case scenario, Jamal was able to quickly recognize that Kevin's wound was the result of being struck by the ball cart and that there was low likelihood of broken bones. By the time he reached Kevin, Jamal had determined that the child could be moved without worry. But even though the bleeding was managed with bandaging, Jamal encouraged the family to seek medical advice since a head injury was involved.

Taking Action

In an early childhood setting, the initial assessment of an accident should take less than 30 seconds. From the first recognition of a problem, teachers begin to assume their roles in emergency response. At this point the supporting teacher redirects the remaining children to an appropriate activity away from the injured child. The teacher who is the lead responder conducts the following activities:

- *Identify and address any immediate dangers to yourself or the victim.* Ensure there is no danger of electrocution. Sweep broken glass away. Do not move the child if there is potential for spine or head injury.
- *Try to get a response.* Is the child unconscious, asleep, or playing? Try to rouse the child. Say the child's name and ask, "Are you all right?"
- *Check to see if the child is breathing.* Look for signs of regular breathing.

If the child is breathing, conduct the activities below. If the child is breathing, and you are alone, phone for emergency assistance right away, then continue your observation and conduct first aid as needed.

- *Check quickly for injuries.* Run hands gently over the body. Look for signs of injury.
- *Stop the bleeding.* Apply direct pressure to the wound. Use clean gauze to cover the wound. If possible, hold the bleeding area higher than the heart to slow blood flow. Hold firm against pressure points to stop excessive bleeding if necessary.
- *Treat for shock.* Lay the child down and elevate the feet. Keep the child evenly warm. If the child is breathing and appears stable, move the child into a recovery position by placing the child on one side. This assists with breathing and helps prevent choking if the child vomits.
- *Speak calmly and reassure the child.* Let the child know you are going to stay very near.

- *Stay with the child at all times.* Do not leave the child unattended. Travel with the child to the emergency medical facility if needed. Stay with the child until you can release responsibility to the child's parent or guardian.
- *Provide the child's medical information to emergency personnel.* Describe any allergies, medications the child is taking, and health concerns such as diabetes or asthma. If the child has a special health concern, the child's physician's name and contact information should be shared.
- *Call the child's parent or guardian.* When the child's care has been transferred to emergency responders, contact the child's family. Report the cause of the accident and the first aid and medical care that has been provided. Give information about who is providing emergency care and tell where the child has been transported for medical assistance. Do not attempt to diagnose the situation or offer medical advice or guidance. Direct the family to the medical provider for professional assistance and follow-up.

The teacher's responsibility in this scenario is to obtain emergency assistance, provide immediate first-aid and temporary care, and stay with the child until responsibility can be transferred to the emergency responder or the parent, guardian, or other authorized individual.

If the child is unresponsive and not breathing, it should be assumed that cardiac arrest has occurred and CPR is needed.

Conducting CPR

The most common reasons a child might experience cardiac arrest are SIDS, congenital malformations, injuries from motor vehicle accidents, choking, and drowning. The first aid approach for treating a child who is not breathing follows a sequenced approach called CAB: chest compressions, airway, and breathing/ventilation (Berg et al., 2010).

C = Chest Compressions

Chest compressions help oxygen-rich blood flow and circulate to the body's vital organs. If a child is unresponsive and not breathing, the AHA (Berg et al., 2010) recommends giving 30 chest compressions right away, followed by two breaths (and repeat) for children and infants. If the teacher is not trained in rescue breathing (ventilation) or is unable to do so, the chest compressions should be continued. This is called, "hands only" CPR (Berg et al., 2010). Trained individuals are prepared to administer chest compressions using the general process described below.

For a child (Berg et al., 2010):

- Place the child on a hard surface such as the floor. Call out to another teacher or child to call 911.
- Kneel over the child, placing the heel of one hand at the midpoint of the child's breast.
- Keeping the elbows locked, apply 30 downward compressions. Depress the chest hard, about 2 inches, and fast, at a rate of at least 100 compressions per minute.
- After each compression, allow the chest to recoil as the heart fills with blood.

For infants (Berg et al., 2010):

- Lay the baby on a hard surface. Call out to another teacher or child to call 911.
- Use two fingers positioned on the center of the chest just below an imaginary "line" between the two nipples.
- Give 30 downward compressions. Depress the chest hard, about 1½ inches, at a fast rate of 100 compressions per minute.
- After each compression, allow the heart to refill with blood as the chest recoils.

A = Airway

After giving the 30 chest compressions, ensure the child's airway is open. Lift the child's chin, and gently press back on the forehead to tip the child's head back naturally. This lifts the tongue off the throat, opening the airway (Berg et al., 2010; Heller & Zieve, 2011b).

If the child or baby is unconscious, these moves can often correct the cause of stopped breathing.

B = Breathing/Ventilation

If breathing does not start when the airway is opened, give two rescue breaths (ventilations).

For a child:

- Keeping the child's chin tilted upward, gently pinch the nose closed to ensure that air is guided into the child's lungs.
- Lay a one-way mask across the child's mouth and give two rescue breaths (Berg et al., 2010). At each breath the rise in the chest should be visible.

For an infant:

- Place mouth over the baby's nose and mouth. Give two small rescue breaths by offering a puff-breath or small "mouthful" of air at a rate of about 1 breath per second.
- Reposition the baby if needed to ensure the breaths are effective.

For infants and children:

- Repeat the 30 compressions and 2 rescue breaths cycle for 2 minutes. Then, if you are alone, call 911.
- Continue the "30 and 2" cycle until emergency help arrives.

If a rescue breath does not go in, check that the airway is sufficiently opened and try again.

If breath still does not go in, the airway may be obstructed and must be cleared. Do not give up! Your efforts may save the child's life.

Clearing the Airway

Choking from obstructions in the airway occurs when a child swallows or aspirates (breathes in) a small object, such as food or a toy, that gets stuck in the throat. The blockage stops the flow of air which cuts off oxygen to the brain. First aid is required as soon as possible.

Watch for a child who is:

- Clutching the throat.
- Unable to talk or cough.
- Turning blue—look at skin, lips, nails.
- Unconscious.

Perform emergency actions to clear the airway.

For children (Heller & Zieve, 2011a):

- Stand or kneel behind the child.
- Wrap arms around the child's waist.
- Make a fist with one hand over the other.
- Position the hands just above the navel but below the breastbone.
- Press hard giving quick thrusts inward and upward.
- Continue until the object is dislodged or the child becomes unconscious.
- If the child becomes unconscious, lower the child to the floor, call 911, and begin CPR.
- If the object is visible try to remove it.
- Continue giving CPR until emergency help arrives.

For infants (Heller & Zieve, 2011b):

- Sit down. Place the infant facedown along your forearm. Rest your forearm on your thigh. Hold the infant's jaw with your fingers and support the chest with your hand to stabilize the neck. Keep the head lower than the body.
- Using the heel of your hand give five firm thumps on the middle of the back. Check to see if the item has been dislodged.

- If not, "sandwich" the child between both forearms. Roll the child face up on one forearm, keeping the head lower than the body. Place two fingers just below the nipple line on the middle of the breastbone. Give five quick chest compressions, thrusting in ⅓ to ½ of the depth of the chest.
- Continue giving five back thumps and five chest thrusts until the object is dislodged or emergency personnel arrive.
- If the baby becomes unconscious, administer CPR for 2 minutes then call 911.
- If the object blocking the airway is visible try to remove it.
- Continue giving CPR until emergency help arrives.

● ADMINISTERING FIRST AID

Injuries can, and do, occur in early childhood settings and schools. As a result teachers are likely to be involved in providing some level of first aid assistance for a variety of injuries. **First aid** refers to the set of actions taken to address injuries or illness. First aid has three primary goals:

1. To preserve life.
2. To avoid additional injury.
3. To assist with recovery.

first aid
the actions taken to immediately address illness or injury

First aid in the early childhood setting usually involves uncomplicated, commonsense procedures such as cleaning and bandaging a small cut or placing a cold compress on a bump or strained ankle. These are examples of *basic first aid* that are easily performed and that in most cases do not require formal medical assistance. When teachers administer basic first aid actions, the child's family should be contacted so that parents can participate in determining whether they will seek additional medical assistance.

Some situations are more complex, requiring additional and advanced actions such as providing CPR or wrapping a body part to immobilize an injured area in case of a broken bone. These are examples of injuries that require *emergency first aid*. If an injury requires emergency first aid, teachers should call for emergency medical assistance right away, while providing basic first aid until help arrives. In an emergency, trained medical personnel are needed to reduce any further injury to the child and to avoid the risk of disability or death.

In this section we offer descriptions of injuries and provide teachers with common approaches to basic first aid care. However, obtaining formal training in emergency response procedures from credible sources, such as the certified trainers of the American Heart Association or American Red Cross, is the most important way for teachers to learn to recognize the signs that emergency medical assistance is needed and be prepared to take action until emergency help arrives.

Falls

Falls are a primary cause of injury in young children. Some falls can cause significant injury. Falls from greater heights onto hard surfaces are more likely to result in a head injury or broken bone. If a fall is witnessed or suspected:

- Do not move the child.
- Check the child to ensure the airway is open and the child is breathing.
- Notice the height of the fall and consider the surface on which the child landed. Review the child for potential head injury. Watch for unequal size of pupils; fluid draining from the nose, ears, or mouth; confusion; or drowsiness (Homeier, 2005).
- Review the child for potential broken bones. Watch for a misshapen limb and intense pain and observe if a child is favoring a limb or is unable to move a body part (Vorvick & Zieve, 2009a).
- Treat minor wounds with basic first aid.

In an emergency, first aid is administered until professional medical help can be obtained.

Keep the child still and seek immediate medical help for any suspected head injury or broken bones. Inform the family of the fall, even if the injury appears minor. This way the child can be monitored for any unrecognized injuries (Cronan, 2011a).

Head Injury

Any injury to the head should be considered significant, and should be reported to the child's family as soon as possible. A severe head injury can cause bleeding inside the skull, which can result in brain damage or death. Even if the child begins to play again soon after the head injury, families should be consulted so they can participate directly in determining if medical care is needed. The child should be observed carefully for the next 24 hours.

In case of head injury:

- Lay the child down, positioning the head higher than the feet.
- Observe the child's eyes, looking for unnaturally dilated pupils.
- Notice if the child is disoriented.
- Keep the child calm.

Seek immediate medical assistance if the child is unconscious or if any signs of concussion are evident such as drowsiness; nausea and vomiting; slurred speech; disorientation; fluid seeping from nose, ears, and mouth; or headache (CDC, 2012a; Heller & Zieve, 2012).

Asthma

The most common symptoms of asthma attack in children are a wheezing sound when breathing and frequent episodes of coughing or coughing spasms. In some cases asthma attacks can be acute and life threatening (CDC, 2012b). Watch for:

- Increasing shortness of breath or wheezing.
- Chest tightness or pain.
- High level of distress.

For children with a known asthma condition, treat according to the child's asthma emergency medical plan using the child's nebulizer. Contact the family to report the child's condition and to have the family participate in determining a follow-up plan. Seek medical help immediately if the asthma attack is acute and resembles anaphylaxis (Ben-Joseph, 2011; Kaneshiro & Zieve, 2008).

Anaphylactic Shock: Severe Allergic Reaction

Allergies can result in anaphylactic shock, a life-threatening reaction that causes respiratory distress or circulatory collapse. Severe allergic reactions may result from a wide range of causes including allergy to foods or drugs, insect venom (from bites), pollen, latex, and other possibly unknown causes (Dugdale, Henochowicz, & Zieve, 2008). Reaction can occur quickly or a few hours after exposure. Some children may have known allergies, while others have not yet shown signs of allergic reaction. Signs of anaphylactic shock include:

- Hives that spread.
- Swelling of the eyes or mouth.
- Difficulty breathing and talking.
- Dizziness or mental confusion.
- Abdominal cramping, nausea, and vomiting.

Treat anaphylaxis as follows:

- Call 911 immediately.
- Administer epinephrine injection (EpiPen).
- Lay the child down on her or his back.

- Do not offer any food or drink.
- Monitor the child carefully.
- If breathing stops, administer CPR.

Seek medical assistance immediately. Epinephrine treatment is only temporary. A second injection may be needed if signs of anaphylaxis return (Defelice & Stewart, 2011; Dugdale et al., 2008).

Bleeding from Cuts, Bumps, and Wounds

Follow these steps when treating a child who is bleeding:

- Wear vinyl or nonlatex gloves.
- Cover the wound with a sterile gauze pad.
- Apply direct pressure.
- Have the child sit or lay down.
- Hold the wound higher than the heart.
- If blood fills the gauze, add more layers of gauze. Do not remove the gauze because this will disturb the natural blood clot that is forming.
- When the bleeding stops, wash with water and cover with a clean bandage.

Seek medical help if the wound is dirty or deep, if you cannot stop the bleeding, if any blood seeps from the ears, or if the child vomits blood (Dowshen, 2010; Heller & Zieve, 2011c). The *Health Hint* provides suggestions about how to ensure that teachers have protective gloves readily available.

Nosebleeds

Nosebleeds can be quite common in the early childhood setting. Treat them as follows:

- Have the child sit down and lean forward.
- Use a sterile gauze pad to pinch the nose between the thumb and index finger. Have the child breathe through the mouth.
- Hold this position for 10 minutes or until bleeding stops.

Seek medical help if the nosebleed is the result of an injury to the head or if the bleeding does not stop (Cronan, 2011b; Cunah & Shiel, 2007).

Bites

Bites are one of the top causes of unintentional injury in young children. Bites may be the result of animals, humans, or spiders.

Animal Bites

Teachers should closely supervise children with any animal in the early childhood setting. If injury occurs:

- Apply direct pressure to stop the bleeding if needed.
- Wash the wound for 3–5 minutes using gentle soap and water.
- Cover the wound with a bandage.

HEALTH HINT **Tips for Having Plastic Gloves Ready**

- Install glove dispenser boxes on the wall near the emergency first aid supplies and in the diapering and toileting areas.
- Place a pair of gloves in a plastic bag and carry them in a pocket.

- Package pairs of gloves inside several plastic bags. Tape the bags at various locations around the children's indoor and outdoor spaces where they can be easily seen and readily accessed.
- Include several pairs of gloves in the traveling first aid kit.

Seek medical help immediately if the bite was caused by an animal with unknown immunization for rabies; if the wound is deep and the skin is torn; if the injuries are on the head, face or hands; or if there is sign of infection (Klein, 2010).

Human Bites

Biting among young children is a common challenge for teachers. The human mouth can contain dangerous bacteria and viruses that present a high risk for infection.

Human bites can also transmit bloodborne pathogens. If the bite breaks the skin:

- Apply direct pressure to the wound, using a sterile gauze pad, until the bleeding stops.
- Wash the bite area with soap and water for 3 to 5 minutes.
- Apply a clean bandage.

Contact the child's family and recommend that the family seek medical advice if the bite is on the face, neck, hands, or feet (Heller & Zieve, 2010c).

Spider Bites

Usually spider bites are just an annoyance, but brown recluse (violin shape on back) or black widow (red hourglass shape on back) spider bites can be dangerous. If possible, capture or try to identify the spider. To treat a spider bite:

- Clean the bite area with soap and water.
- Apply a cool compress.
- Watch for signs of chills, fever, nausea, or abdominal pain, which may indicate a serious spider bite reaction.

Seek immediate medical assistance if the bite is known to be from a brown recluse or black widow spider or if signs of a serious bite are observed (Ben-Joseph, 2010; Duldner & Zieve, 2008).

Bruises and Bumps

Bruises are a common injury among young children. Often good comfort care is the best first aid:

- Raise the injured area.
- Wrap a cold pack in cloth; hold it against the bruised area. Do not place the cold pack directly against the skin because this may cause damage by freezing.
- Cover the bruise with a bandage only if the skin is broken and bleeding.
- Rest the bruised area.

Seek medical assistance if the bruised area is extensive or if there is sign of infection (Gavin, 2010; Vorvick & Zieve, 2009b).

Burns

Burns are classified according to the severity of the wound (Heller & Zieve, 2010a):

- *First-degree burn:* The skin looks red.
- *Second-degree burn:* The skin is red, blotchy, and blistered.
- *Third-degree burn:* The skin is charred; may be black or ash white.

  What to do:

- Cool the burned area under cool running water for 5 minutes.
- Cover with a light dry sterile gauze bandage.

A cool cloth and comfort care may be the best first aid for bumps and bruises.

- Do not use ice.
- Do not apply oils or ointment.
- Do not pop any blisters.
- Monitor breathing and treat for shock as needed.

Seek medical assistance for any burn on an infant. For toddlers and older children, seek medical help if the burned area is larger than 3 inches in diameter or if the burn is on the hands, feet, face, groin, or buttocks; over a major joint; or if signs of infection appear (National Institute of General Medicine Sciences, 2008). Notify the child's family as soon as possible.

Drowning

Drowning is the second leading cause of death for children in the early childhood age group (CDC, 2009). The goal of emergency response is to rescue the child from the water source and begin first aid as soon as possible:

- Remove the child from the water without endangering self.
- Check to see if the airway is open.
- Begin rescue breathing as soon as possible.
- Conduct CPR if the child's heart is not beating.
- Keep the child warm and treat for hypothermia and shock.
- Don't give up. Some children have been successfully resuscitated after being in cold water for up to an hour.

Seek medical help right away. Even if resuscitation has revived the child, medical help is needed to ensure that infection, respiratory problems, or other complications do not occur.

Electrical Shock

If a child is severely shocked by electricity:

- Do *not* touch the child. Assess the situation.
- If possible turn off the electricity or move the electrical source away from the child and yourself using a nonconductive product such as cardboard or plastic.
- Call 911 for emergency assistance if the electrical source is a high-voltage wire or if you cannot turn off the electrical source.
- If the child is no longer touching the electrical source, observe the child for breathing and heartbeat. Restore breathing with rescue breathing. If heartbeat has stopped, call 911 and conduct CPR.
- Treat for shock: Lay the child down. Elevate the child's legs.

Call 911 for emergency assistance if the child shows signs of cardiac arrest or heart rhythm problems, stopped breathing, muscle seizure, or pain or if the child is unconscious (Heller & Zieve, 2011d).

Foreign Objects

Children are very involved with their environment and explore their world in ways that make them vulnerable to foreign objects in the eyes, nose, and mouth. The goal of first aid is to carefully remove any object but only if this can be done without causing harm.

To remove a foreign object from an eye:

- Wash hands carefully.
- Have the child sit down and look upward.
- Lift the eyelid away from the eye and look for the object.

- If the object is visible, try gently flushing the eye with water to wash it out.
- *Do not* rub the eye or try to remove items that are lodged in the eyeball.

Seek medical assistance if the object is not removed through tears, if the object is large, or if vision is impaired (Vorvick, 2011).

To remove a foreign object from the nose:

- Determine which nostril holds the foreign object.
- Gently pinch in the other (unobstructed) nostril and have the child blow the nose gently to dislodge the object.
- Do not probe the nose—this may move the object in deeper.

Seek medical assistance if these steps do not dislodge the object (Vorvick, 2011).

Tooth Injury

If a child's baby tooth is injured, apply pressure to stop bleeding, and offer comfort. Call the doctor for guidance. If a child's permanent tooth is knocked out, careful treatment can sometimes restore it:

- Find the tooth.
- Gently rinse tooth in a bowl of water; do not rub or scrape it.
- Place the tooth in the tooth socket in the child's mouth; cover with gauze and hold in place or have the child bite down gently on the gauze. If the tooth cannot be replaced in the socket, then place the tooth in a cup of whole milk (Goss, 2010).

Contact the dentist right away for guidance.

Heat Exhaustion

Heat exhaustion refers to moderate heat-related illness. It may occur when children are engaged in highly active play during very warm days. Dehydration may be a cause. Signs of heat exhaustion include dizziness, nausea, rapid heartbeat, fast shallow breathing, and cramps.

What to do:

- Move child to shady area, lay child down, and remove extra clothing.
- Sponge or spray child with cool water.
- Offer cool water to drink.

Seek medical assistance if symptoms increase (CDC, 2012c, 2012e).

Heatstroke

Heatstroke is the most severe heat-related illness. Without aid, heat stroke can lead to death. Watch for these signs:

- Elevated body temperature (above 104°F [40°C]).
- Hot dry skin.
- Rapid heartbeat.
- Confusion, dizziness, fainting, coma.

What to do:

- Move child to a cool and shady place.
- Call 911 for emergency medical assistance.
- Lay child down and remove extra clothing.
- Cover child with moist cloth or spray with cool water.
- Fan the child to help with cooling.

Seek medical assistance immediately (CDC, 2012c, 2012e).

Seizure

Seizures are the result of abnormal activity in the brain. Some children may have known seizure history and physician-suggested protocols for seizure management. For others the seizure may be a new event. The goal of first aid is to prevent the child from being hurt during a seizure. Watch for these signs:

- Temporary confusion or loss of consciousness.
- Uncontrolled jerking of arms, legs, and head.
- Staring straight ahead; no recognition.

If a seizure occurs:

- Protect the child from harm: Ease the child down to the floor. Clear the area around the child and place something soft under the child's head and gently roll the child onto one side.
- Do not put anything in the child's mouth.
- Do not restrain the child.
- Let the seizure take its course.
- Call the child's family immediately to report the seizure event.

Seek immediate medical help if the seizure lasts more than 5 minutes or if the child is slow to improve or has trouble breathing (Filloux & Goodman, 2010; Dugdale & Zieve, 2010).

Shock

Shock is often associated with injury but can also occur with heatstroke, allergic reactions, infections, poisoning, or other causes. Shock is a sign that the body is struggling. Watch for:

- Cool and clammy skin.
- Weak but rapid pulse.
- Faintness or confusion.

Treatment for shock includes:

- Lay the child down.
- Raise the child's feet if this does not contribute to injury.
- Check for an open airway, regular breathing, and circulation.
- Keep the child calm, comfortable, and warm.
- Do not give the child anything to eat or drink.
- Address any injuries.

Seek medical assistance if these actions do not resolve the concern, or if shock is associated with significant injury (Heller & Zieve, 2010b).

Cleaning Blood Spills

Blood spills can be relatively common in early childhood settings. Skinned knees, bloody noses, and cuts, especially those to the mouth, can cause small blood spills that must be cleaned up in a safe and hygienic way. Cleaning up blood spills is important to prevent the possibility of transmitting communicable disease. The U.S. Occupational Safety and Health Administration and the *National Health and Safety Performance Standards* (AAP et al., 2011) are good sources of information for managing blood spills in the work site and early childhood setting.

Cleaning Blood Spills Indoors

Teachers should wear gloves and other appropriate protection (apron, eye covering) depending on the extent of the blood spill. Do not step on the contaminated area and avoid splashing the spill into eyes, mouth, nose, or unprotected skin. The area should be sprayed thoroughly with disinfecting

FIGURE 15-4 **Procedure for Safely Discarding Protective Gloves**

1. Grasp the palm of the left-hand glove with the fingers of the right-gloved hand. Pull outward and remove the left-hand glove from the hand. Do not reach inside the opposite glove—let only the dirty surfaces touch each other.
2. Grasp the left-hand glove in a ball inside the palm of the gloved right hand.
3. Use a finger of the left hand to reach inside the wrist of the right-hand glove, and peel the right-hand glove off inside out encasing the dirty surfaces of both gloves.
4. Drop the soiled gloves inside a plastic bag. Seal the bag and discard it in an appropriate location.
5. Wash your hands thoroughly.

Source: Based on *Sequence for Removing Personal Protective Equipment: Gloves,* Centers for Disease Control and Prevention. (2012), retrieved May 9, 2012, from http://www.cdc.gov/sars/downloads/ppeposter148.pdf.

solution (1 tablespoon bleach to 1 quart of water) and wiped with absorbent paper towels. This should be repeated a second time. Then the area should be washed with soap and water and wiped with paper towels. Soiled paper towels should be placed in a leakproof plastic bag, being careful to not touch the outside of the bag, and the bag should be closed securely and discarded. Figure 15-4 provides guidance for safely removing and discarding protective gloves. Teachers should wash their hands thoroughly when done (AAP et al., 2011).

Cleaning Blood Spills Outdoors

Teachers should wear appropriate protection and avoid stepping on or splashing the spill. The grass, sand, bark, or sidewalk areas should be sprayed or flooded thoroughly with disinfecting solution (mix 2 quarts bleach with 5 gallons of water). Let stand for 15 minutes, and then spray the area thoroughly with a hose to disperse the solution (Purdue University, 2012).

Cleaning Large Blood Spills

Large spills can be cleaned using absorbent pellet materials. The pellets should be allowed to absorb the spill and then collected and discarded along with other contaminated materials.

Cleaning Upholstery and Carpeting

Upholstery and carpeting should be spot cleaned using a disinfectant product designed for fabrics. Let the solution set for 15 minutes (or as directed) and then blot the area dry. This should be repeated until the spill is no longer visible on the surface (AAP et al., 2011).

Addressing Blood Spill Splatters

If unprotected skin is splashed with a blood product, the skin should be washed with soap and water as soon as possible. If the splash is in the eyes, the eyes should be flushed thoroughly with clean water. Splashes on skin that has cuts or open sores should be washed, and the child's medical provider should be contacted for follow-up (AAP et al., 2011).

● MANAGING DISASTERS

Emergency response is also needed in disaster events. Whether the disaster strikes suddenly or through a series of events, teachers must take decisive action to ensure children's safety.

The first steps in disaster response include the following:

- Remain calm.
- Review the facility for danger.

- Provide first aid for any injury.
- Listen to the radio for reports and guidance.
- Decide whether to take shelter-in-place, lock down, or evacuate.
- Take action.

The decisions related to taking action include whether to shelter-in-place, implement lockdown or evacuate and relocate the children. Specific actions are needed to address the impacts of natural disasters, technological hazards, and disease emergencies. Later, when the disaster emergency has passed, it is important for teachers to complete reports to record what was done to keep children safe and what additional preparedness steps are needed for the future.

Sheltering-in-Place

Sometimes sheltering in place simply involves staying inside the facility. In other situations special measures may be needed. For tornadoes, shelter should be sought in the lowest area in the building such as a basement or interior room. For chemical spills or airborne hazards, doors, windows, and any air vents should be covered with plastic and sealed shut with duct tape (CDC, 2006; Federal Emergency Management Agency (FEMA), Ready.gov, 2012a). If sheltering-in-place is needed, teachers should:

- Assemble children and visitors inside as quickly as possible.
- Go into the identified shelter room.
- Take the emergency kit and water.
- Lock windows and exterior doors to seal them. Cover air vents with plastic, if necessary.
- Engage children in calm and quiet games: reading, playing with manipulative toys.
- Watch TV, check the internet news, or listen to the radio for information.
- Stay in shelter until word is received that it is safe to leave.

In most cases teachers and children need to shelter-in-place only for a few hours. However, if sheltering for a longer period is required, teachers should use the emergency supplies to care for and comfort children. The *Nutrition Note* provides guidance for using stored food and water when taking shelter-in-place.

NUTRITION NOTE Using Emergency Food

- Take an inventory of the kinds and quantity of food you have on hand and in storage.
- Throw away any foods that are spoiled or cans that are swollen or corroded.
- Create a plan for portioning out the foods. Aim to provide fully balanced meals.
- Use any perishable foods you have on hand in the refrigerator, freezer, and cupboards, first.
- Open stored foods carefully. Place leftover foods in resealable bags or containers.
- Canned food can be eaten right out of the can (no heating is required).

- If stored water runs low, the water stored in the hot-water heater can be used. Be sure the gas or electric power is turned off. Open the drain at bottom of the water heater. Turn off the water intake valve at the tank and turn on a hot water faucet in the building to start the water flowing from the water heater drain.
- If needed, boil stream, pond, spring, or rainwater for one full minute and let cool, or treat with 1/8 teaspoon of newly opened unscented household bleach (that contains 6.0% sodium hypochlorite). Stir and let stand for 30 minutes. The water should smell slightly of bleach. If it doesn't, repeat the process.

Source: Based on *Food and Water in an Emergency* (FEMA 447; A5055), August 2004, Jessup, MD: FEMA and Washington, DC: American Red Cross. Retrieved May 11, 2012, from http://www.fema.gov/pdf/library/f&web.pdf.

Implementing Lockdown

lockdown
taking shelter in the children's facility while stopping the access and entry of an intruder

Lockdown is needed when there is a danger to children from entry of an intruder, shooting, or a hostage situation (Illinois Emergency Medical Services for Children [IEMSC], 2006). Teachers work to shelter children from harm inside the classroom or school or child care facility. If lockdown is needed, teachers should:

- Have a program code word or other way to signal the need for lockdown.
- Assemble children in an interior room or corner of the children's classroom.
- Create protection in an interior closet, behind a shelf or a table turned on its side.
- If possible, lock doors and windows; close blinds, turn off lights.
- Stay quiet and still.
- Call 911 to report what was seen or heard.
- Count children to be sure all are present.
- Stay in lockdown until informed that it is "all clear" by emergency personnel.

Lockdown situations are likely to be unpredictable, frightening, and intense. Teachers may need to shelter with children in the setting for several hours. Locating bottled water and small comfort toys in the designated space can support teachers and children until the lockdown is lifted (American Red Cross, 2012a; Curtis, 2008). Gathering courage to remain calm is essential.

Evacuating and Relocating

In this video, a teacher describes the evacuation procedure used in an early childhood setting. What strategies do teachers use to familiarize children with this procedure? How do they keep track of children during evacuation?

Evacuation requires that children be assembled and safely moved to a previously identified location (IEMSC, 2006). The nearby location should be within walking distance and suitable for sheltering for a short time until families can be contacted to pick up their child. Children may also be moved to a relocation site further away if the facility is damaged or dangerous. The relocation site should be identified in advance and appropriate for taking shelter for a longer period of time. A sign identifying the relocation site should be prepared in advance so it can quickly be placed in a conspicuous location at departure. This can serve as a cue for emergency responders or parents in case of a relocation emergency. In some cases, community emergency personnel will direct the group to an evacuation site. If evacuation is needed (FEMA, Ready.gov, 2012a):

- Gather children and exit the classroom safely to the designated assembly location.
- Count to ensure all children and staff are present. Assign each child to an adult.
- If time permits, place a sticker label on each child's coat with the child's name, family name, address, and phone number.
- Take emergency kit and child and staff emergency contact records.
- Post a sign identifying the evacuation relocation site.
- Travel to the emergency evacuation spot along a predetermined route.
- Make contact with emergency personnel if possible and follow directions.
- Listen to the radio for instructions as appropriate.

Because disaster emergencies are unpredictable, support for evacuation is hard to anticipate. In some cases, emergency responders from outside the disaster area are able to arrive quickly to help. In other situations the disaster may be widespread and emergency aid very slow to contact those in need. Teachers may find that their informed care and management makes the difference between life and death for the children and themselves. Preparation, practice, and courage are the resources that teachers carry with them to make a positive impact in such significant situations.

Responding to Natural Disasters

Disasters can be caused by a wide range of natural causes, including tornadoes, hurricanes, earthquakes, storms, floods, and fires. The plan for response is unique to each situation.

Tornadoes

Programs in areas with the potential for tornadoes should install a weather radar warning system. Teachers should listen for storm watch warnings on the radio and modify activities in case safety actions may be needed (FEMA, Ready.gov, 2012b; IEMSC, 2006). If a tornado warning is announced take action as recommended:

- Move children to shelter in an underground space, interior room, or hallway away from windows.
- Take cover under tables or desks.
- If a mobile home is used for family child care, leave and take shelter in a safe location.
- Take a cell phone or cordless phone.
- Remain in the shelter until the warning has ended.

Hurricanes

Teachers should listen for hurricane warnings and keep alert to storm watch systems on radio, TV, or the Internet. If enough time is available, try to return children to their families. If not, follow these precautions (FEMA, Ready.gov, 2012b):

- Close windows and secure the facility as much as possible.
- Turn off propane tanks and unplug unneeded appliances.
- Gather water containers and emergency supplies at the ready.
- Take cover in an interior room or hallway away from windows.
- Lay down on the floor under a table or other sturdy furniture.
- Remain indoors until the hurricane has passed over.
- Evacuate as directed by emergency personnel.

Earthquakes

Earthquakes usually occur without warning. Teachers and children must be prepared to take cover immediately (FEMA, Ready.gov, 2012b):

- If indoors, drop to the ground and take cover under tables or desks. Hold on until shaking stops.
- After shaking stops, evacuate if the facility is unsafe. Be aware that aftershocks may occur.
- If outside when the earthquake occurs, move to an open area away from walls, windows, or electric wires.

Storms

Check emergency broadcasts for storm warnings and travel advisories. Close the children's program if recommended. Return children to families if time allows. If the children must remain at the school or care facility, then (FEMA, Ready.gov, 2012b):

- If a storm warning is issued, gather emergency supplies at the ready.
- Move to an interior space away from windows if high winds are a concern.
- Stay in shelter until the storm is passed.
- Evacuate if needed.

Floods

Keep aware of flood warnings. Close the facility and return children to families if time allows. If not, then (FEMA, Ready.gov, 2012b):

- If there is time, secure the facility: Forward electronic records to a recipient outside the area, move equipment to a higher location, and turn off gas and utilities.
- Evacuate from the facility if there is any chance of flooding or flash flooding.

If an earthquake occurs, take cover under tables or desks and hold on until shaking stops.

Wildfires and Forest Fires

Keep aware of active fires in the area. Follow the guidance of emergency management personnel regarding closure or evacuation. Close the facility and return children to families if time allows. If a fire approaches near the children's setting (FEMA, Ready.gov, 2012b):

- Gather all children inside.
- Close doors and windows.
- Turn off gas and electricity.
- Position sprinklers to spray water against the building and roof.
- Evacuate as soon as possible.

Responding to Technological Hazards

A variety of technological hazards can introduce danger to children's settings. These include situations that disrupt utilities, chemical spills or explosions involving toxic materials, and threats to personal safety.

Disruption of Utilities

The children's program should be closed if water, electricity, heat, and the ability to communicate by telephone are disrupted for more than a short time. When utility disruption occurs without warning:

- Gather children in a secure location that has sufficient light and heat.
- Help children feel secure and comfortable.
- Contact families by cell phone or wireless e-mail to pick up children as needed.

Chemical Spills and Explosions of Hazardous Materials

Assess the situation to determine a plan for shelter and then follow these steps (IEMSC, 2006):

- Do not turn any electrical switches on or off.
- Evacuate immediately moving upwind from the hazard if it is safe to do so.
- Otherwise, shelter-in-place.
- Assemble children in an interior room.
- Cover windows, doors, and air vents.
- Use cell phones or wireless e-mail to communicate with emergency personnel.
- Stay in the shelter until advised by emergency personnel that it is safe to leave.

Industrial activities can introduce technological hazards to nearby early childhood settings.

Attacks and Threats to Personal Safety

Attacks and threats usually occur without warning. Teachers need to be prepared to take appropriate and responsive actions, such as:

- *Explosions:* Take cover from falling debris. Evacuate quickly and calmly.
- *Fire:* Keep low. Get out and stay out. If clothes catch on fire, stop-drop-roll and cover eyes with hands.
- *Missing child or kidnapping:* Call 911 to report a missing child immediately. Provide information about when and where the child was last seen and what the child was wearing. Follow the guidance of emergency personnel.
- *Bomb threat:* Report bomb threats to emergency personnel immediately. Provide details about the threat. Evacuate quickly and calmly.
- *Person with firearms:* Call 911. Implement lockdown procedures. Stay in lockdown until emergency personnel advise that it is safe.

Addressing Disease Emergencies

Health emergencies include situations where communicable disease is widespread, challenging the ability of public health organizations to administer aid to victims and to stop the spread of disease. Some health emergencies, such as pandemic flu, may unfold gradually as health professionals recognize the outbreak and monitor the spread of disease across the world. Other health emergencies are discovered when unusual numbers of people are suddenly struck with acute illness, such as may occur with Severe Acute Respiratory Syndrome (SARS). Health emergencies impact classrooms so teachers must pay special attention to sanitizing the environment, teaching children ways to reduce the spread of disease, and monitoring children's health. Teachers themselves are threatened with contracting disease during health emergencies and must take precautions such as obtaining special immunizations. Teachers should be aware of diseases under emergency watch and be prepared to (FEMA, 2012c):

- Follow the guidance of medical personnel to reduce the exchange and spread of disease.
- Communicate closely with families about symptoms of disease.
- Report identified cases as directed.
- Close the children's program as directed by community health personnel.

Teachers' resilience and courage may be tested to the extreme when disaster strikes. Following the strategies and procedures of the disaster emergency response plan helps teachers keep focused on the goals of achieving safety for children and adults: preserving life, avoiding additional injury, and assisting with recovery. Pandemic disease disasters are a rare occurrence. If they do happen, prepared teachers are ready.

Completing Emergency Response Reports

After the immediate emergency actions have been managed, teachers still need to bring closure to the event. This includes reviewing the setting to see if a blood spill has occurred, cleaning the area safely, and disposing of any soiled toweling and gloves in an appropriate way.

Teachers should also make a record of the event and the emergency response actions by completing an accident or emergency report. This is important to do soon after the event so that all details about the incident and the first aid offered can be recorded while the information is still fresh. Such reflections are important at the classroom and program level to guide future preparations and practices. They are also significant at the federal and policy level. For example, the *Progressive Programs & Practices* feature describes how lessons learned from Hurricane Katrina raised awareness of the need for emergency preparedness planning, promoted the development of resources for teachers, and influenced federal policies.

As well as reflecting on emergency actions, teachers also observe the effects of the emergency on children. Extra efforts may be needed to comfort and support children to help them work through the after-effects of the event.

● SUPPORTING CHILDREN AFTER EMERGENCIES

When the drama of emergency events has passed, teachers face the next step in effective management: focusing on helping children cope with the trauma they have experienced and learn to develop resilience.

Helping Children Cope

After emergencies teachers continue to guide children by being positive role models, reestablishing familiar classroom routines, and supporting children as they process their worries. If tragedies have occurred, teachers are important resources for helping children and families cope with their feelings of loss. As teachers conduct these supportive activities, they also need to recognize their own need for support.

PROGRESSIVE PROGRAMS & PRACTICES

Lessons Learned from Hurricane Katrina

By Cathy Grace, Director (Retired), The Early Childhood Institute, Mississippi State University (MSU)

The Early Childhood Institute (ECI) is a unit of the College of Education at Mississippi State University. The institute was established in 1999 by Cathy Grace, Ed.D. to provide training, technical assistance, and applied research for improved quality and accessibility of early care and education across Mississippi. The institute serves communities statewide through programs which focus on improving the quality of early childhood education, providing professional development for early childhood professionals, and engaging the community in supporting young children.

What Challenge Did You Face?

After Hurricane Katrina hit the Mississippi Gulf Coast in 2005, close to 90% of the early care and education programs were inoperable. At the request of Chevron and state government agencies, ECI spearheaded an early care and education program recovery effort like none ever attempted in the country.

How Did You Meet the Challenge?
What Was the Institute's Role?

Given the degree of community devastation in the coastal communities and extending 200 miles northward, ECI staff went to each licensed early care and education center and assessed their operational condition. The information gathered was transformed via spatial mapping to communicate to government agencies and potential funders the degree of need that existed. Working with Chevron, Save the Children, the MSU Extension Service, and a small foundation based in South Mississippi, ECI enlisted the support of numerous foundations, donors and businesses to provide funds and other resources to reconstruct and refurnish over 200 programs and conduct training for hundreds of staff members.

The work which lasted over two years, moved from repairing and equipping the buildings to providing support to the adult staff members and children suffering from post-traumatic stress syndrome as a result of hurricane Katrina. Through this process national awareness was raised related to the failure of federal agencies to address early care and education programs in emergency planning at the state and local level, to provide mental health counseling to small children and their families, and to provide simple and accessible procedures so program owners could file claims for disaster relief funding.

While the repair to the facilities has been completed, the emotional stress and trauma is still present for some. Recovery may take many more years as residents work to fully heal. Some early care and education teachers on the Gulf Coast lost their homes, and in some cases family members. This created

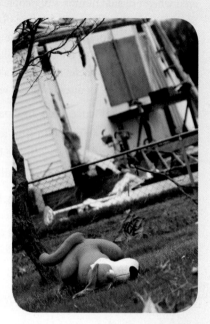

challenges as to how to support the mental health of those who had suffered great loss but had no time to grieve and recover. In emergency situations such as the one Katrina created, early care and education teachers should be considered as first responders and afforded the training and support as such. When communities are in disarray and families in the midst of attempting to secure financial assistance and social services, individuals charged with the care of young children should be supported and given first priority for their own needs to be met so they can meet the needs of children and families in trauma. To address this, ECI contracted with national experts to provide mental health assistance to teachers in early care and education facilities. The support extended to classroom strategies for teachers to use with preschoolers to help the children heal and move forward.

Classroom teachers, depending on the age of children they teach, can do the following to support children to cope with unexpected life events:

- Provide problem solving activities as part of daily instruction;
- Read books that highlight how children, when faced with a problem, determined solutions and resolved the issue;
- Encourage the children to talk to their parents about developing an escape plan in the event of a fire or natural disaster;
- Invite emergency personnel into the classroom so children can meet them and better understand their jobs; and
- Practice emergency drills in a calm and controlled manner so the children will gain confidence and knowledge of what to do in the event of an emergency.

What Was the Outcome?

As a result of the work, by March 2006, 251 centers out of a total 291 were operational in new or renovated facilities and with materials of a higher quality than prior to hurricane Katrina. A partnership with the National Association of Child Care Resource and Referral Agencies resulted in the development of a resource book for early care and education programs that is used across the country to support emergency planning in all types of early childhood programs. Approximately 100 playgrounds were provided to early care programs on the coast and training materials were developed that supported staff in using the newly purchased materials. Changes in federal policies regarding emergency preparedness for children in out-of—home settings have occurred, but further revisions are needed to ensure children and families who are displaced receive the services to which they are entitled. The original reporting of the physical condition of the program facilities and use of spatial mapping and color coding has been replicated in other natural disasters when facility assessments have been conducted.

For more information and photos go to http://earlychildhood.msstate.edu/reports.htm

Being a Confident Role Model

After emergency events, children need to regain their confidence that things will be "all right." Children gain this assurance when they observe their teachers managing the situation calmly, positively, and with appropriate optimism (American Red Cross, 2012b; Centers for Disease Control and Prevention [CDC], 2012d). This means teachers must pay special attention to moving with confidence rather than appearing disorganized. Teachers can acknowledge the difficulties and distress of an emergency situation by stating frankly, "That was scary, wasn't it?" But it is especially important to focus as much as possible on the actions children, teachers, and others performed to resolve the emergency situation, for example by saying, "Wasn't that good that we knew to move up the hill to the community center until the moms and dads could come?" This conveys the message that children and teachers are capable of taking appropriate actions and helps to address feelings of powerlessness.

What if . . .

you had effectively managed an emergency in your classroom, like Jamal in the opening case scenario. How will you tell the other families about the event now that it is over? Do you think the families will blame you for "allowing" the accident to happen?

Acknowledging Children's Feelings

Children are likely to struggle with a variety of feelings if they have either directly or indirectly witnessed or experienced an emergency event. They may need extra assurance and understanding from teachers, including personal contact and hugs. Children may need to talk about the emergency as they try to understand what happened and to help process their fears. After a difficult experience, a child might wonder: *Can it happen again? Could someone I love be hurt? Could I be left alone?* (FEMA, 2010). These concerns need to be validated and addressed with brief and correct information. Teachers should not avoid talking about the event. At the same time teachers must keep from using frightening descriptions when talking about the emergency with the children, with one another, or when talking on the phone in the presence of children. For children who have difficulty talking about their feelings, teachers might offer opportunities for children to create drawings to express their concerns or to tell their story.

Regaining a Sense of Routine and Control

Young children derive great comfort from the routines and rhythms of their day. When routines are disrupted by injury, emergency, or disaster response, children may feel hopeless. They may think that no one is in control. Returning to familiar routines as quickly as possible is one way to begin the process of healing (American Red Cross, 2012b; CDC, 2012d; MacCormack, 2008). Once children are surrounded by their familiar world, they are better able to work through the stresses of the unusual events and to regain a sense of safety and well-being.

Children, like adults, are often able to cope better when they feel the sense of being prepared (FEMA, 2010). This confidence can be supported by engaging children in emergency response preparation. Even after a difficult event, teachers and children can work together to replenish the first aid kit, post a new evacuation plan map, or make a new emergency response plan.

Continuing to Monitor the Effects on Children

Each child copes with extraordinary events in unique and personal ways. Some may be very outward in their expression of worry, sadness, or dismay, whereas others may seem uninterested and unaffected by the events. Children need many opportunities to safely express their concerns. This support should be provided over a long period of time because a child may express worry many weeks after the event (MacCormack, 2008). Tips for helping children cope after distressing situations are provided in Figure 15-5. Teachers should continue to watch for signs that suggest children may need special help to resolve their worries. If the worries interrupt the child's daily behavior a referral for special counseling support may be needed (CDC, 2012d; FEMA, 2010).

Addressing Tragedies

Sometimes emergencies and disasters have tragic outcomes such as the death of a playmate or teacher. Children, families, and teachers all need the opportunity to process their feelings of loss. One approach is for teachers to invite families to join their child while the teacher explains in simple terms what has happened. Describing how much the child or teacher was loved and talking about how the group will miss that person offers opportunity for children and teachers to tell their stories of love and loss.

Turning sad thoughts to productive actions and expressions is a positive next step. Decorating a special remembrance poster with drawings or planting a special tree "for teacher Karla" are options that allow children to express their feelings through action. Managing a sad event with children is one way to model healthy coping strategies and can be supportive for children, families, and teachers alike.

Recognizing That Teachers Need Support, Too

Teachers involved in managing emergencies also need support. Like parents, they carry the dual responsibilities of emergency responder and care provider for children, which can be extremely stressful. Some teachers may feel responsible for injuries, thinking they should have protected the children in some way, or they may wonder if they made the right decisions during an emergency situation (CDC, 2012d). Unsettling events may cause teachers themselves to feel unsafe in the environment. It is important for teachers to be aware of these concerns and access needed supports

---

FIGURE 15-5   Tips for Helping Children Cope After Disasters

❑ Protect children from graphic images—limit television and keep from talking about the event when children can hear.

❑ Offer reassurance—let children know that everyone is working to keep them safe.

❑ Provide children extra time and attention—be available, accessible, and close.

❑ Model positive coping—explain your feelings as appropriate and help children recognize how you are managing your emotions.

❑ Reestablish normal routines and activities—surround the child with familiar activity.

❑ Pay attention to what children say—learn what they are worried about.

❑ Find ways for children to engage in helpful action—have them draw pictures, or send cards or books to share with others.

❑ Recognize different responses—children do not experience events in the same way.

❑ Watch for changes that might signal emotional stress—seek professional counseling for the child, if needed.

Source: Based on *Emergency Preparedness and Response: Coping with Disaster or Traumatic Events*, Centers for Disease Control and Prevention. (2012). Retrieved May 8, 2012, from http://emergency.cdc.gov/mentalhealth/.

to help resolve their feelings and regain their sense of personal confidence and well-being (Government Services Agency, Child Care Division, 2011).

Preparing Children to Be Resilient

Children are active participants in emergency situations and need to be prepared with knowledge and strategies to help them cope. This is accomplished by sharing information about injuries, illness, and emergencies in child-appropriate ways through what is called a "child-centered risk reduction program" (International Save the Children Alliance, 2006). Classroom activities that equip children with the knowledge that helps them be resilient include these:

Planting a tree is a positive action that can help children express their feelings of loss and gain hope for the future.

- Explore the topics of injury and illness through books and dramatic play settings such as a doctor's office or offer appropriate props such as firefighter hats and pieces of hose.
- Use current events to begin discussions with school-age children about emergencies that are being addressed. Put special focus on the ways people help each other in emergencies.
- Conduct emergency drills that teach children what to do and establish a sense of routine about evacuating the classroom.

It is important to infuse these life lessons into everyday activities to help children recognize their competence in participating in the emergency process. Equipping children with appropriate information and skills makes them partners in keeping themselves safe and builds their resilience to face and manage the negative impacts of disastrous events.

▶ Because young children are at high risk of injury or death due to fire, early childhood curriculum should address fire safety. As you watch this **video**, think about specific aspects of fire safety to teach young children.

● SUMMARY

Teaching is a dynamic profession that requires many competencies, including the ability to safely address everyday injuries and identify when injuries are emergencies requiring specialized care. Teachers need to access training on appropriate first aid and CPR practices, and develop a sense of leadership when difficult events occur.

Managing emergencies can be stressful. Developing an emergency response plan and assembling emergency supplies helps teachers prepare to take effective action. When emergency events occur, teachers need to be confident in implementing the emergency plan by administering basic first aid and providing comfort care until emergency assistance can be obtained.

Teachers must also be prepared to manage the impacts of disaster events by knowing how to respond to natural disasters, technological hazards, and pandemic disease situations. They must be ready to supervise children when disaster strikes, to take shelter or lead children to safety, and provide care until the children can be released to their families.

When emergencies and disasters have passed, teachers continue to play an important role in helping children manage the emotional impacts of the distressing events. They do this by being confident role models, acknowledging children's emotions and reestablishing regular routines, and by offering support and positive activities that assist children to develop resilience and regain their confidence in the future.

KEY TERMS

Disaster	Good Samaritan doctrine	Shelter-in-place
Emergency	Lockdown	Universal precautions
First aid		

REVIEW QUESTIONS

1. What signs indicate that emergency medical assistance is needed?
2. What are the three goals of first aid?
3. What is the Good Samaritan doctrine and why is it important?
4. What is the definition of a disaster?
5. Provide examples of how teachers help children cope following traumatic events.

DISCUSSION STARTERS

1. Think about a children's classroom that you have observed. Describe the setting and propose an emergency management plan for the classroom. Discuss some of the supports available for the classroom and identify challenges.
2. Consider a rural and an urban community in your state. Identify and compare some of the similarities and differences in challenges that teachers in those areas may face in accessing emergency assistance.
3. Select an age group—infants, toddlers, preschoolers, or school-age children—and develop activities for teaching the children the appropriate emergency response for different disaster events.

PRACTICE POINTS

1. Imagine that you manage a small child care program in a rural area. You know that first aid training is important, but you have to work every weekday, and no training is available in your small town. What other options for training can you identify?
2. Go to the Federal Emergency Management Agency website listed in the Web Resources. Review the site to learn about emergencies that have been recorded for your area. What disaster emergency management plans could you put in place to prepare yourself and the children in your class for such emergencies?
3. Create a list of emergency supplies needed to support a class group of 18 children and two adults for 3 days. Use the Web Resources to guide your planning. Draft a budget for the needed supplies. Explain how the supplies can be assembled and stored in readiness for emergency evacuation.

WEB RESOURCES

American Academy of Pediatrics, Disaster Planning
www.aap.org/healthtopics/disasters.cfm

American Red Cross
www.redcross.org

Federal Emergency Management Agency
www.fema.gov
www.Ready.gov

Mayo Clinic, First Aid Information
www.mayoclinic.com/health/FirstAidIndex/FirstAidIndex

National Oceanic and Atmospheric Administration's National Weather Service
www.weather.gov

National Resource Center for Health and Safety in Child Care and Early Education
http://nrc.uchsc.edu

MyEducationLab™

Go to Topic 9 (Emergencies and Injuries) in the MyEducationLab (www.myeducationlab.com) for your course, where you can:

- Find learning outcomes for Emergencies and Injuries along with the national standards that connect to these outcomes.
- Complete Assignments and Activities that can help you more deeply understand the chapter content.
- Apply and practice your understanding of the core teaching skills identified in the chapter with the Building Teaching Skills and Dispositions learning units.

- Check your comprehension on the content covered in the chapter by going to the Study Plan in the Book Resources for your text. Here you will be able to take a chapter quiz, receive feedback on your answers, and then access Review, Practice, and Enrichment activities to enhance your understanding of chapter content.

sixteen
Child Abuse and Neglect

learning outcomes

AFTER READING THIS CHAPTER, YOU SHOULD BE ABLE TO:

1. Define child maltreatment and describe different types of child abuse and neglect.

2. Describe some of the physical and behavioral signs of child maltreatment.

3. Explain the term mandated reporter and describe the steps in reporting suspected child maltreatment.

4. Identify other sources of violence and explain their impacts on children and families.

5. Describe some of the strategies that teachers can use to reduce the effects of maltreatment and violence and assist children to build positive coping skills.

6. Discuss ways to prevent child abuse in early childhood settings and help children and families develop protective factors.

Min Jee teaches a small group of children ages 2 to 5 years, who are gathered together from several class groups at the end of the program's service day. The children are involved and busy, and she notices with pleasure that Katherine is drawing with marking pens. Katherine usually spends the end of the day in the book corner alone. Min Jee watches as Katherine carefully outlines a figure of a girl in a pink dress who has curly hair just like her own. Min Jee encourages Katherine by saying softly, "Tell me about your picture." Katherine pauses, and then speaks slowly, "This girl is a special princess. She has a beautiful dress and she likes to dance." Then Katherine looks intensely at Min Jee and says very solemnly, "But I smell and I'm dirty." Leaving her picture on the table Katherine gets up and walks over to the book corner where she curls up against a pillow.

Min Jee is bothered by this statement but it seems to summarize the concerns she has about Katherine. The other children do not want to sit beside Katherine because she smells bad. Though Katherine is anxious to eat at afternoon snack, she struggles to chew and sometimes gives up. Min Jee learns that Katherine's full-day teacher has been concerned about the child's teeth, and has provided the child's mother with information about a volunteer dentist. Min Jee decides to follow up and offers to help the mother call to schedule an appointment. But Katherine's mother responds by saying, "That girl is always causing me trouble. She's just too dumb to brush her teeth." Min Jee reflects on all of these observations and makes a decision. She calls the child protective services hotline to report child maltreatment due to neglect.

Child abuse, neglect, and violence are serious threats to children's safety. They interfere with healthful development by eroding children's trust in others and in their world. These forms of maltreatment and violence inflict cruel injuries, scarring children physically and emotionally, and can cause disability and death (U.S. Department of Health and Human Services, Administration for Children and Families, Administration on Children, Youth and Families [HHS/ACF], Children's Bureau, 2011). However, in spite of these overwhelming negative impacts, child maltreatment is sometimes disregarded by those who confuse maltreatment with parental discipline practices, or overlooked by those who have the notion that child maltreatment "doesn't happen here."

Young children are vulnerable, unable to defend or protect themselves, and may not know where to go for help. Teachers play an important role in keeping children safe from maltreatment and by reporting maltreatment when it is suspected. In this chapter we discuss the different types of child maltreatment, provide guidance for teachers to recognize the signs of maltreatment, and outline the steps to take if maltreatment is suspected. We also present strategies to prevent and reduce maltreatment and to address the effects of all forms of violence in children's lives.

UNDERSTANDING CHILD MALTREATMENT

Childhood is a unique and special time of development. The vulnerability of the young child suggests that children have the right to expect safe and kind care to meet their basic needs. In turn, the child's "task" during childhood is to explore the world, grow, develop, and learn. During the early years of development, young children are particularly impressionable and can be seriously affected by negative experiences. Many behaviors of parents, teachers, caregivers, and others enhance the child's development, but sometimes these people mistreat children. In this section we define child maltreatment, discuss the history that brought child maltreatment to the public's notice, and describe the different kinds of maltreatment, their risk factors, and impacts on individuals and their communities.

Defining Child Maltreatment

Child maltreatment is a collective term that encompasses all aspects of harmful or injurious behaviors toward children, including abuse and neglect. **Child abuse** specifically involves *harmful acts*, whereas **child neglect** refers to *failure to protect* a child from harm. A formal definition of child maltreatment was first established by the federal government as recently as 1974 through legislation called the Child Abuse Prevention and Treatment Act (CAPTA), and was reaffirmed through the CAPTA Reauthorization Act of 2010. The law defines child maltreatment as follows:

> Any recent act or failure to act on the part of a parent or caretaker which results in death, serious physical or emotional harm, sexual abuse, or exploitation, or an act or failure to act which presents an imminent risk of serious harm. (Administration for Children and Families (ACF), 2010)

The federal definition is considered a minimum explanation of acts or behaviors that constitute maltreatment, and in some cases does not specifically define what acts constitute abuse. Each state is allowed to further define child maltreatment in state law. This means that the actual definition of child maltreatment may vary from state to state, and that the state definition may be stricter and more detailed than the federal definition.

Teachers must know the laws for the state in which they work in order to effectively assume their professional responsibilities. In the opening scenario, Min Jee had reviewed the statutes for

MyEducationLab™

Visit the MyEducationLab for *Nutrition, Health, and Safety for Young Children* to enhance your understanding of chapter concepts with a personalized Study Plan. You'll also have the opportunity to hone your teaching skills through video-based Assignments and Activities, as well as Building Teaching Skills and Dispositions lessons.

child maltreatment
a collective term that encompasses all aspects of harmful or injurious behaviors toward children, including abuse and neglect

child abuse
child maltreatment that involves harmful *acts* toward children

child neglect
child maltreatment that refers to failure to protect a child from harm

her state when she was hired, so she knew what to watch for and what to do. State-specific information is available through the State Statutes Search provided online by the Child Welfare Information Gateway, a service of the U.S. Department of Health and Human Services.

Understanding the History of Child Abuse Prevention

Throughout history children have been used and exploited, suffering the cruelty of forced labor, long work days, and dangerous environments. Early on, the treatment of children was considered a family matter and there was no formal recognition of child maltreatment. Efforts to protect children from abuse first emerged from the success of the Society for the Prevention of Cruelty to Animals (SPCA). In 1874, Henry Bergh, who had founded the SPCA, was approached about a little girl named Mary Ellen who was being severely beaten. It was hoped that his work with the SPCA could be used to help the child. Bergh was successful in bringing the case to court. The proceedings highlighted the seriousness of the abuse, which caused the jurors to weep aloud at the sight of the girl. As a result, in 1874 the New York Society for the Prevention of Cruelty to Children was founded (New York Society for the Prevention of Cruelty to Children, 2008).

The frequency and severity of nonaccidental injuries to children caused by their parents and other adults was not fully understood until Henry Kempe, a physician, changed the course of history with his articles describing maltreatment as "the battered child syndrome" (Kempe, Silverman, Steele, Droegemueller, & Silver, 1962). Subsequently the landmark Child Abuse Prevention and Treatment Act of 1974 (Public Law 93-247) was written into law. The act provided federal funding for research and a variety of prevention and treatment services that are in place today. The act also sparked greater attention to children's safety, such as protecting children from environmental hazards.

Over time child maltreatment has become better understood, leading to more specific definitions for each type of maltreatment and the expectation that state and local agencies should investigate and manage reports of abuse. However, historic tensions continue. Some people deny that child maltreatment is a concern in their community or consider it a problem of "other" economic or cultural groups. Others believe their communities are doing too little to protect children from maltreatment. Even as these tensions persist, the reports of child maltreatment continue to increase, and the ill treatment of children continues to threaten children's growth and development.

Types of Child Maltreatment

The formal definitions of child maltreatment vary from state to state. However, four primary types of child maltreatment are typically identified (Centers for Disease Control and Prevention [CDC], 2010):

1. Physical abuse.
2. Neglect.
3. Sexual abuse and exploitation.
4. Emotional abuse.

Physical Abuse

Physical abuse includes any injury that is caused by physical force, including hitting, kicking, shaking, burning, or using other kinds of force against a child (CDC, 2010). Other injuries caused by physical abuse may include welts, cuts, bruises, broken bones, sprains, and bites that are inflicted on a child. Physical abuse can also include poisoning by forcing children to drink huge quantities of water or laxatives. Patterns of particular kinds of physical abuse have been assigned specific names:

- *Battered child syndrome:* Battered child syndrome refers to the physical signs that indicate a pattern of abuse has occurred over a period of time (Mannheim & Kaneshiro, 2011). The child may demonstrate injuries at various stages of healing.
- *Shaken baby syndrome:* Shaken baby syndrome refers to a type of traumatic brain injury that is caused by intentional and violent shaking, hitting, or impacting a child's head (National Institute of Neurological Disorders and Stroke, National Institutes of Health, 2010). Injuries associated with shaken baby syndrome include internal bleeding, blood clots, injury to the brain, blindness, and death. Children of any age can be damaged by being shaken or hit on the head.
- *Munchausen's syndrome by proxy:* This type of maltreatment occurs when the parent, usually the mother, causes the child to become ill, induces the symptoms of disease, or fabricates illness claiming the child has symptoms that do not exist. The child may undergo frequent medical procedures to address the false symptoms. This form of abuse is usually identified by medical personnel who notice variations from typical disease characteristics (Kaneshiro & Dugdale, 2011).

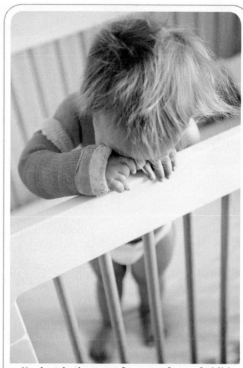

Neglect is the most frequent form of child maltreatment.

Neglect

Neglect is defined as a failure to meet the child's basic needs, including food, housing, clothing, medical care, and education (CDC, 2010). When identifying neglect, the focus is on what the responsible adult does *not* do to appropriately care for the child. Neglect is further clarified through four distinct categories:

- *Physical neglect:* Physical neglect refers to deprivation of the basic necessities of food, clothing, and shelter or not providing sufficient supervision such that the child's safety and health are compromised (Child Welfare Information Gateway [CWIG], 2008a; Children's Bureau & DePanfilis, 2006).
- *Medical neglect:* Medical neglect involves failure to provide for the medical and health care needs of a child in spite of having sufficient resources to do so, or refusing care for the child when medical help is offered (CWIG, 2008a; HHS/ACF, 2011). This is the type of neglect that Min Jee recognized when she noticed Katherine's unmet need for dental care and saw how it was interfering both with her ability to eat and her overall health. Medical neglect also refers to cases where parents do not access medical care for their child due to religious beliefs. Religious beliefs are typically honored and are not considered neglect except in cases where the child's life is in danger. A checklist of signs of medical neglect is provided in the *Health Hint.*

> ## What if . . .
> you were told by another parent that a family was restricting a child's food because of religious or cultural practices such as fasting? How would you explore this with the family to learn more?

- *Educational neglect:* Educational neglect includes failure to provide for the basic education or special education needs of a child (CWIG, 2008a).
- *Emotional neglect:* This category encompasses failure to act on behalf of the child's emotional needs. It includes not interacting with or being responsive to a child's needs and not protecting a child from threats, bullying, or other fearful situations. It also includes ignoring a child's use of alcohol or drugs (CWIG, 2008a).

Sexual Abuse and Exploitation

Sexual abuse refers to engaging an infant or child in any sexual act including fondling, rape, or exposing a child to sexual activities (CDC, 2010). It also includes indecent exposure and showing a child pornographic materials. Exploitation involves actions that take advantage of a child in a sexual manner such as coercion to participate in prostitution or pornography (CWIG, 2008a).

HEALTH HINT   Signs of Medical Neglect

✓ Child has chronic and severe diaper rash or infections that are not treated.

✓ Child's injury is not cared for; for example, a child who experiences a fall or blow to the head that could typically cause a fracture or concussion is not taken for medical assessment.

✓ Child is inappropriately medicated without guidance from a medical professional.

✓ Child's special health needs, such as diabetes or allergies, are not addressed.

Emotional Abuse

Emotional abuse refers to acts that cause injury to a child's self-worth or emotional, psychological, or mental stability. It includes verbal abuse such as threatening, ridiculing, calling names, shaming, and withholding love (CDC, 2010). Emotional abuse also includes making demands that are beyond the child's ability or developmental level to achieve; threat of harm such as exposure to or involvement in domestic violence; patterns of terrorizing, isolating, or rejecting a child; selling a child for sexual purposes; and deserting or abandoning a child (CWIG, 2008a; HHS/ACF, 2011).

Maltreatment may include overlapping kinds of abuse and neglect. For example, physical abuse, emotional abuse, and emotional neglect may occur together. Some states use an "other" category to describe situations in which several kinds of abuse occur in combination, and some identify additional categories such as parental substance abuse and abandonment as specific categories of child maltreatment (CWIG, 2008a).

Incidence of Child Maltreatment

The National Child Abuse and Neglect Data System collects and summarizes reported cases of child abuse and neglect and examines the findings made by state child protective agency investigations (U.S. Department of Health and Human Services, Administration for Children and Families (HHS/ACF), Children's Bureau, 2011). This information helps teachers understand the kinds of maltreatment that may be evident among children in the classroom. In 2010, 3.3 million referrals of suspected maltreatment were made involving 5.9 million children. Of these, 2 million cases were screened-in for follow up investigation with 436,321 cases of maltreatment ultimately confirmed nationwide (HHS/ACF, 2011). The following trends were revealed:

- Neglect is the most frequent form of child maltreatment, accounting for nearly 75% of the confirmed cases, followed by physical abuse (17%), sexual abuse (9%), and emotional abuse (7%) (HHS/ACF, 2011). The incidence of these forms of maltreatment by child age group is shown in Figure 16-1. The count exceeds 100% in each age group because individual children may have suffered several kinds of maltreatment.

- While the majority of confirmed cases of maltreatment involve children with no history of previous abuse (75%), about 25% of children suffer repeated abuse (HHS/ACF, 2011).

- Child maltreatment can cause permanent disability and death. In 2010, over 1,500 fatalities occurred due to maltreatment (HHS/ACF, 2011). The majority of the deaths (nearly 80%) occurred among children under the age of 4 years. The causes of the fatalities were attributed to a combination of types of maltreatment (40%) or exclusively to neglect (32%). The fatality rate was higher among boys than girls (HHS/ACF, 2011).

FIGURE 16-1

Child Victims of Maltreatment, Percent of Incidence by Age and Type of Maltreatment, 2010

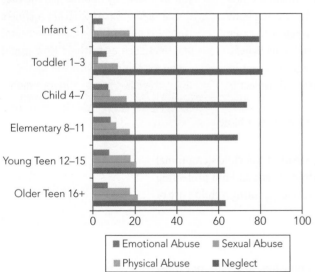

Source: Based on U.S. Department of Health and Human Services. Administration for Children and Families, National Child Abuse and Neglect Data System. *FAM7.B Child Maltreatment: Percentage of Substantiated Maltreatment Reports of Children Ages 0–17 By Maltreatment Type and Age. 2010.* Retrieved October 31, 2012 from http://www.childstats.gov/americaschildren/tables/fam7b.asp.

- The maltreatment and death rates vary according to age, gender, and race. The incidence of maltreatment is higher among older children, while death due to maltreatment occurs more frequently among younger children (see Figure 16-2) (HHS/ACF, 2011).

In spite of these sobering statistics, there is doubt about whether the magnitude of the problem of child maltreatment is sufficiently understood. Several reasons are cited for this challenge (Chalk, Gibbons, & Scarupa, 2002):

- Many instances of abuse are never reported to child protective agencies, leaving questions about how many cases go unreported.
- Only a small percentage of the incidents that are reported are actually substantiated due either to lack of follow-up or insufficient evidence.
- State definitions of maltreatment vary, making it difficult to compare data.

The actual number of children who are abused or neglected or who are at risk for maltreatment is likely to be much higher than the reported numbers. This suggests that more reliable methods of counting the incidence of maltreatment are needed.

Perpetrators of Abuse and Neglect

The people who commit acts of abuse or harm children from neglect are called **perpetrators**. Perpetrators include parents, other immediate family members, relatives, the unmarried partner of a parent, foster parents, child care providers, family friends, and other children (HHS/ACF, 2011). However, patterns of abuse and neglect indicate that those who have the most frequent contact with the child perpetrate the majority of the maltreatment. Such trends identify the following:

- Maltreatment is more often committed by the biological parent (81%), most often by the child's mother, with fewer instances by stepparents and adoptive parents (HHS/ACF, 2011).
- The racial distribution of those who perpetrate child maltreatment is similar to that of child victims. More offenses are committed by Caucasians (nearly 49%), followed by Hispanics (20%) and African Americans (nearly 19%) (HHS/ACF, 2011).
- Child death from maltreatment is most often caused by the child's parents (70%), usually by the mother alone or by the mother and father together (HHS/ACF, 2011).

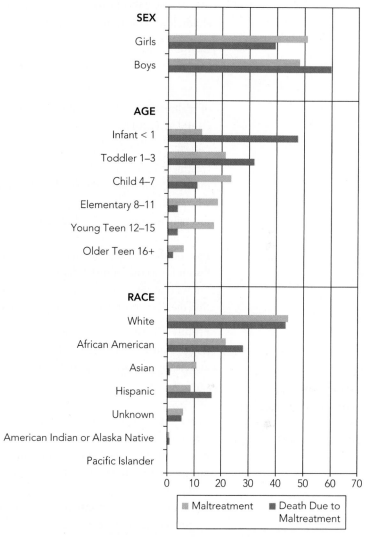

FIGURE 16-2

Percentage of Child Victims of Maltreatment and Death Due to Maltreatment by Gender, Age, and Race, 2010

Source: Based on U.S. Department of Health and Human Services, Administration for Children and Families, Administration on Children, Youth, and Families (HHS/ACF), Children's Bureau. (2011). *Child Maltreatment 2010.* Available from http://www.acf.hhs.gov/programs/cb/stats_research/index.htm#can.

Because parents and family members are frequently the perpetrators of maltreatment, it is important for teachers to serve as healthy role models for adult and child interactions.

perpetrators
people who commit acts of abuse or harm children by neglecting them

Risk Factors Associated with Maltreatment

Various risk factors are associated with the likelihood that a child will be maltreated, including children's age, gender, race, disability, and family factors. Factors associated with the likelihood that an adult will inflict abuse or commit acts of neglect include personal and situational factors and triggers that may spark acts of maltreatment.

Child Risk Factors for Maltreatment

A review of the confirmed cases of child maltreatment identifies the factors discussed next as being associated with a greater likelihood of abuse or neglect.

Age Younger children have the highest risk for maltreatment. Being born prematurely may put a child at greater risk for abuse. Twenty-seven percent of confirmed cases occur among children under the age of 4. Nearly 24% of cases occur among children 4 to 7 years of age (HHS/ACF, 2011). The majority of children who die from maltreatment (over 73%) are under the age of 4 years (HHS/ACF, 2011).

Gender More than half (51%) of abused children are girls. However, the fatality rate due to maltreatment is slightly higher among infant boys (nearly 60%) (HHS/ACF, 2011).

Race and Culture Maltreatment occurs among all racial and cultural groups. Of the victims of maltreatment, 45% are White Non-Hispanic, 22% are African American, and 21% are Hispanic (HHS/ACF, 2011).

Disability and Special Developmental Needs Nearly 16% of children who are victims of maltreatment have a disability including those who have behavior problems, emotional disturbance, or medical conditions (HHS/ACF, 2011). It is anticipated that the number of children with disabilities who suffer abuse is underreported, primarily because many children with disabilities have not been formally identified through diagnostic assessment. Children with disabilities as well as typically developing children who display challenging behaviors or have chronic illness may also be at greater risk for abuse. These factors are important for teachers to recognize. For example, Malika, a home visitor for a community Healthy Start program, thinks about this when she goes on home visits. She knows that new parents may feel particularly isolated and ill equipped to cope with the discovery that their newborn has a developmental delay. She prepares with referral information to share.

Family Factors Risk factors in the home can put children at risk for abuse. Of the children identified as maltreated in 2010, 25% were exposed to domestic violence, 18% were exposed to drug abuse, and nearly 11% were exposed to alcohol abuse in the home (HHS/ACF, 2011).

Adult Risk Factors for Maltreating Children

There is no one description of an adult who is at risk for abusing children. And, while risk factors provide insight into the possibility of abuse, not all adults who experience these situations abuse children. Teachers consider these adult risk factors for maltreating children as they develop and share resources to support families of young children. Factors that have been identified as potentially putting adults at risk for committing violent acts against children include personal attributes, stresses or situations that increase the risk for abuse, and susceptibility to triggers that might set off abusive events (Goldman, Salus, Wolcott, & Kennedy, 2003). The impact of these risks can also compound, such that when more risks are evident the likelihood for maltreatment increases.

Personal Risk Factors Personal risk factors are associated with negative experiences in an adult's early life as well as individual aspects that may disrupt the adult's ability to appropriately care for the child. Experiences that may put an adult at risk for perpetrating abuse include having experienced punitive parenting or abuse as a child. Issues such as depression, poor impulse control, or substance abuse problems are also considered personal risk factors for abusing a child. These issues are thought to reduce the adult's ability to cope with a child's behaviors or situations that, although they may be difficult, are typical aspects of caring for young children. In the opening case scenario, Min Jee might wonder if Katherine's mother suffers from depression and low self-esteem, as these could be risk factors in the neglect that Min Jee suspects.

Situational Risk Factors Situational factors are conditions or circumstances that are common among those who commit acts of violence toward children. Social isolation, or being a young or single parent, or a victim of domestic violence are examples of situational factors that can put an

FIGURE 16-3   Risk for Maltreatment Among the Families of Enlisted Soldiers

Military families face a variety of challenges including making frequent moves, experiencing times of single parenting while the soldier parent is being trained or is on assignment, and managing the impacts of combat-related deployment.

A research investigation explored the incidence of parent-perpetrated child maltreatment among families of enlisted U.S. Army soldiers during combat-related deployment and times when the parent soldier was not deployed. When soldier-fathers were deployed, the incidence of physical abuse doubled and the rate of neglect was four times greater than when the soldier father was not deployed. To address these challenges, the army provides support services for families affected by combat deployment including assistance centers that link families to support agencies.

Source: "Child Maltreatment in Enlisted Soldiers' Families during Combat-Related Deployments," by D. Gibbs, S. Martin, L. Kupper, and R. Johnson, 2007 (August), *Journal of the American Medical Association*, 298(5). Retrieved July 22, 2012, from http://jama .jamanetwork.com/article.aspx?articleid=208223.

adult at risk for harming a child. Stressful circumstances may cause an adult to be cut off from positive social connections and social support. Limited access to advice, relief, or respite from challenging conditions may cause violent and abusive behaviors to escalate. Figure 16-3 describes the risk for maltreatment among military families who face long periods of time when one parent is absent during deployment.

Triggering Factors   Triggers are conditions that set off a series of events that may increase the risk for abuse. Triggers might include difficult child behaviors, such as excessive crying, discipline, or teaching situations (such as pressuring a child during toilet training) that have gotten out of control, or adult arguments that carry over to behaviors acted out against a child.

Understanding the Effects of Maltreatment

Maltreatment can negatively affect children, families, and society for a lifetime, if not for generations (Child Welfare Information Gateway [CWIG], 2008b). However, not all children suffer long-term effects. The impacts vary according to the characteristics of the abuse and the services available in the community to help children and families cope.

Impacts on Children

Some effects of maltreatment are temporary and fleeting, such as bruises, whereas other experiences cause permanent physical and emotional scars. Child age and the type, frequency, and duration of the maltreatment are factors associated with long-term effects.

Maltreatment that is frequent and continual significantly increases a child's experience of a form of stress called *toxic stress*. Toxic stress disrupts the body's hormones and brain chemical systems. This negatively impacts brain development, impairing learning, behavior, and health (National Scientific Council on the Developing Child, 2005, 2010). Toxic stress is especially alarming when experienced by infants and toddlers who are most vulnerable, have the greatest risk for maltreatment, and consequently are in the greatest danger for long-term damage.

Children who have suffered brain injuries, such as those seen in cases of shaken baby syndrome, may suffer permanent brain damage or death because of bruising of the brain and intracranial bleeding (CWIG, 2008b). In addition, children who experience maltreatment are more likely to suffer as adults from depression (JAMA and Archives Journals, 2007) and physical health concerns such as allergies, arthritis, asthma, high blood pressure, and ulcers (CWIG, 2008b; Springer, Sheridan, Kuo, & Carnes, 2007).

Impacts on Communities

Communities are also affected by maltreatment because they must fund child welfare agencies, investigate reports, and provide social services for children and families when maltreatment occurs (Children's Bureau & DePanfilis, 2006). These direct costs are estimated a $24 billion per year (CWIG, 2008b). Other impacts include higher rates of crime, juvenile delinquency, and disability and mental illness in children who have been mistreated. For example, children who were abused are more than 11 times as likely to be arrested for juvenile crime, and nearly 3 times as likely to be arrested for violence when they are adults (CWIG, 2008b; English, Widom, & Brandford, 2004).

● IDENTIFYING CHILD MALTREATMENT

Teachers like Min Jee interact closely with children, observing their growth and development and building relationships of trust that allow children to bring forward their worries and concerns. Teachers must be intentional about watching for the physical and behavioral signs of maltreatment. This involves understanding cultural perspectives related to treatment of children and recognizing the difference between guidance and abuse.

Recognizing the Signs of Child Maltreatment

Children display the signs of child maltreatment in various ways that astute teachers learn to recognize. The signs may be obvious and observable or exhibited through very subtle changes in the child's behavior. The behaviors of the parent may also be signs that maltreatment is occurring (Crosson-Tower, 2002).

Teachers need to consider all the ways in which maltreatment may be evident and use this information to determine if there is reasonable cause to suspect that abuse has occurred or is occurring. For example, at a Head Start teachers' meeting Celia has just shared her frustrations about working with a child whose behavior has regressed. Some of the other teachers respond to her descriptions saying, "That sounds like neglect!" When Celia reflects on it, she decides they are right. How did she miss it? Figure 16-4 lists child and parent signs that may signal maltreatment.

Physical Signs

Some signs of maltreatment are definite and unambiguous. Teachers are able to observe marks, movements, or other visible signs that signal abuse or neglect are occurring. Special attention should be given to details.

Observable Marks   Some signs of maltreatment can be clearly visible and observed during the teacher's daily interactions with children. The marks of physical abuse may be evident in the form of bruises, burns, or scalds. They may be easily viewed on the child's face, neck, or hands; revealed on the legs and torso when changing a baby's diaper; or seen on the arms when children pull up their sleeves to play in the sensory bin. Teachers must look closely and weigh whether the marks observed seem logical for the kinds of injuries children typically experience and for the usual activities of the child. For example, a skinned knee is a common result from a fall on the sidewalk, but a series of circular burns on the leg would be unusual to see. The teacher should watch for:

- Marks that are unusual or different from the injuries a child might logically receive during the course of everyday play.
- Marks that are patterned, such as in the shape of a hand or object or a series of striped marks caused by being hit with a strap.
- Marks in various stages of healing, suggesting the possibility of repeated physical abuse (CWIG, 2007).

For example, Teacher Mandy is alarmed to notice dark bruise-colored marks all over Krissy's arms. They look like Krissy has been poked repeatedly with a blunt object. As she studies them closely,

FIGURE 16-4 Signs of Maltreatment

Physical Abuse

Child PHYSICAL Signs

- ✓ Bruises, welts, and marks, possibly in varying stages of healing
- ✓ Burns and marks in the shape of objects: cigarette, handprints, wooden spoons
- ✓ Bald spots from severe hair pulling
- ✓ Unexplained or recurrent injuries
- ✓ Unexplained broken bones
- ✓ Child reports being hit by parent

Child BEHAVIOR Signs

- ✓ Limping or protecting body parts
- ✓ Recurrent complaints of headache or belly ache or other pains
- ✓ Child protests when it is time to go home; seems frightened of the parent
- ✓ Child's behavior changes; is more withdrawn or aggressive

Parent BEHAVIOR Signs

- ✓ Parent cannot explain child's injuries or offers unconvincing or conflicting explanations
- ✓ Parent reports that child harmed self
- ✓ Parent shows little interest or concern for child
- ✓ Parent instructs teacher to use harsh discipline with child

Emotional Abuse

Child PHYSICAL Signs

- ✓ Unexplained delayed physical, intellectual, or emotional development
- ✓ Otherwise unexplained persistent habits such as rocking, sucking on fingers, head banging
- ✓ Self-destructive actions (hitting self)
- ✓ General destructive actions

Child BEHAVIOR Signs

- ✓ Apathy and depression: low affect, empty facial expression
- ✓ Fear of parent
- ✓ Extreme fears or phobias
- ✓ Extreme behavior: overly passive or aggressive
- ✓ Cruelty to others; laughing at others' pain

Parent BEHAVIOR Signs

- ✓ Parent belittles the child
- ✓ Parent rejects the child
- ✓ Parent minimizes concerns for the child

Sexual Abuse

Child PHYSICAL Signs

- ✓ Pain, itching, bruises, or bleeding around the genitalia
- ✓ Stained or bloody underclothing
- ✓ Discharge from vagina or urinary openings
- ✓ Difficulty walking or sitting

Child BEHAVIOR Signs

- ✓ Acting out sexual behaviors that are too sophisticated for age
- ✓ Asking others to do sexual acts
- ✓ Acting in a sexual or seductive manner
- ✓ Showing an inordinate fear of males (or females)
- ✓ Child reports sexual abuse

Parent BEHAVIOR Signs

- ✓ Parent is controlling and jealous of others
- ✓ Parent is isolated or secretive

Neglect

Child PHYSICAL Signs

- ✓ Poor hygiene such as dirty hair, skin, and clothes; smells of urine or feces
- ✓ Unaddressed medical or dental needs
- ✓ Dress that is inappropriate for the weather
- ✓ Failure to grow and thrive

Child BEHAVIOR Signs

- ✓ Begging for food
- ✓ Hoarding food
- ✓ Fatigue or listlessness
- ✓ Child craves attention, even eliciting negative attention

Parent BEHAVIOR Signs

- ✓ Parent is indifferent and uninterested in the child
- ✓ Parent is depressed or seems apathetic
- ✓ Parent does not provide age-appropriate supervision for long periods of time

Source: Based on Child Welfare Information Gateway (CWIG). (2007). *Recognizing Child Abuse and Neglect: Signs and Symptoms.* Retrieved June 3, 2012, from http://www.childwelfare.gov/pubs/factsheets/signs.cfm.

Krissy says, "See! I was playing 101 Dalmatians last night and those are my spots. I made them with markers, but they are hard to wash off." In this case the spots are harmless.

Observable Movements Movements can also suggest abuse. For example when Teacher Carolyn first notices 6-year-old Ennis limping, she asks him what has happened. Looking down he answers, "Um, I fell down." Teachers may observe a child limping or protecting a sore arm, or the child might complain of a headache or other soreness. Teachers should not investigate or try to "prove" that maltreatment has occurred. However, it is within the realm of a teacher's responsibility to show sympathy for a child's injury and to ask, "How did it happen?" or say, "Show me where it hurts." Soreness and some injuries may be easily explained by overexertion or typical accidents, but a child's unlikely explanation may be a signal that maltreatment has occurred (CWIG, 2007).

Visible Signs of Neglect Neglect can also be observed through recognizable patterns that suggest that the parent is ignoring a child's needs. The child may be consistently hungry, dirty, dressed inappropriately for the weather (even when the family has resources for appropriate garments), or the child may have unaddressed medical or dental needs, such as Katherine in the opening case scenario (CWIG, 2007).

Child Statements A child might also directly tell the teacher about an incident of maltreatment. Trina might say, "I don't want to go home; my mom hits me with a spoon." Dustin, her teacher, should believe what she says. Young children are considered to be very reliable sources for reporting abusive situations, and at the very minimum the child is expressing worry or fear. It is best if Dustin responds to Trina's statement without shock. He should reassure her that the incident was not her fault and tell her that there are people who can help. When she returns to play, Dustin should immediately report Trina's statement to the appropriate child protective services or law enforcement agency, and make special efforts to demonstrate support and understanding to Trina.

Hiding Signs of Maltreatment Teachers should also be alert to indications that a parent or child is trying to hide the signs of maltreatment. For example, Brandie might dress her son Jacob in excessive layers of clothing to cover the marks of abuse, or William might report that he does not know how his daughter Sophia's injury occurred. In some cases a child may be coached to explain marks of abuse through unlikely stories, or the child may be threatened that their pet or a family member will be hurt if they tell what happened. Children who have been sexually abused are often caught up in a web of secrecy and threats that lead them to hide the signs of abuse.

Child Behavioral Signs

Maltreatment can also be expressed through a child's behavior, for example, in the themes of play or by changes in the child's mood and level of activity (CWIG, 2007). Behavioral indicators can be more ambiguous and harder to connect clearly to maltreatment. These signs should be considered together with other observations of the child and parent when considering whether abuse is occurring. Some behavioral indicators are discussed next.

Communicating Through Play Children sometimes reveal signs of maltreatment through play, for example, by repeatedly acting out abusive situations in the housekeeping area or doll house. Sami might hit and spank the dolls excessively or make cruel threats. Laurie may not understand the sexual abuse that she has experienced; sometimes it is not until years later when a child's greater maturity helps them understand the meaning of the actions they have experienced (London, Bruck, Ceci, & Shuman, 2005). However, Laurie may demonstrate signs of sexual abuse by showing physical discomfort when walking or sitting, or by inviting others to engage in secretive games that suggest awareness of sexual actions beyond her maturity. Teachers may also find that children demonstrate their experiences by depicting the abuse in drawings or by building clay structures that communicate situations of maltreatment.

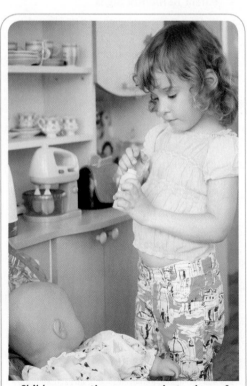

Children sometimes communicate signs of maltreatment through play.

Change in Mood A child's change in mood may be a signal. A typically happy child who suddenly becomes excessively withdrawn or sad, or a typically congenial child who suddenly becomes overly aggressive, argumentative, or resistant may be experiencing abuse or neglect (CWIG, 2007).

Change in Activity Level A change in the child's typical level or style of activity should also raise concern (CWIG, 2007). For example, Madison, who is usually a leader, might suddenly prefer to play alone. Or Logan, who is typically very active, may lose interest in the games he used to enjoy and appear listless and lethargic. These changes may be signs of abuse or neglect.

Parent Behaviors

The daily interactions that teachers observe between parents and their children may reveal behaviors or a style of interaction that, when consistently demonstrated, suggests risk for abuse. These include negative interactions such as (CWIG, 2007):

- Belittling the child.
- Describing the child in negative ways, such as "evil," "bad," or "worthless."
- Ignoring the child and showing lack of interest or concern.
- Not attending to the child's needs when they have been identified.
- Having unreasonable expectations for the child's behavior or performance.

The suspicion of child maltreatment is often based not on just one signal but on the combination of indications including observable signs, behaviors of the child or parent, as well as interactions between the child and parent (CWIG, 2007). Teachers need to be alert to the many ways in which maltreatment is communicated and the signs that it is being hidden, and reflect on all they know about the child and family when determining whether there is reasonable cause to suspect maltreatment.

> **What if . . .**
> you were teaching full time during the day and taking classes at the community college in the evening? How would you ensure that you have the time to appropriately reflect on the observations for the day and remain alert to the signs of maltreatment?

Considering Cultural Perspectives

Teachers must also be aware of the cultural traditions practiced among the families in their class and understand how these may impact perceptions of maltreatment. Definitions of child abuse, perspectives about the vulnerability of children, and child-rearing practices are highly influenced by culture (Roer-Strier, 2001).

There is no common international standard for child maltreatment by which cultural practices are judged. For example, the Western practice of placing an infant in her own bed to sleep would be considered cruel by some cultures. Some cultures tend to use mild physical punishment such as spanking with more frequency than others, but does this constitute abuse? A practice called "coin rubbing" is used by Southeast Asian families as a traditional cure for fevers, chills, and headaches (Renteln, 2010). Heated metal coins are rubbed against the child's body, typically leaving circular bruises or scrape marks. The purpose is to enhance the child's health and, although the practice causes bruises to the child, the intent is different from what is typically considered abuse.

Some cultures allow young children more freedom and autonomy than typical Western cultures, permitting young children to move freely and with little supervision or allowing a child to stay home alone. These might be viewed as signs of neglect. When Jessica is confused about how to interpret such behaviors in her classroom, she makes a call to the child protective services agency to discuss her concern. The protective services worker can help clarify steps to take when the parenting practices are unfamiliar and the potential for child maltreatment is not easily understood. Being culturally sensitive is appropriate and important, but it does not mean overlooking signs of child maltreatment (Renteln, 2010).

Reflecting on Family Disciplinary Practices

Child guidance and disciplinary practices are heavily influenced by regional, cultural, and religious perspectives. Some approaches are permissive; others are stricter than typical practices used in the early childhood classroom. Some parents may use spanking as a disciplinary approach while others

What if . . .

you observed a parent interacting harshly with a child and using threats that seemed to be escalating? How would you intervene to redirect the situation? How might you begin a conversation with the parent about more effective ways to gain the child's cooperation?

consider spanking to be inappropriate. While spanking is not recommended, it is not generally defined as child maltreatment unless it is frequent, out of proportion to the situation, or intense. Examples of inappropriate spanking may include spanking with a solid object such as a belt or hairbrush or other forms of corporal punishment. Teachers strive to be supportive of families, but this does not mean overlooking parental use of disciplinary actions that are detrimental to a child's health and well-being. A child protective services worker is an important resource when teachers find it difficult to interpret harsh family disciplinary practices.

● REPORTING CHILD MALTREATMENT

It is standard practice in early childhood classrooms for teachers to observe children on a daily basis looking for signs of general health, illness, or stress. These observations may also reveal the possibility that abuse or neglect is occurring or has occurred. Teachers need to be prepared to report maltreatment as soon as it is suspected.

Understanding Reporting Responsibilities

Reporting child maltreatment is a serious and important responsibility. Because of their proximity to children and the large amounts of time they spend with them, teachers may be the first to become aware that maltreatment could be occurring. Teachers, by the nature of the profession, have a legal obligation and professional and ethical duty to report suspected child abuse and neglect.

Legally Mandated Reporters

mandatory reporters persons who because of the nature of their employment have close and frequent contact with young children are required by state law to report suspected child maltreatment

Teachers and others employed in positions that have close and frequent contact with children are legally identified as **mandatory reporters**. Mandatory reporters are required by law to immediately report their "reasonable suspicions" of child maltreatment to law enforcement or the local child protective services agency. Each state identifies the professions that are mandatory reporters. They typically include (CWIG, 2008b):

- Medical personnel such as physicians, nurses, dentists, optometrists, and psychologists.
- Law enforcement personnel.
- Employees in licensed child care and early education programs.
- Teachers and other school employees.
- Social workers, counselors, and therapists.
- Clergy.
- Attorneys.
- Firefighters.

More than three fifths of the reports of child maltreatment are made by mandatory reporters such as these, primarily educational and law enforcement professionals (HHS/ACF, 2011). Another 28% of cases are reported by nonprofessional sources such as parents, relatives, friends, neighbors, and sports coaches. Indeed, the involvement of "everyday citizens" is important in reporting and stopping child maltreatment.

Professional and Ethical Responsibilities

Teachers also have a *professional and ethical responsibility* to protect children in their care. That is, they have a duty to take honest and moral action to protect a child from further abuse. The Code of Ethical Conduct and Statement of Commitment of the NAEYC (2011) confirms this ethical responsibility:

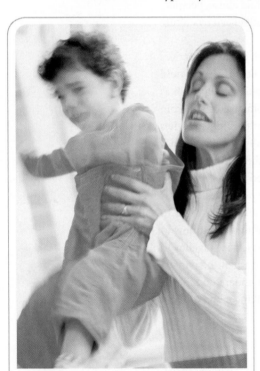

Stressors can compound, increasing the potential for maltreatment.

P-1.1—Above all, we shall not harm children. We shall not participate in practices that are emotionally damaging, physically harmful, disrespectful, degrading, dangerous, exploitative, or intimidating to children. *This principle has precedence over all others in this Code.*

P-1.8—We shall be familiar with the risk factors for and symptoms of child abuse and neglect, including physical, sexual, verbal, and emotional abuse and physical, emotional, educational, and medical neglect. We shall know and follow state laws and community procedures that protect children against abuse and neglect (p. 3).

By taking on the responsibility to care for and educate children, teachers also pledge themselves to advocate for the health and safety of each child by reporting suspected cases of abuse. This is an important aspect of professionalism.

Sometimes, however, teachers may struggle with their own discomfort in discussing or addressing child abuse and neglect. Teachers cite various reasons for having difficulty in reporting suspected maltreatment (Kenny, 2001):

- Worry about retribution from the family if they learn that the teacher has made a report.
- Concern that they will disrupt the family by reporting suspected maltreatment.
- A mistaken notion that they can "help" the family better by withholding information or delaying such a report.
- Lack of trust in child protective services.
- Lack of knowledge about the signs of child maltreatment or how to report suspected abuse.
- Worry about making a mistake or being wrong especially when there are no observable signs of abuse.

Not reporting suspected child maltreatment is harmful to children and it is against the law. It abandons children to the despair of neglect and abuse, the long-term negative effects they create, and may even jeopardize the child's life. Teachers can gain confidence in their ability to appropriately participate in protecting children by knowing the signs of maltreatment, who to contact, and how to make a report.

Responding Appropriately When Abuse Is Suspected

When observations suggest maltreatment has occurred, or when a child reveals that abuse has occurred, teachers need to be ready to respond with calm confidence. Children should immediately be reassured that they will be kept safe. They should be allowed to fully express worry, fear, and any other emotions that surround their experience. The teacher's response should be warm and encouraging, and it should clearly communicate that the teacher believes what is being said. It is important to avoid showing alarm or dismay about anything the child says. Figure 16-5 provides guidance for teachers regarding what they should and should not do when a child discloses situations of maltreatment.

Reporting Suspected Abuse and Neglect

When maltreatment is suspected, teachers need to be ready to make a report and assume their responsibilities in the protective services process.

Making a Report

When preparing to make a report, teachers should briefly record what was observed and what the child said that led to the suspicion of maltreatment. This helps keep the details of the concern clear. A call from a private location should then be made to report the suspected abuse or neglect. It is important to clearly state the purpose of the report and, when possible, provide basic information about the child and family. Figure 16-6 provides an example of information to share when making a protective services call. Teachers can contact the National Child Abuse Hotline (1-800-4-A-CHILD) to learn more about making a child abuse report.

FIGURE 16-5   What Should Teachers Do When a Child Discloses Abuse?

Do this:

Be prepared:
- ✓ Understand your responsibility as a reporter.
- ✓ Know your program policy about reporting.
- ✓ Know the signs of child maltreatment.
- ✓ Know who to call for help.

Take action if needed.

Allow the child to talk or show what happened without interruption or questions.

Believe what the child says.

Reassure the child that it was a good thing to come to you and that you will find the right people to help.

Redirect the child to play.

Report immediately by calling child protective services or law enforcement.

Keep the child with you unless authorities agree the child may be released to the parent.

Write down what the child told you as soon as possible.

Continue to support the child.

Do NOT do this:

Do not ignore a child's report of abuse.

Do not promise not to tell. You must report abuse. Tell the child you will find people to help.

Do not act shocked. Don't correct or criticize the child's choice of words or language. Just receive the information with confidence.

Do not express doubt or disbelief or try to talk the child out of what he or she is saying.

Do not ask a lot of questions. Act quickly to mobilize the system that will investigate and protect the child.

Do not entice the child to disclose. Do not offer rewards or suggest negative consequences if the child does not tell.

Do not conduct an investigation. Document the information and investigators will take over from there.

Do not call the child's parents. Let law enforcement or child protective services decide at what point the parents should be involved. Investigations can be ruined and children endangered by informing family members.

Source: Based on practice (author).

Steps in Protective Service

Once a report has been made, the protective services or law enforcement agency will determine if the situation warrants investigation and follow-up. An investigation may include interviews with the child, teacher, and family (Children's Bureau & DePanfilis, 2006). Sometimes teachers are asked to participate in the interview with the child to provide familiarity and support. For example, Abby participated with law enforcement when Leon was being interviewed about injuries he obtained during a weekend visit to his dad's house. Her presence helped Leon talk about the experience. The information gathered through the assessment process determines whether there is reasonable cause to believe that maltreatment has occurred and whether there is continuing threat of harm.

When Maltreatment Is Confirmed

If it is established that maltreatment has occurred, the protective and law enforcement workers move quickly to protect the child from immediate harm. Child protection workers consider whether the child can safely remain in the family home. If it is determined that the child's safety is at risk by remaining in the home, an out-of-home placement is identified and temporary shelter may be arranged with a safe relative or an appropriate foster family. Meanwhile, the child protective services agency creates a service plan with the child's family. Goals are outlined to provide support and training for the parents, to address the issues that contributed to the

FIGURE 16-6 Steps in Reporting Maltreatment

1. Provide your name and contact information.
   Say: *My name is Min Jee Kim. I am a teacher at the Northside Child Development Center. My phone number is XXX-XXX-XXXX.*
2. State the purpose for your call and what maltreatment you suspect has occurred.
   Say: *I'm calling to make a report. I suspect a child is being neglected.*
3. Give the name of child, age, and birth date if known.
   Say: *The child's name is Katherine Goss. She is four years old. Her birthday is March 4, 2009.*
4. Give the name and address of the family.
   Say: *Her parents are Lynn and Calvin Goss. They live at 3579 Canal Street, Our City and State.*
5. Tell what you observed.
   Say: *This child is consistently dirty and has severe dental needs, and Katherine told me she does not want to go home because her mom hits her when she wets her pants.*
6. Provide other relevant information.
   Say: *We referred the mom to community dental services to help the child, but she won't go. The dad recently lost his job and I think that he may have an alcohol problem. I know that toilet training has been a challenge for this child.*

Source: Based on practice (author).

maltreatment and to improve the capacity of the parents to safely care for the child's well-being in the future.

Guidance for Teachers

Teachers should not contact parents or other family members to inform them that a report has been made. This is important for several reasons (Office on Child Abuse and Neglect, Caliber Associates, & Crosson-Tower, 2003):

- Doing so may put the child in danger of retribution, especially if the child is the one who disclosed the abuse.
- The parent may flee with the child.
- The parent may try to coach the child to deny the abuse.
- There may be risk for suicide by the perpetrator following reports of sexual abuse.

The child protective or law enforcement agency will direct teachers about how to appropriately interact with the family immediately following a report of maltreatment. Although reports to law enforcement and child protective services are confidential, a parent may suspect that the report came from the teacher. If approached, teachers should be prepared to discuss the situation with the parent in a calm and professional manner. The focus of the conversation should be on establishing the understanding that teachers want to help keep children healthy and safe, and that teachers have a responsibility to make a report if they suspect abuse.

If a discussion with a parent feels threatening in any way, teachers should know who in their school or program they can contact to provide support (Office on Child Abuse and Neglect et al., 2003). Likewise a family child care provider should have a neighbor or nearby friend or family member to call on for support. Usually, listening to the parent's concerns and treating the parent with respect helps to diffuse difficult situations such as these and can be crucial in building a relationship of support to help keep the child safe in the future.

What if . . .
you suspected that a child has been maltreated? What aspects of reporting abuse do you feel would be most difficult or challenging? How would you overcome these worries?

● BEING AWARE OF OTHER FORMS
OF VIOLENCE IN CHILDREN'S LIVES

Violence has become a reality in the lives of many children today. It is so prevalent that some experts consider violence to be a "public health epidemic" (Dahlberg & Mercy, 2009; Mitchum, 2011). Zero to Three: National Center for Infants, Toddlers and Families, maintains that "the United States is the most violent industrialized country in the world" (2009, p. 1). Violence enters children's lives from various sources, putting children at risk for its negative effects.

Identifying Sources of Violence

The potential for any child to witness or be affected by violence is very high. Violence is evident in nearly every part of the environment: the home, school, and community. Although children's exposure to these sources of violence may vary, it would be difficult to find a child who has not experienced at least some source of violence.

Domestic Violence

Young children are often witnesses to violence within the home. Domestic violence refers to a pattern of abusive behavior used by a partner in a relationship to gain power and control over the other. It includes both verbal and physical abuse and may involve insults, intimidation, threats, hitting, and fatal assault with weapons. Domestic violence is the most prevalent form of violence to which children are exposed (U.S. Department of Justice, 2011; Swaner, et al., 2011). It is estimated that three to ten million children are witness to domestic violence each year (Child Welfare Information Gateway, 2009). Besides being traumatized by seeing and hearing the violent acts of others, children in homes where domestic violence occurs are also more likely to experience other forms of abuse (Finkelhor, Turner, Ormrod, Hamby, & Kracke, 2009). This compounds the potential negative impact of violence on children.

Media Violence

▶ This **video** shows a group of girls and a teacher engaged in dramatic play based on the theme of restaurant. Notice that when the teacher leaves, the girls' play changes to include power objects. Do you think that their play could have been influenced by exposure to media?

Nearly every child in the United States today is touched in some way by the violence depicted through media sources such as television, movies, the Internet, electronic games, and music. It is estimated that a typical child watches television 28 hours per week and by the age of 18 has seen 200,000 acts of violence and 16,000 dramatized murders (American Psychological Association [APA], 2004). Cartoons often depict more than 80 acts of aggression or cruelty an hour, which is 50 to 60 times more violent acts than adult prime-time programs (APA, 2004). This is especially damaging because most acts of violence depicted go unaddressed and are not corrected. Even children as young as 14 months are more likely to imitate the violent and aggressive behaviors they view on TV since punishment is not shown as a consequence. The sounds of violence can also pervade children's experience even when they are not watching television by the sounds of programs that adults watch when children are playing or in bed.

Research links exposure to violence from media sources with increased aggressive and antisocial behaviors (Fitzpatrick, Barnett, & Pagani, 2012), fears about the world, and desensitization to both fantasy and real violence (APA, 2004; Huesmann, Moise-Titus, Podolski, & Eron, 2003; National Association for the Education of Young Children [NAEYC], 1997). Increases in nightmares, sleep disturbances, and depression have also been associated with exposure to media violence. To address these issues, Claire, a second-grade teacher, encourages families to turn off the TV. Every year she provides families with a stream of ideas about what to do besides watching TV.

Community Violence

Many children live in neighborhoods that exhibit high levels of community violence and frequent exposure to the use of guns, knives, drugs, and random violence (Osofsky, 1999; Shonkoff & Phillips, 2000). These children are able to describe witnessing shootings and beatings, and may see them as everyday and ordinary events (Osofsky, 1999). Community violence also includes the signs of aggression and vandalism that children see, such as broken windows, and the sounds associated with violence, such as yelling in the street and police sirens. Exposure to violence of these kinds negatively impacts children. Many suffer psychological trauma that persists into adulthood (Luthar & Goldstein, 2004). Thinking of this, Karl plays soft music from different cultures in his kindergarten class to direct children's attention away from the sounds outside that may disturb them.

Other Forms of Violence

Other forms of violence, such as gang violence, drug use, and assault, may also be part of children's experiences while growing up. Young children may witness gang violence in the neighborhood or be the unintended victims of violence associated with drug use. Children may become involved in gangs or social groups that are founded on violence, especially if they have older siblings who participate in these activities. They may be trained by older children to threaten or inflict violence on younger children. Teachers need to be alert to ways that violence can directly or indirectly impact young children, and aware to recognize the potential impacts of violence.

Understanding the Effects of Violence

Violence impacts everyone: children, families, and teachers. Its negative influence is measurable and long lasting (APA, 2004; Luthar & Goldstein, 2004).

Impacts on Children

The effects of violence on very young children's behavior and development are just beginning to be understood. Research has revealed that experiencing violence directly or indirectly affects children of all ages (Shonkoff & Phillips, 2000). Even before children can talk, the negative consequences of witnessing domestic or community violence are demonstrated through children's temper tantrums, fears, and difficulty separating from parents (Osofsky, 2004). Sleep disturbances such as fear of going to bed, aggressive or withdrawn behaviors, and disruption in parent and child attachment are also associated with exposure to violence (Rice & Groves, 2005). Some children who witness violence in the community even show symptoms of posttraumatic stress disorder similar to the responses of those who experience violence in war zones (National Center for Posttraumatic Stress Disorder, 2007).

Witnessing violence also interrupts normal brain development. Kindergarten and school-age children, who are able to understand the intentionality of acts of violence, often have trouble concentrating and paying attention due to fears and intrusive thoughts. Children who are not able to trust in the safety of their surroundings may withdraw and have trouble building social attachments. They may also become disassociated with their surroundings, eventually losing the ability to develop care and empathy for others (APA, 2004). These experiences take social and emotional development off course and ultimately negatively impact the child's ability to learn.

Teachers can offer hope for these children through strategies that mediate the impacts of violence. Marion, a teacher of 3-year-olds, remembers two brothers that attended her class. They had been so traumatized by violence in their neighborhood that when they first joined her class they would lay on the floor right in front of the door. They didn't cry, but they didn't play. She helped them transition into typical play by bringing toys to them and allowing them to gain trust slowly. Sonya uses storyboards to help her first graders review the actions of the characters in a story. She teaches words to describe inappropriate behaviors and provides opportunities for the children to offer creative alternatives for the poor decisions or aggressive actions of the characters.

Impacts on Parents

Domestic and community violence traumatize parents as well as children. Parents who witness or experience such violence are challenged to cope and manage their own fears while at the same time realizing that they might not be able to keep their child safe (Osofsky, 1999; Margolin & Gordis, 2004). These parents may respond by becoming overprotective, not allowing the child to be away from them. They

> **What if . . .**
> a child in your class reported that he had witnessed acts of violence and was afraid to go outside? How would you assist this child?

> **What if . . .**
> you observed children dramatizing violent acts in their play? How would you redirect the children's play to themes of empowerment?

Domestic and community violence disrupt a basic function of the family by challenging a mother's ability to keep her child safe.

may become numb to the effects of violence and may experience extreme sadness and depression. This can create an overwhelming sense of helplessness and hopelessness that is unavoidably communicated to the child. Over time the parent may become emotionally unavailable, less responsive to the child's needs, and unable to be a source of comfort to the child (Osofsky, 1999). As a result, the parent becomes unable to provide supportive care for the child, which disrupts the parent–child relationship.

Parents living in violent environments need to find ways to manage their own trauma before they are able to support their children. Teachers play an important role in this effort by offering information for parents about social service supports and by strengthening the parent–child relationship through positive experiences in the early childhood setting. Maria keeps a stack of information cards on her desk that provide information for social service supports in her community. Because she has these readily available, parents recognize that many people need extra support now and then.

Impacts on Teachers

Adults who work with young children who have been impacted by violence also experience its negative effects. Learning about a child's tragic stories can evoke many feelings including anger, fear, and anxiety. Teachers may express these "secondhand" effects of violence through physical symptoms such as headaches and stomach upsets, as well as emotional distress, exhaustion, and sadness (Rice & Groves, 2005). In addition, teachers are called on to help children cope with their negative experiences, while also managing the child's expressions of distress through behaviors such as aggression toward others, fears and clinginess, or regression in toileting or language development.

Teachers may need extra support and assistance from their supervisors to help them manage children's needs while coping with their own stresses (Osofsky, 1999; Rice & Groves, 2005). In the opening case scenario Min Jee recognized the signs of maltreatment and knew how to make a report. However, after doing so, she reflected on her actions and wondered if she should have noticed and addressed her concerns sooner. She feels guilty that she didn't protect Katherine from the effects of abuse and neglect. Min Jee may need to seek support from others to help her resolve her feelings about this situation and focus on planning ways to support Katherine and her mother in the future.

● ADDRESSING THE EFFECTS OF MALTREATMENT AND VIOLENCE

A caring and supportive relationship is crucial in helping children and parents manage the effects of traumatic events. Teachers are a source of safety, caring support, and reassurance for the child and family (Office on Child Abuse and Neglect et al., 2003). They are able to create classroom environments and offer activities that help children and families cope with the effects of maltreatment and violence while helping to boost resilience for the future.

Implementing Supportive Strategies for Children

To improve children's positive long-term outcomes after negative experiences, teachers focus special attention on supports for the child in the classroom. This includes providing continuity, focusing on children's needs, and assisting children to manage their emotions in appropriate ways.

Providing Continuity

Disruption in the child's familiar daily routine may be a consequence related to maltreatment or experiences of violence. The child may be placed in the temporary care of a family member or foster care provider who is unaware of the child's regular schedule. By encouraging the protective services agency to continue the child's participation in the early childhood setting, teachers help support the child's familiar routine, which contributes to the child's positive coping process. Often services for children who have experienced traumatic events include positive socialization experiences such as those provided by early childhood programs (Office on Child Abuse and Neglect et al., 2003).

Focusing on Needs

Not every child who experiences maltreatment or violence responds the same. This can complicate treatment planning. Teachers learn to support children's coping strategies by acknowledging each child's individual needs and challenges. Children may need to:

- Overcome fear and regain the ability to trust.
- Dispel a sense of helplessness.
- Regain self-esteem.
- Feel safe and supported.
- Build a sense of autonomy, or independence.
- Feel in control and competent.

These needs can be addressed through interventions offered by skilled practitioners as well as through the child's participation in a high-quality early childhood education program (Cohen, Groves, & Kracke, 2009). Caring teachers work to address children's needs in ways that are developmentally appropriate.

The Infant Teachers provide extra time for holding and caring for infants who have experienced maltreatment or violence. They smile and speak kindly and gently when playing. They pay special attention to the infant's cues for hunger, need to sleep, or interest in play, helping to reestablish the baby's trust.

The Toddler Toddlers may need extra support to experience positive interactions. Allowing the toddler to play without having to share a toy for an extra period of time may help the child relax, boosting the child's sense of autonomy and control. Teachers might encourage the child to explore a new task, such as crawling through an interesting obstacle course, to help the child regain interest in play and develop a refreshed sense of competence.

The Preschooler Preschoolers can benefit from opportunities to immerse themselves in positive play, where they can retreat from their fears, relax, and pursue their own interests. Interesting dramatic play settings, extended play periods in the sensory bin materials or sandbox, and positive interest from the teacher are ways to build the child's sense of safety and personal control.

The Kindergarten and School-Age Child Teachers can support school-age children in two somewhat opposing ways. On the one hand, children in this age group may be interested in expressing and discussing their fears and feelings of violation from maltreatment or abuse. Inviting children to share their concerns with the teacher at appropriate times is one approach. At the same time children in this age group may wish to retreat from the experience and simply immerse themselves in play and exploration. In the opening case scenario, Min Jee noticed that Katherine recognized that she was dirty. Min Jee helped Katherine gain self-care skills by presenting activities in group time about how to brush your teeth, how to wash your hands and face, and how to comb your hair. Activities such as these assist children to gain a sense of control and competence.

Providing Appropriate Outlets for Expressing Emotions

All children benefit from the opportunity to explore and express their emotions. Children who have experienced violence or have been maltreated need access to a variety of appropriate opportunities for the open and free expression of their feelings and ideas. Expressive activities can be provided across the curriculum, including:

- Providing dramatic play props that support dramatization of everyday home life, including cooking, cleaning, and shopping props.
- Creating a designated space for children to build and keep their block structure from one day to the next until the children are ready to disassemble it.

 Dramatic play encourages children to express and work through their emotions. As you watch this **video**, consider how play around the theme of hospital may help children resolve their anxiety. What kinds of insights might the teacher gain by observing children's hospital play?

Children who have experienced traumatic events benefit from a variety of activities that allow them to express and process their emotions.

- Exploring feelings through children's literature and small-group discussions.
- Guiding children to draw, dictate, or write a story about a child solving a problem and, hence, gaining strength and confidence.
- Offering music and opportunity for children to play a rhythm instrument or to dance and move to a variety of musical styles as a method of expressing their feelings.

Reducing the Child's Sense of Isolation

Children who have experienced maltreatment or violence often feel set apart or emotionally isolated from other children. Supportive approaches include offering activities that encourage interactive play and that build social skills such as group games, team projects, and dramatic play. For example, when Min Jee sees Katherine alone in the library corner, she invites her to join the children who are playing with play dough. Min Jee offers Katherine a basket of cookie cutters to share with others at the table.

Creating Opportunities for Appropriate Problem Solving

Children who have been victimized may have experienced feelings of being trapped or not in control. They need support to regain a sense of confidence and competence. Teachers encourage this by offering the child appropriate opportunities to make choices and by guiding the child through reasonable problem-solving situations that build a sense of accomplishment. Activities to accomplish this include:

- Providing new physical challenges, such as offering the toddler an interesting new target for beanbags or presenting a preschooler with a variety of appropriate challenges on the child-sized balance beam.
- Involving the preschool child in selection of the snack menu or the books for story time for the following week.
- Creating opportunities for school-age children to assist in making decisions for the classroom, such as choosing books to purchase or selecting the games for gym time.

Addressing Violence in Children's Play Themes

Children may engage in play about violence, especially if this has been a part of their experience. Children are also easily attracted to strong characters depicted in the media, such as superheroes, and are interested in the excitement of games that involve chasing others and using pretend weapons. Children use play to explore and understand events, and play involving violent themes may have value in therapeutic settings (Levin, 2003). However, in the early childhood setting teachers worry that engaging in play that has violent themes may be detrimental. Teachers are concerned that:

- Once violent play gets started it is hard to stop; children get out of control.
- Other children may be scared or traumatized by viewing the play violence.
- Acting out violent acts reinforces violent behaviors and may teach children to be violent.
- Playing the same fantasy role over and over may interrupt children's social connection with other children and distracts children from other skill development.

There is no simple solution to meeting both children's needs and teacher concerns. However, some basic strategies can be implemented for all age groups of young children (Levin, 2003).

Recognizing Violent Themes in Play   Teachers should be observant and try to understand the topic children are exploring through play. Simply banning such play denies children the opportunity to process difficult topics in a developmentally appropriate way; also, it rarely works and is often counterproductive because children may respond by hiding the play themes and perhaps even lying about their play (Levin, 2003). Instead, teachers should offer interesting challenges to divert interest away from violent play and explore alternative ways to meet children's needs. For example, Noemi recognizes that Aaron and Kip tend to act out shooting themes in their play. She brings a variety of beanbags out to the play yard and helps the boys create targets for a challenge course. Later, Noemi guides the children to write creative stories and draw pictures about events that interest them. In this way Aaron and Kip are provided an active alternative in the play yard and an opportunity to explore the violent themes that interest them in ways that do not disturb the other children.

Ensuring Everyone Is Safe   Children engaged in play with violent themes may frighten others. Safety limits are needed to address the concerns of the other children. Involving all children in the development of the safety limits is a useful teaching approach. Noemi plans a group time for the discussion and guides the children to identify what to say when they don't want to play the scary games.

Meeting Children's Needs   Teachers need to be purposeful in planning activities that provide alternative and appropriate ways for children to explore frightening topics. Through painting, drawing, building with clay, and dictating stories, children who have experienced trauma are able to outwardly express emotions in ways that are less threatening than speaking about them (Malchiodi, 2001, 2008). It is also important to rotate the toys and materials that are available for play to ensure that children have interesting alternatives and are not falling back on violent play themes as a sign of boredom.

Promoting Healthy Play   Violent play themes sometimes emerge as children imitate the violent actions they have experienced. This is called *imitative play*. Children involved in imitative play act out the same violent events and themes over and over again. For example, Warren and Kyle might persist in play in which one child pretends to be waiting for a bus while the other sneaks up behind him and "shoots" him. Children engaged in imitative play seem stuck and unable to move beyond these repetitive themes. If these play themes persist in their focus on violence and death, the special assistance of a counselor or mental health specialist might be helpful. Teachers should work closely with families to share strategies for managing a child's worries and guiding the child to engage in *imaginative play*.

> ### What if . . .
> a small group of parents approached you with a complaint that they had observed children acting out violent themes in the play yard? How would you respond?

Imaginative play is play that explores a variety of scenarios, with the play partners demonstrating creative ways for keeping safe or withstanding the effects of violence. Tony, Karen, and Enrique pick up their play theme each day at recess, but the ideas and activities change. What began as play focused on police and shootings evolves to firefighters saving people and animals, and then changes to play about being a veterinarian. Teachers can encourage these empowering themes by offering ideas for resolving conflicts and giving suggestions about how the "characters" might take charge and manage the dramatic theme in appropriate ways. This approach guides children to continue to move on to new play themes.

Building Conflict Resolution Skills

Learning to resolve disagreements in positive and productive ways helps children build the skills they need to cope with and resolve future difficulties. Conflict resolution approaches offer concrete alternatives to using force or violence to address problems. Activities that help children develop these skills include:

- Reading books about children who solve problems.
- Using puppets to act out a challenge, such as figuring out how to divide an apple.
- Planning activities that require problem solving, such as setting out cut-and-paste activities for four children, while providing only two pairs of scissors and two glue sticks.
- Teaching children the language of conflict resolution and modeling how to solve a problem, such as naming the problem, identifying possible solutions, and selecting a mutually agreeable result (Office on Child Abuse and Neglect et al., 2003).

 This **video** shows a teacher helping a group of children work through a conflict. What strategies are used by the teacher in order to enhance the children's understanding of each other's perspectives and resolve the conflict?

Recognizing Overlooked Victims

When violence occurs in the family, everyone is affected, and sometimes there may be overlooked victims. Children may have witnessed the abuse of a sibling or they may have been required to participate in the abuse in some way. Children may have been coached to cover up the abuse, or they may feel guilty that they were not able to protect the other child from maltreatment. Similarly a parent may suffer from guilt, feeling that he should have recognized and protected the child from maltreatment by another adult. These overlooked victims may need support to express and manage their emotions.

Supporting Families

Teachers are a source of support for families who have been affected by maltreatment and other forms of violence. They make a positive contribution by creating welcoming environments and offering activities such as (Office on Child Abuse and Neglect et al., 2003):

- Providing information about typical child development and positive parenting.
- Conducting activities that help families develop social contacts, reducing the family's sense of isolation.
- Encouraging families to be involved in community service projects to help develop a sense of contribution, confidence, and connection to the community in which they live.

Teachers can also help families identify their strengths and available resources. For example, Alicia tells parents about the strong points she observes, such as picking their children up on time, and encourages families to recognize their friends as positive resources. Sometimes simply being friendly can offer the encouragement that families need to face the process of healing from traumatic events (NAEYC, 2004).

What if . . .

you knew that the mother of a child in your class was a victim of domestic violence? You can see that she wants to develop friendships with other parents. How would you help her to get acquainted?

Building Coping Skills and Resilience

In spite of the serious effects of child maltreatment and violence, not all children demonstrate poor development. Some children who have experienced acts of violence display considerable ability to cope and are able to thrive following interventions that restore their sense of confidence. This characteristic is called **resilience** (Children's Bureau & DePanfilis, 2006). Various factors appear to be associated with a child's ability to be resilient.

resilience
the ability to cope with negative experiences

Personal Characteristics

Specific aspects of the child's temperament or personality style that are associated with resilience include optimism, humor, intelligence, and positive self-esteem (Fraser & Terzian, 2005). These characteristics mediate the negative effects of maltreatment and support the child's ability to think positively and to heal from the emotional trauma.

Aspects of the Experience

The ability to be resilient is affected by various aspects of the experience. For example, resilience following maltreatment is impacted by the following:

- *Age of the child:* Younger children tend to be more resilient and more responsive to appropriate therapies following experiences of abuse or neglect (National Scientific Council on the Developing Child, 2005).
- *Relationship of the child to the abuser:* Children who know their abuser find it harder to cope with the effects of maltreatment. An extreme sense of betrayal is experienced when the abuse is perpetrated by someone the child knows, such as a parent, family member, or friend (Office on Child Abuse and Neglect et al., 2003).
- *Kind, frequency, and severity of maltreatment:* Children are better able to cope with the effects of maltreatment when it is less invasive and less emotionally involved. For example, a child who experiences a single incidence of abuse may be better able to cope than a child who has been neglected over a long period of time (Children's Bureau & DePanfilis, 2006).

POLICY POINT **Public Policy Strategies to Reduce Child Maltreatment**

- Enact policies that allow parents to take leave from work after the birth or adoption of a child, and provide financial supports for those who wish to stay home with their newborn but are not financially able to do so.
- Provide supports for parents who struggle with the challenges of working and raising their children, especially those who work low-wage jobs or irregular work hours, and those whose children have special health or developmental challenges.
- Increase access to mental health care for young children and families.
- Provide resources for parents and early childhood teachers to manage children's challenging behaviors.
- Make quality early childhood programs accessible for low-income families.

Source: Based on *Excessive Stress Disrupts the Architecture of the Developing Brain* (Council Working Paper #3), National Scientific Council on the Developing Child, 2005, Cambridge, MA: Center on the Developing Child at Harvard University. Retrieved July 21, 2012, from http://developingchild.harvard.edu/library/reports_and_working_papers/wp3.

Social Support Resources

Children who are surrounded by warm and reassuring environments fare better than those who are isolated or not supported (Child Welfare Information Gateway, 2004). The extended family members, caring and responsive teachers, and other positive role models can assist the child to form an optimistic vision of the future (Fraser & Terzian, 2005). For example, when Mitch teaches a child who has experienced abuse or violence, he helps the child make a paper journal booklet. Once a week he and the child sit down together, open the booklet, and each draws a picture on his side of the book. They talk and enjoy the time together.

Positive Community Influences

Aspects of the broader community also support children's resilience. These include access to health care, social service resources, stable neighborhoods, and safe schools (Fraser & Terzian, 2005). Children in communities that have accessible resources such as these are more likely to have their physical and emotional health needs met, thus reducing the long-term negative effects of maltreatment.

In spite of this knowledge, however, and the increasing scientific evidence about the long-term negative effects of child maltreatment, little is being done to systematically provide the resources or strategies needed to reduce maltreatment or address its consequences (Center on the Developing Child at Harvard University, 2007). The *Policy Point* provides examples of public policies that could improve this situation.

● PREVENTING MALTREATMENT AND PROTECTING CHILDREN FROM VIOLENCE

Prevention is the most effective way to reduce maltreatment. For teachers this involves understanding the risks for abuse and neglect and taking prevention measures in the early childhood setting. Teachers also help children and families build protective skills that reduce the risk for abuse, and serve as advocates for reducing maltreatment in their communities.

Prevention Measures for the Classroom

A variety of prevention activities occur in early childhood settings. These include careful hiring of teachers, making special arrangements in the environment, being sensitive to children's needs, and recognizing teacher risk factors for abuse.

Safe Hiring Practices

Teachers of young children must be competent and safe. Even though early education teachers them-selves make up a small percentage (less than 1%) of those who abuse children (HHS/ACF, 2011), it is alarming to note that maltreatment does occur in early childhood settings. To address this, great care must be taken during the hiring process. Prospective teachers should be prepared to earnestly participate in the process, understanding that this is an important abuse prevention strategy. For example, the hiring process may involve:

- Reviewing the applicant's education and work history to clarify competency for work with young children.
- Conducting interviews that reveal personal temperament traits and dispositions that suggest a good fit for work with young children.
- Conducting criminal background checks before new teachers are hired.
- Checking references to screen for any concerns about appropriateness for hire.
- Observing applicants working with children to recognize skills.

People who have the potential to abuse children are often drawn to work in settings where they have frequent contact and access to them (Koralek, 1992). Careful screening during the hiring process helps to eliminate these concerns.

Arranging the Environment

The way the classroom or home care environment is arranged helps reduce the chance of abuse and pro-tects teachers from claims of suspected abuse (Rice & Groves, 2005). Furniture and equipment should be positioned so there is a clear view of all the indoor and outdoor spaces, with no hidden areas. Diaper-changing and toileting areas should be open so that adults can be observed for appropriate interaction.

Following Safety Guidelines

Program and school safety policies are designed to keep children safe and eliminate the possibility that abuse could occur. Teachers need to understand and follow these guidelines. For example, some settings may require that teachers and volunteers are never alone with children. The *Safety Segment* provides examples of program policies and practices that should be in place to ensure children's safety from maltreatment and protect teachers from potential allegations of abuse.

Touching Children Appropriately

Many early childhood settings have policies related to touching children. Some prohibit teachers from holding children on their laps or hugging a child, others may have "no touch" policies. Imple-menting "no touch" policies to reduce the risk of abuse is an extreme measure, especially because touch is an essential component of interaction and responsive care for very young children. More appropriate approaches guide teachers to touch children in ways that are suitable for the setting. Holding hands, patting a child on the back, or putting an arm around a child's shoulder are ways teachers can show care through safe touch. Teachers must also be mindful of cultural variations in acceptable ways to touch. In addition, it is important to recognize and respect that children always have the right to say they do not want to be touched (Koralek, 1992; NAEYC, 2004).

Being Aware of a Teacher's Potential for Abuse

On occasion even well-seasoned teachers may experience frustration and find it difficult to manage children's behaviors. Teachers who frequently exhibit frustration and poor management may show signs that they could abuse children, such as (Koralek, 1992):

- Yelling at or belittling children for mistakes.
- Responding inappropriately to challenging behaviors such as grabbing or jerking the child.
- Expressing personal frustrations to a child.
- Showing unusual or inappropriate interest in a particular child or seeking to be alone with a child.

Source: Based on *Caregivers of Young Children: Preventing and Responding to Child Maltreatment*, by D. Koralek, 1992, Washington, DC: U.S. Department of Health & Human Services, retrieved July 21, 2012, from http://www.childwelfare.gov/pubs/usermanuals/caregive/caregive.pdf; and *Building Circles—Breaking Cycles* (Publication DD2), 2004, Washington, DC: National Association for the Education of Young Children.

Supervisors watch for these kinds of behaviors as signs of inappropriateness for working with children and intervene as needed. It is also important for teachers to be aware of their own behaviors and recognize when they may need additional supports, such as rest breaks and new strategies to ensure they can keep children safe.

Building Protective Factors

Child abuse prevention also involves supporting children and families to develop *protective factors*. Protective factors are buffers that reduce the potential for abuse or neglect. These factors are associated with a decreased incidence of child maltreatment, making them important contributors to abuse prevention (CWIG, 2004).

Protective Factors for Children

High-quality early childhood settings provide opportunities for children to experience safety and security in an environment where all people are treated with respect and dignity (Cohen & Knitzer, 2004). Such experiences help children form secure relationships, increase their interest in problem solving, and promote the development of language, healthy physical development, and positive social skills (Cohen, Onunaku, Clothier, & Poppe, 2006). These protective factors also enhance children's abilities to develop interests and hobbies, practice self-control, and learn to both seek help and gain independence and autonomy (CWIG, 2004). In her classroom, Jen sets up project-based activities that evolve across the week. Jen takes pictures for the project's story poster so children can reflect on how they worked through the steps of their activity.

As children grow through the preschool and elementary years, they can also learn personal safety skills through appropriate and purposefully planned activities. Activities might focus on lessons such as:

- Don't go with strangers.
- Who to go to for help.
- What are "good" secrets and what are "bad" secrets.
- Safe touch—it's ok to say "don't touch me."

The *Teaching Wellness* feature provides examples of ways to teach children about safe touch and how to say "Stop!"

Protective Factors for Families

Protective factors for families include knowing about community support resources and how to access them, and building positive parenting skills. Many early childhood programs, such as Head Start, have a specific commitment to supporting families through planned parent education and family service

> **What if . . .**
> you witnessed another teacher threatening, belittling, or yelling at a child? What would you do?

TEACHING WELLNESS   Keeping Me Safe

LEARNING OUTCOME   **Children will understand the concepts of friendly and not friendly touch, and know that they can choose if they want to be touched.**

Safety watch: Be aware of children's feelings as they participate. Listen if they wish to tell about a time they were hurt or not touched in a friendly way. Provide reassurance and help guide the conversation back to the group discussion as needed. Follow up if children describe instances that may suggest possible maltreatment.

INFANTS AND TODDLERS

- **Goal:** Children will imitate gentle touch.
- **Materials:** Small doll or stuffed animal.
- **Vocabulary focus:** Words that convey friendly touch (gentle, soft, kind, nice) and unfriendly touch (too hard, hurts, not nice).
- **Activity plan:** Sit with the infant or toddler on the floor. Create play interactions between the child and the doll or animal. Hold the prop kindly and demonstrate gentle touching. Point to the eyes, ears, nose, and say, "This is how I touch gently" or "This hug is my friendly touch." Reinforce these concepts in everyday interactions.

- **How to adjust the activity:** Reinforce these concepts with all babies during everyday play. Overcome language barriers with body language; smile and provide positive encouragement when a child demonstrates friendly touching, or if unfriendly touching of toys or people is demonstrated, make a frowning face, and speak words and use a tone that indicates, "We don't hit; hitting hurts." Then smile and use a friendly voice and gestures demonstrating, "This is the way to be gentle. See, this is a friendly way to touch."
- **Did you meet your goal?** Do children begin to imitate the gentle touching that you model? Do toddlers begin to use words like *gentle, kind, nice, friendly*?

PRESCHOOLERS AND KINDERGARTNERS

- **Goal:** Children will describe friendly and unfriendly touch, and know how to respond appropriately when the child does not want to be touched.
- **Materials:** Paper cut into 5" × 8" card, marking pen, two boxes or containers, one labeled with a smiling face and one with a frowning face.
- **Vocabulary focus:** Words that convey friendly touch (gentle, kind, reassuring, friendly); words that describe hurtful and unfriendly touch (pain, uncomfortable, scary); phrases that communicate dislike and stop (I don't like that, stop that, go away!).
- **Activity plan:** At group time, gather the children and introduce the definitions of friendly and unfriendly touch. Say, "Friendly touching is touch that cares for us and make us feel good like hugging or patting or giving a high-five." Talk about unfriendly touching, the kind that hurts—like hitting or kicking. Provide a few examples, and write each word on a paper card. Then ask the children to suggest words that describe friendly touch. Write each word on a card. If children describe a scenario, such as, "Friendly touch is when your friend hugs you," write the scenario on a card. Ask the children to give examples of unfriendly touching. Now lay the cards face down and give each child a turn to pick up a card. Read the word and ask the child if the word (or scenario) describes friendly or unfriendly touch. Ask the child to

place friendly words or scenarios in the "smiling face" box, and unfriendly words or scenarios in the "frowning face" box. Tell children that unfriendly touching is not ok, and that children can stop unfriendly touching. Invite the children to identify ways they can say "no" if they do not want to be touched such as saying, "You need to stop. I don't like that. That hurts!" Tell children that they can get help by telling their teacher or parents about the unfriendly touching. Now ask each child to choose one of the unfriendly word or scenario cards. Invite the child to show how they could say "no" to the unfriendly touching. Close the activity by reminding children about friendly and unfriendly touching, and that it is ok to say "no" if the child does not want to be touched.
- **How to adjust the activity:** Ask parents who speak the home languages of children in the class to assist you with the activity. Teach the words for friendly and unfriendly touching (or good and bad touch) in each child's language as well as English. Remember that children may need frequent reminders about friendly and unfriendly touching during their everyday play. Children with special learning needs may benefit from repeating this activity periodically.
- **Did you meet your goal?** Are children able to describe friendly and unfriendly touch? Can they model appropriate responses to each kind of touch?

SCHOOL-AGE CHILDREN

- **Goal:** Children will be able to describe a variety of friendly and unfriendly touches, and articulate when a friendly touch might become an unfriendly touch.
- **Materials:** Small pieces of paper, marking pens.

- **Vocabulary focus:** Words that describe friendly (kind, caring, nice, gentle, tender, soft, good) and unfriendly (harsh, hard, rough, mean, bad, hurtful) touch.

- **Activity plan:** Create game cards by having children write down different kinds of friendly and unfriendly kinds of touch on small pieces of paper. Fold the papers and place them in the middle of the group. Have the children take turns selecting and reading from one of the papers. Ask the other children to "vote," by raising their hands, whether the touch is a friendly or unfriendly touch. Ask the children to explain why they voted the way they did. As appropriate, introduce the notion that some kinds of touching can be friendly, but if done too hard, can be unfriendly or hurtful, such as hugging or tickling too hard. Guide discussion about friendly touching that might become unfriendly touching if it is too hard or too rough.

- **How to adjust the activity:** Using the same cards have the children role-play responding to friendly and unfriendly touch. Encourage all children to participate, providing opportunity for all children to learn the messages through acting out scenarios. Guide children to use dramatic motions as well as language. Ensure that each child has the opportunity to fully participate.

- **Did you meet your goal?** Are children able to describe friendly and unfriendly touch? Can children tell when friendly touch begins to feel like an unfriendly touch? Are children able to role-play appropriate responses to friendly and unfriendly touch?

Source: Based on *Teaching Touching Safety Rules*, Committee for Children. (2012). Seattle, WA: Author. Retrieved July 21, 2012, from http://www.cfchildren.org/advocacy/child-safety/teaching-touching-safety-rules.aspx.

approaches. Schools may have a family social service worker who assists families to access resources that help to bolster these protective factors, but often the early childhood teacher is seen as the most accessible and trusted resource for parents. Strategies that help families develop the protective factors that reduce the potential for maltreatment include (Children's Bureau & DePanfilis, 2006):

- Arranging times to talk with families to explore and recognize their strengths and use them as the foundation for future growth.
- Guiding families to identify their needs, recognize their current network of supports and resources, and engage in problem solving about how to address challenges.
- Linking parents to available resources and providing them with access to these supports.
- Modeling and offering guidance techniques for children's challenging behaviors.
- Helping families know who to call in times of crisis.

Knowledge of the resources in the community, and familiarity with the individuals who work in those settings, reinforce teachers in this role of social support provider. Building relationships with social services providers also helps those agencies to be receptive to referrals from the teacher. Brenda participates in a local child and family network group. This provides a chance to meet other early childhood teachers and family services workers and talk about community, child, and family needs. The *Nutrition Note* describes an example in which collaboration with a local dietitian helps families develop protective factors, helping to resolve a situation of potential medical neglect.

Contributing to Community Abuse Prevention Efforts

Effective child abuse prevention relies on community efforts. However, sometimes energizing the public around the topic of abuse is difficult because it requires people to think about an

NUTRITION NOTE   Community Partners Help Develop Protective Factors

Teachers play an important role in linking families to community support agencies. Programs such as the Women, Infants, and Children (WIC) program can help families access food and support them to address a child's special nutritional needs. For example, a child with an iron deficiency is at risk for poor growth and learning challenges.

A parent who offers the child a vegetarian diet may not be aware of the growing child's need for an iron-rich diet, resulting in anemia. WIC dietitians teach the parent how to offer a diet that will address the child's need for iron-rich foods. This knowledge builds protective factors that reduce the potential for medical neglect.

uncomfortable subject. A lack of common understanding about the prevalence of abuse in the community and disagreement about appropriate parenting practices can also hinder community efforts. Early childhood teachers are logical partners for such initiatives because they have knowledge and experience that equip them to speak strongly about the challenges that families face and the negative effects of maltreatment and violence (Kracke & Cohen, 2008).

A positive approach to child abuse prevention is often the best approach. This involves placing the focus on supporting and strengthening all families and raising healthy children (Washington Council for Prevention of Child Abuse, 2005). Successful child abuse prevention efforts focus on (Thomas, Leicht, Hughes, Madigan, & Dowell, 2003):

- Providing support programs for parents, especially first-time parents.
- Enhancing family relationships.

PROGRESSIVE PROGRAMS & PRACTICES

Building Bonds by Supporting Breastfeeding Behind Bars

By Farzana Siddiqui, Community Action Head Start, Washington County, OR

Community Action of Washington County, Oregon, operates an innovative Early Head Start program at Coffee Creek Correctional Facility. Over 75% of inmates at this women's prison have children, and some inmates are pregnant when they enter the facility. Through a partnership with the Oregon Department of Corrections (DOC), eight children under age 3 and their incarcerated mothers meet for two half-day classes each week in an Early Head Start classroom on the prison grounds. Qualified teachers help mothers learn parenting skills, bond with their children to prepare for parenting after prison, and conduct monthly visits with the children's caregivers.

Prenatal and labor and delivery services are provided to inmates through the current Corrections system, but Early Head Start, DOC, and Health Department staff identified some gaps, which led to the formation of a Prenatal Services Group.[1] The work of this group, which required no additional funds, improved support for nursing mothers and helped establish consistency in how inmates are treated by officers when they are moved to the hospital for delivery.

The current system was reviewed and several challenges were identified. Pregnant inmates were housed in the Medium Security Facility until their deliveries. Mothers delivered their babies at a community hospital and then returned to prison while their infants were cared for by family members or foster parents. Breastfeeding and expressing breast milk was allowed, but logistically difficult. To breast-feed, mothers had to visit with their babies during normal visiting hours, but these visits counted against the mother's monthly allowance of visit points. This forced the mothers to choose between bonding with their babies during visiting hours or visiting with other family members. Mothers who expressed breast milk were only allowed to use hand pumps, and family members had to supply coolers and cold packs for transporting the breast milk.

Through the new Early Head Start collaboration women may now use machine breast pumps provided by the Women, Infants and Children (WIC) program, and Baby Bonding visits to breast-feed no longer count against the mother's total visit points. For example, one mother serving a short sentence entered prison early in her pregnancy. After she delivered her son a volunteer brought him to the prison to visit her, which affirmed her role as a mother. She was able to pump milk and to participate in substance abuse treatment in the Minimum facility. A DHS worker brought her son to the Coffee Creek Child Development Center Early Head Start, where mother and child established their relationship and she was able to breast-feed her baby. The mother is now out of prison, has been reunited with her son, and they have a strong parent–child relationship.

[1]This group included Sharon Bolmeier, Community Head Start Family Support Teacher; Sue Omel, RN, MS, MTH, Washington County Dept of Health and Human Services Supervisor; Cally Wolery, Nurse Manager at Coffee Creek; Becky Wiggin, Executive Support at Coffee Creek; and Carol Thompson, RN, Nurse at Coffee Creek.

- Teaching parenting skills.
- Providing access to emergency care and shelter for domestic violence protection.

It is important to frame the actions of child abuse prevention as part of the many ways in which communities contribute to the positive growth and development of children, such as by providing libraries, parks, schools, and youth sports and recreation programs. Effective prevention messages must also be culturally relevant and appropriate, so that all members of the community participate in the goal to raise safe and healthy children (Fontes, 2005). The *Progressive Programs & Practices* feature describes an innovative effort initiated by an Early Head Start Program at a women's correctional institution. Collaborative approaches such as this engage the community in positive and supportive child abuse prevention efforts.

● SUMMARY

Many young children suffer from harmful acts of abuse or the failure of families to protect them from harm. Teachers need to be aware of the different types of maltreatment and understand that the effects of abuse can be long lasting. Maltreatment is expressed through both physical and behavioral signs. Children may have visible marks, show the effects through play, or tell teachers about the abuse.

Teachers and others who work closely with young children are mandated to report when maltreatment is suspected. To prepare, teachers need to recognize the signs of maltreatment, know how to make a report, and understand their role in the protective service process.

Children are exposed to many other sources of violence that can negatively affect their ability to learn and thrive. Teachers need to be prepared with strategies to help children cope and to manage difficult behaviors.

Teachers play a supportive role in helping children who have witnessed violence to attain coping skills that help them to be resilient in difficult times. This is an important step in guiding children to build trust in people and the world.

Child abuse prevention efforts encompass actions taken in the early childhood setting, including hiring safe teachers who know how to appropriately nurture and care for children. Teachers are also important resources for their communities as they convey the importance of child abuse prevention in building safe communities and enhancing the development of healthy children.

KEY TERMS

Child abuse	Child neglect	Perpetrators
Child maltreatment	Mandatory reporters	Resilience

REVIEW QUESTIONS

1. Define physical abuse and neglect. Describe how these forms of maltreatment are different. Give four examples of abuse and four of neglect.
2. Describe some of the physical and behavioral signs of maltreatment.
3. It is good practice to ensure that families understand that teachers are mandatory reporters of suspected maltreatment. How would you share this information with families in your class?
4. What are some of the types of violence that children experience? Name three and describe how they impact young children.
5. Provide three examples of ways teachers can support children in coping with the effects of violence.

DISCUSSION STARTERS

1. Reflect on your own experiences as a child and perhaps as a parent. What is your perception about why child maltreatment occurs? Scan the local media for your area to identify a case of child maltreatment in the news. Discuss the case with others in your class. Identify supports or strategies that might have helped prevent the maltreatment from occurring.

2. Most teachers find some children's styles or behaviors to be annoying and frustrating, such as clinging, crying, or whining, always having a runny nose, or demonstrating challenging and aggressive behaviors. Identify the style or behavior that you find most frustrating. What steps have you taken (or would you take) to learn how to better manage these frustrating behaviors? Talk with others about your ideas and supports that may be available.

3. Making reports of suspected abuse or neglect can be very stressful because it means that teachers must recognize when they have reasonable suspicion that maltreatment has occurred. What aspects of child maltreatment do you feel would be the most difficult to recognize? What would be the most difficult part of making a report for you? What agency would you call to make a report?

PRACTICE POINTS

1. Refer to Figure 16-1. Speculate about why the incidence of each form of maltreatment varies according to children's age. Discuss your reasoning with others. Test your thinking by exploring authoritative resources.

2. Spend time reviewing the children's television programming that is available in your area. What aspects of violence stand out to you? Are the characters performing the aggressive or violent acts held accountable for their behaviors? What lessons about violence are communicated in the programs that you reviewed? What activities would you implement in your early childhood classroom to reduce the impact of such messages?

3. Gather information about the incidence and prevalence of abuse and neglect in your community. Identify the resources that are available to support children who are victims of maltreatment and their families. What specific kinds of services are available to children and parents? Is there a cost associated with getting this help? Are there other barriers that might keep some families from benefiting?

WEB RESOURCES

American Humane Society
www.americanhumane.org/protecting-children

Child Trends
www.childtrends.org

Child Welfare Information Gateway
www.childwelfare.gov

Family Violence Prevention Fund
http://endabuse.org/userfiles/file/Children_and_Families/DomesticViolence.pdf

National Center on Shaken Baby Syndrome
www.dontshake.org

New York Society for the Prevention of Cruelty to Children
www.nyspcc.org

MyEducationLab™

Go to Topic 12 (Child Abuse and Neglect) in the MyEducationLab (www.myeducationlab.com) for your course, where you can:

- Find learning outcomes for Child Abuse and Neglect along with the national standards that connect to these outcomes.
- Complete Assignments and Activities that can help you more deeply understand the chapter content.
- Apply and practice your understanding of the core teaching skills identified in the chapter with the Building Teaching Skills and Dispositions learning units.

- Check your comprehension on the content covered in the chapter by going to the Study Plan in the Book Resources for your text. Here you will be able to take a chapter quiz, receive feedback on your answers, and then access Review, Practice, and Enrichment activities to enhance your understanding of chapter content.

appendix

Dietary Reference Intakes (DRIs): Recommended Dietary Allowances and Adequate Intakes, Vitamins

Food and Nutrition Board, Institute of Medicine, National Academies

Life Stage Group	Vitamin A (µg/d)[a]	Vitamin C (mg/d)	Vitamin D (µg/d)[b,c]	Vitamin E (mg/d)[d]	Vitamin K (µg/d)	Thiamin (mg/d)	Riboflavin (mg/d)	Niacin (mg/d)[e]	Vitamin B6 (mg/d)	Folate (µg/d)[f]	Vitamin B12 (µg/d)	Pantothenic Acid (mg/d)	Biotin (µg/d)	Choline (mg/d)[g]
Infants														
0 to 6 mo	400*	40*	10	4*	2.0*	0.2*	0.3*	2*	0.1*	65*	0.4*	1.7*	5*	125*
6 to 12 mo	500*	50*	10	5*	2.5*	0.3*	0.4*	4*	0.3*	80*	0.5*	1.8*	6*	150*
Children														
1–3 y	300	15	15	6	30*	0.5	0.5	6	0.5	150	0.9	2*	8*	200*
4–8 y	400	25	15	7	55*	0.6	0.6	8	0.6	200	1.2	3*	12*	250*
Males														
9–13 y	600	45	15	11	60*	0.9	0.9	12	1.0	300	1.8	4*	20*	375*
14–18 y	900	75	15	15	75*	1.2	1.3	16	1.3	400	2.4	5*	25*	550*
19–30 y	900	90	15	15	120*	1.2	1.3	16	1.3	400	2.4	5*	30*	550*
31–50 y	900	90	15	15	120*	1.2	1.3	16	1.3	400	2.4	5*	30*	550*
51–70 y	900	90	15	15	120*	1.2	1.3	16	1.7	400	2.4[h]	5*	30*	550*
>70 y	900	90	20	15	120*	1.2	1.3	16	1.7	400	2.4[h]	5*	30*	550*
Females														
9–13 y	600	45	15	11	60*	0.9	0.9	12	1.0	300	1.8	4*	20*	375*
14–18 y	700	65	15	15	75*	1.0	1.0	14	1.2	400[i]	2.4	5*	25*	400*
19–30 y	700	75	15	15	90*	1.1	1.1	14	1.3	400[i]	2.4	5*	30*	425*
31–50 y	700	75	15	15	90*	1.1	1.1	14	1.3	400[i]	2.4	5*	30*	425*
51–70 y	700	75	15	15	90*	1.1	1.1	14	1.5	400	2.4[h]	5*	30*	425*
>70 y	700	75	20	15	90*	1.1	1.1	14	1.5	400	2.4[h]	5*	30*	425*
Pregnancy														
14–18 y	750	80	15	15	75*	1.4	1.4	18	1.9	600[j]	2.6	6*	30*	450*
19–30 y	770	85	15	15	90*	1.4	1.4	18	1.9	600[j]	2.6	6*	30*	450*
31–50 y	770	85	15	15	90*	1.4	1.4	18	1.9	600[j]	2.6	6*	30*	450*
Lactation														
14–18 y	1,200	115	15	19	75*	1.4	1.6	17	2.0	500	2.8	7*	35*	550*
19–30 y	1,300	120	15	19	90*	1.4	1.6	17	2.0	500	2.8	7*	35*	550*
31–50 y	1,300	120	15	19	90*	1.4	1.6	17	2.0	500	2.8	7*	35*	550*

NOTE: This table (taken from the DRI reports, see www.nap.edu) presents Recommended Dietary Allowances (RDAs) in **bold type** and Adequate Intakes (AIs) in ordinary type followed by an asterisk (*). An RDA is the average daily dietary intake level; sufficient to meet the nutrient requirements of nearly all (97-98 percent) healthy individuals in a group. It is calculated from an Estimated Average Requirement (EAR). If sufficient scientific evidence is not available to establish an EAR, and thus calculate an RDA, an AI is usually developed. For healthy breastfed infants, an AI is the mean intake. The AI for other life stage and gender groups is believed to cover the needs of all healthy individuals in the groups, but lack of data or uncertainty in the data prevent being able to specify with confidence the percentage of individuals covered by this intake.

[a] As retinol activity equivalents (RAEs). 1 RAE = 1 µg retinol, 12 µg β-carotene, 24 µg α-carotene, or 24 µg β-cryptoxanthin. The RAE for dietary provitamin A carotenoids is two-fold greater than retinol equivalents (RE), whereas the RAE for preformed vitamin A is the same as RE.

[b] As cholecalciferol. 1 µg cholecalciferol = 40 IU vitamin D.

[c] Under the assumption of minimal sunlight.

[d] As α-tocopherol. α-Tocopherol includes RRR-α-tocopherol, the only form of α-tocopherol that occurs naturally in foods, and the 2R-stereoisomeric forms of α-tocopherol (RRR-, RSR-, RRS-, and RSS-α-tocopherol) that occur in fortified foods and supplements. It does not include the 2S-stereoisomeric forms of α-tocopherol (SRR-, SSR-, SRS-, and SSS-α-tocopherol), also found in fortified foods and supplements.

[e] As niacin equivalents (NE). 1 mg of niacin = 60 mg of tryptophan; 0–6 months = preformed niacin (not NE).

[f] As dietary folate equivalents (DFE). 1 DFE = 1 µg food folate = 0.6 µg of folic acid from fortified food or as a supplement consumed with food = 0.5 µg of a supplement taken on an empty stomach.

[g] Although AIs have been set for choline, there are few data to assess whether a dietary supply of choline is needed at all stages of the life cycle, and it may be that the choline requirement can be met by endogenous synthesis at some of these stages.

[h] Because 10 to 30 percent of older people may malabsorb food-bound B12, it is advisable for those older than 50 years to meet their RDA mainly by consuming foods fortified with B12 or a supplement containing B12.

[i] In view of evidence linking folate intake with neural tube defects in the fetus, it is recommended that all women capable of becoming pregnant consume 400 µg from supplements or fortified foods in addition to intake of food folate from a varied diet.

[j] It is assumed that women will continue consuming 400 µg from supplements or fortified food until their pregnancy is confirmed and they enter prenatal care, which ordinarily occurs after the end of the periconceptional period—the critical time for formation of the neural tube.

SOURCES: *Dietary Reference Intakes for Calcium, Phosphorous, Magnesium, Vitamin D, and Fluoride* (1997); *Dietary Reference Intakes for Thiamin, Riboflavin, Niacin, Vitamin B6, Folate, Vitamin B12, Pantothenic Acid, Biotin, and Choline* (1998); *Dietary Reference Intakes for Vitamin C, Vitamin E, Selenium, and Carotenoids* (2000); *Dietary Reference Intakes for Vitamin A, Vitamin K, Arsenic, Boron, Chromium, Copper, Iodine, Iron, Manganese, Molybdenum, Nickel, Silicon, Vanadium, and Zinc* (2001); *Dietary Reference Intakes for Water, Potassium, Sodium, Chloride, and Sulfate* (2005); and *Dietary Reference Intakes for Calcium and Vitamin D* (2011). These reports may be accessed via www.nap.edu.

Dietary Reference Intakes (DRIs): Recommended Dietary Allowances and Adequate Intakes, Elements
Food and Nutrition Board, Institute of Medicine, National Academies

Life Stage Group	Calcium (mg/d)	Chromium (µg/d)	Copper (µg/d)	Fluoride (mg/d)	Iodine (µg/d)	Iron (mg/d)	Magnesium (mg/d)	Manganese (mg/d)	Molybdenum (µg/d)	Phosphorus (mg/d)	Selenium (µg/d)	Zinc (mg/d)	Potassium (g/d)	Sodium (g/d)	Chloride (g/d)
Infants															
0 to 6 mo	200*	0.2*	200*	0.01*	110*	0.27*	30*	0.003*	2*	100*	15*	2*	0.4*	0.12*	0.18*
6 to 12 mo	260*	5.5*	220*	0.5*	130*	11	75*	0.6*	3*	275*	20*	3	0.7*	0.37*	0.57*
Children															
1–3 y	700	11*	340	0.7*	90	7	80	1.2*	17	460	20	3	3.0*	1.0*	1.5*
4–8 y	1,000	15*	440	1*	90	10	130	1.5*	22	500	30	5	3.8*	1.2*	1.9*
Males															
9–13 y	1,300	25*	700	2*	120	8	240	1.9*	34	1,250	40	8	4.5*	1.5*	2.3*
14–18 y	1,300	35*	890	3*	150	11	410	2.2*	43	1,250	55	11	4.7*	1.5*	2.3*
19–30 y	1,000	35*	900	4*	150	8	400	2.3*	45	700	55	11	4.7*	1.5*	2.3*
31–50 y	1,000	35*	900	4*	150	8	420	2.3*	45	700	55	11	4.7*	1.5*	2.3*
51–70 y	1,000	30*	900	4*	150	8	420	2.3*	45	700	55	11	4.7*	1.3*	2.0*
>70 y	1,200	30*	900	4*	150	8	420	2.3*	45	700	55	11	4.7*	1.2*	1.8*
Females															
9–13 y	1,300	21*	700	2*	120	8	240	1.6*	34	1,250	40	8	4.5*	1.5*	2.3*
14–18 y	1,300	24*	890	3*	150	15	360	1.6*	43	1,250	55	9	4.7*	1.5*	2.3*
19–30 y	1,000	25*	900	3*	150	18	310	1.8*	45	700	55	8	4.7*	1.5*	2.3*
31–50 y	1,000	25*	900	3*	150	18	320	1.8*	45	700	55	8	4.7*	1.5*	2.3*
51–70 y	1,200	20*	900	3*	150	8	320	1.8*	45	700	55	8	4.7*	1.3*	2.0*
>70 y	1,200	20*	900	3*	150	8	320	1.8*	45	700	55	8	4.7*	1.2*	1.8*
Pregnancy															
14–18 y	1,300	29*	1,000	3*	220	27	400	2.0*	50	1,250	60	12	4.7*	1.5*	2.3*
19–30 y	1,000	30*	1,000	3*	220	27	350	2.0*	50	700	60	11	4.7*	1.5*	2.3*
31–50 y	1,000	30*	1,000	3*	220	27	360	2.0*	50	700	60	11	4.7*	1.5*	2.3*
Lactation															
14–18 y	1,300	44*	1,300	3*	290	10	360	2.6*	50	1,250	70	13	5.1*	1.5*	2.3*
19–30 y	1,000	45*	1,300	3*	290	9	310	2.6*	50	700	70	12	5.1*	1.5*	2.3*
31–50 y	1,000	45*	1,300	3*	290	9	320	2.6*	50	700	70	12	5.1*	1.5*	2.3*

NOTE: This table (taken from the DRI reports, see www.nap.edu) presents Recommended Dietary Allowances (RDAs) in **bold type** and Adequate Intakes (AIs) in ordinary type followed by an asterisk (*). An RDA is the average daily dietary intake level; sufficient to meet the nutrient requirements of nearly all (97-98 percent) healthy individuals in a group. It is calculated from an Estimated Average Requirement (EAR). If sufficient scientific evidence is not available to establish an EAR, and thus calculate an RDA, an AI is usually developed. For healthy breastfed infants, an AI is the mean intake. The AI for other life stage and gender groups is believed to cover the needs of all healthy individuals in the groups, but lack of data or uncertainty in the data prevent being able to specify with confidence the percentage of individuals covered by this intake.

SOURCES: *Dietary Reference Intakes for Calcium, Phosphorous, Magnesium, Vitamin D, and Fluoride* (1997); *Dietary Reference Intakes for Thiamin, Riboflavin, Niacin, Vitamin B₆, Folate, Vitamin B₁₂, Pantothenic Acid, Biotin, and Choline* (1998); *Dietary Reference Intakes for Vitamin C, Vitamin E, Selenium, and Carotenoids* (2000); and *Dietary Reference Intakes for Vitamin A, Vitamin K, Arsenic, Boron, Chromium, Copper, Iodine, Iron, Manganese, Molybdenum, Nickel, Silicon, Vanadium, and Zinc* (2001); *Dietary Reference Intakes for Water, Potassium, Sodium, Chloride, and Sulfate* (2005); and *Dietary Reference Intakes for Calcium and Vitamin D* (2011). These reports may be accessed via www.nap.edu.

references

Chapter 1

Alemango, S., Niles, S., Shafer-King, P., & Miller, W. (2008). Promoting health and preventing injury among preschool children: The role of parenting stress. *Early Childhood Research & Practice, 10*(2).

Allard, Patricia, & Greene, Judith. (2011). *Children on the outside: Voicing the pain and human costs of parental incarceration. Justice strategies.* Retrieved March 2012, from http://www.justicestrategies.org/sites/default/files/publications/JS-COIP-1-13-11.pdf

American Academy of Pediatrics, American Public Health Association, National Resource Center for Health and Safety in Child Care and Early Education. (2011). *Caring for our children: National health and safety performance standards; Guidelines for early care and education programs* (3rd ed.). Elk Grove Village, IL: American Academy of Pediatrics; Washington, DC: American Public Health Association. Also available at http://nrckids.org

American Academy of Pediatrics. (2007, April). *AAP: Healthy Child Care America: Health and Safety E-news for caregivers and teachers.* Retrieved June 2012, from http://www.healthychildcare.org/ENewsApr07.html#habits

American Academy of Pediatrics. *Healthy Child Care America.* Retrieved June 8, 2012, from http://www.healthychildcare.org/about.html#1

American Association for Health Education. (2007). Health Education Standards.

American Psychological Association. (2012). *Changing diet and exercise for kids.* Retrieved March 13, 2012, from http://www.apa.org/topics/children/healthy-eating.aspx#

America's Children: Key National Indicators of Well-Being. 2009. *Emotional and behavioral difficulties.* For further information, visit http://childstats.gov Retrieved June 2012, from http://www.childstats.gov/pdf/ac2009/ac_09body2.pdf

Bloom B., Cohen R. A., & Freeman G. (2011). Summary health statistics for U.S. children: National Health Interview Survey, 2010. National Center for Health Statistics. *Vital Health Stat, 10*(250).

Bronfenbrenner, Urie. 1979. *The ecology of human development: Experiments by nature and design.* Cambridge, MA: Harvard University Press. ISBN 0-674-22457-4

Center on the Developing Child at Harvard University. (2007). *A science-based framework for early childhood policy: Using evidence to improve outcomes in learning, behavior, and health for vulnerable children.* http://www.developingchild.harvard.edu

Centers for Disease Control. (2012). Childhood Obesity Facts. Retrieved May 22, 2012, from http://www.cdc.gov/obesity/data/childhood.html

Council on Communications and Media. (2011). Children, adolescents, obesity, and the media. *Pediatrics, 128*(1), 201–208.

Dolinoy, D. C., Das, R., Weidman, J. R., & Jirtle, R. L. (2007). Metastable epialleles, imprinting, and the fetal origins of adult diseases. *Pediatric Research, 61*(5 Pt 2), 30R–37R.

Douglas-Hall, A., & Chau, M. (2008). *Basic facts about low-income children birth to age 6.* New York: National Center for Children in Poverty, Mailman School of Public Health, Columbia University. Retrieved online December 2008, at http://www.nccp.org/publications/pub_847.html

Faulk, C., & Dolinoy, D. C. (2011). Timing is everything: The when and how of environmentally induced changes in the epigenome of animals. *Epigenetics, 6*(7), 791–797.

Federal Interagency Forum on Child and Family Statistics. *America's children: Key national indicators of wellbeing, 2012; Demographic background.* Retrieved December 2012, from http://www.childstats.gov/americaschildren/demo.asp

Federal Interagency Forum on Child and Family Statistics, *America's children: Key national indicators of wellbeing, 2011; Immunizations.* Retrieved December 2012, from www.childstats.gov/pubs/pubs.asp?PlacementID=2&SlpgID=22

Food and Nutrition Service of the USDA. (2011). *DRI tables: Dietary guidance.* Retrieved March 13, 2012, from http://fnic.nal.usda.gov/nal_display/index.php?info_center=4&tax_level=3&tax_subject=256&topic_id=1342&level3_id=5140

Glaze, L. E., & Maruschak, L. M. (2010). Parents in Prison and Their Minor Children. *Bureau of Justice Report.* Retrieved March 2012, from http://www.bjs.gov/content/pub/pdf/pptmc.pdf

Hawley, T. (2000). *Starting smart: How early experiences influence brain development.* Ounce of Prevention Fund and ZERO TO THREE. Retrieved June 2012, from http://www.zerotothree.org/site/DocServer/startingsmart.pdf?docID=2422

Howes, C., Burchinal, M., Pianta, R., Bryant, D., Early, D., Clifford, R., & Barbarin, O. (2008). Ready to learn? Children's pre-academic achievement in pre-kindergarten programs. *Early Childhood Research Quarterly, 23*(3), 27–50.

Let's Move. (2012). Retrieved June 2012, from http://www.letsmove.gov/

Liu, J., Bennett, K. J., Harun, N., & Probst, J. C. (2008). Urban-rural differences in overweight status and physical inactivity among US children aged 10–17 years. *The Journal of Rural Health: Official Journal of the American Rural Health Association and the National Rural Health Care Association, 24*(4), 407–415.

Massachusetts Institute of Technology. (2006). Researchers provide first evidence for learning mechanism in brain. *ScienceDaily.* Retrieved March 22, 2009, from http://www.sciencedaily.com/releases/2006/08/060824222608.htm

National Association for the Education of Young Children. (1999). *Working together to keep children healthy.* Retrieved from http://www.naeyc.org/ece/1999/14.asp

National Association for the Education of Young Children. (2009a). *Developmentally appropriate practices.* Retrieved from http://www.naeyc.org/about/positions/pdf/PSDAP.pdf

National Association for the Education of Young Children. (2009b). *NAEYC Radio presents . . . Why playful learning is more effective.* Retrieved June 2012, from http://www.naeyc.org/newsroom/pressreleases/20090609

National Association for the Education of Young Children. (2009c). *Where we stand: On responding to linguistic and cultural diversity.* Retrieved June 2012, from http://www.naeyc.org/files/naeyc/file/positions/diversity.pdf

National Association for the Education of Young Children. (2011). *Code of ethical conduct and statement of commitment.* Retrieved online April 2012, from http://www.naeyc.org/positionstatements/ethical_conduct

National Association for the Education of Young Children & National Association of Early Childhood Specialists in State Departments of Education. (2002). *Early learning standards: Creating the conditions for success.* Retrieved March 2009, from http://naeyc.org/about/positions/pdf/position_statement.pdf

National Governors Association Center for Best Practices & Council of Chief State School Officers. (2010). *Common Core State Standards.* National Governors Association Center for Best Practices, Council of Chief State School Officers, Washington DC.

National Institute of Child Health and Human Development, & National Institutes of Health (NIH). (2012). *National Children's Study.* Retrieved June 2012, from http://www.nationalchildrensstudy.gov

National Institute of Mental Health. (2011). *Child Mental Health Awareness: Brain Development*

During Childhood and Adolescence Fact Sheet. Retrieved December 2012, from www.nimh.nih .gov/health/publications/brain-development-during-childhood-and-adolescence/index.shtml

National Scientific Council on the Developing Child. (2006). *Early exposure to toxic substances damages brain architecture: Working Paper No. 4.* Retrieved June 2012, from www.developingchild .harvard.edu

National Scientific Council on the Developing Child. (2007). *The timing and quality of early experiences combine to shape brain architecture: Working Paper No. 5.* Retrieved from www .developingchild.harvard.edu

National Scientific Council on the Developing Child. (2010). *Early experiences can alter gene expression and affect long-term development: Working Paper No. 10.* Retrieved June 2012, from www.developingchild.harvard.edu

Nord, M., Coleman-Jensen, A., Andrews, M., & Carlson, S. (2010). *Household food security in the United States, 2009* (Economic Research Report 108). Washington, DC: U.S. Department of Agriculture, Economic Research Service (pp. 68). Retrieved from http://www.ers.usda .gov/Publications/ERR108

Nutrition and the epigenome. 2012. Retrieved March 2, 2012, from http://learn.genetics.utah .edu/content/epigenetics/nutrition/

Ogden, C., & Carroll, M. (2010). *Prevalence of obesity among children and adolescents: United States, trends 1963–1965 through 2007–2008.* NCHS Health E-Stat. Retrieved June 2012, from http://www.cdc.gov/nchs/data/hestat/obesity_ child_07_08/obesity_child_07_08.htm#table1

Ogden, C. L., Carroll, M. D., & Flegal, K. M. (2008). High body mass index for age among US children and adolescents, 2003–2006. *Journal of the American Medical Association, 299*(20), 2401.

Ogden C. L., Carroll, M. D., Kit, B. K., & Flegal, K. M. (2012). *Prevalence of obesity in the United States, 2009–2010. NCHS data brief, no 82.* Hyattsville, MD: National Center for Health Statistics.

Partnership for 21st Century Skills. (2011). Retrieved online June 2012 from http://www.p21 .org/index.php

Piaget, J. (1929). *The child's conception of the world.* New York: Harcourt, Brace Jovanovich.

Simopoulos, A. P., & Milner, J. (2010). Personalized nutrition: Translating nutrigenetic/nutrigenomic research into dietary guidelines. *World Review of Nutrition and Dietetics Volume 101,* Switzerland: S. Karger AG. Retrieved March 13, 2012, from http://content.karger.com/ProdukteDB/ produkte.asp?Aktion=showproducts&search What=books&ProduktNr=253821

Sorte, J., & Daeschel, I. (2006). Health in Action: A program approach to fighting obesity in young children. *Young Children, 61*(3), 40–48.

Strain, P. S., & Dunlap, G. D. (2012) *Being an evidence-based practitioner.* Center for Evidence-based Practices: Young Children with Challenging Behavior. Recommended Practices. Retrieved June 2012 from http://challengingbehavior.org/ do/resources/documents/rph_practitioner.pdf

The Source for Learning. (2012). *Correlation of the Head Start framework to the Common Core State Standards in kindergarten.* Retrieved March 2012, from http://www.sourceforlearning.org/ projects.cfm?newsid=68

U.S. Department of Agriculture. (2011). *USDA's MyPlate—home page.* Retrieved June 2012, from http://www.choosemyplate.gov/

U.S. Department of Agriculture Food & Nutrition Service. (2012). *Child Nutrition Reauthorization: The Healthy Hunger Free Kids Act of 2010.* (PL111-296). Retrieved June 2012, from http:// www.fns.usda.gov/cnd/governance/legislation/ cnr_2010.htm

U.S. Department of Education. (2001). No Child Left Behind Act of 2001 (Public Law 107-110). Retrieved June 2012 from http://www2.ed.gov/ policy/elsec/leg/esea02/beginning.html#sec1

U.S. Department of Education. (2007). *History: Twenty-five years of progress in educating children with disabilities through IDEA.* Retrieved July 2009, from http://www.ed.gov/policy/ speced/leg/idea/history.html

U.S. Department of Education, Building the Legacy: IDEA 2004; Individuals with Disabilities Education Act. http://idea.ed.gov/

U.S. Department of Education, Office of Planning, Evaluation and Policy Development. (2010). *ESEA Blueprint for Reform,* Washington, DC. Retrieved March 2012, from http://www2 .ed.gov/policy/elsec/leg/blueprint/

U.S. Department of Education, National Center for Education Statistics (2011) *Digest of Education Statistics, 2010* (NCES 2011-015), Chapter 2.

U.S. Department of Health & Human Services. (2003). *A national call to action to promote oral health.* Rockville, MD: U.S. Department of Health and Human Services, Public Health Service, Centers for Disease Control and Prevention, National Institutes of Health, National Institute of Dental and Craniofacial Research. NIH Publication No. 03-5303, May 2003. Retrieved June 2012, from http://www.nidcr.nih .gov/datastatistics/surgeongeneral/ nationalcalltoaction/nationalcalltoaction.htm

U.S. Department of Health & Human Services. (2003). *National call to action to promote oral health.* Rockville, MD: U.S. Department of Health and Human Services, National Institutes of Health, National Institute of Dental and Craniofacial Research. NIH Publication 03-5303. Retrieved March 2009, from http://www.cdha .org/downloads/NationalCallToAction.pdf

U.S. Department of Health & Human Services. (2012). *Healthy people 2020.* Retrieved June 2012, from http://www.healthypeople.gov/2020/ about/default.aspx

U.S. Department of Health & Human Services, & U.S. Department of Agriculture. (2011). *Dietary guidelines for Americans, 2010.* Retrieved June 2012, from http://health.gov/dietaryguidelines/ 2010.asp

Vygotsky, L. S. (1962). *Thought and language.* Cambridge, MA: MIT Press.

Wang, J., Wu, Z., Li, D., Li, N., Dindot, S. V., Satterfield, M. C., et al. (2012). Nutrition, epigenetics, and metabolic syndrome. *Antioxidants and Redox Signaling,* March 9, 2012.

World Health Organization. (2010). *Strengthening our response.* Fact Sheet No. 220. Retrieved March 2012, from http://www.who.int/ mediacentre/factsheets/fs220/en/

World Health Organization. (2011). Mental health: A state of well-being. *Fact file: 10 facts on mental health.* Retrieved June 2012, from http://www .who.int/features/factfiles/mental_health/en/ index.html

Chapter 2

Adams, I. (2011). Family mealtimes: A wealth of benefits. *Cooperative Extension Service, University of Kentucky College of Agriculture, FCS3-552,* March 6, 2012.

American Dietetic Association. (2011). Position of the American Dietetic Association: Benchmarks for nutrition in child care. *111*(4), 607–615.

American Dietetic Association. (2012). *Pediatric nutrition care manual.* Retrieved February 22, 2012, from http://peds.nutritioncaremanual .org

American Dietetic Association Foundation. (2011). *Family nutrition and physical activity report from the Academy of Nutrition and Dietetics.* Retrieved March 19, 2012, from http://www .eatright.org/foundation/fnpa/

Baker, R. D., Greer, F. R., & The Committee on Nutrition. (2010). Diagnosis and prevention of iron deficiency and iron-deficiency anemia in infants and young children (0–3 years of age). *Pediatrics, 126*(5), 1040–1050.

Beard, J. L. (2008). Why iron deficiency is important in infant development. *Journal of Nutrition, 138*(12), 2534–2536.

Bernal, A. J., & Jirtle, R. L. (2010). Epigenomic disruption: The effects of early developmental exposures. *Birth Defects Research. Part A, Clinical and Molecular Teratology, 88*(10), 938–944.

Boone-Heinonen, J., Gordon-Larsen, P., Kiefe, C. I., Shikany, J. M., Lewis, C. E., & Popkin, B. M. (2011). Fast food restaurants and food stores: Longitudinal associations with diet in young to middle-aged adults: The CARDIA study. *Archives of Internal Medicine, 171*(13), 1162–1170.

Brotanek, J. M., Gosz, J., Weitzman, M., & Flores, G. (2008). Secular trends in the prevalence of iron deficiency among U.S. toddlers, 1976–2002. *Archives of Pediatric Adolescent Medicine, 162*(4), 374–381.

Centers for Disease Control and Prevention. (2010). *Growth charts.* Retrieved March 29, 2012, from http://www.cdc.gov/growthcharts/

Cepeda-Lopez, A. C., Osendarp, S. J., Melse-Boonstra, A., Aeberli, I., Gonzalez-Salazar, F., Feskens, E., et al. (2010). Does obesity increase risk for iron deficiency anemia. *American Journal of Clinical Nutrition, 2012* (March 22).

Chenhall, C. (2010). *Improving cooking and food preparation skills: A synthesis of the evidence to inform program and policy development.* Government of Canada.

Child Trends. (2012). *Food insecurity: child trends databank*. Retrieved March 6, 2012, from http://www.childtrendsdatabank.org/?q=node/365

Coleman, K. J., Geller, K. S., Rosenkranz, R. R., & Dzewaltowski, D. A. (2008). Physical activity and healthy eating in the after-school environment. *The Journal of School Health, 78*(12), 633–640.

Coleman-Jensen, A., Nord, M., Andrews, M., Carlson, S., & U.S. Department of Agriculture. (2011). Household food security in the United States in 2010. *USDA–Economic Research Service*, (Economic Research Report No. (ERR-125)).

Committee to Review Dietary Reference Intakes for Vitamin D Food and Nutrition Board, & Institute of Medicine of the National Academies. (2011). In C. Taylor, A. L. Yaktine, & H. B. Del Valle (Eds.), *Dietary reference intakes for calcium and vitamin D*. Washington, DC: National Academies Press.

Faulk, C., & Dolinoy, D. C. (2011). Timing is everything: The when and how of environmentally induced changes in the epigenome of animals. *Epigenetics, 6*(7), 791–797.

Food Research and Action Center. (2011). *FRAC brief: Food insecurity and obesity understanding the connections*. Retrieved April 7, 2012, from http://org2.democracyinaction.org/o/5118/p/salsa/web/common/public/content?content_item_KEY=5634#1

Food Research and Action Center. (2012). *Food hardship in America 2011*. Retrieved March 21, 2012, from http://frac.org/pdf/food_hardship_2011_report.pdf

Fretham, S. J., Carlson, E. S., & Georgieff, M. K. (2011). The role of iron in learning and memory. *Advances in Nutrition (Bethesda, Md.), 2*(2), 112–121.

Georgia State University. (2004). *New education for New Americans project: Multicultural nutrition and diabetic handouts*. Retrieved April 15, 2012, from http://monarch.gsu.edu/multiculturalhealth

Georgieff, M. K. (2011). Long-term brain and behavioral consequences of early iron deficiency. *Nutrition Reviews, 69*, S43–S48.

Health Canada. (2011). *Canada's food guide*. Retrieved April 14, 2012, from http://www.hc-sc.gc.ca/fn-an/food-guide-aliment/order-commander/index-eng.php

Holick, M. F. (2010). The vitamin D deficiency pandemic: A forgotten hormone important for health. *Public Health Reviews, 32*, 267.

Institute of Medicine. (2009). *Use of dietary reference intakes in nutrition labeling-Institute of Medicine* Retrieved April 9, 2012, from http://www.iom.edu/Activities/Nutrition/DRINutritionLabeling.aspx

Jarratt, J., & Mahaffie, J. B. (2007). The profession of dietetics at a critical juncture: A report on the 2006 environmental scan for the American Dietetic Association. *Journal of the American Dietetic Association, 107*(7), S39.

Johns Hopkins Children's Center. (2012a). *Failure to thrive*. Retrieved March 22, 2012, from http://www.hopkinschildrens.org/tpl_rlinks_nav1up.aspx?id=5112

Johns Hopkins Children's Center. (2012b). *Failure to thrive*. Retrieved March 22, 2012, from http://www.hopkinsmedicine.org/healthlibrary/conditions/adult/pediatrics/failure_to_thrive_90,P02297/

Kenney, E. L., Henderson, K. E., Humphries, D., & Schwartz, M. B. (2011). Practice-based research to engage teachers and improve nutrition in the preschool setting. *Childhood Obesity, 7*(6), 475–479.

Kraak, V. I., Story, M., & Wartella, E. A. (2012). Government and school progress to promote a healthful diet to American children and adolescents: A comprehensive review of the available evidence. *American Journal of Preventive Medicine, 42*(3), 250–262.

Krukowski, R. A., Eddings, K., & West, D. S. (2011). The children's menu assessment: Development, evaluation, and relevance of a tool for evaluating children's menus. *Journal of the American Dietetic Association, 111*(6), 884–888. doi:10.1016/j.jada.2011.03.018

Lee, V., Srikantharajah, J., & Mikkelsen, L. (2010). *Fostering physical activity for children and youth: Opportunities for a lifetime of health*. Retrieved April 5, 2012, from http://www.convergencepartnership.org/atf/cf/{245A9B44-6DED-4ABD-A392-AE583809E350}/Convergence_Physical Activity_final.pdf

Looker, A. C., Johnson, C. L., Lacher, D. A., Pfeiffer, C. M., Schleicher, R. L., & Sempos, C. T. (2011). *Vitamin D status: United States, 2001–2006. NCBI* (NCHS Data Brief. 2011 No. 59). Hyattsville, MD 20782, USA: Centers for Disease Control and Prevention's National Center for Health Statistics, Division of Health and Nutrition Examination Surveys.

McDonald's Corporation. (2012). *McDonald's momentum delivers another year of strong results for 2011 press release*. Retrieved March 18, 2012, from http://phx.corporate-ir.net/phoenix.zhtml?c=97876&p=irol-newsArticle&ID=1651870&highlight=

Meinke, M., & University of Nebraska-Lincoln Extension in Lancaster County. (2009). *Think what you drink*. Retrieved January 25, 2009, from http://lancaster.unl.edu/NEP/thinkdrink.shtml

Murphy, D. (2012). The more we eat together: State data on frequency of family meals. *Child Trends Fact Sheet, Publication # 2012–03*(January), March 6, 2012.

National Association for Sport and Physical Education. (2009). *Active start: A statement of physical activity guidelines for children from birth to age 5*. Retrieved January 2, 2011, from http://www.aahperd.org/naspe/standards/nationalGuidelines/ActiveStart.cfm

National Institutes of Health, Office of Dietary Supplements. (2011). *Vitamin D—health professional fact sheet*. Retrieved March 27, 2012, from http://ods.od.nih.gov/factsheets/VitaminD-HealthProfessional/

Nevin-Folino, N. L. (2003; updated 2008). *Pediatric manual of clinical dietetics* (2nd ed.).

United States of America: American Dietetic Association.

Nutrition and the epigenome. (2012). Retrieved March 2, 2012, from http://learn.genetics.utah.edu/content/epigenetics/nutrition/

O'Dea J. A., & Eriksen M. P. (Eds.). (2010). *Childhood obesity prevention: International research, controversies and interventions*. New York: Oxford University Press.

Odgen, C., Carroll, M., & Centers for Disease Control and Prevention. (2010). *Prevalence of obesity among children and adolescents: United States, trends 1963–1965 through 2007–2008*. Retrieved March 12, 2012, from http://www.cdc.gov/nchs/data/hestat/obesity_child_07_08/obesity_child_07_08.htm#figure1

Ogden, C. L., Carroll, M. D., Kit, B. K., & Flegal, K. M. (2012). Prevalence of obesity and trends in body mass index among U.S. children and adolescents, 1999–2010. *The Journal of the American Medical Association, 307*(5), 483–490.

Olshansky, S. J., Passaro, D. J., Hershow, R. C., Laydon, J., Brody, J., Carnes, B. J., et al. (2005). Peering into the future of American longevity. *Discovery Medicine, 5*(26), 130–134.

Otten, J. J., Pitzi-Hellwig, J., & Meyers, L. D. (Ed.). (2006). *Dietary reference intakes, the essential guide to nutrient requirements*. Washington, DC: National Academies Press.

Queen Samour, P., & King, K. (2012). *Pediatric nutrition* (4th ed.). Sudbury, MA: Jones & Bartlett Learning, LLC.

Quets, G., & Spota, A. (2011). *NYC Hunger experience: Sacrifice and support*. New York: Food Bank for New York City.

Reedy, J., Krebs-Smith, S. M., & Bosire, C. (2010). Evaluating the food environment: Application of the healthy eating index-2005. *American Journal of Preventive Medicine, 38*(5), 465–471.

Schneeman, B., Trumbo, P., Ellwood, K., & Satchell, F. (2006). The regulatory process to revise nutrient labeling relative to the dietary reference intakes. *The American Journal of Clinical Nutrition, 83*(5), 1228S–1230S.

Schwimmer, J. B., Burwinkle, T. M., & Varni, J. W. (2003). Health-related quality of life of severely obese children and adolescents. *The Journal of the American Medical Association, 289*(14), 1813–1819.

Shine Dyer, J., & Rosenfeld, C. R. (2011). Metabolic imprinting by prenatal and postnatal overnutrition. *Seminars in Reproductive Medicine, 29*, 266–277.

Sloan, E. (2012). What, when, and where America eats. *Food Technology, 66*(1), 21–32.

Southeastern Michigan Dietetic Association. (2004). *SEMDA web site: food pyramid*. Retrieved April 15, 2012, from http://www.semda.org/info/pyramid.asp?ID=15

Spear, B. (2006). The need for family meals. *Journal of the American Dietetic Association, 106*(2), 218–219.

Spruyt, K., & Gozal, D. (2012). A mediation model linking body weight, cognition, and sleep-disordered breathing. *American Journal of Respiratory and Critical Care Medicine, 185*(2), 199–205.

Story, M. (2009). The third school nutrition dietary assessment study: Findings and policy implications for improving the health of U.S. children. *Journal of the American Dietetic Association, 109*(2), S7.

Sweitzer, S. J., Briley, M. E., Roberts-Gray, C., Hoelscher, D. M., Harrist, R. B., Staskel, D. M., et al. (2010). Lunch is in the bag: Increasing fruits, vegetables, and whole grains in sack lunches of preschool-aged children. *Journal of the American Dietetic Association, 110*(7), 1058–1064. doi:10.1016/j.jada.2010.04.010

Sweitzer, S. J., Briley, M. E., & Robert-Grey, C. (2009). Do sack lunches provided by parents meet the nutritional needs of young children who attend child care? *Journal of the American Dietetic Association, 109*(1), 141–144.

University of Washington. (2012). *Childhood obesity FAQs.* Retrieved April 5, 2012, from http://www.washington.edu/earlychildhood/faqs/childhood-obesity-faqs

U.S. Department of Agriculture. (2011). *ChooseMyPlate.gov choking hazards.* Retrieved October 30, 2011, from http://www.choosemyplate.gov/preschoolers/FoodSafety/chokinghazards.html

U.S. Department of Agriculture. (2012). *ChooseMyPlate.gov.* Retrieved April 14, 2012, from http://www.choosemyplate.gov/

U.S. Department of Agriculture, Economic Research Service. (2011). *ERS/USDA briefing room child nutrition programs.* Retrieved March 28, 2012, from http://www.ers.usda.gov/Briefing/ChildNutrition/

U.S. Department of Agriculture, Food and Nutrition Service. (2012a). *FNS supplemental nutrition assistance program (SNAP).* Retrieved March 23, 2012, from http://www.fns.usda.gov/snap/

U.S. Department of Agriculture, Food and Nutrition Service. (2012b). *Links to state agency approved food lists.* Retrieved March 23, 2012, from http://www.fns.usda.gov/wic/Contacts/stateagencyfoodlists.htm

U.S. Department of Agriculture, Food and Nutrition Service. (2012c). Nutrition standards in the national school lunch and breakfast programs. *Federal Register, 77*(17).

U.S. Department of Health and Human Services. (2012). *Nutrition and weight status—Healthy People 2020.* Retrieved March 22, 2012, from http://www.healthypeople.gov/2020/topicsobjectives2020/objectiveslist.aspx?topicId=29

U.S. Department of Health and Human Services, & U.S. Department of Agriculture. (2011). *Dietary guidelines for Americans, 2010.* Retrieved April 10, 2012, from http://www.health.gov/dietaryguidelines/2010.asp

U.S. Department of Labor U.S. Bureau of Labor Statistics. (2011). *Women in the labor force: A data book (2011 edition).* Retrieved March 16, 2012, from http://www.bls.gov/cps/wlf-databook2011.htm

U.S. Food and Drug Administration (2011a). Consumer updates: A glimpse at 'gluten-free' food labeling. Retrieved April 9, 2012, from http://www.fda.gov/ForConsumers/ConsumerUpdates/ucm265212.htm

U.S. Food and Drug Administration. (2011b). *Food labeling guide: Appendix G: Daily values for infants, children less than 4 years of age, and pregnant and lactating women.* Retrieved April 9, 2012, from http://www.fda.gov/Food/GuidanceComplianceRegulatoryInformation/GuidanceDocuments/FoodLabelingNutrition/FoodLabelingGuide/ucm064930.htm

U.S. Food and Drug Administration. (2011c). *Food labeling guide: Claims.* Retrieved April 9, 2012, from http://www.fda.gov/Food/GuidanceComplianceRegulatoryInformation/GuidanceDocuments/FoodLabelingNutrition/FoodLabelingGuide/ucm064908.htm#structfunct

U.S. Food and Drug Administration. (2011d). Food labeling guide: Nutrition labeling; questions L1 through L153. Retrieved April 9, 2012, from http://www.fda.gov/Food/GuidanceComplianceRegulatoryInformation/GuidanceDocuments/FoodLabelingNutrition/FoodLabelingGuide/ucm064904.htm#kidlabel

U.S. Food and Drug Administration. (2011e). Labeling & nutrition: New menu and vending machines labeling requirements. Retrieved March 17, 2012, from http://www.fda.gov/Food/LabelingNutrition/ucm217762.htm

U.S. Food and Drug Administration. (2012). *How to understand and use the nutrition facts label.* Retrieved April 8, 2012, from http://www.fda.gov/Food/ResourcesForYou/Consumers/NFLPM/ucm274593.htm

U.S. National Library of Medicine, National Institutes of Health. (2010). *Iron deficiency anemia—children: MedlinePlus medical encyclopedia.* Retrieved March 21, 2012, from http://www.nlm.nih.gov/medlineplus/ency/article/007134.htm

U.S. National Library of Medicine, National Institutes of Health. (2012). *Slipped capital femoral epiphysis: MedlinePlus medical encyclopedia.* Retrieved April 4, 2012, from http://www.nlm.nih.gov/medlineplus/ency/article/000972.htm

Wagner, C. L., Greer, F. R., & the Section on Breastfeeding and Committee on Nutrition. (November 2008). Prevention of rickets and vitamin D deficiency in infants, children, and adolescents. *Pediatrics, 122*(5), 1142–1152.

Wood, Y., & Child and Nutrition Division, Food and Nutrition Service. (2008). *Strategies for creating a healthier school environment.* Retrieved April 19, 2012, from http://www.extension.iastate.edu/NR/rdonlyres/1EF27CB9-3E0C-4875-A232-47BFDA05E296/76661/ICNsessionSchoolHealthEnvironment1.pdf

Ziegler, E. E. (2011). Consumption of cow's milk as a cause of iron deficiency in infants and toddlers. *Nutrition Reviews, 69* (Supplement), S37–S42.

Chapter 3

Abrams, S. A. (2011). Dietary guidelines for calcium and vitamin D: A new era. *Pediatrics, 127*(3), 566–568.

American Academy of Nutrition and Dietetics. (2011). *Pediatric Nutrition Care Manual.* Retrieved May 1, 2012, from http://peds.nutritioncaremanual.org

American Academy of Nutrition and Dietetics. (2012a). *Nutrition Care Manual.* Retrieved May 6, 2012, from http://www.nutritioncaremanual.org

American Academy of Nutrition and Dietetics. (2012b). Use of nutritive and nonnutritive sweeteners. *Journal of the Academy of Nutrition and Dietetics, 112*(5), 739–758.

American Academy of Pediatrics, American Public Health Association, National Resource Center for Health and Safety in Child Care and Early Education. (2011). *Caring for Our Children Third Edition, National Resource Center for Health and Safety in Child Care and Early Education, American Academy of Pediatrics,* Elk Grove Village, IL, 3rd edition.

American Academy of Pediatrics, Hassink, S. (2012). *Low fat diets for babies.* Retrieved May 19, 2012, from http://www.healthychildren.org/English/ages-stages/baby/feeding-nutrition/Pages/Low-Fat-Diets-For-Babies.aspx

American Dental Association. (2010). *Baby bottle tooth decay—American Dental Association.* Retrieved April 22, 2012, from http://www.ada.org/3034.aspx

American Dietetic Association. (2008). Position of the American Dietetic Association: Nutrition guidance for healthy children ages 2 to 11 years. *Journal of the American Dietetic Association, 108*(6), 1038–1047.

American Heart Association. (2012a). *About cholesterol.* Retrieved May 10, 2012, from http://www.heart.org/HEARTORG/Conditions/Cholesterol/AboutCholesterol/About-Cholesterol_UCM_001220_Article.jsp

American Heart Association. (2012b). *Dietary recommendations for healthy children.* Retrieved May 19, 2012, from http://www.heart.org/HEARTORG/GettingHealthy/NutritionCenter/Dietary-Recommendations-for-Healthy-Children_UCM_303886_Article.jsp

Anderson, J., & Young, L. (2012). *Water-soluble vitamins.* Retrieved May 22, 2012, from http://www.ext.colostate.edu/pubs/foodnut/09312.html

Ball, J. W., Bindler, R., & Cowen, K. J. (2010). *Child health nursing: Partnering with children and families* (2nd ed.). Upper Saddle River, NJ: Pearson Education, Inc.

Benton, D. (2008). Sucrose and behavioral problems. *Critical Reviews in Food Science and Nutrition, 48*(5), 385–401.

Berg, J. M., Tymoczko, J. L., & Stryer, L. (2008). *Biochemistry* (6th ed.). New York: W. H. Freeman and Company.

Birch, E. E., Carlson, S. E., Hoffman, D. R., Fitzgerald-Gustafson, K. M., Fu, V. L., Drover, J. R., et al. (2010). The DIAMOND (DHA intake and measurement of neural development) study: A double-masked, randomized controlled clinical trial of the maturation of infant visual acuity as a function of the dietary level of docosahexaenoic acid. *American Journal of Clinical Nutrition, 91*(4), 848–859.

California Department of Education. (2011). *Nutrition education resource guide–healthy eating & nutrition education*. Retrieved May 26, 2012, from http://www.cde.ca.gov/ls/nu/he/nerg.asp

Campanozzi, A., Boccia, G., Pensabene, L., Panetta, F., Marseglia, A., Strisciuglio, P., et al. (2009). Prevalence and natural history of gastroesophageal reflux: Pediatric prospective survey. *Pediatrics, 123*(3), 779–783.

Centers for Disease Control and Prevention. (2011). *Q & A's—fact sheets—community water fluoridation—oral health*. Retrieved April 22, 2012, from http://www.cdc.gov/fluoridation/fact_sheets/cwf_qa.htm#3

Centers for Disease Control and Prevention Division of Oral Health. (2011). *Children's oral health—topics—oral health*. Retrieved April 22, 2012, from http://www.cdc.gov/oralhealth/topics/child.htm

Davis, N. (2012). Raising HDL not a sure route to countering heart disease. *Broad Institute of MIT and Harvard*. Retrieved May 19, 2012, from http://www.broadinstitute.org/news/4164

Dee, D. L., Sharma, A. J., Cogswell, M. E., Grummer-Strawn, L. M., Fein, S. B., & Scanlon, K. S. (2008). Sources of supplemental iron among breastfed infants during the first year of life. *Pediatrics, 122*(Supplement 2), 98–104.

Drake, V. J. (2011). *Linus Pauling Institute at Oregon State University: Multivitamin/mineral supplements*. Retrieved May 20, 2012, from http://lpi.oregonstate.edu/infocenter/multivitamin-mineral.html

Goodman, B. E. (2010). Insights into digestion and absorption of major nutrients in humans. *Advances in Physiology Education, 34*(2), 44–53.

Harvard School of Public Health. (2012). *Fats and cholesterol: Out with the bad, in with the good—what should I eat?* Retrieved May 11, 2012, from http://www.hsph.harvard.edu/nutritionsource/what-should-you-eat/fats-full-story/index.html#fats-and-heart-disease

Higdon, J., & Drake, V. J. (2009). *Micronutrient information center: Phytochemicals*. Retrieved May 25, 2012, from http://lpi.oregonstate.edu/infocenter/phytochemicals.html

Higdon, J., & Drake, V. J. (2012). *An evidence-based approach to vitamins and minerals* (2nd ed.). New York: Thieme Publishing Group.

Hirsch, G., Edelstein, B., Frosh, M., & Anselmo, T. (2012). A simulation model for designing effective interventions in early childhood caries. *Preventing Chronic Disease*. doi: 9:110219

Holick, M. F., Binkley, N. C., Bischoff-Ferrari, H. A., Gordon, C. M., Hanley, D. A., Heaney, R. P., et al. (2012). Guidelines for preventing and treating vitamin D deficiency and insufficiency revisited. *Journal of Clinical Endocrinology & Metabolism, 97*(4), 1153–1158.

Hurrell, R., & Egli, I. (2010). Iron bioavailability and dietary reference values. *The American Journal of Clinical Nutrition, 91*(5), 1461S–1467S.

International Food Information Council. (2009). *Food insight: Sugar alcohols fact sheet*. Retrieved May 1, 2012, from http://www.foodinsight.org/Resources/Detail.aspx?topic=Sugar_Alcohols_Fact_Sheet

Jensen, M. K., Rimm, E. B., Furtado, J. D., & Sacks, F. M. (2012). Apolipoprotein C-III as a potential modulator of the association between HDL-cholesterol and incident coronary heart disease. *Journal of the American Heart Association, 1*(2).

Jonnalagadda, S. S., Harnack, L., Hai Liu, R., McKeown, N., Seal, C., Liu, S., et al. (2011). Putting the whole grain puzzle together: Health benefits associated with whole grains—summary of American Society for Nutrition 2010 satellite symposium. *Journal of Nutrition, 141*(5), 1011S–1022S. doi: 10.3945/jn.110.132944

Kleinman, R. K. (Ed.). (2009). *Pediatric nutrition handbook* (6th ed.). United States: American Academy of Pediatrics.

Linus Pauling Institute at Oregon State University. (2012). *Essential fatty acids*. Retrieved May 8, 2012, from http://lpi.oregonstate.edu/infocenter/othernuts/omega3fa/index.html#activities

Mahan, L., Escott-Stump, S., & Raymond, J. L. (Eds.). (2012). *Krause's food and the nutrition care process* (13th ed.). St. Louis: Elsevier Saunders.

Mayo Clinic. (2011). *Cavities/tooth decay: Prevention*. Retrieved April 22, 2012, from http://www.mayoclinic.com/health/cavities/DS00896/DSECTION=prevention

Mennella, J. A., Ziegler, P., Briefel, R., & Novak, T. (2006). Feeding infants and toddlers study: The types of foods fed to Hispanic infants and toddlers. *Journal of the American Dietetic Association, 106*(Supplement 1), 96–106.

Millichap, J. G., & Yee, M. M. (2012). The diet factor in Attention-Deficit/Hyperactivity Disorder. *Pediatrics, 129*(2), 330–337.

National Institute of Diabetes and Digestive and Kidney Diseases, National Institutes of Health. (2008). *National digestive diseases information clearinghouse: Your digestive system and how it works*. Retrieved April 30, 2012, from http://digestive.niddk.nih.gov/ddiseases/pubs/yrdd/

Oregon Department of Education. (2012). *CACFP memos*. Retrieved May 25, 2012, from http://www.ode.state.or.us/search/page/?id=3282

Otten, J. J., Pitzi-Hellwig, J., & Meyers, L. D. (Ed.). (2006). *Dietary Reference Intakes, the essential guide to nutrient requirements*. Washington, DC: National Academies Press.

Queen Samour, P., & King, K. (2012). *Pediatric nutrition* (4th ed.). Sudbury, MA: Jones & Bartlett Learning, LLC.

Reed, K. A., Warburton, D., & McKay, H. A. (2007). Determining cardiovascular disease risk in elementary school children: Developing a healthy heart score. *Journal of Sports Science and Medicine, 6*(1), 142.

Reuter-Rice, K., & Bolick, B. (2012). *Pediatric acute care: A guide for interprofessional practice*. Burlington MA: Jones & Bartlett Publishers.

Ridker, P. M. (2012). Hyperlipidemia as an instigator of inflammation: Inaugurating new approaches to vascular prevention. *Journal of the American Heart Association, 1*(1), 3–5.

Roberts, M. W., & Wright, J. T. (2012). Nonnutritive, low caloric substitutes for food sugars: Clinical implications for addressing the incidence of dental caries and overweight/obesity. *International Journal of Dentistry, 2012*.

Rosen, C. J., Abrams, S. A., Aloia, J. F., Brannon, P. M., Clinton, S. K., Durazo-Arvizu, R. A., et al. (2012). IOM committee members respond to endocrine society vitamin D guideline. *The Journal of Clinical Endocrinology and Metabolism, 97*(4), 1146–1152.

Sapone, A., Bai, J., Ciacci, C., Dolinsek, J., Green, P. H., Hadjivassiliou, M., et al. (2012). Spectrum of gluten-related disorders: Consensus on new nomenclature and classification. *BMC Medicine, 10*(1), 13. doi: 10.1186/1741-7015-10-13

Sapone, A., Lammers, K. M., Casolaro, V., Cammarota, M., Giuliano, M. T., De Rosa, M., et al. (2011). Divergence of gut permeability and mucosal immune gene expression in two gluten-associated conditions: Celiac disease and gluten sensitivity. *BMC Medicine, 9*(1), 23. doi: 10.1186/1741-7015-9-23

Shills, M., Shike, M., Ross, A., Caballero, B., & Cousins, R. (Eds.). (2006). *Modern nutrition in health and disease* (10th ed.). Baltimore, MD: Lippincott Williams & Wilkins.

Simopoulos, A. P. (2011). Evolutionary aspects of diet: The omega-6/Omega-3 ratio and the brain. *Molecular Neurobiology, 44*(2), 303–315. doi: 10.1007/s12035-010-8162-0

Sizer, F., & Whitney, E. (2011). *Nutrition concepts and controversy* (12th ed.). Belmont CA: Wadsworth Cengage Learning.

Task Force on Sudden Infant Death Syndrome. (2011). SIDS and other sleep-related infant deaths: Expansion of recommendations for a safe infant sleeping environment. *Pediatrics*. doi: 10.1542/peds.2011-2285

University of Maryland School of Medicine. (2012). *Celiac disease FAQ: Celiac research*. Retrieved May 1, 2012, from http://www.celiaccenter.org/faq.asp#symptoms

U.S. Department of Agriculture. (2010). *Conclusion statement: Is intake of sugar-sweetened beverages associated with adiposity in children? (DGAC 2010)*. Retrieved May 5, 2012, from http://www.nel.gov/conclusion.cfm?conclusion_statement_id=250242

U.S. Department of Agriculture. (2012). *Choose MyPlate.gov*. Retrieved April 14, 2012, from http://www.choosemyplate.gov/

U.S. Department of Health and Human Services, & U.S. Department of Agriculture. (2011). *Dietary Guidelines for Americans 2010*. Retrieved April 10, 2012, from http://www.health.gov/dietaryguidelines/2010.asp

U.S. Geological Survey. (2012). *Water properties: The water in you*. Retrieved May 25, 2012, from http://ga.water.usgs.gov/edu/propertyyou.html

U.S. Library of Medicine, & National Institute of Health. (2012). *Fat: MedlinePlus medical encyclopedia*. Retrieved May 8, 2012, from http://www.nlm.nih.gov/medlineplus/ency/article/002468.htm

U.S. National Library of Medicine National Institutes of Health. (2011). *Amino acids: MedlinePlus medical encyclopedia*. Retrieved May 6, 2012, from http://www.nlm.nih.gov/medlineplus/ency/article/002222.htm

U.S. National Library of Medicine, National Institutes of Health. (2012). *Small intestine disorders: MedlinePlus*. Retrieved May 30, 2012, from http://www.nlm.nih.gov/medlineplus/smallintestinedisorders.html

Vandenplas, Y., Rudolph, C. D., Di Lorenzo, C., Hassall, E., Liptak, G., Mazur, L., et al. (2009). Pediatric gastroesophageal reflux clinical practice guidelines: Joint recommendations of the North American Society for Pediatric Gastroenterology, Hepatology, and Nutrition (NASPGHAN) and the European Society for Pediatric Gastroenterology, Hepatology, and Nutrition (ESPGHAN). *Journal of Pediatric Gastroenterology and Nutrition, 49*(4), 498–547.

Voight, B. F., Peloso, G. M., Orho-Melander, M., Frikke-Schmidt, R., Barbalic, M., Jensen, M. K., et al. (2012). Plasma HDL cholesterol and risk of myocardial infarction: A Mendelian randomization study. *The Lancet.* doi: 10.1016/S0140-6736(12)60312-2

Weber, C., & Noels, H. (2011). Atherosclerosis: Current pathogenesis and therapeutic options. *Nature Medicine, 17*(11), 1410–1422. doi: 10.1038/nm.2538

World Health Organization. (2012). *Micronutrient deficiencies*. Retrieved May 26, 2012, from http://www.who.int/nutrition/topics/vad/en/

Yang, Y., Lucas, B., & Feucht, S., (Eds.). (2010). *Nutrition interventions for children with special health care needs* (3rd ed.). Olympia, WA: Washington State Department of Health.

Chapter 4

Academy of Nutrition and Dietetics. (2012). *Pediatric Nutrition Care Manual*. Retrieved June 4, 2012, from http://peds.nutritioncaremanual.org

Adler, J., & Dickinson, C. J. (2009). Thickened formula is only moderately effective in the treatment of gastroesophageal reflux in healthy infants. *The Journal of Pediatrics, 154*(5), 774.

Allali, F., El Aichaoui, S., Saoud, B., Maaroufi, H., Abouqal, R., & Hajjaj-Hassouni, N. (2006). The impact of clothing style on bone mineral density among postmenopausal women in Morocco: A case-control study. *BMC Public Health, 6*.

Al-Oballi Kridli, S. (2011). Health beliefs and practices of Muslim women during Ramadan.

American Journal of Maternal/Child Nursing, 36(4), 216–224.

American Academy of Pediatrics. (2011). *Vitamins for breastfed babies*. Retrieved June 3, 2012, from http://www.healthychildren.org/English/ages-stages/baby/breastfeeding/pages/Vitamins-for-Breastfed-Babies.aspx

American Academy of Pediatrics. (2012). Breast-feeding and the use of human milk. *Pediatrics, 129*(3), e827–e841.

American Academy of Pediatrics. (2012a). *Ages and stages baby 0–12 months: Feeding and nutrition*. Retrieved June 23, 2012, from http://www.healthychildren.org/English/ages-stages/baby/feeding-nutrition/Pages/default.aspx

American Academy of Pediatrics. (2012b). *Ages and stages baby 0–12 months: Feeding and nutrition—water and juice*. Retrieved June 23, 2012, from http://www.healthychildren.org/English/ages-stages/baby/feeding-nutrition/Pages/default.aspx

American Academy of Pediatrics. (2012c). *Health Issues: Botulism*. Retrieved June 14, 2012, from http://www.healthychildren.org/English/healthissues/conditions/infections/Pages/Botulism.aspx

American Academy of Pediatrics. (2012d). *Ages and stages baby 0–12 months feeding and nutrition-Cereal in a bottle: Solid food shortcuts to avoid*. Retrieved June 14, 2012, from http://www.healthychildren.org/English/ages-stages/baby/feeding-nutrition/pages/Cereal-in-a-Bottle-Solid-Food-Shortcuts-to-Avoid.aspx

American Academy of Pediatrics. (2012e). *Childhood nutrition*. Retrieved July 1, 2012, from http://www.healthychildren.org/English/healthy-living/nutrition/Pages/Childhood-Nutrition.aspx

American Academy of Pediatrics. (2012f). Policy statement: Breastfeeding and the use of human milk. *Pediatrics, 129*(3), e827–e841.

American Academy of Pediatrics. (2012g). *Press release: Low-income moms under stress may overfeed infants*. Retrieved June 22, 2012, from http://www.aap.org/en-us/about-the-aap/aap-press-room/Pages/Low-Income-Moms-Under-Stress-May-Overfeed-Infants.aspx

American Academy of Pediatrics, American Public Health Association, and National Resource Center for Health and Safety in Child Care and Early Education. (2011). *Caring for our children: National health and safety performance standards;guidelines for early care and education programs* (3rd ed.). Elk Grove Village, IL: American Academy of Pediatrics.

American Dietetic Association. (2009). Position of the American Dietetic Association: Promoting and supporting breastfeeding. *Journal of the American Dietetic Association, 109*(11), 1926–1942.

Avery, A., Zimmermann, K., Underwood, P. W., & Magnus, J. H. (2009). Confident commitment is a key factor for sustained breastfeeding. *Birth (Berkeley, Calif.), 36*(2), 141–148.

Baker, R. D., Greer, F. R., & The Committee on Nutrition. (2010). Diagnosis and prevention of

iron deficiency and iron-deficiency anemia in infants and young children (0–3 years of age). *Pediatrics, 126*(5), 1040–1050.

Berseth, C. L., Mitmesser, S. H., Ziegler, E. E., Marunycz, J. D., & Vanderhoof, J. (2009). Tolerance of a standard intact protein formula versus a partially hydrolyzed formula in healthy, term infants. *Nutrition Journal, 8*, 27.

Bhatia, J., & Greer, F. (2008). Use of soy protein-based formulas in infant feeding. *Pediatrics, 121*(5), 1062–1068.

Black, M. M., & Aboud, F. E. (2011). Responsive feeding is embedded in a theoretical framework of responsive parenting. *The Journal of Nutrition, 141*(3), 490–494.

Blossfied, I., Collins, A., & Delahunty, C. (2007). Texture preferences of 12-month-old infants and the role of early experiences. *Food Quality and Preference, 18*(2), 396.

Butte, N., Cobb, K., Dwyer, J., Graney, L., Heird, W., & Rickard, K. (2004). The start healthy feeding guidelines for infants and toddlers. *Journal of the American Dietetic Association, 104*, 442–454.

California Department of Public Health. (2011). *Welcome to the infant botulism treatment and prevention program*. Retrieved July 1, 2012, from http://www.infantbotulism.org/general/faq.php#

Cattaneo, A., Williams, C., Pallás-Alonso, C. R., Hernández-Aguilar, M. T., Lasarte-Velillas, J. J., Landa-Rivera, L., et al. (2011). ESPGHAN's 2008 recommendation for early introduction of complementary foods: How good is the evidence? *Maternal & Child Nutrition, 7*(4), 335–343.

Centers for Disease Control and Prevention. (2009). *Viral hepatitis: FAQ for the public*. Retrieved June 27, 2012, from http://www.cdc.gov/hepatitis/B/bFAQ.htm

Centers for Disease Control and Prevention. (2010). *Breastfeeding: Frequently asked questions (FAQs)* Retrieved June 3, 2012, from http://www.cdc.gov/breastfeeding/faq/

Centers for Disease Control and Prevention. (2011a). *Breastfeeding Report Card—United States, 2011*. Retrieved June 2, 2012, from http://www.cdc.gov/breastfeeding/data/reportcard.htm

Centers for Disease Control and Prevention. (2011b). *Breastfeeding: Data: Breastfeeding among U.S. children born 2000–2008, CDC national immunization survey*. Retrieved June 1, 2012, from http://www.cdc.gov/breastfeeding/data/NIS_data/index.htm

The Children's Hospital at Westmead. (2003). *Oral hypersensitivity*. Retrieved June 25, 2012, from http://www.chw.edu.au/rehab/brain_injury/information_sheets/swallowing/oral_hypersensitivity.htm

Corbet, S. J., & Poon, C. C. (2008). Toxic levels of mercury in Chinese infants eating fish congee. *The Medical Journal of Australia, 88*(1), 59–60.

Coulthard, H., Harris, G., & Emmett, P. (2009). Delayed introduction of lumpy foods to children during the complementary feeding period affects child's food acceptance and feeding at 7 years of age. *Maternal & Child Nutrition, 5*(1), 75–85.

Dattilo, A. M., Birch, L., Krebs, N. F., Lake, A., Taveras, E. M., & Saavedra, J. M. (2012). Need for early interventions in the prevention of pediatric overweight: A review and upcoming directions. *Journal of Obesity, 2012,* 123023. doi:10.1155/2012/123023

Dee, D. L., Li, R., Lee, L., & Grummer-Strawn, L. M. (February 2007). Associations between breastfeeding practices and young children's language and motor skill development. *Pediatrics, 119*(Supplement 1), S92–S98.

Dellwo Houghton, M., & Graybeal, T. E. (2001). Breast-feeding practices of Native American mothers participating in WIC. *Journal of the American Dietetic Association, 101*(2), 245–247.

Diamant, A. (2005). *The new Jewish baby book: Names, ceremonies, & customs—A guide for today's families* (2nd ed.). Woodstock, Vermont: Jewish Lights Publishing.

Division of Communicable Disease Control, California Department of Public Health. (2010). *Infant botulism treatment and prevention program.* Retrieved June 12, 2012, from http://www.infantbotulism.org/

Division of Communicable Disease Control, Center for Infectious Diseases, California Department of Public Health. (2011). *Epidemiological summaries of selected general communicable disease in California 2001–2008.* Retrieved June 12, 2012, from http://www.cdph.ca.gov/programs/sss/Documents/Epi-Summaries-CA-2001-2008-083111.pdf

Eidelman, A. I., Schandler, R. J., & American Academy of Pediatrics. (2012). Executive summary: Breastfeeding and the use of human milk. *Pediatrics, 129*(2), 600–603.

Eisner, T. (2011). *Necrotizing enterocolitis: Medline Plus medical encyclopedia.* Retrieved May 31, 2012, from http://www.nlm.nih.gov/medlineplus/ency/article/001148.htm

Food and Drug Administration. (2011). *Infant formula.* Retrieved June 5, 2012, from http://www.fda.gov/food/foodsafety/product-specificinformation/infantformula/default.htm

Gaur, A. H., Dominguez, K. L., Kalish, M. L., Rivera-Hernandez, D., Donohoe, M., Brooks, J. T., et al. (2009). Practice of feeding premasticated food to infants: A potential risk factor for HIV transmission. *Pediatrics, 124*(2), 658–666.

Geraghty, S. R., Khoury, J. C., Morrow, A. L., & Lanphea, B. P. (2008). Reporting individual test results of environmental chemicals in breastmilk: Potential for premature weaning. *Breastfeeding Medicine, 3*(4), 207–213.

Gill, S. L. (2009). Breastfeeding by Hispanic women. *Journal of Obstetric, Gynecologic, and Neonatal Nursing, 38*(2), 244–252.

Grummer-Strawn, L. M., Scanlon, K. S., & Fein, S. B. (2008). Infant feeding and feeding transitions during the first year of life. *Pediatrics, 122*(2), S36.

Guxens, M., Mendez, M. A., Molto-Puigmarti, C., Julvez, J., Garcia-Esteban, R., Forns, J., et al. (2011). Breastfeeding, long-chain polyunsaturated fatty acids in colostrum, and infant mental development. *Pediatrics, 128*(4), e880–889. doi:10.1542/peds.2010-1633

Haggerty, L. L. (2011). Maternal supplementation for prevention and treatment of vitamin D deficiency in exclusively breastfed infants. *Breastfeeding Medicine, 6*(3), 137–144.

Heinig, M. J., Follett, J. R., Ishii, K. D., Kavanagh-Prochaska, K., Cohen, R., & Panchula, J. (2006). Barriers to compliance with infant-feeding recommendations among low-income women. *Journal of Human Lactation, 22*(1), 27–38.

Horodynskia, M. A., Calcaterab, M., & Carpenter, A. (2012). Infant feeding practices: Perceptions of Native American mothers and health paraprofessionals. *Health Education Journal, 71*(3), 327–339.

Huh, S. Y., Rifas-Shiman, S. L., Taveras, E. M., Oken, E., & Gillman, M. W. (2011). Timing of solid food introduction and risk of obesity in preschool-aged children *Pediatrics, 127*(3), e544–551.

Hurley, K. M., & Black, M. M. (2011). Introduction to a supplement on responsive feeding: Promoting healthy growth and development for infants and toddlers. *The Journal of Nutrition, 141*(3), 489.

Hurley, K. M., Cross, M. B., & Hughes, S. O. (2011). A systematic review of responsive feeding and child obesity in high-income countries. *The Journal of Nutrition,* doi:10.3945/jn.110.130047

Irani, C., Germanos, M., Kazma, H., & Merhej, V. (2006). Food allergy in Lebanon: Is sesame the "Middle Eastern" peanut? *The Journal of Allergy and Clinical Immunology, 117*(2), S38.

Isaacs, E. B., Fischl, B. R., Quinn, B. T., Chong, W. K., Gadian, D. G., & Lucas, A. (2010). Impact of breast milk on IQ, brain size and white matter development. *Pediatric Research, 67*(4), 357–362. doi:10.1203/PDR.0b013e3181d026da

Katz, S. H. (Ed.). (2003). *Baby food: Encyclopedia of food & culture.* New York: Charles Scribner's Sons.

Kittler, P. G., Sucher, K., & Nelms, M. (2012). *Food and culture* (6th ed.). Belmont, CA: Wadsworth Publishing.

Kleinman, R. K. (Ed.). (2009). *Pediatric nutrition handbook* (6th ed.). Elk Grove Village, IL: American Academy of Pediatrics.

Koletzko, B., von Kries, R., Monasterolo, R. C., Subías, J. E., Scaglioni, S., Giovannini, M., et al. (2009). Can infant feeding choices modulate later obesity risk? *The American Journal of Clinical Nutrition, 89*(5), 1502S–1508S.

Kramer M. S., Aboud, F., Mironova, E., Vanilovich, I., Platt, R. W., Matush, L., et al. (2008). Breastfeeding and child cognitive development: New evidence from a large randomized trial. *Archives of General Psychiatry, 65*(5), 578–584.

Li, M., Bauer, L. L., Chen, X., Wang, M., Kuhlenschmidt, T. B., Kuhlenschmidt, M. S., et al. (2012). Microbial composition and in vitro fermentation patterns of human milk oligosaccharides and prebiotics differ between formula-fed and sow-reared piglets. *The Journal of Nutrition, 142*(4), 681–689.

Lozoff, B. (2011). Early iron deficiency has brain and behavior effects consistent with dopaminergic dysfunction. *The Journal of Nutrition, 141*(4), 740S–746S.

Mahan, L., Escott-Stump, S., & Raymond, J. L. (Eds.). (2012). *Krause's food and the nutrition care process* (13th ed.). St. Louis: Elsevier Saunders.

Mayo Clinic. (2011). *Infant choking: How to keep your baby safe.* Retrieved July 2, 2012, from http://www.mayoclinic.com/health/infant-choking/MY01224/

McDowell, M. M., Wang, C., & Kennedy-Stephenson, J. (2008). Breastfeeding in the United States: Findings from the national health and nutrition examination survey, 1999–2006. *NCHS Data Brief, 2009*(No.5).

Mennella, J. A., Jagnow, C. P., & Beauchamp, G. K. (2001). Prenatal and postnatal flavor learning by human infants. *Pediatrics, 107*(6), e88.

Mennella, J. A., Lukasewycz, L. D., Castor, S. M., & Beauchamp, G. K. (2011). The timing and duration of a sensitive period in human flavor learning: A randomized trial. *The American Journal of Clinical Nutrition, 93*(5), 1019–1024.

Mennella, J. A., Ziegler, P., Briefel, R., & Novak, T. (2006). Feeding infants and toddlers study: The types of foods fed to Hispanic infants and toddlers *Journal of the American Dietetic Association, 106*(1 Suppl 1), S96–106.

National Association for the Education of Young Children. (2012). *Academy for early childhood program accreditation: Standard 5: NAEYC accreditation criteria for health standard.* Retrieved June 2, 2012, from http://www.naeyc.org/files/academy/file/AllCriteriaDocument.pdf

National Institute of Dental and Craniofacial Research, & National Institute of Health. (2011). *A healthy mouth for your baby.* Retrieved June 11, 2012, from http://www.nidcr.nih.gov/OralHealth/Topics/ToothDecay/AHealthyMouthforYourBaby.htm

National Resource Center for Health and Safety in Child Care and Early Education, University of Colorado Denver. (2011). *National resource center for health and safety in child care and early education: Achieving a state of healthy weight: A national assessment of obesity prevention terminology in child care regulations 2010.* Aurora, CO. Retrieved June 2, 2012, from http://nrckids.org/regulations_report_2010.pdf

Nemours. (2012). *Formula feeding FAQs: Starting solids and milk.* Retrieved June 12, 2012, from http://kidshealth.org/parent/pregnancy_newborn/formulafeed/formulafeed_solids.html

Ogbuanu, C., Glover, S., Probst, J., Liu, J., & Hussey, J. (2011). The effect of maternity leave length and time of return to work on breastfeeding. *Pediatrics, 127*(6), e1414–e1427.

Oregon Department of Education. (2009). *USDA child and adult care food program child care center manual.* Salem, Oregon.

Pak-Gorstein, S., Haq, A., & Graham, E. A. (2009). Cultural influences on infant feeding practices. *Pediatrics in Review, 30*(3), e11–21.

Perneczky, R., Wagenpfeil, S., Lunetta, K. L., Cupples, L. A., Green, R. C., DeCarli, C., et al. (2010). Head circumference, atrophy, and cognition: Implications for brain reserve in Alzheimer disease. *Neurology, 75*(2), 137–142. doi:10.1212/WNL.0b013e3181e7ca97

Phelan, S., Hart, C., Phipps, M., Abrams, B., Schaffner, A., Adams, A., et al. (2011). Maternal behaviors during pregnancy impact offspring obesity risk. *Experimental Diabetes Research, 2011*, 985139. doi:10.1155/2011/985139

Przyrembel, H. (2012). Timing of introduction of complementary food: Short- and long-term health consequences. *Annals of Nutrition and Metabolism, 60*(Supplement 2), 8–20.

Queen Samour, P., & King, K. (2012). *Pediatric nutrition* (4th ed.). Sudbury, MA: Jones & Bartlett Learning, LLC.

Rajendran, A. (2011). *Annaprashana in Bengali culture – rice eating ceremony*. Retrieved June 25, 2012, from http://www.hindu-blog.com/2010/05/annaprashana-in-bengali-culture-rice.html

Ramachandran, A. (2004). *Congee: Asia's comfort food: Things Asian*. Retrieved 7/31/2009, from http://www.thingsasian.com/stories-photos/2953

Retnakaran, R., Ye, C., Hanley, A. J. G., Connelly, P. W., Sermer, M., Zinman, B., et al. (2012). Effect of maternal weight, adipokines, glucose intolerance and lipids on infant birth weight among women without gestational diabetes mellitus. *Canadian Medical Association Journal*, doi:10.1111/j.1463-1326.2012.01607

Roed, C., Skovby, F., & Lund, A. M. (2009). Severe vitamin B12 deficiency in infants breast fed by vegans [Abstract]. *Ugeskr Laeger, 171*(43), 3099–3101.

Shaikh, U., & Ahmed, O. (2006). Islam and infant feeding. *Breastfeeding Medicine, 1*(3), 164.

Sinclair, D., & Dangerfield, S. D. (1998). *Human growth after birth* (6th ed.). Oxford: Oxford University Press.

Sparks, P. J. (2011). Racial/Ethnic differences in breastfeeding duration among WIC-eligible families. *Women's Health Issues, 21*(5), 374–382.

United States Breastfeeding Committee. (2011). *Workplace support in federal law: Breastfeeding Promotion Act 2011*. Retrieved June 3, 2012, from http://www.usbreastfeeding.org/Employment/WorkplaceSupport/WorkplaceSupportinFederalLaw/tabid/175/Default.aspx

U.S. Department of Agriculture. (2009). *Infant nutrition and feeding: A guide for use in the WIC and CSF programs*. Retrieved February 16, 2012, from http://www.nal.usda.gov/wicworks/Topics/FG/CompleteIFG.pdf

U.S. Department of Agriculture, Food and Nutrition Service. (2000). *Issues related to feeding infants in the CACFP*. Retrieved May 31, 2012, from http://www.fns.usda.gov/cnd/Care/Regs-Policy/InfantMeals/2000-04-20.htm

U.S. Department of Agriculture, Food and Nutrition Service. (2012a). *Interim rule—revisions to the WIC food packages*. Retrieved June 17, 2012, from http://www.fns.usda.gov/wic/regspublished/foodpackages-interimrule.htm

U.S. Department of Agriculture, Food and Nutrition Service. (2012b). *WIC food package regulatory requirements* Retrieved June 23, 2012, from http://www.fns.usda.gov/wic/benefitsandservices/foodpkgregs

.htm#INFANT_FOOD_FRUITS_and_VEGETABLES

U.S. Department of Health and Human Services. (2012). *Affordable care act rules on expanding access to preventive services for women*. Retrieved June 30, 2012, from http://www.healthcare.gov/news/factsheets/2011/08/womensprevention08012011a.html

University of Illinois College of Agricultural, Consumer and Environmental Sciences. (2012). *New infant formula ingredients boost babies' immunity by feeding their gut bacteria*. Retrieved May 31, 2012, from http://nutrsci.illinois.edu/content/new-infant-formula-ingredients-boost-babies-immunity-feeding-their-gut-bacteria

World Health Organization. (2010). *Infant and Young Child Feeding Fact Sheet*. Retrieved July 2, 2012, from http://www.who.int/mediacentre/news/statements/2011/breastfeeding_20110115/en/index.html

World Health Organization. (2011). *Exclusive breastfeeding for six months best for babies everywhere*. Retrieved June 17, 2012, from http://www.who.int/mediacentre/news/statements/2011/breastfeeding_20110115/en/index.html

World Health Organization, & UNICEF. (2003). *Global strategy for infant and young child feeding*. Geneva, Switzerland: World Health Organization.

Worobey, J., Lopez, M. I., & Hoffman, D. J. (2009). Maternal behavior and infant weight gain in the first year. *Journal of Nutrition Education and Behavior, 41*(3), 169–175.

Wright, A. L., & Schanler, R. J. (2001). The resurgence of breastfeeding at the end of the second millennium. *The Journal of Nutrition, 131*(2), 421S–425S.

Yang Y., Lucas B., & Feucht S. (Ed.). (2010). *Nutrition interventions for children with special health care needs* (3rd ed.). Olympia, WA: Washington State Department of Health.

Chapter 5

Academy of Nutrition and Dietetics. (2012). *Pediatric nutrition care manual*. Retrieved June 4, 2012, from http://peds.nutritioncaremanual.org

American Academy of Family Physicians. (2012). *Breastfeeding, family physicians supporting (position paper)*. Retrieved July 3, 2012, from http://www.aafp.org/online/en/home/policy/policies/b/breastfeedingpositionpaper.html

American Academy of Pediatrics. (2012). *Health issues-eating disorders*. Retrieved July 29, 2012, from http://www.healthychildren.org/English/health-issues/conditions/emotional-problems/pages/Eating-Disorders.aspx

American Dietetic Association. (2011). Position of the American Dietetic Association: Benchmarks for nutrition in child care. *Journal of the American Dietetic Association, 111*(4), 607–615.

American Dietetic Association and the American Dietetic Association Foundation. (2011). The state of family nutrition and physical activity: Are we making progress. *Journal of the American Dietetic Association, 111*(4), F1–F30.

Anderson, S. E., & Whitaker, R. C. (2009). Prevalence of obesity among U.S. preschool children in different racial and ethnic groups. *Archives of Pediatrics Adolescent Medicine, 163*(4), 344–348.

Ball, S. C., Benjamin, S. E., & Ward, D. S. (2008). Dietary intakes in North Carolina child-care centers: Are children meeting current recommendations? *Journal of the American Dietetic Association, 108*(4), 718–721.

Benjamin Neelon, S. E., Vaughn, A., Ball, S. C., McWilliams, C., & Ward, D. S. (2012). Nutrition practices and mealtime environments of North Carolina child care centers. *Childhood Obesity, 8*(3), 216–223.

Benton, D., & Jarvis, M. (2007). The role of breakfast and a mid-morning snack on the ability of children to concentrate at school. *Physiology & Behavior, 90*(2–3), 382–385.

Birch, L. L., Fisher, J. O., & Davison, K. K. (2003). Learning to overeat: Maternal use of restrictive feeding practices promotes girls' eating in the absence of hunger. *The American Journal of Clinical Nutrition, 78*(2), 215–220.

Brotanek, J. M., Schroer, D., Valentyn, L., Tomany-Korman, S., & Flores, G. (2009). Reasons for prolonged bottle-feeding and iron deficiency among Mexican-American toddlers: An ethnographic study. *Academic Pediatrics, 9*(1), 17–25.

Burger, K. S., Fisher, J. O., & Johnson, S. L. (2011). Mechanisms behind the portion size effect: Visibility and bite size. *Obesity, 19*(3), 546–551. doi:10.1038/oby.2010.233

Butte, N. F., Fox, M. K., Briefel, R., R., Siega-Riz, A. M., Dwyer, J. T., Deming, D. M., et al. (2010). Nutrient intakes of U.S. infants, toddlers, and preschoolers meet or exceed dietary reference intakes. *Journal of the American Dietetic Association, 110*(12, Supplement), S27–S37.

Centers for Disease Control and Prevention. (2012). *Nutrition-facts—adolescent and school health*. Retrieved July 26, 2012, from http://www.cdc.gov/healthyyouth/nutrition/facts.htm

Chefs Move to Schools. (2012). *Chefs move to schools*. Retrieved July 28, 2012, from http://www.chefsmovetoschools.org/

Committee to Review Child and Adult Care Food Program Meal Requirements, & Institute of Medicine. (2011). In S. P. Murphy, A. L. Yaktine, C. W Suitor, & S. Moats, *Child and Adult Care Food Program: Aligning dietary guidance for all*. Washington DC: National Academies Press.

Cooke, L. J., Haworth, C., & Wardle, J. (2007). Genetic and environmental influences on children's food neophobia. *American Journal of Clinical Nutrition, 86*(2), 428–433.

Coppinger, T., Jeanes, Y. M., Hardwick, J., & Reeves, S. (2012). Body mass, frequency of eating and breakfast consumption in 9–13-year-olds. *Journal of Human Nutrition and Dietetics, 25*(1), 43–49.

Davis, A. M., Cocjin, J., Mousa, H., & Hyman, P. (2010). Empirically supported treatments for feeding difficulties in young children. *Current Gastroenterology Reports, 12*(3), 189–194.

Deshmukh-Taskar, P. R., Nicklas, T. A., O'Neil, C. E., Keast, D. R., Radcliffe, J. D., & Cho, S. (2010). The relationship of breakfast skipping and type of breakfast consumption with nutrient intake and weight status in children and adolescents: The national health and nutrition examination survey 1999–2006. *Journal of the American Dietetic Association, 110*(6), 869–878. doi:10.1016/j.jada.2010.03.023

Dwyer, J. T., Butte, N. F., Deming, D. M., Siega-Riz, A. M., & Reidy, K. C. (2010). Feeding infants and toddlers study 2008: Progress, continuing concerns, and implications. *Journal of the American Dietetic Association, 110*(12 (Supplement)), S60–S67.

Erinosho, T. O., Hales, D. P., McWilliams, C. P., Emunah, J., & Ward, D. S. (2012). Nutrition policies at child-care centers and impact on role modeling of healthy eating behaviors of caregivers. *Journal of the Academy of Nutrition and Dietetics, 112*(1), 119–124. doi:10.1016/j.jada.2011.08.048

Field, A. E., Javaras, K. M., Aneja, P., Kitos, N., Camargo, C. A., Jr., Taylor, C. B., et al. (2008). Family, peer, and media predictors of becoming eating disordered. *Archives of Pediatrics & Adolescent Medicine, 162*(6), 574–579.

Fishel, A. (2010). *The power of table talk*. Retrieved July 23, 2012, from http://thefamilydinnerproject .org/the-power-of-table-talk/

Fisher, J. O., Liu, Y., Birch, L. L., & Rolls, B. J. (2007). Effects of portion size and energy density on young children's intake at a meal. *American Journal of Clinical Nutrition, 86*(1), 174–179.

Food Research & Action Center. (2010). *School breakfast program*. Retrieved July 26, 2012, from http://www.frac.org/html/federal_food_ programs/programs/sbp.html

Fox, M., Devaney, B., Reidy, K., Razafindrakoto, C., & Ziegler, P. (2006). Relationship between portion size and energy intake among infants and toddlers: Evidence of self-regulation. *The Journal of American Dietetic Association, 106*(1 Suppl 1), S77–S83.

Frankel, L. A., Hughes, S. O., O'Connor, T. M., Power, T. G., Fisher, J. O., & Hazen, N. L. (2012). Parental influences on children's self-regulation of energy intake: Insights from developmental literature on emotion regulation. *Journal of Obesity, 2012.* doi:10.1155/2012/327259

Harding, C., Faiman, A., & Wright, J. (2010). Evaluation of an intensive desensitization, oral tolerance therapy and hunger provocation program for children who have had prolonged periods of tube feeds. *International Journal of Evidence Based Health Care, 8*(4), 268–276.

Hayes, J. E., Wallace, M. R., Knopik, V. S., Herbstman, D. M., Bartoshuk, L. M., & Duffy, V. B. (2011). Allelic variation in TAS2R bitter receptor genes associates with variation in sensations from and ingestive behaviors toward common bitter beverages in adults. *Chemical Senses, 36*(3), 311–319.

Huber, D. (2009). Making a difference in early childhood obesity. *Child Care Exchange.*

Ishige, R. (2012). *The dietary culture of Asia.* Retrieved July 16, 2012, from http://asiasociety .org/print/1646

Johnson, L., van Jaarsveld, C. H. M., & Wardle, J. (2011). Individual and family environment correlates differ for consumption of core and non-core foods in children. *British Journal of Nutrition, 105*(6), 950–959.

Johnson-Askew, W. L., Gordon, L., & Sockalingam, S. (2011). Practice paper of the American Dietetic Association: Addressing racial and ethnic health disparities. *Journal of the American Dietetic Association, 111*(3), 446–456. doi:10.1016/j.jada.2011.01.024

Kleinman, R. K. (Ed.). (2009). *Pediatric nutrition handbook* (6th ed.). United States: American Academy of Pediatrics.

Knaapila, A., Silventoinen, K., Broms, U., Rose, R. J., Perola, M., & Kaprioand, J. T. (2011). Food neophobia in young adults: Genetic architecture and relation to personality, pleasantness and use frequency of foods, and body mass index—A twin study. *Behavior Genetics, 2012*(7/7/2012), 512–521.

Knaapila, A., Tuorila, H., Silventoinen, K., Keskitalo, K., Kallela, M., Wessman, M., et al. (2007). Food neophobia shows heritable variation in humans. *Physiology & Behavior, 91*(5), 573–578.

Let's Move. (2010). *Let's move!* Retrieved July 28, 2012, from http://www.letsmove.gov/

Luitel, A. (2006). Food and eating customs differ around the world. *Silver International Newspaper,* retrieved July 23, 2012, from http:// silverinternational.mbhs.edu/v202/V20.2.05a .eatingcustoms.html

Mahan, L., Escott-Stump, S., & Raymond, J. L. (Eds.). (2012). *Krause's food and the nutrition care process* (13th ed.). St. Louis, MO: Elsevier Saunders.

Maritz, J. (2011). *Parmalat pushing into Africa; powdered milk remains a challenge.* Retrieved July 16, 2012, from http://www.howwemadeitinafrica .com/parmalat-pushing-into-africa-powdered- milk-remains-a-challenge/8475/

Martinez, J. M., & Shelnutt, K. P. (2010). *FCS8902/ FY1154: Raising healthy children: The role of snacking.* Retrieved July 26, 2012, from http:// edis.ifas.ufl.edu/fy1154

McConahy, K., Smiciklas-Wright, H., Mitchell, D., & Picciano, M. (2004). Portion size of common foods predicts energy intake among preschool-aged children. *Journal of the American Dietetic Association, 104*(6), 975–979.

Monneuse, M., Hladik, C. M., Simmen, B., & Pasquet, P. (2011). Changes in food neophobia and food preferences during a weight reduction session: Influence of taste acuity on the individual trajectory. In V. R. Preedy, R. R. Watson, & C. R. Martin (Eds.), *Handbook of behavior, food and nutrition* (chapter 111). New York: Springer.

Montana Team Nutrition Program. (2009). *Challenges, benefits and essential factors for success in implementing a recess before lunch schedules in Montana elementary schools.* Retrieved July 27,

2012, from http://www.opi.mt.gov/pdf/ SchoolFood/RBL/08RBLSurveySumRpt.pdf

Muthayya, S., Thomas, T., Srinivasan, K., Rao, K., Kurpad, A. V., van Klinken, J. W., et al. (2007). Consumption of a mid-morning snack improves memory but not attention in school children. *Physiology & Behavior, 90*(1), 142–150.

National Association for the Education of Young Children. (2012). *Academy for early childhood program accreditation: Standard 5: NAEYC accreditation criteria for health standard.* Retrieved June 2, 2012, from http://www.naeyc.org/files/ academy/file/AllCriteriaDocument.pdf

National Food Service Management Institute. (2012). *New meal pattern.* Retrieved July 27, 2012, from http://nfsmi.org/ResourceOverview .aspx?ID=425

Nova. (2009). *The science of picky eaters.* Retrieved July 6, 2012, from http://www.pbs.org/wgbh/ nova/body/science-picky-eaters.html

Ochs, E. S., & Shohet, M. (2006). The cultural structuring of mealtime socialization. *New Directions for Child and Adolescent Development, 111,* 35–49.

O'Connell, M. L., Henderson, K. E., Luedicke, J., & Schwartz, M. B. (2012). Repeated exposure in a natural setting: A preschool intervention to increase vegetable consumption. *Journal of the Academy of Nutrition and Dietetics, 112*(2), 230–234. doi:10.1016/j.jada.2011.10.003

Oregon Department of Education. (2009). *USDA child and adult care food program child care center manual.* Salem, Oregon.

Orlet Fisher, J., Rolls, B. J., & Birch, L. L. (2003). Children's bite size and intake of an entree are greater with large portions than with age-appropriate or self-selected portions. *The American Journal of Clinical Nutrition, 77*(5), 1164–1170.

Piernas, C., & Popkin, B. M. (2011). Increased portion sizes from energy-dense foods affect total energy intake at eating occasions in US children and adolescents: Patterns and trends by age group and sociodemographic characteristics, 1977–2006. *The American Journal of Clinical Nutrition, 94*(5), 1324–1332.

Pinhas, L., Morris, A., Crosby, R. D., & Katzman, D. K. (2011). Incidence and age-specific presentation of restrictive eating disorders in children: A Canadian paediatric surveillance program study. *Archives of Pediatrics & Adolescent Medicine, 165*(10), 895–899.

Queen Samour, P., & King, K. (2012). *Pediatric nutrition* (4th ed.). Sudbury, MA: Jones & Bartlett Learning, LLC.

Rainville. A. Wolf, K. N., & Carr, D. H. (2006). Recess placement prior to lunch in elementary schools: What are the barriers? *Journal of Child Nutrition & Management—School Nutrition Association, 30*(2).

Rampersaud, G. C. (2009). Benefits of breakfast for children and adolescents: Update and recommendations for practitioners. *American Journal of Lifestyle Medicine, 3*(2), 86.

Rampersaud, G. C., Pereira, M. A., Girard, B. L., Adams, J., & Metzl, J. D. (2005). Breakfast habits, nutritional status, body weight, and academic performance in children and adolescents. *Journal of the American Dietetic Association, 105*(5), 743.

Ramsay, S. A., Branen, L. J., Fletcher, J., Price, E., Johnson, S. L., & Sigman-Grant, M. (2010). "Are you done?" child care providers' verbal communication at mealtimes that reinforce or hinder children's internal cues of hunger and satiation. *Journal of Nutrition Education and Behavior, 42*(4), 265–270.

Ritchie, L. D., Boyle, M., Chandran, K., Spector, P., Whaley, S. E., James, P., et al. (2012). Participation in the child and adult care food program is associated with more nutritious foods and beverages in child care. *Childhood Obesity, 8*(3), 224–229.

Rolls, B., Engell, D., & Birch, L. (2000). Serving portion size influences 5-year-old but not 3-year-old children's food intakes. *The Journal of the American Dietetic Association, 100*(2), 232–234.

Satter, E. (2008). *Secrets of feeding a healthy family-how to raise good eaters, how to cook* (2nd ed.). Madison: Kelsey Press.

Satter, E. (2012a). *The picky eater.* Retrieved July 7, 2012, from http://www.ellynsatter.com/the-picky-eater-i-43.html

Satter, E. (2012b). *3 to 5 years: Feeding your preschooler.* Retrieved July 24, 2012, from http://www.ellynsatter.com/to-years-feeding-your-preschooler-i-32.html

Satter, E. (2012c). *Children know how much they need to eat.* Retrieved July 24, 2012, from http://www.ellynsatter.com/children-know-how-much-they-need-to-eat-i-36.html

Schwartz, C., Issanchou, S., & Nicklaus, S. (2009). Developmental changes in the acceptance of the five basic tastes in the first year of life. *The British Journal of Nutrition, 102*(9), 1375–1385.

Snow, C. E., & Beals, D. E. (2006). Mealtime talk that supports literacy development. *New Directions for Child and Adolescent Development,* (111), 51–66.

Stein, M. T., Boies, E. G., & Snyder, D. M. (2004). Parental concerns about extended breastfeeding in a toddler. *Pediatrics, 114*(5), 1506–1509.

Sustainable Schools Project. (2012). *Sustainable schools project.* Retrieved July 30, 2012, from http://www.sustainableschoolsproject.org/

Tan, C. C., & Holub, S. C. (2011). Children's self-regulation in eating: associations with inhibitory control and parents' feeding behavior. *Journal of Pediatric Psychology, 36*(3), 340–345.

U.S. Department of Agriculture. (2012a). *ChooseMyPlate.gov.* Retrieved April 14, 2012, from http://www.choosemyplate.gov/

U.S. Department of Agriculture. (2012b). *Getting started with MyPlate.* Retrieved July 28, 2012, from http://www.cnpp.usda.gov/Publications/MyPlate/GettingStartedWithMyPlate.pdf

U.S. Department of Agriculture Food and Nutrition Service. (2011a). (CACFP Memo No. 21-2011 revised). Retrieved July 28, 2012, from http://www.fns.usda.gov/cnd/care/regs-policy/policymemo/2011/CACFP-21-2011.pdf

U.S. Department of Agriculture, Food and Nutrition Service. (2011b). *Child and Adult Care Food Program.* Retrieved September 12, 2011, from http://www.fns.usda.gov/cnd/care/cacfp/aboutcacfp.htm

U.S. Department of Agriculture Food and Nutrition Service. (2012). *Summer food service program.* Retrieved July 28, 2012, from http://www.fns.usda.gov/cnd/summer/sponsors/waiver.html

U.S. Department of Agriculture Food and Nutrition Service. (2012a). *Healthier US school challenge.* Retrieved July 28, 2012, from http://www.fns.usda.gov/tn/HealthierUS/index.html

U.S. Department of Agriculture Food and Nutrition Service. (2012b). *Team nutrition homepage.* Retrieved July 28, 2012, from http://www.fns.usda.gov/tn/

U.S. Department of Health and Human Services, & U.S. Department of Agriculture. (2011). *Dietary Guidelines for Americans, 2010.* Retrieved April 10, 2012, from http://www.health.gov/dietaryguidelines/2010.asp

U.S. Food and Drug Administration. (2012a). *Final rule: Nutrition standards in the national school lunch and school breakfast programs* Retrieved July 26, 2012, from http://www.fns.usda.gov/cnd/Governance/Legislation/nutrition standards.htm

U.S. Food and Drug Administration. (2012b). *Healthy Hunger-Free Kids Act.* Retrieved July 27, 2012, from http://www.fns.usda.gov/cnd/Governance/Legislation/CNR_2010.htm

U.S. Food and Drug Administration. (2012c). *Healthy meals resource system.* Retrieved July 29, 2012, from http://healthymeals.nal.usda.gov/

U.S. Food and Drug Administration. (2012d). *School breakfast program.* Retrieved July 26, 2012, from http://www.fns.usda.gov/cnd/breakfast/

U.S. Food and Drug Administration Food and Nutrition Service. (2009). *WICworks sharing gallery—overview of the new food packages.* Retrieved July 8, 2012, from http://www.nal.usda.gov/wicworks/Sharing_Center/CO/Overview.pdf

U.S. Food and Drug Administration Food and Nutrition Service. (2011). *Local school wellness policy.* Retrieved July 29, 2012, from http://www.fns.usda.gov/tn/healthy/wellnesspolicy.html

U.S. Food and Drug Administration Food and Nutrition Service. (2012). *USDA farm to school.* Retrieved July 28, 2012, from http://www.fns.usda.gov/cnd/F2S/Default.htm

Van Horn, L. (2012). Socioeconomic, ethnic, cultural, and other influences on eating behavior: Complex considerations. *Journal of the Academy of Nutrition and Dietetics, 112*(5), 598–598. doi:10.1016/j.jand.2012.04.003

Zero to Three. (n.d.). *It's too mushy! It's too spicy! The peas are touching the chicken! (or, how to handle your picky eater).* Retrieved July 5, 2012, from http://www.zerotothree.org/site/PageServer?pagename=ter_key_health_picky

Zuercher, J. L., & Kranz, S. (2012). Toddlers and preschoolers consume more dietary fiber when high-fiber lunch menus are served. *Childhood Obesity, 8*(1), 71–75.

Chapter 6

Academy of Nutrition and Dietetics. (2012). *Pediatric Nutrition Care Manual.* Retrieved February 22, 2012, from http://peds.nutritioncaremanual.org

Affenito, S. (2007). Breakfast: A missed opportunity. *Journal of the American Dietetic Association, 107*(4), 565–569.

Allen, J. H., Benson, C., Shuman, M., & Skees-Gregory, D. (2011). *Making food service sustainable: Portland State University's experience.* Retrieved October 6, 2011, from http://www.pdx.edu/sites/www.pdx.edu.sustainability/files/sus_sustainable_food_service.pdf

American Academy of Pediatrics, American Public Health Association, National Resource Center for Health and Safety in Child Care and Early Education. (2011). *Caring for our children National Resource Center for Health and Safety in Child Care and Early Education* (3rd ed.). Elk Grove Village, IL: American Academy of Pediatrics.

American Diabetes Association. (2011a). Diabetes care in the school and day care setting. *Diabetes Care, 34*(1), S70–74.

American Diabetes Association. (2011b). *Food and fitness.* Retrieved October 24, 2011, from http://www.diabetes.org/food-and-fitness/food/

American Diabetes Association. (2012). Diabetes care in the school and day care setting. *Diabetes Care, 35*(1), S76–S80.

American Dietetic Association. (2004). *Conclusion statement: Is intake of fruits and vegetables related to adiposity in children?* Retrieved October 1, 2011, from http://www.adaevidencelibrary.com/conclusion.cfm?conclusion_statement_id=41

American Dietetic Association. (2010a). *Executive summary of recommendations: Pediatric weight management.* Retrieved October 30, 2011, from http://www.adaevidencelibrary.com/topic.cfm?cat=3013

American Dietetic Association. (2010b). Position of the American Dietetic Association: Providing nutrition services for people with developmental disabilities and special health care needs. *Journal of the American Dietetic Association, 110*(2), 296.

American Dietetic Association. (2011a). *Pediatric Nutrition Care Manual.* Retrieved October 24, 2011, from http://www.nutritioncaremanual.org/auth.cfm

American Dietetic Association. (2011b). Position of the American Dietetic Association: Benchmarks for nutrition in child care. *Journal of the American Dietetic Association, 111*(4), 607–615.

American Dietetic Association. (2011c). *Cultural food practices. Pediatric Nutrition Care Manual.* Retrieved from http://peds.nutritioncaremanual.org

Anderson, J. (2009). *Birthing green students.* Retrieved October 6, 2011, from http://www.sherwoodgazette.com/sustainable/story.php?story_id=124456510676248000

Annema, N., Heyworth, J. S., McNaughton, S. A., Iacopetta, B., & Fritschi, L. (2011). Fruit and vegetable consumption and the risk of proximal colon, distal colon, and rectal cancers in a case-control study in Western Australia. *Journal of the American Dietetic Association, 111*(10), 1479–1490.

August, G. P., Caprio, S., Fennoy, I., Freemark, M., Kaufman, F. R., Lustig, R. H., et al. (2008). Prevention and treatment of pediatric obesity: An endocrine society clinical practice guideline based on expert opinion. *Journal of Clinical Endocrinology and Metabolism, 93*(12), 45–76.

Beauchamp, G. K., & Mennella, J. A. (2011). Flavor perception in human infants: Development and functional significance. *Digestion, 83 Supplement* 1, 1–6.

Berni Canani, R., Di Costanzo, M., & Troncone, R. (2011). The optimal diagnostic workup for children with suspected food allergy. *Nutrition, 27*(10), 983–987.

Birch, L. L., & Anzman-Frasca, S. (2011). Promoting children's healthy eating in obesogenic environments: Lessons learned from the rat. *Physiology & Behavior, 104*(4), 641–645.

Carlsen, M. H., Halvorsen, B. L., Holte, K., Bohn, S. K., Dragland, S., Sampson, L., et al. (2010). The total antioxidant content of more than 3100 foods, beverages, spices, herbs and supplements used worldwide. *Nutrition Journal, 9*(3). doi:10.1186/1475-2891-9-3 or retrieved January 1, 2013 from http://www .nutritionj.com/content/9/1/3.

Connecticut State Department of Education, Bureau of Health/Nutrition, Family Services and Adult Education. (2010). *Action guide for child care nutrition and physical activity policies.* Retrieved October 15, 2011 from http://www .sde.ct.gov/sde/cwp/view.asp?a=2678&Q=322594

Cooke, L. J., Haworth, C. M., & Wardle, J. (2007). Genetic and environmental influences on children's food neophobia. *American Journal of Clinical Nutrition, 86*(2), 428–433.

Davis, M. M., Gance-Cleveland, B., Hassink, S., Johnson, R., Paradis, G., & Resnicow, K. (2007). Recommendations for prevention of childhood obesity. *Pediatrics, 120* (Supplement 4), S229–S253.

Edwards, G. M. (2003). The health cost of soul food: Introduction. *Topic in Advanced Practice Nursing, 3*(2). Retrieved from http://www.medscape.com/ viewarticle/453335

Ewing, J. & The Ohio State University. (2010). *The Ohio State University fact sheet: Cultural diversity: Eating in America-African American HYG-5250-95-R10.* Retrieved October 31, 2011, from http://ohioline.osu.edu/hyg-fact/5000/ pdf/5250.pdf

Ferdman, R., McClenahan, J. M., & Falco, J. (2010). Food allergy prevention: To eat or not to eat. *Infant, Child, & Adolescent Nutrition, 2*(6), 340.

Flock, M. R., & Kris-Etherton, P. M. (2011). Dietary guidelines for Americans 2010: Implications for cardiovascular disease. *Current Atherosclerosis Reports, 13*(6), 499.

Food Allergy Anaphylaxis Network. (2011). *About food allergy—FAAN.* Retrieved October 18, 2011, from http://www.foodallergy.org/section/ about-food-allergy

Food and Nutrition Service & United States Department of Agriculture. (2001). Accommodating children with special dietary needs in the school nutrition program: Guidance for school food service staff. Retrieved February, 29, 2012, from http://www.fns.usda.gov/cnd/guidance/ special_dietary_needs.pdf

Forestell, C. A., & Mennella, J. A. (2007). Early determinants of fruit and vegetable acceptance. *Pediatrics, 120*(6), 1247–1254.

Ghaddar, S., Brown, C. J., Pagán, J. A., & Díaz, V. (2010). Acculturation and healthy lifestyle habits among Hispanics in United States-Mexico border communities. *Revista Panamericana De Salud Pública, 28*(3).

Green Mountain Technologies, 2012. *Earth tub: Green mountain technologies.* Retrieved February 29, 2012, from http://www.compostingtechnology .com/invesselsystems/earthtub/

Greer, F. R., Sicherer, S. H., Burks, A. W., & the Committee on Nutrition and Section on Allergy and Immunology. (2008). Effects of early nutritional interventions on the development of atopic disease in infants and children: The role of maternal dietary restriction, breastfeeding, timing of introduction of complementary foods, and hydrolyzed formulas. *Pediatrics, 121*(1), 183–191.

Guidetti, M., & Cavazza, N. (2008). Structure of the relationship between parents' and children's food preferences and avoidances: An explorative study. *Appetite, 50*(1), 83–90.

Gupta, R. S., Springston, E. E., Warrier, M. R., Smith, B., Kumar, R., Pongracic, J., et al. (2011). The prevalence, severity, and distribution of childhood food allergy in the United States. *Pediatrics, 128*(1) e9–e17. Retrieved from http://pediatrics.aappublications .org/content/128/1/e9.full

Harris, G. (2008). Development of taste and food preferences in children. *Current Opinion in Clinical Nutrition and Metabolic Care, 11*(3), 315–319.

Harvard School of Public Health. (2011a). *Health gains from whole grains—what should I eat?— the nutrition source.* Retrieved October 3, 2011, from http://www.hsph.harvard.edu/ nutritionsource/what-should-you-eat/health- gains-from-whole-grains/

Harvard School of Public Health. (2011b). *The nutrition source—vegetables and fruits: Get plenty every day—what should I eat?* Retrieved October 1, 2011, from http://www.hsph.harvard .edu/nutritionsource/what-should-you-eat/ vegetables-full-story/index.html

Head Start Performance Standards Title 45, Volume 4, U.S.C. Section 1304.23. (1998). http://edocket .access.gpo.gov/cfr_2007/octqtr/45cfr1304.23 .htm

Hesketh, K. D., & Campbell, K. J. (2010). Interventions to prevent obesity in 0–5 year olds: An updated systematic review of the literature. *Obesity, 18 Supplement* 1, S27–S35.

Hill, P., & The Ohio State University. (2010). *The Ohio State University fact sheet: Cultural diversity: Eating in America-Asian HYG-5253-95-R10.* Retrieved October 31, 2011, from http://ohioline .osu.edu/hyg-fact/5000/pdf/5253.pdf

Hoyland, A., Dye, L., & Lawton, C. L. (2009). A systematic review of the effect of breakfast on the cognitive performance of children and adolescents. *Nutrition Research Reviews, 22*(2), 220–243.

Institute of Medicine. (2008). *Nutrition standards and meal requirements for national school lunch and breakfast programs phase I. Proposed approach for recommending revisions.* Washington, DC: National Academies Press.

Islamic Food and Nutrition Council of America. (2011). *IFANCA: What is halal?* Retrieved October 31, 2011, from http://www.ifanca.org/ halal/

Kleinman, R. K. (Ed.). (2009). *Pediatric nutrition handbook* (6th ed.). Elk Grove Village, IL: American Academy of Pediatrics.

Kulkarni, K. D. (2004). Food, culture, and diabetes in the United States. *Clinical Diabetes, 22*(4), 190–192.

Liu, R. H. (2003). Health benefits of fruit and vegetables are from additive and synergistic combinations of phytochemicals. *The American Journal of Clinical Nutrition, 78*(3), 517S–520S.

Llargues, E., Franco, R., Recasens, A., Nadal, A., Vila, M., Perez, M. J., et al. (2011). Assessment of a school-based intervention in eating habits and physical activity in school children: The AVall study. *Journal of Epidemiology and Community Health, 65*(10), 896–901.

Martinez, S., Hand, M., DePra, M., Pollack, S., Ralston, K., Smith, T., et al. (2010). *Local food systems: Concepts, impacts and issues,* No. 97, U.S. Department of Agriculture Economic Research Service.

Mennella, J. A., Ziegler, P., Briefel, R., & Novak, T. (2006). Feeding infants and toddlers study: The types of foods fed to Hispanic infants and toddlers. *Journal of the American Dietetic Association, 106* (Supplement 1), S96–S106.

Mier, N., Piziak, V., Kjar, D., Castillo-Ruiz, O., Velazquez, G., Alfaro, M. E., et al. (2007). Nutrition provided to Mexican-American preschool children on the Texas-Mexico border. *Journal of the American Dietetic Association, 107*(2), 311–315.

Murphy, S. P., Yaktine, A. L., Suitor, C. W., & Moats, S. (Eds.) (2011). Committee to Review Child and Adult Care Food Program Meal Requirements, Institute of Medicine. *Child and Adult Care Food Program: Aligning dietary guidance for all.* Washington, DC: National Academies Press.

National Association for the Education of Young Children. (2012). *Academy for early childhood program accreditation: Standard 5: NAEYC accreditation criteria for health standard.* Retrieved September 30, 2012, from http://lms.naeyc.org/icohere/custompages/ naeycsearch/search_framer .cfm?t=1319069982686

National Diabetes Education Program. (2011). *Overview of diabetes in children and adolescents* Retrieved February 22, 2012, from http://ndep .nih.gov/media/youth_factsheet.pdf

National Resource Center for Health and Safety in Child Care and Early Education. (2010). *Preventing childhood obesity in early care and education programs*. Retrieved October 1, 2011, from http://nrckids.org/CFOC3/PREVENTING_OBESITY/index.htm

National Resource Center for Health and Safety in Child Care and Early Education, University of Colorado Denver. (2011). *Achieving a state of healthy weight: A national assessment of obesity prevention terminology in child care regulations 2010*. Retrieved October 1, 2011, from http://nrckids.org/regulations_report_2010.pdf

Nemours. (2011). *All about allergies*. Retrieved October 16, 2011, from http://kidshealth.org/parent/medical/allergies/allergy.html

Nevin-Folino, N. L. (2003; updated 2008). *Pediatric manual of clinical dietetics* (2nd ed.). United States of America: American Dietetic Association.

NIAID-sponsored expert panel, Boyce, J. A., Assa'ad, A., Burks, A. W., Jones, S. M., Sampson, H. A., et al. (2010). Guidelines for the diagnosis and management of food allergy in the United States: Report of the NIAID-sponsored expert panel. *Journal of Allergy and Clinical Immunology, 126*(6 Suppl), S1–S58.

Nolan, J. E., & The Ohio State University. (2010). *The Ohio State University fact sheet: Cultural diversity: Eating in America-Middle Eastern HYG-5256-95-R10*. Retrieved October 31, 2011, from http://ohioline.osu.edu/hyg-fact/5000/pdf/5256.pdf

O'Connell, M. L., Henderson, K. E., Luedicke, J., & Schwartz, M. B. (2012). Repeated exposure in a natural setting: A preschool intervention to increase vegetable consumption. *Journal of the Academy of Nutrition and Dietetics, 112*(2), 230–234.

The Ohio State University. (2010). *The Ohio State University fact sheet: Cultural diversity: Eating in America-Mexican American HYG-5255-R10*. Retrieved October 31, 2011, from http://ohioline.osu.edu/hyg-fact/5000/pdf/5255.pdf

Oliveira, P. (2005). *Connecticut child care center operating budget basics: Calculating your bottom line*. Retrieved October 8, 2011, from http://www.ctkidslink.org/publications/ece05operating06.pdf

Rampersaud, G. C. (2008). Benefits of breakfast for children and adolescents: Update and recommendations for practitioners. *American Journal of Lifestyle Medicine, 3*(2), 86.

Samour, P. Q., & King, K. (Eds.) (2012). *Pediatric nutrition* (4th ed.). Sudbury, MA: Jones & Bartlett Learning, LLC.

Satter, E. (2011). *The child who doesn't eat fruits and vegetables*. Retrieved October 2, 2011, from http://www.ellynsatter.com/the-child-who-doesnt-eat-fruits-and-vegetables-i-42.html

Schwartz, C., Chabanet, C., Lange, C., Issanchou, S., & Nicklaus, S. (2011). The role of taste in food acceptance at the beginning of complementary feeding. *Physiology & Behavior, 104*(4), 646–652.

Sizer, F., & Whitney, E. (2011). *Nutrition concepts and controversy* (12th ed.). United States: Wadsworth Cengage Learning.

Skelton, J. A., & Beech, B. M. (2011). Attrition in paediatric weight management: A review of the literature and new directions. *Obesity Reviews, 12*(5), e273–e281.

Stallings, V. A., Suitor, C. W., & Taylor, C. (Eds.). Food and Nutrition Board, Institute of Medicine. (2010). *School meals: Building blocks for healthy children*. Washington, DC: National Academies Press.

United Nations Department of Social and Economic Affairs Division for Sustainable Development. (2009). *UN division for sustainable development—initiative details page*. Retrieved July 6, 2009, from http://webapps01.un.org/dsd/caseStudy/public/displayDetailsAction.do?code=8

U.S. Department of Agriculture. (2009). *Infant nutrition and feeding: A guide for use in the WIC and CSF programs*. Retrieved February 23, 2012, from http://www.nal.usda.gov/wicworks/Topics/FG/CompleteIFG.pdf

U.S. Department of Agriculture. (2010). *Topic: Dietary intake and childhood adiposity*. Retrieved October 30, 2011, from http://www.nel.gov/topic.cfm?cat=3068

U.S. Department of Agriculture. (2011a). *USDA's MyPlate*. Retrieved September 30, 2011, from http://www.choosemyplate.gov/

U.S. Department of Agriculture. (2011b). *Choose MyPlate.gov choking hazards*. Retrieved October 30, 2011, from http://www.choosemyplate.gov/preschoolers/FoodSafety/chokinghazards.html

U.S. Department of Agriculture. (2012). Health and Nutrition Information for preschoolers. Retrieved December 17, 2012, from http://www.choosemyplate.gov/preschoolers.html

U.S. Department of Agriculture, Food and Nutrition Service. (2006). *Healthy school meals resource system: Special diets—vegetarian diets and other variations—Jewish schools and institutions*. Retrieved November 1, 2011, from http://healthymeals.nal.usda.gov/hsmrs/Special_Diets_jewish_for_print.htm

U.S. Department of Agriculture, Food and Nutrition Service. (2011). Nutrition standards in the national school lunch and school breakfast programs. *Federal Register, 76*(9), Retrieved September 12, 2011, from http://www.fns.usda.gov/cnd/governance/regulations/2011-01-13.pdf

U.S. Department of Agriculture, Food and Nutrition Service. (2011a). *CACFP policy memos*. Retrieved September 13, 2011, from http://www.fns.usda.gov/cnd/care/regs-policy/policymemoranda.htm

U.S. Department of Agriculture, Food and Nutrition Service. (2011b). *Child and adult care food program*. Retrieved September 12, 2011, from http://www.fns.usda.gov/cnd/care/cacfp/aboutcacfp.htm

U.S. Department of Agriculture, Food and Nutrition Service. (2011c). *Child nutrition labeling*. Retrieved October 9, 2011, from http://www.fns.usda.gov/cnd/CNlabeling/default.htm

U.S. Department of Agriculture, Food and Nutrition Service. (2011d). *Schools & child nutrition program: Eligibility requirements and how to apply*. Retrieved September 30, 2011, from http://www.fns.usda.gov/fdd/programs/schcnp/schcnp_eligibility.htm

U.S. Department of Agriculture, Food and Nutrition Service. (2012a). *Final rule: Nutrition standards in the national school lunch and school breakfast programs*. Retrieved February 14, 2012, from http://www.fns.usda.gov/cnd/Governance/Legislation/nutritionstandards.htm

U.S. Department of Agriculture, Food and Nutrition Service. (2012b). *National School Lunch Program*. Retrieved September 30, 2012, from http://www.fns.usda.gov/cnd/lunch/

U.S. Department of Agriculture Nutrition Evidence Library. (2010). *Evidence summary: In adults, what is the relationship between the intake of vegetables and fruits, not including juice, and cardiovascular disease?* Retrieved October 1, 2011, from http://www.nel.gov/evidence.cfm?evidence_summary_id=250366&highlight=fruits and vegetables&home=1

U.S. Department of Health and Human Services Food and Nutrition Service, & Administration for Children and Families. (2008). *Head Start program performance standards and other regulations–Head Start*. Retrieved September 30, 2012, from http://eclkc.ohs.acf.hhs.gov/hslc/Head Start Program/Program Design and Management/Head Start Requirements/Head Start Requirements

U.S. Department of Health and Human Services, Administration for Children and Families. (2011). *Administration for children and families*. Retrieved September 29, 2011, from http://www.acf.hhs.gov/index.html

U.S. Department of Health and Human Services, & U.S. Department of Agriculture. (2011). *Dietary Guidelines for Americans, 2010*. Retrieved September 30, 2011, from http://health.gov/dietaryguidelines/2010.asp#overview

U.S. Food and Drug Administration. (2009). *Guidance, compliance & regulatory information: Approaches to establish thresholds for major food allergens and for gluten in food*. Retrieved October 19, 2011, from http://www.fda.gov/Food/LabelingNutrition/FoodAllergensLabeling/GuidanceComplianceRegulatoryInformation/ucm106108.htm#ii

U.S. National Library of Medicine, the National Institutes of Health. (2010). *Allergic reactions: MedlinePlus medical encyclopedia*. Retrieved October 16, 2011, from http://www.nlm.nih.gov/medlineplus/ency/article/000005.htm

Vos, M. B., & Welsh, J. (2010). Childhood obesity: Update on predisposing factors and prevention strategies. *Current Gastroenterology Reports, 12*(4), 280–287.

Wardle, J., & Cooke, L. (2008). Genetic and environmental determinants of children's food preferences. *British Journal of Nutrition, 99 Supplement* 1, S15–S21.

Weight realities division of the Society of Nutrition Education, Center for Weight and Health, U.C. Berkeley. (2003). Guidelines for obesity prevention programs: Promoting healthy weight in children. *Journal of Nutrition Education and Behavior, 35*(1), 1–4.

WIC Works Resource Team. (2010). *WIC works resource system*. Retrieved October 1, 2011, from http://www.nal.usda.gov/wicworks/

Zhang, Y., Fein, E. B., & Fein, S. B. (2011). Feeding of dietary botanical supplements and teas to infants in the United States. *Pediatrics, 127*(6), 1060–1066.

Chapter 7

American Academy of Pediatrics. (2010). Prevention of choking among children. *Pediatrics, 125*(3), 601–607.

American Academy of Pediatrics. (2011). *Storing and preparing expressed breast milk.* Retrieved January 27, 2012, from http://www .healthychildren.org/English/ages-stages/baby/ breastfeeding/pages/Storing-and-Preparing-Expressed-Breast-Milk.aspx

American Academy of Pediatrics. (2012). *Health issues: Choking prevention.* Retrieved January 28, 2012, from http://www.healthychildren.org/ English/health-issues/injuries-emergencies/ pages/Choking-Prevention.aspx

American Academy of Pediatrics, American Public Health Association, National Resource Center for Health and Safety in Child Care and Early Education. (2011). *Caring for our children: National health and safety performance standards; guidelines for early care and education programs* (3rd ed.). Elk Grove Village, IL: American Academy of Pediatrics.

American Red Cross. (2012). *Be red cross ready— get a kit, make a plan, be informed.* Retrieved January 30, 2012, from www.redcross.org/www-files/Documents/pdf/Preparedness/ checklists/Be_Red_Cross_Ready.pdf

B.C. First Nations Head Start. (2003). *B.C. First Nations Head Start using traditional foods.* Retrieved January 29, 2012, from http://www .bcfnhs.org/downloads/sixComponents/culture/ CULT_Traditional_Foods.pdf

Brown, A. L. (2011). *Understanding food: Principles and preparation* (4th ed.). Belmont, CA: Wadsworth Cengage Learning.

Buchholz, U., Bernard, H., Werber, D., Böhmer, M. M., Remschmidt, C., Wilking, H., et al. (2011). German outbreak of Escherichia coli O104:H4 associated with sprouts. *New England Journal of Medicine, 365*(19), 1763–1770.

Centers for Disease Control and Prevention. (2008). Preliminary FoodNet data on the incidence of infection with pathogens transmitted commonly through food—10 states, 2007. *Morbidity and Mortality Weekly Report, 57*(14), July 24, 2008.

Centers for Disease Control and Prevention. (2010). *Norovirus: Technical fact sheet.* Retrieved December 5, 2011, from http://www.cdc.gov/ ncidod/dvrd/revb/gastro/norovirus-factsheet .htm.

Centers for Disease Control and Prevention. (2011a). *CDC—foodborne outbreak investigations–key players in foodborne outbreak response.* Retrieved December 26, 2011, from http:// www.cdc.gov/outbreaknet/investigations/ key_players.html

Centers for Disease Control and Prevention. (2011b). *Prevention–listeriosis.* Retrieved January 29, 2012, from http://www.cdc.gov/ listeria/prevention.html

Centers for Disease Control and Prevention. (2011c). Vital signs: Incidence and trends of infection with pathogens transmitted commonly through food—foodborne diseases active surveillance network, 10 U.S. sites, 1996–2010. *Morbidity and Mortality Weekly Report, 60*(22).

Centers for Disease Control and Prevention (2012a). *E. coli.* Retrieved October 8 2012, from http://www.cdc.gov/ecoli/outbreaks.html

Centers for Disease Control and Prevention. (2012bd). *Food safety at CDC: Questions and answers about foodborne illness (sometimes called "Food poisoning").* Retrieved October 8, 2012, from http://www.cdc.gov/foodsafety/ facts.html#howmanycases

Colorado State University Extension. (2006). *Sushi: Minimizing the food safety risk.* Retrieved February 5, 2012, from http://www.ext.colostate .edu/safefood/newsltr/v10n3s01.html

Environmental Services Department, Maricopa County Arizona. (2011). *Food safety manual for the food service worker.* Retrieved November 28, 2011, from http://www.maricopa.gov/envsvc/ envhealth/Pdf/Engbook.pdf

Federal Emergency Management Agency. (2012). *Build a kit.* Retrieved January 30, 2012, from http://www.ready.gov/.htm

Food Safe Schools. (2004). *Food safety for the local health department.* Retrieved December 4, 2011, from http://www.foodsafeschools.org/ healthdepartment.php

Garden-Robinson, J. (2012). *Food safety basics: A reference guide for foodservice operators– FN572: NDSU.* Retrieved January 23, 2012, from http://www.ag.ndsu.edu/extension/ pubs/landing-pages/food-and-nutrition/ food-safety-basics-fn572

Goodrich, R. M., Schneider, K. R., Schmidt, R. H. & University of Florida, IFAS Extension. (2008). *HACCP: An overview.* Retrieved December 9, 2011, from http://edis.ifas.ufl.edu/fs122

Hunting, K. L., & Gleason, B. L. (2012). *Essential case studies in public health, putting public health into practice.* Burlington, MA: Jones & Bartlett Learning.

Iowa State University Extension. (2009). *HACCP in schools.* Retrieved December 8, 2011, from http://www.extension.iastate.edu/HRIM/ HACCP/haccpinschools.htm

Iowa State University Extension. (2010). *School foodservice standard operating procedures.* Retrieved December 13, 2011, from http:// www.extension.iastate.edu/HRIM/HACCP/ schoolfoodservice.htm

Jones, T. F., Ingram, L. A., Fullerton, K. E., Marcus, R., Anderson, B. J., McCarthy, P. V., et al. (2007). A case-control study of the epidemiology of sporadic salmonella infection in infants. *Pediatrics, 118*(6), 23–80.

Kids Health: The Nemours Foundation. (2012). *Food safety for your family.* Retrieved January 8, 2012, from http://kidshealth.org/parent/firstaid_ safe/home/food_safety.html#

Krueger, L. (2008). *Working together to accommodate children with special needs.* Retrieved January 29, 2012, from dpi.wi.gov/fns/ppt/ ms_sdn_2.pp

Marriott, N. G., & Gravani, R. B. (2006). *Principles of food sanitation* (5th ed.). New York: Springer Science+Business, Media, Inc.

Mayo Clinic. (2010). *Food-borne illness: First aid.* Retrieved November 20, 2011, from http://www.mayoclinic.com/health/ first-aid-food-borne-illness/FA00043

McSwane, D., Rue, N. R., & Linton, R. (2005). *Essentials of food safety and sanitation* (4th ed.). Upper Saddle River, NJ: Pearson.

National Association for the Education of Young Children. (2012). *Standard 5: NAEYC accreditation criteria for health standard.* Retrieved December 16, 2012, from http:// www.naeyc.org/files/academy/file/AllCriteria Document.pdf

National Food Service Management Institute. (2005). *Food safety standard operating procedures (SOPs).* Retrieved January 22, 2012, from http://www.nfsmi.org/documentlibraryfiles/ PDF/20080213012315.pdf

National Food Service Management Institute. (2009). *Food safety fact sheet: Thawing foods.* Retrieved January 23, 2012, from http://www .nfsmi.org/DocumentSearch.aspx?q=thawing food

National Restaurant Association. (2010). *Servsafe coursebook* (5th ed.). Chicago, IL: National Restaurant Association Educational Foundation.

Nevada Department of Education. (2010). *Child nutrition and school health CACFP guide for registered food vendors.* Retrieved January 8, 2012, from http://www.doe.nv.gov/CACFP.htm

New York State Department of Health. (2006). *Food defense strategies—A self-assessment guide for food service operators.* Retrieved February 1, 2012, from http://www.health.state.ny.us/ environmental/indoors/food_safety/food_ defense_strategies.htm

Orange County North Carolina. *Environmental health inspection services FAQ.* Retrieved December 26, 2011, from http://www.co.orange.nc.us/envhlth/ inspections/InspectionServicesFAQ.asp

Pelton, S. I. (2011). *Watch for foodborne illness. Pediatric News, 45*(7), 4–5.

Riggins, L. D., & Barrett, B. (2008). Benefits and barriers to following HACCP-based food safety programs in childcare centers. *Food Protection Trends, 28*(1), 12/10/11-37-44.

Safe minimum cooking temperatures FoodSafety.gov. Retrieved January 4, 2012, from http://www .foodsafety.gov/keep/charts/mintemp.html

Savolainen-Kopra, C., Haapakoski, J., Peltola, P. A., Ziegler, T., Korpela, T., Anttila, P., et al. (2012). Hand washing with soap and water together with behavioral recommendation prevents infection in common work environment: An open cluster-randomized trial. *Trials, 13*(1).

Schmidt, R. H., & Newslow, D. L. (2009). *Hazard analysis critical control points (HACCP)— principle 3: Establish critical limits and principle 4: Monitoring critical control points (CCPs).* Retrieved December 13, 2011, from http://edis .ifas.ufl.edu/FS141

Talaat, M., Afifi, S., Dueger, E., El-Ashry, N., Martin, A., Kandeel, A., et al. (2011). Effects of hand hygiene campaigns on incidence of laboratory-confirmed influenza and absenteeism in schoolchildren, Cairo, Eygpt. *Emerging Infectious Disease Journal, 17*(4), 619–625.

U.S. Department of Agriculture, Food and Nutrition Service. (2009a). Rules and regulations: School food safety inspections. *Federal Register, 74*(169).

U.S. Department of Agriculture Food and Nutrition Service. (2009b). *USDA recipes for child care.* Retrieved December 13, 2011, from http://www.fns.usda.gov/tn/Resources/childcare_recipes.html

U.S. Department of Agriculture Food Safety and Inspection Service. (2011). *Fact sheet: Cleanliness helps prevent foodborne illness.* Retrieved December 31, 2011, from http://www.fsis.usda.gov/factsheets/Cleanliness_Helps_Prevent_Foodborne_Illness/index.asp

U.S. Department of Agriculture Food Safety and Inspection Service. (2011a). *About FSIS: Agency history.* Retrieved December 8, 2011, from http://www.fsis.usda.gov/About_FSIS/Agency_History/index.asp#1953

U.S. Department of Agriculture Food Safety and Inspection Service. (2011b). *Fact sheet on clostridium botulinum.* Retrieved November 30, 2011, from http://www.fsis.usda.gov/factsheets/Clostridium_botulinum/index.asp

U.S. Department of Agriculture Food Safety and Inspection Service. (2011d). *Fact sheet: Safe food handling.* Retrieved January 8, 2012, from http://www.fsis.usda.gov/Fact_Sheets/Danger_Zone/index.asp

U.S. Department of Agriculture Food Safety and Inspection Service. (2011e). *Is it done yet? recommended internal temperatures.* Retrieved January 24, 2012, from http://www.fsis.usda.gov/is_it_done_yet/brochure_text/index.asp#SMIT

U.S. Department of Health and Human Services. (2011). *What does the new food safety law mean for you?* Retrieved December 3, 2011, from http://www.foodsafety.gov/blog/fsma.html

U.S. Department of Health and Human Services, Food and Drug Administration. (2011). *Federal Register, 76*(149). Retrieved December 3, 2011, from http://www.gpo.gov/fdsys/pkg/FR-2011-08-03/pdf/2011-19620.pdf

U.S. Department of Health and Human Services Food and Drug Administration Center for Food Safety and Applied Nutrition. (2006). *A manual for the voluntary use of HACCP principles for operators of food service and retail establishments. Chapter 2—the process approach for managing food safety.* Retrieved December 31, 2011, from http://www.fda.gov/Food/FoodSafety/RetailFoodProtection/ManagingFoodSafetyHACCPPrinciples/Operators/ucm077998.htm#diagram

U.S. Department of Health and Human Services U.S. Food and Drug Administration. (2011). *Consumer updates: Food bill aims to improve safety.* Retrieved December 3, 2011, from http://www.fda.gov/ForConsumers/ConsumerUpdates/ucm237758.htm

U.S. Department of Health and Human Services, Public Health Service, U.S. Food and Drug Administration. (2011). *Food code 2009.* Retrieved December 13, 2011, from http://www.fda.gov/Food/FoodSafety/RetailFoodProtection/FoodCode/FoodCode2009/ucm186451.htm#part3-5

U.S. Department of Homeland Security. (2010). *FEMA: Food.* Retrieved February 2, 2012, from http://www.fema.gov/plan/prepare/food.shtm

U.S. Environmental Protection Agency. (2011a). *The EPA and food security: Pesticides.* Retrieved December 28, 2011, from http://www.epa.gov/pesticides/factsheets/securty.htm

U.S. Environmental Protection Agency. (2011b). *Food irradiation, radiation protection.* Retrieved December 1, 2011, from http://www.epa.gov/radiation/sources/food_irrad.html

U.S. Environmental Protection Agency. (2011c). *Food safety.* Retrieved December 1, 2011, from http://epa.gov/radiation/sources/food_safety.html

U.S. Food and Drug Administration. (2008). *FDA updates health information advisory on melamine contamination.* Retrieved February 5, 2012, from http://www.fda.gov/NewsEvents/Newsroom/PressAnnouncements/2008/ucm116955.htm

U.S. Food and Drug Administration. (2010). *Retail food risk factor studies: FDA trend analysis report on the occurrence of foodborne illness risk factors in selected institutional foodservice, restaurant, and retail food store facility types (1998–2008).* Retrieved January 1, 2012, from http://www.fda.gov/Food/FoodSafety/RetailFoodProtection/FoodborneIllnessandRiskFactorReduction/RetailFoodRiskFactorStudies/ucm223293.htm#executive_summary

U.S. Food and Drug Administration. (2011a). *Food defense and emergency response: Guidance for industry, retail food stores and food service establishments: Food security preventive measures guidance.* Retrieved January 30, 2012, from http://www.fda.gov/Food/GuidanceComplianceRegulatoryInformation/GuidanceDocuments/FoodDefenseandEmergencyResponse/ucm082751.htm

U.S. Food and Drug Administration. (2011b). *Hazard analysis and critical control point principles and application guidelines.* Retrieved December 11, 2011, from http://www.fda.gov/Food/FoodSafety/HazardAnalysisCriticalControlPointsHACCP/HACCPPrinciplesApplicationGuidelines/default.htm#execsum

U.S. Food and Drug Administration. (2011c). *Once baby arrives: Food safety for mothers to be.* Retrieved January 27, 2012, from http://www.fda.gov/food/resourcesforyou/healtheducators/ucm089629.htm

U.S. Food and Drug Administration. (2012a). *Consumers: Food allergies: What you need to know.* Retrieved October 8, 2012, from http://www.fda.gov/food/resourcesforyou/consumers/ucm079311.htm

U.S. Food and Drug Administration. (2012b). *FDA food code.* Retrieved December 16, 2012, from http://www.fda.gov/Food/FoodSafety/RetailFoodProtection/FoodCode/default.htm

U.S. Food and Drug Administration, Center for Food Safety and Nutrition. (2008). *Bad bug book: Introduction to foodborne pathogenic microorganisms and natural toxins.* Retrieved February 5, 2012, from http://www.cfsan.fda.gov/~mow/intro.html

Wallace, C. A., Sperber, W. H., & Mortimore, S. E. (2010). *Food safety for the 21st century: Managing HACCP and food safety throughout the global supply chain.* United Kingdom: Wiley-Blackwell.

Washington State Department of Health. (2011). *BE AWARE these foods may cause choking in toddlers—health education resource exchange (H.E.R.E.).* Retrieved January 29, 2012, from http://here.doh.wa.gov/materials/be-aware-these-foods-may-cause-choking-in-toddlers

Wisconsin Department of Public Instruction. (2011). *Materials & resources for the national school lunch program: Guidelines for contracting vended meals.* Retrieved January 7, 2012, from http://dpi.wi.gov/fns/market1.html

Zhang, X., Bai, J., Ma, P., Ma, J., Wan, J., & Jiang, B. (2010). Melamine-induced infant urinary calculi: A report on 24 cases and a 1-year follow-up. *Urological Research, 38*(5), 391–395.

Chapter 8

American Academy of Pediatrics, American Public Health Association, National Resource Center for Health and Safety in Child Care and Early Education. (2011). *Caring for our children: National health and safety performance standards: Guidelines for out-of-home childcare programs* (3rd ed.). Elk Grove Village: American Academy of Pediatrics.

Bershad, C., & Blaber, C. (2011). *Realizing the promise of the whole-school approach to children's mental health. A practical guide for schools.* National Center for Mental Health Promotion and Youth Violence Prevention. Education Development Center.

Bright Futures at Georgetown University. (n.d.). *Bright futures.* Retrieved September 20, 2011, from http://www.brightfutures.org/physicalactivity/frontmatter/index.html

Bronfenbrenner, U. (1979). *The ecology of human development: Experiments by nature and design.* Cambridge, MA: Harvard University Press.

Burgden, E., Martinez, A., Greene, B., & Eig, K. (2011). *Safe at school and ready to learn: A comprehensive policy guide for protecting students with life-threatening food allergies.* National School Board Association.

Centers for Disease Control and Prevention. (2011, September 15). *Healthy youth! Nutrition, physical activity, and childhood obesity; Local wellness policy tools and resources.* Retrieved Septmber 30, 2011, from http://www.cdc.gov/HealthyYouth/healthtopics/wellness.htm

Connecticut State Department of Education. (2010). *ACTION GUIDE for child care nutrition and physical activity policies best practices for creating a healthy child care environment.*

Cutts, D., Meyers, A., Black, M., Casey, P. C., Cook, J., & Geppert, J. (2011, August). U.S. housing insecurity and the health of very young children. *American Journal of Public Health, 101*(8), 1508–1514.

Dowda, M. E. (2009). Policies and characteristics of the preschool environment and physical activity of young children. *Pediatrics, 123,* e123–e266.

Gubbels, J., Kremers, S., van Kann, D., & Stafleu, A. (2011). Interaction between physical environment, social environment, and child characteristics in determining physical activity at child care. *Health Psychology, 30*(1), 84–90.

Institute of Medicine. (2003). *Crossing the quality chasm: A new health system for the 21st century.* Washington, DC.

Lapin, B., & Smith, J. (2008). *Dental care: The often neglected part of health care.* School of the 21st Century; Yale University.

Marrs, J.-A., Trumbley, S., & Malik, G. (2011, January–February). Early childhood caries: Determining the risk factors and assessing the prevention strategies for nursing intervention. *Pediatric Nursing, 37*(1), 9–16.

Seith, D., & Isakson, E. (2011). *Who are America's poor children? Examining health disparities among children in the United States.* National Center for Child Poverty.

Seith, D., & Kalof, C. (2011). *Who are America's poor children? Examining health disparities by race and ethnicity.* National Center for Child Poverty.

Spector, R. (2009). *Cultural diversity in health and illness.* Upper Saddle River, NJ: Pearson.

Sun, Y., & Sundell, J. (2011, Oct). Early daycare attendance increases the risk for respiratory infections and asthma in children. *Journal of Asthma, 48*(8), 790–796.

Trost, S., Ward, D., & Senso, M. (2010, March). Effects of child care policy and environment on physical activity. *Medicine and Science in Sports and Exercise, 42*(3), 520–525.

U.S. Department of Health and Human Services. (2009). *Head Start program performance standards.* Retrieved September 30, 2011, from http://eclkc.ohs.acf.hhs.gov/hslc/resources/ECLKC_Bookstore/Chapter XIII Performance Standards without Guidance.html

World Health Organization. (1948). *Preamble to the Constitution of the World Health Organziation as adopted by the International Health Conference, New York, 19 June–22 July 1946 by the representatives of 61 states (Official records of the World Health Organization, no. 2, p. 100) and entered into force on 7 April 1948.*

World Health Organization. (2011). *Health impact assessment.* Retrieved September 30, 2011, from World Health Organization: http://www.who.int/hia/evidence/doh/en/index4.html

Chapter 9

American Academy of Pediatrics. (2009). *Red Book 2009. Report of the Committee on Infectious Diseases.* In L. Pickering, C. Baker, D. Kimberlin, & S. Long (Eds.). Elk Grove Village, IL.

American Academy of Pediatrics. (n.d.). *National Center for Medical Home Implementation.* Retrieved December 10, 2011, from http://www.medicalhomeinfo.org

American Academy of Pediatrics, American Public Health Association, National Resource Center for Health and Safety in Child Care and Early Education. (2011). *Caring for our children: National health and safety performance standards: Guidelines for out-of-home childcare programs* (3rd ed). Elk Grove Village: American Academy of Pediatrics.

American Dental Association. (2011). *Give kids a smile.* Retrieved December 16, 2011, from http://www.ada.org/givekidsasmile.aspx

Basch, C. (2011, October). Vision and the achievement gap among urban minority youth. *Journal of School Health, 81*(10), 599–605.

Batis, C., Hernandez-Barrera, L., Barquera, L., Rivera, J., & Popkin, B. (2011). Food acculturation drives dietary differences among Mexicans, Mexican Americans, and non-Hispanic whites. *Journal of Nutrition, 141*(10), 1898–1906.

Borse, N., Gilchrist, J., Dellinger, A., Rudd, R., Ballestros, M., & Sleet, D. (2008). *CDC childhood injury report: Patterns of unintentional injuries among 0–19 year olds in the US, 2000–2006.* CDC National Center for Injury Prevention and Control, Atlanta.

Centers for Disease Control and Prevention. (2009). *Toy.* Retrieved December 17, 2011, from http://www.cdc.gov/nceh/lead/tips.toys.htm

Centers for Disease Control and Prevention. (2010). Use of World Health Organization and CDC growth charts for children ages 0–59 months in the United States. *MMWR, 59*(RR-9), 1–13.

Centers for Disease Control and Prevention. (2011). *Epidemiology and prevention of vaccine-preventable diseases* (12th ed.). Washington DC: Public Health Foundation.

Child and Adolescent Health Measurement Initiative. (2007). *2007 National Survey of Children's Health, data resource center for child and adolescent health.* Retrieved December 15, 2011, from http://www.nschdata.org

Dave, J., Evans, A., Saunders, R., Watkins, K., & Pfeiffer, K. (2009, April). Associations among food insecurity, acculturation, demographic factors, and fruit and vegetable intake at home in Hispanic children. *Journal of the American Dietetic Association, 109*(4), 697–701.

Early Head Start National Resource Center. (2009). *Developmental screening, assessment, and evaluation: Key elements for individualized curricula in early Head Start programs.* Technical Assistance Paper No. 4.

Heward, W. (2013). *Exceptional children: An introduction to special education* (10th ed.). Upper Saddle River, NJ: Pearson.

Kaczmarski, J., DeBate, R., Marhefka, S., & Dale, E. (2011). State-mandated school-based BMI screening and parent notification: A descriptive case study. *Health Promotion Practice, 12*, 797–801.

Kentucky Cabinet for Health and Family Services. (2011, June 21). *The Health Insurance Portability Act of 1996.* Retrieved November 30, 2011, from http://chfs.ky.gov/dcbs/dcc/hipaa/htm

Melchior, M. E. (2011). Maternal depression, socioeconomic position, and temperament in early childhood: The EDEN mother-child cohort. *Journal of Affective Disorders, 137*(1–3), 165–169.

National Conference of State Legislatures. (2011, December 10). *States with religious and philosophical exemptions from school immunization requirements.* Retrieved from http://www.ncsl.org/programs/health/SchoolExempLawsChart.htm

Omer, S., Salmon, D., Orenstein, W., deHart, M., & Halsey, N. (2009, May 7). Vaccine refusal, mandatory immunization and the risks of vaccine-preventable diseases. *New England Journal of Medicine, 360*(19), 1981–1988.

Prevent Blindness America. (2011). *Signs of possible eye problems in children.* Retrieved December 13, 2011, from http://preventblindness.org/children/trouble_signs.html

Russ, S., White, K., Dougherty, D., & Forsman, I. (2010). Preface: Newborn hearing screening in the United States: Historical perspective and future directions. *Pediatrics, 126*, S3–S6.

Shelov, S., & Remer, T. (2009). Caring for your baby and young child: Birth to Age 5. Fifth Edition. *American Academy of Pediatrics.* Elk Grove Village, IL.

Thomas, A., & Chess, S. (1977). *Temperament and development.* New York: Brunner-Mazel.

Warniment, C., Tsang, K., & Galazka, S. (2010). Lead poisoning in children. *American Family Physician, 81*(6), 751–757.

Chapter 10

American Academy of Pediatrics. (2012). *Red Book 2009 Report of the Committee on Infectious Diseases.* In L. Pickering, C. Baker, D. Kimberlin, & S. Long (Eds.). Elk Grove Village, IL.

American Academy of Pediatrics, American Public Health Association, National Resource Center for Health and Safety in Child Care and Early Education. (2011). *Caring for our children: National health and safety performance standards: Guidelines for out-of-home childcare programs* (3rd ed). Elk Grove Village: American Academy of Pediatrics.

Ball, J., Bindler, R., & Cowen, K. (2012). Chapter 19: Infectious and communicable diseases. In J. Ball, & R. Bindler, *Child health nursing: Partnering with children and families* (5th ed., pp. 574–586). Upper Saddle River, NJ: Pearson.

Ben-Arye, E., Traube, Z., Schachter, L., Haimi, M., Levy, M., Schiff, E., et al. (2011, January). Integrative pediatric care: Parents' attitudes toward communication of physicians and CAM practitioners. *Pediatrics, 127*(1), e84–e95.

Bozzetoo, S., Carraro, S., Giordano, G., Boner, A., & Baraldi, E. (2012). Asthma, allergy and respiratory infections: The vitamin D hypothesis. *Allergy*, 10–17.

Centers for Disease Control and Prevention. (2010, August 9). *Personal prevention of MRSA skin infections.* Retrieved January 24, 2012, from http://www.cdc.gov/mrsa/prevent/personal.html

Centers for Disease Control and Prevention. (2010). *CDC health information for international travel 2010.* Atlanta: U.S. Department of Health and Human Services, Public Health Service.

Centers for Disease Control and Prevention. (2011). *Epidemiology and prevention of vaccine-preventable diseases.* Washington DC: Public Health Foundation.

Frankowski, B., & Bocchini, J. (2010, August). Clinical Report–Head Lice. *Pediatrics, 126*(2).

La Crosse County Environmental Health. (n.d.). *Hand washing*. Retrieved June 3, 2012, from http://www.co.la-crosse.wi.us/health/environmental/docs/handwsh.htm

Pappas, D., & Hendley, J. (2012, January). *Patient information: The common cold in children*. Retrieved January 24, 2012, from http://www.uptodate.com/contents/patient-information-the-common-cold-in-children

Sweet, K., Sutherland, W., Ehresmann, K., & Lynfield, R. (2011, August 1). Hepatitis A infection in recent international adoptees and their contacts in Minnesota, 2007–2009. *Pediatrics, 128*(2), e333–e338.

Chapter 11

American Academy of Pediatrics, American Public Health Association, National Resource Center for Health and Safety in Child Care and Early Education. (2011). *Caring for our children: National health and safety performance standards: Guidelines for out-of-home childcare programs* (3rd ed). Elk Grove Village: American Academy of Pediatrics.

American Diabetes Association. (2012, January). Diabetes care in the school and day care setting. *Diabetes Care, 35*(Supplement), S76–S80.

American Speech-Language Hearing Association. (n.d.). *Early hearing detection & intervention action center*. Retrieved April 10, 2012, from http://www.asha.org/advocacy/federal/ehdi

Ball, J., Bindler, R., & Cowen, K. (2012). Chapter 20. Alterations in respiratory function. In *Principles of pediatric nursing* (5th ed., pp. 574–586). Upper Saddle River, NJ: Pearson.

Bugis, B. (2012). Early childhood caries and the impact of current U.S. Medicaid program: An overview. *International Journal of Dentistry*, 1–7.

California Dental Association. (2011, Oct). Advancing the practice of dental disease management. *California Dental Association Journal, 39*(10), 679–766.

Centers for Disease Control. (2012, March 13). *Asthma and schools*. Retrieved April 1, 2012, from http://www.cdc.gov/HealthyYouth/asthma

Council on School Health. (2008). Role of the school nurse in providing school health services. *Pediatrics, 121*(5), 1052–1056.

Division for Early Childhood & National Association for the Education of Young Children. (2009, April). *Early childhood inclusion*. Retrieved March 15, 2012, from www.naeyc.org/files/naeyc/file/positions/DEC_NAEYC_EC_updatedKS.pdf

Environmental Protection Agency. (2010). *Managing asthma in the school environment*.

Floet, A., Scheiner, C., & Grossman, L. (2010). Attention-Deficit/Hyperactivity Disorder. *Pediatrics in Review, 31*, 56–69.

Forrest, C., Bevans, K., Riley, A., Crespo, R., & Louis, T. (2011, August). School outcomes of children with special health care needs. *Pediatrics, 128*(2), 303–312.

Healthy People 2020. (2012, May 18). *HealthPeople.gov educational and community-based programs*. Retrieved June 6, 2012, from http://healthypeople.gov/2020/topicsobjectives2020/objectiveslist.aspx?topicid=11

Heward, W. (2013). *Exceptional children: An introduction to special education*. Upper Saddle River, NJ: Pearson.

Kawashita, K. S. (2011, July). Early childhood caries. *International Journal of Dentistry, 11*, 1–7.

Kramer, M. (2012, December 21). Breastfeeding and allergy: The Evidence. *Annals Nutrition Metabolism, 59*(Suppl 1), 20–26.

Kuo, D., Cohen, E., Agrawal, R., Barry, J., & Casey, P. (2011). A national profile of caregiver challenges among more medically complex children with special health care needs. *Archives of Pediatric and Adolescent Medicine, 165*(11), 1020–1026.

Lindley, L., & Mark, B. (2010, February). Children with special health needs: Impact of health care expenditures on family financial burden. *Journal of Child and Family Studies, 19*(1), 79–89.

Lollar, D., Hartzell, M., & Evans, M. (2012, February). Functional difficulties and health conditions among CSHCN. *Pediatrics*, e714–e722.

Milgrom, H., & Leung, D. (2011). Chapter 137. Allergic rhinitis. In R. Kliegman, B. Stanton, J. Geme, & R. Behrman, *Kliegman: Nelson textbook of pediatrics* (pp. 775–777). Philadelphia, PA: Elsevier Saunders.

National Center for Child Poverty. (2011). *Who are America's poor children? Examining health disparities by race and ethnicity*.

Oswald, D., Bodurtha, J. W., Gilles, D., Christon, L., & Ogston, P. (2011). Disparities in the clinical encounter. Virginia's African American children with special health care needs. *ISRN Pediatrics*, 1–8.

Paintner, A., Williams, A., & Burd, L. (2012, January). Fetal alcohol spectrum disorders–Implications for child neurology. Part 2: Diagnosis and management. *Journal of Child Neurology*, 1–8.

Parish, S., Rose, R., Dababnah, S., Yoo, J., & Cassiman, S. (2012). State-level income inequality and family burden of US families raising children with special health care needs. *Social Science & Medicine, 74*, 399–407.

Schwartz, I., Billingsley, F., & McBride, B. (n.d.). *Including children with autism in inclusive preschools: Strategies that work*. Retrieved April 3, 2012, from http://www.newhorizons.org/spneeds/inclusion/information/schwartz2.htm

Shah, S., Kublaoui, J., & White, P. (2009). Screening for type 2 diabetes in obese youth. *Pediatrics, 124*(2), 573–579.

Silvers, L., Frampton, C., Wickens, K., Pattemore, P., Ingham, T., Fishwick, D., et al. (2012). Breastfeeding protects against current asthma up to 6 years of age. *Journal of Pediatrics, 160*(6), 991–996.

Strickland, B., van Dyck, P., Kogan, M., Lauver, C., Blumber, S., & Bethell, C. (2011, Feb). Assuring and ensuring comprehensive system of services for children with special health care needs: A public health approach. *American Journal of Public Health, 101*(2), 224–231.

Turnbull, A., Turnbull, R., Wehmeyer, M., & Shogren, K. (2013). Chapter 8. Understanding students with attention-deficit/hyperactivity disorder. In *Exceptional lives: Special education in today's schools* (pp. 172–193). Upper Saddle River, NJ: Pearson.

U.S. Department of Education. (n.d.). *Building the legacy: IDEA 2004*. Retrieved March 15, 2012, from http://idea.ed.gov/explore/home

U.S. Department of Health and Human Services. (2012, March 22). *Healthy People 2020*. Retrieved March 27, 2012, from http://www.healthypeople.gov/2020/topicsobjectives2020/objectiveslist.aspx?topicid=26

U.S. Department of Health and Human Services, Health Resources and Services Administration, Maternal and Child Health Bureau. (2008). *The national survey of children with special health care needs. Chartbook 2005–2006*. Retrieved March 15, 2012, from http://mchb.hrsa.gov/cshcn05

Wankoff, L. (2011, August). Warning signs in the development of speech, language, and Communication: When to refer to a speech-language pathologist. *Journal of Child and Adolescent Psychiatric Nursing, 24*(3), 175–184.

Chapter 12

American Academy of Pediatrics. (2009). *Caring for your baby and young child birth to age 5* (5th ed.). (S. Shelov, & T. Remer Altmann, Eds.). Bantam Books.

Ball, J., Bindler, R., & Cowen, K. (2013). Child health nursing partnering with children and families. In *Child Health Nursing Partnering with Children and Families* (pp. 1415–1417). Upper Saddle River: Pearson.

Bershad, C., & Blaber, C. (2011). *Realizing the promise of the whole-school approach to children's mental health. A practical guide for schools*. National Center for Mental Health Promotion and Youth Violence Prevention. Education Development Center.

Biringen, A., Altenhofen, S., Aberle, J., Baker, M., Brosal, A., Bennett, S., et al. (2012). Emotional availability, attachment, and intervention in center-based child care for infants and toddlers. *Development and Psychopathology, 24*, 23–34.

Bowlby, J. (1969). *Attachment and loss: Volume 1: Attachment*. New York: Basic Books.

Brennan, E., Bradley, J., Ama, S., & Cawood, N. (2003). *Setting the pace: Model inclusive child care centers serving families of children with emotional and behavioral challenges*. Portland, OR: Portland State University, Research and Training Center on Family Support and Children's Mental Health.

Center on the Developing Child at Harvard University. (2010). *The foundations of lifelong health are built in early childhood*. Retrieved from http://developingchild.harvard.edu/index.php/resources/reports_and_working_papers/foundations-of-lifelong-health/

Committee on the Rights of the Child. (1991). *Official Records of the General Assembly, Forty-Seventh Session, Supplement No. 41*. Retrieved

May 4, 2012, from http://www.ohchr.org/Documents/Publications/FactSheet10Rev.1en.pdf

Egertson, H. (2006). In praise of butterflies: Linking self-esteem and learning. *Young Children, 61*(6), 58–60.

Engelbright Fox, J. (n.d.). *Early childhood news.* Retrieved May 10, 2012, from http://earlychildhoodnews.com/earlychildhood/article_view.asp?x.ArticleID=240

Ewing Marion Kauffman Foundation. (2002). *Set for success: Building a strong foundation for school readiness based on the social-emotional development of young children.* Kansas City, MO: Kauffman Early Education Exchange.

Fox, L., & Duda, M. (2008). *What are kids trying to tell us?* Retrieved May 10, 2012, from http://csefel.vanderbilt.edu/resources/training_kits.html

Heller, S., Boothe, A., Keyes, A., Nagle, G., Sidell, M., & Rice, J. (2011). Implementation of a mental health consultation model and its impact on early childhood teachers' efficacy and competency. *Infant Mental Health Journal, 32*(2), 143–164.

Homer, R., Albin, R., Sprague, W., & Storey, J. N. (n.d.). *Functional assessment and program development for problem behavior.* Retrieved May 10, 2012, from www.vanderbilt.edu/csefel/modules-archive/module3a/handouts/4.html

Hyson, M., & Taylor, J. (2011, July). Caring about caring: What adults can do to promote young children's prosocial skills. *Young Children.* 74–83.

Kendziora, K., Weissberg, R., Ji, P., & Dusenbury, L. (2011). *Strategies for social and emotional learning: Preschool and elementary grade student learning standards and assessment.* Newton, MA: National Center for Mental Health Promotion and Youth Violence Prevention, Education Development Center.

Kruizinga, I., Jansen, W., Carter, A., & Raat, H. (2011). Evaluation of an early detection tool for social-emotional and behavioral problems in toddlers: The brief Infant Toddler Social and Emotional Assessment—A cluster randomized trial. *BMC Public Health, 11*(494), 1–6.

Milteer, R., Ginsburg, K., Council on Communications and Media Committee on Psychosocial Aspects of Child and Family Health, & Mulligan, D. (2012). The importance of play in promoting healthy child development and maintaining strong parent-child bond: Focus on children in poverty. *Pediatrics, 129,* e204–e213.

National Institute of Mental Health. (2009, April 7). *Bipolar Disorder in Children and Teens: A Parent's Guide.* Retrieved January 11, 2013, from www.nimh.nih.gov/health/publications/bipolar-disorder-in-children-and-teens.shtml

Prager, L. (June 2009). Depression and suicide in children and adolescents. *Pediatrics in Review.* Vol. 30. No. 6. 199–206.

Quach, J., Hisock, H., Ukoumunne, O. C., & Wake, M. (2011, Oct). A brief sleep intervention improves outcomes in the school entry year: a randomized controlled trial. *Pediatrics, 128*(4): 692–701.

Sawyer, M. G., Harchak, T., Wake, M., & Lynch, J. (2011, Oct) Four-year prospective study of BMI

and mental health problems in young children. *Pediatrics, 128*(4): 677–84.

Shonkoff, J., & Garner, A. (2012, Jan). The lifelong effects of early childhood adversity and toxic stress. *Pediatrics, 129*(1), e232–e246.

Smith, S., Stagman, S., Blank, S., Ong, C., & McDow, K. (2011). *Building strong systems of support for young children's mental health.* New York: National Center for Children in Poverty.

Spenrath, M., Clarke, M., & Kutcher, S. (2011, November). The science of brain and biological development: Implications for mental health research, practice and policy. *Journal of the Canadian Academy of Child and Adolescent Psychiatry, 20*(4), 298–304.

Stagman, S., & Cooper, J. (2010). *Children's mental health; What every policymaker should know.* New York: National Center for Children in Poverty.

Turnbull, A., Turnbull, R., Wehmeyer, M., & Shogren, K. (2013). Understanding students with attention-deficit/hyperactivity disorder. *In Exceptional Lives: Special Education in Today's Schools* (pp. 172–193). Upper Saddle River, NJ.

U.S. Public Health Service. (2000). *Report of the Surgeon General's Conference on Children's Mental Health: A National Action Agenda.* U.S. Department of Health and Human Services.

Zeanah, C., Berlin, L., & Boris, N. (2011). Practitioner Review: Clinical applications of attachment theory and research for infants and young children. *Journal of Child Psychology and Psychiatry, 52*(8), 819–833.

Zero to Three. (n.d.). *Early Childhood Mental Health.* Retrieved May 5, 2012, from http://www.zerotothree.org/child-development/early-childhood-mental-health/

Chapter13

Agran, P. F., Anderson, C., Winn, D., Trent, R., Walton-Haynes, L., & Thayer, S. (2003) Rates of pediatric injuries by 3-month intervals for children 0 to 3 years of age. *Pediatrics, 111*(6), 3683–3692.

American Academy of Dermatology. (2005). *Sun protection for children.* Schaumburg, IL: Author. Retrieved September 5, 2012, from http://www.aad.org/public/publications/pamphlets/sun_sunprotection.html

American Academy of Pediatrics. (2001). Prevention of agricultural injuries among children and adolescents. *Pediatrics, 108*(4), 1016–1019.

American Academy of Pediatrics, American Public Health Association, & National Resource Center for Health and Safety in Child Care and Early Education. (2011). *Caring for our children: National health and safety performance standards; Guidelines for early care and education programs* (3rd ed.). Elk Grove Village, IL: American Academy of Pediatrics; Washington, DC: American Public Health Association. Also available at http://nrckids.org.

Borse, N., Gilchrist, J., Dellinger, A., Rudd, R., Ballesteros, M., & Sleet, D. (2008, December). *CDC childhood injury report: patterns of unintentional*

injuries among 0-19 year olds in the United States, 2000–2006. U.S. Department of Health and Human Services, Centers for Disease Control and Prevention, National Center for Injury Prevention and Control, Division of Unintentional Injury Prevention. Atlanta, GA.

Bureau of Labor Statistics, U.S. Department of Labor. (2010). *Occupational outlook handbook: 2008–09 edition, Teachers–preschool–kindergarten, elementary, middle, and secondary.* Retrieved July 21, 2012, from http://www.bls.gov/OCO

Caronongan, P., Kirby, G., Malone, L., & Boller, K. (2011). *Defining and measuring quality: An in-depth study of five child care quality rating and improvement systems.* OPRE Report #2011-29. Washington, DC: Office of Planning, Research and Evaluation, Administration for Children and Families, U.S. Department of Health and Human Services. Retrieved July 21, 2012, from http://www.acf.hhs.gov/programs/opre/cc/childcare_quality/five_childcare/five_childcare.pdf

Center on the Developing Child at Harvard University. (2012). *The science of neglect: The persistent absence of responsive care disrupts the developing brain: working paper 12.* Retrieved from www.developingchild.harvard.edu

Centers for Disease Control and Prevention. Retrieved July 20, 2012, from http://www.cdc.gov/mmwr/preview/mmwrhtml/mm61e0416a1.htm

Centers for Disease Control and Prevention. (2008). *10 leading causes of injury death by age group highlighting unintentional injury deaths, United States, 2008.* Retrieved July 21, 2012, from http://www.cdc.gov/Injury/wisqars/pdf/Leading_Causes_injury_Deaths_Age_GRoup_Highlighting_Unintentional_Injury%20Deaths_US_2008-a.pdf

Centers for Disease Control and Prevention. (2009). *10 leading causes of injury deaths by age group highlighting unintentional injury deaths, United States–2009.* Retrieved July 18, 2012, from http://www.cdc.gov/injury/wisqars/LeadingCauses.html

Centers for Disease Control and Prevention (2010). *National estimates of the 10 leading causes of nonfatal injuries treated in hospital emergency departments, United States–2010.* Office of Statistics and Programming, National Center for Injury Prevention and Control. Retrieved July 18, 2012, from http://www.cdc.gov/injury/wisqars/LeadingCauses.html

Cohen, J., Onunaku, N., Clothier, S., & Poppe, J. (2005). *Helping young children succeed: Strategies to promote early childhood social and emotional development.* Retrieved May 31, 2007, from the National Conference of State Legislatures website: http://www.zerotothree.org/site/DocServer/helping_young_children_succeed_final.pdf?docID=1725&AddInterest=1157

Copple, C., & Bredekamp, S. (2009). *Developmentally appropriate practice in programs serving children from birth through age 8.* National Association for the Education of Young Children.

Currie, J. M., & Hotz, V.J. (2004). Accidents will happen? Unintentional injury, maternal employment, and child care policy. *Journal of Health Economics, 23,* 25–59.

Danseco, E. R., Miller, T. R., & Spicer, R. S. (2000). Incidence and costs of 1987–1994 childhood injuries: Demographic breakdowns. *Pediatrics, 105*(2), e27. Online at: http://pediatrics.aappublications .org/cgi/content/full/105/2/e27

Edwards, C., Gandini, L., & Forman, G. (1993). *The hundred languages of children: The Reggio Emilia approach to early childhood education.* Norwood, NJ: Ablex Publishing.

Greenman, J. B. (2005, May). Places for childhood in the 21st century: A conceptual framework. In *Young children: Beyond the journal.*

Katz, L. G., & Cesarone, B. (Eds.). (1994). *Reflections on the Reggio Emilia approach.* Urbana, IL: ERIC Clearinghouse on Elementary and Early Childhood Education.

Maine Bureau of Insurance. (2012). *A consumer's guide to . . . Child care liability insurance.* Retrieved July 21, 2012, from http://maine.gov/ pfr/insurance/consumer/daycare.html

Maslow, A. (1954). *Motivation and personality.* New York: Harper & Row.

Moore Johnson, S. (2006). *The workplace matters: Teacher quality, retention, and effectiveness* (Best Practices Working Papers). Washington, DC: National Education Association. Retrieved from http://www.nea.org/research/bestpractices/ images/wcreport.pdf

Montessori, M. (1966). *The secret of childhood.* Notre Dame, IN: Fides.

National Association of Child Care Resource and Referral Agencies [NACCRRA]. (2008). *Leaving children to chance: NACCRRA's ranking of state standards and oversight of small family child care homes.* Retrieved January 6, 2012, from: http://www.naccrra.org/publications/ naccrra-publications/leaving-children-to-chance

National Association for the Education of Young Children. (1998). *Licensing and public regulation of early childhood programs.* Retrieved September 14, 2009, from http://208.118.177.216/ about/positions/pdf/PSLIC98.PDF

National Association for the Education of Young Children. (2007). *NAEYC early childhood program standards and accreditation criteria: The mark of quality in early childhood education.* Washington, DC: Author.

National Association for the Education of Young Children (NAEYC). (2008). *Overview of the NAEYC Early Childhood Program Standards.* Retrieved January 6, 2012, from http://www.naeyc .org/files/academy/file/OverviewStandards.pdf

National Association for the Education of Young Children. (2011). *Code of ethical conduct and statement of commitment.* Retrieved July 13, 2012, from http://www.naeyc.org/ positionstatements/ethical_conduct

National Association for Regulatory Administration [NARA]. (2010). *National child care licensing study.* 2008. Retrieved July 21, 2012, from http:// www.naralicensing.drivehq.com/2008_Licensing_ Study/1005_2008_Child%20Care%20Licensing% 20Study_Full_Report.pdf

National Child Care Information and Technical Assistance Center & National Association for Regulatory Administration [NARA]. (2010). *The 2008 child care licensing study.* Retrieved from http://www.naralicensing.org/Licensing_Study

National Head Start Facilities Information Services. (2002). *Region IV Head Start quality improvement center.* Bowling Green, KY: Author.

National Institute of Child Health & Human Development (NICHD). (2006). *SIDS: "Back to Sleep" campaign.* National Institutes of Health. Retrieved from http://www.nichd.nih.gov/sids/

National Institute of Child Health & Human Development (NICHD). (2012). *Back to sleep public education campaign.* National Institute of Child Health & Human Development. Retrieved July 21, 2012, from https://www.nichd.nih.gov/sids/

Nemours Foundation. (2012). *KidsHealth for parents: Playground safety.* Retrieved July 21, 2012, from http://www.kidshealth.org/parent/ firstaid_safe/outdoor/playground.html

New, R. S. (1993). *Reggio Emilia: Some lessons for U.S. educators.* Retrieved from http://ceep. crc .uiuc.edu/eecearchive/digests/1993/new93.html

Pate, R., Pfeiffer, K. A., Trost, S. G., Ziegler, P., & Dowda, M. (2004). Physical activity among children attending preschools. *Pediatrics, 114*(5), 1258–1263.

Perri, F. S. (2006). *You're being investigated . . . Now What?* Redleaf National Institute, the National Center for the Business of Family Child Care. Retrieved from http://www.redleafinstitute.org

Phelan, K. J., Khoury, J., Kalkwarf, H., & Lanphear, B. (2005). Most childhood injuries occur at home. *Public Health Reports.* Retrieved January 6, 2012, from http://www.childrenscolorado.org/wellness/ info/news/41169.aspx

Ritchie, S., & Weller, B. (Eds.). (2005). *Physical environment: A guide to the NAEYC early childhood program standard and related accreditation criteria.* Washington, DC: National Association for the Education of Young Children.

Rivkin, M. S. (1995). *The great outdoors: Restoring children's right to play outside.* Washington, DC: National Association for the Education of Young Children.

Savage, M. A., Kawanabe, I. T., Mejeur, J., Goehring, J. B., & Reed, J. B. (2002). *Protecting children: A guide to child traffic safety laws.* Washington, DC: National Conference of State Legislatures.

Shonkoff, J. P., & Phillips, D. A. (Eds.). (2000). *From neurons to neighborhoods: The science of early childhood development.* National Research Council and Institute of Medicine. Committee on Integrating the Science of Early Childhood Development. Board on Children, Youth, and Families, Commission on Behavioral and Social Sciences and Education. Washington, DC: National Academy Press.

Sussman, C., & Gillman, A. (2007). *Building early childhood facilities—What states can do to create supply and promote quality* (NIEER Preschool Policy Report). New Brunswick, NJ: National Institute for Early Education Research. Retrieved July 2, 2012, from http://www.nieer.org/resources/ research/Facilities.pdf

Tarr, P. (2001). Aesthetic codes in early childhood classrooms: What art educators can learn from Reggio Emilia. *Art Education, 54*(3) 33–39.

Telep, V. (2009). *Tips on toys.* (Pub. #350-063). Blacksburg: Virginia State University Cooperative Extension. Retrieved July 21, 2012, from http:// pubs.ext.vt.edu/350/350-063/350-063.html

Trancik, A. M., & Evans, G. W. (1995). Spaces fit for children: Competency in the design of daycare center environments. *Children's Environments, 12*(3), 43–58.

U.S. Census Bureau. U.S. Department of Commerce, 2010. *Who's minding the kids? Child care arrangements, Spring 2010.* Retrieved July, 2012, from http://www.census.gov/hhes/childcare/data/ sipp/2010/tables.html

U.S. Consumer Product Safety Commission. (1999). *Consumer product safety commission staff study of safety hazards in child care settings.* Washington, DC: Author. Retrieved July 12, 2012, from http:// www.cpsc.gov/library/ccstudy.html

U.S. Consumer Product Safety Commission. (2008, April). *Public playground saftey handbook* (Publication No. 325). Retrieved July 21, 2012, from http://www.cpsc.gov/CPSCPUB/PUBS/325.pdf

U.S. General Services Administration. (2003, July). *Child care center design guide.* Washington, DC: Author. Retrieved July 2, 2012, from http://www .gsa.gov/graphics/pbs/designguidesmall.pdf

Wrigley, J., & J. Dreby. (2005). Fatalities and the Organization of Child Care in the United States, 1985–2003. *American Sociological Review, 70,* 729–757. Retrieved July 21, 2012, from http:// fcd-us.org/resources/fatalities-and-organization- child-care-united-states-1985-2003?destination= resources%2Fsearch%3Fpage%3D23

Wyatt, J. (2001). *Just what is adequate liability coverage?* Redleaf National Institute, the National Center for the Business of Family Child Care. Retrieved April 15, 2007, from http://www .redleafinstitute.org

York, S. (1991). *Roots and wings: Affirming culture in early childhood programs.* St. Paul, MN: Redleaf Press.

Chapter 14

Alter, P. J., & Conroy, M. (2007). *Recommended practices: Preventing challenging behavior in young children: Effective practices.* Center for Evidence-Based Practice. Retrieved from www .challengingbehavior.org

American Academy of Pediatrics, American Public Health Association, and National Resource Center for Health and Safety in Child Care and Early Education. (2011). *Caring for our children: National Health and Safety Performance Standards: Guidelines for out-of-home child care programs* (2nd ed.). Elk Grove Village, IL: American Academy of Pediatrics and Washington, DC: American Public Health Association. Also available at: http://nrc.uchsc.edu

Bales, D., Wallinga, C., & Coleman, M. (2005). *The teaching basic health and safety in the early childhood classroom curriculum.* University of Georgia.

Bluth, L. (1993). Transporting infants, toddlers and preschool children with disabilities. *School Business Affairs, 59*(4), 13–16.

Bowlby, J. (1982). *Attachment and loss: Vol. 1. Attachment* (2nd ed.). New York: Basic Books.

Carson, K. (2006). Family mealtimes: More than just eating together. *Journal of the American Dietetic Association, (106)*, 532–533.

Centers for Disease Control and Prevention, National Center for Injury Prevention and Control. (2006). *Web-based injury statistics query and reporting system (WISQARS)*. Available online at: http://www.cdc.gov/ncipc/wisqars

Early Childhood Learning and Knowledge Center (ECLKC). (2008). Office of Head Start, U.S. Department of Health and Human Services Administration for Children and Families. For guidance about safe transportation of young children in Head Start (ages 3 to 5 years) and Early Head Start (ages infant to 3 years). Retrieved February 1, 2012, from http://eclkc.ohs.acf.hhs.gov/hslc

Fox, L., & Garrison, S. (2009). Helping children learn to manage their own behavior: What Works Brief #7. Center for Social and Emotional Foundations for Early Learning. Retrieved July 17, 2012, from http://csefel.vanderbilt.edu/resources/what_works.html

French, K. (2004). Supporting a child with special health care needs. *Young Children, 59*(2), 62–63.

Gartrell, D. (2006). Guidance matters: The beauty of class meetings. *Young Children, 61*(6) 1–3.

Gartrell, D., & Gartrell, J. J. (2008). Guidance matters: Understanding bullying. *Young Children. 63*(3), 54–57.

Gilliam, W. S. (2005). Prekindergartners left behind: Expulsion rates in state prekindergarten programs. *Policy Briefs*. Foundation for Child Development. Retrieved July 13, 2012, from http://www.challengingbehavior.org/explore/policy_docs/prek_expulsion.pdf

Hanline, M. F., Nunes, D., & Worthy, M. B. (2007). Augmentative and alternative communication in the early childhood years. *Young Children, 62*(4), 78–82.

Hemmeter, M., Ostrosky, M., Artman, K., & Kinder, K. (2008, May). Planning transitions to prevent challenging behavior. Beyond the Journal: *Young Children* on the Web. National Association for the Education of Young Children. Retrieved January 9, 2013, from http://journal.naeyc.org/btj/200805/pdf/BTJ_Hemmeter_Transitions.pdf

Kern, P., & Wakeford, L. (2007). Supporting outdoor play for young children: The zone model of playground supervision. *Young Children. 62*(5), 12–18.

Nast, P. (2012). Establishing classroom rules. *Classroom Management*. National Education Association. Retrieved July 13, 2012, from http://www.nea.org/tools/establishing-classroom-rules.html

National Association for the Education of Young Children (NAEYC). (2006). *NAEYC accreditation classroom observation tool*. Washington, DC: NAEYC.

National Association for the Education of Young Children. (2009). *Developmentally appropriate practice in early childhood programs serving children birth through 8*. Washington DC: NAEYC.

National Association for the Education of Young Children (NAEYC). (2011a). *Code of ethical conduct and statement of commitment*. Retrieved July 13, 2012, from http://www.naeyc.org/positionstatements/ethical_conduct

National Association for the Education of Young Children (NAEYC). (2011b). *Q & A highlights: What can I do when a child bites?* Retrieved July 13, 2012, from http://www.naeyc.org/event/challenging-behaviors/highlights

National Education Association. (2002–2006). *Classroom management*. Retrieved July 13, 2012, from http://www.nea.org/tools/ClassroomManagement.html

National Highway Traffic Safety Administration. (1999, February). *Guidelines for the safe transportation of pre-school age children in school buses*. Retrieved July 13, 2012, from http://www.nhtsa.dot.gov/people/injury/buses/Guide1999/prekfinal.htm

National Highway Traffic Safety Administration. (2011). School transportation related crashes. *Traffic safety facts: 2009 data*. NHTSA National Center for Statistics and Analysis. Publication 811396. Retrieved July 17, 2012, from http://www-nrd.nhtsa.dot.gov/Pubs/811396.pdf

National Safety Council. (2009). *School bus safety: Infants, toddlers, and preschoolers*. Retrieved July 17, 2012, from http://www.nsc.org/news_resources/Resources/Documents/School_Bus_Safety_Infants_Toddlers_and_Pre-schoolers.pdf

Olson, M. (2007). Strengthening families: Community strategies that work. *Young Children, 62*(2), 26–32.

Savage, M., Kawanabe, I., Mejeur, J., Goehring, J., & Reed, J. (2002). *Protecting children: A guide to traffic safety laws*. National Conference of State Legislatures. Retrieved February 1, 2012, from http://www.nhtsa.gov/staticfiles/nti/enforcement/pdf/ProtectingChildren.pdf

Start Safe Kids USA. (2009). *Start safe fire safety. Start safe fire: A fire and burn prevention safety program for preschoolers and their families*. Retrieved July 17, 2012, from http://www.safekids.org/educators/Start-safe/fire-safety/

Strain, P. S., & Dunlap, G. 2006. *Recommended practices: Being an evidence-based practitioner*. Tampa: University of South Florida, Louis de la Parte Florida Mental Health Institute, Center for Evidence-based Practice: Young Children with Challenging Behavior.

U.S. Consumer Products Safety Commission. (2012). *Water safety tips*. Publication 210. Retrieved February 1, 2012, from http://www.cpsc.gov/cpscpub/pubs/210.pdf

Wittmer, D. S., & Petersen, S. H. (2008). Issues in infant/toddler programs. In S. Feeney, (Ed.), Issues in Early Childhood Education. Upper Saddle River, NJ: Merrill Prentice Hall.

Chapter 15

American Academy of Pediatrics, American Public Health Association, National Resource Center for Health and Safety in Child Care and Early Education. (2011). *Caring for our children: National health and safety performance standards; Guidelines for early care and education programs* (3rd ed.). Elk Grove Village, IL: American Academy of Pediatrics; Washington, DC: American Public Health Association. Also available at http://nrckids.org

American Red Cross. (2012a). *Red Cross helps kids build preparedness backpacks*. Retrieved May 7, 2012, from www.redcross.org

American Red Cross. (2012b). *Recovering after disaster: Recovering emotionally*. Retrieved May 7, 2012, from www.redcross.org

Ben-Joseph, E. P. (2010). Hey! A black widow spider bit me! *KidsHealth*. Nemours Foundation. Retrieved May 7, 2012, from http://kidshealth.org/kid/ill_injure/bugs/black_widow.html#

Ben-Joseph, E. P. (2011). Asthma. *KidsHealth*. Nemours Foundation. Retrieved May 7, 2012, from http://kidshealth.org/kid/asthma_basics/what/asthma.html#

Berg, M. D., Schexnayder, S. M., Chameides, L., Terry, M., Donoghue, A., Hickey, R. W., Berg, R. A., Sutton, R. M., & Hazinski, M. F. (2010). Part 13: Pediatric basic life support: 2010 American Heart Association Guidelines for Cardiopulmonary Resuscitation and Emergency Cardiovascular Care. *Circulation, 122*(suppl 3), S862–S875.

Centers for Disease Control and Prevention. (2006). *Emergency preparedness: Chemical spills*. Retrieved July 18, 2012, from http://www.bt.cdc.gov/planning/shelteringfacts.asp

Centers for Disease Control and Prevention. (2009). *10 leading causes of injury deaths by age group highlighting unintentional injury deaths, United States – 2009*. Office of Statistics and Programming, National Center for Injury Prevention and Control. Retrieved July 18, 2012, from http://www.cdc.gov/injury/wisqars/LeadingCauses.html

Centers for Disease Control and Prevention. (2012a). *Injury prevention and control: Traumatic brain injury (TBI)*. Retrieved July 19, 2012, from http://www.cdc.gov/traumaticbraininjury/severe.html

Centers for Disease Control and Prevention. (2012b). *Asthma. Basic information*. Retrieved July 18, 2012, from http://www.cdc.gov/asthma/faqs.htm

Centers for Disease Control and Prevention. (2012c). *NIOSH workplace safety and health topics: Heat stress*. Retrieved July 18, 2012, from http://www.cdc.gov/niosh/topics/heatstress/

Centers for Disease Control and Prevention. (2012d). *Emergency preparedness and response: Coping with disaster or traumatic events*. CDC Emergency Risk Communication Branch (ERCB), Division of Emergency Operations (DEO), Office of Public Health Preparedness and Response (OPHPR). Retrieved July 18, 2012, from http://emergency.cdc.gov/mentalhealth/

Centers for Disease Control and Prevention. (2012e). *Emergency Preparedness & Response. Frequently Asked Questions (FAQ) About Extreme Heat*. Retrieved January 9, 2013, from http://www.bt.cdc.gov/disasters/extremeheat/faq.asp

Cronan, K. M. (2011b). Nosebleeds. *KidsHealth*. Nemours Foundation. Retrieved May 7, 2012, from http://kidshealth.org/parent/firstaid_safe/emergencies/nose_bleed.html#

Cronan, K. M. (2011b). Nosebleeds. *KidsHealth.* Nemours Foundation. Retrieved May 7, 2012, from http://kidshealth.org/parent/firstaid_safe/emergencies/nose_bleed.html#

Cunah, J. P., & Shiel, W. C. (2007). *Nosebleed.* Retrieved from http://www.medicinenet.com/nosebleed/article.htm

Curtis, N. (2008). Emergency response planning for child care providers. Montgomery County, MD: Child Care Resource and Referral Agency. Retrieved July 18, 2012, from http://www.montgomerycountymd.gov/content/hhs/phs/APC/childcaremanual.pdf

Defelice, M., & Stewart, S. M. (2011). Nut or peanut allergy. *KidsHealth.* Nemours Foundation. Retrieved May 7, 2012, from http://kidshealth.org/kid/nutrition/diets/nut_allergy.html#

Dowshen, S. (2010). Dealing with cuts. *KidsHealth.* Nemours Foundation. Retrieved May 18, 2012, from http://kidshealth.org/parent/firstaid_safe/emergencies/bleeding.html

Dugdale, D. C., Henochowicz, S. L., & Zieve, D. (2008). *Anaphylaxes.* MedlinePlus. U.S. National Library of Medicine & National Institutes of Health. Retrieved from http://www.nlm.nih.gov/medlineplus/ency/article/000844.htm

Dugdale, D. C., & Zieve, D. (2010). *Febrile Seizures.* MedlinePlus. U.S. National Library of Medicine & National Institutes of Health. Retrieved January 9, 2013, from http://www.nlm.nih.gov/medlineplus/ency/article/000028.htm; http://www.nlm.nih.gov/medlineplus/ency/article/000980.htm

Duldner, J. E., & Zieve, D. (2008). *Insect bites and stings.* Medline Plus. U.S. National Library of Medicine & National Institutes of Health. Retrieved from http://www.nlm.nih.gov/medlineplus/ency/article/000033.htm

Federal Emergency Management Agency FEMA). (2010). *Helping children cope with disaster.* Retrieved April 25, 2012, from http://www.fema.gov/rebuild/recover/cope_child.shtm

Federal Emergency Management Agency (FEMA). (2012a). *Hazardous materials incidents.* Retrieved July 18, 2012, from http://www.ready.gov/hazardous-materials-incidents

Federal Emergency Management Agency (FEMA). (2012b). *Natural disasters.* Retrieved July 18, 2012, from http://www.ready.gov/natural-disasters

Federal Emergency Management Agency (FEMA). (2012c). *Pandemic.* Retrieved July 18, 2012, from http://www.ready.gov/pandemic

Filloux, F., & Goodman, M. (2010). Seizures. *KidsHealth.* Nemours Foundation. Retrieved January 9, 2012, from http://kidshealth.org/parent/firstaid_safe/emergencies/seizure.html#

Gavin, M. L. (2010). What's a bruise? *KidsHealth.* Nemours Foundation. Retrieved May 7, 2012, from http://kidshealth.org/kid/talk/qa/bruise.html

Goss, L. A. (2010). Tooth injuries. *KidsHealth.* Nemours Foundation. Retrieved May 18, 2012, from http://kidshealth.org/parent/firstaid_safe/emergencies/tooth_injury.html

Government Services Agency, Child Care Division. (2011). *Child Care Emergency Preparedness Toolbox.* Retrieved April 25, 2012, from http://www.gsa.gov/graphics/pbs/Child_Care_Emergency_Preparedness_Toolbox.pdf

Heller, J. L., & Zieve, D. (2010a). *Burns.* MedLinePlus. U.S. National Library of Medicine & National Institutes of Health. Retrieved May 18, 2012, from http://www.nlm.nih.gov/medlineplus/ency/article/000030.htm

Heller, J. L., & Zieve, D. (2010b). *Shock.* MedLinePlus. U.S. National Library of Medicine & National Institutes of Health. Retrieved May 18, 2012, from http://www.nlm.nih.gov/medlineplus/ency/article/000039.htm

Heller, J. L., & Zieve, D. (2010c). *Human bites.* Medline Plus. U.S. National Library of Medicine & National Institutes of Health. Retrieved July 18, 2012, from http://www.nlm.nih.gov/medlineplus/ency/article/000035.htm

Heller, J. L., & Zieve, D. (2011a). *Choking first aid: Adults and children over age 1.* MedlinePlus. U.S. National Library of Medicine & National Institutes of Health. Retrieved May 18, 2012, from http://www.nlm.nih.gov/medlineplus/ency/presentations/100222_5.htm

Heller, J. L., & Zieve, D. (2011b). *Choking first aid: Infant under 1 year.* MedlinePlus. U.S. National Library of Medicine & National Institutes of Health. Retrieved May 18, 2012, from http://www.nlm.nih.gov/medlineplus/ency/presentations/100221_3.htm

Heller, J. L., & Zieve, D. (2011c) *Bleeding.* MedlinePlus. U.S. National Library of Medicine & National Institutes of Health. Retrieved May 18, 2012, from http://www.nlm.nih.gov/medlineplus/ency/presentations/100221_3.htm

Heller, J. L., & Zieve, D. (2011d) *Electrical Injury.* MedlinePlus. U.S. National Library of Medicine & National Institutes of Health. Retrieved January 9, 2013, from http://www.nlm.nih.gov/medlineplus/ency/article/000028.htm; http://www.nlm.nih.gov/medlineplus/ency/article/000053.htm

Heller, J. L., & Zieve, D. (2012) *Head injury first aid.* MedlinePlus. U.S. National Library of Medicine & National Institutes of Health. Retrieved January 9, 2013, from http://www.nlm.nih.gov/medlineplus/ency/article/000028.htm

Homeier, B. P. (2005). Falls. *KidsHealth.* Nemours Foundation. Retrieved January 9, 2012, from http://kidshealth.org/teen/safety/first_aid/falls_sheet.html

Illinois Emergency Medical Services for Children. (2006). *Emergency preparedness planning guide for child care centers.* Retrieved May 2, 2012, from ttp://www.chtc.org/dl/handouts/20061114/20061114-2.pdf

International Save the Children Alliance. (2006). *Two years later: Rebuilding lives after the tsunami: The children's road to recovery.* London: Author. Retrieved July 18, 2012, from http://www.savethechildren.org/atf/cf/%7B9def2ebe-10ae-432c-9bd0-df91d2eba74a%7D/savechild_tsunami_report.pdf

Kaneshiro, N. K., & Zieve, D. (2008). *Signs of an asthma attack.* MedlinePlus. U.S. National Library of Medicine & National Institutes of Health. Retrieved from http://www.nlm.nih.gov/medlineplus/ency/patientinstructions/000062.htm

Klein, J. (2010). Rabies. *KidsHealth.* Nemours Foundation. Retrieved May 7, 2012, from http://kidshealth.org/kid/health_problems/infection/rabies.html

MacCormack, C. (2008). *How to help children cope after the tornadoes in the south: Ten tips from Save the Children.* Westport, CT: Save the Children. Retrieved July 18, 2012, from www.savethechildren.org/newsroom/2008/how-to-help-children-cope.html

National Association of Child Care Resource and Referral Agencies (NACCRRA) and Save the Children. (2010). *Protecting children in child care during emergencies.* Retrieved April 16, 2012, from http://www.naccrra.org/sites/default/files/publications/naccrra_publications/2012/protectingchildreninchildcareemergencies.pdf

National Commission on Children and Disasters. (2010, October). *2010 Report to the President and Congress.* AHRQ Publication No. 10-M037. Rockville, MD: Agency for Healthcare Research and Quality.

National Institute of General Medical Sciences. (2008). *Burns fact sheet.* Retrieved from http://www.nigms.hih.gov/Publications/Factsheet_Burns.htm

Purdue University. (2012). *Radiological and environmental management: Blood spill procedures.* West Lafayette, IN: Author. Retrieved January 9, 2013, from http://www.purdue.edu/rem/eh/bsp.htm

Rosenbaum, S., Harty, M., & Sheer, J. (2008, March–April). State laws extending comprehensive legal liability protections for professional health-care volunteers during public health emergencies. *Public Health Report, 123*(2), 238–241. PMC2239336. Association of Schools of Public Health. Retrieved May 13, 2012, from http://www.ncbi.nlm.nih.gov/pmc/articles/PMC2239336/

Schwartz, A. (2009). *Head Start Emergency Preparedness Manual.* Office of Head Start, Administration for Children and Families, U.S. Department of Health and Human Services. Retrieved July 18, 2012, from http://eclkc.ohs.acf.hhs.gov/hslc/tta-system/health/ep/Head_Start_Emergency_Preparedness_Manual.pdf

Siegel, J. D., Rhinehart, E., Jackson, M., Chiarello, L., & the Healthcare Infection Control Practices Advisory Committee. (2007). *Guideline for isolation precautions: Preventing transmission of infectious agents in healthcare settings.* Retrieved May 15, 2012, from http://www.cdc.gov/ncidod/dhqp/pdf/isolation2007.pdf

Vorvick, L. J. (2011). *Eye—foreign object in.* MedlinePlus. U.S. National Library of Medicine & National Institutes of Health. Retrieved July 18, 2012, from http://www.nlm.nig.gov/medlineplus/ency/article/002084.htm

Vorvick, L. J., & Zieve, D. (2009a). *Broken bones.* Medline Plus. U.S. National Library of Medicine & National Institutes of Health. Retrieved from http://www.nlm.nih.gov/medlineplus/ency/article/000001.htm

Vorvick, L. J., & Zieve, D. (2009b). *Bruises.* Medline Plus. U.S. National Library of Medicine & National Institutes of Health. Retrieved from http://www.nlm.nih.gov/medlineplus/ency/article/007213.htm

Chapter 16

Administration for Children and Families. (2010). The Child Abuse and Prevention and Treatment Act. (PL 111-320) Reauthorization of CAPTA, 2012. U.S. Department of Health & Human Services, Retrieved June 2012, from http://www.acf.hhs.gov/programs/cb/laws_policies/cblaws/capta/capta2010.pdf

American Psychological Association. (2004). *Violence in the media—Psychologists help protect children from harmful effects*. Retrieved July 21, 2012, from http://www.apa.org/research/action/protect.aspx

Center on the Developing Child at Harvard University. (2007, August). *A science-based framework for early childhood policy: Using evidence to improve outcomes in learning, behavior and health for vulnerable children.* Cambridge, MA: Author. Retrieved July 21, 2012, from http://developingchild.harvard.edu/files/7612/5020/4152/Policy_Framework.pdf

Centers for Disease Control and Prevention (CDC). (2010). Understanding Child Maltreatment Fact Sheet. Retrieved June 2012, from http://www.cdc.gov/ViolencePrevention/pdf/CM-FactSheet-a.pdf

Chalk, R., Gibbons, A., & Scarupa, H. J. (2002). The multiple dimensions of child abuse and neglect: New insights into an old problem (child Trends Research Brief). Washington, DC: Child Trends. Retrieved July 22, 2012, from http://www.childtrends.org/files/child abuserb.pdf

Child Welfare Information Gateway (2004). *Risk and protective factors for child abuse and neglect.* Washington, DC: Author. Retrieved July 12, 2012, from http://www.childwelfare.gov/can/factors

Child Welfare Information Gateway. (2007). Recognizing Child Abuse and Neglect: Signs and Symptoms. Retrieved June 3, 2012, from http://www.childwelfare.gov/pubs/factsheets/signs.cfm

Child Welfare Information Gateway. (2008a). *What is child abuse and neglect? Factsheets.* Retrieved July 22, 2012, from http://www.childwelfare.gov/pubs/factsheets/whatiscan.cfm

Child Welfare Information Gateway. (2008b). *Long-term consequences of child abuse and neglect.* Retrieved June 3, 2012, from: http://www.childwelfare.gov/pubs/factsheets/long_term_consequences.pdf

Child Welfare Information Gateway. (2009). *Domestic violence and the child welfare system. Bulletins for professionals.* Retrieved June 2012, from http://www.childwelfare.gov/pubs/factsheets/domesticviolence.cfm

Children's Bureau & DePanfilis, D. (2006). *Child neglect: A guide for prevention assessment and intervention.* User Manual Series. Retrieved July 21, 2012, from http://www.childwelfare.gov/pubs/usermanuals/neglect/index.cfm

Cohen, E., & Knitzer, J. (2004, January). *Young children living with domestic violence: The role of early childhood programs.* Iowa City: University of Iowa.

Cohen, E., Groves, B., & Kracke, K. (2009) *Understanding children's exposure to violence.* Issue Brief: #1. The Safe Start Center Series on Children Exposed to Violence. Retrieved July 18, 2012, from http://www.safestartcenter.org/pdf/IssueBrief1_UNDERSTANDING.pdf

Cohen, J., Onunaku, N., Clothier, S., & Poppe, J. (2006). *Helping young children succeed: Strategies to promote early childhood social and emotional development* (Early Childhood Research and Policy Report). Washington, DC: National Conference of State Legislatures and Zero to Three.

Crosson-Tower, C. (2002). How can we recognize child abuse and neglect? In *When children are abused: An educator's guide to intervention* (pp. 8–34). Boston, MA: Allyn & Bacon.

Dahlberg L. L., & Mercy, J. A. (2009, February). History of violence as a public health issue. *AMA Virtual Mentor, 11*(2), 167–172. Available online at http://virtualmentor.ama-assn.org/2009/02/mhst1-0902.html

English, D. J., Widom, C. S., & Brandford, C. (2004). Another look at the effects of child abuse. *National Institute of Justice Journal, 251,* 23–24.

Finkelhor, D., Turner, H., Ormrod, R., Hamby, S., & Kracke, K. (2009). Children's exposure to violence: A comprehensive national survey. *Juvenile Justice Bulletin.* Office of Justice Programs. U.S. Department of Justice. Retrieved June 2012, from https://www.ncjrs.gov/pdffiles1/ojjdp/227744.pdf

Fitzpatrick, C., Barnett, T., & Pagani, L. S. (2012). Early exposure to media violence and later child adjustment. *Journal of Development and Behavioral Pediatrics, 33*(4), 291–297. Retrieved June 2012, from http://www.ncbi.nlm.nih.gov/pubmed/22481072

Fontes, L. A. (2005). Child maltreatment prevention and parent education. In *Child abuse and culture: Working with diverse families* (pp. 76–199). New York: Guilford Press.

Fraser, M. W., & Terzian, M. A. (2005). Risk and resilience in child development: Principles and strategies of practice. In G. P. Mallon & P. M. Hess (Eds.), *Child welfare for the 21st century: A handbook of practices, policies, and programs* (pp. 55–71) New York: Columbia University Press.

Goldman, J., Salus, M. K., Wolcott, D., & Kennedy, K. Y. (2003). *A coordinated response to child abuse and neglect: The foundation for practice.* Author(s): Office on Child Abuse and Neglect, Children's Bureau. Retrieved June 2012, from http://www.childwelfare.gov/pubs/usermanuals/foundation/foundatione.cfm

Huesmann, L. R., Moise-Titus, J., Podolski, C., & Eron, L. D. (2003). Longitudinal relations between children's exposure to TV violence and their aggressive and violent behavior in young adulthood: 1977–1992. *Developmental Psychology, 30*(2), 201–221. Available online at http://www.apa.org/journals/releases/dev392201.pdf

JAMA and Archives Journals. (2007, January 3). Child abuse and neglect associated with increased risk of depression among young adults. *Science Daily.* Retrieved January 9, 2013 from http://www.sciencedaily.com/releases/2007/01/070102092229.htm

Kaneshiro, N. K., & Dugdale, D. C. (2011). *Munchausen syndrome by proxy.* MedlinePlus. National Institutes of Health. Retrieved June 2012 from http://www.nlm.nih.gov/medlineplus/ency/article/001555.htm

Kempe, C.H., Silverman, F. N., Steele, B. F. Droegemueller, W., & Silver, H. K. (1962). The battered-child syndrome. *Journal of the American Medical Association, 181*(1), 17–24.

Kenny, M. C. (2001). Child abuse reporting: Teachers' perceived deterrents. *Child Abuse and Neglect, 25*(1), 81–92.

Koralek, D. (1992). *Caregivers of young children: Preventing and responding to child maltreatment.* Washington, DC: U.S. Department of Health & Human Services. Retrieved July 21, 2012, from http://www.childwelfare.gov/pubs/usermanuals/caregive/caregi.pdf

Kracke, K., & Cohen, E. P. (2008). The Safe Start Initiative: Building and disseminating knowledge to support children exposed to violence. *Journal of Emotional Abuse, 1*(2), 155–174.

Levin, D. (2003, March). *Beyond banning war and superhero play: Meeting children's needs in violent times.* Washington, DC: National Association for the Education of Young Children.

London, K., Bruck, M., Ceci, S., & Shuman, D. (2005). Disclosure of child sexual abuse: What does research tell us about the ways the children tell? *Psychology, Public Policy, and Law, 11*(1), 194–226.

Luthar, S., & Goldstein, A. (2004). Children's exposure to community violence: Implications for understanding risk and resilience. *Journal of Clinical Child and Adolescent Psychology, 33*(3), 499–505. Retrieved June 2012, from http://www.ncbi.nlm.nih.gov/pubmed/15271607

Malchiodi, C. A. (2001). Using drawing as intervention with traumatized children. *Trauma and Loss: Research and Interventions, 1*(1). Gross Pointe Woods, MI: National Institute of Trauma and Loss in Children. Retrieved July 21, 2012, from http://www.tlcinst.org/drawinginterevention.html

Malchiodi, C. A. (2008). When trauma happens, children draw. The healing arts: The restoring power of imagination. *Psychology Today.* Retrieved July 21, 2012, from http://www.psychologytoday.com/blog/the-healing-arts/200805/when-trauma-happens-children-draw-part-i

Mannheim, J. K., & Kaneshiro, N. K. (2011). *Child abuse: Physical.* PubMed. National Institutes of Health. Retrieved June 2012, from http://www.ncbi.nlm.nih.gov/pubmedhealth/PMH0002519/

Margolin, G., & Gordis, E. (2004). Children's Exposure to Violence in the Family and Community. *Current Directions in Psychological Science, 13*(4). American Psychological Society. Retrieved June 2012, from http://www.psy.miami.edu/faculty/dmessinger/c_c/rsrcs/rdgs/

peers_social_general/margolin.exposure2 violence.curdir.04.pdf.

Mitchum, R. (2011). Public health epidemics without diseases. *Science Life*. University of Chicago. Retrieved June 2012, from http://sciencelife.uchospitals.edu/2011/02/03/public-health-epidemics-without-diseases/

National Association for the Education of Young Children. (1997). *Early years are learning years: Media violence and young children.* Available online at http://npin.org/library/pre1998/n00154/n00154.html

National Association for the Education of Young children. (2004). *Building circles–Breaking Cycles* (Publication DD2). Author.

National Association for the Education of Young Children. (2011). *Code of ethical conduct and statement of commitment.* Retrieved July 24, 2012, from http://www.naeyc.org/files/naeyc/file/positions/Ethics%20Position%20Statement2011.pdf

National Center for Posttraumatic Stress Disorder. (2007). *Community violence: The effects on children and teens.* U.S. Department of Veteran's Affairs. Retrieved July 21, 2012, from www.ptsd.va.gov

National Institute of Neurological Disorders and Stroke, National Institutes of Health. (2010). *NINDS Shaken baby syndrome information page.* Retrieved June 2012, from http://www.ninds.nih.gov/disorders/shakenbaby/shakenbaby.htm

National Scientific Council on the Developing Child. (2005). *Excessive stress disrupts the architecture of the developing brain* (Council Working Paper #3). Cambridge, MA: Center on the Developing Child at Harvard University. Retrieved July 21, 2012, from http://developingchild.harvard.edu/library/reports_and_working papers/wp3

National Scientific Council on the Developing Child. (2010). *Persistent fear and anxiety can affect young children's learning and development: Working paper no. 9.* Retrieved from www.developingchild.harvard.edu

New York Society for the Prevention of Cruelty to Children. (2008). *The catalyst: 1870–1874.* New York: Author. Retrieved July 22, 2012, from http://www.nyspcc.org/nyspcc/history/the_catalyst

Office on Child Abuse and Neglect, Caliber Associates, & Crosson-Tower, C. (2003). *The role of educators in preventing and responding to child abuse and neglect.* User manual series. Retrieved July 21, 2012, from http://www.childwelfare.gov/pubs/usermanuals/educator/educatorc.cfm

Osofsky, J. (1999). The impact of violence on children. *The Future of Children, 9*(3), 33–49.

Osofsky, J. (Ed.). (2004). *Young children and trauma: Intervention and treatment.* New York: Guilford Publications.

Renteln, A. D. (2010). *Corporal punishment and the cultural defense.* Retrieved June 3, 2012, from http://scholarship.law.duke.edu/cgi/viewcontent.cgi?article=1572&context=lcp

Rice, K., & Groves, B. (2005). *Hope & healing; A caregivers' guide to helping young children affected by trauma.* Washington, DC: Zero to Three.

Roer-Strier, D. (2001) Reducing risk for children in changing cultural contexts: Recommendations for intervention and training. *Child Abuse and Neglect, 25*(2), 231–248.

Shonkoff, J., & Phillips, D. (Eds.). (2000). *From neurons to neighborhoods: The science of early childhood development.* Washington DC: National Academy Press.

Springer, K. W., Sheridan, J., Kuo, D., & Carnes, M. (2007). Long-term physical and mental health consequences of childhood physical abuse: Results from a large population-based sample of men and women. *Child Abuse & Neglect, 31*, 517–530.

Swaner, R., Kohn, J. Rempel, M., Campbell, M., Jaffe, P., & Wolfe, D. (2011). *The U.S. Attorney General's Defending Childhood Initiative: Formative evaluation of the Phase I Demonstration Program.* Retrieved June 2012, from https://www.ncjrs.gov/pdffiles1/nij/grants/236563.pdf

Thomas, D., Leicht, D., Hughes, C., Madigan, A., & Dowell., K. (2003). *Emerging practices in the prevention of child abuse and neglect.* Wayne, PA: Caliber Associates. Retrieved July 21, 2012, from http://www.childwelfare.gov/preventing/programs/whatworks/report/report.pdf

U.S. Department of Health and Human Services, Administration for Children and Families, Administration on Children, Youth and Families (HHS/ACF), Children's Bureau. (2011). *Child maltreatment 2010.* Available from http://www.acf.hhs.gov/programs/cb/stats_research/index.htm#can

U.S. Department of Health and Human Services. Administration for Children and Families, National Child Abuse and Neglect Data System. (2009). *FAM7.B Child maltreatment: Percentage of substantiated maltreatment reports of children ages 0–17 by maltreatment type and age. 2009.* Retrieved July 22, 2012, from http://www.childstats.gov/americaschildren/tables/fam7b.asp?popup=true

U.S. Department of Justice. (2011). *Fact Sheets: Domestic violence.* Retrieved June 2012, from http://www.ojp.usdoj.gov/newsroom/factsheets/ojpfs_domesticviolence.html

Washington Council for Prevention of Child Abuse. (2005). *Reframing child abuse messages.* Seattle: Author.

Zero to Three. (2009). *Research summary: Children exposed to violence.* Retrieved July 22, 2012, from http://www.zerotothree.org/site/DocServer/Children_Exp_to_Violence.pdf?docID=2502

Note: Page numbers follow by "b" indicate boxed material; "f" for illustrations and "t" for tables.

Standard	Key Elements of the Standard	Chapter and Topic
3: Observing, Documenting and Assessing to Support Young Children & Families	3a. Understanding the goals, benefits, and uses of assessment 3b. Knowing about and using observation, documentation, and other appropriate assessment tools and approaches 3c. Understanding and practicing responsible assessment to promote positive outcomes for each child 3d. Knowing about assessment partnerships with families and with professional colleagues	1: Using Evidence-Based Practices, p. 22 2: Recognizing Undernutrition, p.50, and Overnutrition, p. 53 4: Linking Developmental Skills to Feeding, p. 135 6: Fig. 6-13: Eating and Feeding Evaluation: Children with Special Needs, p. 255 8: What Determines Children's Health and Illness?, p. 274 8: Children's Health in the Context of Their Environments, p. 276 8: Policy Point: Characteristics of the Preschool Environment that Influence Physical Activity, p. 277 8: Nutrition Note: Policies Relevant to Nut Allergies, p. 282 8: Policies Promoting Oral Health, p. 282 8: Teaching Wellness: Brushing My Teeth Keeps My Smile Healthy, p. 283 9: entire chapter, p. 290 10: Conducting Daily Health Checks, p. 332 12: Making Referrals, p. 406 13: Individual Child Risk Profile, p. 429 14: Gathering Information at Enrollment, p. 471 15: Continuing to Monitor the Effects on Children, p. 532 16: Impacts on Children, p. 543
4: Using Developmentally Effective Approaches to Connect with Children and Families	4a. Understanding positive relationships and supportive interactions as the foundation of one's work with children 4b. Knowing and understanding effective strategies and tools for early education 4c. Using a broad repertoire of developmentally appropriate teaching/ learning approaches 4d. Reflecting on one's own practice to promote positive outcomes for each child	1: Engaging in Developmentally Appropriate Practices, p. 23 All chapters: Teaching Wellness features 4: Understanding the Feeding Relationship p. 125 5: Fig. 5-2: Strategies for Encouraging the Selective Eater, p. 156 5: Fig. 5-3: The Division of Feeding Responsibility, p. 158 5: Table 5-1: Developmental Influences on Toddlers' Eating and Relevant Teacher Strategies, p. 161 8: Influencing Health and Wellness in the Early Childhood Setting, p. 276 12: Understanding Successful Integration, p. 409 12: Curricula and Instruction, p. 414 13: Fig. 13-2 The Classroom Is a Refuge from Threats to Children's Physical and Emotional Safety, p. 425 14: Creating Familiar Routines, p. 473 15: Preparing Children to Be Resilient, p. 533 16: Social Support Resources, p. 559
5: Using Content Knowledge to Build Meaningful Curriculum	5a. Understanding content knowledge and resources in academic disciplines 5b. Knowing and using the central concepts, inquiry tools, and structures of content areas or academic disciplines 5c. Using one's own knowledge, appropriate early learning standards, and other resources to design, implement, and evaluate meaningful, challenging curricula for each child	1: Understanding How Children Learn, p. 18 1: Fig. 1-7 Steps in Scaffolding Children's Learning, p. 21 All chapters: Teaching Wellness features 2: Using the ChooseMyPlate Food Guidance System, p. 66 3: Teaching Nutrition Concepts, p. 103 5: Fig. 5-9: Sample Wellness Policy Guidelines, p. 179 5: Using an Integrated Nutrition Curriculum, p. 184 6: Progressive Programs & Practices: Healthful Leaning in an Edible Schoolyard, p. 207 10: Teaching Children Preventive Health Practices, p. 334 11: Teaching Wellness: Same and Special, p. 363 13: Progressive Programs & Practices: Safety Measures in a Gardening Experience, p. 466 14: Making Safety Relevant to Children's Lives, p. 497 15: Implementing Emergency Drills with Children, p. 509 16: Protective Factors for Children, p. 561